Helmut Satzinger & Danijela Stefanović

Egyptian Root Lexicon

Lingua Aegyptia

Studia Monographica

Herausgegeben von

Frank Kammerzell, Gerald Moers und Kai Widmaier

Band 25

Institut für Archäologie
Humboldt Universität
Berlin

Widmaier Verlag
Hamburg

Institut für Ägyptologie
Universität Wien
Wien

Egyptian Root Lexicon

Helmut Satzinger & Danijela Stefanović

Widmaier Verlag · Hamburg
2021

Titelaufnahme:
Helmut Satzinger & Danijela Stefanović,
Egyptian Root Lexicon
Hamburg: Widmaier Verlag, 2021
(Lingua Aegyptia – Studia Monographica; Bd. 25)
ISSN 0946-8641
ISBN 978-3-943955-25-5
DOI: https://doi.org/10.37011/studmon.25

Gedruckt auf säurefreiem, archivierfähigem Papier.
Druck und Verarbeitung: Hubert & Co., Göttingen
Printed in Germany

www.widmaier-verlag.de

Table of contents

Preface vii

I Introduction 1
I.1 Reduplication of root consonants 5
I.1.2 The significance of reduplication 9
I.2 Initial root consonants j and w 10
I.3 Various linguistic changes 11
I.4 Palatalisation of velars 11
I.5 Doublets 12
I.6 Debuccalisation 13
I.7 The Aleph problem 15
I.8 The Ayin problem 15
I.9 The structure of the root lexicon 16
I.9.1 Instructions for readers 17
I.10 Conclusion 18

II Roots
II.1 ꜣ 19
II.2 j 30
II.3 y 65
II.4 ᶜ 66
II.5 w 91
II.6 b 125
II.7 p 147
II.8 f 160
II.9 m 165
II.10 n 196
II.11 r 230
II.12 h 242
II.13 ḥ 251
II.14 ḫ 285
II.15 ẖ 311
II.16 z 319
II.17 s 332
II.18 š 368
II.19 ḳ 391
II.20 k 404
II.21 g 414
II.22 t 425
II.23 ṯ 438
II.24 ḏ 449
II.25 ḏ 462

Root index – numerical 478
Root index – alphabetical 512
Lexeme index 547
Index of roots of Semitic origin 703

Selected bibliography 711

Preface

The idea of an Egyptian root lexicon goes back to a conversation between me and the Soviet scholar Alexandr Militarev (Милитарёв), at the Fifth International Hamito-Semitic Congress held in Vienna in 1987 (convenor Hans Mukarovsky). When I complained, that Semitists, when doing comparative work, committed many mistakes in respect to Egyptian roots and historical phonology, Militaev answered: "Why don't you write an Egyptian root lexicon?"

Since then I was always aware of this idea, but my obligations as a head of the Egyptian and Near Eastern Department in the Vienna art museum, not to mention the University, kept me from really pursuing such a project; I merely managed to make several trial runs in direction of an Egyptian root lexicon. It was clear that I could not achieve it in this way, and the closer the date of my retirement from the museum work came (2003), the more my hopes developed for a realisation in the following period. But even then, when I was retired, work would not proceed, and I saw clearly that I needed help. That means, I had to launch a project.

The project "Egyptian Root Lexicon" was funded by Austrian Science Fund (FWF Der Wissenschaftsfonds) in 2016, and launched in 2017. The major collaborators were Kristina Hutter (University of Vienna, 2017 – initial databank entries) and Danijela Stefanović (University of Belgrade / University of Vienna, 2020-2021 – work on the databank entries and on the structure of the lexicon), and partially also Alfred Hutter (University of Vienna, 2018).

The project team is grateful to the Institute of Egyptology, University of Vienna, and Prof. Dr. Christiana Köhler for hosting the Root Lexicon. Due to cooperation with the project Strukturen und Transformationen des Wortschatzes der Ägyptischen Sprache. Text- und Wissenskultur im Alten Ägypten, and especially with Dr. Simon D. Schweitzer, many technical issues were easily solved as well as accession to relevant Thesaurus Linguae Aegyptiae (TLA) data.

Helmut Satzinger

I Introduction

Almost 40 years ago Harry S. Smith, in his paper "The treatment of roots in the lexicography of ancient Egyptian,"[1] addressed some of the key issues, including the question: Why is a root lexicon needed?

Smith noted that in Semitic lexicography, it is accepted that words should be listed under the roots from which they are formed, in order that the whole range of meaning which a root is capable of developing may be displayed. However, this has not been done in the major dictionaries of the Egyptian language, with the significant exception of W. E. Crum, A Coptic Dictionary. The practice of listing every "word" separately, whatever its status, does not help students of Egyptian to appreciate the basic meanings of Egyptian roots and the diachronic processes by which derived meanings were acquired; nor is it helpful to comparative research, either synchronic or diachronic, particularly by those who come to Egyptian from other linguistic disciplines. Among the disconcerting effects of the mentioned, Smith lists the following:

(i) Under the vocables ẖꜥ, ẖꜥi̯, ẖꜥw Berlin *Wörterbuch* lists 24 separate words or expressions (III, 239–243). To the Egyptologist it is clear that all of these derive their meaning from the basic root 'meaning' "rise". ... They may not however be so explicit to others. There are instances, indeed, where there are in appearance at least several roots exhibiting the same consonantal skeleton ... Here the *Wörterbuch* helps by grouping derivatives so as to follow each "root", but with no indication at all on what grounds it has been decided that the "roots" were indeed separate in the Egyptian mind or at what period ...

(ii) Substantive and adjective deverbal nouns formed with the preformative m- are separated in the dictionaries from their roots, e.g. wrḥ "anoint" (I, 334, 6) and mrḥ·t "ointment" (II, 111, 1), ṯwnw "fighting bull" (V, 3,59, 9) and mṯwn "bullring" (II, 175, 12). In these instances, the Wb. gives cross-references, which it by no means always does; imagine, however, a dictionary of any Semitic language in which mim-performatives were all listed separately from their roots!

(iii) The derived themes of the verb are not listed with the simplex. The causatives with preformative s- are the most obvious example, but an iterative like hdhd "plunder, ravage" (II, 506, 9) is listed separately from its simplex hd "advance, attack" (II, 504, 8), from its n- preformative adjective nhd "savage, fierce", from its iterative with prefixed n-, nhdhd "throb" and a syncopated form thereof nhdh "throbbing" (all II, 288). Likewise, fẖ "loose" (1, 578, 5), sfẖ "release" (IV, 116, 2) and snfẖfẖ "untie (mummy bandages)" have to be individually sought.

(iv) The princip(le) of root formation deduced for *Ursemitisch*, by which biconsonantal roots were expanded into triconsonantal roots, can be shown to have been operative to at least a limited extent in Egyptian at some stage, as

1 Smith 1982: 71–73. The Egyptian roots have been in the focus of lexicography in a very limited extent and an unsystematic way. Up till now there exists no inventory of roots. Some of the roots have been treated within individual articles and one monograph: Brunner (1965) - kꜣp, ṯb; Graefe (1971) - bjꜣ; Ward (1975; 1978) - bꜣ; (1986) - gb; Friedman (1985) (ꜣẖ); Frandsen (1992) - nfr; Koemoth (1993) - wꜥb; Jansen-Winkeln (1996) - ꜣẖ; Cannata (2006) - ḳs; also, of course, in sections of grammars and similar works.

> obvious examples such as ḳbb and ḳbḥ "be cool" (V, 22, 6 and V, 26, 4) show. Some examples may however be more subtle; sšm "lead" (IV, 28-0, 6) is no doubt the causative of šm "go" (IV, 462, 7) as Wb. suggests, but is šms "follow" (IV, 482, 7) also connected or not?

The same corpus of ideas motivated the work on the present Root Lexicon. The root is the core of the word, once all affixes are removed. If a root is shared by several lexemes, it may be said that it is the common denominator of this word family.

In a language like Egyptian, a root has to do more with consonants than with vowels. Whereas it is said, in general, that roots typically consist of one syllable (e.g. *root-*, *typ-*, *lab-*), more rarely – and (or) secondarily – of two syllables (e.g. *gener-*); in Egyptian, as also in Semitic, also in Berber, it is the consonants that are counted, rather than the syllables. They are named *radicals*, that is 'root sounds' (the root of this word being *radic-*). The number of radicals is most often (in two thirds of the cases) three, less often four, more rarely two.

If the root is the (fictive) element, or form, in which the whole word family is founded, the stem is the form in which anyone of the members of the family – the lexemes – manifests itself; apart, however, from conjugational elements and gender / number morphemes. The Egyptian stem of the word for 'god' would be, when singular, *nāṯir-* (whence Coptic ⲛⲟⲩⲧⲉ); when plural, *nVṯūr-* (whence Coptic ⲛ̄ⲧⲏⲣ); when feminine singular, *nVṯār-* (whence Coptic ⲛ̄ⲧⲱⲣⲉ). In contrast to the roots, the stems will not feature in this dictionary (although it is not always clear how the "subroots," a category introduced here, can be delimited from the stems).

There is a difference between verbs and other parts of speech. In Egyptian, as also in Semitic, also in Berber, the vocalization of *verbs* follows very few patterns. The root of a verb encompasses appurtenance to a specific type or paradigm. *Nouns*, however, can follow more numerous vocalization patterns. Anyway, Egyptian is transmitted without vowels in the hieroglyphic and hieratic scripts, hence this aspect is not of practical relevance. In languages like Egyptian, Semitic or Berber, verbs follow a certain limited number of patterns. For example, the typical infinitive of Coptic 3-radical verbs, either CōCəC (ⲥⲱⲧⲙ̄ < *sḏm*) or CCoC (ⲙ̄ⲧⲟⲛ < *mdn*); weak verbs, either *CīCə* (ϩⲓⲥⲉ < *ḥz(j)·t*) or *CCai* (ⲥϩⲁⲓ < *zḫꜣ*); etc.); or in Arabic, the three patterns of the perfect, 3rd masculine singular: CaCaCa (جَعَلَ *jaʕala* 'he did'), or, more rarely, CaCiCa (لَعِبَ *laʕiba* 'he played'), or CaCuCa (وَزُنَ *wazuna* 'he was heavy'). Appurtenance to one such pattern is an integral part of the respective root.

This has also a bearing on the question of the vowels: prior to Coptic times, Egyptian is transmitted without vowels. Actually, the consonantal script – which only makes sense for a root-inflecting language like Egyptian, Semitic or Berber – is an invention of Egypt. For example, the whole family of the root of snb 'healthy,' or of ʿnḫ 'to live,' is spelt with the same basic signs (𓋴𓈖𓃀, 𓋹𓈖𓐍, respectively), no matter what individual form, in its particular vocalization, is featuring in a given form; similarly, in Arabic and Hebrew – سلم *s-l-m*, שלם *š-l-m*, etc. – apart from all *scriptio plena* phenomena. The Semitic alphabet scripts (Phoenician, Aramaic/Hebrew, Arabic, Sabaean, etc.) are later, and are originally created after the example of the Egyptian so-called syllabic script, a phonetic medium which Egypt developed for rendering neologisms and proper names.

The roots of the language are not in the same conventional order (the Egyptological "alphabet") as the lexemes in the standard dictionaries; there are various linguistic circumstances that prevent lexemes from automatically appearing in the order of the roots.

In Indo-European languages (and others, like e.g. the Fenno-Ugric) it is mainly the prefixes of the verb that make the lexeme appear at a place different from that of the basic root (*ankommen, bekommen* etc., vs. *kommen*; cf. Hungarian *kimegy* ['kimɛɟ] 'goes out', *bemegy* 'goes in', *felmegy* 'goes up', *elmegy* 'goes away', vs. *megy* 'goes'). Another factor of separating lexemes from their roots is apophony (Ablaut; cf. *Sprache, sprechen, Spruch* etc.). Also, in Egyptian many verbs derive from basic roots by prefixes (often of common Afroasiatic origin). Consequently, words with such prefixes will appear in the normal dictionary in completely different places than the respective simplex verb. However, there are many cases where such "deep roots" have the same consonants as the lexemes, apart from endings like *·t* (feminine nouns), *·w* (masculine abstracts, etc.). In other cases, the form of the lexeme differs from the root in respect to the beginning of the word, like when the lexeme displays a prefix. Such prefixes include s- (causative, etc.), n- (reflexive, etc.), m- (instrumental, etc.).

117680[2] ḫni̯ 'to rest; to dwell,' but: 500096 s-ḫni̯ 'to bring to rest'(causative); the root is ḫni̯ in both cases (DRID 1000621)[3].
500096 s-ḫni̯ 'to bring to rest,' but: 75720 m-s-ḫn 'abode (of gods)' (locative; with double prefix, viz. m- and s-); again, the root is ḫni̯ in both cases (DRID 1000621).
123230 ẖni̯ 'to go by boat,' but: 74610 m-ẖn·t 'ferry-boat' (instrumental); the root is ẖni̯ in both cases (DRID 1000620).

Apart from these transparent prefixes there seem to be numerous older root prefixes and suffixes whose semantic character or functions are not at all clear, including root prefixes like ꜥ-, w-, r-, ḥ-, b-, d-, ꜥ-; root suffixes like -n, -ꜣ, -ꜥ, -r, -ḥ, -b.

Among the attested prefixes, the prefix s- is the best known as its causative meaning is often clear, and there are also correspondences in all Afro-Asiatic language families (e.g., Hebrew with its hiphʕal, as also the Arabic stem IV, *ʔafʕala* – the correspondence of Afroasiatic *s* with Hebrew *h* and Arabic *ʔ* is exceptional, but has a partial parallel in the pronouns of the 3rd person, like Hebrew *hū, hī, hɛm, hen*; Arabic *huwa, hiya, hum, hunna, humā*).

The best attested semantic effect of the *s* prefix is causative and/or factitive meaning.

140950 s-ḥn-ḥn 'to make retreat'— cf. 105940 ḥn 'to obstruct,' 106930 ḥn-ḥn 'to be detained'
149910 s-dḥ 'to bring low'— cf. 180350 dḥ or 180480 dḥ-dḥ 'to be low'
146370 s-ḳd-d 'to let sleep'— cf. 162650 ḳd-d 'sleep'
143240 s-ḫt-ḫt 'to drive back'— cf. 121510 ḫti̯, 121890 ḫt-ḫt 'to retreat'
150420 s-ḏwi̯ 'to slender'— cf. 182860 ḏw 'bad'; 91360 n-ḏwj·t 'defamation'
149370 s-ṯḥn 'to make bright'— cf. 176570 ṯḥn 'to be bright'
138250 s-n-šm-šm 'to sharpen'— cf. 88670 n-šm 'to cut off'
146770 s-km 'to make complete' — cf. 164370 km 'to complete'
133780 s-fḫ 'to loosen; to release'; 137390 s-n-fḫ-fḫ 'to loosen'— cf. 63970 fḫ, 63980 fḫ-ḫ 'to loosen'

2 The figures preceding the lexemes refer to the ID's in the TLA.
3 DRID for "ID of a Deep Root" of this lexicon.

Prefix n-, which is also attested in Afroasiatic comparison, is equally frequent.

It is true that in some cases a great number of lexemes can be found that are obviously derived from one and the same root, like dšr (DRID 1000280) 'to be / become red' with ca. 25 words dšr, or dšr·t, or dšr·w, etc., all of the semantic field 'red.' There are, however, many cases that do not show such a clear relationship, as the meaning of the lexemes does not prima vista seem to derive from that of the root in question. Their affinity to the posited root is less evident, or even – on the basis of our limited knowledge – not evident at all (and be it because we do not know the exact meaning of a word). Such examples of the root dšr are: a substance (med.); an oil; a tree and its wood; etc. However, little harm is done if they are joined to the other lexemes on suspicion, if their affinity can at least be imagined.

In not few cases the basic root can be subdivided into several categories. This can lead to recognition of homonyms, or quasi-homonyms, with a seemingly divergent meaning. For example, wsḫ 'to be(come) broad' is the nucleus of a clearly defined word family (e.g., verbal nouns, verbal adjectives, and other items). Lexemes, in which the basic meaning is clearly discernable, are: 49800 wsḫ 'to be wide; to be broad'; 400135 'broad; proud; famous'; 49820 'breadth; width'; 49850 wsḫ·t 'breadth.'

There are, however, also lexemes with a derived meaning whose basic meaning is still clearly discernable: 49830 wsḫ 'broad collar'; 49840 wsḫ 'barge'; 49860 wsḫ·t 'barge'; 49870 'broad hall, court'; 49940 'bowl'; etc.

The root wsḫ 'wide' (DRID 1002723) undoubtedly applies for all members of the family (add to this the Semitic correspondances, like Arabic wasiʕ 'wide'). To this list may have to be added items that are morphologically modified, e.g. with a root prefix like s-: 130740 swsḫ 'to widen; to extend'.

However, if the first consonant is the week sound w-, which proves to be unstable, the affiliation of the lexeme to the root is not so obvious anymore:

> 141540 sḫ·w 'breadth' (there is no certain ratio discernable why root-initial w- is preserved or lost).

Furthermore, such a truncated stem can be the base of other lexemes, including those with root prefix s-:

> 141550 sḫ·w 'courtyard'; 1341480 sḫ·t 'marshland; country,' hence 141500 sḫ·tj 'peasant'; 'fieldworker'; 'fowler.'
> 855127 ssḫ 'to widen; to extend' (it is a doublet of 130740 swsḫ)

As the given examples show, and as it has been attested in not few cases, the basic root ("deep root") can be subdivided into several categories (so-to-say "subroot"). This can lead to an understanding of homonyms with a seemingly divergent meaning. Thus, from wsḫ 'to become broad' derives sḫ·t 'marshland; country'; from this subcategory derives sḫ·tj 'peasant; fieldworker; fowler.' A direct derivation of sḫ·tj 'peasant' from wsḫ 'to become broad' would, on the other hand, remain inexplicable.

It is important to note that the root affixes present a problem for the identification of roots. It is crucial to distinguish affixes from root consonants. But not every word starting with s-, n-, d-, etc. contains the respective prefix: the consonant in question may equally well be the first consonant of the root. This is an issue that asks for a scrutinizing procedure and a critical attitude.

I.1 Reduplication of Root Consonants

In Egyptian, there are a number of verbs that are derived from two-radical verbal roots, by total reduplication, such as:

AB → AB-AB

> 136220 sn 'to join' | 138150 sn-sn 'to fraternize'

In this case, both verbs have been documented since the Pyramid Texts. In many other cases, the reduplicated stem is attested later than the base stem, e. g.

> 90910 nḏ 'to ask, to question' (since Pyr.) | 91600 nḏ-nḏ 'to ask for advice' (since Lit. MK).
> 119610 ḫr 'to fall' (since Pyr.) | 12042S0 ḫr-ḫr 'to destroy' (= 'to make fall'; Late Egyptian).
> 158990 ḳꜣ 'high' (since Pyr.) |159560 ḳꜣ-ḳꜣ 'to rise (of pylons)' (P. Harris I 4,1-2: nꜣy·s-bḫnw m jnr ḥr ḳꜣḳꜣ r ḥr·t 'their stone pylons rise to the sky'; Late Egn.).
> 37500 ꜥm 'to swallow' (since Pyr.) | 37810 ꜥm-ꜥm 'to devour' (late Ethiopian).

Examples such as the first show that this stem formation is already old and was laid out in the older stages of the language.

In addition to the total reduplication AB-AB, there is also a partial one, AB-A:AB: AB-A: AB-AB

However, it should be noted that the basic stem is not always attested. For example:

> *nk (cf. nk·t 'wound') | 89330 nk-n 'to injure', 'to suffer' | *nk-nk 'to injure' (cf. 89390 nk-nk·t 'injured eye').

As can be observed in the given example with AB-A, there is also a full reduplication AB-AB, which makes it plausible to posit a basic root *AB, even if no such verbal form appears in the texts. The same is true for 41120 ꜥš-ꜥ, 41130 ꜥš-ꜥš 'throat, 41140 ꜥš-ꜥš 'to choke'; 85860 n-hd-h 'trembling, horror'; 85870 n-hd-hd 'to tremble.'

If, on the other hand, neither a basic form AB nor a form AB-AB is attested for a verb of the root structure ABA, it is not appropriate to trace it back to a basic root AB. Such cases include the frequent verb 40110 ꜥḥꜥ 'to stand up', as also 87260 nḫn 'to be young', 168000 grg 'to establish'.

However, there is also a completely different type of partial reduplication, namely a doubling of only the second radical. The reduplication of type AB-A can be regarded as a truncated full reduplication AB-AB. The reduplication of type AB-B is, on the other hand, only the reduplication of the second consonant. It is here necessary to clarify whether we are indeed dealing with a lexical reduplication, or with a morphological one (ABB as reduplicated form of ABi̯ or AB).

AB: AB-B: AB-AB

> 63970 fḫ 'to loosen; 133780 s-fḫ 'to loosen, to release' | 63980 fḫ-ḫ 'to loosen'; 857662 s-fḫ-ḫ 'to solve, release'|*fḫ-fḫ; 137390 s-n-fḫ-fḫ 'to loosen, to release'.

165890 kt 'small' (cf. 600036 n-kt 'something of, a little', 89460 n-kt·w 'pieces': 165880 kt-t 'to be small' | kt-kt-šrj, name of a small dog (šrj 'small').

*ḳd 'to sleep'; cf. 162470 ḳd·t 'sleep' | 162650 ḳd-d 'to sleep'; cf. 89190 n-ḳd-d 'to sleep'; 146370 s-ḳd-d 'to make sleep.'

It may be mentioned, however, that otherwise the verbs IIae geminatae cannot be traced back to a two-radical root. Although the verbs ABB can also appear in the form AB, this can be explained by syncope. The subjunctive **ḳ(V)bá* 'so (that) will become cool' (> Copt. **-кво**), is ***ḳVbbá* from ****ḳVbVbá*. Until proven otherwise, the form ABB of verbs IIae geminatae must be regarded as the basic root of the respective verb. After all, compare the verb ḳbb 'to be cool' with the synonym ḳb-ḥ (apparently, a two-radical stem with ḥ-suffix).

Three-radical roots are the most frequently attested type of verbal roots. They are, however, often to be derived from two-radical ones by means of a root suffix. Among the examples that follow, there are ones with root suffix -n, -ᶜ, -b. In the cases where three-radical verbs correspond to reduplicated two-radical verbs (ABC ~ ABAB) the third consonant is either -n, or -ᶜ, or –b. It is here obviously a root suffix, and not a radical.

AB | AB-C (C = *n*/ᶜ/*b*) | AB-AB

The basic stem is often not – at least not as a verb – documented:

*sf | 133530 sf-ꜣ 'to hate'; 'to neglect; to be slow' | 133650 sf-n 'to cause trouble (phonetic variance ꜣ – n)
*ṯḥ (cf. 176530 ṯḥ·w 'joy') | 176580 ṯḥ-n 'to shine; to illuminate; to exhilarate'; 149370 s-ṯḥ-n 'to let shine' (sṯḥn ḥr 'to cheer someone up') | 90620 n-ṯḥ-ṯḥ 'to smile'.
* ᶜḏ | 42190 ᶜḏ-b 'to shout of joy, to rejoice' | 42160 ᶜḏ- ᶜḏ 'to shout of joy, rejoice loudly'.
*nm (cf. Semitic nwm 'to sleep') | 84220 nm-ᶜ 'to sleep' | *nm-nm 'to sleep'; cf. 84320 nm-nmw 'state of sleeping'.
*ẖꜣ: 113560 ẖꜣ-ᶜ 'to throw' | 114220 ẖꜣ-ẖꜣ 'to winnow'.

Partial reduplicating AB-A is also documented:

AB: AB-n | AB-A | AB-AB

142440 zẖ-n 'to happen' | 142990 zẖ-z 'to run, to hurry' | 143040 zẖ-zẖ, id.[4]

In addition to basic stems AB (two radicals) there are also IIIae infirmae stems ABi̯/u̯, which can be extended to new lexemes by reduplicating. The situation is very similar to that of the two-radicals. It should be noted here that the weak radical (i̯ or u̯) does not normally appear in the reduplicated forms.

4 This does not include 142970 sẖẖ 'to hurry through', because it is actually 141760 s-ẖꜣẖ, to 860497 ẖꜣẖ 'to go fast'.

ABi̯ (ABu̯) | ABAB.

146710 ski̯ 'to destroy'; cf. 146720 ski̯ 'to go down' | 147010 sk-sk 'to hack, to destroy'.
119 ꜣfi̯ 'to eat greedily' | 10420 ꜣf-ꜣf, id.
96210 ršu̯ 'to rejoice' | 96270 rš-rš, id.
85620 n-hm 'to shout'; 98380 hm 'cry of jubilation' | 98480 hm-hm 'to roar (bull)'; 85630 n-hm-hm 'to roar'; cf. the causative 137810 s-n-hm-hm 'to shout for joy'.
121510 ḫti̯ 'to recede'; 121890 ḫt-ḫt, id.; cf. the causative 143240 s-ḫt-ḫt 'to drive back.'
99480 htj 'to drill with a push drill' | 99500 ht-ht 'to drill a well'.
155490 šni̯ 'to dispute'; 88780 n-šni̯ 'to rage' | 88840 n-šn-šn 'to rage against someone'.
136590 zni̯ 'get close to' | 138190 zn-zn 'to split, to break' | 88210 n-zn-zn 'to detach completely (from)'.
166950 gbi̯ 'to become weak' | 167050 gb-gb 'to throw down.'
115570 ḫbi̯ 'to reduce' | 858554 ḫb-ḫb 'to push away'; 87190 n-ḫb-ḫb 'to open (the door); cf. the causative 137960 s-n-ḫb-ḫb 'to draw back (the door bolt)'.
46280 wni̯ 'to hurry; bypassing; not to pay attention' | 46490 wn-wn 'to move back and forth; wandering through.'

As with roots of two-radicals, there are very isolated forms with partial reduplication AB-A in the verbs IIIae infirmae.

ABi̯ | AB-A | AB-AB

37500 ꜥmi̯ 'to smear (a stopper)' | 37670 ꜥm-ꜥ 'to rub; to smear' | 37790 ꜥm-ꜥm, id.
155460 šni̯ 'to dispute'; 'to suppress a turmoil' | 156240 šn-š and 156260 šn-šn 'to destroy'.

Similar cases (AB-B and AB-n, respectively):

136590 zni̯ 'by; pass; separate (from)' | 137550 zn-n 'to pass' | 88200 n-zn-zn 'to pass away'.
153350 šbi̯ 'to mix; mix (under); to replace' | 153490 šb-n 'to mix' | 153570 šb-šb, id.

There are a very few attestations where the weak radical of a form ABi̯ is preserved in writing. In such cases the second and weak third radicals are duplicated.

ABi̯ | ABj-Bj

89200 nki̯[5] 'to copulate' | 89280 nkj-kj 'to fertilize (a female)'.

5 According to the identification of ϥ-ⲛⲁⲅⲧ in the Old-Coptic Schmidt papyrus, as *ϥⲛⲁⲕⲧ 'he cohabits with me,' the verb is *ⲛⲓⲕⲉ, therefore IIIae infirmae nki̯, rather than two-radical *nk, as is generally assumed.

98720 hni̯ ‘to rejoice’ | 98680 hnj-nj ‘to rejoice.’
82580 nbj ‘to be aflame’ | 82720 hbj-bj ‘to be hot’ (med.); probably denominal, from 82590 nbj ‘flame.’

There is another verb of this reduplicated structure: 141020 sḥj-ḥj ‘to scour, to roam’ (?); however, no suitable simplex verb seems to be attested.

With some stem formations of IIIae infirmae roots, the second radical can be reduplicated. Here, the weak third radical is omitted. The same applies if the root is enlarged by a suffix, like -n, instead of the reduplication.

ABi̯; ABC (C = n): AB-B | AB-AB

153350 šbi̯ ‘to mix’; 153490 šb-n ‘to mix’ | 153430 šb-b ‘to mix together’ | 153570 šb-šb ‘to mix’.

The total reduplication of a strong three-radical root is rarely attested.

ABC: ABC-ABC

500020 nḏm ‘to be sweet, pleasant’ | 91590 nḏm-nḏm ‘to have sexual intercourse’; cf. 91580 nḏm-nḏm ‘sexual pleasure’.
112780 ḥḏn ‘to be unwilling; to be annoying; to resist’ | 859147 ḥḏn-ḏn, 112810 ḥḏn-ḥḏn ‘to be unwilling’ (?)
182120 ḏꜣf ‘to burn’ | 182140 ḏꜣf-ḏꜣf ‘to burn someone’.

The basic root of n-ḥr-n-ḥr ‘to rejoice’ has two radicals (AB), as the following derivation of the type AB-AB shows: ḥr-ḥr ‘to rejoice’. Thus, there is the full reduplication of an n-stem *n-ḥr. Similar is n-ḏd-n-ḏd ‘duration,’ but here the basic root is IIIae infirmae: ḏdi̯ ‘to last’.

The most common extension of three radical roots is through a reduplication of the second and third radicals.

ABC | ABC-BC

86830 nẖꜣ ‘to bristle up (of female breasts)’ | 86880 nẖꜣ-ẖꜣ, id.; causative 137940 s-nẖꜣ-ẖꜣ ‘to delight (heart)’.
143250 sẖd ‘to be upside down’ | 143310 sẖd-ẖd, id.
163340 kꜣp ‘to hide’ | 163490 kꜣp-ꜣp ‘to hide, to cover’.
59960 pn^{c} ‘to turn’ (doublet 60090 pnz, basic meaning ‘to twist’) | 60010 pn^{c}-n^{c} ‘to turn several times, turn around one’s own axis’.
88670 nšm ‘to cut off’: *nšm-šm ’to cut well (knife)’; causative 138250 s-nšm-šm ‘to sharpen (teeth)’.
98720 hni̯ ‘to rejoice’ | 98680 hnj-nj ‘to rejoice.
101610 ḫꜣg ‘to be glad’ | 101630 ḫꜣgꜣg, 107340 ḫngg ‘to rejoice’ (with variation ꜣ : n); Coptic ϩⲗⲟϭ ‘to take delight’, which shows the basic L sound.
1001226 km ‘to complete’; 1001226 s-km ‘to make complete’ | *s-km-km, id.; see m s-km-km ‘totally’.
177620 dꜣ ‘to tremble’; 149660 s-dꜣ, id. | 149690 s-dꜣ-dꜣ, id.

In a derived lexeme, combinations of more than one of these phenomena may be extant.

Total or partial reduplication, prefix n-, prefix s-:

162450 ḳdd 'to sleep': 89190 n-ḳdd, id.: 146370 s-ḳdd 'to make sleep'
63970 fẖ 'to loosen': 137390 s-n-fẖfẖ, id.; basically 'to cause to become loose'

I.1.2 The significance of reduplication

The semantic aspect of root reduplication is inconsistent. In some cases, the root has an intensive meaning: 'to swallow' > 'to devour' (DRID 1002994 ꜥm); 'to think' > 'to plan, to think' (DRID 1002758 wꜣ); 'to turn around' > pnꜥnꜥ 'to turn several times' (plurality; DRID 1001788 pnꜥ). In some cases, the meaning is causative: 'to fall' > 'to make fall' (DRID 1000706 ẖr); 'to hide' > 'to hide, to cover' (DRID 1001277 kꜣp). In many other cases, the dictionaries give for the reduplicated form the same meaning as for the simple form; however, in-depth philological efforts can often prove a nuance of intensity or plurality.[6]

Intensity:

64220 fd 'to wipe, to wipe away'— 64300 fd-fd 'to apply (ointment)'
158990 ḳꜣ 'high'— 159560 ḳꜣ- ḳꜣ 'to tower up (of pylons).'
136590 zni̯ 'to redeem (from evil); to separate'— 1002819 zn-zn 'to split, break';
1002819 n-zn-zn 'to detach' completely.
89200 nki̯ 'to copulate' — 89280 nkj-kj 'to impregnate'
115410 ẖb 'to destroy'; 115490 ẖb-ꜣ 'to destroy; to diminish' — 115760 ẖb-ẖb 'to slay'.
90760 n-db 'to drink' — 178940 db-db 'to slurp (blood)'.

Plurality of contents:

98020 hbu̯ 'to enter (place)' — 98200 hb-hb 'to transgress'.
46280 wni̯ 'to hurry' — 46490 wn-wn 'to move back and forth'.
60920 pri̯ 'to come out, go out' — 61220 pr-pr 'to jump around'.
69720 mn 'to displace' — 70710 mn-mn 'to move'; 84330 n-mn-mn 'to go here and there; cf. 70730 mn-mn·t 'herd; cattle'.
113560 ẖꜣ-ꜥ 'to throw' — 114220 ẖꜣ-ẖꜣ 'to winnow'.
59960 pnꜥ 'to turn around' — 60010 pnꜥ-nꜥ 'to turn several times, to turn around its own axis'.

6 The semantic characteristics of intensity and causativity (i.e. characteristics of the Semitic D-stems) can be reconciled by the concept of plurality. Intensity of meaning implies a plurality of the process (iterative, frequentative, etc.), or a plurality of actants (agents and/or patients). In the case of causativity, the number of actants is increased by exactly one, namely an 'over-agent', to which the basic agent is assigned as patient: 'he lives': 1 actant; 'I revive him': 2 actants; whereas in 'You (pl.) drink a cup of water' there are 2 actants (1 agent, *you*, and 1 patient, *cup of water*), in 'He will make you drink a cup of water' (cf. ⲡⲉⲧⲛⲁⲥⲉ ⲧⲏⲩⲧⲛ̄ ⲛ̄ⲟⲩⲁⲡⲟⲧ ⲙ̄ⲙⲟⲟⲩ Mk. 9, 41), there are 3 actants, *he, you, cup of water*. Passivation, on the other hand, reduces the number of actants by eliminating the agent and conferring the subject position to the patient. 'You drink the cup of water': 2 actants, *you, cup of water;* 'the cup of water is drunk': 1 actant, *cup of water*.

Causative/factitive:

> 50040 wš 'to be empty, to be destroyed' — 50310 wš-wš 'to smash, break up'.
> 119610 ẖr 'to fall' — 120420 ẖr-ẖr 'to destroy'.
> 105920 ḥn 'to be fresh' — 106960 ḥn-ḥn 'to maintain the vitality'.
> 66940 mꜣwi̯ 'to renew yourself' — 67140 mꜣ-mꜣwi̯ 'to renew'.
> 163340 kꜣp 'to hide' — 163490 kꜣp-ꜣp 'to hide, cover'.

Reflexive or passive:

> 85210 nh 'to shake' — 85660 nh-nh 'to quake (of fear)' (cf. tꜣ r-ḏr·f ḥr nhnh n snḏ n jdt·f 'the whole country trembles (is shaking) for fear of his wrath').

In respect to reduplication one must beware of confounding lexical and morphological reduplication (the latter wrongly called *gemination* in traditional Egyptological terminology). Thus, lexical reduplication has no bearing on morphological categories, whereas morphological reduplication may be incompatible with other morphological features. šspp ꜥ·f 'his arm will be seized' is passive and cannot therefore be sḏm·n·f in the same time. s-fẖfẖ, in s-fẖfẖ·n Gb 'Geb has totally released,' is a lexical reduplication (deep root fẖ 'to loosen') and nothing prevents it from assuming a TAM form like sḏm·n·f.[7]

I.2 Initial root consonants j and w

Roots with initial consonants *j* and *w* display special features.[8] Initial j- may be a verbal morphological prefix, particularly in Old Egyptian and in Late Egyptian. It may also replace an initial ꜣ- in spelling (especially in the Graeco-Roman period, like jẖjẖ for ꜣẖꜣẖ, 'to shine'), or it may be a root prefix (cf. doublets like jꜥr ~ ꜥr, 'to mount up'). Furthermore, -jꜣ- may alternate with -ꜥ- (jꜣš ~ ꜥš 'to call, to read'), etc.

Initial w- may get lost in some forms, as in sẖ·t 'width,' of wsẖ 'to be wide' (by the way, an isogloss with Arabic, which here even has, by chance, the same root: سعة *siʿa*^{tun} 'width' ~ وسِع *wasiʿa* 'he was wide')

---

7 "However, there is no general ban on the combination of a reduplicated stem with TAM markers, since pluractionals [= 4-rad. verbs of pattern ABAB] are compatible with the Perfect suffix -n" (Bendjaballah & Reintges 2009: 136). That would mean, in the usual terminology: verbs of a stem with root reduplication are just verbs as any other, they may display the same forms as others (and can accordingly form a sḏm·n·f or any other TAM-form).

8 About two thirds of the Egyptian verbal roots have three root consonants, or radicals (most others are roots of two consonants). In numerous cases the third consonant is a weak one – if the third consonant is weak it is transcribed as i̯, u̯; if the verb shows, however, the morphology of a strong verb, the third consonant is rendered as j, w).The typical infinitive and stative forms of the IIIae infirmae verbs display vocalizations that are different from the strong verbs (infinitive, stative 3ms): strong verb, sḏm: sāḏam, satpu, but weak verb, msi̯: mīsit, masu. When weak verbs develop derived stems, the weak consonants are usually disregarded: n-šni̯ 'to rage' (intrans.); n-šn-šn 'to rage against someone (r)' (intrans.) – šni̯ 'to quarrel' (cf. the transitive verb šni̯ ẖ.t 'to argue about sth.' = 'to litigate'); 'subjugate'; šn-šn 'to destroy.'

I.3 Various linguistic changes

The conservative nature of the Egyptian script will obscure phonetic changes to a certain extent. The reader must nevertheless be aware of them, as certain phenomena are not explicable otherwise. The history of the Egyptian language is the background story of the phonetic development. Some important innovations go obviously back to the later part of the fourth millennium, the late prehistoric period, or the Third Naqāda ('Negade') period. It is then that the palatalization of the velar sounds began – a process that lasted obviously in parts until the end of the Old Kingdom. The earliest coherent texts, among them the Pyramid Texts, are from the Late Old Kingdom (Dynasties 5–6). Some innovations appear in the Late Old Kingdom and the following First Intermediate Period. In particular, the direct speeches of the estate personnel and others (kind of speech balloons) in the mastaba tombs of the Old Kingdom show occasionally first traces of Later Egyptian (Late Egyptian, Demotic, Coptic); some such features appear also in literary texts of the late Middle Kingdom, like the definite article.

At the beginning of the Middle Kingdom (Dynasties 11 to 13) there is obviously an endeavour to bring the language back to the high standards of the Old Kingdom, which seems to have been regarded as classical. On the other hand, the spoken language had developed further on in the meantime.

After the Second Intermediate Period, in the early New Kingdom (Dynasty 18), the language of the Middle Kingdom was being cultivated. Nevertheless, traces of the vernacular language began to appear in the texts. The break through happened in the Amarna period, towards the end of the Dynasty 18, when under Pharaoh Amenhotep IV Akhenaten Egypt had to subordinate to the new state doctrine of a crass naturalism – extended even to the language: it had to become adapted to the spoken idiom. The result is a language called 'Late Egyptian' (also, 'Neo-Egyptian').

In the meantime, a lot had happened that influenced the language. In the Second Intermediate Period a West Semitic population from Northern Syria, that settled in the Eastern Delta, had acquired the rule over Egypt (Hyksos kings, Dynasty 15). From this time on, many foreign things made their first appearance in Egypt, like the horse and the horse-driven chariot, numerous crops (apple, pomegranate etc.), and with them their terms entered the Egyptian language – they are mostly of Canaanite (hence Semitic) origin.

I.4 Palatalisation of velars

During the long history of Egyptian language, which is just briefly outlined here, numerous important changes occurred. A lexicon that covers a time span of several thousand years must cope with substantial sound changes in the language. Phonemes do not always have the same realization at different periods and/or in different areas or idioms.

In many, though not all cases, the velar stops k, ḳ, and g very early became palatal affricates, namely ṯ (= č), ḏ (= ç̌), and again ḏ. There are, however, cases where the older form was also preserved in some function, like kb·wj 'foot soles' displaying a root kb that is a variant of that of ṯbw, ṯbw·t, ṯb·t, with a similar meaning. The problem for the root lexicon is that one will not find kb·wj on the same page of the dictionary as the realisations of root ṯb. Such phonetic doublets, involving palatalization and its absence, are found with all velar sounds. They are most numerous for ẖ versus ḏ, and for ẖ versus š. In the rare cases where both palatalized and non-palatalized consonants are attested this may be indicated as kb = ṯb.

86760 nẖ 'to protect' versus 90940 nḏ, id. — the deep root is noted as nẖ = nḏ (DRID 1001552)

154890 šmm 'to become hot' versus * ẖmm, id. (cf. Coptic ϧⲙⲟⲙ / ϩⲙⲟⲙ, id.) — the deep root is noted as šmm = *ẖmm (DRID 1002159).

I.5 Doublets

Phonetic doublets are pairs of words wherefrom one part shows a root consonant in a modified form. It is probable that they resulted from sound changes that did not affect the whole linguistic area, so that the older articulation persisted in dialectal forms. An important phenomenon is the process of palatalisation of velar occlusives that obviously took place in the centuries around and after the beginning of Egyptian dynastic history.

k : ṯ (= č)

Pronoun =k (2sm) : =ṯ (2sf), =ṯn (2p)
sk, Old Kingdom form of sṯ, jsṯ
kw, Old Kingdom variant of ṯw
kb·wj 'soles (of foot)': ṯb·w, ṯb·wt, id.
nk·t 'fetter': nṯ 'to tie up,' jnṯ 'to fetter', jnṯ·t 'fetter'

ḳ : ḏ (= ç̣)

dḳw 'flour': dḏw 'to mill'
ḳn 'to thresh' : ḏn, id.
ḳnb 'to bind; to bend; to subjugate' : ḏnb 'to be crooked'; 'to deflect'
sḳr 'to strike' : sḳr written with the determinative of sḏr 'to lie down'

g : ḏ

gnẖ 'wing' : ḏnḥ 'wing'[9]
gꜣf 'to bake' : ḏꜣf 'to burn,' ḏꜣfḏꜣf, id.
wg 'plank'[10] : wḏ, wḏy·t, a wooden part of the ship
wgꜣ 'inundation' (read wg ?) : wḏnw 'flood' (perhaps with variation ꜣ : n)
gn 'twig',[11] Coptic B ϭⲁⲗ, id.
gꜣb·t, Coptic ϭⲱⲱⲃⲉ, 'leaf' : ḏbꜣ·w 'leaves'[12]

ẖ : š

ẖꜥḳ 'to shave' : šꜥḳ, Pyr. Text spelling of ẖꜥḳ
mẖn.t 'ferry-boat' : mšn.t, Pyr. Text spelling variant of mẖn.t
ẖkr 'to decorate' : škr, Pyr. Text spelling of ẖkr
ẖꜣ·t 'corps' : šꜣ·t, Pyr. Text spelling of ẖꜣ·t
*zẖꜣ, Coptic sẖai (B ⲥϧⲁⲓ, A ⲥϩⲉⲓ), 'to write' zš(ꜣ), rare phonetic spelling of *zẖꜣ
*ẖmm, Coptic ẖmom (B ϧⲙⲟⲙ, A ϩⲙⲁⲙ), 'to become warm'
nẖ 'to spit; spittle' : ꜣš 'to spit' (with variation ꜣ : n); nš 'spittle'

9 Cf. Arab. ǵanāḥ, id.
10 Spelling wgꜣ only NK.
11 Late Egn. ḏ-l (spelt ḏ-nr)
12 Since Dynasty 18; read ḏ(ꜣ)b·w

ẖ : ḏ (= č̣)

nẖ ‘to protect’ : nḏ ‘to protect
ʿẖ ‘to burn’ : ‘brazier’ ʿḏ ‘to burn’; ‘brazier’
wꜣẖi̯ ‘to become green’ : wꜣḏ ‘to become green’
wꜣẖy ‘colonnade’ : wꜣḏ ‘column’; wꜣḏy·t ‘colonnade’
mẖꜣ ‘to make fast; to bind; rope’ : mḏꜣ ‘to fetter’?
ẖꜣm ‘troops’ : ḏꜣm ‘troops, youth’

ẖ : š

zẖz ‘to tear out’ zšš ‘to tear out’
ẖfʿ ‘to grasp’ : šfd ‘to grasp’ (with variation ʿ: d)
sꜣẖ ‘to repuls’ : sꜣš ‘to repuls’
ẖpt ‘to be discontented; discontent’ : špt ‘to be angry’
ẖpw, spelling variant of špw ‘blindness’
jẖ·t ‘thing’ jš ·t·f, Old Kingdom spelling of ‘his thing’

The oscillation between š and ẖ is not only a matter of sound change but also of development of the hieroglyphic script. The Pyramid Texts have <š> (represented by the one-consonant sign 𓈙 or any of the two- or three-consonant signs that contain this consonant) in several cases where later texts have 𓄡 <ẖ>. This has led Egyptology to the erroneous assumption that 𓄡 <ẖ> is the symbol of a phoneme of palatal articulation [ç], similar to that of 𓈙 <š> [ʃ]. Studies in Early dynastic spellings have shown, however, that hieroglyph 𓄡 <ẖ> is a late-comer. In early and traditional texts, 𓈙 <š> is not used for š [ʃ], but rather for the ẖ phoneme, with its original phonetic value [x]. But at Early dynastic times, the phoneme ẖ [x] became palatalized to turn into [ʃ] in many cases (parallel to k becoming ṯ [c], etc.). A new sign was created for the cases where the old velar articulation persisted (we do not seem to know the conditions for this): 𓄡 <ẖ> now served for the value [x],[13] whereas 𓈙 <š> was now exclusively used for rendering the new [ʃ] sound. By the way, in the second wave of palatalization, in pre-Coptic times, the remaining <ẖ> phoneme was not to become palatalized (whereas <ẖ> usually reappears as a [ʃ] sound in most Coptic idioms). This development, partly graphic, partly phonetic, has to be studied separately from the question of root doublets, with ẖ and š, respectively, like ẖpꜣ ‘navel’, and its spelling in the Pyramid Texts, <špꜣ>.

I.6 Debuccalisation

Debuccalisation is a sound change in which an oral consonant leaves its original place of articulation, and moves towards the glottis (typically [h], [ɦ], or [ˀ]; here, in Egyptian, [ʿ] and [ˀ].

13 Hence, 𓄡 <ẖ> is phonetic [x], whereas 𓐍 <ḫ> is originally voiced, phonetic [ɣ]. Cf. correspondances like Egyptian wsẖ and Semitic wšʿ, both ‘to be broad,’ with a voiced laryngeal. NB In Egyptian the laryngeals merged with the velars, whereas in Aramaic and Hebrew the velars merged with the laryngeals.

Debuccalisation of Dentals / Alveolars to ꜥ

d (=ṭ) : ꜥ

db ‘horn’ ꜥb, id.
dbdb ‘to pound (of the heart)’ : ꜥbb ‘to knock (on door)’ (root √db)
šfd ‘to grasp’ : ẖfꜥ, id. (with variation ẖ : š)

s/ts : ꜥ

pnz ‘to distort’ : pnꜥ ‘to turn around’; pnꜥnꜥ ‘to rotate’
jz ‘tomb’ : jꜥ, id.
zbš ‘to drown’ : ꜥbš, id.

r : ꜥ

ḏrb·t ‘charcoal’: ḏꜥb·t, id.
ḏḥr ‘leather’ ḏḥꜥ, id.

Debuccalisation of Velars / Laryngeals to j

g : j

pꜥg ‘to spit’ (doublet of psg) : pꜥi̯ ‘to spit’

ḳ : j

ḳbḥ 1) ‘to become cool’; jbḥ ‘to sprinkle water’
2) ‘to pour a libation’ jbḥ·w ‘libationer
ḳnd ‘to rage; to be come angry’ : jnd ‘to be vexed; to be sad’

ẖ : j

snwẖ ‘to cook’ : snw(i̯?) ‘to cook’
ẖnm ‘to become friendly’ : jꜣm ‘to become pleasant’ (with variation ꜣ : n)

ẖ : j

s(w)tẖ, god Seth : swti̯, id.

“Debuccalisation” describes a type of process, or rather its result, but it is not an explanation for it. In Egyptian, the situation is rather complex, as it involves dialectal differences. In some area of Predynastic Egyptian, the Proto-Egyptian consonants remained as they were: *the conservative dialect*. In others – in the idiom that was to become the standard, which also means: for which the hieroglyphic writing was being developed – the voiced stops and fricatives underwent grave changes: *the progressive dialect*. An important change concerned the voiced stops. *b* obviously became [β], as it is probably still in Coptic. Consequently, d and g should have become [ð] and [ɣ], respectively. But the development did not stop at that: the articulation of [ð] moved backward to [ʕ], and that of [ɣ] probably to [ˀ] (spelled <j> or <i̓>).

What is spelled <d>, <ḏ>, and <g> in hieroglyphic – hence looking in their transcriptions like voiced consonants – is not what it suggests: not voiced sounds, but probably glottalised “emphatics,” necessarily unvoiced (glottalisation is only possible with lax vocal cords, hence with unvoiced consonants). Some scholars who are aware of this, like W. Schenkel, transcribe them as ṭ and ç̣ instead of d and ḏ, respectively.

What is spelled <ẖ>, on the other hand, is originally not an unvoiced fricative [x], but rather its voiced counterpart, [ɣ] (typically corresponding to Semitic *^{c} or *ġ=ɣ): it was only about the time of the beginning of the Middle Kingdom that it was realised as voiceless [x].

It seems to have occurred that words of the conservative idiom were loaned into the standard language. They may have contained phonemes that do not exist anymore in the progressive idiom, so the next-similar phoneme had to be chosen.

From the lexemes ᶜ3b 'to offer' (ᶜ3b·t 'offerings' already in the Pyramid Texts), d3p 'to offer' (Pyramid Texts), and drp, id. (from MK onward), we can reconstruct an original root *dlb 'to offer' (on the Semitic side, one may compare Arabic ṭalaf^{un}, 'present'). This remained as such in the conservative idiom, but developed into ᶜ3b [^{c}-$^{?}$-β] in the progressive idiom. For some reason or other, the conservative form *dlb was loaned by the progressive idiom. However, this did not possess a phoneme /d/ (which had become /^{c}/), nor a phoneme /l/ (which had become /$^{?}$/), nor a phoneme /b/ (which had become /β/); the next-best choice was /ṭ/ (transcribed d anyway) for /d/, and /p/ for /b/. As for /l/, the pyramid Texts write <3> (obviously pronounced [l] or [r] in this corpus), whereas later literacy spelled it with <r>: d3p, later drp.

I.7 The Aleph problem

Other phonetic doublets involve an equally substantial sound change. It has long been observed that <3>, generally assumed to be the expression of a glottal stop, quite often stands in an etymological relationship to Semitic *l* or *r*. As late as in the execration texts of the Middle Kingdom, the Egyptian <3> graphemes are clearly used to render Canaanite *l* and *r* (as in  3wš3mm = (u)rušalimum 'Jerusalem'). On the other hand, <3> is clearly the expression of a weak sound, like the glottal stop [ʔ]. On this background it is not unexpected that there are doublets where <3> in one item corresponds to <r> in the other. More numerous are, however, the doublets that contrast <3> in one item to <n> in the other; in these cases, hieroglyph 𓈖 obviously represents the l sound, whereas 𓄿 may be the expression of a sound like the glottal stop [ʔ]. Examples:

> d3p 'to offer' | 180220 drp, id. (cf. Arabic طَلَفَ ṭalafa 'he presented') — the deep root is noted as d3p = drp (DRID 1000271).
> 159240 ḳ3b 'to fold over': 161330 ḳnb (=ḳlb) 'to bind; to bend; to subjugate' (cf. Arabic قَلَبَ qalaba 'he turned around') — the deep root is noted as ḳ3b = ḳnb (DRID 1001884).

If a word is attested partly with 3, partly with n or with r, respectively, the deep root will here be noted by both of them, as in "b3 = bn 'to erect."

I.8 The Ayin problem

Another type of doublets is in conformity with O. Rössler's well-founded thesis that Egyptian ʿ reflects Proto-Afroasiatic/Hamito-Semitic alveolar and dental sounds, including d, z, ð. Actually, arguments have in the meantime been forwarded for assuming that Egyptian ᶜ does phonetically correspond in some words to Semitic d, z, or ð, in others however to Semitic ᶜAyin. In the New Kingdom it was normally realized as some kind of ᶜAyin. Semitic ᶜ is, according to all we know, not essentially different from what it is, e.g., in Arabic: a voiced laryngeal fricative. When, in the New Kingdom, a Semitic word with ᶜ is taken over by Egyptian, it is rendered by Egyptian <ᶜ>, as in 41770 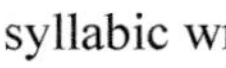 ᶜgrt 'wagon' (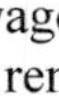, the Late Egyptian spelling of the word ᶜ3 'big,' serves in the syllabic writing to render ᶜAyin plus vowel).

I.9 The structure of the root lexicon

The raw material for this work is the Egyptian lexicon. It is most completely recorded – as far as it is attested at all in modern works – in the Thesaurus Linguae Aegyptiae (TLA) of the Berlin Academy of Sciences, in the frame of the project "Strukturen und Transformationen des Wortschatzes der ägyptischen Sprache. Text- und Wissenskultur im Alten Ägypten" (formerly Ägyptisches Wörterbuch). It contains the most complete collection of data of the printed Wörterbuch, plus many additional bibliographical data, plus many new items from these, etc.

The list of Egyptian lexical roots (i.e., the deep roots) established here is based on a perusal of the complete Egyptian lexicon. Wherever it can be ascertained that there is more than one reflex of a particular root, the basic form (deep root) was identified. All derived roots are determined in respect to the type of derivation and the semantic character. There are, of course, many cases where it is not cogent that a root is derived from another one, or what is the root of a given lexeme, or what is the meaning of a given root. A case in question are many of the assumed derivations by means of the "ancient" affixes, as mentioned above, of which the affix character is often still waiting to be proven by exactly this kind of evidence, viz. of a root inventory.

The lexemes are identified by the ID (unique digital marker), as is established in the TLA. Facing the vast orthographic diversity and having in mind that the lexeme is not the main focus of our work (but is just the source corpus for extracting roots) we refer to the lexemes by the TLA ID for all further information, like hieroglyphic spelling (in its major variants), nuances of meaning, earliest attestations and bibliography, data that can be easily retrieved from the TLA[14] via the ID. This data base provides the full wealth of the Wörterbuch slips (on which the Berlin dictionary is based), apart from the bibliography, enriched for all the items provided, inter alia, by the TLA studies of the past years, etc. It needs to be mentioned that the present dictionary is based on the material of the TLA. There are a few cases where recent research has yielded arguments for a different reading in some cases. This includes the reading of tp 'head' as dp,[15] and the reading of mr 'pyramid' as mḥr.[16] Etymologies of šmᶜ and mḥ.wj, "Upper resp. Lower Egypt," are plausibly explained (as "narrow" and "full" = "broad") by R. Müller-Wollermann[17] and W. Schenkel.[18] In a forthcoming online data base these data will be mentioned under

14 TLA: https://aaew.bbaw.de/tla/index.html.
15 Werning 2004; Peust 2006.
16 Quack 2003b; Collombert 2010.
17 Müller-Wollermann 1987.
18 Schenkel 2005.

"Remarks." Here, however, we refrained from replacing the traditional readings by new ones since our corpus is the TLA.

In assigning roots to given lexemes, there is a strong temptation to subsuming in an uncritical way as many lexemes as possible under one root. However, one should here critically and realistically proceed in regard to the meaning. For the present work, we operated with two classes of roots: a "deep root", and a not-so-deep subroot, intermediary between the lexeme and the deep root. Even if the deep root and the not-so-deep root are identical in many cases, this concept offers a possibility to differentiate between a truly abstract root and a more concrete subcategory (cf. the following).

- TLA ID 143230 sẖt·w 'meat of snared wild-fowl' (?); this is obviously derived from
- RID (= Root ID) 0002350 sẖt 'to trap,' for its part derived from
- DRID (= Deep Root ID) 1002104 sẖt 'to make ready,' (yielding inter alia lexeme TLA ID 854548 sẖt, id.)

Both deep roots and subroots are marked by numerical identifiers (that is DRID and RID) which are both assigned to the respective lexeme by this dictionary. Consequently, the root lexicon data are organized upon three different identity numbers: TLA ID for every single lexeme (this ID is taken over from TLA), RID consisting of 7 digits starting with 0, marking the subroot, and DRID also consisting of 7 digits starting with 1, referring to the deep root.

There are arguments for assuming that a reduplication form ABAB is based upon an unreduplicated root, viz. AB. Accordingly, reduplication is normally shown in the subroot only, but not in the deep root.

The prefixes are also not marked, neither in deep nor in subroot. There are verbs which are attested, so far, just as causatives, with prefix s-. In such cases, the envisaged – although non-attested – simplex is marked in the deep root field with the asterisk *. The same rule applies for verbal nouns whose verbal root is not attested.

Hapax legomena words are often isolates – they don't share their root with other attested words. In this case they are excluded from the lexicon, though with two exceptions: when a given lexeme (although hapax) indisputably could be linked with an established deep root, and also in the case of Semitic lexemes. Purely grammatical elements are also excluded.

On the other hand, we completely refrained from rendering account of the "prehistory" of the roots: we completely ignored their Afroasiatic etymologies. In spite of all endeavours in this field, in the course of many decades of research, this field is still not ripe for an exploitation of this ultimate character. Hopefully, studies on the roots like the present one will pave the road for such endeavour.

I.9.1 Instructions for readers

The core entries of the lexicon, that is the deep roots, are arranged numerically. Within the first line of the main entry, a reader will find 1) the numerical marker of the deep root (DRID 1xxxxxx), 2) transliteration, and 3) meaning.

1) **DRID 1001215** 2) kfi̯ 3) to open

The subsequent line of the main entry provides 1) the numerical marker of the subroot (RID 0xxxxxx), 2) transliteration, and 3) meaning.

1) **RID 0001387** 2) kfi̯ 3) to open

What follows is the list of lexemes. Every lexeme is provided with 1) TLA ID, 2) transliteration and 3) meaning. E.g.:

1) ID Lexeme 164100 2) kf 3) knife

In cases where several subroots are identified within a deep root, the sub-entries are clearly marked:

DRID 1001226 **km to complete**

RID 0001403	km to complete			
	ID Lexeme	164370	km	to complete
		164380	km	completion; duty; profit
		164450	km.t	completion; final account?
		164580	kmy.t	conclusion (of a book)
		146770	skm	to make complete; to finish
RID 0001404	km to grow old			
	ID Lexeme	146790	skm	balding; greying (of the hair)
		146780	skm	to grow old; to be wise
		869969	skm	gray-haired one
		501142	skm.w	gray-haired one
		146830	skm.yw	The old ones
RID 0001405	kmkm destruction			
	ID Lexeme	65650	skmkm	destruction

I.10 Conclusion

Lexicography of a dead language is struggling with considerable difficulties, since the only means for determining form and semantics of a word is the analysis of the texts in which it occurs. In a dead language this process is much less direct and more complicated than in a living language, with native speakers and possibly indigenous traditions of linguistic analysis, grammatical or lexicographical.

Knowledge of the history of a word and its family is helpful in determining its exact meaning. In addition to its practical aspect, lexicography has also a theoretical (philosophical) aspect: the roots as an integral part of the lexicon. Furthermore, knowledge of the roots (and comparison with roots in related languages) is a means to elucidate phenomena in social anthropology and social history.

II Roots

II.1 ꜣ

DRID	**1001022**		**ꜣ not**		
	RID	**0003206**	ꜣ not		
		ID Lexeme	3	ꜣ	[particle of negation]
DRID	**1001737**		**ꜣwr = nwr to tremble**		
	RID	**0003267**	ꜣwr to tremble		
		ID Lexeme	856496	ꜣwr, ꜣwj	trembling
			55	ꜣwr	to tremble
	RID	**0001939**	nwr to tremble		
		ID Lexeme	81340	nwr	to shake; to tremble
			136830	snwr	to make tremble (med.) (or similar)
DRID	**1002864**		**ꜣ moment**		
	RID	**0003205**	ꜣ moment		
		ID Lexeme	6	ꜣ.t	strength
			5	ꜣ.t	moment; instant; time
DRID	**1002865**		**ꜣ vulture**		
	RID	**0003207**	ꜣ vulture		
		ID Lexeme	1	ꜣ	vulture; bird (gen.)
DRID	**1002866**		**ꜣb family**		
	RID	**0003208**	ꜣb family		
		ID Lexeme	67	ꜣb.t	family
			88	ꜣb.tjw	household; family member
DRID	**1002867**		**ꜣb to cease to do**		
	RID	**0003210**	ꜣb to cease to do		
		ID Lexeme	858405	ꜣb	to avoid; to have ceased
			852472	ꜣb	to cease to do (aux./modal)
			856201	ꜣb	to cease; to avoid; to tarry
			72	ꜣb	to cease; to separate; to avoid; to linger
			79	ꜣb.w	cessation
			400754	jꜣb	to draw back (from); to avoid
			126630	sꜣb	to make tarry
DRID	**1002868**		**ꜣb to mark**		
	RID	**0003209**	ꜣb to brand		
		ID Lexeme	10270	ꜣb	fingernail
	RID	**0003211**	ꜣbb to keep apart		

		ID Lexeme	85	ꜣbb	to separate; to move away; to keep apart
	RID	0003216	ꜣbu̯ to brand		
		ID Lexeme	61	ꜣb.w	brand; branding iron
			66	ꜣb.t	brand
			60	ꜣbu̯	to brand (cattle, slaves)
DRID	**1002869**		**ꜣbd month**		
	RID	**0003211**	ꜣbd month		
		ID Lexeme	93	ꜣbd	month
			95	ꜣbd	[a priest serving for the lunar month]
			500043	ꜣbd	Abed (one of those who support the heavenly cow)
			96	ꜣbd	Abed (the moon)
			94	ꜣbd.w	Abedu (festival on the 2nd day of the lunar month)
			99	ꜣbd.w	Abedu (2nd day of the lunar month)
			97	ꜣbd.w	monthly
DRID	**1002870**		**ꜣbẖ to mix**		
	RID	**0003212**	ꜣbẖ to mix		
		ID Lexeme	91	ꜣbẖ	to mingle; to unite
			90	ꜣbẖ	to link; to be linked
			89	ꜣbẖ	to mix; to join; to be merged with
			359	ꜣbẖ	to burn; to cook
			450623	ꜣbẖ	linker
			92	ꜣbẖ.t	[a med. liquid]
DRID	**1002871**		**ꜣbi̯ to wish**		
	RID	**0003213**	ꜣbi̯ to be glad		
		ID Lexeme	126640	sꜣbi̯	to gladden (the heart)
			10310	ꜣbꜣb	to be delighted
	RID	**0003214**	ꜣbi̯ to wish		
		ID Lexeme	73	ꜣbi̯	to wish for; to covet
			10340	ꜣb.w	wish; vow
			84	ꜣb.wt	appearance; aspect
			68	ꜣb.t	wish(es); vow?
DRID	**1002872**		**ꜣbj leopard**		
	RID	**0003215**	ꜣbj leopard		
		ID Lexeme	74	ꜣbj	leopard
			75	ꜣbj.t	female leopard
DRID	**1002873**		**ꜣbw [medical substance]**		
	RID	**0003217**	ꜣbw [medical substance]		

ID Lexeme	82	ꜣbw	[a med. substance]	

DRID 1002874 ꜣbw elephant

RID 0003218 ꜣbw elephant

ID Lexeme	80	ꜣbw	elephant
	63	ꜣbw	tusk; ivory

DRID 1002875 ꜣd to be aggressive

RID 0003219 ꜣd to be aggressive

ID Lexeme	343	ꜣd	to rage; to be angry
	342	ꜣd	to rage; to attack
	344	ꜣd	to attack; to anger (someone); to be aggressive
	356	ꜣd.w	Furious one
	346	ꜣd.w	anger; aggression
	353	ꜣd.w	aggressor (lit. furious one, of a crocodile)

DRID 1002876 ꜣd to decay

RID 0003220 ꜣd to decay

ID Lexeme	348	ꜣd	to decay
	351	ꜣd	to fail (of the heart)

DRID 1002877 ꜣd to smear

RID 0003221 ꜣd to smear

ID Lexeme	349	ꜣd	to smear (a vessel with clay)
	350	ꜣd.w	lining (of a pot with clay); smoothing

DRID 1002878 ꜣf to hail

RID 0003225 ꜣfꜣf to hail

ID Lexeme	117	ꜣfꜣf	to hail

DRID 1002879 ꜣfi̯ to eat (greedily)

RID 0003222 ꜣfi̯ to eat (greedily)

ID Lexeme	121	ꜣfꜥ	gluttony
	122	ꜣfꜥ	greedy one
	119	ꜣfi̯	to eat (greedily)
	10420	ꜣfꜣf	to eat (greedily)

DRID 1002880 ꜣfr to boil

RID 0003223 ꜣfr to boil

ID Lexeme	851320	ꜣfr	to heat (something); to boil; to simmer
	126	ꜣfr	to boil; to simmer
	125	ꜣfr	to boil (something); to heat
	120	ꜣfy.t	warmth; heat

DRID	**1002881**	**ꜣg to plant**			
	RID	**0003226**	ꜣg to plant		
		ID Lexeme	309	ꜣg	to plant
			320	ꜣgg.t	sheaf (of flax stalks)
			127520	sꜣg	to cover with vegetation
DRID	**1002882**	**ꜣgb to shudder?**			
	RID	**0003227**	ꜣgbgb to shudder?		
		ID Lexeme	318	ꜣgbgb	to shudder?
DRID	**1002883**	**ꜣgbi̯ to flood**			
	RID	**0003228**	ꜣgbi̯ to flood		
		ID Lexeme	314	ꜣgb.w	flood; abundance
			860570	ꜣgb.w	flood
			313	ꜣgbi̯	to overflow; to flood
			10630	ꜣgbgb	[noun (a food?)]; abundance?
			127530	sꜣgb	to irrigate
			860554	ꜣgb.t	flood
DRID	**1002884**	**ꜣḥ [a mash]**			
	RID	**0003229**	ꜣḥ [a mash]		
		ID Lexeme	186	ꜣḥ	[a mash]; [dough (med.)]
DRID	**1002885**	**ꜣḫ beneficial**			
	RID	**0003233**	ꜣḫ glorious		
		ID Lexeme	200	ꜣḫ	to be glorious; to be beneficial; to be useful
			600475	ꜣḫ	glorious; beneficial; glorified
			217	ꜣḫ.t	glory; what is beneficial
			220	ꜣḫ.t	uraeus; diadem
			219	ꜣḫ.t	glorious ones (gods)
			127110	sꜣḫ	to glorify; to make excellent
			127120	sꜣḫ	spiritual state; glorified state
			869123	sꜣḫ.w	glorification
			127160	sꜣḫ.t	one who glorify
	RID	**0003235**	ꜣḫ shining		
		ID Lexeme	221	ꜣḫ.t	glossy eye (of a god)
			222	ꜣḫ.t	shining one (Hathor cow)
			232	ꜣḫ.t	horizon (metaph. for palace, tomb, temple)
			227	ꜣḫ.t	horizon
			237	ꜣḫ.tj	horizon-dweller
			852800	ꜣḫ.tj	of the horizon
			853669	ꜣḫ.tj	both glossy eyes (of a god)
			239	ꜣḫ.tjw	Horizon-Dwellers
			240	ꜣḫ.tjt	horizon-dweller (Hathor in Dendera)

		247	ꜣḫꜣḫ	Akhakhu (a constellation)
		20860	jꜣḫ.t	radiant one (Hathor)
		20880	jꜣḫ.w	radiance; (sun)shine
		854996	jꜣḫ.w	radiant
		20850	jꜣḫ	to shine
RID	**0003237**	ꜣḫ useful		
	ID Lexeme	500721	ꜣḫ.y	Effective one
		231	ꜣḫ.t	[a knife?]
		866282	ꜣḫꜣḫ	equipment; accessories; part of a ship
		248	ꜣḫꜣḫ	[ship's equipment (mast?; ropes?)]
RID	**0004211**	ꜣḫ magic; ritual recitations		
	ID Lexeme	253	ꜣḫ.w	(magical) power; mastery
		127220	sꜣḫ.w	(ritual) recitations
		127150	sꜣḫ.t	(ritual) recitations
RID	**0004212**	ꜣḫ Akh-spirit		
	ID Lexeme	500678	ꜣḫ	Akh-spirit
		203	ꜣḫ	akh-spirit; glorified spirit (the deceased)
		218	ꜣḫ.t	akh-spirit; glorified spirit (the deceased)

DRID 1002886 ꜣḫ bones

RID	**0003230**	ꜣḫ bones		
	ID Lexeme	246	ꜣḫꜣḫ	bones

DRID 1002887 ꜣḥ field

RID	**0003231**	ꜣḥ field		
	ID Lexeme	856256	ꜣḥ	abundance
		185	ꜣḥ	field
		856369	ꜣḥ.w	flood
		191	ꜣḥ.t	field; arable land
		850622	ꜣḥ.t	Field (a domain)
		197	ꜣḥy	inundation?; to inundate?
		196	ꜣḥꜣḥ	to bury in the ground

DRID 1002888 ꜣḫ flame

RID	**0003232**	ꜣḫ flame		
	ID Lexeme	856498	ꜣḫ	flame; fire
		223	ꜣḫ.t	flame; fire

DRID 1002889 ꜣḫ ibis

RID	**0003234**	ꜣḫ ibis		
	ID Lexeme	230	ꜣḫ.t	(crested) ibis

DRID 1002890 ꜣh pain

RID	**0003236**	ꜣh to be troubled		

		ID Lexeme	169	ꜣh	to be miserable
			170	ꜣh	to make miserable
			175	ꜣh.w	sufferer; anxious one
			174	ꜣh.w	pain
			126930	sꜣhh.w	grumbler?
DRID	**1002891**	**ꜣhd to be weak**			
	RID	**0003239**	ꜣhd to be weak		
		ID Lexeme	182	ꜣhd	weakness
			181	ꜣhd	to be weak; to be exhausted
			184	ꜣhd	Exhausted one
			126940	sꜣhd	to cause to quake
DRID	**1002892**	**ꜣḫi to be well watered**			
	RID	**0003240**	ꜣḫi to be well watered		
		ID Lexeme	198	ꜣḫ	papyrus thicket
			251	ꜣḫ.y	plants
			215	ꜣḫ.w	[a field crop?]
			228	ꜣḫ.t	field; arable land
			216	ꜣḫ.t	akhet-season (inundation)
			853579	ꜣḫ.tj	well-watered
			863198	ꜣḫ.tj	the first day of Akhet season
			199	ꜣḫi	to grow green; to flourish; to be inundated
	RID	**0001352**	jꜣḫi to be flooded		
		ID Lexeme	20870	jꜣḫi	to be flooded
			857083	jꜣḫ.w	papyrus thicket; inundated area
	RID	**0003241**	ꜣḫꜣḫ to be verdant		
		ID Lexeme	245	ꜣḫꜣḫ	to make verdant; to make grow green
			244	ꜣḫꜣḫ	to be verdant; to be inundated
			243	ꜣḫꜣḫ	to be verdant; to make green
			127200	sꜣḫꜣḫ	to make green
DRID	**1002893**	**ꜣẖʿ to scratch**			
	RID	**0003242**	ꜣẖʿ to scratch		
		ID Lexeme	258	ꜣẖʿ	to scratch; to carve
			259	ꜣẖʿ	stonecutter
		ID Lexeme	261	ꜣẖʿ.t	scratch
DRID	**1002895**	**ꜣj bandage**			
	RID	**0003243**	ꜣj bandage		
		ID Lexeme	10	ꜣj.wj	pair of bandages
DRID	**1002896**	**ꜣjs brain**			
	RID	**0003244**	ꜣjs brain		
		ID Lexeme	13	ꜣjs	brain; viscera

DRID 1002897 ꜣk to bend

RID 0003245 ꜣk to bend

ID Lexeme		
401	ꜣk	to be bent; to bend (the elbow)
306	ꜣk.wt	[a symptom of illness]

DRID 1002898 ꜣm to burn up

RID 0003246 ꜣm to burn up

ID Lexeme		
130	ꜣm	to burn up
129	ꜣm	to burn (something); to destroy
128	ꜣm	to burn; to burn up
861178	ꜣm.w	ember (illness)
142	ꜣm.w	(scorching) heat; ember
143	ꜣm.wt	burning
853103	ꜣm.tj	Burnt one (Seth)
137	ꜣmj	Fiery? one (sun god)
126750	sꜣm	to let burn up

DRID 1002899 ꜣmj to mix

RID 0003247 ꜣmj to mix

ID Lexeme		
141	ꜣmꜥ.t	[a mash (med.)]
136	ꜣmj	to mix

DRID 1002900 ꜣmm to seize

RID 0003248 ꜣmm to seize

ID Lexeme		
133	ꜣm	seizer (hieracosphinx, as a manifestation of Horus)
132	ꜣm	seizer (Horus as a lion (at Edfu), the king)
501096	ꜣm.w	Seizer
856380	ꜣmm	Seizer
144	ꜣmm	to seize; to grasp
145	ꜣmm	grip?; grasp
148	ꜣmm.w	gripings; spasms (gynecological term)
146	ꜣmm.t	grasp; grip

DRID 1002901 ꜣms [a scepter]

RID 0003249 ꜣms [a scepter]

ID Lexeme		
852756	ꜣms	to wield the ames-sceptre
150	ꜣms	[a club shaped scepter; ames-scepter]
854912	ꜣms.y	belonging to the ames-sceptre

DRID 1002902 ꜣmꜥ bearing (techn.)

RID 0003250 ꜣmꜥ bearing (techn.)

ID Lexeme		
140	ꜣmꜥ.t	socket (for a door hinge)
139	ꜣmꜥ.t	ramus (of the lower jaw);

forked bone

DRID 1002903 ꜣpd bird

RID	**0003251**	ꜣpd bird		
	ID Lexeme	111	ꜣpd	poultry fat
		107	ꜣpd	bird (gen.); fowl (coll.)
		108	ꜣpd	bird (a constellation)
		110	ꜣpd	to rush forward
		115	ꜣpd.wt	poultry

DRID 1002904 ꜣḳ to perish

RID	**0003252**	ꜣḳ to perish		
	ID Lexeme	290	ꜣḳ	to perish; to come to naught
		294	ꜣḳ.yt	loss
		291	ꜣḳ.w	devastation; ruin
		127390	sꜣḳ	to ruin, to devastate so./sth.

DRID 1002905 ꜣḳḥ* to strengthen?

RID	**0003253**	ꜣḳḥ* to strengthen?		
	ID Lexeme	127490	sꜣḳḥ	to strengthen?

DRID 1002906 ꜣr need

RID	**0003254**	ꜣr need		
	ID Lexeme	156	ꜣr	need?
		164	ꜣrr	disappointment?
		10460	ꜣrr	to be frustrated?
		126820	sꜣr	needy man
		126810	sꜣr	wish; need
		126870	sꜣr.t	wish

DRID 1002907 ꜣr to supersede

RID	**0003255**	ꜣr to supersede		
	ID Lexeme	155	ꜣr	to drive away; to oppress
		856454	ꜣrw.t	excrement?
		856455	ꜣrw.t	displacement; repression?

DRID 1002908 ꜣs to hurry

RID	**0003256**	ꜣs to hurry		
	ID Lexeme	268	ꜣs	to overtake (somebody); to hasten
		267	ꜣs	to rush; to run
		266	ꜣs	to rush; to make rush
		273	ꜣs.t	splinter
		269	ꜣsꜣs	hastily; in a hurry

DRID 1002909 ꜣs vulture

RID	**0003257**	ꜣs vulture		

ID Lexeme 854105 ꜣz Az-vulture

DRID 1002910 ꜣšr to roast
RID 0003258 ꜣšr to roast

ID Lexeme 288	ꜣšr	roast meat
287	ꜣšr	to roast
289	ꜣšr.t	roast joint
127320	sꜣšr.t	[a pastry]

DRID 1002911 ꜣt to enter?
RID 0003259 ꜣt to enter?

ID Lexeme 850151	ꜣt	to enter? (a place)

DRID 1002912 ꜣtf crown
RID 0003260 ꜣtf crown

ID Lexeme 328	ꜣtf	to be equipped (with donations)
326	ꜣtf	atef-crown (crown of the gods)
854488	ꜣtf	to be crowned
327	ꜣtf	to be crowned
331	ꜣtf	[designation of a serpent (in the name of Atfet)]
333	ꜣtf.tj	Crowned-one with the atef-crown (Osiris)

DRID 1002913 ꜣtf incense
RID 0003261 ꜣtf incense

ID Lexeme 329	ꜣtf	incense (gen.)

DRID 1002914 ꜣṯi̯ to take care
RID 0003262 ꜣṯi̯ to take care

ID Lexeme 336	ꜣṯ.yt	nurse; attendant
338	ꜣṯ.w	administrator (gen.); foreman; tutor?
855659	ꜣṯ.w	administrator; steward;
337	ꜣṯ.wtj	one relating to rearing (nurse? nursling?)
334	ꜣṯ.t	bier; bed
335	ꜣṯi̯	to mind (a child); to rear (a child); to care (for); to bring up

DRID 1002915 ꜣtj [a part of the solar bark]
RID 0003263 ꜣtj [a part of the solar bark]

ID Lexeme 321	ꜣtj	[a part of the solar bark]

DRID 1002916 ꜣṯp to load
RID 0003264 ꜣṯp to load

ID Lexeme 323	ꜣṯp	[a box]

			340	ꜣṯp	to load (a ship)
			341	ꜣṯp.y	laden one
			324	ꜣṯp.w	load; cargo
			325	ꜣṯp.wt	load; cargo
DRID	**1002917**	**ꜣwi̯ to be long**			
	RID	**0003265**	ꜣwi̯ to be dead		
		ID Lexeme	858947	ꜣw	to be dead
			863783	ꜣw	dead one
			32	ꜣw	death
	RID	**0003266**	ꜣwi̯ to be long		
		ID Lexeme	31	ꜣw	length
			400588	ꜣw	long
			39	ꜣw.t	gift(s); offering(s)
			38	ꜣw.t	slaughter?; long knife?
			37	ꜣw.t	length; span
			51	ꜣwi̯	to extend; to present (something)
			50	ꜣwi̯	to be extended (in width, in length)
			49	ꜣwi̯	to extend; to be extended (in width, in length)
			858406	ꜣwꜣw	to be elongated; long extended; double long
			856494	ꜣwꜣw.tj	long one [designation of a person]
			66170	mꜣ.t	flute
			66230	mꜣ.tj	[pair of endings (of tendons?)]
			66850	mꜣw.t	stalk
			66870	mꜣw.t	rays; beams
			66840	mꜣw.t	shaft; staff
			500095	mꜣw.tj	Radiant one
			126530	sꜣwi̯	to gladden
			126540	sꜣwi̯	to keep an eye on
			126520	sꜣwi̯	to lengthen; to gladden
DRID	**1002918**	**ꜣyt to be pale**			
	RID	**0003268**	ꜣyt to be pale		
		ID Lexeme	14	ꜣyt	to be pale (of face)
DRID	**1002919**	**ꜣẖb to swallow**			
	RID	**0003238**	ꜣẖb to swallow		
		ID Lexeme	262	ꜣẖb	to swallow
			263	ꜣẖb.y	Swallower
			500723	ꜣẖb.yt	Swallower
DRID	**1002920**	**ꜣzb to burn**			
	RID	**0003269**	ꜣzb to burn		
		ID Lexeme	852777	ꜣzb	to burn; to glow
			278	ꜣzb	the burning One (gate keeper of the netherworld)

			280	ꜣzb.jw	Asebiu (11th gate of the netherworld)
			279	ꜣsb.t	Asbet (a serpent goddess)
			856527	ꜣzb.t	the burning one
DRID	**1002921**	**ꜣzẖ to harvest**			
	RID	**0003270**	ꜣzẖ to harvest		
		ID Lexeme	265	ꜣzẖ	harvest
			264	ꜣzẖ	to reap; to harvest
			281	ꜣzẖ	sickle
DRID	**1002922**	**ꜣꜣ ruin?**			
	RID	**0003271**	ꜣꜣ ruin?		
		ID Lexeme	7	ꜣꜣ	ruin (or similar)
DRID	**1002923**	**ꜣꜥb damage**			
	RID	**0003272**	ꜣꜥb damage		
		ID Lexeme	28	ꜣꜥb.t	oppression
DRID	**1002924**	**ꜣꜥw bag**			
	RID	**0003273**	ꜣꜥw bag		
		ID Lexeme	26	ꜣꜥw	(leather) bag
DRID	**1002925**	**ꜣꜥꜥ = nꜥꜥ to be smooth**			
	RID	**0001960**	nꜥꜥ to be smooth		
		ID Lexeme	80360	nꜥ	kindness; compassion
			80340	nꜥi̯	to be mild; to pity
			80470	nꜥꜥ	smooth cloth
			80460	nꜥꜥ	to be smooth; to smooth
			80480	nꜥꜥ	the best (of something) (field); a unblemished one (animal)
			450172	snꜥꜥ	powder? (i.e., something ground fine); mixture
			136700	snꜥꜥ	to make smooth; to grind
	RID	**0003275**	ꜣꜥꜥ to coat with plaster		
		ID Lexeme	16	ꜣꜥꜥ	to coat with plaster; to repair
			27	ꜣꜥ.w	[building component?]; [construction material?]
DRID	**1002926**	**ꜣꜥꜥ to blame**			
	RID	**0003274**	ꜣꜥꜥ to blame		
		ID Lexeme	17	ꜣꜥꜥ	to accuse; to blame; to injure, to harm
			35680	ꜥꜥ.t	accusation

II.2 j

DRID	**1000934**	**j to say**			
	RID	**0001101**	j to say		
		ID Lexeme	500024	j	to say
			854785	j.j	address; name
			21270	jj	spell?; to say?
			21280	jj	to agree?
DRID	**1000935**	**jb [a sistrum]**			
	RID	**0001102**	jb [a sistrum]		
		ID Lexeme	23330	jb	[a sistrum]
DRID	**1000936**	**jb [a tree]**			
	RID	**0001103**	jb [a tree]		
		ID Lexeme	23320	jb	[a leaf tree]
DRID	**1000937**	**jb = jbr unguent, oil**			
	RID	**0001104**	jb = jbr unguent, oil		
		ID Lexeme	23550	jbꜣ.t	[an unguent]
DRID	**1000938**	**jb chapel**			
	RID	**0001105**	jb chapel		
		ID Lexeme	863642	jb.t	chapel
DRID	**1000939**	**jb goat**			
	RID	**0001106**	jb goat		
		ID Lexeme	23340	jb	kid; goat
DRID	**1000940**	**jb heart**			
	RID	**0001107**	jb heart		
		ID Lexeme	23370	jb	to wish; to suppose; to think
			23290	jb	heart; mind; wish; character
			23460	jb.wj	double-heart amulet
	RID	**0001113**	jbjb joy		
		ID Lexeme	23650	jbjb	darling
			857087	jbjb	satisfaction; joy
DRID	**1000941**	**jb purification booth**			
	RID	**0001108**	jb purification booth; refuge		
		ID Lexeme	450607	jb.w	purification booth; refuge
DRID	**1000942**	**jbh gneiss**			
	RID	**0001109**	jbh gneiss		
		ID Lexeme	23820	jbh.tj	gneiss
DRID	**1000943**	**jbḥ to be flooded**			

	RID	**0001110**	jbḥ to stream (with liquid); to be flooded		
		ID Lexeme	23850	jbḥ	to be wet; to be flooded
			23860	jbḥ.w	libationer
DRID	**1000944**		**jbḥ tooth**		
	RID	**0001111**	jbḥ tooth		
		ID Lexeme	23830	jbḥ	tooth
			23840	jbḥ	to laugh (lit. to bare the teeth)
DRID	**1000945**		**jbi̯ to be thirsty**		
	RID	**0001112**	jbi̯ to be thirsty		
		ID Lexeme	23400	jb	farmer
			23430	jb.t	thirst
			23360	jb	thirsty man
			23640	jbi̯	to be thirsty
DRID	**1000946**		**jbn alum**		
	RID	**0001114**	jbn alum		
		ID Lexeme	23770	jbn.w	alum; vitriolic salts (gen.)
DRID	**1000947**		**jbr stallion**		
	RID	**0001115**	jbr stallion		
		ID Lexeme	23790	jbr	stallion
DRID	**1000948**		**jbs headdress**		
	RID	**0001116**	jbs headdress		
		ID Lexeme	23910	jbs	ibes-headdress
DRID	**1000949**		**jbšt [a bread]**		
	RID	**0001117**	jbšt [a bread]		
		ID Lexeme	23960	jbšt	[a kind of bread or biscuit]
DRID	**1000950**		**jbṯ trap**		
	RID	**0001118**	jbṯ trap		
		ID Lexeme	24000	jbṯ.tj	fowler
			851571	jbṯ	to catch (in a trap)
			857088	jbṯ	birdtrap
			23990	jbṯ.t	bird-trap
DRID	**1000951**		**jbzꜣ [an oil plant]**		
	RID	**0001119**	jbzꜣ [an oil plant]		
		ID Lexeme	23920	jbzꜣ	[an (ethereal?) oil]
			23930	jbzꜣ	[a plant (med.)]
DRID	**1000952**		**jbꜣ maned sheep**		
	RID	**0001120**	jbꜣ maned sheep		
		ID Lexeme	23600	jbꜣ.w	maned sheep

DRID	**1000953**	**jbꜣ to dance**			
	RID	**0001121**	jbꜣ to dance		
		ID Lexeme	23520	jbꜣ	to dance
			23540	jbꜣ	dancer
			23630	jb.yt	[a servant (dancer?) of Neith)]
			23570	jbꜣ.yt	dancer (a bird? an insect?)
			23580	jbꜣ.yt	dancer (figurative for an oar)
			23530	jbꜣ.w	dance; entertainment
			23560	jbꜣ.t	dancer
			23510	jbꜣ	playing piece (for a board game)
			861020	sjbꜣ	make dance
DRID	**1000954**	**jd pleasant scent**			
	RID	**0001122**	jd pleasant scent		
		ID Lexeme	33840	jd.t	(pleasant) scent; perfume; dew; exudation
DRID	**1000955**	**jd uterus**			
	RID	**0001123**	jd uterus		
		ID Lexeme	500032	jd.t	cow; female animal (gen.)
			850291	jd.t	uterus; womb
	RID	**0001124**	jd youth		
		ID Lexeme	33780	jd.w	male child; youth
			33910	jdy.t	girl
DRID	**1000956**	**jdb riverbank**			
	RID	**0001126**	jdb riverbank		
		ID Lexeme	33970	jdb	river plot (arable land along the river bank)
			33960	jdb	riverbank; shore; edge
			854494	jdb	shore; shore land; acre; open land
			34010	jdb.w	edge (of a wound, of the mouth) (med.)
			400868	jdb.wj	the two banks (Egypt)
			33980	jdb.wj	the one of the two banks (the king)
DRID	**1000957**	**jdg kerchief**			
	RID	**0001127**	jdg kerchief		
		ID Lexeme	34270	jdg	kerchief
DRID	**1000958**	**jdḫ marsh**			
	RID	**0001128**	jdḫ marsh		
		ID Lexeme	34220	jdḫ.y	man of the Delta
			34230	jdḫ.yt	woman of the Delta
			34240	jdḫ.w	marshes of the Delta
DRID	**1000959**	**jdi̯ to be deaf**			
	RID	**0001129**	jdi̯ to be deaf		

ID Lexeme 33890 jdi̯ to be deaf; to deafen

DRID 1000960 jdi̯ to cense
RID 0001131 jdi̯ to cense
ID Lexeme 33900 jdi̯ to cense; to libate

DRID 1000961 jdi̯ to subjugate
RID 0001130 jdi̯ to be subjugated
ID Lexeme 128640 sjdi̯ to mortify; to make powerless
33830 jdi̯ to be subjugated; to subjugate

DRID 1000962 jdm linen
RID 0001132 jdm linen
ID Lexeme 34030 jdm.j high quality linen
34040 jdm.jt high quality linen

DRID 1000963 jdn ear
RID 0001133 jdn ear
ID Lexeme 34070 jdn ear

DRID 1000964 jdn granary
RID 0001134 jdn granary
ID Lexeme 34060 jdn.t silo; granary

DRID 1000965 jdn to replace
RID 0001136 jdn to replace
ID Lexeme 34080 jdn to replace; to dominate
34120 jdn.w deputy; adjutant (mil.)
855690 jdn.w representative; deputy
34090 jdn.t deputy (Nephthys)
34110 jdnjw [a mat]

DRID 1000966 jdr heart
RID 0001137 jdr heart
ID Lexeme 34190 jdr heart

DRID 1000967 jdr to bind together
RID 0001138 jdr to bind together
ID Lexeme 400987 jdr to bind together; to stitch (med.)
34150 jdr herd
34180 jdr bindings; (surgical) seam
34140 jdr belt; girdle
34200 jdr.yt punishment, fetters

DRID 1000968 jdꜣ to smooth
RID 0001138 jdꜣ to smooth
ID Lexeme 33870 jdꜣ to smooth

DRID	**1000969**		**jf [bone marrow]**		
	RID	**0001139**	jf [bone marrow]		
		ID Lexeme	24530	jf.t	[bone marrow]
DRID	**1000970**		**jfd to run**		
	RID	**0001140**	jfd to run		
		ID Lexeme	69480	mfd	to traverse (a land)
			24610	jfd	to flee; to move quickly
DRID	**1000971**		**jfn to go back**		
	RID	**0001141**	jfn to go back		
		ID Lexeme	24540	jfn	to turn round; to turn to
DRID	**1000972**		**jgn gladness**		
	RID	**0001142**	jgn gladness		
		ID Lexeme	32760	jgn	gladness
DRID	**1000973**		**jḥ [a tree]**		
	RID	**0001143**	jḥ [a tree]		
		ID Lexeme	30630	jḥ.w	[an unknown fruit (med.)]
			30430	jḥ	[a tree]
DRID	**1000975**		**jh cow**		
	RID	**0001144**	jh cow		
		ID Lexeme	30130	jh.t	Ihet (heavenly cow)
DRID	**1000976**		**jḥ crocodile**		
	RID	**0001145**	jḥ crocodile		
		ID Lexeme	862886	jḥ	crocodile
DRID	**1000977**		**jẖ item**		
	RID	**0001146**	jẖ item		
		ID Lexeme	114520	ẖy	how?
			114510	ẖy	oh!
			114570	ẖy...ẖy	just as ... so
			855913	jẖ.tjt	proportion of?; portion ?
			850967	jẖ.t	something; some
			30750	jẖ.t	thing; goods; offerings
	RID	**0001153**	jẖ what?		
		ID Lexeme	30740	jẖ	what? [interrog. pron.]
	RID	**0001274**	jšst what?		
		ID Lexeme	32050	jšst	what?
	RID	**0001398**	kj other		
		ID Lexeme	853259	ktẖ	other
DRID	**1000978**		**jḥ ox**		
	RID	**0001147**	jḥ land-tax		
		ID Lexeme	30700	jḥ.tjt	land-tax

	RID	**0001148**	jḥ ox		
		ID Lexeme	30410	jḥ	ox; cattle
			30400	jḥ	[a weight (tauroform)]
			30480	jḥ.t	cow
			30660	jḥ.w	stable; pen (for livestock)
DRID	**1000979**	**jh stable**			
	RID	**0001149**	jh stable		
		ID Lexeme	30190	jh.y	[a building]
			30210	jh.w	camp; pen (for livestock)
DRID	**1000980**	**jḥ thigh**			
	RID	**0001150**	jḥ thigh		
		ID Lexeme	30490	jḥ.tj	thighs
DRID	**1000981**	**jḥ to weep?**			
	RID	**0001151**	jḥ to weep?		
		ID Lexeme	30460	jḥ	to weep?; to sleep?
DRID	**1000982**	**jẖ to worship**			
	RID	**0001152**	jẖ to worship		
		ID Lexeme	30850	jẖ	to worship; to rejoice at/in/over
DRID	**1000983**	**jḫḫ darkness**			
	RID	**0001154**	jḫḫ darkness		
		ID Lexeme	30960	jḫḫ.w	twilight (morning and evening); darkness
DRID	**1000984**	**jhj to wail**			
	RID	**0001155**	jhj to wail		
		ID Lexeme	30160	jhj	Oho!
			30180	jhj	to wail
			853243	jhj	plaintive cry; oh!; pain
DRID	**1000985**	**jhm [a resin?]**			
	RID	**0001156**	jhm [a resin?]		
		ID Lexeme	30300	jhm.t	[a resin, or balm]
DRID	**1000986**	**jhm sigh**			
	RID	**0001157**	jhm sigh		
		ID Lexeme	30290	jhm	jubilation
			855874	jhm	[shout]
			856210	jhm	to sigh
			850149	jhm	suffering; pain
			30280	jhm	to mourn; to suffer
			855873	jhm	sigh
			850287	jhm.t	suffering

DRID 1000987 jhm to walk slowly

RID	**0001158**	jhm to walk slowly		
	ID Lexeme	97650	hꜣmw	to slow down?
		851873	sjhm	to restrain; to refrain
		30270	jhm	to walk slowly; to restrain

DRID 1000988 jhmz rope

RID	**0001159**	jhmz rope		
	ID Lexeme	857099	jhmz.t	rope
		30340	jhms.t	cord

DRID 1000989 jḫr form

RID	**0001160**	jḫr form		
	ID Lexeme	30940	jḫr	form; image

DRID 1000990 jhr tent

RID	**0001161**	jhr tent		
	ID Lexeme	30350	jhr	tent

DRID 1000991 jhy joy

RID	**0001162**	jhy joy		
	ID Lexeme	30170	jhy	joy; rejoicing
		861314	jhy	jubilant [designation of a person]
		30360	jhhj	jubilation
		30370	jhhj	festival (of jubilation)

DRID 1000992 jḥy to make music

RID	**0001163**	jḥy to make music		
	ID Lexeme	851597	jḥy	musician (a priest)
		860508	jḥy	music
		30560	jḥy	to make music
		857101	jḥy.w	sistrum player
		30610	jḥy.t	musician (a priestess)

DRID 1000993 jjr horned animal

RID	**0001164**	jjr horned animal		
	ID Lexeme	21420	jjr	stag?; ram?

DRID 1000994 jki̯ to hack

RID	**0001165**	jk quarry		
	ID Lexeme	32450	jk.y	stonemason
		32480	jk.w	quarry
RID	**0001166**	jki̯ to attack		
	ID Lexeme	855152	jk.w	potentate
		32420	jki̯	to attack; to bow
		858979	jkjk	[rhythmical muscle contraction]

DRID 1000996 jkm shield

RID	**0001167**	jkm shield		
	ID Lexeme	32550	jkm	shield; protection

DRID 1000997 jkn bad?

RID	**0001168**	jkn bad?		
	ID Lexeme	32630	jkn	[a negative characteristic (of the heart, tongue)]

DRID 1000998 jkn to scoop out

RID	**0001169**	jkn to scoop out		
	ID Lexeme	854493	jkn	to scoop
		32590	jkn	to draw (water)
		32570	jkn	to hoe; to scoop out; to hack
		855875	jkn	tomb?; digger? hole?
		32600	jkn	to seize; to take hold of
		32640	jkn.w	hoe (made of wood)
		32580	jkn.t	hole; hollow (demon's habitation?)
		128600	sjkn	to destroy

DRID 1000999 jm clay

RID	**0001170**	jm clay		
	ID Lexeme	24690	jm	mud; clay

DRID 1001000 jm in

RID	**0001171**	jm in		
	ID Lexeme	64365	m	in; on (temp.)
		400007	m	in; to; on; from (spatial)
		400082	m	in; of; (consisting) of
		500292	m	like; as; as (predication)
		64364	m	by means of; through (instrumental)
		400080	m	together with
		25120	jm.j	what is within; who is within
		25130	jm.j	being in
		863007	jm.jt	bed?
		400138	jm.jt	insides; content
		25400	jm.wtj	in the midst of; between

DRID 1001001 jm pupil (eye)

RID	**0001172**	jm pupil (eye)		
	ID Lexeme	24650	jm	pupil (of the eye)

DRID 1001002 jm pus (med.)

RID	**0001173**	jm pus (med.)		
	ID Lexeme	25970	jm.w	pus (med.)

DRID	**1001003**		**jm rib**		
	RID	**0001174**	jm rib, side		
		ID Lexeme	24670	jm	side; form; rib area
			25110	jm.y	one who is formed
DRID	**1001005**		**jm strong**		
	RID	**0001181**	jmjm strong?		
		ID Lexeme	25950	jmjm	to conduct (plans) effectively
			852257	jmjm	to become strong
DRID	**1001006**		**jm there**		
	RID	**0001176**	jm there		
		ID Lexeme	24640	jm	there
			25160	jm.y	belonging to
DRID	**1001007**		**jm to wail**		
	RID	**0001177**	jm to wail		
		ID Lexeme	24660	jm	to groan
			24700	jm	mourner (a bird)
			851359	jm.y	the lamenting one (Osiris)
			25980	jm.w	lamentation; wailing
			866387	jm.w	Mourner
			24790	jm.t	choking?
			857154	jm.tj	Mourner
			25940	jmjm	to bewail
DRID	**1001008**		**jmḥ to suck**		
	RID	**0001178**	jmḥ to suck		
		ID Lexeme	26400	jmḥ	to suck; to drink
DRID	**1001009**		**jmi̯ not to be**		
	RID	**0001179**	jmi̯ not to be		
		ID Lexeme	64410	m	[imperative of the negative verb]
			851305	jm.w	senselessness
			25170	jmi̯	not to be (negative verb)
DRID	**1001010**		**jmi̯ to give**		
	RID	**0001180**	jmi̯ to give		
		ID Lexeme	25180	jmi̯	give!
			550022	jmi̯	cause (that)!
			851706	jmi̯	give!; cause (that)!
			25900	jmi̯.tw	get (that)!
			600062	jmi̯.tw	give! take it over!
DRID	**1001011**		**jmk to putrefy**		
	RID	**0001183**	jmk to putrefy		
		ID Lexeme	26490	jmk	putrefaction
			26480	jmk	to putrefy

DRID 1001012 jmn right

RID 0001184 jmn right

ID Lexeme 26080 jmn right (hand); western

500247	jmn.t	right eye
26130	jmn.t	[object represented in the imenet-hieroglyph]
26140	jmn.t	right side; west; land of the dead
26360	jmn.tj	Western-one (a mirror)
852036	jmn.tj	Westerner
26160	jmn.tj	west wind
26151	jmn.tj	west
500176	jmn.tj	one belonging to the netherworld
26150	jmn.tj	western
26220	jmn.tjw	westerners; the dead
26180	jmn.tjt	west

DRID 1001013 jmn to hide

RID 0001185 jmn to hide

ID Lexeme			
	26030	jmn	to hide; to be hidden
	26050	jmn	hidden one (a priest)
	855893	jmn	the hidden one
	26040	jmn	hidden one (of several god)
	500080	jmn	hidden; concealed
	26290	jmn.y	one who hides himself (ram-headed sun god)
	26310	jmn.w	hidden one (a demon)
	26230	jmn.wj	two hidden ones (testicles of the deceased for limb deification)
	26090	jmn.t	secret; what is hidden
	26100	jmn.t	hidden place (of the netherworld); secret place

DRID 1001014 jmr to be deaf

RID 0001186 jmr to be deaf

ID Lexeme 26370 jmr to be deaf

DRID 1001015 jms dill

RID 0001187 jms dill

ID Lexeme 26440 jms.t dill

DRID 1001016 jmw boat

RID 0001188 jmw boat

ID Lexeme 25990 jmw boat (gen.)

DRID 1001017 jmꜣẖ backbone

RID 0001189 jmꜣẖ backbone

ID Lexeme 25040 jmꜣẖ backbone; spinal canal

DRID 1001018 jmꜣḫ well supplied

RID	**0001190**	jmꜣḫ well supplied		
	ID Lexeme	25030	jmꜣḫ	[a kind of incense]
		25050	jmꜣḫ	to be provided for; to be revered; to revere
		25070	jmꜣḫ	revered one
		25060	jmꜣḫ	provision; dignity
		25090	jmꜣḫ.w	revered one; one who is provided for (the deceased)
		25100	jmꜣḫ.wt	revered one; one who is provided for (the deceased)
		855892	jmꜣḫ.t	provides; blessedness

DRID 1001019 jn [a garment]

RID	**0001191**	jn [a garment]		
	ID Lexeme	26620	jn.t	type of a garment

DRID 1001020 jn by (of agent)

RID	**0001192**	jn by (of agent)		
	ID Lexeme	26660	jn	by (of agent)

DRID 1001023 jn pain

RID	**0001193**	jn pain		
	ID Lexeme	27110	jn.wt	(physical) pain (med.)

DRID 1001024 jn refrain

RID	**0001194**	jn refrain? (of a song)		
	ID Lexeme	26900	jn.yt	refrain? (of a song)

DRID 1001025 jn tilapia

RID	**0001195**	jn tilapia		
	ID Lexeme	26760	jn.t	tilapia (Nile perch)

DRID 1001026 jn today?

RID	**0001196**	jn today?		
	ID Lexeme	26740	jn	today?

DRID 1001027 jn valley

RID	**0001197**	jn valley		
	ID Lexeme	26780	jn.t	(desert) valley

DRID 1001028 jnb [a plant]

RID	**0001198**	jnb [a plant]		
	ID Lexeme	27250	jnbꜣ	Inba-plant
		27200	jnb	[a plant]

DRID 1001029 jnb ax

RID	**0001199**	jnb ax		
	ID Lexeme	68460	mjnb	ax (tool, weapon)
		68300	mjnb.yt	ax
DRID	**1001030**	**jnb lynx**		
RID	**0001200**	jnb lynx		
	ID Lexeme	27140	jnb	lynx
		27160	jnb.t	lynx pelt?
DRID	**1001031**	**jnb wall**		
RID	**0001201**	jnb wall		
	ID Lexeme	27180	jnb	wall; fence; enclosure
		27190	jnb	to surround (with walls)
		27210	jnb.w	[a field]
		27230	jnb.t	fortification; fence
DRID	**1001032**	**jnbꜣ to be mute**		
RID	**0001202**	jnbꜣ to be mute		
	ID Lexeme	27260	jnbꜣ	to be mute
DRID	**1001033**	**jnd to be sad**		
RID	**0001203**	jnd to be sad		
	ID Lexeme	28050	jnd	to be vexed; to be sad; to be sick
		28070	jnd	afflicted man
		28060	jnd	misery
		857164	jnd.t	grief, sorrow
		128490	sjnd	to make sad
DRID	**1001034**	**jnf discharge**		
RID	**0001204**	jnf discharge		
	ID Lexeme	27380	jnf	discharge (of the divine eye) (incense?)
		27400	jnf.w	discharge (from the eyes) (med.)
DRID	**1001035**	**jnḥ to surround**		
RID	**0001205**	jnḥ to surround		
	ID Lexeme	27710	jnḥ	to surround; to enclose; to border
		27700	jnḥ	eyebrow
		27730	jnḥ.w	frame (of a picture)
DRID	**1001036**	**jnhmn pomegranate**		
RID	**0001206**	jnhmn pomegranate		
	ID Lexeme	27690	jnhmn	pomegranate
DRID	**1001037**	**jnḥꜣs husks (of lotus)**		
RID	**0001207**	jnḥꜣs husks (of lotus)		
	ID Lexeme	850243	jnḥꜣs	husks (of lotus)

DRID	**1001038**	**jni̯ to fetch**			
	RID	**0001208**	jni̯ to fetch		
		ID Lexeme	26870	jni̯	to bring; to bring away; to buy
			450200	jnn	bearer (of offerings)
			27050	jn.w	messenger; supplier; bearer
			27040	jn.w	gifts; produce; tribute
			860234	jn.w	captive
			27100	jn.wt	ferry
			27090	jn.wt	freight?
			861712	jn.t	the one who brings
DRID	**1001039**	**jnj [a plant]**			
	RID	**0001209**	jnj [a plant]		
		ID Lexeme	852305	jnj.w	[a plant]
			26950	jnj.t	[a plant used as fuel]
			26930	jnj.t	seed (med.)
DRID	**1001040**	**jnj to delay**			
	RID	**0001210**	jnj to delay		
		ID Lexeme	26720	jnj	to tarry; to delay
			128360	sjni̯	to wait
DRID	**1001041**	**jnk I**			
	RID	**0001211**	jnk I		
		ID Lexeme	27940	jnk	I [indepen. pron., 1st per. sing.]
DRID	**1001042**	**jnm [wine jug?]**			
	RID	**0001212**	jnm [wine jug?]		
		ID Lexeme	27430	jnm.t	[a vintage?]; [wine jug?]; [wineskin]
DRID	**1001043**	**jnm skin?**			
	RID	**0001213**	jnm skin?		
		ID Lexeme	27420	jnm	skin (of a man); hide (of an animal); skin color
			27440	jnm.yt	skin-wearer (unknown goddess)
	RID	**0001214**	jnm to devour?		
			128480	sjnm	to devour
DRID	**1001044**	**jnn fishing net**			
	RID	**0001215**	jnn fishing net		
		ID Lexeme	27480	jnn.t	cordage
			854705	jn.wtj	the one belonging to the fishnet
DRID	**1001045**	**jnn to cut**			
	RID	**0001216**	jnn to cut		
		ID Lexeme	26730	jn	knife

		26970	jnjn	to cut up
		26980	jnjn.t	knife
		850234	jnn	to cut; to cut up

DRID 1001046 jnnk thyme?

RID	**0001218**	jnnk thyme?		
	ID Lexeme	27520	jnnk	[a plant (thyme?)]

DRID 1001047 jnp royal child

RID	**0001219**	jnp royal child		
	ID Lexeme	27350	jnp.w	royal child (prince, princess)
		852341	jnp.w	prince (Osiris)

DRID 1001048 jnp to lie down

RID	**0001221**	jnp to lie down (on the stomach)		
	ID Lexeme	27310	jnp	to be laid down?; to lie down (on the stomach)?
		27320	jnp	to decay

DRID 1001049 jnḳ to encompass

RID	**0001222**	jnḳ to encompass		
	ID Lexeme	27880	jnḳ	to encompass; to embrace; to unite
		27950	jnḳj.w	[cordage (naut.)]
		27910	jnḳ.t	net (lit. encloser)
		27920	jnḳ.tj	one who is in the net (Osiris)

DRID 1001050 jnḳfḳf [a wooden part of a chariot]

RID	**0001223**	jnḳfḳf [a wooden part of a chariot]		
	ID Lexeme	27930	jnḳfḳf.t	[a wooden part of a chariot]

DRID 1001051 jnr stone

RID	**0001224**	jnr stone		
	ID Lexeme	27550	jnr	Iner-plate (a unit of measure)
		27560	jnr	stone; (block of) stone (gen.)
		27540	jnr	stone (Apophis)

DRID 1001052 jnrm oak

RID	**0001225**	jnrm oak		
	ID Lexeme	27670	jnrm	oak

DRID 1001053 jns lower leg

RID	**0001226**	jns lower leg		
	ID Lexeme	27820	jns.t	lower leg (calf); shin

DRID 1001054 jns red (blood)

RID	**0001227**	jns red (blood)		
	ID Lexeme	27800	jns	red (blood)

			27810	jns	to paint (eyes) red
			27860	jnṡ	testicles
			31550	jns	hide?; bag? (of hide)
			27780	jns	a red one [a priestess (of Bastet)]
			27840	jns.j	red(-dyed) linen; red(-dyed) bandages
			27850	jns.yt	Red (eye of Horus)
			31360	js.wj	testicles
			858082	ns	bloodbath (or similar)
DRID	**1001056**		**jntj to repel**		
	RID	**0001228**	jntj to repel		
		ID Lexeme	28000	jntnt	to hinder
			27980	jntj	to drive back; to withdraw
DRID	**1001063**		**jn^{c} chin**		
	RID	**0001229**	jn^{c} chin		
		ID Lexeme	38310	^{c}n^{c}n	chin
			27000	jn^{c}	chin
			27010	jn^{c}.t	chin
DRID	**1001064**		**jp hippopotamus**		
	RID	**0001230**	jp hippopotamus		
		ID Lexeme	856426	jp.t	hippopotamus
DRID	**1001065**		**jp inner area**		
	RID	**0001231**	jp inner area		
		ID Lexeme	24130	jp.t	[(secret? lockable?) chamber]
			24180	jp.t	ipet (the sky)
			24140	jp.t	women's apartments; inner chamber
	RID	**0001236**	jpjp [an implement]		
		ID Lexeme	24300	jpjp	[an implement made of alabaster]
DRID	**1001066**		**jp to count**		
	RID	**0001232**	jp to count		
		ID Lexeme	859124	jp	accounting; estimation
			856683	jp	[designation of a person]
			24070	jp	to count; to assess; to be cognizant of
			24080	jp	stairway
			24330	jp.w	account; inventory; list
			24340	jp.w	account; inventory; list
			24120	jp.t	oipe (a dry measure); [a measuring vessel]
			24110	jp.t	number; census
			855599	jpp	to search

24410	jpp.t	pellet; pill (med.)
128130	sjp	to assign; to revise; to inspect
854810	sjpp	to examine
858645	sjp.tj	inventory; register
97121	sjp	to deliver
128140	sjp	inspection; inventory
854525	sjp	to transfer; to deliver; to revise; to examine; to visit
128160	sjp.tj	inspection; inventory

DRID 1001067 jpd [unit of measure for baked goods]

RID 0001233 jpd [unit of measure for baked goods]

ID Lexeme	24500	jpd	[unit of measure for baked goods]

DRID 1001068 jpd furniture

RID 0001234 jpd furniture

ID Lexeme	24510	jpd.w	furniture (gen.)

DRID 1001069 jpḥ pig

RID 0001235 jpḥ pig

ID Lexeme	24440	jpḥ	[a pig]

DRID 1001070 jpt bread

RID 0001237 jpt bread

ID Lexeme	24490	jpt	[bread, biscuit]

DRID 1001071 jpꜣ red dye (madder)

RID 0001238 jpꜣ red dye (madder)

ID Lexeme	24250	jpꜣ	red dye (madder)

DRID 1001072 jḳḥ to enter

RID 0001239 jḳḥ to enter

ID Lexeme	32340	jḳḥ	to illumine
	32330	jḳḥ	to enter; to go (to)
	32360	jḳḥ.w	axe; battleaxes

DRID 1001073 jḳr [a serpent]

RID 0001240 jḳr [a serpent]

ID Lexeme	855063	jḳr.t	[a snake]
	32300	jḳr.w	[a serpent]

DRID 1001074 jḳr to be excellent

RID 0001241 jḳr to be excellent

ID Lexeme	850289	jḳr	trustworthy man
	32240	jḳr	to be excellent; to be (trust)worthy
	32250	jḳr	excellent one (Thoth)
	400077	jḳr	orderly; very
	400076	jḳr	excellent; useful

			32260	jḳr	[a piece of furniture]
			32290	jḳr.w	virtue; excellence
			32280	jḳr.w	worthy ones (the blessed dead)
			32270	jḳr.t	excellent lady (Wadjet)
			857175	jḳr.tj	excellent one
			32320	jḳrt	[a food]
			128590	sjḳr	to enrich; to make excellent
DRID	**1001075**	**jr eye**			
	RID	**0001242**	jr eye		
		ID Lexeme	28200	jr	sight (personified as a god)
			29550	jr.w	eye witness
			28300	jr.wj	pair of eyes
			28290	jr.t	eye (of a god); eye (of heaven, metaph. for the sun and moon)
			28250	jr.t	eye
DRID	**1001076**	**jr lion**			
	RID	**0001243**	jr lion		
		ID Lexeme	28180	jr	lion?; wild beast?
DRID	**1001077**	**jr milk cow**			
	RID	**0001244**	jr milk cow		
		ID Lexeme	28600	jr.yt	milk cow
DRID	**1001078**	**jr towards**			
	RID	**0001245**	jr towards		
		ID Lexeme	91900	r	[preposition]
			863008	jr.j	glossary
			28570	jr.t	companion
			28580	jr.t	purpose (of something); duty
			858843	jr.j	all; altogether
			28500	jr.j	pertaining to; belonging to
			859370	jr.j	accordingly; corresponding
			28510	jr.j	fellow; companion
			851428	jr.j	belonging to [adjective of the preposition jr/r]
			850583	jr.j	thereof; thereto (possessive adjective, mostly invariable)
			853686	jr.w	crew of boat
DRID	**1001079**	**jrdb ἀρτάβη**			
	RID	**0001246**	jrdb ἀρτάβη		
		ID Lexeme	850062	jrdb	artabe (a measure of volume)
DRID	**1001080**	**jrḫ [a semi-precious stone]**			
	RID	**0001247**	jrḫ [a semi-precious stone]		
		ID Lexeme	29890	jrḫ	[a translucent semi-precious stone]

DRID	**1001081**		**jri̯ to do**		
	RID	**0001248**	jri̯ to do		
		ID Lexeme	28590	jr.yt	act; ceremony
			28610	jr.yt	assessment (in grain)
			29610	jr.w	creation; form
			29600	jr.w	duty; rite
			29620	jr.w	delivery; cattle tax
			500286	jr.w	creator (Re)
			29590	jr.w	maker (of ...); trader (in ...)
			850272	jr.wt	deed
			29640	jr.wt	doers (women)
			852806	jr.tj	doer
			28550	jri̯	to do; to make; to create; to act as
			600080	jri̯	[aux. (as conjugation bearer with following infinitive)]
			28220	jri̯	to eat
			852348	jri̯	to cause that
			400112	jri̯	to engender; to bear
			851809	jri̯	to do
			28560	jry	knife
			401153	jrr	adversary
			401154	jrr.t	adversary
DRID	**1001082**		**jrj ram**		
	RID	**0001249**	jrj ram		
		ID Lexeme	28540	jrj	ram
DRID	**1001083**		**jrjr guide**		
	RID	**0001250**	jrjr guide		
		ID Lexeme	29530	jrjr	guide; leader
DRID	**1001084**		**jrkt (tree) trunk**		
	RID	**0001251**	jrkt (tree) trunk		
		ID Lexeme	29930	jrkt	(tree) trunk; (wooden) beam
DRID	**1001085**		**jrp wine**		
	RID	**0001252**	jrp wine		
		ID Lexeme	29740	jrp	wine
			450472	jrp	wine jug
			29750	jrp	grape vine
			29810	jrp.y	winemaking?
			852779	jrp.j	belonging to vine
DRID	**1001086**		**jrḳbs rock crystal**		
	RID	**0001253**	jrḳbs rock crystal		
		ID Lexeme	29910	jrḳb.t	mirror (of rock crystal)
			29900	jrḳbs	rock crystal

DRID	**1001087**	**jrt a vegetal purple dye**			
	RID	**0001254**	jrt a vegetal purple dye		
		ID Lexeme	29990	jrt.w	red color (from plants)
			30010	jrt.w	condition; (bluish) discoloration (med.)
			30000	jrt.w	[a purple cloth]
			29980	jrt.w	[a plant (med.)]; [a vegetal (blue) dye]
			866495	jrt.wj	blue
DRID	**1001088**	**jrt distress**			
	RID	**0001255**	jrt distress		
		ID Lexeme	30020	jrt.w	distress
DRID	**1001089**	**jrṯ milk 0001256**			
	RID	**0001256**	jrṯ milk		
		ID Lexeme	30090	jrṯ.t	milky sap (of the sycamore) (med.)
			854491	jrṯ.t	milk (from mother, from animals, from sycamore)
			30080	jrṯ.t	milk (from mother or from animals)
			29970	jrt.j	belonging to milk; sucking calf
DRID	**1001090**	**js like**			
	RID	**0001257**	js like		
		ID Lexeme	852270	js	like (postposition)
	RID	**0001276**	jsw equivalent		
		ID Lexeme	31290	jsw	people (with marketable value)
			31330	jsw	payment; equivalent
DRID	**1001091**	**jš meal**			
	RID	**0001258**	jš meal		
		ID Lexeme	31960	jš.tt	food; meal
DRID	**1001092**	**js to call**			
	RID	**0001259**	js to call		
		ID Lexeme	500202	js	to summon
			860673	js.t	calculation; estimation
	RID	**0001823**	njs to call upon		
		ID Lexeme	80220	njs	calling
			80210	njs	to call upon; to reckon (math.)
			854165	njs	Calling one
			80240	njs.w	one who calls
DRID	**1001093**	**jsbr juniper?**			
	RID	**0001260**	jsbr juniper?		
		ID Lexeme	31430	jsbr	[a Syrian plant (juniper?)]

DRID	**1001094**	**jsbr whip**		
RID	**0001261**	jsbr whip		
	ID Lexeme	31420	jsbr	whip
DRID	**1001095**	**jsbt seat**		
RID	**0001262**	jsbt seat		
	ID Lexeme	31390	jsbt	seat (gen.); chair; base
DRID	**1001096**	**jsbw hut?**		
RID	**0001263**	jsbw hut?		
	ID Lexeme	600286	jsbw	shelter?; hut?
DRID	**1001097**	**jšd [a tree (Balanites aegyptiaca?)]**		
RID	**0001264**	jšd [a tree (Balanites aegyptiaca?)]		
	ID Lexeme	32140	jšd	ished-tree (Balanites aegyptiaca?)
		32150	jšd	[ished-fruit]
		32160	jšd.t	ished-tree (a sacred tree in Heliopolis)
		32170	jšd.t	ished-fruit; fruit (gen.)
DRID	**1001098**	**jsd to sit?**		
RID	**0001265**	jsd to sit?		
	ID Lexeme	31860	jsd	[verb (to sit)]
		76160	msd.t	thigh; haunch
DRID	**1001099**	**jsd to spit**		
RID	**0001266**	jsd to spit		
	ID Lexeme	31850	jsd	to spew?
		31870	jsd	spittle
DRID	**1001100**	**jšf to burn**		
RID	**0001267**	jšf to burn		
	ID Lexeme	31980	jšf	to burn; to scorch (a town)
DRID	**1001101**	**jsp to starve**		
RID	**0001268**	jsp to starve		
	ID Lexeme	31480	jsp	to ache with hunger
DRID	**1001102**	**jspt quiver (for arrows)**		
RID	**0001269**	jspt quiver (for arrows)		
	ID Lexeme	31490	jspt	quiver (for arrows)
DRID	**1001103**	**jsḳ to linger**		
RID	**0001270**	jsḳ to linger		
	ID Lexeme	31730	jsḳ	to linger; to wait; to hold back
DRID	**1001104**	**jsr rushes**		

	RID	**0001271**	jsr rushes	
		ID Lexeme	31630 jsr	rushes
DRID	**1001105**	**jšš image?**		
	RID	**0001272**	jšš image?	
		ID Lexeme	32100 jšš	image (or similar)
DRID	**1001106**	**jšš to bring out**		
	RID	**0001273**	jšš to bring out	
		ID Lexeme	32090 jšš	to carry; to support
			32070 jšš	to spew
			854492 jšš	to transport
			32080 jšš	spittle
			32060 jšš	[a product (from Punt)]
			31970 jš.w	expectoration
DRID	**1001107**	**jstn to bind**		
	RID	**0001275**	jstn to bind	
		ID Lexeme	855287 jstn	hanger
			31800 jstn	to strap up; to bind
DRID	**1001109**	**jswt long plank**		
	RID	**0001277**	jswt long plank	
		ID Lexeme	31380 jswt	long plank (of coniferous wood)
DRID	**1001110**	**jt barley**		
	RID	**0001278**	jt barley	
		ID Lexeme	32830 jt	barley; grain (gen.)
DRID	**1001111**	**jṯ which**		
	RID	**0001279**	jṯ which	
		ID Lexeme	33490 jṯ	which?; where?
DRID	**1001112**	**jtḥ to drag**		
	RID	**0001280**	jtḥ to drag	
		ID Lexeme	852569 jtḥ	prisoners
			33410 jtḥ	to pull; to drag
			33420 jtḥ	fortress; prison
			857209 jtḥ.w	rope
DRID	**1001113**	**jṯi̯ to seize**		
	RID	**0001281**	jṯi̯ to seize	
		ID Lexeme	33560 jṯi̯	to take; to seize
			33630 jṯ.w	thief; conqueror
DRID	**1001114**	**jtj father**		
	RID	**0001282**	jtj father	

	ID Lexeme	32820	jtj	father; grandfather
		32910	jty	to be king; to rule as king
		32930	jty	sovereign; ruler; lord
		32940	jty.t	queen; sovereign

DRID 1001115 jṯm [metal part of a whip]

RID	**0001283**	jṯm [metal part of a whip]		
	ID Lexeme	33680	jṯm	[metal part of a whip (ferrule?)]

DRID 1001117 jtn disc 0001285

RID	**0001285**	jtn disc		
	ID Lexeme	33100	jtn	to shine; to illuminate
		33090	jtn	sun disk (a mirror)
		33080	jtn	disk (of the sun, of the moon)
		859436	jtn	light
		33160	jtn.j	one who belongs to the sun disk
		33150	jtn.wj	the two disks (sun and moon)

DRID 1001118 jtn fluffy

RID	**0001286**	jtn fluffy		
	ID Lexeme	33170	jtnw	hairy; fluffy

DRID 1001119 jtn ground

RID	**0001287**	jtn ground		
	ID Lexeme	862928	jtn	resting place; perch
		33120	jtn, jwtn	ground; earth; dust
		33190	jtn.w	obscurities; riddles

DRID 1001121 jṯn to resist

RID	**0001289**	jṯn to resist		
	ID Lexeme	850318	jṯn	to resist
		33130	jṯn	to oppose
		33180	jṯn.w	opponent
		128630	sjṯn	to subordinate?, to compel?
		869129	sjṯn.w	to be rebellious

DRID 1001122 jṯr captive

RID	**0001290**	jṯr captive		
	ID Lexeme	33720	jṯr	captive

DRID 1001123 jtr iteru

RID	**0001291**	jtr iteru		
	ID Lexeme	33360	jtr.w	iteru (a measure of distance); mile
		33390	jtr.w	season(s)
		33370	jtr.w	river; canal; the Nile
		33290	jtr.t	row (of chapels)
		33310	jtr.tj	the two rows of shrines (Egypt, as the totality of shrines)

		33320	jtr.tj	both sides; vicinity (of someone)
DRID	**1001124**	**jtr papyrus?**		
RID	**0001292**	jtr papyrus?		
	ID Lexeme	33260	jtr	papyrus; aquatic plant (for cordage)
RID	**0001293**	jtr shabti box		
	ID Lexeme	33300	jtr	shabti box
DRID	**1001125**	**jṯṯ = ḥṯṯ to fly up**		
RID	**0000933**	ḥṯṯ to fly up		
	ID Lexeme	112130	ḥṯṯ	to lift someone
RID	**0001294**	jṯṯ to fly up		
	ID Lexeme	33740	jṯṯ	to fly
		33750	jṯṯ.t	flutter? [a symptom of illness]
DRID	**1001126**	**jṯꜣ to capture**		
RID	**0001295**	jṯꜣ to capture		
	ID Lexeme	33530	jṯꜣ	to steal; to capture; to carry off
		874337	jṯꜣ	clot; lump
		33540	jṯꜣ	thief
DRID	**1001127**	**jw not to be**		
RID	**0001298**	jw not to be		
	ID Lexeme	856668	jw.tj	without
		23140	jw.tj	non-existent one
		23150	jw.tjw	those who are not (the dead)
		550302	jw.tjt	what does not exist
		22040	jwt.j	wrongdoer (Seth)
		23190	jwt.w	what is putrefied
RID	**0001300**	jwi̯ to separate		
	ID Lexeme	21960	jw	to separate
		21940	jw	island
		400636	jw.w	boatless man
		857228	jw.w	boatlessness (person)
		856211	jwi̯	to separate
		22260	jwi̯	to strand; to leave (someone) boatless
RID	**0001299**	jw to be evil		
	ID Lexeme	450616	jw	to be evil
		21990	jw	evil; mischief
		22310	jw.yt	wrongdoing
RID	**0001302**	jwd to separate		
	ID Lexeme	23240	jwd.t	parting
		23220	jwd	to separate; to lie between; charged to
		23230	jwd	to catch in a net

DRID	**1001129**	**jw dog**		
RID	**0001296**	jw dog		
	ID Lexeme	855612	jw.t	she-dog
		21970	jw	dog
RID	**0001310**	jwjw dog		
	ID Lexeme	22340	jwjw	dog
		855041	jwjw	juju (dog)
DRID	**1001130**	**jw small livestock?**		
RID	**0001297**	jw small livestock?		
	ID Lexeme	21950	jw	livestock?
DRID	**1001132**	**jw to bewail**		
RID	**0001301**	jw to wail		
	ID Lexeme	22000	jw	to wail
		550312	jw.yt	mourning
		22480	jw.w	wailing
		650070	msyw.t	accusation
		128050	sjwi̯	to say something loudly (hence: to announce (someone); to complain; to praise)
RID	**0001306**	jwḥ to wail		
	ID Lexeme	23030	jwḥ	to weep; to mourn
		23040	jwḥ.yt	mourner (Isis)
RID	**0001311**	jwjw to bewail		
	ID Lexeme	22350	jwjw	to bewail
DRID	**1001134**	**jwf meat**		
RID	**0001303**	jwf meat		
	ID Lexeme	500729	jwf	meat; flesh
		22520	jwf	flesh; meat
DRID	**1001135**	**jwh to carry**		
RID	**0001304**	jwh to carry		
	ID Lexeme	22990	jwh	to carry; to load
DRID	**1001136**	**jwḥ to destroy**		
RID	**0001305**	jwḥ to destroy		
	ID Lexeme	23010	jwḥ	to destroy; to dispel
		23020	jwḥ	[an evil activity]
		128120	sjwḥ	to be violent
DRID	**1001137**	**jwḥ to wet**		
RID	**0001305**	jwḥ to wet		
	ID Lexeme	23000	jwḥ	to sprinkle (with water); to moisten
		23050	jwḥ.w	inundation

		128060	sjw	[a waterway in the heavens])
		128110	sjwḥ	to flood
		68680	mᶜwḥ.w	oar

DRID 1001138 jwi̯ to come

RID	**0001307**	jwi̯ to come		
	ID Lexeme	21310	jy	one who comes (Horus)
		21360	jy.wj	welcome!
		500291	jy.tj	welcome
		21450	jy.tjw	[the naos-bearers?]
		21340	jy.t	what comes (euphemism for trouble)
		857227	jw.w	arrival
		21930	jwi̯	to come; to return
		851688	jwi̯	[aux./modal]

DRID 1001140 jwj building

RID	**0001309**	jwj building		
	ID Lexeme	22320	jwy.t	house; sanctuary; quarter (of a town)

DRID 1001141 jwms untruth

RID	**0001312**	jwms untruth		
	ID Lexeme	22550	jwms	untruth

DRID 1001142 jwn bow

RID	**0001313**	jwn bow		
	ID Lexeme	22670	jwn.t	[a bow (weapon)]
		861025	jwn.tj	bowman

DRID 1001143 jwn colour

RID	**0001314**	jwn colour		
	ID Lexeme	22570	jwn	colour; essence
		400106	jwn	character; reputation
		22840	jwn.w	colorful one (the sun god)

DRID 1001144 jwn support

RID	**0001315**	jwn support		
	ID Lexeme	22560	jwn	to carry (in procession)?
		22620	jwn	pillar (Osiris and other gods)
		22610	jwn	pillar; column
		500162	jwn	pillar (of the moon)
		22600	jwn	support (designation for the wind, as a support of the sky)
		22780	jwn.j	back pillar? (of a statue)
		22800	jwn.yt	columned hall; columned court
		22910	jwnn	sanctuary (gen.)

DRID	**1001145**		**jwn to unite**		
	RID	**0001316**	jwn to unite		
		ID Lexeme	22590	jwn	to unite
			22580	jwn	nest?
			22640	jwn.w	heap(s)
			22680	jwn.t	[something made of cloth (bag?) (clothing?)]
			22700	jwn.tjw	[temple musicians]
			860332	jwn.tjt	[group of persons]
DRID	**1001146**		**jwr [roast meat]**		
	RID	**0001317**	jwr [roast meat]		
		ID Lexeme	22960	jwr	[roast meat (as an offering)]
DRID	**1001147**		**jwr beans**		
	RID	**0001318**	jwr beans		
		ID Lexeme	22980	jwr.yt	beans
DRID	**1001148**		**jwr to become pregnant**		
	RID	**0001319**	jwr to become pregnant		
		ID Lexeme	22930	jwr	to conceive; to become pregnant
			22940	jwr	pregnancy
			22970	jwr.t	pregnant woman
			128090	sjwr	to make pregnant; to make conceive
			857670	sjwr.tj	one who is engendered
DRID	**1001149**		**jws scales**		
	RID	**0001320**	jws scales		
		ID Lexeme	23100	jws.w	scales
DRID	**1001150**		**jwšš dough**		
	RID	**0001321**	jwšš dough		
		ID Lexeme	23110	jwšš	[mash (med.)]; [dough (med.)]
DRID	**1001151**		**jwsw truly**		
	RID	**0001322**	jwsw truly		
		ID Lexeme	855125	jwsw	truly
			864329	jwsw	as; how; like; same, truly
			851437	jsw	truly
DRID	**1001152**		**jwy to irrigate**		
	RID	**0001323**	jwy to irrigate		
		ID Lexeme	22270	jwy	to irrigate
DRID	**1001153**		**jwꜣ cattle**		
	RID	**0001324**	jwꜣ cattle		

		ID Lexeme	22160	jwꜣ	steer; ox; cattle
			22200	jwꜣ.t	cow
			22220	jwꜣ.t	[loaf of bread shaped like a cow's head]
			22210	jwꜣ.t	cattle

DRID 1001154 jwꜣ help

RID	**0001325**	jwꜣ help			
		ID Lexeme	851074	jwꜣ.w	helper
			22230	jwꜣ.yt	helper

DRID 1001155 jwꜣ throat

RID	**0001327**	jwꜣj throat			
		ID Lexeme	22240	jwꜣy.t	throat

DRID 1001156 jwꜣ to take away

RID	**0001326**	jwꜣ to take away			
		ID Lexeme	22250	jwꜣ.w	removal
			22180	jwꜣ	to take away; to rob; to Replace

DRID 1001157 jwʿ haunch

RID	**0001328**	jwʿ haunch			
		ID Lexeme	22360	jwʿ	meat on the bone; haunch?

DRID 1001158 jwʿ to inherit

RID	**0001329**	jwʿ to inherit			
		ID Lexeme	22380	jwʿ	to inherit
			859266	jwʿ.w	heritage; heir
			22460	jwʿ.w	heir
			857231	jwʿ.w	heritage; heir
			22470	jwʿ.w	bracelet (for the upper arm, part of the Gold-of-favor); reward
			22410	jwʿ.wt	heiress
			22420	jwʿ.wt	inheritance
			859431	jwʿ.wt	throne
			859471	sjwʿ	throne
			128080	sjwʿ	to inherit something

DRID 1001159 jwʿ troops

RID	**0001330**	jwʿ troops			
		ID Lexeme	22440	jwʿ.yt	troops

DRID 1001160 jz old

RID	**00013311**	jz old			
		ID Lexeme	31040	jz	old, used
			852306	jz	to be old

		31250	js	to ruin
		31160	js	old one? (priest of Hathor)
		31270	jz.ywt	old clothes; rags
		31050	jz.w	old (primeval) ones
		31320	jz.wt	the old; ancient writings; ancient times
		873113	jz.wtj	patriarchal one
		850288	jz.wtjw	ancestors (those of ancient times)
		31100	jz.t	age; decline
		31210	jsy	shortage; loss (in weight)

DRID 1001161 jz reed

RID	**0001332**	jz reed		
	ID Lexeme	31310	jz.w	reed

DRID 1001162 jz = j^c tomb

RID	**0001333**	jz tomb		
	ID Lexeme	31010	jz	tomb
		31020	jz	workshop; (council) chamber
		500964	jz.w	Izu-instrument (in the netherworld)
		31780	jz.t	silo; granary
		31070	jz.t	palace; palatial precinct
		31060	jz.t	boundary stone; landmark
RID	**0001375**	j^c tomb		
	ID Lexeme	21480	j^c	tomb

DRID 1001163 jz windpipe?

RID	**0001334**	jz windpipe?		
	ID Lexeme	31090	jz.t	windpipe?; throat?

DRID 1001164 jzf disorder

RID	**0001335**	jzf disorder		
	ID Lexeme	852226	zf	to be fake; to do an injustice
		31500	jzf.t	disorder; chaos; wrongdoing
		31510	jzf.tj	evildoer; enemy

DRID 1001165 jzj cord?

RID	**0001336**	jzj cord?		
	ID Lexeme	31260	jzj	band?; thong?

DRID 1001166 jzj to be light (of weight)

RID	**0001337**	jzj to be light (of weight)		
	ID Lexeme	31240	jzj	to be light (of weight)
		128550	sjzj	to lessen (a burden)

DRID 1001167 jzkn zenith?

	RID	**0001338**	jzkn zenith?		
		ID Lexeme	31770	jzkn	[a region of the sky]; zenith?
DRID	**1001168**	**jzn bolt**			
	RID	**0001339**	jzn bolt		
		ID Lexeme	31540	jzn	to bolt (open and closed)
			31570	jzn.yt	lock; bolt
DRID	**1001169**	**jzp to hew**			
	RID	**0001340**	jzp to hew		
		ID Lexeme	64510	jzp	slope
			31460	jzp	to hew (wood)
DRID	**1001170**	**jzr tamarisk**			
	RID	**0001341**	jzr tamarisk		
		ID Lexeme	31610	jzr	tamarisk
			31600	jzr	[a scepter (of tamarisk wood)]
			31620	jzr.t	tamarisk wood
DRID	**1001171**	**jzzj to catch**			
	RID	**0001342**	jzzj to catch		
		ID Lexeme	143730	ss	net
			31700	jzzj	to catch (in the bird net)
			31720	jzz.yt	clap net (for fowling)
DRID	**1001172**	**jꜣ [a plant]**			
	RID	**0001343**	jꜣ [a plant]		
		ID Lexeme	20170	jꜣ.t	[a plant]
DRID	**1001173**	**jꜣb left**			
	RID	**0001344**	jꜣb left		
		ID Lexeme	20530	jꜣb.j	left side; left arm
			20610	jꜣb.j	left; eastern
			854362	jꜣb.w	east
			20550	jꜣb.t	east
			20560	jꜣb.t	left eye
			860353	jꜣb.t	diadem of Lower Egypt
			20580	jꜣb.tj	east wind
			20570	jꜣb.tj	eastern; left
			866300	jꜣb.ty	eastern
			20670	jꜣb.tjw	easterners
			20590	jꜣb.tjt	east
DRID	**1001174**	**jꜣbys foundation**			
	RID	**0001345**	jꜣbys foundation		
		ID Lexeme	20620	jꜣbys	foundation; treasure

DRID	**1001175**	**jꜣd cord**			
	RID	**0001346**	jꜣd cord		
		ID Lexeme	21120	jꜣd	[a cord (on a door bolt)]
			21190	jꜣd.t	net (gen.)
DRID	**1001176**	**jꜣd dew**			
	RID	**0001347**	jꜣd dew		
		ID Lexeme	21170	jꜣd.t	meadow; field
			21180	jꜣd.t	dew; (pleasant) scent; water
DRID	**1001177**	**jꜣd to climb**			
	RID	**0001348**	jꜣd to climb		
		ID Lexeme	21130	jꜣd	to climb
DRID	**1001178**	**jꜣd to suffer**			
	RID	**0001349**	jꜣd to suffer		
		ID Lexeme	21140	jꜣd	to be miserable; to torture
			21150	jꜣd	miserable one; sufferer; evildoer
			21220	jꜣd.w	plague
			21160	jꜣd.t	lack; need
DRID	**1001179**	**jꜣf claw**			
	RID	**0001350**	jꜣf claw		
		ID Lexeme	20710	jꜣf.t	claw (of a predatory bird)
DRID	**1001182**	**jꜣḫi̯ to sweep (the harvest)**			
	RID	**0001353**	jꜣḫi̯ to sweep (the harvest)		
		ID Lexeme	250	jꜣḫi̯	to sweep (the harvest) together
DRID	**1001184**	**jꜣi̯ to rise**			
	RID	**0001354**	jꜣi̯ to raise		
		ID Lexeme	20050	jꜣi̯	to praise; to adore; to pray
			20360	jꜣ.w	praise
			600170	jꜣ.wt	praised
	RID	**0001355**	jꜣi̯ to rise		
		ID Lexeme	20350	jꜣ.w	hill?
			20220	jꜣ.wt	the mounds (designation for Egypt)
			20090	jꜣ.t	spine; back (as body part)
			20140	jꜣ.t	[an offering]
			20100	jꜣ.t	standard (for images of deities)
			20120	jꜣ.t	place; mound
			20110	jꜣ.t	[a place]
			20200	jꜣ.tjt	cadaster?
DRID	**1001185**	**jꜣj [braid]**			
	RID	**0001356**	jꜣj [braid]		

		ID Lexeme	20320	jꜣj.w	[designation of the braid (“dancer”)]
DRID	**1001186**		**jꜣk old**		
	RID	**0001357**	jꜣk old		
		ID Lexeme	21000	jꜣk	old (experienced) man
			851551	jꜣk.t	age; seniority
DRID	**1001187**		**jꜣkb to mourn**		
	RID	**0001358**	jꜣkb to mourn		
		ID Lexeme	21010	jꜣkb	to mourn
			21020	jꜣkb	mourning
			855868	jꜣkb.y	mourner
			21050	jꜣkb.yt	mourning woman
			852392	jꜣkb.ty	the two mourning women
DRID	**1001188**		**jꜣm to be pleasant**		
	RID	**0001359**	jꜣm to be pleasant		
		ID Lexeme	24820	jꜣm	to be pleasant; to be friendly
			550093	jꜣm	friendly; popular
			24840	jꜣm	pleasing form
			24830	jꜣm	charm; graciousness; sacrifice
			24970	jꜣm.yt	charming one (Hathor)
			24990	jꜣm.w	radiance of the sun
			25000	jꜣm.w	[the color red]; [a red mineral]
			859048	jꜣm.wtj	pleasant one
			856489	jꜣm.wtj	the pleasant one
			25020	jꜣm.wtj	charming one (Amun)
			24920	jꜣm.t	priestess (at Edfu)
			24900	jꜣm.t	courtesy
			128310	sjꜣm	to make well-disposed
	RID	**0001361**	jꜣm tree		
		ID Lexeme	24810	jꜣm	[a broadleaf tree with fruits]; jam-timber
			24960	jꜣm.jt	leaves of the iam-tree
			850689	jꜣm.t	[fruit of the iam-tree]
DRID	**1001189**		**jꜣm to bind**		
	RID	**0001360**	jꜣm to bind		
		ID Lexeme	20730	jꜣm	to bind (animals for slaughter)
			25010	jꜣm.w	tent; camp
			24880	jꜣm.t	female (ibex and of other game animals)
DRID	**1001190**		**jꜣḳ to dominate**		
	RID	**0001362**	jꜣḳ to rise		
		ID Lexeme	20970	jꜣḳ	to command

		857075	jꜣḳ	climber [snake]
		20980	jꜣḳ	to rise
		67450	mjꜣḳ.t	ladder

DRID 1001191 jꜣḳ vegetables

RID	**0001363**	jꜣḳ vegetables		
	ID Lexeme	20990	jꜣḳ.t	leek; vegetables (gen.)

DRID 1001192 jꜣꜣ = jꜣr = ꜥr rush

RID	**0001364**	jꜣr rush?		
	ID Lexeme	20770	jꜣr	[a plant (med.)]
		857080	jꜣr.wt	rush thicket?
		20810	jꜣr.w	rush (a flatsedge)
		39160	ꜥr	rush; reed
RID	**0001373**	jꜣꜣ reed		
	ID Lexeme	20010	j	[leaf of the reed]

DRID 1001193 jꜣr to mourn

RID	**0001365**	jꜣr to mourn		
	ID Lexeme	20760	jꜣr	mourning
		857076	jꜣr	dull eyes
		20790	jꜣr.t	[discharge (of an animal, med.)
		20780	jꜣr.t	[a head covering (braid of hair?)]
		20750	jꜣrr	to be faint (of heart); to be dim (of eye)
		857081	jꜣrr	dimness

DRID 1001194 jꜣrr vine

RID	**0001366**	jꜣrr vine		
	ID Lexeme	20830	jꜣrr.wt	grapevine; grapes; raisins
RID	**0001371**	jꜣꜣ = jꜣꜣr vine?		
	ID Lexeme	20250	jꜣꜣ	[an agricultural crop (wine?)]

DRID 1001195 jꜣs to be bald

RID	**0001367**	jꜣs to be bald		
	ID Lexeme	20900	jꜣs	to be bald
		20910	jꜣs	bald one (a priest of Hathor)
		866315	jꜣs	bald one

DRID 1001196 jꜣṯ to injure

RID	**0001368**	jꜣṯ to injure		
	ID Lexeme	21070	jꜣṯ	pain; to injure; to be injured
		855639	jꜣṯ	wildernesses
		21090	jꜣṯ.w	mutilation; theft
		21100	jꜣṯ.w	place of judgment
		21080	jꜣṯ.t	injury

			127960	sjꜣṯ	to cheat; to mutilate (somebody)
			127970	sjꜣṯ.j	cheater; mutilator
			127980	sjꜣṯj	[sacred leg of Osiris]
DRID	**1001197**	**jꜣwi̯ to be old**			
	RID	**0001369**	jꜣw to be old		
		ID Lexeme	20490	jꜣw	old age
			20380	jꜣw	old man
			20390	jꜣw.t	old age
			20400	jꜣw.t	old woman
			20410	jꜣy.wt	old ones (also of gods)
			20480	jꜣwi̯	to be old
	RID	**0007032**	jꜣw to be rewarded		
		ID Lexeme	20420	jꜣw.t	[a cult object]
			860195	jꜣw.t	office insignia
			20430	jꜣw.t	function; office; dignity
			20450	jꜣw.tj	office holder
DRID	**1001198**	**jꜣꜣ twig**			
	RID	**0001370**	jꜣꜣ [a tree]		
		ID Lexeme	20260	jꜣꜣ.t	rod (as a mace, as a scepter)
			857684	jꜣꜣ.t	[tree]
			20270	jꜣꜣ.t	twig; rod
	RID	**0001372**	jꜣꜣ pillar		
		ID Lexeme	450238	jꜣꜣ	support?
DRID	**1001202**	**jꜥ pearl necklace**			
	RID	**0001374**	jꜥ pearl necklace		
		ID Lexeme	21460	jꜥ.t	pearl necklace; pearl net
DRID	**1001203**	**jꜥb to unite**			
	RID	**0001376**	jꜥb to unite		
		ID Lexeme	21660	jꜥb	to rake(?) together; to comb?
			21680	jꜥb	to unite; to be united; to hand over to
			21650	jꜥb.t	bunch? (of offerings); heap? (of offerings)
	RID	**0003290**	ꜥbb to use a pitchfork		
		ID Lexeme	36860	ꜥbb	to use a pitchfork
DRID	**1001204**	**jꜥf to squeeze**			
	RID	**0003323**	ꜥf [a measure]		
		ID Lexeme	37260	ꜥf	[a measure (sack, basket)]
	RID	**0003324**	ꜥf brewer		
		ID Lexeme	37440	ꜥf.tj	brewer
	RID	**0003332**	ꜥfi̯ to squeeze		
		ID Lexeme	37240	ꜥfi̯	to squeeze (out)

	RID	0001377	jʿf to squeeze		
		ID Lexeme	863041	jʿf	squeezed
			21710	jʿf	to wring out (clothes); to press out (grapes)
			864191	jʿf	squeezer
DRID	1001205		**jʿḥ moon**		
	RID	0001378	jʿḥ moon		
		ID Lexeme	21810	jʿḥ	moon
DRID	1001206		**jʿi̯ to wash**		
	RID	0001379	jʿi̯ to wash		
		ID Lexeme	21470	jʿ	bowl; basin (for washing)
			21560	jʿ	(gold) washer
			850185	jʿ.w	washing; breakfast
			21550	jʿi̯	to wash
			21570	jʿy.t	[a med. liquid, related to beer]
			21530	jʿj.t	purifier? (Nephthys)
			68590	mʿ	basin for washing the feet
DRID	1001207		**jʿn grief**		
	RID	0001380	jʿn grief		
		ID Lexeme	21750	jʿn.w	grief; woe!
DRID	1001208		**jʿnʿ baboon**		
	RID	0001381	jʿnʿ baboon		
		ID Lexeme	850186	jʿnʿ	baboon
			850335	jʿnʿ	baboon (Thoth)
			21730	jʿnʿ.t	baboon
DRID	1001209		**jʿr to rise**		
	RID	0001382	jʿr to rise		
		ID Lexeme	21770	jʿr	to mount up; to touch; to bring up
			21800	jʿry.t	god's dwelling
			21780	jʿr.t	(divine) serpent; uraeus
			21790	jʿr.tj	one who belongs to the two uraei
			22	ꜣʿʿ.w	approach
	RID	0003418	ʿr to make ascend		
		ID Lexeme	128980	sʿr	to make ascend
			129010	sʿr	[a constellation]
			129020	sʿry	ewer on a stand
			128000	sjʿr	to make ascend; to present
			128010	sjʿr.t	[epithet of the snake goddess of Buto; uraeus]
	RID	0003419	ʿr to rise		
		ID Lexeme	39150	ʿr	stairway
			856410	ʿr	ascender

			39300	ꜥr.yt	lintel
			39330	ꜥr.yt	ascender (the flood)
			39320	ꜥr.yt	heaven?; roof? [designation of the sky?]
			851628	ꜥr.w	proximity
			39210	ꜥr.t	(lotus) stalk; stem
	RID	**0003420**	ꜥr to roll		
		ID Lexeme	39230	ꜥr.t	scroll (of papyrus, of leather)
	RID	**0003428**	ꜥrr gate		
		ID Lexeme	39570	ꜥrr.wt	gate; hall; (center for) administration
	RID	**0003432**	ꜥrꜥr to accomplish		
		ID Lexeme	39360	ꜥrꜥr	to accomplish (something); to supply
	RID	**0003433**	ꜥrꜥr to rise		
		ID Lexeme	39370	ꜥrꜥr	to rise up (of the inundation)
DRID	**1001210**	**jꜥꜣ donkey**			
	RID	**0001383**	jꜥꜣ donkey		
		ID Lexeme	34840	jꜥꜣ	donkey
			35270	ꜥꜣ.w	donkey-loads?
			21520	jꜥꜣ.t	jenny (she-ass)
DRID	**1001211**	**jꜥꜣ to cover**			
	RID	**0001384**	jꜥꜣ to cover		
		ID Lexeme	21510	jꜥꜣ	cloak; kilt?
			855671	jꜥꜣ	to cover; to withdraw, to hide (from view)
DRID	**1001212**	**jꜥꜣ to speak a foreign language**			
	RID	**0001385**	jꜥꜣ to speak a foreign language		
		ID Lexeme	850019	jꜥꜣ	to speak a foreign language; to interpret
			450319	jꜥꜣ.w	a person who speaks a foreign language; interpreter

II.3 y

RID	**1002784**		**ybr stream**		
	RID	**0003116**	ybr stream		
		ID Lexeme	23800	ybr	stream
DRID	**1002785**		**yd^{c} skilled**		
	RID	**0003117**	yd^{c} skilled		
		ID Lexeme	33920	yd^{c}	skilled, smart
DRID	**1002786**		**ym sea**		
	RID	**0003118**	ym sea		
		ID Lexeme	24730	ym	sea

II.4 ^{c}

DRID	**1001055**	**^{c}f there**		
	RID	**0003325**	^{c}f there	
		ID Lexeme	500157 ^{c}f	there
DRID	**1001057**	**^{c}n here**		
	RID	**0003384**	^{c}n here	
		ID Lexeme	38000 ^{c}n	here
DRID	**1001058**	**^{c}ꜣ here**		
	RID	**0003454**	^{c}ꜣ here	
		ID Lexeme	34790 ^{c}ꜣ	here; there; yonder
DRID	**1002927**	**^{c} item**		
	RID	**0003276**	^{c} act (juridical)	
		ID Lexeme	34480 ^{c}	act; deed
			800062 ^{c}y	legitimate claim
	RID	**0003277**	^{c} arm	
		ID Lexeme	34320 ^{c}	arm; hand
			34410 ^{c}	dike; riverbed
			34590 ^{c}.wj	hand-shaped clappers
	RID	**0003278**	^{c} house	
		ID Lexeme	34460 ^{c}	house
			34540 ^{c}.t	room; department; dwelling
	RID	**0001518**	mj^c [a house?]	
		ID Lexeme	68200 mj^c.t	[a house?]
	RID	**0003279**	^{c} item	
		ID Lexeme	34400 ^{c}	trace; track
			34510 ^{c}	person
			34380 ^{c}	document
			34360 ^{c}	portion; piece
			34390 ^{c}	shaft; pole
			34340 ^{c}	region; side; administrative area
			36060 ^{c}.wj	[parts of a net (dual)]
			34560 ^{c}.t	piece rope; cord (at door or ship's mast)
			34550 ^{c}.t	member; limb
			854495 ^{c}.t	part (of something)
			855770 ^{c}.t	limb; part of meet
			34370 ^{c}j	cup; bowl
	RID	**0003280**	^{c} state	
		ID Lexeme	34350 ^{c}	condition; state (of affairs)
DRID	**1002928**	**^{c}b = db to push**		
	RID	**0003281**	^{c}b enemy	
		ID Lexeme	36280 ^{c}b	enemy; victim

RID	**0003283**	ᶜb horn			
	ID Lexeme	850983	ᶜb	(wooden) arch	
		36250	ᶜb	horn (of hoofed animals); sting (of a scorpion)	
		856342	ᶜb.j	horned	
		500827	ᶜb.wj	Two-horns	
		36800	ᶜb.wt	staff of office; pitchfork	
		36810	ᶜb.wtj	horned one (the king, Osiris)	
		36820	ᶜb.wtt	horned one (tutelary goddess of Upper Egypt)	
		36430	ᶜb.t	[abet-utensil for the Opening-of-the-mouth ceremony]	
		36390	ᶜb.t	female worker of horn	
RID	**0003288**	ᶜbb to knock			
	ID Lexeme	36850	ᶜbb	to knock? (on the door)	
RID	**0000194**	db to push			
	ID lexeme	178290	db	horn; tusk	
		90750	ndb	to wound (with the horns)	
RID	**0000200**	dbdb to beat			
	ID lexeme	178930	dbdb	to attack?	
		178910	dbdb	to beat (of the heart) (med.)	
		178920	dbdb	to stab; to cut up	
RID	**0000580**	ḥdb to crush down			
	ID Lexeme	111340	ḥtp	[harmful action?]	
		112200	ḥdb	to overthrow; to prostrate; to halt (at)	
		112210	ḥdb.yt	Bunch of beaten enemies	
		112220	ḥdb.w	[a symptom of a urological disorder]	

DRID	**1002930**	**ᶜb lettuce**			
	RID	**0003285**	ᶜb lettuce		
		ID Lexeme	36750	ᶜb.w	lettuce

DRID	**1002931**	**ᶜb meal**			
	RID	**0003286**	ᶜb meal		
		ID Lexeme	852141	ᶜb	meal
			36440	ᶜb.t	meal (or similar)

DRID	**1002932**	**ᶜb to purify**			
	RID	**0003287**	ᶜb to purify		
		ID Lexeme	36320	ᶜb	purifier (priest)
			36310	ᶜb	to purify; to be pure
			36350	ᶜb	[a sanctuary]
			36760	ᶜb.w	pitchfork wielder?
			36740	ᶜb.w	purification; purity
			36780	ᶜb.w	purifier

			36690	ꜥbꜥb.t	purification?
			128750	sꜥb	to cleanse; to purify
	RID	0003284	ꜥb impurity		
		ID Lexeme	36340	ꜥb	to dirty; to pollute
			36300	ꜥb.w	calamity; sinfulness; impurity; infection
DRID	**1002934**	**ꜥbb to smooth**			
	RID	**0003289**	ꜥbb to smooth		
		ID Lexeme	36840	ꜥbb	to smooth? (while making pottery)
DRID	**1002935**	**ꜥbd servant**			
	RID	**0003291**	ꜥbd servant		
		ID Lexeme	36970	ꜥbd	servant
DRID	**1002936**	**ꜥbḥ to fill a jug**			
	RID	**0003292**	ꜥbḥ to fill a jug		
		ID Lexeme	36900	ꜥbḥ	to fill (a jug) to the brim
DRID	**1002937**	**ꜥbẖn frog**			
	RID	**0003293**	ꜥbẖn frog		
		ID Lexeme	36910	ꜥbẖn	frog
			855106	ꜥbẖn.w	Frogs
DRID	**1002938**	**ꜥbš [a wine jug]**			
	RID	**0003294**	ꜥbš [a wine jug]		
		ID Lexeme	36920	ꜥbš	[a wine jug]
DRID	**1002939**	**ꜥbš to drown**			
	RID	**0003295**	ꜥbš to drown		
		ID Lexeme	36930	ꜥbš	to drown
DRID	**1002940**	**ꜥbꜣ a bird**			
	RID	**0003296**	ꜥbꜣ a bird		
		ID Lexeme	36580	ꜥbꜣ	pigeon
DRID	**1002941**	**ꜥbꜣ rope**			
	RID	**0003297**	ꜥbꜣ rope		
		ID Lexeme	36610	ꜥbꜣ.yt	rope; fetter
DRID	**1002942**	**ꜥbꜣ to interact**			
	RID	**0003298**	ꜥbꜣ to act		
		ID Lexeme	854498	ꜥbꜣ	to influence; to interfere
			36490	ꜥbꜣ	to command (a ship)
			500725	ꜥbꜣ	Aba-scepter
			36480	ꜥbꜣ	[aba-scepter]

		68700	mꜥbꜣ	[a spear]
		857653	sꜥbꜣ	to instruct
		128810	sꜥbꜣ	to be frightened (fig.)
RID	**0003300**	ꜥbꜣ to provide		
	ID Lexeme	36530	ꜥbꜣ	offering table; altar
		866762	ꜥbꜣ	to present, to lead
		36500	ꜥbꜣ	to provide (someone with something); to be provided with
		36600	ꜥbꜣ.yt	altar
		128780	sꜥb	to equip; to adorn
		128790	sꜥb	ornament
RID	**0003299**	ꜥbꜣ thirty		
	ID Lexeme	68690	mꜥbꜣ	thirty
		68740	mꜥbꜣ.yt	tribunal of 30 (judicial body)
		68720	mꜥbꜣ.w	the thirty (squares, of the board game senet)
		855925	mꜥbꜣ.t	thirty-ships

DRID 1002943 ꜥbꜣ to shine

RID	**0003301**	ꜥbꜣ to shine		
	ID Lexeme	36550	ꜥbꜣ	to glitter; to shine; to illuminate
		36560	ꜥbꜣ	light
		36570	ꜥbꜣ	shining one (the king, Horus)

DRID 1002944 ꜥbꜥ to boast

RID	**0003302**	ʿbʿ = ʿb to boast		
	ID Lexeme	36270	ʿb	to boast
		36640	ꜥbꜥ	[phallus]
		850348	ꜥbꜥ	boasting
		36630	ꜥbꜥ	to boast
		36670	ꜥbꜥb	to shine
		36650	ꜥbꜥb	fame; glory
		36660	ꜥbꜥb	to boast; to be excited
		856350	ꜥbꜥb	Boasting one
		36880	ꜥbb.t	javelin; spear
		500350	ꜥbb.tjw	One with the spear

DRID 1002945 ꜥḏ [part of a building (architrave?)]

RID	**0003303**	ꜥḏ [part of a building (architrave?)]		
	ID Lexeme	42150	ꜥḏ.yt	[part of a building (architrave?)]

DRID 1002946 ꜥḏ mongoose

RID	**0003306**	ꜥḏ mongoose		
	ID Lexeme	42030	ꜥḏ	mongoose
		859992	ꜥḏ.t	female mongoose

DRID 1002947 ꜥḏ spin

RID	**0003308**	ꜥḏ spin		

		ID Lexeme	41880	ꜥḏ	spin; (wooden) spool
DRID	**1002948**	**ꜥḏ to be whole**			
	RID	**0003304**	ꜥḏ fat		
		ID Lexeme	41980	ꜥḏ	pieces of fat (from an animal)
			42050	ꜥḏ.t	fat mass (of the heart)
	RID	**0003305**	ꜥḏ measure		
		ID Lexeme	855236	mꜥḏ.t	[grain measure]
	RID	**0003307**	ꜥḏ profit		
		ID Lexeme	855237	mꜥḏꜣ	profit
	RID	**0003309**	ꜥḏ to be whole		
		ID Lexeme	41890	ꜥḏ	to be whole; to be safe
			42040	ꜥḏ.t	slaughter
			129380	sꜥḏ	to make hale
DRID	**1002949**	**ꜥḏ to burn**			
	RID	**0003310**	ꜥḏ to burn		
		ID Lexeme	41950	ꜥḏ	to burn; to roast
DRID	**1002950**	**ꜥḏ to perceive (with ear, nose)**			
	RID	**0003311**	ꜥḏ to perceive (with ear, nose)		
		ID Lexeme	41910	ꜥḏ	to perceive (with ear, nose)
DRID	**1002951**	**ꜥḏ to rejoice**			
	RID	**0003312**	ꜥḏ to rejoice		
		ID Lexeme	860913	ꜥḏ.w	joyous thing
			42160	ꜥḏꜥḏ	to rejoice; to exult
DRID	**1002952**	**ꜥḏ to slaughter**			
	RID	**0003313**	ꜥḏ to slaughter		
		ID Lexeme	41940	ꜥḏ	to hack; to slaughter
			855765	ꜥḏ.wt	splitten tongue
			42280	ꜥḏ.tjw	Executioners
			68990	mꜥḏ	slaughtering block
DRID	**1002953**	**ꜥḏd youth**			
	RID	**0003314**	ꜥḏd youth		
		ID Lexeme	860671	ꜥḏd	to be childlike; to be boyish
			42290	ꜥḏd	youth; (boy) servant
			42300	ꜥḏd.t	girl; maid; virgin
DRID	**1002954**	**ꜥḏi̯ to sift**			
	RID	**0003315**	ꜥḏi̯ to sift		
		ID Lexeme	42000	ꜥḏi̯	to sift (the grain from the chaff)
DRID	**1002955**	**ꜥḏn [a bracelet]**			
	RID	**0003316**	ꜥḏn [a bracelet]		

		ID Lexeme	42220	^{c}ḏn.t	[a bracelet]
DRID	**1002956**		**^{c}dn wheat?**		
	RID	**0003317**	^{c}dn wheat?		
		ID Lexeme	41850	^{c}dn	[a cereal (wheat?)]
DRID	**1002957**		**^{c}ḏr [a part of a chariot]**		
	RID	**0003318**	^{c}ḏr [a part of a chariot]		
		ID Lexeme	42250	^{c}ḏr	[part of a chariot]
DRID	**1002958**		**^{c}ḏr helper**		
	RID	**0003319**	^{c}ḏr helper		
		ID Lexeme	42240	^{c}ḏr	helper
DRID	**1002959**		**^{c}dt conspiracy?**		
	RID	**0003320**	^{c}dt conspiracy?		
		ID Lexeme	41860	^{c}dt	conspiracy?
DRID	**1002960**		**^{c}ḏꜣ to do wrong**		
	RID	**0003321**	^{c}ḏꜣ to be guilty		
		ID Lexeme	42100	^{c}ḏꜣ	injustice; falsehood
			42120	^{c}ḏꜣ	wrongdoer; guilty man
			42110	^{c}ḏꜣ	to be guilty of; to be wrong
			129390	s^{c}ḏꜣ	to ruin
	RID	**0001087**	ḥ^{c}ḏꜣ to rob		
		ID Lexeme	868409	ḥ^{c}ḏꜣ.wt	robbery
			102240	ḥ^{c}ḏꜣ	to rob
			102250	ḥ^{c}ḏꜣ	robbery
DRID	**1002961**		**^{c}f to be greedy**		
	RID	**0003326**	^{c}f to be greedy		
		ID Lexeme	37360	^{c}f^{c}	greedy one (designation of crocodiles)
			862931	^{c}f^{c}f	crocodile
DRID	**1002962**		**^{c}fḏ chest**		
	RID	**0003327**	^{c}fḏ chest		
		ID Lexeme	37490	^{c}fḏ.t	chest; cabin (of a ship)
DRID	**1002963**		**^{c}fd nail**		
	RID	**0003328**	^{c}fd nail		
		ID Lexeme	37480	^{c}fd	nail; peg
	RID	**0003329**	^{c}fd to lead		
		ID Lexeme	37460	^{c}fd	to lead (the way)
DRID	**1002964**		**^{c}ff to fly**		
	RID	**0003330**	^{c}ff to fly		

		ID Lexeme	37330	ᶜfj	bee
			37370	ᶜff	to fly
DRID	**1002965**	**ᶜff to hum**			
	RID	**0003331**	ᶜff to hum		
		ID Lexeme	500940	ᶜff	to hum
DRID	**1002966**	**ᶜfn = ᶜfꜣ to envelop**			
	RID	**0003333**	ᶜfn to envelop		
		ID Lexeme	37380	ᶜfn	to cover; to be covered
			37390	ᶜfn	[a covering (package, pouch)]
			37410	ᶜfn.w	boot?; leather sock?
			37420	ᶜfn.wj	He with the headcloth
			37400	ᶜfn.t	headcloth ("wrapping")
			857654	sᶜfn	to cover; to veil
	RID	**0003336**	ᶜfꜣ to envelop?		
		ID Lexeme	37310	ᶜfꜣ.y	encampment (of Bedouins)
DRID	**1002967**	**ᶜft collection of spells**			
	RID	**0003334**	ᶜft collection of spells		
		ID Lexeme	500067	ᶜft.t	collection of spells (relating to the hereafter)
DRID	**1002968**	**ᶜfꜣ to demolish**			
	RID	**0003335**	ᶜfꜣ to demolish		
		ID Lexeme	37280	ᶜfꜣ	to demolish; to devour
			37290	ᶜfꜣ.t	ripped out body part
DRID	**1002969**	**ᶜgn ringstand**			
	RID	**0003337**	ᶜgn ringstand		
		ID Lexeme	41730	ᶜgn	ringstand
DRID	**1002970**	**ᶜgrt wagon (drawn by oxen)**			
	RID	**0003338**	ᶜgrt wagon (drawn by oxen)		
		ID Lexeme	41770	ᶜgrt	wagon (drawn by oxen)
DRID	**1002971**	**ᶜgsw belt**			
	RID	**0003339**	ᶜgsw belt		
		ID Lexeme	41800	ᶜgsw	belt
DRID	**1002972**	**ᶜgꜣ [an ointment]**			
	RID	**0003340**	ᶜgꜣ [an ointment]		
		ID Lexeme	41680	ᶜgꜣ	[an ointment (for ritual anointing)]
DRID	**1002973**	**ᶜgꜣ claw**			
	RID	**0003341**	ᶜgꜣ claw		
		ID Lexeme	41690	ᶜgꜣ.t	claw (lion, bird)

DRID 1002974 ꜥgꜣ to capsize

RID 0003342 ꜥgꜣ to capsize

ID Lexeme			
	41660	ꜥgꜣ	to capsize; to drown
	41510	ꜥqw	to capsize
	129360	sꜥgꜣ	to make capsize

DRID 1002975 ꜥḥ cultivated land

RID 0003343 ꜥḥ cultivated land

ID Lexeme			
	40490	ꜥḥ.wtj	cultivator; tenant
	39880	ꜥḥ.t	cultivated land

DRID 1002976 ꜥḥ palace

RID 0003344 ꜥḥ palace

ID Lexeme			
	39850	ꜥḥ	palace
	39890	ꜥḥ.t	palace

DRID 1002977 ꜥḥ to catch

RID 0003345 ꜥḥ to catch

ID Lexeme			
	39820	ꜥḥ	to capture; to catch (e.g., game, with a net)
	39810	ꜥḥ	cord; rope; wick
	39870	ꜥḥ.t	net (stretched for the hunt)
	30590	jḥy	sack; net; rope

DRID 1002978 ꜥḥ to wipe away

RID 0003346 ꜥḥ to wipe away

ID Lexeme			
	39830	ꜥḥ	to wipe away

DRID 1002979 ꜥḫi̯ to burn

RID 0003347 ꜥḫi̯ to burn

ID Lexeme			
	40500	ꜥḫ	brazier
	40610	ꜥḫ.w	[an illness]
	500481	ꜥḫ.w	Burning one
	40620	ꜥḫ.wt	braziers
	40520	ꜥḫi̯	to burn; to evaporate
	129230	sꜥḫ	to burn up

DRID 1002980 ꜥḫi̯ to fly

RID 0003348 ꜥḫi̯ to fly

ID Lexeme			
	40730	ꜥḫ	[a bird]
	866810	ꜥḫ.t	flight
	40740	ꜥḫ.t	wing
	40750	ꜥḫ.t	aviary?
	40760	ꜥḫi̯	to fly (away)

DRID 1002981 ꜥḫi̯ to raise up

RID 0003349 ꜥḫi̯ to raise up

		ID Lexeme	40550	ꜥḫ.t	accumulation (of fluid)
			40570	ꜥḫi̯	to raise up; to rise up
			40720	ꜥḫḫ	griffin (fig. for the king and gods)
			129220	sꜥḫi̯	to make rise (the heavens)
DRID	**1002982**	**ꜥẖm leaf**			
	RID	**0003350**	ꜥẖm leaf		
		ID Lexeme	40830	ꜥẖm.w	leaves; twigs [of a plant]
DRID	**1002983**	**ꜥḫm to extinguish**			
	RID	**0003351**	ꜥḫm to extinguish		
		ID Lexeme	40630	ꜥḫm	to quench; to extinguish
DRID	**1002984**	**ꜥḫm to fly**			
	RID	**0003352**	ꜥḫm to fly		
		ID Lexeme	40650	ꜥḫm	to fly
DRID	**1002985**	**ꜥẖm to inspire fear**			
	RID	**0003353**	ꜥẖm to inspire fear		
		ID Lexeme	40790	ꜥẖm	to cause to shudder; to inspire awe
			858543	ꜥẖm	hawk; eagle
			40780	ꜥẖm	(cult) image of a falcon; (cult) image (gen.)
			40810	ꜥẖm	Horrifier (crocodile demon)
DRID	**1002986**	**ꜥḫm wick?**			
	RID	**0003354**	ꜥḫm wick?		
		ID Lexeme	40640	ꜥḫm	[a combustible material (wick?)]
DRID	**1002987**	**ꜥẖn to close (the eyes)**			
	RID	**0003355**	ꜥẖn to close (the eyes)		
		ID Lexeme	40840	ꜥẖn	to close (the eyes)
DRID	**1002988**	**ꜥḥꜣ to fight**			
	RID	**0003356**	ꜥḥꜣ to fight		
		ID Lexeme	39990	ꜥḥꜣ	fighter (hippopotamus)
			39980	ꜥḥꜣ	Nile perch
			39930	ꜥḥꜣ	fighting; battle
			39950	ꜥḥꜣ	unfavorable; inauspicious (of calendar days); militant
			39940	ꜥḥꜣ	warrior
			39970	ꜥḥꜣ	Fighter (Bes-like demon)
			39920	ꜥḥꜣ	to fight
			40050	ꜥḥꜣ.w	weapons (gen.); arrows
			40030	ꜥḥꜣ.wj	the two fighters (Horus and Seth)
			40080	ꜥḥꜣ.wj	to argue
			40060	ꜥḥꜣ.wj	fighter; warrior; man

		40070	ꜥḥꜣ.wj	male
		856368	ꜥḥꜣ.wtt	warship
		40010	ꜥḥꜣ.t	battleground
		40020	ꜥḥꜣ.t	fighter (leonine goddess)
		856367	ꜥḥꜣ.t	fight
		40000	ꜥḥꜣ.t	warship
		860219	mꜥḥꜣ	guy
		68910	mꜥḥꜣ	fighter (with the arm)
		858895	mꜥḥꜣ	fighter?
		852719	sꜥḥꜣ	make ready for battle; let fight
DRID	**1002989**	**ꜥḥꜥ boat**		
RID	**0003357**	ꜥḥꜥ boat		
	ID Lexeme	40210	ꜥḥꜥ	boat (gen.)
		859328	ꜥḥꜥ.w	fleet
DRID	**1002990**	**ꜥḥꜥ to stand**		
RID	**0003359**	ꜥḥꜥ to stand		
	ID Lexeme	40120	ꜥḥꜥ	position (of a star)
		40110	ꜥḥꜥ	to stand; to stand up
		40200	ꜥḥꜥ	attendant; helper
		851887	ꜥḥꜥ	to stand up
		40230	ꜥḥꜥ	height
		851686	ꜥḥꜥ	to get ready to do (something)
		858623	ꜥḥꜥ	door leaves
		40100	ꜥḥꜥ	mast
		854135	ꜥḥꜥ	Standing one
		40360	ꜥḥꜥ.y	midday
		40380	ꜥḥꜥ.yt	midday (6th hour of the day)
		40370	ꜥḥꜥ.yt	attendant
		860380	ꜥḥꜥ.yt	Helpers (female)
		40390	ꜥḥꜥ.yt	Ahait (south pillar of the sky)
		40420	ꜥḥꜥ.w	stela
		40450	ꜥḥꜥ.w	stander (snake god)
		40430	ꜥḥꜥ.w	nape (of the neck); spinal ridge
		40470	ꜥḥꜥ.w	obstacles?
		40440	ꜥḥꜥ.w	heron
		866804	ꜥḥꜥ.w	Stand-by, Helper
		40410	ꜥḥꜥ.w	station; position; standstill
		40460	ꜥḥꜥ.w	Helper
		501057	ꜥḥꜥ.t	Stander
		500527	ꜥḥꜥ.tj	He who belongs to the tomb
		68920	mꜥḥꜥ.t	funerary chapel (for offerings or a stela); cenotaph
		129190	sꜥḥꜥ	to erect; to set up; to make stand
RID	**0003358**	ꜥḥꜥ quantity		
	ID Lexeme	40160	ꜥḥꜥ	amount; number; quantity
		40240	ꜥḥꜥ	treasure; storehouse

			40180	ʿḥʿ	[a measure for beer]
			40130	ʿḥʿ	to lack; to be lacking; to wait
			40170	ʿḥʿ	multitude (of people)
			40150	ʿḥʿ	uncertain (of calendar days)
			40480	ʿḥʿ.w	lifetime; time; duration
			40280	ʿḥʿ.w	heap(s); quantity (math.)
			40260	ʿḥʿ.t	quantity (math.)

DRID 1002991 ʿj to jubilate

RID	**0003362**	ʿjʿj to jubilate			
	ID Lexeme	859363	ʿjʿj	to jubilate; to rejoice	
RID	**0003360**	ʿj to jubilate			
	ID Lexeme	35580	ʿy	to rejoice	

DRID 1002992 ʿjn limestone

RID	**0003361**	ʿjn limestone		
	ID Lexeme	35630	ʿjn	to face with limestone
		35620	ʿjn	limestone
		38340	ʿn.w	limestone?; pebbles?

DRID 1002993 ʿk end of a rod/stick

RID	**0003363**	ʿk end of a rod/stick		
	ID Lexeme	41570	ʿk.t	end of a rod/stick

DRID 1002994 ʿm to swallow

RID	**0003364**	ʿm to swallow		
	ID Lexeme	37510	ʿm	to know; to come to know
		37500	ʿm	to swallow; to devour; to absorb
		500299	ʿm.w	Devourer
		128850	sʿm	to inlay; to overlay (with gold)
		128840	sʿm	to swallow; to wash down (medicine)
		862961	sʿm.w	remedy to be swallowed
RID	**0003379**	ʿmʿm to swallow		
	ID Lexeme	37790	ʿmʿm	to devour
		37810	ʿmʿm	to devour
		37830	ʿmʿm.w	shrew mouse

DRID 1002995 ʿmd to be weak

RID	**0003365**	ʿmd to be weak		
	ID Lexeme	37960	ʿmd	to be weak (of heart, body parts)

DRID 1002996 ʿmḏ to turn away

RID	**0003366**	ʿmḏ to turn away		
	ID Lexeme	37990	ʿmḏ	to turn away (from something)

DRID 1002997 ʿmdy supports (chariot parts)

	RID	**0003367**	ꜥmdy supports (chariot parts)	
		ID Lexeme	37980 ꜥmdy	supports (chariot parts)
DRID	**1002998**	**ꜥmj to smear**		
	RID	**0003368**	ꜥmj to smear	
		ID Lexeme	37640 ꜥmj	ointment (med.)
			850352 ꜥmj	to smear; to seal
			37740 ꜥmꜥ.t	mud; Nile mud
			37780 ꜥmꜥm	to rub (feet)
			37820 ꜥmꜥm.t	mud; Nile mud; muddy ground
			850353 ꜥmr	ointment
DRID	**1002999**	**ꜥmnt to box**		
	RID	**0003369**	ꜥmnt to box	
		ID Lexeme	37880 ꜥmnt	to box
DRID	**1003000**	**ꜥmḳ to couple**		
	RID	**0003370**	ꜥmḳ to couple	
		ID Lexeme	37930 ꜥmḳ	to mount (sexually); to couple
DRID	**1003001**	**ꜥmr baker**		
	RID	**0003371**	ꜥmr baker	
		ID Lexeme	37890 ꜥmr	(temple) bakery
			37910 ꜥmr	baker
DRID	**1003002**	**ꜥmt clouds**		
	RID	**0003372**	ꜥmt clouds	
		ID Lexeme	37940 ꜥmt	clouds (or similar)
DRID	**1003003**	**ꜥmw [a fruit]**		
	RID	**0003373**	ꜥmw [a fruit]	
		ID Lexeme	37840 ꜥmw	[a very juicy fruit? (med.)]
DRID	**1003004**	**ꜥmꜣ [a part of a body]**		
	RID	**0003374**	ꜥmꜣ [a part of a body]	
		ID Lexeme	37610 ꜥmꜣ.t	[a part of body (spec. of Osiris]
DRID	**1003005**	**ꜥmꜣ [a plant]**		
	RID	**0003375**	ꜥmꜣ [a plant]	
		ID Lexeme	37600 ꜥmꜣ	[a plant (a very juicy fruit?) (med.)]
DRID	**1003006**	**ꜥmꜣ to turn sour**		
	RID	**0003377**	ꜥmꜣ to turn sour	
		ID Lexeme	37690 ꜥmꜥ	[a kind of beer]
			37570 ꜥmꜣ	to turn sour (of beer)
			37580 ꜥmꜣ	[a beer jug]

DRID 1003007 ꜥmꜥ sexually immature?

RID 0003378 ꜥmꜥ sexually immature?

ID Lexeme		
37680	ꜥmꜥ	uncircumcised? person; youngling?; impure one?
37730	ꜥmꜥ.t	virgin

DRID 1003008 ꜥmꜥꜣ to throw

RID 0003380 ꜥmꜥꜣ to throw

ID Lexeme		
37750	ꜥmꜥꜣ	to throw (a throw stick)
856379	ꜥmꜥꜣ.wj	thrower of a throw stick?
37760	ꜥmꜥꜣ.t	throw stick; casting net

DRID 1003009 ꜥmꜥꜥ kernel

RID 0003382 ꜥmꜥꜥ kernel

ID Lexeme		
37770	ꜥmꜥꜥ	kernel (of grain); (date) pip (med.)

DRID 1003010 ꜥn [eye, as a character in writing]

RID 0003383 ꜥn [eye, as a character in writing]

ID Lexeme		
38060	ꜥn	[eye, as a character in writing]

DRID 1003011 ꜥn ring

RID 0003385 ꜥn ring

ID Lexeme		
38140	ꜥn.t	(metal) ring

DRID 1003012 ꜥn talon

RID 0003386 ꜥn talon

ID Lexeme		
38120	ꜥn.t	adze
38130	ꜥn.t	claw; talon; thumb
38150	ꜥn.t	[smallest unit for measuring time]

DRID 1003013 ꜥn writing board

RID 0003387 ꜥn writing board

ID Lexeme		
38020	ꜥn	writing board; writing tablet

DRID 1003014 ꜥnb alfa grass

RID 0003388 ꜥnb alfa grass

ID Lexeme		
38370	ꜥnb	alfa grass

DRID 1003015 ꜥnb to close

RID 0003389 ꜥnb to close

ID Lexeme		
38390	ꜥnb	to close (the mouth); to enclose
38400	ꜥnb.yt	bundle; basket (measure for papyrus and bread)

DRID 1003016 ꜥnḏ [an unguent]

RID 0003390 ꜥnḏ [an unguent]

ID Lexeme		
39110	ꜥnḏ.w	[a jar]
39120	ꜥnḏ.w	[an unguent]; [an oil]

DRID 1003017 ᶜnḏ to be diminished

RID	0003391	ᶜnḏ to be diminished		
	ID Lexeme	39040	ᶜnḏ	to be few; to be diminished
		500588	ᶜnḏ	few; deficient
		39030	ᶜnḏ	[a part of a wing]
		859790	ᶜnḏ	to weaken; to decimate
		39050	ᶜnḏ.t	the few (people)
		863022	sᶜnḏ	narrowing; reduction; decrease
		128970	sᶜnḏ	to lessen
RID	0004244	ᶜnḏ diminished sunlight		
		854281	ᶜnḏ.w	sunshine
		39100	ᶜnḏ.w	light of the sun; dawn
		853792	mᶜnḏ.t	morning bark (Nephthys)
		68850	mᶜnḏ.t	Manedjet (day bark of the sun god)

DRID 1003018 ᶜnḫ alabaster

RID	0003392	ᶜnḫ alabaster		
	ID Lexeme	38620	ᶜnḫ.w	blocks of Egyptian alabaster

DRID 1003019 ᶜnḫ ankh-sign

RID	0003393	ᶜnḫ ankh-sign		
	ID Lexeme	500274	ᶜnḫ	ankh (symbol of life)
		38640	ᶜnḫ	[ankh-vessel (for libations)]
		38600	ᶜnḫ	Ankh beetle (solar beetle)
		38900	ᶜnḫ.y	living one
		500892	ᶜnḫ.jt	She-who-belongs-to-the-sign-of-life?

DRID 1003020 ᶜnḫ to bind

RID	0003394	ᶜnḫ to bind		
	ID Lexeme	38520	ᶜnḫ	(sandal strap)
		38650	ᶜnḫ	wing of a door
		38660	ᶜnḫ	[a document]
		38590	ᶜnḫ	garland; bouquet
		38580	ᶜnḫ	captive (lit. bound one)
		860270	ᶜnḫ.t	wing of a door
		68820	mᶜnḫ.t	tassel (as necklace)
		68830	mᶜnḫ.t	staff
		68840	mᶜnḫ.tj	he with the tassel

DRID 1003021 ᶜnḫ goat

RID	0003395	ᶜnḫ goat		
	ID Lexeme	38680	ᶜnḫ	goat; herd (gen.)
		38760	ᶜnḫ.t	goat; herds (gen.); flocks (gen.)

DRID 1003022 ᶜnḫ to live

RID	0003396	ᶜnḫ to live		

	ID Lexeme	38540	ᶜnẖ	life
		38530	ᶜnẖ	to live; to be alive
		38670	ᶜnẖ	livelihood
		38550	ᶜnẖ	[in formulae, to introduce an oath]
		38710	ᶜnẖ	water of life (given by Isis)
		38720	ᶜnẖ	earth; land
		38610	ᶜnẖ	life (the inundation)
		400614	ᶜnẖ	living person; inhabitant; member (of a group); soldier
		38630	ᶜnẖ	mirror
		38920	ᶜnẖ.w	stars
		38910	ᶜnẖ.w	the living ones
		38930	ᶜnẖ.wj	pair of ears
		856399	ᶜnẖ.wt	living one
		852886	ᶜnẖ.t	living person (female)
		38780	ᶜnẖ.t	the west (lit. (place) of life)
		38740	ᶜnẖ.t	living eye (of a god)
		38730	ᶜnẖ.t	living one (Hathor-Isis)
		38750	ᶜnẖ.t	grain
		128960	sᶜnẖ.t	she who preserves (maat) (as a designation of the seat of the king)
RID	**0007861**	sᶜnẖ to represent life		
	ID Lexeme	128930	sᶜnẖ	to sculpt
		128920	sᶜnẖ	sculptor
RID	**0007862**	sᶜnẖ to make live		
	ID Lexeme	128910	sᶜnẖ	to make live; to perpetuate; to nourish
		128940	sᶜnẖ	one who sustains
		128950	sᶜnẖ	endowment; revernue
		851895	sᶜnẖ.w	Life sustainer
RID	**0007863**	ᶜnẖ	to swear	
	ID Lexeme	38560	ᶜnẖ	oath
		38570	ᶜnẖ	to swear

DRID	**1003023**	**ᶜnḥb [a bird]**			
	RID	**0003397**	ᶜnḥb [a bird]		
		ID Lexeme	38510	ᶜnḥb.t	pied kingfisher

DRID	**1003024**	**ᶜni̯ to be good**			
	RID	**0003398**	ᶜni̯ to be good		
		ID Lexeme	38070	ᶜni̯	to be beautiful; to be kind; to be pleasing
			38080	ᶜn	good one
			400159	ᶜn	beautiful; kind
			600622	ᶜn.w	beauty
			38350	ᶜn.w	ornament (or part?) (of a metal vessel)
			38180	ᶜn.wt	beauty

			38160	ʿn.t	beautiful one (Hathor, Nekhbet)
			38110	ʿn.t	diadem (or similar)
			68770	mʿn	to embellish?
			853997	sʿn.w	Glorifying one
			128900	sʿni̯	to embellish
DRID	**1003025**	**ʿnn singing**			
	RID	**0003399**	ʿnn singing		
		ID Lexeme	860115	ʿnn	singing
DRID	**1003026**	**ʿnn to return**			
	RID	**0003400**	ʿnn to return		
		ID Lexeme	38050	ʿn	again; already; further
			861167	ʿn	prolapse
			38300	ʿnʿn	to complain
			38290	ʿnʿn	to refuse
			38040	ʿnn	to return; to turn back; to invert
			38450	ʿnn.w	coil; intestines
			38480	ʿnn.t	rope (lit. what is coiled)
	RID	**0003401**	ʿnn to twist		
		ID Lexeme	38460	ʿnn.wj	Twice-Coiled (a snake)
			68780	mʿn	to twist; to be twisted
			68800	mʿnn	rope (of two twisted skeins)
			68810	mʿnn	[torture device (for twisting limbs)]
			68790	mʿnn	to twist; to be coiled round
			501049	mʿnn.wj	The two entwined ones (snakes)
DRID	**1003027**	**ʿnnw [a tree]**			
	RID	**0003402**	ʿnnw [a tree]		
		ID Lexeme	38440	ʿnnw	[a (fruit) tree]
			850686	ʿnnw.t	fruit of the anenu-tree
DRID	**1003028**	**ʿnḳ to flow**			
	RID	**0003403**	ʿnḳ to flow		
		ID Lexeme	38960	ʿnḳ	to flow (of the inundation)
			860384	ʿnḳ.t	[flood]
DRID	**1003029**	**ʿnt myrrh**			
	RID	**0003404**	ʿnt myrrh		
		ID Lexeme	39010	ʿnt.w	myrrh
			856389	ʿnt.wj	one belonging to the myrrh
DRID	**1003030**	**ʿpi̯ to fly**			
	RID	**0003405**	ʿpi̯ to fly		
		ID Lexeme	36870	ʿbb	winged one (winged scarab, Horus)
			36980	ʿp	[a serpent (Apophis?)]

		37010	ꜥp.y	winged one (sun as a winged scarab, Horus)
		854185	ꜥp.y	wing
		37020	ꜥp.yw	flying ones (enemies)
		37030	ꜥp.yt	winged one (female sun disk, Hathor)
		37000	ꜥpi̯	to fly
		37070	ꜥpp	winged one (sun disk)
		128820	sꜥpi̯	to allow to pass by
RID	**0003406**	ꜥpi̯ to stride		
	ID Lexeme	37050	ꜥp.w	striding (and similar)
		36990	ꜥpi̯	to stride (through, by)

DRID	**1003031**	**ꜥpnn water newt**		
RID	**0003407**	ꜥpnn water newt		
	ID Lexeme	37080	ꜥpnn.t	water newt?; slug?

DRID	**1003032**	**ꜥpr to provide**		
RID	**0003408**	ꜥpr to provide		
	ID Lexeme	37090	ꜥpr	to equip; to be equipped
		37120	ꜥpr	garment
		37110	ꜥpr	[a cult object (presented by the king to a god)]
		37100	ꜥpr.w	crew (of a ship); gang (of workmen)
		37180	ꜥpr.w	equipment
		37190	ꜥpr.w	jewellery
		37150	ꜥpr.t	[a jar, also used as a bread mold]
		37140	ꜥpr.t	equipment (of offerings)

DRID	**1003033**	**ꜥḳ cormorant**		
RID	**0003409**	ꜥḳ cormorant		
	ID Lexeme	41240	ꜥḳ	cormorant (onomatopoeic)

DRID	**1003034**	**ꜥḳ to enter**		
RID	**0003410**	ꜥḳ to enter		
	ID Lexeme	41180	ꜥḳ	to enter; to have entrée; to usher (someone) in; to set (of stars)
		851300	ꜥḳ	advisor; trusted friend
		41440	ꜥḳ.y	one who has access (a priest)
		41430	ꜥḳ.y	ceremonial entrance (of the king)
		859008	ꜥḳ.yt	servant
		41450	ꜥḳ.yt	servant (lit. one who enters)
		41190	ꜥḳ.w	friend(s); confidant(s)
		41470	ꜥḳ.w	loaves (of bread); income
		500254	ꜥḳ.t	entry (to the netherworld)
		550196	ꜥḳ.t	entering

41460 ꜥḳꜥḳ to enter; to reach
129320 sꜥḳ [designation of the temple porter]
129310 sꜥḳ to make enter; to send in
861169 sꜥḳ something at the beginning?
129350 sꜥḳ.y recruit?; conscript?

RID 0003700 mꜥḳ to skewer
ID Lexeme 68950 mꜥḳ skewer
68970 mꜥḳ roast on a skewer
68960 mꜥḳ to roast on a skewer

DRID 1003035 ꜥḳꜣ [a transport ship]
RID 0003411 ꜥḳꜣ [a transport ship]
ID Lexeme 41410 ꜥḳꜣ.y [a transport ship]

DRID 1003036 ꜥḳꜣ to be accurate
RID 0003412 ꜥḳꜣ to be accurate
ID Lexeme 41360 ꜥḳꜣ ship's cordage; tow rope
41370 ꜥḳꜣ to use the tow rope
41330 ꜥḳꜣ precisely; correctly
41340 ꜥḳꜣ correctness; straightness
41350 ꜥḳꜣ opposite; in view of
41380 ꜥḳꜣ [a priest]
866813 ꜥḳꜣ [rudder]
400768 ꜥḳꜣ correct; exact
41310 ꜥḳꜣ to be accurate; to make accurate
41320 ꜥḳꜣ one who is correct; one who is straightforward
41420 ꜥḳꜣ.yt accuracy; correctness
851308 ꜥḳꜣꜣ luck?
129340 sꜥḳꜣ to direct; to set on the way

DRID 1003037 ꜥr [a tree]
RID 0003413 ꜥr [a tree]
ID Lexeme 39430 ꜥr.w [a tree]

DRID 1003038 ꜥr goat
RID 0003414 ꜥr goat
ID Lexeme 853603 ꜥr nanny (she-goat)?
39170 ꜥr goat

DRID 1003039 ꜥr hind part
RID 0003415 ꜥr hind part
ID Lexeme 39250 ꜥr.t hind parts (of humans); hindquarters (of animals)

DRID 1003040 ꜥr jaw
RID 0003416 ꜥr jaw

		ID Lexeme	39240	ꜥr.t	jaw
DRID	**1003041**	**ꜥr stone**			
	RID	**0003417**	ꜥr stone		
		ID Lexeme	39180	ꜥr	pebble; stone
			39200	ꜥr	seed (or pit of a fruit)
DRID	**1003042**	**ꜥrḏ to terrify (the enemy)**			
	RID	**0003421**	ꜥrḏ to terrify (the enemy)		
		ID Lexeme	39800	ꜥrḏ	to terrify (the enemy); to hold on to
DRID	**1003043**	**ꜥrf to wrap**			
	RID	**0003422**	ꜥrf to wrap		
		ID Lexeme	112590	ꜥrf	[silver processing method (for barks of gods)]
			39500	ꜥrf	to pack (up); to wrap
			39510	ꜥrf	to squeeze?
			39490	ꜥrf	bag
DRID	**1003044**	**ꜥrḳ to complete**			
	RID	**0003423**	ꜥrḳ to be wise		
		ID Lexeme	39640	ꜥrḳ	to be wise; to be understanding; to understand
			39750	ꜥrḳ.yt	cleverness
	RID	**0003424**	ꜥrḳ to complete		
		ID Lexeme	39680	ꜥrḳ	end; extremity
			39630	ꜥrḳ	to complete; to stop (doing something)
			39740	ꜥrḳ.y	month's end (i.e., the last day)
			856688	ꜥrḳ.t	end
			129040	sꜥrḳ	to destroy (enemies)
			129030	sꜥrḳ	to complete; to end
			129050	sꜥrḳ	Wring out (laundry)
DRID	**1003047**	**ꜥrḳ to tie on**			
	RID	**0003426**	ꜥrḳ to tie on		
		ID Lexeme	39610	ꜥrḳ	ankle
			39700	ꜥrḳ	bandage
			39620	ꜥrḳ	to tie on; to don (a garment)
			39670	ꜥrḳ	[an item of chariot equipment (sack or basket)]
			39600	ꜥrḳ	to bend; to pull together
			39660	ꜥrḳ	sack
			39690	ꜥrḳ	corner; turning; bend; angle
			854499	ꜥrḳ	to tie round; to bend
			39760	ꜥrḳ.w	welts (med.)

			852049 mᶜrḳ	[a garment?]
	RID	0003425	ᶜrḳ to swear	
		ID Lexeme	39650 ᶜrḳ	to swear (an oath); to abjure
			854608 ᶜrḳ	oath
DRID	**1003048**		**ᶜrḳwr silver**	
	RID	**0003427**	ᶜrḳwr silver	
		ID Lexeme	39770 ᶜrḳwr	silver
DRID	**1003049**		**ᶜrš to sneeze**	
	RID	**0003429**	ᶜrš to sneeze	
		ID Lexeme	39580 ᶜrš	[something negative relating to the nose (sneezing?)]
DRID	**1003050**		**ᶜršn lentils**	
	RID	**0003430**	ᶜršn lentils	
		ID Lexeme	39590 ᶜršn	lentils
DRID	**1003051**		**ᶜrt [a body of water in Upper Egypt]**	
	RID	**0003431**	ᶜrt [a body of water in Upper Egypt]	
		ID Lexeme	39790 ᶜrt.j	[a body of water in Upper Egypt]
DRID	**1003052**		**ᶜš [a beer jug]**	
	RID	**0003434**	ᶜš [a beer jug]	
		ID Lexeme	40950 ᶜš	[a beer jug]
DRID	**1003053**		**ᶜš [a food]**	
	RID	**0003435**	ᶜš [a food]	
		ID Lexeme	40910 ᶜš	[meal of the soldiers?]
			40960 ᶜš	[a food (fruit?)]
DRID	**1003054**		**ᶜš coniferous wood**	
	RID	**0003436**	ᶜš coniferous wood	
		ID Lexeme	450173 ᶜš	resin; oil (of a coniferous tree)
			40940 ᶜš	Lebanese fir tree; [coniferous wood (of Lebanon)]
DRID	**1003055**		**ᶜš throat**	
	RID	**0003442**	ᶜšᶜš to strangle	
		ID Lexeme	41130 ᶜšᶜš	throat
			41140 ᶜšᶜš	to strangle
DRID	**1003056**		**ᶜš = jꜣš to summon**	
	RID	**0003437**	ᶜš to summon	
		ID Lexeme	40900 ᶜš	call; invocation; announcement
			40890 ᶜš	to summon
			41150 ᶜš.wt	crying (of a child)

			41100	ꜥš.wt	crying fit (of a child)
			129280	sꜥšꜣ	policeman; escort
			129270	sꜥšꜣ	to repel
			129290	sꜥšꜣ	protective rite
DRID	**1003057**	**ꜥši̯ to moan**			
	RID	**0003438**	ꜥši̯ to moan		
		ID Lexeme	40930	ꜥši̯	to moan
DRID	**1003058**	**ꜥšḳ to oppress**			
	RID	**0003439**	ꜥšḳ to oppress		
		ID Lexeme	41170	ꜥšḳ	to oppress
DRID	**1003059**	**ꜥšꜣ lizard**			
	RID	**0003440**	ꜥšꜣ lizard		
		ID Lexeme	41040	ꜥšꜣ	lizard; gecko
DRID	**1003060**	**ꜥšꜣ to be numerous**			
	RID	**0003441**	ꜥšꜣ to be numerous		
		ID Lexeme	41011	ꜥšꜣ	a lot; numerous; common
			41020	ꜥšꜣ	quantity; multitude
			41010	ꜥšꜣ	to be numerous; to be rich
			450171	ꜥšꜣ	miscellaneous?
			450155	ꜥšꜣ	very; often
			41050	ꜥšꜣ.wt	multitude; mass of people
			41060	ꜥšꜣ.tj	a lot; many
			129260	sꜥšꜣ	to make numerous; to multiply
			858699	sꜥšꜣ.w	mass of people
DRID	**1003061**	**ꜥṯḫ to press out**			
	RID	**0003443**	ꜥṯḫ to press out		
		ID Lexeme	600223	ꜥṯḫ	brewer
			41820	ꜥṯḫ	to sieve; to press
DRID	**1003062**	**ꜥw crane**			
	RID	**0003444**	ꜥw crane		
		ID Lexeme	35840	ꜥw	crane
DRID	**1003063**	**ꜥw herd**			
	RID	**0003445**	ꜥw herd		
		ID Lexeme	35870	ꜥw.t	herds (gen.); flocks
			35860	ꜥw.t	scepter; crook (of a shepherd)
			36240	ꜥw.tj	shepherd; scepter bearer
DRID	**1003064**	**ꜥwg to be hot**			
	RID	**0003446**	ꜥwg to be hot		
		ID Lexeme	860376	ꜥwg	heat?

	RID	0003447	ꜥwg to roast		
		ID Lexeme	41620	ꜥg.t	roasted (of grain)
			36210	ꜥwg	to roast (grain)
DRID	1003065		ꜥwꜣi̯ = ꜥwn to rob		
	RID	0003448	ꜥwn to plunder		
		ID Lexeme	36110	ꜥwn	to deceive; to plunder
			36200	ꜥwn	to deceive; to rob
			36190	ꜥwn.w	plunderer
			855231	ꜥwn.tj	greedy one
	RID	0003451	ꜥwꜣi̯ to rob		
		ID Lexeme	856493	ꜥwꜣ	robbery
			401143	ꜥwꜣ	robbing
			850342	ꜥwꜣ.y	robber
			35990	ꜥwꜣ.y	Robber (a demon)
			862907	ꜥwꜣ.yt	robber (female)
			36010	ꜥwꜣ.yt	robber
			36040	ꜥwꜣ.w	reaper
			35960	ꜥwꜣ.t	robbery
			863015	ꜥwꜣ.tj	robber; enemy
			36000	ꜥwꜣi̯	to harvest
			854497	ꜥwꜣi̯	to get something done (or similar); to eliminate something (or similar)
			35980	ꜥwꜣi̯	to rob
			401151	mꜥwꜣ	[provider?]
DRID	1003066		ꜥwn to wail		
	RID	0003449	ꜥwn to wail		
		ID Lexeme	36120	ꜥwn	to wail
DRID	1003067		ꜥwꜣ to rot		
	RID	0003450	ꜥwꜣ to rot		
		ID Lexeme	35950	ꜥwꜣ	foulness
			35940	ꜥwꜣ	to rot; to perish
			36020	ꜥwꜣ.yt	fermented substance (med.)
			35970	ꜥwꜣꜣ	fermented bread
			128740	sꜥwꜣ	to let ferment
DRID	1003069		ꜥyn well		
	RID	0003451	ꜥyn well		
		ID Lexeme	862932	ꜥyn	well
DRID	1003070		ꜥꜣ column		
	RID	0003452	ꜥꜣ column		
		ID Lexeme	34800	ꜥꜣ	column; pillar; beam
			450393	ꜥꜣ	columns?; vertical timbers? (naut.)
			128690	sꜥꜣ	gunwale; thole board

DRID	**1003071**	**ꜥꜣ door**			
	RID	**0003453**	ꜥꜣ door		
		ID Lexeme	34810	ꜥꜣ	door; leaf (of double doors)
			34820	ꜥꜣ	doorkeeper
			39280	ꜥr.tj	pair of door leaves
DRID	**1003072**	**ꜥꜣ linen**			
	RID	**0003455**	ꜥꜣ linen		
		ID Lexeme	450396	ꜥꜣ	linen; cloth?
			34920	ꜥꜣ.t	linen; cloth
DRID	**1003073**	**ꜥꜣb to please**			
	RID	**0003455**	ꜥꜣb to please		
		ID Lexeme	863741	ꜥb	to kill; to sacrifice
			35310	ꜥꜣb	to be pleasing
			35320	ꜥꜣb	to bestow; to offer (prayer / sacrifice)
			35330	ꜥꜣb.t	offering
DRID	**1003074**	**ꜥꜣb washing jug**			
	RID	**0003456**	ꜥꜣb washing jug		
		ID Lexeme	35340	ꜥꜣb.t	washing jug
DRID	**1003075**	**ꜥꜣḏ edge**			
	RID	**0003457**	ꜥꜣḏ edge		
		ID Lexeme	41960	ꜥḏ	edge; margin (of cultivated land, of the desert)
			35520	ꜥꜣḏ	edge; margin (of cultivated land, of desert)
DRID	**1003076**	**ꜥꜣḏ to be pale**			
	RID	**0003458**	ꜥꜣḏ to be pale		
		ID Lexeme	35550	ꜥꜣḏ	to be pale; to turn pale
			861807	ꜥꜣḏ.y	Shining one?
			35540	ꜥꜣḏ.w	(grey) mullet (Mugilidae)
			850355	ꜥꜣḏ.w	(grey) mullet (sun god)
			852713	ꜥꜣḏ.wj	Canal of the two (grey) mullet (in the 2nd nome of Lower Egypt); Canal of the two (grey) mullet (in the 20th nome of Upper Egypt); Canal of the two (grey) mullet (in the 17th nome of Upper Egypt)
			80390	nꜥꜣḏ.t	[excrement of a person suffering from a stomach problem]
DRID	**1003077**	**ꜥꜣg to beat**			
	RID	**0003459**	ꜥꜣg to beat		

	ID Lexeme	35460	ꜥꜣg	to squeeze (dates)
		35470	ꜥꜣg	to thrash; to mistreat
		854496	ꜥꜣg	to edit, to handle something (forcibly)
		35500	ꜥꜣg.yt	secretion; resin (med.)
		35480	ꜥꜣg.t	hoof (of an ox or donkey)
DRID	**1003078**	**ꜥꜣi̯ to be great**		
RID	**0003460**	ꜥꜣi̯ to be great		
	ID Lexeme	34770	ꜥꜣ	greatness
		450158	ꜥꜣ	great; much; long; old; noble
		34760	ꜥꜣ	great one; elder; noble one
		851497	ꜥꜣ	great one (various gods)
		35240	ꜥꜣ.w	greatness
		35250	ꜥꜣ.w	difference (math.); excess
		34780	ꜥꜣ.w	exceedingly; very
		855762	ꜥꜣ.t	very?
		34860	ꜥꜣ.t	something great; something difficult
		34850	ꜥꜣ.t	great one (goddesses)
		34880	ꜥꜣ.t	gemstone; precious material
		34930	ꜥꜣ.t	rule
		34900	ꜥꜣ.t	swelling; tumor
		34890	ꜥꜣ.t	stone vessel
		35510	ꜥꜣ.tjt	lot (quantity); amount
		34750	ꜥꜣi̯	to be great; to become great; to be rich; to grow up
		35090	ꜥꜣj	rejoicing
		35120	ꜥꜣj	phallus?
		35080	ꜥꜣy	(glowing) fire
		35100	ꜥꜣy.t	temple; shrine
		35110	ꜥꜣy.t	heaven; roof
		128670	sꜥꜣ	great
		856445	sꜥꜣ	pregnancy (amniotic sac)
		128680	sꜥꜣ	frightening
		128660	sꜥꜣi̯	to make great; to increase
DRID	**1003079**	**ꜥꜣm throw stick**		
RID	**0003461**	ꜥꜣm throw stick		
	ID Lexeme	35390	ꜥꜣm	throw stick; boomerang
		35400	ꜥꜣm	Asian
		35420	ꜥꜣm.w	[a plant (med.)]
		35440	ꜥꜣm.wt	[a cultivated plant]
		35410	ꜥꜣm.t	Asian (female)
DRID	**1003081**	**ꜥꜣꜥ to squirt**		
RID	**0003463**	ꜥꜣꜥ to squirt		
	ID Lexeme	856333	ꜥꜣꜥ	Ejaculator
		35140	ꜥꜣꜥ	water hole; wet ground

			35160	ꜥꜣꜥ	to ejaculate; to beget
			35170	ꜥꜣꜥ	semen; poison
			35180	ꜥꜣꜥ	[an illness?]; [an influence causing illness?]
			35230	ꜥꜣꜥ.y	begetter (sun god)
			35640	ꜥꜥ	sweat; spit
			35800	ꜥꜥm	Nile flood
DRID	**1003082**		**ꜥꜥj to be fearful**		
	RID	**0003464**	ꜥꜥj to be fearful		
		ID Lexeme	35710	ꜥꜥj	to be fearful
DRID	**1003083**		**ꜥꜥnj to enclose**		
	RID	**0003465**	ꜥꜥnj to enclose		
		ID Lexeme	35810	ꜥꜥnj	tent; encampment
			35820	ꜥꜥnj	to enclose
DRID	**1003084**		**ꜥꜥw to be agitated**		
	RID	**0003466**	ꜥꜥw to be agitated		
		ID Lexeme	35750	ꜥꜥw	to be agitated; to flutter (of the heart)
DRID	**1003085**		**ꜥꜥw to sleep**		
	RID	**0003467**	ꜥꜥw to sleep		
		ID Lexeme	35740	ꜥꜥw	to sleep (invariably negated)
			35760	ꜥꜥw	sleep

II.5 w

DRID	**1000974**		**w not**		
	RID	**0002904**	w not		
		ID Lexeme	42360	w	[particle of negation]
DRID	**1002602**		**w district**		
	RID	**0002903**	w district		
		ID lexeme	42350	w	district; region
			860534	w.t	district; region
DRID	**1002603**		**wbd to burn**		
	RID	**0002905**	wbd to burn		
		ID lexeme	45410	wbd	to burn; to heat
			45420	wbd	soot? (med.)
			860817	wbd.t	burning one
			45430	wbd.t	burning; burn
DRID	**1002604**		**wbg to be green**		
	RID	**0002906**	wbg to be green		
		ID lexeme	45390	wbg	blossom; to turn green
			860373	wbg	to open
			130070	swbg	make blossom
DRID	**1002605**		**wbẖ = wbg to shine**		
	RID	**0002907**	wbẖ to shine		
		ID lexeme	45270	wbẖ	to shine; to brighten; to be bright
			858119	wbẖ.t	the bright one
			45280	wbẖ.t	clarity (of the eye)
			45310	wbẖ.t	[a mineral (from Asia Minor)]
			45290	wbẖ.t	clean clothing
			857996	swbẖ	to shine; to illuminate
	RID	**0003600**	wbg to shine		
		ID lexeme	45380	wbg	to shine; to illuminate
			45400	wbg.wj	shining one?
			858114	wbg.t	fire; heat; sexual arousal?
DRID	**1002606**		**wbn to rise up**		
	RID	**0002908**	wbn to rise up		
		ID lexeme	854500	wbn	rise; overflow
			45050	wbn	to shine; to rise (of the sun); coming out
			45070	wbn	spring (“what comes forth”)
			45060	wbn	overflowing (from the grain)
			45150	wbn.j	shining one (the sun god)
			45160	wbn.w	sunrays
			45170	wbn.w	the east (“sunrise”)

				45100	wbn.t	the one who comes out (first hour of the day)
				45090	wbn.t	one who shines
				45110	wbn.t	webenet (mummy bindings of the head)
				45120	wbn.t	Webenet (place of sunrise)
				45230	wbnn.j	shining one (the sun god)
				45220	wbnbn	to arise
				131780	sbn	to crown
DRID	**1002607**		**wbn wound**			
	RID	**0002909**	wbn wound			
		ID lexeme		45190	wbn.w	open wound; injury
				858117	wbn.w	hole; wound
DRID	**1002609**		**wbs = bzi̯ to come out**			
	RID	**0002911**	wbs to come out			
		ID lexeme		45370	wbs	swell (of water, of the inundation); flood
				45350	wbs	to heap up (corn and sheaves)
				858118	wbs	to arise
				854501	wbs	to come out
				45340	wbs	herbs; greenery
				45330	wbs	to come out; to sprout; to make sprout
	RID	**0000134**	bzi̯ flow forth			
		ID lexeme		57180	bz	product (of the fields, of the mountains)
				57350	bz.y	Emerging one (manifestation of Re)
				57370	bz.w	swelling; turgidity (of stomach)
				57340	bzi̯	to flood out; to emerge; to come forth
				57400	bs.w	result; consequence
DRID	**1002610**		**wbꜣ to open**			
	RID	**0002912**	wbꜣ to open			
		ID lexeme		855697	wbꜣ	butler; servant; steward
				44930	wbꜣ	butler; servant; steward
				44940	wbꜣ	opposite; in front of
				44890	wbꜣ	to open; to drill
				44910	wbꜣ	(open) forecourt
				44900	wbꜣ	to deflower
				44920	wbꜣ	to pour out (a drink)
				45030	wbꜣ.yt	female butler; servant
				45020	wbꜣ.yt	forecourt (of a temple)
				44950	wbꜣ.t	opening
				130040	swbꜣ	to open (someone's face)

DRID	**1002611**	**wḏ to assign**		
RID	**0002915**	wḏ to assign		
ID lexeme		51990	wḏ	stela
		51970	wḏ	to command; to assign
		52350	wḏ.yw	pilots? (of Re's solar bark)
		51980	wḏ.w	command; decree
		52050	wḏ.t	post (for the steering-oar)
		52040	wḏ.t	command; decree
		863063	wḏ.t	stele
		52770	wḏḏ.t	what is commanded
		130950	swḏ	to hand over; to bequeath

DRID	**1002612**	**wḏb to turn around**		
RID	**0002916**	wḏb to turn around		
ID lexeme		52620	wḏb	to turn back; to fold over; to revert
		52610	wḏb	[folded cloth]
		52640	wḏb	shore; river bank
		500450	wḏb.jw	those belonging to the Two Banks
		550444	wḏb.w	donation (of produce)
		869216	swḏb	to bring back; to answer
		852149	swḏb	to wound; to twine

DRID	**1002613**	**wdd gall bladder**		
RID	**0002917**	wdd gall bladder		
ID lexeme		51940	wdd	gall bladder

DRID	**1002614**	**wdd to cook**		
RID	**0002918**	wdd to cook		
ID lexeme		51950	wdd	to cook

DRID	**1002615**	**wdfi̯ to delay**		
RID	**0002919**	wdfi̯ to delay		
ID lexeme		28800	wdf	period (of time); delay
		51620	wdfi̯	to hesitate (and similar)
		130930	swdf	to delay; to make (someone) wait

DRID	**1002616**	**wḏḥ fruit**		
RID	**0002920**	wḏḥ fruit		
ID lexeme		52740	wḏḥ	fruit
		52750	wḏḥ	to bear fruit?; to ripen?; to be planted
		550246	wḏḥ.t	fruit; yield

DRID	**1002617**	**wdḥ to pour**		
RID	**0002921**	wdḥ to pour		
ID lexeme		51870	wdḥ	to pour out; to water
		861174	wdḥ	clyster (med.); git; sprue

			51880	wdḥ	to melt (metal, glass)
			854504	wdḥ	to pour; to water; to melt (metal); to manufacture (glass)
			51920	wdḥ.w	distribution (of offerings)
			858795	wdḥ.w	offering; sacrifice
			400433	wdḥ.w	altar; offering stand
			51900	wdḥ.w	offering jug
DRID	**1002618**	**wḏḥ to wean**			
	RID	**0002922**	wḏḥ to wean		
		ID lexeme	52730	wḏḥ	weaned child
			52720	wḏḥ	to wean (the infant)
DRID	**1002619**	**wdi̯ to place**			
	RID	**0002923**	wdi̯ to place		
		ID lexeme	501070	wd.w	Slinger
			51490	wd.t	shift (of contagious matter, infection?)
			51510	wdi̯	to put; to place
			858907	wdi̯	to cause that
			500186	wdi̯	to push; to throw
	RID	**0002931**	wdwd to bandage		
		ID Lexeme	130920	swdwd	to bandage; to wrap
	RID	**0001731**	ndj to fell		
		ID Lexeme	90690	ndj	to fell (someone or something)
DRID	**1002620**	**wḏi̯ to travel**			
	RID	**0002924**	wḏi̯ to travel		
		ID lexeme	52300	wḏi̯	to send out; to depart
			858121	wḏ	stand of the rudder
			856154	wḏ.yt	steering gear
			52330	wḏ.yt	journey; campaign; expedition
			52590	wḏ.w	[cattle rambling around freely]
DRID	**1002621**	**wḏj perch**			
	RID	**0002925**	wḏj perch		
		ID lexeme	52320	wḏj	perch; bulti-fish (tilapia nilotica)
DRID	**1002622**	**wdn [a sacred baboon]**			
	RID	**0002926**	wdn [a sacred baboon]		
		ID lexeme	51730	wdn	[a sacred baboon]
DRID	**1002623**	**wdn to be heavy**			
	RID	**0002927**	wdn to be heavy		
		ID lexeme	51740	wdn	heavy one (hippopotamus)
			51650	wdn	to lay down; to set (the royal titles)
			51660	wdn	to install; to enthrone

51670 wdn to be heavy; to weigh
51690 wdn to offer; to sacrifice
850424 wdn offering
51710 wdn basket (for offering bread)
51640 wdn to cast down (enemies)?
51700 wdn offering; sacrificial ritual
51830 wdn.w offerer
51810 wdn.w burden
51820 wdn.w weight (on a plumb line)
51770 wdn.t offering courtyard
856881 wdn.t offering stand
51750 wdn.t heavy block of stone
51760 wdn.t offering
130940 swdn to give oneself airs?

DRID 1002624 wḏn width
RID 0002928 wḏn width
ID lexeme 52690 wḏn width?
52710 wḏn.w flood

DRID 1002625 wḏnj [oboe?]
RID 0002929 wḏnj [oboe?]
ID lexeme 52700 wḏnj [reed instrument (oboe?)]

DRID 1002626 wdp attendant
RID 0002930 wdp attendant
ID lexeme 860398 wdp.w steward
51600 wdp.w butler; attendant
855519 wdp.w butler; attendant
51610 wdp.wyt serving maid

DRID 1002627 wḏꜣ to be intact
RID 0002932 wḏꜣ notification
ID lexeme 852937 swḏꜣ notification; communication
RID 0002933 wḏꜣ room in a temple
ID lexeme 52120 wḏꜣ room in a temple
RID 0002934 wḏꜣ storehouse
ID lexeme 52110 wḏꜣ storehouse
RID 0002935 wḏꜣ temple roof
ID lexeme 52170 wḏꜣ.t heaven; temple roof
RID 0002936 wḏꜣ to be intact
ID lexeme 52090 wḏꜣ to be whole; to be intact
52100 wḏꜣ wellbeing
858128 wḏꜣ intact one
182070 wḏꜣ magical protection?
450203 wḏꜣ.w remainder
52280 wḏꜣ.w amulet; protective spell
450146 wḏꜣ.wt remainder

		52150	wḏꜣ.t	wedjat measure (parts of the Wdjat eye as a measure for grain)
		52210	wḏꜣ.t	remainder; deficiency (from deliveries)
		52140	wḏꜣ.t	Wedjat eye (Horus eye); eye
		130960	swḏꜣ	to make whole; to protect
		857716	swḏꜣ	protective spell
		150240	sḏꜣ	to be healthy; to be safe and sound
		150310	sḏꜣ.w	protection

DRID 1002628 wḏꜣ to go

RID	**0002937**	wḏꜣ to go		
	ID lexeme	52130	wḏꜣ	to proceed; to pass (away); to walk (in a procession)
		853562	wḏꜣ.w	departed ones (the dead)
		52200	wḏꜣ.t	road; way
		130970	swḏꜣ	to convey; to go
		130980	swḏꜣ	to pass away (to die)
		500597	sḏꜣ	end? (of the kingdom of the dead)
		150220	sḏꜣ	to take away
		150210	sḏꜣ	to go; to travel

DRID 1002629 wḏꜥ to separate

RID	**0002938**	wḏꜥ freshwater clam		
	ID lexeme	850426	wḏꜥ.yt	freshwater clam
		858135	wḏꜥ.w	scribe’s ink well (made of shell?)
		52480	wḏꜥ.wt	scribe’s ink-shell (made of shell?)
RID	**0002939**	wḏꜥ to judge		
	ID lexeme	52380	wḏꜥ	He who hears well?
		52390	wḏꜥ	judgement
		52400	wḏꜥ	the judged one (Seth)
		52460	wḏꜥ.t	judgement; sentence
		500452	wḏꜥ.tj	He who belongs to the judgment
RID	**0002940**	wḏꜥ to separate		
	ID lexeme	52420	wḏꜥ	demoiselle crane
		52540	wḏꜥ	judge
		450154	wḏꜥ	piece; fragment
		52360	wḏꜥ	to separate; to judge; to appoint
		858134	wḏꜥ.w	knife, separator
		52550	wḏꜥ.w	[a part or a processing state of dates (med.)]
		52570	wḏꜥ.w	discharge
		52560	wḏꜥ.w	irrigation canal?; canal?; net?
		52500	wḏꜥ.wt	severed limb
		52450	wḏꜥ.t	separator? (a knife?)
		450079	wḏꜥ.t	ration; piece
		52470	wḏꜥ.t	divorced woman
		858132	wḏꜥ.tj	splitter?

DRID 1002630 wfꜣ lung

RID	**0002941**	wfꜣ lung		
	ID lexeme	45860	wfꜣ	lung

DRID 1002631 wfꜣ to support

RID	**0002942**	wfꜣ to support		
	ID lexeme	45870	wfꜣ	to discuss; to support

DRID 1002632 wg plank

RID	**0002943**	wg plank		
	ID lexeme	850420	wg	board; plank
		50830	wg.yt	a plank (naut.)?
		50720	wgj	board; plank

DRID 1002633 wgb to shout

RID	**0002944**	wgb to shout		
	ID lexeme	50850	wgb	to cry out; to shout
		147160	sgb	shrieking; shouting
		147150	sgb	to shriek; to shout

DRID 1002634 wgg to be weak

RID	**0002945**	wgg to be weak		
	ID lexeme	850126	wgg	to be weak
		50940	wgg	shortage; famine?; weakness
		850421	wgg.t	harmfulness; complaint
		130820	swgg	to deprive (someone of something); to damage

DRID 1002635 wgi̯ to chew

RID	**0002946**	wgi̯ to chew		
	ID lexeme	50820	wg.yt	twaddle?
		50840	wg.wt	lower jaw
		50750	wgꜣ	[crushed grain or fruit]
		50790	wgi̯	to chew

DRID 1002636 wgm to grind

RID	**0002947**	wgm to grind		
	ID lexeme	50880	wgm	powder; crushed grain; flour
		50870	wgm	to grind (grain) (or similar)
		855631	swgm	powder; grind

DRID 1002637 wgp to crush

RID	**0002948**	wgp to crush		
	ID lexeme	50860	wgp	to crush; to destroy; to break

DRID 1002638 wgs to cut open

RID	**0002949**	wgs to gut		

		ID lexeme	50900	wgs	to cut open; to gut (animals)
			50910	wgs	(gutted?) bird
			858137	wgs	Slaughterer
			50930	wgs.w	slaughter (fish and fowl)
DRID	**1002639**	**wgꜣ flood**			
	RID	**0002950**	wgꜣ flood		
		ID lexeme	50760	wgꜣ	inundation; flood
DRID	**1002640**	**wḥ kin**			
	RID	**0002951**	wḥ kin		
		ID lexeme	48730	wḥ.yt	family; kin; tribe
			48650	wḥ.wt	settlement; village
DRID	**1002641**	**wḥ to bark**			
	RID	**0002967**	wḥwḥ to bark		
		ID lexeme	48980	wḥwḥ	to bark (of a dog)
DRID	**1002642**	**wẖ to be dark**			
	RID	**0002952**	wẖ to be dark		
		ID lexeme	49050	wẖ	to be dark
			49060	wẖ	darkness; night
			49080	wẖ.t	darkness
			851131	swẖ	evening offering?
			130680	swẖꜣ	to spend the night
			141650	sẖꜣ	darken
DRID	**1002643**	**whb to pierce**			
	RID	**0002953**	whb to pierce		
		ID lexeme	48390	whb	to pierce
			48400	whb	hole (med.)
DRID	**1002644**	**wẖd to suffer**			
	RID	**0002954**	wẖd to suffer		
		ID lexeme	49370	wẖd	forbearance; patience
			49350	wẖd	to endure; to suffer
			49360	wẖd	to suffer; to endure
			851445	wẖd	to suffer
			49400	wẖd.y	sufferer
			49410	wẖd.w	pain (med.); disease trigger
			49390	wẖd.t	disease trigger
DRID	**1002645**	**wḥf to burn**			
	RID	**0002955**	wḥf to burn		
		ID lexeme	853374	wḥf	to burn
DRID	**1002646**	**whi̯ to fail**			
	RID	**0002956**	whi̯ to fail		

		ID lexeme	852973	wh	unsuccessful one (Seth)
			856687	wh	sinner
			48360	wh.yw	unsuccessful ones (designation for enemy)
			851908	wh.t	failure
			48330	whi̯	to escape; to miss; to fail
			48340	whj	failure
DRID	**1002647**	**wḫj diarrhoea**			
	RID	**0002957**	whj diarrhoea		
		ID lexeme	48370	whj	(bloody) diarrhea
DRID	**1002648**	**wḥm bull’s leg**			
	RID	**0002958**	wḥm bull’s leg		
		ID lexeme	48470	wḥm	bull’s leg (a piece of furniture)
			48430	wḥm.t	bull’s leg; hoof
DRID	**1002649**	**whm to burn**			
	RID	**0002959**	whm to burn		
		ID lexeme	48420	whm	to burn
			48480	whm	heat
DRID	**1002650**	**wḥm to repeat**			
	RID	**0002960**	wḥm to repeat		
		ID lexeme	48440	wḥm	to repeat (gen.)
			851319	wḥm	to repeat (something said)
			48460	wḥm	tongue (lit. repeater)
			600562	wḥm	further; again
			851318	wḥm	to repeat (to do); [aux./modal]
			48530	wḥm.yt	repetition
			855699	wḥm.w	speaker; transmitter
			48540	wḥm.w	speaker; herald; transmitter
			48990	wḥm.wtj	repeater
DRID	**1002651**	**whn to fall apart**			
	RID	**0002961**	whn to fall apart		
		ID lexeme	48560	whn	to tear down; to decay; to fall apart
DRID	**1002652**	**whn* to be fragile**			
	RID	**0002962**	whnn crown (of the head)		
		ID lexeme	48590	whnn	crown (of the head)
			48610	whnn.wtj	the two who are on the crown of the head
DRID	**1002654**	**wẖr to process**			
	RID	**0002964**	wẖr to process		
		ID lexeme	49340	wẖr.yt	carpenter’s tools (gen.)

			49330	wḫr.t	carpenter’s workshop; shipyard
			49320	wḫr	to work, to process (wood); to struggle; to care (for someone)
	RID	**0002963**	wḫr to answer a prayer?		
		ID lexeme	49310	wḫr	to answer a prayer?
DRID	**1002655**	**whs to be casual**			
	RID	**0002965**	whs to be casual		
		ID lexeme	48640	whs	to slacken; to be worn out
DRID	**1002656**	**wḥs to cut**			
	RID	**0002966**	wḥs to cut		
		ID lexeme	49010	wḥs	to cut (off, down); to remove
			49020	wḥs.wt	predators?
DRID	**1002657**	**wḥꜣ [a skin disease]**			
	RID	**0002969**	wḥꜣ [a skin disease]		
		ID lexeme	48670	wḥꜣ	[a skin disease (rash?)]
DRID	**1002658**	**wḥꜣ cauldron**			
	RID	**0002970**	wḥꜣ cauldron		
		ID lexeme	48690	wḥꜣ.t	cauldron
DRID	**1002659**	**wḫꜣ claw?**			
	RID	**0002971**	wḫꜣ claw?		
		ID lexeme	49280	wḫꜣ.w	claws?
DRID	**1002660**	**wḫꜣ column**			
	RID	**0000999**	ḫꜣ hall		
		ID lexeme	113180	ḫꜣ	hall; office
			49090	wḫꜣ	columned hall
			49200	wḫꜣ	column; supporting pillar
			49210	wḫꜣ	columned hall (a figure in dancing)
			850417	wḫꜣ.yt	columned hall
DRID	**1002661**	**wḫꜣ to be foolish**			
	RID	**0002974**	wḫꜣ to be foolish		
		ID lexeme	49160	wḫꜣ	foolishness
			49150	wḫꜣ	fool
			49170	wḫꜣ	to be foolish
			851604	swḫꜣ	to talk wrong; invalidity; ineffectiveness
			130690	swḫꜣ	to harm
DRID	**1002662**	**wḥꜣ to cut down**			
	RID	**0002968**	wḥwḥ to disappear		

	ID lexeme	48970	wḥwḥ	to disappear; fading (of inscriptions)
RID	**0002973**	wḥꜣ oasis		
	ID lexeme	48700	wḥꜣ.t	oasis
		48710	wḥꜣ.tjw	oasis dweller
RID	**0002975**	wḥꜣ to cut down		
	ID lexeme	101090	ḥꜣ.w	grape harvest
		400572	wḥꜣ	stone worker
		48660	wḥꜣ	to quarry (stone); to tear out; to pick; to gather
		48720	wḥꜣ.y	harvest; crop

DRID	**1002663**		**wẖꜣ to empty**		
	RID	**0002976**	wẖꜣ to empty		
		ID lexeme	49100	wẖꜣ	to empty out; to shake out
			49110	wẖꜣ	blowing (of a storm)
DRID	**1002664**		**wẖꜣ to hang down**		
	RID	**0002977**	wẖꜣ to hang down		
		ID lexeme	858478	wẖꜣ	hang down
			49230	wẖꜣ	lotus flower
DRID	**1002665**		**wẖꜣ to seek**		
	RID	**0002978**	wẖꜣ to seek		
		ID lexeme	49120	wẖꜣ	to seek; to get; to desire
			49180	wẖꜣ	official letter; decree
			49290	wẖꜣ.wt	scout; patrol
DRID	**1002666**		**wẖꜣ to smoothen?**		
	RID	**0002979**	wẖꜣ to smoothen?		
		ID lexeme	49260	wẖꜣ	to smoothen?
DRID	**1002667**		**wḥꜥ scorpion**		
	RID	**0002983**	wḥꜥ scorpion		
		ID lexeme	48840	wḥꜥ	to sting (of scorpion)
			48880	wḥꜥ.t	scorpion; scorpion venom
DRID	**1002668**		**wḥꜥ to fish and fowl**		
	RID	**0002980**	wḥꜥ [a duck]		
		ID lexeme	48870	wḥꜥ.t	[a duck (greater white-fronted goose)]
	RID	**0002981**	wḥꜥ catfish		
		ID lexeme	48830	wḥꜥ.w	catfish (Synodontis schall)
	RID	**0002982**	wḥꜥ Nile pike		
		ID lexeme	850415	wḥꜥ.t	Nile pike
	RID	**0002984**	wḥꜥ to fish and fowl		
		ID lexeme	48820	wḥꜥ	Weha-festival (temple foundation

festival)
48790 wḥꜥ fisher and fowler
48810 wḥꜥ provision
860971 wḥꜥ fisherman and fowler
875450 wḥꜥ fisherman and fowler
48800 wḥꜥ to fish and fowl
855698 wḥꜥ fisherman and fowler

DRID 1002669 wḥꜥ to solve
RID 0002985 wḥꜥ to offer
ID lexeme 48770 wḥꜥ to offer; to sacrifice
48850 wḥꜥ to destroy? (a tomb)
48760 wḥꜥ to loosen; to explain; to establish; return home
48860 wḥꜥ explanation; commentary
858138 wḥꜥ Detached one
48900 wḥꜥ.t supplies; provisions

DRID 1002670 wj mummy case
RID 0002987 wj mummy case
ID lexeme 44010 wj mummy case

DRID 1002671 wjꜣ = wjn weak
RID 0002988 wjn to reject
ID lexeme 44040 wjꜣ without (doing); apart from (something)
44030 wjꜣ to push aside; to reject
859663 wjn crime
44120 wjn to push aside; to reject
RID 0002990 wjꜣ weakness
ID lexeme 44060 wjꜣ.t [a symptom of a heart ailment]
44090 wjꜣw.yt senility (of heart)
RID 0002991 wjꜣwjꜣ to be powerless
ID lexeme 44100 wjꜣwjꜣ to be unsuccessful; to be powerless
600207 wjꜣwjꜣ helplessness; weakness

DRID 1002672 wjꜣ boat
RID 0002989 wjꜣ solar boat
ID lexeme 861064 wjꜣ team; crew
44020 wjꜣ ship; processional bark

DRID 1002674 wmt to be thick
RID 0002992 wmt to be thick
ID lexeme 45930 wmt thickness (as dimension)
45950 wmt thickness (of a wall); reveal (of a doorway); gateway
45920 wmt to be thick

		45960	wmt	thick garment; thick cloth
		45970	wmt	fortification wall; surrounding walls
		45940	wmt	concentration, density (of enemies)
		45990	wmt.t	surrounding wall
		46000	wmt.t	thickness; size (of humans)
		130080	swmt	to make thick
DRID	**1002675**	**wn enclosure?**		
RID	**0002993**	wn enclosure?		
	ID lexeme	46140	wn.t	[a sanctuary (in the temple)]
		46150	wn.t	fortress
DRID	**1002676**	**wn error**		
RID	**0002994**	wn error		
	ID lexeme	46080	wn	error; fault; blame
DRID	**1002677**	**wn hare**		
RID	**0002995**	wn hare		
	ID lexeme	46110	wn	hare
DRID	**1002678**	**wn to be bald**		
RID	**0002996**	wn to be bald		
	ID lexeme	46100	wn	to be bald
		46300	wn.yt	stripped of eyebrows
		874151	wn.w	baldness?
DRID	**1002679**	**wn to open**		
RID	**0002997**	wn to open		
	ID lexeme	46060	wn	to open
		46070	wn	opening (of a door)
		46350	wn.w	doorkeeper
		46170	wn.wt	doors?
		46160	wn.t	wenet-priestess (in the nome of Beni Hasan, the 16th nome of Upper Egypt)
		867440	wn.t	something opened; opening; sanctuary?
		130130	swn	to open
DRID	**1002680**	**wn to threaten**		
RID	**0003020**	wnwn to threaten		
	ID lexeme	46500	wnwn	to threaten
DRID	**1002681**	**wnb blossom**		
RID	**0002998**	wnb blossom		
	ID lexeme	42890	wꜣnb	[a plant (med.)]

		46580	wnbwnb	flower; blossom

DRID 1002682 wnḏ cavity

RID	**000299**	wnḏ cavity		
		47220	wnḏ.wt	hold (of a ship); cavity
		47170	wnḏ.t	hollow; depression

DRID 1002683 wnḏ herd

RID	**0003000**	wnḏ herd		
	ID lexeme	47210	wnḏ.w	goats
		47200	wnḏ.w	short-horned cattle
		47230	wnḏ.wt	people
		47190	wnḏ.wt	cattle; herd

DRID 1002684 wnḏ quantity

RID	**0003001**	wnḏ quantity		
	ID lexeme	47240	wnḏ.ww	units (of produce, of things, of people)
		47250	wnḏ.ww	offerings

DRID 1002685 wnf to resolve

RID	**0003002**	wnf to resolve		
	ID lexeme	46660	wnf	to be glad; to rejoice
		856220	wnf	loosen
		69290	mwnf	guard; protector; assistance
		130340	swnf	to make (the heart) rejoice

DRID 1002686 wnẖ to clothe

RID	**0003003**	wnẖ to clothe		
	ID lexeme	46960	wnẖ	plank (naut.)
		46920	wnẖ	to clothe; to coat
		46980	wnẖ.yt	mummy bandage
		46990	wnẖ.w	clothing
		47000	wnẖ.wj	two strips of cloth
		46970	wnẖ.t	clothing; strip of cloth; bandage
		71170	mnẖ.t	cloth; garment; mummy bandage
		851035	mnẖ.t	clothing (feast)
		500997	mnẖ.tj	Clothed one

DRID 1002687 wnẖ to loosen

RID	**0003004**	wnẖ to loosen		
	ID lexeme	46930	wnẖ	dislocation (med.)
		856221	wnẖ	to move yourself, to loosen

DRID 1002688 wni̯ to bind

RID	**0003005**	wni̯ to bind		
	ID lexeme	46130	wn.t	rope; cord

		46320	wni̯	to tow; to bind
DRID	**1002689**	**wni̯ to hurry**		
RID	**0003006**	wni̯ to hurry		
	ID lexeme	46280	wni̯	to hurry; to pass by; to neglect
		850325	swni̯	to drive on?; to make hurry?
RID	**0003014**	wnr to move along?		
	ID lexeme	46900	wnr	to move along?
RID	**0003021**	wnwn to traverse		
	ID lexeme	46490	wnwn	to move to and fro; to traverse
		46550	wnwnw.t	She who moves to and fro (a serpent)
DRID	**1002690**	**wnj light**		
RID	**0003007**	wnj light		
	ID lexeme	46290	wny	light
DRID	**1002691**	**wnm diadem**		
RID	**0003008**	wnm diadem		
	ID lexeme	860354	wnm.t	diadem of Upper Egypt
DRID	**1002692**	**wnm to eat**		
RID	**0003009**	wnm right		
	ID lexeme	46770	wnm.j	right (side)
		600035	wnm.j	right side; right
		46780	wnm.j	the right side (division of Theban necropolis workmen)
		46790	wnm.j	right hand
		500929	wnm.t	the right one
		46750	wnm.t	right eye (of a deity)
		46760	wnm.t	right eye (mostly Nekhbet as the crown goddess of Upper Egypt
RID	**0003010**	wnm to eat		
	ID lexeme	46730	wnm	fattened ox?
		46710	wnm	to eat
		46720	wnm	food; to take (medicine)
		46800	wnm.yt	devourer (fire)
		852396	wnm.yt	devourer (flame)
		46820	wnm.w	devourer
		46810	wnm.w	food
		46740	wnm.t	food; fodder
		858159	wnm.t	the one who eats
		137410	snm	greed
		137400	snm	to feed (someone); to consume (food); to eat
		137490	snm.w	food supply
		137470	snm.t	food supply

DRID	**1002693**		**wnn to exist**		
	RID	**0003011**	wnn to exist		
		ID lexeme	863618	wn	existing one
			858148	wn	one who exist
			855526	wn	[particle introducing existential sentences]
			46040	wn	[substantive (essence, being or similar)]
			853887	wn.w	wealth? ("what is (with someone)")
			851210	wn.t	because (conj.)
			851212	wn.t	indeed (emphasis after independent pronouns);
			46050	wnn	to exist; to be
			858160	wnn	the one who exists
			501130	wnn.w	the child (sun god, king)
			46860	wnn.yw	those who exist
			850407	wnn.w	child (in the womb)
			550416	wnn.t	indeed; really (emphasis after independent pronouns);
			46830	wnn.t	that which exists
			852791	swn	condition?
DRID	**1002694**		**wnp to stab**		
	RID	**0003012**	wnp to stab		
		ID lexeme	46600	wnp	to stab; to fetter
			46610	wnp	stabber (a priest at Edfu)
			46620	wnp	stabber (Horus of Edfu)
			46650	wnp.w	triumph ("stabbing" the enemies)
DRID	**1002695**		**wnpj to harvest (flax)?**		
	RID	**0003013**	wnpj to harvest (flax)?		
		ID lexeme	46630	wnpj	to harvest (flax)?
DRID	**1002696**		**wnš grape**		
	RID	**0003015**	wnš grape		
		ID lexeme	47040	wnš	grape; raisin
			47060	wnš.t	wine
DRID	**1002697**		**wnš jackal**		
	RID	**0003016**	wnš jackal		
		ID lexeme	47030	wnš	jackal headed sled
			47020	wnš	jackal
			47070	wnš.jw	wolfhound
			47050	wnš.t	female jackal
			854772	wnš.tj	One belonging to the female jackal
			47080	wnšnš	to hurry

DRID	**1002698**	**wnw hour**		
RID	**0003017**	wnw hour		
	ID lexeme	500287	wn.t	Hour
		46570	wnw.t	hour-star
		46430	wnw.t	service; hourly service (of priests)
		46420	wnw.t	hour
		46440	wnw.t	hour goddess (designation of the uraeus serpent)
		500359	wnw.tj	He who belongs to the hour
		46450	wnw.tj	hour-watcher (a priest)
RID	**0003018**	wnw night's rest?		
	ID lexeme	46370	wnw	night's rest?
RID	**0003019**	wnwn to observe (the stars)		
	ID lexeme	46510	wnwn	to observe (the stars)
		46520	wnwn.w	star watcher

DRID	**1002699**	**wp horn**		
RID	**0003022**	wp horn		
	ID lexeme	45530	wp.t	horns; brow; top (of the head)
		851599	wp.t	mountain peak
		860179	wp.t	horned cattle (cattle; cows)

DRID	**1002700**	**wp quantity?**		
RID	**0003023**	wp quantity?		
	ID lexeme	45740	wp.wt	crowd of women (for greeting and similar)
		45550	wp.wt	entry; list; inventory
		45730	wp.wt	members of a household; household list

DRID	**1002701**	**wpi̯ to open**		
RID	**0003024**	wpi̯ to judge		
	ID lexeme	45700	wp.w	judge (usually Thoth)
		45480	wp.w	judge
		45540	wp.t	judge's decision; judgment
RID	**0003025**	wpi̯ to open		
	ID lexeme	852648	wp	disclosure; specification
		45520	wp.w	bread; food (as offerings)
		45460	wp.w	knife ("separator")
		45510	wp.w	butchered animal (as an offering)
		45720	wp.w	1st day of the lunar month ("opener")
		858187	wp.w	exclusion
		45490	wp.w	festival (gen.); festive mood
		45690	wp.w	Wepu ("corps opener"?)
		858180	wp.t	Opening one
		45640	wpi̯	to divide; to separate judicially; to open; to decide

			45680	wpw	except for; but
			45750	wpw.t	message; task; issue (gen.)
			45760	wpw.tj	messenger
			855093	wpw.tj	messenger
			858185	wpw.tjt	messenger
DRID	**1002702**	**wpr side lock**			
	RID	**0003026**	wpr side lock		
		ID lexeme	45780	wpr.t	side lock of a child
			45790	wpr.t	wepret-priestess
DRID	**1002703**	**wps to burn up**			
	RID	**0003027**	wps to burn up		
		ID lexeme	45800	wps	to burn up (the bad one)
			858189	wps.t	flame
			45810	wps.t	She who burns up (the enemies)
DRID	**1002704**	**wpš to illuminate**			
	RID	**0003028**	wpš to illuminate		
		ID lexeme	45830	wpš	light (or similar)
			45820	wpš	to spread (natron, gypsum); to illuminate
DRID	**1002705**	**wr [a sacred body of water?]**			
	RID	**0003029**	wr [a sacred body of water?]		
		ID lexeme	47510	wr.t	[a sacred body of water?]
DRID	**1002706**	**wr swallow**			
	RID	**0003030**	wr swallow		
		ID lexeme	47260	wr	swallow
DRID	**1002707**	**wrḏ to be weary**			
	RID	**0003031**	wrḏ to be weary		
		ID lexeme	48260	wrḏ	to be weary; to grow weary
			48300	wrḏ.w	weariness
			500889	wrḏ.w	Weary one
			48290	wrḏ.w	weary one
			48270	wrḏ.t	weariness
			130520	swrḏ	to make (someone) weary
DRID	**1002708**	**wrh to dance**			
	RID	**0003032**	wrh to dance		
		ID lexeme	48010	wrh	to dance
DRID	**1002709**	**wrḥ to smear**			
	RID	**0003032**	wrḥ to smear		
		ID lexeme	48030	wrḥ	to anoint; to smear

			48040	wrḥ	ointment
			48050	wrḥ	ointment vessel (a measure)
			855572	wrḥ.j	belonging to the ointment
			48080	wrḥ.w	anointer (a priest)
			48060	wrḥ.t	ointment
			72800	mrḥ	pitch
			72790	mrḥ	to anoint
			72820	mrḥ	to paint
			72840	mrḥ.t	fat (gen.); unguent
			855555	mrḥ.tj	oil trader
			130500	swrḥ	to anoint

DRID	**1002710**	**wrm to mount up**			
	RID	**0003033**	wrm to mount up		
		ID lexeme	450145	wrm	to draw oneself up; to mount up
			47820	wrm	erected one (lofty figure)
			47810	wrm	high flood
			850411	wrm.yt	[a symptom of illness]
			47850	wrm.t	pergola; roof
			854805	wrm.t	erected one; figure

DRID	**1002711**	**wrm* to wind**			
	RID	**0003034**	wrm* to wind		
		ID lexeme	850412	wrm.w	windings

DRID	**1002712**	**wrr to be great**			
	RID	**0003035**	wrr to be great		
		ID lexeme	47300	wr	very; fast
			47320	wr	large amount of; quantity of
			47340	wr	great one (a bull)
			47350	wr	[a vessel for oil?]; [a quality of oil?]
			856163	wr	great one (a serpent)
			851429	wr	greatest one (various gods)
			47271	wr	great; a lot; rich; important
			400685	wr	the elder (qualifying personal names)
			47330	wr	Great one (hippopotamus, as a manifestation of Seth)
			47310	wr	how much? how many? (interrogative)
			47290	wr	greatness
			47280	wr	great one
			47760	wr.yt	great flood; high waters
			47720	wr.yt	[a sacral building (tomb, embalming hall)]
			47730	wr.yt	door posts
			852271	wr.w	great one

		47780	wr.w	great waters (water place, pond)
		855586	wr.w	Great ones
		47520	wr.t	Great (a body of water in the nome of Latopolis)
		450429	wr.t	Weret-canal
		47500	wr.t	[a sacred bark]
		47460	wr.t	great one (crown of Lower Egypt)
		450161	wr.t	very
		47430	wr.t	great thing; greatness
		47420	wr.t	great one (various goddesses)
		47440	wr.t	great one (a cow)
		47450	wr.t	great one (uraeus)
		47490	wr.t	great flame (on the altar)
		850963	wr.t	great one (ruler, noble woman)
		47480	wr.t	great one (eye of Horus)
		865109	wr.tj	the two great ones (uraeus serpents)
		860633	wrwr	Exceedingly great one
		47270	wrr	to be great; to be large
		47980	wrr.w	great waters
		47990	wrr.w	great ones
		47920	wrr.t	great one (crown of Upper Egypt)
		47940	wrr.t	great one ("spiral" at the front of the Red Crown of Upper Egypt)
		867530	wrr.t	[Epithet of Nut]
		130430	swr	to increase; to make great

DRID 1002713 wrrj wagon

RID	**0003036**	wrrj wagon		
	ID lexeme	47970	wrry.t	wagon; chariot

DRID 1002714 wrs headrest

RID	**0003037**	wrs headrest		
	ID lexeme	48110	wrs	mast-support (naut.)
		48090	wrs	headrest

DRID 1002715 wršu̯ to be awake

RID	**0003038**	wršu̯ to be awake		
	ID lexeme	48150	wrš	time period (used alongside year)
		852796	wrš	guard; watching over
		48200	wrš.y	keeper of the daily watch; guard
		500125	wrš.w	who guards
		854709	wrš.w	one having daily service; guard
		854413	wrš.ww	Awakened ones
		48170	wrš.t	festival participants
		600301	wrš.t	morning watch; day watch
		48180	wrš.t	guardhouse
		48130	wršu̯	to spend the day; to be awake,

				to dwell
		852476	wršu̯	spend the day on (a quest);

DRID 1002716 ws height (math.)

RID	**0003039**	ws height (math.)		
	ID lexeme	49430	ws	height (of a pyramid) (math.)

DRID 1002717 ws to be empty

RID	**0003040**	ws to be empty		
	ID lexeme	49420	ws	to finish; to lack; to be empty
		49480	wsj	(small) window; chink

DRID 1002718 wš to destroy

RID	**0003040**	wš to be empty		
	ID lexeme	50040	wš	to be empty; to be destroyed; to destroy
		50070	wš	(vacant) place; gap; interruption
RID	**0003041**	wš to destroy		
	ID lexeme	858205	wš.w	whose hair falls out
		50080	wš.t	splinter
		450165	wš.t	destruction (possibly break)
RID	**0003062**	wšwš to smash		
	ID lexeme	50310	wšwš	to smite; to smash; to break

DRID 1002719 wš to push

RID	**0003042**	wš to push		
	ID lexeme	50060	wš	to push one's way through

DRID 1002720 wšb small bead?

RID	**0003043**	wšb small bead?		
	ID lexeme	50470	wšb.yt	small beads (or similar)

DRID 1002721 wšb to feed

RID	**0003044**	wšb to feed		
	ID lexeme	153210	šb	piece of meat
		153330	šb.w	food; main meal
		153260	šb.t	meat offering
		153320	šb.tjw	[primordial creative beings]
		50320	wšb	to feed on (something)
		88610	nšbšb	to refresh oneself?
		153460	šbb	a bit to eat
RID	**0003045**	wšb to react		
		50340	wšb	to answer; to answer for; take revenge; to react
		854083	wšb	fighting bull (Month)
		50350	wšb	answer

			50360	wšb	fighting bull
			50400	wšb	representation?; image?
			50460	wšb.yt	answer; statement
			50480	wšb.yt	loan (“answer”)
			50420	wšb.t	fighting cow; mourner? (Isis)
			50410	wšb.t	mourner
			50500	wšb.w	answerer; defender
			50510	wšb.w	response; return
DRID	**1002722**	**wšd to question**			
	RID	**0003046**	wšd to question		
		ID lexeme	50700	wšd	to address (someone); to question; to greet
DRID	**1002723**	**wsẖ to be broad**			
	RID	**0003047**	wsẖ to be broad		
		ID lexeme	49840	wsẖ	cargo-boat
			49800	wsẖ	to be wide; to be broad; to extend
			49820	wsẖ	breadth; width
			49830	wsẖ	broad collar
			400135	wsẖ	broad; proud; famous
			49850	wsẖ.t	breadth (as a measure)
			49880	wsẖ.t	[heaven(s)?]
			49860	wsẖ.t	barge; sacred bark
			49870	wsẖ.t	broad hall; court; chapel
			49890	wsẖ.tj	one of the broad hall (a priest)
			130740	swsẖ	to widen; to extend
			141550	sẖ.w	courtyard
			141540	sẖ.w	breadth
			142960	sẖẖ	width; breadth
			855127	ssẖ	to widen; to extend
	RID	**0002329**	sẖ marshland		
		ID Lexeme	859040	sẖ.t	field
			141480	sẖ.t	field; marshland; country
			141510	sẖ.tj	he who belongs to the marshland
			141500	sẖ.tj	peasant; fieldworker
			141870	sẖ.tjw	[a kind of cattle]
			141520	sẖ.tjt	[cow goddess]
			141860	sẖ.tw	[god of fields]
			75640	msẖ.t	[a body of water?]
DRID	**1002724**	**wsḥ to burn**			
	RID	**0003048**	wsḥ to burn		
		ID lexeme	49790	wsḥ	heat (or similar)
			49780	wsḥ	to burn; to heat
DRID	**1002726**	**wši̯ to reduce**			
	RID	**0003049**	wši̯ to reduce		

	ID lexeme	50250	wši̯	to reduce to bits; to shred; to empty
DRID	**1002727**	**wsi̯ to saw**		
RID	**0003050**	wsi̯ to saw		
	ID lexeme	500233	ws.w	sawer
		49450	ws.t	sawdust (med.)
		49470	wsi̯	to saw; to cut
DRID	**1002728**	**wšm awn**		
RID	**0003051**	wšm awn		
	ID lexeme	50600	wšm	awn (of an ear of grain)
		858212	wšm.y	One belonging to the awn
DRID	**1002729**	**wšm to mix**		
RID	**0003052**	wšm to mix		
	ID lexeme	50540	wšm	to stir, to mix; to blend
DRID	**1002730**	**wšm to slaughter**		
RID	**0003053**	wšm to slaughter		
	ID lexeme	50580	wšm	slaughtering knife
		50570	wšm	to slay; to kill
DRID	**1002731**	**wsn to procreate**		
RID	**0003054**	wsn to procreate		
	ID lexeme	49570	wsn	to procreate; to fertilize
		49580	wsn.j	procreator
DRID	**1002732**	**wšn to sacrifice**		
RID	**0003055**	wšn to sacrifice		
	ID lexeme	50620	wšn	to wring (the necks of birds); to sacrifice
		50630	wšn.w	the catch (of fishing and fowling); sacrifice
		88730	nšn	[offering of birds]
DRID	**1002733**	**wsr oar**		
RID	**0003056**	wsr oar		
	ID lexeme	49620	wsr	oar
DRID	**1002734**	**wsr to be strong**		
RID	**0003057**	wsr to be strong		
	ID lexeme	49490	wsy	very; how (emphatic)
		49640	wsr	[Weser-scepter]
		851401	wsr	powerful one (various gods)
		49610	wsr	powerful one
		49590	wsr	powerful; strong

			500010	wsr	to be powerful; to be strong; to strengthen
			49630	wsr	powerful one (phallus of Osiris)
			49600	wsr.w	strength; wealth
			49760	wsr.wt	power
			853977	wsr.tj	the two uraei
			858216	wsr.tj	powerful one
			49680	wsr.t	mighty one (fire)
			49700	wsr.t	front hawser; prow rope (naut.)
			49710	wsr.t	powerful one (rich woman)
			858850	wsr.t	powerful one
			49660	wsr.t	stake (in the hereafter); canid head symbol
			49650	wsr.t	neck
			49690	wsr.t	power (eye)
			130730	swsr	to make strong; to make rich
DRID	**1002735**		**wšr to dry**		
	RID	**0003058**	wšr to dry		
		ID lexeme	70028	wšr	to be absent; to lack; without
			50650	wšr	dry land; dry area
			854502	wšr	to dry; to parch; to lack; to be bald
			50640	wšr	to dry; to parch
			401162	wšr.t	dry land?
			50680	wšr.t	[an affliction of the eyes (dryness?)]
			861722	swšr.w	drying; drying agent
			130790	swšr	to parch; to dry
DRID	**1002736**		**wstn [a body of water?]**		
	RID	**0003060**	wstn [a body of water?]		
		ID lexeme	50000	wstn	[a body of water?]
DRID	**1002737**		**wstj official writings**		
	RID	**0003059**	wstj official writings		
		ID lexeme	49980	wstj	official writings
DRID	**1002738**		**wsṯn to stride unhindered**		
	RID	**0003061**	wsṯn to stride unhindered		
		ID lexeme	50030	wsṯn	to stride unhindered
DRID	**1002739**		**wšꜣ darkness**		
	RID	**0003063**	wšꜣ darkness		
		ID lexeme	500633	wšꜣ.yt	One belonging to the midnight hour
			50230	wšꜣ.w	darkest part of the night; darkness
DRID	**1002740**		**wšꜣ slander**		

	RID	**0003064**	wšꜣ slander		
		ID lexeme	50220	wšꜣ.w	slanders (or similar)
DRID	**1002741**	**wšꜣ to fatten**			
	RID	**0003065**	wšꜣ to fatten		
		ID lexeme	50110	wšꜣ	to fatten (animals)
			50120	wšꜣ	feeder (of animals)
			50140	wšꜣ	to treat (a tooth)
			50200	wšꜣꜣ.w	fattened animals
			50160	wšꜣ.t	[a fattened fowl (wigeon duck?)]
DRID	**1002742**	**wšꜣ to pour out**			
	RID	**0003066**	wšꜣ to pour out		
		ID lexeme	50130	wšꜣ	to pour out
DRID	**1002743**	**wšꜥ to chew**			
	RID	**0003067**	wšꜥ to chew		
		ID lexeme	50270	wšꜥ	to chew; to eat
			50300	wšꜥ.w	itching ("eating" as an illness)
			50290	wšꜥ.t	itching spot (med.)
DRID	**1002744**	**wt to bandage**			
	RID	**0003068**	wt to bandage		
		ID lexeme	51060	wt	embalmed one
			51000	wt	innermost coffin
			50990	wt	mummy bandages; bandages
			50980	wt	to bandage; to bind
			855700	wt.j	embalmer
			51010	wt.j	bandager (of wounds)
			51100	wt.j	fettered one
			51020	wt.j	embalmer
			851721	wt.y	embalmer (Anubis)
			500412	wt.t	fetterer
			500271	wtꜣ.w	those who are wrapped (gods in the netherworld)
			51140	wtwt	binding; fetter
			130880	swt	embalmed? [epithet of Osiris]
DRID	**1002745**	**wt to move around**			
	RID	**0003074**	wtwt to move around		
		ID lexeme	854337	nwtwt	to totter
			130890	swtwt	to walk about; to travel
			600319	swtwt	journey
DRID	**1002746**	**wtẖ to flee**			
	RID	**0003069**	wtẖ to flee		
		ID lexeme	51230	wtẖ	to flee

			51240	wtẖ.w	fugitive
DRID	**1002747**	**wti̯ to be old**			
	RID	**0003070**	wti̯ to be old		
		ID lexeme	51120	wt.w	eldest son
			51080	wt.t	Oldest one (a serpent goddess)
			852193	wt.t	Oldest one (a serpent goddess as a place in the netherworld)
			850422	wti̯	to be old; to be great
			51130	wtw.tj	eldest son
			130860	swti̯	to make great
DRID	**1002748**	**wtmt to tumble**			
	RID	**0003071**	wtmt to tumble		
		ID lexeme	51150	wtmt	to stick firmly?
			51160	wtmtm	to collapse?; to stagger?
DRID	**1002749**	**wtn to pierce**			
	RID	**0003072**	wtn to pierce		
		ID lexeme	51170	wtn	to pierce; to break through
			859103	wtn	opening; drill; tunnel
DRID	**1002750**	**wtṯ to create**			
	RID	**0003073**	wtṯ to create		
		ID lexeme	51290	wtṯ	semen
			51280	wtṯ	to create; to beget
			51270	wtṯ	creator? (Osiris)
			51320	wtṯ.w	offspring; son
			51310	wtṯ.w	creator; father
			858220	wtṯ.t	offspring
DRID	**1002751**	**wṯz = ṯzi̯ to lift up**			
	RID	**0003075**	wṯz to lift up		
		ID lexeme	450102	wṯz	standard
			51350	wṯz	carrying chair
			51340	wṯz	to announce; to extol; to slander
			51330	wṯz	to lift up; to carry; to raise; to boast
			51380	wṯz	one who elevates (something, ritually)
			500475	wṯz	He who elevates
			854313	wṯz.w	elevation
			51460	wṯz.w	accuser (who elevates (the accusation))
			853631	wṯz.wt	betrayal; accusations
			51360	wṯz.t	throne
			858710	wṯz.t	sky; heavens

		858222	wṯz.t	flame
		51370	wṯz.t	Throne (of Horus) (town and nome of Edfu)
RID	**0002872**	ṯzi̯ to rise		
	ID Lexeme	176880	ṯz	taxes; dues; delivery
		176890	ṯz	support
		176840	ṯz	sandbank
		176900	ṯz.w	reprehensible
		177260	ṯz.w	extension (of the neck); accumulation (med.)
		176980	ṯz.t	taxes
		177000	ṯz.t	rank
		177010	ṯz.t	heaven; roof
		176960	ṯz.t	ridge (of hills); (mountain) range
		177040	ṯz.t	image of an enemy (to be destroyed)
		177020	ṯz.t	mourning woman
		177030	ṯz.t	complaint; accusation
		860615	ṯz.t	One who is elevated
		176920	ṯz.t	[a case for a sekhem-scepter]
		855640	ṯz.t	transport
		176990	ṯz.t	chest (on legs?)
		177070	ṯz.tj	one who is in the chest (Osiris)
		177100	ṯz.tjw	image of an enemy (to be destroyed)
		860994	ṯz.tjt	image of an enemy (to be destroyed)
		177200	ṯzi̯	to raise; to elevate
		600467	ṯzi̯	to rise up; to go up (to a place)
		854581	ṯzi̯	to elevate
		852063	ṯzi̯	to elevate
		177210	ṯzi̯	to blame; to suspend
		177220	ṯzi̯	to accumulate (things)
		852151	sṯz	staff; support
		149470	sṯz.w	clouds
		149460	sṯz.w	raising up
		149420	sṯzi̯	to make (bulls) fervent
		149390	sṯzi̯	to raise; to lift up
		149400	sṯzi̯	to bring up (vomit?) (med.)

DRID 1002752 ww to make music

RID	**0003076**	ww to make music		
	ID lexeme	44850	ww	to sing?; to make music?
		44870	ww	[a singing or music-making woman?
		44880	ww.t	Uut (singing Hathor)

DRID 1002753 wzf to be idle

	RID	0003077	wzf to be idle		
		ID lexeme	49520	wzf	to be idle; to be sluggish; to neglect (something)
			49530	wzf	laziness; idleness
			49540	wzf	[address of a fisherman?]
			49550	wzf.w	idler; sluggard
			650064	wzf.t	neglect; sluggishness; laziness
DRID	**1002754**	**wzš to urinate**			
	RID	**0003078**	wzš to urinate		
		ID lexeme	49950	wzš	to urinate; to discharge
			858227	wzš.wt	bilge-water
			49970	wzš.t	urine
DRID	**1002755**	**wzṯ to decay**			
	RID	**0003079**	wzṯ to decay		
		ID lexeme	50020	wzṯ	to be decayed; to be devastated
			858228	wzṯ	decay; decline; dissolution
DRID	**1002756**	**wꜣ [a plant]**			
	RID	**0003102**	wꜣwꜣ [a plant]		
		ID lexeme	42740	wꜣwꜣ.t	[a plant]
DRID	**1002757**	**wꜣ cord**			
	RID	**0003080**	wꜣ cord		
		ID lexeme	42380	wꜣ	rope; cord; string
			855535	wꜣ.j	one belonging to the cord
			42470	wꜣ.t	cord; ribbon
			42720	wꜣwꜣ.t	rope
DRID	**1002758**	**wꜣ to plan**			
	RID	**0003081**	wꜣ to conspire		
		ID lexeme	42390	wꜣ	[verb (to resist?)]
			42430	wꜣ	conspiracy?; disloyalty?
			42420	wꜣ	to ponder; to brood; to conspire
			866828	wꜣ	conspirer
			42600	wꜣ.y	one pondering evil (a demon associated with illness)
			42670	wꜣ.wtj	conspirator
			42480	wꜣ.t	evil
			43520	wꜣ.tj	captive?
			42630	wꜣ.w	woe!; don't you dare!
			44110	wy	woe!; don't you dare!
			44310	wꜥꜣ	to revile
			44340	wꜥꜣ.w	Slanderer (gatekeeper in the netherworld)
	RID	**0003103**	wꜣwꜣ to plan		

	ID lexeme	42690	w3w3	evil plan?
		42680	w3w3	to plan; to consider (often with neg. connotations)

DRID 1002760 w3b root

RID	**0003082**	w3b root		
	ID lexeme	42770	w3b	root; socket; base
		42790	w3b	cord (naut.?); cloth?
		42810	w3b.t	lower part of the red crown (base)
		42800	w3b.t	hill; knoll; mound

DRID 1002761 w3ḏ to be green

RID	**0002913**	wḏ [a body of water?]		
	ID lexeme	52030	wḏ	[a body of water?]
RID	**0002914**	wḏ palm fiber		
	ID lexeme	52000	wḏ	palm fiber (for making rope)
RID	**0003083**	w3ḏ column		
	ID lexeme	43550	w3ḏ	papyrus column
		853825	w3ḏ	papyrus pillar
		43900	w3ḏ.yt	columned hall
RID	**0003084**	w3ḏ papyrus		
	ID lexeme	43560	w3ḏ	[a papyrus shaped amulet]
		43530	w3ḏ	papyrus (also as a symbol for Lower Egypt)
		858094	w3ḏ	papyrus plant
		850387	w3ḏ.t	stern; bow (of a ship)
RID	**0003085**	w3ḏ to be green		
	ID lexeme	43610	w3ḏ	fresh grain
		43570	w3ḏ	fresh spices
		43620	w3ḏ	green stone (gen.); malachite
		600304	w3ḏ	green; fresh; young
		43640	w3ḏ	cylindrical bead (made of green stone)
		43650	w3ḏ	[a kind of (water?) fowl]
		43600	w3ḏ.y	green plants
		43920	w3ḏ.w	raw meat
		43910	w3ḏ.w	green eye paint; green pigment
		861183	w3ḏ.w	wadju (a pasture ground)
		851899	w3ḏ.wt	raw foods
		851140	w3ḏ.t	green stone
		43750	w3ḏ.t	green one (crown of Lower Egypt)
		43700	w3ḏ.t	vegetables; greens
		43710	w3ḏ.t	[a fruit]
		43720	w3ḏ.t	green cloth
		859343	w3ḏ.tj	oasis region
		850386	w3ḏ.tj	two green stones
		43780	w3ḏ.tj	vegetable gardener
		43790	w3ḏ.tj	the two uraei; the two crowns

		43990	wꜣḏḏ.t	vegetation; green plants
		76170	msꜣḏ.t	nostril
		129930	swꜣḏ	to make green; to make prosper
RID	**0003086**	wꜣḏ to be lucky		
	ID lexeme	43590	wꜣḏ	fortunate man
		43930	wꜣḏ.w	success; happiness
		861578	wꜣḏ.t	flourishing one
RID	**0003087**	wꜣḏ to be young		
	ID lexeme	43540	wꜣḏ	child; son
RID	**0003088**	wꜣḏwꜣḏ to make green		
	ID lexeme	43950	wꜣḏwꜣḏ	green plants
		43940	wꜣḏwꜣḏ	to become green; to make green
		129960	wꜣḏwꜣḏ	to make green

DRID	**1002762**	**wꜣg to be joyful loudly**		
RID	**0003089**	wꜣg to be joyful loudly		
	ID lexeme	43500	wꜣg	to shout (for joy); to rejoice
		858107	wꜣg	bull for Wag-festival
		43510	wꜣg	Wag-festival (funerary festival)
		43490	wꜣgi̯	to provision (for a feast); to rejoice?

DRID	**1002763**	**wꜣḥ to lay down**		
RID	**0003090**	wꜣḥ to lay down		
	ID lexeme	43020	wꜣḥ	wreath; garland (of flowers, gold)
		853147	wꜣḥ	to refrain (from something); to decrease; to ease [aux./modal]
		43010	wꜣḥ	to lay down; to endure; to offer; to leave behind
		43190	wꜣḥ.yt	precinct
		43200	wꜣḥ.yt	yield (of the harvest); grain
		43060	wꜣḥ.wt	donation; oblations (or similar)
		43050	wꜣḥ.t	[a fem. mourner]
		43070	wꜣḥ.t	way station (on a processional way)
		856152	wꜣḥ.tj	one who brings offerings
		67240	mꜣḥ	wreath; grape; garland
		73440	mḥ	to coil around (of snakes); entwine (garlands); adorn
		129860	swꜣḥ	to make endure; to endure

DRID	**1002764**	**wꜣẖi̯ to flood**		
RID	**0003091**	wꜣẖi̯ to flood		
	ID lexeme	43230	wꜣẖ	fresh plants; verdure
		852765	wꜣẖ	abundance; flood
		43240	wꜣẖ	Fresh-water (a canal in the netherworld)
		854332	wꜣẖ.tj	[designation of the deceased]

			43270	wꜣẖy	pillared hall; columned hall
			43260	wꜣẖi̯	to flood; to make verdant; to rejoice; available in abundance
			129890	swꜣẖi̯	to make green; to refresh
DRID	**1002765**	**wꜣi̯ to move to**			
	RID	**0003092**	wꜣi̯ to be far (away from)		
		ID lexeme	42641	wꜣ	far; remote
			42640	wꜣ.w	long ago; far away
			42550	wꜣi̯	to be far (away from); to remove oneself
			129790	swꜣ.w	district; area; vicinity
			129770	swꜣ.t	past
			129800	swꜣi̯	keep (sb./sth.) away
	RID	**0003093**	wꜣi̯ to move to		
		ID lexeme	42440	wꜣ	[a transportation boat]
			42650	wꜣ.w	wave (of the sea); surge; floodwater
			853183	wꜣ.t	the way (domain)
			42490	wꜣ.t	road; way; path; side
			42560	wꜣi̯	to come to (do) (aux./modal)
			29300	swꜣ.w	journey
			129830	swꜣ.w	passerby (a demon)
			855623	swꜣ.wt	passerby (a female demon)
			129820	swꜣ.tjw	ones who pass by
			129740	swꜣi̯	to pass
DRID	**1002766**	**wꜣi̯ to parch**			
	RID	**0003094**	wꜣi̯ to parch (grain)		
		ID lexeme	42410	wꜣi̯	to parch (grain)
	RID	**0003103**	wꜣwꜣ to burn		
		ID lexeme	858473	wꜣwꜣ	to be fiery
			42760	wꜣwꜣ.w	sunlight
			858112	wꜣwꜣ.w	Fiery one
			42730	wꜣwꜣ.t	fire; ember; glow (or similar)
DRID	**1002767**	**wꜣp sheep**			
	RID	**0003095**	wꜣp sheep		
		ID lexeme	42850	wꜣp.t	sheep
DRID	**1002768**	**wꜣr reed**			
	RID	**0003097**	wꜣr reed		
		ID lexeme	42960	wꜣr	reed flute?; reed
DRID	**1002769**	**wꜣr to dance (or similar)**			
	RID	**0003098**	wꜣr to dance (or similar)		
		ID lexeme	42940	wꜣr	to dance (or similar)

DRID	**1002770**	**wꜣr to tie**		
RID	**0003096**	wꜣr cord		
	ID lexeme	42920	wꜣr	to tie up (the bag)
		42990	wꜣr.w	[a girdle]
		42980	wꜣr.t	rope; cord

DRID	**1002771**	**wꜣš to be powerful**		
RID	**0003099**	wꜣš to be powerful		
	ID lexeme	43430	wꜣš	honor; respect
		855544	wꜣš	prestigious one
		43420	wꜣš	to be powerful; to worship (someone)
		500606	wꜣš.yw	Honorable ones
		43460	wꜣš.wt	honorable ones? (female beings)
		43480	wꜣšš	bruise; hematoma? (med.)
		129900	swꜣš	to pay honor to; to praise

DRID	**1002772**	**wꜣs to rule**		
RID	**0003100**	wꜣs to rule		
	ID lexeme	43310	wꜣs	to rule; to be powerful; to be happy
		43300	wꜣs	dominion; power; well-being
		43290	wꜣs	[was-scepter]
		43400	wꜣs.yt	She of the Was-scepter
		43340	wꜣs.t	[a garment (for a divine image)]

DRID	**1002773**	**wꜣsi̯ to be ruined**		
RID	**0003101**	wꜣsi̯ to be ruined		
	ID lexeme	43410	wꜣsi̯	to be ruined (buildings); to be fallen down; to go down
DRID	**1002774**	**wꜥ goat**		
RID	**0003104**	wꜥ goat		
	ID lexeme	44240	wꜥ.tj	goat

DRID	**1002775**	**wꜥ one**		
RID	**0003109**	wꜥi̯ to be alone		
	ID lexeme	600041	wꜥ	one (of many); some (of a material)
		852351	wꜥ	the only one; the lonely one
		400101	wꜥ	one; sole one
		44150	wꜥ	one; sole
		600043	wꜥ	a; an (indef. article)
		855693	wꜥ.w	solder; sailor
		44390	wꜥ.w	soldier; sailor
		44180	wꜥ.t	sole one (uraeus)
		600045	wꜥ.t	(sole) one; the only thing
		861109	wꜥ.t	palace

44190 w^{c}.t sole one (Hathor of Dendera)
44170 w^{c}.t sole one (solar eye)
44250 w^{c}.tj [a lion]
852751 w^{c}.tj the only one; the lonely one
44230 w^{c}.tj sole; single
855564 w^{c}.tj unique one
865709 w^{c}.tj one-sided
44370 w^{c}.tjw one (numerical concept)
44270 w^{c}.tjt sole one (name of the uraeus)
44360 w^{cc}.w loneliness; solitude
44350 w^{c}i̯ to be alone; to be (the only) one
130000 sw^{c}i̯ to leave alone

DRID 1002776 w^{c} to kill

RID 0003105 w^{c} harpoon
ID lexeme 44140 w^{c} harpoon

RID 0003113 w^{c}w^{c} to cut down
ID lexeme 44420 w^{c}w^{c} to cut down (an enemy)

DRID 1002777 w^{c}b to be pure

RID 0003106 w^{c}b to be pure
ID lexeme 44470 w^{c}b to serve as priest
44480 w^{c}b pure place
44450 w^{c}b pure one; free one
852709 w^{c}b [a water stream?]
44440 w^{c}b purity; purification
860551 w^{c}b pure one
855694 w^{c}b wab-priest
44460 w^{c}b wab-priest
44430 w^{c}b to purify; to be pure; to be free (to be unused)
853177 w^{c}b the pure (domain)
850111 w^{c}b Pure one (Gebel Barkal)
44490 w^{c}b piece of meat (for offering)
400114 w^{c}b pure
44620 w^{c}b.w pure garment (for the gods and the dead)
44580 w^{c}b.wt priestly duty (for the month)
44530 w^{c}b.t pure garment (for gods)
44540 w^{c}b.t pure place (embalming place, workshop for crafts); sanctuary; tomb
44520 w^{c}b.t w^{c}b-priestess
44560 w^{c}b.t meat; flesh (for offerings)
44570 w^{c}b.t food offerings (lit. what is pure)
858088 w^{c}b.t cleansing; purification
44550 w^{c}b.t pure place (heavens)
130010 sw^{c}b to cleanse; to purify

			130020	swᶜb	[designation for natron]
DRID	**1002778**	**wᶜf to bend down**			
	RID	**0003107**	wᶜf to bend down		
		ID lexeme	44640	wᶜf	to bend (something) down; to prostrate; to be bent; to bend into shape
DRID	**1002779**	**wᶜḥ chufa**			
	RID	**0003108**	wᶜḥ chufa		
		ID lexeme	44830	wᶜḥ	chufa (sedge with edible tuber)
DRID	**1002780**	**wᶜn juniper**			
	RID	**0003110**	wᶜn juniper		
		ID lexeme	44660	wᶜn	juniper tree
DRID	**1002781**	**wᶜr leg**			
	RID	**0003112**	wᶜr to flee		
		ID lexeme	44680	wᶜr	to flee; to hurry
			44690	wᶜr	fugitive
			44810	wᶜr.w	hurry
			44730	wᶜr.t	flight; escape
			44740	wᶜr.t	leg
DRID	**1002782**	**wᶜr partition**			
	RID	**0003111**	wᶜr partition		
		ID lexeme	44750	wᶜr.t	part; department; administrative district
			44760	wᶜr.t	district (of the necropolis)
			44780	wᶜr.t	[a body of water in the hereafter]
			44720	wᶜr.t	[part of a ship]
			44770	wᶜr.t	[a celestial region]
DRID	**1002783**	**wᶜꜣ torch**			
	RID	**0003115**	wᶜꜣ torch		
		ID lexeme	44320	wᶜꜣ	candle; torch
			856148	wᶜꜣ	star (or similar)

II.6 b

DRID 1000001 b lips
RID 0000002 b lips
ID lexeme 859225 b.tj lips

DRID 1000002 b leg
RID 0000001 b foot, leg?
ID lexeme 856528 b’ leg

DRID 1000003 bb throat, neck
RID 0000003 bb throat, neck
ID lexeme 55370 bb.t throat
55430 bb.yt region of the collar bones?
859345 bb.t collar; necklace
55340 bb collar
55420 bb.wj the two collar bones
RID 0000004 bb to strangle?
ID lexeme 550424 bb [verb (a way to die)]

DRID 1000004 bbn to wriggle along
RID 0000006 bbn to wriggle along
ID lexeme 550450 bbn to wriggle along

DRID 1000005 bḏ ball, corn
RID 0000007 bḏ ball
ID lexeme 82960 nbḏbḏ to hop, to jump (of the Horus eye)
58530 bḏ ball; pellet
RID 00000012 bḏn ball?
ID lexeme 856547 bḏn.w ball?

DRID 1000006 bd emmer
RID 0000008 bd emmer
ID lexeme 58430 bd.t emmer

DRID 1000007 bd natron
RID 0000009 bd fragrance
ID lexeme 58510 bdd fragrance
RID 0000019 bd natron
ID lexeme 58410 bd to purify (with natron)
58400 bd natron (granulated soda)
RID 0000011 bd to shine
ID lexeme 58429 bd to illumine; to shine

DRID 1000009 bḏn stick
RID 0000013 bḏn stick

	ID lexeme	58630	bd̲n	stick; cudgel

DRID 1000010 bdš to be weak

RID	**0000014**	bdš to be weak		
	ID lexeme	58470	bdš	to be weak; to be inert
		856548	bdš.j	weary one
		856550	bdš.w	weariness; fatigue
		856549	bdš.t	weariness; fatigue
		132290	sbdš	to make weak
		58490	bdš.t	Weary one

DRID 1000011 bd̲ꜣ pad

RID	**0000016**	bd̲ꜣ pad		
	ID lexeme	58590	bd̲ꜣ	stiff roll of fabric; pad (used med.)

DRID 1000012 bd̲ꜣ mold

RID	**0000015**	bd̲ꜣ mold		
	ID lexeme	58570	bd̲ꜣ	bread mould; mould (pot made of fired clay)

DRID 1000014 bfn scorpion

RID	**0000018**	bfn scorpion		
	ID lexeme	55460	bfn	[a scorpion]
		55490	bfn.t	[a scorpion (fem.)]

DRID 1000015 bgs to injure

RID	**0000019**	bgs to injure		
	ID lexeme	450143	bgs	to injure; to be injured; to be disloyal
		58060	bgs.w	damage; harm; turmoil
		856672	bgs.w	rebel
		132230	sbgs	to hurt; to damage

DRID 1000016 bgz = bgs throat

RID	**0000020**	bgz = bgs throat		
	ID lexeme	58050	bgz	throat

DRID 1000017 bgꜣ to be shipwrecked

RID	**0000021**	bgꜣ to be shipwrecked		
	ID lexeme	58010	bgꜣ.w	shipwrecked man
		850481	bgꜣ	to be shipwrecked

DRID 1000018 bgꜣ to shout

RID	**0000022**	bgꜣ to shout		
	ID lexeme	855211	bgꜣ	to howl
		58000	bgꜣ.w	shouting

DRID	**1000019**	**bḥ bead**		
RID	**0000026**	bḥbḥ bead		
	ID lexeme	855369	bḥbḥ	lapis lazuli beads
DRID	**1000020**	**bḫ to force**		
RID	**0000024**	bḫ to force		
	ID lexeme	56800	bḫ	to do compulsory labor; to force
		550264	bḫ.w	compulsory labor
		858410	bḫ	to capture?
DRID	**1000021**	**bšw flint**		
RID	**0000116**	bšw flint		
	ID lexeme	57620	bšw	[a shiny flint]
DRID	**1000022**	**bḥd to settle down?**		
RID	**0000027**	bḥd Edfou		
	ID lexeme	56970	bḥd.t	Edfu
		858626	bḥd.t	Behdet (court M in Edfou)
		850566	bḥd.tj	Behdety (winged sun disk)
		858498	bḥd.tj	One of Edfu
		400311	bḥd.tj	One of Edfou (Horus)
		56980	bḥd.tjt	One of Edfu (Hathor)
RID	**0000028**	bḥd to settle down?		
	ID lexeme	858853	bḥd	to settle down
		56990	bḥd.w	throne; seat
		858715	bḥd.w	a place of throne
		858694	bḥd.t	necropolis of primordial gods
DRID	**1000023**	**bhd to sniff**		
RID	**0000029**	bhd to sniff		
	ID lexeme	56770	bhd	to fumigate; to smoke thoroughly
		56750	bhd	perfume
		854508	bhd	to inhale; to breath in; to smoke thoroughly
		56760	bhd	to inhale (fragrance); to breath in
DRID	**1000025**	**bḫḫ to glow**		
RID	**0000031**	bḫḫ to glow		
	ID lexeme	57080	bḫḫ	to glow
		57100	bḫḫ.w	fiery breath
		500324	bḫḫ.y	Glowing one (gate in the netherworld)
		501079	bḫḫ.t	Glowing One
RID	**0000030**	bḫḫ pellets of natron		
	ID lexeme	57070	bḫḫ	pellets of natron
DRID	**1000026**	**bḫn greywacke**		

	RID	**0000032**	bḫn greywacke		
		ID lexeme	57020	bḫn	greywacke (crystalline dark gray sandstone)
DRID	**1000027**		**bḥn = bfn to bark**		
	RID	**0000033**	bḥn to bark		
		ID lexeme	56850	bḥn	dog (“barker”)
			56860	bḥn	to bark
	RID	**0000017**	bfn dog		
		ID lexeme	55470	bfn	to bark
			55480	bfn	dog
DRID	**1000028**		**bḫn to watch**		
	RID	**0000034**	bḫn to watch		
		ID lexeme	859887	bḫn	[a screen made of wattle]
			859593	bḫn	to watch
			57030	bḫn	fortified house; castle; stronghold; fortress
			57040	bḫn	pylon (headdress of Hathor and upper part of the sistrum)
			57060	bḫn.t	pylon; gateway
			132010	sbḫn	mat
DRID	**1000029**		**bḥni̯ to cut**		
	RID	**0000035**	bḥni̯ to cut		
		ID lexeme	103650	ḥbn	to kill
			56830	bḥni̯	to cut (up, off); to punish
			856553	bḥn	biting snake
			56840	bḥn	dismemberment (punishment)
			56870	bḥn.t	knife
DRID	**1000030**		**bḥs to hunt**		
	RID	**0000036**	bḥs to hunt		
		ID lexeme	56920	bḥs	to hunt
DRID	**1000031**		**bḥz calf**		
	RID	**0000037**	bḥz calf		
		ID lexeme	56890	bḥz	calf
			56910	bḥz.t	calf (female)
DRID	**1000032**		**bhꜣ to move back**		
	RID	**0000038**	bhꜣ fan		
		ID lexeme	56680	bh.t	fan
			56690	bhꜣ	fan
	RID	**0000039**	bhꜣ to flee		
		ID lexeme	56720	bhꜣ.w	fugitive
			56700	bhꜣ	to make turn back; to flee

		131890	sbhꜣ	to make to flee
DRID	**1000033**	**bj bee**		
RID	**0000040**	bj bee		
	ID lexeme	54530	bj.w	wasp?; bee?; hornet ?
		54200	bj.t	bee
		54210	bj.t	honey
		860123	bj.t	honey
		54220	bj.t	Bit (red crown of Lower Egypt)
		852172	bj.t	Bit (crown goddess of Lower Egypt)
		54240	bj.tj	King of Lower Egypt
		853220	bj.tj	King of Lower Egypt (various gods)
		54230	bj.tj	beekeeper; honey gatherer
		54260	bj.tjt	Queen
		852663	bjt	King of Lower Egypt
		54250	bjtj	to be king of Lower Egypt
RID	**0000044**	bjbj bee		
	ID lexeme	54570	bjbj	[an insect (wasp?)]
DRID	**1000034**	**bj cheer**		
RID	**0000045**	bjbj cheer		
	ID lexeme	54560	bjbj	cheer; acclamation
DRID	**1000035**	**bj clapnet**		
RID	**0000041**	bj clapnet		
	ID lexeme	54110	bj.t	clapnet
DRID	**1000036**	**bj groats**		
RID	**0000042**	bj groats		
	ID lexeme	54120	bj	groats (coarsely ground cereals)
DRID	**1000037**	**bj processional bark**		
RID	**0000043**	bj processional bark		
	ID lexeme	54100	bj.t	processional bark
DRID	**1000038**	**bjdj [an affliction of the eye]**		
RID	**0000046**	bjdj [an affliction of the eye]		
	ID lexeme	54750	bjdj	[an affliction of the eye]
DRID	**1000039**	**bjk falcon**		
RID	**0000047**	bjk falcon		
	ID lexeme	54690	bjk	falcon ship
		54680	bjk	falcon
		500418	bjk	falcon
		54700	bjk.t	falcon (female)

			54710	bjk.t	falcon (Hathor and other goddesses)
			851580	bjk.t	Falcon town

DRID	**1000040**		**bjn evil**		
	RID	**0000049**	bjn to be bad		
		ID lexeme	54600	bjn	to be bad; to be evil
			54610	bjn	evil one
			855485	bjn	Evil one (Seth)
			54620	bjn	bad things
			54605	bjn	bad; evil
			54660	bjn.w	bad deeds
			54640	bjn.t	evil
			131680	sbjn	to alienate; to talk down

DRID	**1000041**		**bjn harp**		
	RID	**0000048**	bjn harp		
		ID lexeme	54650	bjn.t	harp

DRID	**1000042**		**bjꜣ astonishing**		
	RID	**0000050**	bjꜣ astonishing		
		ID lexeme	54340	bjꜣ	example; model
			54480	bjꜣ.yt	wonders; marvels
			54490	bjꜣ.ytj	marvelous one (Amun)
			54440	bjꜣ.w	marvelous things
			54410	bjꜣ.t	character; mood
			54400	bjꜣ.t	amazement; confusion
			54470	bjꜣi̯	to marvel (at)

DRID	**1000043**		**bjꜣ ore**		
	RID	**0000051**	bjꜣ ore		
		ID lexeme	860878	bjꜣ.tj	ore (gen.); copper
			54430	bjꜣ.tjt	brazen one; steadfast one (Thebes as the oldest city)
			54160	bj.t	(Egyptian) alabaster (of Hatnub)
			54300	bjꜣ	mineral of meteoric origin (gen.); ore
			54460	bjꜣ.j	valuable; brazen; metal
			54510	bjꜣ.w	mine; mining region
			54380	bjꜣ.t	mining region
			54500	bjꜣ.w	ore mining
			1856570	bjꜣ.wj	cymbals
			856573	bjꜣ.wt	firmament
			54390	bjꜣ.t	crystalline sandstone (Quartzite)
			54140	by	stone mason
			54290	bjꜣ	ore (gen.); metal; meteoric iron; copper
			873149	bjꜣ.j	bronze, celestial

860355 bjꜣ spear

DRID 1000044 bjꜣi̯ to be far from

RID 0000052 bjꜣi̯ to be far from?

ID lexeme
54350 bjꜣ (processional) way
54280 bjꜣ shell (of the primeval egg)
54330 bjꜣi̯ to be far from; to remove oneself from

RID 0006000 bjꜣi̯ heaven, sky
54320 bjꜣ brazen heavenly waters; firmament
856572 bjꜣ.w belonging to the heavenly waters
852220 bjꜣ.y One belonging to the sky

DRID 1000045 bkj [tree]

RID 0000054 bkj a tree

ID lexeme
57900 bkj [a (pear?) tree]
57910 bkj [a fruit (of the pear tree?)]

DRID 1000047 bkn excrement (med.)

RID 0000055 bkn excrement (med.)

ID lexeme
57920 bkn excrement (med.)

DRID 1000048 bkr throne

RID 0000056 bkr throne

ID lexeme
57930 bkr throne

DRID 1000049 bkꜣ pregnancy

RID 0000057 bkꜣ to be pregnant

ID lexeme
57840 bkꜣ.t pregnant woman
57860 bkꜣ.t sprout (of a rush); embryo?
57850 bkꜣ.t mother cow
57830 bkꜣ morning; morrow
57820 bkꜣ to be (become) pregnant; to make pregnant
57880 bkꜣ.tj [the two testicles]
132190 sbkꜣ to make pregnant
23970 jbkꜣ pregnant one (designation for a sow)

DRID 1000050 bnr = bl outside

RID 0000058 bnr = bl outside

ID lexeme
55920 bnr.w outside; exterior
56340 br open field (at necropolis); outside?

DRID 1000051 bn white wagtail

RID 0000062 bn white wagtail

		ID lexeme	55520	bn	white wagtail; species of heron
DRID	**1000052**	**bd natron**			
	RID	**0000010**	bd natron		
		ID lexeme	854363	bd.w	Natron God
DRID	**1000053**	**bn not**			
	RID	**0000061**	bn not		
		ID lexeme	55500	bn	[particle of negation]
DRID	**1000054**	**bꜣ = bn to overflow**			
	RID	**0000088**	bnu̯ to go out		
		ID lexeme	55510	bnu̯	to escape; to depart
			82770	nbnb	[coming of the inundation]
			103690	ḥbnbn	to slide down
			55750	bnbn	to beget; to ejaculate
			55770	bnbn	to flow out (Nile); to swell
	RID	**0000087**	bnu̯ to flow out		
		ID lexeme	131820	sbn.t	nursing cow; breastfeeding one
	RID	**0000154**	bꜣbꜣ	to overflow	
		ID lexeme	53430	bꜣbꜣ	to distribute; to pour out
			53450	bꜣbꜣ.t	fresh flood water; whirlpool
	RID	**0000155**	bꜣbꜣ to throb, to pulse?		
		ID lexeme	82490	nbꜣbꜣ	to throb?
			137180	snbꜣbꜣ	to make restless?
			103550	ḥbꜣbꜣ	to waddle (goose)
DRID	**1000055**	**bnd bad situation**			
	RID	**0000072**	bnd to fare badly		
		ID lexeme	56200	bnd	to fare badly
DRID	**1000056**	**bnḏ discharge**			
	RID	**0000069**	bnḏ discharge		
		ID lexeme	856577	bnḏ.t	landing (naut.)
			56260	bnḏ	to discharge (from the body)
DRID	**1000057**	**bnd garden bed; cucumber?**			
	RID	**0000070**	bnd garden bed; cucumber?		
		ID lexeme	850454	bnd.t	cucumber garden; cucumber
DRID	**1000058**	**bnd = *bnʿ = bʿn to wrap**			
	RID	**0000184**	bʿn to mount		
		ID lexeme	54940	bʿn	to mount (stones, in gold)
	RID	**0000073**	bnd to wrap		
		ID lexeme	56240	bnd	clothing; garment
			56220	bnd	to wrap; to clothe

		54090	bꜣḏ.y	[part of sandals (lacing?)]

DRID 1000059 bnf gall-bladder

RID	**0000074**	bnf gall-bladder		
	ID lexeme	55810	bnf	gall-bladder

DRID 1000060 bng to be happy

RID	**0000075**	bng to be happy		
	ID lexeme	56150	bng	to have abundance (of food)?

DRID 1000061 bngzyt [a kind of a musical instrument]

RID	**0000076**	bngzyt [a kind of a musical instrument]		
	ID lexeme	56160	bngzyt	[a musical instrument]

DRID 1000062 bnj to be sweet

RID	**0000077**	bnj to be sweet		
	ID lexeme	56040	bnj	confectioner
		854286	bnj	pleasant
		55950	bnj	sweetness (milk)
		55960	bnj	sweetness (canal)
		400993	bnj	sweet
		55930	bnj	date
		55940	bnj	to be sweet
		850457	bny	[a fruit (corn)]
		56070	bnj.w	sweetness; popularity
		55570	bnj.w	date juice
		867728	bnj.wt	sweetness
		56050	bnj.t	popularity
		55990	bnj.t	date wine
		55980	bnj.t	date palm
		56000	bnj.t	sweets
		56010	bnj.tj	confectioner
		56080	bnjbnj	sweet
		93990	rbnbn	to be pleased
		131850	sbnj	to make pleasant

DRID 1000063 bnn threshold?

RID	**0000079**	bnn threshold?		
	ID lexeme	55910	bnn.t	threshold?

DRID 1000064 bnš doorpost

RID	**0000083**	bnš doorpost		
	ID lexeme	56120	bnš	doorpost

DRID 1000065 bnš flower crown?

RID	**0000084**	bnš flower crown?		
	ID lexeme	56130	bnš	flower crown?

DRID 1000066 bns to pierce
RID 0000085 bns to pierce
ID lexeme 56100 bns to pierce; to gore

DRID 1000067 bnw millstone
RID 0000090 bnw millstone
ID lexeme 55620 bnw miller?
55650 bnw.t millstone

DRID 1000068 bḳ behold
RID 0000094 bḳ behold
ID lexeme 850452 bḳ to spot; to catch sight of

DRID 1000069 bḳ to be hostile
RID 0000095 bḳ to be hostile
ID lexeme 57710 bḳbḳ recalcitrance?
57670 bḳ to be stubborn; to be rebellious; to be hostile

DRID 1000070 bḳn to stride
RID 0000096 bḳn to stride
ID lexeme 57730 bḳn to stride
57760 bḳnḳn standards
861481 bḳnḳn.w standards

DRID 1000071 bḳy to open?
RID 0000098 bḳy to open?
ID lexeme 57700 bḳy to open?; to stay?

DRID 1000072 bḳ^{c} pool
RID 0000099 bḳ^{c} pool
ID lexeme 53790 bḳ^{c} depression (where flood water collects and stagnates)

DRID 1000073 br mullet
RID 0000102 br mullet
ID lexeme 56320 br [a mullet]

DRID 1000074 br transport ship
RID 0000103 br transport ship
ID lexeme 56310 br transport ship

DRID 1000075 brg [a kind of a semi-precious stone]
RID 0000105 brg [a kind of a semi-precious stone]
ID lexeme 56610 brg.t [a semi-precious stone (beryl?)]

DRID 1000076 brg be happy

	RID	**0000106**	brg be happy		
		ID lexeme	56600	brg	to be happy; to be content
DRID	**1000077**	**brk gift**			
	RID	**0000107**	brk = mrk to offer		
		ID lexeme	56560	brk	gift
			56540	brk	to offer
			73000	mrk	to provide; to offer; to present
DRID	**1000078**	**brkt pool**			
	RID	**0000108**	brkt pool		
		ID lexeme	56570	brkt	pool
DRID	**1000079**	**brḳ to sparkle**			
	RID	**0000109**	brḳ to sparkle		
		ID lexeme	56530	brḳ	to sparkle
DRID	**1000080**	**brt agreement**			
	RID	**0000110**	brt agreement		
		ID lexeme	56650	brt	agreement; pact
DRID	**1000081**	**brtj [semi-precious stone]**			
	RID	**0000111**	brtj [a kind of a semi-precious stone]		
		ID lexeme	56660	brtj	[a semi-precious stone]
DRID	**1000083**	**bši̯ to spit out**			
	RID	**0000112**	bši̯ to spit out		
		ID lexeme	57550	bš	vomiting
			57610	bš.w	vomit
			57600	bši̯	to spit out; to spew
			132060	sbš	to make vomit; become clear, sober
			132090	sbš.w	something disgusting; emetic
DRID	**1000084**	**bsk entrails**			
	RID	**0000113**	bsk entrails		
		ID lexeme	57520	bsk	entrails; heart
			57530	bsk	to cut out; to eviscerate
DRID	**1000085**	**bsn = msn to pierce**			
	RID	**0000114**	bsn = msn to pierce		
		ID lexeme	75420	msn	swimmer on the harpoon leash
			75490	msn	to hammer
			75500	msn.j	knife
			75510	msn.w	hapooner
			857373	msn.w	Harpooner
			858629	msn.t	Mesenet (room I in Edfu)

			75480	msn.tj	harpooner (priest at Edfu)
			75470	msn.tj	harpooner (epithet of Horus and the king)
			57470	bsn.t	etching needle; burin

DRID	**1000086**	**bšṯ to rebel**			
	RID	**0000115**	bšṯ to rebel		
		ID lexeme	57640	bšṯ	to be rebellious
			57650	bšṯ.w	rebels
			57660	bšṯ.w	rebellion
DRID	**1000087**	**bšꜣ ax**			
	RID	**0000117**	bšꜣ ax		
		ID lexeme	57580	bšꜣ	ax
DRID	**1000088**	**bšꜣ malted barley**			
	RID	**0000118**	bšꜣ malted barley		
		ID lexeme	57570	bšꜣ	[malted barley (for beer production)]
DRID	**1000089**	**bt mold**			
	RID	**0000119**	bt mold		
		ID lexeme	58120	bt	[a mold for making Osiris figures]
DRID	**1000090**	**bṯ running**			
	RID	**0000121**	bṯ	to run	
		ID lexeme	854510	bṯ	to run; to leave (somebody)
			859834	bṯ	to gather
			58280	bṯ	to run
			58290	bṯ	to leave (somebody)
			58310	bṯ.y	reed worker
DRID	**1000091**	**bt womb**			
	RID	**0000122**	bt womb		
		ID lexeme	856565	bt.t	womb
DRID	**1000092**	**btk to slaughter (enemies)**			
	RID	**0000124**	btk to slaughter (enemies)		
		ID lexeme	58230	btk	rebel (or similar)
			58250	btk	to slaughter (enemies)
			58220	btk	squalor; dirt
DRID	**1000093**	**btk to escape?**			
	RID	**0000123**	btk to escape?		
		ID lexeme	58270	btktk	to escape (or similar)
			58260	btk	expectoration?

				58240	btk	to be grieved? (of the heart)
DRID	**1000094**	**bṯn to resist**				
	RID	**0000125**		bṯn to resist		
		ID lexeme		58350	bṯn	to resist; to disobey
				58380	bṯn.w	rebel
DRID	**1000095**	**btꜣ wrongdoing**				
	RID	**0000126**		btꜣ to accuse		
		ID lexeme		58150	btꜣ	wrongdoer
				58140	btꜣ	to make (oneself) guilty
				58130	btꜣ.w	crime; offence; delict
				58170	btꜣ.t	disadvantage
DRID	**1000096**	**bw abomination?**				
	RID	**0000129**		bw to abominate?		
		ID lexeme		82730	nbw	sin
				55150	bw.t	disgust; abomination; crime; iniquity
				55320	bwi̯	to abhor; to detest
				55170	bw.tj	detested one
DRID	**1000097**	**bw not**				
	RID	**0000127**		bw not		
		ID lexeme		55130	bw	[particle of negation]
DRID	**1000098**	**bw place**				
	RID	**0000128**		bw place		
		ID lexeme		858690	bw	[for building abstract nouns]
				55110	bw	place; position
				55120	bw	item (in counting)
DRID	**1000099**	**bwn spearheads**				
	RID	**0000130**		bwn spearheads		
		ID lexeme		55330	bwn	spearheads (of fishing spear)
DRID	**1000100**	**bwꜣ to be high**				
	RID	**0000132**		bwꜣ to be high		
		ID lexeme		131720	sbwꜣ	to raise (up)
				850444	bwꜣ	hill
	RID	**0000131**		bwꜣ to be esteemed		
		ID lexeme		500315	bwꜣ	sublimity
				55270	bwꜣ	noble one
				55260	bwꜣ	to be high; to be esteemed
				53330	bwꜣ.w	hill ?
				55280	bwꜣ.t	hill; swamp thicket
				55300	bwꜣ.t	mighty deeds?

DRID	**1000101**		**bz flame**		
	RID	**0000135**	bzi̯ to burn		
		ID lexeme	856590	bz	flame; fire
			856589	bz.y	Flaming one
			856591	bzi̯	to burn
			500361	bs.y	Flaming one
			57360	bs.yt	Flaming one
			858439	nbs	burning
			82830	nbsbs	to catch fire; to inflame

DRID	**1000102**		**bz secret**		
	RID	**0000133**	bz secret		
		ID lexeme	57170	bz	secret; initiation
			850478	bz	secret image (cult statue)
			57160	bzi̯	to introduce (someone); to enter
			854509	bzi̯	to introduce (someone); to enter; to emerge; to come forth

DRID	**1000104**		**bzn to consider**		
	RID	**0000138**	bznw to consider		
		ID lexeme	57480	bznw	to consider; to notice

DRID	**1000105**		**bzn gypsum**		
	RID	**0000136**	bzn gypsum		
		ID lexeme	57460	bzn	gypsum; natron
		ID lexeme	855785	bznw	gypsum

DRID	**1000106**		**bzꜣ to protect**		
	RID	**0000139**	bzꜣ to protect		
		ID lexeme	850476	bzꜣ.t	protectress (Isis)
			57220	bs	[golden amulet]
			57330	bsꜣ.w	besau-pendant, sporran (as protection made of beads)
			57300	bzꜣ	protection
			57290	bzꜣ	[an offering object (“protection” that is being handed over)]
			57310	bzꜣ	to protect
			500726	bzꜣ	Protection

DRID	**1000107**		**bꜣ black stork?**		
	RID	**0000140**	bꜣ black stork? jabiru?		
		ID lexeme	52810	bꜣ	[a bird (a stork)]

DRID	**1000108**		**bꜣ boat**		
	RID	**0000141**	bꜣ boat		
		ID lexeme	53310	bꜣ.w	a cargo boat

DRID	**1000109**	**bꜣ leopard**		
RID	**0000145**	bꜣ leopard		
	ID lexeme	52880	bꜣ	leopard skin garment
		52860	bꜣ	leopard
		52870	bꜣ	leopard skin
DRID	**1000110**	**bꜣ pot**		
RID	**0000147**	bꜣ pot		
	ID lexeme	53320	bꜣ.w	[a pot; a jar]
DRID	**1000111**	**bꜣ ram**		
RID	**0000148**	bꜣ ram		
	ID lexeme	52850	bꜣ	Ba (sacred ram of Mendes); ram god
DRID	**1000112**	**bꜣ soul**		
RID	**0000150**	bꜣ soul		
	ID lexeme	850437	bꜣ.w	ba-souls (community of gods)
		53020	bꜣ.wj	the two bas (pairs of gods)
		52830	bꜣ	to endow with a ba(-soul) by to be ba-like, immanent
		52820	bꜣ	to be a ba-mighty; to be endowed with a ba(-soul) by to be ba-like, immanent
		854507	bꜣ	to be ba-mighty; to make ba-mighty by to be ba-like, immanent
		53300	bꜣ.w	might; ba-power
		52840	bꜣ	ba (might, power as part of the personality) by spirit
		53270	bꜣ.yt	She who belongs to Ba (Osiris) (a demon)
		53030	bꜣ.wj	Bawi (decanal star)
		53280	bꜣ.yw	Those belonging to the Ba (Ra)
		500106	bꜣ.y	He who is endowed with a Ba(-soul)
DRID	**1000113**	**bꜣ throat**		
RID	**0000152**	bꜣ throat		
	ID lexeme	850443	bꜣ.t	throat
DRID	**1000114**	**bꜣ to hack open**		
RID	**0000144**	bꜣ to hack open		
	ID lexeme	52890	bꜣ	to hack up (the earth); to open up; chop up
		52920	bꜣ	[head disease (bald spot, hole)]
		53420	bꜣbꜣ	hole; cavern
		850440	bꜣ.t	tomb; hole

			53190	bꜣ.y	hole
			854365	bꜣꜣ.j	inhabitants of holes
			860481	bꜣbꜣ.t	[building]
			53380	bꜣwj	battlefield (of bulls)
DRID	**1000115**	**bꜣ = bn spherical object**			
	RID	**0000104**	brbr small bowl		
		ID lexeme	56450	brbr	knob (upper part of the Upper Egyptian White Crown)
	RID	**0000100**	br basket		
		ID lexeme	56380	br	basket
	RID	**0000101**	br eyeball		
		ID lexeme	56480	brr	blind man
			56270	br	eyeball; eye
			56370	br	[a bead of pigment?]
			56360	br	tuft (of an ox's tail)
			56280	br	to see
	RID	**0000730**	ḥnbꜣ ball		
		ID lexeme	106630	ḥnbꜣbꜣ	ball-shaped (of a swelling; med.)
	RID	**0000078**	bnn little ball		
		ID lexeme	55850	bnn	globule (of myrrh); bead
			501072	bnn	Spherical One
			55890	bnn.t	ball
	RID	**0000142**	bꜣ bush		
		ID lexeme	52960	bꜣ.t	bush; shrub
			859756	bꜣ.tj	The Two Bushes (designation of Egypt)
	RID	**0000149**	bꜣ small ball		
		ID lexeme	52970	bꜣ.t	[a cereal]
			53120	bꜣꜣ	eye
	RID	**0000005**	bbj [a semi-precious stone]		
		ID lexeme	850446	bbj	[a semi-precious stone (beads?)]
	RID	**0000060**	bn little ball		
		ID lexeme	55550	bn.tj	nipples; breasts (dual)
DRID	**1000116**	**bꜣ = bn to erect**			
	RID	**0000146**	bꜣ pole		
		ID lexeme	82430	nbꜣ	carrying pole
			82470	nbꜣ.t	[post (used at foundation ceremony]
			600644	bꜣbꜣ	lance
			52990	bꜣ.t	[a wooden instrument (pestle, masher)]
			53260	bꜣ.y	wooden peg ?; wooden post ?
			850441	bꜣ.w	[a wooden instrument (pestle, masher)]
			52980	bꜣ.t	[a scepter of Hathor]
	RID	**0000153**	bꜣbꜣ [a serpent]		

	ID lexeme	867707	b3b3.j	[a serpent]
RID	**0000080**	bnn to erect		
	ID lexeme	55830	bnn	to beget; to be erected
		55840	bnn	[phallus?]
		55880	bnn	to repulse (the Nine Bows)
		850952	bnn.wt	virility; potency
		131810	sbnn	to fertilise
		857658	sbnn.wt	virility
RID	**0000161**	b3ḥ phallus		
	ID lexeme	53530	b3ḥ.yt	under-kilt? (as phallus protection); [fabric name]
		53520	b3ḥ	[a measure (solid measure?)]
		850447	b3ḥ	to beget
		53510	b3ḥ	phallus
RID	**0000092**	bnw phoenix		
	ID lexeme	867722	bnw	phoenix bnw, byn
		55590	bn.w	Phoenix (benu-bird)
RID	**0000093**	bnw potency?		
	ID lexeme	856575	bnw	potency
RID	**0000089**	bnw inflammation		
	ID lexeme	55640	bnw.t	inflammation; swelling
		55660	bnw.t	heat; oestrum (oestrous phase of female mammal)
RID	**0000091**	bnw perch?		
	ID lexeme	55700	bnw.t	[perch? for a bird]
RID	**0000059**	bn baboon		
	ID lexeme	873152	bn.tj	Benti (baboon as a son of the sun god)
		867725	bn.tjj	baboonish
		56180	bn.ty	Benti (baboon as a son of the sun god)
RID	**0000175**	b33 engender		
	ID lexeme	53140	b33.wt	virility
RID	**0000065**	bnbn obelisk		
	ID lexeme	500134	bnbny.tj	One belonging to the obelisk (sun god)
		55720	bnbn	Benben (sacred stone); obelisk
		500131	bnbn	House of the obelisk (myth. locality in the netherworld)
		850461	bnbn	Benben bnbn
		856233	bnbn	Benben Sanctuary in Heliopolis
RID	**0000064**	bnbn (wooden) beam		
	ID lexeme	55740	bnbn	[a beam (made of cedarwood)]
RID	**0000081**	b3 = bn to overflow		
	ID lexeme	55820	bnn	to overflow (of a granary); to swell
RID	**0000063**	bnbn a conical object		

		ID lexeme	55730	bnbn	[a conical loaf of bread]
			851819	bnbn.t	[a loaf of bread]
			500647	bnbn.tj	He who belongs to the conical loaf
			55800	bnbn.t	pyramidion (capstone of pyramid and obelisk)
	RID	**0000067**	bnbn to be erected		
		ID lexeme	55780	bnbn	to point upwards; to be erected
	RID	**0000082**	bnn upright		
		ID lexeme	55860	bnn	Benen (a serpent)
DRID	**1000118**	**bꜣḏ = pꜣḏ spheric shape**			
	RID	**0000156**	bꜣḏ myrrh		
		ID lexeme	54080	bꜣḏ	Myrrhe [substantive (something to rub)]
			54050	bꜣḏ	[name for myrrh or similar]
	RID	**0000157**	bꜣḏ ringlet?		
		ID lexeme	854444	bꜣḏ.t	ringlet (or similar)
	RID	**0002034**	pꜣḏ knee		
		ID Lexeme	59440	pꜣḏ	to kneel; to run
			59460	pꜣḏ	knee; kneecap
DRID	**1000120**	**bꜣg coagulate**			
	RID	**0000158**	bꜣg coagulate		
		ID lexeme	53970	bꜣg	to congeal? (med.)
DRID	**1000121**	**bꜣgi̯ to be weak**			
	RID	**0000159**	bꜣgi̯ to be weak		
		ID lexeme	131450	sbꜣgi̯	to make weary
			856543	bꜣgg.t	weakness; impotence
			53980	bꜣg	weakness; weariness
			856542	bꜣgg	weakness; impotence
			53990	bꜣgi̯	to be weary
			869222	sbꜣg	to make weary
DRID	**1000122**	**bꜣgs to stab**			
	RID	**0000160**	bꜣgs to stab		
		ID lexeme	54020	bꜣgs.w	dagger
			54010	bꜣgs	to dagger; to stab to death
			54000	bꜣgs	[a plant (thornbush?)]
DRID	**1000123**	**bꜣẖ sunrise / sunset?**			
	RID	**0000023**	bẖ to bring forth		
		ID lexeme	57110	bẖ	to give birth; to bring forth
	RID	**0000025**	bẖ to shine?		
		ID lexeme	57120	bẖ	to shine
			57140	bẖbẖ	arrogance
	RID	**0000162**	bꜣẖ sunset		

	ID lexeme	850449	bꜣẖ	to sink; to set
		53570	bꜣẖ.w	Bakhu (in Libya); western mountains
RID	**0000163**	bꜣẖ to rise		
	ID lexeme	53550	bꜣẖ	to rise (of the sun); to shine brightly
		53580	bꜣẖ.t	white of the eye?
		500779	bꜣẖ.yt	She of the Eastern Mountains
		850448	bꜣẖ.w	Bakhu (myth. locality in the east where the sun rises)

DRID 1000124 bꜣi̯ to be moist

RID	**0000164**	bꜣi̯ to be moist		
	ID lexeme	53340	bꜣ.w	moisture (of the human body); perspiration
		53170	bꜣi̯	to be moist
		53180	bꜣ.y	foot wash basin

DRID 1000125 bꜣk ramp

RID	**0000165**	bꜣk ramp		
	ID lexeme	53840	bꜣk	platform; ramp; tribune

DRID 1000126 bꜣk servant

RID	**0000166**	bꜣk servant		
	ID lexeme	53800	bꜣk	to work; to pay dues; to render (services)
		53830	bꜣk	servant; underling
		53890	bꜣk.w	taxes; deliveries; pay
		53940	bꜣk.wt	servants
		53820	bꜣk.w	labour; task; performance
		53860	bꜣk.t	duties; produce
		53920	bꜣkꜣ.t	plot; district; town
		53960	bꜣkbꜣk.t	equipment?
		53930	bꜣk.w	workers
		53870	bꜣk.t	servant

DRID 1000127 bꜣni̯ sleep

RID	**0000167**	bꜣni̯ slumber		
	ID lexeme	852854	bꜣni̯	to lie dormant; slumber; drowse
		867710	bꜣn(i)	the sleepy one

DRID 1000128 bꜣḳ moringa tree

RID	**0000168**	bꜣḳ moringa tree, moringa oil		
	ID lexeme	53700	bꜣḳ	moringa tree?; olive tree?
		53720	bꜣḳ	oil of the moringa tree (ben oil)?; olive oil?
		53750	bꜣḳ.t	oil of the moringa tree?; olive oil?

		53760	bꜣḳ.t	[an oil jar]

DRID 1000129 bꜣḳ to be bright

RID	**0000169**	bꜣḳ to be bright		
	ID lexeme	53730	bꜣḳ	to be bright; to be clear; to be healthy
		53770	bꜣḳ.t	Dazzling-Eye (Egypt)
		53780	bꜣḳ.t	clear character; wellbeing
		861298	sbꜣḳ	Illuminating One
		855476	sbꜣḳ	to look at (god)
		131430	sbꜣḳ	to make bright; to make serene
		132160	sbꜣḳ.t	heavenly eye (sun, moon)
		131440	sbꜣḳḳ	to substantiate; to witness; certify; to commend

DRID 1000130 bꜣs bowl

RID	**0000171**	bꜣs unguent; bowl		
	ID lexeme	53650	bꜣs.t	beaker; pail
		53600	bꜣs	[a jar (for unguent)]
		850451	bꜣs	measure of capacity (1/2 hin)

DRID 1000131 bꜣs to cut out

RID	**0000170**	bꜣs to cut out		
	ID lexeme	53620	bꜣs	to cut out; to devour

DRID 1000132 bꜣš vessel

RID	**0000172**	bꜣš vessel (for oil, unguent?)		
	ID lexeme	53680	bꜣš	jar (measure for unguent)

DRID 1000133 bꜣw hill

RID	**0000173**	bꜣw hill		
	ID lexeme	850444	bꜣw	hill
		53390	bꜣwj	offering stand?
		53370	bꜣw.tjw	those belonging to the mound (grave)

DRID 1000134 bꜣy malt

RID	**0000174**	bꜣy (a fruit with grains)		
	ID lexeme	53160	bꜣy	malt (soaked grain)
		53150	bꜣy	[a kind of sweet baked goods]
		53210	bꜣy.t	[a kind of sweet baked goods]
		53440	bꜣbꜣ.t	[a cereal]

DRID 1000135 b^{c} to deal with water

RID	**0000176**	b^{c} to bathe		
	ID lexeme	860858	b^{c}	to bubble; to bathe
RID	**0000179**	b^{c}b^{c} to bubble		

	ID lexeme	54910	bᶜbᶜ	glazer (faience craftsman)
		54900	bᶜbᶜ	to bubble; to bath, to drink
RID	**0000180**	bᶜbᶜ to drink		
	ID lexeme	856540	bᶜbᶜ	drink
RID	**0000178**	bᶜ to produce (water)		
	ID lexeme	54920	bᶜbᶜ.t	inundation; current of water; stream (swirl)
		54860	bᶜy	[a term for flood]
		54830	bᶜ	to engender; to produce; to yield

DRID 1000137 bᶜ to disregard

RID	**0000177**	bᶜ to disregard		
	ID lexeme	54820	bᶜ	to disregard; to neglect
		54790	bᶜ	Esteemed One

DRID 1000140 bᶜḥi̯ to inundate

RID	**0000181**	bᶜḥi̯ to inundate		
	ID lexeme	55020	bᶜḥ	[term for birds (metaphor for abundance?)]
		55030	bᶜḥ	grapevine?
		55040	bᶜḥ	stream of semen (of Sobek, metaphor for the inundation)
		55080	bᶜḥi̯	to be flooded; to flood; to inundate; to have in abundance
		55000	bᶜḥ	inundated farmland
		54990	bᶜḥ.w	flood; inundation
RID	**0005000**	bᶜḥi̯ abundant		
		131690	sbᶜḥi̯	to make abundant
		854994	bᶜḥ.w	abundance
		55060	bᶜḥ.t	abundance
		860254	bᶜḥ.t	Abundance

DRID 1000141 bᶜj rod of palm

RID	**0000182**	bᶜj rod of palm		
	ID lexeme	54870	bᶜj	rod of palm

DRID 1000142 bᶜn neck

RID	**0000183**	bᶜn neck		
	ID lexeme	54950	bᶜn.t	neck; throat
		500364	bᶜn.tj	He with the neck

DRID 1000143 bᶜr Baal

RID	**0000187**	bᶜr to fight		
	ID lexeme	54980	bᶜr	to fight
		54960	bᶜr	Baal
		860150	bᶜr.t	Baalat

DRID 1000144 bᶜr big water

RID 0000185 bᶜr big water

ID lexeme 54970 bᶜr sea; river

II.7 p

DRID	**1001759**	**p base**		
RID	**0001961**	p base		
	ID Lexeme	58650	pj	base; pedestal; throne
DRID	**1001760**	**p heaven**		
RID	**0001962**	p heaven		
	ID Lexeme	58710	p.t	heaven(s)
		859338	p.t	sky
		855565	p.tjw	heavenly ones
DRID	**1001761**	**pꜣḏ incense cone**		
RID	**0001963**	pꜣḏ incense cone		
	ID Lexeme	63190	pḏ	to cure; to burn incense
		59470	pꜣḏ	pellet (or cone) (of incense)
		875714	pꜣd.w	[a med. substance]
		863029	pꜣḏ.tjt	[a med. substance]
DRID	**1001762**	**pḏ to stretch**		
RID	**0001964**	pḏ to stretch		
	ID Lexeme	63220	pḏ	[part of a fisher's net?]
		63200	pḏ	[measure for ink colour, pigment]
		63170	pḏ	to stretch out; to spread out
		63360	pḏ.w	[food offering (lit. what is spread out)]
		852799	pḏ.w	wide ground; [cult site of Sokar]
		63370	pḏ.w	flood; pond
		63380	pḏ.wj	lateral walls
		501074	pḏ.tj	Archer
		63250	pḏ.t	[designation for the sky]
		63240	pḏ.t	[a measure for incense]
		63230	pḏ.t	[a measure for linen]
		63290	pḏ.t	troop (of soldiers)
		63280	pḏ.t	bow-people
		63270	pḏ.t	bow
		63260	pḏ.tj	(slaughtered) ox (an offering)
		63310	pḏ.tj	archer
		63300	pḏ.tj	barbarian (bow-man)
		501065	pḏ.tjt	Archer
		63390	pdpḏ	to be diffused (of perfume)
DRID	**1001763**	**pḏi̯ to grind**		
RID	**0001965**	pḏi̯ to grind		
	ID Lexeme	63350	pḏi̯	to grind; to sharpen
DRID	**1001764**	**pdr measure?**		

RID	**0001966**	pdr measure?		
	ID Lexeme	63090	pdr	sack (or measure)

DRID	**1001765**	**pds to flatten**		
RID	**0001967**	pds to flatten		
	ID Lexeme	858692	pds	door leaf
		63120	pds	to flatten; to destroy
		63110	pds	box (for clothing, for documents)
		63140	pds.t	[a kind of wood?]
		63130	pds.t	small ball; pill
		63160	pdsw.t	delta coast

DRID	**1001766**	**pgg frog**		
RID	**0001968**	pgg frog		
	ID Lexeme	62880	pgg.t	frog (amulet) (med.)

DRID	**1001767**	**pgꜣ box**		
RID	**0001970**	pgꜣ box		
	ID Lexeme	62800	pgꜣ	[a chest?]

DRID	**1001768**	**pgꜣ to open**		
RID	**0001969**	pgꜣ bowl		
	ID Lexeme	62790	pgꜣ	bowl
		62840	pgꜣ.w	washing utensil; bowl
RID	**0001971**	pgꜣ to open		
	ID Lexeme	854511	pgꜣ	opening; open space; battlefield
		62730	pgꜣ	to unfold; to open up
		62760	pgꜣ	opening
RID	**0001972**	pgꜣ to slaughter		
	ID Lexeme	62770	pgꜣ	battlefield
		62780	pgꜣ	to slaughter (the enemy)

DRID	**1001769**	**pḥ lion**		
RID	**0001973**	pḥ lion		
	ID Lexeme	61630	pḥ.tj	strong
		61640	pḥ.tj	lion
		860512	pḥ.tj	Strong one
		61400	pḥ.tj	physical strength
		855240	pḥ.tj	strength
		61620	pḥ.tj	to be strong

DRID	**1001770**	**pḥ sheaf**		
RID	**0001974**	pḥ sheaf		
	ID Lexeme	61390	pḥ.t	sheaf (of grain)

DRID	**1001771**	**pḥ to reach**		
RID	**0001975**	pḥ to reach		

61370	pḥ	to reach; to attack
61380	pḥ.w	marshland; hinterland
61470	pḥ.w	the far north
856007	pḥ.wj	marshes
61510	pḥ.wj	rear
61490	pḥ.wj	back; end
61520	pḥ.wjt	anus; rectum
859978	pḥ.wjt	back; end
61550	pḥ.ww	ends (of the country); end (of the world)
61570	pḥ.ww	northern end
860884	pḥ.wt	marshland
61480	pḥ.wt	anchor rope of ships
857519	pḥ.wtj	rear
857520	pḥ.wtjt	anchor rope of ships; stern warp
500483	pḥ.tjw	Those located at the end?
500336	pḥ.tjt	to reach the shore
83190	npḥ.w	[part of human lower abdomen]; udder (of cows)
132970	spḥ	to attain
132960	spḥ	to postpone, to avert (death)

DRID 1001772 pḥḏ to split

RID 0001976 pḥḏ to split

ID Lexeme

61660	pḥḏ	to split
61650	pḥḏ.tj	separator (a serpent)

DRID 1001773 phr [a pond]

RID 0001978 phr [a pond]

ID Lexeme

61340	phr.t	[a body of water]

DRID 1001774 pẖr to turn round

RID 0001979 pẖr to turn round

ID Lexeme

858691	pẖr	circumferential walkway (part of a building)
859793	pẖr	one who crosses
61910	pẖr	area; rural district; circuit; country estate?
61920	pẖr	circulation of offerings; offerings
61900	pẖr	to go around; to turn round; to circulate; to encircle; to traverse
62080	pẖr.yt	orbital period of stars; period
62090	pẖr.w	flushing (of water)?
854399	pẖr.wj	[a boat]
61940	pẖr.t	frontier patrol
867803	pẖr.t	circuit; area; vicinity
855329	pẖr.t	journey

			61930	pẖr.t	ambulatory (a space in a temple)
			857548	pẖr.t	circulation of offerings
			61960	pẖr.t	[a kilt]
			61950	pẖr.t	remedy (gen.)
			61990	pẖr.tj	traveller (or similar)
			133040	spẖr	to copy; to register; to draw
			133030	spẖr	to brandish (weapons); to cause to circulate (the wind)
			133050	spẖr.w	writing; record
			859348	pẖr.tjw	one wandering around
DRID	**1001775**	**pḥrr to run**			
	RID	**0001980**	pḥrr to run		
		ID Lexeme	61600	pḥrr	runner
			61590	pḥrr	to run
DRID	**1001776**	**pẖꜣ [a cereal]**			
	RID	**0001981**	pẖꜣ [a cereal]		
		ID Lexeme	61710	pẖꜣ	[a cereal]
DRID	**1001777**	**pẖꜣ to split**			
	RID	**0001977**	pẖpẖ to tear		
		ID Lexeme	61870	pẖpẖ	to course (of poison in the body); to tear; to pull out
			61880	pẖpẖ	storm; tempest (or similar)
	RID	**0001982**	pẖꜣ to equip		
		ID Lexeme	61750	pẖꜣ	to equip
			61800	pẖꜣ.t	field
	RID	**0001983**	pẖꜣ to split		
		ID Lexeme	61780	pẖꜣ	(wooden) bird trap
			61760	pẖꜣ	plank
			61730	pẖꜣ	to separate; to open (med.); to split
			61770	pẖꜣ	log
			61790	pẖꜣ.t	ankle shackle
			133010	spẖꜣ	to purge; to make (the skin) sleek?
	RID	**0001984**	pẖꜣ uraeus		
		ID Lexeme	61810	pẖꜣ.t	[designation of the Uraeus]
DRID	**1001778**	**pj flea**			
	RID	**0001985**	pj flea		
		ID Lexeme	59500	py	flea
DRID	**1001779**	**pj to knead (clay)**			
	RID	**0001987**	pjpj to knead (clay)		
		ID Lexeme	59540	pjpj	to knead (clay)
DRID	**1001780**	**pjpj keel?**			

	RID	**0001986**	pjpj keel?		
		ID Lexeme	59080	pꜣjp.t	keel? (naut.)
			59550	pjpj.t	keel?, standard
DRID	**1001781**	**pjs to tread in**			
	RID	**0001988**	pjs to tread in		
		ID Lexeme	858452	pjs	to tread in; to stamp
DRID	**1001782**	**pn mouse**			
	RID	**0001989**	pn mouse		
		ID Lexeme	60020	pn.w	mouse
DRID	**1001783**	**png to divide**			
	RID	**0001991**	png to divide		
		ID Lexeme	60150	png	to divide
DRID	**1001784**	**pnn to twist**			
	RID	**0001992**	pnn to twist		
		ID Lexeme	59940	pn	spindle
			60060	pnn	to twist, to reel (a thread)
			60030	pnn	to strew (powder)
DRID	**1001785**	**pnḳ = pnḏ to scoop**			
	RID	**0001990**	pnḏ to scoop		
		ID Lexeme	867779	pnḏ	to scoop (out)
			60140	pnḳ	bailer
			60130	pnḳ	to scoop (out); to water
DRID	**1001786**	**pnt to squeeze**			
	RID	**0001994**	pnt to squeeze		
		ID Lexeme	60160	pnt	to squeeze
DRID	**1001787**	**pnz = pn^{c} to turn round**			
	RID	**0001995**	pnz to turn round		
		ID Lexeme	60090	pnz	to twist; to pull out
			60070	pnz	to cut off; to pull out
			60110	pns	earth ("turned around", as material)
			60120	pns.t	clump (form of a remedy)
	RID	**0001996**	pn^{c} to invert		
		ID Lexeme	59960	pn^{c}	to turn upside down; to capsize; to reverse; to curve
			59970	pn^{c}.y	incorrectness; wrongness
			59990	pn^{c}.yt	threshold; doorstep
			59980	pn^{c}.yt	cataract
			60000	pn^{c}.wt	[an injustice; something wrong]
			60010	pn^{c}n^{c}	to turn over several times; to roll

				around
		132800	spn^{c}	to overturn
DRID	**1001789**	**pḳ flood**		
	RID	**0001997**	pḳ flood	
		ID Lexeme	860385 pḳ	[flood]
			62700 pḳj	[an irrigated area in Delta]
DRID	**1001790**	**pḳr [a fragrant ingredient]**		
	RID	**0001998**	pḳr [a fragrant ingredient]	
		ID Lexeme	62720 pḳr	[a fragrant ingredient in kyphi preparation]
DRID	**1001791**	**pr beans**		
	RID	**0001999**	pr beans	
		ID Lexeme	60970 prj	beans
DRID	1001792	pr house		
	RID	**0002000**	pr house	
		ID Lexeme	60220 pr	house (gen.); palace; temple; tomb; administration
			550304 pr	household; domestic staff
			61040 pr.y	domestic servant
			860218 pr.y	field service person
			61010 pr.yt	houses; properties
			60340 pr.t	domestic servant (fem.)
			60320 pr.t	people; servants (of a god)
DRID	**1001793**	**prḏ to separate**		
	RID	**0002001**	prḏ to separate	
		ID Lexeme	61320 prḏ	to separate
DRID	**1001794**	**prẖ to blossom**		
	RID	**0002002**	prẖ to blossom	
		ID Lexeme	61250 prẖ	blossom; sprout
			61240 prẖ	to blossom; to unfurl
DRID	**1001795**	**pri̯ to come forth**		
	RID	**0002003**	pri̯ to come forth	
		ID Lexeme	60260 pr	outlay; issuing office?
			857528 pr	one who is going out
			450627 pr	square (on a game board)
			60940 pr.y	lone fighter
			60950 pr.y	ferocious bull
			500375 pr.yw	Emerging ones
			501005 pr.yt	One who comes out
			61170 pr.w	field (after the inundation)

			61150	pr.w	deliveries
			61140	pr.w	coming out; procession
			61160	pr.w	surplus; excess
			60300	pr.t	peret-season (winter)
			60280	pr.t	procession (of a god)
			60270	pr.t	Issuing point of provisions
			60310	pr.t	fruit (of a plant); seed; posterity (metaph.)
			60330	pr.t	mourning; sadness
			863195	pr.tj	first day of peret-season
			859428	prj.t	fetter (or similar)
			60990	prj	battlefield
			60920	pri̯	to come forth; to go forth
			60980	pry	bandage; strip (of linen)
			61020	pry.t	[designation of the female part of the house]
			61230	prpr	to enjoy (food) (or similar)
			857531	prr	one who is going forth
			83140	npr	grain
			83170	npr.t	step (of the stairs); stairs
			83160	npr.t	edge; bank
			500571	npr.tjw	inhabitant of the shores
			500251	npn	corn
			83110	npn.t	grain
			132930	spri̯	to make come out
	RID	**0002005**	prpr to jump around		
		ID Lexeme	61220	prpr	to jump around (or similar)

DRID **1001796** **prš juniper berries?**

	RID	**0002006**	prš juniper berries?		
		ID Lexeme	61260	prš	[red ochre or ochre containing earth (med.)]; juniper berries?

DRID **1001797** **prš to smash**

	RID	**0002007**	prš to smash		
		ID Lexeme	61270	prš	to smite; to smash; to tear

DRID **1001798** **prṯ to break?**

	RID	**0002008**	prṯ to break?		
		ID Lexeme	61290	prṯ	to break?

DRID **1001799** **pr^{c} to be accessible?**

	RID	**0002009**	pr^{c} to be accessible?		
		ID Lexeme	61130	pr^{c}	to be accessible?

DRID **1001800** **ps measure?**

	RID	**0002010**	ps measure?

		ID Lexeme	62150	ps	[a jug (used as a measure for beverages)]
			62140	ps	[measure for herbs, weed]
			62190	ps.w	ratio (of grain to the product, for baking, for brewing)
			59270	pꜣz.wt	brewers

DRID 1001801 psḏ nine

RID	**0002011**	psḏ nine			
	ID Lexeme	62450	psḏ	nine	
		62460	psḏ.j	[linen (nine-strand fabric)]	
		62500	psḏ.t	Divine Ennead	
		62490	psḏ.t	Nine Bows peoples	
		550381	psḏ.t	ennead	
		859664	psḏ.t	teeth	

DRID 1001802 psḏ pelican

RID	**0003490**	psḏ pelican		
	ID Lexeme	62520	psḏ.tj	pelican

DRID 1001803 psḏ spine

RID	**0002013**	psḏi̯ to turn the back		
	ID Lexeme	62400	psḏ	spine; backbone; back
		62470	psḏ	keel arch? (naut.)
		62540	psḏ.y	helper (or similar)
		62530	psḏ.wj	double back plate
		62410	psḏi̯	to distance oneself from; to turn the back
		62550	psḏn	threshing floor

DRID 1001804 psḏ to shine

RID	**0002012**	psḏ to shine		
	ID Lexeme	500184	psḏ	shining
		854201	psḏ	shining one
		62420	psḏ	to shine
		62430	psḏ	light
		857533	psḏ.t	light
		62480	psḏ.t	shining one
		62510	psḏ.t	shining one

DRID 1001805 psḏn new moon

RID	**0002014**	psḏn new moon		
	ID Lexeme	62560	psḏn.tjw	new moon; festival of the new moon
		850569	psḏn.tjw	new moon day

DRID 1001806 psg to spit

RID	**0002015**	psg to spit		
	ID Lexeme	62350	psg	spittle
		62360	psg	spittoon
		62340	psg	to spit on; to spit at
DRID	**1001807**	**psẖ mat?**		
RID	**0002016**	psẖ mat?		
	ID Lexeme	857538	psẖ	platform on the ship's bow
DRID	**1001808**	**psi̯ to cook**		
RID	**0002017**	psi̯ to cook		
	ID Lexeme	62120	ps	cook; baker
		62130	ps	[a kind of bread]
		857535	ps.wt	cooking pot
		501112	ps.t	cook
		62170	ps.t	cooking
		62180	psi̯	to cook; to bake; to heat
DRID	**1001809**	**pšj comb**		
RID	**0002018**	pšj comb		
	ID Lexeme	62600	pšj	comb
DRID	**1001810**	**pšj pustule?**		
RID	**0002019**	pšj pustule?		
	ID Lexeme	62590	pšj	pustule?
DRID	**1001811**	**pšn to split**		
RID	**0002020**	pšn to split		
	ID Lexeme	62620	pšn	fissure; fracture (med.)
		62640	pšn	[designation for an adversary]
		62610	pšn	to split
DRID	**1001812**	**psš to divide**		
RID	**0002021**	psš to divide		
	ID Lexeme	857536	psš	share; portion
		62680	psš	to spread
		450149	psš	[a fishtail-shaped knife of flint (used in the Opening-of-the-mouth ritual]
		62280	psš	to divide; to share
		851900	psš.w	referee; associate; partner
		62290	psš.t	half; share; portion
		867812	psš.t	portion
		62300	psš.t	carpet; matting
		854402	psš.tj	[designation of a servant]
		62310	psš.tj	the two parts (of the land, Upper and Lower Egypt)

DRID	**1001813**	**pt to tread**		
RID	**0002025**	ptpt to tread		
	ID Lexeme	857539	ptpt	resigning one
		62890	ptpt	to tread; to trample
RID	**0002028**	ptt to tread?		
	ID Lexeme	63040	ptt	[condition of cultivatable fields]

DRID	**1001814**	**ptḥ to create**		
RID	**0002023**	ptḥ to create		
	ID Lexeme	63000	ptḥ	to form; to create

DRID	**1001815**	**ptẖ to prostrate**		
RID	**0002024**	ptẖ to prostrate		
	ID Lexeme	63010	ptẖ	to prostrate (oneself, before so.)
		133160	sptẖ	to make writhe (on the ground, like a snake)
		133170	sptẖ.w	serpent; reptile

DRID	**1001816**	**ptr bandage?**		
RID	**0002026**	ptr bandage?		
	ID Lexeme	62960	ptr	strip (of cloth)

DRID	**1001817**	**ptr to see**		
RID	**0002027**	ptr to see		
	ID Lexeme	62930	ptr	window of heaven
		62910	ptr	behold! [interjection]
		857541	ptr	look; sight
		857540	ptr	Onlooker
		62900	ptr	to see; to behold
		62950	ptr	Beholder
		62920	ptr	who? what?

DRID	**1001818**	**pw who?**		
RID	**0002029**	pw who?		
	ID Lexeme	59750	pw	who?

DRID	**1001819**	**pzẖ to be confused**		
RID	**0002030**	pzẖ to be confused		
	ID Lexeme	62240	pzẖ	to be confused; to confuse

DRID	**1001820**	**pzḥ to bite**		
RID	**0002031**	pzḥ to bite		
	ID Lexeme	62230	pzḥ	bite; sting
		62220	pzḥ	to bite; to sting

DRID	**1001821**	**pzz to travail**		
RID	**0002032**	pzz to travail		

ID Lexeme		62260	pzz	to labour; to exert oneself
		62270	pzz	undertaking
DRID	**1001822**	**pꜣ? [a bread]**		
RID	**0002033**	pꜣ? [a bread]		
ID Lexeme		83000	npꜣ.t	[a small cake]
DRID	**1001824**	**pꜣḫ [a plant]**		
RID	**0002035**	pꜣḫ [a plant]		
ID Lexeme		59190	pꜣḫ	[plant (med.)]
DRID	**1001825**	**pꜣḫ to scratch**		
RID	**0002036**	pꜣḫ to scratch		
ID Lexeme		59200	pꜣḫ	to scratch out (eyes)
		856006	pꜣḫ.w	scratching
		856425	pꜣḫ.t	lion
DRID	**1001826**	**pꜣḫd to be turned over**		
RID	**0002038**	pꜣḫd to be turned over		
ID Lexeme		59230	pꜣḫd	to be turned upside down; to be turned over
		856050	spꜣḫd	to turn upside down
DRID	**1001827**	**pꜣi̯ to fly**		
RID	**0002039**	pꜣi̯ to fly		
ID Lexeme		857055	jpꜣ	flyer
		500384	pꜣ.y	Flying up one
		59070	pꜣ.yw	birds (lit. what flies)
		855525	pꜣ.yw	Flying ones
		59040	pꜣy.t	birds (lit. what flies)
		867764	pꜣw.w	duck
		58780	pꜣi̯	to fly
		854651	npꜣ	to shiver; to tremble
		132700	spꜣ.w	swarm (birds)
		132670	spꜣi̯	to make fly
RID	**0002041**	pꜣpꜣ to flutter?		
ID Lexeme		83010	npꜣpꜣ	to flutter? (with the meaning to shake)
RID	**0002045**	pꜣu̯ to have done		
ID Lexeme		58790	pꜣu̯	to have done (something in the past); to be primeval
		58800	pꜣw	original state (of being)
		59150	pꜣw.t	primeval goddess
		58830	pꜣw.t	primeval times
		59160	pꜣw.t	burden (metaph.) (med.)
		59170	pꜣw.tj	primeval
		861271	pꜣw.tj	Primeval one

500060 pꜣw.tj primeval god
59140 pꜣw.tjw primeval gods
RID **0002046** pꜣy to copulate
ID Lexeme 59030 pꜣy to beget; to copulate

DRID **1001828** **pꜣjs granules**
RID **0002040** pꜣjs granules
ID Lexeme 852309 pꜣjs [pellets, granules? (drug)]

DRID **1001829** **pꜣḳi̯ to be thin**
RID **0002042** pꜣḳi̯ to be thin
ID Lexeme 59310 pꜣḳ [a thin biscuit]
857504 pꜣḳ [a kind of a cake]
59350 pꜣḳ.t potsherd; flake (of stone); carapace (also metaph. for the skull)
59340 pꜣḳ.t thin sheet of metal
59330 pꜣḳ.t fine linen
59360 pꜣḳ.t ladder?
59300 pꜣḳi̯ to be thin

DRID **1001830** **pꜣs [scribe's water-pot]**
RID **0002043** pꜣs [scribe's water-pot]
ID Lexeme 59250 pꜣs (scribe’s) water-pot

DRID **1001831** **pꜣṯṯ baboon**
RID **0002044** pꜣṯṯ baboon
ID Lexeme 873158 pꜣṯṯ baboon
59420 pꜣṯṯ Patjetj (baboon)

DRID **1001832** **pꜣz to suffer**
RID **0002048** pꜣz to suffer
ID Lexeme 59240 pꜣz to suffer
59260 pꜣz.wt faint (or similar)

DRID **1001833** **p^{c} [a food]**
RID **0002049** p^{c} [a food]
ID Lexeme 59620 p^{c}.t [a kind of pastry]
850684 p^{c}.t [a fruit?]; [a cereal?]

DRID **1001834** **p^{c} area**
RID **0002050** p^{c} area
ID Lexeme 59650 p^{c}.t [bank; area of land]

DRID **1001835** **p^{c} fire**
RID **0002051** p^{c} fire
ID Lexeme 59660 p^{c}.w fire; flame
59630 p^{c}.t Flaming one

	RID	**0002057**	$p^{c}p^{c}$ to shine		
		ID Lexeme	59680	$p^{c}p^{c}$	to shine
DRID	**1001836**		**p^{c} people**		
	RID	**0002052**	p^{c} people		
		ID Lexeme	59610	p^{c}.t	people; humankind; (social) upper class
	RID	**0002056**	$p^{c}p^{c}$ to be born		
		ID Lexeme	59670	$p^{c}p^{c}$	to bear; to be born
DRID	**1001837**		**p^{c} to spit out**		
	RID	**0002053**	p^{c} to spit out		
		ID Lexeme	59600	p^{c}	to spew; to spray (sparks)
			59700	$p^{c}p^{c}$.yt	what is spat out?
DRID	**1001838**		**p^{c}g to spit**		
	RID	**0002054**	p^{c}g to spit		
		ID Lexeme	858449	p^{c}g	spit
DRID	**1001839**		**p^{c}n to be clever**		
	RID	**0002055**	p^{c}n to be clever		
		ID Lexeme	59710	p^{c}n	to be clever (or similar)
			857503	p^{c}n	Clever one
DRID	**1001840**		**p^{c}ȝ = p^{c}r quail**		
	RID	**0002058**	p^{c}ȝ quail		
		ID Lexeme	401147	p^{c}ȝ.t	quail

II.8 f

DRID	**1000334**		**fd [an oil]**			
	RID	**00004123**		fd [an oil]		
		ID Lexeme		64300	fdfd	to apply (an ointment)
				64250	fd	[a kind of an oil]
DRID	**1000335**		**fd four**			
	RID	**0000414**		fd four		
		ID Lexeme		858706	jfd	to be complete on all four sides
				24570	jfd	rectangle; square (plot of land)
				24560	jfd	(the) four (sides; corners; pillars of heaven; cardinal directions
				24600	jfd	rectangle (block of stone)
				24590	jfd.j	sheet; garment (rectangle piece of linen)
				850571	jfd.w	four
				64310	jfd.nw	[a piece of writing?]
				852782	jfd.nw	fourth
				24620	jfd.t	four (in number)
				859052	jfdi̯	to quadruplicate
DRID	**1000336**		**fd to sweat**			
	RID	**0000415**		fd to sweat		
		ID Lexeme		64240	fd	to sweat
				64260	fd.t	sweat
DRID	**1000337**		**fdi̯ to tear out**			
	RID	**0000416**		fdi̯ to tear out		
		ID Lexeme		64190	ftt	to obliterate (an inscription)
				64280	fdi̯	to uproot
DRID	**1000338**		**fdḳ to trench**			
	RID	**0000417**		fdḳ to trench		
		ID Lexeme		858978	fdḳdḳ	to cut up (completely); to destroy
				64320	fdḳ	to sever; to hack into pieces
				64330	fdḳ	slice; portion
DRID	**1000339**		**fgn to defecate**			
	RID	**0000418**		fgn to defecate		
		ID Lexeme		64120	fgn	to defecate
DRID	**1000340**		**fḫ to loosen**			
	RID	**0000419**		fḫ to loosen		
		ID Lexeme		116710	fḫfḫ	to shatter (a statue)
				63970	fḫ	to loosen; to move along; to destroy; to cease (doing)

			63990	fḫ.t	wig?
			63980	fḫḫ	to loosen
			69350	mfḫ	sledge
			69360	mfḫ	to sift (grain)
			133820	sfḫ	waste
			133790	sfḫ	what is laid aside; offering
			133780	sfḫ	to loosen; to release
			97050	sfḫ	[ceremony of the mortuary cult]
			133800	sfḫ	excretion; urine
			133830	sfḫ	strap (of sandals)
			133840	sfḫ.y	watch; guardhouse
			857661	sfḫ.t	excretion; urine
			852044	sfḫḫ	to loosen; to release
			857662	sfḫfḫ	to release
			137390	snfḫfḫ	to loosen; to release
			133920	sfg	to be hidden
DRID	**1000341**		**fjṯ = pjṯ to laugh**		
	RID	**0000420**	fjṯ = pjṯ to laugh		
		ID Lexeme	63740	fjṯ	to deride; to be scornful
			59580	pjṯꜣ	to mock
DRID	**1000342**		**fjw to become disgusted at**		
	RID	**0000421**	fjw to become disgusted at		
		ID Lexeme	63730	fjw	to be disgusted?
DRID	**1000343**		**fkꜣ turquoise**		
	RID	**0000422**	fkꜣ turquoise		
		ID Lexeme	69440	mfkꜣ.t	Land of turquoise (on the Sinai, Wadi Maghara); Mefkat (in the Delta, Terenouthis, Kom Abu Billu)
			69410	mfkꜣ.t	turquoise
			69390	mfkꜣ.t	Turquoise (Hathor)
	RID	**0007898**	fkꜣ turquoise-like		
		ID Lexeme	854425	mfkꜣ.tj	Turquoise-like one
			69470	mfkꜣ.tjw	Turquoise coloured ones
			69420	mfkꜣ.t	green of plants
			69460	mfkꜣ.t	turqouise-coloured (metaph. for papyrus)
			69370	mfkꜣ	turquoise-like
DRID	**1000344**		**fn to be weak**		
	RID	**0000423**	fn to be weak		
		ID Lexeme	63810	fn	to be weak
			133660	sfn.w	annoying
			133650	sfn	to cause trouble

DRID 1000345 fnḏ to snort?

RID 0000424 fnḏ to snort?

ID Lexeme	63920	fnḏ	nose
	63930	fnḏ	to rage against
	63960	fnḏ.j	One with the beak (Thoth)
	861782	fnḏ.j	One with the beak
	863810	nfdw.t	[illness]

DRID 1000346 fnẖ cord?

RID 0000425 fnẖ cord?

ID Lexeme	63850	fnẖ	cord?

DRID 1000347 fnẖ to make smooth

RID 0000426 fnẖ to make smooth

ID Lexeme	855573	fnẖ	carpenter
	63840	fnẖ	carpenter; joiner
	63860	fnẖ	to be smart (or similar)

DRID 1000348 fnṯ maggot

RID 0000427 fnṯ maggot

ID Lexeme	63900	fnṯ	to become maggoty
	63890	fnṯ	snake; worm; maggot

DRID 1000349 fqꜣ to reward

RID 0000428 fqꜣ to reward

ID Lexeme	64020	fqꜣ	reward; gift
	64000	fqꜣ	cake (or similar)
	106401	fqꜣ	to reward

DRID 1000350 ft to be disgusted

RID 0000429 ft to be disgusted

ID Lexeme	64130	ft	to be disgusted; to become weary

DRID 1000351 ft to leap

RID 0000430 ft to leap

ID Lexeme	64170	ftft	to leap; to spring (plants)
	64200	ftt	[fibrous veg. matter (med.]
	64210	ftt.w	jumper, diver (name for fish(es))

DRID 1000352 fṯṯꜣ to decay

RID 0000431 fṯṯꜣ to decay, rot?

ID Lexeme	858417	fṯṯꜣ	to decay, rot?

DRID 1000353 fꜣ dust?

RID 0000432 fꜣ dust?

ID Lexeme	63430	fꜣ.t	dust?

DRID	**1000354**	**fꜣ threat**		
RID	**0000433**	fꜣ threat		
ID Lexeme		63650	fꜣ.w	threat
DRID	**1000355**	**fꜣg to cut (meat)**		
RID	**0000434**	fꜣg to cut off		
ID Lexeme		63700	fꜣg	to cut off (the foreleg)
DRID	**1000356**	**fꜣg to eradicate**		
RID	**0000435**	fꜣg to eradicate?		
ID Lexeme		64050	fkꜣ	to jump out quickly
		64040	fkꜣ	to uproot; to eradicate
DRID	**1000357**	**fꜣi̯ to lift**		
RID	**0000436**	fꜣi̯ to lift		
ID Lexeme		63570	fꜣ	weight
		63520	fꜣ.y	cloth
		63500	fꜣ.y	[something (a rope?) made of Wedj-plants]
		63490	fꜣ.y	bearer
		63510	fꜣ.y	[something made of semiprecious stone (string or the like, used as bracelet, necklace or for stringing amulets)]
		63630	fꜣ.w	deliveries of food (offerings) (and similar)
		63660	fꜣ.w	carrying service
		63640	fꜣ.w	power; authority; reputation
		63410	fꜣ.t	serving food
		63420	fꜣ.t	freight (of a boat); yield (or similar)
		856728	fꜣ.t	a part of a ship (rope?)
		63480	fꜣi̯	to weigh
		63460	fꜣi̯	to lift; to carry; to raise
		874892	fꜣi̯	to hoist (the sails)
		63400	fꜣi̯	[verb referring to the decay of the corpse (to raise, to bloat)
		852484	fꜣi̯	to set about (doing)
		63530	fꜣy.t	bearers (of a divine image)
		63550	fꜣy.t	portable shrine (for gods)
		63560	fꜣy.t	raising
DRID	**1000358**	**fꜣk to be bald**		
RID	**0000437**	fꜣk to be bald		
ID Lexeme		63690	fꜣk	man with a shaved head
		856729	fꜣk	bald spot

			63680	fꜣk	to be bald; to be shorn
			64080	fk.ty	one with a shaved head (a priest)
	RID	**0000438**	fꜣk to be empty		
		ID Lexeme	133910	sfkk	[verb (to suffer? to punish?)]
			64060	fk	to be empty; to be wasted; to be bald
DRID	**1000359**	**fꜥg claw**			
	RID	**0000439**	fꜥg claw		
		ID Lexeme	858995	fꜥg	[temple of Nekhbet in Elkab]
			63770	fꜥg	claw
			63780	fꜥg.jt	[epithet of Nekhbet]; [priestess of Nekhbet]
DRID	**1000360**	**fꜥy hair**			
	RID	**0000440**	fꜥy hair		
		ID Lexeme	852956	fꜥꜣ	hair

II.9 m

DRID	**1001281**	**m who?**		
RID	**0001469**	m who?		
ID Lexeme		64430	m	who?; what?
		83990	njm	who?

DRID	**1001282**	**mḏ oil**		
RID	**0001470**	mḏ oil		
ID Lexeme		78390	mḏ.t	oil, unguent (used in cult)
		78400	mḏ.tj	person who prepares unguent

DRID	**1001283**	**mḏ ten**		
RID	**0001471**	mḏ ten		
ID Lexeme		78340	mḏ	ten
		850603	mḏ.tj	[a boat ("Tener"?)]

DRID	**1001284**	**mḏ to be deep**		
RID	**0001472**	mḏ to be deep		
ID Lexeme		78360	mḏ	deep; to be deep
		78610	mḏw.t	depth; height
		78380	mḏ.t	byre
		136060	smḏ	to make deep

DRID	**1001285**	**mḏd to align**		
RID	**0001473**	mḏd to align		
ID Lexeme		78370	mḏ.t	binding; hobble
		78770	mḏd	to hit; to press hard; to follow (something); to pierce
		78780	mḏd	dues (taxes and services)
		868028	mḏd.w	preparation; measure
		857343	mḏd.wt	adjustment
		78790	mḏd.t	share, stake
		600635	smḏd	to make obedient

DRID	**1001286**	**mḏḥ carpenter**		
RID	**0001474**	mḏḥ carpenter		
ID Lexeme		78700	mḏḥ	to hew (wood); to timber
		78740	mḏḥ	carpenter
		855574	mḏḥ.w	carpenter
		78710	mḏḥ.t	carpentry

DRID	**1001287**	**mḏḥ to make ready**		
RID	**0001475**	mḏḥ to make ready		
ID Lexeme		78690	mḏḥ	to wind around (the head); to be entwined
		854517	mḏḥ	to make ready all around

			78680	mḏḥ	bandeau; band
			78670	mḏḥ	belt; strip of cloth
DRID	**1001288**	**mdn to rest**			
	RID	**0001476**	mdn to rest		
		ID Lexeme	78220	mdn	to rest; to be relaxed
			600462	mdn	rest; quite; calm
			854403	mdns	quite; calm; silence; rest
DRID	**1001289**	**mḏḳ [a vessel]**			
	RID	**0001477**	mḏḳ [a vessel]		
		ID Lexeme	78750	mḏḳ	[a vessel (for beer)] (syll.)
			78760	mḏḳ.t	[a vessel (for beer and oil)] (syll.)
DRID	**1001290**	**mḏri̯ to turn**			
	RID	**0001478**	mḏri̯ to turn		
		ID Lexeme	78640	mḏri̯	to fall over
			78650	mḏri̯	to turn (to)
			26530	jmḏr	rampart, circumvallation
DRID	**1001291**	**mḏrn [a metal tool]**			
	RID	**0001479**	mḏrn [a metal tool]		
		ID Lexeme	78660	mḏrn	[a metal tool]
DRID	**1001292**	**mdw staff**			
	RID	**0001480**	mdw staff		
		ID Lexeme	78130	mdw	staff; sacred staff (standard)
			500649	mdw.y	He who belongs to the staff
DRID	**1001293**	**mdwi̯ to speak**			
	RID	**0001481**	mdwi̯ to speak		
		ID Lexeme	78150	mdw	word; speech; matter
			78210	mdw.w	caller (who sets the rhythm for work); speaker
			550067	mdw.t	[for forming abstract nouns]
			78030	mdw.t	word; speech; matter
			78180	mdw.tj	speaker
			78140	mdwi̯	to speak; to badmouth; to claim
DRID	**1001294**	**mḏꜣb to scoop**			
	RID	**0001482**	mḏꜣb to scoop		
		ID Lexeme	78580	mḏꜣb	to scoop
			78590	mḏꜣb.t	scoop (for bailing a boat)
			78600	mḏꜣb.t	[part of the ship]
DRID	**1001295**	**mḏꜥ to subdue**			
	RID	**0001483**	mḏꜥ to subdue		

		ID Lexeme	855235 mḏꜥ	to subdue
DRID	**1001296**	**mfkꜣ to be glad**		
	RID	**0001484**	mfkꜣ to be glad	
		ID Lexeme	69430 mfkꜣ.t	joy
			69380 mfkꜣ	to be glad; to rejoice
DRID	**1001297**	**mgr to roast**		
	RID	**0001485**	mgr to roast	
		ID Lexeme	600648 mgr	to roast; to grill
DRID	**1001298**	**mgrt cave**		
	RID	**0001486**	mgrt cave	
		ID Lexeme	77240 mgrt	cave
DRID	**1001299**	**mgꜣ youthful soldier**		
	RID	**0001487**	mgꜣ youthful soldier	
		ID Lexeme	77170 mgꜣ	youthful soldier
DRID	**1001300**	**mḥ cubit**		
	RID	**0007868**	mḥ cubit	
		ID Lexeme	73350 mḥ	child
			73330 mḥ	ell; cubit; cubit rod (yardstick)
DRID	**1001301**	**mḥ north**		
	RID	**0001487**	mḥ north	
		ID Lexeme	73860 mḥ.yt	north wind
			73940 mḥ.w	Lower Egypt
			73470 mḥ.w	(crown of) Lower Egypt
			860404 mḥ.w	grain of Lower Egypt
			74000 mḥ.wj	Lower Egyptian; northern
			73560 mḥ.tj	northern
			73561 mḥ.tj	north
			73580 mḥ.tjw	northerners
			500788 mḥ.tjt	She of the north
			73570 mḥ.tjt	north
DRID	**1001302**	**mḥ to fill**		
	RID	**0001488**	mḥ to fill	
		ID Lexeme	73400 mḥ	nest
			73290 mḥ	to fill; to be full
			73300 mḥ	to hold; to seize
			852598 mḥ	to do (something) diligently (with infinitive); to start (doing somethings)
			854514 mḥ	to be full; to fill; to hold; to seize;

				to line (with stone)
		73310	mḥ	to inlay (with stone)
		73810	mḥ.y	filler (of the eye) (Thoth)
		850371	mḥ.w	filling
		73490	mḥ.t	full eye
		73970	mḥw	plot of land
		857351	mḥw.t	fullness; filling

DRID 1001303 mẖ to respect

RID	**0001489**	mẖ to respect		
	ID Lexeme	74200	mẖ	to respect (someone) (or similar)

DRID 1001304 mḥḏrt fish pond

RID	**0001490**	mḥḏrt fish pond		
	ID Lexeme	74170	mḥḏrt	fish pond

DRID 1001305 mḥi̯ to be in water

RID	**0001491**	mḥi̯ to be in water		
	ID Lexeme	73760	mḥ.j	water (of the Nile); flood
		73880	mḥ.yt	fishes (gen.)
		73920	mḥ.w	drowned one?
		851362	mḥ.w	one floating on the water (Osiris)
		73960	mḥ.w	hunter; fish spearer
		73550	mḥ.t	[part of a wooden boat (strap?)]
		73520	mḥ.t	marshes of the Delta
		860274	mḥ.t	field
		73840	mḥy.t	flood
		73850	mḥy.t	papyrus
		73740	mḥi̯	to be in water; to swim; to float; to drown; to sail
		135530	smḥ	[large transport ship]
		135520	smḥ	to finish; to complete a boat
		135540	smḥ	branch
		856080	smḥ	[a kind of a ship]
		859472	smḥi̯	[an action concerning the ship]
		135570	smḥi̯	to water; to flood; to let swim

DRID 1001306 mḥi̯ to care for

RID	**0001492**	mḥi̯ to care for		
	ID Lexeme	73370	mḥ	care
		73720	mḥ.y	caretaker; guardian
		73360	mḥi̯	to care for; to be concerned about
		74030	mḥw.tj	son (as heir); advocate

DRID 1001307 mhi̯ to forget

RID	**0001493**	mhi̯ to forget

		ID Lexeme	73050	mh.t	forgetfulness; negligence
			73070	mhi̯	to forget; to be forgetful
			135500	smhi̯	to cause to forget

DRID 1001308 mḥj to flee

RID	0001494		mḥj to flee		
		ID Lexeme	73780	mḥj	to flee
			73950	mḥw	refugee

DRID 1001309 mḥn to encircle

RID	0001495		mḥn to encircle		
		ID Lexeme	74060	mḥn	to coil; to encircle
			857353	mḥn	encircling one; uraeus serpent
			859277	mḥn	coil
			74080	mḥn	Serpent (a game, a board game)
			74070	mḥn	Encircler (a serpent)
			860556	mḥn.j	belonging to the serpent board game
			74110	mḥn.yt	encircler (king's uraeus)
			853213	mḥn.yt	uraeus (designation of various goddesses)

DRID 1001310 mhr braver

RID	0001496		mhr braver		
		ID Lexeme	73270	mhr	associates of Seth
			73260	mhr	braver [military officer commanding troops and handling logistics]

DRID 1001311 mḫt [a chariot part]

RID	0001497		mḫt [a chariot part]		
		ID Lexeme	74480	mḫt	[chariot parts]

DRID 1001312 mḫtb golden armband

RID	0001498		mḫtb golden armband		
		ID Lexeme	74490	mḫtb.t	armband [a golden ornament]
			74500	mḫtbtb	armband

DRID 1001313 mhw a positive social characteristic

RID	0001500		mhw a positive social characteristic		
		ID Lexeme	73140	mhw.t	[a positive social characteristic]

DRID 1001314 mḫꜣ to bind

RID	0001501		mḫꜣ to bind		
		ID Lexeme	74220	mḫ	to suffocate; to dam
			74230	mḫꜣ	to make fast; to bind
			74250	mḫꜣ	wreath (or similar) of figs (as

					measure)
			74260	mḫꜣ	builder's hut; wood depot (of the temple of Amun)
			74240	mḫꜣ	fetter; rope
	RID	**0001675**	mḫꜣ to make fast		
		ID Lexeme	67270	mḫꜣ	corn sheaf
			500717	mꜣḫ.y	He of the corn sheaf?
DRID	**1001315**	**mḥꜥ flax**			
	RID	**0001502**	mḥꜥ flax		
		ID Lexeme	854482	mḥꜥ.w	flax fibre
			450266	mḥꜥ.w	flax
DRID	**1001316**	**mj [a (funerary) boat]**			
	RID	**0001503**	mj [a (funerary) boat]		
		ID Lexeme	67900	mj.t	[a (funerary) boat]
DRID	**1001317**	**mj come**			
	RID	**0001504**	mj come		
		ID Lexeme	860703	mj	Come!
			67770	mj	Come!
DRID	**1001318**	**mj = mr like**			
	RID	**0001505**	mj like		
		ID Lexeme	67830	mj	as if; if (conjunction)
			67820	mj	like; according to
			68170	mj.y	likewise
			867905	mj.w	likewise; the same
			68230	mj.wj	such a one
			867914	mj.wtj	equal
			67960	mj.tjt	the like; the same
			851710	mj.tj	alike; similar
			67930	mj.tj	the equal (of); the like (of)
			67940	mj.tj	copy
			67950	mj.tj	likeness (of statues)
			68220	mj.tw	the same (as)
	RID	**0002398**	smj cordage		
		ID Lexeme	134920	smj.w	cordage
	RID	**0007861**	smj to report		
		ID Lexeme	851903	smj.t	indictment
			134880	smj.tj	regulator
DRID	**1001319**	**mj road**			
	RID	**0001506**	mj road		
		ID Lexeme	67910	mj.t	path; road
DRID	**1001320**	**mj take**			

RID **0001507** mj take
ID Lexeme 67780 mj take!

DRID 1001321 mj to bring
RID 0001508 mj to bring
ID Lexeme 67760 mj to bring

DRID 1001322 mjdꜣ [kind of meat]
RID 0001509 mjdꜣ [kind of meat]
ID Lexeme 68580 mjdꜣ [edible part of a butchered bull]

DRID 1001323 mjm [a plant]
RID 0001510 mjm [a plant]
ID Lexeme 68310 mjm.t [a plant (med.)]

DRID 1001324 mjmj dura
RID 0001511 mjmj dura
ID Lexeme 68320 mjmj [a cereal (durra?)]

DRID 1001325 mjn today
RID 0001512 mjn today
ID Lexeme 850961 mjn today
68330 mjn today
68360 mjn.t daily diet

DRID 1001326 mjn water
RID 0001513 mjn water
ID Lexeme 68350 mjn [grape juice]; mash
68370 mjn.t [a water]
68380 mjn.t country estate; area, field
500433 mjn.tjw those belonging to the irrigation basins

DRID 1001327 mjw cat
RID 0001515 mjw cat
ID Lexeme 68250 mjw tomcat
857359 mjw.j tomcat-like
856483 mjw.t lament; mourning; grief
854443 mjw.t cat
68280 mjw.tj cat-like one

DRID 1001328 mjz liver
RID 0001517 mjz liver
ID Lexeme 68520 mjz.t liver

DRID 1001330 mk [a boat]
RID 0001519 mk [a boat]

	ID Lexeme	76810	mk	to drive (boat)
		76800	mk	[a boat]

DRID 1001331 mk correct position

RID	**0001520**	mk correct position		
	ID Lexeme	76890	mk.t	(correct) position; (proper) place
		76900	mk.t	place of execution (or similar)

DRID 1001332 mk to sustain

RID	**0001521**	mk to sustain		
	ID Lexeme	858664	mk	sustain
		76840	mk.w	sustenance; food

DRID 1001333 mkḥꜣ back of the head

RID	**0001522**	mkḥꜣ back of the head		
	ID Lexeme	77100	mkḥꜣ	back of the head
RID	**0001523**	mkḥꜣ to neglect		
	ID Lexeme	77110	mkḥꜣ	to neglect; not care about

DRID 1001334 mki̯ to protect

RID	**0001524**	mki̯ to protect		
	ID Lexeme	76920	mk.t	overlay
		858560	mk.t	protectress
		76820	mki̯	to overlay (with gold and similar)
		77020	mki̯	to protect; to ward off; to respect
		77030	mkw	protector
		76930	mkw.tj	protector
		76880	mkw.t	protection; magical protection
		77120	mks	[a scepter]; [a cult object of the king (document bag?)]

DRID 1001335 mkmr fishnet

RID	**0001525**	mkmr fishnet		
	ID Lexeme	77040	mkmr.t	fishnets

DRID 1001336 mkr merchant

RID	**0001526**	mkr [a boat]		
	ID Lexeme	77050	mkr	[a boat]
		77060	mkr.j	merchant

DRID 1001337 mktr [a tower]

RID	**0001529**	mktr [a tower]		
	ID Lexeme	77140	mktr	tower

DRID 1001338 mkꜣ to be brave

RID	**0001530**	mkꜣ to be brave		
	ID Lexeme	76970	mkꜣ	to attend to something

DRID 1001339 mkꜣ to flatten

RID	**0001531**	mkꜣ to flatten		
	ID Lexeme	857360	mkꜣ	pedestal; base
		76980	mkꜣ	to flatten; to level
		76990	mkꜣ.t	supporting base; bier
		77010	mkꜣ.tj	the one on the bier (Osiris)

DRID 1001340 mmj giraffe

RID	**0001532**	mmj giraffe		
	ID Lexeme	69540	mmj	giraffe

DRID 1001341 mn [a bowl]

RID	**0001533**	mn [a bowl]		
	ID Lexeme	69880	mn.tj	[bowl]

DRID 1001342 mn [a fabric]

RID	**0001534**	mn [a fabric]		
	ID Lexeme	69640	mn	[a kind of fabric]
		69650	mn.wy	[a measure for fabric]

DRID 1001343 mn hot fire

RID	**0001535**	mn hot fire		
	ID Lexeme	69820	mn.t	melting fire
		69940	mn.wj	coal fire

DRID 1001344 mn jug

RID	**0001536**	mn jug		
	ID Lexeme	69630	mn	[a jug (for wine, beer)]; [bowl (incense burner)]
		500968	mn.w	jug

DRID 1001345 mn quartz

RID	**0001538**	mn quartz		
	ID Lexeme	70490	mn.w	quartz; [a semiprecious stone (of different colour)]

DRID 1001346 mn thigh

RID	**0001539**	mn thigh		
	ID Lexeme	69800	mn.t	thigh (of a human); haunch (of an animal); tights (gen.)
		69890	mn.tj	lap (that the child sits on)

DRID 1001347 mn to be ill

RID	**0001540**	mn to be ill		
	ID Lexeme	69660	mn	to be ill; to suffer (from); to injure
		69670	mn	sufferer

		70400	mn.w	suffering
		69770	mn.t	disease; suffering
		69930	mn.tj	Miserable one (serpent)

DRID 1001348 mn to move

RID	**0001541**	mn to displace		
	ID Lexeme	69720	mn	to displace
RID	**0001565**	mnmn to beget		
	ID Lexeme	70720	mnmn	to beget
		859929	mnmn.y	begetter
RID	**0001566**	mnmn to move		
	ID Lexeme	70710	mnmn	to move about; to shift; to fluctuate
		500804	mnmn.w	the one who moves
		70730	mnmn.t	herd; cattle
		135340	smnmn	to make move

DRID 1001349 mn to stay

RID	**0001542**	mn to stay		
	ID Lexeme	69590	mn	to remain; to endure; to be established
		69600	mn	remaining is; amount left is
		70110	mn	to ascertain; to examine
		853600	mn	remainder; equation; compensation
		859627	mn	battle ground
		70130	mn.y	corveé laborer (carrying stones)
		70510	mn.w	thread
		70480	mn.w	mace
		70420	mn.w	monument(s)
		70560	mn.wy	rich in monuments
		69840	mn.t	sky; heaven
		69760	mn.t	the like; contents
		69900	mn.tj	mountain ranges (to the east and west of the Nile)
		70220	mny.t	root
		70430	mnw	statue
		70790	mnn.w	fortress
		70820	mnn.t	[part of a tomb]; [part of a granite sarcophagus]
		70800	mnnw	annals
		854325	jmn	stay
		26300	jmn.yt	what endures (offerings)
		26330	jmn.w	enduring one (bull)
		84730	nn.wt	roots
		135150	smn	image (of a god)
		135210	smn	to resign from office
		135110	smn	to stay; to dwell; to last
		135160	smn	value; price (of grain)
		851677	smn	to stay; to remain

		135120	smn	order; attachment; fixture
		135100	smn	to make firm; to make endure; to establish; to strengthen
		135170	smn	[designation for offering]
		135270	smn.w	rungs of the ladder
		135280	smn.w	supports (of the sky)
		865235	smn.t	sky; heaven
		135230	smn.t	establishment
		135250	smn.tj	explorer; prospector
		135330	smnw	ordinance?
		854830	smnn	to establish; to erect; to fasten; to fix
		135080	zmn	to linger?; to remain?
		450451	zmn	to examine (the quality of bread)

DRID 1001350 mn tree?

RID	**0001543**	mn tree		
	ID Lexeme	70450	mn.w	trees; plantation
		70470	mn.w	[waterway with plants]

DRID 1001351 mnbj throne

RID	**0001544**	mnbj throne		
	ID Lexeme	69980	mnbj.t	lion couch; estrade

DRID 1001352 mnḏ cheek?

RID	**0001545**	mnḏ cheek?		
	ID Lexeme	71730	mnḏ.t	walls (of a crucible) (lit. cheek)
		71721	mnḏ.t	cheek; eye; eyebrow

DRID 1001353 mnḏ chest

RID	**0001546**	mnḏ chest		
	ID Lexeme	71720	mnḏ	chest; breast; udder
		857571	mnḏ.j	bib

DRID 1001354 mnd tribute

RID	**0001547**	mnd tribute		
	ID Lexeme	71710	mnd.t	tax; gifts; tribute

DRID 1001355 mnfꜣ soldiers

RID	**0001549**	mnfꜣ soldiers		
	ID Lexeme	70670	mnfꜣ.t	infantry; soldiers

DRID 1001356 mnḥ evil fate

RID	**0001550**	mnḥ evil fate		
	ID Lexeme	70970	mnḥ	evil fate

DRID 1001357 mnḥ papyrus plant

RID	**0001551**	mnḥ papyrus plant		
	ID Lexeme	70930	mnḥ	papyrus plant
		71010	mnḥ.j	papyrus shaped

DRID 1001358 mnḫ to be effective

RID	**0001552**	mnḫ to be effective		
	ID Lexeme	400111	mnḫ	splendid; excellent
		71080	mnḫ	to be splendid; to make splendid; to be effective
		400110	mnḫ	effective; splendid
		856481	mnḫ	splendid one
		71100	mnḫ	[designation for food]
		850986	mnḫ.j	properly; neatly
		71240	mnḫ.w	excellence; virtues
		850987	mnḫ.t	neatly
		71140	mnḫ.t	excellence
		71160	mnḫ.t	excellent one
		135360	smnḫ	to make excellent; to make effective; to embellish; to endow
		135370	smnḫ	appearance, shape (of the moon)
		135380	smnḫ.t	Semenkhet (one who makes excellent)
		135390	smnḫ.t	food; offerings

DRID 1001359 mnḫ to chisel

RID	**0001553**	mnḫ to chisel		
	ID Lexeme	71060	mnḫ	chisel
		71070	mnḫ	to chisel

DRID 1001360 mnḫ to rejoice

RID	**0001554**	mnḫ to rejoice		
	ID Lexeme	71110	mnḫ	to rejoice
		70950	mnḫ	to rejoice (or similar)

DRID 1001361 mnḥ to slaughter

RID	**0001555**	mnḥ to slaughter		
	ID Lexeme	70960	mnḥ	to slay; to butcher
		860311	mḥwn	butcher
		71020	mnḥy.t	Menhit (Slaughteress (uraeus goddess))
		26340	jmnḥ	butcher
		26350	jmnḥ.y	Butcher (a demon)
		860783	jmnḥ.yw	Butcher Demon

DRID 1001362 mnḫ to string

RID	**0001556**	mnḫ to string		
	ID Lexeme	71130	mnḫ	string of the amulet?

		71120	mnẖ	to string (beads); to put on (an amulet)
DRID	**1001363**	**mnḥ tribute**		
	RID	**0001557**	mnḥ tribute	
	ID Lexeme	71050	mnḥ.t	gift; tribute
DRID	**1001364**	**mnḥ wax**		
	RID	**0001558**	mnḥ wax	
	ID Lexeme	70920	mnḥ	wax
DRID	**1001365**	**mnḥ youth**		
	RID	**0001559**	mnḥ youth	
	ID Lexeme	70940	mnḥ	youth; stripling; young animal
		858862	mnḥ	to make young; to become young
		600248	mnḥ.tj	army tenants
DRID	**1001366**	**mjni̯ to land**		
	RID	**0001560**	mjni̯ to land	
	ID Lexeme	401137	mjn	landing (i.e. death; dying)
		863006	mnj.w	daybed
		70140	mjn.t	mooring post; post
		854448	mjn.tjw	those belonging to the poles
		70080	mjni̯	to protect
		70070	mjni̯	to gift; to connect, to bind (man and woman)
		70060	mjni̯	to moor; to steer; to die (metaph.)
		854513	mjni̯	to stake
		68450	mjnw.t	harbor
DRID	**1001367**	**mnj herdsman**		
	RID	**0001561**	mnj herdsman	
	ID Lexeme	854852	mjn.t	stake
		70160	mnj.t	pasture (for geese)
		70250	mny.tj	[a farmer]
		70310	mnj.w	herdsman
		855126	mnj.w	shepherd
		861591	mnj.w	shepherd
		70340	mnjwj	[epithet of Anubis]
DRID	**1001368**	**mnj necklace**		
	RID	**0001562**	mnj necklace	
	ID Lexeme	70180	mnj.t	Menat (Hathor)
		70190	mnj.t	[singer (at Dendera and Edfu)]
		70170	mnj.t	menat-necklace
DRID	**1001369**	**mnj shrine**		

	RID	**0001563**	mnj shrine		
		ID Lexeme	854999	mnj.wj	the one of the shrine
			70320	mnj.w	[a shrine]
DRID	**1001371**		**mnn mina**		
	RID	**0001567**	mnn mina		
		ID Lexeme	70780	mnn	mina (a measure of weight)
DRID	**1001372**		**mnnn asphalt**		
	RID	**0001568**	mnnn asphalt		
		ID Lexeme	70810	mnnn	asphalt; resin; pitch
DRID	**1001373**		**mnpḥ animal skin?**		
	RID	**0001569**	mnpḥ animal skin?		
		ID Lexeme	70630	mnpḥ	skin / fur of the white saber antelope [a gown]
DRID	**1001374**		**mnḳ to complete**		
	RID	**0001570**	mnḳ to complete		
		ID Lexeme	71400	mnḳ	to complete; to retaliate; to grant
			71410	mnḳ	to reward
DRID	**1001375**		**mnḳry [a pendant]**		
	RID	**0001571**	mnḳry [a pendant]		
		ID Lexeme	71530	mnḳry.t	[pendant in the shape of a snake's head]
DRID	**1001376**		**mnš cartouche**		
	RID	**0001572**	mnš cartouche		
		ID Lexeme	71340	mnš	[(cartouche-shaped) wooden bowl]
			71350	mnš	to brand (with the cartouche)
			71330	mnš	cartouche
DRID	**1001377**		**mnsꜣ to cause ejaculation?**		
	RID	**0001573**	mnsꜣ to cause ejaculation?		
		ID Lexeme	84480	nms.w	[illness of the vulva]
			71310	mnsꜣ	to cause ejaculation
			854465	mnsꜣ	ejaculation
DRID	**1001378**		**mnt diorite**		
	RID	**0001574**	mnt diorite		
		ID Lexeme	71580	mnt.t	diorite (diorite-gneiss)
DRID	**1001379**		**mnṯ grain sieve?**		
	RID	**0001575**	mnṯ grain sieve?		
		ID Lexeme	71630	mnṯ	grain sieving?

DRID 1001380 mnty doorkeeper
RID 0001576 mnty doorkeeper
ID Lexeme 71610 mnty doorkeeper

DRID 1001381 mntꜣ grove
RID 0001577 mntꜣ grove
ID Lexeme 71590 mntꜣ holly grove of the abaton
71600 mntꜣ.j one belonging to the grove (Osiris)

DRID 1001382 mnw pigeon
RID 0001578 mnw pigeon
ID Lexeme 851863 mn.w [birds (pigeons?)]
69780 mn.t swallow; pigeon?
70550 mnw.t pigeon

DRID 1001383 mnwr to purify
RID 0001579 mnwr to purify
ID Lexeme 70580 mnwr incense
70600 mnwr country in the east
70590 mnwr to purify

DRID 1001384 mnz leg
RID 0001580 mnz leg
ID Lexeme 71270 mnz.tj legs

DRID 1001385 mn^c property
RID 0001581 mn^c property
ID Lexeme 70390 mn^c.t property

DRID 1001386 mn^c to nurse
RID 0001582 mn^c to nurse
ID Lexeme 70350 mn^c to nurse; to bring up
854729 mn^c.j Nurses' Lake (in the sky)
70380 mn^c.j nurturer; educator
70370 mn^c.t milk cow
70360 mn^c.t nurse

DRID 1001387 mḳ to rest
RID 0001583 mḳmḳ to rest
ID Lexeme 856670 mḳmḳ to think
76660 mḳmḳ to sleep, to rest

DRID 1001388 mḳn washboard?
RID 0001584 mḳn washboard?
ID Lexeme 76680 mḳn.t washboard?

DRID 1001389 mḳr [a staff]

RID	**0001585**	mḳr [a staff]		
	ID Lexeme	76690	mḳr	staff; rod

DRID	**1001390**	**mḳr [a vessel]**			
	RID	**0001586**	mḳr [a vessel]		
		ID Lexeme	76710	mḳr	[a vessel (situla?)]

DRID	**1001391**	**mḳs to comminute?**			
	RID	**0001587**	mḳs to comminute?		
		ID Lexeme	76770	mḳs	to comminute?
			76780	mḳs.t	disintegration

DRID	**1001392**	**mr [chest; box (for linen)]**			
	RID	**0001588**	mr [chest; box (for linen)]		
		ID Lexeme	72090	mr.t	[chest; box (for linen)]

DRID	**1001393**	**mr board**			
	RID	**0001589**	mr board		
		ID Lexeme	72080	mr.t	board

DRID	**1001394**	**mr bull**			
	RID	**0001590**	mr bull		
		ID Lexeme	71940	mr	bull
			72490	mr.y	fighting bull; bull
			72030	mr.t	black cow

DRID	**1001395**	**mr canal**			
	RID	**0001591**	mr canal		
		ID Lexeme	71850	mr	pasture
			71840	mr	canal
			863036	mr	canal (med.)
			650038	mr.ytj	one who lives on the shore [designation for crocodiles]
			72540	mry.t	bank; shore; quay
			72630	mrw	dam; harbour
			72740	mrr.t	street; block of houses

DRID	**1001396**	**mr desert**			
	RID	**0001592**	mr desert		
		ID Lexeme	72640	mr.w	desert

DRID	**1001370**	**mnkby [a pendant]**			
	RID	**0001564**	mnkby [a pendant]		
		ID Lexeme	71540	mnkby.t	[pendant in the shape of a snake's head]

DRID	**1001397**	**mr eye**

	RID	**0001593**	mr eye		
		ID Lexeme	72070	mr.t	eye
DRID	**1001398**	**mr milk jug**			
	RID	**0001594**	mr milk jug		
		ID Lexeme	71890	mr	milk jug
DRID	**1001399**	**mr pyramid**			
	RID	**0001595**	mr pyramid		
		ID Lexeme	71780	mr	pyramid
DRID	**1001400**	**mr throat**			
	RID	**0001596**	mr throat		
		ID Lexeme	72060	mr.t	throat; gullet (or similar)
DRID	**1001401**	**mr to be ill**			
	RID	**0001597**	mr to be ill		
		ID Lexeme	71790	mr	to ache; to be ill; to suffer
			851222	mr	ill; distressing; painful
			71800	mr	a sick man
			71810	mr	illness; pain
			72000	mr.t	illness; evil
			135440	smr	to cause pain; to make ill
DRID	**1001402**	**mr to bind**			
	RID	**0001598**	mr to bind		
		ID Lexeme	71870	mr	hoe
			71880	mr	to bind
			71900	mr	to attach (oneself to)
			855067	mr	bond; fetter
			71860	mr.w	servants; underlings; weavers; parties
			72120	mr.w	strips of cloth; bundle; bunch (as a measure of vegetables)
			72040	mr.wt	meret-serfs; underlings (coll.); weavers
			72010	mr.t	bundle of clothes?
			26380	jmr.w	a material used for bandaging?
			855047	mꜣr	to bind; to fetter
DRID	**1001403**	**mr to strand**			
	RID	**0001599**	mr to strand		
		ID Lexeme	72510	mr	to run aground; to strand
DRID	**1001404**	**mrḥ lance**			
	RID	**0001600**	mrḥ lance		
		ID Lexeme	72830	mrḥ	lance

DRID	**1001405**	**mrḥ to decay**		
RID	**0001601**	mrḥ to decay		
	ID Lexeme	72810	mrḥ	to decay; to pass away

DRID	**1001406**	**mrḫm the one who works with the salt**		
RID	**0001602**	mrḫm the one who works with the salt		
	ID Lexeme	854479	mrḫm	the one who works with the salt

DRID	**1001407**	**mri̯ to love**		
RID	**0001603**	mri̯ to love		
	ID Lexeme	856667	mr	love
		72480	mr.y	beloved
		400005	mr.y	the beloved (of)
		550321	mr.yt	the beloved one
		72470	mri̯	to love; to wish
		72550	mry.tj	beloved one
		851631	mry.tj	the beloved one
		72650	mrw.t	love; popularity; wish
		859329	mrw.tj	beloved
		72660	mrw.tj	beloved
		72680	mrw.tjt	the beloved one (various goddesses)
		72560	mrw.tjt	beloved one
		72750	mrr.tj	beloved one (of the king)

DRID	**1001408**	**mrj groom**		
RID	**0001604**	mrj groom		
	ID Lexeme	72520	mrj	groom

DRID	**1001409**	**mrj speed**		
RID	**0001605**	mrj speed		
	ID Lexeme	859104	mrj	speed

DRID	**1001410**	**mrjjnt [a kind of a container]**		
RID	**0001606**	mrjjnt [a kind of a container]		
	ID Lexeme	72580	mrjjnt	a container?

DRID	**1001411**	**mrkbt chariot**		
RID	**0001607**	mrkbt chariot		
	ID Lexeme	73010	mrkbt	chariot

DRID	**1001412**	**mrḳḏn [a kind of a metal tool]**		
RID	**0001608**	mrḳḏn [a kind of a metal tool]		
	ID Lexeme	72980	mrḳḏn	[a metal tool]

DRID	**1001413**	**mrḳḥt to catch?**
RID	**0001609**	mrḳḥt to catch?

		ID Lexeme	72970	mrkḫt	[catch?]; [retreat?]

DRID	**1001414**		**mrr flame?**		
	RID	**0001610**	mrr flame?		
		ID Lexeme	72730	mrr	flame
			72770	mrr.yt	lumps (of incense)
DRID	**1001415**		**mrš to be bright red**		
	RID	**0001611**	mrš to be bright red		
		ID Lexeme	72960	mrš	to be bright red
DRID	**1001416**		**mrsw cider?**		
	RID	**0001612**	mrsw cider?		
		ID Lexeme	72950	mrsw	[a kind of a vessel for cider?]
			72940	mrsw	cider?
DRID	**1001417**		**mrt chin**		
	RID	**0001613**	mrt chin		
		ID Lexeme	73040	mrt	chin
DRID	**1001418**		**mrw cedar**		
	RID	**0001614**	mrw cedar		
		ID Lexeme	72620	mrw	cedar (from Lebanon)
DRID	**1001420**		**ms levy**		
	RID	**0001616**	ms levy		
		ID Lexeme	74780	ms	grain (as levy)
DRID	**1001421**		**mš to cut open**		
	RID	**0001617**	mš to cut open		
		ID Lexeme	76250	mš	to cut open; to gut (fish)
			76260	mš	[pond? fish processing site?]
DRID	**1001422**		**ms to venerate**		
	RID	**0001618**	ms to venerate		
		ID Lexeme	74810	ms	to venerate
DRID	**1001423**		**msbb to turn towards**		
	RID	**0001619**	msbb to turn towards		
		ID Lexeme	75270	msbb	to turn towards; to serve; to debate
DRID	**1001424**		**mšd ford**		
	RID	**0001620**	mšd ford		
		ID Lexeme	76620	mšd.t	ford (on the Orontes)
DRID	**1001425**		**mšd(d) comb**		
	RID	**0001622**	mšd(d) comb		

		ID Lexeme	76630	mšdd.t	comb
DRID	**1001426**		**msḏi̯ to hate**		
	RID	**0001623**	msḏi̯ to hate		
		ID Lexeme	650045	msḏ.w	rival?
			76210	msḏi̯	to hate; to dislike
			76220	msḏ.yt	that which is hateful; hate
			76240	msḏḏ.t	[designation for a rival]
DRID	**1001427**		**msẖ [a vessel]**		
	RID	**0001624**	msẖ [a vessel]		
		ID Lexeme	75630	msẖ	[a large vessel, for oil and wine]
			75740	msẖ.t	[a measure for oil]; [large vessel for wine and oil]
DRID	**1001428**		**mjtr [kind of court person]**		
	RID	**0001514**	mjtr [kind of court person]		
		ID Lexeme	850152	mjtr	miter (a worker in the palace)
			68570	mjtr.t	miteret (women's title)
DRID	**1001429**		**knḥ to darken**		
	RID	**0001410**	knḥ to darken		
		ID Lexeme	164900	knḥ	to grow dark; to make dark
			164910	knḥ	porch; shrine
			164920	knḥ.w	darkness
DRID	**1001430**		**msi̯ to give birth**		
	RID	**0001625**	msi̯ to give birth		
		ID Lexeme	74750	ms	child
			74740	ms	creator
			74770	ms	calf
			74980	ms.yt	foal
			74990	ms.yt	supper (a festival)
			75050	ms.w	produce
			74830	ms.t	apron (made of jackal skin)?
			74840	ms.t	dame; maid
			74950	msi̯	to give birth; to create
			75060	msw.t	descendants
			75080	msw.t	manifestation (or similar)
			75070	msw.t	birth; childbirth
			855388	msw.tj	descendant
			75020	msjw.t	she who gives birth (mother)
			135670	sms	nestling
			135700	smsi̯	to deliver; to create
			135710	sms.yt	she who delivers
			856048	sms.w	creation

DRID 1001431 mškb [title of an official]

RID	**0001626**	mškb [title of an official]		
	ID Lexeme	76540	mškb	[title of an official]

DRID 1001432 msktw bracelet

RID	**0001627**	msktw bracelet		
	ID Lexeme	75930	msktw	bracelet

DRID 1001433 mskꜣ animal skin

RID	**0001628**	mskꜣ animal skin		
	ID Lexeme	75890	mskꜣ	leather; hide

DRID 1001434 msn to spin

RID	**0001629**	msn to spin		
	ID Lexeme	75410	msn	spinner (epithet of goddess)
		75400	msn	to spin; to twist
		75450	msn.t	[type of fabric]

DRID 1001435 mšp to endeavour?

RID	**0001630**	mšp to endeavour?		
	ID Lexeme	76420	mšp	to endeavour?; to strive?

DRID 1001436 msḳ a metalworking activity

RID	**0001631**	msḳ a metalworking activity		
	ID Lexeme	75860	msḳ	[weapon?]
		75870	msḳ	[metalworking activity (to emboss?)]

DRID 1001437 mšr [a piece of furniture]

RID	**0001632**	mšr [a piece of furniture]		
	ID Lexeme	76450	mšr	[a piece of furniture (table?)]

DRID 1001438 mšr evening

RID	**0001633**	mšr evening		
	ID Lexeme	76440	mšr	to happen in the evening
		76470	mšr.w	evening; (evening) twilight; supper
		76500	mšr.wt	dinner
		135810	smšr	to spend the evening; to have dinner

DRID 1001439 mšrr to attach

RID	**0001634**	mšrr to attach		
	ID Lexeme	76510	mšrr	to attach; to affix

DRID 1001440 mšrw [plain]

RID	**0001635**	mšrw [plain]		
	ID Lexeme	76490	mšrw	[plain; wetland]

DRID 1001441 mšš [a wood]

RID 0001636 mšš [a wood]

ID Lexeme 76520 mšš [part of a boat]

860933 mšš [wood]

DRID 1001442 mss robe

RID 0001637 mss robe

ID Lexeme 75810 mss ribbon?; belt?

600233 mss tunic; shirt (Galabiya)

75820 mss.t tunic (Galabjya)

DRID 1001443 msṯ offspring

RID 0001638 msṯ offspring

ID Lexeme 76030 msṯ.w offspring

76040 msṯ.wt Offspring (Hathor)

76110 msṯ.wt offspring

854735 msṯ.wtj offspring

868004 msṯ.wtjt offspring

DRID 1001444 msṯ to carry?

RID 0001639 msṯ to carry?

ID Lexeme 800070 msṯ.t (work) obligations

DRID 1001445 mstḥ trap

RID 0001640 mstḥ trap

ID Lexeme 76080 mstḥ trap; snare

DRID 1001446 mstj basket

RID 0001641 mstj basket

ID Lexeme 76020 mstj [a small galley propelled by oars]

76010 mstj [a basket]

DRID 1001447 mstr [an apron]

RID 0001642 mstr [an apron]

ID Lexeme 76070 mstr.t [apron from the fabric]

DRID 1001448 mstr chancellery

RID 0001643 mstr chancellery

ID Lexeme 76060 mstr office; chancellery

DRID 1001449 mstꜣ [a liquid]

RID 0001644 mstꜣ [a liquid]

ID Lexeme 75980 mstꜣ [a liquid]

DRID 1001450 msw supper

RID 0001645 msw supper

ID Lexeme 75090 msw.t supper

DRID 1001451 mšꜣ leather part of chariot

RID 0001646 mšꜣ leather part of chariot

ID Lexeme	76280	mšꜣy	[a chariot part (made of leather)]

DRID 1001452 mšꜣb watering place

RID 0001647 mšꜣb watering place

ID Lexeme	76290	mšꜣb	watering place

DRID 1001453 mš^{c} to march

RID 0001648 mš^{c} to march

ID Lexeme	76330	mš^{c}	to march
	76320	mš^{c}	expedition; campaign
	76360	mš^{c}	commissions; processes (gen.); rules
	600594	mš^{c}	journey; march
	76300	mš^{c}	workforce; combat force
	400345	mš^{c}	member of a workforce
	76380	mš^{c}.w	traveler
	76370	mš^{c}.t	combat force
	139150	mš^{c}y.tj	envoy; messenger

DRID 1001454 mt to discuss

RID 0001652 mtmt to discuss

ID Lexeme	77540	mtmt	to discuss
	77550	mtmt	gossip

DRID 1001455 mtḥn girl

RID 0001650 mtḥn girl

ID Lexeme	77810	mtḥn.t	girl

DRID 1001456 mtj to be correct

RID 0001651 mtj to be correct

ID Lexeme	77320	mt	suppository (med.)
	77680	mtj	correctness
	853566	mtj	reliable one
	77440	mtj	cord?
	77430	mtj	right quantity
	77420	mtj	correct; precise
	400854	mtj	to be precise; to be correct; to be modest
	858168	mtj	very
	77460	mtj.t	rectitude of the character
	868013	mtj.t	suitability

DRID 1001457 mtn knife?

RID 0001653 mtn knife?

ID Lexeme	77580	mtn	to cut into pieces

	77590	mtnj.t	ax; knife

DRID 1001458 mṯn to assign

RID 0001654 mṯn to assign

ID Lexeme			
	77950	mṯn	to assign
	77610	mṯn	to inscribe; to name
	77570	mṯn	tax list
	77560	mṯn	to reward; to recompense
	77600	mṯnw	products (of lands)

DRID 1001459 mṯpr [a tool]

RID 0001655 mṯpr [a tool]

ID Lexeme			
	77940	mṯpr.t	[a tool (chisel?)]

DRID 1001460 mtr flood

RID 0001656 mtr flood

ID Lexeme			
	77690	mtr	flood; floodwaters

DRID 1001461 mtr midday

RID 0001657 mtr midday

ID Lexeme			
	77710	mtr.t	midday

DRID 1001462 mtr to be present

RID 0001658 mtr to be present

ID Lexeme			
	77650	mtr	presence; vicinity
	77640	mtr	to be present; to witness; to instruct
	77780	mtr.w	[solders (scouts)]
	77760	mtr.w	witness
	77770	mtr.w	testimony
	77700	mtr.t	testimony; admonition; instruction
	135940	smtr	to examine; to make inquiry
	135900	smtr	judge (or similar)
	135950	smtr	inquiry; interrogation

DRID 1001463 mtw semen (sperm)

RID 0001659 mtw semen (sperm)

ID Lexeme			
	77490	mtw.t	poison
	77480	mtw.t	semen (sperm); son (metaph.)
	854515	mtw.t	liquid
	851469	mtw.tj	Poisonous One (gatekeeper in the netherworld)

DRID 1001464 mṯꜣ to challenge

RID 0001660 mṯꜣ to challenge

ID Lexeme			
	77880	mṯꜣ	insolent person
	77850	mṯꜣ	[designation for the followers

				of Seth]
		77860	mṯꜣ	to challenge
DRID	**1001465**	**mtꜣ to skewer**		
RID	**0001661**	mtꜣ to skewer		
ID Lexeme		77380	mtꜣ	to skewer
		77400	mtꜣy.t	[a skewer]
DRID	**1001466**	**mṯꜣi̯ to deliver**		
RID	**0001662**	mṯꜣi̯ to deliver		
ID Lexeme		77890	mṯꜣi̯	to deliver; to present
DRID	**1001467**	**mw dancer**		
RID	**0001663**	mw dancer		
ID Lexeme		69100	mw.w	[a kind of a ritual dancers]
DRID	**1001468**	**mw water**		
RID	**0001664**	mw water		
ID Lexeme		69000	mw	water
		859785	mw	field of water
		69210	mw	seed (metaphorically for son)
		69200	mw.y	urine; (bodily) fluid
		69240	mw.yt	moisture; urine
		69230	mwj	[pun with water]
		69220	mwi̯	to wet; to be wet
RID	**0001665**	mwmw raw?		
ID Lexeme		69280	mwmw	raw, uncooked?
DRID	**1001469**	**mwt to die**		
RID	**0001666**	mwt to die		
ID Lexeme		550415	mt	[something unpleasant (poison?)]
		69310	mwt	death
		69320	mwt	dead person; spirit of the dead
		69300	mwt	to die; to be dead; to vanish
		69330	mwt.t	dead person; spirit of a dead person
DRID	**1001470**	**mwꜥd council**		
RID	**0001667**	mwꜥd council		
ID Lexeme		853912	mwꜥd	council
DRID	**1001471**	**mz to bring**		
RID	**0001668**	mz to bring		
ID Lexeme		74720	mz	floral offerings
		74710	mz	carrier
		74700	mz	to bring about; to approach; to go; to proceed to
		135630	smz	to go (somewhere)

RID **0001670** mzmz to put on?
ID Lexeme 75380 mzmz to put on?

DRID **1001472** **mzḥ crocodile**
RID **0001669** mzḥ crocodile
ID Lexeme 75590 mzḥ crocodile
854101 mzḥ Crocodile
75600 mzḥ.t female crocodile

DRID **1001473** **m’w mother**
RID **0001671** m’w mother
ID Lexeme 69040 mw.t mother
69080 mw.t trough (of a coffin, of a sarcophagus)
69060 mw.t weight of the scale

DRID **1001474** **mꜣ [a plant]**
RID **0001672** mꜣ [a plant]
ID Lexeme 66140 mꜣ [a plant]

DRID **1001475** **mꜣ antelope**
RID **0001673** mꜣ antelope
ID Lexeme 66130 mꜣ antelope

DRID **1001476** **mꜣ sickle**
RID **0001674** mꜣ sickle
ID Lexeme 66120 mꜣ bow (of a boat)

DRID **1001478** **mꜣh door**
RID **0001676** mꜣh door
ID Lexeme 67220 mꜣh.t door

DRID **1001479** **mꜣẖ to burn?**
RID **0001677** mꜣẖ to burn?
ID Lexeme 67280 mꜣẖ to burn (up) (of heart, lit. to be afraid)

DRID **1001480** **mꜣḥ to clap**
RID **0001678** mꜣḥ to clap
ID Lexeme 67230 mꜣḥ to clap (the hands)
67250 mꜣḥ clapper
450626 mꜣḥ.t clapper?; clapping?

DRID **1001481** **mꜣj lion**
RID **0001679** mꜣj lion
ID Lexeme 66380 mꜣj sphinx
66400 mꜣj Lion (a star constellation)
66370 mꜣj lion
857335 mꜣj.j lion alike

		66420	mꜣj.t	lioness
DRID 1001482		**mꜣ doum palm**		
RID	**0001680**	mꜣmꜣ doum palm		
	ID Lexeme	67120	mꜣmꜣ	doum palm (Hyphaene thebaica Mart)
		854417	mꜣmꜣ.t	doum palm (Hyphaene thebaica Mart)
		857336	mꜣmꜣ.t	He of the doum-palm (mꜣmꜣ.t=f)
		67130	mꜣmꜣw	fruits of the doum palm
DRID 1001483		**mꜣnw western mountain**		
RID	**0001681**	mꜣnw western mountain		
	ID Lexeme	67160	mꜣnw	western mountains; realm of the dead; the west
		855933	mꜣnw.j	belonging to the western mountains
DRID 1001484		**mꜣr place of joy**		
RID	**0001682**	mꜣr place of joy		
	ID Lexeme	67210	mꜣr.w	maru-temple (lit. viewing place, associated with the solar cult); pavilion
DRID 1001485		**mꜣr to oppress**		
RID	**0001683**	mꜣr to oppress		
	ID Lexeme	851853	mꜣr	bandage?; fetter?
		67180	mꜣr	misery
		67170	mꜣr	wretched person
		67190	mꜣr	to dispossess; to wrong (someone)
		134770	smꜣr	to impoverish
DRID 1001486		**mꜣš [a duck]**		
RID	**0001684**	mꜣš [a duck]		
	ID Lexeme	854630	mꜣš	[a duck]
		854631	mꜣš.t	[a duck]
DRID 1001487		**mꜣs knee**		
RID	**0001685**	mꜣs knee		
	ID Lexeme	67320	mꜣs	to sink down (of heart)
		67330	mꜣs	[a dance posture]
		67310	mꜣs	to kneel
		67410	mꜣs.yw	kneelers
		67380	mꜣs.t	garment of fur?; knee-length kilt?
		67390	mꜣs.t	shoal; sandbank
		67370	mꜣs.t	knee (of a human); hock (of

					an animal)
			67420	mꜣs.tjw	those belonging to the knees?
DRID	**1001488**	**mꜣṯ granite**			
	RID	**0001687**	mꜣṯ granite		
		ID Lexeme	67580	mꜣṯ	granite
DRID	**1001489**	**mꜣṯ to praise**			
	RID	**0001688**	mꜣṯ to praise		
		ID Lexeme	67600	mꜣṯ	to praise
DRID	**1001490**	**mꜣṯr to mourn**			
	RID	**0001689**	mꜣṯr to mourn		
		ID Lexeme	67660	mꜣṯr	to mourn for (a dead person)?
			67650	mꜣṯr.t	mourner
			67670	mꜣṯr.t	auricula tree (Calatropis procera)
			67550	mꜣty.t	mourner
DRID	**1001491**	**mꜣwḏ to carry**			
	RID	**0001690**	mꜣwḏ to carry		
		ID Lexeme	67710	mꜣd.yw	waiters (servers of food)
			67020	mꜣwḏ	staff; pole; supporting rod
			67030	mꜣwḏ	drudgery; soccage
			67050	mꜣwḏ	to carry or sim.
			67010	mꜣwḏ	[label beside a cage of captured animals]; to carry?
			67040	mꜣwḏ	(carrying, counterbalancing) arms
DRID	**1001492**	**mꜣwi̯ to be new**			
	RID	**0001691**	mꜣwi̯ to be new		
		ID Lexeme	66960	mꜣw	Renewed one
			66810	mꜣw	new condition
			66150	mꜣw	new
			859725	mꜣw	new
			66820	mꜣw.t	new
			66830	mꜣw.t	new land
			66860	mꜣw.t	refrain
			66880	mꜣw.tj	newcomer; novice
			66900	mꜣw.tj	[designation for testicles]
			66950	mꜣwi̯	to lighten
			66940	mꜣwi̯	to be new; to become new
			134750	smꜣwi̯	to renew; to renovate
DRID	**1001493**	**mꜣwr to write**			
	RID	**0001692**	mꜣwr to write		
		ID Lexeme	66970	mꜣwr	to write

DRID	**1001494**	**mꜣwṯ to think**		
RID	**0001693**	mꜣwṯ to think		
	ID Lexeme	853873	mꜣwt	thought?
		854441	mꜣwṯ	(sad) thoughts
		500899	mꜣwṯ	the mindful one
		67590	mꜣwṯ	to think (up)
		500747	mꜣwṯ.jt	the mindful one

DRID	**1001495**	**mꜣz to slaughter?**		
RID	**0001694**	mꜣz to slaughter?		
	ID Lexeme	68160	mjꜣz	spine(s) (or similar)
		67300	mꜣz	to slaughter
		67290	mꜣz	knife

DRID	**1001496**	**mꜣꜣ to see**		
RID	**0001468**	m behold		
	ID Lexeme	64440	m	behold!
RID	**0001695**	mꜣꜣ to see		
	ID Lexeme	66270	mꜣꜣ	to see; to look
		66280	mꜣꜣ	sight; seeing; supervision; diagnosis
		66220	mꜣ.tj	eyes (sun and moon as heavenly eyes)
		854706	mꜣ.w	sight
		851912	mꜣ.w	one who sees
		857334	mꜣꜣ.wt	sight; view
		857333	mꜣꜣ.wt	sight
		134570	smꜣꜣ	to make see

DRID	**1001497**	**mꜣꜥ [a wood]**		
RID	**0001696**	mꜣꜥ [a wood]		
	ID Lexeme	66800	mꜣꜥ.w	[a (wooden) part of a ship]
		66680	mꜣꜥ.w	[a kind of wood]

DRID	**1001498**	**mꜣꜥ bank**		
RID	**0001697**	mꜣꜥ bank		
	ID Lexeme	66550	mꜣꜥ	bank
		850060	mꜣꜥ	place (site)
		66560	mꜣꜥ	[Maa-canal (waters in the heavens)]

DRID	**1001499**	**mꜣꜥ to be just**		
RID	**0001698**	mꜣꜥ favorable wind		
	ID Lexeme	66790	mꜣꜥ.w	favorable wind
RID	**0001699**	mꜣꜥ to be just		
		66480	mꜣꜥ	to be just; to be true; to do right
		66470	mꜣꜥ	a just man

			66460	mꜣꜥ	just; correct; true
			854512	mꜣꜥ	to be true; to do right; to offer; to lead
			852260	mꜣꜥ	The Right one?
			400136	mꜣꜥ	to offer; to present
			400137	mꜣꜥ	to guide; to lead
			500171	mꜣꜥ	to run a straight line; to coil
			500218	mꜣꜥ	correctly; truthfully
			854782	mꜣꜥ.j	the leading one
			860536	mꜣꜥ	floodwater
			66770	mꜣꜥ.w	validity; rightness; regularity
			66780	mꜣꜥ.w	products (of foreign lands); presentation
			96860	mꜣꜥ.w	guidance
			66620	mꜣꜥ.t	right order; truth; righteousness
			66630	mꜣꜥ.t	Maat
			500390	mꜣꜥ.t	Maat figure
			66640	mꜣꜥ.t	Maat (solar barque)
			66650	mꜣꜥ.tj	the two truths
			66670	mꜣꜥ.tj	Maaty (canal at the Giza plateau)
			66660	mꜣꜥ.tj	just; righteous (of the blessed dead); vindicated
			859759	mꜣꜥ.tj	truthful one
			66760	mꜣꜥ.t(j)	[name of a mirror]
			500312	mꜣꜥ.tj	just men; the righteous (of the blessed dead); vindicated one
			134630	smꜣꜥ	to do right; to put in order; to correct
			134640	smꜣꜥ	to pray (to)
			134650	smꜣꜥ	prayer(s)
	RID	**0001700**	mꜣꜥ to steer		
		ID Lexeme	66510	mꜣꜥ	to sail
	RID	**0007865**	mꜣꜥ bank		
		ID Lexeme	66530	mꜣꜥ	temple (of the head)
	RID	**0001706**	mꜥꜣꜥ uprights (of a ladder)		
		ID Lexeme	68620	mꜥꜣꜥ	uprights (of a ladder)
DRID	**1001500**	**mꜥ [a boat]**			
	RID	**0001701**	mꜥ [a boat]		
		ID Lexeme	68600	mꜥ.t	[a boat]
DRID	**1001501**	**mꜥkꜣ to be brave**			
	RID	**0001702**	mꜥkꜣ to be brave		
		ID Lexeme	850573	mꜥkꜣ	to be brave
DRID	**1001502**	**mꜥḳ undergarment?**			
	RID	**0001703**	mꜥḳ undergarment?		
		ID Lexeme	41210	mꜥḳ	undergarment?

DRID	**1001503**	**m^{c}r to be successful**			
	RID	**0001704**	m^{c}r to be successful?		
		ID Lexeme	68890	m^{c}r	[a book]
			400955	m^{c}r	to be fortunate; to be successful
			68860	m^{c}r	fortunate; impeccable
			135020	sm^{c}r	to cleanse; to make fortunate; to dress
	RID	**0001705**	m^{c}r to cloth		
		ID Lexeme	860240	m^{c}r	to cloth; to dress
			68870	m^{c}r	[a garment of gods]

DRID	**1001879**	**mryn noble person**			
	RID	**0009711**	mryn noble person		
		ID Lexeme	72570	mryn	noble person

DRID	**1002154**	**mn person**			
	RID	**0007899**	mn man		
			69610	mn	so and so; someone; man (gen.)
			69750	mn.t	so and so; someone (fem.); woman (gen.)

DRID	**1003901**	**mk festival**			
	RID	**0003701**	mk festival		
		ID Lexeme	76850	mk	festival

II.10 n

DRID	**1001505**	**n not**		
RID	**0011707**	n not		
	ID Lexeme	26700	jn	[negation]

DRID	**1001506**	**n red crown**		
RID	**0001708**	n red crown		
	ID Lexeme	79000	n.t	Red Crown (of Lower Egypt)
		868037	n.t	[serpent]
		26880	jnj	Ini (Red Crown)
		857163	jnw	red crown

DRID	**1001507**	**n to**		
RID	**0001709**	n to		
	ID Lexeme	78870	n	to
		850787	n.j	to
		79970	n.j	therefore
		78990	n.t	item
		89860	n.tj	the one who is (exists) – crocodile (a name for Sobek)
		550018	n.tjt	that (conj.)

DRID	**1001508**	**nb basket**		
RID	**0001710**	nb basket		
	ID Lexeme	81920	nb.wt	Islands (of the Aegean)
		853384	nb.wtj	inhabitants of the Aegean (Basket countries)
		81730	nb.t	basket
		857406	nb.t	isle
		500999	nb.tj	He who belongs to the basket

DRID	**1001509**	**nb every**		
RID	**0001711**	nb every		
	ID Lexeme	81660	nb	every; all

DRID	**1001510**	**nb lord**		
RID	**0001712**	nb lord		
	ID Lexeme	858944	nb	lord
		81650	nb	lord; master; possessor (owner)
		81910	nb.wj	the two lords (Horus and Seth)
		81740	nb.t	lady; mistress
		400065	nb.tj	the two ladies (king's title "Nebty")
		860538	nb.tj	queen
		81830	nb.tj	the consort of Osirs (in Edfou)
		81850	nb.tj	the one belonging to the two

				mistresses (the king)
		81810	nb.tj	uraeus pair
		81800	nb.tj	The two ladies (Nekhbet and Wadjet)
		852407	nb.tj	The two ladies (the two crowns of Upper and Lower Egypt)
DRID	**1001511**	**nbḏ evil**		
RID	**0001713**	nbḏ evil		
	ID Lexeme	82940	nbḏ	evil one (Apophis, Seth)
		82930	nbḏ	evil; destructive
		855650	nbḏ.t	destructiveness
		852315	nbd.t	dice snake
DRID	**1001512**	**nbd to braid**		
RID	**0001714**	nbd to braid		
	ID Lexeme	82880	nbd	[an instrument]
		82870	nbd	basketwork
		82850	nbd	to wind around; to coil
		82860	nbd	tresses; curls
		82890	nbd	to band (with metal)
		82920	nbd.j	plaiter; hairdresser
		82910	nbd.t	plait (of hair); tresses
DRID	**1001513**	**nbi̯ to create**		
RID	**0001715**	nbi̯ to create		
	ID Lexeme	82560	nb	creator; builder
		82700	nby.w	protector
		82760	nbnb	to protect
		500438	nbnb	Protector
DRID	**1001514**	**nbw gold**		
RID	**0001721**	nbw gold		
	ID Lexeme	82670	nb.yw	Swimmers (in the netherworld)
		81680	nbw	gold
		450654	nbw	golden one (deceased, as Osiris in relation to Hathor)
		81690	nbw	Gold (Hathor)
		81700	nbw	gold (the sun)
		81710	nbw	grain; golden grain
		854316	nbw.j	golden
		450625	nbw.j	belonging to gold
		81780	nbw.t	Ombos
		81770	nbw.t	[a heavenly cow, associated with Hathor]
RID	**0001716**	nbi̯ to gild		
	ID Lexeme	81670	nb	broad collar
		857417	nb.wt	melting; pouring
		82540	nbw	goldsmith

			854847	nb.tj	gilded one (Nemti)
			82520	nbi̯	to melt (metal); to cast (metal)
			82550	nbi̯	to fashion; to model; to gild
DRID	**1001515**		**nbi̯ to swim**		
	RID	**0001717**	nb to swim		
		ID Lexeme	82500	nb.y	swimmer (Osiris)
			81760	nb.t	soft parts (of the body)
			82530	nbi̯	to swim
DRID	**1001516**		**nbj flame**		
	RID	**0001718**	nbj flame		
		ID Lexeme	82590	nbj	flame
			82580	nbj	to be aflame
			861790	nbj	Burning one
			500727	nbj.wj	The two flames
			500455	nbj.t	Flame
			82650	nbj.t	flame
			861201	nbj.t	the flaming one
			82720	nbjbj	to be hot (med.)
DRID	**1001517**		**nbj reed**		
	RID	**0001719**	nbj reed		
		ID Lexeme	82640	nbj.t	reed
DRID	**1001518**		**nbj spit**		
	RID	**0001720**	nbj spit		
		ID Lexeme	82620	nbj	saliva
DRID	**1001519**		**nh to protect**		
	RID	**0011615**	nh to protect		
			85200	nh	to protect
			859452	nh	protecting snake
			85240	nh.t	protection
			85280	nh.t	magic book
			850633	nh.t	Sycamore (place and/or sanctuary of Hathor at Giza)
			85250	nh.t	guardian snakes
			85220	nh.t	protection; refuge (metaph. of persons)
			85260	nh.t	[protective substance (med.)]
			867941	mnh.w	rampart
DRID	**1001520**		**nbꜣ to plait**		
	RID	**0001722**	nbꜣ to plait		
		ID Lexeme	82460	nbꜣ	spindle
			82480	nbꜣ	to tie?

		155420	nbꜣ	wig?; hair of a wig?; braid?
		82440	nbꜣ	[horn-shaped object]
DRID	**1001521**	**nḏ thread**		
RID	**0001723**	nḏ thread		
	ID Lexeme	90960	nḏ	thread
		857423	nḏ.t	rope
		89830	nty	[a fabric?]
DRID	**1001522**	**nḏ to ask**		
RID	**0001724**	nḏ to appoint		
	ID Lexeme	90920	nḏ	to confer (an office); to appoint
		91060	nḏ	appointment (for something)
RID	**0001725**	nḏ to ask		
	ID Lexeme	90910	nḏ	to ask for (advice); to consult
		857425	nḏ.wt	questions
		91030	nḏ.tj	agitator?
RID	**0001735**	nḏnḏ to consult		
	ID Lexeme	91610	nḏnḏ	advice; counsel
		91600	nḏnḏ	to consult (with someone); to ask (for advice)
DRID	**1001523**	**nḏ to grind**		
RID	**0001726**	nḏ to grind		
	ID Lexeme	90900	nḏ	flour
		90880	nḏ	to grind; to crush
		90890	nḏ.w	miller
		91340	nḏ.wt	grinding woman (i.e. fem. miller)
		91040	nḏ.wt	maid servants (or similar)
		91020	nḏ.t	cosmetic palette
		850683	nḏ.t	flour
DRID	**1001525**	**ndb base**		
RID	**0001728**	ndb base		
	ID Lexeme	859000	ndb	the whole earth
		90810	ndb.wt	foundations (or similar)
DRID	**1001527**	**ndb wind**		
RID	**0001730**	ndb wind		
	ID Lexeme	90780	ndb	wind (or similar)
		90790	ndb.yt	bunt? (of a sail)
DRID	**1001529**	**ndm throne**		
RID	**0001732**	ndm throne		
	ID Lexeme	90850	ndm	throne (or similar)
DRID	**1001530**	**nḏm to be sweet**		

	RID	**0001548**	mnḏm basket	
		ID Lexeme	71740 mnḏm	basket
	RID	**0001733**	nḏm to be sweet	
		ID Lexeme	91460 nḏm	to sit down; to settle; to be pleased
			500020 nḏm	to be sweet; to be pleasant
			91420 nḏm	sweetness; pleasantness
			91400 nḏm	carob tree; fruit of the carob tree
			91410 nḏm	sweet; pleasing
			850399 nḏm	pleasingly
			91480 nḏm.t	kindness (or similar)
			91470 nḏm.t	[a fruit?]
			138840 snḏm	seat; dwelling
			138820 snḏm	to make pleasant; to revive
			138830 snḏm	to make oneself comfortable; to rest
			138850 snḏm.t	one who is installed? (Hathor, as the uraeus at the forehead of the king)
			851678 snḏm	to make pleasant; to rest
	RID	**0001734**	nḏmnḏm to copulate	
		ID Lexeme	28980 nḏmm.t	sexual pleasure
			91580 nḏmnḏm	sexual pleasure
			91590 nḏmnḏm	to copulate with
DRID	**1001531**	**nḏr carpenter**		
	RID	**0001736**	nḏr to do carpentry	
		ID Lexeme	91650 nḏr	chip; ostracon
			91630 nḏr	to smooth (wood); to carpenter
			91690 nḏr.wt	[part of a bed (frame?)]
DRID	**1001532**	**nḏri̯ to follow**		
	RID	**0001737**	nḏri̯ to follow	
		ID Lexeme	861185 nḏri̯	to follow
			854151 nḏr.wt	the moving ones
DRID	**1001534**	**nḏs to be small**		
	RID	**0001739**	nḏs to be small	
		ID Lexeme	91770 nḏs	junior; commoner
			865685 nḏs	at the low level
			91760 nḏs	small; little; weak
			853877 nḏs	to be small
			91810 nḏs.w	low estate
			91790 nḏs.t	littleness (or similar)
			91771 nḏs.t	the younger
			91800 nḏs.tj	[epithet of Osiris]
			138870 snḏs	diminishment; decrease; reduction
DRID	**1001535**	**nḏꜣ water**		

RID **0001740** nḏꜣ thirst

ID Lexeme 91240 nḏꜣ thirst

91230 nḏꜣ to parch (with thirst)

RID **0001741** nḏꜣ water

ID Lexeme 91290 nḏꜣḏꜣ [to be watery? (med.)]

91300 nḏꜣḏꜣ [designation for water]

91260 nḏꜣ.t irrigation; water

138810 snḏꜣḏꜣ.w [watery substance (med.)]

DRID 1001536 nf breath

RID **0001742** nf breath

ID Lexeme 83260 nf breath

855709 nf.w sailor

83420 nf.wj sailor; skipper (title)

868085 nf.t wind

83300 nf.t fan

83310 nf.t [a disease of cattle]

83430 nfnf flood water(s)

83380 nfi̯ to blow (on); to breathe

83390 nfj darkness?; fog?

83350 nfꜣ to blow (from the nose)

857440 nfꜣ.w snorter

857437 nfw.t wind; breath

855995 snf one which makes you breathe

137270 snfi̯ to let breathe; to comfort

137280 snfi̯ to empty; to unload

DRID 1001537 nf that, yonder

RID **0001743** nf that, yonder

ID Lexeme 83270 nf that (demons. pron.)

RID **0001744** nf to be evil

ID Lexeme 83280 nf wrong; wrong-doing

858443 nf to be evil

850750 nf.y wrongful

DRID 1001538 nfr [a jar]

RID **0001745** nfr [a jar]

ID Lexeme 83650 nfr jar

DRID 1001539 nfr fire

RID **0001747** nfr fire

ID Lexeme 83590 nfr.t fire, glow

DRID 1001540 nfr prow-rope?

RID **0001754** nfr prow-rope?

ID Lexeme 83730 nfr.t prow-rope? (naut.)

DRID 1001541 nfr tiller

	RID	**0001755**	nfr tiller		
		ID Lexeme	83890	nfr.yt	tiller (naut.)
DRID	**1001542**	**nfr to be perfect**			
	RID	**0001746**	nfr bracelet		
		ID Lexeme	70690	mnfr.t	bracelet; anklet
	RID	**0001748**	nfr grain		
		ID Lexeme	83540	nfr	grain
	RID	**0001749**	nfr horse		
		ID Lexeme	83580	nfr	horse
	RID	**0001750**	nfr lotus		
		ID Lexeme	83610	nfr	lotus (of Nefertem)
	RID	**0001751**	nfr non-existant		
		ID Lexeme	550123	nfr	[negative word]
			83880	nfr.yt	end; limit
			83940	nfr.w	deficiency
	RID	**0001752**	nfr pelvis		
		ID Lexeme	83750	nfr.t	pelvis (anatomical)
	RID	**0001753**	nfr phallus		
		ID Lexeme	83560	nfr	phallus
	RID	**0001756**	nfr to be perfect		
		ID Lexeme	83470	nfr	to be good; to be perfect
			83630	nfr	nefer (crown of Upper Egypt)
			83480	nfr	to make beautiful
			83500	nfr	good one; beautiful one
			83510	nfr	good
			83520	nfr	beauty; goodness
			83550	nfr	wine; beer
			854519	nfr	to be good; to be beautiful
			851970	nfr	the perfect one
			550034	nfr	good; beautiful; perfect; finished
			400458	nfr	well; happily
			854664	nfr.yt	Neferyt (cow goddess)
			83600	nfr.w	radiance of the sun
			859229	nfr.w	offering
			400468	nfr.w	goodness; good being
			400467	nfr.w	beauty
			83920	nfr.w	good things; valuables
			854638	nfr.w	good things; precious; beauty; the goodness; good being
			83930	nfr.w	ground-level; base
			83530	nfr.w	best quality (relating to cloth)
			857449	nfr.wt	beauty
			857448	nfr.wt	bark of goodness
			83660	nfr.t	beautiful one
			83700	nfr.t	[netherworld]
			83680	nfr.t	what is good
			853340	nfr.t	beautiful one

			857446	nfr.t	[designation for the sky]
			83690	nfr.t	grave
			83720	nfr.t	[crown of Upper Egypt]
			137360	snfr	ornamentation
			137350	snfr	to make beautiful; to embellish
	RID	**0001758**	nfr young		
		ID Lexeme	83670	nfr.t	maiden
			83910	nfr.w	young men (of the army); recruits
			852023	nfr	young man, recruit
			83710	nfr.wt	cows
DRID	**1001543**		**nfr windpipe?**		
	RID	**0001757**	nfr windpipe?		
		ID Lexeme	83460	nfr	[heart with windpipe (hieroglyph)]
DRID	**1001544**		**nfr to loosen**		
	RID	**0001759**	nfr to loosen		
		ID Lexeme	83950	nfr	to slacken; to loosen
			83960	nftft	to leap (away)
DRID	**1001545**		**nfꜥ to remove**		
	RID	**0001760**	nfꜥ to remove		
		ID Lexeme	83400	nfꜥ	to take out; to remove
DRID	**1001546**		**ngg to cackle**		
	RID	**0001761**	ngg to cackle		
		ID Lexeme	500623	ng.y	cackler
			89720	ngg	to cackle; to screech
			857451	ngg	cackler
DRID	**1001547**		**ngi̯ to break (sth.)**		
	RID	**0001762**	ngi̯ to break (sth.)		
		ID Lexeme	89490	ng.t	breach (in a dam)
			89570	ngꜣ.yt	defloration
			860299	ngy.t	crime
			89630	ngi̯	to break open
			138500	sngꜣ	to despoil
DRID	**1001548**		**ngs to overflow**		
	RID	**0001763**	ngs to overflow		
		ID Lexeme	89700	ngs	to overflow
			89710	ngsgs	to overflow
DRID	**1001549**		**ngꜣ cow**		
	RID	**0001764**	ngꜣ cow		
		ID Lexeme	89590	ngꜣ.w	long-horned cattle

DRID	**1001550**	**ngꜣ to kill**		
	RID	**0001765**	ngꜣ to kill	
		ID Lexeme	89500 ngꜣ	to kill; to cut up
DRID	**1001551**	**nḥ guinea-fowl**		
	RID	**0001766**	nḥ guinea-fowl	
		ID Lexeme	85900 nḥ	guinea-fowl? (as a divine being)
DRID	**1001552**	**nḫ = nḏ to protect**		
	RID	**0001727**	nḏ to protect	
		ID Lexeme	90940 nḏ	to protect
			90950 nḏ	protector
			854522 nḏ	to protect; to punish
			853694 nḏ	protector
			90930 nḏ	to punish; to bring to justice
			91110 nḏ.w	protection
			550362 nḏ.t	subjects
			90990 nḏ.t	protectress (Isis; Hathor)
			91000 nḏ.t	protection
			864989 nḏ.tj	protector
			91080 nḏ.tj	protector
			853693 nḏ.tj j	protector
			91090 nḏ.tjt	protectress
			90700 ndj	[a name for the sun god]
	RID	**0001767**	nḫ to protect	
		ID Lexeme	86760 nḫ	to protect; to help
			400968 nḫ	protection
			86780 nḫ	to confirm (the special status of land ownership)
			85390 nḫ.y	[name of a book as an amulet]
			854700 nḫ.w	protector
			868178 nḫ.w	safely
			86990 nḫ.w	protector; defender (divine epithet)
			86960 nḫy.t	protector (goddesses)
	RID	**0001793**	nḫnḫ to protect	
		ID Lexeme	179900 dnḫnḫ	to protect
DRID	**1001553**	**nh to shake**		
	RID	**0001768**	nh to shake	
		ID Lexeme	85210 nh	to shake
	RID	**0001794**	nhnh to quake	
		ID Lexeme	85660 nhnh	to quake (with fear)
DRID	**1001554**	**nḫ to skid**		
	RID	**0001795**	nḫnḫ to skid	
		ID Lexeme	87380 nḫnḫ	to skid; to slam

DRID 1001555 nḫb heifer?

RID	**0001769**	nḫb heifer?		
	ID Lexeme	856238	nḫb	heifer?

DRID 1001556 nḫb lotus

RID	**0001770**	nḫb lotus		
	ID Lexeme	87020	nḫb	lotus

DRID 1001557 nḥb = nḥm lotus bud

RID	**0001771**	nḥb lotus bud		
	ID Lexeme	86330	nḥb.wt	lotiform columns
		86230	nḥb.t	lotus blossom; lotus bud
		86220	nḥb.t	lotus-bud scepter
		86350	nḥb.tj	one with lotus-bud scepter
RID	**0011771**	nḥm lotus bud		
	ID Lexeme	86440	nḥm.t	lotus bud

DRID 1001558 nḥb neck

RID	**0001772**	nḥb neck		
	ID Lexeme	86210	nḥb.t	neck; nape of the neck
		500854	nḥb.yt	unifier

DRID 1001559 nḥb to assign

RID	**0001773**	nḥb to assign		
	ID Lexeme	87040	nḥb	to assign; to decide
		87050	nḥb	stipulation
		87060	nḥb	fresh field (freshly determined arable land)
		87100	nḫb.t	titulary (of the king); designation

DRID 1001560 nḫb to illuminate

RID	**0001774**	nḫb to illuminate		
	ID Lexeme	857493	nḫb	blazing one
		858447	nḫb	to burn; to illuminate
		87110	nḫb	blazing one
		87170	nḫbw	night lighting?

DRID 1001561 nḥb to equip

RID	**0001775**	nḥb to equip		
	ID Lexeme	86140	nḥb	to harness an animal
		86180	nḥb	taxable people
		86130	nḥb	to give; to loan
		86160	nḥb	to cause (strife); to establish (a festival)
		86150	nḥb	yoke
		86260	nḥb.w	yoke oxen

DRID 1001562 nḥd [a medical ingredient]

RID	**0001776**	nḥd [a medical ingredient]		
	ID Lexeme	86730	nḥd	[an ingredient (med.)]
		86740	nḥd.t	[kind of myrrh]

DRID 1001563 nhḏ scribe's palette

RID	**0001777**	nhḏ scribe's palette		
	ID Lexeme	70910	mnhḏ	scribe's palette

DRID 1001564 nḥd to be strong

RID	**0001778**	nḥd to be strong		
	ID Lexeme	86700	nḥd	to be strong
		858085	nḥd	to roar; to bellow out; to raise one's voice
		86750	nḥḏ.t	fang(s); tooth (teeth)

DRID 1001565 nhd to tremble

RID	**0001780**	nhd to tremble		
	ID Lexeme	85810	nhd	to tremble; to be infuriated
		85820	nhd	weakness, trembling
		85840	nhd	Dreadful one
		85860	nhdh	to be horrified
		85850	nhdh	tremor; horror (or similar)
		85870	nhdhd	to tremble (med.)
		137830	snhd	cause to palpitate?

DRID 1001566 nḥḥ eternity

RID	**0001781**	nḥḥ eternity		
	ID Lexeme	86580	nḥḥ	eternally
		86570	nḥḥ	eternity
		86590	nḥḥ	eternity

DRID 1001567 nḥḥ hippopotamus

RID	**0001782**	nḥḥ hippopotamus		
	ID Lexeme	86610	nḥḥ	hippopotamus
		854342	nḥḥ.wt	hippopotamus?

DRID 1001568 nḥḥ olive oil

RID	**0001783**	nḥḥ olive oil		
	ID Lexeme	86600	nḥḥ	olive oil

DRID 1001569 nḫi̯ to endure

RID	**0001784**	nḫi̯ to endure		
	ID Lexeme	86930	nḫi̯	to endure
		87470	nḫḫ	to become old; to endure
		87460	nḫḫ	enduring one; adolescent
		87480	nḫḫ	old one

		87440	nḫḫ	to be new born
		87500	nḫḫ	Enduring-one (a star)
		858448	nḫḫ	cling to?
		87450	nḫḫ	youth
		852228	nḫjḫi̯	to endure; to survive; to grow older
		137930	snḫ	to bring up (a child); to make young; cause to be protected
		137950	snḫy.t	age
		138000	snḫḫ	to rejuvenate

DRID 1001570 nḫi̯ to escape

RID	**0001785**	nḫi̯ to escape		
	ID Lexeme	85380	nḫi̯	to avoid; to escape
		85420	nḫ.w	loss; lack

DRID 1001571 nḫi̯ to request

RID	**0001786**	nḫi̯ to request		
	ID Lexeme	86920	nḫi̯	to lament; to complain
		87000	nḫ.wt	lamentation; complaint

DRID 1001572 nḥi̯ to pray for

RID	**0001787**	nḥi̯ to pray for		
		85880	nḥ	request; prayer
		86050	nḥi̯	to ask for; to pray for
		86070	nḥ.y	supplicator
		85940	nḥ.wj	as is required
		85920	nḥ.t	prayer; plea

DRID 1001573 nẖ = nš spittle

RID	**0001788**	nẖ spittle		
	ID Lexeme	87710	nẖ	spittle
		855192	nẖ	spittle
		87700	nẖi̯	to spit out; to eject
		87780	nẖẖ	spittle
		87730	nẖw.t	what is spit out
		138040	snẖ.t	phlegm
RID	**0001788**	nš spittle		
	ID Lexeme	88410	nš spittle	
		88890	nšš.w	damp air

DRID 1001574 nhi̯* to register

RID	**0001789**	nhi̯* to register		
	ID Lexeme	137770	snh	registry; revision
		137750	snh.t	the registrant?
		137760	snhi̯	to register; to assemble (i.e. to muster (troops))

DRID 1001575 nhj some

RID	**0001790**	nhj some		
	ID Lexeme	85370	nhj	some; a little

DRID 1001576 nḥm to protect

RID	**0001791**	nḥm to protect		
	ID Lexeme	86430	nḥm	to take away; to rescue
		86450	nḥm.w	rescuer
		650030	nḥm.n	surely; assuredly
		137920	snḥm	to prevent

DRID 1001577 nḫn to be a child

RID	**0001792**	nḫn to be a child		
	ID Lexeme	87260	nḫn	to be a child; to become a young child
		861819	nḫn.w	Child
		859268	nḫn.w	child
		87250	nḫn.w	child
		87330	nḫn.w	childhood; youth
		87320	nḫn.w	brood (of Renenutet)
		87280	nḫn.t	little girl
		87300	nḫn.t	youth (abstract)
		87290	nḫn.t	little girl (Hathor)
		117780	ḫn.w	child
		137970	snḫn	to make young; to educate
		137980	snḫn	to guide (so. with sayings)
		856049	snḫn.w	rejuvenating one

DRID 1001578 nḥni̯ to rejoice

RID	**0001796**	nḥni̯ to rejoice		
	ID Lexeme	86480	nḥni̯	to rejoice

DRID 1001579 nḥp to create

RID	**0001799**	nḥp to create		
	ID Lexeme	86370	nḥp	to shape; to create
		450065	nḥp	potter's wheel
		86380	nḥp	creator (divine epithet)
		86360	nḥp	potter's wheel
		86390	nḥp	molded
		45000	nḥp.t	ball of dung
		86420	nḥp.tj	potter

DRID 1001580 nhp to protect

RID	**0001802**	nhp to protect		
	ID Lexeme	85500	nhp	to protect
		85480	nhp	to look after
		865367	nhp	lid

		85510	nhp	protector
		859453	nhp	protection
		85520	nhp	Protector
		853113	nhp.w	guardian
DRID	**1001581**	**nhp to revive**		
RID	**0001798**	nhp morning		
	ID Lexeme	85470	nhp	to rise early in the morning
		85450	nhp	to jump up; to revive; to cast down
		85570	nhp.w	early morning
		70880	mnhp	morning
RID	**0001800**	nhp to jump		
	ID Lexeme	98250	hp	to wrest from; escape
		85440	nhp	to get away from; to escape from
		854520	nhp	to leap; jump away
		137790	snhp	to set in motion (med.)
RID	**0001803**	nhp virility		
	ID Lexeme	85540	nhp	generative power?; virility?
		85460	nhp	to beget; to copulate
		70860	mnhp	begetter (divine epithet)
		70870	mnhp	[an aphrodisiac plant]
		70890	mnhp	phallus with rump (for procreation)
		137800	snhp	to promote sexual activity
DRID	**1001582**	**nḥr [a bread]**		
RID	**0001804**	nḥr [a bread]		
	ID Lexeme	86520	nḥr.w	[a kind of bread]
DRID	**1001583**	**nẖr canal**		
RID	**0001805**	nẖr canal		
	ID Lexeme	87400	nẖr	stream?; canal?
DRID	**1001584**	**nhr sacred well?**		
RID	**0001806**	nhr sacred well?		
	ID Lexeme	85760	nhr.ty	sacred well?
DRID	**1001585**	**nhr terror**		
RID	**0001807**	nhr terror		
	ID Lexeme	85710	nhr	terrifer (Seth)
		854745	nhr	dread, terror
		85720	nhr.t	wickedness (of Seth)
DRID	**1001586**	**nhr to flee?**		
RID	**0001808**	nhr to flee?		
	ID Lexeme	85690	nhr	to flee?; to sail?
		85700	nhr	fugitive

DRID 1001587 nḥš a medical ingredient

RID	**0001809**	nḥš a medical ingredient		
	ID Lexeme	86670	nḥš	[an ingredient (med.)]

DRID 1001588 nḥs to sting

RID	**0001810**	nḥs to sting		
	ID Lexeme	86630	nḥs	to sting

DRID 1001589 nḫt to be strong

RID	**0001811**	nḫt to be strong		
	ID Lexeme	87590	nḫt	Mighty one (a constellation)
		87550	nḫt	[something on which the risen king should stand for]
		858952	nḫt	strong one
		87560	nḫt	to be strong; to strengthen
		550230	nḫt	able; very
		400031	nḫt	strong; victorious
		87580	nḫt	strong one
		87690	nḫt.j	giant
		87630	nḫt.w	stronghold(s)
		87640	nḫt.w	captives; hostages
		87620	nḫt.w	strength; victory
		872162	nḫt.t	stiffness (limbs)
		87600	nḫt.t	stiffness (of joints) (med.)
		87610	nḫt.t	reinforcements
		86680	nḫti̯	to trust; to be confident
		138010	snḫt	to make strong; to strengthen
		138020	snḫt.w	stiffness (med.)

DRID 1001591 nhzi̯ to be awake

RID	**0001813**	nhzi̯ to be awake		
	ID Lexeme	868169	nhzj	wakeful one
		85790	nhzi̯	to awaken; to be awake
		85770	nhz	one who is awaken
		70900	mnhz	watcher
		137820	snhzi̯	to wake

DRID 1001592 nḥꜣ [an illness]

RID	**0001814**	nḥꜣ [an illness]		
	ID Lexeme	85980	nḥꜣ	[an illness]
		86000	nḥꜣ.t	trachoma; a sadness

DRID 1001593 nḥꜣ to be fierce

RID	**0001815**	nḥꜣ to be fierce		
	ID Lexeme	500898	nḥꜣ	flame?
		85950	nḥꜣ	to be fierce; to be unruly; abnormal

			852179	nḥꜣ	dangerous waters
			85960	nḥꜣ	fierce one
			137900	nḥꜣ	to frustrate?; to make dangerous
DRID	**1001594**		**nḥꜣ to exile**		
	RID	**0001816**	nḥꜣ to exile		
		ID Lexeme	864992	nḥꜣ	to exile
			500444	nḥꜣ	the expeller
			85350	nḥꜣ.w	those who are in silence
DRID	**1001595**		**nḫꜣ to hang down**		
	RID	**0001817**	nḫꜣ to hang down		
		ID Lexeme	86830	nḫꜣ	to be pendulous (of the female breasts); dangle
			86810	nḫꜣ	flagellum
			86850	nḫꜣ.w	fish-shaped pendant (jewelry)
			86890	nḫꜣḫꜣ	flagellum
			86880	nḫꜣḫꜣ	to be pendulous (of the breasts); dangle
DRID	**1001596**		**njk to punish**		
	RID	**0001819**	njk to punish		
		ID Lexeme	80270	njk	to punish; to be punished
			80280	njk	evil-doer
			80290	njk	Punisher
			500905	njk.yt	Punisher
			80300	njk.t	Punisher (a knife)
			136680	snjk	to destroy
DRID	**1001597**		**njs papyrus blossom?**		
	RID	**0001822**	njs papyrus blossom?		
		ID Lexeme	854375	njs	[papyrus blossom?]
DRID	**1001598**		**njt to hesitate**		
	RID	**0001824**	njt to hesitate		
		ID Lexeme	80310	njtjt	to hesitate; to hinder
DRID	**1001599**		**njw ostrich**		
	RID	**0001825**	njw ostrich		
		ID Lexeme	80010	njw	ostrich
DRID	**1001600**		**njw to be festive**		
	RID	**0001826**	njw to be festive		
		ID Lexeme	80110	njwjw	to be festive
DRID	**1001601**		**njꜣ ibex**		
	RID	**0001827**	njꜣ ibex		
		ID Lexeme	79960	njꜣ.w	ibex

			857469	njꜣ.wj	like an ibex
DRID	**1001602**	**nkftr [an oil]**			
	RID	**0001828**	nkftr [an oil]		
		ID Lexeme	89320	nkftr	[an oil]
DRID	**1001603**	**nki̯ to copulate**			
	RID	**0001829**	nki̯ to copulate		
		ID Lexeme	89200	nk	to copulate (all nuances)
			89240	nk.w	fornicator
			89420	nkk	homosexual
			89280	nkjkj	to make pregnant
DRID	**1001604**	**nkn hide**			
	RID	**0001830**	nkn hide		
		ID Lexeme	89350	nkn	hide (as material of a shield)
DRID	**1001605**	**nkn to injure**			
	RID	**0001831**	nkn to injure		
		ID Lexeme	89220	nk.t	injured eye
			89330	nkn	to wound
			89340	nkn	harm; injury
			89360	nkn	one who injures
			857472	nkn.t	injury (injured eye)
			89430	nkn.t	wounded eye
			855985	nkn.t	wounded eye
			859629	nkn.t	knife
			857674	snkn	injure; damage
			401300	snkn.t	injury; hindrance
			138480	snk(n)tj.w	harmful ones [a divine being]
DRID	**1001606**	**nkp [a plant]**			
	RID	**0001832**	nkp [a plant]		
		ID Lexeme	89300	nkp.t	[an edible plant]
DRID	**1001607**	**nm dwarf**			
	RID	**0001833**	nm dwarf		
		ID Lexeme	84070	nm.t	dwarf
			852814	nmj	Dwarf
			84270	nmw	dwarf
DRID	**1001608**	**nm fermentation?**			
	RID	**0001834**	nm fermentation?		
		ID Lexeme	84030	nm	winery (winepress?); brewery
			84020	nm	[a large vessel, for grain and beverages]

DRID 1001609 nm produce of the fields (as offerings)

RID	**0001835**	nm produce of the fields (as offerings)		
	ID Lexeme	84040	nm	produce of the fields (as offerings)

DRID 1001610 nm to rob

RID	**0001836**	nm to rob		
	ID Lexeme	84010	nm	to rob; to steal
		400947	nm.t	something occupied?
RID	**0002461**	snm to grab		
	ID Lexeme	137430	snm	to grab

DRID 1001611 nm to sleep

RID	**0001842**	nmj to sleep		
	ID Lexeme	84170	nmj.t	bier; bed
		84320	nmnm.w	sleeping
RID	**0001852**	nm^{c} to sleep		
	ID Lexeme	84220	nm^{c}	to (go to) sleep
		70700	mnm.t	bed

DRID 1001612 nmḥ to be poor

RID	**0001837**	nmḥ to be poor		
	ID Lexeme	84350	nmḥ	to be poor
		853886	nmḥ	poverty
		500415	nmḥ	orphan?
		84360	nmḥ.yt	free woman (of lower social status)
		84340	nmḥ.w	orphanhood
		84370	nmḥ.w	poor man; orphan; free man (of lower social status)
		137540	snmḥ	prayer
		137520	snmḥ	[fraud on the scales]
		137530	snmḥ	to pray; to make supplication

DRID 1001613 nmḥf nephrite

RID	**0001838**	nmḥf nephrite		
	ID Lexeme	79200	nmḥf	nephrite [stone for heart scarabs]

DRID 1001614 nmi̯ to traverse

RID	**0001839**	nmi̯ to traverse		
	ID Lexeme	854368	nmj	Wanderer? (a snake)
		84130	nmi̯	to traverse; to travel
		84180	nmj.w	[a kind of a boat]
		854369	nmj.t	Wanderer? (a snake)
		84300	nmnm	to move to and fro; to quiver
RID	**0001843**	nmnm to sneak		
	ID Lexeme	106760	ḥnmnm	to sneak
		856849	ḥnmnm.w	Sneaker (snake)

	RID	**0001844**	nmnm to speak badly of sb.		
		ID Lexeme	106770	ḥnmnm	to speak badly of sb.
	RID	**0001861**	nnm to stray		
		ID Lexeme	84980	nnm	to stray

DRID	**1001615**	**nmj to butcher**			
	RID	**0001840**	nmj to butcher		
		ID Lexeme	84000	nm	knife (for butchering)
			84050	nm.t	place of slaughter
			868130	nm.tj	butcher
			84090	nm.tjw	Executioner
			84160	nmj	[transitive verb] (what Seth did to Osiris)

DRID	**1001616**	**nmj to shout**			
	RID	**0001841**	nmj to shout		
		ID Lexeme	84140	nmj	to shout
			500352	nmj.y	Shouter
			137420	snm	to be sad
			500524	snm	mourning; grief

DRID	**1001617**	**nms [a jug]**			
	RID	**0001845**	nms [a jug]		
		ID Lexeme	84450	nms.t	[a jug]

DRID	**1001618**	**nms a weight unit**			
	RID	**0001846**	nms a weight unit		
		ID Lexeme	84460	nms.t	ingot (of standard weight and/or form) (or similar)
			84470	nms.t	[a kind of a weight unit]

DRID	**1001619**	**nms to wrap (in bandages)**			
	RID	**0001847**	nms to wrap (in bandages)		
		ID Lexeme	84380	nms	cloth; nemes-headcloth (of the king)
			84390	nms	to wrap (in bandages) (ritual)
			84400	nms	[cult object (document case?)]
			84440	nms	to dazzle; to illumine
			84110	nms.yt	Those who wear a hood

DRID	**1001620**	**nmt to stride**			
	RID	**0001848**	nmt to stride		
		ID Lexeme	84500	nmt	stride
			84490	nmt	to go; to stride through
			84510	nmt.t	stride; course
			858693	nmt.t	location

DRID 1001621 nmt white quartzite

RID	**0001849**	nmt white quartzite		
	ID Lexeme	84530	nmt.t	[a kind of a stone vessel]
		84520	nmt.t	[a stone used for vessels (white quartzite?)]
		84540	nmtj	[a stone used for vessels (white quartzite?)]

DRID 1001622 nm^{c} to be biased

RID	**0001850**	nm^{c} to be biased		
	ID Lexeme	84240	nm^{c}	to be biased

DRID 1001623 nm^{c} to cover?

RID	**0001851**	nm^{c} to cover?		
	ID Lexeme	84230	nm^{c}	to lay out (a bed, with linen); to face (a wall with limestone)

DRID 1001624 nn [food]

RID	**0001853**	nn [food]		
	ID Lexeme	84610	nn	[a kind of a food]

DRID 1001625 nn child

RID	**0001854**	nn child		
	ID Lexeme	79820	ny	[noise made by a newborn child as a sign of its viability (med.)]
		84560	nn.w	child
		854644	nnj	to be youthful; to be a child
RID	**0001925**	nw to be weak		
	ID Lexeme	80770	nw	wrong?; weakness?
		80760	nw	to be weak

DRID 1001626 nn heaven

RID	**0001855**	nn heaven		
	ID Lexeme	84660	nn.t	lower heaven
		858207	nn.t	one of the lower heaven
		855547	nn.tj	what belongs to the lower heaven
		500177	nn.tjw	those of the lower heaven

DRID 1001627 nn not

RID	**0001707**	n not		
	ID Lexeme	400261	n	[particle in discontinuous negation n ... js]
		78890	n	[particle of negation]
		850806	n	[particle of negation]
		850808	ny	while not (particle of negation)
		851923	nn	[particle of negation (Late Middle Egyptian)]

			851961	nn	[particle of negation]
			84550	nn	[negative word, distinct from n]
	RID	**0001818**	ni̯ to refuse		
		ID Lexeme	79810	ni̯	to rebuff; to drive away
			79830	nj.t	wrong-doing
			500462	nj.tjw	The evil one
			180060	njw.y	lance; spear
			80190	njnj	injury?
	RID	**0001821**	njnj to move		
		ID Lexeme	852225	njnj	to turn away
			80170	njnj	to turn away from; to move
DRID	**1001628**	**nn schist? [a stone for making divine statues]**			
	RID	**0001856**	nn schist? [a stone for making divine statues]		
		ID Lexeme	84890	nn	schist? [a stone for making divine statues]
DRID	**1001629**	**nn-wn is not**			
	RID	**0001537**	mn nonexistent		
		ID Lexeme	69570	mn	nonexistence; loss
			69560	mn	nonexistent [particle (expression for nonexistence)]
DRID	**1001630**	**nni̯ to be tired**			
	RID	**0001857**	nni̯ to be tired		
		ID Lexeme	84870	nn.yt	weary one (a dead person)
			854307	nn.y	tired one
			854132	nn.yw	Tired ones
			84900	nn.yw	inert ones (the dead)
			84820	nni̯	to be weary; to be inert; to subside
			84940	nnj.w	bed
			84700	nnw	weariness
			84720	nnw.t	inertia [noun (a condition)]
			137630	snni̯	to calm; to soothe
DRID	**1001631**	**nni̯ to turn back**			
	RID	**0001858**	nni̯to turn back		
		ID Lexeme	84710	nn.w	[designation of a person]
	RID	**0001217**	jnn to turn (away)		
		ID Lexeme	27500	jnn	to turn round
DRID	**1001632**	**nni̯ to writhe**			
	RID	**0001859**	nni̯ to writhe		
		ID Lexeme	84860	nn.y	to bow down
			84670	nn.t	[a plant used to make baskets]
			84680	nn.t	rope?; coils?
			84960	nn.t	hanging net

			80180	njnj	greeting (as posture)
			84840	nny	[a serpent]
DRID	**1001634**		**nnjb resin**		
	RID	**0001860**	nnjb resin		
		ID Lexeme	84920	nnjb	[an aromatic tree (styrax?)]
DRID	**1001635**		**nnšm spleen**		
	RID	**0001862**	nnšm spleen		
		ID Lexeme	85010	nnšm	spleen
DRID	**1001636**		**np hem**		
	RID	**0001864**	npnp hem		
		ID Lexeme	83120	npnp.t	hem
DRID	**1001637**		**npḏ to slaughter**		
	RID	**0001863**	npḏ to slaughter		
		ID Lexeme	83220	npḏ	to slaughter
			83240	npḏ.y	knife
			857477	npḏ(w)	slaughterer
			857479	npḏ.t	butcher's knife
DRID	**1001638**		**npꜣ to make wet**		
	RID	**0001865**	npꜣ to make wet		
		ID Lexeme	82990	npꜣ	to water; to make wet
DRID	**1001639**		**npꜣ umbilical cord**		
	RID	**0001866**	npꜣ umbilical cord		
		ID Lexeme	82980	npꜣ	umbilical cord
			82970	npꜣ	umbilical cord (Apophis)
DRID	**1001640**		**nḳf to beat**		
	RID	**0001867**	nḳf to beat		
		ID Lexeme	89080	nḳf	to beat; to tear (heart)
DRID	**1001641**		**nḳr to sieve**		
	RID	**0001868**	nḳr to sieve		
		ID Lexeme	89140	nḳr	gold dust (or similar)
			89120	nḳr	to sieve
			89130	nḳr	sieve
			89160	nḳr	sprinkler (of gold) (Horus of Edfu)
			89150	nḳr	to sprinkle (with gold)
DRID	**1001642**		**nḳᶜ to scratch**		
	RID	**0001869**	nḳᶜ to scratch		
		ID Lexeme	88990	nḳᶜ	to scratch
			88980	nḳᶜ	[a specially formed loaf]

		89040	nḳ^c.wt	notched sycamore fig
		854710	nḳ^c.wt	the cutting (as pain)

DRID 1001643 nr time

RID	**0001870**	nr time		
	ID Lexeme	85100	nr	specific moment; date
		858633	nr.t	year

DRID 1001644 nrḫ to blaspheme

RID	**0001871**	nrḫ to blaspheme		
	ID Lexeme	600265	nrḫ	to blaspheme; to abuse verbally

DRID 1001645 nri̯ to fear

RID	**0001872**	nri̯ to fear		
	ID Lexeme	85150	nr.w	terrible one (with ref. to gods and the king)
		85160	nr.w	fear
		85070	nri̯	to fear (someone); to overawe
		85180	nrw.t	sprain; dislocation (med.)
		85170	nrw.t	fear
		857481	nrw.tj	terrible one
		868160	nrw.tjt	terrible one
		137710	snri̯	to terrify
		137730	snr.tj	sudden blindness?

DRID 1001646 nri̯ to protect

RID	**0001873**	nri̯ to protect		
	ID Lexeme	85030	nr	[s scepter (or similar)]
		85020	nr	herdsman; protector
		859210	nr.t	[amulet]
		85040	nr.t	vulture
		858897	nr.t	vulture
		85120	nry.t	sanctuary (or similar)
		85080	nry	to be defensive?
		85090	nri̯	to protect; to tend

DRID 1001647 ns [a plant]

RID	**0001874**	ns [a plant]		
	ID Lexeme	87890	ns.ty	seedlings?
		87990	ns.tjw	[a plant]

DRID 1001648 nš grain

RID	**0001875**	nš grain		
	ID Lexeme	860462	nš	grain
		88490	nš	grain (of sand)
		88440	nš	to gather (grain) together

DRID 1001649 nš hairdressing

RID 0001876 nš hairdressing

ID Lexeme	88390	nš	to comb
	88500	nš.t	hairdresser
	88400	nšw.t	hairdressing

DRID 1001650 ns knife

RID 0001877 ns knife

ID Lexeme	88190	ns	to carve
	88020	nsw.t	[injury to a vertebra of the neck]

RID 0001898 nsꜣ knife

ID Lexeme	87950	nsꜣ	knife

DRID 1001651 nš to expel

RID 0001878 nš to expel

ID Lexeme	88510	nš.w	[a discharge (med.)]
	88460	nš	to drive away; to expel
	854521	nš	to haul out
	138230	snš	to unstopp (the ears)

DRID 1001652 ns to go (to)

RID 0001879 ns to go (to)

ID Lexeme	87810	ns	to sink in
	87820	ns	to go; to travel

DRID 1001653 nš to shudder

RID 0001880 nš to shudder

ID Lexeme	88470	nš	to shudder

DRID 1001654 ns tongue

RID 0001881 ns tongue

ID Lexeme	87800	ns tongue	
	88030	ns.wt	[a javelin]
	860949	ns.tjw	[javelin]
	860950	ns.tjt	[javelin]
	88000	nsw	to lick sth.?
	136360	sn.w	tongue

DRID 1001655 nsbi̯ to devour

RID 0001882 nsbi̯ to devour

ID Lexeme	500306	nsb.w	flame
	854283	nsb.tj	one who licks
	88100	nsbi̯	to devour; to lick
	88130	nsby.t	to devour; to lick
	88140	nsbs	to burn, to consume?

DRID 1001656 nšḏ to comminute

RID 0001883 nšḏ to comminute

		ID Lexeme	450164	nšḏ	to comminute
			88900	nšd	to lacerate; to tear

DRID 1001657 nsi̯ to open

RID	0001885	nsi̯ to open			
	ID Lexeme	860386	ns.t	[flood]	
		856262	nsi̯	to open (or similar)	

DRID 1001658 nsj [a demon?]

RID	0001886	nsj [a demon?]			
	ID Lexeme	87960	nsj	[a demon responsible for an illness]	
		87970	nsy.t	[an illness caused by a demon]	

DRID 1001659 nsk to put in proper array

RID	0001887	nsk to put in proper array			
	ID Lexeme	88380	nsk	to put in proper array	

DRID 1001662 nšp gate

RID	0001891	nšp gate			
	ID Lexeme	88640	nšp	gate (or similar)	

DRID 1001663 nšp to breath

RID	0001892	nšp to breath			
	ID Lexeme	88620	nšp	to inhale; to pant?	

DRID 1001664 nsḳ to sting

RID	0001893	nsḳ to sting			
	ID Lexeme	88370	nsḳ	to stab, to sting; to bite	
		859063	nsḳ	needling	

DRID 1001665 nsr to burn

RID	0001894	nsr to burn			
	ID Lexeme	500414	nsr	Burning one	
		88250	nsr	rage; wrath	
		88270	nsr	to burn up; to shrivel	
		88280	nsr	fire; flame	
		88300	nsr.t	flame	
		70013	nsrsr	Island of Fire	
		88340	nsrsr	the burning one	

DRID 1001666 nss to damage sth.

RID	0001895	nss to damage sth.			
	ID Lexeme	88350	nss	to do damage to (or similar)	

DRID 1001667 nssḳ hair loss?

RID	0001896	nssḳ hair loss?			
	ID Lexeme	88360	nssḳ	[an affliction of the head (hair	

loss?)]

DRID	**1001668**	**nsw king**			
	RID	**0001897**	nsw king		
		ID Lexeme	852664	nzw	king; king of Upper Egypt
			88070	nsw.y	to rule as king
			88050	nsw.y	serfs
			88090	nsw.yt	kingship
			88080	nsw.yt	queen
			851639	nswt	king (of Upper Egypt)
			88040	nswt	king; king of Upper Egypt

DRID	**1001669**	**nsꜣ rowlock**			
	RID	**0001899**	nsꜣ rowlock		
		ID Lexeme	87930	nsꜣ.wj	rowlocks

DRID	**1001700**	**nṯ to tie up**			
	RID	**0001901**	nṯ to tie up		
		ID Lexeme	90180	nṯ	to tie together; to fetter
			90670	nṯṯ	to bind; to tie up (foes)
			90680	nṯṯ	rope; cord
			501051	nṯṯ.t	the bound one
			850245	jnṯ	to fetter, to tie up
			28040	jnṯ	[part of a ship]
			500884	jnṯ.t	fettered one
			28030	jnṯ.t	fetter
			28020	jnṯ.tj	the two fetters (manifestation of Re)
			500354	jnṯ.tjw	fettered ones

DRID	**1001701**	**nṯ tongue**			
	RID	**0001900**	nṯ spittle		
		ID Lexeme	90200	nṯ	spittle?
	RID	**0001902**	nṯ tongue		
		ID Lexeme	90190	nṯ	tongue
	RID	**0001908**	nṯnṯ spittle		
		ID Lexeme	854712	nṯnṯ	spittle

DRID	**1001702**	**nṯb to parch**			
	RID	**0001903**	nṯb to parch		
		ID Lexeme	852755	nṯb	to parch

DRID	**1001703**	**nṯḫ [a musical instrument]**			
	RID	**0001904**	nṯḫ [a musical instrument]		
		ID Lexeme	90630	nṯḫ	[a musical instrument]
DRID	**1001704**	**nṯi̯ to be oppressed**			
	RID	**0001905**	nṯi̯ to be oppressed		

		ID Lexeme	89820	nti̯	to be oppressed
DRID	**1001705**	**nṯn dirt**			
RID	**0001906**	nṯn dirt			
		ID Lexeme	90250	nṯn.t	dirt (or similar)
DRID	**1001706**	**ntn skin**			
RID	**0001907**	ntn skin			
		ID Lexeme	90050	ntn.t	diaphragm
			90060	ntn.t	skin
DRID	**1001707**	**nṯr [a beer]**			
RID	**0001909**	nṯr [a beer]			
		ID Lexeme	90460	nṯr.j	beer; beer jug
DRID	**1001708**	**nṯr [a plant]**			
RID	**0001910**	nṯr [a plant]			
		ID Lexeme	90270	nṯr	[a plant]
DRID	**1001709**	**nṯr god**			
RID	**0001911**	nṯr god			
		ID Lexeme	90260	nṯr	god
			90450	nṯr.j	heart (of gods; of kings)
			90420	nṯr.j	holy palace
			90470	nṯr.j	the divine one (designation of a censer)
			90480	nṯr.j	Canal of the god (waters in the netherworld)
			90490	nṯr.j	[a kind of divine cloth]
			90400	nṯri̯	to be divine; to make divine
			90570	nṯr.j	Divine (a phyle of funerary priests)
			860853	nṯr.j	(divine) fabric
			400281	nṯr.j	divine; sacred
			90410	nṯr.j	divine one; sacred one
			859230	nṯr.j	[amulet]
			90500	nṯr.j	magic cord
			90560	nṯr.y	[a mirror]
			90580	nṯr.jw	[a priest of Re]
			90590	nṯr.jw	mistress of the stars (Isis-Sothis)
			854110	nṯr.jt	divine one
			90550	nṯr.jt	[a festival, preliminary to the festival of Sokar]
			90530	nṯr.jt	[a divine staff]
			851539	nṯr.wj	the two gods (Horus and Seth, Ra and Tatenen)
			90610	nṯr.wt	divine state

		90320	nṯr.t	divine eye
		90290	nṯr.t	[a garment, perhaps made of a feline's pelt]
		90310	nṯr.t	sacred-eye(s)
		90280	nṯr.t	goddess
		853664	nṯr.tj	the two divine eyes
		90330	nṯr.tj	Two Goddesses (double uraeus)
		90340	nṯr.tj	[adze used in the Opening-of-the-mouth ritual]
		71550	mnkr.t	bull's tail (royal regalia)
		138650	snṯr	to cense; to purify
		138670	snṯr	incense
		138660	snṯr	censing?
		138690	snṯri̯	to make divine
RID	**0001912**	nṯr natron		
	ID Lexeme	90540	nṯr.yt	[a substance related to natron (med.)]
		90520	nṯri̯	to purify (with natron); to be pure (through natron)
		90510	nṯr.j	natron
DRID	**1001710**	**ntš to besprinkle**		
RID	**0001913**	ntš to besprinkle		
	ID Lexeme	90100	ntš	to besprinkle
DRID	**1001711**	**ntꜣi̯ to hurry**		
RID	**0001914**	ntꜣi̯ to hurry		
	ID Lexeme	89790	ntꜣi̯	to run; to hurry?
DRID	**1001712**	**nṯꜥ to divorce**		
RID	**0001915**	nṯꜥ to divorce		
	ID Lexeme	90220	nṯꜥ	to desert; to divorce
DRID	**1001713**	**ntꜥ to organize**		
RID	**0001916**	ntꜥ to organize		
	ID Lexeme	89970	ntꜥ	to organize
DRID	**1001714**	**nw [a jug]**		
RID	**0001917**	nw [a jug]		
	ID Lexeme	80020	njw	[a jug]
DRID	**1001715**	**nw [a substance]**		
RID	**0001918**	nw [a substance]		
	ID Lexeme	80790	nw	[pleasant-smelling substance, from Punt]
DRID	**1001716**	**nw [a vessel]**		
RID	**0001919**	nw [a vessel]		

		ID Lexeme	80710	nw	[a (bronze) vessel]
DRID	**1001717**	**nw adze**			
	RID	**0001920**	nw adze		
		ID Lexeme	80970	nw.t	adze
DRID	**1001718**	**nw hunter**			
	RID	**0001921**	nw hunter		
		ID Lexeme	80830	nw	hunter; scout
			30510	nw	to hunt
			80740	nw	desert?
			855708	nw	hunter
			450471	nw.t	quarry (taken hunting); product (of the desert)
DRID	**1001719**	**nw light**			
	RID	**0001922**	nw light		
		ID Lexeme	81060	nw.t	ray of light
DRID	**1001720**	**nw sky**			
	RID	**0001923**	nw sky		
		ID Lexeme	80950	nw.t	sky; temple roof (metaph.)
			81020	nw.t	oval; mist ball of scarab?
DRID	**1001722**	**nw this**			
	RID	**0001924**	nw this		
		ID Lexeme	500046	nw	this; these (demons. pron., pl.)
			80730	nw	this (demons. pron.)
DRID	**1001723**	**nw time**			
	RID	**0001924**	nw time		
		ID Lexeme	80840	nw	time; moment
			80850	nw	to spend time (to do sth.)
			81040	nw.t	time
			81300	nw.tjw	God of hours
DRID	**1001724**	**nw to clothe**			
	RID	**0001926**	nw to clothe		
		ID Lexeme	79620	nꜣy.t	weaving workshop
			80870	nw	to clothe; to wrap
			80980	nw.t	thread; yarn (for weaving); cord
			80990	nw.t	[a kind of cloth]
			81010	nw.t	bundle (of flax)
DRID	**1001725**	**nw water**			
	RID	**0001927**	nw water		

		ID Lexeme	79020	n.t	water; flood
			500671	n.tjt	She of the western floods
			80080	njwy	come to a standstill (the flood)
			84930	nw	water
			81240	nw.y	water (gen.); (flood) water(s)
			81260	nw.yt	water; flood; wave
			500005	nw.w	primeval waters
			500006	nw.w	Nun
			854860	nw.wj	one who belongs to the primordial water
			855999	nwnw.t	floodwater
			84620	nn	[flood water]
			84590	nn	Darkness (god)
			84580	nn	darkness
			84910	nn.yw	[a beverage]
			84650	nn.t	Darkness (goddess)

DRID	**1001726**		**nwḏ antilope**		
	RID	**0001928**	nwḏ antilope		
		ID Lexeme	81640	nwḏ.w	antelope

DRID	**1001727**		**nwḏ inaccuracy**		
	RID	**0001929**	nwḏ inaccuracy		
		ID Lexeme	81600	nwd.w	inaccuracy (or similar)
			81560	nwd.t	weakness; inaccuracy

DRID	**1001728**		**nwḏ to move**		
	RID	**0001930**	nwḏ to move		
		ID Lexeme	81520	nwd	agility
			81620	nwḏ	to dangle
			81610	nwd.y	Waverer
			857491	nwḏ.wt	Dangler
			81570	nwd.t	swaddling clothes
			136880	snwḏ	to thrust aside

DRID	**1001729**		**nwdi̯ to press out**		
	RID	**0001931**	nwdi̯ to press out		
		ID Lexeme	81550	nwd	unguent cook
			81540	nwdi̯	to press out (oil); to cook (unguent)
			81580	nwd.t	oil-press bark
			81590	nwd.t	ointment
			852185	nwd.tj	unguent cook

DRID	**1001730**		**nwḥ to bind**		
	RID	**0001932**	nwḥ to bind		
		ID Lexeme	81410	nwḥ	to bind (enemies)

			81400	nwḥ	rope (gen.)
			81420	nwḥ	twisted (of the horns)?
			81430	nwḥ	to copulate
DRID	**1001731**	**nwḫ to boil**			
	RID	**0001933**	nwḫ to boil		
		ID Lexeme	81460	nwḫ	to boil; to be scorched
			136860	snwḫ	to boil; to burn
DRID	**1001732**	**nwḥ to drink**			
	RID	**0001934**	nwḥ to drink		
		ID Lexeme	81440	nwḥ	to drink; to make drunk
			81450	nwḥ	drunkenness
			136840	snwḥ	to make drunk
			136850	snwḥ	to impassion
DRID	**1001734**	**nwi̯ to return**			
	RID	**0001936**	nwi̯ to return		
		ID Lexeme	80880	nw	to return; to bring back
			854081	nwi̯	to return
DRID	**1001735**	**nwi̯ to take care of**			
	RID	**0001937**	nwi̯ to take care of		
		ID Lexeme	81230	nwi̯	to take care of; to collect
DRID	**1001736**	**nwn to dishevel**			
	RID	**0001938**	nwn to dishevel		
		ID Lexeme	81320	nwn	Disheveled-one
			81310	nwn	to dishevel (the hair, in mourning)
DRID	**1001738**	**nws crown?**			
	RID	**0001940**	nws crown?		
		ID Lexeme	81480	nws	[a crown worn by Re]
DRID	**1001739**	**nwṯ to tremble**			
	RID	**0001941**	nwṯ to tremble		
		ID Lexeme	81500	nwṯ	to tremble
DRID	**1001740**	**nwz ingot**			
	RID	**0001942**	nwz ingot		
		ID Lexeme	81470	nwz	ingot; lump?; sheet? (as a measure (by weight) of metal)
DRID	**1001741**	**nwꜣ adze**			
	RID	**0001943**	nwꜣ adze		
		ID Lexeme	81180	nwꜣ	adze (instrument for the Opening-of-the-mouth ritual)

DRID	**1001742**	**nwꜣ to see**			
	RID	**0001944**	nwꜣ to see		
		ID Lexeme	79690	nꜣw	Naw (foreign troops? scouts? hunters?)
			80800	nwꜣ	to see; to look; to watch
			80810	nwꜣ	sight
			136750	snwꜣ	to see
	RID	**0001935**	nwi̯ to call		
		ID Lexeme	80750	nwi̯	to call (gesture of greeting (or similar))

DRID	**1001743**	**nzp knife**			
	RID	**0001945**	nzp knife		
		ID Lexeme	88180	nzp	wounds
			88160	nzp	knife

DRID	**1001744**	**nzp to smooth out**			
	RID	**0001946**	nzp to smooth out		
		ID Lexeme	88150	nzp	to smooth out (bread when baked)

DRID	**1001745**	**nzr flame**			
	RID	**0001947**	nzr flame		
		ID Lexeme	88240	nzr.t	Flame
			860581	nzr.t	the fiery one

DRID	**1001746**	**n’ urban area**			
	RID	**0001948**	n’ urban area		
		ID Lexeme	80890	n’.t	town; city
			868052	n’.t	town residents
			80910	n’.t	the city
			81070	n’.tj	town; local
			81110	n’.tjw	townsmen
			868055	n’.tjt	female resident of an urban area
			81090	n’.tjt	the one from town

DRID	**1001747**	**nꜣb = nꜣp tress**			
	RID	**0001949**	nꜣb tress		
		ID Lexeme	79730	nꜣp	tresses
			857392	nꜣp.t	tress
			79710	nꜣp.t	tresses (or similar)
			79720	nꜣb.tj	[one with the tress who is in Amduat]

DRID	**1001748**	**nꜣš cursed**			
	RID	**0001950**	nꜣš cursed		
		ID Lexeme	79740	nꜣš	cursed
			852810	nꜣš.wtj	[a serpent?]

DRID	**1001749**	**nꜣw breath**		
	RID	**0001951**	nꜣw breath	
		ID Lexeme	79680 nꜣw	breath
			79930 njꜣ	[illness affecting the nose (head cold?) (med.)]
			650032 njꜣj	fan?
DRID	**1001750**	**nᶜ to announce? (death)**		
	RID	**0001952**	nᶜ to announce? (death)	
		ID Lexeme	80350 nᶜ	to announce? (death)
DRID	**1001751**	**nᶜg door crack?**		
	RID	**0001953**	nᶜg door crack?	
		ID Lexeme	80690 nᶜg	door crack?
DRID	**1001752**	**nᶜg to pulverize**		
	RID	**0001954**	nᶜg to pulverize	
		ID Lexeme	80680 nᶜg	to pulverize (med.)
			80700 nᶜg.w	flour (or similar)
DRID	**1001753**	**nᶜẖ bundle**		
	RID	**0001955**	nᶜẖ bundle	
		ID Lexeme	80640 nᶜẖ	bundle (unit of measure)
DRID	**1001754**	**nᶜi̯ to travel**		
	RID	**0001956**	nᶜi̯ to travel	
		ID Lexeme	860446 nᶜ.y	One who travels there
			80380 nᶜ.t	traveler
			80450 nᶜy.t	mooring post
			80530 nᶜw.tj	traveler (sun god)
			80410 nᶜi̯	to travel
			136690 snᶜi̯	to be mobile
DRID	**1001755**	**nᶜi̯ to twist**		
	RID	**0001957**	nᶜi̯ to twist	
		ID Lexeme	80420 nᶜi̯	to twist (a rope)
			80430 nᶜ.y	ropemaker
			852793 nᶜw	a kind of a snake ("twister")
			80510 nᶜw	the twister (personification of the snake)
			857388 nᶜw.t	a kind of a serpent
			857389 nᶜw.tj	a kind of a snake
DRID	**1001756**	**nᶜr catfish**		
	RID	**0001958**	nᶜr catfish	
		ID Lexeme	80570 nᶜr	catfish

DRID 1001757 n^{c}rn unite of soldiers

RID 0001959 n^{c}rn unite of soldiers

ID Lexeme	80630	n^{c}rn	soldiers; special detachment

DRID 1001758 n^{c}š to be strong

RID 0001960 n^{c}š to be strong

ID Lexeme	80650	n^{c}š	to be strong
	865238	sn^{c}š	to strengthen

II.11 r

DRID	**1001926**	**rbš to arm oneself**			
	RID	**0002150**	rbš to arm oneself		
		ID Lexeme	94010	rbš	cuirass (of leather)
			855625	rbš	to arm oneself
DRID	**1001927**	**rd [a grain]**			
	RID	**0002157**	rdrd [a grain]		
		ID Lexeme	97210	rḏrḏ	[term for grain]
			97170	rdrd	[a kind of bread]
DRID	**1001928**	**rd foot**			
	RID	**0002151**	rd foot		
		ID Lexeme	96600	rd	foot; footprint
			96640	rd.wj	obligation; functions; transfer; position; art; wise
DRID	**1001929**	**rd to grow**			
	RID	**0002153**	rd to grow		
		ID Lexeme	96620	rd	plants
			96610	rd	to grow
			96720	rd.yt	plant; herb
			96630	rd.w	[a growing bird]
			854724	rd.t	plant
			139920	srd	to make grow; to plant
			139930	srd	[a plant]
			139910	srd	to gleen
			139960	srdd	[sprout? young branch?]
			875723	srdd	collection
DRID	**1001930**	**rḏi̯ to give**			
	RID	**0002154**	rḏi̯ to give		
		ID Lexeme	550028	rḏi̯	to cause; to allow
			96700	rḏi̯	to give; to put; to place
			851711	rḏi̯	to give; to cause
			177820	ḏ.y	gift; provision
DRID	**1001931**	**rdn laudanum**			
	RID	**0002156**	rdn laudanum		
		ID Lexeme	852318	rdn.y	laudanum
DRID	**1001932**	**rḏw fluidity**			
	RID	**0002158**	rḏw fluidity		
		ID Lexeme	97200	rḏw	fluidity
			856561	rḏw	forewaters
			857620	rḏw.t	efflux

		856754	ḥrḏw	efflux

DRID	**1001933**	**rg compartment**		
RID	**0002159**	rg compartment		
	ID Lexeme	96520	rg.t	compartment

DRID	**1001934**	**rgi̯ to finish**		
RID	**0002160**	rgi̯ to finish		
	ID Lexeme	856676	rgi̯	to stop; to remove

DRID	**1001935**	**rḥ comrade**		
RID	**0002161**	rḥ comrade		
	ID Lexeme	95540	rḥ.w	comrades; mates
		95550	rḥ.wj	the two rivals (Horus and Seth)
		859001	rḥ.t	dame; mistress
		95510	rḥ.tj	two women

DRID	**1001936**	**rdm**	**[a plant]**	
RID	**0002155**	rdm	[a plant]	
	ID Lexeme	97150	rdm.t	cypress grass

DRID	**1001937**	**rḥ to burn**		
RID	**0002163**	rḥ to burn		
	ID Lexeme	95560	rḥḥ	to burn
		95580	rḥrḥ	to be cheerful (of heart)
		859231	nrḥrḥ	to inflame; to irritate

DRID	**1001938**	**rḫ to know**		
RID	**0002164**	rḫ to know		
	ID Lexeme	95640	rḫ	knowledge; opinion
		860504	rḫ	knowledgeable one
		852475	rḫ	know how to do; be able to do
		95620	rḫ	to know
		95650	rḫ	to know (sexually)
		95630	rḫ	wise man
		95790	rḫ.j	acquaintance
		95660	rḫ.t	wise one
		95670	rḫ.t	acquaintance
		95800	rḫy.t	amount
		95860	rḫḫ.j	well-known; famous
		800020	mrḫ.t	memorial stone
		72910	mrḫ.t	[an astronomical instrument]
		72920	mrḫ.t	[observation with an astronomical instrument?]
		139610	srḫ	[something from gods as protection against disease]

		139620	srẖ	[designation of Thot]
		139600	srẖ	(bad) reputation; accusation
		139670	srẖ	memorial stone
		856423	srẖ	reliquary
		139590	srẖ	to make known (information); to complain; to accuse
		851146	srẖ	authority
		139660	srẖ	palace facade; throne
		139680	srẖ.y	accuser
RID	0002162	rẖ subjects (of the king)		
	ID Lexeme	95820	rẖ.yt	common folk; humankind; subjects (of the king)

DRID 1001939 rẖ weaver

RID	0002165	rẖ weaver		
	ID Lexeme	854485	rẖ.tj	two women weavers
		95690	rẖ.tj	[designation of Isis and Nephthys]

DRID 1001941 rḥb [a vessel]

RID	0002166	rḥb [a vessel]		
	ID Lexeme	95570	rḥb	[a vessel]

DRID 1001942 rhb embers

RID	0002167	rhb embers		
	ID Lexeme	95420	rhb	embers

DRID 1001943 rhd [a caldron]

RID	0002168	rhd [a caldron]		
	ID Lexeme	95500	rhd.t	caldron (of metal)

DRID 1001944 rhn to lean (on)

RID	0002169	rhn to lean (on)		
	ID Lexeme	95430	rhn	to lean (on); to rely (on)
		95440	rhn	to have (no) success at?

DRID 1001945 rhni̯ to wade

RID	0002170	rhni̯ to wade		
	ID Lexeme	95450	rhni̯	to wade
		95460	rhni̯	to flee

DRID 1001946 rhnj criosphinx

RID	0002171	rhnj criosphinx		
	ID Lexeme	95470	rhnj	ram (of Amun); criosphinx

DRID 1001947 rhnj waste

RID	0002172	rhnj waste		

		ID Lexeme	95480	rhnj	waste
DRID	**1001948**	**rḥs [a baked good]**			
	RID	**0002175**	rḥs [a baked good]		
		ID Lexeme	95610	rḥs	[a kind of baked goods]
DRID	**1001949**	**rḫs to slaughter**			
	RID	**0002176**	rḫs to slaughter		
		ID Lexeme	95870	rḫs	to slaughter; to butcher
DRID	**1001950**	**rḫt list**			
	RID	**0002177**	rḫt list		
		ID Lexeme	95680	rḫt	list; amount
DRID	**1001951**	**rḫt to wash (clothes)**			
	RID	**0002178**	rḫt to wash (clothes)		
		ID Lexeme	95890	rḫt	to wash (clothes)
			95930	rḫt.j	washer
			855716	rḫt.j	washer
			868307	rḫt.wt	washerwoman
DRID	**1001952**	**rj coil?**			
	RID	**0002179**	rj coil?		
		ID Lexeme	852803	rj.t	coil?
DRID	**1001953**	**rj heaven**			
	RID	**0002180**	rj heaven		
		ID Lexeme	93220	ry.t	heaven
DRID	**1001954**	**rj ink**			
	RID	**0002181**	rj ink		
		ID Lexeme	93190	ry.t	ink
DRID	**1001955**	**rj pus**			
	RID	**0002182**	rj pus		
		ID Lexeme	93200	ry.t	pus (or similar)
DRID	**1001956**	**rj side**			
	RID	**0002183**	rj side		
		ID Lexeme	93230	rj.t	side
DRID	**1001957**	**rk [a plant]**			
	RID	**0002187**	rkrk [a plant]		
		ID Lexeme	96430	rkrk	astragalus?
DRID	**1001958**	**rk time**			
	RID	**0002184**	rk time		

		ID Lexeme	96390	rk	time
DRID	**1001959**		**rk to creep**		
	RID	**0002188**	rkrk to creep		
		ID Lexeme	401172	rkrk	to creep
			873167	rkrk.yt	creep
DRID	**1001960**		**rk to stop**		
	RID	**0002185**	rk to stop		
		ID Lexeme	96400	rk	to stop
DRID	**1001961**		**rkḥ fire**		
	RID	**0002186**	rkḥ to light (a fire)		
		ID Lexeme	96450	rkḥ	fire
			96440	rkḥ	to light (a fire); to burn up
			96460	rkḥ	Burning (a festival)
			96370	rkḥ.y	Fiery one
			96380	rkḥ.yt	Burning one (2nd night hour)
			861200	rkḥ.t	Burning one
			501113	rkḥ.t	burning one (designation for goddesses)
			73020	mrkḥ.t	pyre; stake
DRID	**1001962**		**rks harnessed team**		
	RID	**0002189**	rks harnessed team		
		ID Lexeme	96490	rks	harnessed team
DRID	**1001963**		**rm fish**		
	RID	**0002190**	rm fish		
		ID Lexeme	94160	rm	fish (gen.)
DRID	**1001964**		**rm to chastize**		
	RID	**0002195**	rmrm to chastize		
		ID Lexeme	94470	rmrm	to chastize
			94480	rmrm	Chastizer
DRID	**1001965**		**rmi̯ to weep**		
	RID	**0002191**	rmi̯ to weep		
		ID Lexeme	94190	rm.y	Weeper (sun god)
			94210	rm.yt	Weeper (i.e. mourner)
			94200	rm.yt	tear
			94230	rm.w	weeper
			94220	rm.w	weeping
			855602	rm.wt	weeping
			94180	rmi̯	to weep; to beweep
			500090	rmy.tj	Tearful (Osiris)
			858630	rmm	weeping
			139540	srm.t	[a body of water]

			139510	srmi̯	to make weep
DRID	**1001966**	**rmn arm**			
	RID	**0002192**	rmn arm		
		ID Lexeme	29840	jrm	together with
			94250	rmn	side; half
			854523	rmn	upper arm; shoulder; side; half
			94260	rmn	side (of rowing women)
			94240	rmn	upper arm; shoulder
			94300	rmn	[measure of area (1/2 aroura)]
			94340	rmn	rank
			94280	rmn	[a measure of length]
			94290	rmn	[measure of length (5 palms)]
			94420	rmn.yt	domain; department
			854764	rmn.w	Carrier
			856017	rmn.w	companion
			857627	rmn.wj	arms of balance
			501058	rmn.wj	Double-Arm
			94430	rmn.wt	of the same rank; equal
			94440	rmn.wtj	carrier; companion
			868286	rmn.wtj	companion
			856018	rmn.wtt	companion
			94360	rmn.t	[part of the reliquary shrine of Osiris]
			94410	rmny.t	domain; land of a domain
			94490	rmrm.t	[a field]
	RID	**0002193**	rmni̯ to carry		
		ID Lexeme	94320	rmn	support (i.e. column; pillar)
			94310	rmn	bearer; support
			94400	rmni̯	to carry; to support
	RID	**0002194**	rmni̯ to decay		
		ID Lexeme	94330	rmn	to decay (of walls)
DRID	**1001967**	**rmṯ human being**			
	RID	**0002196**	rmṯ human being		
		ID Lexeme	94530	rmṯ	human being; man
			450402	rmṯ	people; personnel
			94550	rmṯ.t	humankind; people
			853446	rmṯ.t	women
DRID	**1001968**	**rn name**			
	RID	**0002197**	rn name		
		ID Lexeme	94700	rn	name
DRID	**1001969**	**rnn joy**			
	RID	**0002198**	rnn joy		
		ID Lexeme	95040	rnn	to rejoice; to praise

			95220	rnn.wt	joy; exultation
			95150	rnn.t	fortune
DRID	**1001970**		**rnn to bring up**		
	RID	**0002199**	rnn to bring up		
		ID Lexeme	93660	rwny.t	heifer
			94720	rn	young one (of animals)
			94810	rn.y	calf
			94740	rn.t	young one (fem.) (of animals)
			94830	rnw.t	motherless girl
			95080	rnn	youth
			95060	rnn	[a kind of cattle]
			854524	rnn	to embrace
			95090	rnn	to embrace
			95100	rnn	to nurse; to rear (a child)
			95130	rnn.t	maiden
			95120	rnn.t	young hippos
			95140	rnn.t	wet nurse; attendant
			95110	rnn.t	cows; heifers
DRID	**1001971**		**rnpi̯ to be young**		
	RID	**0002201**	rnpi̯ to be young		
		ID Lexeme	852345	rnp	youth
			94900	rnp	colt
			94870	rnp	fresh water
			94910	rnp	young bull (Montu)
			94880	rnp	youth
			94860	rnp	rejuvenation
			94950	rnp.wj	youth
			94850	rnp.wj	youthful; vigorous
			95030	rnp.wt	fresh things (plants and fruit)
			94920	rnp.t	year
			500284	rnp.t	yearly sustenance; festival of the year
			95000	rnpi̯	to be young; to become young (again)
			139560	srnpi̯	to make young; to rejuvenate
DRID	**1001972**		**rns beads?**		
	RID	**0002202**	rns beads?		
		ID Lexeme	95230	rns	[beads (or similar)]
DRID	**1001973**		**rpw image of a woman**		
	RID	**0002203**	rpw image of a woman		
		ID Lexeme	94110	rpw.t	figure of a woman; statue of a woman
			94030	rpw.t	Repit (a goddess); woman of high status; statue (of a woman)

		851932	rpw.tj	the two ladies (Isis and Nephthys)

DRID 1001974 rpw to rot

RID	**0002204**	rpw to rot		
	ID Lexeme	94100	rpw	to rot
		857633	rpw.w	putrefaction

DRID 1001975 rḳ opponent

RID	**0002205**	rḳ opponent		
	ID Lexeme	96300	rḳ	counterweight
		96340	rḳ.w	enmity
		96330	rḳ.w	opponent
		96350	rḳw.t	resistance (of a swelling?)
		96310	rḳ.t	intractable
		96290	rḳi̯	to turn aside; to defy
		855367	rḳrḳ	resistance
		857634	rḳḳ.t	enmity; resentment?
RID	**0002206**	rḳi̯ to stop		
	ID Lexeme	856232	rḳrḳ	to stop; to remove; to leave

DRID 1001976 rr swine

RID	**0002207**	rr swine		
	ID Lexeme	95350	rr.j	swine (gen.); boar
		95300	rr.t	sow

DRID 1001977 rr time

RID	**0002208**	rr time		
	ID Lexeme	95240	rr	time

DRID 1001978 rrm mandrake?

RID	**0002209**	rrm mandrake?		
	ID Lexeme	95400	rrm.t	mandrake?

DRID 1001979 rš coryza

RID	**0002210**	rš coryza		
	ID Lexeme	96170	rš coryza	

DRID 1001980 rs south

RID	**0002211**	rs south		
	ID Lexeme	96011	rs.j	south
		96010	rs.j	southern
		96070	rs.jw	southerners
		96120	rs.w	south wind
		500787	rs.wt	Southern
		96150	rs.wt	south
		856024	rs.wtj	Southerner

DRID	**1001981**	**rs to watch**			
	RID	**0002212**	rs to watch		
		ID Lexeme	852848	rs	guard (place where Re and Osiris are being protected)
			95940	rs	to wake; to watch
			95950	rs	guard; watchman
			96110	rs.w	the watch (of sentries); vigilance
			500430	rs.w	Guarding Ones
			96130	rs.wt	dream (“wakening (in sleep)”)
			95960	rs.t	captured enemies?
			96030	rsj	entirely; quite; at all
			96060	rsy.t	the watch (of sentries); guard post
			96040	rsy.t	guardian (of goddesses)
			139720	srs	to awake; to wake up
			139700	srs.t	[epithet of Sachmet]
DRID	**1001983**	**ršj peak**			
	RID	**0002214**	ršj peak		
		ID Lexeme	96200	ršj	peak; summit
DRID	**1001984**	**ršu̯ to rejoice**			
	RID	**0002215**	ršu̯ to rejoice		
		ID Lexeme	96180	rš.w	joy
			96220	rš.wt	joy
			96210	ršu̯	to rejoice
			96280	ršrš	joy
			96270	ršrš	to rejoice
			139760	sršu̯	to make happy
DRID	**1001985**	**rtḥ to bake**			
	RID	**0002216**	rtḥ to bake		
		ID Lexeme	800009	rtḥ	to bake
			96530	rtḥ	baker
			96560	rtḥ.t	bakery
			96570	rtḥ.tj	baker
DRID	**1001986**	**rtḥ to restrain**			
	RID	**0002217**	rtḥ to restrain		
		ID Lexeme	96550	rtḥ	fortification
			96540	rtḥ	to confine; to restrain
			500234	rtḥ.tj	Metal craftsmen?
DRID	**1001987**	**rw lion**			
	RID	**0002219**	rw lion		
		ID Lexeme	93390	rw	lion
			860603	rw	lion
			500396	rw	Lion

		857644	rw.t	Lioness
		861786	rw.tj	Pair of Lions
		500389	rw.tj	pair of lions
RID	**0002230**	rwrw lion		
	ID Lexeme	93680	rwrw.t	den (of a lion)
DRID	**1001988**	**rw straw**		
RID	**0002221**	rw straw		
	ID Lexeme	857648	rw	straw, reed
		93630	rwy.t	straw
DRID	**1001989**	**rwḏ bowstring**		
RID	**0002222**	rwḏ bowstring		
	ID Lexeme	93760	rwḏ	bowstring; cord
		93860	rwḏ.t	bowstring?; whip's lash?
		96710	rdy.t	cord
DRID	**1001990**	**rwd stairway**		
RID	**0002223**	rwd stairway		
	ID Lexeme	93730	rwd	stairway; tomb shaft
		93800	rwd	stairway; tomb shaft
		97130	rdw	stairway; steps
DRID	**1001991**	**rwḏ to be strong**		
RID	**0002224**	rwḏ to be firm		
	ID Lexeme	93780	rwḏ	to be firm; to prosper; to succeed
		400633	rwḏ	strong; firm
		860132	rwḏ	neat; efficient
		93790	rwḏ	firmness; strength
		93830	rwḏ	shore
		93880	rwḏ.t	hard stone (gen.); sandstone
		857845	srwẖ	to foster
		139310	srwẖ	to foster; to treat (med.)
		139340	srwḏ	to make endure; to make strong
		139330	srwd.t	awesomeness?
		851109	srwḏ.t	equipment?
RID	**0002225**	rwḏ to control		
	ID Lexeme	93840	rwḏ	to control; to administer
		93850	rwḏ.w	agent; inspector
		93870	rwḏ.t	success (or similar)
DRID	**1001992**	**rwḥ to trespass**		
RID	**0002226**	rwḥ to trespass		
	ID Lexeme	600032	rwḥ	to trespass
DRID	**1001993**	**rwhꜣ evening**		

	RID	**0002227**	rwhꜣ evening		
		ID Lexeme	93690	rwhꜣ	evening
DRID	**1001994**	**rwi̯ to dance**			
	RID	**0002228**	rwi̯ to dance		
		ID Lexeme	93450	rw.t	dance (or similar)
			856025	rw.tj	dancer
			856215	rwi̯	to dance
			93570	rwj.t	[a dance]
DRID	**1001995**	**rwi̯ to depart**			
	RID	**0002218**	rw gateway		
		ID Lexeme	93610	rw.yt	[administrative building]; [law court]
			93420	rw.t	gateway; door
			93410	rw.t	(false)door
			93430	rw.t	tribunal
			93590	rwy.t	[part of a false-door (architrave)]
	RID	**0002220**	rw outside		
		ID Lexeme	93440	rw.t	outside
			93490	rw.tj	stranger
			650022	rw.tj	outside
	RID	**0002229**	rwi̯ to depart		
		ID Lexeme	853689	rwi̯	to cease from
			93540	rwi̯	to go away; to expel; to drive off
			851902	rw.wt	departure
			93600	rwy.t	[discharge? (med.)]
			139260	srw	to turn
			139300	srwi̯	to remove
			139180	sr	to sever?
DRID	**1001996**	**rzf catch**			
	RID	**0002231**	rzf catch		
		ID Lexeme	96160	rzf	the catch (fish and fowl); disarray
DRID	**1001997**	**rꜥ goose**			
	RID	**0002232**	rꜥ goose		
		ID Lexeme	92640	rꜥ	goose (gen.)
DRID	**1001998**	**rꜥ mouth**			
	RID	**0002233**	rꜥ item		
		ID Lexeme	92590	rꜥ	item; part
			92680	rꜥ	activity; action
			92630	rꜥ	stock of; item (in lists)
			92600	rꜥ	[small measure of capacity]
			92610	rꜥ	a third
			600203	rꜥ.wj	two-thirds

	RID	**0002234**	r’ mouth		
		ID Lexeme	92620	r’	water's edge
			92570	r’	opening; door
			92580	r’	utterance; speech
			92560	r’	mouth
			92690	r’.w	openings? [part of a ship]
DRID	**1001999**	**r^c sun**			
	RID	**0002235**	r^c sun		
		ID Lexeme	400015	r^c	Re
			93340	r^{c}y.t	Raet (fem. counterpart of the sun god Re)
			862769	r^{c}y.t	sun goddess
			853477	r^{c}w	sun (the king)
			93290	r^{c}w	sun
			860277	r^{c}w.w	Re-Gods

II.12 h

DRID	**1000458**	**hbj ibis**			
	RID	**0000554**	hbj ibis		
		ID Lexeme	854102	hbj	Ibis
			98120	hbj	ibis
			98090	hbj.t	ibis (fem.)
DRID	**1000459**	**hbn [a vessel]**			
	RID	**0000555**	hbn [a vessel]		
		ID Lexeme	98170	hbn.t	[a bulbous vessel (also a measure of capacity)]
DRID	**1000460**	**hbn antelope**			
	RID	**0000556**	hbn antelope		
		ID Lexeme	98160	hbn	[an antelope]
DRID	**1000462**	**hbnj ebony**			
	RID	**0000558**	hbnj ebony		
		ID Lexeme	98180	hbnj	ebony
DRID	**1000464**	**hbḳ to pound**			
	RID	**0000560**	hbḳ to pound		
		ID Lexeme	98230	hbḳ	thicket?
			98220	hbḳ	to beat up; to triturate
DRID	**1000470**	***hbu̯ to abuse?**			
	RID	**0000568**	*hbu̯ to abuse?		
		ID Lexeme	140120	shbu̯	to abuse?
DRID	**1000471**	**hbu̯ to step**			
	RID	**0000550**	hbhb to remove		
		Lexeme ID	98210	hbhb	to pervade (med.); to remove (enemies)
	RID	**0000551**	hbhb to traverse		
		Lexeme ID	98200	hbhb	to traverse; to tread
	RID	**0000569**	hbu̯ to dance		
		Lexeme ID	30250	jhb.t	dancer
			30240	jhb	(ritual) dancer
			30220	jhb	dance
			30230	jhb	dancing song
			176	jhb	to dance
			98080	hbu̯	dance
	RID	**0000570**	hbu̯ to step		
		Lexeme ID	98010	hbu̯	plow
			98020	hbu̯	to tread; to traverse; to trample
			853107	hb	the trampled one (Seth)

		98150	hb.w	intrusion
		860419	hb.t	netherworld
		98070	hb.t	place of execution
DRID	**1000478**	**hd to confront**		
RID	**0000579**	hd to confront		
	ID Lexeme	99610	hd	to quarry (stone)
		862904	hd	One who returns whack
		99620	hd	assault
		99600	hd	to attack; to prevail over
		854527	hd	to confront; to attack; to break
		99640	hd.t	thorn? (of the acacia)
		140230	shd	to punish; to curb
		869357	shd	to punish
		140240	shd.t	coercion
RID	**0000585**	hdhd to charge		
	ID Lexeme	99730	hdhd	to charge (of the army)
DRID	**1000482**	**hdd famine?**		
RID	**0000582**	hdd famine?		
	ID Lexeme	99740	hddw.t	famine?
DRID	**1000487**	**hdm throne**		
RID	**0000591**	hdm throne		
	ID Lexeme	99680	hdm.w	footstool; throne
DRID	**1000488**	**hdn [a plant]**		
RID	**0000592**	hdn [a plant]		
	ID Lexeme	865385	hdn	hand broom
		99700	hdn	[a plant (rabbit ear?)]
		99710	hdn.j	[epithet of Thot]
DRID	**1000493**	**hdr [collar]**		
RID	**0000597**	hdr [collar]		
	ID Lexeme	97750	hdr.t	[a collar]
DRID	**1000498**	**hf to hull**		
RID	**0000601**	hf to hull		
	ID Lexeme	98350	hf	to hull (med.)
DRID	**1000516**	**hhi̯ to be fiery**		
RID	**0000622**	hhi̯ to be fiery		
	ID Lexeme	99260	hh	blast (of fire); heat (of fire)
		99310	hhi̯	to be fiery
DRID	**1000517**	**hhj to be deaf**		
RID	**0000623**	hhj to be deaf		

		ID Lexeme	99290	hhj	to deafen; to benumb
			99300	hhy.t	[a form of deafness (med.)]
DRID	**1000518**	**hj onomatopoetic**			
	RID	**0000624**	hj onomatopoetic		
		ID Lexeme	97850	hj.w	Hiu (a hostile serpent, ass, gazelle)
			97860	hj.w	Monster (donkey); evil snake
			97800	hj.w	[Seth as an ass and as a gazelle]
DRID	**1000519**	**hj to contort**			
	RID	**0000625**	hj to contort		
		ID Lexeme	97810	hy	to make fast (the tow-rope)
DRID	**1000520**	**hj to rejoice**			
	RID	**0000626**	hj to rejoice		
		ID Lexeme	853667	hj	to cheer; to whoop
			501126	hy	Cheering one
			97760	hy	[interjection]
			97780	hy	joy; gladness
			600455	hjhj	to rejoice
			856804	hjhj	cheer; rejoicing; acclamation
			99270	hh	to exult
DRID	**1000522**	**hjms to approach humbly**			
	RID	**0000631**	hjms to approach humbly		
		ID Lexeme	97880	hjms	to approach humbly
DRID	**1000524**	**hjw [creature threatening the dead]**			
	RID	**0000633**	hjw [creature threatening the dead]		
		ID Lexeme	97870	hjw.t	[creature threatening the dead]
DRID	**1000528**	**hkr [serpent]**			
	RID	**0000639**	hkr [serpent]		
		ID Lexeme	99400	hkj	[a serpent]
			99410	hkr.t	[a female serpent]
DRID	**1000538**	**hm fare**			
	RID	**0000649**	hm fare		
		ID Lexeme	856827	hm.tt	cartage; remuneration
			98420	hm.t	cartage; remuneration
DRID	**1000544**	**hm saliva**			
	RID	**0000655**	hm saliva		
		ID Lexeme	98460	hmh	saliva (or similar)
DRID	**1000547**	**hm to be hot**			
	RID	**0000658**	hm to be hot		

		ID Lexeme	98370	hm	to be hot (diseased state)
DRID	**1000549**	**hm to shout aloud**			
	RID	**0000660**	hm to rejoice		
		ID Lexeme	85610	nhm	gladness; rejoicing
			85580	nhm	to rejoice
			56090	bnhm	jubilation
	RID	**0000661**	hm to roar		
		ID Lexeme	85620	nhm	to tremble; quake; shout
			98380	hm	roar (warlike)
	RID	**0000667**	hmhm to rejoice		
		ID Lexeme	98490	hmhm	[a crown]
			137810	snhmhm	to rejoice
	RID	**0000668**	hmhm to roar		
		ID Lexeme	85630	nhmhm	to roar (or similar)
			98480	hmhm	to roar; to rumble
			98470	hmhm	roar
			98500	hmhm.t	roar; war-cry
			98510	hmhm.tj	Roarer
			98520	hmhm.tj	[a term for evil creatures]
DRID	**1000561**	**hms cord**			
	RID	**0000677**	hms cord		
		ID Lexeme	98530	hms	cord
DRID	**1000565**	**hmṯ [serpent]**			
	RID	**0000681**	hmṯ [serpent]		
		ID Lexeme	98540	hmṯ	[a serpent]
			98550	hmṯ.t	[a serpent]
DRID	**1000595**	**hn sweet**			
	RID	**0000713**	hn sweet		
		ID Lexeme	859652	hnꜣ	sweet
			98660	hnꜣ.y	[a sweet]
			98790	hnwy.t	[part of the djaret-fruit (med.)]
DRID	**1000619**	**hni̯ to rejoice**			
	RID	**0000746**	hni̯ to rejoice		
		ID Lexeme	855962	nhn.y	rejoicing?; acclamation?
			98670	hnj.wt	Rejoicing one
			98730	hn.w	jubilation
			855841	hn.y	bark of jubilation
			98720	hni̯	to rejoice
	RID	**0000749**	hnjnj to rejoice		
		ID Lexeme	98680	hnjnj	to rejoice
	RID	**0000744**	hnhn to rejoice		
		ID Lexeme	98860	hnhn	to rejoice

DRID	**1000636**	**hnn fallow deer**		
RID	**0000764**	hnn fallow deer		
	ID Lexeme	98830	hnn	fallow deer
		98840	hnn.t	doe

DRID	**1000641**	**hnn to incline**		
RID	**0000769**	hnn to incline		
	ID Lexeme	97670	hꜣn.w	waves; flood
		853106	hn	one who is bowing down (Seth)
		98810	hnn	to nod; to assent to
		97660	hꜣnꜣ	O that...!

DRID	**1000666**	**hnw box**		
RID	**0000797**	hnw box		
	ID Lexeme	73180	mhn	box
		98700	hnw	[a jar]; hin (unit of measure, ca. 1/2 liter)
		98650	hnw.y	[epithet of Anubis]
		98560	hnw	box; cavity (of the body, chest, skull)

DRID	**1000668**	**hnw kin**		
RID	**0000799**	hnw kin		
	ID Lexeme	98760	hnw	supporter; relative

DRID	**1000674**	**hp regulation**		
RID	**0000805**	hp regulation		
	ID Lexeme	98260	hp	cord (for determining guide-lines in construction)
		98240	hp	law; regulation
		853896	hp	to act rightly?; to act according to regulations?
		140150	shp.w	behavioral norm
		140140	shp	to govern (the Two Lands)

DRID	**1000688**	**hḳ to crack?**		
RID	**0000821**	hḳ to crack?		
	ID Lexeme	859894	hḳ	[illness]
		99360	hḳ	to break, to crack?

DRID	**1000691**	**hḳs to damage**		
RID	**0000824**	hḳs to damage		
	ID Lexeme	99370	hḳs	to damage; to harm
		99390	hḳs.wtt	injured eye

DRID	**1000698**	**hr highland**
RID	**0000831**	hr highland

ID Lexeme 98920 hr wooded highlands?

DRID 1000705 hr to dispel completely
RID 0000841 hr to dispel completely
ID Lexeme 98910 hr to dispel completely

DRID 1000714 hri̯ to milk
RID 0000854 hri̯ to milk
ID Lexeme 73250 mhr suckling; child
73210 mhr milk jar
73240 mhr milker (dairy worker)
73220 mhr to milk; to suckle
73090 mhj.t milch-cow
73160 mhwj [a liquid (med.)]
99010 hrj to milk?

DRID 1000717 hrm to include
RID 0000856 hrm to include
ID Lexeme 99210 hrm to include; to close

DRID 1000720 hrp to sink
RID 0000859 hrp to sink
ID Lexeme 99170 hrp to sink; to be immersed
99180 hrp.yw Drowned ones
140200 shrp to plunge; to immerse

DRID 1000729 hrṯṯ to do stealthily
RID 0000868 hrṯṯ to do stealthily
ID Lexeme 99250 hrṯṯ to do stealthily

DRID 1000730 hru̯ to be pleased
RID 0000869 hru̯ to be pleased
ID Lexeme 99050 hru̯ to be pleased; to be at peace; to be content
400109 hru̯ peaceful; pleasing; content
98990 hr.t contentment; peace
140180 shru̯ to make content; to satisfy
851901 shrr peacemaker ('who makes content')
RID 0000851 hrhr to satisfy
ID Lexeme 85750 nhrhr be satisfied with oneself
856208 hrhr to satisfy oneself

DRID 1000732 hrw day
RID 0000871 hrw day
ID Lexeme 99060 hrw day
99070 hrw due today (grain for harvesting)
99160 hrw.yt journal; legal document

DRID	**1000751**		**hskt [bad way of walking]**		
	RID	**0000890**	hskt [bad way of walking]		
		ID Lexeme	99350	hskt	[bad way of walking]
DRID	**1000752**		**hsmḳ storming (of the king joining battle)**		
	RID	**0000891**	hsmḳ storming (of the king joining battle)		
		ID Lexeme	99340	hsmḳ	storming (of the king joining battle)
DRID	**1000759**		**ht [an animal]**		
	RID	**0000898**	ht [an animal]		
		ID Lexeme	99460	ht.w	[an animal (in spells)]
			99450	ht.t	[a female animal (in spells)]
DRID	**1000766**		**ht to dig**		
	RID	**0000909**	htht to dig		
		ID Lexeme	99520	htht	[a canal]
			99500	htht	to dig up
			99480	htj	to bore (with a drill)
			99490	hty.t	borer (bit) (of a carpenter's drill)
DRID	**1000769**		**ht to wander**		
	RID	**0000906**	ht to wander		
		ID Lexeme	854727	ht	to wander about
	RID	**0000912**	htht to traverse		
		ID Lexeme	99530	htht	to traverse (the heavens); to rush
			853568	shtht	to dispel; to scatter
DRID	**1000796**		**hw to run**		
	RID	**0000948**	hwhw to run away		
		ID Lexeme	97940	hwhw	to run away
DRID	**1000799**		**hw sailing?**		
	RID	**0000942**	hw sailing?		
		ID Lexeme	97980	hw.tj	sailor; ship's hand, crew
DRID	**1000813**		**hwš to disregard**		
	RID	**0000959**	hwš to disregard		
		ID Lexeme	600374	hwš	to miss; to disregard
DRID	**1000815**		**hwt to burn**		
	RID	**0000961**	hwt to burn		
		ID Lexeme	97960	hwt	flame; fire
			97990	hwt.wt	burning (med.)
			854725	hwt	to burn
DRID	**1000816**		**hwt to lament**		
	RID	**0000962**	hwt to lament		

	ID Lexeme	97950	hwt	to lament; to complain
		97970	hwt	lamentation(s)
DRID	**1000817**	**hwṯn [a fish]**		
RID	**0000964**	hwṯn [a fish]		
	ID Lexeme	98000	hwṯn	[a fish]
DRID	**1000822**	**hyn territory**		
RID	**0000971**	hyn territory		
	ID Lexeme	97890	hyn	[a kind of land or boundary]
		860377	hyn	dwelling; house
DRID	**1000841**	**h’ courtyard**		
RID	**0000991**	h’ courtyard		
	ID Lexeme	97220	h’	courtyard
DRID	**1000847**	**hꜣ blaze**		
RID	**0000996**	hꜣ blaze		
	ID Lexeme	97270	hꜣ	blaze
		97440	hꜣy.t	bakery (or similar)
DRID	**1000851**	**hꜣ husband**		
RID	**0001001**	hꜣ husband		
	ID Lexeme	97400	hꜣj	to beget
		97770	hꜣj	husband
DRID	**1000855**	**hꜣ pavillon**		
RID	**0001005**	hꜣ pavillon		
	ID Lexeme	97430	hꜣy.t	ceiling; heaven
		97420	hꜣy.t	portal; portico
DRID	**1000863**	**hꜣ wild bird**		
RID	**0001014**	hꜣ wild bird		
	ID Lexeme	852142	hꜣ.w	wild birds
DRID	**1000870**	**hꜣb to send**		
RID	**0001021**	hꜣb to send		
	ID Lexeme	550085	hꜣb	letter; communication
		97610	hꜣb.w	messenger
		97580	hꜣb	to send
		856771	hꜣb.t	journey
DRID	**1000881**	**hꜣi̯ period**		
RID	**0001038**	hꜣi̯ period		
	ID Lexeme	854526	hꜣw	proximity; surrounding; time; issue; property
		97470	hꜣw	time; life-time

DRID	**1000882**		**h3i̯ to descend**		
	RID	**0001039**	h3i̯ to descend		
		ID Lexeme	73130	mhw.t	family; kin
			73150	mhw.tj	kin
			853536	hꜣ.y	descended one
			856774	h3.w	descent
			97260	h3.w	corvée; duty
			97500	h3.w	corvée worker
			97290	h3.tjw	crew (phyle) on duty
			856765	h33	Descending one
			97360	h3i̯	to attack (the enemy)
			97350	h3i̯	to descend; to fall; to strike
			860784	h3i̯	to throw; to strike
			97460	h3w	neighborhood; environment
			550026	h3w	affairs; belongings
			97490	h3w	need
			97900	hyt.t	burial chamber?
			140050	shꜣ	to confound; to defraud
			140080	sh3.t	drum
			853090	sh3.tj	he was made fall (Seth)
			140090	sh3i̯	to bring down; to make fall
			140020	sh3	to damage
			140060	sh3	to confound; to defraud
			858549	sh3	to confound; to defraud
			140010	sh3	turmoil

DRID	**1000892**		**h3r herd**		
	RID	**0001061**	h3r herd		
		ID Lexeme	97680	h3r.t	herd (of desert animals)
DRID	**1000893**		**h3m poultry**		
	RID	**0001052**	h3m poultry, aviary		
		ID Lexeme	97630	h3m.w	poultry
DRID	**1000904**		**h3w kin**		
	RID	**0001073**	h3w kin		
		ID Lexeme	97480	h3w	kindred

II.13 ḥ

DRID	**10000478**		**ḥ flax?**		
	RID	**00005356**	ḥ flax?		
		ID Lexeme	99780	ḥ	[a quality of cloth]
			99770	ḥ	[hieroglyph depicting a wick of twisted flax]
DRID	**1000449**		**ḥb stairway?**		
	RID	**0000537**	ḥb stairway?		
		ID Lexeme	103370	ḥb	[stairway?]
			103360	ḥb	target
DRID	**1000455**		**ḥbḏ to open**		
	RID	**0000544**	ḥbḏ to open		
		ID Lexeme	103950	ḥbḏ	to open (mouth)
DRID	**1000463**		**ḥbnn [a bread]**		
	RID	**0000559**	ḥbnn [a bread]		
		ID Lexeme	103710	ḥbnn.wt	[a kind of bread]
			866501	jḥbnn.t	[bread]
DRID	**1000466**		**ḥbs to cover**		
	RID	**0000562**	ḥbs [a priest]		
		ID Lexeme	103790	ḥbs.t	priestess (in the nome of Hieracon)
			103780	ḥbs	priest (in the nome of Athribis)
	RID	**0000563**	ḥbs to cover		
		ID Lexeme	103750	ḥbs	garment; clothing
			103740	ḥbs	to clothe; to cover
			103760	ḥbs	lid
			851898	ḥbs.w	clothes
			103920	ḥbs.wt	cloth
	RID	**0000566**	ḥbs to protect		
		ID Lexeme	103900	ḥbs.yt	protégé
			140660	sḥbs	cover (face with balm)
DRID	**1000474**		**ḥḏ [a medicine]**		
	RID	**0000574**	ḥḏ [a medical substance]		
		ID Lexeme	863031	ḥḏ.w	[a med. substance]
			112720	ḥḏ.w	[a med. substance (aromatic resin?)]
			112510	ḥḏ.t	[a med. substance]
			112490	ḥḏ.t	[a med. plant]
			112480	ḥḏ.t	[a plant]
DRID	**1000476**		**ḥḏ mace**		
	RID	**0000577**	ḥḏ mace		

	ID Lexeme	112290	ḥḏ	mace
		856130	sḥḏ	inspector
		141280	sḥḏ	inspector
		141310	sḥḏ.t	chest
		141300	sḥḏ.t	inspector

DRID 1000477 ḥḏ to be white

RID	**0000578**	ḥḏ to be white		
	ID Lexeme	112380	ḥḏ	white land
		859467	ḥḏ	oryx
		112301	ḥḏ	to be white; to be bright
		112320	ḥḏ	light
		112370	ḥḏ	jawbone
		112350	ḥḏ	bones
		112300	ḥḏ	white; bright
		112330	ḥḏ	silver; silver (as medium of exchange)
		112360	ḥḏ	[a goose or duck]
		112340	ḥḏ	chapel
		112190	ḥḏ.y	the shining one
		112730	ḥḏ.w	milk
		112710	ḥḏ.w	onions
		501050	ḥḏ.t	White Crown (personified)
		112410	ḥḏ.t	daylight
		112420	ḥḏ.t	white cloth; white clothing
		112460	ḥḏ.t	milk; [a beverage, lit. white stuff]
		112430	ḥḏ.t	White One (goddesses)
		112450	ḥḏ.t	white (of the eye)
		859672	ḥḏ.t	honey
		112520	ḥḏ.t	White one (hippopotamus goddess)
		112440	ḥḏ.t	White (crown of Upper Egypt)
		112160	ḥḏ.t	white one (woman grinding grain)
		112530	ḥḏ.t	the white one [mark of the sacred animal]
		112540	ḥḏ.tj	white sandals
		112760	ḥḏw.y	[a kind of a fabric]
		112770	ḥḏw.yt	lamp (or similar]
		855217	ḥḏw.yt	spawn
		112740	ḥḏw.t	light
		112750	ḥḏw.tj	One who belongs to light (sun god)
		112900	ḥḏḏ	(rays of) light
		112880	ḥḏḏ.t	[festival of light]
		112920	ḥḏḏ.tj	[eyes of the sun]
		112940	ḥḏḏw.t	(rays of) light; beams
		112890	ḥḏḏwj	to shine
		141270	sḥḏ	clearing (by burning)

		141250	sḥḏ	to make bright; to illuminate; to shine
		141260	sḥḏ	light
		857664	sḥḏ	brightness
		141320	sḥḏ.w	illuminator (sun god)
		141340	sḥḏ.w	[a symptom of illness]
		141290	sḥḏ.t	illuminator (Hathor)
		141360	sḥḏy.t	palace; shrine (i.e. god's palace)
		141370	sḥḏw.t	light
		500718	sḥḏw.tj	He who belongs to light

DRID 1000483 ḥdg to kill

RID	**0000583**	ḥdg to kill		
	ID Lexeme	112240	ḥdg	to kill
		112250	ḥdg	from attacking (the lion)

DRID 1000485 ḥḏi̯ to damage

RID	**0000588**	ḥḏi̯ to damage		
	ID Lexeme	853560	ḥḏ.w	destroyer
		112400	ḥḏ	damage
		112660	ḥḏi̯	to injure; to destroy; to be lacking
		112680	ḥḏ.yt	slaughter; execution; damage
		500435	sḥḏi̯	to punish
RID	**0000587**	ḥḏḥḏ to kill		
	ID Lexeme	860607	ḥḏḥḏ	to kill

DRID 1000486 ḥḏi̯ to spread out

RID	**0000589**	ḥḏi̯ to spread out		
	ID Lexeme	101790	ḥꜣd	to be overwhelmed
		112170	ḥdy	to spread out
		112180	ḥdy	to become limp

DRID 1000489 ḥḏn to be angry

RID	**0000593**	ḥḏn to be angry		
	ID Lexeme	112780	ḥḏn	to resist; to become angry; to be angry
		112790	ḥḏn.w	reluctance
		859147	ḥḏnḏn	to rage
		112820	ḥḏnḏn	Rage
		112970	ḥḏnḏn.t	angry one? (Anukis)
		141390	sḥḏn	to vex

DRID 1000490 ḥdḳ to cut off

RID	**0000594**	ḥdḳ to cut off		
	ID Lexeme	112230	ḥdḳ	to cut off
RID	**0000595**	ḥdḳḳ rat?		
	ID Lexeme	871199	ḥdḳḳ	rat? [rodent]

DRID	**1000492**	**ḥḏr [animal]**			
	RID	**0000596**	ḥḏr [animal]		
		ID Lexeme	112830	ḥḏr	[a small animal (hyena?)]
			112860	ḥḏr.t	[a small animal (hyena?)]
DRID	**1000495**	**ḥḏy west wind**			
	RID	**0000599**	ḥḏy west wind		
		ID Lexeme	112700	ḥḏy	west wind
DRID	**1000497**	**ḥf to hear?**			
	RID	**0000606**	ḥfḥf to hear?		
		ID Lexeme	104530	ḥfḥf	to hear?
DRID	**1000500**	**ḥfdi̯ to climb**			
	RID	**0000603**	ḥfdi̯ to climb		
		ID Lexeme	856800	ḥfd.w	climber?
			104560	ḥfdi̯	to climb; to fly
DRID	**1000501**	**ḥfdi̯ to settle**			
	RID	**0000604**	ḥfdi̯ to settle		
		ID Lexeme	104570	ḥfd	to sit; to settle
DRID	**1000502**	**ḥfk to drink milk**			
	RID	**0000607**	ḥfk to drink milk		
		ID Lexeme	104540	ḥfk	to drink (milk from a cow's udder)
			860183	nḥfk	to extract milk
DRID	**1000506**	**ḥfꜣ to crawl**			
	RID	**0000611**	ḥfꜣ to crawl		
		ID Lexeme	500777	ḥfꜣ	Reverer
			104340	ḥfꜣ	to snake; to twist
			501179	ḥfꜣ.yw	those who come crawling
			104390	ḥfꜣ.w	snake (gen.)
			104360	ḥfꜣ.wt	snakes; worms (coll.)
			65150	ḥfꜣ.t	crawling posture; humble posture
			104370	ḥfꜣ.t	worm
			501180	ḥfꜣy.t	those who come crawling
			104470	ḥfn.w	[a snake]
			854345	ḥfnn	[designation of a person?]
			104490	ḥfnn.t	[a snake]
			140680	sḥfꜣ	[wooden part of boat or house]
	RID	**0000614**	ḥfꜣ to swarm		
		ID Lexeme	104430	ḥfn	tadpole
	RID	**0000608**	ḥfn hundred thousand		
		ID Lexeme	104460	ḥfn.w	hundred thousand
			104440	ḥfn	one hundred thousand

DRID 1000508 ḥfꜣ = ḥfn = ḥnf to praise

RID	**0000613**	ḥfꜣ to praise		
	ID Lexeme	106720	ḥnf	to worship
		104350	ḥfꜣ	to revere; to praise

DRID 1000512 ḥgꜣ festivity

RID	**0000618**	ḥgꜣ festivity		
	ID Lexeme	110940	ḥgꜣ	joys
		110970	ḥgꜣ.w	festival place

DRID 1000513 ḥḥ million

RID	**0000619**	ḥḥ million		
	ID Lexeme	500031	ḥḥ	Heh (divine being(s) who support the heavens)
		109260	ḥḥ	Heh (subdivision of a phyle)
		853978	ḥḥ	Heh (symbol of time)
		109250	ḥḥ	million

DRID 1000521 ḥj to seek

RID	**0000627**	ḥj to seek		
	ID Lexeme	141020	sḥjḥj	to scour, to roam?
RID	**0000628**	ḥjḥj to go		
	ID Lexeme	109290	ḥḥi̯	to go; to tread
RID	**0000630**	ḥjḥj to seek		
	ID Lexeme	101930	ḥjḥj	to seek
		141010	sḥḥ	to be engaged (as servant)

DRID 1000523 ḥjp to run

RID	**0000632**	ḥjp to run		
	ID Lexeme	103960	ḥjp	to run; to hasten
		104020	ḥjp.t	steering oar
		104030	ḥjp.t	course
		104070	ḥp.tj	[designation of gods]
		104130	ḥpw.tj	runner
		104140	ḥpp	to be held back
		104160	ḥpḥp	to be held back

DRID 1000525 ḥkn lion?

RID	**0000637**	ḥkn lion?		
	ID Lexeme	855173	ḥkn	Necklace (depicting a lioness)
		110790	ḥkn	door-bolt (in the shape of a lion)

DRID 1000526 ḥkn oil or unguent

RID	**0000635**	ḥkn [medical substance]		
	ID Lexeme	110760	ḥkn	activity of drug preparation [verb]
		110770	ḥkn	[a med. substance]

			110870	ḥkn.w	[a sacred oil]
			110800	ḥkn.w	[a med. substance]
DRID	**1000527**	**ḥkn to praise**			
	RID	**0000638**	ḥkn to praise		
		ID Lexeme	110740	ḥkn	to praise
			110850	ḥkn.y	the praised one
			400259	ḥkn.w	Praiser
			110860	ḥkn.w	praise
			110810	ḥkn.w	One who praises
			110830	ḥkn.wtt	Praiser (a serpent)
			500676	ḥkn.t	Praiser
			860344	ḥknkn	to exult
DRID	**1000530**	**ḥkꜣ to perform magic**			
	RID	**0000641**	ḥkꜣ to perform magic		
		ID Lexeme	110680	ḥkꜣ	to bewitch
			500345	ḥkꜣ.yw	Bewitchers
			162370	ḥkꜣ.yt	magician
			110661	ḥkꜣ.w	magic spell
			110660	ḥkꜣ.w	magic; magical power
			110700	ḥkꜣ.w	magician
			110710	ḥkꜣ.w	The magical one (crown of Upper Egypt)
			110720	ḥkꜣw.t	magic
DRID	**1000531**	**ḥnr = ḥl to darken**			
	RID	**0000642**	ḥnr = ḥl to darken		
		ID Lexeme	106860	ḥnr	to squint?
			854746	ḥnr	clouding; darkening
			106890	ḥnry	[nickname of the goddess Hathor]
DRID	**1000533**	**ḥm [a weapon at a chariot]**			
	RID	**0000644**	ḥm [a weapon at a chariot]		
		ID Lexeme	105250	ḥmy.t	[a weapon at a chariot]
DRID	**1000535**	**ḥm [plant]**			
	RID	**0000646**	ḥm [plant]		
		ID Lexemes	104880	ḥm.w	[a plant (fenugreek?)]
DRID	**1000536**	**ḥm coward**			
	RID	**0000647**	ḥm coward		
		ID Lexemes	104630	ḥm	coward
			105820	ḥm.tj	coward
DRID	**1000539**	**ḥm forty**			
	RID	**0000650**	ḥm forty		

		ID Lexemes	105320 ḥm.w	

DRID	**1000540**		**ḥm frit**	
	RID	**0000651**	ḥm frit	
		ID Lexemes	104800 ḥm.t	

DRID	**1000541**		**ḥm majesty**	
	RID	**0000652**	ḥm majesty	
		ID Lexemes	104690 ḥm	
			104830 ḥm.t	

DRID	**1000542**		**ḥm misfortune**	
	RID	**0000653**	ḥm misfortune	
		ID Lexemes	104750 ḥm.t	

DRID	**1000545**		**ḥm servant**	
	RID	**0000656**	ḥm servant	
		ID Lexemes	104680 ḥm	servant
			868343 ḥm	servant
			104820 ḥm.t	servants
			104810 ḥm.t	servant

DRID	**1000546**		**ḥm though**	
	RID	**0000657**	ḥm though	
		ID Lexemes	104600 ḥm	though; verily

DRID	**1000548**		**ḥm to copulate**	
	RID	**0000659**	ḥm to copulate	
		ID Lexemes	104620 ḥm	to copulate [forbidden indecent act]

DRID	**1000550**		**ḥm to steer**	
	RID	**0000662**	ḥm to steer	
		ID Lexemes	104650 ḥm	to steer
			105210 ḥm.y	helmsman
			105240 ḥm.yt	steering oar
			105300 ḥmw	steering oar
	RID	**0000663**	ḥm to tread	
		ID Lexemes	876725 ḥm	backlog
			853105 ḥm	the downtrodden (Seth)
			104661 ḥm	[a club (weapon)]
			104660 ḥm	[a club (for beating the wash)]
			104700 ḥm	to tread
			104840 ḥm.t	stake
			500232 ḥm.t	a drill

DRID	**1000551**		**ḥm woman**	

RID	**0000664**	ḥm woman		
	ID Lexemes	860606	ḥm.t	woman
		104730	ḥm.t	woman; wife
		105270	ḥmy.t	the woman

DRID 1000552 ḥmḏ vinegar

RID	**0000665**	ḥmḏ vinegar		
	ID Lexemes	105840	ḥmḏ	vinegar; wine of a poor quality

DRID 1000554 ḥmi̯ to flood

RID	**0000670**	ḥmi̯ to flood		
	ID Lexemes	140750	sḥmy.t	flooding
		31670	jsḥm	[a body of water?]

DRID 1000556 ḥmi̯ to repel

RID	**0000672**	ḥmi̯ to repel		
	ID Lexemes	105200	ḥmi̯	to drive back; to repel
		104860	ḥm	[verb associated with curing an illness?]
		104740	ḥm.t	One who push back
		105540	ḥmmy	[a magical creature]
		70018	ḥmḥm	to withdraw; inhibit (of step)
		105630	ḥmḥm	flight?
		140700	sḥmi̯	to put a stop to

DRID 1000558 ḥmn several

RID	**0000674**	ḥmn several		
	ID Lexemes	105580	ḥmn	a number of; several; some
		854643	ḥmn	several; some

DRID 1000559 ḥmr donkey

RID	**0000675**	ḥmr donkey		
	ID Lexemes	854615	ḥmr	donkey

DRID 1000560 ḥmr throne

RID	**0000676**	ḥmr throne		
	ID Lexemes	105590	ḥmr	seat; throne

DRID 1000564 ḥmsi̯ to sit down

RID	**0000680**	ḥmsi̯ to sit down		
	ID Lexeme	105690	ḥms	phallus
		105670	ḥms	sloth
		105700	ḥms	base (of a vessel)?
		857287	ḥms	court session
		851289	ḥms.y	commensal
		105740	ḥms.t	the one who sits

		105730	ḥms.t	seat (i.e. rank; status)
		105720	ḥms.t	session
		852032	ḥms.t	Hemset [a kind of a pendant]
		105680	ḥmsi̯	one who sits
		856442	ḥmsi̯	to start doing something (aux /modal)
		105780	ḥmsi̯	to sit; to sit down; to occupy
		853281	ḥmsi̯	the one who sits
		857667	sḥmsi̯	to sit; to let yourself be seated
		30680	jḥms	(household) servant

DRID 1000567 ḥmt ore

RID	**0000683**	ḥmt ore		
	ID Lexemes	450114	ḥmt	copper; copper ore; ore (gen.)
		855732	ḥmt.j	miner; metal-worker
		865673	ḥmt.j	cupreous
		600034	ḥmt.j	miner; metal-worker
RID	**0000687**	ḥmtj cymbals		
	ID Lexemes	105830	ḥmtj	(a pair of) cymbals (or gongs?)

DRID 1000570 ḥmu̯ to be skilled

RID	**0000688**	ḥmu̯ to be skilled		
	ID Lexemes	105280	ḥmy.t	[a stone implement]
		105330	ḥmu̯	to be skilled; to be skillful
		105470	ḥmu̯.w	skillful
		105500	ḥmw.w	crafts
		450166	ḥmw.w	manufacture
		105480	ḥmw.w	craftsman; carpenter
		105380	ḥmw.t	skilled one; expert
		104790	ḥmw.t	workshop
		105360	ḥmw.t	craftsmen
		105350	ḥmw.t	skill; craft; craftsmanship
		855575	ḥmw.tj	craftsman
		105390	ḥmw.tj	craftsman
		140740	sḥmu̯	to let one become skilled

DRID 1000571 ḥmw abrasive sand?

RID	**0000689**	ḥmw abrasive sand?		
	ID Lexemes	860957	ḥmw.t	abrasive sand?

DRID 1000572 ḥmw weapon

RID	**0000690**	ḥmw weapon		
	ID Lexemes	856207	ḥmw	weapon

DRID 1000574 ḥmz to slaughter

RID	**0000692**	ḥmz to slaughter		
	ID Lexemes	105640	ḥmz	to slaughter

DRID	**1000575**	**ḥmꜣ [plant]**		
RID	**0000693**	ḥmꜣ [plant]		
	ID Lexemes	105100	ḥmꜣ.yt	[a plant (fenugreek?)]
		105080	ḥmꜣ.w	[a plant (fenugreek?)]
DRID	**1000576**	**ḥmꜣ ball**		
RID	**0000694**	ḥmꜣ ball		
	ID Lexemes	105090	ḥmꜣ.w	[swelling? tumor? (med.)]
		105030	ḥmꜣ	ball
		105180	ḥmꜣ	ball-like
DRID	**1000577**	**ḥmꜣ salt**		
RID	**0000695**	ḥmꜣ salt		
	ID Lexemes	105070	ḥmꜣ.t	salt
		105170	ḥmꜣ.tj	salty places? [of heavenly paths]
DRID	**1000578**	**ḥmꜣg [scales]**		
RID	**0000696**	ḥmꜣg [scales]		
	ID Lexemes	105140	ḥmꜣg	[scales]
DRID	**1000579**	**ḥmꜣg garnet?**		
RID	**0000697**	ḥmꜣg garnet?		
	ID Lexemes	105160	ḥmꜣg.t	[a red-colored, semi-precious stone (garnet?)]
DRID	**1000580**	**ḥmꜣg to surround**		
RID	**0000698**	ḥmꜣg to surround		
	ID Lexemes	105120	ḥmꜣg	to encompass
		105130	ḥmꜣg	[epithet of Osiris]
DRID	**1000581**	**ḥmꜣṯ a cord?**		
RID	**0000699**	ḥmꜣṯ a cord?		
	ID Lexemes	105190	ḥmꜣṯṯ	[a cord?]
DRID	**1000584**	**ḥn [bird]**		
RID	**0000702**	ḥn [bird]		
	ID Lexemes	105950	ḥn	[a bird]
		106080	ḥn.tj	kingfisher?
DRID	**1000585**	**ḥn [jar] 0000703**		
RID	**0000703**	ḥn [jar]		
	ID Lexemes	106280	ḥn.w	jar; chattel(s)
DRID	**1000591**	**ḥn pelican**		
RID	**0000708**	ḥn pelican		
	ID Lexeme	500197	ḥn.t	Pelican Goddess
		106020	ḥn.t	pelican

DRID	**1000598**	**ḥn to be fresh**			
	RID	**0000716**	ḥn to be fresh		
		ID Lexeme	105860	ḥn	to grow (of lotus)
			856836	ḥn	[waters, or basin?]
			105920	ḥn	to be fresh; to provide with
			106060	ḥn.t	[waters (in the sky)]
			106050	ḥn.t	pool; lake
			106090	ḥn.t	palm; irrigation channel
			855121	ḥn.tj	the one belonging to the Henet waters
			105850	ḥnj	[a plant of the marshes (sedge?)]
			875732	ḥnw	[plant]
	RID	**0000742**	ḥnḥn to grow		
		ID Lexeme	106960	ḥnḥn	vitality
			857000	ḥnḥn	dawdler
			106970	ḥnḥn.t	[a swelling (med.)]
DRID	**1000599**	**ḥn to block**			
	RID	**0000717**	ḥn to block		
		ID Lexeme	105890	ḥn	to obstruct
			106310	ḥnw	obstruction?
			106360	ḥnw.t	casket
			106390	ḥnw.t	[obstruction? (med.)]
			106460	ḥnwy.t	Grain usury
	RID	**0000740**	ḥnḥn to block		
		ID Lexeme	106950	ḥnḥn	from forgetting (or the like of the name)
DRID	**1000602**	**ḥn to hurry**			
	RID	**0000720**	ḥn to hinder		
		ID Lexeme	105940	ḥn	to draw back from
			140880	sḥn	to repel
			860652	sḥn.tj	one who hurries back
	RID	**0000721**	ḥn to hurry		
		ID Lexeme	105930	ḥn	to go speedily; to journey
			854531	ḥn	to go speedily; to journey
			106150	ḥn.w	rising? (of the wind)
	RID	**0000743**	ḥnḥn to hinder		
			106930	ḥnḥn	to hinder; to detain
			106940	ḥnḥn	[an affliction of the legs (med.)]
			500885	ḥnḥn.yt	She who is detained
			140950	sḥnḥn	to let it retreat
DRID	**1000603**	**ḥn to jubilate**			
	RID	**0000722**	ḥn to jubilate		
		ID Lexeme	105980	ḥn	to hail

		106330	ḥn.w	jubilation
DRID	**1000604**	**ḥn to look at**		
RID	**0000723**	ḥn to look at		
	ID Lexeme	105970	ḥn	to look at (or similar)
DRID	**1000605**	**ḥn to protect**		
RID	**0000718**	ḥn to command		
	ID Lexeme	851162	ḥn	order, mission
		853138	ḥn.w	military commander
		854850	ḥn.wt	mistress
		106350	ḥn.wt	mistress; lady
		868460	ḥn.wt	order
		853139	ḥn.wtj	servant
		106000	ḥn.t	orders; command
		107440	ḥn.tw	commander (mil.)
		140790	sḥn	order; commission
		140820	sḥn	commander (Thoth)
		140810	sḥn	commander; officer
		140780	sḥn	to command; to provide
RID	**0000725**	ḥn to protect		
	ID Lexeme	105880	ḥn	[a protective container]
		105900	ḥn	to equip; to protect; to command
		865700	ḥn.w	ribs
		106030	ḥn.t	[sanctuary of Neith]
		106120	ḥn.tj	ends; limits
		106320	ḥnw	[a crown]
		140850	sḥn	[structure associated with Min-Horus]
		140800	sḥn	benefit; endowment; allocation
		140870	sḥn	crown
		140860	sḥn	to crown; to adorn
		140930	sḥn.yt	product
		140890	sḥn.t	[structure associated with Min, with Amun]
DRID	**1000606**	**ḥnb solar?**		
RID	**0000726**	ḥnb solar?		
	ID Lexeme	106580	ḥnb.w	[designation of the sun's rays]
		106660	ḥnb.w	[a kind of a solar bark]
DRID	**1000607**	**ḥnb to measure**		
RID	**0000727**	ḥnb to measure		
	ID Lexeme	106470	ḥnb	to survey
		106480	ḥnb	arable land
		500215	ḥnb.y	Measurer
		106540	ḥnb.t	measured parcel of land; meadow; garden

			106530	ḥnb.t	bread ration
			500651	ḥnb.tj	who belongs to the lot of land
			500853	ḥnb.tjt	one which belongs to the lot of land
			106570	ḥnb.tjt	farmland?
DRID	**1000608**	**ḥnb to repel**			
	RID	**0000728**	ḥnb to repel		
		ID Lexeme	106490	ḥnb	to drive away (from)
			106680	ḥnbb	wind
			106690	ḥnbb	to slay (offering animals)
DRID	**1000616**	**ḥkk to swallow**			
	RID	**0000634**	ḥkk to swallow sth.		
		ID Lexeme	110910	ḥkk	to swallow sth. (or similar)
DRID	**1000617**	**ḥngg gullet**			
	RID	**0000737**	ḥngg gullet		
		ID Lexeme	868472	ḥng	slaver
			107350	ḥngg	gullet
DRID	**1000623**	**ḥnk to braid**			
	RID	**0000751**	ḥnk to braid		
		ID Lexeme	107150	ḥnk	papyrus float
			856846	ḥnk	pigtailer
			107240	ḥnk.yt	bed; bed linens?
			107050	ḥnk.yt	with braided hair
			107220	ḥnk.t	braided lock of hair
			856847	ḥnk.tj	pigtailer
			107040	ḥnk.tj	He with (braided) side lock
			107300	ḥnk.tj	braided one (uraeus)
			854751	ḥnk.tj	provided with a hair braid; pigtailed
			853605	ḥnk.tjw	Those with braided hair (pl.)
			856848	ḥnk.tjt	pigtailed
			107310	ḥnk.tyt	one with braided hair (Hathor; Isis; Nephthys)
			853606	ḥnk.tyty	the two with braided hair (Isis and Nephthys)
DRID	**1000624**	**ḥnk to present**			
	RID	**0000752**	ḥnk to present		
		ID Lexeme	107180	ḥnk	donated land; donation
			107120	ḥnk	[an offering vessel]
			107140	ḥnk	[kind of an offering]
			107110	ḥnk	to present (a gift); to offer
			107160	ḥnk	cluster? (of dates) (as a unit of

					measure)
			107250	ḥnk.yt	(diplomatic) gifts
			107260	ḥnk.w	scale-pan (of a balance)
			107210	ḥnk.t	bedchamber
			107200	ḥnk.t	companion
			107190	ḥnk.t	offerings; donation
			855703	mḥnk	intimate?
			74120	mḥnk	rewarded person; intimate

DRID 1000626 ḥnm go around?

RID	**0000753**	ḥnm go around?		
	ID Lexeme	106740	ḥnmw	go around?

DRID 1000633 ḥnmm mankind

RID	**0000761**	ḥnmm mankind		
	ID Lexeme	106750	ḥnmm.t	sunfolk (of Heliopolis); humankind

DRID 1000635 ḥnn blossom of date palm

RID	**0000763**	ḥnn blossom of date palm		
	ID Lexeme	106820	ḥnn	[part of a date (med.)]

DRID 1000638 ḥnn phallus

RID	**0000766**	ḥnn phallus		
	ID Lexeme	500658	ḥnn.j	He with the phallus
		106810	ḥnn	phallus

DRID 1000640 ḥnn to hoe

RID	**0000768**	ḥnn to hoe		
	ID Lexeme	858516	ḥnḥn	to tear up
		106800	ḥnn	to hoe
		106790	ḥnn	hoe

DRID 1000644 ḥnḳ to ferment

RID	**0000772**	ḥnḳ to ferment		
	ID Lexeme	110300	ḥnq.t	beer
		107070	ḥnḳ	foam; ferment?

DRID 1000651 ḥnrg to quake

RID	**0000779**	ḥnrg to quake		
	ID Lexeme	106910	ḥnrg	to quake; to be embarrassed

DRID 1000654 ḥns to be narrow

RID	**0000783**	ḥns to be narrow		
	ID Lexeme	106990	ḥns	narrow; constricted
		400975	ḥns	to be narrow; to be constricted
		140960	sḥns	to narrow

DRID 1000659 ḥnt scale?

RID 0000789 ḥnt scale?

ID Lexeme		
855842	ḥnt	scale?; spike?

DRID 1000660 ḥnti̯ to be greedy

RID 0000791 ḥnti̯ to be greedy

ID Lexeme		
851645	ḥnty	Greedy One (crocodile)
107400	ḥnti̯	to be covetous; to be greedy
851907	ḥnt	greed
107390	ḥntj	greedy one (enemy of gods manifested as a crocodile) (of Seth and other gods)

DRID 1000661 ḥnṯi̯ to butcher

RID 0000792 ḥnṯi̯ to butcher

ID Lexeme		
855001	ḥnṯ.t	slaughter
858541	ḥnṯ.tj	butcher
107480	ḥnṯ.tj	butcher
500355	ḥnṯ.tjw	Those who butcher
107470	ḥnṯi̯	to butcher (animals); to kill (enemies)

DRID 1000663 ḥntꜣ porcupine?

RID 0000794 ḥntꜣ porcupine?

ID Lexeme		
107370	ḥntꜣ	breastbone; sternum
107360	ḥntꜣ	an animal (porcupine?) (med.)
107410	ḥntj	an animal with spines (porcupine?) (med.)
106140	ḥntj	[a boat]

DRID 1000664 ḥntꜣsw lizard

RID 0000795 ḥntꜣsw lizard

ID Lexeme		
107380	ḥntꜣsw	lizard

DRID 1000665 ḥnw [jug]

RID 0000796 ḥnw [jug]

ID Lexeme		
106340	ḥnw.t	[a jug (for beer, for wine)]

DRID 1000667 ḥnw horn

RID 0000798 ḥnw horn

ID Lexeme		
106370	ḥnw.t	horn
856857	ḥnw.tj	Horned one

DRID 1000670 ḥny spear

RID 0000801 ḥny spear

ID Lexeme		
106190	ḥny.t	spear; javelin

DRID 1000672 ḥnᶜ together with

RID	**0000803**	ḥnᶜ together with		
	ID Lexeme	106200	ḥnᶜ	together with
		106240	ḥnᶜ	therewith
		850800	ḥnᶜ	[preposition]
		550300	ḥnᶜ	and
		850771	ḥnᶜ.j	therewith; nearby
		106260	ḥnᶜ.w	accumulation (in a description of a med. condition)

DRID 1000676 ḥpd to open

RID	**0000807**	ḥpd to open		
	ID Lexeme	104320	ḥpd	to open (the mouth)
		62990	ptḥ	to open

DRID 1000677 ḥpg to dance

RID	**0000808**	ḥpg to dance		
	ID Lexeme	104200	ḥpg	to dance

DRID 1000685 ḥpt to embrace

RID	**0000818**	ḥpt to embrace		
	ID Lexeme	104050	ḥp.t	[crown; diadem]
		104080	ḥp.tj	[extreme limits (of the earth)]
		104230	ḥpt	to embrace; to enclose
		104240	ḥpt	reel? (of thread; of twine)
		104220	ḥpt	embrace; armful
		104300	ḥpt.w	mast step (naut.)
		104290	ḥpt.w	crosspieces at the door
		500325	ḥpt.w	Embracer
		140670	sḥpt	embrace

DRID 1000689 ḥḳr to be hungry

RID	**0000822**	ḥḳr to be hungry		
	ID Lexeme	110570	ḥḳr	famine
		110550	ḥḳr	hungry man
		110560	ḥḳr	hunger
		110540	ḥḳr	to be hungry; to fast (med.)
		110600	ḥḳr.w	famine
		110590	ḥqr.t	those who are hungry
		141100	sḥqr	to starve; to make hungry

DRID 1000692 ḥqꜣ bushel

RID	**0000825**	ḥqꜣ bushel		
	ID Lexeme	600004	ḥqꜣ.tj	double-bushel (20 hin)
		110440	ḥqꜣ.t	bushel (a corn measure, 10 hin)

DRID 1000693 ḥqꜣ to rule

RID	**0000826**	ḥqꜣ to rule		
	ID Lexeme	853727	ḥqꜣ	ruler
		110360	ḥqꜣ	ruler; chief
		110340	ḥqꜣ	to rule; to govern
		110420	ḥqꜣ.t	uraeus
		110430	ḥqꜣ.t	[a priest]
		110380	ḥqꜣ.t	(crook-like) scepter
		110390	ḥqꜣ.t	ruler
		110400	ḥqꜣ.t	rulership
		141090	sḥqꜣ	to install as ruler
DRID	**1000695**	**ḥr canal?**		
RID	**0000828**	ḥr canal?		
	ID Lexeme	108370	ḥr	canal?
DRID	**1000697**	**ḥr face**		
RID	**0000830**	ḥr face		
	ID Lexeme	107510	ḥr	face; sight
		107600	ḥr	face (a mirror)
		107760	ḥr.w	people
		86177	ḥr.wj	two faces
		86500	nḥr	to be like; to resemble
RID	**0000833**	ḥr on, upon		
	ID Lexeme	400091	ḥr	at (the time of); in (temp.duration)
		107530	ḥr	because
		400090	ḥr	on; upon; up
		107580	ḥr	diameter
		108310	ḥr.j	supervisor; chieftain
		108320	ḥr.j	[part of the head]
		108450	ḥr.j	Lid (of a smoking device)
		108300	ḥr.j	being upon; being above; uppermost
		108330	ḥr.j	the upper (Mortuary temple with pyramid)
		108480	ḥr.jw	[those who are above (birds)]
		108470	ḥr.jw	[those who are above (stars)]
		108380	ḥr.jt	topmost
		108990	ḥr.w	upper part; top
		107670	ḥr.t	heaven
		107710	ḥr.t	offering table
		107660	ḥr.t	path
		107640	ḥr.t	tomb; necropolis
		107680	ḥr.t	roof (of a temple)
		107650	ḥr.t	high inundation
		107630	ḥr.t	upper side
		500280	ḥr.tj	Heavenly one
RID	**0000867**	ḥrti̯ to travel overland		
	ID Lexeme	107720	ḥrti̯	to travel overland

DRID	**1000699**	**ḥr lump of lapis lazuli**		
RID	**0000832**	ḥr lump of lapis lazuli		
	ID Lexeme	107740	ḥr.tt	lump (of semi-precious stone)
DRID	**1000701**	**ḥr rope**		
RID	**0000835**	ḥr rope		
	ID Lexeme	856905	ḥr.t	rope
		107540	ḥr	steering rope
DRID	**1000703**	**ḥꜣi̯ to uncover**		
RID	**0001044**	ḥꜣi̯ to uncover		
	ID Lexeme	100710	ḥꜣi̯	to bare; to be naked
		100790	ḥꜣ.yt	nakedness
		101050	ḥꜣ.w	naked man
		100900	ḥꜣ.wtj	naked man
		140390	sḥꜣi̯	to strip; to reveal
DRID	**1000704**	**ḥr to be ready**		
RID	**0000840**	ḥr to be ready		
	ID Lexeme	107560	ḥr	to be ready (to do something); to make ready
DRID	**1000707**	**ḥr to guard**		
RID	**0000849**	ḥrḥr to guard		
	ID Lexeme	109180	ḥrḥr	to guard; to keep
DRID	**1000708**	**ḥr to rejoice**		
RID	**0000850**	ḥrḥr to rejoice		
	ID Lexeme	861073	nḥrnḥr	to rejoice
		86560	nḥrḥr	to rejoice
DRID	**1000712**	**ḥri̯ to be distant**		
RID	**0000852**	ḥri̯ to be distant		
	ID Lexeme	856921	ḥr.t	the distant one
		108340	ḥri̯	to be far (from); to remove (oneself)
		108350	ḥri̯	to fly (to heaven)
		140990	sḥrr.t	one who is removed
		140970	sḥr	he who exorcises evil (protector of Osiris)
		856046	sḥr	to remove
		140980	sḥri̯	(to drive away; to exorcise (evil); to make distant)
DRID	**1000713**	**ḥri̯ to frighten**		
RID	**0000853**	ḥri̯ to frighten		

	ID Lexeme	859816	ḥr.yw	enemies
		108390	ḥr.yt	fear; dread
		109010	ḥr.w	terror; dread, respect
		108360	ḥri̯	to dread; to instill dread

DRID 1000715 ḥrj melting oven

RID 0000873 ḥry melting oven

ID Lexeme	108400	ḥry.t	melting oven

DRID 1000718 ḥrp dagger

RID 0000857 ḥrp dagger

ID Lexeme	109060	ḥrp	dagger; short sword

DRID 1000722 ḥrr flower

RID 0000861 ḥrr flower

ID Lexeme	500497	ḥrr.tj	He who belongs to the flower
	109110	ḥrr.t	flower
	109080	ḥrr	to roar

DRID 1000725 ḥrr worm

RID 0000864 ḥrr worm

ID Lexeme	109120	ḥrr.t	small creeping and/or crawling creatures (generic term); worm (med.)

DRID 1000727 ḥrs carnelian

RID 0000866 ḥrs carnelian

ID Lexeme	109210	ḥrst	to make red (eyes, with rage); to be red (eyes, with rage)
	109190	ḥrs.t	carnelian
	109200	ḥrs.t	rage

DRID 1000734 ḥry dung

RID 0000872 ḥry dung

ID Lexeme	108410	ḥry.t	dung

DRID 1000736 ḥs defecate?

RID 0000875 ḥs defecate?

ID Lexeme	74140	mḥs	[an external illness affecting the head]
	74150	mḥs	sterile; impotent
	74160	mḥsḥs	[designation of a person]
	858423	ḥs	to stain
	109370	ḥs	excrement

DRID 1000738 ḥs to be closed

RID 0000877 ḥs to be closed

		ID Lexeme	600609 ḥs	closed (with a string)
DRID	**1000739**	**ḥs to be cold**		
	RID	**0000878**	ḥs to be cold	
		ID Lexeme	109690 ḥs	to be cold
			109700 ḥs	he who is cold
			109710 ḥs.y	frost, cold
DRID	**1000740**	**ḥsb cross band**		
	RID	**0000879**	ḥsb cross band	
		ID Lexeme	109850 ḥsb	cross band
DRID	**1000741**	**ḥsb to break**		
	RID	**0000880**	ḥsb to break	
		ID Lexeme	109830 ḥsb	fracture (of a bone) (med.)
			109820 ḥsb	to break
DRID	**1000742**	**ḥsb to count**		
	RID	**0000881**	ḥsb to count	
		ID Lexeme	450206 ḥsb	accounting; distribution
			109880 ḥsb	enlistee (for compulsory work)
			109860 ḥsb	one quarter of an aroura
			860396 ḥsb	ground
			109870 ḥsb	to count; to reckon; to distribute
			109940 ḥsb.w	accounting; reckoning
			109950 ḥsb.w	square fields (to be drawn on the floor)
			109960 ḥsb.w	worker
			868520 ḥsb.t	calculation
			109910 ḥsb.t	portion (of quota achieved)
			550010 ḥsb.t	quota
DRID	**1000744**	**ḥsb to slaughter**		
	RID	**0000883**	ḥsb to slaughter	
		ID Lexeme	109890 ḥsb	to slaughter
			109840 ḥsb	[to hunt with a throwstick]
			450272 ḥsb.w	Slaughtered(-steer) (11th nome of Lower Egypt)
			109920 ḥsb.t	knife
DRID	**1000750**	**ḥsi̯ to sing**		
	RID	**0000889**	ḥsi̯ to sing	
		ID Lexeme	109680 ḥsi̯	to sing; to make music
			109430 ḥs.w	singer
			855743 ḥs.w	singer
			855744 ḥs.t	singer
			109400 ḥs.t	singer

			109390	ḥs.t	song; singing
DRID	**1000753**		**ḥsḳ to cut off**		
	RID	**0000892**	to cut off		
		ID Lexeme	110220	ḥsḳ.t	knife
			110210	ḥsḳ	"the cutter" (demon)
			110230	ḥsḳ	"what is cut off" (the head)
			110200	ḥsḳ	to cut off (the head); to cut out (the heart)
			856932	ḥsḳ	butcher
DRID	**1000757**		**ḥsꜣ thread**		
	RID	**0000896**	ḥsꜣ thread		
		ID Lexemes	109550	ḥsꜣ	thread
DRID	**1000760**		**ḥt [part of the eye]**		
	RID	**0000899**	ḥt [part of the eye]		
		ID Lexemes	861075	ḥtj.t	[part of the eye]
			111010	ḥt	[part of the eye (duct?)]
DRID	**1000762**		**ḥt comb**		
	RID	**0000901**	ḥt comb		
		ID Lexemes	111000	ḥt	comb [verb describing an activity related to the hair]
DRID	**1000764**		**ḥṯ hyena**		
	RID	**0000903**	ḥṯ hyena		
		ID Lexemes	851409	ḥṯ.w	The Hyenas (domain)
			112040	ḥṯ.t	hyena
DRID	**1000767**		**ḥṯ to place in**		
	RID	**0000905**	ḥṯ to place in		
		ID Lexemes	112030	ḥṯ	[a block of stone of a particular shape or size (facing block?)]
			112010	ḥṯ	to overlay; to inlay
DRID	**1000776**		**ḥtj smoke**		
	RID	**0000918**	ḥtj smoke		
		ID Lexemes	111130	ḥtj	smoke (rising from the offering table)
DRID	**1000777**		**ḥtm [an animal]**		
	RID	**0000920**	ḥtm [an animal]		
		ID Lexemes	111680	ḥtm.t	[animal native to Syria (hyena? bear?)]
DRID	**1000778**		**ḥtm chair**		

	RID	**0000921**	ḥtm chair	
		ID Lexemes	111700 ḥtm.t	chair
DRID	**1000779**	**ḥtm to destroy**		
	RID	**0000922**	ḥtm to destroy	
		ID Lexemes	111640 ḥtm	what should be destroyed [Seth as hippopotamus]
			111600 ḥtm	to destroy; to be destroyed
			111590 ḥtm	to provide with; to complete
			500195 ḥtm	destruction
			858510 ḥtm	provider
			111620 ḥtm	destroyer
			111630 ḥtm	the one to be destroyed (designation of the serpent hostile to the sun god)
			111610 ḥtm	to pay (a debt)
			97540 ḥtm	ravaging; destroying
			111760 ḥtm.yw	Destroyed ones
			111750 ḥtm.yt	place of execution (in the netherworld)
			853539 ḥtm.yt	annihilation?
			853092 ḥtm.w	destroyer
			111740 ḥtm.wt	The Destroying one
			111770 ḥtm.wt	She who provides
			111720 ḥtm.tj	[designation of Apophis]
			141190 sḥtm	to destroy
			141210 sḥtm.w	destroyer
			857668 sḥtm.wt	destruction
DRID	**1000782**	**ḥtp blood**		
	RID	**0000925**	ḥtp blood	
		ID Lexeme	111330 ḥtp	blood
DRID	**1000783**	**ḥtp to rest**		
	RID	**0000926**	ḥtp to offer	
		ID Lexeme	856944 ḥtp	god of offering
			400524 ḥtp	offering (gen.)
			111300 ḥtp	basket
			111310 ḥtp	floral offering
			854532 ḥtp	food offerings
			111320 ḥtp	incense
			111210 ḥtp	offering table
			859941 ḥtp	to make gift
			111220 ḥtp	food offerings
			111530 ḥtp.y	priest
			111520 ḥtp.y	Provided with offerings
			500890 ḥtp.wj	Two offering tables
			111380 ḥtp.t	priestess

			111360	ḥtp.t	offerings
			111410	ḥtp.t	bundle (of herbs) as offering
			111400	ḥtp.t	bowl (for bread)
			111430	ḥtp.tjw	[ones who have to do with offerings]
			500212	ḥtp.tjw	[ones who are provided with offerings (the blessed dead)]
			141140	sḥtp	[a kind of incense]
			141160	sḥtp	offering table
			141150	sḥtp	[a kind of bread]
			863435	sḥtp	[a part of a plant]
			141170	sḥtp.y	arm-like censer
	RID	**0000927**	ḥtp to please		
		ID Lexeme	852773	ḥtp	the content one
			111250	ḥtp	mercy
			111290	ḥtp	Contented One
			111230	ḥtp	to be pleased; to be content; to make content; to set (of the sun)
			111560	ḥtp.yw	the peaceful one
			111550	ḥtp.yt	Merciful One
			111260	ḥtp.w	peace; contentment
			111370	ḥtp.t	peace
			141120	sḥtp	to propitiate; to please; to satisfy
			141180	sḥtp.y	the pleased one [name of the deceased Osiris]
	RID	**0000928**	ḥtp to rest		
		ID Lexeme	500193	ḥtp.w	setting (of the sun)
DRID	**1000785**	**ḥtr to bind together**			
	RID	**0000930**	ḥtr to bind together		
		ID Lexeme	111810	ḥtr	team of horses; steeds; chariotry
			600012	ḥtr	pair
			111880	ḥtr	bird cage
			111840	ḥtr	revenue; wages
			111790	ḥtr	twin
			111800	ḥtr	yoke of oxen; team (gen.)
			111850	ḥtr	lashings
			111860	ḥtr	to bind together
			111830	ḥtr	to tax; to assess
			111910	ḥtr.w	tax collector
			111820	ḥtr.w	door jambs
	RID	**0000929**	ḥtr [basketwork]		
		ID Lexeme	600478	ḥtr	[basketwork]
DRID	**1000786**	**ḥts to accomplish**			
	RID	**0000931**	ḥts to accomplish		
		ID Lexeme	111960	ḥts	to bury; to conceal
			111940	ḥts	to complete

		111930	ḥts	[object given by the king to a god in ritual scene]

DRID 1000787 ḥṯṯ armpit?

RID	**0000932**	ḥṯṯ armpit?		
	ID Lexeme	112150	ḥṯṯ.t	mast-step? (naut.)
		112140	ḥṯṯ.t	armpit

DRID 1000789 ḥtw throat

RID	**0000935**	ḥtw throat		
	ID Lexeme	111170	ḥty.t	Breather
		111160	ḥty.t	throat
		869408	ḥty.t	needle
		111100	ḥty.t	end piece (terminal; of a broad collar?)
		855517	ḥtw	throat

DRID 1000790 ḥṯꜣ [a bread]

RID	**0000936**	ḥṯꜣ [a bread]		
	ID Lexeme	112070	ḥṯꜣ	[a kind of bread]

DRID 1000791 ḥtꜣ sail

RID	**0000937**	ḥtꜣ sail		
	ID Lexeme	111070	ḥtꜣ.w	sail
		111080	ḥtꜣ.wt	sail

DRID 1000792 ḥtꜣ to be shabby

RID	**0000938**	ḥtꜣ to be shabby		
	ID Lexeme	111060	ḥtꜣ.w	blotches (on the face) (med.)
		111040	ḥtꜣ	shabby; worn (of clothing, for example)

DRID 1000793 ḥw [the great sphinx of Giza]

RID	**0000939**	ḥw [the great sphinx of Giza]		
	ID Lexeme	102300	ḥw	[the great sphinx of Giza]

DRID 1000794 ḥw food

RID	**0000940**	ḥw food		
	ID Lexeme	102280	ḥw	food
		854333	ḥw	The Food

DRID 1000795 ḥw house

RID	**0000941**	ḥw house		
	ID Lexeme	852043	ḥw.wtj	one who belongs to estates
		99790	ḥw.t	(larger) house; estate (administrative unit); temple (“mansion”)

		102410	ḥw.t	verse
		852042	ḥw.tj	one who belongs to the estate
		857035	ḥw.tj(t)	He / She of the mansion
		102440	ḥw.tjw	those belonging to an estate

DRID 1000798 ḥw utterance

RID	**0000965**	ḥww to proclaim		
	ID Lexeme	500190	ḥw	Hu ("Utterance")
		102270	ḥw	utterance
		102260	ḥww	to proclaim
		855147	ḥww.t	report; announcement
		103000	ḥww.tj	messenger

DRID 1000805 ḥwi̯ to strike

RID	**0000949**	ḥwi̯ to collect		
	ID Lexeme	140560	sḥw	grouping (of personnel); assembly
		140550	sḥw	collection; assemblage; summary
		140500	sḥw	wrapping
		140540	sḥwi̯	to collect; to assemble
RID	**0000950**	ḥwi̯ to flow		
	ID Lexeme	102760	ḥy	flood
		100770	ḥꜣy.t	sheet of shallow inundation water overlying the ground
		100690	ḥꜣy	to overflow
		100700	ḥꜣy	flood
		855566	ḥw.t	rain
		102400	ḥw.t	rain; flood
		102750	ḥwi̯	to rain
		102740	ḥwi̯	to flow; to flood
		109240	ḥḥ	inundation water
RID 0000952		ḥwi̯ to strike		
	ID Lexeme	100680	ḥꜣy	to come
		100960	ḥꜣy.w	[designation of a bird of prey]
		100920	ḥꜣy.tj	[designation of the two royal serpents]
		868373	ḥꜣy.tj	[a person who is hostile]
		101880	ḥy	inspector
		855342	ḥw	striking one
		102320	ḥw	driver; slugger; shepherd
		102800	ḥw.yt	chipped (from the millstone); stone flour (in medical use)
		102790	ḥw.yt	stroke; blow
		102450	ḥw.w	(class of) bulls; cattle (gen.)
		102420	ḥw.t	pig
		102360	ḥw.t	One who beats
		99810	ḥw.tt	mine; quarry

		102730	ḥwi̯	to strike; to drive; to tread
		854530	ḥwi̯	to beat; bump; to enter; flow; water; rain; consecrate
		102840	ḥwi̯	to gather (crops, the harvest)
		30620	jḥjḥ	[a noise in the water (bubble?)]
RID	**0000963**	ḥwtf to rob		
	ID Lexeme	103270	ḥwtf	to rob; to plunder
RID	**0000966**	ḥww washer?		
	ID Lexeme	102990	ḥww	washer?

DRID	**1000807**	**ḥwj happy song**		
RID	**0000953**	ḥwj happy song		
	ID Lexeme	102770	ḥwj	happy song

DRID	**1000808**	**ḥwn a cut of meat**		
RID	**0000954**	ḥwn a cut of meat		
	ID Lexeme	103070	ḥwn	[a cut of meat]

DRID	**1000809**	**ḥwn to be young**		
RID	**0000955**	ḥwn to be young		
	ID Lexeme	74010	mḥwn	poultry farm
		103060	ḥwn	childhood; youth
		103030	ḥwn	young man (priest's title in Dendera)
		103040	ḥwn	to become young; to be rejuvenated
		103050	ḥwn	youthful
		103020	ḥwn.w	child; youth; young man
		103110	ḥwn.w	young crocodile
		857045	ḥwn.w	pupil
		500417	ḥwn.w	the young one
		852272	ḥwn.wt	pupil
		855867	ḥwn.wt	young lioness
		103090	ḥwn.wt	young lioness (Tefnut)
		103080	ḥwn.wt	girl; maiden
		500613	ḥwn.wt	maiden (goddesses)
		103100	ḥwn.wtj	the two maidens (uraei)
		140580	sḥwn	to constrict
		140590	sḥwn	rejuvenate (the moon)

DRID	**1000811**	**ḥwrw to be weak**		
RID	**0000957**	ḥwrw to be weak		
	ID Lexeme	103200	ḥwrw	to speak evil?
		103190	ḥwrw	to be wretched; to be weak
		400950	ḥwrw	wretched; weak
		103150	ḥwrw	humble man; wretch
		103220	ḥwrr	poverty?
		140600	ḥwrw	to vilify; to reproach

		852704	ḥwrw	curse

DRID	**1000812**	**ḥwr^c to rob**		
RID	**0000958**	ḥwr^c to rob		
	ID Lexeme	103170	ḥwr^c	to rob; to plunder
		103180	ḥwr^c	robber (Seth, as a crocodile)
		856681	ḥwr^c	robber

DRID	**1000819**	**ḥwꜣ to rot**		
RID	**0000968**	ḥwꜣ to rot		
	ID Lexeme	102640	ḥwꜣ	to rot; to putrefy
		102660	ḥwꜣ.w	stench (of putrefication)
		102700	ḥwꜣ.wtj	He who belongs to the stench of putrefaction
		857040	ḥwꜣꜣ	putrefaction
		102680	ḥwꜣꜣ.t	rotten materials
		863039	sḥwꜣ.w	putrefaction product
		140530	sḥwꜣ	to make decay; to despair

DRID	**1000820**	**ḥw^c to be short**		
RID	**0000969**	ḥw^c to be short		
	ID Lexeme	102920	ḥw^c	to be short
		102930	ḥw^c	dwarf (“short man”)
		852813	ḥw^c	the short one
		140570	sḥw^c	to shorten (time)

DRID	**1000824**	**ḥz forearm**		
RID	**0000972**	ḥz forearm		
	ID Lexeme	109350	ḥz.t	forearm; animal leg

DRID	**1000826**	**ḥz water jar**		
RID	**0000974**	ḥz water jar		
	ID Lexeme	109330	ḥz.t	water jar; ewer (in ritual use)

DRID	**1000829**	**ḥzi̯ to praise**		
RID	**0000978**	ḥzi̯ to praise		
	ID Lexeme	109630	ḥz.y	statue
		856479	ḥz.y	the praised one
		109750	ḥz.y	praised one
		109660	ḥz.yt	praised one
		109760	ḥz.w	praised one
		852082	ḥz.w	spell
		109620	ḥzi̯	to praise; to favor
		109670	ḥzy.tj	favorite
		109800	ḥzw.t	favor; praise
		68730	ḥzw.tj	favorite
		110180	ḥzz.t	what is praise worthy

		141040	sḥzi̯	to enchant, to invoke

DRID	**1000830**	**ḥzi̯ to turn back**		
RID	**0000979**	ḥzi̯ to turn back		
	ID Lexeme	109640	ḥzi̯	to turn back; to turn away (the evil-doer)
DRID	**1000831**	**ḥzk [a priest]**		
RID	**0000980**	ḥzk [a priest]		
	ID Lexeme	110250	ḥzk.w	[a priest of Osiris in Abydos]
DRID	**1000832**	**ḥzmn amethyst**		
RID	**0000981**	ḥzmn amethyst		
	ID Lexeme	400018	ḥzmn	Amethyst-region (Wadi el-Hudi)
		110070	ḥzmn	amethyst
DRID	**1000833**	**ḥzmn bronze**		
RID	**0000982**	ḥzmn bronze		
	ID Lexeme	110060	ḥzmn	bronze
DRID	**1000834**	**ḥzmn to eat**		
RID	**0000983**	ḥzmn to eat		
	ID Lexeme	110050	ḥzmn	to drink; to eat
		110110	ḥzmn.w	[a meal]
DRID	**1000835**	**ḥzp garden**		
RID	**0000984**	ḥzp garden		
	ID Lexeme	109990	ḥzp	[corn Osiris]
		109980	ḥzp	garden (plot); meadow
		858669	ḥzp.t	garden product
DRID	**1000838**	**ḥzꜣ dough**		
RID	**0000988**	ḥzꜣ dough		
	ID Lexeme	109510	ḥzꜣ	dough; paste; mucus (med.)
		109500	ḥzꜣ	Nil god?; god of dough?
DRID	**1000839**	**ḥzꜣ to be wild**		
RID	**0000989**	ḥzꜣ to be wild		
	ID Lexeme	852665	ḥzꜣ	to be wild
		109520	ḥzꜣ	fierce
DRID	**1000843**	**ḥꜣ [a waterfowl]**		
RID	**0000993**	ḥꜣ [a waterfowl]		
	ID Lexeme	100250	ḥꜣ.t	[a kind of waterfowl]
DRID	**1000846**	**ḥꜣ behind**		
RID	**0000995**	ḥꜣ behind		
	ID Lexeme	73700	mḥꜣ	back of the head

			100110	ḥꜣ	back of the head
			100100	ḥꜣ	[relating to the foundation of buildings]
			100120	ḥꜣ	back (of something); exterior
			100130	ḥꜣ	behind; around
			100150	ḥꜣ	behind (in prepositions)
			400511	ḥꜣ	round about
			100140	ḥꜣ	(a)round
			100230	ḥꜣ	to stretch out (wings protectively)
			100660	ḥꜣ.j	surrounding; being behind
			100670	ḥꜣ.y	protector; helper
			101060	ḥꜣ.w	increase; surplus
			800061	ḥꜣ.w	except
			100850	ḥꜣy.t	rectangle?
			140380	sḥꜣ.w	[symptom of illness affecting the uterus]
DRID	**1000849**	**ḥꜣ front**			
	RID	**0000998**	ḥꜣ front		
		ID Lexeme	101180	ḥꜣ.wtj	first
			101200	ḥꜣ.wtjw	ancestors
			100380	ḥꜣ.t	Forward (a phyle)
			100350	ḥꜣ.t	[designation for wine]
			100360	ḥꜣ.t	[an amulet shaped like the forepart of a lion]
			100340	ḥꜣ.t	[choice (cuts of meat)]
			100310	ḥꜣ.t	forepart; beginning; foremost; best
			100320	ḥꜣ.t	before
			873176	ḥꜣ.t	bow, forepart
			100290	ḥꜣ.t	food?
			868364	ḥꜣ.tj	being in front
			101040	ḥꜣ.tjw	[fine-quality linen]
			100450	ḥꜣ.tjt	prow rope
			100440	ḥꜣ.tjt	best oil
			101130	ḥꜣw.t	face (of a god)
	RID	**0001013**	ḥꜣ water		
		ID Lexeme	100370	ḥꜣ.t	[designation for water]
			100330	ḥꜣ.t	[waters]
	RID	**0001045**	ḥꜣj bandage		
		ID Lexeme	863014	ḥꜣy.t	bandage
DRID	**1000850**	**ḥꜣ heart**			
	RID	**0001000**	ḥꜣ heart		
		ID Lexeme	100400	ḥꜣ.tj	heart
			100410	ḥꜣ.tj	[heart-shaped medal, for non-military achievement]
			863789	ḥꜣ.tjj	vessel ('belonging to the heart')
	RID	**0001032**	ḥꜣḥꜣ heart		

ID Lexeme 101510 ḥꜣḥꜣ [heart ailment]

DRID 1000861 ḥꜣ to land?

RID 0001010 ḥꜣ to land?

ID Lexeme 100180	ḥꜣ	to go ashore; to run aground (naut.)

DRID 1000862 ḥꜣ tomb

RID 0001012 ḥꜣ tomb

ID Lexeme 500463	ḥꜣ	He who belongs to the tomb
100280	ḥꜣ.t	tomb
100870	ḥꜣy.t	[room in a temple, shrine or sanctuary]
100880	ḥꜣy.t	embalming hall

DRID 1000869 ḥꜣb to catch

RID 0001020 ḥꜣb to catch

ID Lexeme 550435	ḥꜣb	bird catcher
850109	ḥꜣb	to fish
103350	ḥꜣb	catch (of fish, of fowl)
859013	ḥꜣb.t	bird catcher

DRID 1000871 ḥꜣb turquoise

RID 0001022 ḥꜣb turquoise

ID Lexeme 103340	ḥꜣb	turquoise

DRID 1000872 ḥꜣb festival

RID 0001023 ḥꜣbi̯ to be festive

ID Lexeme 103300	ḥꜣb	festival
103290	ḥꜣb	tent; kiosk
876143	ḥꜣb	triumph
868376	ḥꜣb.j	participants of a festival
103590	ḥꜣb.yt	festival offerings
103570	ḥꜣb.yt	festival pavilion
550080	ḥꜣb.ytj	one who is festive
401173	ḥꜣb.wj	pair of gods
103420	ḥꜣb.t	[part of a tomb; niche; festival kiosk]
856772	ḥꜣb.t	triumphant
103410	ḥꜣb.t	program (for a ritual service)
103310	ḥꜣbi̯	to triumph
103560	ḥꜣbi̯	to be in festival
854980	ḥꜣbi̯	to make a festival
140620	sḥꜣbi̯	to make festive
859386	ḥbn	to triumph

DRID 1000873 ḥꜣbi̯ to mourn

RID **0001024** ḥꜣbi̯ to mourn

ID Lexeme		
851405	ḥb	grief; sorrow
103320	ḥꜣbi̯	to mourn

DRID 1000875 ḥꜣd agitation

RID **0001026** ḥꜣd agitation

ID Lexeme		
101820	ḥꜣd.t	agitation

DRID 1000877 ḥꜣd to trap

RID **0001028** ḥꜣd to trap

ID Lexeme		
101770	ḥꜣd	trap (esp. for fish)
101780	ḥꜣd	to trap (fish)
101800	ḥꜣd.t	[a basket (also as a measure of capacity for vegetables)]
101810	ḥꜣd.t	basket; container (as a unit of capacity for vegetables)

DRID 1000879 ḥꜣg = ḥng to be glad

RID **0001030** ḥꜣg to be glad

ID Lexeme		
101610	ḥꜣg	to be glad
101630	ḥꜣgꜣg	to rejoice
107340	ḥngg	to rejoice

DRID 1000884 ḥꜣi̯ to mourn

RID **0001041** ḥꜣi̯ to mourn

ID Lexeme		
100060	ḥꜣ	lament?
856776	ḥꜣ.w	mourner
100260	ḥꜣ.t	worry
100650	ḥꜣi̯	to mourn; to screech; to dance (at the funeral)
100760	ḥꜣy.t	Mourner
100890	ḥꜣy.ty	the two mourners (Isis and Nephthys)
500559	ḥꜣy.ty	mourner
140400	sḥꜣ.w	wailers
856045	sḥꜣ.wt	group of wailers

DRID 1000886 ḥꜣi̯ to support

RID **0001043** ḥꜣi̯ to support

ID Lexeme		
856205	ḥꜣi̯	to support

RID **0001035** ḥꜣḥꜣ to support

ID Lexeme		
868391	ḥꜣḥꜣ	to support

DRID 1000887 ḥꜣj light

RID **0001046** ḥꜣj light

ID Lexeme		
100750	ḥꜣy	one who shines (sun god)
100730	ḥꜣy	to illumine; to light up

			100740	ḥꜣy	light
			100780	ḥꜣy.t	what shines (the sky)
			100800	ḥꜣy.t	light
			100810	ḥꜣy.t	one who shines (Hathor)
			100910	ḥꜣy.tj	the two lights (sun and moon)
			100930	ḥꜣy.tj	He who belongs to what shines (sun god)
			100940	ḥꜣy.tjt	one who shines (goddesses; Hathor)
			101750	ḥꜣ.tw	those who shine (demons)
			102830	ḥwy.tj	shining light
DRID	**1000889**	**ḥꜣk to truncate**			
	RID	**0001048**	ḥꜣk to truncate		
		ID Lexeme	101570	ḥꜣk	to truncate
DRID	**1000890**	**ḥꜣḳ to plunder**			
	RID	**0001059**	ḥꜣḳ to plunder		
		ID Lexeme	101540	ḥꜣḳ	captive (taken in war)
			101530	ḥꜣḳ	plunder
			101520	ḥꜣḳ	to plunder; to capture
			858991	ḥꜣq.w	booty maker
			101560	ḥꜣq.w	plunderer
			101550	ḥꜣq.t	plunder
DRID	**1000892**	**ḥꜣm path**			
	RID	**0001051**	ḥꜣm path		
		ID Lexeme	101450	ḥꜣm.t	path, road (or similar)
DRID	**1000895**	**ḥꜣm to catch**			
	RID	**0001054**	ḥꜣm to catch		
		ID Lexeme	101420	ḥꜣm	(yield of the) net; catch
			101400	ḥꜣm	to fish; to catch
			853529	ḥꜣm.w	fisherman
			101440	ḥꜣm.t	[designation for fishnet]
DRID	**1000898**	**ḥꜣp to hide**			
	RID	**0001057**	ḥꜣp to hide		
		ID Lexeme	501184	ḥꜣp	Veiled one
			101310	ḥꜣp	[secret place?]
			101300	ḥꜣp	to hide; to keep secret
			101320	ḥꜣp	[a priest]
			101370	ḥꜣp.wtj	scout
			101330	ḥꜣp.t	hiding place
			140410	sḥꜣp	to conceal
DRID	**1000899**	**ḥꜣt to blur**			

	RID	0001068	ḥꜣt to blur	
		ID Lexeme	101640 ḥꜣt	to be bleared (of the eyes)
			101680 ḥꜣtj	covering; garment
			101670 ḥꜣtj	[eye illness (bleariness)]
			858803 ḥꜣtj	to wrap; to coat; to encompass
			101690 ḥꜣtj	cloudiness
			856783 ḥꜣtj.j	the one who is blurred
DRID	**1000906**	**ḥꜣwj pole?**		
	RID	**0001075**	ḥꜣwj pole?	
		ID Lexeme	101270 ḥꜣwy.t	stake?; pole?; box?
DRID	**1000911**	**ḥꜣᶜ = ḥꜣy turmoil**		
	RID	**0001080**	ḥꜣᶜ turmoil	
		ID Lexeme	100990 ḥꜣᶜ.y	turmoil
			101000 ḥꜣᶜ.yt	turmoil
			856766 ḥꜣᶜ.wtj	creator of strive
			101010 ḥꜣᶜᶜ	to touch (of a boat on land)
	RID	**0004210**	ḥꜣy turmoil	
		ID Lexeme	100820 ḥꜣy.t	malady
			100840 ḥꜣy.t	restlessness (from sleep)
DRID	**1000914**	**ḥᶜ limb**		
	RID	**0001082**	ḥᶜ limb	
		ID Lexeme	859149 ḥᶜ	flesh
			450197 ḥᶜ.w	[a cut of meat (offering)]
			101950 ḥᶜ.w	flesh; limbs; body; self
			854529 ḥᶜ.w	flesh; limbs; body; self
DRID	**1000915**	**ḥᶜ staff**		
	RID	**0001083**	ḥᶜ staff	
		ID Lexeme	102130 ḥᶜ.w	staff
DRID	**1000917**	**ḥᶜb [an enemy]**		
	RID	**0001085**	ḥᶜb [an enemy]	
		ID Lexeme	102170 ḥᶜb.y	[designation for enemies]
DRID	**1000918**	**ḥᶜb to play**		
	RID	**0001086**	ḥᶜb to play	
		ID Lexeme	102160 ḥᶜb	to play
DRID	**1000923**	**ḥᶜnẖ to rotate**		
	RID	**0001092**	ḥᶜnẖ to rotate	
		ID Lexeme	102220 ḥᶜnẖ	to rotate, to turn, to twist?
DRID	**1000924**	**ḥᶜp flood**		
	RID	**0001093**	ḥᶜpj flood	

		ID Lexeme	102190 ḥꜥpj	the Nile; flood

DRID	**1000929**		**ḥꜥtj bed**	
	RID	**0001097**	ḥꜥtj bed	
		ID Lexeme	859513 ḥꜥtj	throne
			102230 ḥꜥtj	bed

DRID	**1000930**		**ḥꜥw fleet**	
	RID	**0001098**	ḥꜥw fleet	
		ID Lexeme	101990 ḥꜥw	fleet; cargo boat

DRID	**1000931**		**ḥꜥꜣ child**	
	RID	**0001099**	ḥꜥꜣ child	
		ID Lexeme	102050 ḥꜥꜣ	child

DRID	**1001128**		**ḥꜣk trapeze**	
	RID	**0001049**	ḥꜣk trapeze	
		ID Lexeme	101600 ḥꜣk.t	trapeze
			101580 ḥꜣk	[the shorter parallel side of the trapeze]

II.14 ḫ

DRID	**1000447**	**ḫ fire**			
	RID	**0000535**	ḫ fire		
		ID Lexeme	113020	ḫ.t	fire; flame
			113040	ḫ.tj	Fiery one (a serpent)
			868574	ḫ.tj	fiery
			113050	ḫ.tjt	fiery one (serpent, Sachmet)
DRID	**1000451**	**ḫb to slay**			
	RID	**0000540**	ḫb to slay		
		ID Lexeme	115410	ḫb	to annihilate
			115450	ḫb.t	place of execution
			115460	ḫb.t	fire
			851557	ḫb.tj	executed one
			115950	ḫb.tjw	Foe (also as a designation of Apophis)
			115610	ḫby.t	massacre
			115640	ḫbb	massacre
			115750	ḫbḫb	to trample; to slay
			115760	ḫbḫb	to slay
			500400	ḫbḫb.t	destruction
			115940	ḫbt	to punish (the enemy)
			854000	ḫbt.j	The one belonging to the flame
			113880	ḫꜣbb	slayers
DRID	**1000452**	**ḫb to slink into**			
	RID	**0000541**	ḫb to slink into		
		ID Lexeme	115720	ḫbḫ	to slink into
			861711	ḫbḫb	to slink into
			141980	sḫbḫ	to slink into
DRID	**1000454**	**ḫbḏ to hate**			
	RID	**0000543**	ḫbḏ to hate		
		ID Lexeme	852759	ḫbḏ	hateful one
			855504	ḫbḏ	to damage
			115990	ḫbḏ	to be displeased with; to be hateful
			858259	ḫbḏ.w	hateful one
			115980	ḫbḏ.t	what is hateful
DRID	**1000456**	**ḫbi̯ to dance**			
	RID	**0000552**	ḫbi̯ to dance		
		ID Lexeme	115380	ḫb	dancer
			401139	ḫb.t	dance
			115560	ḫbi̯	to dance
			115600	ḫby.t	dancers
			401138	ḫbb	dance

87090 nḫbi̯ to dance

DRID 1000457 ḫbi̯ to reduce

RID 0000545 ḫbḫb to draw back
ID Lexeme 137960 snḫbḫb to draw back (the door bolt)

RID 0000546 ḫbḫb to hobble
ID Lexeme 115730 ḫbḫb to hobble

RID 0000547 ḫbḫb to make leave
ID Lexeme 854354 sḫbḫb to cause to part

RID 0000548 ḫbḫb to move
ID Lexeme 858554 ḫbḫb to move; push away

RID 0000549 ḫbḫb to open
ID Lexeme 87190 ḫbḫb to open (door; door-bolt)

RID 0000553 ḫbi̯ to reduce
ID Lexeme 115430 ḫb.t reduction? (med.)
115570 ḫbi̯ to deduct; to reduce
115590 ḫbi̯ to gather (tribute); to exact (dues)

DRID 1000461 ḫbn crime

RID 0000557 ḫbn to commit a crime
ID Lexeme 115670 ḫbn.t crime; guilt; falseness
115680 ḫbn.tj criminal
115660 ḫbn to distort; to be criminal

DRID 1000465 ḫbr to join together

RID 0000561 ḫbr to join together
ID Lexeme 115700 ḫbr business, trading partner
859942 ḫbr to join together

DRID 1000467 ḫbs to hack

RID 0000564 ḫbs to hack
ID Lexeme 115830 ḫbs to plough (through water)
115820 ḫbs plough lands
115860 ḫbs [a bird (cormorant?)]
115810 ḫbs to hack up (the earth); to plough
115910 ḫbs.yt hoe

DRID 1000468 ḫbs to illuminate

RID 0000565 ḫbs to illuminate
ID Lexeme 113860 ḫbs (artificial) light (lamp; candle)
115800 ḫbs to illuminate

DRID 1000469 ḫbs wrongdoing

RID 0000567 ḫbs wrongdoing
ID Lexeme 115850 ḫbs wrongdoer (or similar)
115840 ḫbs violence?

DRID	**1000472**	**ḫbz tail**			
	RID	**0000571**	ḫbz tail		
		ID Lexeme	115780	ḫbz.t	tail
			115920	ḫbz.wt	divine beard
			115870	ḫbz.wtjw	bearded man
DRID	**1000473**	**ḫbꜣ to hack**			
	RID	**0000572**	ḫbꜣ in spite of		
		ID Lexeme	115510	ḫbꜣ	in spite of?
			115540	ḫbꜣ.tw	despite
	RID	**0000573**	ḫbꜣ to hack		
		ID Lexeme	115500	ḫbꜣ	loss
			115490	ḫbꜣ	to destroy; to diminish
DRID	**1000475**	**ḫd land register?**			
	RID	**0000576**	ḫd land register?		
		ID Lexeme	121980	ḫd.t	land register (or similar)
DRID	**1000484**	**ḫdi̯ to flow**			
	RID	**0000590**	ḫdi̯ to travel downstream		
		ID Lexeme	121950	ḫd	[canal in the Memphite nome]
			121940	ḫd	stream
			859285	ḫd	north
			122010	ḫdi̯	to flow
			122000	ḫdi̯	to travel downstream; to travel northwards
			143270	sḫdi̯	to flow to sth.
			143260	sḫdi̯	to make sail northwards
	RID	**0003469**	ḫdi̯ to be upside down		
		ID Lexeme	143300	sḫd.w	Those who are upside down (the damned, in the netherworld)
			143250	sḫd	to be upside down
			876569	sḫd	Upside-down walker
	RID	**0000584**	ḫdḫd to be upside down		
		ID Lexeme	143310	sḫdḫd	to be upside down
DRID	**1000496**	**ḫf to flow**			
	RID	**0000600**	ḫf to flow		
		ID Lexeme	855088	ḫf	to flood
			87200	nḫf	to pour
			87210	nḫf	cold sweat
	RID	**0000605**	ḫfḫf to cause to overflow		
		ID Lexeme	116700	ḫfḫf	to cause to overflow
			116730	ḫfḫf.w	Place of origin (of the north wind)
			116720	ḫfḫf.t	outburst
			116740	ḫfḫfj	to stream

DRID	**1000499**		**ḫf to see sth.**		
	RID	**0000602**	ḫf to see sth.		
		ID Lexeme	116580	ḫf	to see; to perceive
DRID	**1000504**		**ḫfnn [fruit]**		
	RID	**0000609**	ḫfnn [fruit]		
		ID Lexeme	116690	ḫfnn.wt	[fruits]
DRID	**1000505**		**ḫft vis-à-vis**		
	RID	**0000610**	ḫft vis-à-vis		
		ID Lexeme	400129	ḫft	when; at the time of
			400128	ḫft	at the time of; at the same time
			116760	ḫft	in front of (someone)
			400127	ḫft	in accordance with (a command)
			116761	ḫft	[preposition]
			116770	ḫft	when; while
			116800	ḫft.j	enemy
			856170	ḫft.jj	hostile; enemy
			116840	ḫft.w	accordingly
			116810	ḫft.t	enemy
DRID	**1000507**		**ḫfꜣ to feed**		
	RID	**0000612**	ḫfꜣ to feed		
		ID Lexeme	854806	ḫfꜣ	to feed
			116610	ḫfꜣ.t	food
DRID	**1000509**		**ḫfꜣi̯ to lighten**		
	RID	**0000615**	ḫfꜣi̯ to lighten		
		ID Lexeme	116590	ḫfꜣi̯	to lighten
			854697	ḫfꜣ.t	candlestick?; lamp?
DRID	**1000510**		**ḫfꜣꜣ riverbank**		
	RID	**0000616**	ḫfꜣꜣ riverbank		
		ID Lexeme	116620	ḫfꜣꜣ.t	riverbank
DRID	**1000511**		**ḫfꜥ to grasp**		
	RID	**0000617**	ḫfꜥ to grasp		
		ID Lexeme	116670	ḫfꜥ.t	Seizer (a serpent)
			116640	ḫfꜥ	fist; grasp
			116630	ḫfꜥ	to seize; to grasp
			116650	ḫfꜥ	bundle (i.e. a fist-full, of arrows)
DRID	**1000514**		**ḫḫ neck**		
	RID	**0000620**	ḫḫ neck		
		ID Lexeme	120510	ḫḫ	neck; throat
			860285	ḫḫ	neck; collar
			120530	ḫḫ	to weigh

DRID 1000532 ẖnr = ẖl to sting

RID 0000643 ẖnr = ẖl to sting

ID Lexeme	118380	ẖnr	fangs

DRID 1000537 ẖm dust

RID 0000648 ẖm dust

ID Lexeme	116870	ẖm	dusted one?
	116880	ẖm	[pulverized ingredient in incense]
	116860	ẖm	to be dry (as dust)
	117110	ẖm	[stone worker]
	860314	ẖm.w	dry grains
	117160	ẖm.w	dust

DRID 1000543 ẖm not to know

RID 0000654 ẖm not to know

ID Lexeme	116930	ẖm	shrine; sanctuary
	856275	ẖm	[a relic]
	116910	ẖm	to not know; to be ignorant of
	116920	ẖm	ignorant man
	117170	ẖm.w	those who do not know (Egypt) (i.e. Egypt's foes)
	116960	ẖm.w	sacred images
	116970	ẖm.wt	sacred images?; sacred beings?
	857242	jẖm.t	ignorant? [designation of a person]
	852146	sẖm	[a kind of a building (place of worship?)]
	142100	zẖm	sanctuary
	135620	smẖꜣ	to correct (a manuscript)
	135600	smẖ	to forget; to ignore

RID 0000666 ẖmẖm not to know

ID Lexeme	858766	ẖmẖm	to not know; to negate

DRID 1000553 ẖmi̯ to consume

RID 0000669 ẖmi̯ to consume

ID Lexemes	117050	ẖmi̯	to consume; eat

DRID 1000555 ẖmi̯ to oppose

RID 0000671 ẖmi̯ to oppose

ID Lexeme	500449	jẖm.tjw	Those who belong to the riverbank
	30870	jẖm.t	bank (of a river, of a fortress)
	858267	ẖm	destruction
	117070	ẖm.yw	overthrower
	868634	ẖm.wt	destruction
	117020	ẖmi̯	to overthrow; to demolish; to oppose
	400986	ẖmꜥ.w	debris
	858271	ẖmm	destroyer

142230 sẖm to founder?

DRID 1000557 ẖmn eight
RID 0000673 ẖmn eight
ID Lexeme
858273 ẖmnnw.t eight-thread garment
117250 ẖmn.yw Ogdoad (of Hermopolis)
854321 ẖmn.nw the eighth one
117200 ẖmn.j 8-thread weave (a quality of linen)
117220 ẖmn.t ogdoad
117240 ẖmn eight

DRID 1000566 ẖmt companion?
RID 0000682 ẖmt companion?
ID Lexemes
860850 ẖmt companion

DRID 1000568 ẖmt three
RID 0000684 ẖmt three
ID Lexemes
117290 ẖmt to treble; to do thrice
117320 ẖmt [a part of the bark "the third"]
117280 ẖmt.w three
117380 ẖmt.nj [a liquid diluted by a third?]
117400 ẖmt.nw [third month of the year]
117390 ẖmt.nw third one
117410 ẖmt.nw third

DRID 1000569 ẖmt to stab
RID 0000685 ẖmt to stab
ID Lexemes
117310 ẖmt to stab
117300 ẖmt spear; harpoon

DRID 1000534 ẖmt to think
RID 0000686 ẖmt to think
ID Lexemes
117360 ẖmt the thinker?
117340 ẖmt to plan; to intend

DRID 1000573 ẖmy sand-fly?
RID 0000691 ẖmy sand-fly?
ID Lexemes
117080 ẖmy sand-fly

DRID 1000582 ẖmꜣꜣ to shrivel
RID 0000700 ẖmꜣꜣ to shrivel
ID Lexemes
116990 ẖmꜣꜣ to be convulsed?; to have a convulsion?

DRID 1000583 ẖmᶜi̯ to seize
RID 0000701 ẖmᶜi̯ to seize
ID Lexemes
117130 ẖmᶜ.t blade (or handle?) (of an oar)

		117090 ḫmꜥi̯	to seize; to grasp	
DRID	**1000589**	**ḫn disgusting**		
RID	**0000710**	ḫn rebel		
	ID Lexemes	117500 ḫn	rebel	
		117510 ḫn	revolting	
RID	**0000724**	ḫn to lour		
	ID Lexemes	108100 ḫn	to lour	
DRID	**1000590**	**ḫn extra gift**		
RID	**0000706**	ḫn extra gift		
	ID Lexemes	117570 ḫn.t	extra gift	
DRID	**1000592**	**ḫn porter**		
RID	**0000709**	ḫn porter		
	ID Lexeme	850588 ḫn.w	porter	
DRID	**1000593**	**ḫn speech**		
RID	**0000711**	ḫn speech		
	ID Lexeme	117520 ḫn	speech; utterance; matter	
DRID	**1000597**	**ḫn to be foolish**		
RID	**0000715**	ḫn to be foolish		
	ID Lexemes	117540 ḫn	to be foolish	
		854618 ḫn	fool	
DRID	**1000600**	**ḫn to direct**		
RID	**0000719**	ḫn to direct		
	ID Lexemes	117490 ḫn	to direct (one's hand against)	
DRID	**1000610**	**ḫnḏ shin**		
RID	**0000731**	ḫnḏ shin		
	ID Lexemes	119560 ḫnḏ	shin; (bull's) shank	
DRID	**1000611**	**ḫnd to bend**		
RID	**0000732**	ḫnd to bend		
	ID Lexemes	119540 ḫnd.w	seat (stool, chair, throne); stairway	
		119490 ḫnd.w	bent timbers (naut.)	
		119470 ḫnd.wt	the (female) weavers	
		119450 ḫnd	to plait; to (en)twine	
		119420 ḫnd	to bend (a staff, during manufacture)	
DRID	**1000612**	**ḫnd to tread**		
RID	**0000732**	ḫnd to tread		
	ID Lexemes	119480 ḫnd.w	"Runner" (job designation)	
		119430 ḫnd	to tread	

		119440	ẖnd	lower leg (calf)

DRID 1000613 ẖnf to take sth.

RID	**0000734**	ẖnf to take sth.		
	ID Lexemes	117960	ẖnf	to take sth.

DRID 1000614 ẖnfi̯ to burn

RID	**0000735**	ẖnfi̯ to burn		
	ID Lexemes	854701	ẖnfi̯	to burn
		868655	ẖnf.t	fire
		118020	ẖnf.w	[a baked goods]
		118030	ẖnf.wt	[a baked goods]
		118010	ẖnfy	fire

DRID 1000615 ẖnfꜣ arrogance?

RID	**0000736**	ẖnfꜣ arrogance?		
	ID Lexemes	117990	ẖnfꜣ	arrogance?
		118000	ẖnfꜣ	to be aggressive?

DRID 1000618 ẖni̯ to make music

RID	**0000745**	ẖni̯ to make music		
	ID Lexemes	117740	ẖn.w	music-maker
		118490	ẖnr.yt	female musician belonging to the ẖnr
		851029	ẖnr	person belonging to the ẖnr
		118350	ẖnr	the institution of ẖnr
		860452	ẖn	dance; music
		858931	ẖn.ywt	those making music
		117700	ẖn.yt	music makers
		117750	ẖn.w	percussionist (of Hathor)
		861112	ẖn.wt	music-maker (sistrum player) (of Hathor)
		117820	ẖn.wt	music-maker (sistrum player) (of Hathor)
		117690	ẖni̯	to make music
		117460	ẖn	choral singing (clap beat)
		142570	sẖn	dance?

DRID 1000621 ẖni̯ to settle

RID	**0000748**	ẖni̯ to settle		
	ID Lexemes	75710	msẖn	residence (of gods)
		75720	msẖn.t	abode (of gods); birthplace; birth bricks
		117790	ẖn.w	storeroom
		117550	ẖn.t	the quiet place
		117680	ẖni̯	to flatten; to settle; to stop
		500096	sẖni̯	to alight; to rest; to dwell

		142600	sḫn.t	daybed
		851680	sḫni̯	to alight; to rest
		855049	sḫni̯	to lie down (with so.); to sleep (with so.)
		142660	sḫni̯	to alight; to bring to rest
		142510	sḫn	resting-place
		142520	sḫn	to go to law; to contend
		142690	sḫn.yw	resting
		87350	nḫn.wy	opponents
		87230	nḫn	[a kind of a sacred place]
RID	**0000741**	ḥnḫn to establish oneself		
	ID Lexeme	118580	ḥnḫn	to establish oneself

DRID 1000628 ḫnm jasper

RID	**0000755**	ḫnm jasper		
	ID Lexeme	74400	mḫnm.t	jasper
		118140	ḫnm.t	jasper

DRID 1000629 ḫnm to enjoy

RID	**0000756**	ḫnm to enjoy		
	ID Lexeme	118110	ḫnm.t	harlot
		118270	ḫnms	[a beer]
		118250	ḫnms	friendship
		850992	ḫnm	friendly; glad
		118260	ḫnms	friend
		118240	ḫnms	to be friendly with
		118290	ḫnms.t	friend
		118060	ḫnm	friend
		850984	ḫnm.w	friendly
		118050	ḫnm	to gladden; to be glad
RID	**0000758**	ḫnm to scent		
	ID Lexeme	118070	ḫnm	to treat (with an ointment) (med.)
		118230	ḫnm.w	smell
		854533	ḫnm	to scent; breathe in; delight; be happy; enjoy
		118120	ḫnm.t	kiss ("smell")
		118040	ḫnm	to breathe in (a pleasant smell)
		851531	sḫnm	smell

DRID 1000630 ḫnm to rear

RID	**0000757**	ḫnm to rear		
	ID Lexeme	118200	ḫnm.tj	nurse (who rears a divine child)
		118220	ḫnm.tjt	nurse (as applied to goddesses)
		118130	ḫnm.t	nurse
		118080	ḫnm	to rear (of goddesses who rear divine children)
		868658	ḫnm	infant
		857705	ḫnm.t	nurse

		118090	ẖnm	keeper of a divine child
		856001	nẖnm	altar?
DRID	**1000634**	**ẖnms mosquito**		
RID	**0000762**	ẖnms mosquito (or gnat?)		
	ID Lexeme	118280	ẖnms	mosquito (or gnat?)
DRID	**1000637**	**ẖnn fowl**		
RID	**0000765**	ẖnn fowl		
	ID Lexeme	118310	ẖnn.t	fowl
DRID	**1000642**	**ẖnp [baked good]**		
RID	**0000770**	ẖnp [baked good]		
	ID Lexeme	117880	ẖnp	[a kind of baked goods]
DRID	**1000643**	**ẖnp to consume**		
RID	**0000771**	ẖnp to consume		
	ID Lexeme	117870	ẖnp	to drink water
		117850	ẖnp	to steal; to catch; to present
		117860	ẖnp	to take in air (i.e. breathe)
DRID	**1000645**	**ẖnr rein**		
RID	**0000773**	ẖnr rein		
	ID Lexeme	118360	ẖnr	reins
DRID	**1000646**	**ẖnr = ẖl spike**		
RID	**0000774**	ẖnr spike		
	ID Lexeme	118370	ẖnr	spike (for splitting stone); Chisel
DRID	**1000647**	**ẖnr to be hoarse**		
RID	**0000775**	ẖnr to be hoarse		
	ID Lexeme	118410	ẖnr	to be hoarse
DRID	**1000648**	**ẖnr = ẖl to scatter**		
RID	**0000776**	ẖnr = ẖl to scatter		
	ID Lexeme	118390	ẖnr	to scatter; to disperse
DRID	**1000649**	**ẖnr to seclude**		
RID	**0000777**	ẖnr to seclude		
	ID Lexeme	118470	ẖnr.t	labour camp; fortress; council chamber
		118500	ẖnr.tt	plotting
		401029	ẖnr.tj	official of the labor camp
		118330	ẖnr	prisoner
		118340	ẖnr	criminal
		118320	ẖnr	to restrain

DRID	**1000650**	**ḫnrf = ḫlf insult**		
RID	**0000778**	ḫnrf = ḫlf insult		
	ID Lexeme	118530	ḫnrf	insult; abuse
DRID	**1000652**	**ḫnrj roar**		
RID	**0000780**	ḫnrj roar		
	ID Lexeme	118510	ḫnrj	roar
DRID	**1000653**	**ḫnš [a plant]**		
RID	**0000781**	ḫnš [a plant]		
	ID Lexeme	854821	ḫnš	[plant]
DRID	**1000655**	**ḫnš to stink**		
RID	**0000784**	ḫnš to stink		
	ID Lexeme	856666	ḫnš	stinker
		853385	ḫnš	sweating
		118730	ḫnš	to stink
		142700	sḫnš	to make stink
DRID	**1000656**	**ḫns two-sided item**		
RID	**0000782**	ḫns Janus-faced		
	ID Lexeme	854079	ḫns	To and Fro canal
		856230	ḫns.wj	skin of the double bull
		118620	ḫns	[a gold amulet]
		450240	ḫns	rolled-up curtain (of matting)
		118630	ḫns	double doors
DRID	**1000657**	**ḫnt face**		
RID	**0000785**	ḫnt best quality		
	ID Lexeme	118890	ḫnt.jt	something of the best quality
		854822	sḫnt.jw	excellent linen fabric
RID	**0000786**	ḫnt face		
	ID Lexeme	118790	ḫnt	brow; face; front
		850802	ḫnt	in front of
		118820	ḫnt	(head) cold; congestion (med.)
RID	**0000787**	ḫnt front		
	ID Lexeme	74410	mḫnt	forehead; front
		119340	ḫnt.jw	gods who are in front
		119050	ḫnt.j	foremost; in front
		119350	ḫnt.w	earlier; previously
		119130	ḫnti̯	to be in front of
		119070	ḫnt.j	entrance hall
		118900	ḫnt.jt	beginning of something
		859638	ḫnt.jt	one in front
		119040	ḫnt	in front of; foremost of; out of
		142720	sḫnti̯	to advance; to promote
		119120	ḫnt.j	canal

		119110	ẖnt.j	one who is in front
		119030	ẖnt.j	what is in front (gen.)
		119090	ẖnt.j	[characteristic of a crocodile]
		854347	ẖnt.j	something located frontally
		500014	ẖnt	in (some time)
RID	**0000790**	ẖnt south		
	ID Lexeme	119060	ẖnt.j	forepart; south
		119140	ẖnti̯	to sail upstream; to travel southwards
		119330	ẖnt.jw	person from the far south
		119150	ẖnt.yt	voyage southwards
		142740	sẖnti̯	to take southwards

DRID 1000658 ẖnt jar-stand

RID	**0000788**	ẖnt jar-stand		
	ID Lexeme	118780	ẖnt	jar-stand; sideboard (for food as well as drink)

DRID 1000662 ẖntš to be glad

RID	**0000793**	ẖntš to be glad		
	ID Lexeme	119390	ẖntš	to be glad; to make glad
		119380	ẖntš	to walk about freely
		119400	ẖntš	joy
		142760	sẖntš	to make rejoice

DRID 1000669 ẖnw dorsal fin (synodontis)

RID	**0000800**	ẖnw dorsal fin (synodontis)		
	ID Lexeme	117800	ẖnw	dorsal fin (synodontis))

DRID 1000671 ẖnz to travel through

RID	**0000802**	ẖnz to travel through		
	ID Lexeme	118700	ẖnz.w	Wanderer
		500246	ẖnz	to move in two directions
		118590	ẖnz	to traverse (a region); to travel through

DRID 1000675 ẖpd back side

RID	**0000806**	ẖpd back side		
	ID Lexeme	116550	ẖpd	buttock(s); rear part
		116570	ẖpd.t	[rear part of a quail (med.)]

DRID 1000678 ẖpi̯ to travel

RID	**0000809**	ẖpi̯ to travel		
	ID Lexeme	116070	ẖp.y	the moving one
		116130	ẖp.yw	[gods who follow Osiris]
		858305	ẖp.yt	death
		116000	ẖp	the deceased

		116060	ẖpi̯	to die; to do away with
		116120	ẖpj.w	passing away
		858304	ẖp.t	journey
		500265	ẖpi̯	to fly up
		116050	ẖpi̯	to travel; to encounter (someone)
		116150	ẖpp	passerby; stranger
		141990	sẖpi̯	to conduct; to bring
		142030	sẖp.wt	swimmer on harpoon
		142020	sẖp.w	bringers (of cattle, of boxes)

DRID 1000680 ẖpp seeds

RID	**0000811**	ẖpp lotus		
	ID Lexeme	116190	ẖppwj	flowers (lotus?)
RID	**0000812**	ẖpp seeds		
	ID Lexeme	116200	ẖppwj	[pellets? of myrrh]

DRID 1000681 ẖpp to be strange

RID	**0000813**	ẖpp to be strange		
	ID Lexeme	116160	ẖpp	strange
		859324	ẖpp	to be strange
		116170	ẖpp.w	strange words
		116180	ẖpp.wt	strange things

DRID 1000682 ẖpr to exist

RID	**0000814**	ẖpr to exist		
	ID Lexeme	854383	ẖpr	to create
		116230	ẖpr	to come into being; to become; to occur
		500446	ẖpr	to begin (doing)
		70024	ẖpr	to bring into being; to bring about
		116360	ẖpr.y	creator (a divine serpent)
		116300	ẖpr.w	mode of being; form; transformation
		116290	ẖpr.w	those who live now
		116270	ẖpr.t	event (lit. that which happens); that which comes into being
		116340	ẖprj	child
		122920	ẖpy	sun disk encircled by a pair of ureai
		142060	sẖpr	offspring; ward
		142050	sẖpr	to create; to bring into being; to rear (a child)
		142070	sẖpr.w	creature
		600610	sẖpr.w	increment; acquisitions
RID	**0000815**	ẖprr scarab		
	ID Lexeme	500094	ẖprr	scarab
		116410	ẖprr	[dung beetle; scarab]

DRID 1000683 ḫprš Blue Crown

RID	**0000816**	ḫprš Blue Crown		
	ID Lexeme	116420	ḫprš	Blue Crown

DRID 1000684 ḫpš to subjugate

RID	**0000817**	ḫpš to subjugate		
	ID Lexeme	116480	ḫpš	armory
		116470	ḫpš	to conquer
		116460	ḫpš	scimitar; battle ax
		116510	ḫpš	"he whose arm is strong" (the creator god)
		116450	ḫpš	strong arm; power; strength
		116440	ḫpš	Great Bear (the constellation)
		116430	ḫpš	foreleg; thigh
		116500	ḫpš	to be efficient
		116520	ḫpš.y	armed with a sword (king)

DRID 1000694 ḫr at

RID	**0000827**	ḫr at		
	ID Lexeme	500185	ḫr.t	state; wish
		854534	ḫr.t	matter; requirement; possession; essence; wish
		119860	ḫr.j	located at
RID	**0000838**	ḫr then		
	ID Lexeme	119600	ḫr	also, but, then etc.
		30920	jḫr	and; further
RID	**0000844**	ḫr with		
	ID Lexeme	80012	ḫr	to (someone)
		850795	ḫr	with

DRID 1000700 ḫr road

RID	**0000834**	ḫr road		
	ID Lexeme	119570	ḫr	street; road; quarter

DRID 1000702 ḫr sistrum

RID	**0000836**	ḫr sistrum		
	ID Lexeme	119950	ḫr.tw	sistrum

DRID 1000706 ḫr to fall

RID	**0000839**	ḫr to be hostile		
	ID Lexeme	858315	ḫrḫr	fighter?
		119960	ḫr.w	enemy
		119970	ḫr	hostile
		119910	ḫrw.yw	troops
		120110	ḫrw.yt	enemy
		142790	sḫr	foe
		120090	ḫrw.yw	hostility; war

			120080	ḫrw.yt	hostility; war
	RID	**0000842**	ḫr to fall		
		ID Lexeme	119610	ḫr	to fall; to fell
			858314	ḫrḫr.t	destruction?
			120440	ḫrḫr.t	destruction
			120490	ḫr.tj	[sic lege] to kill
			120420	ḫrḫr	to upset; to overturn
			119980	ḫr.w	low-lying land
			120100	ḫrwrw	discord
			142780	sḫr	to overthrow; to cast down
			142840	sḫr.t	overthrow, massacre
			142820	sḫr	Waste (from crops)
			119890	ḫr.yt	animals for sacrifice; butchery
			87390	nḫr	[something harmful]
			550175	mḫr.yt	storehouse
			855370	mḫr.w	storage (domain)
			119620	ḫr	tomb; necropolis
			860283	ḫr.jt	descendant
	RID	**0000847**	ḫrḫr to be sad		
		ID Lexeme	87420	nḫrḫr	to be sad
	RID	**0000848**	ḫrḫr to drive back		
		ID Lexeme	142930	sḫrḫr	to drive back (lions)
DRID	**1000711**	**ḫrd veils**			
	RID	**0000846**	ḫrd veils		
		ID Lexeme	120500	ḫrd	veils; thin cloth
DRID	**1000719**	**ḫrp to administer**			
	RID	**0000858**	ḫrp to administer		
		ID Lexeme	120160	ḫrp	to bring; to provide
			120150	ḫrp	to govern; to control; to administer
			120250	ḫrp.w	mallet
			120320	ḫrp.wt	dues; taxes
			120170	ḫrp	to be forward of
			855078	ḫrp	director
			120190	ḫrp	director
			120180	ḫrp	to set out (in the morning)
			120140	ḫrp	[herep-scepter]
			120210	ḫrp.t	levy (in the form of cattle)
			120230	ḫrp.t	steering rope
			120220	ḫrp.t	taxpayers
DRID	**1000721**	**ḫrḳ slippery ground**			
	RID	**0000860**	ḫrḳ slippery ground		
		ID Lexeme	120480	ḫrḳ.t	slippery ground
DRID	**1000724**	**ḫrr watercourse**			

	RID	0000863	ẖrr watercourse	
		ID Lexeme	859155 ẖrr	watercourse; channel
DRID	**1000726**		**ẖrš bundle**	
	RID	**0000865**	ẖrš bundle	
		ID Lexeme	120460 ẖrš	bundle(s)
			120470 ẖrš.t	bundle
DRID	**1000731**		**ẖru̯ to say**	
	RID	**0000870**	ẖru̯ to say	
		ID Lexeme	600211 ẖru̯	to say; to tell
			120010 ẖrw	voice; sound; quarrel
			860993 ẖrw.y	noise maker
			120070 ẖrw.y	noisy one
			119940 ẖr.tw	utterance; oracle
			120400 ẖrr	Noisy one
			856179 ẖrw	noisy one
			852555 ẖrw	The voice (a domain)
DRID	**1000735**		**ẖry myrrh?**	
	RID	**0000874**	ẖry myrrh?	
		ID Lexeme	119870 ẖry	[myrrh]
DRID	**1000737**		**ẖs rubbing stone**	
	RID	**0000876**	ẖs rubbing stone	
		ID Lexeme	120610 ẖs	rubbing stone (for removing body hair); razor
DRID	**1000743**		**ẖšb to mutilate**	
	RID	**0000882**	ẖšb to mutilate	
		ID Lexeme	121160 ẖšb	to mutilate
DRID	**1000745**		**ẖsbḏ lapis lazuli**	
	RID	**0000884**	ẖsbḏ lapis lazuli	
		ID Lexeme	120740 ẖsbḏ	serpent of the lapis lazuli colour
			120730 ẖsbḏ	artificial lapis lazuli
			860286 ẖsbḏ	to make blue coloured
			859153 ẖsbḏ	[a plant of lapis lazuli color]
			120760 ẖsbḏ.tj	one of the lapis lazuli colour
			120710 ẖsbḏ.t	one of the lapis lazuli colour (Hathor; Isis)
			120700 ẖsbḏ	lapis lazuli; substitutes for lapis lazuli (faience, glass)
			120720 ẖsbḏ	lapis lazuli-like; of blue colour
DRID	**1000746**		**ẖsbḏ [a kilt]**	
	RID	**0000885**	ẖsbḏ [a kilt]	
		ID Lexeme	121120 ẖsbḏ	[a kilt]

DRID	**1000747**	**ḫsḏḏ to grow mouldy**		
RID	**0000886**	ḫsḏḏ to grow mouldy		
	ID Lexeme	121130	ḫsḏḏ	to grow mouldy
DRID	**1000748**	**ḫsf to confront?**		
RID	**0000887**	ḫsf to confront?		
	ID Lexeme	74470	mḫsf	peg
		501073	ḫsf.w	Repeller
		650004	ḫsf	to punish
		120791	ḫsf	to oppose (in court)
		120910	ḫsf	[door of heaven]
		120900	ḫsf.w	approach
		858321	ḫsf.w	refuse?
		120880	ḫsf.t	punishment
		120960	ḫsfi̯	to sail upstream
		120870	ḫsf	answer (to a letter)
		450465	ḫsf	to spin (yarn)
		120780	ḫsf	spindle
		851854	ḫsf	offender
		120800	ḫsf	to meet (someone); to draw near; to answer
		120790	ḫsf	to repel
		120810	ḫsf	to turn round
		120830	ḫsf	to remove body hair
		854547	sḫsf	to collate; check; oppose; face
		143020	sḫsf	collation
		143010	sḫsf	to collate
		143030	sḫsf	to oppose
DRID	**1000749**	**ḫšḫš rubble**		
RID	**0000888**	ḫšḫš rubble		
	ID Lexeme	121170	ḫšḫš	rubble
DRID	**1000754**	**ḫsr to dispel**		
RID	**0000893**	ḫsr to dispel		
	ID Lexeme	121030	ḫsr	to dispel; to drive away
		858331	ḫsr	one who distributes
DRID	**1000761**	**ḫt behind**		
RID	**0000900**	ḫt behind		
	ID Lexeme	121550	ḫt.y	Retreating One
		121230	ḫt	through; throughout
		853931	ḫti̯	to rove around
		121510	ḫti̯	to retreat
		121590	ḫt.w	followers
		868709	ḫt.j	located behind it

		143210	sḫti̯	to rush; to run
		143130	sḫti̯	to recede
		143120	sḫti̯	to take back
	RID	**0000913**	ḫtḫt to turn back	
		ID Lexeme	121890 ḫtḫt	to turn back; to drive away
			143240 sḫtḫt	to drive back
DRID	**1000763**	**ḫt crop**		
	RID	**0000902**	ḫt crop	
		ID Lexeme	121620 ḫt.wj	crop, cereal?
DRID	**1000765**	**ḫt plot**		
	RID	**0000904**	ḫt plot	
		ID Lexeme	121220 ḫt	[an administrative unit (land register?)]
			121290 ḫt.t	parcel (measured and registered in the cadaster)
DRID	**1000768**	**ḫṯ to pound**		
	RID	**0000911**	ḫṯḫṯ to pound	
		ID Lexeme	121930 ḫṯḫṯ	to pound
DRID	**1000770**	**ḫt wood**		
	RID	**0000907**	ḫt wood	
		ID Lexeme	121210 ḫt	[rod (linear measure of 100 cubits)]
			121300 ḫt.wt	wooden things
			121270 ḫt	[an ethereal oil]
			121200 ḫt	wood (gen.); tree; stick
DRID	**1000772**	**ḫti̯ platform**		
	RID	**0000914**	ḫti̯ platform	
		ID Lexeme	121610 ḫt.w	threshing floor
			121600 ḫt.w	dais; platform; terrace
DRID	**1000773**	**ḫti̯ to carve**		
	RID	**0000915**	ḫti̯to carve	
		ID Lexeme	121520 ḫti̯	to carve; to inscribe
			121910 ḫt.t	carving; inscription
DRID	**1000775**	**ḫti̯ to see**		
	RID	**0000917**	ḫti̯ to see	
		ID Lexeme	121540 ḫti̯	to see
DRID	**1000780**	**ḫtm to seal**		
	RID	**0000923**	ḫtm to seal	
		ID Lexeme	855928 mḫtm	ring

74510	mẖtm.t	pinfold
74520	mẖtm.t	sealed box
121710	ẖtm	to seal; to put a seal on
121700	ẖtm	ring
150290	ẖtm	precious
121720	ẖtm	chest (that can be sealed shut); storehouse (sealed)
859355	ẖtm	bread; offering meal
121730	ẖtm	lock
121750	ẖtm	seal
121740	ẖtm	fortress
121790	ẖtm	(images of gods) with inscriptions
121690	ẖtm	seal; sealing; sealing cylinder
121850	ẖtm.yt	closure?
150350	ẖtm.w	sealer
121780	ẖtm.w	inscriptions
121840	ẖtm.w	seal maker; sealer?
121830	ẖtm.t	contract
850597	ẖtm.t	treasure (lit. what is sealed)
855793	ẖtm.tj	sealer
850589	ẖtm.tj	sealer
850146	ẖtm.tjt	sealer

DRID 1000781 ẖṯn garlic?

RID	**0000924**	ẖṯn garlic?		
	ID Lexeme	121920	ẖṯn	garlic?

DRID 1000797 ẖw unique

RID	**0000943**	ẖw unique		
	ID Lexeme	113070	ẖw	oneness; uniqueness

DRID 1000800 ẖwd carrying chair

RID	**0000944**	ẖwd carrying chair		
	ID Lexeme	115360	ẖwd.t	carrying chair
		115350	ẖwd	palanquin

DRID 1000801 ẖwd to be rich

RID	**0000945**	ẖwd to be rich		
	ID Lexeme	115330	ẖwd	richness
		115310	ẖwd	to be rich; to enrich
		115320	ẖwd	rich man
		141970	sẖwd	to make rich

DRID 1000802 ẖwd to fish

RID	**0000946**	ẖwd to fish		
	ID Lexeme	122050	ẖḏw	[fish]
		115370	ẖwḏ.w	[a category of fisherman]

115340	ḫwd	to fish? (with a net)

DRID 1000803 ḫwḫ [a boat]

RID 0000947 ḫwḫ [a boat]

ID Lexeme		
115240	ḫwḫ.t	[a boat]

DRID 1000804 ḫwi̯ to protect

RID 0000951 ḫwi̯ to protect

ID Lexeme		
112980	ḫ	to be young
114450	ḫy	child
852398	ḫy	child
874154	ḫy.t	little girl
114530	ḫy.t	shelter
113000	ḫy.t	little girl
858339	ḫw	Protector
856185	ḫw	protégé; child
114930	ḫw	[a fan]
114940	ḫw	protection
856186	ḫw	protector
115000	ḫw.t	heavens
114970	ḫw.t	protection; exemption (from assessment)
114990	ḫw.t	king's palace; sanctuary
859220	ḫw.tj	protector
115020	ḫw.tjw	Protective deities
114920	ḫwi̯	to be exempt from
852623	ḫwi̯	to prevent (from doing something)
115110	ḫwi̯	to protect; to prevent
115130	ḫwy.t	[flywhisk (lit. protector)]
115150	ḫww	baseness; wrongdoing
141880	sḫwi̯	to protect
876563	sḫwi̯	cause to protect

DRID 1000810 ḫwn to hurt

RID 0000956 ḫwn to hurt

ID Lexemes		
115170	ḫwn	to pierce
115180	ḫwn	to be hurtful
141930	sḫwn	to dispute
141950	sḫwn.w	riot

DRID 1000814 ḫws to slaughter

RID 0000960 ḫws to slaughter

ID Lexeme		
115260	ḫws	to slaughter (offering animal)

DRID 1000818 ḫwzi̯ to build

RID 0000967 ḫwzi̯ to build

ID Lexeme		
115270	ḫwzi̯	to pound; to build

			115290	ẖwz.w	[a kind of a structure - hut]
			141960	sẖwzi̯	to equip
DRID	**1000821**	**ẖyi̯ to be high**			
	RID	**0000970**	ẖyi̯ to be high		
		ID Lexeme	114470	ẖy	height
			114480	ẖy	high-lying land
			114490	ẖy	Flood (the "high")
			858998	ẖy.t	acclamation
			114550	ẖy.t	sky; roof
			114540	ẖy.t	size (of a figure)
			114560	ẖy.t	[goddess who lifts up the sky]
			114460	ẖyi̯	to be high; to mount up
			141780	sẖyi̯	to raise up
DRID	**1000823**	**ẖz [a myrrh]**			
	RID	**0000985**	ẖzz [a myrrh]		
		ID Lexeme	121060	ẖzz	[a myrrh]
			121050	ẖzẖz	[a myrrh]
DRID	**1000825**	**ẖz ritual**			
	RID	**0000973**	ẖz ritual		
		ID Lexeme	120580	ẖz	ritual
DRID	**1000827**	**ẖzd to decay**			
	RID	**0000975**	ẖzd to decay		
		ID Lexeme	121090	ẖzd	putrefaction (in the limbs of Osiris)
			121080	ẖzd	swelling (boil?)
DRID	**1000836**	**ẖzꜣ [a plant]**			
	RID	**0000986**	ẖzꜣ [a plant]		
		ID Lexeme	120670	ẖzꜣ.w	[part of a plant (med.)]; [oak apple?]
			120680	ẖzꜣ.w	[a plant used for fuel]
DRID	**1000837**	**ẖzꜣ carrying pole**			
	RID	**0000987**	ẖzꜣ carrying pole		
		ID Lexeme	450162	ẖzꜣ	carrying pole
DRID	**1000840**	**ẖzꜣj bribe**			
	RID	**0000990**	ẖzꜣj bribe		
		ID Lexeme	120650	ẖzꜣj	bribe
DRID	**1000842**	**ẖꜣ [a water]**			
	RID	**0000992**	ẖꜣ [a water]		
		ID Lexeme	113190	ẖꜣ	[Waters in the sky]

DRID	**1000845**		**ḫꜣ an element of dressing**		
	RID	**0000994**	ḫꜣ an element of dressing		
		ID Lexeme	113280	ḫꜣ.t	khat-headcloth
			113270	ḫꜣ.t	[a collar-like necklace]

DRID	**1000852**		**ḫꜣ illness**		
	RID	**0001002**	ḫꜣ illness		
		ID Lexeme	855596	ḫꜣ.tj	demon causing illness
			113640	ḫꜣ.tjw	demons of diseases; demons with knifes
			113480	ḫꜣ.t	disease; illness
			86820	nḫꜣ	knife (of flint)

DRID	**1000854**		**ḫꜣ meat**		
	RID	**0001004**	ḫꜣ meat		
		ID Lexeme	113650	ḫꜣ.w	meat (as an offering)

DRID	**1000856**		**ḫꜣ plant category**		
	RID	**0001006**	ḫꜣ plant category		
		ID Lexeme	113330	ḫꜣ.w	ingredients (plants; flowers)
			113320	ḫꜣ.w	herbs; plants
			113100	ḫꜣ	leaf

DRID	**1000857**		**ḫꜣ thousand**		
	RID	**0001008**	ḫꜣ thousand		
		ID Lexeme	113110	ḫꜣ	thousand
			113310	ḫꜣ.w	[Decans]

DRID	**1000858**		**ḫꜣ to be young**		
	RID	**0001009**	ḫꜣ to be young		
		ID Lexeme	113140	ḫꜣ	to be young

DRID	**1000865**		**ḫꜣb hippopotamus**		
	RID	**0001015**	ḫꜣb hippopotamus		
		ID Lexeme	113810	ḫꜣb	hippopotamus (often for Seth)
	RID	**0001016**	ḫꜣb infant		
		ID Lexeme	856167	ḫꜣb.w	infant (human, or animal)

DRID	**1000868**		**ḫꜣb to be humble**		
	RID	**0001018**	ḫꜣb to be humble		
		ID Lexeme	113820	ḫꜣb	to bend; to bow (in submission)

DRID	**1000874**		**ḫꜣḏ [a bread]**		
	RID	**0001025**	ḫꜣḏ [a bread]		
		ID Lexeme	114410	ḫꜣḏ.w	[a kind of dough]; [a flat loaf]
			114430	ḫꜣḏ.t	[a bread mold?]

DRID	**1000876**	**ḫꜣd to pluck**			
	RID	**0001027**	ḫꜣd to pluck		
		ID Lexeme	114400	ḫꜣd	to disintegrate
			114390	ḫꜣd	to be dull?; be indifferent?; to dissolve
			114380	ḫꜣd	to pluck (fowl)
DRID	**1000878**	**ḫꜣf to twist?**			
	RID	**0001029**	ḫꜣf to be twisted?		
		ID Lexeme	856222	ḫꜣf	to be twisted?
DRID	**1000880**	**ḫꜣḫ to hurry**			
	RID	**0001031**	ḫꜣḫ to hurry		
		ID Lexeme	860497	ḫꜣḫ	the fast one
			114170	ḫꜣḫ	to come in haste; to be fast
			114190	ḫꜣḫ.w	fast ones
			141760	sḫꜣḫ	to hasten
			850124	sḫꜣḫ.tj	courier
DRID	**1000883**	**ḫꜣi̯ to measure**			
	RID	**0001040**	ḫꜣi̯ to measure		
		ID Lexeme	121630	ḫt.jw	[a kind of measurement]
			74300	mḫꜣ.t	balance
			74280	mḫꜣ	to make level; to match; to be like
			74290	mḫꜣ	to skewer
			74340	mḫꜣ.wt	customs stations on the river
			74330	mḫꜣ.wt	result (of weighing)
			113230	ḫꜣ	road; path
			113430	ḫꜣ.y	measurements
			113520	ḫꜣ.y	weighing house?
			113220	ḫꜣ.y	[measure of area]; [measure of capacity]
			113660	ḫꜣ.w	grain assessor
			868508	ḫꜣ.w	grain knife
			113690	ḫꜣ.w	bowl
			113420	ḫꜣj	measuring cord
			113410	ḫꜣi̯	to measure
			113400	ḫꜣi̯	to examine (a wound) (med.)
DRID	**1000895**	**ḫꜣrt wadi**			
	RID	**0001064**	ḫꜣrt wadi		
		ID Lexeme	114160	ḫꜣrt	wadi
DRID	**1000896**	**ḫꜣs foreign land**			
	RID	**0001065**	ḫꜣs foreign land		
		ID Lexeme	853199	ḫꜣs.wt	The foreign countries (domain)
			114300	ḫꜣs.t	hill-country; foreign land; desert

			114320 ḫꜣs.tj	foreigner; desert dweller
			860224 ḫꜣs.tjt	foreign woman
DRID	**1000897**		**ḫꜣnn doum palm**	
	RID	**0001056**	ḫꜣnn doum palm	
		ID Lexeme	114080 ḫꜣnn	[part of the doum palm's fruit]
			114090 ḫꜣnn.t	[variety of the doum palm]
DRID	**1000900**		**ḫꜣtb to spare**	
	RID	**0001069**	ḫꜣtb to spare	
		ID Lexeme	114360 ḫꜣtb	to spare
DRID	**1000901**		**ḫꜣtrw mongoose**	
	RID	**0001070**	ḫꜣtrw mongoose	
		ID Lexeme	114370 ḫꜣtrw	mongoose
DRID	**1000902**		**ḫꜣw altar**	
	RID	**0001071**	ḫꜣw altar	
		ID Lexeme	113720 ḫꜣw.t	altar
DRID	**1000903**		**ḫꜣw hide (of animals)**	
	RID	**0001072**	ḫꜣw hide (of animals)	
		ID Lexeme	113710 ḫꜣw.t	hide (of animals)
			113680 ḫꜣw	hide (of animals)
DRID	**1000905**		**ḫꜣwj evening**	
	RID	**0001074**	ḫꜣwj evening	
		ID Lexeme	113760 ḫꜣwj	evening traveler
			113750 ḫꜣwj	night; evening
DRID	**1000907**		**ḫꜣyb shadow**	
	RID	**0001076**	ḫꜣyb shadow	
		ID Lexeme	113540 ḫꜣyb.t	shadow
DRID	**1000908**		**ḫꜣz to climb**	
	RID	**0001077**	ḫꜣz to climb	
		ID Lexeme	114280 ḫꜣz.t	[a snake]
			114270 ḫꜣz	climb
DRID	**1000910**		**ḫꜣ to throw**	
	RID	**0001079**	ḫꜣꜥ to throw	
		ID Lexeme	862789 ḫꜣꜥ	end
			113560 ḫꜣꜥ	to throw; to abandon; to dispatch
			113630 ḫꜣꜥ	[a siege device]
	RID	**0001135**	ḫꜣꜥ to get ready	
		ID Lexeme	141750 sḫꜣꜥ	to get ready
	RID	**0001036**	ḫꜣḫꜣ to tousle?	
		ID Lexeme	874331 nḫꜣḫꜣ	to tousle?

	RID	**0001037**	ḫꜣḫꜣ to winnow	
		ID Lexeme	114230 ḫꜣḫꜣ	winnowing field [a field in the hereafter]
			114220 ḫꜣḫꜣ	to winnow, to scatter
DRID	**1000912**	**ḫꜥ [a tool]**		
	RID	**0001081**	ḫꜥ [a tool]	
		ID Lexeme	114640 ḫꜥ	[a hoe]
			600592 ḫꜥ.w	[a basket?]
			114680 ḫꜥ.w	(equipment (weapons, tackle, for the tomb); implements (gen.))
DRID	**1000913**	**ḫꜥ clew**		
	RID	**0001082**	ḫꜥ clew	
		ID Lexeme	114630 ḫꜥ	clew (of yarn, as a measure of quantity)
DRID	**1000920**	**ḫꜥi̯ to appear**		
	RID	**0001088**	ḫꜥi̯ to appear (in glory)	
		ID Lexeme	75700 msḫꜥ	splendor (of gods)
			114620 ḫꜥ	Festival
			114610 ḫꜥ	mound
			114760 ḫꜥ.y	the one who appears in glory
			114870 ḫꜥ.w	[place of punishment for evil ones]
			114860 ḫꜥ.w	[characteristic of crocodile]
			114850 ḫꜥ.w	crowns
			114840 ḫꜥ.w	rising (of stars); appearance (of gods)
			850114 ḫꜥ.w	one who appears
			114670 ḫꜥ.t	primeval hill
			114740 ḫꜥi̯	to appear (in glory); to be shining
			114750 ḫꜥi̯	to give birth
			114800 ḫꜥj.t	daily revenue?
			114790 ḫꜥy.t	the one who appears
			141800 sḫꜥ	appearance (of gods in procession)
			141830 sḫꜥi̯	to make appear; to appear
	RID	**0001089**	ḥꜥi̯ to rejoice	
		ID Lexeme	102060 ḥꜥi̯	to rejoice; to be happy
			102070 ḥꜥ.y	Rejoicer (sun god)
			852771 ḥꜥjꜥi̯	to cheer; to be excited
			861326 ḥꜥꜥ.t	the joyful one
			102120 ḥꜥꜥ.wt	joy; rejoicing
			854761 ḥꜥ.w	exultation
			868406 ḥꜥ.wt	jubilance
			140470 sḥꜥꜥ	to make glad
			140460 sḥꜥi̯	to acclaim
DRID	**1000921**	**ḫꜥm throat**		

	RID	**0001090**	ḫꜥm throat		
		ID Lexeme	114880	ḫꜥm	throat; neck
DRID	**1000927**		**ḫꜥr leather**		
	RID	**0001095**	ḫꜥr leather		
		ID Lexeme	600161	ḫꜥr	leather
DRID	**1000928**		**ḫꜥr to be furious**		
	RID	**0001096**	ḫꜥr to be furious		
		ID Lexeme	114900	ḫꜥr	to knock down (the enemy)
			861236	ḫꜥr	fierceness
			114890	ḫꜥr	to rage
			853078	ḫꜥr.tj	the furious one
			141850	sḫꜥr	to enrage
DRID	**1001213**		**ḫꜣm to bend (the arm)**		
	RID	**0001053**	ḫꜣm to bend (the arm)		
		ID lexeme	114010	ḫꜣm	to bend (the arm); to bow down
DRID	**1003086**		**ḫꜣt to become ecstatic**		
	RID	**0001067**	ḫꜣt to become ecstatic		
		ID Lexeme	113800	ḫꜣt	to become ecstatic
			853908	ḫꜣt	the ecstatic one

II.15 ẖ

DRID	**1000446**	**ẖ belly**			
	RID	**0000543**	ẖ body		
		ID Lexeme	74690	mẖt.w	bowel; entrails
			122070	ẖ	belly of an animal
			122120	ẖ.t	Wording (of a document)
			122090	ẖ.t	body (of gods; of men); generation
			122110	ẖ.t	section (of a building)
			122080	ẖ.t	body; belly; womb
			122100	ẖ.t	mass (of a substance)
DRID	**1000453**	**ẖb to subdue**			
	RID	**0000542**	ẖb to subdue		
		ID Lexeme	122840	ẖb	to down; to subdue
DRID	**1000479**	**ẖd to examine**			
	RID	**0000910**	htẖt to examine		
		ID Lexeme	124910	htẖt	inquirers (mil.)
			124920	htẖt	to examine
	RID	**0000586**	ẖdẖd	to examine	
		ID Lexeme	124990	ẖdẖd	to examine
DRID	**1000481**	**ẖdb to kill**			
	RID	**0000581**	ẖdb to kill		
		ID Lexeme	124950	ẖdb	to kill
			124890	ẖtb	to overthrow
DRID	**1000494**	**ẖdr to feel uncomfortable?**			
	RID	**0000598**	ẖdr to feel uncomfortable?		
		ID Lexeme	124980	ẖdr	to feel uncomfortable?
DRID	**1000529**	**ẖkr to adorn**			
	RID	**0000640**	ẖkr to be adorned		
		ID Lexeme	143700	sxkr	to decorate; to adorn
			124740	ẖkr	adornment
			124760	ẖkr	the adorned one
			124730	ẖkr	to adorn; to be adorned
			856568	ẖkr.y	jewellery maker
			124840	ẖkr.yt	[designation of the white crown]
			124850	ẖkr.yt	insignia
			124790	ẖkr.t	adornment (uraeus)
DRID	**1000562**	**ẖms incense**			
	RID	**0000678**	ẖms incense		
		ID Lexeme	123020	ẖms	[incense]
DRID	**1000563**	**ẖms to bend**			

	RID	**0000679**	ẖms to bend	
		ID Lexeme	123000 ẖms	to bend (the back, in respect)
			123030 ẖms	spear point
			123010 ẖms	ear of grain
DRID	**1000586**	**ẖn [water]**		
	RID	**0000704**	ẖn [water]	
		ID Lexemes	850909 ẖnw.t	desert fountain; cistern?
			123290 ẖnw	[a body of water]
			123800 ẖnnn	irrigation basin?
DRID	**1000587**	**ẖn bag?**		
	RID	**0000705**	ẖn bag?	
		ID Lexemes	100970 ẖn	[a bandage (med.)]
DRID	**1000588**	**ẖn covering**		
	RID	**0000707**	ẖn interior	
		ID Lexemes	123080 ẖn	[a sack]
			123090 ẖn	tent
			123180 ẖn.w	provisions
			123140 ẖn.t	hide; skin; tube (of skin) (med.)
			865688 ẖn.tj	dermal layer
			123270 ẖnw	interior
			854537 ẖnw	interior; living place; residence
			123280 ẖnw	home; abode
			123250 ẖnw.jw	what belong to the household
			200018 ẖnw.tj	inner
			123390 ẖnw.tj	inner layer (of the skin)
			123320 ẖnw.tjw	people who wear animal skin
DRID	**1000594**	**ẖn statue**		
	RID	**0000712**	ẖn statue	
		ID Lexeme	123860 ẖn.tj	statue
DRID	**1000596**	**ẖn to approach**		
	RID	**0000714**	ẖn to approach	
		ID Lexeme	123110 ẖn	to approach
			853897 ẖn	related party; friend
	RID	**0000739**	ẖnẖn to approach	
		ID Lexeme	123820 ẖnẖn	to the side of, in the company of
			123810 ẖnẖn	to approach
DRID	**1000609**	**ẖnbb to mingle**		
	RID	**0000729**	ẖnbb to mingle	
		ID Lexeme	123400 ẖnbb	to mingle with people; to enter
DRID	**1000620**	**ẖni̯ to row**		

	RID	**0000747**	ẖni̯ to row		
		ID Lexeme	74610	mẖn.t	ferry-boat
			74630	mẖn.tj	ferryman
			500731	ẖn.w	Oarsman
			123300	ẖn.w	oarsman
			123130	ẖn.w	oarsman
			858280	ẖn.t	ferryboat
			123160	ẖn.t	water-procession
			123230	ẖni̯	to convey by water; to row
			123240	ẖny.t	crew of rowers
			858290	ẖnn	rower
DRID	**1000622**		**ẖnk [garment]**		
	RID	**0000750**	ẖnk [garment]		
		ID Lexemes	858288	ẖnk.t	[a garment]
			123850	ẖnk	[a garment]
DRID	**1000625**		**ẖnm [an oil]**		
	RID	**0001797**	nẖnm [an oil]		
		ID Lexemes	87760	nẖnm	[one of the seven sacred oils]
DRID	**1000631**		**ẖnm to unite**		
	RID	**0000759**	ẖnm to unite		
		ID Lexemes	123450	ẖnm	to build; to construct
			123420	ẖnm	to join; to unite with
			123430	ẖnm	housemate; dependants
			500383	ẖnm.ww	creators
			123500	ẖnm.t	nurse
			123520	ẖnm.t	one who unites (waxing moon)
			123540	ẖnm.t	strainer
			123570	ẖnm.tj	nostrils
	RID	**0000754**	ẖnm group of animals		
		ID Lexemes	123580	ẖnm.w	herd
			854538	ẖnm.w	[group of animals]
			123440	ẖnm.w	marsh fowl; swarm (of waterfowl)
DRID	**1000632**		**ẖnm water facility**		
	RID	**0000760**	ẖnm water facility		
		ID Lexemes	123550	ẖnm.t	well; watering place
			123560	ẖnm.t	basin? (for irrigation)
			123530	ẖnm.t	[dwelling of the sacred crocodile in Ombos]
			123690	ẖnmj.t	[water in the nome of Hierakonpolis]
			854483	mẖnm.t	pool
DRID	**1000639**		**ẖnn septic?**		

RID	**0000767**	ẖnn septic?		
	ID Lexeme	143580	sẖnn	to arouse; to stir up
		143600	sẖnn	to make decompose (med.)
		143610	sẖnn	ruin?
		123760	ẖnn.w	disturbance
		123730	ẖnn.w	brawler
		123700	ẖnn	to trouble; to decay (med.)
		123740	ẖnn	dust; rubble
		123720	ẖnn	to be inflamed (med.); to decay
		123060	ẖn	to be swollen (from the stomach)
DRID	**1000673**	**ẖp figure**		
RID	**0000804**	ẖp figure		
	ID Lexeme	122870	ẖp.w	figure; image
DRID	**1000679**	**ẖpn to be bulged**		
RID	**0000810**	ẖpn to be bulged		
	ID Lexeme	122970	ẖpn	to be fat
		855580	ẖpn.t	fattened (domestic) fowl
		142040	sẖpn	to fatten (cattle)
		153720	špn.t	voluptuous woman
		153750	špnn	poppy seeds?
		153700	špn	[a kind of an illness of the urinary tract]
		851309	špn	to be well fed
		153710	špn	[a plant (poppy?)]
		76430	mšpn.t	[a skin illness]
DRID	**1000686**	**ẖpꜣ navel**		
RID	**0000819**	ẖpꜣ navel		
	ID Lexeme	122890	ẖpꜣ	pellet?
		122880	ẖpꜣ	navel
		122910	ẖpꜣw.t	scar (as a result of a tumour)
DRID	**1000687**	**ẖp^{c} to chew**		
RID	**0000820**	ẖp^{c} to chew		
	ID Lexeme	122930	ẖp^{c}	to chew (med.)
		122950	ẖp^{c}.w	[a med. substance to be chewed]
DRID	**1000690**	**ẖḳs to be injured**		
RID	**0000823**	ẖḳs to be injured		
	ID Lexeme	124710	ẖḳs	to be injured
		124720	ẖḳs.t	injured eye (of Horus)
DRID	**1000709**	**ẖr under**		
RID	**0000843**	ẖr under		
	ID Lexeme	74650	mẖr	granary; storehouse

74660	mẖr	pasture
74670	mẖr.w	deposit
74680	mẖr.w	necessities; provisions; offerings
851509	ẖr	as a result (reason); [causal]
852288	ẖr	storeroom
850794	ẖr	under
857322	ẖr.j	descendant
124220	ẖr.j	being under: lower
851459	ẖr.y	beneath
124240	ẖr.jw	humankind
860469	ẖr.jw	reptile
123930	ẖr.jw	relatives; underlings (of a household)
869000	ẖr.jt	lower sky
124420	ẖr.w	base; bottom; under-side
124430	ẖr.wj	testicles
123940	ẖr.t	belongings; share; requirements
123950	ẖr.t	hereafter
859943	ẖr.t	country of provisions
124470	ẖr.tjw	basement

DRID 1000710 ẖrd child

RID 0000845 ẖrd child

ID Lexeme		
124480	ẖrd	child
854539	ẖrd	child; young people
124510	ẖrd	to be a child
124500	ẖrd	daughter
124490	ẖrd	young (of an animal)
124540	ẖrd.w	childhood
858312	ẖrd.wt	childhood
124520	ẖrd.t	childhood
143690	sẖrd	to rejuvenate

DRID 1000716 ẖrm causeway?

RID 0000855 ẖrm causeway?

ID Lexeme 854473 ẖrm.t causeway?

DRID 1000755 ẖss corner (of a building)

RID 0000894 ẖss corner (of a building)

ID Lexeme 124670 ẖss corner (of a building)

DRID 1000756 ẖsw eyelid

RID 0000895 ẖsw eyelid

ID Lexeme 124660 ẖsw eyelid

DRID 1000758 ẖsꜣ to be unanointed

RID 0000897 ẖsꜣ to be unanointed

		ID Lexeme	124570	ẖsꜣ	to be unanointed
			857922	ẖsꜣ	wig
			124630	ẖsꜣ	“unanointed one“?; “weak one”? (Osiris)
			124590	ẖsꜣ.yt	[a kind of a balsam]
DRID	**1000771**		**ẖtb to dip into**		
	RID	**0000908**	ẖtb to dip into		
		ID Lexeme	124900	ẖtb	to dip into (med.)
DRID	**1000774**		**ẖti̯ to pluck (plants)**		
	RID	**0000916**	ẖti̯ to pluck (plants)		
		ID Lexeme	122170	ẖ.tj	bast
			123890	ẖt	[a part of a plant]
			124930	ẖti̯	to pluck (plants)
DRID	**1000788**		**hṯt to scream**		
	RID	**0000934**	hṯt to scream		
		ID Lexeme	99560	hṯt	Screamer (baboon)
			99580	hṯt	screaming; noise
			99570	hṯt	to scream (of baboons; of monkeys); to rejoice
			855103	hṯt.w	baboons
DRID	**1000828**		**ẖzi̯ to be weak**		
	RID	**0000977**	ẖzi̯ to be weak		
		ID Lexeme	124610	ẖz	coward; vile person
			400267	ẖz	weak; vile
			852832	ẖz	the miserable one (Seth)
			124640	ẖz.yt	cowardice
			124680	ẖz.tj	the weak one (Osiris)
			124600	ẖzi̯	to be weak
DRID	**1000848**		**ẖꜣ corpse**		
	RID	**0000997**	ẖꜣ corpse		
		ID Lexeme	122360	ẖꜣ.yt	heap of corpses
			122220	ẖꜣ.t	corpse
			858232	ẖꜣ.tj	he of the corpses
			122240	ẖꜣ.tjw	enemy
			500114	ẖꜣ.tyw	those of the corpse
DRID	**1000853**		**ẖꜣ marsh**		
	RID	**0001003**	ẖꜣ marsh		
		ID Lexeme	122270	ẖꜣ.t	marshes; lagoon
			122210	ẖꜣ.t	oxyrhynchus fish
			852200	ẖꜣ.tj	mash dweller
			858233	ẖꜣ.tjwt	marsh dweller

		122430	ẖꜣ.tjwt	marsh dwellers
RID	0001033	ẖꜣẖꜣ marsh		
	ID Lexeme	122620	ẖꜣẖꜣ.wt	marsh; lagoon

DRID 1000860 ẖꜣ to disturb

RID	0001007	ẖꜣ storm		
	ID Lexeme	122690	ẖꜣ.tj	storm
		865226	ẖꜣ.tjj	stormy
		122610	ẖꜣẖꜣ.tj	storm
RID	0001011	ẖꜣ to pound		
	ID Lexeme	122400	ẖꜣ	to break up; to batter
		122410	ẖꜣ.w	rubbed (i.e. hammered) copper
		122230	ẖꜣ.t	[a mineral (lit. quarried thing]
		122280	ẖꜣ.t	quarry
RID	0001034	ẖꜣẖꜣ to disturb		
	ID Lexeme	858446	nẖꜣẖꜣ	to disturb
		138050	snẖꜣẖꜣ	to disturb

DRID 1000867 ẖꜣb to be crooked

RID	0001017	ẖꜣb to be crooked		
	ID Lexeme	122440	ẖꜣb	to be crooked
		122460	ẖꜣb	clavicle
		122450	ẖꜣb	sickle
		122510	ẖꜣb.yw	Those who belong to the sickle
		122470	ẖꜣb.t	'curl' (at the front of the red crown)
		122480	ẖꜣb.t	crookedness
		855503	ẖꜣb.tj	[characteristic of the red crown]
		122490	ẖꜣb.tj	crooked one (Seth)
		122500	ẖꜣb.tjt	[characteristic of the red crown]
		122520	ẖꜣbb	falseness, dishonesty

DRID 1000885 ẖꜣi̯ = šꜣi̯ to resist

RID	0001042	ẖꜣi̯ to resist		
	ID Lexeme	863351	ẖꜣꜣ	game?
		650052	ẖꜣꜣ	stake
		122370	ẖꜣy.t	palisade; stake
		122350	ẖꜣi̯	to resist

DRID 1000888 ẖꜣk to be cunning

RID	0001047	ẖꜣk to be cunning		
	ID Lexeme	122650	ẖꜣk	to be cunning; to be hostile
		122670	ẖꜣk	sorrow; pain

DRID 1000891 ẖꜣr bag (of leather)

RID	0001060	ẖꜣr bag (of leather)		
	ID Lexeme	122580	ẖꜣr	[a dry measure (for grain)];

sack; bag (of leather)

DRID	**1000894**	**ẖꜣr widow**		
RID	**0001063**	ẖꜣr widow		
	ID Lexeme	122600	ẖꜣr.t	widow
		858929	ẖꜣr.tj	the two widows

DRID	**1000897**	**ẖꜣs hole**		
RID	**0001066**	ẖꜣs hole		
	ID Lexeme	122630	ẖꜣs.t	hole in the earth
		858250	ẖꜣs.w	lustral basin?

DRID	**1000899**	**ẖꜣpi̯ to flow freely**		
RID	**0001058**	ẖꜣpi̯ to flow freely		
	ID Lexeme	122530	ẖꜣpi̯	to flow freely
		122540	ẖꜣp.t	storm

DRID	**1000909**	**ẖꜣꜣ to decide**		
RID	**0001078**	ẖꜣꜣ to be decided		
	ID Lexeme	122320	ẖꜣꜣ	to be decided

DRID	**1000916**	**ẖꜥ to empty**		
RID	**0001084**	ẖꜥ to empty		
	ID Lexeme	854536	ẖꜥ	to disgrace (a woman); to empty (so./sth.); deprive
		122720	ẖꜥ	to empty sth. /so.
		122740	ẖꜥꜥ	[a jug]
		122760	ẖꜥꜥ.w	piece; ration
		122770	ẖꜥw	[a jug]

DRID	**1000922**	**ẖꜥm to approach**		
RID	**0001091**	ẖꜥm to approach		
	ID Lexeme	122780	ẖꜥm	to approach; to reach

DRID	**1000926**	**ẖꜥḳ to shave**		
RID	**0001094**	ẖꜥḳ to shave		
	ID Lexeme	122810	ẖꜥḳ	barber
		855324	ẖꜥḳ	barber
		122830	ẖꜥḳ	razor
		122800	ẖꜥḳ	to shave
		122820	ẖꜥḳ.t	skin (shed by a snake)
		865712	mẖꜥḳ.t	razor
		74580	mẖꜥḳ.t	razor

II.16 z

DRID	**1002787**	**z door bolt**		
RID	**0003119**	z door bolt		
	ID Lexeme	125000	z	door bolt
DRID	**1002788**	**z person**		
RID	**0003120**	z person		
	ID Lexeme	125010	z man	
		125040	z.t	woman
		852654	jz.t	crew member
		859857	jz.t	(one of a) team
		31080	jz.t	crew; gang (of workmen)
		31120	jz.tj	boat crew (of the gods)
RID	**0003144**	zj who?		
	ID Lexeme	127760	zy	who? what?
DRID	**1002789**	**zb board?**		
RID	**0003121**	zb board?		
	ID Lexeme	852468	zb.w	[something wooden (board, beams)]
DRID	**1002790**	**zb heir**		
RID	**0003122**	zb heir		
	ID Lexeme	131050	zb.t	heir
DRID	**1002791**	**zbi̯ to go**		
RID	**0003123**	zbi̯ to go		
	ID Lexeme	131500	zb.y	uraeus?
		400805	zb.t	expedition
		131030	zb.t	cargo; transport
		131040	zb.t	wrong; evil
		131020	zb.t	reward; remuneration
		858725	zb.tj	one who passes by (serpent)
		131700	zb.tjw	oppressors
		131460	zbi̯	to go; to conduct; to send; to attain
		131670	zbi̯.tw	in order that
		143910	szbi̯	to send
		855456	zbb	leader; chief
RID	**0003127**	zbzb to drive away		
	ID Lexeme	132050	zbzb	to drive away
DRID	**1002792**	**zbn [a fish]**		
RID	**0003124**	zbn [a fish]		
	ID Lexeme	131830	zbn.w	[a fish]
DRID	**1002793**	**zbn to slip**		

RID	**0003125**	zbn to slip		
	ID Lexeme	131760	zbn	to slip; to steer (a ship) of course; to make fall
		852805	zbn	walking path; running route
		131840	zbnbn	to wander

DRID 1002794 zbṯ to laugh

RID	**0003126**	zbṯ to laugh		
	ID Lexeme	853499	sbj	joke
		143940	szbṯ	to make laugh
		131660	zbṯ	laughter
		132270	zbṯ	to laugh

DRID 1002795 zbꜣ flute

RID	**0003128**	zbꜣ flute		
	ID Lexeme	450260	zbꜣ	flutist
		131160	zbꜣ	to blow (i.e. play a woodwind instrument)

DRID 1002796 zf to be mild

RID	**0003129**	zf to be mild		
	ID Lexeme	133390	zf	to be mild; to be merciful
		851877	zf	friendliness; mildness
		853454	zf.w	the mild one
		133500	sf.t	friendliness; mildness
		133630	zfn	gentleness
		133620	zfn	to be gentle; to be merciful; to make calm
		143990	szf	to sound friendly
		133700	zfn.y	gentle one
		133690	zfn.w	kind person

DRID 1002797 zf = zfṯ to slaughter

RID	**0003130**	zf to slaughter		
	ID Lexeme	133410	zf	to cut up; to slaughter
		133400	zf	knife; sword
		133590	zf.j	one who cuts
		856190	zf.wt	slice
		133420	zf.t	sword; knife
RID	**0003131**	zfzf to slaughter		
	ID Lexeme	133860	zfzf	to break
		133850	zfzf	bad slaughter
RID	**000422**	zfṯ to slaughter		
	ID Lexeme	133950	zfṯ	butcher
		133940	zfṯ	to slaughter; to cut off
		133960	zfṯ	slaughter
		854261	zfṯ	butcher
		134010	zfṯ.yw	Butcher

133980 zfṯ.t sacrifice

DRID 1002798 zḥ [a bird]
RID 0003140 zḥzḥ [a bird]
ID Lexeme 141050 zḥzḥ [a bird]
855028 zḥzḥ (to sound like Zehzeh bird)

DRID 1002799 zḥ hall
RID 0003132 zḥ hall
ID Lexeme 140260 zḥ council; counsel
140250 zḥ tent; hall
140420 zḥ.y counselor; a man of good council

DRID 1002800 zḫ to hurry
RID 0003133 zḫ to hurry
ID Lexeme 142990 zḫz to run; to hurry
143000 zḫz.w runner
143040 zḫzḫ to run; to hurry

DRID 1002801 zḥ to trample
RID 0003134 zḥ to trample
ID Lexeme 140270 zḥ.t herd of sheep (treading seed into the earth)
141060 zḥzḥ to rub down; to trample
141080 zḥzḥ.y trampler

DRID 1002802 zẖi̯ to be deaf
RID 0003135 zẖi̯ to be deaf
ID Lexeme 143410 zẖ.y deaf person
855579 zẖ.yt deaf one (woman)
550303 zẖi̯ to make deaf
854862 zẖi̯ to be deaf
143400 zẖi̯ to be deaf

DRID 1002803 zḫi̯ to strike
RID 0003136 zḫi̯ to strike
ID Lexeme 141420 zḫ.t blow
141430 zḫ.tj smiter (king in battle)
141400 zḫi̯ to hit; to smite; to beat

DRID 1002804 zḫni̯ to encompass
RID 0003137 zḫni̯ to encompass
ID Lexeme 142460 zḫn random event
142450 zḫn to unite
142490 zḫn stock?
142470 zḫn [a part of the body of an offering animal]

		856200	zẖn	seeker
		142480	zẖn	reed-float
		142540	zẖn	swelling
		853457	zẖn.w	[a kind of a prediction]
		860491	zẖn.w	[the name of an area]
		142630	zẖn.w	companion
		142620	zẖn.w	search
		142640	zẖn.w	comprehensive one
		142500	zẖn.t	pole; support
		142610	zẖn.tj	inventory
		142440	zẖni̯	to embrace; to seek out; to meet
		142680	zẖni̯	the one who extends
DRID	**1002805**	**zẖz to tear**		
	RID	**0003139**	zẖz to tear	
	ID Lexeme	142980	zẖz	to tear out (the eye of Horus); to pull up (papyrus)
DRID	**1002806**	**zẖꜣ = zš to write**		
	RID	**0003142**	zẖꜣ to write	
	ID Lexeme	144250	zẖꜣ	scribe's equipment
		600375	zẖꜣ	to write; to paint
		144670	zẖꜣ.yt	writings
		144680	zẖꜣ.yt	female scribe
		550055	zẖꜣ.w	scribe
		450097	zẖꜣ.w	writing; record; depiction
		855553	zẖꜣ.w	scribe
		600376	zẖꜣ.w	writing material
		856031	zẖꜣ.w	a god who writes
		144270	zš	writing; writings
DRID	**1002807**	**zj to go**		
	RID	**0003143**	zj to go	
	ID Lexeme	856192	zj	departure
		127740	zj	to go
	RID	**0002368**	sjsj to go	
	ID Lexeme	128560	sjsj	to hurry
DRID	**1002808**	**zjn to rub**		
	RID	**0003145**	zjn to rub	
	ID Lexeme	128320	zjn	to rub (in); to rub (out)
DRID	**1002809**	**zk to dig**		
	RID	**0003146**	zk to dig	
	ID Lexeme	146380	zk	to dig out (a pool)
		146970	zkzk	[a snake]

DRID 1002810 zkr to travel

RID	**0003147**	zkr to travel		
	ID Lexeme	146900	zkr	to journey?

DRID 1002811 zmn natron

RID	**0003148**	zmn natron		
	ID Lexeme	110030	ḥzmn	to cleanse; to purify
		110040	ḥzmn	menstruation
		600346	ḥzmn	one who works with natron
		110020	ḥzmn	natron
		110130	ḥzmn.y	washstand pitcher
		110100	ḥzmn.w	one who cleans his mouth with natron
		110090	ḥzmn.t	menstruating woman
		135070	zmn	natron [element used during the ritual]
		134960	smjn	natron

DRID 1002812 zmy desert

RID	**0003149**	zmy desert		
	ID Lexeme	134780	zmy.t	desert; necropolis
		500423	zmy.tj	One who belongs to the two deserts

DRID 1002813 zmzr [a gate]

RID	**0003150**	zmzr [a gate]		
	ID Lexeme	855515	zmzr.w	[a gate]

DRID 1002814 zmꜣ to unite

RID	**0003151**	zmꜣ to unite		
	ID Lexeme	134220	zmꜣ	to beget
		134180	zmꜣ	to unite; to join
		859249	zmꜣ	to eat
		134170	zmꜣ	lung
		134230	zmꜣ	Unifier
		134280	zmꜣ	bed
		134580	zmꜣ.y	compeer
		134610	zmꜣ.yw	confederates; associates; enemies
		134600	zmꜣ.yt	band; troop
		134620	zmꜣ.yt	hogging beam?
		134900	smj.w	[a god's bark]
		134680	zmꜣ.w	combination; alloy (in reference to metals)
		134450	zmꜣ.w	branches; twigs
		134740	zmꜣ.wj	darkness
		134710	zmꜣ.wtj	[characteristic of a king]
		134720	zmꜣ.wtj	confederate

			134310	zmꜣ.t	[throne]
			134320	zmꜣ.tj	testicles
			861285	zmꜣ.tj	Compeer
			134350	zmꜣ.tj	road; path
DRID	**1002815**	**znb to overthrow**			
	RID	**0003152**	znb to overthrow		
		ID Lexeme	136890	znb	battlement
			136900	znb	to overthrow; to destroy
			137000	snb	to burn
			137030	snb	to build
			136910	znb.t	rampart
DRID	**1002816**	**znbꜣ to get out of control**			
	RID	**0003153**	znbꜣ to get out of control		
		ID Lexeme	851036	znbꜣ	failure?
			137170	znbꜣ	to get out of control
DRID	**1002817**	**znf blood**			
	RID	**0003154**	znf blood		
		ID Lexeme	137260	znf	to bleed
			137250	znf	blood
			500159	znf.yw	bloody ones
DRID	**1002818**	**znḥm locust**			
	RID	**0003155**	znḥm locust		
		ID Lexeme	858385	znḥm	Locust
			137910	znḥm	locust; grasshopper
DRID	**1002819**	**zni̯ to pass**			
	RID	**0003156**	zni̯ to cut		
		ID Lexeme	136140	zn	plowshare
			136120	zni̯	to cut off
			138190	znzn	to cut through
			138100	znzn.t	conflagration
			88210	nznzn	to destroy
	RID	**0003157**	zni̯ to open		
		ID Lexeme	136070	zn	to open
			136150	zn.t	senet (board game)
			144070	szn	to open (doors)
	RID	**0003158**	zni̯ to pass		
		ID Lexeme	136650	zn.yw	those who passed away
			136590	zni̯	to pass (by); to go (by); to separate
			854546	zni̯	get close to; surpass; pass; happen; to separate (from); cut off; cut off; be similar to
			137560	znn	chariot soldier; warrior

88200 nznzn to pass away
RID 0003159 zni̯ to resemble
ID Lexeme 850921 zn cutting edge (of the sword)?; sharpening?
136180 zn.tj likeness
136080 zni̯ to come close to; to exceed; to resemble
136670 snj.w [a measure of value]; piece of silver (of specific weight)
137580 znn image; likeness
137570 znn copy (of a document); record
144060 szn to cause to resemble?

DRID 1002820 znš = zꜣš = zš to open
RID 0003160 znš to open
ID Lexeme 144300 zš to open
144310 zš threshold
144320 zš to spread; to strew
855474 znš to open
858387 znš gate; corner
RID 0003200 zꜣš to open
ID Lexeme 127290 zꜣš to open (ears)

DRID 1002821 znṯ to be rebellious
RID 0003161 znṯ to be rebellious
ID Lexeme 138530 znṯ to be rebellious; to be lustful
138610 znṯ.w rebels

DRID 1002822 zp matter
RID 0003162 zp matter
ID Lexeme 132300 zp matter; affair; conduct
132310 zp time; occasion
854543 zp case; matter; essence; time
132320 zp remedy; means
132480 zp.w case of illness

DRID 1002823 zp to tousle
RID 0003164 zpz to tousle
ID Lexeme 133090 zpz The tousled one
133080 zpz to tousle
RID 0003165 zpzp to tousle
ID Lexeme 133120 zpzp to tousle
133130 zpzp [a kind of illegal deed]

DRID 1002824 zpi̯ to remain
RID 0003163 zpi̯ to remain
ID Lexeme 132330 zp remainder; remnant

			132730	zp.yt	remainder; remnant
			860460	zp.w	harvest grain
			132380	zp.t	threshing floor; heap of grain
			132710	zpi̯	to remain over; to be left out (excluded); to be left (abandoned)
			132740	zpy.t	gobbet
			132780	zpp	remainder
			132790	zpp.y	remainder
DRID	**1002825**	**zpꜣ to wriggle**			
	RID	**0003166**	zpꜣ to wriggle		
		ID Lexeme	132340	zp	worm-like clot
			132620	zpꜣ	writhing; to be wrinkled (or similar)
			132660	zpꜣ	[verb of movement, applied to the intestines (med.)]
			132630	zpꜣ	centipede
			132650	zpꜣ	carrying chair; steps
			857288	zpꜣ.t	centipede
			132720	zpy	[as an element during Osiris mysteries]
DRID	**1002826**	**zr pellet**			
	RID	**0003167**	zr pellet		
		ID Lexeme	139130	zr.w	pellets of incense
DRID	**1002827**	**zr ram**			
	RID	**0003168**	zr ram		
		ID Lexeme	138890	zr	double-ram gate (in heavens)
			138880	zr	ram
			139040	sr	sheep fat?
			856198	zr.wj	the two rams
			138910	zr.t	a decan star
			138900	zr.t	sheep; ewe
DRID	**1002828**	**zrm [a beer]**			
	RID	**0003169**	zrm [a beer]		
		ID Lexeme	139490	zrm.t	[beer made of dates]
DRID	**1002829**	**zrt knife**			
	RID	**0003170**	zrt knife		
		ID Lexeme	858394	zrt.w	knife
DRID	**1002830**	**zš [a rope]**			
	RID	**0003171**	zš [a rope]		
		ID Lexeme	144380	zš	a rope

DRID	**1002831**	**zš to pass**		
	RID	**0003172**	zš to pass	
		ID Lexeme	144350 zš	to cause to pass away (e.g., anger, through the sound of the sistrum)
			859855 zš	run
			144330 zš	to pass (by)
DRID	**1002832**	**zši̯ to tear out**		
	RID	**0003172**	zši̯ to tear out	
		ID Lexeme	850590 zši̯	to tear out; to pull out
			145600 zšš	to tear out (papyrus)
			854863 mzš	to core sth; to dissolute
DRID	**1002833**	**zšj to nest**		
	RID	**0003173**	zšj to nest	
		ID Lexeme	144430 zš.w	swamp fowl
			144360 zš	marsh land; pond; nest
			144660 zšj	to nest
DRID	**1002834**	**zšn lotus**		
	RID	**0003174**	zšn lotus	
		ID Lexeme	145220 zšn	lotus blossom
			865373 zšn	Lotus flower application (made of copper)
			145440 zšn.t	lotus-bark [a kind of a boat]
			856199 zšn.t	lotus pond
			145420 sšn.t	lotus pond
			145390 zšnn	Lotus flower
			145450 sšntj	bird of the lotus pond
DRID	**1002835**	**zšp to polish**		
	RID	**0003175**	zšp to polish	
		ID Lexeme	144840 zšp	polisher
			144830 zšp	to polish; to smooth
DRID	**1002836**	**zšš sistrum**		
	RID	**0003176**	zšš sistrum	
		ID Lexeme	500365 zšš	one who rattles
			859774 zšš	sistrum
			145610 zšš	to play the sistrum
			145620 zšš.t	sistrum
DRID	**1002837**	**zšzš [a rope]**		
	RID	**0003177**	zšzš [a rope]	
		ID Lexeme	145590 zšzš.t	a rope
DRID	**1002838**	**zw wheat**		

RID	**0003178**	zw wheat	
ID Lexeme	129420	zw.t	[a kind of a wheat]
	850978	zw.tjt	[a kind of a wheat]
	75040	mzw.t	[an offering of grain]
DRID	**1002839**	**zwn [a vessel]**	
RID	**0003179**	zwn [a vessel]	
ID Lexeme	130250	zwn.w	[a vessel]
DRID	**1002840**	**zwn arrow**	
RID	**0003180**	zwn arrow	
ID Lexeme	130090	zwn	arrow
DRID	**1002841**	**zwnu̯ to suffer**	
RID	**0003181**	zwnu̯ to suffer	
ID Lexeme	853383	swn	one who suffer; needy one
	130230	swn.yt	the suffering
	130260	zwn.w	physician
	855957	zwn.w	physician
	130270	zwnu̯	to suffer
	137670	znnj	bad luck
	137660	znnj	to suffer; to be distressed
	143890	szwnu̯	to destroy; to punish
DRID	**1002842**	**zwr to drink**	
RID	**0003182**	zwr to drink	
ID Lexeme	130360	zwr	to drink
	130390	zwr	drinking bowl?
	130370	zwr	drinking bowl
	600362	zwr	drinking bout; carousal
	130410	zwr.t	watering place
	130400	zwr.t	[a beverage]
	860650	zwr.tj	one who slurps
	75220	mzwr	drinking place
	143900	szwr	to soak
DRID	**1002843**	**zwrw [a bird]**	
RID	**0003183**	zwrw [a bird]	
ID Lexeme	130490	zwrw.t	[a bird]
DRID	**1002844**	**zwš to lump**	
RID	**0003184**	zwš to twist	
ID Lexeme	130760	zwš	strip; ball (of material)
	130770	zwš	massing (as an illness symptom)
	129910	zwš	rope (on harpoon)
	130750	zwš	to lump; to twist together
	450010	zwš.t	[a rope]

DRID	**1002845**	**zwṯ to roll**		
	RID	**0003185**	zwṯ to roll	
		ID Lexeme	130910 zwṯ	to roll (a flour ball, fattening geese)
DRID	**1002846**	**zwꜣ to chop**		
	RID	**0003186**	zwꜣ to chop	
		ID Lexeme	129730 zwꜣ	to cut (down, off)
			855501 zwꜣ.t	chopper
DRID	**1002847**	**zz to burn**		
	RID	**0003187**	zz to burn	
		ID Lexeme	143720 ss	to burn
			143740 zz.w	dust?; ashes?
			855601 zz.wj	the one belonging to the ashes
DRID	**1002848**	**zzḥ to destroy**		
	RID	**0003188**	zzḥ to destroy	
		ID Lexeme	144140 zzḥ	to destroy (enemies)
DRID	**1002849**	**zzḥꜣ vessel**		
	RID	**0003189**	zzḥꜣ vessel	
		ID Lexeme	144150 zzḥꜣ	vessel (gen.)
DRID	**1002850**	**zzi̭ to punish**		
	RID	**0003190**	zzi̭ to punish	
		ID Lexeme	856224 zzi̭	to punish
DRID	**1002851**	**zꜣ duck**		
	RID	**0003191**	zꜣ duck	
		ID Lexeme	125060 z.t	northern pintail duck
			74930 mzꜣ.t	[a goose]
DRID	**1002852**	**zꜣ eighth of an aroura**		
	RID	**0003192**	zꜣ eighth of an aroura	
		ID Lexeme	125520 zꜣ	eighth of an aroura
DRID	**1002853**	**zꜣ son**		
	RID	**0003193**	zꜣ son	
		ID Lexeme	125510 zꜣ	son
			125900 zꜣ.wtt	sons and daughters
			125630 zꜣ.t	daughter
			860541 zꜣ.t	daughter
			125660 zꜣ.tj	son (in: son of Geb; of the king)
			125650 zꜣ.tj	the two daughters
DRID	**1002854**	**zꜣb jackal**		

RID	**0003194**	zꜣb jackal		
	ID Lexeme	126620	zꜣb	dignitary
		126610	zꜣb	to traverse (like a jackal)
		126600	zꜣb	jackal
		852031	zꜣb.wt	wisdom
RID	**0003195**	zꜣb to flow		
	ID Lexeme	126590	zꜣb	to flow; to drip

DRID 1002855 zꜣg [a mythological animal]

RID	**0003196**	zꜣg [a mythological animal]		
	ID Lexeme	127510	zꜣg.t	[a fabulous animal (griffin?)]

DRID 1002856 zꜣi̯ to linger

RID	**0003197**	zꜣi̯ to linger		
	ID Lexeme	126320	zꜣi̯	to linger; to creep
		401125	zꜣꜣ.y	sneaker
		143770	szꜣi̯	to discard (clothing)
		852807	zꜣw.tj	sneaker?

DRID 1002857 zꜣr [a plant]

RID	**0003198**	zꜣr [a plant]		
	ID Lexeme	126790	zꜣr.t	[a garden plant]

DRID 1002858 zꜣr bond

RID	**0003199**	zꜣr bond		
	ID Lexeme	126890	zꜣr	bonds

DRID 1002860 zꜣt incense

RID	**0003201**	zꜣt incense		
	ID Lexeme	127550	zꜣt.t	incense

DRID 1002861 zꜣṯ to make libation

RID	**0003202**	zꜣṯ to make libation		
	ID Lexeme	127630	zꜣṯ	libation stone
		127610	zꜣṯ	to pour out; to make a libation
		127620	zꜣṯ	libation
		127650	zꜣṯ.w	ground; floor; earth
		853160	zꜣṯ.w	Offering (domain)

DRID 1002862 zꜣu̯ to protect

RID	**0003203**	zꜣu̯ to protect		
	ID Lexeme	125581	zꜣ	phyle (of priests)
		125600	zꜣ	protection
		854541	zꜣ	phyle (of priests)
		125610	zꜣ	amulet
		125550	zꜣ	to ward
		125580	zꜣ	troop (of soldiers, of workmen)
		126300	zꜣ.w	guardian

126280	zꜣ.w	magician
400556	zꜣ.w	one belonging to the phyle
855948	zꜣ.w	guardian
126390	zꜣ.wt	custody
126410	zꜣ.wtj	guardian
861593	zꜣ.wtj	guardian
126190	zꜣy.t	protectress
858344	zꜣꜣ	guardian
851821	zꜣu̯	to prevent (aux., modal)
126290	zꜣu̯	to guard; to heed; to guard against
126310	zꜣw	captive? [abusive name of Apophis]
126400	zꜣw.t	lumbal area

DRID 1002863 zꜣw to break

RID	**0003204**	zꜣw to break		
	ID Lexeme	126330	zꜣw	to break; to be broken
		126360	zꜣw	beam; baulk
		857007	zꜣw.t	beam

II.17 s

DRID	**1000145**	**stnw charburner?**		
RID	**0002589**	stnw charburner?		
	ID lexeme	148350	stnw.y	charburner?
DRID	**1001880**	**snrw = slw [a product of Nubia]**		
RID	**0002236**	snrw = slw [a product of Nubia]		
	ID lexeme	137720	snrw	[basket, or sim.]
DRID	**1002000**	**s [a goose]**		
RID	**0002236**	s [a goose]		
	ID lexeme	125090	s	[a goose]
DRID	**1002002**	**s folded cloth**		
RID	**0002238**	s folded cloth		
	ID lexeme	856026	s	folded cloth
DRID	**1002003**	**s seat**		
RID	**0002240**	s seat		
	ID lexeme	125140	s.t	[in abstract sense]
		400492	s.t	throne
		400493	s.t	residence
		125100	s.t	place; seat; position (rank)
		854540	s.t	place; seat; position (rank); throne; living place
		125120	s.tj	successor; deputy
		125130	s.tjt	successor?
		87880	ns.t	Base (part of brick ramp)
		87870	ns.t	seat; throne
		851582	ns.tj	what belongs to the thorn
		857004	ns.tjw	those belonging to thrones
DRID	**1002006**	**sb [edible part of cattle]**		
RID	**0002243**	sb [edible part of cattle]		
	ID lexeme	131090	sb	[edible part of cattle]
DRID	**1002008**	**sb reed**		
RID	**0002245**	sb reed		
	ID lexeme	131120	sb.t	reed
DRID	**1002013**	**sbḥ to cry out**		
RID	**0002250**	sbḥ to cry out		
	ID lexeme	140630	sbḥ	wind
		131910	sbḥ	cry; shriek
		131900	sbḥ	to cry out

DRID	**1002014**	**sbḫ to enclose**		
RID	**0002251**	sbḫ to enclose		
	ID lexeme	131960	sbḫ	to spread (poison in the limbs)
		131940	sbḫ	to enclose (with the arms); to enfold (in the arms)
		131950	sbḫ	pot
		131970	sbḫ.t	portal; portico
		131980	sbḫ.t	pylon-shaped pectoral amulet
		132000	sbḫ.tj	he who belongs to the portal
DRID	**1002017**	**sbj to rebel**		
RID	**0002254**	sbj to rebel		
	ID lexeme	131520	sbj	to rebel against
		131530	sbj	rebel
		131610	sbj.w	hostility
		131560	sbj.t	outrage
		131550	sbj.t	rebels
		131570	sby.t	head wind
		143920	ssbj	to provoke (a revolt); to incite
DRID	**1002018**	**sbn bandage**		
RID	**0002256**	sbn bandage		
	ID lexeme	131770	sbn	bandage (especially of mummies)
DRID	**1002021**	**sbḳ leg**		
RID	**0002259**	sbḳ leg		
	ID lexeme	132110	sbḳ	leg
DRID	**1002022**	**sbḳ to be wise**		
RID	**0002260**	sbḳ to be wise		
	ID lexeme	401163	sbḳ	splendid; wise
		501137	sbḳ	wise one
		132120	sbḳ	to become knowing; to be wise
		143930	ssbḳ	to honor someone
DRID	**1002023**	**sbr branch**		
RID	**0002261**	sbr branch		
	ID lexeme	131870	sbr	shoots (of a tree); clusters (of grapes)
DRID	**1002024**	**sbt [a plant]**		
RID	**0002264**	sbt [a plant]		
	ID lexeme	132240	sbt.t	flower
		132250	sbtty.t	[a kind of a plant]
DRID	**1002025**	**sbtj wall**		
RID	**0002265**	sbtj wall		

		ID lexeme	132260	sbtj	wall; rampart
DRID	**1002026**	**sbꜣ gate**			
	RID	**0002266**	sbꜣ gate		
		ID lexeme	131200	sbꜣ	door; doorway; portal
			500386	sbꜣ.y	he of the portal
			869219	sbꜣ.t	gate
DRID	**1002027**	**sbꜣ star**			
	RID	**0002267**	sbꜣ star		
		ID lexeme	131270	sbꜣ	sun shade
			854091	sbꜣ	star amulet
			131180	sbꜣ	star
			131400	sbꜣ.yw	the starry ones
			131380	sbꜣ.yt	the starry one
			131280	sbꜣ.t	star
			131370	sbꜣy	to be star-like; to sparkle like a star
DRID	**1002028**	**sbꜣ to teach**			
	RID	**0002268**	sbꜣ to teach		
		ID lexeme	131240	sbꜣ	surveying instrument?
			131230	sbꜣ	pupil
			856678	sbꜣ	wise; smart
			131220	sbꜣ	to learn
			131210	sbꜣ	to teach; to tend
			863201	sbꜣ.yt	[observation instrument]
			131390	sbꜣ.yt	teaching; instruction; punishment
			131330	sbꜣ.w	teaching
			131320	sbꜣ.w	teacher; instructor
			860917	sbꜣ.wtj	teacher
			131420	sbꜣ.wtj	the punisher?
			131310	sbꜣ.tj	pupil
			131740	sbbꜣ.yw	instructor
DRID	**1002029**	**sd column (of a text)**			
	RID	**0002269**	sd column (of a text)		
		ID lexeme	149570	sd	section; column (of a text)
DRID	**1002031**	**sḏ fire**			
	RID	**0002271**	sḏ fire		
		ID lexeme	150140	sḏ.t	fire; flame
DRID	**1002032**	**sḏ foster child**			
	RID	**0002272**	sḏ foster child		
		ID lexeme	858943	sḏ.tj	child
			150150	sḏ.tj	child; foster child
			869996	sḏ.tjt	girl; foster child (female)

		150160	sḏ.tjt	girl; foster child (female)
DRID	**1002034**	**sḏ loincloth**		
	RID	**0002274**	sḏ loincloth	
		ID lexeme	600584 sḏ.w	loincloth
DRID	**1002035**	**sd tail**		
	RID	**0002276**	sd tail	
		ID lexeme	149520 sd	tail
DRID	**1002036**	**sd to be clothed**		
	RID	**0002277**	sd to be clothed	
		ID lexeme	149540 sd	to be clothed
			76130 msd	to clothe
			76140 msd.t	clothing
DRID	**1002037**	**sḏ to break**		
	RID	**0002278**	sḏ to break	
		ID lexeme	150120 sḏ	fracture (of a bone); rupture (med.)
			150110 sḏ	to break; set out; to solve; dissolve
			857754 sḏ	Breaker
			150130 sḏ.t	water breakthrough
DRID	**1002038**	**sdb [a garment]**		
	RID	**0002279**	sdb [a garment]	
		ID lexeme	149760 sdb	[a kind of a garment]
			149750 sdb	[fringed hem of a linen sheet]
DRID	**1002039**	**sḏb evil**		
	RID	**0002280**	sḏb evil	
		ID lexeme	150450 sḏb	obstacle; impediment; evil
DRID	**1002040**	**sdb to be softened**		
	RID	**0002281**	sdb to be softened	
		ID lexeme	856299 sdb	to be softened
DRID	**1002042**	**sḏḏ image**		
	RID	**0002283**	sḏḏ image	
		ID lexeme	151000 sḏḏ	image; form
DRID	**1002043**	**sdf [a unit of measure, for figs]**		
	RID	**0002284**	sdf [a unit of measure, for figs]	
		ID lexeme	149810 sdf	[a unit of measure, for figs]
DRID	**1002044**	**sḏḥ shin**		
	RID	**0002285**	sḏḥ shin	
		ID lexeme	150900 sḏḥ	shin; lower leg

DRID	**1002048**	**sdm eye-paint**		
RID	**0002289**	sdm eye-paint		
ID Lexeme		149840	sdm	eye-paint
		149830	sdm	to paint (the eyes)
		76200	msdm.j	one who prepares eye-paint
		76190	msdm.t	black eye paint (galena)

DRID	**1002049**	**sḏm to hear**		
RID	**0002291**	sḏm to hear		
ID Lexeme		150560	sḏm	to hear; to listen
		863378	sḏm	servant
		150590	sḏm	servant
		150570	sḏm	questioning
		150680	sḏm.j	hearer
		150700	sḏm.yw	judges (lit. listeners)
		150690	sḏm.yt	gossip
		851875	sḏm.w	the hearer

DRID	**1002050**	**sḏn to carry**		
RID	**0002292**	sḏn to carry		
ID Lexeme		150710	sḏn	to lift up; to carry

DRID	**1002051**	**sḏnf ibex**		
RID	**0002293**	sḏnf ibex		
ID Lexeme		150730	sḏnf	ibex

DRID	**1002052**	**sḏr [a med. liquid]**		
RID	**0002294**	sḏr [a med. liquid]		
ID Lexeme		150760	sḏr	[a med. liquid]

DRID	**1002054**	**sḏr to sleep**		
RID	**0002296**	sḏr to sleep		
ID Lexeme		150870	sḏr	sleeper
		852797	sḏr	sleeping one
		851684	sḏr	to spend the night; [aux./modal]
		150800	sḏr	appartment (of the Residence)
		150750	sḏr	mat
		150740	sḏr	to lie; to sleep; spend the night
		150820	sḏr.yt	sleeping place; (state of being) bedridden; intercourse
		150840	sḏr.yt	intercourse
		150890	sḏr.yt	defeat
		150830	sḏr.yt	(state of being) bedridden
		851893	sḏr.w	the sleeping ones
		150850	sḏr.t	(festival of) laying (Osiris to rest)
		150860	sḏr.t	sleeping draught
		76230	msḏr	ear

860133 msḏr.t ear

DRID 1002055 sdꜣ cattle egret
RID 0002297 sdꜣ cattle egret
ID Lexeme 149650 sdꜣ cattle egret

DRID 1002056 sḏꜣ to amuse (trans.)
RID 0002298 sḏꜣ to amuse (trans.)
ID Lexeme 150230 sḏꜣ to amuse (trans.)
108200 sḏꜣs to be prosperous

DRID 1002057 sḏꜣ to seal
RID 0002299 sḏꜣ to seal
ID Lexeme 150280 sḏꜣ [necklace with seal cylinder]
150320 sḏꜣ.wt seal; sealing
150300 sḏꜣ.t valuables; treasure (lit. what is sealed)
144240 ssḏꜣ.t protective spell

DRID 1002059 sḏꜣm hoe
RID 0002301 sḏꜣm hoe
ID Lexeme 150410 sḏꜣm.t hoe

DRID 1002060 sḏꜣm to speak boastfully
RID 0002302 sḏꜣm to speak boastfully
ID Lexeme 150390 sḏꜣm to speak boastfully (of something)

DRID 1002061 sf to burn?
RID 0002303 sf to burn?
ID Lexeme 144010 ssf ashes
144000 ssf to burn up
133880 sfsf ashes
133870 sfsf to burn

DRID 1002062 sf yesterday
RID 0002304 sf yesterday
ID Lexeme 851674 sf yesterday
133440 sf yesterday

DRID 1002064 sfẖ seven
RID 0002306 sfẖ seven
ID Lexeme 133760 sfẖ seven
857771 sfẖ.wj seven wave cloth
854324 sfẖ.nw seventh

DRID 1002065 sfi̯ to mix
RID 0002307 sfi̯ to mix

	ID Lexeme	133580	sfi̯	to mix
		133890	sfsf	to offer [water]

DRID 1002069 sfṯ [an oil]

RID	**0002314**	sfṯ [an oil]?		
	ID Lexeme	128290	sjft	[a kind of jar]
		133990	sfṯ	[one of the seven sacred oils]

DRID 1002071 sfy child

RID	**0002316**	sfy child		
	ID Lexeme	133600	sfy	child; lad; son

DRID 1002072 sfꜣ to neglect

RID	**0002317**	sfꜣ to neglect		
	ID Lexeme	133520	sfꜣ	to hate
		133530	sfꜣ	to neglect; to be slow
		874520	sfꜣ.w	hated; something you don't want to eat
		133560	sfꜣ.t	hatred

DRID 1002074 sg sacking

RID	**0002319**	sg sacking		
	ID Lexeme	34680	sg	sacking

DRID 1002075 sg to open a way

RID	**0002320**	sg to open a way		
	ID Lexeme	147080	sg	to open a way; to break a trail

DRID 1002076 sgbyn [a body of water]

RID	**0002321**	sgbyn [a body of water]		
	ID Lexeme	147180	sgbyn	[a body of water]

DRID 1002077 sgmḥ (cult) spear

RID	**0002322**	sgmḥ (cult) spear		
	ID Lexeme	147210	sgmḥ	(cult) spear (of Horus at Edfu)

DRID 1002080 sgr fortress

RID	**0002325**	sgr fortress		
	ID Lexeme	147280	sgr	fortress

DRID 1002081 sẖ [a beverage]

RID	**0002326**	sẖ [a beverage]		
	ID Lexeme	143340	sẖ.t	[a kind of a beverage]

DRID 1002082 sẖ barley

RID	**0002327**	sẖ barley		
	ID Lexeme	143330	sẖ.t	barley [a kind of a cereal]

DRID	**1002083**	**sḫ gallbladder**		
	RID	**0002328**	sḫ gallbladder	
		ID Lexeme	141440 sḫ.w	gallbladder
DRID	**1002085**	**sḥ royal dome**		
	RID	**0002330**	sḥ royal dome	
		ID Lexeme	140280 sḥ	royal dome
DRID	**1002086**	**sẖb to slurp**		
	RID	**0002331**	sẖb to slurp	
		ID Lexeme	143480 sẖb	to swallow (something liquid); to quaff
			143490 sẖb.w	drinking portion
DRID	**1002087**	**sḥd star**		
	RID	**0002332**	sḥd star	
		ID Lexeme	141220 sḥd	[a star]
			141230 sḥd	to be covered with stars
			141240 sḥd.w	[part of heaven]
DRID	**1002088**	**sḫd to rebuke**		
	RID	**0002333**	sḫd to rebuke	
		ID Lexeme	143280 sḫd	to rebuke
			856669 sḫd	blame
			143290 sḫd.y	evildoer
			863945 sḫd.yt	evildoer
DRID	**1002089**	**sḫf to write down**		
	RID	**0002334**	sḫf to write down	
		ID Lexeme	142080 sḫf	to write down
DRID	**1002090**	**sḫm [watery area in heaven]**		
	RID	**0002335**	sḫm [watery area in heaven]	
		ID Lexeme	142120 sḫm	[watery area in heaven]
DRID	**1002091**	**sḫm sistrum**		
	RID	**0002336**	sḫm sistrum	
		ID Lexeme	142200 sḫm	to play sistrum
			142190 sḫm	sistrum
			142380 sḫm.yt	sistrum player
			142390 sḫmjj	sistrum player
DRID	**1002092**	**sẖm to be hasty**		
	RID	**0002337**	sẖm to be hasty	
		ID Lexeme	143540 sẖm	to be hasty; to be impetuous
DRID	**1002093**	**sḫm to be mighty**		

RID	**0002338**	sḫm to be mighty		
	ID Lexeme	500441	sḫm	power
		142150	sḫm	sword
		854304	sḫm	the mighty one
		142140	sḫm	(divine) power; (divine) image
		142130	sḫm	sekhem-scepter
		855216	sḫm	book of spells
		400331	sḫm	mighty
		142180	sḫm	might
		142160	sḫm	to be mighty
		142170	sḫm	to be mighty; to prevail over
		851679	sḫm	to be mighty; to prevail over
		142400	sḫm.w	powerful beings (i.e. cult images)
		142300	sḫm.wj	[name for two mirrors]
		142240	sḫm.t	power; might
		858646	sḫm.t	powerful one
		142270	sḫm.t	[term for fire]
		142280	sḫm.tj	two powerful ones (the double crown)
		142290	sḫm.tj	mighty
		859592	sḫm.tj	two powerful ones
		144160	ssḫm	to strengthen

DRID 1002094 sḥm to crush

RID	**0002339**	sḥm to crush		
	ID Lexeme	870269	sḥm	resolution
		140730	sḥm	contusion
		140710	sḥm	to pound; to crush
		140720	sḥm	trituration (mixture of finely powdered substances) (med.)
		140770	sḥm.y	pestle
		869369	sḥm.t	mortar

DRID 1002095 sḫmḫ to amuse

RID	**0002340**	sḫmḫ to amuse		
	ID Lexeme	142410	sḫmḫ	to amuse

DRID 1002096 sḫn [a divine bark]

RID	**0002341**	sḫn [a divine bark]		
	ID Lexeme	142550	sḫn	[a divine bark]

DRID 1002097 sḫnš to irritate

RID	**0002342**	sḫnš to irritate		
	ID Lexeme	142710	sḫnš	to irritate

DRID 1002098 sḫp to laud

RID	**0002343**	sḫp to laud

		ID Lexeme	142000	sẖp	to laud
DRID	**1002100**	**sẖr lumber**			
	RID	**0002345**	sẖr lumber		
		ID Lexeme	850926	sẖr	lumber; wooden utensils
DRID	**1002101**	**sẖr plan**			
	RID	**0002346**	sẖr plan		
		ID Lexeme	142800	sẖr	plan; condition; nature; conduct
			861829	sẖr.y	counselor
			142890	sẖr.y	advisor
			142870	sẖr.y	captain; plan maker
			142880	sẖr.y	advisor
			142830	sẖr.t	roll of papyrus; scroll
DRID	**1002102**	**sẖt [a stretch of water]**			
	RID	**0002347**	sẖt [a stretch of water]		
		ID Lexeme	143090	sẖt	[a stretch of water]
DRID	**1002103**	**sẖt to form**			
	RID	**0002348**	sẖt to form		
		ID Lexeme	97070	sẖt	brick
			143060	sẖt	to weave; to form (bricks, in a mould)
			143200	sẖt.j	castrated one
			143110	sẖt.j	weaver
			143190	sẖt.j	weaver
DRID	**1002104**	**sẖt to make ready**			
	RID	**0002349**	sẖt to make ready		
		ID Lexeme	854548	sẖt	to make ready
			143070	sẖt	to grasp (something)
			75750	msẖ.t	arm
			75760	msẖt.w	[adze (as used in the Opening-of-the-mouth ritual)]
	RID	**0002350**	sẖt to trap		
		ID Lexeme	143050	sẖt	to trap (with a net, a snare)
			450571	sẖt	bird trap; net; noose
			143180	sẖt.j	bird catcher
			143220	sẖt.jt	bird catcher
			143230	sẖt.w	flesh of snared wild-fowl?
			857936	sẖt.t	trapping place
DRID	**1002105**	**sḥw dirt**			
	RID	**0002351**	sḥw dirt		
		ID Lexeme	140480	sḥw	dirt

DRID 1002106 sḫwꜣ to deny

RID	**0002352**	sḫwꜣ to deny		
	ID Lexeme	141920	sḫwꜣ	to deny

DRID 1002107 sḫꜣ [a piece of nautical equipment]

RID	**0002353**	sḫꜣ [a piece of nautical equipment]		
	ID Lexeme	141660	sḫꜣ	[a piece of nautical equipment (rope?)]

DRID 1002108 sḥꜣ donkey

RID	**0002354**	sḥꜣ donkey		
	ID Lexeme	140370	sḥꜣ.t	herd of donkeys
		450655	sḥꜣ.tj	donkey boy

DRID 1002109 sḫꜣ to remember

RID	**0002355**	sḫꜣ to remember		
	ID Lexeme	141620	sḫꜣ	to remember
		141700	sḫꜣ.w	memorandum
		141690	sḫꜣ.w	remembrance; memory; memorial
		75650	msḫꜣ	to rejoice
		75670	msḫꜣ	[a sacred beetle]
		75690	msḫꜣꜣ.t	[a sacred beetle]; clearing goddess

DRID 1002110 sẖꜣk to strain

RID	**0002356**	sẖꜣk to strain		
	ID Lexeme	143390	sẖꜣk	to strain; to squeeze out
		143620	sẖnk.t	sieve

DRID 1002111 sẖꜣꜣ hauling

RID	**0002357**	sẖꜣꜣ hauling		
	ID Lexeme	143360	sẖꜣ	to pull
		143370	sẖꜣ.t	to pull?
		450518	sẖꜣꜣ	to land (a boat); to row
		860102	msẖꜣ	waterway

DRID 1002112 sẖꜥ hare

RID	**0002358**	sẖꜥ hare		
	ID Lexeme	855191	sẖꜥ	Hare (Seth)
		143470	sẖꜥ.t	hare

DRID 1002113 sẖꜥ to gild

RID	**0002359**	sẖꜥ to gild		
	ID Lexeme	143440	sẖꜥ	to gild
		143460	sẖꜥ	[an amuletic pendant?]

DRID 1002114 sj to limp?

RID	**0002360**	sj to limp?

ID Lexeme 127800 sj to limp?

DRID 1002115 sjd tray
RID 0002361 sjd tray
ID Lexeme 128650 sjd tray; tray with a “heap” (of bread)

DRID 1002116 sjf to insult
RID 0002362 sjf to insult
ID Lexeme 128260 sjf to insult

DRID 1002117 sjm haze
RID 0002363 sjm haze
ID Lexeme 128300 sjm fog, haze, humidity (or sim.)

DRID 1002118 sjn clay
RID 0002364 sjn clay
ID Lexeme 128340 sjn clay (material for seals)
128410 sjn.t sealing (of clay); clay vessel

DRID 1002119 sjn to hurry
RID 0002365 sjn to hurry
ID Lexeme 128380 sjn the fast one
128370 sjn to run; to hurry; to bring (something) quickly
128430 sjn courier
854358 sjn hurry
128400 sjn.t canoe (fast-moving boat)

DRID 1002120 sjr [activity connected with the heart]
RID 0002366 sjr [activity connected with the heart]
ID Lexeme 128500 sjr [activity connected with the heart]

DRID 1002121 sjs six
RID 0002367 sjs six
ID Lexeme 128520 sjs six
128530 sjs.j six-weave linen
857784 sjs.w house of six chambers?
857783 sjs.nwt Sixth-day festival

DRID 1002122 sjtj trial
RID 0002369 sjtj trial
ID Lexeme 171100 sjtj trial (when calculating)

DRID 1002123 sjꜣ [a falcon]
RID 0002370 sjꜣ [a falcon]
ID Lexeme 127920 sjꜣ.w [sacred falcon]
127900 sjꜣ.t [a bird-shaped amulet]

DRID	**1002124**	**sjꜣ fringed cloth**			
	RID	**0002371**	sjꜣ fringed cloth		
		ID Lexeme	127890	sjꜣ.t	[a fringed cloth of linen]
			856069	sjꜣ.tj	the one with a fringed cloth
DRID	**1002125**	**sjꜣ to recognize**			
	RID	**0002372**	sjꜣ to recognize		
		ID Lexeme	500191	sjꜣ	knowledge (personification)
			127840	sjꜣ	to recognize; to perceive
			127850	sjꜣ	perception; mind
			75010	msjꜣ.t	appreciation; characteristic
DRID	**1002126**	**sk [a toilette utensil]**			
	RID	**0002373**	sk [a toilette utensil]		
		ID Lexeme	146690	sk.j	[a toilette utensil]
DRID	**1002127**	**sk complain**			
	RID	**0002374**	sk complain		
		ID Lexeme	146420	sk	accusation
			75910	mskj	rumor?
DRID	**1002128**	**sk flour**			
	RID	**0002375**	sk flour		
		ID Lexeme	146730	sk.j	flour
DRID	**1002129**	**sk lance**			
	RID	**0002376**	sk lance		
		ID Lexeme	146460	sk	lance
DRID	**1002130**	**sk to be a star in the sky**			
	RID	**0002377**	sk to be a star in the sky		
		ID Lexeme	146410	sk	to be a star in the sky
	RID	**0002384**	sksk to illumine		
		ID Lexeme	146990	sksk	light
			147000	sksk	[baboon worshiping the sun]
			146980	sksk	to illumine
DRID	**1002131**	**sk to wipe**			
	RID	**0002378**	sk to wipe		
		ID Lexeme	146400	sk	to wipe (out, away)
DRID	**1002132**	**ski̯ to perish**			
	RID	**0002379**	ski̯ to perish		
		ID Lexeme	75920	msk.tjt	nocturnal solar bark
			853782	msk.tjt	nocturnal solar bark
			858508	sk	sinking
			852792	sk	ruin
			859239	sk.yt	Battlefield

			146580	sk.w	fray; battle
			146520	sk.t	[a headache]
			146540	sk.tj	[a boat]
			146570	sk.tj	military officer
			146710	ski̯	to destroy
			146720	ski̯	to pass (time)
			146700	ski̯	to perish
			854552	ski̯	to perish; to destroy
			146430	ski̯	to grind
			147010	sksk	to destroy
			147040	skt	[a military officer (scout?) (guard?)]
DRID	**1002133**		**skn to be greedy**		
	RID	**0002380**	skn to be greedy		
		ID Lexeme	858372	zkn	to be greedy
			146870	skn	to make unpopular (or similar)
			650002	skn	greedy one
			146840	skn	to be greedy; to be voracious
DRID	**1002135**		**skp to filter**		
	RID	**0002382**	skp to filter		
		ID Lexeme	146760	skp	to filter
DRID	**1002137**		**skꜣ to plough**		
	RID	**0002385**	skꜣ to plough		
		ID Lexeme	146610	skꜣ	to plough; to cultivate
			146630	skꜣ	plough ox
			146620	skꜣ	crops
			146490	skꜣ	plough ass
			600215	skꜣ.t	plough land
DRID	**1002141**		**sm herbs**		
	RID	**0002386**	sm herbs		
		ID Lexeme	134940	sm.y	weeded
			134870	sm.yt	herbage
			134140	sm.w	plants; vegetables; pasture
			500646	sm.wj	one who belongs to the plants
			134120	sm.t	Straw mat
DRID	**1002144**		**sm to respect**		
	RID	**0002389**	sm to respect		
		ID Lexeme	854837	sm	pleasure
			853500	sm	situation?
			134050	sm	deed; event; pastime
			134060	sm	occasion? attention? worry?
			134090	sm	altar

		134030	sm	to respect
		134080	sm	high priest of Ptah at Memphis
		134100	sm	image; likeness
		134020	sm	sem-priest
		856043	sm	sem-priest
		854545	sm	to respect; to provide; to help
		134070	sm	to be happy
		134040	sm	to help; to provide
		134790	sm.y	respected one
		134150	sm.wj	[a kind of a priest]
		134130	sm.t	respect
		135780	smsm	to praise

DRID 1002146 smd [a star]

RID	**0002390**	smd [a star]		
	ID Lexeme	135990	smd	[a star]

DRID 1002147 smd bead

RID	**0002391**	smd bead		
	ID Lexeme	136040	smd.t	beads

DRID 1002148 smd edge

RID	**0002392**	smd eyebrow		
	ID Lexeme	135970	smd	eyebrow
		136020	smd.t	something written at the edge

DRID 1002149 smd personnel

RID	**0002393**	smd personnel		
	ID Lexeme	136030	smd.t	personnel; staff; underlings
		136050	smd.t	workplace?; service?

DRID 1002150 smd sistrum

RID	**0002394**	smd sistrum		
	ID Lexeme	136000	smd	sistrum

DRID 1002151 smd slab

RID	**0002395**	smd slab		
	ID Lexeme	136010	smd.t	slab

DRID 1002152 smḥ left

RID	**0002396**	smḥ left		
	ID Lexeme	135580	smḥ.j	left; left side
		135590	smḥ.j	left hand
		600521	smḥ.j	left

DRID 1002155 smj soured milk

RID	**0002399**	smj soured milk		

	ID Lexeme	134840	smj	cream; soured milk
DRID	**1002156**	**smj to report**		
RID	**0002400**	smj to report		
	ID Lexeme	134810	smj	reporter
		134910	smj	shouting (of the infant)
		134830	smj	report; accusation
		134820	smj	to report
		134890	smj.t	the one who prosecutes
DRID	**1002157**	**smj whips**		
RID	**0002401**	smj whips		
	ID Lexeme	134930	smj	whips
DRID	**1002158**	**smk beam**		
RID	**0002402**	smk beam		
	ID Lexeme	135830	smk.t	beam; girder
DRID	**1002160**	**smn [a goose]**		
RID	**0002404**	smn [a goose]		
	ID Lexeme	135180	smn	Nile goose
DRID	**1002161**	**smn lion**		
RID	**0002405**	smn lion		
	ID Lexeme	135220	smn.t	lioness
DRID	**1002162**	**smn mourner**		
RID	**0002406**	smn mourner		
	ID Lexeme	857574	smn.tjt	mourning woman
		135260	smn.tjt	mourning woman
DRID	**1002163**	**šmr bow**		
RID	**0002407**	šmr bow		
	ID Lexeme	154970	šmr.t	bow (weapon)
		154980	šmr.tj	bowman
DRID	**1002164**	**smr friend**		
RID	**0002408**	smr friend		
	ID Lexeme	856044	smr	friend; courtier
		135420	smr	friend; courtier
		135480	smr.t	friend; companion (the queen)
		869276	smr.t	female friend
DRID	**1002165**	**sms [a cut of beef]**		
RID	**0002409**	sms [a cut of beef]		
	ID Lexeme	135650	sms	[a cut of beef]

DRID	**1002167**		**sms mallet**		
	RID	**0002411**	sms mallet		
		ID Lexeme	135640	sms	mallet
DRID	**1002168**		**sms to become old**		
	RID	**0002412**	sms to become old		
		ID Lexeme	135730	sms	to be old; to become old
			135660	sms	seniority
			500187	sms.w	the oldest one
			135720	sms.w	oldest; older
			856128	sms.w	elder
			400263	sms.w	elder
			852249	sms.w	elder
			861521	sms.w	the older one
			856246	sms.ww	old ones
			869285	sms.t	the old one
			135690	sms.t	the eldest (daughter)
			135760	smsm	the oldest
DRID	**1002170**		**smswn libation**		
	RID	**0002415**	smswn [a vessel]		
		ID Lexeme	135740	smswn	[myrrh vessel]
	RID	**0002416**	smswn libation		
		ID Lexeme	135750	smswn	libation water
DRID	**1002171**		**smt to hear**		
	RID	**0002417**	smt to hear		
		ID Lexeme	135890	smt	The hearing one
			135840	smt	to hear; to overhear
			856082	smt.t	The hearing one (Spy)
			135930	smtmt	listen, listen around
DRID	**1002172**		**smwn surely**		
	RID	**0002418**	smwn surely		
		ID Lexeme	135040	smwn	probably; surely
DRID	**1002174**		**smꜣ stolist**		
	RID	**0002420**	smꜣ stolist		
		ID Lexeme	852746	smꜣ	stolist
			860895	smꜣ.tj	stolist
DRID	**1002175**		**smꜣ to slaughter**		
	RID	**0002421**	smꜣ to slaughter		
		ID Lexeme	134360	smꜣ	scalp; temple (of the head)
			134380	smꜣ	sacrifice; sacrificial steer
			134370	smꜣ	to slaughter
			856077	smꜣ.t	killing knife

	RID	**0002423**	smꜣ wild cattle	
		ID Lexeme	134390 smꜣ	wild bull
			854781 smꜣ	wild bull
			134440 smꜣ.t	wild cow
			134430 smꜣ.t	wild cow
DRID	**1002177**	**sm^{c} stake**		
	RID	**0002424**	sm^{c} rope	
		ID Lexeme	135000 sm^{c}	rope (from plant fibers)
			134980 sm^{c}	stake (for pushing the ship)
			860824 sm^{c}	to push
			134990 sm^{c}	[term for the legs of the falcon ("stake")]
			135010 sm^{c}.t	staff [a scepter]
DRID	**1002181**	**sn [an offering]**		
	RID	**0002428**	sn [an offering]	
		ID Lexeme	136350 sn.w	gift (from the field)
			136340 sn.w	bread; offerings
			136470 sn.wt	offerings?
DRID	**1002183**	**sn brother**		
	RID	**0002430**	sn brother	
		ID Lexeme	136230 sn	brother
			136310 sn.w	siblings
			136800 sn.wt	brethren; siblings
			136260 sn.t	sister; beloved
			851924 sn.tj	the two sisters (mostly Isis and Nephthys)
			138180 snsn	close friend
	RID	**0002438**	sn to be together	
		ID Lexeme	136220 sn	to join
			136200 sn	two-pronged fork
			136210 sn.w	two
			136370 sn.w	doors; gates
			853665 sn.wj	The two (two gods as a couple)
			136390 sn.wj	twin calves
			136380 sn.wj	the two; the two contenders
			136500 sn.nw	to be second
			136480 sn.nw	the second
			136490 sn.nw	second best; inferior
			550359 sn.nw	second (companion, fellow); replica
			857809 sn.nwt	companion
			136300 sn.tj	testicles
			138150 snsn	to associate with; to fraternize
			138160 snsn	brotherhood (characterization of the relationship between rulers)

DRID	**1002184**	**sn flag pole**		
RID	**0002432**	sn flag pole		
	ID Lexeme	136280	sn.t	flag pole
DRID	**1002187**	**sn serpentine**		
RID	**0002436**	sn serpentine		
	ID Lexeme	136440	sn.wt	serpentine
		136430	sn.wt	senu-sanctuary
		136270	sn.t	polishing stone
DRID	**1002188**	**sn to smell**		
RID	**0002439**	sn to smell		
	ID Lexeme	136240	sn	to smell; to kiss
		136760	snw	[a pleasant-smelling plant]
		144080	ssn	to breathe; to smell
		137650	snn.wt	veneration
RID	**0002468**	snsn to smell		
	ID Lexeme	138130	snsn	to smell; to breathe
		138170	snsn	rotten; stink (from the corpse)
		138140	snsn	breathe
		138210	snsn.t	smell; perfume
DRID	**1002190**	**snb [a boat]**		
RID	**0002441**	snb [a boat]		
	ID Lexeme	137090	snb.t	[a boat (papyrus skiff)]
RID	**0002442**	snb [a plant]		
	ID Lexeme	136960	snb	fringe
		136970	snb	[a plant associated with Lower Egypt (papyrus?)]
DRID	**1002192**	**snb heaven**		
RID	**0002444**	snb heaven		
	ID Lexeme	137080	snb.t	heaven; sky
DRID	**1002193**	**snb to be healthy**		
RID	**0002445**	snb to be healthy		
	ID Lexeme	136940	snb	to heal
		851676	snb	to be healthy; to heal
		137040	snb	air; breath
		136930	snb	to be healthy
		136950	snb	health
		137190	snbb	to exchange greetings
		137200	snbb	to cool (by the wind)
		144100	snnb	to heal; to keep healthy
DRID	**1002197**	**snḏ to fear**		
RID	**0002449**	snḏ to fear		

		ID Lexeme	138750	snḏ	dreadful one
			138720	snḏ	roast goose
			138730	snḏ	to fear
			138740	snḏ	fear
			138790	snḏ.w	frightened one; timid one
			138770	snḏ.t	fear
			138780	snḏ.t	frightening one (Hathor)
			144110	ssnḏ	to frighten
DRID	**1002198**		**snf previous year**		
	RID	**0002450**	snf previous year		
		ID Lexeme	137300	snf	previous year
DRID	**1002199**		**snḥ to tie up**		
	RID	**0002451**	snḥ to tie up		
		ID Lexeme	137850	snḥ	to tie up; to fetter
			500330	snḥ	fetter(s)
			137890	snḥ.tt	fettering
			75520	msnḥ	to turn around
DRID	**1002202**		**sni̯ to free**		
	RID	**0002454**	sni̯ to free		
		ID Lexeme	136630	sni̯	to loosen; to free oneself from something
			136740	snw	poverty
			136730	snw	to free oneself from someone
DRID	**1002207**		**snk to be dark**		
	RID	**0002459**	snk to be dark		
		ID Lexeme	138360	snk	the dark one
			138350	snk	to be dark
			138330	snk	to sink (into darkness)
			138380	snk	greed (of water)
			138450	snk.y	dark one (the sun god in the netherworld)
			138440	snk.w	darkness
			857572	snk.wj	who belongs to darkness
			138400	snk.t	the dark one
			138410	snk.t	darkness
			852150	snk.t	longing?
			138420	snk.tj	darkness
			138430	snk.t.t	[a name of a female deity]
DRID	**1002208**		**snm storm**		
	RID	**0002460**	snm storm		
		ID Lexeme	137440	snm	flood of rain

DRID	**1002211**	**snḳ to suckle**		
	RID	**0002463**	snḳ to suckle	
		ID Lexeme	137160 snḳ	breast (of a nurse)
			138280 snḳ	to suckle
DRID	**1002212**	**sns hairdresser?**		
	RID	**0002465**	sns hairdresser?	
		ID Lexeme	138060 sns	hairdresser?
DRID	**1002213**	**snsi̯ to praise**		
	RID	**0002466**	snsi̯ to praise	
		ID Lexeme	138070 sns.w	praise
			138090 snsi̯	to worship; to praise
	RID	**0002467**	snsn to praise	
		ID Lexeme	138110 snsn	to worship
			138120 snsn	praise
DRID	**1002215**	**snṯi̯ to establish**		
	RID	**0002470**	snṯ body	
		ID Lexeme	138550 snṯ	limbs, body
			138630 snṯy.t	body (i.e., group?) (of the dead)
	RID	**0002473**	snṯi̯ to establish	
		ID Lexeme	138560 snṯ	custom
			138540 snṯ	foundation (of a temple); (ground) plan (of a temple)
			138640 snṯ.y	deckhouse; cabin (of a cult bark)
			138580 snṯ.t	foundation; plan (for a building)
			450241 snṯ.t	[shrine on a cult bark]
			138620 snṯi̯	to found
			75560 msntj	foundation ditch
DRID	**1002221**	**snꜥḥ angler**		
	RID	**0002480**	snꜥḥ angler	
		ID Lexeme	136720 snꜥḥ.w	angler
			136710 snꜥḥ.t	fishhook
DRID	**1002222**	**sp lips**		
	RID	**0002481**	sp lips	
		ID Lexeme	132450 sp.t	base (column, stele)
			132440 sp.t	lips; edge; bank; shore
			31450 jsp.t	language; speech
DRID	**1002226**	**spd to be sharp**		
	RID	**0002485**	spd [a wood]	
		ID Lexeme	133260 spd	[a kind of a wood]
	RID	**0002486**	spd to be sharp, efficient	
		ID Lexeme	133180 spd	sharp

		500142	spd	to be sharp; to make sharp
		133290	spd	efficacious one (sun god)
		133190	spd	sharp; skilled
		133210	spd	[a kind of an object]
		133280	spd	efficacy?
		500143	spd	to be effective; to be skilled
		857835	spd.w	sharpness
		855077	spd.w	the sharp one
		133300	spd.t	triangle
		133320	spd.t	[women in the entourage of a goddess]
		851287	spd.t	efficacy
RID	**0002487**	spd to equip		
	ID Lexeme	133240	spd	provision; grain ration
		143970	sspd	to make ready; to supply
		143960	sspd	to enliven
		133370	spdd	to equip
DRID	**1002227**	**spi̯ to bind together**		
RID	**0002488**	spi̯ to bind together		
	ID Lexeme	132750	spi̯	to bind together (a papyrus boat or skiff)
		132950	spḥ	to lasso
		133000	spḥ.w	lasso catcher (demon)
		132990	spḥ.w	lasso
		132980	spḥ.t	ribs (of the deceased, of an offering animal)
DRID	**1002229**	**spr [a vegetable]**		
RID	**0002489**	spr [a vegetable]		
	ID Lexeme	132850	spr	[a vegetable]
DRID	**1002230**	**spr rib**		
RID	**0002490**	spr rib		
	ID Lexeme	132820	spr	rib
		132920	spr.wt	ship's rib?
DRID	**1002231**	**spr sheet (of metal)**		
RID	**0002491**	spr sheet (of metal)		
	ID Lexeme	132860	spr	sheet (of metal)
DRID	**1002232**	**spr to reach**		
RID	**0002492**	spr to reach		
	ID Lexeme	132840	spr	to appeal to
		132830	spr	to arrive at; to reach
		852612	spr	achieve (to do); ability (to do)
		132900	spr.w	petitioner

		132890	spr.w	request
		132870	spr.t	plea; petition
		132880	spr.tj	petitioner
		75330	mspr.t	frame?
		75360	mspr.tjw	[a kind of a worker]

DRID 1002233 sps to build

RID	**0002493**	sps to build		
	ID Lexeme	133110	sps	to build

DRID 1002234 sps to dance

RID	**0002494**	sps to dance		
	ID Lexeme	133100	sps	to dance

DRID 1002238 spt to slaughter

RID	**0002498**	spt to slaughter		
	ID Lexeme	133150	spt	to slaughter

DRID 1002239 spꜣ nome

RID	**0002499**	spꜣ nome		
	ID Lexeme	132420	spꜣ.t	nome; district
		132430	spꜣ.t	nome; district
		854544	spꜣ.t	nome; district; estate district; desert
		854859	spꜣ.tj	what belongs to a nome

DRID 1002240 sḳ fish trap

RID	**0002500**	sḳ fish trap		
	ID Lexeme	145950	sḳ.t	fish trap

DRID 1002242 sḳ to cut

RID	**0002502**	sḳ to cut		
	ID Lexeme	145940	sḳ	to cut (flowers)

DRID 1002244 sḳr to strike

RID	**0002504**	sḳr to strike		
	ID Lexeme	146190	sḳr	to strike; to step out; to present
		146210	sḳr	wound; injury
		854551	sḳr	to strike; to step out; to present
		146200	sḳr	captive; prisoner
		146220	sḳr	to unbolt

DRID 1002246 sr [a goose]

RID	**0002506**	sr [a goose]		
	ID Lexeme	139140	sr.w	grey goose
		139090	sr.t	grey goose

DRID 1002247 sr captive (noble) woman
RID 0002507 sr captive (noble) woman
ID Lexeme 139900 sr.t [srt] captive (noble) woman

DRID 1002248 sr nobleman
RID 0002518 sri̯ to be in charge
ID Lexeme 138920 sr nobleman; official
855554 sr nobleman; official
852375 sr the one who is in charge
860970 sr.y order
857005 sr.w the noble one
139060 sr.t body of magistrates
860190 sr.t the noble one
138930 sri̯ to be noble; to lead; to command
139270 srw [command to hire people]

DRID 1002250 sr thorn
RID 0002509 sr thorn
ID Lexeme 139120 sr.t metal (hair?) pin
139070 sr.t thorn; spine

DRID 1002251 sr to announce
RID 0002510 sr to announce
ID Lexeme 855669 sr prophesier
138940 sr giraffe
138990 sr tambourine-like drum
139000 sr to strike a drum
138950 sr to foretell; to make known
863037 sr to cough
139220 sry.t cough
139740 srsr to proclaim; to comfort

DRID 1002252 sr to visit
RID 0002511 sr to visit
ID Lexeme 138970 sr to visit

DRID 1002253 srḏ to chisel
RID 0002512 srḏ to chisel
ID Lexeme 139970 srḏ to chisel; to hammer

DRID 1002254 srf to be warm
RID 0002513 srf to be warm
ID Lexeme 857841 srf the hot one
139380 srf to warm; to be warm
550417 srf warm
133730 srf griffin
139390 srf warmth

				139450	srf.t	rash? (as a symptom of illness)
				857844	srf.t	warm bread
DRID	**1002255**		**srf to rest**			
	RID	**0002514**		srf to rest		
		ID Lexeme		139420	srf	[term for water]
				139400	srf	property
				139410	srf	to make rest; to rest
				139430	srf	to refresh
				650020	srf	rest; relief
DRID	**1002258**		**srḫ stalks (of onions)**			
	RID	**0002517**		srḫ stalks (of onions)		
		ID Lexeme		139580	srḫ.t	stalks (of onions); bunches (of onions) (as a unit of measure)
DRID	**1002259**		**sri̯ to spread**			
	RID	**0002519**		sri̯ to spread		
		ID Lexeme		138980	sr	hair (of a woman, of an nimal)
				139020	sr	to spread
				139010	sr	dirt ?
				139240	sr.w	anklet
DRID	**1002260**		**srj standard**			
	RID	**0002520**		srj standard		
		ID Lexeme		139210	sry.t	standard
DRID	**1002262**		**srḳ scorpion**			
	RID	**0002523**		srḳ scorpion		
		ID Lexeme		139870	srḳ.t	scorpion
				139850	srḳ.t	Selkis
				139860	srḳ.t	Selkis (constellation in the northern sky)
DRID	**1002263**		**srḳ to open**			
	RID	**0002525**		srḳ to open		
		ID Lexeme		139810	srḳ	to rip open; to slay
				139770	srḳ	to open; to make inhale
				139890	srḳ.y	breather
				139880	srḳ.w	breathing
DRID	**1002273**		**sšd shrine**			
	RID	**0002535**		sšd shrine		
		ID Lexeme		145910	sšd.t	shrine (of the falcon)
	RID	**0002538**		sšd window?		
		ID Lexeme		145880	sšd	window?

DRID 1002274 sšd to flash

RID 0002536 sšd to flash

ID Lexeme
145830 sšd thunderbolt
145850 sšd to whistle (to make the sound of the harpoon flying through the air and striking the foe)
500150 sšd flash; lightening
145840 sšd to tremble; flash; to lighten fast

DRID 1002275 sšd to tie

RID 0002537 sšd to tie

ID Lexeme
145890 sšd leather pouch
145860 sšd bandage; headdress; diadem
145870 sšd to tie (jewelry ribbon); decorate (with)

DRID 1002277 sskꜣ [an ingredient]

RID 0002539 sskꜣ [an ingredient]

ID Lexeme
144190 sskꜣ [an ingredient in unguent]
852028 sskꜣ from the drug Seseka intoxicated

DRID 1002278 sskꜣ temple (a body part)

RID 0002540 sskꜣ temple (a body part)

ID Lexeme
144180 sskꜣ temple

DRID 1002280 ssm horse

RID 0002542 ssm horse

ID Lexeme
144020 ssm.t horse

DRID 1002284 sšm whetstone

RID 0002546 sšm whetstone

ID Lexeme
145080 sšm butcher (lit. one of the whetstone)
145070 sšm whetstone
855520 sšm butcher (lit. one of the whetstone)

DRID 1002285 sšn [a fish]

RID 0002547 sšn [a fish]

ID Lexeme
145340 sšn.w [a kind of a fish]

DRID 1002286 sšn to spin

RID 0002548 sšn to spin

ID Lexeme
145240 sšn to spin; to weave; to twist
145270 sšn storm
145330 sšn.w cordage (naut.)
145320 sšn.t rope

DRID 1002287 sšp cucumber?

RID 0002549 sšp cucumber?

		ID Lexeme	144920	sšp.t	cucumber?
DRID	**1002288**	**sšp to be bright**			
	RID	**0002550**	sšp to be bright		
		ID Lexeme	144880	sšp	[term for wine]
			859240	sšp	milk
			144870	sšp	[a bright cloth]; [a bright garment]
			144860	sšp	light
			144850	sšp	to be bright; to make bright
			854743	sšp	[a shining object]
			144940	sšp.y	bright one
			857856	sšp.t	brightness
			144930	sšp.t	[a kind of a golden amulet]
			144900	sšp.t	bright one (Hathor)
			144910	sšp.t	[term for heaven]
			857855	sšp.t	bright (white) cloth
DRID	**1002289**	**sšr grain**			
	RID	**0002551**	sšr grain		
		ID Lexeme	851818	sšr	grain
DRID	**1002290**	**sšr linen**			
	RID	**0002552**	sšr linen		
		ID Lexeme	145530	sšr.w	a linen fabric
DRID	**1002293**	**sšr to stroke**			
	RID	**0002555**	sšr to stroke		
		ID Lexeme	854550	sšr	to stroke; to milk
			145460	sšr	to stroke; to spread (with something)
			145490	sšr	[an offering (what's milked?)]
			145470	sšr	to milk
DRID	**1002297**	**sšš to level**			
	RID	**0002559**	sšš to level		
		ID Lexeme	145660	sššj	to prepare a bed
	RID	**0002558**	sšš road		
		ID Lexeme	145650	sšš.t	road; path
DRID	**1002298**	**sst ankle**			
	RID	**0002560**	sst ankle		
		ID Lexeme	144200	sst	ankle
DRID	**1002299**	**sštꜣ [a fruit]**			
	RID	**0002561**	sštꜣ [a fruit]		
		ID Lexeme	850976	sštꜣ	[a fruit]

DRID 1002300 ssw to enclose
RID 0002562 ssw to enclose
ID Lexeme 143860 ssw to enclose?
143840 ssw enclosure

DRID 1002306 sṯ [a bread mold]
RID 0002569 sṯ [a bread mold]
ID Lexeme 148610 sṯ.t [bread mold]
148630 sṯ.t [bread]

DRID 1002307 sṯ [a jug]
RID 0002570 sṯ [a jug]
ID Lexeme 148600 sṯ.t [jug, for beer]; [jug, as a measure of capacity]

DRID 1002308 sṯ [a material]
RID 0002571 sṯ [a material]
ID Lexeme 148640 sṯ.t [a kind of a material]

DRID 1002309 st [necklace]
RID 0002572 st [necklace]
ID Lexeme 859280 st necklace?
450483 st necklace stringer

DRID 1002310 st jar stand
RID 0002573 st jar stand
ID Lexeme 147850 st.yw jar stand

DRID 1002311 sṯ jfragrance
RID 0002574 sṯ jfragrance
ID Lexeme 148990 sṯj fragrance; stench

DRID 1002317 stḥ to open
RID 0002581 stḥ to open
ID Lexeme 148500 stḥ to open (a door, a door bolt)

DRID 1002318 sti̯ to catch sight of
RID 0002582 sti̯ to catch sight of
ID Lexeme 147670 sti̯ to look at intently

DRID 1002319 sti̯ to knot
RID 0002583 sti̯ to knot
ID Lexeme 147640 sti̯ to knot

DRID 1002320 sṯi̯ to pluck (fowl)
RID 0002584 sṯi̯ to pluck (fowl)
ID Lexeme 149480 sṯi̯ to pluck (fowl)

DRID 1002321 sti̯ to send out

RID 0002585 sti̯ to send out

ID Lexeme	500262	st.y	the blazing one
	855635	st.yt	sperm
	861260	st.yt	descendants
	147420	st.w	the firing one
	148680	sṯ.w	sower
	147890	st.w	arrow; dart
	147900	st.w	target
	148660	sṯ.t	censing
	147400	st.t	[a slimy substance (med.)]
	147630	sti̯	to pour
	147610	sti̯	to pour
	147600	sti̯	to scatter
	147590	sti̯	to throw
	147570	sti̯	to shoot; to throw; to pour
	147660	sti̯	to illumine; to light up
	147620	sti̯	to shoot out (semen)
	147650	sti̯	to kindle; to set fire to; to glitter
	147790	sty	shooter
	147730	stj.t	shrine; temple
	147910	stw.t	light; rays
	500329	stw.tj	radiant one

DRID 1002322 stj leg (esp. of Osiris)

RID 0002586 stj leg (esp. of Osiris)

ID Lexeme	147710	stj	leg (esp. of Osiris)

DRID 1002325 stp [a cloth]

RID 0002590 stp [a cloth]

ID Lexeme	148100	stp	strip (of cloth); rag

DRID 1002326 stp goose?

RID 0002591 stp goose?

ID Lexeme	148060	stp	goose, or similar

DRID 1002327 stp incident

RID 0002592 stp incident

ID Lexeme	148150	stp.t	incident

DRID 1002328 stp to choose

RID 0002593 stp to choose

ID Lexeme	148090	stp	choice; select
	855636	stp	to drip; to absorb liquid
	148070	stp	to pick out; to choose
	858700	stp.w	selected pieces of meat
	148170	stp.w	choice

		148140	stp.t	choice things
		550337	stp.t	cut (of meat)
RID	**0002594**	stp to extract		
	ID Lexeme	855648	stp	to rapture
		853590	stp	to be ruined
		148030	stp	to work with the adze
		148080	stp	to refuse; to resist (med.)
		148050	stp	to set off; to cut up
		853082	stp.tj	the disassembled one (Seth)

DRID 1002329 sṯp to leap up

RID	**0002595**	sṯp to leap up		
	ID Lexeme	149150	sṯp	to leap up
		76120	msṯp.t	sled (for transporting coffin or shrine); portable shrine

DRID 1002330 str to make jewelry

RID	**0002596**	str to make jewelry		
	ID Lexeme	148400	str	to make jewelry
		148470	str.w	necklace maker

DRID 1002331 sṯr to wrap up

RID	**0002597**	sṯr to wrap up		
	ID Lexeme	149340	sṯr	to wrap up
		149360	sṯr.t	upper eyelid

DRID 1002333 sṯꜣ [a body of water]

RID	**0002599**	sṯꜣ [a body of water]		
	ID Lexeme	148780	sṯꜣ	[a body of water]

DRID 1002334 sṯꜣ [a jar]

RID	**0002600**	sṯꜣ [a jar]		
	ID Lexeme	148700	sṯꜣ	jar

DRID 1002335 sṯꜣ offering

RID	**0002601**	sṯꜣ offering		
	ID Lexeme	148830	sṯꜣ.t	offering

DRID 1002336 sṯꜣ secretion (med.)

RID	**0002602**	sṯꜣ secretion (med.)		
	ID Lexeme	148790	sṯꜣ	secretion (med.)

DRID 1002338 sṯꜣ to drag

RID	**0002604**	sṯꜣ to drag		
	ID Lexeme	148750	sṯꜣ	passage; cavern; ramp
		148730	sṯꜣ	to pull; to flow; to move to
		148720	sṯꜣ	to drag; to pull; to usher in

		858980	sṯꜣ	[a dance position]
		148740	sṯꜣ	(stretchable (dough) (med.)
		148870	sṯꜣ.w	dragging
		148860	sṯꜣ.w	attack; wounding
		148850	sṯꜣ.t	necropolis
		148810	sṯꜣ.t	hole
		148840	sṯꜣ.t	aroura
RID	**0002605**	sṯꜣ to weave		
	ID Lexeme	148760	sṯꜣ	to weave; to spin
		148770	sṯꜣ	[a kind of cloth]
RID	**0002606**	sṯꜣ tower		
	ID Lexeme	148910	sṯꜣ.yw	tower
		501144	sṯꜣ.t	tower
RID	**0002607**	sṯꜣ tower		
	ID Lexeme	148920	sṯꜣ.tjw	tower
RID	**0002598**	sṯꜣ [a (wooden) chest on a sled]		
	ID Lexeme	148820	sṯꜣ.t	[a (wooden) chest on a sled]

DRID	**1002340**	**sw [a plant]**		
RID	**0002609**	sw [a plant]		
	ID Lexeme	129470	sw	[a plant]
		129610	sw.t	sedge plant
DRID	**1002341**	**sw 1/16 arure**		
RID	**0002610**	sw 1/16 arure		
	ID Lexeme	863861	sw	1/16 arure (area measurement)
DRID	**1002342**	**sw a piece of meat**		
RID	**0002611**	sw a piece of meat		
	ID Lexeme	129630	sw.t	a piece of meat (of beef, as an offering)
		129670	sw.tjt	[full replacement for the horus eye?]
		129810	swꜣjt	[a piece of meat]
DRID	**1002343**	**sw danger**		
RID	**0002612**	sw danger		
	ID Lexeme	129620	sw.t	danger?
		129520	sww	to be harmful
DRID	**1002348**	**sw time**		
RID	**0002618**	sw time		
	ID Lexeme	129450	sw	time; day; date
		129460	sw	day (of the month, in dates)
		854542	sw	time; day; date; day of the month
DRID	**1002351**	**swbb to draw back**		

	RID	**0002621**	swbb to draw back		
		ID Lexeme	130060	swbb	to draw back
DRID	**1002352**		**swgꜣ to be foolish**		
	RID	**0002622**	swgꜣ to be foolish		
		ID Lexeme	130800	swgꜣ	to be foolish
			130810	swgꜣ	underaged child
DRID	**1002353**		**swḥ egg**		
	RID	**0002623**	swḥ egg		
		ID Lexeme	130630	swḥ.t	egg
			130650	swḥ.t	(inner) coffin
DRID	**1002354**		**swḥ to enwrap**		
	RID	**0002624**	swḥ to enwrap		
		ID Lexeme	130570	swḥ	to enwrap
			130560	swḥ	a kind of garment
DRID	**1002355**		**swḥ wind**		
	RID	**0002625**	swḥ wind		
		ID Lexeme	130600	swḥ	wind
DRID	**1002356**		**swhi̯ to praise**		
	RID	**0002626**	swhi̯ to praise		
		ID Lexeme	130540	swhi̯	to praise; to yell
DRID	**1002357**		**swhꜣ to break**		
	RID	**0002627**	swhꜣ to break		
		ID Lexeme	650021	swhꜣ	to break (naut.)
DRID	**1002362**		**swn fortress**		
	RID	**0002632**	swn fortress		
		ID Lexeme	130170	swn.w	tower; fortress
DRID	**1002363**		**swn pond**		
	RID	**0002633**	swn pond		
		ID Lexeme	130190	swn.w	fish pond
DRID	**1002364**		**swn to flatter**		
	RID	**0002634**	swn to flatter		
		ID Lexeme	859730	swn	compliment; flattery
			130330	swnwn	flattery
			130320	swnwn	to flatter
DRID	**1002365**		**swn to recognize**		
	RID	**0002635**	swn to recognize		
		ID Lexeme	130350	swnn	[epithet of Horus]
			130140	swn	to know of something
			130150	swn	to recognize

DRID	**1002366**	**swn to trade**		
RID	**0002636**	swn to trade		
	ID Lexeme	130110	swn	to trade; to buy
		130160	swn.t	trade; price
DRID	**1002367**	**swr [a chariot equipment]**		
RID	**0002637**	swr [a chariot equipment]		
	ID Lexeme	130450	swr	[chariot equipment]
DRID	**1002368**	**swr bead**		
RID	**0002638**	swr bead		
	ID Lexeme	130470	swr.t	barrel bead (of carnelian) (an amulet)
DRID	**1002369**	**swt wind**		
RID	**0002639**	swt wind		
	ID Lexeme	130850	swt	gust of wind
DRID	**1002370**	**swy [a crocodile]**		
RID	**0002640**	swy [a crocodile]		
	ID Lexeme	129980	swy	[a name for a crocodile]
DRID	**1002378**	**sꜣ back**		
RID	**0002648**	sꜣ back		
	ID Lexeme	125680	sꜣ	outside
		125710	sꜣ	stall; byre
		125670	sꜣ	back; back (of something)
		600052	sꜣ	after
		125980	sꜣ	flush (of water)
		125790	sꜣ	to lay on back?
RID	**0002656**	sꜣ wall		
	ID Lexeme	858698	sꜣ	wall
		125890	sꜣ.wt	building (“walls”)
		125800	sꜣ.t	wall
RID	**0002677**	sꜣsꜣ to drive back		
	ID Lexeme	127250	sꜣsꜣ	to drive back; to repel
		127270	sꜣsꜣ	to force (a boat over the rapids)
		127260	sꜣsꜣ	to apply (oil to someone)
DRID	**1002380**	**sꜣ gold**		
RID	**0002650**	sꜣ gold		
	ID Lexeme	125880	sꜣ.wj	gold two-thirds fine
DRID	**1002387**	**sꜣb colorful**		
RID	**0002658**	sꜣb colorful		
	ID Lexeme	126650	sꜣb	colorful
		126720	sꜣb.w	[a bird with colorful plumage]

		126680	sꜣb.t	speckled snake
		126670	sꜣb.t	dappled cow

DRID 1002390 sꜣd to strangulate

RID	**0002662**	sꜣd to strangulate		
	ID Lexeme	127670	sꜣd	to strangulate

DRID 1002391 sꜣḥ to reach

RID	**0002663**	sꜣḥ to reach		
	ID Lexeme	126990	sꜣḥ	neighbors
		126950	sꜣḥ	(human) toe
		127000	sꜣḥ	to endow
		127050	sꜣḥ	framework
		126960	sꜣḥ	toes
		127010	sꜣḥ	grant of land
		126980	sꜣḥ	to reach; to arrive (at a place)
		127090	sꜣḥ.yt	those who approach
		65440	sꜣḥ.t	in the vicinity of

DRID 1002392 sꜣẖm a bat

RID	**0002664**	sꜣẖm a bat		
	ID Lexeme	127230	sꜣẖm.w	[a bat]

DRID 1002393 sꜣi̯ to be sated

RID	**0002665**	sꜣi̯ to be sated		
	ID Lexeme	126440	sꜣ.w	satiety
		125840	sꜣ.t	satiety
		650033	sꜣi̯	to prepare; to equip
		126200	sꜣi̯	to be sated; to sate
		140040	shꜣ	satiation
		143780	ssꜣ	provisions; sustenance
		143800	ssꜣi̯	to satisfy

DRID 1002395 sꜣm unkempt hair

RID	**0002667**	sꜣm unkempt hair		
	ID Lexeme	126780	sꜣm.t	disheveled hair (a sign of mourning)

DRID 1002397 sꜣp lotus

RID	**0002669**	sꜣp lotus		
	ID Lexeme	126730	sꜣp	to create a pond
		126740	sꜣp.t	lotus leaf
		860926	sꜣp.t	incense holder (in the form of a lotus leaf)
		139370	srp.t	lotus leaf
		139360	srp.t	lotiform fan

DRID 1002399 sꜣḳ to join

	RID	**0002671**	sꜣḳ to join	
		ID Lexeme	127400 sꜣḳ	assembler [a divine ferryman]
			127330 sꜣḳ	to pull together; to be wary of
			127340 sꜣḳ	incense roaster?
			127380 sꜣḳ	mat
			857738 sꜣḳ.tj	assembler
			127430 sꜣḳ.tj	[construction worker]
DRID	**1002401**		**sꜣr to sieve**	
	RID	**0002673**	sꜣr to sieve	
		ID Lexeme	866969 sꜣ.w	divided by cutting?
			126840 sꜣr	to sieve
DRID	**1002404**		**sꜣṯ cargo boat**	
	RID	**0002679**	sꜣṯ cargo boat	
		ID Lexeme	127640 sꜣṯ	cargo boat; tow boat
DRID	**1002405**		**sꜣt to defile**	
	RID	**0002681**	sꜣt to defile	
		ID Lexeme	127590 sꜣt	dirt
			127570 sꜣt	to defile
DRID	**1002406**		**sꜣt to dislocate**	
	RID	**0002680**	sꜣt to be dislocated	
		ID Lexeme	127560 sꜣt	to be dislocated (med.)
DRID	**1002407**		**sꜣw niche?**	
	RID	**0002682**	sꜣw niche?	
		ID Lexeme	126450 sꜣw	[part of a construction]
DRID	**1002409**		**sꜣꜣ = sꜣr to be wise**	
	RID	**0002684**	sꜣꜣ to be wise	
		ID Lexeme	126220 sꜣꜣ	the wise one
			853654 sꜣꜣ	the wise one
			126170 sꜣꜣ	wise man
			851310 sꜣꜣ	wisdom
			126160 sꜣꜣ	to be wise; to be prudent; to understand
			865547 sꜣr	the wise one
			126800 sꜣr	to be wise
			850780 sꜣ.t	prudence; wisdom
			126860 sꜣr.t	understanding; wisdom
DRID	**1002414**		**sꜥ to damage?**	
	RID	**0002694**	sꜥsꜥ to damage?	
		ID Lexeme	129240 sꜥsꜥ	to damage?
DRID	**1002415**		**šꜥḏ to cut**	

	RID	**0002688**	šᶜḏ to cut	
		ID Lexeme	152610 šᶜd	sword
			152600 šᶜd	to cut (off, down)
			450452 šᶜḏ	to cut off
			152630 šᶜd	log; beam
DRID	**1002416**	**sᶜḥ to dignify**		
	RID	**0002689**	sᶜḥ to dignify	
		ID Lexeme	129130 sᶜḥ	mummy; form
			129110 sᶜḥ	to mark; to wrap in bandages; to be venerated
			129100 sᶜḥ	bandage (around the head)
			129120 sᶜḥ	noble; dignitary
			129070 sᶜḥ	rank; dignity
			129090 sᶜḥ	[special neck ornament of the high priests of Memphis]
			129150 sᶜḥ.tj	the two noble ones (Isis and Nephthys)
DRID	**1002418**	**sᶜr scrub country?; barley field?**		
	RID	**0002691**	sᶜr scrub country?; barley field?)	
		ID Lexeme	129000 sᶜr	scrub country?; barley field?
DRID	**1002420**	**sᶜr wool**		
	RID	**0002693**	sᶜr wool	
		ID Lexeme	129060 sᶜr.t	wool
DRID	**1002859**	**sꜣẖ to ram**		
	RID	**0012663**	sꜣẖ to ram	
		ID Lexeme	127100 sꜣẖ	to ram (the neck vertebra)
			127130 sꜣẖ	knife
			127170 sꜣẖ.t	[characteristic of a knife]
DRID	**1003089**	**sᶜb to cut**		
	RID	**0002687**	sᶜb to cut	
		ID Lexeme	128760 sᶜb	to saw off (wood); to castrate (cattle)
			128770 sᶜb	castrated bull

II.18 š

DRID	**1002001**	**š chair**			
	RID	**0002237**	š chair		
		ID lexeme	151020	š	chair; support
DRID	**1002003**	**š lake**			
	RID	**0002239**	š lake		
		ID lexeme	151050	š	basin; offering bowl
			151010	š	lake; district; garden (with pool)
			854557	š	lake; district; garden (with pool)
			152180	šy	[euphemism for crocodile]
DRID	**1002004**	**š workplace?**			
	RID	**0002241**	š workplace?		
		ID lexeme	151030	š	work?; workplace?
DRID	**1002005**	**šb [a ritual object]**			
	RID	**0002242**	šb [a ritual object]		
		ID lexeme	153300	šb.t	[ritual object, which king offers to a goddess]
DRID	**1002007**	**šb melon?**			
	RID	**0002244**	šb melon?		
		ID lexeme	153290	šb.t	[an edible vegetable (cucumber?) (melon?)]
DRID	**1002009**	**šb rib**			
	RID	**0002246**	šb rib		
		ID lexeme	153380	šb.tj	rib-joints (as food)
DRID	**1002010**	**šbb mastic**			
	RID	**0002247**	šbb mastic		
		ID lexeme	153220	šb	[an aromatic plant]
			153450	šbb	mastic
DRID	**1002011**	**šbb tube**			
	RID	**0002248**	šbb tube		
		ID lexeme	153410	šbb	tube, i.e. reed
			153420	šbb	gullet; esophagus
			153600	šbd	stick (to beat)
DRID	**1002015**	**šbi̯ = šbn to mix**			
	RID	**0002252**	šbi̯ to replace		
		ID lexeme	856686	šb.w	remuneration, payment; retribution
			153250	šb.t	value; price; wage
			153270	šb.t	[a mash (med.)]

		153350	šbi̯	to mix; to mingle; to replace
		153430	šbb	to mix; to mash
RID	**0002255**	šbn [ingredients in kyphi]		
	ID lexeme	153520	šbn	[ingredients in kyphi]
RID	**0002257**	šbn to mix		
	ID lexeme	153500	šbn	mixed; various
		153490	šbn	to mix; to mingle
		153510	šbn	[multicolored components of neck collar etc.]
RID	**0002258**	šbn various?		
	ID lexeme	153530	šbn.t	various?
RID	**0002262**	šbšb to brew		
	ID lexeme	153570	šbšb	to brew; to mix
		153580	šbšb	brewer?
		153470	šbb.t	(beer) mash
		870035	šbb.t	brew?
RID	**0002263**	šbšb to regulate		
	ID Lexeme	153560	šbšb	to regulate

DRID	**1002016**	**šbj shebyu-necklace**		
RID	**0002253**	šbj shebyu-necklace		
	ID lexeme	153370	šby.w	shebyu-necklace

DRID	**1002030**	**šḏ dough**		
RID	**0002270**	šḏ dough		
	ID lexeme	158970	šḏ.t	a dough (for baking bread)

DRID	**1002033**	**šd leather**		
RID	**0002273**	šd leather		
	ID Lexeme	158470	šd	cushion (of leather)
		158640	Sd.w	skin; water skin

DRID	**1002034**	**šd mortar**		
RID	**0002275**	šd mortar		
	ID Lexeme	158530	šd	vulva
		158520	šd	mortar
		158880	šdwj	[inner animal body part]

DRID	**1002045**	**šdi̯ to dig**		
RID	**0002286**	šdi̯ to dig		
	ID Lexeme	158510	šd	[a kind of timber used for building boats]
		158540	šd	potter
		158780	šd.y	field; meadow; parcel of land
		158770	šd.y	ditch
		158820	šd.yt	flooded parcel of land
		158860	šd.w	field; meadow; parcel of land

		158650	šd.w	lacings? (naut.)
		857753	šd.w	artificial lake; pool
		158870	šd.wt	field; meadow; parcel of land
		158600	šd.t	well; water hole
		860727	šd.tj	excavators
		158810	šdy.t	rubble
		158720	šdi̯	to dig; to carve
		158940	šdšd	[bolster-like protuberance on the front of divine standard]
DRID	**1002046**	**šdi̯ to educate**		
RID	**0002287**	šdi̯ to educate		
	ID Lexeme	158480	šd	tutor
		158550	šd	liturgies
		158500	šd	[a kind of a messenger]
		158490	šd	young brood (of birds)
		869177	šd	magician; reciter
		158740	šdi̯	to read; to recite
		158750	šdi̯	to suckle; to educate
		158800	šdy.t	nurse (a divine cow; also epithet of Hathor)
DRID	**1002047**	šdi̯ **to take**		
RID	**0002288**	šdi̯ to take		
	ID Lexeme	158730	šdi̯	to rescue
		158710	šdi̯	to take; remove; remove; to offer (gifts)
		450163	sšdi̯	to make leave; to remove
		158960	šddt	payment; expenditure
		88910	nšd	to pick (plants)
		88940	nšd.y	jeweler; lapidary
RID	**0002288**	šdi̯ to take		
	ID Lexeme	158850	šd.y	catch (of fish; of fowl)
RID	**0001621**	māšd to apply		
	ID Lexeme	76580	mšd	to apply
RID	**0001884**	nšd to maul		
	ID Lexeme	71390	mnšd	The tearer? (Apophis)
DRID	**1002053**	**šdr ravine**		
RID	**0002295**	šdr ravine		
	ID Lexeme	158900	šdr.t	ravine; chasm
DRID	**1002063**	**šfd to grasp**		
RID	**0002305**	šfd to grasp		
	ID Lexeme	154280	šfd	to grasp; to seize
		154290	šfd.w	sheet of papyrus; scroll of papyrus
		154310	šfdy.t	bier

DRID	**1002066**	**šfi̯ to respect**		
	RID	**0002308**	šfi̯ to respect	
		ID Lexeme	860289 šf	having the ram's had; handsome
			154030 šf	respect?; honor?
			859866 šfi̯	to respect
			154090 šf.yt	truth [synonym for maat]
			154080 šf.yt	majesty; respect
			154110 šf.ytj	respected one
			154050 šf.t	ram (of Amun, of Khnum)
	RID	**0002311**	šfšf respect	
		ID Lexeme	154240 šfšf.t	respect; awe
			154230 šfšf.t	ram's head
			154260 šfšf.tj	greatly-respected one
DRID	**1002067**	**šfn to touch**		
	RID	**0002309**	šfn to touch	
		ID Lexeme	154190 šfn	to touch
DRID	**1002068**	**šfn undergrowth**		
	RID	**0002310**	šfn undergrowth	
		ID Lexeme	154200 šfn.w	bushes; undergrowth
DRID	**1002070**	**šfu̯ to swell**		
	RID	**0002315**	šfu̯ to swell	
		ID Lexeme	154060 šf.w	[a substance (slime?) (med.)]
			154170 šf.wt	swelling
			154160 šfu̯	to swell; to be swollen
			154250 šfšf.t	[a med. substance]
			88650 nšf.wt	liquids?; liquid food?
			852795 nšf	fang?
			88660 nšfšf	to drip
DRID	**1002073**	**šfꜥ to fight**		
	RID	**0002318**	šfꜥ to fight	
		ID Lexeme	154130 šfꜥ	to fight
DRID	**1002078**	**šgr [a body of water]**		
	RID	**0002323**	šgr [a body of water]	
		ID Lexeme	157910 šgr	[a body of water (ditch? dyke?)]
DRID	**1002079**	**šgr [a wooden box]**		
	RID	**0002324**	šgr [a wooden box]	
		ID Lexeme	157900 šgr	[a wooden box]
DRID	**1002099**	**šḥq dust cloud**		
	RID	**0002344**	šḥq dust cloud	
		ID Lexeme	156900 šḥq	dust cloud

DRID 1002134 škn watering place
RID 0002381 škn watering place
ID Lexeme 157860 škn watering place

DRID 1002136 škr [a mineral]
RID 0002383 škr [a mineral]
ID Lexeme 157870 škr [a mineral]

DRID 1002138 šlf to be disheveled
RID 0002464 šnrf to be disheveled
ID Lexeme 156220 šnrf to be disheveled

DRID 1002139 šlg snow
RID 0002524 šrḳ snow
ID Lexeme 139820 srḳ snow

DRID 1002140 šlm peace
RID 0002522 šrm peace
ID Lexeme 156800 šrm to lay down (weapons); to seek peace
156780 šrm peace; greeting
156790 šrm to lay down arms; to seek peace

DRID 1002142 šm in law
RID 0002387 šm in law
ID Lexeme 856309 šm father in law
154440 šm.t mother in law

DRID 1002143 šm omen
RID 0002388 šm omen
ID Lexeme 853456 šm.w [a kind of spells]; omen; oracle

DRID 1002145 šm to cut off
RID 0001889 nšm to cut off
ID Lexeme 88670 nšm to cut off
RID 0002414 šmšm to sharpen
ID Lexeme 138250 snšmšm to sharpen

DRID 1002153 šmi̯ to go
RID 0002397 šmi̯ to go
ID Lexeme 154350 šm servant (of a deity)
154670 šm.y corridor (in a temple)
154650 šm.yt stake; palisade
856079 šm.w one who goes, servant
450456 šm.w waterway
859179 šm.wj legs; walking tools
154400 šm.t walking; gait; business

154410	šm.t	path (on land, in the sky)
154420	šm.t	[walk with statues]
154340	šmi̯	to go; to traverse
852485	šmi̯	go (to do)
154640	šmy	storehouse
154450	šmw	movements
154940	šmm.t	stable; storehouse
154930	šmm.t	street
861166	nšm.y	flow
145060	sšm	swab
145000	sšm	division; specification
144990	sšm	guidance; state of affairs; conduct
145010	sšm	manifestation (of a god); nature (of a god)
145120	sšm.w	statue; image; likeness
145030	sšm.w	leader (a god)
145140	sšm.w	leader; guide
145130	sšm.w	retinue
145190	sšm.wt	leader; guide (uraeus, goddesses)
859775	sšm.t	[a kind of a bark]
145090	sšm.t	guidance; proof (math.)
144980	sšmi̯	to lead; to guide

DRID 1002159 šmm = *ḫmm to be hot

RID 0002403 šmm to be hot

ID Lexeme

154660	šm.yt	heat; summer
154850	šm.w	shemu-season (summer)
154460	šm.w	heat
154860	šm.w	harvest; crop
154880	šm.ww	summer ships
154430	šm.t	fever; inflammation
151770	šꜣm	to be hot; to burn
154900	šmm	hot one
154890	šmm	to be hot; to become hot (feverish)
145200	sšmm	to warm (someone); to head (something)
154910	šmm	heat
154920	šmm.t	fever; inflammation

DRID 1002166 šms [instrument of punishment]

RID 0002410 šms [instrument of punishment]

ID Lexeme

155010	šms.t	[instrument of punishment]

DRID 1002169 šms to follow

RID 0002413 šms to follow

ID Lexeme

155000	šms	to follow; to accompany; to bring
155040	šms.w	following; suite
155030	šms.w	retainer

	853223	šms.w	retainer, follower
	155060	šms.wt	following; suite
	155020	šms.t	retainer (fem.)
	870050	šms.t	follower (fem.)

DRID 1002173 šmꜣ flower

RID 0002419 šmꜣ flower

ID Lexeme	154590	šmꜣ.w	flowers

DRID 1002176 šmꜣ to wander

RID 0002422 šmꜣ to wander

ID Lexeme	863021	šmꜣ	to be strange; be abnormal
	154540	šmꜣ	to wander; to move around
	154550	šmꜣ	to stray around
	854558	šmꜣ	to wander; move around; stray around
	154570	šmꜣ	foreigner (i.e., a non-Egyptian); wanderer
	154610	šmꜣ.y	strangeness; abnormality (a symptom of the disease)

DRID 1002178 šmᶜ to be slender

RID 0002425 šmᶜ to be slender

ID Lexeme	600027	šmᶜ	thin (linen) cloth; [a thin material]
	154710	šmᶜ	to be slender
	154720	šmᶜ	thin; slender
	154750	šmᶜ.t	thin (linen) cloth

DRID 1002180 šmᶜ Upper Egypt

RID 0002427 šmᶜ Upper Egypt

ID Lexeme	154800	šmᶜ	Upper Egyptian grain
	154700	šmᶜ	[heraldic plant of Upper Egypt (flowering sedge?)]
	154730	šmᶜ	to make music
	154790	šmᶜ.j	Upper Egyptian
	154810	šmᶜ.yt	musician
	154770	šmᶜ.w	musician; singer; chantress
	154840	šmᶜ.w	oil of Upper Egypt
	154690	šmᶜ.w	crown of Upper Egypt
	154740	šmᶜ.t	snake (ureus) of Upper Egypt

DRID 1002182 šn bad

RID 0002429 šn bad

ID Lexeme	155270	šn	bad

DRID 1002185 šn hundred

RID 0002433 šn hundred

	ID Lexeme	155320	šn.t	hundred
DRID	**1002186**	**šn rope**		
RID	**0002435**	šn rope		
	ID Lexeme	155930	šn.w	rope
		155940	šn.w	net(s)
DRID	**1002189**	**šn tree**		
RID	**0002440**	šn tree		
	ID Lexeme	155240	šn	tree (gen.)
		155250	šn	tree (gen.)
		450467	šnj	[a tree or fruits of this tree]
		156000	šn.wj	tree garden
		156020	šn.wt	date palm inflorescence?
DRID	**1002191**	**šnb chest**		
RID	**0002443**	šnb chest		
	ID Lexeme	156060	šnb.t	chest; front fuselage; throat
		156070	šnb.tj	falcon (also Horus) [in a form of breast amulet]
DRID	**1002194**	**šnb trumpet**		
RID	**0002446**	šnb trumpet		
	ID Lexeme	156030	šnb	trumpet; tube (for kohl)
DRID	**1002195**	**šnḏ acacia**		
RID	**0002447**	šnḏ acacia		
	ID Lexeme	156500	šnḏ	acacia
		156510	šnḏ.t	acacia
		156520	šnḏ.t	acacia thorn (med.)
DRID	**1002196**	**šnḏ kilt**		
RID	**0002448**	šnḏ kilt		
	ID Lexeme	156540	šnḏ.wt	king's kilt; kilt (gen.)
		156530	šnḏ.tj	wearer of the kilt [a kind of a priest]
DRID	**1002200**	**šni̯ to be round**		
RID	**0002452**	šni̯ to be round		
	ID Lexeme	155200	šn	circuit of the world
		155190	šn	[indefinitely huge number]
		155210	šn	ocean
		155170	šn	shen-ring
		155220	šn	[a body of water, in compounds]
		155180	šn	[protective symbol behind figures of the king]
		155350	šn.w	circuit; circumference

			155400	šn.wt	encircling?
			855502	šn.t	circling
			155450	šni̯	to be round; to surround; to encircle
			155560	šni̯	[a vessel]
			155950	šnw	food offering
			155970	šnw.t	granary; storeroom
			156280	šnt.t	enclosure
			852227	sšni̯	to make it round?
	RID	**0003462**	šni̯ to conjure		
		ID Lexeme	155500	šni̯	to curse; to exorcise; to conjure
			155300	šn.t	spell; conjuration
	RID	**0002431**	šn crocodile		
		ID Lexeme	155590	šn	crocodile
			155230	šni̯	to be infested (with crocodiles)
	RID	**0002434**	šn jaw		
		ID Lexeme	156010	šn.wt	the jaws?
	RID	**0002475**	šnw court		
		ID Lexeme	857817	šnw.tj	courtier?
			155980	šnw.t	court; entourage (of the king, of a god)
DRID	**1002201**	**šni̯ to fight**			
	RID	**0002453**	šni̯ to fight		
		ID Lexeme	155760	šn^{c}	storm cloud
			155460	šni̯	to fight; to quarrel
			155520	šnj	to knock down
			155470	šnj	to compel
			155570	šnj.t	hailstorm; storm
			156150	šnn	illness; grief
			857825	šnn.t	quarrel
			32000	jšnn	war cry
	RID	**0002469**	šnšn to tear up		
		ID Lexeme	156240	šnš	to tear up
			156260	šnšn	to tear up
DRID	**1002203**	**šni̯ to dispute**			
	RID	**0002455**	šni̯ to inquire		
		ID Lexeme	155490	šni̯	to inquire; to question (someone)
			155280	šni̯	to pass in review
			155580	šni̯	inquirer
			854559	šni̯	to ask; examine; look through; check; recite; discuss; summon
			155380	šn.w	summoners; reciter
			852182	šn.w	official inquiry
			853888	šn.w	tax inspection; fee
			155370	šn.w	official inquiry
	RID	**0001890**	nšni̯ to rage		

	ID Lexeme	88480	nš	rager? (hippopotamus as a Sethian animal)
		88800	nšn	raging one (Seth; Montu)
		88810	nšn	sharp (or similar)
		88790	nšn.j	storm; rage
		88760	nšn.t	furious one (Hathor-Sakhmet)
		88750	nšn.t	fury
		88770	nšn.tj	raging
		88780	nšni̯	to rage; to be furious
		88830	nšnš	to tear up (documents)
		88840	nšnšn	to rage (against enemies)
		138260	snšn	to frighten
		138270	snšnš	to extricate (oneself)

DRID	**1002204**	**šni̯ to stink**		
RID	**0002456**	šni̯ to stink		
	ID Lexeme	856218	šni̯	to stink
		155530	šni̯	(something) rotten (of fish) (med.)
		156250	šnš	to be smelly; to be brackish

DRID	**1002205**	**šni̯ to suffer**		
RID	**0002457**	šni̯ to suffer		
	ID Lexeme	853480	šn	weak one; disabled?
		155360	šn.w	troubles; need
		155340	šn.tj	two (grieving) sisters (Isis and Nephthys)
		155480	šni̯	to suffer
		145260	sšn	anger
		853573	sšni̯	to grieve?
		156380	šntj	[an affliction of the liver]
RID	**0002910**	šni̯ to demolish		
		145250	sšn	to demolish; to tear down
		145380	sšn.yt	ruins (used as material for building)
		860879	sšn.w	ruins (used for building)

DRID	**1002206**	**šnj hair**		
RID	**0002458**	šnj hair		
	ID Lexeme	155510	šnj	hair
		155390	šnj.w	grass
		156340	šntj	hair
RID	**0002471**	šnt heron		
	ID Lexeme	156350	šntj	heron

DRID	**1002210**	**šnp reed**		
RID	**0002462**	šnp reed		
	ID Lexeme	156090	šnp	[a reed]
		156110	šnp	[woven shenep-reeds (as a mat, a

				garment)]

DRID	**1002214**	**šnṯ to oppose**		
RID	**0002472**	šnṯ to oppose		
	ID Lexeme	156410	šnṯ	abuse
		156400	šnṯ	to revile; to oppose; to punish
		155330	šnṯ	policeman; hundreds
		156460	šnṯ.j	Rebel (Seth)
		156470	šnṯ.y	enemy; foe
		156480	šnṯ.y	enmity
		156420	šnṯ.w	shield?
		156490	šnṯ.yw	enemies; foes
		156430	šnṯ.t	strife; quarrel
		856055	sšnṯ	to cause a quarrel

DRID	**1002216**	**šntꜣy widow**		
RID	**0002474**	šntꜣy widow		
	ID Lexeme	156300	šntꜣy.t	widow
		156310	šntꜣy.t	Shentayet (a heavenly cow)

DRID	**1002217**	**šn^{c} [a small fish]**		
RID	**0002476**	Sno [a small fish]		
	ID Lexeme	155770	Sno	[a small fish]

DRID	**1002218**	**šn^{c} breast**		
RID	**0002477**	šn^{c} breast		
	ID Lexeme	155740	šn^{c}	breast

DRID	**1002219**	**šn^{c} to hold back**		
RID	**0002478**	šn^{c} to hold back		
	ID Lexeme	155700	šn^{c}	water spout in lion-form
		155720	šn^{c}	enemy
		155750	šn^{c}	constipation (med.)
		854560	šn^{c}	to hold; to hold back; to be shy
		155690	šn^{c}	to hold back
		155680	šn^{c}	to turn back; to detain
		155870	šn^{c}.w	police task
		155900	šn^{c}.w	storehouse; [establishment where food was prepared for distribution]
		155780	šn^{c}.w	personnel (of the storehouse)
		155840	šn^{c}.w	deckhouse
		155850	šn^{c}.w	policeman?; gard
		155860	šn^{c}.w	hindrance
		155910	šn^{c}.wt	[a kind of forced labor]
		155830	šn^{c}.t	storehouse
		155540	šny	[a workman]

DRID	**1002220**	**šn^{c} to value**			
RID	**0002479**	šn^{c} to value			
	ID Lexeme	155810	šn^{c}	[unit of value, equivalent to a weight of silver]	
		550094	šn^{c}	to value	
		155920	šn^{c}.tj	[unit of value, equivalent to a weight of silver]	
DRID	**1002223**	**šp to be blind**			
RID	**0002482**	šp to be blind			
	ID Lexeme	153620	šp	to be blind; to blind	
		857832	šp.w	blindness	
		854346	šp.w	blind person	
		153660	šp.t	blindness	
		116140	ẖp.w	[an eye disease]	
RID	**0002660**	šꜣb to be blind			
	ID Lexeme	151640	šꜣb	to be blind?	
DRID	**1002224**	**šp to flow out**			
RID	**0002483**	šp to flow out			
	ID Lexeme	153630	šp	to flow out; to depart	
		153670	šp.t	intestinal disease [an affliction of the anus (hemorrhoids?)]	
DRID	**1002225**	**šp to throw?**			
RID	**0002484**	šp to throw?			
	ID Lexeme	153650	šp	to throw; to bound?	
DRID	**1002228**	**špn [a beverage]**			
RID	**0002489**	špn [a beverage]			
	ID Lexeme	153740	špn.t	[a jug, as a measure for beer]	
		153730	špn.t	[a beverage]	
DRID	**1002235**	**špsi̯ to be dignified**			
RID	**0002495**	špsi̯ to be dignified			
	ID Lexeme	153820	šps	statue; likeness	
		153810	šps	tomb-chapel	
		400546	šps.j	splendid; noble	
		153890	šps.j	libation vase	
		153870	šps.w	noble	
		153880	šps.w	glory; riches; costly offerings	
		858556	šps.w	[a priestly title]	
		855194	šps.ww	the nobles	
		859274	šps.wt	noble women	
		856427	šps.t	statue; image	
		153850	šps.t	magnificent one	
		153860	šps.t	[a ritual jar]	

			153840	šps.t	noblewoman
			858557	šps.t	[a female priestly title]
			169300	šps.t	favorite
			851690	špsi̯	to be dignified; to honor
			153780	špsi̯	be dignified
			153900	špss	noble (an esteemed person)
			550395	špss	noble; splendid
			153910	špss	to be dignified
			153920	špss	to make splendid; to enrich
			851689	špss	to be dignified
			153940	špss	riches; wealth; precious things
			153950	špss.t	noblewoman
DRID	**1002236**		**špt to be angry**		
	RID	**0002496**	špt to be angry		
		ID Lexeme	153970	špt	to be angry
			153980	špt	anger; discontent
DRID	**1002237**		**špt to blow up**		
	RID	**0002497**	špt to blow up		
		ID Lexeme	852498	špj	to blow up; fill with air
			153960	špt	hedgehog fish
			153990	šptj	to be blown up (med.)
			154000	špty.t	(urinary) bladder
DRID	**1002241**		**šḳ ring**		
	RID	**0002501**	šḳ ring		
		ID Lexeme	157790	šḳ	ring
			157810	šḳ	[a container for arrows (quiver?)]
DRID	**1002243**		**šḳb rhinoceros**		
	RID	**0002503**	šḳb rhinoceros		
		ID Lexeme	157820	šḳb	rhinoceros
DRID	**1002245**		**šr [a body of water]**		
	RID	**0002505**	šr [a body of water]		
		ID Lexeme	156560	šr	[a body of water]
DRID	**1002249**		**šr nose**		
	RID	**0002508**	šr nose		
		ID Lexeme	156610	šr.t	nose; nostril(s)
DRID	**1002256**		**šrgḥ feelings**		
	RID	**0002515**	šrgḥ feelings		
		ID Lexeme	859156	šrgḥ	feelings
DRID	**1002257**		**šrḥ brook**		
	RID	**0002516**	šrḥ brook		

	ID Lexeme	156860	šrḥ	brook; stream
		860883	srḥ.w	stream?

DRID 1002261 šrj to block

RID	**0002521**	šrj to block		
	ID Lexeme	156670	šrj	to stop; to block up
		156730	šrw.t	constipation

DRID 1002264 šrr to be small

RID	**0002526**	šrr to be small		
	ID Lexeme	600257	šrj	little
		400731	šrj	the little; the younger (junior)
		156650	šrj	child; son; lad
		853893	šrj	the minor one
		156680	šrj.t	girl; daughter
		853881	šrj.t	junior (after personal name)
		156570	šrr	to be little; to be meagre
		156820	šrr	little
		852250	šrr.j	the little one; child; son
		145540	sšrr	to reduce
		857709	sšrr.t	a kind of loaf

DRID 1002265 šrr to shout

RID	**0002527**	šrr to shout		
	ID Lexeme	156840	šrr	to cry out; to shout

DRID 1002266 šrš to be quick

RID	**0002528**	šrš to be quick		
	ID Lexeme	156870	šrš	to be quick; to rush

DRID 1002267 šs [green pigment]

RID	**0002529**	šs [green pigment]		
	ID Lexeme	157140	šs.yt	[green pigment (med.)]

DRID 1002268 šs alabaster

RID	**0002530**	šs alabaster		
	ID Lexeme	156950	šs	alabaster; alabaster vessels
		157000	šs.t	alabaster (and objects made of alabaster)

DRID 1002269 šš fool

RID	**0002531**	šš fool		
	ID Lexeme	856310	šš	incompetent
		861315	šš	fool

DRID 1002270 šš nest

RID	**0002532**	šš nest		

		ID Lexeme	854815	šš	nest
DRID	**1002271**	**šs rope**			
	RID	**0002533**	šs rope		
		ID Lexeme	156930	šs	rope
			157750	šš	to turn (rope)
			144410	sš.t	rope
DRID	**1002272**	**šš to build**			
	RID	**0002534**	šš to build		
		ID Lexeme	157760	šš	to build (temple)
DRID	**1002279**	**šsm [something of the dead that is to be released]**			
	RID	**0002541**	šsm [something of the dead that is to be released]		
		ID Lexeme	157460	šsm	[something of the dead that is to be released]
DRID	**1002281**	**šsm leather scroll?**			
	RID	**0002543**	šsm leather scroll?		
		ID Lexeme	157470	šsm	leather scroll?
DRID	**1002282**	**šsm to be inflamed**			
	RID	**0002544**	šsm to be inflamed		
		ID Lexeme	157480	šsm	to be red; to be inflamed
			157530	šsm.wt	inflammation (med.)
DRID	**1002283**	**šsm to be strong**			
	RID	**0002545**	šsm to be strong		
		ID Lexeme	157490	šsm	to be strong; effective
DRID	**1002291**	**šsr to kill**			
	RID	**0002553**	šsr to kill		
		ID Lexeme	858464	šsr	to shoot down
			157580	šsr	to slay
			157560	šsr	arrow
			157590	šsr	sacrificial bull
DRID	**1002292**	**šsr to shine**			
	RID	**0002554**	šsr to shine		
		ID Lexeme	157670	šsr	to shine
DRID	**1002294**	**šsr to utter**			
	RID	**0002556**	šsr to utter		
		ID Lexeme	157640	šsr	to utter; to express
			157650	šsr	utterances; specifications
	RID	**0012556**	šsr sanctuary		
		ID Lexeme	157680	šsr.t	sanctuary

DRID	**1002296**	**šsr work**		
RID	**0002557**	šsr work		
	ID Lexeme	145520	šsr	thing; action; method
		157600	šsr	[to prepare the fireplace?]
DRID	**1002301**	**šsꜣ [an antilope]**		
RID	**0002563**	šsꜣ [an antilope]		
	ID Lexeme	157080	šsꜣ	bubalis antilope
DRID	**1002302**	**šsꜣ nightfall**		
RID	**0002564**	šsꜣ nightfall		
	ID Lexeme	157060	šsꜣ.t	nightfall
DRID	**1002303**	**šsꜣ to be skillful**		
RID	**0002565**	šsꜣ to be skillful		
	ID Lexeme	157030	šsꜣ	to be wise; to be skilled; to be conversant with
		157100	šsꜣ.w	diagnosis; prescription
		157110	šsꜣ.w	tongue
		157090	šsꜣ.w	wisdom; skill
		145550	sšsꜣ	to make wise
DRID	**1002304**	**sšꜣ to beseech**		
RID	**0002567**	sšꜣ to beseech		
	ID Lexeme	144590	sšꜣ	to beseech
		144640	sšꜣ	to beseech
DRID	**1002305**	**sšꜣ to change sb.'s mind**		
RID	**0002568**	sšꜣ to change sb.'s mind		
	ID Lexeme	144610	sšꜣ	to change sb.'s mind
DRID	**1002313**	**št tax payer?**		
RID	**0002576**	št tax payer?		
	ID Lexeme	859883	št	tax payer?
DRID	**1002312**	**št stroke oar?**		
RID	**0002575**	št stroke oar?		
	ID Lexeme	158220	štj.w	stroke oar?
		158200	šty.t	leader; stroke (of a bank of oarswomen)
DRID	**1002314**	**šṯ to decorate**		
RID	**0002577**	šṯ to decorate		
	ID Lexeme	158410	šṯ	satchel
		158380	šṯ	to decorate; to cloth
		158390	šṯ	vestment; garment
		76570	mšṯ	[a piece of jewelry]

DRID	**1002315**		**šṯ turtle**		
	RID	**0002579**	šṯ turtle		
		ID Lexeme	158430	šṯ.w	turtle
			857862	šṯ.wj	the turtle like one
			857865	šṯ.wt	she-tortoise
			158450	šṯw.t	domed roof
DRID	**1002316**		**štb to enclose**		
	RID	**0002580**	štb to enclose		
		ID Lexeme	158300	štb	crate? (for fowl)
			158290	štb	to shut in; to enclose
DRID	**1002323**		**šṯj rectum**		
	RID	**0002587**	šṯj rectum		
		ID Lexeme	158440	šṯy.t	[sanctuary of Sokar]
			856429	šṯy.t	rectum
DRID	**1002324**		**štm to be hostile**		
	RID	**0002588**	štm to be hostile		
		ID Lexeme	158360	štm	rebellion; hostility
			158350	štm	to be quarrelsome; to be hostile
DRID	**1002332**		**šlm delivery**		
	RID	**0008692**	šrm delivery		
		ID Lexeme	156810	šrm.t	delivery; provisions
DRID	**1002337**		**štꜣ to be hidden**		
	RID	**0002603**	štꜣ to be hidden		
		ID Lexeme	158010	štꜣ	hidden water
			158000	štꜣ	copse; scrub
			157940	štꜣ	to be secret; to be hidden; to be mysterious
			400452	štꜣ	secret; hidden; mysterious
			158030	štꜣ	small child
			157960	štꜣ	quarry; mine; hill
			158150	štꜣ.y	the hidden one
			600289	štꜣ.yt	cellar; hidden room
			158160	štꜣy.t	secret? (related to the underworld)
			158120	štꜣ.w	secrets; (religious) mysteries
			857997	štꜣ.wt	mysterious one (fem.)
			158100	štꜣ.t	egg
			158050	štꜣ.t	secrets
			158090	štꜣ.t	womb; belly
			158080	štꜣ.t	hidden one (Nekhbet and others)
			158260	štjw	[term for the underworld]
			158180	šty	[term for the deceased]
			145790	sštꜣ	to clothe; to swaddle
			145710	sštꜣ	(secret) image (of a god)

			145690	sštꜣ	secret
			145700	sštꜣ	secret; confidential matter; (religious) mystery
			145680	sštꜣ	to make secret; to be secret
			145780	sštꜣ	libation water
			145730	sštꜣ	[a mummy bandage]
			145800	sštꜣ.y	mysterious one (the sun god)
DRID	**1002339**	**šw [a jug]**			
	RID	**0002608**	šw [a jug]		
		ID Lexeme	152780	šw	[a jug, for beer]
DRID	**1002344**	**šw feather**			
	RID	**0002613**	šw feather		
		ID Lexeme	152830	šw.t	feather; plumage
			860191	šw.tj	the double plume; Two Feather Crown
			854197	šw.tjt	the feathered one
			153100	šwy.w	[decoration? of a coffin]
DRID	**1002345**	**šw protection**			
	RID	**0002614**	šw protection		
		ID Lexeme	152770	šw	protection; sunshade
			152850	šw.t	neighbors; helpers?
	RID	**0002615**	šw shadow		
		ID Lexeme	152900	šw.t	ship's shade?
			152880	šw.t	shadow
			152910	šw.tjt	fan-bearer
DRID	**1002346**	**šw side**			
	RID	**0002616**	šw side	152840	
		ID Lexeme	šw.t	side (as a part of the body)	
DRID	**1002347**	**šw sunlight**			
	RID	**0002617**	šw sunlight		
		ID Lexeme	152760	šw	to shine (with light)
			152750	šw	sunlight; sun
DRID	**1002349**	**šwb [a jar]**			
	RID	**0002619**	šwb [a jar]		
		ID Lexeme	153130	šwb.tj	[a jar]
DRID	**1002350**	**šwb persea tree**			
	RID	**0002620**	šwb persea tree		
		ID Lexeme	153110	šwb	persea tree
DRID	**1002358**	**šwi̯ to be empty**			

RID	**0002628**	šwi̯ to be empty		
	ID Lexeme	152680	šw	needy man
		600209	šw	need; lack
		152700	šw	blank sheet of papyrus
		152870	šw.t	blank sheet of papyrus (med.)
		450167	šw.t	emptiness
		152890	šw.t	empty eye
		152720	šwi̯	to be empty; to be devoid of
		152670	šwi̯	to be empty; to be devoid of
		144810	sšwi̯	to empty
RID	**0002629**	šwi̯ to dry		
	ID Lexeme	855583	šw	dryness
		152740	šw	dry pieces of wood?
		152940	šw.w	hay; dry rush grass
		152920	šw.w	dry land
		153070	šwy.t	desert; dry spot
		152730	šwi̯	dried; dry
		153160	šwšy.t	dryness; drought
		144800	sšwi̯	to dry
RID	**0002641**	šwꜣ to be poor		
	ID Lexeme	152970	šwꜣ	to be poor
		600647	šwꜣ.w	poverty
		153020	šwꜣ.w	poor man
		153010	šwꜣ.t	impoverishment
		144780	sšwꜣ	to deprive (someone of something)
DRID	**1002360**	**šwi̯ to raise up**		
RID	**0002630**	šwi̯ to raise up		
	ID Lexeme	153030	šwi̯	to soar up; to raise up
		860999	šwj.w	ascent
		144790	sšwi̯	to lift up
DRID	**1002361**	**šwj trade**		
RID	**0002631**	šwj trade		
	ID Lexeme	857563	šwy.t	trade
		153090	šwy.tj	merchant; trader
DRID	**1002372**	**šz bowl**		
RID	**0002642**	šz bowl		
	ID Lexeme	156910	šz	bowl
		88870	nšz	drop of poison
		852769	nšzz.t	droplet
DRID	**1002373**	**šzm [a belt]**		
RID	**0002643**	šzm [a belt]		
	ID Lexeme	157410	šzm.t	[a belt]

DRID	**1002374**	**šzm malachite**		
	RID	**0002644**	šzm malachite	
		ID Lexeme	157430 šzm.t	malachite
DRID	**1002375**	**šzp lashing (naut.)**		
	RID	**0002646**	šzp lashing (naut.)	
		ID Lexeme	157290 šzp.t	lashing (naut.)
			157280 šzp.t	leather straps
DRID	**1002376**	**šzp to receive**		
	RID	**0002647**	šzp to receive	
		ID Lexeme	157180 šzp	gift?
			157200 šzp	palm (measure of length)
			157210 šzp	image; likeness; sphinx
			853890 šzp	receipt; commencement
			157170 šzp	to be acceptable
			157160 šzp	to receive; to take possession of
			157390 šzp.yw	the imprisoned one
			157320 šzp.w	core
			157250 šzp.t	chamber; summer house
			153640 šp	prize
DRID	**1002377**	**šꜣ [a fruit]**		
	RID	**0002676**	šꜣšꜣ [a fruit]	
		ID Lexeme	151960 šꜣšꜣ	[a fruit (med.)]
			152060 šꜣšꜣꜥ	[kernels, fruit]
DRID	**1002379**	**šꜣ excrement (med.)**		
	RID	**0002649**	šꜣ excrement (med.)	
		ID Lexeme	151290 šꜣ.w	excrement (med.)
			861168 mšꜣ.t	[body part (anus?)]
DRID	**1002381**	**šꜣ marsh**		
	RID	**0002651**	šꜣ marsh	
		ID Lexeme	151110 šꜣ	marsh; meadow
			151120 šꜣ	tree (gen.); vine(s)
			151150 šꜣ	wine (jars?)
			151130 šꜣ	plants; vine(s)
			151280 šꜣ.w	coriander
			151330 šꜣ.wt	coriander
			151320 šꜣwy.t	[a kind of a plant]
DRID	**1002382**	**šꜣ order**		
	RID	**0002652**	šꜣ order	
		ID Lexeme	151220 šꜣ	to command; to ordain
			151400 šꜣ.yt	what is ordained; taxes; dues
			860007 šꜣ.w	Fate

			151560	šꜣ.w	worth; suitable
			852483	šꜣ.w	to be useful
			151310	šꜣ.w	weight; worth
			151300	šꜣ.w	destiny
			856308	šꜣ.wtj	value; power
DRID	**1002383**	**šꜣ shallow?**			
	RID	**0002653**	šꜣ shallow?		
		ID Lexeme	151200	šꜣ	to go aground (naut.)
			151600	šꜣ.wt	shallows
			151260	šꜣ.t	flat-bottomed boat
DRID	**1002384**	**šꜣ talon**			
	RID	**0002654**	šꜣ talon		
		ID Lexeme	151250	šꜣ.t	talon; foot (of a bird of prey)
DRID	**1002385**	**šꜣ upper chest**			
	RID	**0002655**	šꜣ upper chest		
		ID Lexeme	151240	šꜣ.t	upper chest
	RID	**0002678**	šꜣšꜣj upper chest		
		ID Lexeme	152040	šꜣšꜣy.t	upper chest; bosom
			152050	šꜣšꜣy.t	[a necklace]
DRID	**1002386**	**šꜣb [a boat]**			
	RID	**0002657**	šꜣb [a boat]		
		ID Lexeme	151670	šꜣb.t	[a boat]
DRID	**1002388**	**šꜣb food**			
	RID	**0002659**	šꜣb food		
		ID Lexeme	151690	šꜣb.w	meals; food
			153120	šꜣb.tj	shabti
DRID	**1002389**	**šꜣd to dig**			
	RID	**0002661**	šꜣd to dig		
		ID Lexeme	152150	šꜣd	to dig; to dig out
			857732	šꜣd.t	pit
DRID	**1002394**	**šꜣj pig**			
	RID	**0002666**	šꜣj pig		
		ID Lexeme	856056	šꜣ	animal (of Seth)
			151350	šꜣj	pig
			151410	šꜣj.t	sow
DRID	**1002396**	**šꜣm dirty item?**			
	RID	**0002668**	šꜣm dirty item?		
		ID Lexeme	151800	šꜣm.w	dirty laundry
			151810	šꜣm.w	[a med. liquid]

			151820	šꜣmy.t	water (of the laundryman) (med.)
DRID	**1002398**		**šꜣḳ [a container]**		
	RID	**0002670**	šꜣḳ [a container]		
		ID Lexeme	152070	šꜣḳ	(leather) bag?
			152100	šꜣḳ	container for arrows (box?) (quiver?)
DRID	**1002400**		**šꜣr [an eye affliction]**		
	RID	**0002672**	šꜣr [an eye affliction]		
		ID Lexeme	151860	šꜣr.w	[an eye affliction]
DRID	**1002402**		**šꜣš to avoid**		
	RID	**0002674**	šꜣš to avoid		
		ID Lexeme	151950	šꜣš	to avoid; to go through
DRID	**1002403**		**šꜣs to travel**		
	RID	**0002675**	šꜣs to travel		
		ID Lexeme	151900	šꜣs	to travel; to go; to tread on
			151920	šꜣs.w	striding
			151910	šꜣs.t	journeyings
DRID	**1002408**		**šꜣw to cauterize**		
	RID	**0002683**	šꜣw to cauterize		
		ID Lexeme	151570	šꜣw	to cauterize (med.)
DRID	**1002410**		**šꜣᶜ storeroom**		
	RID	**0002684**	šꜣᶜ storeroom		
		ID Lexeme	151480	šꜣᶜ	container (for storage of grain)
			152450	šᶜy.t	[a storeroom]
			151550	šꜣᶜ.t	storeroom
DRID	**1002411**		**šꜣᶜ to begin**		
	RID	**0002684**	šꜣᶜ to begin		
		ID Lexeme	151460	šꜣᶜ	to begin; to be the first (to do something)
			857729	šꜣᶜ	beginning
			151510	šꜣᶜ	primeval waters [canal in the 15th nome of Upper Egypt]
			151470	šꜣᶜ	until
			851685	šꜣᶜ	to begin; to start
			853916	šꜣᶜ	until
			151530	šꜣᶜ.t	primeval goddess (e.g. Hathor, Seshat)
			860546	šꜣᶜ.t	primordial land
			853914	šꜣᶜ.tw	until that (conj.); as soon as (conj.)

DRID 1002412 šꜣꜥzḫ [a plant]

RID	**0002685**	šꜣꜥzḫ [a plant]		
	ID Lexeme	400814	šꜣꜥzḫ	[a spice?, from Punt]

DRID 1002413 šꜥ to cut off

RID	**0002686**	šꜥ to cut off		
	ID Lexeme	152290	šꜥ	field ("detached")
		152250	šꜥ	[scribe's implement]
		152200	šꜥ	to cut; to cut off
		152300	šꜥ.t	slaughtering; terror; evil
		152350	šꜥ.t	document; letter; book
		152310	šꜥ.t	knife
		500026	šꜥ.tj	butcher
		857058	jšꜥ.t	slaughtering knife
		76340	mšꜥ	to cut off
		76390	mšꜥ.t	[provisions?]
		143450	sẖꜥ	dagger
		157770	šš.t	knife

DRID 1002417 šꜥr gate

RID	**0002690**	šꜥr gate		
	ID Lexeme	152540	Sor	prison; gate

DRID 1002419 šꜥr to promise

RID	**0002692**	šꜥr to promise		
	ID Lexeme	859187	šꜥr	to promise
		152550	šꜥr	calculation; scheme; threat; promise

DRID 1002421 šꜥy sand

RID	**0002695**	šꜥy sand		
	ID Lexeme	152500	šꜥ.wtj	wash basin
		152370	šꜥ.t	[a med. substance (barley dough?)]
		152280	šꜥy	sand
		152420	šꜥy	to be grainy (sandy)
		152430	šꜥy.t	sandbank

II.19 ḳ

DRID	**1001841**	**ḳb [a kind of a woodworking]**		
	RID	**0002059**	ḳb [a kind of a woodworking]	
		ID Lexeme	160040 ḳb	[a kind of a woodworking for coffins]
DRID	**1001842**	**ḳb prevalence**		
	RID	**0002060**	ḳb prevalence	
		ID Lexeme	160110 ḳb.w	prevalence
DRID	**1001843**	**ḳbb throat**		
	RID	**0002061**	ḳbb throat	
		ID Lexeme	160220 ḳbb.t	throat
DRID	**1001844**	**ḳbb = ḳbḥ to be cool**		
	RID	**0002062**	ḳbb to be cool	
		ID Lexeme	160070 ḳb	to pour a libation
			160100 ḳb.t	[a term for a temple]; naos
			160090 ḳb.t	coolness
			160130 ḳby	[a kind of a jar (for water, for beer)]
			550102 ḳbb	cool; calm
			160170 ḳbb	to be cool; to be calm
			160180 ḳbb	coolness; calmness
			160190 ḳbb	cool wind
			870143 ḳbb.wt	cool water
			160200 ḳbb.t	cool water
			32720 jgb	air; wind
			71500 mnḳb	cool place; palace
			71490 mnḳb	fan
			146060 sḳbb	to cool; to refresh
			146080 sḳbb.wj	cool room (for food); bathroom
			146050 sḳb.w	cooling
	RID	**0002064**	ḳbḥ to be cool	
		ID Lexeme	160260 ḳbḥ	to pour a libation; to present libations
			160270 ḳbḥ	water pourer
			860401 ḳbḥ	water pourer
			160280 ḳbḥ	to die
			160250 ḳbḥ	to be cool; to cool
			854563 ḳbḥ	to be cool; to cool; to pour a libation; to present libations
			160380 ḳbḥ	[a watery area in heaven]
			160400 ḳbḥ.yt	libation vessel
			160350 ḳbḥ.w	watery region (mythological)
			160410 ḳbḥ.w	Cool one

			160340	ḳbḥ.w	watery region (habitat of birds)
			160360	ḳbḥ.w	water fowl
			160330	ḳbḥ.w	libation water; water
			160320	ḳbḥ.w	libation vase
			160310	ḳbḥ.w	coolness
			854352	ḳbḥ.wj	one who belongs to the watery area
			859947	ḳbḥ.wj	temple (in Egypt)
			854779	ḳbḥ.wj	what belongs to the watery area
			146110	sḳbḥ	to refresh; to give ease to
DRID	**1001845**		**ḳbḥ lower leg**		
	RID	**0002063**	ḳbḥ lower leg		
		ID Lexeme	160230	ḳbḥ	lower leg (with foot)
DRID	**1001847**		**ḳb^c to joke**		
	RID	**0002065**	ḳb^c to joke		
		ID Lexeme	160150	ḳb^c	to joke
DRID	**1001848**		**ḳd [a tree]**		
	RID	**0002066**	ḳd [a tree]		
		ID Lexeme	162480	ḳd.t	[a coniferous, resin-producing tree]
DRID	**1001849**		**ḳd kite**		
	RID	**0002067**	ḳd kite		
		ID Lexeme	162490	ḳd.t	kite (a measure of weight)
DRID	**1001850**		**ḳḏ plaster**		
	RID	**0002068**	ḳḏ plaster		
		ID Lexeme	162680	ḳḏ	plasterer
			162670	ḳḏ	gypsum; plaster
DRID	**1001851**		**ḳḏ thorn bush**		
	RID	**0002069**	ḳḏ thorn bush		
		ID Lexeme	162690	ḳḏ	thorn bush
DRID	**1001852**		**ḳd to form**		
	RID	**0002070**	ḳd to form		
		ID Lexeme	162420	ḳd	to form; to fashion; to build
			162430	ḳd	nature; form; character
			860726	ḳd.tj	builder
			861184	ḳd.w	potter; builder; sculptor
			162500	ḳd.w	potter; builder; sculptor
			162560	ḳdw.w	essence; character
			162550	ḳdw.t	drawings; outlines
			32390	jḳd.w	builder

		855558	jḳd.w	builder
		146310	sḳd	Boat builder?; woodcutter?
		146290	sḳd	slope (of a pyramid)
		146300	sḳd	to make build
DRID	**1001853**	**ḳḏ to run**		
RID	**0002071**	ḳḏ to run		
	ID Lexeme	162700	ḳḏ	to go around; to run
DRID	**1001854**	**ḳdb to rent**		
RID	**0002072**	ḳdb to rent		
	ID Lexeme	162570	ḳdb	to rent (a field)
		550092	ḳdb	rent; lease
		862838	ḳdb.yt	[term used for marking a field (lend on lease)]
DRID	**1001855**	**ḳdd to sleep**		
RID	**0002073**	ḳdd to sleep		
	ID Lexeme	162470	ḳd.t	sleep
		162650	ḳdd	sleep
		162450	ḳdd	to sleep
		89190	nḳdd	to sleep
		146370	sḳdd	to let sleep
DRID	**1001856**	**ḳdf to collect**		
RID	**0002074**	ḳdf to collect		
	ID Lexeme	162590	ḳdf	altar; table
		162580	ḳdf	to pick; to collect
		162600	ḳdfw	gleanings
DRID	**1001857**	**ḳdi̯ to go around**		
RID	**0002075**	ḳdi̯ to go around		
	ID Lexeme	162440	ḳd	circuit
		162530	ḳdi̯	to go around; to surround; to return
		162540	ḳdw.t	surroundings
		162660	ḳdd	to carry out a revision
		146280	sḳd	oarsman
		857677	sḳd	to sail
		146340	sḳd.wt	journey; sailing
		146330	sḳd.t	ship crew
		146360	sḳdi̯	to travel; to travel (by boat)
RID	**0002077**	ḳdḳd to stroll		
	ID Lexeme	859424	ḳdḳd	to stroll
DRID	**1001858**	**ḳḏm to grasp**		
RID	**0002076**	ḳḏm to grasp		
	ID Lexeme	600590	ḳḏm	handful (as a measure)

863669 ḳḏmḏm to grasp

DRID 1001859 ḳdr incense

RID 0002078 ḳdr incense

ID Lexeme 162620 ḳdr.t incense

DRID 1001860 ḳfn to bake

RID 0002079 ḳfn to bake

ID Lexeme 160490 ḳfn to build
160480 ḳfn [a baked good]
160470 ḳfn to bake; to clot (blood)
160510 ḳfn.y baker
146120 sḳfn to bake (bread)

DRID 1001861 ḳfn to bend down

RID 0002080 ḳfn to bend down

ID Lexeme 160450 ḳfn to bend down
160460 ḳfn to bend, grasp someone's hand

DRID 1001862 ḳfꜣ reputation

RID 0002082 ḳfꜣ reputation

ID Lexeme 160440 ḳfꜣ.t fame; reputation

RID 0002081 ḳfḳf call

ID Lexeme 160530 ḳfḳf.t call; name

DRID 1001863 ḳḥ light

RID 0002083 ḳḥ light

ID Lexeme 162090 ḳḥ light
859650 ḳḥ (solar) ring halo
859649 ḳḥ bright
162120 ḳḥ.t [part of heaven]
162130 ḳḥj [characteristic of the Moon]

DRID 1001864 ḳḥ to break

RID 0002084 ḳḥ to break

ID Lexeme 600384 ḳḥ to break stones (as punishment)

RID 0002086 ḳḥḳḥ to hammer

ID Lexeme 162150 ḳḥḳḥ to hammer; to chisel
162160 ḳḥḳḥ.w worker with hammer (metalworker working in the quarry)

DRID 1001865 ḳḥn cauldron?

RID 0002085 ḳḥn cauldron?

ID Lexeme 162140 ḳḥn cauldron?

DRID 1001866 ḳj shape

RID 0002087 ḳj shape

ID Lexeme 159670 ḳj form; shape; nature

DRID 1001867 ḳjs to vomit
RID 0002088 ḳjs to vomit
ID Lexeme 159730 ḳjs vomit
159720 ḳjs to vomit; to spew out
857590 ḳjs.w vomiting
159760 ḳjs.wt efflux

DRID 1001868 ḳm [timpani]
RID 0002093 ḳmḳm [timpani]
ID Lexeme 160850 ḳmḳm [a kind of a timpani]

DRID 1001869 ḳm to be sad
RID 0002089 ḳm to be sad
ID Lexeme 32220 jḳm.w sadness; sorrow
89100 nḳm to be sad; to suffer
89110 nḳm.t sadness

DRID 1001870 ḳmd to be concerned
RID 0002090 ḳmd to be concerned
ID Lexeme 600643 ḳmd lamentation
160870 ḳmd to mourn
160860 ḳmd to think of; to be concerned

DRID 1001871 ḳmḥ [a bread]
RID 0002091 ḳmḥ [a bread]
ID Lexeme 160840 ḳmḥ.w [a kind of bread]

DRID 1001872 ḳmḥ twig
RID 0002092 ḳmḥ twig
ID Lexeme 860192 ḳmḥ barb of harpoon
160830 ḳmḥ twig; foliage

DRID 1001873 ḳmꜣ rush
RID 0002095 ḳmꜣ rush
ID Lexeme 160630 ḳmꜣ reeds

DRID 1001874 ḳrs to bury
RID 0008851 ḳrs to bury
161940 ḳrs to bury
161950 ḳrs burial
161980 ḳrs.w coffin
854326 ḳrs.wt burial
161960 ḳrs.t burial
161970 ḳrs.tjt burial equipment

DRID 1001875 ḳmꜣ to mourn

	RID	**0003491**	ḳmꜣ to mourn		
		ID Lexeme	160610	ḳmꜣ	to mourn
			160680	ḳmꜣ.tj	the two mourners
DRID	**1001876**		**ḳmꜣ to throw**		
	RID	**0003492**	ḳmꜣ to throw		
		ID Lexeme	854564	ḳmꜣ	to throw; create; produce; devise; hammer (metal); float
			160550	ḳmꜣ	to throw
			160540	ḳmꜣ	throw stick
			160560	ḳmꜣ	[method of preparing qemechu bread]
			160700	ḳmꜣ.w	winnower
			853627	ḳmꜣ.w	something thrown (into the water)
	RID	**0002096**	ḳmꜣ to create		
		ID Lexeme	160590	ḳmꜣ	form; appearance; nature
			160640	ḳmꜣ	(sacred) bull
			160580	ḳmꜣ	creator
			160600	ḳmꜣ	to hammer out (metal)
			160570	ḳmꜣ	to create; to produce; to devise
			870263	ḳmꜣ.y	young?
			857592	ḳmꜣ.w	creator (or creation)
			160660	ḳmꜣ.t	product
			160760	ḳmꜣ.tj	[a garment? of the king at the sed-festival]
			160750	ḳmꜣ.tj	image of the god in the temple
	RID	**0002097**	ḳmꜣ to wrestle		
		ID Lexeme	160650	ḳmꜣ	to wrestle
			160710	ḳmꜣ.w	[a class of soldier]
DRID	**1001878**		**ḳn = ḏn [a plant]**		
	RID	**0002098**	ḳn [a plant]		
		ID Lexeme	160960	ḳn	plant of the field
			161090	ḳn.w	[ref. for sterile arable land]
			856566	ḳn.t	[a plant (med.)]
			161140	ḳnj	[a plant (med.)]
	RID	**0002099**	ḳn mat		
		ID Lexeme	160980	ḳn	mat
	RID	**0000271**	ḏn mat		
		ID Lexeme	852090	ꜥḏn	mat
			859933	ꜥḏn	mat
DRID	**1001881**		**ḳn = ḏn to finish**		
	RID	**0002101**	ḳn to finish		
		ID Lexeme	161010	ḳn	to keep away (from so./sth.)
			160990	ḳn	to complete; to finish
			852594	ḳn	cease (to do)
			600621	ḳn	end; first quality

			851298	ḳn.t	achievement?
			161050	ḳn.t	whole grain size?
	RID	**0000274**	ḏn to finish		
		ID Lexeme	852089	ꜥḏn	to finish
DRID	**1001882**	**ḳn to beat**			
	RID	**0002102**	ḳn to injure		
		ID Lexeme	160910	ḳn	to beat; to injure
			870158	ḳn.t	damage; injury
			161220	ḳnj	to hurt?
			160970	ḳnj.w	evil deed; injury; lack
			161250	ḳnj.t	[an injury to the eye (med.)]
	RID	**0002112**	ḳnḳn to beat		
		ID Lexeme	855208	ḳnḳn	chastisement
			161450	ḳnḳn	to beat; to pound up (med.)
			161460	ḳnḳn	[a cut of meat]
			161500	ḳnḳn.yt	mallet?
DRID	**1001883**	**ḳn to weave**			
	RID	**0002103**	ḳn to weave		
		ID Lexeme	161000	ḳn	to weave
			161280	ḳn.yw	weaver
DRID	**1001884**	**ḳꜣb = ḳnb to fold**			
	RID	**0002104**	ḳnb to bend		
		ID Lexeme	161330	ḳnb	to bind; to bend; to subjugate
			161350	ḳnb.t	court (of magistrates)
			161340	ḳnb.t	corner; angle
			161390	ḳnb.tj	magistrate; an officer of a court
			161380	ḳnb.tj	what belongs to the court
	RID	**0002135**	ḳꜣb to double		
		ID Lexeme	857580	ḳꜣb	belly, intestine
			650065	ḳꜣb	interior; middle
			159260	ḳꜣb	windings
			159270	ḳꜣb	intestines
			159240	ḳꜣb	to fold over; to wind
			159250	ḳꜣb	to double; to multiply
			854562	ḳꜣb	to fold over; to wind; to double; to multiply
			870119	ḳꜣb	coil, bend
			858177	ḳꜣb?	to mortify?
			159340	ḳꜣb.y	one who winds [a kind of a snake]
			500988	ḳꜣb.yt	twisted one
			159300	ḳꜣb.t	knee?
			146000	sḳꜣb	to double
	RID	**0002136**	**ḳꜣd to creep?**		
		ID Lexeme	159620	ḳꜣd	[a kind of a plant]

857581 ḳꜣd [a kind of a bird]
159660 ḳꜣd.yt [a small animal (med.)]
159650 ḳꜣd.t [a creeper plant (med.)]

DRID 1001885 ḳnd to rage

RID 0002105 ḳnd to rage

ID Lexeme
161540 ḳnd raging one (esp. Horus, Sobek)
161530 ḳnd to rage; to become angry
161530 ḳnd anger
146180 sḳnd to enrage

DRID 1001886 ḳni̯ to be strong

RID 0002100 ḳn numerous

ID Lexeme
161060 ḳn.w many; numerous
161070 ḳn.w the many

RID 0002106 ḳni̯ to be fat

ID Lexeme
160900 ḳn fat (med.)
870155 ḳn to be fat
161020 ḳn.t fat (symptom of an eye illness)
160890 ḳni̯ fat; to be fat
146140 sḳni̯ to make fat; to enrich

RID 0002107 ḳni̯ to conquer

ID Lexeme
160940 ḳn strong warrior
160950 ḳn strong lion (a water spout shaped like a lion's head)
550122 ḳn strong; brave; capable
856313 ḳn force; bravery
161230 ḳn.yt bodyguard
161030 ḳn.t valor; strength
161160 ḳni̯ to conquer; to make strong
854565 ḳni̯ to be brave; to be strong; to make strong; to be capable; to conquer
161150 ḳni̯ to be brave; to be strong; to be capable
850878 ḳnn predominance
161510 ḳnḳn.wj Beater [a divine being (scribe of Osiris)]
146130 sḳn to harm
550241 sḳni̯ to make strong

DRID 1001888 ḳnj [a bird]

RID 0002108 ḳnj [a bird]

ID Lexeme
161310 ḳnj.w [term for bird(s) of the marshes]

DRID 1001889 ḳnj carrying chair

RID 0002109 ḳnj carrying chair

ID Lexeme
161290 ḳnj.w chair; throne; carrying chair
161320 ḳnj.w portable shrine

DRID	**1001890**	**ḳnj to embrace**		
	RID	**0002110**	ḳnj to embrace	
		ID Lexeme	161300 ḳnj	sheaf; bundle
			161200 ḳnj	[a ceremonial garment]
			161180 ḳnj	embrace
			161170 ḳnj	to embrace
			853381 ḳnj.w	sheaf carrier
DRID	**1001891**	**ḳnj yellow**		
	RID	**0002111**	ḳnj yellow	
		ID Lexeme	161260 ḳnj.t	yellowish [characterist (figurative term for a mineral)]
			161270 ḳnj.t	[a yellow pigment]
DRID	**1001892**	**ḳḳ doum nuts**		
	RID	**0002113**	ḳḳ doum nuts	
		ID Lexeme	162280 ḳḳ	nuts; doum-palm nuts
DRID	**1001893**	**ḳḳ to eat**		
	RID	**0002114**	ḳḳ to eat	
		ID Lexeme	162310 ḳḳ	to eat
DRID	**1001894**	**ḳr to hurry**		
	RID	**0002120**	ḳrḳr to hurry	
		ID Lexeme	89170 nḳrḳr	to hurry
DRID	**1001895**	**ḳr to roll sth.**		
	RID	**0002121**	ḳrḳr to roll sth	
		ID Lexeme	162000 ḳrḳr	to spread over (of the inundation)
			161990 ḳrḳr	quivering?
			857704 ḳrḳr.t	beads; lump
			146260 sḳrḳr	to roll around (in bed, of a feverish patient)
DRID	**1001896**	**ḳrḏn ax**		
	RID	**0002115**	ḳrḏn ax	
		ID Lexeme	162060 ḳrḏn	ax; pick ax
DRID	**1001897**	**ḳrf to contract**		
	RID	**0002116**	ḳrf to contract	
		ID Lexeme	161690 ḳrf	to contract; to draw together
			851023 ḳrf	bag
			161730 ḳrf.w	(facial) wrinkles (med.)
			161710 ḳrf.t	bag
			161720 ḳrf.t	contractions (med.)
DRID	**1001898**	**ḳrḥ uterus?**		

	RID	**0002117**	ḳrḥ uterus?	
		ID Lexeme	161910 ḳrḥ.t	[primordial goddess in a form of a serpent]
			161890 ḳrḥ.t	pottery; pot
			161900 ḳrḥ.t	primeval creature; ancestor
			161920 ḳrḥ.t	uterus? stomach?
DRID	**1001899**	**ḳrm ashes**		
	RID	**0002118**	ḳrm ashes	
		ID Lexeme	161740 ḳrm.t	ashes
DRID	**1001900**	**ḳrn foreskin**		
	RID	**0002119**	ḳrn foreskin	
		ID Lexeme	161760 ḳrn.t	foreskin; uncircumcised penis
DRID	**1001901**	**ḳrr [a boat]**		
	RID	**0002122**	ḳrr [a boat]	
		ID Lexeme	161790 ḳrr	[a boat]
DRID	**1001902**	**ḳrr cavern**		
	RID	**0002123**	ḳrr cavern	
		ID Lexeme	161610 ḳr.tj	the twin caverns (at Elephantine, considered the twin sources of the Nile)
			161870 ḳrr	He of the cavern
			161860 ḳrr.t	cavern
			854566 ḳrr.t	hole; cavern
			161850 ḳrr.t	hole
			161840 ḳrr.t	offering place (at the tomb)
			161620 ḳrr.tj	rotary pan
			500137 ḳrr.tj	He of the cavern
			852048 ḳrḳr.t	hole
DRID	**1001903**	**ḳrr cloud**		
	RID	**0002124**	ḳrr cloud	
		ID Lexeme	161770 ḳrr	storm; storm cloud
			161830 ḳrr	[storm-snake?]
DRID	**1001904**	**ḳrr frog**		
	RID	**0002125**	ḳrr frog	
		ID Lexeme	161780 ḳrr	frog
DRID	**1001905**	**ḳrr to burn**		
	RID	**0002126**	ḳrr to burn	
		ID Lexeme	860315 ḳr	[to blacken?]
			161810 ḳrr	to fire (pottery); to cook (food)
			161820 ḳrr	burnt offering

DRID	**1001906**	**ḳrṯ [a young animal]**			
	RID	**0002127**	ḳrṯ [a young animal]		
		ID Lexeme	859143	ḳrṯ	[a kind of a young animal]
DRID	**1001907**	**ḳr^{c} shield**			
	RID	**0002128**	ḳr^{c} shield		
		ID Lexeme	161670	ḳr^{c}.w	shield
			161680	ḳr^{c}.w	shield bearer
DRID	**1001908**	**ḳs bone**			
	RID	**0002129**	ḳs bone		
		ID Lexeme	162190	ḳs	harpoon tip
			162200	ḳs	bone
			860563	ḳs	to harpoon; to bone
			855576	ḳs.tj	sculptor; carver
	RID	**0000097**	bḳs spine		
		ID Lexeme	57780	bḳs.w	spine
DRID	**1001909**	**ḳsn to be difficult**			
	RID	**0002130**	ḳsn to be difficult		
		ID Lexeme	858513	ḳsn	the bad one
			162230	ḳsn	painful; irksome; difficult
			856685	ḳsn	difficulty; bad luck; annoyance; exertion
			550033	ḳsn	to be difficult; to be in difficulty
			162240	ḳsn.t	trouble; misfortune
			146270	sḳsn	to make sth. miserable
DRID	**1001910**	**ḳwpr henna**			
	RID	**0002131**	ḳwpr henna		
		ID Lexeme	159950	ḳwpr	henna
DRID	**1001911**	**ḳwr cargo loader**			
	RID	**0002132**	ḳwr cargo loader		
		ID Lexeme	159980	ḳwr	barge; cargo boat
			860227	ḳwr.j	stevedores (from ships); unloader (from ships)
DRID	**1001912**	**ḳwr gold worker?**			
	RID	**0002133**	ḳwr gold worker?		
		ID Lexeme	159970	ḳwr	gold worker?; miner?
DRID	**1001913**	**ḳꜣb chest**			
	RID	**0002134**	ḳꜣb chest		
		ID Lexeme	159290	ḳꜣb.t	chest
DRID	**1001915**	**ḳꜣd to cry**			

	RID	**0002137**	ḳꜣd to cry	
		ID Lexeme	159630 ḳꜣd	to cry
DRID	**1001916**		**ḳꜣḥ to bind**	
	RID	**0002138**	ḳꜣḥ to bind	
		ID Lexeme	159420 ḳꜣḥ	to bind
			858209 ḳꜣḥ	to tame (horse)
			858208 ḳꜣḥ	saddle
DRID	**1001917**		**ḳꜣḥ to plaster**	
	RID	**0002139**	ḳꜣḥ to plaster	
		ID Lexeme	159410 ḳꜣḥ	Nile clay; mortar (of clay)
			159450 ḳꜣḥ.yt	Nile clay
			146010 sḳꜣḥ	to whitewash; to plaster
DRID	**1001918**		**ḳꜣi̯ to be high**	
	RID	**0002140**	ḳꜣi̯ to be high	
		ID Lexeme	158990 ḳꜣ	tall; high; loud
			158980 ḳꜣ	the high one
			861034 ḳꜣ.yt	[palanquin]
			159160 ḳꜣ.yt	high field; high-lying land; height
			854776 ḳꜣ.tj	that belongs to the high one
			159060 ḳꜣꜣ	hill; high ground
			159010 ḳꜣw	height; length; volume (of voice)
			400393 ḳꜣw	foreman?
			856012 ḳꜣw.w	swelling?
			857583 ḳꜣj.t	High Boat
			159110 ḳꜣi̯	to be tall; to be high; to be loud
			161420 ḳnr	desert; desert edge
			145970 sḳꜣ	pedestal (for chapels); gallery
			145980 sḳꜣ	increase; rising
			145960 sḳꜣi̯	to make high; to exalt
	RID	**0002143**	ḳꜣḳꜣ to look upwards	
		ID Lexeme	159560 ḳꜣḳꜣ	to look upwards
			870140 ḳꜣḳꜣ	hill
DRID	**1001919**		**ḳꜣj [a beverage]**	
	RID	**0002141**	ḳꜣj [a beverage]	
		ID Lexeme	159120 ḳꜣj	[a beverage]
DRID	**1001920**		**ḳꜣr bolt**	
	RID	**0002144**	ḳꜣr bolt	
		ID Lexeme	159380 ḳꜣr.t	door bolt
DRID	**1001921**		**ḳꜣri̯ to stay near**	
	RID	**0002145**	ḳꜣri̯ to stay	
		ID Lexeme	159370 ḳꜣr	sack; bundle

			858170	ḳꜣr	vagabond
			850645	ḳꜣri̯	to stay; to deposit
			858171	ḳꜣrr	vagabond
DRID	**1001922**	**ḳꜣs to bind**			
	RID	**0002146**	ḳꜣs to bind		
		ID Lexeme	859476	ḳꜣs	binder
			159490	ḳꜣs	rope ladder
			159480	ḳꜣs	rope (as fetters, as rigging (naut.))
			159470	ḳꜣs	to bind (a victim); to string (a bow)
			146020	sḳꜣs	to bind; to fetter
DRID	**1001923**	**ḳꜣw flour**			
	RID	**0002142**	ḳꜣj cereals		
		ID Lexeme	159150	ḳꜣj	seeds (as feed for fowl)
	RID	**0002147**	ḳꜣw flour?, cake?		
		ID Lexeme	159230	ḳꜣw	flour? cake?
DRID	**1001924**	**ḳꜣꜥ to spew**			
	RID	**0002148**	ḳꜣꜥ to spew		
		ID Lexeme	159200	ḳꜣꜥ	to vomit; to pour out
			159210	ḳꜣꜥ.w	vomit; spit out
			146030	sḳꜣꜥ	to make pour forth; to vomit (med.)
DRID	**1001925**	**ḳꜥḥ to bend**			
	RID	**0002149**	ḳꜥḥ to bend		
		ID Lexeme	159810	ḳꜥḥ	to bend (the hand, the arm)
			159830	ḳꜥḥ	arm; shoulder
			159900	ḳꜥḥ	[papyrus sheet]
			159840	ḳꜥḥ.w	corner; bend
			159910	ḳꜥḥ.t	shoulder (of beef)
			159930	ḳꜥḥ.t	side?
			159920	ḳꜥḥ.t	district
DRID	**1002371**	**ḳmy resin**			
	RID	**0002094**	ḳmy resin		
		ID Lexeme	160810	ḳmy	[anointing oil]
			160800	ḳmy.t	gum; resin
			860755	ḳmy.tj	what belongs to gum mountain

II.20 k

DRID	**1001214**	**kff to suck**			
	RID	**0001100**	kff to suck		
		ID Lexeme	164250	kff	to suck (med.)
DRID	**1001215**	**kfi̯ to open**			
	RID	**0001387**	kfi̯ to open		
		ID Lexeme	164100	kf	knife
			500353	kf.y	Revealing one
			164080	kf.t	trustworthiness?
			863016	kf.t	flap (of a wound)
			164200	kfi̯	to uncover; to remove
			164210	kfi̯	to gape (wound)
			858347	kfi̯	to open
	RID	**0001388**	kfkfꜣ to be discrete		
		ID Lexeme	853452	kfkfꜣ	to be discrete
	RID	**0001390**	kfꜣ to be discrete		
		ID Lexeme	164130	kfꜣ	to be discrete
DRID	**1001216**	**kfꜣ rear part**			
	RID	**0001389**	kfꜣ rear part		
		ID Lexeme	164110	kfꜣ	hinter-parts; base; bottom (of a jar)
			164120	kfꜣ	root [a part of a plant (med.)]
			855920	kfꜣ	trunk
			164170	kfꜣ.t	pedestal?
DRID	**1001217**	**kfꜥ to plunder**			
	RID	**0001391**	kfꜥ to plunder		
		ID Lexeme	163880	kfꜥ	to requisition
			164220	kfꜥ	to plunder; to capture
			164230	kfꜥ	booty; captives
DRID	**1001218**	**kḥ to become old**			
	RID	**0001393**	kḥkḥ to become old		
		ID Lexeme	859037	kḥkḥ	old man
			165310	kḥkḥ	to become old; to grow old
			863735	kḥkḥ	the old one
			165330	kḥkḥ.t	the old one (fem.)
DRID	**1001219**	**khb to push violently**			
	RID	**0001392**	khb to push violently		
		ID Lexeme	165230	khb	raging one (Seth)
			165220	khb	to harm (someone); to be violent; to roar
DRID	**1001220**	**kḥs chair**			

	RID	0001394	kḥs chair	
		ID Lexeme	854765 kḥs	chair
DRID	**1001221**	**khꜣ to rage furiously**		
	RID	**0001395**	khꜣ to cast a shadow	
		ID Lexeme	165190 khꜣ	to cast a shadow
	RID	**0001396**	khꜣ to rage furiously	
		ID Lexeme	165180 khꜣ	to rage furiously
			854569 khꜣ	to rage furiously; to cast a shadow; to raise (the voice); to utter (a bellow)
			165200 khꜣ	to raise (the voice); to utter (a bellow)
DRID	**1001222**	**kj [a monkey]**		
	RID	**0001397**	kj [a monkey]	
		ID Lexeme	163830 ky	[a monkey]
			163750 ky.t	[a monkey]
DRID	**1001223**	**kj to shout**		
	RID	**0001399**	kj to shout	
		ID Lexeme	163730 kj	to yell; to lament
			163740 kj.t	shout of acclamation
			163800 kj.w	shout of acclamation
			163810 kjw	summons
DRID	**1001224**	**kjw to bow**		
	RID	**0001400**	kjw to bow	
		ID Lexeme	163820 kjw	to bow
DRID	**1001225**	**kki̯ to be dark**		
	RID	**0001401**	kki̯ to be dark	
		ID Lexeme	165620 kki̯	to be dark; to shade
			165700 kk.w	[a term for a flood water]
			165680 kk.w	darkness
			855319 kk.wtj	dark one [a kind of a snake]
			165710 kk.wt	darkness
			147030 skki̯	to eclipse
DRID	**1001226**	**km to complete**		
	RID	**0001403**	km to complete	
		ID Lexeme	164370 km	to complete
			164380 km	completion; duty; profit
			164450 km.t	completion; final account?
			164580 kmy.t	conclusion (of a book)
			146770 skm	to make complete; to finish
	RID	**0001404**	km to grow old	

	ID Lexeme	146790	skm	balding; greying (of the hair)
		146780	skm	to grow old; to be wise
		869969	skm	gray-haired one
		501142	skm.w	gray-haired one
		146830	skm.yw	The old ones
RID	**0001405**	kmkm destruction		
	ID Lexeme	65650	skmkm	destruction

DRID 1001227 kmm to be black

RID	**0001402**	km to be black		
	ID Lexeme	164300	km	pile of burning charcoals
		164320	km	black
		401218	km	black
		164330	km	pupil (lit. black (of the eye))
		164340	km	black leather
		164590	km.y	[a kind of a serpent]
		164560	km.y	black one (Osiris, Min)
		164430	km.t	Black-land (Egypt)
		850767	km.t	black (arable) land
		164470	km.t	[a big jar made of granite]
		164420	km.t	black cattle (divine herd)
		164440	km.tj	Egyptians
		146800	skm	to make dark; to blacken
RID	**0001406**	kmm to be black		
	ID Lexeme	164310	kmm	to be black; to be dark
		164311	kmm	black; dark

DRID 1001228 kmr [a dancer]

RID	**0001407**	kmr [a dancer]		
	ID Lexeme	164650	kmr	[a dancer]

DRID 1001229 kmrj ivory

RID	**0001408**	kmrj ivory		
	ID Lexeme	164660	kmrj	tusks; ivory

DRID 1001230 knj to be dissatisfied

RID	**0001411**	knj to be dissatisfied		
	ID Lexeme	164710	kn.t	dislike (of someone)?
		164720	knj	to complain; to lament
		164730	knj	to call; to complain
		854568	knj	to complain; to lament; to call; to complain
		164750	knj.w	slander
		164770	knw.y	complainers
		500242	knw.t	female complainer

DRID 1001231 knm to wrap

	RID	**0001412**	knm darkness		
		ID Lexeme	164780	knm	to wrap in
			164830	knm.t	darkness
			164870	knm.tj	one belonging to darkness
			164880	knm.tj	the dark one (star)
DRID	**1001232**		**knnr lyre**		
	RID	**0001414**	knnr lyre		
		ID Lexeme	164760	knnr	lyre
DRID	**1001233**		**kns abdominal region**		
	RID	**0001415**	kns abdominal region		
		ID Lexeme	164950	kns	abdominal region
DRID	**1001234**		**knt [a garment (cloak?)]**		
	RID	**0001416**	knt [a garment (cloak?)]		
		ID Lexeme	165010	knt	[a garment (cloak?)]
DRID	**1001235**		**kp = kb palm of hand, sole of foot**		
	RID	**0001386**	kb palm of hand, sole of foot		
		ID Lexeme	163950	kb.wj	soles
	RID	**0001417**	kp palm of hand, sole of foot		
		ID Lexeme	164020	kp	palm (of the hand); sole (of the foot)
			164030	kp	sole (of the foot)
	RID	**0001418**	kp waterhole		
		ID Lexeme	858346	kp	waterhole
DRID	**1001236**		**kr [a boat]**		
	RID	**0001419**	kr [a boat]		
		ID Lexeme	165030	kr	[a small boat (cargo ship)]
DRID	**1001237**		**kr heap of stones**		
	RID	**0001425**	krkr heap of stones		
		ID Lexeme	165140	krkr	heap of stones
DRID	**1001238**		**kr horn**		
	RID	**0001420**	kr horn		
		ID Lexeme	165040	kr.tj	horns (at the crown of Amun)
DRID	**1001239**		**kr saddle**		
	RID	**0001421**	kr saddle		
		ID Lexeme	600048	kr	saddle (for a donkey)
DRID	**1001240**		**krḥt [a basket]**		
	RID	**0001422**	krḥt [a basket]		
		ID Lexeme	165090	krḥt	basket; bushel

DRID	**1001241**	**krj prison**		
	RID	**0001423**	krj prison	
		ID Lexeme	165050 krj	prison
DRID	**1001242**	**krk bed**		
	RID	**0001424**	krk bed	
		ID Lexeme	165130 krk	couch; bed
DRID	**1001243**	**krm [a jewelry]**		
	RID	**0001426**	krm [a jewelry]	
		ID Lexeme	165070 krm.t	[jewelry of Nubian slaves]
DRID	**1001244**	**krp to efface**		
	RID	**0001427**	krp to efface	
		ID Lexeme	165060 krp	to efface (inscriptions)
DRID	**1001245**	**krs bag**		
	RID	**0001428**	krs bag	
		ID Lexeme	165100 krs	sack
DRID	**1001246**	**krs to jump**		
	RID	**0001429**	krs to jump	
		ID Lexeme	165110 krs	to jump
DRID	**1001247**	**krṯ cords (for whip)**		
	RID	**0001430**	krṯ cords (for whip)	
		ID Lexeme	165170 krṯ	whip cords?; cloth strips?
DRID	**1001248**	**krt to cut**		
	RID	**0001431**	krt to cut	
		ID Lexeme	165160 krt	slaughter
DRID	**1001249**	**krṯ young animal**		
	RID	**0001432**	krṯ young animal	
		ID Lexeme	859143 krṯ	young animal
DRID	**1001250**	**ks [a basket]**		
	RID	**0001434**	ksks [a basket]	
		ID Lexeme	165540 ksks	[a footed basket]
			600025 ksks.t	[a basket]
DRID	**1001251**	**ks to dance**		
	RID	**0001435**	ksks to dance	
		ID Lexeme	165530 ksks	(Nubian) dancer
			165520 ksks	to dance; to perform
			165550 ksks.t	dancer

DRID	**1001252**	**ksi̯ to bow**		
RID	**0001433**	ksi̯ to bow		
	ID Lexeme	165390	kz	[to hang down arms?]
		165430	ksi̯	to bow down; to bend down; to be prostrate
		857304	ksw.t	bowing, reverence
		165450	ks.w	bowing(s); obedience
		146940	sksi̯	to make bow down
DRID	**1001253**	**ksm to oppose**		
RID	**0001436**	ksm to oppose		
	ID Lexeme	165490	ksm	antagonist
		165480	ksm	to defy; to browbeat; to profane (a temple)
DRID	**1001254**	**kšw [a plant]**		
RID	**0001437**	kšw [a plant]		
	ID Lexeme	165590	kšw	[a plant]
DRID	**1001255**	**kt dark**		
RID	**0001438**	ktkt dark		
	ID Lexeme	165850	ktkt	eclipse
RID	**0001439**	ktkt quiet		
	ID Lexeme	500007	ktkt	quiet
DRID	**1001256**	**kt to tremble**		
RID	**0001440**	ktkt to tremble		
	ID Lexeme	165810	ktkt	to tremble; quake; steal
		165840	ktkt	to beat
DRID	**1001257**	**kṯm boasting**		
RID	**0001441**	kṯm boasting		
	ID Lexeme	165950	kṯm	divination; omen; decision (based on augury)
DRID	**1001258**	**ktm gold**		
RID	**0001442**	ktm gold		
	ID Lexeme	165800	ktm.t	gold
DRID	**1001259**	**kṯn charioteer**		
RID	**0001443**	kṯn charioteer		
	ID Lexeme	165960	kṯn	charioteer
DRID	**1001260**	**ktp scimitar**		
RID	**0001444**	ktp scimitar		
	ID Lexeme	165790	ktp	sword

DRID	**1001261**	**ktt to be small**		
RID	**0001445**	ktt to be small		
	ID Lexeme	165910	kt.t	louse?
		169320	kt.t	little girl
		165890	ktt	little one
		165900	ktt	trifle
		165730	ktt	small; trifling
		165880	ktt	to be small; to be trifling
		138490	snktkt	gossip?
DRID	**1001262**	**ktw cauldron**		
RID	**0001446**	ktw cauldron		
	ID Lexeme	165770	ktw.t	cauldron(s)
		165760	ktw.t	hearth stones; cauldron
DRID	**1001263**	**kwšn [part of harness]**		
RID	**0001447**	kwšn [part of harness]		
	ID Lexeme	163920	kwšn	[part of a chariot harness]
DRID	**1001264**	**kj other**		
RID	**0001398**	kj other		
	ID Lexeme	400645	ky	another
		163760	ky	another
		853029	ky.t	another one
		162830	ky.t	another
		163840	kj.wj	others; the masses
		500393	kj.wj	foes; hostile forces
		855087	kj.wj	enmity
DRID	**1001265**	**kz to run freely?**		
RID	**0001448**	kz to run freely?		
	ID Lexeme	165370	kz	to run freely?
DRID	**1001266**	**kꜣ life force**		
RID	**0001449**	kꜣ bull		
	ID Lexeme	162940	kꜣ	to appear as a bull?
		162950	kꜣ	male serpent; bull-snake (i.e. a powerful serpent)
		162930	kꜣ	bull
		500667	kꜣ	bull (manifestation of gods, also of king)
		862899	kꜣ.t	cow
		851433	kꜣ	bull
RID	**0001450**	kꜣ food		
	ID Lexeme	860293	mnkꜣ	provider
		162890	kꜣ	food; provisions
RID	**0001451**	kꜣ life force		

		ID Lexeme	162870	kꜣ	ka; spirit; essence
			162900	kꜣ	name
			850254	kꜣ.j	what belongs to Ka
			860248	kꜣ.t	female Ka
	RID	**0001459**	kꜣkꜣ to revive?		
		ID Lexeme	89270	nkꜣkꜣ	to revive?
DRID	**1001267**		**kꜣ vagina**		
	RID	**0001452**	kꜣ vagina		
		ID Lexeme	162990	kꜣ.t	vagina; vulva
DRID	**1001268**		**kꜣ work**		
	RID	**0001453**	kꜣ work		
		ID Lexeme	859747	kꜣ.wj	worker
			163070	kꜣ.wj	works
			853549	kꜣ.wtj	worker; porter
			163280	kꜣ.wtj	worker; porter
			163010	kꜣ.t	work
			163020	kꜣ.t	work; product
			163290	kꜣwt	to carry; to support
DRID	**1001269**		**kꜣf flint**		
	RID	**0001454**	kꜣf flint		
		ID Lexeme	164090	kꜣf	flint
DRID	**1001270**		**kꜣhs to be rough**		
	RID	**0001455**	kꜣhs to be rough		
		ID Lexeme	165240	kꜣhs	to be harsh; to be overbearing
DRID	**1001271**		**kꜣi̯ to swell**		
	RID	**0001456**	kꜣi̯ to swell		
		ID Lexeme	875705	kꜣ	[appearance of wound secretions]
			163270	kꜣw.t	blister
			163720	kꜣkꜣ.t	blister (med.)
DRID	**1001272**		**kꜣi̯ to think**		
	RID	**0001457**	kꜣi̯ to think		
		ID Lexeme	162840	kꜣ	so; then
			400415	kꜣ	[formative element of verbal forms]
			162850	kꜣ	to say
			162980	kꜣ.t	thought
			163220	kꜣi̯	to think about; to plan
			89260	nkꜣ	to consider; to think (about sth.)
DRID	**1001273**		**kꜣj [a boat]**		
	RID	**0001458**	kꜣj [a boat]		

	ID Lexeme	163240	kꜣj	[a Nubian boat]
DRID	**1001274**	**kꜣm garden**		
RID	**0001460**	kꜣm garden		
	ID Lexeme	163520	kꜣm	vineyard
		163550	kꜣm.wtt	ear of wheat?; [barley?]
		163590	kꜣn.w	vineyard
		163600	kꜣn.w	gardener; vintner
		163650	kꜣr.y	gardener
DRID	**1001275**	**kꜣmn to be blind**		
RID	**0001461**	kꜣmn to be blind		
	ID Lexeme	163580	kꜣmn	blind person
		163570	kꜣmn	to be blind; to blind
DRID	**1001277**	**kꜣp to cover**		
RID	**0001462**	kꜣp to catch		
	ID Lexeme	163370	kꜣp	to catch birds?
		163460	kꜣp.w	birdcatcher
RID	**0001463**	kꜣp to cover		
	ID Lexeme	163380	kꜣp	royal nursery (institution for schooling elite youths)
		163330	kꜣp	shelter
		163340	kꜣp	to cover; to roof over
		854567	kꜣp	to cover; to roof over; to hide
		163360	kꜣp	to hide; to take cover
		850651	kꜣp	bandaging material
		163430	kꜣp.w	roof; cover; lid
		163440	kꜣp.w	Hidden-one (a demon causing illness)
		163470	kꜣp.w	hidden one (crocodile)
		163410	kꜣp.t	linen cover (for a pot) (med.)
		163490	kꜣpꜣp	to cover up
		146670	skꜣp	to cover
RIP	**0001482**	kꜣp to cense		
	ID Lexeme	163300	kꜣp	censer
		163310	kꜣp	to cense; to fumigate
		163320	kꜣp	incense
		163400	kꜣp.t	incense
		163390	kꜣp.t	incense burning
DRID	**1001278**	**kꜣr chapel**		
RID	**0001464**	kꜣr chapel		
	ID Lexeme	856212	kꜣri̯	to be enshrined
		163620	kꜣr, kꜣj	chapel; shrine
DRID	**1001279**	**kꜣy excrement?**		
RID	**0001466**	kꜣy excrement?		

		ID Lexeme	163250 kꜣy.t	excrement (of a gazelle, of a lizard) (med.)
DRID	**1001280**		**kꜣꜣ leopard-patterned**	
	RID	**0001467**	kꜣꜣ leopard-patterned	
		ID Lexeme	163200 kꜣꜣ	leopard-patterned?
DRID	**1002576**		**kbs basket**	
	RID	**0009545**	kbs basket	
		ID Lexeme	164010 kbs	basket

II.21 g

DRID	**1000361**	**gb to incline**		
	RID	**0000441**	gb to incline	
		ID Lexeme	166860 gb	to incline; to bow
	RID	**0000444**	gbgb floatsam	
		ID Lexeme	855595 gbgb	floatsam
DRID	**1000362**	**gbb [a goose]**		
	RID	**0000442**	gbb [a goose]	
		ID Lexeme	167000 gbb	[a goose]
DRID	**1000363**	**gbb earth**		
	RID	**0000443**	gbb earth	
		ID Lexeme	167010 gbb	Geb
			167020 gbb	earth
			167030 gbb	field
			854570 gbb	ground; field
DRID	**1000364**	**gbi̯ to damage**		
	RID	**0000445**	gbi̯ to damage	
		ID Lexeme	166960 gb.w	damage
			166950 gbi̯	to be weak; to be deficient; to damage; to cheat
			850911 gbb	fatigue
			167060 gbgb	to be lame
			167070 gbgb	a lame person
			167090 gbgb.t	heap of corpses
			89670 ngbgb	to turn aside
			89660 ngb	to refract; to remove
			167050 gbgb	to overthrow (the enemy)
DRID	**1000365**	**gbꜣ arm**		
	RID	**0000446**	gbꜣ arm	
		ID Lexeme	166910 gbꜣ	side (of a room)
			166900 gbꜣ	arm
			166930 gbꜣ	to accompany, to walk side by side?
DRID	**1000366**	**gbꜣ payment**		
	RID	**0000447**	gbꜣ payment	
		ID Lexeme	166940 gbꜣ.w	payment
DRID	**1000367**	**gbꜣ to blind**		
	RID	**0000448**	gbꜣ to blind	
		ID Lexeme	166920 gbꜣ	to blind
DRID	**1000368**	**gḏ arm**		

RID 0000449 gḏ arm
ID Lexeme 168780 gḏ arms

DRID 1000369 gḏm to grasp
RID 0000450 gḏm to grasp
ID Lexeme 168790 gḏm to grasp

DRID 1000370 gg kidney
RID 0000452 gg kidney
ID Lexeme 168710 gg.t kidneys

DRID 1000371 ggwi̯ to be amazed
RID 0000453 ggwi̯ to be amazed
ID Lexeme 855817 g.wt the amazement; the stare
852232 ggw.t the amazement; the stare
856740 ggw.w the amazement; the stare
852231 ggwi̯ to marvel; to be amazed
147100 sgi̯ to be amazed; to stare
147140 sg.wt astonishment
855608 gi̯ to be astonished

DRID 1000372 gḥs gazelle
RID 0000454 gḥs gazelle
ID Lexeme 168230 gḥs.t gazelle
168210 gḥs gazelle

DRID 1000373 gj [a plant]
RID 0000455 gj [a plant]
ID Lexeme 166660 gj.w [an aromatic plant]
166650 gy.t [a plant]

DRID 1000374 gjf monkey
RID 0000455 gjf monkey
ID Lexeme 166670 gjf vervet (long-tailed monkey)
166680 gjf.t vervet (long-tailed monkey)

DRID 1000375 gm ibis
RID 0000456 gm ibis
ID Lexeme 167160 gm.t black ibis

DRID 1000376 gm power
RID 0000457 gm power
ID Lexeme 167150 gm power
167370 gmgm to smash; to break; to tear

DRID 1000377 gm weak
RID 0000458 gm weak

	ID Lexeme	167180	gm.w	weakness; daze
		855819	gm.wt	weakness
RID	**0000459**	gmgm feel, grope		
	ID Lexeme	167380	gmgm	to feel; to fumble around
DRID	**1000378**	**gmḫ strand of hair**		
RID	**0000460**	gmḫ strand of hair		
	ID Lexeme	167310	gmḫ.t	plaited hair
		167330	gmḫ.t	widow
DRID	**1000379**	**gmḫ to see**		
RID	**0000462**	gmḫs [a bird of prey]		
	ID Lexeme	167360	gmḫs.w	[a bird of prey]
RID	**0000461**	gmḫ to see		
		167270	gmḫ	to catch sight of; to look
		167290	gmḫ	[specially shaped stone as part of a doorway]
		167280	gmḫ	[a term used for eye]
		147200	sgmḫ	to make see; to glimpse
DRID	**1000380**	**gmi̯ to find**		
RID	**0000464**	gmi̯ to find		
	ID Lexeme	167210	gmi̯	to find; to discover
		89680	ngmgm	to conspire
DRID	**1000381**	**gmꜣ temple (of the head)**		
RID	**0000465**	gmꜣ temple (of the head)		
	ID Lexeme	167200	gmꜣ	temple (of the head) (med.)
DRID	**1000382**	**gn [a plant]**		
RID	**0000466**	gn [a plant]		
	ID Lexeme	167580	gnn	[an edible plant (legume?)]
		167700	gngn.t	[a plant of the Wadi Natrun]
DRID	**1000383**	**gn base**		
RID	**0000467**	gn base		
	ID Lexeme	167470	gn.w	stand
		450115	gn	stand
DRID	**1000384**	**gn respect**		
RID	**0000468**	gn to be respected		
	ID Lexeme	167410	gn	strongman
		167400	gn	to be respected; to be mighty
DRID	**1000385**	**gn to record***		
RID	**0000469**	gn to record*		
	ID Lexeme	167490	gn.wt	annals; records

167440 gn.t record

DRID 1000386 gnf repel
RID 0000470 gnf repel
ID Lexeme 167520 gnf to rebuff; to repel

DRID 1000387 gngntj lute
RID 0000471 gngntj lute
ID Lexeme 167720 gngntj lute

DRID 1000388 gnẖ to fix
RID 0000473 gnẖ to fix?
ID Lexeme 167650 gnẖ to serve; to be subjected
167620 gnẖ to stud; to mount
167630 gnẖ to stick; to fix
167660 gnẖ.t star

DRID 1000389 gnẖ wing
RID 0000474 gnẖ wing
ID Lexeme 167640 gnẖ wing(s)

DRID 1000390 gnn soft
RID 0000475 gnn to be weak
ID Lexeme 600572 gnn to be weak; to be soft
167540 gnn to be weak; to be soft
167550 gnn weak one
856747 gnn.w weakness
167610 gnn.w fat
167590 gnn.t the weak one (delivering woman)
167600 gnn.t weakness
147250 sgnn [additive in beer preparation]
147220 sgnn to make weak; to enfeeble
RID 0000476 gnn to soft
ID Lexeme 167560 gnn [soft part of a plant product (med.)]
147240 sgnn oil; ointment
147230 sgnn to anoint; to perfume

DRID 1000391 gnš to select
RID 0000477 gnš to select
ID Lexeme 167690 gnš to select; to distinguish

DRID 1000392 gns violence
RID 0000478 gns violence
ID Lexeme 167670 gns outrage; violence

DRID 1000393 gp cloud

	RID	**0000480**	gp to inundate	
		ID Lexeme	167120 gp	to overflow; to inundate
	RID	**0000479**	gp to be clouded	
		ID Lexeme	167100 gp	to be clouded (med., fig. for a heart condition)
			167130 gp	to overcloud; to be cloudy
			32730 jgp	rain cloud
			857093 jgp	cloud
DRID	**1000394**	**gr also**		
	RID	**0000481**	gr also	
		ID Lexeme	167790 gr.t	furthermore
			167740 gr	also; furthermore
			167730 gr	also; furthermore
DRID	**1000395**	**gr kidney**		
	RID	**0000482**	gr kidney	
		ID Lexeme	168180 gr.tj	kidneys
DRID	**1000396**	**gr silence**		
	RID	**0000483**	gr to be silent	
		ID Lexeme	866516 jgr	the silent one
			32790 jgr.w	Silent ones
			32770 jgr.t	Silence (realm of the dead, the necropolis)
			857053 jgr.tj	the silent one
			167750 gr	to be silent; to end
			167760 gr	silence
			167770 gr	fishes
			167800 gr.w	silent one
			167970 grqr	gossiper?
			147270 sgr	silence; stillness
			147260 sgr	to silence
DRID	**1000397**	**grb property**		
	RID	**0000484**	grb property	
		ID Lexeme	860251 grb	property
DRID	**1000398**	**grb to cut (wood)**		
	RID	**0000485**	grb to cut (wood)	
		ID Lexeme	167830 grb	to cut (a piece of wood serving as a chariot part)
DRID	**1000399**	**grg exaltation**		
	RID	**0000486**	grg exaltation	
		ID Lexeme	168060 grg	exaltation

DRID	**1000400**	**grg lie**			
	RID	**0000490**	grg to lie		
		ID Lexeme	168040	grg	lie; falsehood
			168050	grg	rumors
			168150	grg.y	liar
			168100	grg.t	liar (female)
			77220	mgrg	liar (Seth)

DRID	**1000401**	**grg rib**			
	RID	**0000487**	grg rib		
		ID Lexeme	168160	grgy.t	rib

DRID	**1000402**	**grg to prepare**			
	RID	**0000488**	grg to establish		
		ID Lexeme	168020	grg	equipment
			168000	grg	to establish; to equip; to organize
			168010	grg	to be ready
			168030	grg	settlement
			853430	grg.w	The foundations (domain)
			168170	grg.t	dowry
			550075	grg.t	settlement; foundation; newly arable land
			168080	grg.t	catch
			147310	sgrg	yard arm? (naut.)
			147320	sgrg	to make ready
	RID	**0000489**	grg to hunt		
		ID Lexeme	167980	grg	to hunt; to lay (a trap)
			167990	grg	hunter
			168120	grg.t	trap; net

DRID	**1000403**	**grḥ night**			
	RID	**0000491**	grḥ dark, night?		
		ID Lexeme	167910	grḥ	[one of the 8 primordial gods]
			167920	grḥ	night
			167950	grḥ.yt	darkness

DRID	**1000404**	**grḥ to finish**			
	RID	**0000492**	grḥ to finish		
		ID Lexeme	167880	grḥ	to complete; to be satisfied with; to finish
			167890	grḥ	tax arrears
			167900	grḥ	ending
			147300	sgrḥ	to pacify; to make peaceful; to satisfy

DRID	**1000405**	**grm to drag away**	
	RID	**0000493**	grm to drag away

ID Lexeme 167860 grm to drag away

DRID 1000406 grt husk?
RID 0000494 grt husk?
ID Lexeme 863678 grt husk?

DRID 1000407 gs half
RID 0000495 gs half
ID Lexeme 168250 gs side
168250 gs side
854572 gs side; half
168260 gs half
168320 gs.y neighbor
168330 gs.w half-loaf (offering)
168680 gs.tj (testicles)

DRID 1000408 gš liquid
RID 0000498 gš to pour off
ID Lexeme 858492 gš to pour off; to pour away
168700 gš [a body of water]
858493 gš [dregs or lees]
865331 gš [vessel]

DRID 1000409 gš migrating bird
RID 0000496 gš migrating bird
ID Lexeme 168690 gš migrating bird

DRID 1000410 gs to anoint
RID 0000497 gs to anoint
ID Lexeme 168280 gs to anoint
168340 gs.w ointment

DRID 1000411 gs to mourn
RID 0000497 gs to mourn
ID Lexeme 168240 gs to mourn
858490 gs.t mourner

DRID 1000412 gs to regulate
RID 0000500 gsgs to regulate
ID Lexeme 168630 gsgs to put in order; to regulate

DRID 1000413 gs to treat (leather)
RID 0000499 gs to treat (leather)
ID Lexeme 855556 gs to treat (leather)
168290 gs leather-worker

DRID 1000414 gsi̯ to run

RID 0000501 gsi̯ to run
ID Lexeme
168310 gs.t run; course
168640 gsgs to overflow
168550 gsi̯ to run

DRID 1000415 gsp basket
RID 0000502 gsp cavetto
ID Lexeme
858729 gsp cavetto
RID 0000503 gsp cornice (arch.)
ID Lexeme
77260 mgsp crate; basket

DRID 1000416 gsp to equip
RID 0000504 gsp to equip
ID Lexeme
500087 gsp to equip?

DRID 1000417 gsr finger ring
RID 0000505 gsr finger ring
ID Lexeme
863456 gsr finger ring

DRID 1000418 gstj scribe's palette
RID 0000506 gstj scribe's palette
ID Lexeme
168670 gstj scribe's palette

DRID 1000419 gsꜣ [an antilope]
RID 0000507 gsꜣ [an antilope]
ID Lexeme
168530 gsꜣ [an antilope]

DRID 1000420 gsꜣ bag
RID 0000508 gsꜣ bag
ID Lexeme
168540 gsꜣ bag
855165 gsꜣ.t [Leather cover (as robe or bag)]

DRID 1000421 gsꜣ to be inclined
RID 0000509 gsꜣ to be inclined
ID Lexeme
168520 gsꜣ.t inclined bed
859413 gsꜣ favorite?
168510 gsꜣ to be inclined; to go wrong
855203 gsꜣ to destroy; to annihilate

DRID 1000422 gt cistern
RID 0000510 gt cistern
ID Lexeme
863681 gt.t cistern

DRID 1000423 gw [a bull]
RID 0000511 gw [a bull]
ID Lexeme
166700 gw [a bull]
RID 0000512 gw [a horse]

		ID Lexeme	166720 gw	[a horse]

DRID 1000425 gw to rejoice

RID	**0000513**	gw to rejoice		
	ID Lexeme	852253	gw	to rejoice
		852091	gw.w	singer
		166020	gꜣ	to chant

DRID 1000426 gwš to be crooked

RID	**0000514**	gwš to be crooked		
	ID Lexeme	166820	gwš	to be crooked; to turn away
		166810	gwš	to be crooked (med.)

DRID 1000427 gwꜣ chest

RID	**0000515**	gwꜣ chest		
	ID Lexeme	858488	gwꜣ.t	sarcophagus (of the Apis bull)
		166760	gwꜣ.t	chest; box

DRID 1000428 gwꜣ to tighten

RID	**0000516**	gwꜣ to tighten		
	ID Lexeme	875741	gw	[bandage]
		166730	gwꜣ	to tighten; to be close
		166740	gwꜣ	to besiege
		850639	gwꜣ	[a tool]
		166770	gwꜣwꜣ	to capture
		166790	gwn	haversack
		166840	gwtn	to bind; to replenish

DRID 1000429 gꜣ [a heron]

RID	**0000517**	gꜣ [a heron]		
	ID Lexeme	166060	gꜣ	[a heron]

DRID 1000430 gꜣ to chatter

RID	**0000521**	gꜣgꜣ to chatter		
	ID Lexeme	77270	mgꜣgꜣ	ululation?
		166600	gꜣgꜣ	to chatter

DRID 1000431 gꜣ to hang

RID	**0000522**	gꜣgꜣ to hang		
	ID Lexeme	89600	ngꜣgꜣ	to be pendulous (of the breasts); swell?

DRID 1000432 gꜣ to wound

RID	**0000518**	gꜣ to wound		
	ID Lexeme	166010	gꜣ	to wound

DRID 1000433 gꜣb arm

	RID	**0000519**	gꜣb arm		
		ID Lexeme	166370	gꜣb.t	arm
			166400	gꜣb.w	[a kind of an employee]
DRID	**1000434**	**gꜣb leaf**			
	RID	**0000520**	gꜣb leaf		
		ID Lexeme	166390	gꜣb.tj	eyelash
			166380	gꜣb.t	leaf; (lotus) petal
DRID	**1000435**	**gꜣf to bake**			
	RID	**0003468**	gꜣf to bake		
		ID Lexeme	166450	gꜣf	to bake
	RID	**0000451**	gfgf [a bread]		
		ID Lexeme	858489	gfgf	[a kind of a bread, or cake]
DRID	**1000436**	**gꜣḥ shoulder**			
	RID	**0000523**	gꜣḥ shoulder		
		ID Lexeme	166490	gꜣḥ	shoulder
DRID	**1000437**	**gꜣḥ to be weary**			
	RID	**0000524**	gꜣḥ to be weary		
		ID Lexeme	166480	gꜣḥ	to be weary
			856733	gꜣḥ.w	fatigue; solidification; exhaustion
			856734	gꜣḥ.w	weariness
DRID	**1000438**	**gꜣḥ to squeeze**			
	RID	**0000525**	gꜣḥ to squeeze		
		ID Lexeme	166470	gꜣḥ	to press out the juice
DRID	**1000439**	**gꜣi̯ to make wet**			
	RID	**0000526**	gꜣi̯ to make wet		
		ID Lexeme	166150	gꜣi̯	to moisten
			166030	gꜣ	to smear (with ointment)
DRID	**1000440**	**gꜣi̯ to overthrow**			
	RID	**0000527**	gꜣi̯ to overthrow?		
		ID Lexeme	166130	gꜣi̯	to revile
			166110	gꜣi̯	to overthrow
			166230	gꜣw	to crash down (the enemy)
	RID	**0000528**	gꜣi̯ to overturn		
		ID Lexeme	32710	jgy.w	overturned ones (beings in the nether world)
DRID	**1000441**	**gꜣj [a jar]**			
	RID	**0000529**	gꜣj [a jar]		
		ID Lexeme	166140	gꜣy	jar; bowl; flask
DRID	**1000442**	**gꜣj [a measure]**			

	RID	**0000530**	gꜣj [a measure]		
		ID Lexeme	860119	gꜣy.t	[a measure]
DRID	**1000443**	**gꜣj naos**			
	RID	**0000531**	gꜣj naos		
		ID Lexeme	166180	gꜣj.t	chapel; shrine
DRID	**1000444**	**gꜣš reed**			
	RID	**0000532**	gꜣš reed		
		ID Lexeme	166570	gꜣš	rush; reed
DRID	**1000445**	**gꜣu̯ to be narrow**			
	RID	**0000533**	gꜣu̯ to be narrow		
		ID Lexeme	166220	gꜣ.w	lack; need
			166250	gꜣ.wt	lack; need
			166280	gꜣ.wt	bundle; dues
			166210	gꜣu̯	to be narrow; to be constricted; to lack; to deprive
			89540	ngꜣ	cord (used to tighten a net)
			89530	ngꜣ	to lack; to be lacking
			89550	ngꜣ.w	absence (of)
			147130	sgꜣu̯	to degrade

II.22 t

DRID	**1002425**	**t' bread**		
RID	**0002699**	t' bread		
	ID lexeme	168810	t'	bread (gen.)
DRID	**1002428**	**tb to recompense**		
RID	**0002702**	tb to recompense		
	ID lexeme	170650	tb	to pay
		170620	tb.t	[a measure]
		170610	tb.t	payment; reward
DRID	**1002429**	**tb to take up?**		
RID	**0002708**	tbtb to take up?		
	ID lexeme	170810	tbtb	to hoist
		170830	tbtb	to carry
DRID	**1002430**	**tbn head**		
RID	**0002703**	tbn head		
	ID lexeme	170670	tbn	head; top
		170690	tbn	bone marrow
DRID	**1002432**	**tbn to drum**		
RID	**0002705**	tbn to drum		
	ID lexeme	170720	tbn	to drum
		170710	tbn	tambourine-like drum
DRID	**1002433**	**tbs heel**		
RID	**0002706**	tbs heel		
	ID lexeme	170750	tbs	heel
DRID	**1002434**	**tbs to stab**		
RID	**0002707**	tbs to stab		
	ID lexeme	170760	tbs	to stab
DRID	**1002435**	**tf to spit out**		
RID	**0002709**	tf to spit out		
	ID lexeme	90030	ntf	to besprinkle; to wet
		171740	tf	to spit out
		171750	tf	spittle
		148250	stf	overflow (of fermenting beer) (or similar)
		148260	stf	water, liquid pouring out
		148240	stf	to pour sth.
RID	**0002716**	tftf to spit out		
	ID lexeme	858891	tftf	to spit out; to trickle

DRID	**1002436**	**tfi̯ to repulse**		
RID	**0002710**	tfi̯ to repulse		
	ID lexeme	171780	tfi̯	to remove forcefully; to repulse
RID	**0002715**	tftf to be confused		
	ID lexeme	171950	tftf	to be confused
DRID	**1002437**	**tfn dent (in metal objects)**		
RID	**0002711**	tfn dent (in metal objects)		
	ID lexeme	171860	tfn	dent (in metal objects)
DRID	**1002438**	**tfn orphan**		
RID	**0002712**	tfn orphan		
	ID lexeme	171830	tfn	orphan
		171870	tfn.t	orphan
DRID	**1002439**	**tfnn to rejoice**		
RID	**0002713**	tfnn to rejoice		
	ID lexeme	171850	tfn	joy
		171900	tfnn	to rejoice; to be glad
		148300	stfnn	to rejoice
DRID	**1002442**	**tfꜣ saw**		
RID	**0002718**	tfꜣ saw		
	ID lexeme	171760	tfꜣ	saw
		876482	jtfꜣ	saw
		858431	jtfꜣ	to saw
DRID	**1002443**	**tḫ fat**		
RID	**0002719**	tḫ fat		
	ID lexeme	173130	tḫ	fat, fattened
DRID	**1002444**	**tḫ lead**		
RID	**0002720**	tḫ lead		
	ID lexeme	173140	tḫ	Plummet? (Thoth?)
		173100	tḫ	plummet (of a balance)
DRID	**1002445**	**tḫ to confuse**		
RID	**0002748**	tḫtḫ to confuse		
	ID lexeme	854420	tḫtḫ	disorder
		173370	tḫtḫ	to confuse; to confound
DRID	**1002447**	**thb reduce (liquid)**		
RID	**0002722**	thb reduce (liquid)		
	ID lexeme	172970	thb.w	concentration (med.)
DRID	**1002449**	**tḫb to moisten**		
RID	**0002724**	tḫb to moisten		

	ID lexeme	173220	tẖb	bloating; blister (med.)
		169640	tẖb	[moist secretion?]
		173210	tẖb	to dip; to moisten; to irrigate

DRID 1002450 tẖb turtle

RID	**0002725**	tẖb turtle		
	ID lexeme	859679	tẖb	turtle

DRID 1002451 tẖbs [a basket]

RID	**0002726**	tẖbs [a basket]		
	ID lexeme	173230	tẖbs	[a basket]

DRID 1002452 tẖi̯ to be drunk

RID	**0002728**	tẖi̯ to be drunk		
	ID lexeme	859951	tẖ	drunkenness
		173120	tẖ	heavy drinking
		173160	tẖ.w	drunkard
		173150	tẖ.t	drunkenness
		173110	tẖi̯	to be drunk; to become drunk

DRID 1002453 tẖi̯ to obstruct

RID	**0002729**	tẖi̯ to obstruct		
	ID lexeme	172900	th	sacrilege; transgression
		172910	th.w	transgressor
		172920	tẖi̯	to go astray; to transgress; to damage
		148480	stẖi̯	to pervert; to cause obstruction

DRID 1002454 thm to cook

RID	**0002730**	thm to cook		
	ID lexeme	173020	thm	to water
		173000	thm	to stir (in the kettle)
		173010	thm	to cook something

DRID 1002455 thm to perforate

RID	**0002731**	thm to perforate		
	ID lexeme	172990	thm	perforation; puncture (wound)
		172980	thm	to perforate (med.); to penetrate; to drive (cattle)

DRID 1002456 tẖn ibis

RID	**0002733**	tẖn ibis		
	ID lexeme	173250	tẖn	ibis (as Thoth's sacred animal)

DRID 1002458 tẖn to damage

RID	**0002735**	tẖn to damage		
	ID lexeme	173320	tẖn	to injure; to damage

		173260	tḫn	injury (to the eye) (med.)
DRID	**1002460**	**tḫn to protect**		
RID	**0002737**	tḫn to enter		
	ID lexeme	173290	tḫn	to enter
RID	**0002738**	tḫn to hide		
	ID lexeme	173270	tḫn	to hide; to be hidden
RID	**0002739**	tḫn to protect		
	ID lexeme	173310	tḫn	door, door leaf
		173280	tḫn	to protect
		173330	tḫnḫn	to spread wings (over so.)
DRID	**1002461**	**tḫn towering cultic structure**		
RID	**0002740**	tḫn towering cultic structure		
	ID lexeme	173240	tḫn	obelisk
		173300	tḫn	high statue?
DRID	**1002464**	**tḫs to slaughter**		
RID	**0002744**	tḫs to slaughter		
	ID lexeme	173350	tḫs	to slaughter; to dismantle
DRID	**1002465**	**tḥs to squash**		
RID	**0002745**	tḥs to squash		
	ID lexeme	173090	tḥs	to squash; to crush; to pulverize
DRID	**1002467**	**tḥwꜣ peas**		
RID	**0002751**	tḥwꜣ peas		
	ID lexeme	852327	tḥwꜣ	peas
DRID	**1002469**	**tj [a chapel]**		
RID	**0002754**	tj [a chapel]		
	ID lexeme	169800	tj.t	[a chamber in temple]
DRID	**1002470**	**tj [a measure of incense]**		
RID	**0002755**	tj [a measure of incense]		
	ID lexeme	169770	tj.t	[a kind of a measure of incense]
DRID	**1002471**	**tj [a mineral]**		
RID	**0002756**	tj [a mineral]		
	ID lexeme	450169	tjꜣ.t	[a mineral]
DRID	**1002472**	**tj [an amulet]**		
RID	**0002757**	tj [an amulet]		
	ID lexeme	169740	tj.t	[Isis blood - symbol]
DRID	**1002473**	**tj fraction**		
RID	**0002758**	tj fraction		

		ID lexeme	169760	tj.t	fraction
			169750	tj.t	lower part of the Udjat eye
DRID	**1002474**	**tj image**			
	RID	**0002759**	tj image		
		ID lexeme	169790	tj.t	image; form; sign
DRID	**1002476**	**tj to pound**			
	RID	**0002753**	ti̯ to trample		
		ID lexeme	169700	ti̯	to trample
	RID	**0002761**	tj to pound		
		ID lexeme	169670	tj.t	pestle
			169700	tj	to pound
	RID	**0002765**	tjtj to trample		
		ID lexeme	858889	tjtj	[term for legs]
			170080	tjtj	to trample
DRID	**1002479**	**tjs to fix**			
	RID	**0002764**	tjs to fix		
		ID lexeme	170030	tjs	to fix; to mount with
DRID	**1002480**	**tjꜣ to shout**			
	RID	**0002767**	tjꜣ to shout		
		ID lexeme	169890	tjꜣ	to moan; to scream; to jubilate
			863156	tjꜣ	song of praise
			852087	tjꜣ	one who celebrates
			169880	tjꜣ	acute pain
DRID	**1002481**	**tk to attack**			
	RID	**0002768**	tkk to attack		
		ID lexeme	850939	tkk	attack
			173740	tkk	to attack; to injure
			173750	tkk	attacker
			854366	tkk	Attacker (a serpent)
			173760	tkk.t	attacker (stinging insect (wasp?))
	RID	**0002772**	tkšš to kick someone		
		ID lexeme	173730	tkšš	to kick someone
	RID	**0002773**	tktk to attack		
		ID lexeme	173780	tktk	attacker
			173770	tktk	to attack
DRID	**1002482**	**tk to be near**			
	RID	**0002769**	tkn to be near		
		ID lexeme	173680	tkn	to be near; to draw near
			860291	tkn.j	assailant
			851306	tkn.w	neighbours
			858012	tkn.w	Approacher

		148550	stkn	to make approach
RID	**0002771**	tks to reach		
	ID lexeme	173710	tks	to reach (a place); to run through
		173720	tks	to be fixed; to settled, to be stigmatized
DRID	**1002484**	**tkꜣ to burn**		
RID	**0002774**	tkꜣ to burn		
	ID lexeme	173610	tkꜣ	to illumine; to burn
		173620	tkꜣ.w	flame; torch; candle
		173660	tkꜣ.t	illumination
DRID	**1002485**	**tl mound**		
RID	**0002808**	ṯnr mound		
	ID lexeme	176080	ṯnr	mound; hill
DRID	**1002487**	**tm not to be**		
RID	**0002775**	tm not to be		
	ID lexeme	171990	tm	not to be; [negative verb]
		171980	tm	to cease; to perish
		854578	tm	to be over
		172240	tm.jw	the vain ones (enemies of Osiris)
		148310	stm	to destroy
RID	**0002778**	tm to be perfect		
	ID lexeme	172010	tm	to complete
		172000	tm	to be complete
		172020	tm	everything
		172070	tm.w	everyone; humankind
		858018	tm.wt	totality; completeness
		148320	stm	to comfort
RID	**0002779**	tm to close		
	ID lexeme	172260	tmm	to close (a wound) (med.)
		172250	tmm	to close (the mouth)
RID	**0002787**	tmtm not to be		
	ID lexeme	172350	tmtm	undoing
RID	**0001284**	jtm to be complete		
	ID Lexeme	858432	jtm	to be overfull; to block up
		33050	jtm.w	breathlessness
		33010	jtm.t	destroyer (a knife)
DRID	**1002488**	**tm sledge**		
RID	**0002776**	tm sledge		
	ID lexeme	172040	tm.t	sledge
DRID	**1002492**	**tmm [a wooden chest]**		
RID	**0002782**	tmm [a wooden chest]		
	ID Lexeme	172270	tmm	[a wooden chest]

DRID	**1002495**	**tmt to powder (med.)**		
RID	**0002785**	tmt to powder (med.)		
	ID Lexeme	172330	tmt.w	powder (med.)
		172320	tmt	to powder (med.)
RID	**0002788**	tmtm to powder (med.)		
	ID Lexeme	172340	tmtm	pulverize (med.)
		862948	tmtm	grinder

DRID	**1002496**	**tmz to turn (the face to someone)**		
RID	**0002789**	tmz to turn (the face to someone)		
	ID Lexeme	172310	tmz	to turn (the face to someone)

DRID	**1002497**	**tmꜣ mat**		
RID	**0002790**	tmꜣ mat		
	ID Lexeme	172160	tmꜣ	sack
		172150	tmꜣ	mat (gen.)
		172210	tmꜣ.yt	mat
		858020	tmꜣ.ytj	who is on the Mat
		172200	tmꜣ.wt	pocket (of skin) (med.)

DRID	**1002498**	**tmꜣ mother**		
RID	**0002791**	tmꜣ mother		
	ID Lexeme	172190	tmꜣ.t	ancestress; mother

DRID	**1002500**	**tmꜣ troop**		
RID	**0002793**	tmꜣ troop		
	ID Lexeme	172170	tmꜣ	troop (of soldiers)

DRID	**1002502**	**tnbẖ to be confused**		
RID	**0002795**	tnbẖ to be confused		
	ID Lexeme	172520	tnbẖ	to be confused

DRID	**1002510**	**tnj to grow old**		
RID	**0002803**	tnj to grow old		
	ID Lexeme	172430	tnj	old man
		172450	tnj	big; outstanding
		172470	tnj	to measure oneself (with so.)
		172440	tnj	(external) signs of age (med.)
		172420	tnj	to grow old; to be old
		172460	tnj	[term for a king in battle]

DRID	**1002512**	**tnm to go astray**		
RID	**0002806**	tnm to go astray		
	ID Lexeme	172550	tnm	furrow
		172530	tnm	to avert; to go astray
RID	**0002807**	tnm* to be mistaken		
	ID Lexeme	148360	stnm	to lead astray; to confuse

		851876	stnm.w	misguided

DRID 1002519 tp [a piece of wood?]

RID	**0002814**	tp [a piece of wood?]		
	ID Lexeme	171490	tp.y	big woods
		108910	tp.jt	[a beam of wood]
		40340	tp.tj	[part of a boat]

DRID 1002520 tp head

RID	**0002815**	tp head		
	ID Lexeme	450189	tp	best (of)
		600413	tp	headman; chief
		600417	tp	at; in; to (temp.)
		600415	tp	major
		170870	tp	person
		170880	tp	beginning (of a period of time)
		170900	tp	on; at the top of; at (local)
		170860	tp	head; beginning (of a region)
		170861	tp	tip; top (of mountain, of a building, etc.)
		600414	tp	principle (to do something); type of calculation (adm.)
		600416	tp	itself, yourself etc.
		171450	tp.j	being upon; having authority over
		171480	tp.j	best linen
		550180	tp.j	first
		171470	tp.j	best
		171460	tp.j	principal; first
		171500	tp.y	the one with the head
		170960	tp.jt	first (fine oil)
		858040	tp.jt	great; top
		170930	tp.jt	uraeus
		170940	tp.jt	White Crown (of Upper Egypt)
		860916	tp.jt	first
		853070	tp.w	(the best) fields
		501083	tp.wj	double-headed one
		170920	tp.t	head (as a part of the body)
		872573	tp.t	fine thread
		170980	tp.tj	first (in a series); best

DRID 1002524 tpj [an ox]

RID	**0002818**	tpj [an ox]		
	ID Lexeme	171520	tpj	[an ox]

DRID 1002525 tpn dagger

RID	**0002819**	tpn dagger		
	ID Lexeme	855071	mtpn.t	dagger sheath

		77520	mtpn.t	dagger sheath

DRID 1002527 tpnn cumin

RID	**0002821**	tpnn cumin		
	ID Lexeme	171690	tpnn	cumin
		171700	tpnn.t	[an ingredient (med.)]

DRID 1002529 tpr to breathe

RID	**0002823**	tpr to breathe		
	ID Lexeme	600420	tpr	to breathe

DRID 1002531 tpꜣ [a fruit]

RID	**0002825**	tpꜣ [a fruit]		
	ID Lexeme	171410	tpꜣ.w	[a fruit]

DRID 1002532 tpꜣ [a part of a skull]

RID	**0002826**	tpꜣ [a part of a skull]		
	ID Lexeme	171390	tpꜣ.w	[an affliction of the head]
		171380	tpꜣ.w	[a part of the skull]

DRID 1002533 tpꜣ [an ingredient]

RID	**0002827**	tpꜣ [an ingredient]		
	ID Lexeme	171400	tpꜣ.w	[an ingredient (med.)]
		171420	tpꜣ.wt	[an ingredient (med.)]

DRID 1002534 tḳr huge

RID	**0002828**	tḳr huge		
	ID Lexeme	173570	tḳr	huge; mighty

DRID 1002537 tr time

RID	**0002831**	tr time		
	ID Lexeme	172710	tr	to be doomed to; to be destined for
		172700	tr	time; season

DRID 1002541 trj door

RID	**0002835**	trj door		
	ID Lexeme	172820	trj	door

DRID 1002542 trj impurity

RID	**0002836**	trj impurity		
	ID Lexeme	172730	tr	misbehavior, unclean
		172830	try.t	impurity

DRID 1002543 trj veneration

RID	**0002837**	trj veneration		
	ID Lexeme	172770	trj	[honorific epithet of the King]

DRID 1002546 trr oven

RID	**0002840**	trr oven		
	ID Lexeme	172850	trr	oven

DRID	**1002547**	**trr to run**			
	RID	**0002841**	trr to run		
		ID Lexeme	172860	trr	to race?; to go for an outing?

DRID	**1002552**	**tr^{c} worm**			
	RID	**0002846**	tr^{c} worm		
		ID Lexeme	860986	tr^{c}	worm (Apophis)

DRID	**1002553**	**tš to crush**			
	RID	**0002847**	tš to crush		
		ID Lexeme	170060	tjšs	to grind; to crush

DRID	**1002555**	**tši̯ to go away**			
	RID	**0002849**	tši̯ to go away		
		ID Lexeme	173450	tš.w	deserters; wanderers
			173490	tši̯	to be absent from; to be missing; to flee
			148540	stši̯	to be carried away

DRID	**1002556**	**tšmm [a crocodile]**			
	RID	**0002850**	tšmm [a crocodile]		
		ID Lexeme	173520	tšmm	[a crocodile]

DRID	**1002557**	**tšꜣ to squash**			
	RID	**0002852**	tšꜣ to squash		
		ID Lexeme	173470	tšꜣ	to squash (grain for beer)
			173480	tšꜣ	to spilt open
	RID	**tštš to squash**			
		ID Lexeme	173540	tštš	to squash; to crush
			173550	tštš	mutilated one

DRID	**1002563**	**twhr (foreign, Asiatic) warrior**			
	RID	**0002859**	twhr (foreign, Asiatic) warrior		
		ID Lexeme	173060	twhr	(foreign, Asiatic) warrior

DRID	**1002567**	**twr to purify**			
	RID	**0002863**	twr to purify		
		ID Lexeme	170390	twr	purifier
			170380	twr	purity; purification
			170400	twr	Pure (a body of water in the hereafter)
			170370	twr	to purify; to be pure

DRID **1002568** **twr to stay away**

	RID	**0002864**	twr to stay away		
		ID Lexeme	170340	twr	to reject; to repulse
			170350	twr	to show respect to
			856122	twr	Respected one
			170360	twr	to stay away (from something); stick to (something)
			147950	stwr	to protect; to keep clean
DRID	**1002569**	**twrj [a staff]**			
	RID	**0002865**	twrj [a staff]		
		ID Lexeme	170420	twrj.t	[a staff]
DRID	**1002570**	**twt to be like**			
	RID	**0002866**	twt to be like		
		ID Lexeme	170460	twt	likeness?
			170480	twt	to be like; to be sufficient; to be complete
			170470	twt	statue; likeness; image
			170520	twt.w	likeness
			855632	twt.wj	the two who are matching
			147970	stwt	to make like; to make resemble
	RID	**0002867**	twti̯ to assemble		
		ID Lexeme	170490	twt	complete
			400242	twt	entire; complete
			170500	twti̯	to collect; to assemble
			147980	stwt	to praise; to smooth over
			148000	stwt	to bring (something)
			148020	stwt.j	outcome
			147990	stwti̯	to collect; to assemble
DRID	**1002572**	**twꜣ [an oil]**			
	RID	**0002868**	twꜣ [an oil]		
		ID Lexeme	170270	twꜣ.wt	[one of the 7 holy oils]
DRID	**1002573**	**twꜣ evil**			
	RID	**0002869**	twꜣ evil		
		ID Lexeme	170240	twꜣ.w	wrong; evil
DRID	**1002574**	**twꜣ to elevate**			
	RID	**0002870**	twꜣ to elevate		
		ID Lexeme	170180	twꜣ	pillar
			170190	twꜣ	[an erected serpent]
			170200	twꜣ	culmination?
			170290	twꜣ	lintel (or jamb?)
			170140	twꜣ	to support; to elevate
			170130	twꜣ	to put a claim (on someone); to appeal (to someone)

		170120	twꜣ	man of low station; inferior
		170150	twꜣ	bearer
		170250	twꜣ.w	swellings (med.)
		851301	twꜣ.w	claim
		147930	stwꜣ	to move
		147940	stwꜣ	to elevate

DRID 1002575 ty steppe

RID	**0002871**	ty steppe		
	ID Lexeme	852604	ty	steppe

DRID 1002580 tꜣ door

RID	**0002876**	tꜣ door		
	ID Lexeme	168910	tꜣ	(main) gateway; (main) door (of a temple)
		169420	tꜣy.t	(main) door (of a temple)

DRID 1002581 tꜣ earth

RID	**0002877**	tꜣ earth		
	ID Lexeme	400576	tꜣ	earth (as a material)
		400577	tꜣ	(arable) land; ground
		854573	tꜣ	earth; land; ground
		450772	tꜣ	[a measure of surface area]
		168860	tꜣ	earth; land; ground
		400096	tꜣ	land (with geo-political reference); Egypt

DRID 1002584 tꜣ to be hot

RID	**0002880**	tꜣ to be hot		
	ID Lexeme	854574	tꜣ	to be hot; to burn
		168890	tꜣ	to be hot
		168900	tꜣ	to burn
		168880	tꜣ	kiln
		859243	tꜣ.yt	bake house?
		169400	tꜣ.yt	heat
		168950	tꜣ.w	heat
		168940	tꜣ.w	hothead
		147450	stꜣ	to heat; to set afire
		147460	stꜣ	flame; lamp
		147490	stꜣ.t	lamp; censer

DRID 1002587 tꜣf pottery kiln

RID	**0002883**	tꜣf pottery kiln		
	ID Lexeme	169480	tꜣf	pottery kiln

DRID 1002588 tꜣḥ to sink

RID	**0002884**	tꜣḥ foe		
	ID Lexeme	169550	tꜣḥ	to kill

			169560	tꜣḥ	rioters (troublemakers by talking)
			169620	tꜣḥ.w	foes
			859158	stꜣḥ	to bewitch; to confuse
	RID	**0002885**	tꜣḥ inhabitant of Delta		
		ID Lexeme	169570	tꜣḥ	inhabitants of Delta
			169580	tꜣḥ.t	female inhabitant of Delta
	RID	**0002886**	tꜣḥ to sink		
		ID Lexeme	169530	tꜣḥ	to sink
			169520	tꜣḥ	to plunge; sink; confuse; to blur
			169590	tꜣḥ.t	dregs (med.)
			169600	tꜣḥ.t	irrigation runnel?
DRID	**1002590**	**tꜣj [a fabric]**			
	RID	**0002889**	tꜣj [a fabric]		
		ID Lexeme	854438	tꜣj.tjt	[a kind of textile, tissue]
			169450	tꜣy.t	fabric; mummy bindings; sail; curtain
			169470	tꜣw	[divine garment]
DRID	**1002591**	**tꜣj to resist**			
	RID	**0002890**	tꜣj to resist		
		ID Lexeme	169390	tꜣy	to resist
			169410	tꜣyt	foe; enemy
DRID	**1002592**	**tꜣm [a worm?]**			
	RID	**0002891**	tꜣm [a worm?]		
		ID Lexeme	169490	tꜣm.w	[noun (worm?); excrements?]
DRID	**1002597**	**tꜣš to demarcate**			
	RID	**0002896**	tꜣš to demarcate		
		ID Lexeme	169650	tꜣš	boundary; border; region
			169660	tꜣš	to demarcate; to divide
DRID	**1003902**	**tḫr [part of chariot]**			
	RID	**0009974**	tḫr [part of chariot]		
		ID Lexeme	173340	tḫr	[part of chariot]

II.23 ṯ

DRID	**1002422**	**ṯ [timber]**		
RID	**0002696**	ṯ [timber]		
	ID lexeme	173890	ṯ.t	timber (for boat building)
		173870	ṯ.t	table (for food)

DRID	**1002423**	**ṯ book**		
RID	**0002697**	ṯ book		
	ID lexeme	173860	ṯ.t	books
		174460	ṯꜣ.w	collection (of writings) (med.)

DRID	**1002424**	**ṯ crew**		
RID	**0002698**	ṯ crew		
	ID lexeme	173850	ṯ.t	clerks; staff
		854579	ṯ.t	staff; crew; clerks
		173840	ṯ.t	people; crew
		177470	ṯt.jw	staff; crew?

DRID	**1002426**	**ṯb cage**		
RID	**0002700**	ṯb cage		
	ID lexeme	175070	ṯb	crate (for fowl)
		170630	tb.t	box

DRID	**1002427**	**ṯb foot sole**		
RID	**0002701**	ṯb foot sole		
	ID lexeme	851384	ṯb	[a bread (sole-shaped)]
		175090	ṯb	to be shod; to provide with sandals
		175120	ṯbw	sole; sandal(s)
		856144	ṯbw	sandalmaker
		175150	ṯbw	sandals
		175160	ṯbw.t	sole (of the foot); sandal

DRID	**1002431**	**ṯbn to be quick**		
RID	**0002704**	ṯbn to be quick		
	ID lexeme	175200	ṯbn	to be quick
		857713	sṯbn	to transport
		175220	ṯbhn	to leap (of animals)

DRID	**1002440**	**ṯfrr lapis lazuli**		
RID	**0002714**	ṯfrr lapis lazuli		
	ID lexeme	855714	ṯfrr	to be blue
		855713	ṯfrr	lapis lazuli
		855712	ṯfrr.t	Tefreret (lapis lazuli land)
		33660	jṯfrr	sky (of the color of Lapis lazuli)

DRID	**1002441**	**ṯftn to rush**		

	RID	**0002717**	ṯftn to rush	
		ID lexeme	855232 ṯftn	to rush; to progress
			175370 ṯftn	to rush
DRID	**1002446**	**ṯḥ to rejoice**		
	RID	**0002721**	ṯḥ to rejoice	
		ID lexeme	176530 ṯḥ.w	joy
	RID	**0002727**	ṯḥḥ to rejoice	
		ID lexeme	176740 ṯḥḥ	to rejoice; to hail
			176750 ṯḥḥw.t	rejoice; exultation
	RID	**0002741**	ṯḥnn to rejoice	
		ID lexeme	176710 ṯḥnn	to rejoice
	RID	**0002749**	ṯḥṯḥ to rejoice	
		ID lexeme	90620 nṯḥṯḥ	to smile
	RID	**0002750**	ṯḥw to rejoice	
		ID lexeme	176520 ṯḥw	to rejoice
DRID	**1002448**	**ṯhb to jump**		
	RID	**0002723**	ṯhb to jump	
		ID lexeme	176460 ṯhb	to jump
DRID	**1002455**	**ṯhm to threaten**		
	RID	**0002732**	ṯhm to threaten	
		ID lexeme	176480 ṯhm	to tempt; to mortify
			176470 ṯhm	to hunt
DRID	**1002457**	**ṯḥn to be bright**		
	RID	**0002734**	ṯḥn to be bright	
		ID lexeme	400374 ṯḥn	to be bright; to gleam; to dazzle
			176570 ṯḥn	to be bright; to gleam; to dazzle
			176590 ṯḥn	brightness
			176600 ṯḥn	[term for flowers]
			176580 ṯḥn	to brighten; to amuse
			176690 ṯḥn.y	dazzling one (the sun god)
			176620 ṯḥn.t	faience; glass
			176610 ṯḥn.t	[a pendant of faience pearls]
			176660 ṯḥn.t	gleamer (goddesses, esp. Hathor)
			176650 ṯḥn.t	[an unguent]; gleamer?
			176720 ṯḥnḥn	to gleam
			149370 sṯḥn	to make bright; to make dazzling
DRID	**1002459**	**ṯḥn to encounter**		
	RID	**0002736**	ṯḥn to encounter	
		ID lexeme	176550 ṯḥn	to open (an infected area) (med.)
			176560 ṯḥn	to encounter; to engage (an enemy, in battle)
DRID	**1002462**	**ṯḥr injury**		

	RID	**0002742**	ṯḥr injury	
		ID lexeme	176730 ṯḥr	injury; mockery
DRID	**1002463**	**ṯḥs [a metal]**		
	RID	**0002743**	ṯḥs [a metal]	
		ID lexeme	176770 ṯḥs.t	[a kind of metal - copper; bronze?]
DRID	**1002466**	**ṯḥs to stretch**		
	RID	**0002746**	ṯḥs to stretch	
		ID lexeme	176760 ṯḥs	to stretch (e.g., leather)
DRID	**1002468**	**ṯḥꜣ lame**		
	RID	**0002747**	ṯḥṯḥ lame	
		ID lexeme	176490 ṯḥṯḥ	lame one
	RID	**0002752**	ṯḥꜣ lame	
		ID lexeme	176450 ṯḥꜣ	lame man
DRID	**1002475**	**ṯj thyme**		
	RID	**0002760**	ṯj thyme	
		ID lexeme	174850 ṯj.t	thyme
DRID	**1002477**	**ṯjf to flee**		
	RID	**0002762**	ṯjf to flee	
		ID lexeme	174800 ṯjf	to flee
DRID	**1002478**	**ṯjs [preparing? dough for beer making]**		
	RID	**0002763**	ṯjs [preparing? dough for beer making]	
		ID lexeme	174820 ṯjs	[preparing? dough for beer making]
DRID	**1002483**	**ṯkr tower gate**		
	RID	**0002770**	ṯkr tower gate	
		ID lexeme	177400 ṯkr	tower gate
DRID	**1002486**	**ṯm [container (measure for cake)]**		
	RID	**0002786**	ṯmṯm [container (measure for cake)]	
		ID lexeme	175630 ṯmṯm	[container?]
DRID	**1002489**	**ṯm to be ashamed**		
	RID	**0002777**	ṯm to be ashamed	
		ID lexeme	175420 ṯm	to be ashamed
DRID	**1002490**	**ṯmḥ [a red ochre]**		
	RID	**0002780**	ṯmḥ [a red ochre]	
		ID lexeme	175520 ṯmḥ.y	[a kind of red ochre]
DRID	**1002491**	**ṯmḥ to turn away?**		

	RID	**0002781**	ṯmḥ to turn away?	
		ID lexeme	175500 ṯmḥ	to avoid; to divide
DRID	**1002493**		**ṯms to be red**	
	RID	**0002783**	ṯms to be red	
		ID lexeme	175540 ṯms	to be red
			175550 ṯms	redness (med., as a symptom of illness)
			175580 ṯms.w	injury; harm
			863012 ṯms.t	[a kind of a plant]
			175570 ṯms.t	red-colored strip of cloth
			854334 ṯms.tj	[term for Horus]
			175600 ṯmss.t	[a kind of a red thing?]
DRID	**1002494**		**ṯms to bury**	
	RID	**0002784**	ṯms to bury	
		ID lexeme	175530 ṯms	to bury; to cover
DRID	**1002499**		**ṯmꜣ to be strong**	
	RID	**0002792**	ṯmꜣ to be strong	
		ID Lexeme	175440 ṯmꜣ	to be strong; to be mighty
DRID	**1002501**		**ṯn guardian**	
	RID	**0002794**	ṯn guardian	
		ID Lexeme	175670 ṯn	warder; guardian; frontier guard
DRID	**1002503**		**ṯnf [a vessel]**	
	RID	**0002796**	ṯnf [a vessel]	
		ID Lexeme	175940 ṯnf.t	[a vessel]
DRID	**1002504**		**ṯnf to drink and dance**	
	RID	**0002797**	ṯnf to drink and dance	
		ID Lexeme	175890 ṯnf	to drink; to dance
DRID	**1002505**		**ṯnf to measure**	
	RID	**0002798**	ṯnf to measure	
		ID Lexeme	175900 ṯnf	[a weight (in recipes, for cereals)]
			175920 ṯnf	to measure; to appraise; to summarize
			175950 ṯnf.yt	sack; bag
DRID	**1002506**		**ṯnḥ to observe**	
	RID	**0002799**	ṯnḥ to observe	
		ID Lexeme	176120 ṯnḥ	to blink; to observe; to wink
DRID	**1002507**		**ṯnḥr [a falcon]**	
	RID	**0002800**	ṯnḥr [a falcon]	

		ID Lexeme	176140	ṯnḥr	[a kind of a falcon]
DRID	**1002508**		**ṯni̯ to rise**		
	RID	**0002801**	ṯni̯ to rise		
		ID Lexeme	401002	ṯn	venerable one
			858936	ṯn	raised one
			175660	ṯn.w	cliffs (along the river, forming a boundary)
			175810	ṯn.w	dignity
			175690	ṯn.t	distinguished; different
			175760	ṯnj	honour; worship
			175750	ṯni̯	ro rise; to distinguish; to be distinguished
			175790	ṯni̯	to observe; to watch closely
			77960	mṯn	road; path; (correct) path (through life) (metaph.)
			77970	mṯn	guide
			77620	mtnw.t	reward; recompense
			855649	sṯn.w	kind of a swelling
			149240	sṯn.w	White Crown
			149310	sṯn.w	height
			149250	sṯn.w	crowned one
			149230	sṯn.t	one who is crowned (Sothis)
			854556	sṯni̯	to raise; to crown; to be highlighted; differ; release (from)
			858663	sṯni̯	to expand
			149280	sṯni̯	to distinguish; to crown
			149290	sṯni̯	to be distinguished (from someone)
DRID	**1002509**		**ṯnj to be weak**		
	RID	**0002802**	ṯnj to be weak		
		ID Lexeme	175780	ṯnj	to be weak
DRID	**1002511**		**ṯnm cauldron**		
	RID	**0002805**	ṯnm cauldron		
		ID Lexeme	175960	ṯnm	cauldron; pit
DRID	**1002514**		**ṯl to be strong**		
	RID	**0002809**	ṯnr to be strong		
		ID Lexeme	176060	ṯnr	mighty one
			176070	ṯnr	might; mighty deeds
			176050	ṯnr	to be strong; to grow strong; to preserve
			550245	ṯnr	strong; energetic; effective
DRID	**1002515**		**ṯlk [a bier]**		

RID 0002810 ṯnrk [a bier]

ID Lexeme 176110 ṯnrk [a kind of a bier]

DRID 1002516 ṯnt [sacred cattle (of Hathor)]

RID 0002811 ṯnt [sacred cattle (of Hathor)]

ID Lexeme 175710 ṯnt.t [sacred cattle (of Hathor)]

DRID 1002517 ṯnṯꜣ dais

RID 0002812 ṯnṯꜣ dais

ID Lexeme 176160	ṯnṯꜣ.t	throne dais
176180	ṯnṯꜣ.t	throne dais
858888	ṯnṯꜣ.tj	the one belonging to the throne dais (Osiris)

DRID 1002518 ṯnw to count

RID 0002813 ṯnw to count

ID Lexeme 175840	ṯnw	each; every
175820	ṯnw	to count; to control
175830	ṯnw	number; quantity
550066	ṯnw	every time that
175870	ṯnw.t	census (of the dead, a religious festival)
175850	ṯnw.t	count; quantity
175860	ṯnw.t	cattle count

DRID 1002521 ṯpg barracks

RID 0002816 ṯpg barracks

ID Lexeme 175290 ṯpg barracks

DRID 1002522 ṯpḥ cave

RID 0002817 ṯpḥ cave

ID Lexeme 175280	ṯpḥ.t	cavern; (snake's) hole; chapel (of a temple)
855316	ṯpḥ.tj	cave dweller

DRID 1002526 ṯpn* to be glad

RID 0002820 ṯpn* to be glad

ID Lexeme 175250 ṯpnpn to be glad

DRID 1002528 ṯpr scribe

RID 0002822 ṯpr scribe

ID Lexeme 175260 ṯpr scribe

DRID 1002530 ṯprṯ (bronze-clad Hittite) chariot

RID 0002824 ṯprṯ (bronze-clad Hittite) chariot

ID Lexeme 175270 ṯprṯ (bronze-clad Hittite) chariot

DRID 1002535 ṯr fine flour

RID	**0002829**	ṯr fine flour		
	ID Lexeme	176430	ṯr.t	finely ground wheat flour

DRID 1002536 ṯr red

RID	**0002830**	ṯr red		
	ID Lexeme	176230	ṯr.w	red (blood)
		176220	ṯr.w	[a mineral, from Elephantine, containing ochre]
		856119	ṯr.wt	redness

DRID 1002538 ṯr willow

RID	**0002832**	ṯr willow		
	ID Lexeme	176280	ṯry.t	[goddess of willow]
		176250	ṯr.t	willow

DRID 1002539 ṯrf [a dance]

RID	**0002833**	ṯrf [a dance]		
	ID Lexeme	176370	ṯrf	[a dance]

DRID 1002540 ṯrẖ* strainer

RID	**0002834**	ṯrẖ* strainer		
	ID Lexeme	77800	mṯrẖ.t	strainer

DRID 1002544 ṯrm to wink

RID	**0002838**	ṯrm to wink		
	ID Lexeme	851501	ṯrm	to move (quickly); to wink; to hurry
		856121	ṯrm	wink
		176380	ṯrm	to blink; to wink; to observe

DRID 1002545 ṯrp [a goose]

RID	**0002839**	ṯrp [a goose]		
	ID Lexeme	176360	ṯrp	to stumble
		176350	ṯrp	white-fronted goose

DRID 1002548 ṯrrj siege mound

RID	**0002842**	ṯrrj siege mound		
	ID Lexeme	176400	ṯrry	siege mound

DRID 1002549 ṯrw* to delight in sth.

RID	**0002843**	ṯrw* to delight in sth.		
	ID Lexeme	176330	ṯrwrw	to delight in sth.

DRID 1002550 ṯryn body armor

RID	**0002844**	ṯryn body armor		
	ID Lexeme	176290	ṯryn	body armor

DRID 1002551 ṯrʿ [a field]
RID 0002845 ṯrʿ [a field]
ID Lexeme 176310 ṯrʿ [a field]

DRID 1002554 ṯs to sit
RID 0002848 ṯs to sit
ID Lexeme 177080 ṯs to sit
177270 ṯsw anticipation?

DRID 1002558 ṯṯ sparrow
RID 0002853 ṯṯ sparrow
ID Lexeme 177580 ṯṯ sparrow

DRID 1002559 ṯt to dissolve
RID 0002854 ṯt to dissolve
ID Lexeme 177440 ṯt to dissolve; to let loose; to remove
RID 0002856 ṯtṯt to quarrel
ID Lexeme 177540 ṯtṯt quarrel
177530 ṯtṯt to quarrel; to scold

DRID 1002560 ṯtf to overflow
RID 0002855 ṯtf to overflow
ID Lexeme 177480 ṯtf to flow; to overflow; to surge (water)
854582 ṯtf to flow; to overflow; to surge (water); to be flooded
177490 ṯtf to overflow; to be flooded
149500 sṯtf to baste

DRID 1002561 ṯw share
RID 0002857 ṯw share
ID Lexeme 174920 ṯw.t share (what belongs (to you))

DRID 1002562 ṯwfj papyrus plant
RID 0002858 ṯwfj papyrus plant
ID Lexeme 174970 ṯwfj papyrus flowers; papyrus marsh

DRID 1002564 ṯwj crown?
RID 0002860 ṯwj crown?
ID Lexeme 174960 ṯwj.t crown?

DRID 1002565 ṯwn = ṯwꜣ to attack
RID 0002861 ṯwn to attack
ID Lexeme 174980 ṯwn to gore; to attack
175020 ṯwn.w fighting bull
77920 mṯwn battlefield
RID 0002870 ṯwꜣ resistance?

		ID Lexeme	174950	ṯwꜣ	resistance
DRID	**1002566**		**ṯwn to reward**		
	RID	**0002862**	ṯwn to reward		
		ID Lexeme	175000	ṯwn	contribution; gift
			175010	ṯwn	to reward
			175030	ṯwn.w	distinction
DRID	**1002577**		**ṯzm hound**		
	RID	**0002873**	ṯzm hound		
		ID Lexeme	855040	ṯzm	greyhound
			177290	ṯzm	hound
			177330	ṯzm.t	hound
DRID	**1002578**		**ṯzm to build**		
	RID	**0002874**	ṯzm to build		
		ID Lexeme	177300	ṯzm	to build
			177340	ṯzm.t	battlements; (defensive) surrounding walls
DRID	**1002579**		**ṯꜣ ball**		
	RID	**0002875**	ṯꜣ ball		
		ID Lexeme	173960	ṯꜣ	pellet; drop
DRID	**1002582**		**ṯꜣ male**		
	RID	**0002878**	ṯꜣ male		
		ID Lexeme	174240	ṯꜣ.y	man; male
			174250	ṯꜣ.y	male
			856255	ṯꜣ.y	the male
			77840	mṯꜣ	phallus
DRID	**1002583**		**ṯꜣ nestling**		
	RID	**0002879**	ṯꜣ nestling		
		ID Lexeme	173950	ṯꜣ	fledgling; chick
			174140	ṯꜣ	nestling (epithet of Horus)
			174150	ṯꜣ.wj	(young) crocodile
			858001	ṯꜣ.t	fledgling
			850972	ṯꜣ.t	the chicks (for children) (coll.)
DRID	**1002585**		**ṯꜣ* vizier**		
	RID	**0002881**	ṯꜣ* vizier		
		ID Lexeme	174090	ṯꜣ.tj	vizier
			174100	ṯꜣ.tjt	female vizier
DRID	**1002586**		**ṯꜣbb corn ear**		
	RID	**0002882**	ṯꜣbb corn ear		
		ID Lexeme	174570	ṯꜣb.t	loan (of grain); agricultural surplus

		174580	ṯꜣbb	corn ear

DRID 1002589 **ṯꜣi̯ to take**

RID	**0002887**	ṯꜣi̯ to reproach		
	ID Lexeme	174280	ṯꜣy	to scold; to reproach
		174290	ṯꜣy	reproach; fault
RID	**0002888**	ṯꜣi̯ to take		
	ID Lexeme	174070	ṯꜣ	to sort out (during the flax harvest)
		174010	ṯꜣ	[part of a chariot (handgrip?)]
		174320	ṯꜣ.yt	tweezer(s)
		174450	ṯꜣ.w	carrier; trainee
		174520	ṯꜣ.wt	theft
		174500	ṯꜣ.wt	stolen goods; stolen property (as a refund value); confiscated
		174260	ṯꜣi̯	to take; to sieze; to don (clothing)
		174470	ṯꜣu̯	to steal
		148900	sṯꜣi̯	to prepare; to form

DRID 1002593 **ṯꜣm to cloak**

RID	**0002892**	ṯꜣm to cloak		
	ID Lexeme	174590	ṯꜣm	to cloak; to cover (with skin) (wound healing)
		174610	ṯꜣm	foreskin
		174600	ṯꜣm	cloak; swaddling clothes;bandages
		856424	mṯꜣ	to cloak
		77910	mṯꜣm	[a woman's garment]
		148940	sṯꜣm	to fertilize farmland
		148950	sṯꜣm	clothing; bindings
		148930	sṯꜣm	to bind up (an injury); to clothe

DRID 1002594 **ṯꜣms to eat**

RID	**0002893**	ṯꜣms to eat		
	ID Lexeme	174650	ṯꜣms	to eat; to devour

DRID 1002595 **ṯꜣpr to swell**

RID	**0002894**	ṯꜣpr to swell		
	ID Lexeme	854336	ṯꜣpr	to swell

DRID 1002596 **ṯꜣr to secure**

RID	**0002895**	ṯꜣr to secure		
	ID Lexeme	174660	ṯꜣr	to protect (someone) from (crocodile)
		174690	ṯꜣr	to make fast [from the good preparation of the headrests]
		174680	ṯꜣr	to exercise protection over
		174700	ṯꜣr	[a shelter]
		174670	ṯꜣr	[act of the King ascending the

					throne]
			174750	ṯꜣr.t	[an enclosed structure]
			174720	ṯꜣr.t	cabin [an enclosed structure]
			174730	ṯꜣr.t	fortress [an enclosed structure]
			174760	ṯꜣr.t	silo; granary
DRID	**1002598**	**ṯꜣw wind**			
	RID	**0002897**	ṯꜣw wind		
		ID Lexeme	450354	ṯꜣw	boatman
			174480	ṯꜣw	air; wind; breath
			174510	ṯꜣw.t	sail
DRID	**1002599**	**ṯꜣz to command**			
	RID	**0002898**	ṯꜣz to command		
		ID Lexeme	176850	ṯꜣz	to command; to be ruler
			177110	ṯꜣz.w	commander
			176970	ṯꜣz.t	detachment; troop; gang (of workmen)
DRID	**1002600**	**ṯꜣz to join**			
	RID	**0002899**	ṯꜣz to join		
		ID Lexeme	176810	ṯꜣz	vertebra; spine
			176820	ṯꜣz	neck
			176930	ṯꜣz.t	vertebra; backbone
			500155	ṯꜣz.t	to put together?; knotted bundle
	RID	**0002900**	ṯꜣz to knot		
		ID Lexeme	176860	ṯꜣz	saying; utterance; phrase
			856104	ṯꜣz	knot
			176940	ṯꜣz.t	[an ivory chariot appurtenance (knob? boss?)]
			176910	ṯꜣz.t	knot
			860525	ṯꜣz.t	[a kind of an amulet]
			862887	ṯꜣzṯꜣz	[a kind of a fabric]
			149430	sṯꜣz	to reknit (something)
	RID	**0002901**	ṯꜣz to spread		
		ID Lexeme	149440	sṯꜣz	to lie stretched out (on the back)
			501071	sṯꜣz.y	lying extended on the back
DRID	**1002601**	**ṯꜣz tooth**			
	RID	**0002902**	ṯꜣz tooth		
		ID Lexeme	176830	ṯꜣz	tooth
			177060	ṯꜣz.t	tooth

II.24 d

DRID	**1000148**	**d hand**		
RID	**0000191**	d hand		
	ID lexeme	33850	jd	hand
DRID	**1000152**	**db riverside**		
RID	**0000195**	db riverside		
	ID lexeme	178360	db.w	bank
DRID	**1000154**	**db to devour**		
RID	**0000201**	dbdb to slurp (blood)		
	ID lexeme	178940	dbdb	to slurp (blood)
RID	**0001729**	ndb to swallow		
	ID Lexeme	90760	ndb	to swallow; to consume (drink and eat)
		90820	ndbdb	to sip
RID	**0002282**	sdb to chew		
	ID lexeme	149770	sdb	to eat; to chew
		856680	sdb	excessive eating
RID	**0008644**	ndb to hear		
	ID Lexeme	90770	ndb	to hear
DRID	**1000157**	**dbb = ḏbb to block**		
RID	**0000199**	dbb to block		
	ID lexeme	178510	dbb.t	constipation
		183610	ḏbb	to close; to block
DRID	**1000160**	**dbḥ to request**		
RID	**0000204**	dbḥ to request		
	ID lexeme	178750	dbḥ	to be in need of; to ask for; to requisition
		861065	dbḥ	the pleading one
		852152	dbḥ.yt	[a plot of land?]
		178830	dbḥ.w	requirements; needs (gen.)
		178840	dbḥ.w	offering foods
		178760	dbḥ.w	requests; necessities
		860366	dbḥ.t	inundation ("need")
		178810	dbḥ.t	altar (for the funerary meal)
		178800	dbḥ.t	need; equipment
		178890	dbḥw	complaint; reclamation
		149780	sdbḥ	to supply; to equip
		149790	sdbḥ	equipment
DRID	**1000161**	**dbj hippopotamus**		
RID	**0000205**	dbj hippopotamus		

		ID lexeme	178320	dbj.t	hippopotamus
			178430	dbj.y	hippopotamus thongs
			178280	dbj	hippopotamus
DRID	**1000163**		**dbn to encircle**		
	RID	**0000207**	dbn to encircle?		
		ID lexeme	178610	dbn	deben (weight); deben (measure, ca. 91g)
			178550	dbn	round
			178620	dbn	clay (also med.)
			178560	dbn	to go round (a place); to travel round; to encircle
			178570	dbn	a kind of a round field
			178580	dbn	round-topped wooden box
			178520	dbn	ring; circle
			178600	dbn	helmet
			178540	dbn	to be round
			178700	dbn.j	He who is in the box (Osiris)
			178660	dbn.w	circumference
			178690	dbn.wj	one who goes round (sun, moon)
			856625	dbn.t	eyebrow?; eyelashes?
			178630	dbn.t	lock of hair
			178650	dbn.tj	two who go round (the sun and moon)
	RID	**0000208**	dbnbn to go around		
		ID lexeme	178720	dbnbn	wanderings; vicissitudes
			178710	dbnbn	to go round (in circles)
DRID	**1000172**	**dd to copulate**			
	RID	**0000221**	dd to copulate		
		ID lexeme	855348	dd	to copulate; to unite
DRID	**1000181**	**dḏw to grind**			
	RID	**0000231**	dḏw to grind		
		ID lexeme	181330	dḏw	to grind
			850682	ḏw	grind; flour
			450193	dwḏw	flour
DRID	**1000183**	**df to tear**			
	RID	**0000233**	df to tear?		
		ID lexeme	600602	ḏf	drop
			183970	ḏfḏ	iris (including the pupil)
			183990	ḏfḏf	droplet
			183980	ḏfḏf	to tear (of the eye); to drip
			184000	ḏfḏf.t	tearing (as an affliction of the eye)
			859909	ḏfḏf.t	droplet
			854641	mḏdf.t	(chisel (used in the Opening of the Mouth ritual))

		71700	mndf.tj	[Creator of the flood]
		90840	ndfdf	to cry; to tear (of the eye of Horus)
DRID	**1000187**	**dg foot print**		
RID	**0000239**	dg to step		
	ID lexeme	181260	dgs	foot print
		181040	dg	to visit; to go
		181250	dgs	to step; to enter
RID	**0000240**	dgdg to step		
	ID lexeme	181270	dgdg	to walk over; to trample down
DRID	**1000188**	**dgi̯ to hide**		
RID	**0000241**	dgi̯ to hide		
	ID lexeme	181130	dgi̯	to hide; to be hidden
		150020	sdg	hidden things
		150010	sdgi̯	to hide
DRID	**10001889**	**dgi̯ to see**		
RID	**0000242**	dgi̯ to see		
	ID lexeme	181150	dg	the one who looks [guardian of Osiris]
		851290	dgꜣ.yt	glimpse
		1181140	dgi̯	to behold; to see
		150040	sdgi̯	to make see
DRID	**1000190**	**dgm ricinus**		
RID	**0000243**	dgm ricinus		
	ID lexeme	181210	dgm	castor-oil (ricinus) plant
		181220	dgm	ricinus oil
DRID	**1000191**	**dgm to feel powerless**		
RID	**0000244**	dgm to feel powerless		
	ID lexeme	181200	dgm	to be speechless; to be unconscious
		181230	dgm.t	unconsciousness
DRID	**1000192**	**dgꜣ rasor**		
RID	**0000245**	dgꜣ rasor		
	ID lexeme	181110	dgꜣ.yt	cut of meat; jerky
		181120	dgꜣ.w	rasor
DRID	**1000194**	**dḥ to be low**		
RID	**0000247**	dḥ to sag		
	ID lexeme	180350	dḥ	to hang down; to be low
		180520	dẖ	to hide
		856646	dḥ.w	prostration; hanging down
		180470	dḥtt	testicles
		29520	sdẖ	to commit sacrilege

		149940	sdẖ	hidden
		149930	sdẖ	to hide
		149910	sdḥ	to reduce; let it sink; drown
		149920	sdḥ	to ease? (misery)
		180360	dḥ	depth; lowest part
RID	**0000249**	dḥdḥ to sag		
	ID lexeme	180480	dḥdḥ	to hang down
		91740	nḏḥḏḥ	[relating to a heart condition (med.)]

DRID 1000195 dẖ to crush

RID	**0000246**	dẖ to crush?		
	ID lexeme	180590	dẖn	to condescend
		180550	dẖ.wt	stone blocks; (piece of) rock
		180530	dẖ	to crush; to prostrate

DRID 1000196 dhn cliff

RID	**0000253**	dhn towering cliff		
	ID lexeme	180330	dhn.t	cliff; mountain spur; rock (cultic)
		859955	dhn.t	(mountain) ridge

DRID 1000197 dhn forehead

RID	**0000252**	dhn to bow		
	ID lexeme	180280	dhn	to bow to; to touch (the ground with the forehead)
		180320	dhn.t	forehead

DRID 1000198 dẖn rhythm

RID	**0000251**	dẖn to beat time		
	ID lexeme	180570	dẖn	to beat time
		180580	dẖn	rhythm maker

DRID 1000199 dhn to appoint

RID	**0000250**	dhn to appoint		
	ID lexeme	180290	dhn	to appoint

DRID 1000200 dḥr to be bitter

RID	**0000254**	dḥr to be bitter		
	ID lexeme	180440	dḥr	to be bitter
		180450	dḥr.t	bitterness; sickness

DRID 1000202 dḥꜣ straw

RID	**0000256**	dḥꜣ straw		
	ID lexeme	180380	dḥꜣ	straw; chop

DRID 1000203 dḥꜣ to pounce

RID	**0000257**	dḥꜣ to pounce		

	ID lexeme	180390	dḥꜣ	to pounce (on something)
DRID	**1000206**	**dj five**		
RID	**0000260**	dj five		
	ID lexeme	177860	dj.wt	five parts
		854323	dj.nw	fifth
		177870	dj.wt	fiver (winnower); troop of five workers
		855796	dj.w	the Five
		177840	dj.w	five
		850975	dj.j	50 square meter fabric
DRID	**1000207**	**dj here**		
RID	**0000370**	dy here		
	ID lexeme	177830	dy	here; there
DRID	**1000208**	**djdj (red) ochre**		
RID	**0000261**	djdj (red) ochre		
	ID lexeme	177900	djdj	(red) ochre
DRID	**1000210**	**dm to be sharp**		
RID	**0000263**	dm to be sharp		
	ID lexeme	600468	dm	to be sharp
		179190	dm	to pronounce (a name); to mention (by name)
		179170	dm	to sharpen
		179180	dm	to pierce; penetrate
		179220	dm.wt	cut; bite; injury (general)
		179210	dm.t	knife
RID	**0002290**	sdm knife		
	ID lexeme	149850	sdm.t	knife (lit. what is sharpened)
DRID	**1000211**	**dm worm**		
RID	**0000264**	dm worm		
	ID lexeme	179200	dm	worm
DRID	**1000213**	**dmj = dmꜣ = dmḏ to unite**		
RID	**0000266**	dmj to attach		
	ID lexeme	179320	dmj	to touch; to be joined to; to cleave to
		179330	dmj	town; quarter of a town; landing place; wharf
		179380	dmj.w	townspeople
		179370	dmj.t	town; quay
		149870	sdmj	to attach (lit. to make touch)
RID	**0000267**	dmꜣ to bind together		
	ID lexeme	179250	dmꜣ	[a colorful apron]

		850991	dmꜣ	to stretch
		179230	dmꜣ	to bind together
		179260	dmꜣ	to clot (med.)
		179310	dmꜣ.w	one who binds
		179290	dmꜣ.t	wing
RID	**0000265**	dmḏ to unite		
	ID lexeme	179420	dmḏ	to unite; to (re)assemble; to be (re)assembled
		179410	dmḏ	two knotted strips of stuff
		179430	dmḏ	total
		179440	dmḏ	summation (in accounts]
		179520	dmḏ.wj	the two united ones
		179530	dmḏ.wt	crowd
		179580	dmḏ.yt	assembly
		179590	dmḏ.yt	[recurring fixed or appointed time]
		550065	dmḏ.yt	grand total
		179470	dmḏ.t	[a golden ring?]
		179460	dmḏ.t	collection (of recipies); pharmacopoeia
		859208	dmḏ.t	[an amulet?]

DRID 1000217 dn family

RID	**0000270**	dn family		
	ID lexeme	179670	dn.wt	families
		179770	dnj.t	family

DRID 1000219 dn to cut

RID	**0000273**	dn to cut off		
	ID lexeme	179760	dn.yt	one who cuts
		179660	dn.w	patch (made of stone in a monolith)
		179620	dn	to cut off; to kill
		180080	dndn	to cut
		78240	mdn	sharpener

DRID 1000225 dn to rage

RID	**0000282**	dndn to rage		
	ID lexeme	854364	dndn	The angry one
		180040	dndn	anger; rage
		180070	dndn	rager (Seth)
		180090	dndn.t	the angry one [Hathor]
		180120	dndny.t	angry one
		184490	ḏnḏn.t	raging fame
RID	**0000278**	dndn to be angry		
		180050	dndn	to be angry; to rage

DRID 1000226 dn to traverse

RID	**0000284**	dndn to traverse

		ID lexeme	180020	dndn	to traverse
DRID	**1000228**	**dng = dꜣg tiny being**			
	RID	**0000286**	dng dwarf		
		ID lexeme	179980	dng	dwarf; pygmy
	RID	**0000386**	dꜣg tiny creature		
		ID Lexemes	859221	dꜣgy.t	bat
DRID	**1000229**	**dng to be deaf**			
	RID	**0000287**	dng to be deaf		
		ID lexeme	179970	dng	to be deaf
DRID	**1000231**	**dnḫs [metal tool]**			
	RID	**0000289**	dnḫs [metal tool]		
		ID lexeme	179890	dnḫs.t	[a metal tool (knife?)]
DRID	**1000232**	**dni̯ share**			
	RID	**0000290**	dni̯ to allocate		
		ID lexeme	179710	dni̯	to allocate (something to so.)
			179800	dnj.t	share; portion
			179850	dnj.w	share; portion
			179810	dny.t	land register
	RID	**0000291**	dni̯ to dam		
		ID lexeme	179680	dni̯	to dam (water); to revet (earthen banks)
			179690	dni̯	to hold back; to restrict
			179700	dni̯	dam; dyke (as boundary of a field)
			179780	dnj.t	dam; dyke
	RID	**0000292**	dni̯ to restrict		
		ID lexeme	149880	sdni̯	to punish
	RID	**0000293**	dni̯ to share out		
		ID lexeme	600586	jdn	arrears (of provisions)
			179630	dni̯	to soak
DRID	**1000234**	**dnj shouting**			
	RID	**0000296**	dnj shouting		
		ID lexeme	179860	dnj.wt	shouting; shriek
DRID	**1000238**	**dnrg a fruit**			
	RID	**0000300**	dnrg a fruit		
		ID lexeme	600464	dnrg	[a fruit (melon?)]
DRID	**1000240**	**dns to be heavy**			
	RID	**0000302**	dns to be heavy		
		ID lexeme	179920	dns	heavy one (Seth, as hippopotamus)
			179910	dns	to be weighty; to be heavy; to be irksome; to be burdensome

				179950	dns.w	weights (of a net)
DRID	**1000241**		**dn’ to refill**			
	RID	**0000303**		dn’ to refill		
		ID lexeme		179640	dn’	to refill (with water)
DRID	**1000242**		**dp boat**			
	RID	**0000304**		dp boat		
		ID lexeme		179040	dp.t	boat (gen.)
				179070	dp.w	steering oar?
				179060	dp.w	boat (gen.)
				179080	dp.w	[a part of a ship's mast?]
DRID	**1000243**		**dp loin**			
	RID	**0000305**		dp loin		
		ID lexeme		179030	dp.t	loin; lumbar region
DRID	**1000244**		**dp lump?**			
	RID	**0000306**		dp lump?		
		ID lexeme		178960	dp	lump? (med.)
DRID	**1000245**		**dp to taste**			
	RID	**0000307**		dp to taste		
		ID lexeme		179020	dp.t	taste
				178970	dp	to taste; to bite into
DRID	**1000246**		**dpẖ execution block?**			
	RID	**0000309**		dpẖ execution block?		
		ID lexeme		179120	dpẖ	execution block?
DRID	**1000249**		**dpy crocodile**			
	RID	**0000311**		dpy crocodile		
		ID lexeme		179100	dpy	crocodile (gen.)
DRID	**1000250**		**dḳ to grind**			
	RID	**0000312**		dḳ to cut		
		ID lexeme		150000	sdḳ	to cut
	RID	**0000313**		dḳ to grind		
				861175	dḳ	to chop; to grind
				180940	dḳ.w	powder; flour
DRID	**1000251**		**dḳr banish?**			
	RID	**0000314**		dḳr banish?		
		ID lexeme		180980	dḳr	to banish?
DRID	**1000252**		**dḳr harvest**			
	RID	**0000315**		dḳr harvest		

	ID lexeme	180950	dḳr	fruit (gen.)
		858413	dḳr	to reap
DRID	**1000253**	**dḳr to attach**		
RID	**0000316**	dḳr to attach		
	ID lexeme	180970	dḳr	to attach
		854588	dḳr	to attach; to dispel
DRID	**1000254**	**dḳrw essence**		
RID	**0000317**	dḳrw essence		
	ID lexeme	181000	dḳrw	essence; essential element? (of a god)
DRID	**1000255**	**dḳw to be barefoot**		
RID	**0000318**	dḳw to be barefoot		
	ID lexeme	180920	dḳw	to be barefoot
DRID	**1000256**	**dḳ^{c} to smoothen**		
RID	**0000319**	dḳ^{c} to smoothen		
	ID lexeme	180930	dḳ^{c}	to shape? (an oar)
DRID	**1000263**	**dr prod**		
RID	**0000324**	dr prod		
	ID lexeme	180180	dr.t	(cattle) prod
DRID	**1000264**	**dr to dress**		
RID	**0000325**	dr to dress		
	ID lexeme	180170	dr	clothing; garment
		180160	dr	to dress
DRID	**1000266**	**dr to remove**		
RID	**0000328**	dr to remove		
	ID lexeme	853086	dr.tj	exterminator (Seth)
		180150	dr	to protect (from)
		180130	dr	to drive away; to repel; to remove
DRID	**1000267**	**dr to spread**		
RID	**0000329**	dr to spread		
	ID lexeme	650023	dr	to spread; to smooth; to overlay
RID	**0000332**	drdr to level		
	ID lexeme	180270	drdrw	leveling
DRID	**1000269**	**drf to paint**		
RID	**0000333**	drf to paint		
	ID lexeme	180250	drf	writing; script; document; papyrus roll

			180240	drf	[to paint black line of the eyebrow]
DRID	**1000271**	**drp to supply**			
	RID	**0000336**	drp to supply		
		ID lexeme	180230	drp.w	offerings
			865577	drp	provider
			859954	drp	a land of supplies
			180220	drp	to offer; to feed; to present
DRID	**1000275**	**ds to be sharp?**			
	RID	**0000340**	ds to be sharp?		
		ID Lexeme	852196	ds	the flint knife (place in the hereafter)
			180620	ds	knife
			180630	ds	to cut; to be sharp
			180610	ds	flint
			860655	dsds	the one who cuts
			78310	mds	knife
			78280	mds	to be sharp; to do violence
			78290	mds	violent one
			78300	mds	to mark
			78320	mds.w	energetic
			855651	mds.t	violence
	RID	**0000341**	dsds be sharp?		
		ID Lexeme	855349	ndsds	to hash?
DRID	**1000280**	**dšr to be red**			
	RID	**0000351**	dšr to be red		
		ID lexeme	180780	dšr	red one (Seth, as a hippopotamus)
			180770	dšr	[a red steer, as an offering]
			180760	dšr	impurity; dirt
			180680	dšr	flamingo
			180700	dšr	reddening (med.)
			180690	dšr	to be red; to become red
			855803	dšr	Red one
			180720	dšr	[a tree and its wood]
			180730	dšr	[a red plant]
			180750	dšr	greed for blood; anger
			856707	dšr	the red one
			550232	dšr	red; angry
			180870	dšr.w	blood; redness
			400757	dšr.w	desert dwellers?
			858938	dšr.w	the red one
			180900	dšr.w	Schrot?
			180880	dšr.w	redfish
			180890	dšr.w	The red one (Seth)
			501048	dšr.t	Red crown of Lower Egypt
			857575	dšr.t	red

			856715	dšr.t	red cow
			180800	dšr.t	mischief; wrath (of the red crown)
			180810	dšr.t	[an oil]
			180820	dšr.t	[a red pot]
			180830	dšr.t	Red (crown of Lower Egypt)
			180850	dšr.t	desert; foreign country
			180840	dšr.t	fire; flame
			180790	dšr.t	blood
			853080	dšr.tj	the one who is reddish (angry Seth)
			180860	dšr.tj	red one (the sun god)
			180910	dšr.tjw	bloody victims?
			854858	dšrr.t	the little red one
			149970	sdšr	to make red
			149980	sdšr.w	reddening

DRID	**1000287**		**dwḫ* to embalm**		
	RID	**0000358**	dwḫ* to embalm		
		ID Lexemes	149740	sdwḫ	to embalm

DRID	**1000292**		**dwn to stretch out**		
	RID	**0000362**	dwn offering		
		ID Lexemes	859682	dwn	libation offering
			178200	dwn	food offerings
	RID	**0000363**	dwn to stretch out		
		ID Lexemes	852346	dwn	usually; regularly; farther
			178160	dwn	to stretch out; to be stretched out (taut); to endow
			855814	dwn.w	extension
			178220	dwn.tj	triumphator
			149730	sdwn	to fall to pieces (of a boat); to spring (of planks)

DRID	**1000293**		**dwr [a basket]**		
	RID	**0000364**	dwr [a basket]		
		ID Lexemes	178260	dwr	[a unit of measure for fruit]

DRID	**1000296**		**dwꜣ rise**		
	RID	**0000367**	dwꜣ to rise early		
		ID Lexemes	177920	dwꜣ	to rise early
			178120	dwꜣ.yt	(early) morning; tomorrow
			400078	dwꜣ.w	in the morning; tomorrow
			600406	dwꜣ.w	tomorrow; the morrow
			178000	dwꜣ.w	(early) morning
			856725	dwꜣ.wj	morning light
			178100	dwꜣ.wj	of the morning
			178110	dwꜣ.wj	morning sun
			177640	dwꜣ.t	netherworld; nether chamber

					(crypt)
			177650	dwꜣ.t	Duat (Heavenly area where the sun rises)
			177670	dwꜣ.t	abyss
			854004	dwꜣ.t	Duat (personified underworld)
			177660	dwꜣ.t	burial chamber; cave
			500223	dwꜣ.tj	(one who) is in the netherworld
			500101	dwꜣ.tj	one who belongs to the netherworld
			500928	dwꜣ.tjt	He of the netherworld
			853472	dwꜣ.tyw	those from the underworld
			178130	dwꜣy.t	garden
			149720	sdwꜣ	to spend the morning (doing something); to make early
	RID	**0000368**	dwꜣ to worship		
		ID Lexemes	177930	dwꜣ	to praise; to worship
			858661	dwꜣ	to enjoy; to appreciate
			178010	dwꜣ.w	song of praise; hymn
			178020	dwꜣ.w	adorer
			1854155	dwꜣ.w	The worshipers
			178030	dwꜣ.wt	[female divine being (dancer)]
			177960	dwꜣ.t	praise
			177970	dwꜣ.t	adoratrice (of a (particular) god)
			177990	dwꜣtj	to praise
DRID	**1000302**	**dꜣ to copulate**			
	RID	**0000374**	dꜣ to copulate		
		ID Lexemes	856558	dꜣ	to copulate
DRID	**1000303**	**dꜣ = ꜥꜣ* to tremble**			
	RID	**0000375**	dꜣ to tremble		
		ID Lexemes	177700	dꜣw.t	trembling
			177620	dꜣ	to tremble (med)
			177610	dꜣ	to escape; to disappear; to pass out?
	RID	**0002300**	sdꜣ to tremble		
		ID Lexeme	149660	sdꜣ	to tremble
			149670	sdꜣ.w	trembling
			149680	sdꜣdꜣ	to tremble; to make tremble
			149690	sdꜣdꜣ	trembling
			31900	jsdd	trembler (an evil spirit)
	RID	**0008460**	sꜥꜣ to tremble		
			128710	sꜥꜣ	to tremble
DRID	**1000304**	**dꜣb fig**			
	RID	**0000378**	dꜣb fig		
		ID Lexemes	859247	dꜣb.yt	[a beverage made from fig]
			177710	dꜣb	fig; fig tree

DRID	**1000311**	**dꜣj linen**		
	RID	**0000391**	dꜣj linen	
		ID Lexemes	600206 dꜣj.w	[a linen garment]
			177680 dꜣj.w	wad of linen; bale of cloth

DRID	**1000319**	**dꜣr to subdue**		
	RID	**0000400**	dꜣr to subdue	
		ID Lexeme	177740 dꜣr	to subdue; to suppress
			853085 dꜣr.tj	Coerced (Seth)

DRID	**1000320**	**dꜣz to bind**		
	RID	**0000401**	dꜣz to bind	
		ID Lexeme	177770 dꜣz	[equipment for bowstring]
			177780 dꜣz	to bind; to tie

II.25 ḏ

DRID	**1000146**	**ḏ cobra**		
	RID	**0000189**	ḏ cobra	
		ID lexeme	181340 ḏ.t	viper; cobra
DRID	**1000147**	**ḏ eternity**		
	RID	**0000188**	ḏ bodily form?	
		ID lexeme	181380 ḏ.t	[a term for the youth of a city]
			181430 ḏ.t	serf
			181350 ḏ.t	body; bodily form; self
			181370 ḏ.t	phallus
	RID	**0000190**	ḏ eternity	
		ID lexeme	852605 ḏ.tj	the eternal one
			181390 ḏ.t	flood
			181420 ḏ.t	estate; funerary endowment
			181400 ḏ.t	eternity
			181401 ḏ.t	eternal
			181440 ḏ.t	djet-servant
DRID	**1000149**	**ḏb army**		
	RID	**0000192**	ḏb army	
		ID lexeme	183410 ḏbj	army
DRID	**1000150**	**ḏb brick**		
	RID	**0000193**	ḏb brick, adobe	
		ID lexeme	183120 ḏb.t	brick; sheet; ingot (also as a unit of measure)
DRID	**1000153**	**ḏb to collect**		
	RID	**0000196**	ḏb to collect	
		ID lexeme	183130 ḏb.w	income
DRID	**1000155**	**ḏb* to make live**		
	RID	**0000197**	ḏb* to make live	
		ID lexeme	150440 sḏb	to make live; to restore (to life)
DRID	**1000156**	**ḏbb [body of water]**		
	RID	**0000198**	ḏbb [body of water]	
		ID lexeme	183600 ḏbb	[a body of water]
DRID	**1000158**	**ḏbg to dive**		
	RID	**0000202**	ḏbg to dive	
		ID lexeme	183660 ḏbqbq	to dive (head-first)
			183670 ḏbg	dive (head-first)
			183680 ḏbgḏq	to dive (head-first)

DRID	**1000159**	**ḏbḥ to fish**		
RID	**0000203**	ḏbḥ to fish		
ID lexeme		183650	ḏbḥ.w	fisherman
DRID	**1000162**	**ḏbn antilope**		
RID	**0000206**	ḏbn antilope		
ID lexeme		183620	ḏbn.w	hartebeest (antelope)
DRID	**1000164**	**ḏbw a piece of meat**		
RID	**0000209**	ḏbw a piece of meat		
ID lexeme		183590	ḏbw	[a cut of meat]
DRID	**1000165**	**ḏbꜣ [a scepter]**		
RID	**0000210**	ḏbꜣ [a scepter]		
ID lexeme		183210	ḏbꜣ	[a scepter]
DRID	**1000166**	**ḏbꜣ harpoon**		
RID	**0000211**	ḏbꜣ harpoon		
ID lexeme		183230	ḏbꜣ	harpoon rope
		183220	ḏbꜣ	harpoon
		183150	ḏbꜣ	papyrus reed float (for fishermen, for harpooners)
DRID	**1000167**	**ḏbꜣ to block?**		
RID	**0000212**	ḏbꜣ to block?		
ID lexeme		183690	ḏbḏb	to crush (by treading)
		183190	ḏbꜣ	to be blocked; to block
		183420	ḏbjjt	fish-nets?
		150480	sḏb	to hold back; prevent
DRID	**1000168**	**ḏbꜣ to change dress**		
RID	**0000215**	ḏbꜣ to fall down		
ID lexeme		178370	ḏbꜣ	to fall down
RID	**0000214**	ḏbꜣ to cloth		
ID lexeme		183250	ḏbꜣ	[a ritual garment]
		183240	ḏbꜣ	[a multi-colored kilt]
		858680	ḏbꜣ	to sew
		183260	ḏbꜣ	[a fabric] strips
		183180	ḏbꜣ	to outfit; to clothe; to adorn
		183300	ḏbꜣ.t	robing room (in the palace)
		183340	ḏbꜣ.tj	adorner?; robing priest
		183400	ḏbꜣy.t	[a dress]
RID	**0000216**	ḏbꜣ to substitute		
ID lexeme		183170	ḏbꜣ	to replace; to reimburse; to repay
		859246	ḏbꜣ.w	burial goods?
		183350	ḏbꜣ.w	compensation; payments

			857428	ḏbꜣ.t	equipment
			183310	ḏbꜣ.t	shrine; sarcophagus
			859244	ḏbꜣ.tj	the equipped one
			858651	ḏbꜣ.tj	rewarder
	RID	**0000213**	ḏbꜣ to change dress		
		ID lexeme	183380	ḏbꜣ.w	leafage
			183370	ḏbꜣ.w	leaves; foliage
DRID	**1000169**	**ḏbꜣ to support**			
	RID	**0000217**	ḏbꜣ to support?		
		ID lexeme	183200	ḏbꜣ	food offerings
			450152	ḏbꜣ.w	[a wooden box]
			183320	ḏbꜣ.t	base (of a shrine)
DRID	**1000170**	**ḏbꜥ finger**			
	RID	**0000219**	ḏbꜥ to seal		
		ID lexeme	183510	ḏbꜥ	seal; signet
			852567	ḏbꜥ	one who seals
			183460	ḏbꜥ	to seal; to lock
			183580	ḏbꜥ.w	sealing; labelling
			183530	ḏbꜥ.wt	seal; seal impression
	RID	**0000218**	ḏbꜥ finger		
		ID lexeme	183450	ḏbꜥ	ten thousand
			183430	ḏbꜥ	finger
			450303	ḏbꜥ	door-hinge tenon?; ring for a door bolt?
			183440	ḏbꜥ	finger (as a measure of length); pinch (as a measure of quantity)
			183480	ḏbꜥ	to point the finger at (in reproach)
			183550	ḏbꜥ.w	blame; reproach
DRID	**1000171**	**ḏḏ flower**			
	RID	**0000220**	ḏḏ flower		
		ID lexeme	186370	ḏḏ	flower; rosette
DRID	**1000173**	**ḏd to say**			
	RID	**0000222**	ḏd to say		
		ID lexeme	185810	ḏd	to say; to tell
			861036	ḏd.w	slanderer
			150940	sḏd	to recount; to talk
			150950	sḏd.w	tale; conversation
DRID	**1000174**	**ḏdb = ḏdm to heap**			
	RID	**0000223**	ḏdb to gather		
		ID lexeme	186160	ḏdb	to collect; to assemble
	RID	**0000229**	ḏdm to heap		
		ID lexeme	186290	ḏdm.t	heaps

			186280	ḏdm	to heap
DRID	**1000175**	**ḏdb = ḏdm to sting**			
RID	**0000224**		ḏdb to sting		
	ID lexeme		186150	ḏdb	sting (of an insect)
			186140	ḏdb	to sting
			186230	ḏdb.y	Piercer (a snake)
			186200	ḏdb.t	scorpion
RID	**0000230**		ḏdm to sting		
	ID lexeme		186270	ḏdm	to be stinging (med.)
			186260	ḏdm	to sting
			501080	ḏdm.yt	Piercer
			150990	sḏdm	to make envious
DRID	**1000176**	**ḏdf to shudder**			
RID	**0000225**		ḏdf to shudder		
	ID lexeme		186240	ḏdf	to stand upright; to shudder
DRID	**1000177**	**ḏdḥ to confine**			
RID	**0000226**		ḏdḥ to confine		
	ID lexeme		859928	ḏdḥ	to block
			186320	ḏdḥ	to shut up; to imprison
			186330	ḏdḥ.w	prison
RID	**0000227**		ḏdḥ to well up		
	ID lexeme		186300	ḏdḥ	to well up
DRID	**1000178**	**ḏdi̯ to endure**			
RID	**0000228**		ḏdi̯ to endure		
	ID lexeme		185890	ḏd	Enduring-one
			185830	ḏd	Djed-column (a symbol of eternity)
			185840	ḏd	column
			185850	ḏd	back bone
			859261	ḏd	The lasting one
			400140	ḏd	stability; duration
			860560	ḏd.w	Enduring-one
			185950	ḏd.t	Osiris' coffin
			185920	ḏd.t	stability; duration
			185910	ḏd.t	Djedet
			186120	ḏdy.t	[Epithet of Isis and Nephthys]
			853876	ḏdi̯	constantly; without interruption (recitation note)
			185870	ḏdi̯	to make endure
			186110	ḏdi̯	to endure
			854356	ḏdjdi̯	to endure
			150980	sḏdi̯	to make permanent
			91860	nḏdnḏd	to endure

			91870	nḏdḏd	to endure
DRID	**1000182**		**ḏdꜣ to grow fat**		
	RID	**0000232**	ḏdꜣ to grow fat		
		ID lexeme	186080	ḏdꜣ	fat
			186100	ḏdꜣ	fat
			186090	ḏdꜣ	to ripen; to swell; to grow fat
			150960	sḏdꜣ	to fatten
DRID	**1000184**		**ḏfi̯ to sink in**		
	RID	**0000234**	ḏfi̯ to sink in		
		ID lexeme	183920	ḏfi̯	to sink in; to descend into chaos
			183810	ḏf	to be ruined (a building)
DRID	**1000185**		**ḏfꜣ to wipe**		
	RID	**0000238**	ḏfꜣ to wipe		
		ID lexeme	183860	ḏfꜣ	to wipe
DRID	**1000186**		**ḏfꜣ = ḏfn to provide?**		
	RID	**0000235**	ḏfn ancestor		
		ID lexeme	183950	ḏfny.t	ancestress
	RID	**0000236**	ḏfn to hurry		
		ID lexeme	863702	ḏfn to hurry	
	RID	**0000237**	ḏfꜣ = ḏfn to provide		
		ID lexeme	183870	ḏfꜣ	to provision
			183850	ḏfꜣ	provision; sustenance
			183910	ḏfꜣ.y	well-provided man
			183890	ḏfꜣ.t	provisions
			183940	ḏfn	provider
			183930	ḏfn	ancestor
			184020	ḏfḏfw	incomplete document?
			150520	sḏfꜣ	temple endowment
			150510	sḏfꜣ	to provide with (food, e.g.); to endow
			150530	sḏfꜣ	to prepare (weapons, for battle)
DROD	**1000193**		**ḏḥ [a monkey]**		
	RID	**0000248**	ḏḥḏḥ [a monkey]		
		ID lexeme	185350	ḏḥḏḥ	[a monkey]
DRID	**1000201**		**ḏḥtj lead (metal)**		
	RID	**0000255**	ḏḥtj lead (metal)		
		ID lexeme	185320	ḏḥtj	lead (metal)
DRID	**1000204**		**ḏḥ^{c} [a plant]**		
	RID	**0000258**	ḏḥ^{c} [a plant]		
		ID lexeme	91710	nḏḥ^{c}ḏḥ^{c}.t [a kind of a plant]	

DRID	**1000205**	**ḏḥ^{c} leather**		
RID	**0000259**	ḏḥ^{c} leather		
	ID lexeme	185280	ḏḥ^{c}	to bind firmly together?
		185270	ḏḥ^{c}	leather; (leather) lacings
DRID	**1000209**	**ḏm sanctuary?**		
RID	**0000262**	ḏm sanctuary?		
	ID lexeme	184030	ḏm.t	[a building as the seat of a god, metaph. for throne]
DRID	**1000215**	**ḏm^{c} papyrus**		
RID	**0000268**	ḏm^{c} papyrus		
	ID lexeme	184040	ḏm^{c}	papyrus (scroll, sheet)
DRID	**1000216**	**ḏm^{c} to be parched**		
RID	**0000269**	ḏm^{c} to be parched		
	ID lexeme	858545	ḏm^{c}	to mourn; to complain
		184060	ḏm^{c}	mourn; misery?
DRID	**1000218**	**ḏn to be hot**		
RID	**0000272**	ḏn to be hot		
	ID lexeme	859927	ḏn	to be hot
		500126	ḏn.tj	[a term for a sun god]
		138860	snḏnḏn	cause to inflame
RID	**0000279**	ḏnḏn to be hot		
	ID lexeme	91620	nḏnḏn	enflame
DRID	**1000220**	**ḏn to thresh**		
RID	**0000274**	ḏn to thresh		
	ID lexeme	184090	ḏn	to thresh
		184220	ḏn.w	threshing floor
RID	**0000283**	ḏnḏn to strike		
	ID lexeme	184480	ḏnḏn	to strike (a percussion instrument)
DRID	**1000221**	**ḏnb dwarf**		
RID	**0000275**	ḏnb dwarf		
	ID lexeme	184250	ḏnb	dwarf
DRID	**1000222**	**ḏnb to turn back**		
RID	**0000276**	ḏnb to turn back		
	ID lexeme	78270	mḏnb.w	boundary, limit
		184240	ḏnb	to bend
		184260	ḏnb	to turn back
DRID	**1000223**	**ḏnd to be angry**		
RID	**0000277**	ḏnd to be angry		
	ID lexeme	184410	ḏnd	anger; rage

		856652	ḏnd	fury
		184420	ḏnd	to be angry
		871064	ḏnd.t	Raging one
DRID	**1000227**	**ḏnḏr brushwood**		
RID	**0000285**	ḏnḏr brushwood		
	ID lexeme	600567	ḏnḏr	brushwood (as fuel)
DRID	**1000230**	**ḏnḥ wing**		
RID	**0000288**	ḏnḥ wing		
	ID lexeme	184380	ḏnḥ	to pinion
		184400	ḏnḥ	oar blade
		184370	ḏnḥ	wing
		184390	ḏnḥ	upper part of the (hind-)leg
		66060	ḏnḥ	[a term for prisoners]
DRID	**1000233**	**ḏnj fifth day**		
RID	**0000295**	dnj fifth day		
	ID Lexeme	179740	dnj [ḏnj] fifth day	
DRID	**1000235**	**ḏnn skull**		
RID	**0000297**	ḏnn skull		
	ID Lexeme	184340	ḏnn.t	skull; head
DRID	**1000236**	**ḏnn to struggle**		
RID	**0000298**	ḏnn to struggle		
	ID Lexeme	184310	ḏnn	to struggle; to be tormented
		184300	ḏnn	breathtaking arrogance; bristling (of hair)
		855207	ḏnn	agony, torture; hard work
DRID	**1000237**	**ḏnr branch**		
RID	**0000299**	ḏnr branch		
	ID Lexeme	184350	ḏnr	branch
		859911	ḏnr	rod; whip
DRID	**1000239**	**ḏnrm to try hard**		
RID	**0000301**	ḏnrm to try hard		
	ID Lexeme	184360	ḏnrm	to try hard
DRID	**1000247**	**ḏpḥ = tpḥ apple**		
RID	**0000308**	ḏpḥ = tpḥ apple		
	ID Lexeme	183730	ḏpḥ	apple
DRID	**1000248**	**ḏpḳ dancer**		
RID	**0000310**	ḏpḳ dancer		
	ID Lexeme	860166	ḏpḳ.t	dancer

		183750	ḏpḳ	dancer
DRID	**1000257**	**ḏr [a precious stone]**		
RID	**0000320**	ḏr [a precious stone]		
	ID Lexeme	184710	ḏr.tt	[a stone for beads]
DRID	**1000258**	**ḏr calf**		
RID	**0000321**	ḏr calf		
	ID Lexeme	184520	ḏr	[a male calf]
		184650	ḏr.t	[small calves]
DRID	**1000259**	**ḏr foreign**		
RID	**0000322**	ḏr foreign		
	ID Lexeme	184610	ḏr	[a grave in a foreign land]
RID	**0000330**	ḏrḏr foreign		
	ID Lexeme	600474	ḏrḏr	to be foreign; to behave hostilely
		650046	ḏrḏr	stranger; foreigner
		185160	ḏrḏr	strange; foreign
DRID	**1000260**	**ḏr hand**		
RID	**0000334**	ḏri̯ to be solid		
	ID Lexeme	184630	ḏr.t	hand; handful (as a measure of volume)
		856247	ḏr.t	hand (Hathor)
		851617	ḏrj	efficient; very; solid
		184860	ḏrj	solid; firm; stout
		184900	ḏrj.t	wall?; floor? [made from ivory and ebony]
		184950	ḏrj.tj	pylon
		184910	ḏry.t	dwelling; chamber
		150790	sḏr	strong
		150770	sḏr	to secure (a city); be steadfast
		850133	ḏri̯	to be hard?; to be stolid?
RID	**0001738**	nḏri̯ to seize		
	ID Lexeme	91640	nḏr	grip
		91680	nḏr.y	seizer
		91660	nḏr.t	imprisonment
		863005	nḏrw.t	contraction?; agglomeration?
		91670	nḏri̯	to hold fast; to seize
DRID	**1000261**	**ḏr kite**		
RID	**0000323**	ḏr kite		
	ID Lexeme	184740	ḏr.w	kite (bird of prey)
		184660	ḏr.t	kite; falcon
		184670	ḏr.t	wailing woman (lit. kite)
		184690	ḏr.tj	falcon
		184700	ḏr.tjt	(fem.) falcon (esp. Hathor)

DRID	**1000262**	**ḏr limit**			
	RID	**0000327**	ḏr to finish		
		ID Lexeme	184570	ḏr	to hinder; to finish
			184550	ḏr	when; because
			184530	ḏr	end; limit; boundary
			184540	ḏr	since (spatial, temp.)
			856665	ḏr	wall
			184560	ḏr	to end up as
			851460	ḏr	until the end; in the end
			185000	ḏr.w	obstacle
			184730	ḏr.w	walls? (of a house)
			184990	ḏr.w	end; limit; boundary
			184980	ḏr.tjw	ancestors; roots
			185060	ḏrw.w	side (of the body); flank
			185010	ḏrw.t	coffin
			185090	ḏrt	necessity; ration
			185030	ḏrwt	façade; hall?
			184990	jḏr	boundary
DRID	**1000265**	**ḏr to drum**			
	RID	**0000326**	ḏr to drum		
		ID Lexeme	184580	ḏr	to beat (a drum)
DRID	**1000268**	**ḏr leaf**			
	RID	**0000331**	ḏrḏr leaf		
		ID Lexeme	185150	ḏrḏ	leaf (med.)
DRID	**1000270**	**ḏrj pigment**			
	RID	**0000335**	ḏrj pigment		
		ID Lexeme	185040	ḏrw.y	paint (gen.); [a pigment]
DRID	**1000272**	**ḏr^{c} plank**			
	RID	**0000337**	ḏr^{c} plank		
		ID Lexeme	184970	ḏr^{c}.t	plank (made of cedar wood)
DRID	**1000273**	**ḏr^{c} to subdue**			
	RID	**0000338**	ḏr^{c} to subdue		
		ID Lexeme	184960	ḏr^{c}	to subdue; to overthrow
DRID	**1000274**	**ḏs person**			
	RID	**0000339**	ḏs person		
		ID Lexeme	185370	ḏs	self
			185360	ḏs	person
			185760	ḏsḏs	alter ego
DRID	**1000276**	**ḏs to burn**			
	RID	**0000342**	ḏsḏs to burn		

	ID Lexeme	91840	nḏsḏs	to burn
DRID	**1000277**	**ḏsf net**		
RID	**0000343**	ḏsf net		
	ID Lexeme	185440	ḏsf	to repair (a net)
		856701	ḏsf	net
DRID	**1000278**	**ḏsr [a plant]**		
RID	**0000344**	ḏsr [a beverage]		
	ID Lexeme	185590	ḏsr.t	[a strong ale (made from the djeseret-plant?)]
		185630	ḏsr.t	[a plant (med.)]
DID	**1000279**	**ḏsr to be raised**		
RD	**0000345**	ḏsr [a piece of furniture]		
	ID Lexeme	185540	ḏsr	[a piece of furniture]
RID	**0000347**	ḏsr [a serpent]		
	ID Lexeme	185510	ḏsr	[a snake]
RID	**0000348**	ḏsr [an incense]		
	ID Lexeme	185520	ḏsr	[an incense]
RID	**0000350**	ḏsr to be raised		
	ID Lexeme	185490	ḏsr	[a priest]
		185500	ḏsr	Splendid-one
		550229	ḏsr	splendid; sacred; holy
		185470	ḏsr	to be holy; to be splendid; to make splendid; to consecrate
		185530	ḏsr	[a staff (or scepter?)]
		856422	ḏsr.w	consecration
		185650	ḏsr.w	splendor; sacredness
		185620	ḏsr.t	[Moon eye]
		856714	ḏsr.t	sacredness
		185640	ḏsr.t	[a table (for offerings)]
		150930	sḏsr	to consecrate; to sanctify
DRID	**1000281**	**ḏsr to seclude**		
RID	**0000352**	ḏsr to seclude		
	ID Lexeme	185460	ḏsr	to clear; to hold (oneself) upright; to separate from; to be separated from
		185560	ḏsr	[a measure of length, equaling 4 palms]
		185720	ḏsr.yt	[10. gate of the underworld]
		185610	ḏsr.t	Shilded one
		871088	ḏsr.t	remote land
RID	**0000349**	ḏsr to be holy		
	ID Lexeme	185600	ḏsr.t	sacred ground

DRID	**1000282**		**ḏswi̯ to call**		
	RID	**0000353**	ḏswi̯ to call		
		ID Lexeme	185420	ḏswi̯	to call; to recite
			185400	ḏsy.t	(loud) lamentation
DRID	**1000283**		**ḏt olive tree**		
	RID	**0000354**	ḏt olive tree		
		ID Lexeme	185770	ḏt	olive tree; olives; olive oil
DRID	**1000284**		**ḏw [a vessel]**		
	RID	**0000355**	ḏw [a vessel]		
		ID Lexeme	450473	ḏw.t	[a vessel]; [a measure of volume]
			183020	ḏwj.w	[a pottery jar]
DRID	**1000285**		**ḏw [an insect]**		
	RID	**0000356**	ḏw [an insect]		
		ID Lexeme	183060	ḏw.t	[a stinging insect]
DRID	**1000286**		**ḏw = ḏw^{c} knife**		
	RID	**0000369**	ḏw^{c} knife		
		ID Lexeme	183040	ḏw^{c}	knife
	RID	**0000357**	ḏw knife		
			182880	ḏw	knife
DRID	**1000288**		**ḏwi̯ to be evil**		
	RID	**0000359**	ḏwi̯ to be evil		
		ID Lexeme	853091	ḏw	The evil one
			600473	ḏw	bad; evil
			853567	ḏw	evil person
			182840	ḏw	evil; bad; sinister
			182860	ḏw	bad
			182900	ḏw.t	evil; dirt
			182910	ḏw.tj	evil one
			858530	ḏwi̯	Evildoer
			600472	ḏwi̯	to be bad; to be evil
			861808	ḏwḏw	The ugly one
			183100	ḏwḏw	bad one
			183090	ḏwḏw	bad
			91360	nḏw.yt	malice?
			91310	nḏ.y	to be hostile towards
			91320	nḏ.yt	badness
			150420	sḏwi̯	to slander
DRID	**1000289**		**ḏwi̯ to call**		
	RID	**0000360**	ḏwi̯ to call		
		ID Lexeme	182980	ḏwi̯	to call
			183010	ḏwj.w	call

DRID	**1000290**	**ḏwi̯ to raise**			
	RID	**0000361**	ḏwi̯ to raise		
		ID Lexeme	182830	ḏw	mountain
			182920	ḏw.wj	two mountain ridges (flanking the river)
			181460	ḏw.wt	papyrus plant (the erected one)
			182890	ḏw.t	mountain
			182990	ḏwi̯	to raise; to lift up
DRID	**1000294**	**ḏws to defame**			
	RID	**0000365**	ḏws to defame		
		ID Lexeme	183050	ḏws	to defame
DRID	**1000295**	**ḏwt twenty (dual?)**			
	RID	**0000366**	ḏwt twenty (dual?)		
		ID Lexeme	183070	ḏwt	twenty
DRID	**1000297**	**ḏꜣ [architectural element]**			
	RID	**0000371**	ḏꜣ [architectural element]		
		ID Lexeme	181790	ḏꜣ.y	cell or wall
			181870	ḏꜣy.t	[a kind of an architectural element]; wall
	RID	**0000376**	ḏꜣ tomb		
		ID Lexeme	181620	ḏꜣ.t	tomb
	RID	**0000384**	ḏꜣḏꜣ to build		
		ID Lexeme	182350	ḏꜣḏꜣ	to build; to install
			182340	ḏꜣḏꜣ	[building in front of a temple (bark station?)]
			182460	ḏꜣḏꜣ.wt	courses (of a brick wall)
DRID	**1000298**	**ḏꜣ ball**			
	RID	**0000373**	ḏꜣ round?		
		ID Lexeme	181950	ḏꜣjw	hump
	RID	**0000383**	ḏꜣḏꜣ circle		
		ID Lexeme	182320	ḏꜣḏꜣ	assembly; council; magistrates (at the judgement of the dead)
			500245	ḏꜣḏꜣ.t	offering table
			182400	ḏꜣḏꜣ.t	surrounding area (med.)
			182390	ḏꜣḏꜣ.t	assembly; council; magistrates (at the judgement of the dead)
	RID	**0004000**	ḏꜣḏꜣ head		
			182330	ḏꜣḏꜣ	head; tip
			872144	ḏꜣḏꜣ.w	pot
			182430	ḏꜣḏꜣtw	(divine) assessor
	RID	**0004000**	ḏꜣḏꜣ harp		
			182410	ḏꜣḏꜣ.t	harp

DRID	**1000299**	**ḏꜣ crossing**		
RID	**0000387**	ḏꜣi̯ to cross sth.?		
	ID Lexeme	181770	ḏꜣ.y	[a large riverboat]
		400687	ḏꜣ.yw	ferryman
		182060	ḏꜣ.w	evening or night
		600463	ḏꜣ.w	foot of mast?
		856599	ḏꜣ.t	crossing
		400952	ḏꜣ.t	[a boat]
		181780	ḏꜣi̯	to cross (a body of water); to ferry
		78430	mḏꜣ	block (of pressed dates as a unit of measure)
		78510	mḏꜣ.w	adversary
		78480	mḏꜣ.t	chisel
		500684	mḏꜣ.t	cover
		78470	mḏꜣ.t	papyrus book; letter; document
		78500	mḏꜣ.t	wooden peg
		78540	mḏꜣj	[an offering]
RID	**0000388**	ḏꜣi̯ to extend?		
	ID Lexeme	181520	ḏꜣ	dja-priest
		181750	ḏꜣi̯	to extend (the arm); to turn to; to oppose
		182070	ḏꜣ.w	magical protection?
		857289	ḏꜣ.wtt	adversary
		181670	ḏꜣ.t	remainder; deficiency
RID	**0000389**	ḏꜣi̯ to oppose		
	ID Lexeme	181960	ḏꜣ.wtj	foe
		181810	ḏꜣ.ywt	offence; wrongdoing; disgusting (gen.)
		181820	ḏꜣ.yt	opponent
		181680	ḏꜣt.t	[a female opponent]
		182370	ḏꜣḏꜣ	foe
		182380	ḏꜣḏꜣ	hostile
		181880	ḏꜣ.yw	opponent
RID	**0000390**	ḏꜣi̯ to reach out		
	ID Lexeme	181740	ḏꜣi̯	to reach out (for food, milk); to devour
		181670	ḏꜣ.t	remainder; deficiency

DRID	**1000300**	**ḏꜣ linen**		
RID	**0000377**	ḏꜣ = ḏnn linen		
	ID Lexeme	181530	ḏꜣ	linen (clothing)
		181850	ḏꜣ.yt	linen (clothing)
		182040	ḏꜣ.w	[linen, for clothing]
		181610	ḏꜣ.t	linen (clothing)
		859910	ḏnn	linen?
		860241	mḏꜣ.t	mummy bandages
		78570	mḏꜣy.t	[a kind of cloth]

DRID 1000301 ḏꜣ rotation
RID 0000372 ḏꜣ fire drill
ID Lexeme 181490 ḏꜣ fire drill
856598 ḏꜣ.t fire drill

DRID 1000305 ḏꜣb to greet
RID 0000379 ḏꜣb to greet
ID Lexeme 182090 ḏꜣb to greet

DRID 1000306 ḏꜣd audience hall
RID 0000380 ḏꜣd audience hall
ID Lexeme 182310 ḏꜣd.w audience hall

DRID 1000307 ḏꜣd to cut
RID 0000381 ḏꜣd to cut
ID Lexeme 182290 ḏꜣd to cut off (offering animal]

DRID 1000308 ḏꜣḏ to wet?
RID 0000382 ḏꜣḏ to wet?
ID Lexeme 861517 ḏꜣḏ.yt wet?

DRID 1000309 ḏꜣf to burn
RID 0000385 ḏꜣf to burn
ID Lexeme 182120 ḏꜣf to burn up
182130 ḏꜣf burned meat (med.)
182140 ḏꜣfḏꜣf to burn up

DRID 1000312 ḏꜣjs to counsel
RID 0000392 ḏꜣjs to counsel
ID Lexeme 182000 ḏꜣjs spell; utterance
181990 ḏꜣjs to negotiate; to counsel
550443 ḏꜣjs.w councilor; sage

DRID 1000313 ḏꜣm = ḏꜣn sexual activity
RID 0000393 ḏꜣm sexual activity
ID Lexeme 182160 ḏꜣm offspring; youths; generation
182170 ḏꜣm young cattle
150380 sḏꜣm to make (land) fertile
150370 sḏꜣm to lie with (a woman)
RID 0000394 ḏꜣn young people?
ID Lexeme 182210 ḏꜣn.w young people

DRID 1000314 ḏꜣp bench
RID 0000395 ḏꜣp bench
ID Lexeme 182110 ḏꜣp bench

DRID 1000315 ḏꜣr helper

RID **0000396** ḏꜣr helper
ID Lexeme 182240 ḏꜣr helper

DRID **1000316** **ḏꜣr requirement**
RID **0000397** ḏꜣr requirement
ID Lexeme 182220 ḏꜣr requirement

DRID **1000317** **ḏꜣr scorpion**
RID **0000398** ḏꜣr scorpion
ID Lexeme 182270 ḏꜣr.t scorpion

DRID **1000318** **ḏꜣr to cook**
RID **0000399** ḏꜣr to cook
ID Lexeme 182230 ḏꜣr to cook (with water)

DRID **1000321** **ḏꜣꜣ braid?**
RID **0000402** ḏꜣꜣ braid?
ID Lexeme 181700 ḏꜣꜣ braid

DRID **1000322** **ḏꜣꜥ frying pan**
RID **0000403** ḏꜣꜥ frying pan
ID Lexeme 182030 ḏꜣꜥ frying pan; gridiron

DRID **1000323** **ḏꜣꜥ vetchling**
RID **0000404** ḏꜣꜥ vetchling
ID Lexeme 182020 ḏꜣꜥ vetchling [a substance (med.)]

DRID **1000324** **ḏꜥ to be stormy?**
RID **0000405** ḏꜥ to be stormy?
ID Lexeme 182540 ḏꜥ to lie desolate
182490 ḏꜥ to be stormy; to break wind (med.)
182480 ḏꜥ storm; wind

DRID **1000325** **ḏꜥ to capture fish**
RID **0000406** ḏꜥ to capture fish
ID Lexeme 182530 ḏꜥ to spear fish
182560 ḏꜥ.wt to spear fish
857429 mḏꜥ.w purse-net

DRID **1000326** **ḏꜥb black**
RID **0000407** ḏꜥb to blacken
ID Lexeme 182660 ḏꜥb.t charcoal
182620 ḏꜥb coal-black
182610 ḏꜥb to blacken

DRID **1000327** **ḏꜥm [a scepter]**
RID **0000408** ḏꜥm [a scepter]

ID Lexeme 182700 ḏᶜm [a scepter]
182750 ḏᶜm.wtj he of the djam-scepter

DRID 1000328 ḏᶜm [a staff]
RID 0000408 ḏᶜm [a staff]
ID Lexeme 860855 ḏᶜm [a staff]

DRID 1000329 ḏᶜm gold
RID 0000409 ḏᶜm gold
ID Lexeme 182710 ḏᶜm fine gold; white gold; electrum
182720 ḏᶜm gold (Hathor)
182730 ḏᶜm golden

DRID 1000330 ḏᶜḳ to shout
RID 0000410 ḏᶜḳ to shout
ID Lexeme 182790 ḏᶜḳ to shout; to call (for help)
182800 ḏᶜḳt shouting

DRID 1000331 ḏᶜr [part of a door (lock)]
RID 0000411 ḏᶜr [part of a door (lock)]
ID Lexeme 850053 ḏᶜr.yt [part of a door (lock)]

DRID 1000332 ḏᶜr to select?
RID 0008211 ḏᶜr to select?
182760 ḏᶜr to seek; to investigate; to take thought of
182770 ḏᶜr to take thought of; to care about
182780 ḏᶜr sieve

DRID 1000333 ḏᶜᶜ twig
RID 0000412 ḏᶜᶜ twig, branch
ID Lexeme 182570 ḏᶜᶜ twig; branch
182580 ḏᶜᶜ [a plant]

Root index – numerical

1000001 b lips
1000002 b leg
1000003 bb throat, neck
1000004 bbn to wriggle along
1000005 bḏ ball, corn
1000006 bd emmer
1000007 bd natron
1000009 bḏn stick
1000010 bdš to be weak
1000011 bḏꜣ pad
1000012 bḏꜣ mold
1000014 bfn scorpion
1000015 bgs to injure
1000016 bgz = bgs throat
1000017 bgꜣ to be shipwrecked
1000018 bgꜣ to shout
1000019 bḥ bead
1000020 bḥ to force
1000021 bšw flint
1000022 bḥd to settle down
1000023 bhd to sniff
1000025 bḫḫ to glow
1000026 bḫn greywacke
1000027 bḥn = bfn to bark
1000028 bḫn to watch
1000029 bḥni̯ to cut
1000030 bḥs to hunt
1000031 bḥz calf
1000032 bhꜣ to move back
1000033 bj bee
1000034 bj cheer
1000035 bj clapnet
1000036 bj groats
1000037 bj processional bark
1000038 bjdj [an affliction of the eye]
1000039 bjk falcon
1000040 bjn evil
1000041 bjn harp
1000042 bjꜣ astonishing
1000043 bjꜣ ore
1000044 bjꜣi̯ to be far from
1000045 bkj [tree]
1000047 bkn excrement (med.)
1000048 bkr throne
1000049 bkꜣ pregnancy
1000050 bnr = bl outside
1000051 bn white wagtail
1000052 bn natron
1000053 bn not
1000054 bꜣ = bn to overflow
1000055 bnd bad situation
1000056 bnḏ discharge
1000057 bnd garden bed; cucumber?
1000058 bnd = *bn^{c} = b^{c}n to wrap
1000059 bnf gall-bladder
1000060 bng to be happy
1000061 bngzyt [a kind of a musical instrument]
1000062 bnj to be sweet
1000063 bnn threshold?
1000064 bnš doorpost
1000065 bnš flower crown?
1000066 bns to pierce
1000067 bnw millstone
1000068 bḳ behold
1000069 bḳ to be hostile
1000070 bḳn to stride
1000071 bḳy to open?
1000072 bḳ^{c} pool
1000073 br mullet
1000074 br transport ship
1000075 brg [a kind of a semi-precious stone]
1000076 brg be happy
1000077 brk gift
1000078 brkt pool
1000079 brḳ to sparkle
1000080 brt agreement
1000081 brtj [semi-precious stone]
1000083 bši̯ to spit out
1000084 bsk entrails
1000085 bsn = msn to pierce
1000086 bšṯ to rebel
1000087 bšꜣ ax

1000088 bšꜣ malted barley
1000089 bt mold
1000090 bṯ running
1000091 bt womb
1000092 btk to slaughter (enemies)
1000093 btk to escape?
1000094 bṯn to resist
1000095 btꜣ wrongdoing
1000096 bw abomination
1000097 bw not
1000098 bw place
1000099 bwn spearheads
1000100 bwꜣ to be high
1000101 bz flame
1000102 bz secret
1000104 bzn to consider
1000105 bzn gypsum
1000106 bzꜣ to protect
1000107 bꜣ black stork?
1000108 bꜣ boat
1000109 bꜣ leopard
1000110 bꜣ pot
1000111 bꜣ ram
1000112 bꜣ soul
1000113 bꜣ throat
1000114 bꜣ to hack open
1000115 bꜣ = bn little spheric object
1000116 bꜣ = bn to erect
1000118 bꜣḏ = pꜣḏ spheric shape
1000120 bꜣg coagulate
1000121 bꜣgi̯ to be weak
1000122 bꜣgs to stab
1000123 bꜣẖ sunrise / sunset
1000124 bꜣi̯ to be moist
1000125 bꜣk ramp
1000126 bꜣk servant
1000127 bꜣni̯ sleep
1000128 bꜣḳ moringa tree
1000129 bꜣḳ to be bright
1000130 bꜣs bowl
1000131 bꜣs to cut out
1000132 bꜣš vessel
1000133 bꜣw hill
1000134 bꜣy malt
1000135 bꜥ to deal with water
1000137 bꜥ to disregard
1000140 bꜥḥi̯ to inundate
1000141 bꜥj rod of palm
1000142 bꜥn neck
1000143 bꜥr Baal
1000144 bꜥr big water
1000145 stnw charburner?
1000146 ḏ cobra
1000147 ḏ eternity
1000148 d hand
1000149 ḏb army
1000150 ḏb brick
1000152 db riverside
1000153 ḏb to collect
1000154 db to devour
1000155 ḏb* to make live
1000156 ḏbb [body of water]
1000157 dbb = ḏbb to block
1000158 ḏbg to dive
1000159 ḏbḥ to fish
1000160 dbḥ to request
1000161 dbj hippopotamus
1000162 ḏbn antilope
1000163 dbn to encircle
1000164 ḏbw a piece of meat
1000165 ḏbꜣ [a scepter]
1000166 ḏbꜣ harpoon
1000167 ḏbꜣ to block
1000168 ḏbꜣ to change dress
1000169 ḏbꜣ to support
1000170 ḏbꜥ finger
1000171 dḏ flower
1000172 dd to copulate
1000173 ḏd to say
1000174 ḏdb = ḏdm to heap
1000175 ḏdb = ḏdm to sting
1000176 ḏdf to shudder
1000177 ḏdḥ to confine
1000178 ḏdi̯ to endure
1000181 dḏw to grind
1000182 ḏdꜣ to grow fat
1000183 df to tear
1000184 ḏfi̯ to sink in

1000185 ḏfꜣ to wipe
1000186 ḏfꜣ = ḏfn to provide
1000187 dg foot print
1000188 dgi̯ to hide
1000189 dgi̯ to see
1000190 dgm ricinus
1000191 dgm to feel powerless
1000192 dgꜣ rasor
1000193 ḏḥ [a monkey]
1000194 dḥ to be low
1000195 dḫ to crush
1000196 dhn cliff
1000197 dhn forehead
1000198 dḫn rhythm
1000199 dhn to appoint
1000200 dḥr to be bitter
1000201 ḏḥtj lead
1000202 dḥꜣ straw
1000203 dḥꜣ to pounce
1000204 ḏḥꜥ [a plant]
1000205 ḏḥꜥ leather
1000206 dj five
1000207 dj here
1000208 djdj (red) ochre
1000209 ḏm sanctuary?
1000210 dm to be sharp
1000211 dm worm
1000213 dmj = dmꜣ = dmḏ to unite
1000215 ḏmꜥ papyrus
1000216 ḏmꜥ to be parched
1000217 dn family
1000218 ḏn to be hot
1000219 dn to cut
1000220 ḏn to thresh
1000221 ḏnb dwarf
1000222 ḏnb to turn back
1000223 ḏnd to be angry
1000225 dn to rage
1000226 dn to traverse
1000227 ḏnḏr brushwood
1000228 dng = dꜣg tiny being
1000229 dng to be deaf
1000230 ḏnḥ wing
1000231 dnḥs [metal tool]
1000232 dni̯ share
1000233 ḏnj fifth day
1000234 dnj shouting
1000235 ḏnn skull
1000236 ḏnn to struggle
1000237 ḏnr branch
1000238 dnrg a fruit
1000239 ḏnrm to try hard
1000240 dns to be heavy
1000241 dn to refill
1000242 dp boat
1000243 dp loin
1000244 dp lump?
1000245 dp to taste
1000246 dpḫ execution block?
1000247 ḏpḥ = tpḥ
1000248 ḏpḳ dancer
1000249 dpy crocodile
1000250 dḳ to grind
1000251 dḳr banish?
1000252 dḳr harvest
1000253 dḳr to attach
1000254 dḳrw essence
1000255 dḳw to be barefoot
1000256 dḳꜥ to smoothen
1000257 ḏr [a precious stone]
1000258 ḏr calf
1000259 ḏr foreign
1000260 ḏr hand
1000261 ḏr kite
1000262 ḏr limit
1000263 dr prod
1000264 dr to dress
1000265 ḏr to drum
1000266 dr to remove
1000267 dr to spread
1000268 ḏr leaf
1000269 drf to paint
1000270 ḏrj pigment
1000271 drp to supply
1000272 ḏrꜥ plank
1000273 ḏrꜥ to subdue
1000274 ḏs person
1000275 ds to be sharp

1000276 ḏs to burn
1000277 ḏsf net
1000278 ḏsr [a plant]
1000279 ḏsr to be raised
1000279 ḏsr to be raised
1000280 dšr to be red
1000281 ḏsr to seclude
1000282 ḏswi̯ to call
1000283 ḏt olive tree
1000284 ḏw [a vessel]
1000285 ḏw [an insect]
1000286 ḏw = ḏwꜥ knife
1000287 dwḫ* to embalm
1000288 ḏwi̯ to be evil
1000289 ḏwi̯ to call
1000290 ḏwi̯ to raise
1000292 dwn to stretch out
1000293 dwr [a basket]
1000294 ḏws to defa
1000295 ḏwt twenty (dual?)
1000296 dwꜣ rise
1000297 ḏꜣ [architectural element]
1000298 ḏꜣ ball?
1000299 ḏꜣ crossing
1000300 ḏꜣ linen
1000301 ḏꜣ rotation
1000302 ḏꜣ to copulate
1000303 ḏꜣ = ꜥꜣ* to tremble
1000304 dꜣb fig
1000305 ḏꜣb to greet
1000306 ḏꜣd audience hall
1000307 ḏꜣd to cut
1000308 ḏꜣḏ to wet?
1000309 ḏꜣf to burn
1000311 dꜣj linen
1000312 ḏꜣjs to counsel
1000313 ḏꜣm = ḏꜣn sexual activity
1000314 ḏꜣp bench
1000315 ḏꜣr helper
1000316 ḏꜣr requirement
1000317 ḏꜣr scorpion
1000318 ḏꜣr to cook
1000319 dꜣr to subdue
1000320 dꜣz to bind
1000321 ḏꜣꜣ braid
1000322 ḏꜣꜥ frying pan
1000323 ḏꜣꜥ vetchling (Platterbse)
1000324 ḏꜥ to be stormy
1000325 ḏꜥ to capture fish
1000326 ḏꜥb black
1000327 ḏꜥm [a scepter]
1000328 ḏꜥm [a staff]
1000329 ḏꜥm gold
1000330 ḏꜥḳ to shout
1000331 ḏꜥr [part of a door (lock)]
1000332 ḏꜥr to select?
1000333 ḏꜥꜥ twig
1000334 fd [an oil]
1000335 fd four
1000336 fd to sweat
1000337 fdi̯ to tear out
1000338 fdḳ to trench
1000339 fgn to defecate
1000340 fḫ to loosen
1000341 fjṯ to laugh
1000342 fjw to become disgusted at
1000343 fkꜣ turquoise
1000344 fn to be weak
1000345 fnḏ to snort
1000346 fnḫ cord?
1000347 fnḫ to make smooth
1000348 fnṯ maggot
1000349 fḳꜣ to rewordt
1000350 ft to be disgusted
1000351 ft to leap
1000352 ftṯꜣ to decay
1000353 fꜣ dust?
1000354 fꜣ threat
1000355 fꜣg to cut (meat)
1000356 fꜣg to eradicate
1000357 fꜣi̯ to lift
1000358 fꜣk to be bald
1000359 fꜥg claw
1000360 fꜥy hair
1000361 gb to incline
1000362 gbb [a goose]
1000363 gbb earth
1000364 gbi̯ to damage

1000365 gbꜣ arm
1000366 gbꜣ payment
1000367 gbꜣ to blind
1000368 gḏ arm
1000369 gḏm to grasp
1000370 gg kidney
1000371 ggwi̯ to be amazed
1000372 gḥs gazelle
1000373 gj [a plant]
1000374 gjf monkey
1000375 gm ibis
1000376 gm power
1000377 gm weak
1000378 gmḥ strand of hair
1000379 gmḥ to see
1000380 gmi̯ to find
1000381 gmꜣ temple (of the head)
1000382 gn [a plant]
1000384 gn respect
1000385 gn to record*
1000386 gnf repel
1000387 gngntj lute
1000388 gnẖ to fix
1000389 gnẖ wing
1000390 gnn soft
1000391 gnš to select
1000392 gns violence
1000393 gp cloud
1000394 gr also
1000395 gr kidney
1000396 gr silence
1000397 grb property
1000398 grb to cut (wood)
1000399 grg exaltation
1000400 grg lie
1000401 grg rib
1000402 grg to prepare
1000403 grḥ night
1000404 grḥ to finish
1000405 grm to drag away
1000406 grt husk
1000407 gs half
1000408 gš liquid
1000409 gš migrating bird
1000410 gs to anoint
1000411 gs to mourn
1000412 gs to regulate
1000413 gs to treat (leather)
1000414 gsi̯ to run
1000415 gsp basket
1000416 gsp to equip
1000417 gsr finger ring
1000418 gstj scribe's palette
1000419 gsꜣ [an antilope]
1000420 gsꜣ bag
1000421 gsꜣ to be inclined
1000422 gt cistern
1000423 gw [a bull]
1000424 gw [a horse]
1000425 gw to rejoice
1000426 gwš to be crooked
1000427 gwꜣ chest
1000428 gwꜣ to tighten
1000429 gꜣ [a heron]
1000430 gꜣ to chatter
1000431 gꜣ to hang
1000432 gꜣ to wound
1000433 gꜣb arm
1000434 gꜣb leaf
1000435 gꜣf [a bread]
1000436 gꜣḥ shoulder
1000437 gꜣḥ to be weary
1000438 gꜣḥ to squeeze
1000439 gꜣi̯ to make wet
1000440 gꜣi̯ to overthrow
1000441 gꜣj [a jar]
1000442 gꜣj [a measure]
1000443 gꜣj naos
1000444 gꜣš reed
1000445 gꜣu̯ to be narrow
1000446 ẖ belly
1000447 ḫ fire
1000448 ḥ flax
1000449 ḥb stairway?
1000450 ḥb target
1000451 ẖb to slay
1000452 ẖb to slink into
1000453 ẖb to subdue

1000454 ḫbḏ to hate
1000455 ḥbḏ to open
1000456 ḫbi̯ to dance
1000457 ḫbi̯ to reduce
1000458 hbj ibis
1000459 hbn [a vessel]
1000460 hbn antilope
1000461 ḫbn crime
1000462 hbnj ebony
1000463 ḥbnn [a bread]
1000464 hbḳ to pound
1000465 ḫbr to join together
1000466 ḥbs to cover
1000467 ḫbs to hack
1000468 ḫbs to illuminate
1000469 ḫbs wrongdoing
1000470 hbu̯ to abuse?
1000471 hbu̯ to step
1000472 ḫbz tail
1000473 ḫbꜣ to hack
1000474 ḥḏ [a medicine]
1000475 ḫd land register?
1000476 ḥḏ mace
1000477 ḥḏ to be white
1000478 hd to confront
1000479 ẖd to examine
1000481 ẖdb to kill
1000482 hdd famine?
1000483 ḥdg to kill
1000484 ḫdi̯ flow
1000485 ḥdi̯ to damage
1000486 ḥdi̯ to spread out
1000487 hdm throne
1000488 hdn [a plant]
1000489 ḥḏn to be angry
1000490 ḥdq to cut off
1000491 ḥdqq rat?
1000492 ḥḏr [animal]
1000493 hdr [collar]
1000494 ẖdr to feel uncomfortable?
1000495 ḥḏy west wind
1000496 ḫf to flow
1000497 ḥf to hear?
1000498 hf to hull
1000499 ḫf to see sth.
1000500 ḥfdi̯ to climb
1000501 ḥfdi̯ to settle
1000502 ḥfk to drink milk
1000504 ḫfnn [fruit]
1000505 ḫft vis-à-vis
1000506 ḥfꜣ to crawl
1000507 ḫfꜣ to feed
1000508 ḥfꜣ = ḥfn = ḥnf to praise
1000509 ḫfꜣi̯ to lighten
1000510 ḫfꜣꜣ riverbank
1000511 ḫfꜥ to grasp
1000512 ḥgꜣ festivity
1000513 ḥḥ million
1000514 ḫḫ neck
1000515 ḫḫ to weigh
1000516 hhi̯ to be fiery
1000517 hhj to be deaf
1000518 hj onomatopoetic
1000519 hj to contort
1000520 hj to rejoice
1000521 ḥj to seek
1000522 hjms to approach humbly
1000523 ḥjp to run
1000524 hjw [creature threatening the dead]
1000525 ḥkn lion?
1000526 ḥkn oil or unguent
1000527 ḥkn to praise
1000528 hkr [serpent]
1000529 ẖkr to adorn
1000530 ḥkꜣ to perform magic
1000531 ḥnr = ḥl to darken
1000532 ḫnr = ḫl to sting
1000533 ḥm [a weapon at a chariot]
1000534 hm [exclamation of satisfaction]
1000535 ḥm [plant]
1000536 ḥm coward
1000537 ḫm dust
1000538 hm fare
1000539 ḥm forty
1000540 ḥm frit
1000541 ḥm majesty
1000542 ḥm misfortune

1000543 ḫm not to know
1000544 hm saliva
1000545 ḥm servant
1000546 ḥm though
1000547 hm to be hot
1000548 ḥm to copulate
1000549 hm to shout aloud
1000550 ḥm to tread
1000551 ḥm woman
1000552 ḥmḏ vinegar
1000553 ḫmi̯ to consume
1000554 ḥmi̯ to flood
1000555 ḫmi̯ to oppose
1000556 ḥmi̯ to repel
1000557 ḫmn eight
1000558 ḥmn several
1000559 ḥmr donkey
1000560 ḥmr throne
1000561 hms cord
1000562 ẖms incense
1000563 ẖms to bend
1000564 ḥmsi̯ to sit down
1000565 hmṯ [serpent]
1000566 ḫmt companion?
1000567 ḥmt ore
1000568 ḫmt three
1000569 ḫmt to stab
1000570 ḥmu̯ to be skilled
1000571 ḥmw abrasive sand?
1000572 ḥmw weapon
1000573 ḫmy sand-fly?
1000574 ḥmz to slaughter
1000575 ḥmꜣ [plant]
1000576 ḥmꜣ ball
1000577 ḥmꜣ salt
1000578 ḥmꜣg [scales]
1000579 ḥmꜣg garnet?
1000580 ḥmꜣg to surround
1000581 ḥmꜣṯ a cord?
1000582 ḫmꜣꜣ to shrivel
1000583 ḫmꜥi̯ to seize
1000584 ḥn [bird]
1000585 ḥn [jar]
1000586 hn [water]
1000587 ẖn bag?
1000588 ẖn covering
1000589 ḫn disgusting
1000590 ḫn extra gift
1000591 ḥn pelican
1000592 ḫn porter
1000593 ḫn speech
1000594 ẖn statue
1000595 hn sweet
1000596 ẖn to approach
1000597 ḫn to be foolish
1000598 ḥn to be fresh
1000599 ḥn to block
1000600 ḫn to direct
1000602 ḥn to hurry
1000603 ḥn to jubilate
1000604 ḥn to look at
1000605 ḥn to protect
1000606 ḥnb solar?
1000607 ḥnb to measure
1000608 ḥnb to repel
1000609 ẖnbb to mingle
1000610 ḫnḏ shin
1000611 ḫnḏ to bend
1000612 ḫnḏ to tread
1000613 ḫnf to take sth.
1000614 ḫnfi̯ to burn
1000615 ḫnfꜣ arrogance?
1000616 ḥkk to swallow
1000617 ḥngg gullet
1000618 ḫni̯ to make music
1000619 hni to rejoice
1000620 ẖni̯ to row
1000621 ḫni̯ to settle
1000622 ẖnk [garment]
1000623 ḥnk to braid
1000624 ḥnk to present
1000625 ẖnm [an oil]
1000626 ḥnm go around?
1000628 ḫnm jasper
1000629 ḫnm to enjoy
1000630 ḫnm to rear
1000631 ẖnm to unite
1000632 ẖnm water facility

1000633 ḥnmm mankind
1000634 ḫnms mosquito
1000635 ḥnn blossom of date palm
1000636 hnn fallow deer
1000637 ḫnn fowl
1000638 ḥnn phallus
1000639 ẖnn septic?
1000640 ḥnn to hoe
1000641 hnn to incline
1000642 ḫnp [baked good]
1000643 ḫnp to consume
1000644 ḥnḳ to ferment
1000645 ḫnr rein
1000646 ḫnr = ḫl spike
1000647 ḫnr to be hoarse
1000648 ḫnr = ḫl to scatter
1000649 ḫnr to seclude
1000650 ḫnrf = ḫlf insult
1000651 ḥnrg to quake
1000652 ḫnrj roar
1000653 ḫnš [a plant]
1000654 ḥns to be narrow
1000655 ḫnš to stink
1000656 ḫns two sided item
1000657 ḫnt face
1000658 ḫnt jar-stand
1000659 ḥnt scale?
1000660 ḥnṯi̯ to be greedy
1000661 ḥnṯi̯ to butcher
1000662 ḫntš to be glad
1000663 ḥntꜣ porcupine?
1000664 ḥntꜣsw lizard
1000665 ḥnw [jug]
1000666 hnw box
1000667 ḥnw horn
1000668 hnw kin
1000669 ḫnw dorsal fin (synodontis)
1000670 ḥny spear
1000671 ḫnz to travel through
1000672 ḥnꜥ together with
1000673 ẖp figure
1000674 hp regulation
1000675 ḫpd back side
1000676 ḥpd to open
1000677 ḥpg to dance
1000678 ḫpi̯ to travel
1000679 ẖpn to be bulged
1000680 ḫpp seeds
1000681 ḫpp to be strange
1000682 ḫpr to exist
1000683 ḫprš Blue Crown
1000684 ḫpš to subjugate
1000685 ḥpt to embrace
1000686 ẖpꜣ navel
1000687 ẖpꜥ to chew
1000688 hḳ to crack?
1000689 ḥḳr to be hungry
1000690 ẖḳs to be injured
1000691 hḳs to damage
1000692 ḥqꜣ bushel
1000693 ḥqꜣ to rule
1000694 ḫr at
1000695 ḥr canal?
1000697 ḥr face
1000698 hr highland
1000699 ḥr lump of lapis lazuli
1000700 ḫr road
1000701 ḥr rope
1000702 ḫr sistrum
1000703 ḥꜣi̯ to uncover
1000704 ḥr to be ready
1000705 hr to dispel completely
1000706 ḫr to fall
1000707 ḥr to guard
1000708 ḥr to rejoice
1000709 ẖr under
1000710 ẖrd child
1000711 ḫrd veils
1000712 ḥri̯ to be distant
1000713 ḥri̯ to frighten
1000714 hri̯ to milk
1000715 ḥrj melting oven
1000716 ẖrm causeway?
1000717 hrm to include
1000718 ḥrp dagger
1000719 ḫrp to administer
1000720 hrp to sink
1000721 ḫrq slippery ground

1000722 ḥrr flower
1000723 ḥrr to roar
1000724 ḫrr watercourse
1000725 ḥrr worm
1000726 ḫrš bundle
1000727 ḥrs carnelian
1000729 hrṯṯ to do stealthily
1000730 hru̯ to be pleased
1000731 ḫru̯ to say
1000732 hrw day
1000734 ḥry dung
1000735 ḫry myrrh?
1000736 ḥs defecate
1000737 ḫs rubbing stone
1000738 ḥs to be closed
1000739 ḥs to be cold
1000740 ḥsb cross band
1000741 ḥsb to break
1000742 ḥsb to count
1000743 ḫšb to mutilate
1000744 ḥsb to slaughter
1000745 ḫsbḏ lapis lazuli
1000746 ḫsdḏ [a kilt]
1000747 ḫsḏḏ to grow mouldy
1000748 ḫsf to confront
1000749 ḫšḫš rubble
1000750 ḥsi̯ to sing
1000751 hskt [bad way of walking]
1000752 hsmḳ storming (of the king joining battle)
1000753 ḥsḳ to cut off
1000754 ḫsr to dispel
1000755 ẖss corner (of a building)
1000756 ẖsw eyelid
1000757 ḥsꜣ thread
1000758 ẖsꜣ to be unanointed
1000759 ht [an animal]
1000760 ḥt [part of the eye]
1000761 ḫt behind
1000762 ḥt comb
1000763 ḫt crop
1000764 ḥt hyena
1000765 ḫt plot
1000766 ht to dig
1000767 ḥt to place in
1000768 ḫṯ to pound
1000769 ht to wander
1000770 ḫt wood
1000770 ḫt wood
1000771 ẖtb to dip into
1000772 ḫti̯ platform
1000773 ḫti̯ to carve
1000774 ẖti̯ to pluck (plants)
1000775 ḫti̯ to see
1000776 ḥtj smoke
1000777 ḥtm [an animal]
1000778 ḥtm chair
1000779 htm to destroy
1000780 ḫtm to seal
1000781 ḫṯn garlic?
1000782 ḥtp blood
1000783 ḥtp to rest
1000785 ḥtr to bind together
1000786 ḥts to accomplish
1000787 ḥṯṯ armpit
1000788 hṯt to scream
1000789 ḥtw throat
1000790 ḥṯꜣ [a bread]
1000791 ḥtꜣ sail
1000792 ḥtꜣ to be shabby
1000793 ḥw [the great sphinx of Giza]
1000794 ḥw food
1000795 ḥw house
1000796 hw to run
1000797 ḫw unique
1000798 ḥw utterance
1000799 hw sailing?
1000800 ḫwd carrying chair
1000801 ḫwd to be rich
1000802 ḫwd to fish
1000803 ḫwḫ [a boat]
1000804 ḫwi̯ to protect
1000805 ḫwi̯ to strike
1000807 ḥwj happy song
1000808 ḥwn a cut of meat
1000809 ḥwn to be young
1000810 ḫwn to hurt
1000811 ḥwrw to be weak

1000812 ḥwrʿ to rob
1000813 hwš to disregard
1000814 ḫws to slaughter
1000815 hwt to burn
1000816 hwt to lament
1000817 hwṯn [a fish]
1000818 ḫwzi̯ to build
1000819 ḥwꜣ to rot
1000820 ḥwʿ to be short
1000821 ḫyi̯ to be high
1000822 hyn territory
1000823 ḫz [a myrrh]
1000824 ḥz forearm
1000825 ḫz ritual
1000826 ḥz water jar
1000827 ḫzd to decay
1000827 ḫzd to decay
1000828 ẖzi̯ to be weak
1000829 ḥzi̯ to praise
1000830 ḥzi̯ to turn back
1000831 ḥzk [a priest]
1000832 ḥzmn amethyst
1000833 ḥzmn bronze
1000834 ḥzmn to eat
1000835 ḥzp garden
1000836 ḫzꜣ [a plant]
1000837 ḫzꜣ carrying pole
1000838 ḥzꜣ dough
1000839 ḥzꜣ to be wild
1000840 ḫzꜣj bribe
1000841 hʾ courtyard
1000842 ḫꜣ [a water]
1000843 ḥꜣ [a waterfowl]
1000844 ṯnj where
1000845 ḫꜣ an element of dressing
1000846 ḥꜣ behind
1000847 hꜣ blaze
1000848 ẖꜣ corpse?
1000849 ḥꜣ front
1000850 ḥꜣ heart
1000851 hꜣ husband
1000852 ḫꜣ illness
1000853 ẖꜣ marsh
1000854 ḫꜣ meat
1000855 hꜣ pavillon
1000856 ḫꜣ plant category
1000857 ḫꜣ thousand
1000858 ḫꜣto be young
1000860 ẖꜣ to disturb
1000861 ḥꜣ to land?
1000862 ḥꜣ tomb
1000863 hꜣ wild bird
1000865 ḫꜣb hippopotamus
1000866 ḫꜣb infant
1000867 ẖꜣb to be crooked
1000868 ḫꜣb to be humble
1000869 ḥꜣb to catch
1000870 hꜣb to send
1000871 ḥꜣb turquoise
1000872 ḥꜣbi̯ festival
1000873 ḥꜣbi̯ to mourn
1000874 ḫꜣḏ [a bread]
1000875 ḥꜣd agitation
1000876 ḫꜣd to pluck
1000877 ḥꜣd to trap
1000878 ḫꜣf to twist?
1000879 ḥꜣg = ḥng to be glad
1000880 ḫꜣḫ to hurry
1000881 hꜣi̯ period
1000882 hꜣi̯ to descend
1000883 ḫꜣi̯ to measure
1000884 ḥꜣi̯ to mourn
1000885 ẖꜣi̯ = šꜣi̯ to resist
1000886 ḫꜣi̯ to support
1000887 ḥꜣj light
1000888 ẖꜣk to be cunning
1000889 ḥꜣk to truncate
1000890 ḥꜣk trapeze
1000891 ẖꜣm [a beer offering]
1000892 hꜣr herd
1000893 hꜣm poultry
1000894 ḫꜣm to bend (the arm)
1000895 ḥꜣm to catch
1000896 ḫꜣm to do something quickly?
1000897 ḫꜣnn doum palm
1000898 ḥꜣp to hide
1000899 ẖꜣpi̯ to flow freely
1000900 ḫꜣtb to spare

1000901 ḫꜣtrw mongoose
1000902 ḫꜣw altar
1000903 ḫꜣw hide (of animals)
1000904 hꜣw kin
1000905 ḫꜣwj evening
1000906 ḥꜣwj pole?
1000907 ḫꜣyb shadow
1000908 ḫꜣz to climb
1000909 ẖꜣꜣ to decide
1000910 ḫꜣ to throw
1000911 ḥꜣꜥ = ḥꜣy turmoil
1000912 ḫꜥ [a tool]
1000913 ḫꜥ clew
1000914 ḥꜥ limb
1000915 ḥꜥ staff
1000916 ẖꜥ to empty
1000917 ḥꜥb [an enemy]
1000918 ḥꜥb to play
1000919 ḥꜥḏꜣ to rob
1000920 ḫꜥi̯ to appear
1000921 ḫꜥm throat
1000922 ẖꜥm to approach
1000923 ḥꜥnẖ to rotate
1000924 ḥꜥp flood
1000925 ḫꜥq to shave
1000926 ẖꜥq to shave
1000927 ḫꜥr leather
1000928 ḫꜥr to be furious
1000929 ḥꜥtj bed
1000930 ḥꜥw fleet
1000931 ḥꜥꜣ child
1000934 j to say
1000935 jb [a sistrum]
1000936 jb [a tree]
1000937 jb = jbr unguent, oil
1000938 jb chapel
1000939 jb goat
1000940 jb heart
1000941 jb purification booth
1000942 jbh gneiss
1000943 jbḥ to be flooded
1000943 jbḥ to be flooded
1000944 jbḥ tooth
1000945 jbi̯ to be thirsty
1000946 jbn alum
1000947 jbr stallion
1000948 jbs headdress
1000949 jbšt [a bread]
1000950 jbṯ trap
1000951 jbzꜣ [an oil plant]
1000952 jbꜣ maned sheep
1000953 jbꜣ to dance
1000954 jd pleasant scent
1000955 jd uterus
1000956 jdb riverbank
1000957 jdg kerchief
1000958 jdḥ marsh
1000959 jdi̯ to be deaf
1000960 jdi̯ to cense
1000961 jdi̯ to subjugate
1000962 jdm linen
1000963 jdn ear
1000964 jdn granary
1000965 jdn to replace
1000966 jdr heart
1000967 jdr to bind together
1000968 jdꜣ to smooth
1000969 jf [bone marrow]
1000970 jfd to run
1000971 jfn to go back
1000972 jgn gladness
1000974 w not
1000975 jh cow
1000976 jḥ crocodile
1000977 jḫ item
1000978 jḥ ox
1000979 jh stable
1000980 jḥ thigh
1000981 jḥ to weep?
1000982 jḫ to worship
1000983 jḫḫ darkness
1000984 jhj to wail
1000985 jhm [a resin?]
1000986 jhm sigh
1000987 jhm to walk slowly
1000988 jhmz rope
1000989 jḫr form
1000990 jhr tent

1000991 jhy joy
1000992 jḥy to make music
1000993 jjr horned animal
1000994 jk to hack
1000996 jkm shield
1000997 jkn bad?
1000998 jkn to scoop out
1000999 jm clay
1001000 jm in
1001001 jm pupil (eye)
1001003 jm rib
1001005 jm strong
1001006 jm there
1001007 jm to wail
1001008 jmḥ to suck
1001009 jmi̯ not to be
1001010 jmi̯ to give
1001011 jmk to putrefy
1001012 jmn right
1001013 jmn to hide
1001014 jmr to be deaf
1001015 jms dill
1001016 jmw boat
1001017 jmꜣḫ backbone
1001018 jmꜣḫ well supplied
1001019 jn [a garment]
1001020 jn by (of agent)
1001022 ꜣ not
1001023 jn pain
1001024 jn refrain
1001025 jn tilapia
1001026 jn today?
1001027 jn valley
1001028 jnb [a plant]
1001029 jnb ax
1001030 jnb lynx
1001031 jnb wall
1001032 jnbꜣ to be mute
1001033 jnd to be sad
1001034 jnf discharge
1001035 jnḥ to surround
1001036 jnhmn pomegranate
1001037 jnḥꜣs husks (of lotus)
1001038 jni̯ to fetch
1001039 jnj [a plant]
1001040 jnj to delay
1001041 jnk I
1001042 jnm [wine jug?]
1001043 jnm skin
1001044 jnn fishing net
1001045 jnn to cut
1001046 jnnk thyme?
1001047 jnp royal child
1001048 jnp to lie down
1001049 jnḳ to encompass
1001050 jnḳfḳf [a wooden part of a chariot]
1001051 jnr stone
1001052 jnrm oak
1001053 jns lower leg
1001054 jns red (blood)
1001055 ꜥf there
1001056 jntj to repel
1001057 ꜥn here
1001058 ꜥꜣ here
1001063 jnꜥ chin
1001064 jp hippopotamus
1001065 jp inner area
1001066 jp to count
1001067 jpd [unit of measure for baked goods]
1001068 jpd furniture
1001069 jpḥ pig
1001070 jpt bread
1001071 jpꜣ red dye (madder)
1001072 jḳḥ to enter
1001073 jḳr [a serpent]
1001074 jḳr to be excellent
1001076 jr lion
1001077 jr milk cow
1001078 jr towards
1001079 jrdb αρτάβη
1001080 jrḫ [a semi-precious stone]
1001081 jri̯ to do
1001082 jrj ram
1001083 jrjr guide
1001084 jrkt (tree) trunk
1001085 jrp wine

1001086 jrḳbs rock crystal
1001087 jrt a vegetal purple dye
1001088 jrt distress
1001089 jrṯ milk
1001090 js like
1001091 jš meal
1001092 js to call
1001093 jsbr juniper?
1001094 jsbr whip
1001095 jsbt seat
1001096 jsbw hut?
1001097 jšd [a tree, (Balanites aegyptiaca?)]
1001098 jsd to sit?
1001099 jsd to spit
1001100 jšf to burn
1001101 jsp to starve
1001102 jspt quiver (for arrows)
1001103 jsḳ to linger
1001104 jsr rushes
1001105 jšš image?
1001106 jšš to bring out
1001107 jstn to bind
1001109 jswt long plank
1001110 jt barley
1001111 jṯ which
1001112 jṯḥ to drag
1001113 jṯi̯ to seize
1001114 jtj father
1001115 jṯm [metal part of a whip]
1001117 jtn disc
1001118 jtn fluffy
1001119 jtn ground
1001121 jṯn to resist
1001122 jṯr captive
1001123 jtr iteru
1001124 jtr papyrus?
1001125 jṯṯ = ḥṯṯ to fly up
1001126 jṯꜣ to capture
1001127 jw not to be
1001129 jw dog
1001130 jw small livestock?
1001132 jw to bewail
1001134 jwf meat
1001135 jwh to carry
1001136 jwḥ to destroy
1001137 jwḥ to moisten
1001138 jwi̯ to come
1001138 jwi̯ to come
1001140 jwj building
1001141 jwms untruth
1001142 jwn bow
1001143 jwn colour
1001144 jwn support
1001145 jwn to unite
1001146 jwr [roast meat]
1001147 jwr beans
1001148 jwr to become pregnant
1001149 jws scales
1001150 jwšš dough
1001151 jwsw truly
1001152 jwy to irrigate
1001153 jwꜣ cattle
1001154 jwꜣ help
1001155 jwꜣ throat
1001156 jwꜣ to take away
1001157 jw^{c} haunch
1001158 jw^{c} to inherit
1001159 jw^{c} troops
1001160 jz old
1001161 jz reed
1001162 jz = j^{c} tomb
1001163 jz windpipe?
1001164 jzf disorder
1001165 jzj cord?
1001166 jzj to be light (of weight)
1001167 jzkn zenith?
1001168 jzn bolt
1001169 jzp to hew
1001170 jzr tamarisk
1001171 jzzj to catch
1001172 jꜣ [a plant]
1001173 jꜣb left
1001174 jꜣbys foundation
1001175 jꜣd cord
1001176 jꜣd dew
1001177 jꜣd to climb
1001178 jꜣd to suffer

1001179 jꜣf claw
1001182 jꜣẖi̯ to sweep (the harvest)
1001184 jꜣi̯ to rise
1001185 jꜣj [braid]
1001186 jꜣk old
1001187 jꜣkb to mourn
1001188 jꜣm to be pleasant
1001189 jꜣm to bind
1001190 jꜣḳ to dominate
1001191 jꜣḳ vegetables
1001192 jꜣꜣ = jꜣr = or rush
1001193 jꜣr to mourn
1001194 jꜣrr vine
1001195 jꜣs to be bald
1001196 jꜣṯ to injure
1001197 jꜣw to be old
1001198 jꜣꜣ twig
1001202 jꜥ pearl necklace
1001203 jꜥb to unite
1001204 jꜥf to squeeze
1001205 jꜥḥ moon
1001206 jꜥi̯ to wash
1001207 jꜥn grief
1001208 jꜥnꜥ baboon
1001209 jꜥr to rise
1001210 jꜥꜣ donkey
1001211 jꜥꜣ to cover
1001212 jꜥꜣ to speak a foreign language
1001214 kff to suck
1001216 kfꜣ rear part
1001217 kfꜥ to plunder
1001218 kḥ to become old
1001219 khb to push violently
1001220 kḥs chair
1001221 khꜣ to rage furiously
1001222 kj [a monkey]
1001223 kj to shout
1001224 kjw to bow
1001225 kki̯ to be dark
1001226 km to complete
1001227 kmm to be black
1001228 kmr [a dancer]
1001229 kmrj ivory
1001230 knj to be dissatisfied
1001231 knm to wrap
1001232 knnr lyre
1001233 kns abdominal region
1001234 knt [a garment (cloak?)]
1001235 kp = kb palm of hand, sole of foot
1001236 kr [a boat]
1001237 kr heap of stones
1001238 kr horn
1001239 kr saddle
1001240 krḥt [a basket]
1001241 krj prison
1001242 krk bed
1001243 krm [a jewelry]
1001244 krp to efface
1001245 krs bag
1001246 krs to jump
1001247 krṯ cords (for whip)
1001248 krt to cut
1001249 krṯ young animal
1001250 ks [a basket]
1001251 ks to dance
1001252 ksi̯ to bow
1001253 ksm to oppose
1001254 kšw [a plant]
1001255 kt dark
1001256 kt to tremble
1001257 kṯm boasting
1001258 ktm gold
1001259 kṯn charioteer
1001260 ktp scimitar
1001261 ktt to be small
1001262 ktw cauldron
1001263 kwšn [part of harness]
1001264 kj other
1001265 kz to run freely?
1001266 kꜣ life force
1001267 kꜣ vagina
1001268 kꜣ work
1001269 kꜣf flint
1001270 kꜣhs to be rough
1001271 kꜣi̯ to swell
1001272 kꜣi̯ to think
1001273 kꜣj [a boat]

1001274 kꜣm garden
1001275 kꜣmn to be blind
1001277 kꜣp to cover
1001278 kꜣr chapel
1001279 kꜣy excrement?
1001280 kꜣꜣ leopard-patterned
1001281 m who?
1001282 mḏ oil
1001283 mḏ ten
1001284 mḏ to be deep
1001285 mḏd to align
1001286 mḏḥ carpenter
1001287 mḏḥ to make ready
1001288 mdn to rest
1001289 mḏḳ [a vessel]
1001290 mḏri̯ to turn
1001291 mḏrn [a metal tool]
1001292 mdw staff
1001293 mdwi̯ to speak
1001294 mḏꜣb to scoop
1001295 mḏʿ to subdue
1001296 mfkꜣ to be glad
1001297 mgr to roast
1001298 mgrt cave
1001299 mgꜣ youthful soldier
1001300 mḥ cubit
1001301 mḥ north
1001302 mḥ to fill
1001303 mḫ to respect
1001304 mḥḏrt fish pond
1001305 mḥi̯ to be in water
1001306 mḥi̯ to care for
1001307 mḥi̯ to forget
1001308 mḥj to flee
1001309 mḥn to encircle
1001310 mhr braver
1001311 mḫt [a chariot part]
1001312 mḫtb golden armband
1001313 mhw a positive social characteristic
1001314 mḫꜣ to constrain
1001315 mḥʿ flax
1001316 mj [a (funerary) boat]
1001317 mj come
1001318 mj = mr like
1001319 mj road
1001320 mj take
1001321 mj to bring
1001322 mjdꜣ [kind of meat]
1001323 mjm [a plant]
1001324 mjmj dura
1001325 mjn today
1001326 mjn water
1001327 mjw cat
1001328 mjz liver
1001329 mjʿ [a house?]
1001330 mk [a boat]
1001331 mk correct position
1001332 mk to sustain
1001333 mkḥꜣ back of the head
1001334 mki̯ to protect
1001335 mkmr fishnet
1001336 mkr merchant
1001337 mktr [a tower]
1001338 mkꜣ to be brave
1001339 mkꜣ to flatten
1001340 mmj giraffe
1001341 mn [a bowl]
1001342 mn [a fabric]
1001343 mn hot fire
1001344 mn jug
1001345 mn quartz
1001346 mn thigh
1001347 mn to be ill
1001348 mn to move
1001349 mn to stay
1001350 mn tree?
1001351 mnbj throne
1001352 mnḏ cheek?
1001353 mnḏ chest
1001354 mnd tribute
1001355 mnfꜣ soldiers
1001356 mnḥ evil fate
1001357 mnḥ papyrus plant
1001358 mnḫ to be effective
1001359 mnḫ to chisel
1001360 mnḥ to rejoice
1001361 mnḥ to slaughter

1001362 mnẖ to string
1001363 mnḥ tribute
1001364 mnḥ wax
1001365 mnḥ youth
1001366 mjni̯ to land
1001367 mnj herdsman
1001368 mnj necklace
1001369 mnj shrine
1001370 mnkby [a pendant]
1001371 mnn mina
1001372 mnnn asphalt
1001373 mnpḥ animal skin?
1001374 mnḳ to complete
1001375 mnḳry [a pendant]
1001376 mnš cartouche
1001377 mnsꜣ to cause ejaculation
1001378 mnt diorite
1001379 mnṯ grain sieve?
1001380 mnty doorkeeper
1001381 mntꜣ grove
1001382 mnw pigeon
1001383 mnwr to purify
1001384 mnz leg
1001385 mnꜥ property
1001386 mnꜥ to nurse
1001387 mḳ to rest
1001388 mḳn washboard?
1001389 mḳr [a staff]
1001390 mḳr [a vessel]
1001391 mḳs to comminute?
1001392 mr [chest; box (for linen)]
1001393 mr board
1001394 mr bull
1001395 mr canal
1001396 mr desert
1001397 mr eye
1001398 mr milk jug
1001399 mr pyramid
1001400 mr throat
1001401 mr to be ill
1001402 mr to bind
1001403 mr to strand
1001404 mrḥ lance
1001405 mrḥ to decay
1001406 mrḥm the one who works with the salt
1001407 mri̯ to love
1001408 mrj groom
1001409 mrj speed
1001410 mrjjnt [a kind of a container]
1001411 mrkbt chariot
1001412 mrḳḏn [a kind of a metal tool]
1001413 mrḳḥt to catch?
1001414 mrr flame
1001415 mrš to be bright red
1001416 mrsw cider?
1001417 mrt chin
1001418 mrw cedar
1001420 ms levy
1001421 mš to cut open
1001422 ms to venerate
1001423 msbb to turn towards
1001424 mšd ford
1001425 mšd(d) comb
1001426 msḏi̯ to hate
1001427 msẖ [a vessel]
1001428 mjtr [kind of court person]
1001429 knḥ to darken
1001430 msi̯ to give birth
1001431 mškb [title of an official]
1001432 msktw bracelet
1001433 mskꜣ animal skin
1001434 msn to spin
1001435 mšp to endeavor?
1001436 msḳ a metalworking activity
1001437 mšr [a piece of furniture]
1001438 mšr evening
1001439 mšrr to attach
1001440 mšrw [plain]
1001441 mšš [a wood]
1001442 mss robe
1001443 msṯ offspring
1001444 msṯ to carry?
1001445 msṯḥ trap
1001446 mstj basket
1001447 mstr [an apron]
1001448 mstr chancellery
1001449 mstꜣ [a liquid]

1001450 msw supper
1001451 mšꜣ leather part of chariot
1001452 mšꜣb watering place
1001453 mšꜥ to march
1001454 mt to discuss
1001455 mtḏj lash
1001456 mtj to be correct
1001457 mtn knife?
1001458 mṯn to assign
1001459 mṯpr [a tool]
1001460 mtr flood
1001461 mtr midday
1001462 mtr to be present
1001463 mtw semen (sperm)
1001464 mṯꜣ to challenge
1001465 mtꜣ to skewer
1001466 mṯꜣi̯ to deliver
1001467 mw dancer
1001468 mw water
1001469 mwt to die
1001470 mwꜥd council
1001471 mz to bring
1001472 mzḥ crocodile
1001473 mʾw mother
1001474 mꜣ [a plant]
1001475 mꜣ antelope
1001476 mꜣ sickle
1001477 mꜣẖ corn sheaf
1001478 mꜣh door
1001479 mꜣẖ to burn?
1001480 mꜣḥ to clap
1001481 mꜣj lion
1001482 mꜣ doum palm
1001483 mꜣnw western mountain
1001484 mꜣr place of joy
1001485 mꜣr to oppress
1001486 mꜣš [a duck]
1001487 mꜣs knee
1001488 mꜣṯ granite
1001489 mꜣṯ to praise
1001490 mꜣṯr to mourn
1001491 mꜣwḏ to carry
1001492 mꜣwi̯ to be new
1001493 mꜣwr to write
1001494 mꜣwṯ to think
1001495 mꜣz to slaughter
1001496 mꜣꜣ to see
1001497 mꜣꜥ [a wood]
1001498 mꜣꜥ bank
1001499 mꜣꜥ to be just
1001500 mꜥ [a boat]
1001501 mꜥkꜣ to be brave
1001502 mꜥḳ undergarment?
1001503 mꜥr to be successful
1001505 n not
1001506 n red crown
1001507 n to
1001508 nb basket
1001509 nb every
1001510 nb lord
1001511 nbḏ evil
1001512 nbd to braid
1001513 nbi̯ to create
1001514 nbw gold
1001515 nbi̯ to swim
1001516 nbj flame
1001517 nbj reed
1001518 nbj spit
1001519 nh to protect
1001520 nbꜣ to plait
1001521 nḏ thread
1001522 nḏ to ask
1001523 nḏ to grind
1001525 ndb base
1001526 ndb to swallow
1001527 ndb wind
1001529 ndm throne
1001530 nḏm to be sweet
1001531 nḏr carpenter
1001532 nḏri̯ to follow
1001534 nḏs to be small
1001535 nḏꜣ water
1001536 nf breath
1001537 nf that, yonder
1001538 nfr [a jar]
1001539 nfr fire
1001540 nfr prow-rope?
1001541 nfr tiller

1001542 nfr to be perfect
1001543 nfr windpipe?
1001544 nfr to loosen
1001545 nfꜥ to remove
1001546 ngg to cackle
1001547 ngi̯ to break (sth.)
1001548 ngs to overflow
1001549 ngꜣ cow
1001550 ngꜣ to kill
1001551 nḥ guinea-fowl
1001552 nḫ = nḏ to protect
1001553 nh to shake
1001554 nḫ to skid
1001555 nḫb heifer?
1001556 nḫb lotus
1001557 nḥb = nḥm lotus bud
1001558 nḥb neck
1001559 nḫb to assign
1001560 nḫb to illuminate
1001561 nḥb to equip
1001562 nḥd [a medical ingredient]
1001563 nhḏ scribe's palette
1001564 nḥd to be strong
1001565 nhd to tremble
1001566 nḥḥ eternity
1001567 nḥḥ hippopotamus
1001568 nḥḥ olive oil
1001569 nḫi̯ to endure
1001570 nhi̯ to escape
1001571 nḫi̯ to request
1001572 nḥi̯ to pray for
1001573 nẖ = nš spittle
1001574 nhi̯* to register
1001575 nhj some
1001576 nḥm to protect
1001577 nḫn to be a child
1001578 nḥni̯ to rejoice
1001579 nḥp to create
1001580 nhp to mourn
1001581 nhp to revive
1001582 nḥr [a bread]
1001583 nḫr canal
1001584 nhr sacred well?
1001585 nhr terror
1001586 nhr to flee?
1001587 nḥš an medical ingredient
1001588 nḥs to sting
1001589 nḫt to be strong
1001590 nḥti̯ to trust
1001591 nhzi̯ to be awake
1001592 nḥꜣ [an illness]
1001593 nḥꜣ to be fierce
1001594 nhꜣ to exile
1001595 nḫꜣ to hang down
1001596 njk to punish
1001597 njs papyrus blossom?
1001598 njt to hesitate
1001599 njw ostrich
1001600 njw to be festive
1001601 njꜣ ibex
1001602 nkftr [an oil]
1001603 nki̯ to copulate
1001604 nkn hide
1001605 nkn to injure
1001606 nkp [a plant]
1001607 nm dwarf
1001608 nm fermentation?
1001609 nm produce of the fields (as offerings)
1001610 nm to rob
1001611 nm to sleep
1001612 nmḥ to be poor
1001613 nmḥf nephrite
1001614 nmi̯ to traverse
1001615 nmj to butcher
1001616 nmj to shout
1001617 nms [a jug]
1001618 nms a weight unit
1001619 nms to wrap (in bandages)
1001620 nmt to stride
1001621 nmt white quartzite
1001622 nmꜥ to be biased
1001623 nmꜥ to cover?
1001624 nn [food]
1001625 nn child
1001626 nn heaven
1001627 nn not
1001628 nn schist? [a stone for making

divine statues]
1001629 nn-wn is not
1001630 nni̯ to be tired
1001631 nni̯ to turn back
1001632 nni̯ to writhe
1001634 nnjb resin
1001635 nnšm spleen
1001636 np hem
1001637 npḏ to slaughter
1001638 npꜣ to make wet
1001639 npꜣ umbilical cord
1001640 nḳf to beat
1001641 nḳr to sieve
1001642 nḳꜥ to scratch
1001643 nr time
1001644 nrḥ to blaspheme
1001645 nri̯ to fear
1001646 nri̯ to protect
1001646 nri̯ to protect
1001647 ns [a plant]
1001648 nš grain
1001649 nš hairdressing
1001650 ns knife
1001651 nš to expel
1001652 ns to go (to)
1001653 nš to shudder
1001654 ns tongue
1001655 nsbi̯ to devour
1001656 nšḏ to comminute
1001657 nsi̯ to open
1001658 nsj [a demon?]
1001659 nsk to put in proper array
1001662 nšp gate
1001663 nšp to breath
1001664 nsḳ to sting
1001665 nsr to burn
1001666 nss to damage sth.
1001667 nssḳ hair loss?
1001668 nsw king
1001669 nsꜣ rowlock
1001700 nṯ to tie up
1001701 nṯ tongue
1001702 nṯb to parch
1001703 nṯḫ [a musical instrument]
1001704 nti̯ to be oppressed
1001705 nṯn dirt
1001706 ntn skin
1001707 nṯr [a beer]
1001708 nṯr [a plant]
1001709 nṯr god
1001710 ntš to besprinkle
1001711 ntꜣi̯ to hurry
1001712 nṯꜥ to divorce
1001713 ntꜥ to organize
1001714 nw [a jug]
1001715 nw [a substance]
1001716 nw [a vessel]
1001717 nw adze
1001718 nw hunter
1001719 nw light
1001720 nw sky
1001722 nw this
1001723 nw time
1001724 nw to clothe
1001725 nw water
1001726 nwḏ antilope
1001727 nwḏ inaccuracy
1001728 nwḏ to move
1001729 nwdi̯ to press out
1001730 nwḥ to bind
1001731 nwḫ to boil
1001732 nwḥ to drink
1001733 nwi̯ to call
1001734 nwi̯ to return
1001735 nwi̯ to take care of
1001736 nwn to dishevel
1001737 ꜣwr = nwr to tremble
1001738 nws crown?
1001739 nwṯ to tremble
1001740 nwz ingot
1001741 nwꜣ adze
1001742 nwꜣ to see
1001743 nzp knife
1001744 nzp to smooth out
1001745 nzr flame
1001746 n’ urban area
1001747 nꜣb = nꜣp tress
1001748 nꜣš cursed

1001749 nꜣw breath
1001750 nᶜ to announce? (death)
1001751 nᶜg door crack?
1001752 nᶜg to pulverize
1001753 nᶜẖ bundle
1001754 nᶜi̯ to travel
1001755 nᶜi̯ to twist
1001756 nᶜr catfish
1001757 nᶜrn unite of soldiers
1001758 nᶜš to be strong
1001759 p base
1001760 p heaven
1001761 pꜣḏ incense cone
1001762 pḏ to stretch
1001763 pḏi̯ to grind
1001764 pdr measure?
1001765 pds to flatten
1001766 pgg frog
1001767 pgꜣ box
1001768 pgꜣ to open
1001769 pḥ lion
1001770 pḥ sheaf
1001771 pḥ to reach
1001772 pḥḏ to split
1001773 phr [a pond]
1001774 pẖr to turn round
1001775 pḥrr to run
1001776 pẖꜣ [a cereal]
1001777 pẖꜣ to split
1001778 pj flea
1001779 pj to knead (clay)
1001780 pjpj keel?
1001781 pjs to tread in
1001782 pn mouse
1001783 png to divide
1001784 pnn to twist
1001785 pnḳ = pnḏ to scoop
1001786 pnt to squeeze
1001787 pnz = pnᶜ to turn round
1001789 pḳ flood
1001790 pḳr [a fragrant ingredient]
1001791 pr beans
1001792 pr house
1001793 prḏ to separate
1001794 prẖ to blossom
1001795 pri̯ to come forth
1001796 prš juniper berries?
1001797 prš to smash
1001798 prṯ to break?
1001799 prᶜ to be accessible?
1001800 ps measure?
1001801 psḏ nine
1001802 psḏ pelican
1001803 psḏ spine
1001804 psḏ to shine
1001805 psḏn new moon
1001806 psg to spit
1001807 psẖ mat?
1001808 psi̯ to cook
1001809 pšj comb
1001810 pšj pustule?
1001811 pšn to split
1001812 pšš to divide
1001813 pt to tread
1001814 ptḥ to create
1001815 ptẖ to prostrate
1001816 ptr bandage?
1001817 ptr to see
1001818 pw who?
1001819 pzẖ to be confused
1001820 pzḥ to bite
1001821 pzz to travail
1001822 pꜣ ? [a bread]
1001824 pꜣẖ [a plant]
1001825 pꜣẖ to scratch
1001826 pꜣẖd to be turned over
1001827 pꜣi̯ to fly
1001828 pꜣjs granules
1001829 pꜣqi̯ to be thin
1001830 pꜣs [scribe's water-pot]
1001831 pꜣṯṯ baboon
1001832 pꜣz to suffer
1001833 pᶜ [a food]
1001834 pᶜ area
1001835 pᶜ fire
1001836 pᶜ people
1001837 pᶜ to spit out
1001838 pᶜg to spit

1001839 pꜥn to be clever
1001840 pꜥꜣ = pꜥr quail
1001841 ḳb [a kind of a woodworking]
1001842 ḳb prevalence
1001843 ḳbb throat
1001844 ḳbb = ḳbḥ to be cool
1001845 ḳbḥ lower leg
1001847 ḳbꜥ to joke
1001848 ḳd [a tree]
1001849 ḳd kite
1001850 ḳḏ plaster
1001851 ḳḏ thornbush
1001852 ḳd to form
1001853 ḳḏ to run
1001854 ḳdb to rent
1001855 ḳdd to sleep
1001856 ḳdf to collect
1001857 ḳdi̯ to go around
1001858 ḳḏm to grasp
1001859 ḳdr incense
1001860 ḳfn to bake
1001861 ḳfn to bend down
1001862 ḳf# reputation
1001863 ḳḥ light
1001864 ḳḥ to break
1001865 ḳḥn cauldron?
1001866 ḳj shape
1001867 ḳjs to vomit
1001868 ḳm [timpani]
1001869 ḳm to be sad
1001870 ḳmd to be concerned
1001871 ḳmḥ [a bread]
1001872 ḳmḥ twig
1001873 ḳmꜣ rush
1001875 ḳmꜣ to mourn
1001874 ḳrs to bury
1001876 ḳmꜣ to throw
1001878 ḳn = ḏn [a plant]
1001879 mryn noble person
1001880 snrw = slw [a product of Nubia]
1001881 ḳn = ḏn to finish
1001882 ḳn to beat
1001883 ḳn to weave
1001884 ḳꜣb = ḳnb to fold
1001885 ḳnb to rage
1001886 ḳni̯ to be strong
1001888 ḳnj [a bird]
1001889 ḳnj carrying chair
1001890 ḳnj to embrace
1001891 ḳnj yellow
1001892 ḳḳ doum nuts
1001893 ḳḳ to eat
1001894 ḳr to hurry
1001895 ḳr to roll sth.
1001896 ḳrḏn ax
1001897 ḳrf to contract
1001898 ḳrḥ uterus?
1001899 ḳrm ashes
1001900 ḳrn foreskin
1001901 ḳrr [a boat]
1001902 ḳrr cavern
1001903 ḳrr cloud
1001904 ḳrr frog
1001905 ḳrr to burn
1001906 ḳrṯ [a young animal]
1001907 ḳrꜥ shield
1001908 ḳs bone
1001908 ḳs bone
1001909 ḳsn to be difficult
1001910 ḳwpr henna
1001911 ḳwr cargo loader
1001912 ḳwr gold worker?
1001913 ḳꜣb chest
1001915 ḳꜣd to cry
1001916 ḳꜣḥ to bind
1001917 ḳꜣḥ to plaster
1001918 ḳꜣi̯ to be high
1001919 ḳꜣj [a beverage]
1001920 ḳꜣr bolt
1001921 ḳꜣri̯ to stay near
1001922 ḳꜣs to bind
1001923 ḳꜣw flour
1001924 ḳꜣꜥ to spew
1001925 ḳꜥḥ to bend
1001926 rbš to arm oneself
1001927 rd [a grain]
1001928 rd foot
1001929 rd to grow

1001930 rḏi̯ to give
1001931 rdn laudanum
1001932 rḏw fluidity
1001933 rg compartment
1001934 rgi̯ to finish
1001935 rḥ comrade
1001936 rdm [a plant]
1001937 rḥ to burn
1001937 rḥ to burn
1001938 rḫ to know
1001939 rḫ weaver
1001941 rḥb [a vessel]
1001942 rhb embers
1001943 rhb [a caldron]
1001944 rhn to lean (on)
1001945 rhni̯ to wade
1001946 rhnj criosphinx
1001947 rhnj waste
1001948 rḥs [a baked good]
1001949 rḫs to slaughter
1001950 rḫt list
1001951 rḫt to wash (clothes)
1001952 rj coil?
1001953 rj heaven
1001954 rj ink
1001955 rj pus
1001956 rj side
1001957 rk [a plant]
1001958 rk time
1001959 rk to creep
1001960 rk to stop
1001961 rkḥ fire
1001962 rks harnessed team
1001963 rm fish
1001964 rm to chastize
1001965 rmi̯ to weep
1001966 rmn arm
1001967 rmṯ human being
1001968 rn name
1001969 rnn joy
1001970 rnn to bring up
1001971 rnpi̯ to be young
1001972 rns beads?
1001973 rpw image of a woman
1001974 rpw to rot
1001975 rḳ opponent
1001976 rr swine
1001977 rr time
1001978 rrm mandrake?
1001979 rš coryza
1001980 rs south
1001981 rs to watch
1001982 rsj entirely
1001983 ršj peak
1001984 ršu̯ to rejoice
1001985 rtḥ to bake
1001986 rtḥ to restrain
1001987 rw lion
1001988 rw straw
1001989 rwḏ bowstring
1001990 rwd stairway
1001991 rwḏ to be strong
1001992 rwḥ to trespass
1001993 rwhꜣ evening
1001994 rwi̯ to dance
1001995 rwi̯ to depart
1001996 rzf catch
1001997 rꜣ goose
1001998 rꜣ mouth
1001999 rꜥ sun
1002000 s [a goose]
1002001 š chair
1002002 s folded cloth
1002003 s seat
1002004 š workplace?
1002005 šb [a ritual object]
1002006 sb [edible part of cattle]
1002007 šb melon?
1002008 sb reed
1002009 šb rib
1002010 šbb mastic
1002011 šbb tube
1002012 šbd stick
1002013 sbḥ to cry out
1002014 sbḫ to enclose
1002015 šbi̯ = šbn to mix
1002016 šbj shebyu-necklace
1002017 sbj to rebel

1002018 sbn bandage
1002021 sbḳ leg
1002022 sbḳ to be wise
1002023 sbr branch
1002024 sbt [a plant]
1002025 sbtj wall
1002026 sbꜣ gate
1002027 sbꜣ star
1002028 sbꜣ to teach
1002029 sd column (of a text)
1002030 šḏ dough
1002031 sḏ fire
1002032 sḏ foster child
1002033 šd leather
1002034 sḏ loincloth
1002035 sd tail
1002036 sd to be clothed
1002037 sḏ to break
1002038 sdb [a garment]
1002039 sḏb evil
1002040 sdb to be softened
1002042 sḏḏ image
1002043 sdf [a unit of measure, for figs]
1002044 sḏḥ shin
1002045 šdi̯ to dig
1002046 šdi̯ to educate
1002047 šdi̯ to take
1002048 sdm eye-paint
1002049 sḏm to hear
1002050 sḏn to carry
1002051 sḏnf ibex
1002052 sḏr [a med. liquid]
1002053 šdr ravine
1002055 sdꜣ cattle egret
1002056 sḏꜣ to amuse (trans.)
1002057 sḏꜣ to seal
1002059 sḏꜣm hoe
1002060 sḏꜣm to speak boastfully
1002061 sf to burn?
1002062 sf yesterday
1002063 šfd to grasp
1002064 sfḫ seven
1002065 sfi̯ to mix
1002066 šfi̯ to respect
1002067 šfn to touch
1002068 šfn undergrowth
1002069 sfṯ [an oil]
1002070 šfu̯ to swell
1002071 sfy child
1002072 sfꜣ to neglect
1002073 šfꜥ to fight
1002074 sg sacking
1002075 sg to open a way
1002076 sgbyn [a body of water]
1002077 sgmḥ (cult) spear
1002078 šgr [a body of water]
1002079 šgr [a wooden box]
1002080 sgr fortress
1002081 sẖ [a beverage]
1002082 sẖ barley
1002083 sḫ gallbladder
1002085 sḥ royal dome
1002086 sẖb to slurp
1002087 sḥd star
1002088 sḫd to rebuke
1002089 sḫf to write down
1002090 sḫm [watery area in heaven]
1002091 sḫm sistrum
1002092 sẖm to be hasty
1002093 sḫm to be mighty
1002094 sḥm to crush
1002095 sḫmḫ to amuse
1002096 sḫn [a divine bark]
1002097 sḫnš to irritate
1002098 sḫp to laud
1002099 šḥq dust cloud
1002100 sẖr lumber
1002101 sḫr plan
1002102 sḫt [a stretch of water]
1002103 sḫt to form
1002104 sḫt to make ready
1002105 sḥw dirt
1002106 sḫwꜣ to deny
1002107 sḫꜣ [a piece of nautical equipment]
1002108 sḥꜣ donkey
1002109 sḫꜣ to remember
1002110 sẖꜣk to strain

1002111 sẖꜣꜣ hauling
1002112 sẖᶜ hare
1002113 sẖᶜ to gild
1002114 sj to limp?
1002115 sjd tray
1002116 sjf to insult
1002117 sjm haze
1002118 sjn clay
1002119 sjn to hurry
1002120 sjr [activity connected with the heart]
1002121 sjs six
1002122 sjtj trial
1002123 sjꜣ [a falcon]
1002124 sjꜣ fringed cloth
1002125 sjꜣ to recognize
1002126 sk [a toilette utensil]
1002127 sk complain
1002128 sk flour
1002129 sk lance
1002130 sk to be a star in the sky
1002131 sk to wipe
1002132 ski̯ to perish
1002133 skn to be greedy
1002134 škn watering place
1002135 skp to filter
1002136 škr [a mineral]
1002137 skꜣ to plough
1002138 šlf to be dishevelled
1002139 šlg snow
1002140 šlm peace
1002141 sm herbs
1002142 šm in law
1002143 šm omen
1002144 sm to respect
1002145 šm to cut off
1002146 smd [a star]
1002147 smd bead
1002148 smd edge
1002149 smd personnel
1002150 smd sistrum
1002151 smd slab
1002152 smḥ left
1002153 šmi̯ to go
1002155 smj soured milk
1002156 smj to report
1002157 smj whips
1002158 smk beam
1002159 šmm = *ẖmm to be hot
1002160 smn [a goose]
1002161 smn lion
1002162 smn mourner
1002163 šmr bow
1002164 smr friend
1002165 sms [a cut of beef]
1002166 šms [instrument of punishment]
1002167 sms mallet
1002168 sms to become old
1002169 šms to follow
1002170 smswn libation
1002171 smt to hear
1002172 smwn surely
1002173 šmꜣ flower
1002174 smꜣ stolist
1002175 smꜣ to slaughter
1002176 šmꜣ to wander
1002177 smᶜ stake
1002178 šmᶜ to be slender
1002179 šmᶜ to make music
1002180 šmᶜ Upper Egypt
1002181 sn [an offering]
1002182 šn bad
1002183 sn brother
1002184 sn flag pole
1002185 šn hundred
1002186 šn rope
1002187 sn serpentine
1002188 sn to smell
1002189 šn tree
1002190 snb [a boat]
1002191 šnb chest
1002192 snb heaven
1002193 snb to be healthy
1002194 šnb trumpet
1002195 šnḏ acacia
1002196 šnḏ kilt
1002197 snḏ to fear
1002198 snf previous year

1002199 snḥ to tie up
1002200 šni̯ to be round
1002201 šni̯ to fight
1002202 sni̯ to free
1002203 šni̯ to dispute
1002204 šni̯ to stink
1002205 šni̯ to suffer
1002206 šnj hair
1002207 snk to be dark
1002208 snm storm
1002210 šnp reed
1002211 snḳ to suckle
1002212 sns hairdresser?
1002214 šnṯ to oppose
1002215 snṯi̯ to establish
1002216 šntꜣy widow
1002217 šnꜥ [a small fish]
1002218 šnꜥ breast
1002219 šnꜥ to hold back
1002220 šnꜥ to value
1002221 snꜥḥ angler
1002222 sp lips
1002223 šp to be blind
1002224 šp to flow out
1002225 šp to throw?
1002226 spd to be sharp
1002227 spi̯ to bind together
1002228 špn [a beverage]
1002229 spr [a vegetable]
1002230 spr rib
1002231 spr sheet (of metal)
1002232 spr to reach
1002233 sps to build
1002234 sps to dance
1002235 špsi̯ to be dignified
1002236 špt to be angry
1002237 špt to blow up
1002238 spt to slaughter
1002239 spꜣ nome
1002240 sḳ fish trap
1002241 šḳ ring
1002242 sḳ to cut
1002243 šqb rhinoceros
1002244 sḳr to strike
1002245 šr [a body of water]
1002246 sr [a goose]
1002247 sr captive (noble) woman
1002248 sr nobleman
1002249 šr nose
1002250 sr thorn
1002251 sr to announce
1002252 sr to visit
1002253 srḏ to chisel
1002254 srf to be warm
1002255 srf to rest
1002256 šrgḥ feelings
1002257 šrḥ brook
1002258 srḥ stalks (of onions)
1002259 sri̯ to spread
1002260 srj standard
1002261 šrj to block
1002262 srḳ scorpion
1002263 srḳ to open
1002264 šrr to be small
1002265 šrr to shout
1002266 šrš to be quick
1002267 šs [green pigment]
1002268 šs alabaster
1002269 šš fool
1002270 šš nest
1002271 šs rope
1002272 šš to build
1002273 sšd shrine
1002274 sšd to flash
1002275 sšd to tie
1002277 sskꜣ [an ingredient]
1002278 sskꜣ temple (a body part)
1002279 šsm [something of the dead that is to be released]
1002280 ssm horse
1002281 šsm leather scroll?
1002282 šsm to be inflamed
1002283 šsm to be strong
1002284 sšm whetstone
1002285 sšn [a fish]
1002286 sšn to spin
1002287 sšp cucumber
1002288 sšp to be bright

1002289 sšr grain
1002290 sšr linen
1002291 šsr to kill
1002292 šsr to shine
1002293 sšr to stroke
1002294 šsr to utter
1002296 sšr work
1002297 sšš to level
1002298 sst ankle
1002299 sštꜣ [a fruit]
1002300 ssw to enclose
1002301 šsꜣ [an antilope]
1002302 šsꜣ nightfall
1002303 šsꜣ to be skillful
1002304 sšꜣ to beseech
1002305 sšꜣ to change sb.'s mind
1002306 sṯ [a bread mold]
1002307 sṯ [a jug]
1002308 sṯ [a material]
1002309 st [necklace]
1002310 st jar stand
1002311 sṯ jfragrance
1002312 št stroke oar?
1002313 št tax payer?
1002314 šṯ to decorate
1002315 šṯ turtle
1002316 štb to enclose
1002317 stẖ to open
1002318 sti̯ to catch sight of
1002319 sti̯ to knot
1002320 sṯi̯ to pluck (fowl)
1002321 sti̯ to send out
1002322 stj leg (esp. of Osiris)
1002323 štj rectum
1002324 štm to be hostile
1002325 stp [a cloth]
1002326 stp goose?
1002327 stp incident
1002328 stp to choose
1002329 sṯp to leap up
1002330 str to make jewelry
1002331 sṯr to wrap up
1002332 šlm delivery
1002333 sṯꜣ [a body of water]
1002334 sṯꜣ [a jar]
1002335 sṯꜣ offering
1002336 sṯꜣ secretion (med.)
1002337 štꜣ to be hidden
1002338 sṯꜣ to drag
1002339 šw [a jug]
1002340 sw [a plant]
1002341 sw 1/16 arure
1002342 sw a piece of meat
1002343 sw danger
1002344 šw feather
1002345 šw protection
1002346 šw side
1002347 šw sunlight
1002348 sw time
1002349 šwb [a jar]
1002350 šwb persea tree
1002351 swbb to draw back
1002352 swgꜣ to be foolish
1002353 swḥ egg
1002354 swḥ to enwrap
1002355 swḥ wind
1002356 swhi̯ to praise
1002357 swhꜣ to break
1002358 šwi̯ to be empty
1002360 šwi̯ to raise up
1002361 šwj trade
1002362 swn fortress
1002363 swn pond
1002364 swn to flatter
1002365 swn to recognize
1002366 swn to trade
1002367 swr [a chariot equipment]
1002368 swr bead
1002369 swt wind
1002370 swy [a crocodile]
1002371 ḳmy resin
1002372 šz bowl
1002373 šzm [a belt]
1002374 šzm malachite
1002375 šzp lashing (naut.)
1002376 šzp to receive
1002377 šꜣ [a fruit]
1002378 sꜣ back

1002379 šꜣ excrement (med.)
1002380 sꜣ gold
1002381 šꜣ marsh
1002382 šꜣ order
1002383 šꜣ shallow?
1002384 šꜣ talon
1002385 šꜣ upper chest
1002386 šꜣb [a boat]
1002387 sꜣb colorful
1002388 šꜣb food
1002389 šꜣd to dig
1002390 sꜣd to strangulate
1002391 sꜣḥ to reach
1002392 sꜣḫm a bat
1002393 sꜣi̯ to be sated
1002394 šꜣj pig
1002395 sꜣm unkempt hair
1002396 šꜣm dirty item?
1002397 sꜣp lotus
1002398 šꜣḳ [a container]
1002399 sꜣḳ to join
1002400 šꜣr [an eye affliction]
1002401 sꜣr to sieve
1002402 šꜣš to avoid
1002403 šꜣs to travel
1002404 sꜣṯ cargo boat
1002405 sꜣt to defile
1002406 sꜣt to dislocate
1002407 sꜣw niche?
1002408 šꜣw to cauterize
1002409 sꜣꜣ = sꜣr to be wise
1002410 šꜣꜥ storeroom
1002411 šꜣꜥ to begin
1002412 šꜣꜥzḫ [a plant]
1002413 šꜥ to cut off
1002414 sꜥ to damage?
1002415 sꜥb to cut
1002416 sꜥḥ to dignify
1002417 šꜥr gate
1002418 sꜥr scrub country
1002419 šꜥr to promise
1002420 sꜥr wool
1002421 šꜥy sand
1002422 ṯ [timber]
1002423 ṯ book
1002424 ṯ crew
1002425 tꜣ bread
1002426 ṯb cage
1002427 ṯb foot sole
1002428 tb to recompense
1002429 tb to take up?
1002430 tbn head
1002431 ṯbn to be quick
1002432 tbn to drum
1002433 tbs heel
1002434 tbs to stab
1002435 tf to spit out
1002436 tfi̯ to repulse
1002437 tfn dent (in metal objects)
1002438 tfn orphan
1002439 tfnn to rejoice
1002440 ṯfrr lapis lazuli
1002441 ṯftn to rush
1002442 tfꜣ saw
1002443 tḫ fat
1002444 tḫ lead
1002445 tḫ to confuse
1002446 ṯḥ to rejoice
1002447 thb reduce (liquid)
1002448 ṯhb to jump
1002449 tḫb to moisten
1002450 tḫb turtle
1002451 tḫbs [a basket]
1002452 tḫi̯ to be drunk
1002453 thi̯ to obstruct
1002454 thm to cook
1002455 thm to perforate
1002456 tḫn ibis
1002457 ṯḥn to be bright
1002458 tḫn to damage
1002459 ṯḥn to encounter
1002460 tḫn to protect
1002461 tḫn towering cultic structure
1002462 ṯḥr injury
1002463 ṯḥs [a metal]
1002464 tḫs to slaughter
1002465 tḥs to squash
1002466 ṯḥs to stretch

1002467 tḥwꜣ peas
1002468 ṯhꜣ lame
1002469 tj [a chapel]
1002470 tj [a measure of incense]
1002471 tj [a mineral]
1002472 tj [an amulet]
1002473 tj fraction
1002474 tj image
1002475 ṯj thyme
1002476 tj to pound
1002477 ṯjf to flee
1002478 ṯjs [preparing? dough for beer making]
1002479 tjs to fix
1002480 tjꜣ to shout
1002481 tk to attack
1002482 tk to be near
1002483 ṯkr tower gate
1002484 tkꜣ to burn
1002485 tl mound
1002486 ṯm [container (measure for cake)]
1002487 tm not to be
1002488 tm sledge
1002489 ṯm to be ashamed
1002490 ṯmḥ [a red ochre]
1002491 ṯmḥ to turn away?
1002492 tmm [a wooden chest]
1002493 ṯms to be red
1002494 ṯms to bury
1002495 tmt to powder (med.)
1002496 tmz to turn (the face to someone)
1002497 tmꜣ mat
1002498 tmꜣ mother
1002499 ṯmꜣ to be strong
1002500 tmꜣ troop
1002501 ṯn guardian
1002502 tnbẖ to be confused
1002503 ṯnf [a vessel]
1002504 ṯnf to drink and dance
1002505 ṯnf to measure
1002506 ṯnḥ to observe
1002507 ṯnḥr [a falcon]
1002508 ṯni̯ to rise
1002509 ṯnj to be weak
1002510 tnj to grow old
1002511 ṯnm cauldron
1002512 tnm to go astray
1002514 ṯl to be strong
1002515 ṯlk [a bier]
1002516 ṯnt [sacred cattle (of Hathor)]
1002517 ṯnṯꜣ dais
1002518 ṯnw to count
1002519 tp [a piece of wood?]
1002520 tp head
1002521 ṯpg barracks
1002522 ṯpḥ cave
1002523 ṯpḥ cave
1002524 tpj [an ox]
1002525 tpn dagger
1002526 ṯpn* to be glad
1002527 tpnn cumin
1002528 ṯpr scribe
1002529 tpr to breathe
1002530 ṯprṯ (bronze-clad Hittite) chariot
1002531 tpꜣ [a fruit]
1002532 tpꜣ [a part of a skull]
1002533 tpꜣ [an ingredient]
1002534 tḳr huge
1002535 ṯr fine flour
1002536 ṯr red
1002537 tr time
1002538 ṯr willow
1002539 ṯrf [a dance]
1002540 trḫ* strainer
1002541 trj door
1002542 trj impurity
1002543 trj veneration
1002544 ṯrm to wink
1002545 ṯrp [a goose]
1002546 trr oven
1002547 trr to run
1002548 ṯrrj siege mound
1002549 ṯrw* to delight in sth.
1002550 ṯryn body armor
1002551 ṯrꜥ [a field]
1002552 trꜥ worm
1002553 tš to crush
1002554 ṯs to sit

1002555 tši̯ to go away
1002556 tšmm [a crocodile]
1002557 tšꜣ to squash
1002558 t̠t̠ sparrow
1002559 t̠t to dissolve
1002560 t̠tf to overflow
1002561 t̠w share
1002562 t̠wfj papyrus plant
1002563 twhr (foreign, Asiatic) warrior
1002564 t̠wj crown?
1002565 t̠wn = t̠wꜣ to attack
1002566 t̠wn to reward
1002567 twr to purify
1002568 twr to stay away
1002569 twrj [a staff]
1002570 twt to be like
1002572 twꜣ [an oil]
1002573 twꜣ evil
1002574 twꜣ to elevate
1002575 ty steppe
1002576 kbs basket
1002577 t̠zm hound
1002578 t̠zm to build
1002579 t̠ꜣ ball
1002580 tꜣ door
1002581 tꜣ earth
1002582 t̠ꜣ male
1002583 t̠ꜣ nestling
1002584 tꜣ to be hot
1002585 t̠ꜣ* vizier
1002586 t̠ꜣbb corn ear
1002587 tꜣf pottery kiln
1002588 tꜣḥ to sink
1002589 t̠ꜣi̯ to take
1002589 t̠ꜣi̯ to take
1002590 tꜣj [a fabric]
1002591 tꜣj to resist
1002592 tꜣm [a worm?]
1002593 t̠ꜣm to cloak
1002594 t̠ꜣms to eat
1002595 t̠ꜣpr to swell
1002596 t̠ꜣr to secure
1002597 tꜣš to demarcate
1002598 t̠ꜣw wind
1002599 t̠ꜣz to command
1002600 t̠ꜣz to join
1002601 t̠ꜣz tooth
1002602 w district
1002603 wbd to burn
1002604 wbg to be green
1002605 wbẖ = wbg to shine
1002606 wbn to rise up
1002607 wbn wound
1002609 wbs = bzi̯ to come out
1002610 wbꜣ to open
1002611 wd̠ to assign
1002612 wd̠b to turn around
1002613 wdd gall bladder
1002614 wdd to cook
1002615 wdfi̯ to delay
1002616 wd̠ḥ fruit
1002617 wdḥ to pour
1002618 wd̠ḥ to wean
1002619 wdi̯ to place
1002620 wd̠i̯ to travel
1002621 wd̠j perch
1002622 wdn [a sacred baboon]
1002623 wdn to be heavy
1002624 wd̠n width
1002625 wd̠nj [oboe?]
1002626 wdp attendant
1002627 wd̠ꜣ to be intact
1002628 wd̠ꜣ to go
1002629 wd̠ꜥ to separate
1002630 wfꜣ lung
1002631 wfꜣ to support
1002632 wg plank
1002633 wgb to shout
1002634 wgg to be weak
1002635 wgi̯ to chew
1002636 wgm to grind
1002637 wgp to crush
1002638 wgs to cut open
1002639 wgꜣ flood
1002640 wḥ kin
1002641 wḥ to bark
1002642 wẖ to be dark
1002643 whb to pierce

1002644 wḫd to suffer
1002645 wḥf to burn
1002646 whi̯ to fail
1002647 whj diarrhoea
1002648 wḥm bull's leg
1002649 whm to burn
1002650 wḥm to repeat
1002651 whn to fall apart
1002652 whn* to be fragile
1002654 wḫr to process
1002655 whs to be casual
1002656 wḥs to cut
1002657 wḥꜣ [a skin disease]
1002658 wḥꜣ cauldron
1002659 wḫꜣ claw?
1002660 wḫꜣ column
1002661 wḫꜣ to be foolish
1002662 wḥꜣ to cut down
1002663 wḫꜣ to empty
1002664 wḫꜣ to hang down
1002665 wḫꜣ to seek
1002666 wḫꜣ to smoothen?
1002667 wḥꜥ scorpion
1002668 wḥꜥ to fish and fowl
1002669 wḥꜥ to solve
1002670 wj mummy case
1002671 wjꜣ = wjn weak
1002672 wjꜣ boat
1002674 wmt to be thick
1002675 wn enclosure?
1002676 wn error
1002677 wn hare
1002678 wn to be bald
1002679 wn to open
1002680 wn to threaten
1002681 wnb blossom
1002682 wnḏ cavity
1002683 wnḏ herd
1002684 wnḏ quantity
1002685 wnf to resolve
1002686 wnḫ to clothe
1002687 wnḫ to loosen
1002688 wni̯ to bind
1002689 wni̯ to hurry
1002690 wnj light
1002691 wnm diadem
1002692 wnm to eat
1002693 wnn to exist
1002694 wnp to stab
1002695 wnpj to harvest (flax)?
1002696 wnš grape
1002697 wnš jackal
1002698 wnw hour
1002699 wp horn
1002700 wp quantity?
1002701 wpi̯ to open
1002702 wpr side lock
1002703 wps to burn up
1002704 wpš to illuminate
1002705 wr [a sacred body of water?]
1002706 wr swallow
1002707 wrḏ to be weary
1002708 wrh to dance
1002709 wrḥ to smear
1002709 wrḥ to smear
1002710 wrm to mount up
1002711 wrm* to wind
1002712 wrr to be great
1002713 wrrj wagon
1002714 wrs headrest
1002715 wršu̯ to be awake
1002716 ws height (math.)
1002717 ws to be empty
1002718 wš to destroy
1002719 wš to push
1002720 wšb small bead?
1002721 wšb to feed
1002722 wšd to question
1002723 wsḫ to be broad
1002724 wsḥ to burn
1002726 wši̯ to reduce
1002727 wsi̯ to saw
1002728 wšm awn
1002729 wšm to mix
1002730 wšm to slaughter
1002731 wsn to procreate
1002732 wšn to sacrifice
1002733 wsr oar

1002734 wsr to be strong
1002735 wšr to dry
1002736 wstn [a body of water?]
1002737 wstj official writings
1002738 wsṯn to stride unhindered
1002739 wšꜣ darkness
1002740 wšꜣ slander
1002742 wšꜣ to pour out
1002743 wšꜥ to chew
1002744 wt to bandage
1002745 wt to move around
1002746 wtḫ to flee
1002747 wti̯ to be old
1002748 wtmt to tumble
1002749 wtn to pierce
1002750 wtṯ to create
1002751 wṯz = ṯzi̯ to lift up
1002752 ww to make music
1002753 wzf to be idle
1002754 wzš to urinate
1002755 wzṯ to decay
1002756 wꜣ [a plant]
1002757 wꜣ cord
1002758 wꜣ to plan
1002760 wꜣb root
1002761 wꜣḏ to be green
1002762 wꜣg to be joyful loudly
1002763 wꜣḥ to lay down
1002764 wꜣḫi̯ to flood
1002765 wꜣi̯ to move to
1002766 wꜣi̯ to parch
1002767 wꜣp sheep
1002768 wꜣr reed
1002769 wꜣr to dance (or similar)
1002770 wꜣr to tie
1002771 wꜣš to be powerful
1002772 wꜣs to rule
1002773 wꜣsi̯ to be ruined
1002774 wꜥ goat
1002775 wꜥ one
1002776 wꜥ to kill
1002777 wꜥb to be pure
1002778 wꜥf to bend down
1002779 wꜥḥ chufa
1002780 wꜥn juniper
1002781 wꜥr leg
1002782 wꜥr partition
1002783 wꜥꜣ torch
1002784 ybr stream
1002785 ydꜥ skilled
1002786 ym sea
1002787 z door bolt
1002788 z person
1002789 zb board?
1002790 zb heir
1002791 zbi̯ to go
1002792 zbn [a fish]
1002793 zbn to slip
1002794 zbṯ to laugh
1002795 zbꜣ flute
1002796 zf to be mild
1002797 zf = zfṯ to slaughter
1002798 zḥ [a bird]
1002799 zḥ hall
1002800 zḫ to hurry
1002801 zḥ to trample
1002802 zẖi̯ to be deaf
1002803 zḫi̯ to strike
1002804 zḫni̯ to encompass
1002805 zḫz to tear
1002806 zẖꜣ = zš to write
1002807 zj to go
1002808 zjn to rub
1002809 zk to dig
1002810 zkr to travel
1002811 zmn natron
1002812 zmy desert
1002813 zmzr [a gate]
1002814 zmꜣ to unite
1002815 znb to overthrow
1002816 znbꜣ to get out of control
1002817 znf blood
1002818 znḥm locust
1002819 zni̯ to pass
1002820 znš = zꜣš = zš to open
1002821 znṯ to be rebellious
1002822 zp matter
1002823 zp to tousle

1002824 zpi̯ to remain
1002825 zpꜣ to wriggle
1002826 zr pellet
1002827 zr ram
1002828 zrm [a beer]
1002829 zrt knife
1002830 zš [a rope]
1002831 zš to pass
1002832 zši̯ to tear out
1002833 zšj to nest
1002834 zšn lotus
1002835 zšp to polish
1002836 zšš sistrum
1002837 zšzš [a rope]
1002838 zw wheat
1002839 zwn [a vessel]
1002840 zwn arrow
1002841 zwnu̯ to suffer
1002842 zwr to drink
1002843 zwrw [a bird]
1002844 zwš to lump
1002845 zwṯ to roll
1002846 zwꜣ to chop
1002847 zz to burn
1002848 zzḥ to destroy
1002849 zzḥꜣ vessel
1002850 zzi̯ to punish
1002851 zꜣ duck
1002852 zꜣ eighth of an aroura
1002853 zꜣ son
1002854 zꜣb jackal
1002855 zꜣg [a mythological animal]
1002856 zꜣi̯ to linger
1002857 zꜣr [a plant]
1002858 zꜣr bond
1002859 sꜣḫ to ram
1002860 zꜣt incense
1002861 zꜣṯ to make libation
1002862 zꜣu̯ to protect
1002863 zꜣw to break
1002864 ꜣ moment
1002865 ꜣ vulture
1002866 ꜣb family
1002867 ꜣb to cease to do
1002868 ꜣb to mark
1002869 ꜣbd month
1002870 ꜣbḥ to mix
1002871 ꜣbi̯ to wish
1002872 ꜣbj leopard
1002873 ꜣbw [medical substance]
1002874 ꜣbw elephant
1002875 ꜣd to be aggressive
1002876 ꜣd to decay
1002877 ꜣd to smear
1002878 ꜣf to hail
1002879 ꜣfi̯ to eat (greedily)
1002880 ꜣfr to boil
1002881 ꜣg to plant
1002882 ꜣgb to shudder?
1002883 ꜣgbi̯ to flood
1002884 ꜣḥ [a mash]
1002885 ꜣḫ beneficial
1002886 ꜣḫ bones
1002887 ꜣḥ field
1002888 ꜣḫ flame
1002889 ꜣḫ ibis
1002890 ꜣh pain
1002891 ꜣḫb to swallow
1002892 ꜣḫi̯ to be well watered
1002893 ꜣḫꜥ to scratch
1002895 ꜣj bandage
1002896 ꜣjs brain
1002897 ꜣk to bend
1002898 ꜣm to burn up
1002899 ꜣmj to mix
1002900 ꜣmm to seize
1002901 ꜣms [a scepter]
1002902 ꜣmꜥ bearing (techn.)
1002903 ꜣpd bird
1002904 ꜣḳ to perish
1002905 ꜣḳḥ* to strengthen?
1002906 ꜣr need
1002907 ꜣr to supersede
1002908 ꜣs to hurry
1002909 ꜣs vulture
1002910 ꜣšr to roast
1002911 ꜣt to enter?
1002912 ꜣtf crown

1002913 ꜣtf incense
1002914 ꜣṯi̯ to take care
1002915 ꜣtj [a part of the solar bark]
1002916 ꜣṯp to load
1002917 ꜣwi̯ to be long
1002918 ꜣyt to be pale
1002920 ꜣzb to burn
1002921 ꜣzẖ to harvest
1002922 ꜣꜣ ruin?
1002923 ꜣꜥb damage
1002924 ꜣꜥw bag
1002925 ꜣꜥꜥ = nꜥꜥ to be smooth
1002926 ꜣꜥꜥ to blame
1002927 ꜥ item
1002928 ꜥb = db to push
1002930 ꜥb lettuce
1002931 ꜥb meal
1002932 ꜥb to purify
1002934 ꜥbb to smooth
1002935 ꜥbd servant
1002936 ꜥbḥ to fill a jug
1002937 ꜥbẖn frog
1002938 ꜥbš [a wine jug]
1002939 ꜥbš to drown
1002940 ꜥbꜣ a bird
1002941 ꜥbꜣ rope
1002942 ꜥbꜣ to interact
1002943 ꜥbꜣ to shine
1002944 ꜥbꜥ to boast
1002945 ꜥḏ [part of a building (architrave?)]
1002946 ꜥḏ mongoose
1002947 ꜥḏ spin
1002948 ꜥḏ to be whole
1002949 ꜥḏ to burn
1002950 ꜥḏ to perceive (with ear, nose)
1002951 ꜥḏ to rejoice
1002952 ꜥḏ to slaughter
1002953 ꜥḏd youth
1002954 ꜥḏi̯ to sift
1002955 ꜥḏn [a bracelet]
1002956 ꜥdn wheat?
1002957 ꜥḏr [a part of a chariot]
1002958 ꜥḏr helper
1002959 ꜥdt conspiracy?
1002960 ꜥḏꜣ to be guilty
1002961 ꜥf to be greedy
1002962 ꜥfḏ chest
1002963 ꜥfd nail
1002964 ꜥff to fly
1002965 ꜥff to hum
1002966 ꜥfn = ꜥfꜣ to envelop
1002967 ꜥft collection of spells
1002968 ꜥfꜣ to demolish
1002969 ꜥgn ringstand
1002970 ꜥgrt wagon (drawn by oxen)
1002971 ꜥgsw belt
1002972 ꜥgꜣ [an ointment]
1002973 ꜥgꜣ claw
1002974 ꜥgꜣ to capsize
1002975 ꜥḥ cultivated land
1002976 ꜥḥ palace
1002977 ꜥḥ to catch
1002978 ꜥḥ to wipe away
1002979 ꜥẖi̯ to burn
1002980 ꜥẖi̯ to fly
1002981 ꜥẖi̯ to raise up
1002982 ꜥẖm leaf
1002983 ꜥẖm to extinguish
1002984 ꜥẖm to fly
1002985 ꜥẖm to inspire fear
1002986 ꜥẖm wick?
1002987 ꜥẖn to close (the eyes)
1002988 ꜥḥꜣ to fight
1002989 ꜥḥꜥ boat
1002990 ꜥḥꜥ to stand
1002991 ꜥj to jubilate
1002992 ꜥjn limestone
1002993 ꜥk end of a rod/stick
1002994 ꜥm to swallow
1002995 ꜥmd to be weak
1002996 ꜥmḏ to turn away
1002997 ꜥmdy supports (chariot parts)
1002998 ꜥmj to smear
1002999 ꜥmnt to box
1003000 ꜥmḳ to couple
1003001 ꜥmr baker
1003002 ꜥmt clouds

1003003 ʿmw [a fruit]
1003004 ʿmꜣ [a part of a body]
1003005 ʿmꜣ [a plant]
1003006 ʿmꜣ to turn sour
1003007 ʿmʿ sexually immature?
1003008 ʿmʿꜣ to throw
1003009 ʿmʿʿ kernel
1003010 ʿn [eye, as a character in writing]
1003011 ʿn ring
1003012 ʿn talon
1003013 ʿn writing board
1003014 ʿnb alfa grass
1003015 ʿnb to close
1003016 ʿnḏ [an unguent]
1003017 ʿnḏ to be diminished
1003018 ʿnḫ alabaster
1003019 ʿnḫ ankh-sign
1003020 ʿnḫ to bind
1003021 ʿnḫ goat
1003022 ʿnḫ to live
1003023 ʿnḥb [a bird]
1003024 ʿni̯ to be good
1003025 ʿnn singing
1003026 ʿnn to return
1003027 ʿnnw [a tree]
1003028 ʿnḳ to flow
1003029 ʿnt myrrh
1003030 ʿpi̯ to fly
1003031 ʿpnn water newt
1003032 ʿpr to provide
1003033 ʿḳ cormorant
1003034 ʿḳ to enter
1003035 ʿḳꜣ [a transport ship]
1003036 ʿḳꜣ to be accurate
1003037 ʿr [a tree]
1003038 ʿr goat
1003039 ʿr hind part
1003040 ʿr jaw
1003041 ʿr stone
1003042 ʿrḏ to terrify (the enemy)
1003043 ʿrf to wrap
1003044 ʿrḳ to complete
1003047 ʿrḳ to tie on
1003048 ʿrḳwr silver
1003049 ʿrš to sneeze
1003050 ʿršn lentils
1003051 ʿrt [a body of water in Upper Egypt]
1003052 ʿš [a beer jug]
1003053 ʿš [a food]
1003054 ʿš coniferous wood
1003055 ʿš throat
1003056 ʿš = jꜣš to summon
1003057 ʿši̯ to moan
1003058 ʿšḳ to oppress
1003059 ʿšꜣ lizard
1003060 ʿšꜣ to be numerous
1003061 ʿṯḫ to press out
1003062 ʿw crane
1003063 ʿw herd
1003064 ʿwg to be hot
1003065 ʿwꜣi̯ = own to rob
1003066 ʿwn to wail
1003067 ʿwꜣ to rot
1003069 ʿyn well
1003070 ʿꜣ column
1003071 ʿꜣ door
1003072 ʿꜣ linen
1003073 ʿꜣb to please
1003074 ʿꜣb washing jug
1003075 ʿꜣḏ edge
1003076 ʿꜣḏ to be pale
1003077 ʿꜣg to beat
1003078 ʿꜣi̯ to be great
1003079 ʿꜣm throw stick
1003081 ʿꜣʿ to squirt
1003082 ʿʿj to be fearful
1003083 ʿʿnj to enclose
1003084 ʿʿw to be agitated
1003085 ʿʿw to sleep
1003086 ḫꜣt to become ecstatic
1003089 sʿb to cut
1003901 mk festival
1003902 ṯḫr [part of chariot]

Root index – alphabetical

ꜣ	
ꜣ moment	1002864
ꜣ vulture	1002865
ꜣ not	1001022
ꜣꜣ ruin?	1002922
ꜣj bandage	1002895
ꜣjs brain	1002896
ꜣyt to be pale	1002918
ꜣꜥw bag	1002924
ꜣꜥꜥ = nꜥꜥ to be smooth	1002925
ꜣꜥꜥ to blame	1002926
ꜣꜥb damage	1002923
ꜣwi̯ to be long	1002917
ꜣwr = nwr to tremble	1001737
ꜣb family	1002866
ꜣb to cease to do	1002867
ꜣb to mark	1002868
ꜣbi̯ to wish	1002871
ꜣbj leopard	1002872
ꜣbw [medical substance]	1002873
ꜣbw elephant	1002874
ꜣbḥ to mix	1002870
ꜣbd month	1002869
ꜣpd bird	1002903
ꜣf to hail	1002878
ꜣfi̯ to eat (greedily)	1002879
ꜣfr to boil	1002880
ꜣm to burn up	1002898
ꜣmj to mix	1002899
ꜣmꜥ bearing (techn.)	1002902
ꜣmm to seize	1002900
ꜣms [a scepter]	1002901
ꜣr need	1002906
ꜣr to supersede	1002907
ꜣh pain	1002890
ꜣhb to be weak	1002891
ꜣḥ [a mash]	1002884
ꜣḥ field	1002887
ꜣḫ beneficial	1002885
ꜣḫ bones	1002886
ꜣḫ flame	1002888
ꜣḫ ibis	1002889
ꜣḫi̯ to be well watered	1002892
ꜣẖꜥ to scratch	1002893
ꜣẖb to swallow	1002919
ꜣz = ꜣs vulture	1002909
ꜣzb to burn	1002920
ꜣzḫ to harvest	1002921
ꜣs to hurry	1002908
ꜣšr to roast	1002910
ꜣḳ to perish	1002904
ꜣḳḥ* to strengthen?	1002905
ꜣk to bend	1002897
ꜣg to plant	1002881
ꜣgb to shudder?	1002882
ꜣgbi̯ to flood	1002883
ꜣt to enter?	1002911
ꜣtj [a part of the solar bark]	1002915
ꜣtf crown	1002912
ꜣtf incense	1002913
ꜣṯi̯ to take care	1002914
ꜣṯp to load	1002916
ꜣd to be aggressive	1002875
ꜣd to decay	1002876
ꜣd to smear	1002877
j	
j to say	1000934
jꜣ [a plant]	1001172
jꜣꜣ twig	1001198
jꜣꜣ = jꜣr = ꜥr rush	1001192
jꜣi̯ to rise	1001184
jꜣj [braid]	1001185
jꜣw to be old	1001197
jꜣb left	1001173
jꜣbys foundation	1001174
jꜣf claw	1001179
jꜣm to be pleasant	1001188
jꜣm to bind	1001189
jꜣr to mourn	1001193
jꜣrr vine	1001194
jꜣḫi̯ to sweep (the harvest)	1001182
jꜣs to be bald	1001195
jꜣḳ to dominate	1001190

jꜣḳ vegetables	1001191
jꜣk old	1001186
jꜣkb to mourn	1001187
jꜣṯ to injure	1001196
jꜣd cord	1001175
jꜣd dew	1001176
jꜣd to climb	1001177
jꜣd to suffer	1001178
jjr horned animal	1000993
jꜥ pearl necklace	1001202
jꜥꜣ donkey	1001210
jꜥꜣto cover	1001211
jꜥꜣ to speak a foreign language	1001212
jꜥi̯ to wash	1001206
jꜥb to unite	1001203
jꜥf to squeeze	1001204
jꜥn grief	1001207
jꜥnꜥ baboon	1001208
jꜥḥ moon	1001205
jꜥr to rise	1001209
jw not to be	1001127
jw dog	1001129
jw small livestock?	1001130
jw to bewail	1001132
jwꜣ cattle	1001153
jwꜣ help	1001154
jwꜣ throat	1001155
jwꜣ to take away	1001156
jwi̯ to come	1001138
jwj building	1001140
jwy to irrigate	1001152
jwꜥ haunch	1001157
jwꜥ to inherit	1001158
jwꜥ troops	1001159
jwf meat	1001134
jwms untruth	1001141
jwn bow	1001142
jwn colour	1001143
jwn support	1001144
jwn to unite	1001145
jwr [roast meat]	1001146
jwr beans	1001147
jwr to become pregnant	1001148
jwh to carry	1001135
jwḥ to destroy	1001136
jwḥ to moisten	1001137
jws scales	1001149
jwsw truly	1001151
jwšš dough	1001150
jb [a sistrum]	1000935
jb [a tree]	1000936
jb = jbr unguent, oil	1000937
jb chapel	1000938
jb goat	1000939
jb heart	1000940
jb purification booth	1000941
jbꜣ maned sheep	1000952
jbꜣ to dance	1000953
jbi̯ to be thirsty	1000945
jbn alum	1000946
jbr stallion	1000947
jbh gneiss	1000942
jbḥ to be flooded	1000943
jbḥ tooth	1000944
jbzꜣ [an oil plant]	1000951
jbs headdress	1000948
jbšt [a bread]	1000949
jbṯ trap	1000950
jp hippopotamus	1001064
jp inner area	1001065
jp to count	1001066
jpꜣ red dye (madder)	1001071
jpḥ pig	1001069
jpt bread	1001070
jpd [unit of measure for baked goods]	1001067
jpd furniture	1001068
jf [bone marrow]	1000969
jfn to go back	1000971
jfd to run	1000970
jm clay	1000999
jm in	1001000
jm pupil (eye)	1001001
jm pus (med.)	1001002
jm rib	1001003
jm strong	1001005
jm there	1001006

jm to wail	1001007
jmꜣẖ backbone	1001017
jmꜣẖ well supplied	1001018
jmi̯ not to be	1001009
jmi̯ to give	1001010
jmw boat	1001016
jmn right	1001012
jmn to hide	1001013
jmr to be deaf	1001014
jmḥ to suck	1001008
jms dill	1001015
jmk to putrefy	1001011
jn [a garment]	1001019
jn by (of agent)	1001020
jn pain	1001023
jn refrain	1001024
jn tilapia	1001025
jn today?	1001026
jn valley	1001027
jni̯ to fetch	1001038
jnj [a plant]	1001039
jnj to delay	1001040
jnꜥ chin	1001063
jnb [a plant]	1001028
jnb ax	1001029
jnb lynx	1001030
jnb wall	1001031
jnbꜣ to be mute	1001032
jnp royal child	1001047
jnp to lie down	1001048
jnf discharge	1001034
jnm [wine jug?]	1001042
jnm skin	1001043
jnn fishing net	1001044
jnn to cut	1001045
jnnk thyme?	1001046
jnhmn pomegranate	1001036
jnr stone	1001051
jnrm oak	1001052
jnḥ to surround	1001035
jnḥꜣs husks (of lotus)	1001037
jns lower leg	1001053
jns red (blood)	1001054
jnḳ to encompass	1001049
jnḳfḳf [a wooden part of a chariot]	1001050
jnk I	1001041
jntj to repel	1001056
jnd to be sad	1001033
jr eye	1001075
jr lion	1001076
jr milk cow	1001077
jri̯ to do	1001081
jrj ram	1001082
jrjr guide	1001083
jrp wine	1001085
jrẖ [a semi-precious stone]	1001080
jrḳbs rock crystal	1001086
jrkt (tree) trunk	1001084
jrt a vegetal purple dye	1001087
jrt distress	1001088
jrṯ milk	1001089
jrdb αρτάβη	1001079
jh cow	1000975
jh stable	1000979
jhj to wail	1000984
jhy joy	1000991
jhm [a resin?]	1000985
jhm sigh	1000986
jhm to walk slowly	1000987
jhmz rope	1000988
jhr tent	1000990
jḥ crocodile	1000976
jḥ [a tree]	1000973
jḥ ox	1000978
jḥ thigh	1000980
jḥ to weep?	1000981
jḥy to make music	1000992
jẖ item	1000977
jẖ to worship	1000982
jẖr form	1000989
jẖẖ darkness	1000983
jz old	1001160
jz reed	1001161
jz windpipe?	1001163
jz = jo tomb	1001162
jzj cord?	1001165
jzj to be light (of weight)	1001166

jzp to hew 1001169
jzf disorder 1001164
jzn bolt 1001168
jzr tamarisk 1001170
jzkn zenith? 1001167
jzzj to catch 1001171
js like 1001090
js to call 1001092
jswt long plank 1001109
jsbw hut? 1001096
jsbr juniper? 1001093
jsbr whip 1001094
jsbt seat 1001095
jsp to starve 1001101
jspt quiver (for arrows) 1001102
jsr rushes 1001104
jsḳ to linger 1001103
jstn to bind 1001107
jsd to sit? 1001098
jsd to spit 1001099
jš meal 1001091
jšf to burn 1001100
jšš image? 1001105
jšš to bring out 1001106
jšd [a tree, (Balanites aegyptiaca?)] 1001097
jḳr [a serpent] 1001073
jḳr to be excellent 1001074
jḳḥ to enter 1001072
jk to hack 1000994
jkm shield 1000996
jkn bad? 1000997
jkn to scoop out 1000998
jgn gladness 1000972
jt barley 1001110
jtj father 1001114
jtn disc 1001117
jtn fluffy 1001118
jtn ground 1001119
jtn obscure 1001059
jtr iteru 1001123
jtr papyrus? 1001124
jtḥ to drag 1001112
jṯ which 1001111
jṯꜣ to capture 1001126
jṯi̯ to seize 1001113
jṯm [metal part of a whip] 1001115
jṯn to resist 1001121
jṯr captive 1001122
jṯṯ = ḥṯṯ to fly up 1001125
jd pleasant scent 1000954
jd uterus 1000955
jdꜣ to smooth 1000968
jdi̯ to be deaf 1000959
jdi̯ to cense 1000960
jdi̯ to subjugate 1000961
jdb riverbank 1000956
jdm linen 1000962
jdn ear 1000963
jdn granary 1000964
jdn to replace 1000965
jdr heart 1000966
jdr to bind together 1000967
jdḥ marsh 1000958
jdg kerchief 1000957

y
ybr stream 1002784
ym sea 1002786
ydꜥ skilled 1002785

ꜥ
ꜥ item 1002927
ꜥꜣ column 1003070
ꜥꜣ door 1003071
ꜥꜣ linen 1003072
ꜥꜣ here 1001058
ꜥꜣi̯ to be great 1003078
ꜥꜣꜥ to squirt 1003081
ꜥꜣb to please 1003073
ꜥꜣb washing jug 1003074
ꜥꜣm throw stick 1003079
ꜥꜣg to beat 1003077
ꜥꜣḏ edge 1003075
ꜥꜣḏ to be pale 1003076
ꜥj to jubilate 1002991
ꜥjn limestone 1002992
ꜥyn well 1003069

ꜥꜥj to be fearful 1003082
ꜥꜥw to be agitated 1003084
ꜥꜥw to sleep 1003085
ꜥꜥnj to enclose 1003083
ꜥw crane 1003062
ꜥw herd 1003063
ꜥwꜣ to rot 1003067
ꜥwꜣi̯ = ꜥwn to rob 1003065
ꜥwn to wail 1003066
ꜥwg to be hot 1003064
ꜥb lettuce 1002930
ꜥb meal 1002931
ꜥb to purify 1002932
ꜥb = db tꜥ push 1002928
ꜥbꜣ a bird 1002940
ꜥbꜣ rope 1002941
ꜥbꜣ to interact 1002942
ꜥbꜣ to shine 1002943
ꜥbꜥ to boast 1002944
ꜥbb to smooth 1002934
ꜥbḥ to fill a jug 1002936
ꜥbẖn frog 1002937
ꜥbš [a wine jug] 1002938
ꜥbš to drown 1002939
ꜥbd servant 1002935
ꜥpi̯ to fly 1003030
ꜥpnn water newt 1003031
ꜥpr to provide 1003032
ꜥf to be greedy 1002961
ꜥf there 1001055
ꜥfꜣ to demolish 1002968
ꜥff to fly 1002964
ꜥff to hum 1002965
ꜥfn = ꜥfꜣ to envelop 1002966
ꜥfḏ chest 1002962
ꜥft collection of spells 1002967
ꜥfd nail 1002963
ꜥm to swallow 1002994
ꜥmꜣ [a part of a body] 1003004
ꜥmꜣ [a plant] 1003005
ꜥmꜣ to turn sour 1003006
ꜥmj to smear 1002998
ꜥmꜥ sexually immature? 1003007
ꜥmꜥꜣ to throw 1003008
ꜥmꜥꜥ kernel 1003009
ꜥmw [a fruit] 1003003
ꜥmnt to box 1002999
ꜥmr baker 1003001
ꜥmt clouds 1003002
ꜥmḳ to couple 1003000
ꜥmd to be weak 1002995
ꜥmdy supports (chariot parts) 1002997
ꜥmḏ to turn away 1002996
ꜥn [eye, as a character in writing] 1003010
ꜥn ring 1003011
ꜥn here 1001057
ꜥn talon 1003012
ꜥn writing board 1003013
ꜥni̯ to be good 1003024
ꜥnb alfa grass 1003014
ꜥnb to close 1003015
ꜥnn singing 1003025
ꜥnn to return 1003026
ꜥnnw [a tree] 1003027
ꜥnḥb [a bird] 1003023
ꜥnẖ alabaster 1003018
ꜥnẖ ankh-sign 1003019
ꜥnẖ to bind 1003020
ꜥnẖ goat 1003021
ꜥnẖ to live 1003022
ꜥnḳ to flow 1003028
ꜥnt myrrh 1003029
ꜥnḏ [an unguent] 1003016
ꜥnḏ to be diminished 1003017
ꜥr [a tree] 1003037
ꜥr goat 1003038
ꜥr hind part 1003039
ꜥr jaw 1003040
ꜥr stone 1003041
ꜥrf to wrap 1003043
ꜥrš to sneeze 1003049
ꜥršn lentils 1003050
ꜥrḳ to complete 1003044
ꜥrḳ to tie on 1003047
ꜥrḳwr silver 1003048
ꜥrt [a body of water in Upper Egypt] 1003051

ꜥrḏ to terrify (the enemy) 1003042
ꜥḥ cultivated land 1002975
ꜥḥ palace 1002976
ꜥḥ to catch 1002977
ꜥḥ to wipe away 1002978
ꜥḥꜣ to fight 1002988
ꜥḥꜥ boat 1002989
ꜥḥꜥ to stand 1002990
ꜥḫi̯ to burn 1002979
ꜥḫi̯ to raise up 1002981
ꜥḫm to extinguish 1002983
ꜥḫm to fly 1002984
ꜥḫm wick? 1002986
ꜥẖi̯ to fly 1002980
ꜥẖm leaf 1002982
ꜥẖm to inspire fear 1002985
ꜥẖn to close (the eyes) 1002987
ꜥš [a beer jug] 1003052
ꜥš [a food] 1003053
ꜥš coniferous wood 1003054
ꜥš throat 1003055
ꜥš = jꜣš to summon 1003056
ꜥšꜣ lizard 1003059
ꜥšꜣ to be numerous 1003060
ꜥši̯ to moan 1003057
ꜥšḳ to oppress 1003058
ꜥḳ cormorant 1003033
ꜥḳ to enter 1003034
ꜥḳꜣ [a transport ship] 1003035
ꜥḳꜣ to be accurate 1003036
ꜥk end of a rod/stick 1002993
ꜥgꜣ [an ointment] 1002972
ꜥgꜣ claw 1002973
ꜥgꜣ to capsize 1002974
ꜥgn ringstand 1002969
ꜥgrt wagon (drawn by oxen) 1002970
ꜥgsw belt 1002971
ꜥṯḫ to press out 1003061
ꜥdn wheat? 1002956
ꜥdt conspiracy? 1002959
ꜥḏ [part of a building (architrave?)] 1002945
ꜥḏ mongoose 1002946
ꜥḏ spin 1002947
ꜥḏ to be whole 1002948
ꜥḏ to burn 1002949
ꜥḏ to perceive (with ear, nose) 1002950
ꜥḏ to rejoice 1002951
ꜥḏ to slaughter 1002952
ꜥḏꜣ to be guilty 1002960
ꜥḏi̯ to sift 1002954
ꜥḏn [a bracelet] 1002955
ꜥḏr [a part of a chariot] 1002957
ꜥḏr helper 1002958
ꜥḏd youth 1002953

w

w district 1002602
w not 1000974
wꜣ [a plant] 1002756
wꜣ cord 1002757
wꜣ to plan 1002758
wꜣi̯ to move to 1002765
wꜣi̯ to parch 1002766
wꜣb root 1002760
wꜣp sheep 1002767
wꜣr reed 1002768
wꜣr to dance (or similar) 1002769
wꜣr to tie 1002770
wꜣḥ to lay down 1002763
wꜣḫi̯ to flood 1002764
wꜣg to be joyful loudly 1002762
wꜣs to rule 1002772
wꜣsi̯ to be ruined 1002773
wꜣš to be powerful 1002771
wꜣḏ to be green? 1002761
wj mummy case 1002670
wjꜣ boat 1002672
wjꜣ = wjn weak 1002671
wꜥ goat 1002774
wꜥ one 1002775
wꜥ to kill 1002776
wꜥꜣ torch 1002783
wꜥb to be pure 1002777
wꜥf to bend down 1002778
wꜥn juniper 1002780
wꜥr leg 1002781

wꜥr partition 1002782
wꜥḥ chufa 1002779
ww to make music 1002752
wbꜣ to open 1002610
wbn to rise up 1002606
wbn wound 1002607
wbḫ = wbg to shine 1002605
wbs = bzi̯ to come out 1002609
wbg to be green 1002604
wbd to burn 1002603
wp horn 1002699
wp quantity? 1002700
wpi̯ to open 1002701
wpr side lock 1002702
wps to burn up 1002703
wpš to illuminate 1002704
wfꜣ lung 1002630
wfꜣ to support 1002631
wmt to be thick 1002674
wn enclosure? 1002675
wn error 1002676
wn hare 1002677
wn to be bald 1002678
wn to open 1002679
wn to threaten 1002680
wni̯ to bind 1002688
wni̯ to hurry 1002689
wnj light 1002690
wnw hour 1002698
wnb blossom 1002681
wnp to stab 1002694
wnpj to harvest (flax)? 1002695
wnf to resolve 1002685
wnm diadem 1002691
wnm to eat 1002692
wnn to exist 1002693
wnḫ to clothe 1002686
wnḫ to loosen 1002687
wnš grape 1002696
wnš jackal 1002697
wnḏ cavity 1002682
wnḏ herd 1002683
wnḏ quantity 1002684
wr [a sacred body of water?] 1002705
wr gold worker? 1001912
wr swallow 1002706
wrm to mount up 1002710
wrm* to wind 1002711
wrr to be great 1002712
wrrj wagon 1002713
wrh to dance 1002708
wrḥ to smear 1002709
wrs headrest 1002714
wršu̯ to be awake 1002715
wrḏ to be weary 1002707
whi̯ to fail 1002646
whj diarrhoea 1002647
whb to pierce 1002643
whm to burn 1002649
whn to fall apart 1002651
whn* to be fragile 1002652
whs to be casual 1002655
wḥ kin 1002640
wḥ to bark 1002641
wḥꜣ [a skin disease] 1002657
wḥꜣ to cut down? 1002662
wḥꜣ cauldron 1002658
wḥꜥ scorpion 1002667
wḥꜥ to fish and fowl 1002668
wḥꜥ to solve 1002669
wḥf to burn 1002645
wḥm bull's leg 1002648
wḥm to repeat 1002650
wḥs to cut 1002656
wḫ to be dark 1002642
wḫꜣ claw? 1002659
wḫꜣ column? 1002660
wḫꜣ to be foolish 1002661
wḫꜣ to empty 1002663
wḫꜣ to hang down 1002664
wḫꜣ to seek 1002665
wḫꜣ to smoothen? 1002666
wḫr to process 1002654
wḫd to suffer 1002644
wzf to be idle 1002753
wzš to urinate 1002754
wzṯ to decay 1002755
ws height (math.) 1002716

ws to be empty 1002717
wsi̯ to saw 1002727
wsn to procreate 1002731
wsḥ to burn 1002724
wsẖ to be broad 1002723
wsr oar 1002733
wsr to be strong 1002734
wstj official writings 1002737
wstn [a body of water?] 1002736
wsṯn to stride unhindered 1002738
wš to destroy 1002718
wš to push 1002719
wšꜣ darkness 1002739
wšꜣ slander 1002740
wšꜣ to fatten 1002741
wšꜣ to pour out 1002742
wši̯ to reduce 1002726
wš^{c} to chew 1002743
wšb small bead? 1002720
wšb to feed 1002721
wšm awn 1002728
wšm to mix 1002729
wšm to slaughter 1002730
wšn to sacrifice 1002732
wšr to dry 1002735
wšd to question 1002722
wg plank 1002632
wgꜣ flood 1002639
wgi̯ to chew 1002635
wgb to shout 1002633
wgp to crush 1002637
wgm to grind 1002636
wgs to cut open 1002638
wgg to be weak 1002634
wt to bandage 1002744
wt to move around 1002745
wti̯ to be old 1002747
wtmt to tumble 1002748
wtn to pierce 1002749
wtẖ to flee 1002746
wṯz = ṯz+ to lift up 1002751
wtṯ to create 1002750
wdi̯ to place 1002619
wdp attendant 1002626
wdfi̯ to delay 1002615
wdn [a sacred baboon] 1002622
wdn to be heavy 1002623
wdḥ to pour 1002617
wdd gall bladder 1002613
wdd to cook 1002614
wḏ to assign 1002611
wḏꜣ to be intact 1002627
wḏꜣ to go 1002628
wḏi̯ to travel 1002620
wḏj perch 1002621
wḏ^{c} to separate 1002629
wḏb to turn around 1002612
wḏn width 1002624
wḏnj [oboe?] 1002625
wḏḥ fruit 1002616
wḏẖ to wean 1002618

b

b lips 1000001
b leg 1000002
bꜣ black stork? 1000107
bꜣ boat 1000108
bꜣ leopard 1000109
bꜣ pot 1000110
bꜣ ram 1000111
bꜣ soul 1000112
bꜣ throat 1000113
bꜣ to hack open 1000114
bꜣ = bn little spheric object 1000115
bꜣ = bn to erect 1000116
bꜣ = bn to overflow 1000054
bꜣi̯ to be moist 1000124
bꜣy malt 1000134
bꜣw hill 1000133
bꜣni̯ sleep 1000127
bꜣẖ sunrise / sunset 1000123
bꜣs bowl 1000130
bꜣs to cut out 1000131
bꜣš vessel 1000132
bꜣg coagulate 1000120
bꜣgi̯ to be weak 1000121
bꜣgs to stab 1000122
bꜣḳ moringa tree 1000128

bꜣḳ to be bright 1000129
bꜣk ramp 1000125
bꜣk servant 1000126
bꜣḏ = pꜣḏ spheric shape 1000118
bj bee 1000033
bj cheer 1000034
bj clapnet 1000035
bj groats 1000036
bj processional bark 1000037
bjꜣ astonishing 1000042
bjꜣ astonishing 1000042
bjꜣ ore 1000043
bjꜣi̯ to be far from 1000044
bjn evil 1000040
bjn harp 1000041
bjk falcon 1000039
bjdj [an affliction of the eye] 1000038
bꜥ to deal with water 1000135
bꜥ to disregard 1000137
bꜥj rod of palm 1000141
bꜥn neck 1000142
bꜥr Baal 1000143
bꜥr big water 1000144
bꜥḥi̯ to inundate 1000140
bw abomination 1000096
bw not 1000097
bw place 1000098
bwꜣ to be high 1000100
bwn spearheads 1000099
bb throat, neck 1000003
bbn to wriggle along 1000004
bfn scorpion 1000014
bn white wagtail 1000051
bn natron 1000052
bn not 1000053
bnj to be sweet 1000062
bnw millstone 1000067
bnf gall-bladder 1000059
bnn threshold? 1000063
bnr = bl outside 1000050
bns to pierce 1000066
bnš doorpost 1000064
bnš flower crown? 1000065
bng to be happy 1000060
bngzyt [a kind of a musical instrument] 1000061
bnd bad situation 1000055
bnd garden bed; cucumber? 1000057
bnd = *bnꜥ = bꜥn to wrap 1000058
bnḏ discharge 1000056
br mullet 1000073
br transport ship 1000074
brḳ to sparkle 1000079
brk gift 1000077
brkt pool 1000078
brg [a kind of a semi-precious stone] 1000075
brg be happy 1000076
brt agreement 1000080
brtj [semi-precious stone] 1000081
bhꜣ to move back 1000032
bhd to sniff 1000023
bḥ bead 1000019
bḥ to force 1000020
bḥn = bfn to bark 1000027
bḥni̯ to cut 1000029
bḥz calf 1000031
bḥs to hunt 1000030
bḥd to settle down? 1000022
bẖn greywacke 1000026
bẖn to watch 1000028
bẖẖ to glow 1000025
bz flame 1000101
bz secret 1000102
bzꜣ to protect 1000106
bzn to consider 1000104
bzn gypsum 1000105
bsn = msn to pierce 1000085
bsk entrails 1000084
bšꜣ ax 1000087
bšꜣ malted barley 1000088
bši̯ to spit out 1000083
bšw flint 1000021
bšṯ to rebel 1000086
bḳ behold 1000068
bq to be hostile 1000069
bḳy to open? 1000071
bḳꜥ pool 1000072

bḳn to stride	1000070
bkꜣ pregnancy	1000049
bkj [tree]	1000045
bkn excrement (med.)	1000047
bkr throne	1000048
bgꜣ to be shipwrecked	1000017
bgꜣ to shout	1000018
bgz = bgs throat	1000016
bgs to injure	1000015
bt mold	1000089
bt womb	1000091
btꜣ wrongdoing	1000095
btk to slaughter (enemies)	1000092
btk to escape?	1000093
bṯ running	1000090
bṯn to resist	1000094
bd emmer	1000006
bd natron?	1000007
bdš to be weak	1000010
bḏ ball, corn	1000005
bḏꜣ pad	1000011
bḏꜣ mold	1000012
bḏn stick	1000009
p	
p base	1001759
p heaven	1001760
pꜣ ? [a bread]	1001822
pꜣi̯ to fly	1001827
pꜣjs granules	1001828
pꜣḫ [a plant]	1001824
pꜣḫ to scratch	1001825
pꜣḫd to be turned over	1001826
pꜣz to suffer	1001832
pꜣs [scribe's water-pot]	1001830
pꜣqi̯ to be thin	1001829
pꜣṯṯ baboon	1001831
pꜣḏ incense cone	1001761
pj flea	1001778
pj to knead (clay)	1001779
pjpj keel?	1001780
pjs to tread in	1001781
pꜥ [a food]	1001833
pꜥ area	1001834
pꜥ fire	1001835
pꜥ people	1001836
pꜥ to spit out	1001837
pꜥꜣ = pꜥr quail	1001840
pꜥn to be clever	1001839
pꜥg to spit	1001838
pw who?	1001818
pn mouse	1001782
pnn to twist	1001784
pnz = pnꜥ to turn round	1001787
pnḳ = pnḏ to scoop	1001785
png to divide	1001783
pnt to squeeze	1001786
pr beans	1001791
pr house	1001792
pri̯ to come forth	1001795
prꜥ to be accessible?	1001799
prḫ to blossom	1001794
prš juniper berries?	1001796
prš to smash	1001797
prṯ to break?	1001798
prḏ to separate	1001793
phr [a pond]	1001773
pḥ lion	1001769
pḥ sheaf	1001770
pḥ to reach	1001771
pḥrr to run	1001775
pḥḏ to split	1001772
pḫꜣ [a cereal]	1001776
pḫꜣ to split	1001777
pẖr to turn round	1001774
pzḥ to bite	1001820
pzḫ to be confused	1001819
pzz to travail	1001821
ps measure?	1001800
psi̯ to cook	1001808
psḫ mat?	1001807
psg to spit	1001806
psḏ nine	1001801
psḏ pelican	1001802
psḏ spine	1001803
psḏ to shine	1001804
psḏn new moon	1001805
pšj comb	1001809

pšj pustule?	1001810
pšn to split	1001811
psš to divide	1001812
pšš to spread	1001060
pḳ flood	1001789
pḳr [a fragrant ingredient]	1001790
pgꜣ box	1001767
pgꜣ to open?	1001768
pgg frog	1001766
pt to tread	1001813
ptr bandage?	1001816
ptr to see	1001817
ptḥ to create	1001814
ptẖ to prostrate	1001815
pdr measure?	1001764
pds to flatten	1001765
pḏ to stretch	1001762
pḏi̯ to grind	1001763
f	
fꜣ dust?	1000353
fꜣ threat	1000354
fꜣi̯ to lift	1000357
fꜣk to be bald	1000358
fꜣg to cut (meat)	1000355
fꜣg to eradicate	1000356
fjw to become disgusted at	1000342
fjṯ = pjṯ to laugh	1000341
fꜥy hair	1000360
fꜥg claw	1000359
fn to be weak	1000344
fnẖ cord?	1000346
fnẖ to make smooth	1000347
fnṯ maggot	1000348
fnḏ to snort	1000345
fẖ to loosen	1000340
fḳꜣ to reword	1000349
fkꜣ turquoise	1000343
fgn to defecate	1000339
ft to be disgusted	1000350
ft to leap	1000351
fṯṯꜣ to decay	1000352
fd [an oil]	1000334
fd four	1000335
fd to sweat	1000336
fdi̯ to tear out	1000337
fdḳ to trench	1000338
m	
m who?	1001281
m’w mother	1001473
mꜣ [a plant]	1001474
mꜣ antelope	1001475
mꜣ sickle	1001476
mꜣ doum palm	1001482
mꜣꜣ to see?	1001496
mꜣj lion	1001481
mꜣꜥ [a wood]	1001497
mꜣꜥ bank	1001498
mꜣꜥ to be just	1001499
mꜣwi̯ to be new	1001492
mꜣwr to write	1001493
mꜣwṯ to think	1001494
mꜣwḏ to carry	1001491
mꜣnw western mountain	1001483
mꜣr place of joy	1001484
mꜣr to oppress	1001485
mꜣh door	1001478
mꜣḥ to clap	1001480
mꜣẖ corn sheaf	1001477
mꜣẖ to burn?	1001479
mꜣz to slaughter	1001495
mꜣs knee	1001487
mꜣš [a duck]	1001486
mꜣṯ granite	1001488
mꜣṯ to praise	1001489
mꜣṯr to mourn	1001490
mj [a (funerary) boat]	1001316
mj come	1001317
mj = mr like	1001318
mj road	1001319
mj take	1001320
mj to bring	1001321
mjꜥ [a house?]	1001329
mjw cat	1001327
mjm [a plant]	1001323
mjmj dura	1001324
mjn today	1001325

mjn water 1001326
mjni̯ to land 1001366
mjz liver 1001328
mjtr [kind of court person] 1001428
mjdꜣ [kind of meat] 1001322
mꜥ [a boat] 1001500
mꜥkꜣ to be brave 1001501
mꜥḳ undergarment? 1001502
mꜥr to be successful 1001503
mw dancer 1001467
mw water 1001468
mwꜥd council 1001470
mwt to die 1001469
mfkꜣ to be glad 1001296
mmj giraffe 1001340
mn [a bowl] 1001341
mn [a fabric] 1001342
mn hot fire 1001343
mn jug 1001344
mn quartz 1001345
mn thigh 1001346
mn to be ill 1001347
mn to move 1001348
mn to stay 1001349
mn tree? 1001350
mnj herdsman 1001367
mnj necklace 1001368
mnj shrine 1001369
mnꜥ property 1001385
mnꜥ to nurse 1001386
mnw pigeon 1001382
mnwr to purify 1001383
mnbj throne 1001351
mnpḥ animal skin? 1001373
mnfꜣ soldiers 1001355
mnn mina 1001371
mnnn asphalt 1001372
mnḥ evil fate 1001356
mnḥ papyrus plant 1001357
mnḥ to rejoice 1001360
mnḥ to slaughter 1001361
mnḥ tribute 1001363
mnḥ wax 1001364
mnḥ youth 1001365
mnẖ to be effective 1001358
mnẖ to chisel 1001359
mnẖ to string 1001362
mnz leg 1001384
mnsꜣ to cause ejaculation 1001377
mnš cartouche 1001376
mnt diorite 1001378
mntꜣ grove 1001381
mnty doorkeeper 1001380
mnṯ grain sieve? 1001379
mnḳ to complete 1001374
mnḳry [a pendant] 1001375
mnkby [a pendant] 1001370
mnd tribute 1001354
mnḏ cheek? 1001352
mnḏ chest 1001353
mr [chest; box (for linen)] 1001392
mr board 1001393
mr bull 1001394
mr canal 1001395
mr desert 1001396
mr eye 1001397
mr milk jug 1001398
mr pyramid 1001399
mr throat 1001400
mr to be ill 1001401
mr to bind 1001402
mr to strand 1001403
mri̯ to love 1001407
mrj groom 1001408
mrj speed 1001409
mrjjnt [a kind of a container]1001410
mryn noble person 1001879
mrw cedar 1001418
mrr flame 1001414
mrḥ lance 1001404
mrḥ to decay 1001405
mrḥm the one who works
with the salt 1001406
mrsw cider? 1001416
mrš to be bright red 1001415
mrḳḥt to catch? 1001413
mrḳḏn [a kind of a metal
tool] 1001412

mrkbt chariot	1001411
mrt chin	1001417
mhi̯ to forget	1001307
mhw a positive social characteristic	1001313
mhr braver	1001310
mḥ cubit	1001300
mḥ north	1001301
mḥ to fill	1001302
mḥi̯ to be in water	1001305
mḥi̯ to care for	1001306
mḥj to flee	1001308
mḥꜥ flax	1001315
mḥn to encircle	1001309
mḥḏrt fish pond	1001304
mḫ to respect	1001303
mḫꜣ to constrain	1001314
mḫt [a chariot part]	1001311
mḫtb golden armband	1001312
mz to bring	1001471
mzḥ crocodile	1001472
ms levy	1001420
ms to venerate	1001422
msi̯ to give birth	1001430
msw supper	1001450
msbb to turn towards	1001423
msn to spin	1001434
msḫ [a vessel]	1001427
mss robe	1001442
msḳ a metalworking activity	1001436
mskꜣ animal skin	1001433
msktw bracelet	1001432
mstꜣ [a liquid]	1001449
mstj basket	1001446
mstr [an apron]	1001447
mstr chancellery	1001448
mstḥ trap	1001445
msṯ offspring	1001443
msṯ to carry?	1001444
msḏi̯ to hate	1001426
mš to cut open	1001421
mšꜣ leather part of chariot	1001451
mšꜣb watering place	1001452
mšꜥ to march	1001453
mšp to endeavor?	1001435
mšr [a piece of furniture]	1001437
mšr evening	1001438
mšrr to attach	1001439
mšrw [plain]	1001440
mšš [a wood?]	1001441
mškb [title of an official]	1001431
mšd ford	1001424
mšd(d) comb	1001425
mḳ to rest	1001387
mḳn washboard?	1001388
mḳr [a staff]	1001389
mḳr [a vessel]	1001390
mḳs to comminute?	1001391
mk festival	1003901
mk [a boat]	1001330
mk correct position	1001331
mk to sustain	1001332
mkꜣ to be brave	1001338
mkꜣ to flatten	1001339
mki̯ to protect	1001334
mkmr fishnet	1001335
mkr merchant?	1001336
mkḥꜣ back of the head	1001333
mktr [a tower]	1001337
mgꜣ youthful soldier	1001299
mgr to roast	1001297
mgrt cave	1001298
mt to discuss	1001454
mtꜣ to skewer	1001465
mtj to be correct	1001456
mtw semen (sperm)	1001463
mtn knife?	1001457
mtr flood	1001460
mtr midday	1001461
mtr to be present	1001462
mtḥn girl	1001455
mṯꜣ to challenge	1001464
mṯꜣi̯ to deliver	1001466
mṯpr [a tool]	1001459
mṯn to assign	1001458
mdw staff	1001292
mdwi̯ to speak	1001293
mdn to rest	1001288

mḏ oil 1001282
mḏ ten 1001283
mḏ to be deep 1001284
mḏꜣb to scoop 1001294
mḏꜥ to subdue 1001295
mḏri̯ to turn 1001290
mḏrn [a metal tool] 1001291
mḏḥ carpenter 1001286
mḏḥ to make ready 1001287
mḏḳ [a vessel] 1001289
mḏd to align 1001285

n
n not 1001505
n red crown 1001506
n to 1001507
n’ urban area 1001746
nꜣw breath 1001749
nꜣb = nꜣp tress 1001747
nꜣš cursed 1001748
njꜣ ibex 1001601
njw ostrich 1001599
njw to be festive 1001600
njs papyrus blossom? 1001597
njk to punish 1001596
njt to hesitate 1001598
nꜥ to announce? (death) 1001750
nꜥi̯ to travel 1001754
nꜥi̯ to twist 1001755
nor catfish 1001756
nꜥrn unite of soldiers 1001757
nꜥẖ bundle 1001753
nꜥš to be strong 1001758
nꜥg door crack? 1001751
nꜥg to pulverize 1001752
nw [a jug] 1001714
nw [a substance] 1001715
nw [a vessel] 1001716
nw adze 1001717
nw hunter 1001718
nw light 1001719
nw sky 1001720
nw this 1001722
nw time 1001723
nw to clothe 1001724
nw water 1001725
nwꜣ adze 1001741
nwꜣ to see 1001742
nwi̯ to call 1001733
nwi̯ to return 1001734
nwi̯ to take care of 1001735
nwn to dishevel 1001736
nwḥ to bind 1001730
nwḥ to drink 1001732
nwẖ to boil 1001731
nwz ingot 1001740
nws crown? 1001738
nwṯ to tremble 1001739
nwdi̯ to press out 1001729
nwḏ antilope 1001726
nwḏ inaccuracy 1001727
nwḏ to move 1001728
nb basket 1001508
nb every 1001509
nb lord 1001510
nbꜣ to plait 1001520
nbi̯ to create 1001513
nbi̯ to swim 1001515
nbj flame 1001516
nbj reed 1001517
nbj spit 1001518
nbw gold 1001514
nbd to braid 1001512
nbḏ evil 1001511
np hem 1001636
npꜣ to make wet 1001638
npꜣ umbilical cord 1001639
npḏ to slaughter 1001637
nf breath 1001536
nf that, yonder 1001537
nfꜥ to remove 1001545
nfr [a jar] 1001538
nfr fire 1001539
nfr prow-rope? 1001540
nfr tiller 1001541
nfr to be perfect 1001542
nfr windpipe? 1001543
nfr to loosen 1001544

nm dwarf 1001607
nm fermentation? 1001608
nm produce of the fields (as offerings) 1001609
nm to rob 1001610
nm to sleep 1001611
nmi̯ to traverse 1001614
nmj to butcher 1001615
nmj to shout 1001616
nmꜥ to be biased 1001622
nmꜥ to cover? 1001623
nmḥ to be poor 1001612
nmḥf nephrite 1001613
nms [a jug] 1001617
nms a weight unit 1001618
nms to wrap (in bandages) 1001619
nmt to stride 1001620
nmt white quartzite 1001621
nn [food] 1001624
nn child 1001625
nn heaven 1001626
nn not 1001627
nn schist? [a stone for making divine statues] 1001628
nn-wn is not 1001629
nni̯ to be tired 1001630
nni̯ to turn back 1001631
nni̯ to writhe 1001632
nnjb resin 1001634
nnšm spleen 1001635
nr time 1001643
nri̯ to fear 1001645
nrḥ to blaspheme 1001644
nh to protect 1001519
nh to shake 1001553
nhꜣ to exile 1001594
nhi̯ to escape 1001570
nhi̯* to register 1001574
nhj some 1001575
nhp to mourn 1001580
nhp to revive 1001581
nhr terror 1001585
nhr to flee? 1001586
nhr sacred well? 1001584
nhzi̯ to be awake 1001591
nhd to tremble 1001565
nhḏ scribe's palette 1001563
nḥ guinea-fowl 1001551
nḥꜣ [an illness] 1001592
nḥꜣ to be fierce 1001593
nḥi̯ to pray for 1001572
nḥb = nḥm lotus bud 1001557
nḥb neck 1001558
nḥb to equip 1001561
nḥp to create 1001579
nḥm to protect 1001576
nḥni̯ to rejoice 1001578
nḥr [a bread] 1001582
nḥḥ eternity 1001566
nḥḥ hippopotamus 1001567
nḥḥ olive oil 1001568
nḥs to sting 1001588
nḥš an medical ingredient 1001587
nḥti̯ to trust 1001590
nḥd [a medical ingredient] 1001562
nḥd to be strong 1001564
nḫ to skid 1001554
nḫ = nḏ to protect 1001552
nḫꜣ to hang down 1001595
nḫi̯ to endure 1001569
nḫi̯ to request 1001571
nḫb heifer? 1001555
nḫb lotus 1001556
nḫb to assign 1001559
nḫb to illuminate 1001560
nḫn to be a child 1001577
nḫr canal 1001583
nḫt to be strong 1001589
nẖ = nš spittle 1001573
nzp knife 1001743
nzp to smooth out 1001744
nzr flame 1001745
ns [a plant] 1001647
ns knife 1001650
ns to go (to) 1001652
ns tongue 1001654
nsꜣ rowlock 1001669
nsi̯ to open 1001657

nsj [a demon?] 1001658
nsw king 1001668
nsbi̯ to devour 1001655
nsr to burn 1001665
nss to damage sth. 1001666
nssḳ hair loss? 1001667
nsḳ to sting 1001664
nsk to put in proper array 1001659
nš grain 1001648
nš hairdressing 1001649
nš to expel 1001651
nš to shudder 1001653
nšp gate 1001662
nšp to breath 1001663
nšḏ to comminute 1001656
nḳꜥ to scratch 1001642
nḳf to beat 1001640
nḳr to sieve 1001641
nki̯ to copulate 1001603
nkp [a plant] 1001606
nkftr [an oil] 1001602
nkn hide 1001604
nkn to injure 1001605
ngꜣ cow 1001549
ngꜣ to kill 1001550
ngi̯ to break (sth.) 1001547
ngs to overflow 1001548
ngg to cackle 1001546
ntꜣi̯ to hurry 1001711
nti̯ to be oppressed 1001704
ntꜥ to organize 1001713
ntn skin 1001706
ntš to besprinkle 1001710
nṯ to tie up 1001700
nṯ tongue 1001701
nṯꜥ to divorce 1001712
nṯb to parch 1001702
nṯn dirt 1001705
nṯr [a beer] 1001707
nṯr [a plant] 1001708
nṯr god 1001709
nṯẖ [a musical instrument] 1001703
ndb base 1001525
ndb wind 1001527
ndm throne 1001529
nḏ thread 1001521
nḏ to ask 1001522
nḏ to grind 1001523
nḏꜣ water 1001535
nḏm to be sweet 1001530
nḏr carpenter 1001531
nḏri̯ to follow 1001532
nḏs to be small 1001534

r

r goose 1001997
r mouth 1001998
rꜥ sun 1001999
rw lion 1001987
rw straw 1001988
rwi̯ to dance 1001994
rwi̯ to depart? 1001995
rwhꜣ evening 1001993
rwḥ to trespass 1001992
rwd stairway 1001990
rwḏ bowstring 1001989
rwḏ to be strong 1001991
rbš to arm oneself 1001926
rpw image of a woman 1001973
rpw to rot 1001974
rj coil? 1001952
rj heaven 1001953
rj ink 1001954
rj pus 1001955
rj side 1001956
rm fish 1001963
rm to chastize 1001964
rmi̯ to weep 1001965
rmn arm 1001966
rmṯ human being 1001967
rn name 1001968
rnpi̯ to be young 1001971
rnn joy 1001969
rnn to bring up 1001970
rns beads? 1001972
rr swine 1001976
rr time 1001977
rrm mandrake? 1001978

rhb embers	1001942
rhn to lean (on)	1001944
rhni̯ to wade	1001945
rhnj criosphinx	1001946
rhnj waste	1001947
rhd [a caldron]	1001943
rḥ comrade	1001935
rḥ to burn	1001937
rḥb [a vessel]	1001941
rḥs [a baked good]	1001948
rtḥ to bake	1001985
rtḥ to restrain	1001986
rḫ to know	1001938
rḫ weaver	1001939
rḫs to slaughter	1001949
rḫt list	1001950
rḫt to wash (clothes)	1001951
rzf catch	1001996
rs south	1001980
rsj entirely	1001982
rš coryza	1001979
ršj peak	1001983
ršu̯ to rejoice	1001984
rḳ opponent	1001975
rk [a plant]	1001957
rk time	1001958
rk to creep	1001959
rk to stop	1001960
rkḥ fire	1001961
rks harnessed team	1001962
rg compartment	1001933
rgi̯ to finish	1001934
rd [a grain]	1001927
rd foot	1001928
rd to grow	1001929
rdm [a plant]	1001936
rdn laudanum	1001931
rḏi̯ to give	1001930
rḏw fluidity	1001932
h	
hʾ courtyard	1000841
hꜣ blaze	1000847
hꜣ husband	1000851
hꜣ pavillon	1000855
hꜣ wild bird	1000863
hꜣi̯ period	1000881
hꜣi̯ to descend	1000882
hꜣw kin	1000904
hꜣb to send	1000870
hꜣm poultry	1000893
hj onomatopoetic	1000518
hj to contort	1000519
hj to rejoice	1000520
hjw [creature threatening the dead]	1000524
hjms to approach humbly	1000522
hyn territory	1000822
hw to run	1000796
hw sailing	1000799
hwš to disregard	1000813
hwt to burn	1000815
hwt to lament	1000816
hwṯn [a fish]	1000817
hbj ibis	1000458
hbu̯ to abuse?	1000470
hbu̯ to step	1000471
hbn [a vessel]	1000459
hbn antilope	1000460
hbnj ebony	1000462
hbḳ to pound	1000464
hp regulation	1000674
hf to hull	1000498
hm fare	1000538
hm saliva	1000544
hm to be hot	1000547
hm to shout aloud	1000549
hms cord	1000561
hmṯ [serpent]	1000565
hn sweet	1000595
hni̯ to rejoice	1000619
hnw box	1000666
hnw kin	1000668
hnn fallow deer	1000636
hnn to incline	1000641
hr highland	1000698
hr to dispel completely	1000705
hri̯ to milk	1000714

hrw day 1000732
hru̯ to be pleased 1000730
hrp to sink 1000720
hrm to include 1000717
hrṯṯ to do stealthily 1000729
hhi̯ to be fiery 1000516
hhj to be deaf 1000517
hsmḳ storming (of the king joining battle) 1000752
hskt [bad way of walking] 1000751
hḳ to crack? 1000688
hḳs to damage 1000691
hkr [serpent] 1000528
ht [an animal] 1000759
ht to dig 1000766
ht to wander 1000769
hṯt to scream 1000788
hd to confront 1000478
hdm throne 1000487
hdn [a plant] 1000488
hdr [collar] 1000493
hdd famine? 1000482
ḥdi̯ to damage 1000485
ḥdi̯ to spread out 1000486

ḥ
ḥ flax 1000448
ḥꜣ [a waterfowl] 1000843
ḥꜣ behind 1000846
ḥꜣ front 1000849
ḥꜣ heart 1000850
ḥꜣ to land? 1000861
ḥꜣ tomb 1000862
ḥꜣi̯ to uncover 1000703
ḥꜣi̯ to mourn 1000884
ḥꜣi̯ to support 1000886
ḥꜣj light 1000887
ḥꜣꜥ = ḥꜣy turmoil 1000911
ḥꜣwj pole? 1000906
ḥꜣb to catch 1000869
ḥꜣp to hide 1000898
ḥꜣb turquoise 1000871
ḥꜣb festival 1000872
ḥꜣbi̯ to mourn 1000873
ḥꜣm to catch 1000895
ḥꜣm path 1000892
ḥꜣk to truncate 1000889
ḥꜣk trapeze 1001128
ḥꜣg = ḥng to be glad 1000879
ḥꜣd agitation 1000875
ḥꜣd to trap 1000877
ḥꜥ limb 1000914
ḥꜥ staff 1000915
ḥꜥꜣ child 1000931
ḥꜥw fleet 1000930
ḥꜥb [an enemy] 1000917
ḥꜥb to play 1000918
ḥꜥp flood 1000924
ḥꜥnẖ to rotate 1000923
ḥꜥtj bed 1000929
ḥꜥḏꜣ to rob 1000919
ḥj to seek 1000521
ḥjp to run 1000523
ḥw [the great sphinx of Giza] 1000793
ḥw food 1000794
ḥw house 1000795
ḥw utterance 1000798
ḥwꜣ to rot 1000819
ḥwꜥ to be short 1000820
ḥwi̯ to strike 1000805
ḥwj happy song 1000807
ḥwn a cut of meat 1000808
ḥwn to be young 1000809
ḥwrꜥ to rob 1000812
ḥwrw to be weak 1000811
ḥb stairway? 1000449
ḥb target 1000450
ḥbnn [a bread] 1000463
ḥbs to cover? 1000466
ḥbḏ to open 1000455
ḥpg to dance 1000677
ḥpt to embrace 1000685
ḥpd to open 1000676
ḥf to hear? 1000497
ḥfꜣ = ḥfn = ḥnf to praise 1000508
ḥfꜣ to crawl 1000506
ḥfk to drink milk 1000502

ḥfdi̯ to climb 1000500
ḥfdi̯ to settle 1000501
ḥm [a weapon at a chariot] 1000533
ḥm [plant] 1000535
ḥm coward 1000536
ḥm forty 1000539
ḥm frit 1000540
ḥm majesty 1000541
ḥm misfortune 1000542
ḥm servant 1000545
ḥm though 1000546
ḥm to copulate 1000548
ḥm to steer 1000550
ḥm woman 1000551
ḥmꜣ [plant] 1000575
ḥmꜣ ball 1000576
ḥmꜣ salt 1000577
ḥmꜣg [scales] 1000578
ḥmꜣg garnet? 1000579
ḥmꜣg to surround 1000580
ḥmꜣṯ a cord? 1000581
ḥmi̯ to flood 1000554
ḥmi̯ to repel 1000556
ḥmw abrasive sand? 1000571
ḥmw weapon 1000572
ḥmu̯ to be skilled 1000570
ḥmn several 1000558
ḥmr donkey 1000559
ḥmr throne 1000560
ḥmz to slaughter 1000574
ḥmsi̯ to sit down 1000564
ḥmt ore 1000567
ḥmḏ vinegar 1000552
ḥn [bird] 1000584
ḥn [jar] 1000585
ḥn to be fresh 1000598
ḥn to block 1000599
ḥn pelican 1000591
ḥn to hurry 1000602
ḥn to jubilate 1000603
ḥn to look at 1000604
ḥn to protect 1000605
ḥny spear 1000670
ḥnꜥ together with 1000672
ḥnw [jug] 1000665
ḥnw horn 1000667
ḥnb solar? 1000606
ḥnb to measure 1000607
ḥnb to repel 1000608
ḥnm go around? 1000626
ḥnmm mankind 1000633
ḥnn blossom of date palm 1000635
ḥnn phallus 1000638
ḥnn to hoe 1000640
ḥnr = ḥl to darken 1000531
ḥnrg to quake 1000651
ḥns to be narrow 1000654
ḥnḳ to ferment 1000644
ḥnk to braid 1000623
ḥnk to present 1000624
ḥngg gullet 1000617
ḥnti̯ to be greedy 1000660
ḥnt scale? 1000659
ḥntꜣ porcupine? 1000663
ḥntꜣsw lizard 1000664
ḥnṯi̯ to butcher 1000661
ḥr canal? 1000695
ḥr face 1000697
ḥr lump of lapis lazuli 1000699
ḥr rope 1000701
ḥr to guard 1000707
ḥr to rejoice 1000708
ḥr to be ready 1000704
ḥri̯ to be distant 1000712
ḥri̯ to frighten 1000713
ḥrj melting oven 1000715
ḥry dung 1000734
ḥrp dagger 1000718
ḥrr flower 1000722
ḥrr to roar 1000723
ḥrr worm 1000725
ḥrs carnelian 1000727
ḥḥ million 1000513
ḥz forearm 1000824
ḥz water jar 1000826
ḥzꜣ dough 1000838
ḥzꜣ to be wild 1000839
ḥzi̯ to praise 1000829

ḥzi̯ to turn back 1000830
ḥzp garden 1000835
ḥzmn amethyst 1000832
ḥzmn bronze 1000833
ḥzmn to eat 1000834
ḥzk [a priest] 1000831
ḥs defecate 1000736
ḥs to be closed 1000738
ḥs to be cold 1000739
ḥsꜣ thread 1000757
ḥsi̯ to sing 1000750
ḥsb cross band 1000740
ḥsb to break 1000741
ḥsb to count 1000742
ḥsb to slaughter 1000744
ḥsḳ to cut off 1000753
ḥḳꜣ bushel 1000692
ḥḳꜣ to rule 1000693
ḥḳr to be hungry 1000689
ḥkꜣ to perform magic 1000530
ḥkn lion? 1000525
ḥkn oil or unguent 1000526
ḥkn to praise 1000527
ḥkk to swallow 1000616
ḥgꜣ festivity 1000512
ḥt [part of the eye] 1000760
ḥt comb 1000762
ḥtꜣ sail 1000791
ḥtꜣ to be shabby 1000792
ḥtj smoke 1000776
ḥtw throat 1000789
ḥtp blood 1000782
ḥtp to rest 1000783
ḥtm [an animal] 1000777
ḥtm chair 1000778
ḥtm to destroy 1000779
ḥtr to bind together 1000785
ḥts to accomplish 1000786
ḥṯ hyena 1000764
ḥṯ to place in 1000767
ḥṯꜣ [a bread] 1000790
ḥṯṯ armpit 1000787
ḥdḳ to cut off 1000490
ḥdḳḳ rat? 1000491
ḥdg to kill 1000483
ḥḏ [a medicine] 1000474
ḥḏ mace 1000476
ḥḏ to be white 1000477
ḥḏy west wind 1000495
ḥḏn to be angry 1000489
ḥḏr [animal] 1000492

ḫ

ḫ fire 1000447
ḫꜣ [a water] 1000842
ḫꜣ an element of dressing 1000845
ḫꜣ illness 1000852
ḫꜣ meat 1000854
ḫꜣ plant category 1000856
ḫꜣ thousand 1000857
ḫꜣ to be young 1000858
ḫꜣ to throw 1000910
ḫꜣi̯ to measure 1000883
ḫꜣyb shadow 1000907
ḫꜣw altar 1000902
ḫꜣw hide (of animals) 1000903
ḫꜣwj evening 1000905
ḫꜣb hippopotamus 1000865
ḫꜣb to be humble 1000868
ḫꜣb infant 1000866
ḫꜣf to twist? 1000878
ḫꜣm to bend (the arm) 1000894
ḫꜣm to do something quickly? 1000896
ḫꜣnn doum palm 1000897
ḫꜣḫ to hurry 1000880
ḫꜣz to climb 1000908
ḫꜣtb to spare 1000900
ḫꜣtrw mongoose 1000901
ḫꜣd to pluck 1000876
ḫꜣḏ [a bread] 1000874
ḫyi̯ to be high 1000821
ḫꜥ [a tool] 1000912
ḫꜥ clew 1000913
ḫꜥi̯ to appear 1000920
ḫꜥm throat 1000921
ḫꜥr leather 1000927
ḫꜥr to be furious 1000928

ḫw unique	1000797
ḫwi̯ to protect	1000804
ḫwn to hurt	1000810
ḫwḫ [a boat]	1000803
ḫwzi̯ to build	1000818
ḫws to slaughter	1000814
ḫwd carrying chair	1000800
ḫwd to be rich	1000801
ḫwd to fish	1000802
ḫb to slay	1000451
ḫb to slink into	1000452
ḫbꜣ to hack	1000473
ḫbi̯ to dance	1000456
ḫbi̯ to reduce	1000457
ḫbn crime	1000461
ḫbr to join together	1000465
ḫbz tail	1000472
ḫbs to hack	1000467
ḫbs to illuminate	1000468
ḫbs wrongdoing	1000469
ḫbḏ to hate	1000454
ḫpi̯ to travel	1000678
ḫpp seeds	1000680
ḫpp to be strange	1000681
ḫpr to exist	1000682
ḫprš Blue Crown	1000683
ḫpš to subjugate	1000684
ḫpd back side	1000675
ḫf to flow	1000496
ḫf to see sth.	1000499
ḫfꜣ to feed	1000507
ḫfꜣꜣ riverbank	1000510
ḫfꜣi̯ to lighten	1000509
ḫfꜥ to grasp	1000511
ḫfnn [fruit]	1000504
ḫft vis-à-vis	1000505
ḫm dust	1000537
ḫm not to know	1000543
ḫmꜣꜣ to shrivel	1000582
ḫmi̯ to consume	1000553
ḫmi̯ to oppose	1000555
ḫmy sand-fly?	1000573
ḫmꜥi̯ to seize	1000583
ḫmn eight	1000557
ḫmt companion?	1000566
ḫmt to think	1000534
ḫmt three	1000568
ḫmt to stab	1000569
ḫn disgusting	1000589
ḫn extra gift	1000590
ḫn porter	1000592
ḫn speech	1000593
ḫn to be foolish	1000597
ḫn to direct	1000600
ḫni̯ to make music	1000618
ḫni̯ to settle	1000621
ḫnw dorsal fin (synodontis)	1000669
ḫnp [baked good]	1000642
ḫnp to consume	1000643
ḫnf to take sth.	1000613
ḫnfꜣ arrogance?	1000615
ḫnfi̯ to burn	1000614
ḫnm jasper	1000628
ḫnm to enjoy	1000629
ḫnm to rear	1000630
ḫnms mosquito	1000634
ḫnn fowl	1000637
ḫnr rein	1000645
ḫnr = ḫl to sting	1000532
ḫnr = ḫl spike	1000646
ḫnr = ḫl to scatter	1000648
ḫnr to be hoarse	1000647
ḫnr to seclude	1000649
ḫnrj roar	1000652
ḫnrf = ḫlf insult	1000650
ḫnz to travel through	1000671
ḫns two-sided item	1000656
ḫnš [a plant]	1000653
ḫnš to stink	1000655
ḫnt face	1000657
ḫnt jar-stand	1000658
ḫntš to be glad	1000662
ḫnd to bend	1000611
ḫnd to tread	1000612
ḫnḏ shin	1000610
ḫr at	1000694
ḫr road	1000700
ḫr sistrum	1000702

ḫr to fall	1000706
ḫry myrrh?	1000735
ḫru̯ to say	1000731
ḫrp to administer	1000719
ḫrr watercourse	1000724
ḫrš bundle	1000726
ḫrḳ slippery ground	1000721
ḫrd veils	1000711
ḫḫ neck	1000514
ḫḫ to weigh	1000515
ḫz [a myrrh]	1000823
ḫz ritual	1000825
ḫzꜣ [a plant]	1000836
ḫzꜣ carrying pole	1000837
ḫzꜣj bribe	1000840
ḫzd to decay	1000827
ḫs rubbing stone	1000737
ḫsbḏ lapis lazuli	1000745
ḫsf to confront	1000748
ḫsr to dispel	1000754
ḫsdḏ [a kilt]	1000746
ḫsḏḏ to grow mouldy	1000747
ḫšb to mutilate	1000743
ḫšḫš rubble	1000749
ḫt behind	1000761
ḫt crop	1000763
ḫt plot	1000765
ḫt wood	1000770
ḫti̯ platform	1000772
ḫti̯ to carve	1000773
ḫti̯ to see	1000775
ḫtm to seal	1000780
ḫṯ to pound	1000768
ḫṯn garlic?	1000781
ḫd land register?	1000475
ḫdi̯ flow	1000484

ẖ

ẖ belly	1000446
ẖꜣ marsh	1000853
ẖꜣ to disturb	1000860
ẖꜣ corpse	1000848
ẖꜣꜣ to decide	1000909
ẖꜣi̯ = šꜣi̯ to resist	1000885
ẖꜣb to be crooked	1000867
ẖꜣpi̯ to flow freely	1000899
ẖꜣr bag (of leather)	1000891
ẖꜣk to be cunning	1000888
ẖꜥ to empty	1000916
ẖꜥm to approach	1000922
ẖꜥḳ to shave	1000926
ẖb to subdue	1000453
ẖp figure	1000673
ẖpꜣ navel	1000686
ẖpꜥ to chew	1000687
ẖpn to be bulged	1000679
ẖḳs to be injured	1000690
ẖms incense	1000562
ẖms to bend	1000563
ẖn [water]	1000586
ẖn bag?	1000587
ẖn covering	1000588
ẖn statue	1000594
ẖn to approach	1000596
ẖni̯ to row	1000620
ẖnbb to mingle	1000609
ẖnm [an oil]	1000625
ẖnm to unite	1000631
ẖnm water facility	1000632
ẖnn septic?	1000639
ẖnk [garment]	1000622
ẖr under	1000709
ẖrm causeway?	1000716
ẖrd child	1000710
ẖzi̯ to be weak	1000828
ẖsꜣ to be unanointed	1000758
ẖsw eyelid	1000756
ẖss corner (of a building)	1000755
ẖkr to adorn	1000529
ẖti̯ to pluck (plants)	1000774
ẖtb to dip into	1000771
ẖd to examine	1000479
ẖdb to kill	1000481
ẖdr to feel uncomfortable?	1000494

z

z door bolt	1002787
z person	1002788

zꜣ duck	1002851
zꜣ eighth of an aroura	1002852
zꜣ son	1002853
zꜣi̯ to linger	1002856
zꜣw to break	1002863
zꜣb jackal	1002854
zꜣu̯ to protect	1002862
zꜣg [a mythological animal]	1002855
zꜣr [a plant]	1002857
zꜣr bond	1002858
zꜣt incense	1002860
zꜣṯ to make libation	1002861
zj to go	1002807
zjn to rub	1002808
zw wheat	1002838
zwꜣ to chop	1002846
zwn [a vessel]	1002839
zwn arrow	1002840
zwnu̯ to suffer?	1002841
zwr to drink	1002842
zwrw [a bird]	1002843
zwš to lump	1002844
zwṯ to roll	1002845
zb board?	1002789
zb heir	1002790
zbꜣ flute	1002795
zbi̯ to go	1002791
zbn [a fish]	1002792
zbn to slip	1002793
zbṯ to laugh	1002794
zp matter	1002822
zp to tousle	1002823
zpꜣ to wriggle	1002825
zpi̯ to remain	1002824
zf to be mild	1002796
zf = zfṯ to slaughter	1002797
zmꜣ to unite	1002814
zmy desert	1002812
zmn natron	1002811
zmzr [a gate]	1002813
zni̯ to pass	1002819
znb to overthrow	1002815
znbꜣ to get out of control	1002816
znf blood	1002817
znḥm locust	1002818
znš = zꜣš = zš to open	1002820
znṯ to be rebellious	1002821
zr pellet	1002826
zr ram	1002827
zrm [a beer]	1002828
zrt knife	1002829
zḥ [a bird]	1002798
zḥ hall	1002799
zḥ to trample	1002801
zḫ to hurry	1002800
zḫi̯ to strike	1002803
zḫni̯ to encompass	1002804
zḫz to tear	1002805
zẖꜣ = zš to write	1002806
zẖi̯ to be deaf	1002802
zz to burn	1002847
zzi̯ to punish	1002850
zzḥ to destroy	1002848
zzḥꜣ vessel	1002849
zš [a rope]	1002830
zš to pass	1002831
zši̯ to tear out	1002832
zšj to nest	1002833
zšp to polish	1002835
zšn lotus	1002834
zšzš [a rope]	1002837
zšš sistrum	1002836
zk to dig	1002809
zkr to travel	1002810
s	
s [a goose]	1002000
s folded cloth	1002002
s seat	1002003
s to watch	1001981
sꜣ back	1002378
sꜣ gold	1002380
sꜣꜣ = sꜣr to be wise	1002409
sꜣi̯ to be sated	1002393
sꜣw niche?	1002407
sꜣb colorful	1002387
sꜣp lotus	1002397
sꜣm unkempt hair	1002395

sꜣr to sieve	1002401
sꜣḥ to reach	1002391
sꜣḫ to ram	1002859
sꜣḫm a bat	1002392
sꜣḳ to join	1002399
sꜣt to defile	1002405
sꜣt to dislocate	1002406
sꜣṯ cargo boat	1002404
sꜣd to strangulate	1002390
sꜥ to damage?	1002414
sꜥb to cut	1002415
sꜥr scrub country?; barley field?	1002418
sꜥr wool	1002420
sꜥḥ to dignify	1002416
sj to limp?	1002114
sjꜣ [a falcon]	1002123
sjꜣ fringed cloth	1002124
sjꜣ to recognize	1002125
sjf to insult	1002116
sjm haze	1002117
sjn clay	1002118
sjn to hurry	1002119
sjr [activity connected with the heart]	1002120
sjs six	1002121
sjtj trial	1002122
sjd tray	1002115
sw [a plant]	1002340
sw 1/16 arure	1002341
sw a piece of meat	1002342
sw danger	1002343
sw time	1002348
swy [a crocodile]	1002370
swbb to draw back	1002351
swn fortress	1002362
swn pond	1002363
swn to flatter	1002364
swn to recognize	1002365
swn to trade	1002366
swhꜣ to break	1002357
swhi̯ to praise	1002356
swḥ egg	1002353
swḥ to enwrap	1002354
swḥ wind	1002355
swr [a chariot equipment]	1002367
swr bead	1002368
swgꜣ to be foolish	1002352
swt wind	1002369
sb [edible part of cattle]	1002006
sb reed	1002008
sbꜣ gate	1002026
sbꜣ star	1002027
sbꜣ to teach	1002028
sbj to rebel	1002017
sbn bandage	1002018
sbr branch	1002023
sbḥ to cry out	1002013
sbḫ to enclose	1002014
sbḳ leg	1002021
sbt [a plant]	1002024
sbtj wall	1002025
sp lips	1002222
spꜣ nome	1002239
spi̯ to bind together	1002227
spr [a vegetable]	1002229
spr rib	1002230
spr sheet (of metal)	1002231
spr to reach	1002232
sps to build	1002233
sps to dance	1002234
spt to slaughter	1002238
spd to be sharp	1002226
sf to burn?	1002061
sf yesterday	1002062
sfꜣ to neglect	1002072
sfi̯ to mix	1002065
sfy child	1002071
sfḫ seven	1002064
sfṯ [an oil]	1002069
sm herbs	1002141
sm to respect	1002144
smꜣ stolist	1002174
smꜣ to slaughter	1002175
smj soured milk	1002155
smj to report	1002156
smj whips	1002157
smꜥ stake	1002177

smwn surely	1002172
smn [a goose]	1002160
smn lion	1002161
smn mourner	1002162
smr friend	1002164
smḥ left	1002152
sms [a cut of beef]	1002165
sms mallet	1002167
sms to become old	1002168
smswn libation	1002170
smk beam	1002158
smt to hear	1002171
smd [a star]	1002146
smd bead	1002147
smd edge	1002148
smd personnel	1002149
smd sistrum	1002150
smd slab	1002151
sn [an offering]	1002181
sn brother	1002183
sn flag pole	1002184
sn serpentine	1002187
sn to smell	1002188
snꜥḥ angler	1002221
sni̯ to free	1002202
snb [a boat]	1001102
snb [a plant]	1002190
snb heaven	1002192
snb to be healthy	1002193
snf previous year	1002198
snḥ to tie up	1002199
snm storm	1002208
snrw = slw [a product of Nubia]	1001888
sns hairdresser?	1002212
snsi̯ to praise	1002213
snḳ to suckle	1002211
snk to be dark	1002207
snṯi̯ to establish	1002215
snḏ to fear	1002197
sr [a goose]	1002246
sr captive (noble) woman	1002247
sr nobleman	1002248
sr thorn	1002250
sr to announce	1002251
sr to visit	1002252
sri̯ to spread	1002259
srj standard	1002260
srf to be warm	1002254
srf to rest	1002255
srḥ stalks (of onions)	1002258
srḳ scorpion	1002262
srḳ to open	1002263
srḏ to chisel	1002253
sḥ royal dome	1002085
sḥꜣ donkey	1002108
sḥw dirt	1002105
sḥm to crush	1002094
sḥd star	1002087
sḫ gallbladder	1002083
sḫꜣ [a piece of nautical equipment]	1002107
sḫꜣ to remember	1002109
sḫwꜣ to deny	1002106
sḫp to laud	1002098
sḫf to write down	1002089
sḫm [watery area in heaven]	1002090
sḫm sistrum	1002091
sḫm to be mighty	1002093
sḫmḫ to amuse	1002095
sḫn [a divine bark]	1002096
sḫnš to irritate	1002097
sḫr plan	1002101
sḫt [a stretch of water]	1002102
sḫt to form	1002103
sḫt to make ready	1002104
sḫd to rebuke	1002088
sẖ [a beverage]	1002081
sẖ barley	1002082
sẖꜣꜣ hauling	1002111
sẖꜣk to strain	1002110
sẖꜥ hare	1002112
sẖꜥ to gild	1002113
sẖb to slurp	1002086
sẖm to be hasty	1002092
sẖr lumber	1002100
ssw to enclose	1002300
ssm horse	1002280

sskꜣ [an ingredient]	1002277
sskꜣ temple (a body part)	1002278
sst ankle	1002298
sšꜣ to beseech	1002304
sšꜣ to beseech?	1002304
sšꜣ to change sb.'s mind	1002305
sšp cucumber	1002287
sšp to be bright	1002288
sšm whetstone	1002284
sšn [a fish]	1002285
sšn to spin	1002286
sšr grain	1002289
sšr linen	1002290
sšr to stroke	1002293
sšr work	1002296
sšš to level	1002297
sštꜣ [a fruit]	1002299
sšd shrine	1002273
sšd to flash	1002274
sšd to tie	1002275
sḳ fish trap	1002240
sḳ to cut	1002242
sḳr to strike	1002244
sk [a toilette utensil]	1002126
sk complain	1002127
sk flour	1002128
sk lance	1002129
sk to be a star in the sky	1002130
sk to wipe	1002131
skꜣ to plough	1002137
ski̯ to perish	1002132
skp to filter	1002135
skn to be greedy	1002133
sg sacking	1002074
sg to open a way	1002075
sgbyn [a body of water]	1002076
sgmḥ (cult) spear	1002077
sgr fortress	1002080
st [necklace]	1002309
st jar stand	1002310
sti̯ to catch sight of	1002318
sti̯ to knot	1002319
sti̯ to send out	1002321
stj leg (esp. of Osiris)	1002322
stp [a cloth]	1002325
stp goose?	1002326
stp incident	1002327
stp to choose	1002328
stnw charburner?	1000145
str to make jewelry	1002330
stḥ to open	1002317
sṯ [a bread mold]	1002306
sṯ [a jug]	1002307
sṯ [a material]	1002308
sṯꜣ [a body of water]	1002333
sṯꜣ [a jar]	1002334
sṯꜣ offering	1002335
sṯꜣ secretion (med.)	1002336
sṯꜣ to drag	1002338
sṯi̯ to pluck (fowl)	1002320
sṯj fragrance	1002311
sṯp to leap up	1002329
sṯr to wrap up	1002331
sd column (of a text)	1002029
sd tail	1002035
sd to be clothed	1002036
sdꜣ cattle egret	1002055
sdb [a garment]	1002038
sdb to be softened	1002040
sdf [a unit of measure, for figs]	1002043
sdm eye-paint	1002048
sḏ to break	1002037
sḏ fire	1002031
sḏ foster child	1002032
sḏ loincloth	1002034
sḏb evil	1002039
sḏꜣ to amuse (trans.)	1002056
sḏꜣ to seal	1002057
sḏꜣm hoe	1002059
sḏꜣm to speak boastfully	1002060
sḏm to hear	1002049
sḏn to carry	1002050
sḏnf ibex	1002051
sḏr [a med. liquid]	1002052
sḏr to sleep	1002054
sḏḥ shin	1002044
sḏḏ image	1002042

š
š chair 1002001
š workplace? 1002004
š lake 1001062
šꜣ [a fruit] 1002377
šꜣ marsh 1002381
šꜣ order 1002382
šꜣ shallow? 1002383
šꜣ talon 1002384
šꜣ upper chest 1002385
šꜣ excrement (med.) 1002379
šꜣj pig 1002394
šꜣꜥ storeroom 1002410
šꜣꜥ to begin 1002411
šꜣꜥzẖ [a plant] 1002412
šꜣw to cauterize 1002408
šꜣb [a boat] 1002386
šꜣb food 1002388
šꜣm dirty item? 1002396
šꜣr [an eye affliction] 1002400
šꜣs to travel 1002403
šꜣš to avoid 1002402
šꜣḳ [a container] 1002398
šꜣd to dig 1002389
šꜥ to cut off 1002413
šꜥy sand 1002421
šꜥr gate 1002417
šꜥr to promise 1002419
šw [a jug] 1002339
šw feather 1002344
šw protection 1002345
šw side 1002346
šw sunlight 1002347
šwi̯ to be empty 1002358
šwi̯ to raise up 1002360
šwj trade 1002361
šwb [a jar] 1002349
šwb persea tree 1002350
šb [a ritual object] 1002005
šb melon? 1002007
šb rib 1002009
šbi̯ = šbn to mix 1002015
šbj shebyu-necklace 1002016
šbb mastic 1002010
šbb tube 1002011
šbd stick 1002012
šp to be blind 1002223
šp to flow out 1002224
šp to throw? 1002225
špn [a beverage] 1002228
špsi̯ to be dignified 1002235
špt to be angry 1002236
špt to blow up 1002237
šfꜥ to fight 1002073
šfi̯ to respect 1002066
šfu̯ to swell 1002070
šfd to grasp 1002063
šfn to touch 1002067
šfn undergrowth 1002068
šm in law 1002142
šm omen 1002143
šm to cut off 1002145
šmꜣ flower 1002173
šmꜣ to wander 1002176
šmi̯ to go 1002153
šmꜥ to be slender 1002178
šmꜥ to make music 1002179
šmꜥ Upper Egypt 1002180
šmm = *ẖmm to be hot 1002159
šmr bow 1002163
šms [instrument of punishment] 1002166
šms to follow 1002169
šn bad 1002182
šn hundred 1002185
šn rope 1002186
šn tree 1002189
šni̯ to be round? 1002200
šni̯ to fight 1002201
šni̯ to dispute 1002203
šni̯ to stink 1002204
šni̯ to suffer 1002205
šnj hair 1002206
šnꜥ [a small fish] 1002217
šnꜥ breast 1002218
šnꜥ to hold back 1002219
šnꜥ to value 1002220

šnb chest 1002191
šnb trumpet 1002194
šnp reed 1002210
šntȝy widow 1002216
šnṯ to oppose 1002214
šnḏ acacia 1002195
šnḏ kilt 1002196
šlf to be disheveled 1002138
šlm delivery 1002332
šlm peace 1002140
šlg snow 1002139
šr nose 1002249
šr [a body of water] 1002245
šrj to block 1002261
šrr to be small 1002264
šrr to shout 1002265
šrḥ brook 1002257
šrš to be quick 1002266
šrgḥ feelings 1002256
šḥḳ dust cloud 1002099
šz bowl 1002372
šzp lashing (naut.) 1002375
šzp to receive 1002376
šzm [a belt] 1002373
šzm malachite 1002374
šs [green pigment] 1002267
šs alabaster 1002268
šš fool 1002269
šs nest 1002270
šs rope 1002271
šs to build 1002272
šsȝ [an antilope] 1002301
šsȝ nightfall 1002302
šsȝ to be skillful 1002303
šsm leather scroll? 1002281
šsm to be inflamed 1002282
šsm to be strong 1002283
šsr to kill 1002291
šsr to shine 1002292
šsr to utter 1002294
šḳ ring 1002241
šḳb rhinoceros 1002243
škn watering place 1002134
škr [a mineral] 1002136
šgr [a body of water] 1002078
šgr [a wooden box] 1002079
št stroke oar? 1002312
št tax payer? 1002313
štȝ to be hidden 1002337
štb to enclose 1002316
štm to be hostile 1002324
šṯ to decorate 1002314
šṯ turtle 1002315
šṯj rectum 1002323
šd leather 1002033
šdi̯ to dig 1002045
šdi̯ to educate 1002046
šdi̯ to take? 1002047
šdr ravine 1002053
šḏ dough 1002030

ḳ

ḳȝi̯ to be high 1001918
ḳȝj [a beverage] 1001919
ḳȝꜥ to spew 1001924
ḳȝw flour 1001923
ḳȝb chest 1001913
ḳȝb = ḳnb to fold 1001884
ḳȝr bolt 1001920
ḳȝri̯ to stay near 1001921
ḳȝḥ to bind 1001916
ḳȝḥ to plaster 1001917
ḳȝs to bind 1001922
ḳȝd to creep 1001061
ḳȝd to cry 1001915
ḳj shape 1001866
ḳjs to vomit 1001867
ḳꜥḥ to bend 1001925
ḳwpr henna 1001910
ḳwr cargo loader 1001911
ḳb [a kind of a woodworking] 1001841
ḳb prevalence 1001842
ḳbꜥ to joke 1001847
ḳbb throat 1001843
ḳbb = ḳbḥ to be cool 1001844
ḳbḥ lower leg 1001845
ḳfn to bake 1001860

ḳfn to bend down 1001861
ḳfꜣ reputation 1001862
ḳm [timpani] 1001868
ḳm to be sad 1001869
ḳmꜣ rush 1001873
ḳmꜣ to mourn 1001875
ḳmꜣ to throw 1001876
ḳmy resin 1002371
ḳmḥ [a bread] 1001871
ḳmḥ twig 1001872
ḳmd to be concerned 1001870
ḳn to beat 1001882
ḳn to weave 1001883
ḳn = ḏn [a plant] 1001878
ḳn = ḏn to finish 1001881
ḳni̯ to be strong 1001886
ḳnj [a bird] 1001888
ḳnj carrying chair 1001889
ḳnj to embrace 1001890
ḳnj yellow 1001891
ḳnd to rage 1001885
ḳr to hurry 1001894
ḳr to roll sth. 1001895
ḳrꜥ shield 1001907
ḳrf to contract 1001897
ḳrm ashes 1001899
ḳrn foreskin 1001900
ḳrr [a boat] 1001901
ḳrr cavern 1001902
ḳrr cloud 1001903
ḳrr frog 1001904
ḳrr to burn 1001905
ḳrḥ uterus? 1001898
ḳrs to bury 1001874
ḳrṯ [a young animal] 1001906
ḳrḏn ax 1001896
ḳḥ light 1001863
ḳḥ to break 1001864
ḳḥn cauldron? 1001865
ḳs bone? 1001908
ḳsn to be difficult 1001909
ḳḳ doum nuts 1001892
ḳḳ to eat 1001893
ḳd [a tree] 1001848
ḳd kite 1001849
ḳd to form 1001852
ḳdb to rent 1001854
ḳdf to collect 1001856
ḳdi̯ to go around 1001857
ḳdr incense 1001859
ḳdd to sleep 1001855
ḳḏ plaster 1001850
ḳḏ thornbush 1001851
ḳḏ to run 1001853
ḳḏm to grasp 1001858

k

kꜣ life force 1001266
kꜣ vagina 1001267
kꜣ work 1001268
kꜣꜣ leopard-patterned 1001280
kꜣi̯ to swell 1001271
kꜣi̯ to think 1001272
kꜣj [a boat] 1001273
kꜣy excrement? 1001279
kꜣp to cover 1001277
kꜣf flint 1001269
kꜣm garden 1001274
kꜣmn to be blind 1001275
kꜣr chapel 1001278
kꜣhs to be rough 1001270
kj [a monkey] 1001222
kj to shout 1001223
kj other 1001264
kjw to bow 1001224
kwšn [part of harness] 1001263
kp = kb palm of hand, sole of foot 1001235
kbs 1002576
kfꜣ rear part 1001216
kfi̯ to open 1001215
kfꜥ to plunder 1001217
kff to suck 1001214
km to complete 1001226
kmrj ivory 1001229
kmm to be black 1001227
kmr [a dancer] 1001228
knj to be dissatisfied 1001230

knm to wrap	1001231
knnr lyre	1001232
knḥ to darken	1001429
kns abdominal region	1001233
knt [a garment (cloak?)]	1001234
kr [a boat]	1001236
kr heap of stones	1001237
kr horn	1001238
kr saddle	1001239
krj prison	1001241
krp to efface	1001244
krm [a jewelry]	1001243
krḥt [a basket]	1001240
krs bag	1001245
krs to jump	1001246
krk bed	1001242
krk to cut	1001248
krṯ cords (for whip)	1001247
krṯ young animal	1001249
khꜣ to rage furiously	1001221
khb to push violently	1001219
kḥ to become old	1001218
kḥs chair	1001220
kz to run freely?	1001265
ks [a basket]	1001250
ks to dance	1001251
ksi̯ to bow	1001252
ksm to oppose	1001253
kšw [a plant]	1001254
kki̯ to be dark	1001225
kt to tremble	1001256
ktw cauldron	1001262
ktp scimitar	1001260
ktm gold	1001258
ktt to be small	1001261
kṯm boasting	1001257
kṯn charioteer	1001259
g	
gꜣ [a heron]	1000429
gꜣ to chatter	1000430
gꜣ to hang	1000431
gꜣ to wound	1000432
gꜣi̯ to make wet	1000439
gꜣi̯ to overthrow	1000440
gꜣj [a jar]	1000441
gꜣj [a measure]	1000442
gꜣj naos	1000443
gꜣu̯ to be narrow	1000445
g#b arm	1000433
gꜣb leaf	1000434
gꜣf to bake	1000435
gꜣḥ shoulder	1000436
gꜣḥ to be weary	1000437
gꜣḥ to squeeze	1000438
gꜣš reed	1000444
gj [a plant]	1000373
gjf monkey	1000374
gw [a bull]	1000423
gw to rejoice	1000425
gwꜣ chest	1000427
gwꜣ to tighten	1000428
gwš to be crooked	1000426
gb to incline	1000361
gbꜣ arm	1000365
gbꜣ payment	1000366
gbꜣ to blind	1000367
gbi̯ to damage	1000364
gbb [a goose]	1000362
gbb earth	1000363
gp cloud	1000393
gm ibis	1000375
gm power	1000376
gm weak	1000377
gmꜣ temple (of the head)	1000381
gmi̯ to find	1000380
gmḥ strand of hair	1000378
gmḥ to see	1000379
gn [a plant]	1000382
gn base	1000383
gn respect	1000384
gn to record*	1000385
gnf repel	1000386
gnn soft	1000390
gnẖ to fix	1000388
gnẖ wing	1000389
gns violence	1000392
gnš to select	1000391

gngntj lute	1000387
gr also	1000394
gr kidney	1000395
gr silence	1000396
grb property	1000397
grb to cut (wood)	1000398
grm to drag away	1000405
grḥ night	1000403
grḥ to finish	1000404
grg exaltation	1000399
grg lie	1000400
grg rib	1000401
grg to prepare	1000402
grt husk?	1000406
gḥs gazelle	1000372
gs half	1000407
gs to anoint	1000410
gs to mourn	1000411
gs to regulate	1000412
gs to treat (leather)	1000413
gsi̯ to run	1000414
gsp basket	1000415
gsp to equip	1000416
gsr finger ring	1000417
gsꜣ [an antilope]	1000419
gsꜣ bag	1000420
gsꜣ to be inclined	1000421
gstj scribe's palette	1000418
gš liquid	1000408
gš migrating bird	1000409
gg kidney	1000370
ggwi̯ to be amazed	1000371
gt cistern	1000422
gḏ arm	1000368
gḏm to grasp	1000369
t	
tʾ bread	1002425
tꜣ door	1002580
tꜣ earth	1002581
tꜣ to be hot	1002584
tꜣj [a fabric]	1002590
tꜣj to resist	1002591
tꜣf pottery kiln	1002587

tꜣm [a worm?]	1002592
tꜣḥ to sink	1002588
tꜣš to demarcate	1002597
tj [a chapel]	1002469
tj [a measure of incense]	1002470
tj [a mineral]	1002471
tj [an amulet]	1002472
tj fraction	1002473
tj image	1002474
tj to pound	1002476
tjꜣ to shout	1002480
tjs to fix	1002479
ty steppe	1002575
twꜣ [an oil]	1002572
twꜣ evil	1002573
twꜣ to elevate	1002574
twr to purify	1002567
twr to stay away	1002568
twrj [a staff]	1002569
twhr (foreign, Asiatic) warrior	1002563
twt to be like	1002570
tb to recompense	1002428
tb to take up?	1002429
tbn head	1002430
tbn to drum	1002432
tbs heel	1002433
tbs to stab	1002434
tp [a piece of wood?]	1002519
tp head	1002520
tpꜣ [a fruit]	1002531
tpꜣ [a part of a skull]	1002532
tpꜣ [an ingredient]	1002533
tpj [an ox]	1002524
tpn dagger	1002525
tpnn cumin	1002527
tpr to breathe	1002529
tf to spit out	1002435
tfꜣ saw	1002442
tfi̯ to repulse	1002436
tfn dent (in metal objects)	1002437
tfn orphan	1002438
tfnn to rejoice	1002439
tm not to be	1002487

tm sledge 1002488
tmꜣ mat 1002497
tmꜣ mother 1002498
tmꜣ troop 1002500
tmm [a wooden chest] 1002492
tmz to turn (the face to someone) 1002496
tmt to powder (med.) 1002495
tnj to grow old 1002510
tnbḫ to be confused 1002502
tnm to go astray 1002512
tl mound 1002485
tr time 1002537
trj door 1002541
trj impurity 1002542
trj veneration 1002543
trꜥ worm 1002552
trḫ* strainer 1002540
trr oven 1002546
trr to run 1002547
thi̯ to obstruct 1002453
thb reduce (liquid) 1002447
thm to perforate 1002455
thm to cook 1002454
tḥwꜣ peas 1002467
tḥs to squash 1002465
tḫ fat 1002443
tḫ lead 1002444
tḫ to confuse 1002445
tḫi̯ to be drunk 1002452
tḫb to moisten 1002449
tḫb turtle 1002450
tḫbs [a basket] 1002451
tḫn to damage 1002458
tḫn to protect 1002460
tḫn towering cultic structure 1002461
tḫr [part of chariot] 1003902
tḫs to slaughter 1002464
tš to crush 1002553
tšꜣ to squash 1002557
tšmm [a crocodile] 1002556
tḳr huge 1002534
tk to attack 1002481
tk to be near 1002482
tkꜣ to burn 1002484

ṯ
ṯ [timber] 1002422
ṯ book 1002423
ṯ crew 1002424
ṯꜣ ball 1002579
ṯꜣ male 1002582
ṯꜣ nestling 1002583
ṯꜣ* vizier 1002585
ṯꜣi̯ to take 1002589
ṯꜣw wind 1002598
ṯꜣbb corn ear 1002586
ṯꜣpr to swell 1002595
ṯꜣm to cloak 1002593
ṯꜣms to eat 1002594
ṯꜣr to secure 1002596
ṯꜣr to secure 1002596
ṯꜣz to command 1002599
ṯꜣz to join 1002600
ṯj thyme 1002475
ṯjf to flee 1002477
ṯjs [preparing? dough for beer making] 1002478
ṯw share 1002561
ṯwj crown? 1002564
ṯwfj papyrus plant 1002562
ṯwn = ṯwꜣ to attack 1002565
ṯwn to reward 1002566
ṯb cage 1002426
ṯb foot sole 1002427
ṯbn to be quick 1002431
ṯpn* to be glad 1002526
ṯpr scribe 1002528
ṯprṯ (bronze-clad Hittite) chariot 1002530
ṯpḥ cave 1002523
ṯpg barracks 1002521
ṯfrr lapis lazuli 1002440
ṯftn to rush 1002441
ṯm [container (measure for cake)] 1002486
ṯm to be ashamed 1002489
ṯmꜣ to be strong 1002499

ṯmḥ [a red ochre]	1002490
ṯmḥ to turn away?	1002491
ṯms to be red	1002493
ṯms to bury	1002494
ṯn guardian	1002501
ṯni̯ to rise	1002508
ṯnj to be weak	1002509
ṯnj where	1000844
ṯnf [a vessel]	1002503
ṯnf to drink and dance	1002504
ṯnf to measure	1002505
ṯnm cauldron	1002511
ṯnḥ to observe	1002506
ṯnḥr [a falcon]	1002507
ṯnt [sacred cattle (of Hathor)]	1002516
ṯnw to count	1002518
ṯntꜣ dais	1002517
ṯl to be strong	1002514
ṯlk [a bier]	1002515
ṯr fine flour	1002535
ṯr red	1002536
ṯr willow	1002538
ṯryn body armor	1002550
ṯrꜥ [a field]	1002551
ṯrw* to delight in sth.	1002549
ṯrp [a goose]	1002545
ṯrf [a dance]	1002539
ṯrm to wink	1002544
ṯrrj siege mound	1002548
ṯhꜣ lame	1002468
ṯhb to jump	1002448
ṯhm to threaten	1002455
ṯhn ibis	1002456
ṯḥ to rejoice	1002446
ṯḥn to be bright	1002457
ṯḥn to encounter	1002459
ṯḥn to encounter	1002459
ṯḥr injury	1002462
ṯḥs [a metal]	1002463
ṯḥs to stretch	1002466
ṯzi̯ to rise	1002576
ṯzm hound	1002577
ṯzm to build	1002578
ṯs to sit	1002554
ṯši̯ to go away	1002555
ṯkr tower gate	1002483
ṯt to dissolve	1002559
ṯtf to overflow	1002560
ṯṯ sparrow	1002558

d

d hand	1000148
dꜣ to copulate	1000302
dꜣ = ꜥꜣ* to tremble	1000303
dꜣj linen	1000311
dꜣb fig	1000304
dꜣr to subdue	1000319
dꜣz to bind	1000320
dj five	1000206
dj here	1000207
djdj (red) ochre	1000208
dwꜣ rise	1000296
dwn to stretch out	1000292
dwr [a basket]	1000293
dwẖ* to embalm	1000287
db riverside	1000152
db to devour	1000154
dbj hippopotamus	1000161
dbb = ḏbb to block	1000157
dbn to encircle	1000163
dbḥ to request	1000160
dp boat	1000242
dp loin	1000243
dp lump?	1000244
dp to taste	1000245
dpy crocodile	1000249
dpẖ execution block?	1000246
df to tear	1000183
dm to be sharp	1000210
dm worm	1000211
dmꜣ to bind together	1000214
dmj = dmꜣ = dmḏ to unite	1000213
dmḏ to unite	1000212
dn family	1000217
dn to cut	1000219
dn to rage	1000225
dn to traverse	1000226

dni̯ share	1000232
dnj shouting	1000234
dnꜥ to refill	1000241
dnrg a fruit	1000238
dnḥs [metal tool]	1000231
dns to be heavy	1000240
dng to be deaf	1000229
dng = dꜣg tiny being	1000228
dr prod	1000263
dr to dress	1000264
dr to remove	1000266
dr to spread	1000267
drp to supply	1000271
drf to paint	1000269
dhn cliff	1000196
dhn forehead	1000197
dhn to appoint	1000199
dḥ to be low	1000194
dḥꜣ straw	1000202
dḥꜣ to pounce	1000203
dḥr to be bitter	1000200
dẖ to crush	1000195
dẖn rhythm	1000198
ds to be sharp	1000275
dšr to be red	1000280
dḳ to grind	1000250
dḳꜥ to smoothen	1000256
dḳw to be barefoot	1000255
dḳr banish?	1000251
dḳr harvest	1000252
dḳr to attach	1000253
dḳrw essence	1000254
dg foot print	1000187
dgꜣ rasor	1000192
dgi̯ to hide	1000188
dgi̯ to see	1000189
dgm ricinus	1000190
dgm to feel powerless	1000191
dḏw to grind	1000181

ḏ

ḏ cobra	1000146
ḏ eternity	1000147
ḏꜣ [architectural element]	1000297
ḏꜣ ball	1000298
ḏꜣ crossing	1000299
ḏꜣ linen	1000300
ḏꜣ rotation	1000301
ḏꜣꜣ braid?	1000321
ḏꜣjs to counsel	1000312
ḏꜣꜥ frying pan	1000322
ḏꜣꜥ vetchling	1000323
ḏꜣb to greet	1000305
ḏꜣp bench	1000314
ḏꜣf to burn	1000309
ḏꜣm = ḏꜣn sexual activity	1000313
ḏꜣr helper	1000315
ḏꜣr requirement	1000316
ḏꜣr scorpion	1000317
ḏꜣr to cook	1000318
ḏꜣd audience hall	1000306
ḏꜣd to cut	1000307
ḏꜣḏ to wet?	1000308
ḏꜥ to be stormy	1000324
ḏꜥ to capture fish	1000325
ḏꜥꜥ twig	1000333
ḏꜥb black	1000326
ḏꜥm [a scepter]	1000327
ḏꜥm [a staff]	1000328
ḏꜥm gold	1000329
ḏꜥr [part of a door (lock)]	1000331
ḏꜥr to select?	1000332
ḏꜥḳ to shout	1000330
ḏw [a vessel]	1000284
ḏw [an insect]	1000285
ḏw = ḏwꜥ knife	1000286
ḏwi̯ to be evil	1000288
ḏwi̯ to call	1000289
ḏws to defame	1000294
ḏwt twenty (dual?)	1000295
ḏb army	1000149
ḏb brick	1000150
ḏb to collect	1000153
ḏb* to make live	1000155
ḏbꜣ [a scepter]	1000165
ḏbꜣ harpoon	1000166
ḏbꜣ to block	1000167
ḏbꜣ to change dress	1000168

ḏbꜣ to support	1000169
ḏbꜥ finger	1000170
ḏbw a piece of meat	1000164
ḏbb [body of water]	1000156
ḏbn antilope	1000162
ḏbḥ to fish	1000159
ḏbg to dive	1000158
ḏpḥ = tpḥ apple	1000247
ḏpḳ dancer	1000248
ḏfꜣ to wipe	1000185
ḏfꜣ = ḏfn to provide?	1000186
ḏfi̯ to sink in	1000184
ḏm sanctuary?	1000209
ḏmꜥ papyrus	1000215
ḏmꜥ to be parched	1000216
ḏn to be hot	1000218
ḏn to thresh	1000220
ḏnj fifth day	1000233
ḏnb dwarf	1000221
ḏnb to turn back	1000222
ḏnn skull	1000235
ḏnn to struggle	1000236
ḏnr branch	1000237
ḏnrm to try hard	1000239
ḏnḥ wing	1000230
ḏnd to be angry	1000223
ḏnḏr brushwood	1000227
ḏr [a precious stone]	1000257
ḏr calf	1000258
ḏr foreign	1000259
ḏr hand	1000260
ḏr kite	1000261
ḏr limit	1000262
ḏr to drum	1000265
ḏr leaf	1000268
ḏrj pigment	1000270
ḏrꜥ plank	1000272
ḏrꜥ to subdue	1000273
ḏḥ [a monkey]	1000193
ḏḥꜥ [a plant]	1000204
ḏḥꜥ leather	1000205
ḏḥtj lead	1000201
ḏs person	1000274
ḏs to burn	1000276
ḏswi̯ to call	1000282
ḏsf net	1000277
ḏsr [a plant]	1000278
ḏsr to be raised	1000279
ḏsr to seclude	1000281
ḏt olive tree	1000283
ḏd to say	1000173
ḏdꜣ to grow fat	1000182
ḏdi̯ to endure	1000178
ḏdb = ḏdm to heap	1000174
ḏdb = ḏdm to sting	1000175
ḏdf to shudder	1000176
ḏdḥ to confine	1000177
ḏḏ flower	1000171

Lexeme index
(Including lexeme ID and DRID)

ꜣ

ꜣ [particle of negation] 3 1001022
ꜣ vulture; bird (gen.) 1 1002865
ꜣ.t strength 6 1002864
ꜣ.t moment; instant; time 5 1002864
ꜣꜣ ruin (or similar) 7 1002922
ꜣj.wj pair of bandages 10 1002895
ꜣꜥ.w [building component?]; [construction material?] 27 1002925
ꜣjs.brain; viscera 13 1002896
ꜣyt to be pale (of face) 14 1002918
ꜣꜥꜥ to coat with plaster; to repair 16 1002925
ꜣꜥꜥ to accuse; to blame; to injure, to harm 17 1002926
ꜣꜥꜥ.w approach 22 1001209
ꜣꜥw (leather) bag 26 1002924
ꜣꜥb.t oppression 28 1002923
ꜣw length 31 1002917
ꜣw to be dead 858947 1002917
ꜣw dead one 863783 1002917
ꜣw long 400588 1002917
ꜣw death 32 1002917
ꜣw.t gift(s); offering(s) 39 1002917
ꜣw.t slaughter?; long knife? 38 1002917
ꜣw.t length; span 37 1002917
ꜣwꜣw to be elongated; long extended; double long 858406 1002917
ꜣwꜣw.tj long one [designation of a person] 856494 1002917
ꜣwi̯ to extend; to present (something) 51 1002917
ꜣwi̯ to be extended (in width, in length) 50 1002917
ꜣwi̯ to extend; to be extended (in width, in length) 49 1002917
ꜣwr to tremble 55 1001737
ꜣwr, ꜣwj trembling 856496 1001737
ꜣb to avoid; to have ceased 858405 1002867
ꜣb cease to do (aux./modal) 852472 1002867
ꜣb to cease; to avoid; to tarry 856201 1002867
ꜣb to cease; to separate; to avoid; to linger 72 1002867
ꜣb fingernail 10270 1002868
ꜣb.w cessation 79 1002867
ꜣb.w brand; branding iron 61 1002868
ꜣb.w wish; vow 10340 1002871
ꜣb.wt appearance; aspect 84 1002871
ꜣb.t wish(es); vow? 68 1002871
ꜣb.t brand 66 1002868
ꜣb.t family 67 1002866
ꜣb.tjw household; family member 88 1002866
ꜣbꜣb to be delighted 10310 1002871
ꜣbi̯ to wish for; to covet 73 1002871
ꜣbj leopard 74 1002872
ꜣbj.t female leopard 75 1002872
ꜣbu̯ to brand (cattle, slaves) 60 1002868
ꜣbw [a med. substance] 82 1002873
ꜣbw elephant 80 1002874
ꜣbw tusk; ivory 63 1002874
ꜣbb to separate; to move away; to keep apart 85 1002868
ꜣbẖ to mingle; to unite 91 1002870
ꜣbẖ to link; to be linked 90 1002870
ꜣbẖ to mix; to join; to be merged with 89 1002870
ꜣbẖ to burn; to cook 359 1002870
ꜣbẖ linker 450623 1002870
ꜣbẖ.t [a med. liquid] 92 1002870
ꜣbd month 93 1002869
ꜣbd [a priest serving for the lunar month] 95 1002869
ꜣbd Abed (one of those who support the heavenly cow) 500043 1002869
ꜣbd Abed (the moon) 96 1002869
ꜣbd.w Abedu (festival on the 2nd day

of the lunar month) 94 1002869
ꜣbd.w Abedu (2nd day of the lunar month) 99 1002869
ꜣbd.w monthly 97 1002869
ꜣpd poultry fat 111 1002903
ꜣpd bird (gen.); fowl (coll.) 107 1002903
ꜣpd bird (a constellation) 108 1002903
ꜣpd to rush forward 110 1002903
ꜣpd.wt poultry 115 1002903
ꜣfꜣf to hail 117 1002878
ꜣfꜣf to eat (greedily) 10420 1002879
ꜣfi̯ to eat (greedily) 119 1002879
ꜣfy.t warmth; heat 120 1002880
ꜣfꜥ gluttony 121 1002879
ꜣfꜥ greedy one 122 1002879
ꜣfr to heat (something); to boil; to simmer 851320 1002880
ꜣfr to boil; to simmer 126 1002880
ꜣfr to boil (something); to heat 125 1002880
ꜣm to burn up 130 1002898
ꜣm seizer (hieracosphinx, as a manifestation of Horus) 133 1002900
ꜣm to burn (something); to destroy 129 1002898
ꜣm to burn; to burn up 128 1002898
ꜣm seizer (Horus as a lion (at Edfu), the king) 132 1002900
ꜣm.w ember (illness) 861178 1002898
ꜣm.w (scorching) heat; ember 142 1002898
ꜣm.w Seizer 501096 1002900
ꜣm.wt burning 143 1002898
ꜣm.tj Burnt one (Seth) 853103 1002898
ꜣmj to mix 136 1002899
ꜣmj Fiery? One (sun god) 137 1002898
ꜣmm to seize; to grasp 144 1002900
ꜣmm grip?; grasp 145 1002900
ꜣmm Seizer 856380 1002900
ꜣmm.w gripings; spasms (gynaecological term) 148 1002900
ꜣmm.t grasp; grip 146 1002900
ꜣms to wield the ames sceptre 852756 1002901
ꜣms [a club shaped scepter; ames-scepter] 150 1002901
ꜣms.y belonging to the ames-sceptre 854912 1002901
ꜣmꜥ.t socket (for a door hinge) 140 1002902
ꜣmꜥ.t ramus (of the lower jaw); forked bone 139 1002902
ꜣmꜥ.t [a mash (med.)] 141 1002899
ꜣr need? 156 1002906
ꜣr to drive away; to oppress 155 1002907
ꜣrw.t excrement? 856454 1002907
ꜣrw.t displacement; repression? 856455 1002907
ꜣrr disappointment? 164 1002906
ꜣrr to be frustrated? 10460 1002906
ꜣh to be miserable 169 1002890
ꜣh to make miserable 170 1002890
ꜣh.w pain 174 1002890
ꜣh.w sufferer; anxious one 175 1002890
ꜣhd to be weak; to be exhausted 181 1002891
ꜣhd weakness 182 1002891
ꜣhd Exhausted One 184 1002891
ꜣḥ [a mash]; [dough (med.)] 186 1002884
ꜣḥ field 185 1002887
ꜣḥ.w flood 856369 1002887
ꜣḥ.t field; arable land 191 1002887
ꜣḥ.t Field (a domain) 850622 1002887
ꜣḥꜣḥ to bury in the ground 196 1002887
ꜣḥy inundation?; to inundate? 197 1002887
ꜣḫ to be glorious; to be beneficial; to be useful 200 1002885
ꜣḫ akh-spirit; glorified spirit (the deceased) 203 1002885
ꜣḫ flame; fire 856498 1002888
ꜣḫ glorious; beneficial; glorified 600475 1002885
ꜣḫ abundance 856256 1002887
ꜣḫ papyrus thicket 198 1002892
ꜣḫ Akh-spirit 500678 1002885
ꜣḫ.y plants 251 1002892
ꜣḫ.y Effective One 500721 1002885

ꜣḫ.w [a field crop?] 215 1002892
ꜣḫ.w (magical) power; mastery 253 1002885
ꜣḫ.t horizon (metaph. for palace, temple, tomb) 232 1002885
ꜣḫ.t glory; what is beneficial 217 1002885
ꜣḫ.t horizon 227 1002885
ꜣḫ.t field; arable land 228 1002892
ꜣḫ.t akh-spirit; glorified spirit (the deceased) 218 1002885
ꜣḫ.t uraeus; diadem 220 1002885
ꜣḫ.t (crested) ibis 230 1002889
ꜣḫ.t flame; fire 223 1002888
ꜣḫ.t shining one (Hathor cow) 222 1002885
ꜣḫ.t akhet-season (inundation) 216 1002892
ꜣḫ.t glossy eye (of a god) 221 1002885
ꜣḫ.t glorious ones (gods) 219 1002885
ꜣḫ.t [a knife?] 231 1002885
ꜣḫ.tj well-watered 853579 1002892
ꜣḫ.tj the first day of Akhet season 863198 1002892
ꜣḫ.tj of the horizon 852800 1002885
ꜣḫ.tj horizon-dweller 237 1002885
ꜣḫ.tj both glossy eyes (of a god) 853669 1002885
ꜣḫ.tjw Horizon-Dwellers 239 1002885
ꜣḫ.tjt horizon-dweller (Hathor in Dendera) 240 1002885
ꜣḫꜣḫ equipment; accessories; part of a ship 866282 1002885
ꜣḫꜣḫ [ship's equipment (mast? ropes?)] 248 1002885
ꜣḫꜣḫ to make verdant; to make grow green 245 1002892
ꜣḫꜣḫ to be verdant; to be inundated 244 1002892
ꜣḫꜣḫ to be verdant; to make green 243 1002892
ꜣḫꜣḫ bones 246 1002886
ꜣḫꜣḫ Akhakhu (a constellation) 247 1002885
ꜣḫi to grow green; to flourish; to be inundated 199 1002892
ꜣḫꜥ to scratch; to carve 258 1002893
ꜣḫꜥ stonecutter 259 1002893
ꜣḫꜥ.t scratch 261 1002893
ꜣḫb to swallow 262 1002891
ꜣḫb.y Swallower 263 1002891
ꜣḫb.yt Swallower 500723 1002891
ꜣz Az-Vulture 854105 1002909
ꜣzb to burn; to glow 852777 1002919
ꜣzb the burning One (gate keeper of the netherworld) 278 1002920
ꜣzb.jw Asebiu (11th gate of the netherworld) 280 1002920
ꜣzb.t the burning one 856527 1002920
ꜣzḫ to reap; to harvest 264 1002921
ꜣzḫ harvest 265 1002921
ꜣzḫ sickle 281 1002921
ꜣs to overtake (somebody); to hasten 268 1002908
ꜣs to rush; to run 267 1002908
ꜣs to rush; to make rush 266 1002908
ꜣs.t splinter 273 1002908
ꜣsꜣs hastily; in a hurry 269 1002908
ꜣsb.t Asbet (a serpent goddess) 279 1002920
ꜣšr roast meat 288 1002910
ꜣšr to roast 287 1002910
ꜣšr.t roast joint 289 1002910
ꜣḳ to perish; to come to naught 290 1002904
ꜣḳ.yt loss 294 1002904
ꜣḳ.w devastation; ruin 291 1002904
ꜣk to be bent; to bend (the elbow) 401 1002897
ꜣk.wt [a symptom of illness] 306 1002897
ꜣg to plant 309 1002881
ꜣgb.w flood; abundance 314 1002883
ꜣgb.w flood 860570 1002883
ꜣgb.t flood 860554 1002883
ꜣgb+ to overflow; to flood 313 1002883
ꜣgbgb [noun (a food?)]; abundance? 10630 1002883
ꜣgbgb to shudder? 318 1002882
ꜣgg.t sheaf (of flax stalks) 320 1002881
ꜣt to enter? (a place) 850151 1002911
ꜣtj [a part of the solar bark] 321 1002915
ꜣtf to be equipped (with donations)

328 1002912
ꜣtf incense (gen.) 329 1002913
ꜣtf atef-crown (crown of the gods) 326 1002912
ꜣtf to be crowned 854488 1002912
ꜣtf to be crowned 327 1002912
ꜣtf [designation of a serpent (in the name of Atfet)] 331 1002912
ꜣtf.tj Crowned-one with the atef-crown (Osiris) 333 1002912
ꜣṯ.yt nurse; attendant 336 1002914
ꜣṯ.w administrator (gen.); foreman; tutor? 338 1002914
ꜣṯ.w administrator; steward; 855659 1002914
ꜣṯ.wtj one relating to rearing (nurse? nursling?) 337 1002914
ꜣṯ.t bier; bed 334 1002914
ꜣṯi̯ to mind (a child); to rear (a child); to care (for); to bring up 335 1002914
ꜣṯp [a box] 323 1002916
ꜣṯp to load (a ship) 340 1002916
ꜣṯp.y laden one 341 1002916
ꜣṯp.w load; cargo 324 1002916
ꜣṯp.wt load; cargo 325 1002916
ꜣd to rage; to be angry 343 1002875
ꜣd to decay 348 1002876
ꜣd to fail (of the heart) 351 1002876
ꜣd to smear (a vessel with clay) 349 1002877
ꜣd to rage; to attack 342 1002875
ꜣd to attack; to anger (someone); to be aggressive 344 1002875
ꜣd.w lining (of a pot with clay); smoothing 350 1002877
ꜣd.w anger; agression 346 1002875
ꜣd.w aggressor (lit. furious one, of a crocodile) 353 1002875
ꜣd.w Furious One 356 1002875

j

j to say 500024 1000934
j [leaf of the reed] 20010 1001192
j.j address; name 854785 1000934
jꜣ.w hill? 20350 1001184
jꜣ.w praise 20360 1001184
jꜣ.wt the mounds (designation for Egypt) 20220 1001184
jꜣ.wt praised 600170 1001184
jꜣ.t [an offering] 20140 1001184
jꜣ.t [a place] 20110 1001184
jꜣ.t standard (for images of deities) 20100 1001184
jꜣ.t place; mound 20120 1001184
jꜣ.t [a plant] 20170 1001172
jꜣ.t spine; back (as body part) 20090 1001184
jꜣ.tjt cadastre? 20200 1001184
jꜣꜣ support? 450238 1001198
jꜣꜣ [an agricultural crop (vine?)] 20250 1001194
jꜣꜣ.t rod (as a mace, as a scepter) 20260 1001198
jꜣꜣ.t [tree] 857684 1001198
jꜣꜣ.t twig; rod 20270 1001198
jꜣi̯ to praise; to adore; to pray 20050 1001184
jꜣj.w [designation of the braid ("dancer")] 20320 1001185
jꜣy.wt old ones (also of gods) 20410 1001197
jꜣw old age 20490 1001197
jꜣw old man 20380 1001197
jꜣw.t old woman 20400 1001197
jꜣw.t [a cult object] 20420 1001197
jꜣw.t office insignia 860195 1001197
jꜣw.t function; office; dignity 20430 1001197
jꜣw.t old age 20390 1001197
jꜣw.tj office holder 20450 1001197
jꜣwi̯ to be old 20480 1001197
jꜣb to draw back (from); to avoid 400754 1002867
jꜣb.j left side; left arm 20530 1001173
jꜣb.j left; eastern 20610 1001173
jꜣb.w east 854362 1001173
jꜣb.t east 20550 1001173
jꜣb.t left eye 20560 1001173

jꜣb.t diadem of Lower Egypt 860353 1001173
jꜣb.tj east wind 20580 1001173
jꜣb.tj eastern; left 20570 1001173
jꜣb.tjt east 20590 1001173
jꜣb.tjw easterners 20670 1001173
jꜣb.ty eastern 866300 1001173
jꜣbys foundation; treasure 20620 1001174
jꜣf.t claw (of a predatory bird) 20710 1001179
jꜣm to bind (animals for slaughter) 20730 1001189
jꜣm charm; graciousness; sacrifice 24830 1001188
jꜣm [a broadleaf tree with fruits]; jam-timber 24810 1001188
jꜣm to be pleasant; to be friendly 24820 1001188
jꜣm riendly; popular 550093 1001188
jꜣm pleasing form 24840 1001188
jꜣm.jt leaves of the iam-tree 24960 1001188
jꜣm.yt charming one (Hathor) 24970 1001188
jꜣm.w tent; camp 25010 1001189
jꜣm.w radiance of the sun 24990 1001188
jꜣm.w [the color red]; [a red mineral] 25000 1001188
jꜣm.wtj the pleasant one 856489 1001188
jꜣm.wtj pleasant one 859048 1001188
jꜣm.wtj charming one (Amun) 25020 1001188
jꜣm.t priestess (at Edfu) 24920 1001188
jꜣm.t courtesy 24900 1001188
jꜣm.t [fruit of the iam-tree] 850689 1001188
jꜣm.t female (ibex and of other game animals) 24880 1001189
jꜣr mourning 20760 1001193
jꜣr dull eyes 857076 1001193
jꜣr [a plant (med.)] 20770 1001192
jꜣr.w rush (a flatsedge) 20810 1001192
jꜣr.wt rush thicket? 857080 1001192
jꜣr.t [discharge (of an animal, med.) 20790 1001193
jꜣr.t [a headcovering (braid of hair?)] 20780 1001193
jꜣrr dimness 857081 1001193
jꜣrr to be faint (of heart); to be dim (of eye) 20750 1001193
jꜣrr.wt grapevine; grapes; raisins 20830 1001194
jꜣẖ to shine 20850 1002885
jꜣẖ.w papyrus thicket; inundated area 857083 1002842
jꜣẖ.w radiance; (sun)shine 20880 1002885
jꜣẖ.w Radiant 854996 1002885
jꜣẖ.t radiant one (Hathor) 20860 1002885
jꜣẖi̯ to be flooded 20870 1002842
jꜣẖi̯ to sweep (the harvest) together 250 1001182
jꜣs bald one (a priest of Hathor) 20910 1001195
jꜣs to be bald 20900 1001195
jꜣs bald one 866315 1001195
jꜣq to command 20970 1001190
jꜣq climber [snake] 857075 1001190
jꜣq to rise 20980 1001190
jꜣq.t leek; vegetables (gen.) 20990 1001191
jꜣk old (experienced) man 21000 1001186
jꜣk.t age; seniority 851551 1001186
jꜣkb to mourn 21010 1001187
jꜣkb mourning 21020 1001187
jꜣkb.ty the two mourning women 852392 1001187
jꜣkb.y mourner 855868 1001187
jꜣkb.yt mourning woman 21050 1001187
jꜣṯ pain; to injure; to be injured 21070 1001196
jꜣṯ wilderness 855639 1001196
jꜣṯ.w mutilation; theft 21090 1001196
jꜣṯ.w place of judgment 21100 1001196
jꜣṯ.t injury 21080 1001196
jꜣd miserable one; sufferer; evildoer 21150 1001178
jꜣd [a cord (on a door bolt)] 21120 1001175

jꜣd to climb 21130 1001177
jꜣd to be miserable; to torture 21140 1001178
jꜣd.w plague 21220 1001178
jꜣd.t meadow; field 21170 1001176
jꜣd.t lack; need 21160 1001178
jꜣd.t net (gen.) 21190 1001175
jꜣd.t dew; (pleasant) scent; water 21180 1001176
jj spell?; to say? 21270 1000934
jj to agree? 21280 1000934
jj stag?; ram? 21420 1000993
jy one who comes (Horus) 21310 1001138
jy.wj welcome! 21360 1001138
jy.t what comes (euphemism for trouble) 21340 1001138
jy.tj welcome 500291 1001138
jy.tjw [the naos-bearers?] 21450 1001138
jʿ tomb 21480 1001162
jʿ bowl; basin (for washing) 21470 1001206
jʿ (gold) washer 21560 1001206
jʿ.w washing; breakfast 850185 1001206
jʿ.t pearl necklace; pearl net 21460 1001202
jʿꜣ cloak; kilt? 21510 1001211
jʿꜣ to cover; to withdraw, to hide (from view) 855671 1001211
jʿꜣ donkey 34840 1001210
jʿꜣ to speak a foreign language; to interpret 850019 1001212
jʿꜣ.w a person who speaks a foreign language; interpreter 450319 1001212
jʿꜣ.t jenny (she-ass) 21520 1001210
jʿi̯ to wash 21550 1001206
jʿj.t purifier? (Nephthys) 21530 1001206
jʿy.t [a med. liquid, related to beer] 21570 1001206
jʿb to rake? together; to comb? 21660 1001203
jʿb to unite; to be united; to hand over to 21680 1001203
jʿb.t bunch? (of offerings); heap? (of offerings) 21650 1001203
jʿf to wring out (clothes); to press out (grapes) 21710 1001204
jʿf squeezer 864191 1001204
jʿf squeezed 863041 1001204
jʿnʿ baboon 850186 1001208
jʿnʿ baboon (Thoth) 850335 1001208
jʿn.w grief; woe! 21750 1001207
jʿnʿ.t baboon 21730 1001208
jʿr to mount up; to touch; to bring up 21770 1001209
jʿr.t (divine) serpent; uraeus 21780 1001209
jʿr.tj one who belongs to the two uraei 21790 1001209
jʿry.t god's dwelling 21800 1001209
jʿḥ moon 21810 1001205
jw dog 21970 1001129
jw to be evil 450616 1001127
jw livestock? 21950 1001130
jw to separate 21960 1001127
jw island 21940 1001127
jw to wail 22000 1001132
jw evil; mischief 21990 1001127
jw.yt wrongdoing 22310 1001127
jw.yt mourning 550312 1001132
jw.w boatless man 400636 1001127
jw.w boatlessness (person) 857228 1001127
jw.w arrival 857227 1001138
jw.w wailing 22480 1001132
jw.t she-dog 855612 1001129
jw.tj without 856668 1001127
jw.tj non-existent one 23140 1001127
jw.tjw those who are not (the dead) 23150 1001127
jw.tjt what does not exist 550302 1001127
jwꜣ steer; ox; cattle 22160 1001153
jwꜣ to take away; to rob; to replace 22180 1001156
jwꜣ.yt helper 22230 1001154
jwꜣy.t throat 22240 1001155
jwꜣ.w helper 851074 1001154

jwꜣ.w removal 22250 1001156
jwꜣ.t cow 22200 1001153
jwꜣ.t [loaf of bread shaped like a cow's head] 22220 1001153
jwꜣ.t cattle 22210 1001153
jwi̯ to come; to return 21930 1001138
jwi̯ to separate 856211 1001127
jwi̯ [aux./modal] 851688 1001138
jwi̯ to strand; to leave (someone) boatless 22260 1001127
jwy to irrigate 22270 1001152
jwy.t house; sanctuary; quarter (of a town) 22320 1001140
jwjw dog 22340 1001129
jwjw to bewail 22350 1001132
jwjw Juju (dog) 855041 1001129
jwꜥ meat on the bone; haunch? 22360 1001157
jwꜥ to inherit 22380 1001158
jwꜥ.yt troops 22440 1001159
jwꜥ.w heritage; heir 859266 1001158
jwꜥ.w heir 22460 1001158
jwꜥ.w heritage; heir 857231 1001158
jwꜥ.w bracelet (for the upper arm, part of the Gold-of-favor); reward 22470 1001158
jwꜥ.wt throne 859431 1001158
jwꜥ.wt inheritance 22420 1001158
jwꜥ.wt heiress 22410 1001158
jwf flesh; meat 22520 1001134
jwf meat; flesh 500729 1001134
jwh to carry; to load 22990 1001135
jwḥ [an evil activity] 23020 1001136
jwḥ to destroy; to dispel 23010 1001136
jwḥ to weep; to mourn 23030 1001132
jwḥ to sprinkle (with water); to moisten 23000 1001137
jwḥ.yt mourner (Isis) 23040 1001132
jwḥ.w inundation 23050 1001137
jwms untruth 22550 1001141
jwn to unite 22590 1001145
jwn color; essence 22570 1001143
jwn to carry (in procession)? 22560 1001144
jwn pillar (Osiris and other gods) 22620 1001144
jwn character; reputation 400106 1001143
jwn pillar; column 22610 1001144
jwn pillar (of the moon) 500162 1001144
jwn nest? 22580 1001145
jwn support (designation for the wind, as a support of the sky) 22600 1001144
jwn.j backpillar? (of a statue) 22780 1001144
jwn.yt columned hall; columned court 22800 1001144
jwn.w heap(s) 22640 1001145
jwn.w colorful one (the sun god) 22840 1001143
jwn.t [something made of cloth (bag?) (clothing?)] 22680 1001145
jwn.t [a bow (weapon)] 22670 1001142
jwn.tj bowman 861025 1001142
jwn.tjt [group of persons] 860332 1001145
jwn.tjw [temple musicians] 22700 1001145
jwnn sanctuary (gen.) 22910 1001144
jwr [roast meat (as an offering)] 22960 1001146
jwr to conceive; to become pregnant 22930 1001148
jwr pregnancy 22940 1001148
jwr.yt beans 22980 1001147
jwr.t pregnant woman 22970 1001148
jws.w scales 23100 1001149
jwsw truly 855125 1001151
jwsw as; how; like; same, truly 864329 1001151
jwšš [mash (med.)]; [dough (med.)] 23110 1001150
jwt.j wrongdoer (Seth) 22040 1001127
jwt.w what is putrefied 23190 1001127
jwd to separate; to lie between; charged to 23220 1001127
jwd to catch in a net 23230 1001127

jwd.t parting 23240 1001127
jb [a leaf tree] 23320 1000936
jb farmer 23400 1000945
jb to wish; to suppose; to think 23370 1000940
jb thirsty man 23360 1000945
jb kid; goat 23340 1000939
jb heart; mind; wish; character 23290 1000940
jb [a sistrum] 23330 1000935
jb.yt [a servant (dancer? of Neith)] 23630 1000953
jb.w purification booth; refuge 450607 1000941
jb.wj double-heart amulet 23460 1000940
jb.t thirst 23430 1000945
jb.t chapel 863642 1000938
jbꜣ dancer 23540 1000953
jbꜣ to dance 23520 1000953
jbꜣ playing piece (for a board game) 23510 1000953
jbꜣ.yt dancer (a bird? an insect?) 23570 1000953
jbꜣ.yt dancer (figurative for an oar) 23580 1000953
jbꜣ.w maned sheep 23600 1000952
jbꜣ.w dance; entertainment 23530 1000953
jbꜣ.t [an unguent] 23550 1000937
jbꜣ.t dancer 23560 1000953
jbi̯ to be thirsty 23640 1000945
jbjb darling 23650 1000940
jbjb satisfaction; joy 857087 1000940
jbn.w alum; vitriolic salts (gen.) 23770 1000946
jbr stallion 23790 1000947
jbh.tj gneiss 23820 1000942
jbḥ tooth 23830 1000944
jbḥ to be wet; to be flooded 23850 1000943
jbḥ to laugh (lit. to bare the teeth) 23840 1000944
jbḥ.w libationer 23860 1000943
jbzꜣ [an (ethereal?) oil] 23920 1000951
jbzꜣ [a plant (med.)] 23930 1000951
jbs ibes-headdress 23910 1000948
jbšt [a kind of bread or biscuit] 23960 1000949
jbkꜣ pregnant one (designation for a sow) 23970 1000049
jbṯ to catch (in a trap) 851571 1000950
jbṯ birdtrap 857088 1000950
jbṯ.t bird-trap 23990 1000950
jbṯ.tj fowler 24000 1000950
jp accounting; estimation 859124 1001066
jp [designation of a person] 856683 1001066
jp to count; to assess; to be cognizant of 24070 1001066
jp stairway 24080 1001066
jp.w account; inventory; list 24330 1001066
jp.w account; inventory; list 24340 1001066
jp.t [(secret? lockable?) chamber] 24130 1001065
jp.t ipet (the sky) 24180 1001065
jp.t women's apartments; inner chamber 24140 1001065
jp.t oipe (a dry measure); [a measuring vessel] 24120 1001066
jp.t hippopotamus 856426 1001064
jp.t number; census 24110 1001066
jpꜣ flyer 857055 1001827
jpꜣ red dye (madder) 24250 1001071
jpjp [an implement made of alabaster] 24300 1001065
jpp to search 855599 1001066
jpp.t pellet; pill (med.) 24410 1001066
jpḥ [a pig] 24440 1001069
jpt [bread, biscuit] 24490 1001070
jpd [unit of measure for baked goods] 24500 1001067
jpd.w furniture (gen.) 24510 1001068
jf.t [bone marrow] 24530 1000969
jfn to turn round; to turn to 24540

1000971
jfd to be complete on all four sides 858706 1000335
jfd rectangle; square (plot of land) 24570 1000335
jfd (the) four (sides; corners; pillars of heaven; cardinal directions) 24560 1000335
jfd rectangle (block of stone) 24600 1000335
jfd to flee; to move quickly 24610 1000970
jfd.j sheet; garment (rectangle piece of linen) 24590 1000335
jfd.w four 850571 1000335
jfd.nw fourth 852782 1000335
jfd.nw [a piece of writing?] 64310 1000335
jfd.t four (in number) 24620 1000335
jfdi̯ to quadruplicate 859052 1000335
jm there 24640 1001006
jm to groan 24660 1001007
jm side; form; rib area 24670 1001003
jm mud; clay 24690 1000999
jm mourner (a bird) 24700 1001007
jm pupil (of the eye) 24650 1001001
jm.j what is within; who is within 25120 1001000
jm.j being in 25130 1001000
jm.y the lamenting one (Osiris) 851359 1001007
jm.y one who is formed 25110 1001003
jm.y belonging to 25160 1001006
jm.jt bed? 863007 1001000
jm.jt insides; content 400138 1001000
jm.w senselessness 851305 1001009
jm.w lamentation; wailing 25980 1001007
jm.w Mourner 866387 1001007
jm.w pus (med.) 25970 1001002
jm.wtj in the midst of; between 25400 1001000
jm.t choking? 24790 1001007
jm.tj Mourner 857154 1001007
jmꜣẖ [a kind of incense] 25030 1001018
jmꜣẖ backbone; spinal canal 25040 1001017
jmꜣẖ to be provided for; to be revered; to revere 25050 1001018
jmꜣẖ revered one 25070 1001018
jmꜣẖ provision; dignity 25060 1001018
jmꜣẖ.w revered one; one who is provided for (the deceased) 25090 1001018
jmꜣẖ.wt revered one; one who is provided for (the deceased) 25100 1001018
jmꜣẖ.t provides; blessedness 855892 1001018
jmi̯ not to be (negative verb) 25170 1001009
jmi̯ give! 25180 1001010
jmi̯ cause (that)! 550022 1001010
jmi̯ give!; cause (that)! 851706 1001010
jmi̯.tw get (that)! 25900 1001010
jmi̯.tw give! take it over! 600062 1001010
jmjm to conduct (plans) effectively 25950 1001005
jmjm to bewail 25940 1001007
jmjm to become strong 852257 1001005
jmw boat (gen.) 25990 1001016
jmn to hide; to be hidden 26030 1001013
jmn right (hand); western 26080 1001012
jmn hidden one (a priest) 26050 1001013
jmn stay 854325 1001349
jmn the hidden one 855893 1001013
jmn hidden one (of several god) 26040 1001013
jmn hidden; concealed 500080 1001013
jmn.y one who hides himself (ram-headed sun god) 26290 1001013
jmn.yt what endures (offerings) 26300 1001349
jmn.w hidden one (a demon) 26310 1001013
jmn.w enduring one (bull) 26330 1001349
jmn.wj two hidden ones (testicles of the

deceased for limb deification) 26230 1001013
jmn.t secret; what is hidden 26090 1001013
jmn.t right eye 500247 1001012
jmn.t [object represented in the imenet-hieroglyph] 26130 1001012
jmn.t hidden place (of the netherworld); secret place 26100 1001013
jmn.t right side; west; land of the dead 26140 1001012
jmn.tj Western-one (a mirror) 26360 1001012
jmn.tj Westerner 852036 1001012
jmn.tj west wind 26160 1001012
jmn.tj west 26151 1001012
jmn.tj one belonging to the netherworld 500176 1001012
jmn.tj western 26150 1001012
jmn.tjt west 26180 1001012
jmn.tjw westerners; the dead 26220 1001012
jmnḥ butcher 26340 1001361
jmnḥ.y Butcher (a demon) 26350 1001361
jmnḥ.yw Butcher demon 860783 1001361
jmr to be deaf 26370 1001014
jmr.w material used for bandaging? 26380 1001402
jmḥ to suck; to drink 26400 1001008
jms.t dill 26440 1001015
jmk putrefaction 26490 1001011
jmk to putrefy 26480 1001011
jmḏr rampart, circumvallation 26530 1001290
jn today? 26740 1001026
jn by (of agent) 26660 1001020
jn knife 26730 1001045
jn [negation] 26700 1001505
jn.yt refrain? (of a song) 26900 1001024
jn.w captive 860234 1001038
jn.w messenger; supplier; bearer 27050 1001038
jn.w gifts; produce; tribute 27040 1001038
jn.wt (physical) pain (med.) 27110 1001023
jn.wt ferry 27100 1001038
jn.wt freight? 27090 1001038
jn.wtj the one belonging to the fishnet 854705 1001044
jn.t tilapia (Nile perch) 26760 1001025
jn.t type of a garment 26620 1001019
jn.t (desert) valley 26780 1001027
jn.t the one who brings 861712 1001038
jnı̯ to bring; to bring away; to buy 26870 1001038
jnj Ini (Red Crown) 26880 1001506
jnj to tarry; to delay 26720 1001040
jnj.w [a plant] 852305 1001039
jnj.t [a plant used as fuel] 26950 1001039
jnj.t seed (med.) 26930 1001039
jnjn to cut up 26970 1001045
jnjn.t knife 26980 1001045
jnᶜ chin 27000 1001063
jnᶜ.t chin 27010 1001063
jnw red crown 857163 1001506
jnb wall; fence; enclosure 27180 1001031
jnb to surround (with walls) 27190 1001031
jnb [a plant] 27200 1001028
jnb lynx 27140 1001030
jnb.w [a field] 27210 1001031
jnb.t lynx pelt? 27160 1001030
jnb.t fortification; fence 27230 1001031
jnbꜣ to be mute 27260 1001032
jnbꜣ Inba-plant 27250 1001028
jnp to be laid down?; to lie down (on the stomach)? 27310 1001048
jnp to decay 27320 1001048
jnp.w royal child (prince, princess) 27350 1001047
jnp.w prince (Osiris) 852341 1001047
jnf discharge (of the divine eye) (incense?) 27380 1001034
jnf.w discharge (from the eyes) (med.) 27400 1001034
jnm skin (of a man); hide (of an animal); skin color 27420 1001043
jnm.yt skin-wearer (unknown goddess) 27440 1001043
jnm.t [a vintage?]; [wine jug?]; [wineskin] 27430 1001042

jnn to cut; to cut up 850234 1001045
jnn bearer (of offerings) 450200 1001038
jnn to turn round 27500 1001631
jnn.t cordage 27480 1001044
jnnk [a plant (thyme?)] 27520 1001046
jnr Iner-plate (a unit of measure) 27550 1001051
jnr stone; (block of) stone (gen.) 27560 1001051
jnr stone (Apophis) 27540 1001051
jnrn oak 27670 1001052
jnhmn pomegranate 27690 1001036
jnḥ to surround; to enclose; to border 27710 1001035
jnḥ eyebrow 27700 1001035
jnḥ.w frame (of a picture) 27730 1001035
jnḥꜣs husks (of lotus) 850243 1001037
jns red (blood) 27800 1001054
jns to paint (eyes) red 27810 1001054
jns testicles 27860 1001054
jns a red one [a priestess (of Bastet)] 27780 1001054
jns.j red(-dyed) linen; red(-dyed) bandages 27840 1001054
jns.yt Red (eye of Horus) 27850 1001054
jns.t lower leg (calf); shin 27820 1001053
jnk I [indepen. pron., 1st per. sing.] 27940 1001041
jnq to encompass; to embrace; to unite 27880 1001049
jnq.t net (lit. encloser) 27910 1001049
jnq.tj one who is in the net (Osiris) 27920 1001049
jnqj.w [cordage (naut.)] 27950 1001049
jnqfqf.t [a wooden part of a chariot] 27930 1001050
jntj to drive back; to withdraw 27980 1001056
jntnt to hinder 28000 1001056
jnṯ to fetter, to tie up 850245 1001700
jnṯ [part of a ship] 28040 1001700
jnṯ.t fettered one 500884 1001700
jnṯ.t fetter 28030 1001700
jnṯ.tj the two fetters (manifestation of Re) 28020 1001700
jnṯ.tjw fettered ones 500354 1001700
jnd to be vexed; to be sad; to be sick 28050 1001033
jnd afflicted man 28070 1001033
jnd misery 28060 1001033
jnd.t grief, sorrow 857164 1001033
jr sight (personified as a god) 28200 1001075
jr lion?; wild beast? 28180 1001076
jr.j glossary 863008 1001078
jr.j all; altogether 858843 1001078
jr.j pertaining to; belonging to 28500 1001078
jr.j accordingly; corresponding 859370 1001078
jr.j fellow; companion 28510 1001078
jr.j belonging to [adjective of the preposition jr/r] 851428 1001078
jr.j thereof; thereto (possessive adjective, mostly invariable) 850583 1001078
jr.yt act; ceremony 28590 1001081
jr.yt milk cow 28600 1001077
jr.yt assessment (in grain) 28610 1001081
jr.w creation; form 29610 1001081
jr.w duty; rite 29600 1001081
jr.w crew of boat 853686 1001078
jr.w delivery; cattle tax 29620 1001081
jr.w creator (Re) 500286 1001081
jr.w maker (of ...); trader (in ...) 29590 1001081
jr.w eye witness 29550 1001075
jr.wj pair of eyes 28300 1001075
jr.wt doers (women) 29640 1001081
jr.wt deed 850272 1001081
jr.t eye (of a god); eye (of heaven, metaph. for the sun and moon) 28290 1001075
jr.t companion 28570 1001078
jr.t eye 28250 1001075
jr.t purpose (of something); duty 28580 1001078
jr.tj doer 852806 1001081
jri̯ to do; to make; to create; to act as 28550 1001081

jri̯ [aux. (as conjugation bearer with following infinitive)] 600080 1001081
jri̯ to eat 28220 1001081
jri̯ to cause that 852348 1001081
jri̯ [for jw of Future III, (with nominal subject)] 853690 1001081
jri̯ to engender; to bear 400112 1001081
jri̯ to do 851809 1001081
jrj ram 28540 1001082
jry knife 28560 1001081
jrjr guide; leader 29530 1001083
jrp wine 29740 1001085
jrp wine jug 450472 1001085
jrp grape vine 29750 1001085
jrp.j belonging to vine 852779 1001085
jrp.y winemaking? 29810 1001085
jrm together with 29840 1001966
jrẖ [a translucent semi-precious stone] 29890 1001080
jrr adversary 401153 1001081
jrr.t adversary 401154 1001081
jrqb.t mirror (of rock crystal) 29910 1001086
jrqbs rock crystal 29900 1001086
jrkt (tree) trunk; (wooden) beam 29930 1001084
jrt.j belonging to milk; sucking calf 29970 1001089
jrt.w distress 30020 1001088
jrt.w red color (from plants) 29990 1001087
jrt.w condition; (bluish) discoloration (med.) 30010 1001087
jrt.w [a purple cloth] 30000 1001087
jrt.w [a plant (med.)]; [a vegetal (blue) dye] 29980 1001087
jrt.wj blue 866495 1001087
jrṯ.t milky sap (of the sycamore) (med.) 30090 1001089
jrṯ.t milk (from mother, from animals, from sycamore) 854491 1001089
jrṯ.t milk (from mother or from animals) 30080 1001089
jrdb artabe (a measure of volume) 850062 1001079
jh.w camp; pen (for livestock) 30210 1000979
jh.t Ihet (heavenly cow) 30130 1000975
jhj Oho! 30160 1000984
jhj to wail 30180 1000984
jhj plaintive cry; oh!; pain 853243 1000984
jhb (ritual) dancer 30240 1000471
jhb dance 30220 1000471
jhb dancing song 30230 1000471
jhb to dance 176 1000471
jhb.t dancer 30250 1000471
jhms.t cord 30340 1000988
jhy joy; rejoicing 30170 1000991
jhy jubilant [designation of a person] 861314 1000991
jhm jubilation 30290 1000986
jhm [shout] 855874 1000986
jhm to sigh 856210 1000986
jhm suffering; pain 850149 1000986
jhm to walk slowly; to restrain 30270 1000987
jhm to mourn; to suffer 30280 1000986
jhm sigh 855873 1000986
jhm.t suffering 850287 1000986
jhm.t [a resin, or balm] 30300 1000985
jhmz.t rope 857099 1000988
jhr tent 30350 1000990
jhhj jubilation 30360 1000991
jhhj festival (of jubilation) 30370 1000991
jḥ ox; cattle 30410 1000978
jḥ to weep?; to sleep? 30460 1000981
jḥ [a weight (tauroform)] 30400 1000978
jḥ crocodile 862886 1000976
jḥ [a tree] 30430 1000973
jh.y [a building] 30190 1000979
jḥ.w [a unknown fruit (med.)] 30630 1000973
jḥ.w stable; pen (for livestock) 30660 1000978
jḥ.t cow 30480 1000978
jḥ.tj thighs 30490 1000980
jḥ.tjt land-tax 30700 1000978
jḥy musician (a priest) 851597 1000992
jḥy music 860508 1000992

jḥy to make music 30560 1000992
jḥy sack; net; rope 30590 1002977
jḥy.w Sistrum player 857101 1000992
jḥy.t musician (a priestess) 30610 1000992
jḥjḥ [a noise in the water (bubble?)] 30620 1000805
jḥbnn.t [bread] 866501 1000463
jḥms (household) servant 30680 1000564
jẖ to worship; to rejoice at/in/over 30850 1000982
jẖ what? [interrog. pron.] 30740 1000977
jẖ.t something; some 850967 1000977
jẖ.t thing; goods; offerings 30750 1000977
jẖ.tjt proportion of?; portion? 855913 1000977
jẖm.t bank (of a river, of a fortress) 30870 1000555
jẖm.t ignorant? [designation of a person] 857242 1000543
jẖm.tjw Those who belong to the riverbank 500449 1000555
jẖr form; image 30940 1000989
jẖr and; further 30920 1000694
jẖẖ.w twilight (morning and evening); darkness 30960 1000983
jz tomb 31010 1001162
jz old, used 31040 1001160
jz workshop; (council) chamber 31020 1001162
jz to be old 852306 1001160
jz.ywt old clothes; rags 31270 1001160
jz.w reed 31310 1001161
jz.w old (primeval) ones 31050 1001160
jz.wt the old; ancient writings; ancient times 31320 1001160
jz.wtj patriarchal one 873113 1001160
jz.wtjw ancestors (those of ancient times) 850288 1000932
jz.t age; decline 31100 1001160
jz.t silo; granary 31780 1001162
jz.t palace; palatial precinct 31070 1001162
jz.t crew member 852654 1002788
jz.t (one of a) team 859857 1002788
jz.t crew; gang (of workmen) 31080 1002788
jz.t windpipe?; throat? 31090 1001163
jz.t boundary stone; landmark 31060 1001162
jz.tj boat crew (of the gods) 31120 1002788
jzj to be light (of weight) 31240 1001166
jzj band?; thong? 31260 1001165
jzp slope 64510 1001169
jzp to hew (wood) 31460 1001169
jzf.t disorder; chaos; wrongdoing 31500 1001164
jzf.tj evildoer; enemy 31510 1001164
jzn to bolt (open and closed) 31540 1001168
jzn.yt lock; bolt 31570 1001168
jzr tamarisk 31610 1001170
jzr [a scepter (of tamarisk wood)] 31600 1001170
jzr.t tamarisk wood 31620 1001170
jzz.yt clap net (for fowling) 31720 1001171
jzzj to catch (in the bird net) 31700 1001171
jzkn [a region of the sky]; zenith? 31770 1001167
js to ruin 31250 1001160
js to summon 500202 1001092
js like (postposition) 852270 1001090
js old one? (priest of Hathor) 31160 1001160
js.wj testicles 31360 1001054
js.t calculation; estimation 860673 1001092
jsy shortage; loss (in weight) 31210 1001160
jsw people (with marketable value) 31290 1001090
jsw payment; equivalent 31330 1001090
jsw truly 851437 1001151
jswt long plank (of coniferous wood) 31380 1001109
jsbw shelter?; hut? 600286 1001096
jsbr [a Syrian plant (juniper?)] 31430 1001093
jsbr whip 31420 1001094
jsbt seat (gen.); chair; base 31390 1001095
jsp to ache with hunger 31480 1001101

jsp.t language; speech 31450 1002222
jspt quiver (for arrows) 31490 1001102
jsn hide?; bag? (of hide) 31550 1001054
jsr rushes 31630 1001104
jsḥm [a body of water?] 31670 1000554
jsq to linger; to wait; to hold back 31730 1001103
jstn hanger 855287 1001107
jstn to strap up; to bind 31800 1001107
jsd [verb (to sit)] 31860 1001098
jsd to spew? 31850 1001099
jsd spittle 31870 1001099
jsdd trembler (an evil spirit) 31900 1000303
jš.w expectoration 31970 1001106
jš.tt food; meal 31960 1001091
jšᶜ.t slaughtering knife 857058 1002413
jšf to burn; to scorch (a town) 31980 1001100
jšnn war cry 32000 1002201
jšst what? 32050 1000977
jšš to carry; to support 32090 1001106
jšš to spew 32070 1001106
jšš image (or similar) 32100 1001105
jšš to transport 854492 1001106
jšš spittle 32080 1001106
jšš [a product (from Punt)] 32060 1001106
jšd ished-tree (Balanites aegyptiaca?) 32140 1001097
jšd [ished-fruit] 32150 1001097
jšd.t ished-tree (a sacred tree in Heliopolis) 32160 1001097
jšd.t ished-fruit; fruit (gen.) 32170 1001097
jḳm.w sadness; sorrow 32220 1001869
jḳr trustworthy man 850289 1001074
jḳr to be excellent; to be (trust)worthy 32240 1001074
jḳr excellent one (Thoth) 32250 1001074
jḳr excellent; useful 400076 1001074
jḳr [a piece of furniture] 32260 1001074
jḳr orderly; very 400077 1001074
jḳr.w virtue; excellence 32290 1001074
jḳr.w worthy ones (the blessed dead) 32280 1001074
jḳr.w [a serpent] 32300 1001073
jḳr.t excellent lady (Wadjet) 32270 1001074
jḳr.t [a snake] 855063 1001073
jḳr.tj excellent one 857175 1001074
jḳrt [a food] 32320 1001074
jḳḫ to illumine 32340 1001072
jḳḫ to enter; to go (to) 32330 1001072
jḳḫ.w axe; battle-axe 32360 1001072
jḳd.w builder 855558 1001852
jḳd.w builder 32390 1001852
jk.y stonemason 32450 1000994
jk.w potentate 855152 1000994
jk.w quarry 32480 1000994
jki̯ to attack; to bow 32420 1000994
jkjk [rhythmical muscle contraction] 858979 1000994
jkm shield; protection 32550 1000996
jkn to scoop 854493 1000998
jkn to draw (water) 32590 1000998
jkn [a negative characteristic (of the heart, tongue)] 32630 1000997
jkn to hoe; to scoop out; to hack 32570 1000998
jkn tomb?; digger? hole? 855875 1000998
jkn to seize; to take hold of 32600 1000998
jkn.w hoe (made of wood) 32640 1000998
jkn.t hole; hollow (demon's habitation?) 32580 1000998
jgy.w overturned ones (beings in the netherworld) 32710 1000440
jgb air; wind 32720 1001844
jgp rain cloud 32730 1000393
jgp cloud 857093 1000393
jgn gladness? 32760 1000972
jgr the silent one 866516 1000396
jgr.w Silent-ones 32790 1000396
jgr.t Silence (realm of the dead, the necropolis) 32770 1000396
jgr.tj the silent one 857053 1000396
jt barley; grain (gen.) 32830 1001110
jty to be king; to rule as king 32910 1001114
jty sovereign; ruler; lord 32930 1001114
jty.t queen; sovereign 32940 1001114
jtj father; grandfather 32820 1001114

jtfꜣ saw 876482 1002442
jtfꜣ to saw 858431 1002442
jtm to be overfull; to block up 858432 1001116
jtm.w breathlessness 33050 1001116
jtm.t destroyer (a knife) 33010 1001116
jtn to shine; to illuminate 33100 1001117
jtn sun disk (a mirror) 33090 1001117
jtn disk (of the sun, of the moon) 33080 1001117
jtn resting place; perch 862928 1001119
jtn to oppose 33130 1001121
jtn light 859436 1001117
jtn.j one who belongs to the sun disk 33160 1001117
jtn.w obscurities; riddles 33190 1001059
jtn.wj the two disks (sun and moon) 33150 1001117
jtn, jwtn ground; earth; dust 33120 1001119
jtnw hairy; fluffy 33170 1001118
jtr papyrus; aquatic plant (for cordage) 33260 1001124
jtr shabti box 33300 1001124
jtr.w iteru (a measure of distance); mile 33360 1001123
jtr.w season(s) 33390 1001123
jtr.w river; canal; the Nile 33370 1001123
jtr.t row (of chapels) 33290 1001123
jtr.tj both sides; vicinity (of someone) 33320 1001123
jtr.tj the two rows of shrines (Egypt, as the totality of shrines) 33310 1001123
jtḥ prisoners 852569 1001112
jtḥ to pull; to drag 33410 1001112
jtḥ fortress; prison 33420 1001112
jtḥ.w rope 857209 1001112
jṯ which?; where? 33490 1001111
jṯ.w thief; conqueror 33630 1001113
jṯꜣ to steal; to capture; to carry off 33530 1001126
jṯꜣ clot; lump 874337 1001126
jṯꜣ thief 33540 1001126
jṯi̯ to take; to seize 33560 1001113
jṯfrr sky (of the color of Lapis lazuli) 33660 1002440
jṯm [metal part of a whip (ferrule?)] 33680 1001115
jṯn to resist 850318 1001121
jṯn.w opponent 33180 1001121
jṯr captive 33720 1001122
jṯṯ to fly 33740 1001125
jṯṯ.t flutter? [a symptom of illness] 33750 1001125
jd hand 33850 1000148
jd.w male child; youth 33780 1000955
jd.t cow; female animal (gen.) 500032 1000955
jd.t (pleasant) scent; perfume; dew; exudation 33840 1000954
jd.t uterus; womb 850291 1000955
jdꜣ to smooth 33870 1000968
jdi̯ to cense; to libate 33900 1000960
jdi̯ to be deaf; to deafen 33890 1000959
jdi̯ to be subjugated; to subjugate 33830 1000961
jdy.t girl 33910 1000955
jdb river plot (arable land along the river bank) 33970 1000956
jdb riverbank; shore; edge 33960 1000956
jdb shore; shoreland; acre; open land 854494 1000956
jdb.w edge (of a wound, of the mouth) (med.) 34010 1000956
jdb.wj the two banks (Egypt) 400868 1000956
jdb.wj the one of the two banks (the king) 33980 1000956
jdm.j high quality linen 34030 1000962
jdm.jt high quality linen 34040 1000962
jdn to replace; to dominate 34080 1000965
jdn ear 34070 1000963
jdn arrears (of provisions) 600586 1000232
jdn.w deputy; adjudant (mil.) 34120 1000965
jdn.w representative; deputy 855690 1000965
jdn.t silo; granary 34060 1000964
jdn.t deputy (Nephthys) 34090 1000965

jdḥ.w marshes of the Delta 34240 1000958
jdḥ.y man of the Delta 34220 1000958
jdḥ.yt woman of the Delta 34230 1000958
jdnjw [a mat] 34110 1000965
jdr to bind together; to stitch (med.) 400987 1000967
jdr herd 34150 1000967
jdr heart 34190 1000966
jdr bindings; (surgical) seam 34180 1000967
jdr belt; girdle 34140 1000967
jḏr boundary 184990 1000262
jdr.yt punishment, fetters 34200 1000967
jdg kerchief 34270 1000957

y

ybr stream 23800 1002784
ym sea 24730 1002786
ydꜥ skilled, smart 33920 1002785

ꜥ

ꜥ act; deed 34480 1002927
ꜥ arm; hand 34320 1002927
ꜥ condition; state (of affairs) 34350 1002927
ꜥ dike; riverbed 34410 1002927
ꜥ document 34380 1002927
ꜥ house 34460 1002927
ꜥ person 34510 1002927
ꜥ portion; piece 34360 1002927
ꜥ region; side; administrative area 34340 1002927
ꜥ shaft; pole 34390 1002927
ꜥ trace; track 34400 1002927
ꜥ.wj [parts of a net (dual)] 36060 1002927
ꜥ.wj hand-shaped clappers 34590 1002927
ꜥ.t limb; part of meet 855770 1002927
ꜥ.t member; limb 34550 1002927
ꜥ.t part (of something) 854495 1002927
ꜥ.t piece rope; cord (at door or ship's mast) 34560 1002927
ꜥ.t room; department; dwelling 34540 1002927
ꜥꜣ column; pillar; beam 34800 1003070
ꜥꜣ columns?; vertical timbers? (naut.) 450393 1003070
ꜥꜣ door; leaf (of double doors) 34810 1003071
ꜥꜣ doorkeeper 34820 1003071
ꜥꜣ great one (various gods) 851497 1003078
ꜥꜣ great one; elder; noble one 34760 1003078
ꜥꜣ great; much; long; old; noble 450158 1003078
ꜥꜣ greatness 34770 1003078
ꜥꜣ here; there; yonder 34790 1001058
ꜥꜣ linen; cloth? 450396 1003072
ꜥꜣ.w difference (math.); excess 35250 1003078
ꜥꜣ.w donkey-loads? 35270 1001210
ꜥꜣ.w exceedingly; very 34780 1003078
ꜥꜣ.w greatness 35240 1003078
ꜥꜣ.t gemstone; precious material 34880 1003078
ꜥꜣ.t great one (goddesses) 34850 1003078
ꜥꜣ.t linen; cloth 34920 1003072
ꜥꜣ.t rule 34930 1003078
ꜥꜣ.t something great; something difficult 34860 1003078
ꜥꜣ.t stone vessel 34890 1003078
ꜥꜣ.t swelling; tumor 34900 1003078
ꜥꜣ.t very? 855762 1003078
ꜥꜣ.tjt lot (quantity); amount 35510 1003078
ꜥꜣi̯ to be great; to become great; to be rich; to grow up 34750 1003078
ꜥꜣj phallus? 35120 1003078
ꜥꜣj rejoicing 35090 1003078
ꜥꜣy (glowing) fire 35080 1003078
ꜥꜣy.t heaven; roof 35110 1003078
ꜥꜣy.t temple; shrine 35100 1003078
ꜥꜣꜥ [an illness?]; [an influence causing illness?] 35180 1003081
ꜥꜣꜥ Ejaculator 856333 1003081
ꜥꜣꜥ semen; poison 35170 1003081
ꜥꜣꜥ to ejaculate; to beget 35160 1003081
ꜥꜣꜥ water hole; wet ground 35140 1003081
ꜥꜣꜥ.y begetter (sun god) 35230 1003081
ꜥꜣb to be pleasing 35310 1003073
ꜥꜣb to bestow; to offer (prayer/sacrifice)

35320 1003073
ꜥꜣb.t offering 35330 1003073
ꜥꜣb.t washing jug 35340 1003074
ꜥꜣm Asian 35400 1003079
ꜥꜣm throw stick; boomerang 35390 1003079
ꜥꜣm.w [a plant (med.)] 35420 1003079
ꜥꜣm.wt [a cultivated plant] 35440 1003079
ꜥꜣm.t Asian (female) 35410 1003079
ꜥꜣg to edit, to handle something (forcibly) 854496 1003077
ꜥꜣg to squeeze (dates) 35460 1003077
ꜥꜣg to thrash; to mistreat 35470 1003077
ꜥꜣg.t hoof (of an ox or donkey) 35480 1003077
ꜥꜣg.yt secretion; resin (med.) 35500 1003077
ꜥꜣḏ edge; margin (of cultivated land, of desert) 35520 1003075
ꜥꜣḏ to be pale; to turn pale 35550 1003076
ꜥꜣḏ.y Shining one? 861807 1003076
ꜥꜣḏ.w (grey) mullet (Mugilidae) 35540 1003076
ꜥꜣḏ.w (grey) mullet (sun god) 850355 1003076
ꜥꜣḏ.wj Canal of the two (grey) mullet (in the 2nd nome of Lower Egypt); Canal of the two (grey) mullet (in the 20th nome of Upper Egypt); Canal of the two (grey) mullet (in the 17th nome of Upper Egypt) 852713 1003076
ꜥj cup; bowl 34370 1002927
ꜥy legitimate claim 800062 1002927
ꜥjꜥj to jubilate; to rejoice 859363 1002991
ꜥy to rejoice 35580 1002991
ꜥjn limestone 35620 1002992
ꜥjn to face with limestone 35630 1002992
ꜥyn well 862932 1003069
ꜥꜥ sweat; spit 35640 1003081
ꜥꜥ.t accusation 35680 1002926
ꜥꜥj to be fearful 35710 1003082
ꜥꜥw sleep 35760 1003085
ꜥꜥw to be agitated; to flutter (of the heart) 35750 1003084
ꜥꜥw to sleep (invariably negated) 35740 1003085
ꜥꜥm Nile flood 35800 1003081
ꜥꜥnj tent; encampment 35810 1003083
ꜥꜥnj to enclose 35820 1003083
ꜥw crane 35840 1003062
ꜥw.t herds (gen.); flocks 35870 1003063
ꜥw.t scepter; crook (of a shepherd) 35860 1003063
ꜥw.tj shepherd; scepter bearer 36240 1003063
ꜥwꜣ foulness 35950 1003067
ꜥwꜣ robbery 856493 1003065
ꜥwꜣ robbing 401143 1003065
ꜥwꜣ to rot; to perish 35940 1003067
ꜥwꜣ.y robber 850342 1003065
ꜥwꜣ.y Robber (a demon) 35990 1003065
ꜥwꜣ.yt fermented substance (med.) 36020 1003067
ꜥwꜣ.yt robber 36010 1003065
ꜥwꜣ.yt robber (female) 862907 1003065
ꜥwꜣ.w reaper 36040 1003065
ꜥwꜣ.t robbery 35960 1003065
ꜥwꜣ.tj robber; enemy 863015 1003065
ꜥwꜣꜣ fermented bread 35970 1003067
ꜥwꜣi̯ to get something done (or similar); to eliminate something (or similar) 854497 1003065
ꜥwꜣi̯ to harvest 36000 1003065
ꜥwꜣi̯ to rob 35980 1003065
ꜥwn to deceive; to plunder 36110 1003065
ꜥwn to deceive; to rob 36200 1003065
ꜥwn to wail 36120 1003066
ꜥwn.w plunderer 36190 1003065
ꜥwn.tj greedy one 855231 1003065
ꜥwg heat? 860376 1003064
ꜥwg to roast (grain) 36210 1003064
ꜥb (wooden) arch 850983 1002928
ꜥb [a sanctuary] 36350 1002932
ꜥb enemy; victim 36280 1002928
ꜥb horn (of hoofed animals); sting (of a scorpion) 36250 1002928
ꜥb to boast 36270 1002944
ꜥb meal 852141 1002931
ꜥb purifier (priest) 36320 1002932
ꜥb to dirty; to pollute 36340 1002932

ꜥb to kill; to sacrifice 863741 1003073
ꜥb to purify; to be pure 36310 1002932
ꜥb.j horned 856342 1002928
ꜥb.w calamity; sinfulness; impurity; infection 36300 1002932
ꜥb.w lettuce 36750 1002930
ꜥb.w pitchfork wielder? 36760 1002932
ꜥb.w purification; purity 36740 1002932
ꜥb.w purifier 36780 1002932
ꜥb.wj Two-horns 500827 1002928
ꜥb.wt staff of office; pitchfork 36800 1002928
ꜥb.wtj horned one (the king, Osiris) 36810 1002928
ꜥb.wtt horned one (tutelary goddess of Upper Egypt) 36820 1002928
ꜥb.t [abet-utensil for the Opening-of-the-mouth ceremony] 36430 1002928
ꜥb.t female worker of horn 36390 1002928
ꜥb.t meal (or similar) 36440 1002931
ꜥbꜣ [aba-scepter] 36480 1002942
ꜥbꜣ Aba-scepter 500725 1002942
ꜥbꜣ light 36560 1002943
ꜥbꜣ offering table; altar 36530 1002942
ꜥbꜣ pigeon 36580 1002940
ꜥbꜣ shining one (the king, Horus) 36570 1002943
ꜥbꜣ to command (a ship) 36490 1002942
ꜥbꜣ to glitter; to shine; to illuminate 36550 1002943
ꜥbꜣ to influence; to interfere 854498 1002942
ꜥbꜣ to present, to lead 866762 1002942
ꜥbꜣ to provide (someone with something); to be provided with 36500 1002942
ꜥbꜣ.yt altar 36600 1002942
ꜥbꜣ.yt rope; fetter 36610 1002941
ꜥbꜥ [phallus] 36640 1002944
ꜥbꜥ boasting 850348 1002944
ꜥbꜥ to boast 36630 1002944
ꜥbꜥb Boasting one 856350 1002944
ꜥbꜥb fame; glory 36650 1002944
ꜥbꜥb to boast; to be excited 36660 1002944
ꜥbꜥb to shine 36670 1002944
ꜥbꜥb.t purification? 36690 1002932
ꜥbb to knock? (on the door) 36850 1002928
ꜥbb to smooth? (while making pottery) 36840 1002934
ꜥbb to use a pitchfork 36860 1001203
ꜥbb winged one (winged scarab, Horus) 36870 1003030
ꜥbb.t javelin; spear 36880 1002944
ꜥbb.tjw One with the spear 500350 1002944
ꜥbḥ to fill (a jug) to the brim 36900 1002936
ꜥbẖn frog 36910 1002937
ꜥbẖn.w Frogs 855106 1002937
ꜥbš [a wine jug] 36920 1002938
ꜥbš to drown 36930 1002939
ꜥbd servant 36970 1002935
ꜥp [a serpent (Apophis?)] 36980 1003030
ꜥp.y wing 854185 1003030
ꜥp.y winged one (sun as a winged scarab, Horus) 37010 1003030
ꜥp.yt winged one (female sun disk, Hathor) 37030 1003030
ꜥp.yw flying ones (enemies) 37020 1003030
ꜥp.w striding (and similar) 37050 1003030
ꜥpi̯ to fly 37000 1003030
ꜥpi̯ to stride (through, by) 36990 1003030
ꜥpnn.t water newt?; slug? 37080 1003031
ꜥpp winged one (sun disk) 37070 1003030
ꜥpr [a cult object (presented by the king to a god)] 37110 1003032
ꜥpr garment 37120 1003032
ꜥpr to equip; to be equipped 37090 1003032
ꜥpr.w crew (of a ship); gang (of workmen) 37100 1003032
ꜥpr.w equipment 37180 1003032
ꜥpr.w jewellery 37190 1003032
ꜥpr.t [a jar, also used as a bread mold] 37150 1003032
ꜥpr.t equipment (of offerings) 37140 1003032
ꜥf [a measure (sack, basket)] 37260 1001204
ꜥf there 500157 1001055
ꜥf.tj brewer 37440 1001204
ꜥfꜣ to demolish; to devour 37280 1002968
ꜥfꜣ.y encampment (of Bedouins) 37310

1002966
ᶜfꜢ.t ripped out body part 37290 1002968
ᶜfᶜ greedy one (designation of crocodiles) 37360 1002961
ᶜfᶜf crocodile 862931 1002961
ᶜff to fly 37370 1002964
ᶜff to hum 500940 1002965
ᶜfi̯ to squeeze (out) 37240 1001204
ᶜfj bee 37330 1002964
ᶜfn [a covering (package, pouch)] 37390 1002966
ᶜfn to cover; to be covered 37380 1002966
ᶜfn.w boot?; leather sock? 37410 1002966
ᶜfn.wj He With The Headcloth 37420 1002966
ᶜfn.t headcloth ("wrapping") 37400 1002966
ᶜft.t collection of spells (relating to the hereafter) 500067 1002967
ᶜfd nail; peg 37480 1002963
ᶜfd to lead (the way) 37460 1002963
ᶜfḏ.t chest; cabin (of a ship) 37490 1002962
ᶜm to know; to come to know 37510 1002994
ᶜm to swallow; to devour; to absorb 37500 1002994
ᶜm.w Devourer 500299 1002994
ᶜmꜢ [a beer jug] 37580 1003006
ᶜmꜢ [a plant (a very juicy fruit?) (med.)] 37600 1003005
ᶜmꜢ to turn sour (of beer) 37570 1003006
ᶜmꜢ.t [a part of body (spec. of Osiris] 37610 1003004
ᶜmj ointment (med.) 37640 1002998
ᶜmj to smear; to seal 850352 1002998
ᶜmᶜ [a kind of beer] 37690 1003006
ᶜmᶜ uncircumcised? person; youngling?; impure one? 37680 1003007
ᶜmᶜ.t mud; Nile mud 37740 1002998
ᶜmᶜ.t virgin 37730 1003007
ᶜmᶜꜢ to throw (a throw stick) 37750 1003008
ᶜmᶜꜢ.t throw stick; casting net 37760 1003008
ᶜmᶜꜢ.wj thrower of a throw stick? 856379 1003008
ᶜmᶜᶜ kernel (of grain); (date) pip (med.) 37770 1003009
ᶜmᶜm to devour 37790 1002994
ᶜmᶜm to devour 37810 1002994
ᶜmᶜm to rub (feet) 37780 1002998
ᶜmᶜm.w shrew mouse 37830 1002994
ᶜmᶜm.t mud; Nile mud; muddy ground 37820 1002998
ᶜmw [a very juicy fruit? (med.)] 37840 1003003
ᶜmnt to box 37880 1002999
ᶜmq to mount (sexually); to couple 37930 1003000
ᶜmr (temple) bakery 37890 1003001
ᶜmr baker 37910 1003001
ᶜmr ointment 850353 1002998
ᶜmt clouds (or similar) 37940 1003002
ᶜmd to be weak (of heart, body parts) 37960 1002995
ᶜmdy supports (chariot parts) 37980 1002997
ᶜmḏ to turn away (from something) 37990 1002996
ᶜn [eye, as a character in writing] 38060 1003010
ᶜn again; already; further 38050 1003026
ᶜn beautiful; kind 400159 1003024
ᶜn good one 38080 1003024
ᶜn here 38000 1001057
ᶜn prolapse 861167 1003026
ᶜn writing board; writing tablet 38020 1003013
ᶜn.w beauty 600622 1003024
ᶜn.w limestone?; pebbles? 38340 1002992
ᶜn.w ornament (or part?) (of a metal vessel) 38350 1003024
ᶜn.wt beauty 38180 1003024
ᶜn.t (metal) ring 38140 1003011
ᶜn.t [smallest unit for measuring time] 38150 1003012
ᶜn.t adze 38120 1003012
ᶜn.t beautiful one (Hathor, Nekhbet) 38160 1003024

ꜥn.t claw; talon; thumb 38130 1003012
ꜥn.t diadem (or similar) 38110 1003024
ꜥni̯ to be beautiful; to be kind; to be pleasing 38070 1003024
ꜥnꜥn chin 38310 1001063
ꜥnꜥn to complain 38300 1003026
ꜥnꜥn to refuse 38290 1003026
ꜥnb alfa grass 38370 1003014
ꜥnb to close (the mouth); to enclose 38390 1003015
ꜥnb.yt bundle; basket (measure for papyrus and bread) 38400 1003015
ꜥnn singing 860115 1003025
ꜥnn to return; to turn back; to invert 38040 1003026
ꜥnn.w coil; intestines 38450 1003026
ꜥnn.wj Twice-coiled (a snake) 38460 1003026
ꜥnn.t rope (lit. what is coiled) 38480 1003026
ꜥnnw [a (fruit) tree] 38440 1003027
ꜥnnw.t fruit of the anenu-tree 850686 1003027
ꜥnḥb.t pied kingfisher 38510 1003023
ꜥnẖ (sandal strap) 38520 1003020
ꜥnẖ [a document] 38660 1003020
ꜥnẖ [ankh-vessel (for libations)] 38640 1003019
ꜥnẖ [in formulae, to introduce an oath] 38550 1003022
ꜥnẖ ankh (symbol of life) 500274 1003019
ꜥnẖ Ankh beetle (solar beetle) 38600 1003019
ꜥnẖ captive (lit. bound one) 38580 1003020
ꜥnẖ earth; land 38720 1003022
ꜥnẖ garland; bouquet 38590 1003020
ꜥnẖ goat; herd (gen.) 38680 1003021
ꜥnẖ life 38540 1003022
ꜥnẖ life (the inundation) 38610 1003022
ꜥnẖ livelihood 38670 1003022
ꜥnẖ living person; inhabitant; member (of a group); soldier 400614 1003022
ꜥnẖ mirror 38630 1003022
ꜥnẖ oath 38560 1003022
ꜥnẖ to live; to be alive 38530 1003022
ꜥnẖ to swear 38570 1003022
ꜥnẖ water of life (given by Isis) 38710 1003022
ꜥnẖ wing of a door 38650 1003020
ꜥnẖ.jt She-who-belongs-to-the-sign-of-life? 500892 1003019
ꜥnẖ.y living one 38900 1003019
ꜥnẖ.w blocks of Egyptian alabaster 38620 1003018
ꜥnẖ.w stars 38920 1003022
ꜥnẖ.w the living ones 38910 1003022
ꜥnẖ.wj pair of ears 38930 1003022
ꜥnẖ.wt living one 856399 1003022
ꜥnẖ.t goat; herds (gen.); flocks (gen.) 38760 1003021
ꜥnẖ.t grain 38750 1003022
ꜥnẖ.t living eye (of a god) 38740 1003022
ꜥnẖ.t living one (Hathor-Isis) 38730 1003022
ꜥnẖ.t living person (female) 852886 1003022
ꜥnẖ.t the west (lit. (place) of life) 38780 1003022
ꜥnẖ.t wing of a door 860270 1003020
ꜥnq to flow (of the inundation) 38960 1003028
ꜥnq.t [flood] 860384 1003028
ꜥnt.w myrrh 39010 1003029
ꜥnt.wj one belonging to the myrrh 856389 1003029
ꜥnḏ [a part of a wing] 39030 1003017
ꜥnḏ few; deficient 500588 1003017
ꜥnḏ to be few; to be diminished 39040 1003017
ꜥnḏ to weaken; to decimate 859790 1003017
ꜥnḏ.w [a jar] 39110 1003016
ꜥnḏ.w [an unguent]; [an oil] 39120 1003016
ꜥnḏ.w light of the sun; dawn 39100 1003017
ꜥnḏ.w sunshine 854281 1003017
ꜥnḏ.t the few (people) 39050 1003017
ꜥr ascender 856410 1001209
ꜥr goat 39170 1003038
ꜥr nanny (she-goat)? 853603 1003038

ꜥr pebble; stone 39180 1003041
ꜥr rush; reed 39160 1001192
ꜥr seed (or pit of a fruit) 39200 1003041
ꜥr stairway 39150 1001209
ꜥr.yt ascender (the flood) 39330 1001209
ꜥr.yt heaven?; roof? [designation of the sky?] 39320 1001209
ꜥr.yt lintel 39300 1001209
ꜥr.w [a tree] 39430 1003037
ꜥr.w proximity 851628 1001209
ꜥr.t (lotus) stalk; stem 39210 1001209
ꜥr.t hind parts (of humans); hindquarters (of animals) 39250 1003039
ꜥr.t jaw 39240 1003040
ꜥr.t scroll (of papyrus, of leather) 39230 1001209
ꜥr.tj pair of door leaves 39280 1003071
ꜥrꜥr to accomplish (something); to supply 39360 1001209
ꜥrꜥr to rise up (of the inundation) 39370 1001209
ꜥrf [silver processing method (for barks of gods)] 112590 1003043
ꜥrf bag 39490 1003043
ꜥrf to pack (up); to wrap 39500 1003043
ꜥrf to squeeze? 39510 1003043
ꜥrr.wt gate; hall; (center for) administration 39570 1001209
ꜥrš [something negative relating to the nose (sneezing?)] 39580 1003049
ꜥršn lentils 39590 1003050
ꜥrḳ [an item of chariot equipment (sack or basket)] 39670 1003047
ꜥrḳ ankle 39610 1003047
ꜥrḳ bandage 39700 1003047
ꜥrḳ corner; turning; bend; angle 39690 1003047
ꜥrḳ end; extremity 39680 1003044
ꜥrḳ oath 854608 1003047
ꜥrḳ sack 39660 1003047
ꜥrḳ to be wise; to be understanding; to understand 39640 1003044
ꜥrḳ to bend; to pull together 39600 1003047
ꜥrḳ to complete; to stop (doing something) 39630 1003044
ꜥrḳ to swear (an oath); to abjure 39650 1003047
ꜥrḳ to tie on; to don (a garment) 39620 1003047
ꜥrḳ to tie round; to bend 854499 1003047
ꜥrḳ.y month's end (i.e., the last day) 39740 1003044
ꜥrḳ.yt cleverness 39750 1003044
ꜥrḳ.w welts (med.) 39760 1003047
ꜥrḳ.t end 856688 1003044
ꜥrḳwr silver 39770 1003048
ꜥrt.j [a body of water in Upper Egypt] 39790 1003051
ꜥrḏ to terrify (the enemy); to hold on to 39800 1003042
ꜥḥ cord; rope; wick 39810 1002977
ꜥḥ palace 39850 1002976
ꜥḥ to capture; to catch (e.g., game, with a net) 39820 1002977
ꜥḥ to wipe away 39830 1002978
ꜥḥ.wtj cultivator; tenant 40490 1002975
ꜥḥ.t cultivated land 39880 1002975
ꜥḥ.t net (stretched for the hunt) 39870 1002977
ꜥḥ.t palace 39890 1002976
ꜥḥꜣ Fighter (Bes-like demon) 39970 1002988
ꜥḥꜣ fighter (hippopotamus) 39990 1002988
ꜥḥꜣ fighting; battle 39930 1002988
ꜥḥꜣ Nile perch 39980 1002988
ꜥḥꜣ to fight 39920 1002988
ꜥḥꜣ unfavorable; inauspicious (of calendar days); militant 39950 1002988
ꜥḥꜣ warrior 39940 1002988
ꜥḥꜣ.w weapons (gen.); arrows 40050 1002988
ꜥḥꜣ.wj the two fighters (Horus and Seth) 40030 1002988
ꜥḥꜣ.wtj fighter; warrior; man 40060 1002988
ꜥḥꜣ.wtj male 40070 1002988
ꜥḥꜣ.wtj to argue 40080 1002988
ꜥḥꜣ.wtt warship 856368 1002988
ꜥḥꜣ.t battleground 40010 1002988

ꜥḥꜣ.t fight 856367 1002988
ꜥḥꜣ.t fighter (leonine goddess) 40020 1002988
ꜥḥꜣ.t warship 40000 1002988
ꜥḥꜥ [a measure for beer] 40180 1002990
ꜥḥꜥ amount; number; quantity 40160 1002990
ꜥḥꜥ attendant; helper 40200 1002990
ꜥḥꜥ boat (gen.) 40210 1002989
ꜥḥꜥ door leaves 858623 1002990
ꜥḥꜥ height 40230 1002990
ꜥḥꜥ mast 40100 1002990
ꜥḥꜥ multitude (of people) 40170 1002990
ꜥḥꜥ position (of a star) 40120 1002990
ꜥḥꜥ Standing One 854135 1002990
ꜥḥꜥ to get ready to do (something) 851686 1002990
ꜥḥꜥ to lack; to be lacking; to wait 40130 1002990
ꜥḥꜥ to stand up 851887 1002990
ꜥḥꜥ to stand; to stand up 40110 1002990
ꜥḥꜥ treasure; storehouse 40240 1002990
ꜥḥꜥ uncertain (of calendar days) 40150 1002990
ꜥḥꜥ.y midday 40360 1002990
ꜥḥꜥ.yt Ahait (south pillar of the sky) 40390 1002990
ꜥḥꜥ.yt attendant 40370 1002990
ꜥḥꜥ.yt Helpers (female) 860380 1002990
ꜥḥꜥ.yt midday (6th hour of the day) 40380 1002990
ꜥḥꜥ.w fleet 859328 1002989
ꜥḥꜥ.w heap(s); quantity (math.) 40280 1002990
ꜥḥꜥ.w Helper 40460 1002990
ꜥḥꜥ.w heron 40440 1002990
ꜥḥꜥ.w lifetime; time; duration 40480 1002990
ꜥḥꜥ.w nape (of the neck); spinal ridge 40430 1002990
ꜥḥꜥ.w obstacles? 40470 1002990
ꜥḥꜥ.w Stand-by, Helper 866804 1002990
ꜥḥꜥ.w stander (snake god) 40450 1002990
ꜥḥꜥ.w station; position; standstill 40410 1002990
ꜥḥꜥ.w stela 40420 1002990
ꜥḥꜥ.n [auxiliary] 40111 1002990
ꜥḥꜥ.t quantity (math.) 40260 1002990
ꜥḥꜥ.t Stander 501057 1002990
ꜥḥꜥ.tj He who belongs to the tomb 500527 1002990
ꜥḫ brazier 40500 1002979
ꜥḫ.w [an illness] 40610 1002979
ꜥḫ.w Burning one 500481 1002979
ꜥḫ.wt braziers 40620 1002979
ꜥḫ.t accumulation (of fluid) 40550 1002981
ꜥḫḫ griffin (fig. for the king and gods) 40720 1002981
ꜥḫi̯ to burn; to evaporate 40520 1002979
ꜥḫi̯ to fly (away) 40760 1002980
ꜥḫi̯ to raise up; to rise up 40570 1002981
ꜥḫm [a combustible material (wick?)] 40640 1002986
ꜥḫm to fly 40650 1002984
ꜥḫm to quench; to extinguish 40630 1002983
ꜥẖ [a bird] 40730 1002980
ꜥẖ.t aviary? 40750 1002980
ꜥẖ.t flight? 866810 1002980
ꜥẖ.t wing 40740 1002980
ꜥẖm (cult) image of a falcon; (cult) image (gen.) 40780 1002985
ꜥẖm hawk; eagle 858543 1002985
ꜥẖm Horrifier (crocodile demon) 40810 1002985
ꜥẖm to cause to shudder; to inspire awe 40790 1002985
ꜥẖm.w leaves; twigs [of a plant] 40830 1002982
ꜥẖn to close (the eyes) 40840 1002987
ꜥš [a beer jug] 40950 1003052
ꜥš [a food (fruit?)] 40960 1003053
ꜥš [meal of the soldiers?] 40910 1003053
ꜥš call; invocation; announcement 40900 1003056
ꜥš Lebanese fir tree; [coniferous wood (of Lebanon)] 40940 1003054
ꜥš resin; oil (of a coniferous tree) 450173

1003054
ꜥš to summon 40890 1003056
ꜥši̯ to moan 40930 1003057
ꜥš.wt crying (of a child) 41150 1003056
ꜥšꜣ a lot; numerous; common 41011 1003060
ꜥšꜣ lizard; gecko 41040 1003059
ꜥšꜣ miscellaneous? 450171 1003060
ꜥšꜣ quantity; multitude 41020 1003060
ꜥšꜣ to be numerous; to be rich 41010 1003060
ꜥšꜣ very; often 450155 1003060
ꜥšꜣ.wt crying fit (of a child) 41100 1003056
ꜥšꜣ.wt multitude; mass of people 41050 1003060
ꜥšꜣ.tj a lot; many 41060 1003060
ꜥšꜥš throat 41130 1003055
ꜥšꜥš to strangle 41140 1003055
ꜥšḳ to oppress 41170 1003058
ꜥḳ advisor; trusted friend 851300 1003034
ꜥḳ cormorant (onomatopoeic) 41240 1003033
ꜥḳ to enter; to have entrée; to usher (someone) in; to set (of stars) 41180 1003034
ꜥḳ.y ceremonial entrance (of the king) 41430 1003034
ꜥḳ.y one who has access (a priest) 41440 1003034
ꜥḳ.yt servant 859008 1003034
ꜥḳ.yt servant (lit. one who enters) 41450 1003034
ꜥḳ.w friend(s); confidant(s) 41190 1003034
ꜥḳ.w loaves (of bread); income 41470 1003034
ꜥḳ.t entering 550196 1003034
ꜥḳ.t entry (to the netherworld) 500254 1003034
ꜥḳꜣ [a priest] 41380 1003036
ꜥḳꜣ [rudder] 866813 1003036
ꜥḳꜣ correct; exact 400768 1003036
ꜥḳꜣ correctness; straightness 41340 1003036
ꜥḳꜣ one who is correct; one who is straightforward 41320 1003036
ꜥḳꜣ opposite; in view of 41350 1003036
ꜥḳꜣ precisely; correctly 41330 1003036
ꜥḳꜣ ship's cordage; tow rope 41360 1003036
ꜥḳꜣ to be accurate; to make accurate 41310 1003036
ꜥḳꜣ to use the tow rope 41370 1003036
ꜥḳꜣ.y [a transport ship] 41410 1003035
ꜥḳꜣ.yt accuracy; correctness 41420 1003036
ꜥḳꜣꜣ luck? 851308 1003036
ꜥḳꜥḳ to enter; to reach 41460 1003034
ꜥḳw to capsize 41510 1002974
ꜥk.t end of a rod/stick 41570 1002993
ꜥg.t roasted (of grain) 41620 1003064
ꜥgꜣ [an ointment (for ritual anointing)] 41680 1002972
ꜥgꜣ to capsize; to drown 41660 1002974
ꜥgꜣ.t claw (lion, bird) 41690 1002973
ꜥgn ringstand 41730 1002969
ꜥgrt wagon (drawn by oxen) 41770 1002970
ꜥgsw belt 41800 1002971
ꜥṯḫ brewer 600223 1003061
ꜥṯḫ to sieve; to press 41820 1003061
ꜥdt conspiracy? 41860 1002959
ꜥḏ edge; margin (of cultivated land, of the desert) 41960 1003075
ꜥḏ mongoose 42030 1002946
ꜥḏ pieces of fat (from an animal) 41980 1002948
ꜥḏ spin; (wooden) spool 41880 1002947
ꜥḏ to be whole; to be safe 41890 1002948
ꜥḏ to burn; to roast 41950 1002949
ꜥḏ to hack; to slaughter 41940 1002952
ꜥḏ to perceive (with ear, nose) 41910 1002950
ꜥḏ.yt [part of a building (architrave?)] 42150 1002945
ꜥḏ.w joyous thing 860913 1002951
ꜥḏ.wt splitten tongue 855765 1002952
ꜥḏ.t Egyptian mongoose female 859992 1002946
ꜥḏ.t fat mass (of the heart) 42050 1002948
ꜥḏ.t slaughter 42040 1002948
ꜥḏ.tjw Executioners 42280 1002952
ꜥḏꜣ injustice; falsehood 42100 1002960

ꜥḏꜣ to be guilty of; to be wrong 42110 1002960
ꜥḏꜣ wrongdoer; guilty man 42120 1002960
ꜥḏi̯ to sift (the grain from the chaff) 42000 1002954
ꜥḏꜥḏ to rejoice; to exult 42160 1002951
ꜥdn [a cereal (wheat?)] 41850 1002956
ꜥḏn mat 852090 1001878
ꜥḏn mat 859933 1001878
ꜥḏn to finish 852089 1001881
ꜥḏn.t [a bracelet] 42220 1002955
ꜥḏr [part of a chariot] 42250 1002957
ꜥḏr helper 42240 1002958
ꜥḏd to be childlike; to be boyish 860671 1002953
ꜥḏd youth; (boy) servant 42290 1002953
ꜥḏd.t girl; maid; virgin 42300 1002953

w

w district; region 42350 1002602
w [particle of negation] 42360 1000974
w.t district; region 860534 1002602
wꜣ [a transportation boat] 42440 1002765
wꜣ conspiracy?; disloyalty? 42430 1002758
wꜣ to ponder; to brood; to conspire 42420 1002758
wꜣ rope; cord; string 42380 1002757
wꜣ [verb (to resist?)] 42390 1002758
wꜣ far; remote 42641 1002765
wꜣ conspirer 866828 1002758
wꜣ.j one belonging to the cord 855535 1002757
wꜣ.y one pondering evil (a demon associated with illness) 42600 1002758
wꜣ.w wave (of the sea); surge; floodwater 42650 1002765
wꜣ.w long ago; far away 42640 1002765
wꜣ.w woe!; don't you dare! 42630 1002758
wꜣ.wtj conspirator 42670 1002758
wꜣ.t the way (domain) 853183 1002765
wꜣ.t road; way; path; side 42490 1002765
wꜣ.t evil 42480 1002758
wꜣ.t cord; ribbon 42470 1002757
wꜣ.tj captive? 43520 1002758
wꜣi̯ to parch (grain) 42410 1002766
wꜣi̯ to come to (do) (aux./modal) 42560 1002765
wꜣi̯ to be far (away from); to remove oneself 42550 1002765
wꜣwꜣ to be fiery 858473 1002766
wꜣwꜣ evil plan? 42690 1002758
wꜣwꜣ to plan; to consider (often with neg. connotations) 42680 1002758
wꜣwꜣ.w Fiery one 858112 1002766
wꜣwꜣ.w sunlight 42760 1002766
wꜣwꜣ.t rope 42720 1002757
wꜣwꜣ.t fire; ember; glow (or similar) 42730 1002766
wꜣwꜣ.t [a plant] 42740 1002756
wꜣb root; socket; base 42770 1002760
wꜣb cord (naut.?); cloth? 42790 1002760
wꜣb.t lower part of the Red Crown (base) 42810 1002760
wꜣb.t hill; knoll; mound 42800 1002760
wꜣp.t sheep 42850 1002767
wꜣnb [a plant (med.)] 42890 1002681
wꜣr reed flute?; reed 42960 1002768
wꜣr to tie up (the bag) 42920 1002770
wꜣr to dance (or similar) 42940 1002769
wꜣr.w [a girdle] 42990 1002770
wꜣr.t rope; cord 42980 1002770
wꜣḥ wreath; garland (of flowers, gold) 43020 1002763
wꜣḥ to refrain (from something); to decrease; to ease[aux./modal] 853147 1002763
wꜣḥ to lay down; to endure; to offer; to leave behind 43010 1002763
wꜣḥ.yt precinct 43190 1002763
wꜣḥ.yt yield (of the harvest); grain 43200 1002763
wꜣḥ.wt donation; oblations (or similar) 43060 1002763
wꜣḥ.t way station (on a processional way) 43070 1002763
wꜣḥ.t [a fem. mourner] 43050 1002763
wꜣḥ.tj one who brings offerings 856152 1002763

wꜣẖ fresh plants; verdure 43230 1002764
wꜣẖ abundance; flood 852765 1002764
wꜣẖ Fresh-water (a canal in the nether world) 43240 1002764
wꜣẖ.tj [designation of the deceased] 854332 1002764
wꜣẖi̯ to flood; to make verdant; to rejoice; available in abundance 43260 1002764
wꜣẖy pillared hall; columned hall 43270 1002764
wꜣs to rule; to be powerful; to be happy 43310 1002772
wꜣs dominion; power; well-being 43300 1002772
wꜣs [was-scepter] 43290 1002772
wꜣs.yt She of the Was-scepter 43400 1002772
wꜣs.t [a garment (for a divine image)] 43340 1002772
wꜣsi̯ to be ruined (buildings); to be fallen down; to go down 43410 1002773
wꜣš honor; respect 43430 1002771
wꜣš prestigious one 855544 1002771
wꜣš to be powerful; to worship (someone) 43420 1002771
wꜣš.yw Honorable ones 500606 1002771
wꜣš.wt honorable ones? (female beings) 43460 1002771
wꜣšš bruise; hematoma? (med.) 43480 1002771
wꜣg to shout (for joy); to rejoice 43500 1002762
wꜣg bull for Wag-festival 858107 1002762
wꜣg Wag-festival (funerary festival) 43510 1002762
wꜣgi̯ to provision (for a feast); to rejoice? 43490 1002762
wꜣḏ child; son 43540 1002761
wꜣḏ fresh grain 43610 1002761
wꜣḏ fresh spices 43570 1002761
wꜣḏ papyrus (also as a symbol for Lower Egypt) 43530 1002761
wꜣḏ papyrus plant 858094 1002761
wꜣḏ papyrus column 43550 1002761
wꜣḏ fortunate man 43590 1002761
wꜣḏ green stone (gen.); malachite 43620 1002761
wꜣḏ green; fresh; young 600304 1002761
wꜣḏ cylindrical bead (made of green stone) 43640 1002761
wꜣḏ [a papyrus shaped amulet] 43560 1002761
wꜣḏ [a kind of (water?) fowl] 43650 1002761
wꜣḏ papyrus pillar 853825 1002761
wꜣḏ.y green plants 43600 1002761
wꜣḏ.yt columned hall 43900 1002761
wꜣḏ.w raw meat 43920 1002761
wꜣḏ.w success; happiness 43930 1002761
wꜣḏ.w green eye paint; green pigmen 43910 1002761
wꜣḏ.w wadju (a pasture ground) 861183 1002761
wꜣḏ.wt raw foods 851899 1002761
wꜣḏ.t green stone 851140 1002761
wꜣḏ.t stern; bow (of a ship) 850387 1002761
wꜣḏ.t flourishing one 861578 1002761
wꜣḏ.t green one (crown of Lower Egypt) 43750 1002761
wꜣḏ.t vegetables; greens 43700 1002761
wꜣḏ.t [a fruit] 43710 1002761
wꜣḏ.t green cloth 43720 1002761
wꜣḏ.tj the two uraei; the two crowns 43790 1002761
wꜣḏ.tj vegetable gardener 43780 1002761
wꜣḏ.tj two green stones 850386 1002761
wꜣḏ.tj Oasis Region 859343 1002761
wꜣdḏ.t vegetation; green plants 43990 1002761
wꜣḏwꜣḏ green plants 43950 1002761
wꜣḏwꜣḏ to become green; to make green 43940 1002761
wj mummy case 44010 1002670
wjꜣ team; crew 861064 1002672
wjꜣ without (doing); apart from (something) 44040 1002671
wjꜣ to push aside; to reject 44030 1002671
wjꜣ ship; processional bark 44020 1002672

wjꜣ.t [a symptom of a heart ailment] 44060 1002671
wjꜣw.yt senility (of heart) 44090 1002671
wjꜣwjꜣ to be unsuccessful; to be powerless 44100 1002671
wjꜣwjꜣ helplessness; weakness 600207 1002671
wjn crime 859663 1002671
wjn to push aside; to reject 44120 1002671
wy woe!; don't you dare! 44110 1002758
wꜥ one (of many); some (of a material) 600041 1002775
wꜥ the only one; the lonely one 852351 1002775
wꜥ one; sole one 400101 1002775
wꜥ one; sole 44150 1002775
wꜥ a; an (indef. article) 600043 1002775
wꜥ harpoon 44140 1002776
wꜥ.w soldier; sailor 44390 1002775
wꜥ.w solder; sailor 855693 1002775
wꜥ.t sole one (solar eye) 44170 1002775
wꜥ.t (sole) one; the only thing 600045 1002775
wꜥ.t palace 861109 1002775
wꜥ.t sole one (Hathor of Dendera) 44190 1002775
wꜥ.t sole one (uraeus) 44180 1002775
wꜥ.tj [a lion] 44250 1002775
wꜥ.tj the only one; the lonely one 852751 1002775
wꜥ.tj sole; single 44230 1002775
wꜥ.tj unique one 855564 1002775
wꜥ.tj goat 44240 1002774
wꜥ.tj one-sided 865709 1002775
wꜥ.tjt sole one (name of the uraeus) 44270 1002775
wꜥ.tjw one (numerical concept) 44370 1002775
wꜥꜣ candle; torch 44320 1002783
wꜥꜣ star (or similar) 856148 1002783
wꜥꜣ to revile 44310 1002758
wꜥꜣ.w Slanderer (gatekeeper in the netherworld) 44340 1002758
wꜥi̯ to be alone; to be (the only) one 44350 1002775
wꜥꜥ.w loneliness; solitude 44360 1002775
wꜥwꜥ to cut down (an enemy) 44420 1002776
wꜥb to serve as priest 44470 1002777
wꜥb pure place 44480 1002777
wꜥb pure one; free one 44450 1002777
wꜥb [a water stream?] 852709 1002777
wꜥb purity; purification 44440 1002777
wꜥb pure one 860551 1002777
wꜥb wab-priest 855694 1002777
wꜥb wab-priest 44460 1002777
wꜥb piece of meat (for offering) 44490 1002777
wꜥb pure 400114 1002777
wꜥb to purify; to be pure; to be free (to be unused) 44430 1002777
wꜥb the pure (domain) 853177 1002777
wꜥb Pure one (Gebel Barkal) 850111 1002777
wꜥb.w pure garment (for the gods and the dead) 44620 1002777
wꜥb.wt priestly duty (for the month) 44580 1002777
wꜥb.t pure garment (for gods) 44530 1002777
wꜥb.t wab-priestess 44520 1002777
wꜥb.t meat; flesh (for offerings) 44560 1002777
wꜥb.t food offerings (lit. what is pure) 44570 1002777
wꜥb.t cleansing; purification 858088 1002777
wꜥb.t pure place (embalming place, workshop for crafts); sanctuary; tomb 44540 1002777
wꜥb.t pure place (heavens) 44550 1002777
wꜥf to bend (something) down; to prostrate; to be bent; to bend into shape 44640 1002778
wꜥn juniper tree 44660 1002780
wꜥr to flee; to hurry 44680 1002781
wꜥr fugitive 44690 1002781
wꜥr.w hurry 44810 1002781

wꜥr.t part; department; administrative district 44750 1002782
wꜥr.t district (of the necropolis) 44760 1002782
wꜥr.t [a body of water in the hereafter] 44780 1002782
wꜥr.t flight; escape 44730 1002781
wꜥr.t [part of a ship] 44720 1002782
wꜥr.t [a celestial region] 44770 1002782
wꜥr.t leg 44740 1002781
wꜥḥ chufa (sedge with edible tuber) 44830 1002779
ww to sing?; to make music? 44850 1002752
ww [a singing or music-making woman?] 44870 1002752
ww.t Uut (singing Hathor) 44880 1002752
wbꜣ butler; servant; steward 855697 1002610
wbꜣ butler; servant; steward 44930 1002610
wbꜣ opposite; in front of 44940 1002610
wbꜣ to open; to drill 44890 1002610
wbꜣ (open) forecourt 44910 1002610
wbꜣ to deflower 44900 1002610
wbꜣ to pour out (a drink) 44920 1002610
wbꜣ.yt forecourt (of a temple) 45020 1002610
wbꜣ.yt female butler; servant 45030 1002610
wbꜣ.t opening 44950 1002610
wbn rise; overflow 854500 1002606
wbn to shine; to rise (of the sun); coming out 45050 1002606
wbn spring ("what comes forth") 45070 1002606
wbn overflowing (from the grain) 45060 1002606
wbn.j shining one (the sun god) 45150 1002606
wbn.w open wound; injury 45190 1002607
wbn.w sunrays 45160 1002606
wbn.w hole; wound 858117 1002607
wbn.w the east ("sunrise") 45170 1002606
wbn.t the one who comes out (first hour of the day) 45100 1002606
wbn.t one who shines 45090 1002606
wbn.t webenet (mummy bindings of the head) 45110 1002606
wbn.t Webenet (place of sunrise) 45120 1002606
wbnbn to arise 45220 1002606
wbnn.j shining one (the sun god) 45230 1002606
wbẖ to shine; to brighten; to be bright 45270 1002605
wbẖ.t the bright one 858119 1002605
wbẖ.t clarity (of the eye) 45280 1002605
wbẖ.t [a mineral (from Asia Minor)] 45310 1002605
wbẖ.t clean clothing 45290 1002605
wbs swell (of water, of the inundation); flood 45370 1002609
wbs to heap up (corn and sheaves) 45350 1002609
wbs to arise 858118 1002609
wbs to come out 854501 1002609
wbs herbs; greenery 45340 1002609
wbs to come out; to sprout; to make sprout 45330 1002609
wbg blossom; to turn green 45390 1002604
wbg to shine; to illuminate 45380 1002605
wbg to open 860373 1002604
wbg.wj shining one? 45400 1002605
wbg.t fire; heat; sexual arousal? 858114 1002605
wbd to burn; to heat 45410 1002603
wbd soot? (med.) 45420 1002603
wbd.t burning one 860817 1002603
wbd.t burning; burn 45430 1002603
wp disclosure; specification 852648 1002701
wp.t horns; brow; top (of the head)) 45530 1002699
wp.t mountain peak 851599 1002699
wp.t judge's decision; judgment 45540 1002701
wp.t horned cattle (cattle; cows) 860179 1002699

wp.t Opening One 858180 1002701
wp.w bread; food (as offerings) 45520 1002701
wp.w judge (usually Thoth) 45700 1002701
wp.w knife (“separator”) 45460 1002701
wp.w butchered animal (as an offering) 45510 1002701
wp.w 1st day of the lunar month (“opener”) 45720 1002701
wp.w judge 45480 1002701
wp.w exclusion 858187 1002701
wp.w festival (gen.); festive mood 45490 1002701
wp.w Wepu (“corps opener”?) 45690 1002701
wp.wt crowd of women (for greeting and similar) 45740 1002700
wp.wt entry; list; inventory 45550 1002700
wp.wt members of a household; household list 45730 1002700
wpi̯ to divide; to separate judicially; to open; to decide 45640 1002701
wpw except for; but 45680 1002701
wpw.t message; task; issue (gen.) 45750 1002701
wpw.tj messenger 45760 1002701
wpw.tj messenger 855093 1002701
wpw.tjt messenger 858185 1002701
wpr.t side lock of a child 45780 1002702
wpr.t wepret-priestess 45790 1002702
wps to burn up (the bad one) 45800 1002703
wps.t flame 858189 1002703
wps.t She who burns up (the enemies) 45810 1002703
wpš light (or similar) 45830 1002704
wpš to spread (natron, gypsum); to illuminate 45820 1002704
wfꜣ to discuss; to support 45870 1002631
wfꜣ lung 45860 1002630
wmt thickness (as dimension) 45930 1002674
wmt thickness (of a wall); reveal (of a doorway); gateway 45950 1002674
wmt to be thick 45920 1002674
wmt thick garment; thick cloth 45960 1002674
wmt fortification wall; surrounding walls 45970 1002674
wmt concentration, density (of enemies) 45940 1002674
wmt.t surrounding wall 45990 1002674
wmt.t thickness; size (of humans) 46000 1002674
wn [substantive (essence, being or similar)] 46040 1002693
wn existing one 863618 1002693
wn one who exist 858148 1002693
wn to open 46060 1002679
wn opening (of a door) 46070 1002679
wn hare 46110 1002677
wn [particle introducing existential sentences] 855526 1002693
wn to be bald 46100 1002678
wn error; fault; blame 46080 1002676
wn [auxiliary] 550129 1002693
wn.yt stripped of eyebrows 46300 1002678
wn.w wealth? (“what is (with someone)”) 853887 1002693
wn.w baldness? 874151 1002678
wn.w doorkeeper 46350 1002679
wn.wt doors? 46170 1002679
wn.t wenet-priestess (in the nome of Beni Hasan, the 16th nome of Upper Egypt) 46160 1002679
wn.t because (conj.) 851210 1002693
wn.t indeed (emphasis after independent pronouns) 851212 1002693
wn.t something opened; opening; sanctuary? 867440 1002679
wn.t [a sanctuary (in the temple)] 46140 1002675
wn.t rope; cord 46130 1002688
wn.t fortress 46150 1002675
wn.t Hour 500287 1002698
wni̯ to hurry; to pass by; to neglect 46280 1002689
wni̯ to tow; to bind 46320 1002688

wny light 46290 1002690
wnw night's rest? 46370 1002698
wnw.t hour-star 46570 1002698
wnw.t service; hourly service (of priests) 46430 1002698
wnw.t hour 46420 1002698
wnw.t hour goddess (designation of the uraeus serpent) 46440 1002698
wnw.tj hour-watcher (a priest) 46450 1002698
wnw.tj He who belongs to the hour 500359 1002698
wnwn to observe (the stars) 46510 1002698
wnwn to threaten 46500 1002680
wnwn to move to and fro; to traverse 46490 1002689
wnwn.w star watcher 46520 1002698
wnwnw.t She who moves to and fro (a serpent) 46550 1002689
wnbwnb flower; blossom 46580 1002681
wnp to stab; to fetter 46600 1002694
wnp stabber (a priest at Edfu) 46610 1002694
wnp stabber (Horus of Edfu) 46620 1002694
wnp.w triumph ("stabbing" the enemies) 46650 1002694
wnpj to harvest (flax)? 46630 1002695
wnf to be glad; to rejoice 46660 1002685
wnf loosen 856220 1002685
wnm food; to take (medicine) 46720 1002692
wnm fattened ox? 46730 1002692
wnm to eat 46710 1002692
wnm.j right (side) 46770 1002692
wnm.j right side; right 600035 1002692
wnm.j the right side (division of Theban necropolis workmen) 46780 1002692
wnm.j right hand 46790 1002692
wnm.yt devourer (fire) 46800 1002692
wnm.yt devourer (flame) 852396 1002692
wnm.w devourer 46820 1002692
wnm.w food 46810 1002692
wnm.t the one who eats 858159 1002692
wnm.t right eye (of a deity) 46750 1002692
wnm.t diadem of Upper Egypt 860354 1002691
wnm.t right eye (mostly Nekhbet as the crown goddess of Upper Egypt) 46760 1002692
wnm.t food; fodder 46740 1002692
wnm.t the right one 500929 1002692
wnn to exist; to be 46050 1002693
wnn [auxilliary] 400006 1002693
wnn the one who exists 858160 1002693
wnn.yw those who exist 46860 1002693
wnn.w the child (sun god, king) 501130 1002693
wnn.w child (in the womb) 850407 1002693
wnn.t indeed; really (emphasis after independent pronouns) 550416 1002693
wnn.t that which exists 46830 1002693
wnr to move along? 46900 1002689
wnẖ plank (naut.) 46960 1002686
wnẖ to clothe; to coat 46920 1002686
wnẖ dislocation (med.) 46930 1002687
wnẖ to move yourself, to loosen 856221 1002687
wnẖ.yt mummy bandage 46980 1002686
wnẖ.w clothing 46990 1002686
wnẖ.wj two strips of cloth 47000 1002686
wnẖ.t clothing; strip of cloth; bandage 46970 1002686
wnš grape; raisin 47040 1002696
wnš jackal headed sled 47030 1002697
wnš jackal 47020 1002697
wnš.jw wolfhound 47070 1002697
wnš.t wine 47060 1002696
wnš.t female jackal 47050 1002697
wnš.tj One belonging to the female jackal 854772 1002697
wnšnš to hurry 47080 1002697
wnḏ.w goats 47210 1002683
wnḏ.w short-horned cattle 47200 1002683
wnḏ.ww units (of produce, of things, of people) 47240 1002684
wnḏ.ww offerings 47250 1002684
wnḏ.wt people 47230 1002683

wnḏ.wt hold (of a ship); cavity 47220 1002682
wnḏ.wt cattle; herd 47190 1002683
wnḏ.t hollow; depression 47170 1002682
wr large amount of; quantity of 47320 1002712
wr very; fast 47300 1002712
wr great one (a bull) 47340 1002712
wr [a vessel for oil?]; [a quality of oil?] 47350 1002712
wr great one (a serpent) 856163 1002712
wr swallow 47260 1002706
wr greatest one (various gods) 851429 1002712
wr great; a lot; rich; important 47271 1002712
wr the elder (qualifying personal names) 400685 1002712
wr Great one (hippopotamus, as a manifestation of Seth) 47330 1002712
wr how much? how many? (interrogative) 47310 1002712
wr greatness 47290 1002712
wr great one 47280 1002712
wr.yt [a sacral building (tomb, embalming hall)] 47720 1002712
wr.yt door posts 47730 1002712
wr.yt great flood; high waters 47760 1002712
wr.w great one 852271 1002712
wr.w great waters (water place, pond) 47780 1002712
wr.w Great Ones 855586 1002712
wr.t [a sacred bark] 47500 1002712
wr.t great one (crown of Lower Egypt) 47460 1002712
wr.t very 450161 1002712
wr.t great thing; greatness 47430 1002712
wr.t great one (various goddesses) 47420 1002712
wr.t great one (a cow) 47440 1002712
wr.t great one (uraeus) 47450 1002712
wr.t great flame (on the altar) 47490 1002712
wr.t great one (ruler, noble woman) 850963 1002712
wr.t great one (eye of Horus) 47480 1002712
wr.t [a sacred body of water?] 47510 1002705
wr.t Great (a body of water in the nome of Latopolis) 47520 1002712
wr.t Weret-canal 450429 1002712
wr.tj the two great ones (uraeus serpents) 865109 1002712
wrwr Exceedingly great one 860633 1002712
wrm to draw oneself up; to mount up 450145 1002710
wrm erected one (lofty figure) 47820 1002710
wrm high flood 47810 1002710
wrm.yt [a symptom of illness] 850411 1002710
wrm.w windings 850412 1002711
wrm.t pergola; roof 47850 1002710
wrm.t erected one; figure 854805 1002710
wrr to be great; to be large 47270 1002712
wrr.w great waters 47980 1002712
wrr.w great ones 47990 1002712
wrr.t great one (crown of Upper Egypt) 47920 1002712
wrr.t great one ("spiral" at the front of the Red Crown of Upper Egypt) 47940 1002712
wrr.t [Epithet of Nut] 867530 1002712
wrry.t wagon; chariot 47970 1002713
wrh to dance 48010 1002708
wrḥ to anoint; to smear 48030 1002709
wrḥ ointment 48040 1002709
wrḥ ointment vessel (a measure) 48050 1002709
wrḥ.j belonging to the ointment 855572 1002709
wrḥ.w anointer (a priest) 48080 1002709
wrḥ.t ointment 48060 1002709
wrs mast-support (naut.) 48110 1002714
wrs headrest 48090 1002714

wrš time period (used alongside year) 48150 1002715
wrš guard; watching over 852796 1002715
wrš.y keeper of the daily watch; guard 48200 1002715
wrš.w who guards 500125 1002715
wrš.w one having daily service; guard 854709 1002715
wrš.ww Awakened ones 854413 1002715
wrš.t festival participants 48170 1002715
wrš.t morning watch; day watch 600301 1002715
wrš.t guardhouse 48180 1002715
wršu̯ to spend the day; to be awake, to dwell 48130 1002715
wršu̯ spend the day on (a quest); [auxiliary] 852476 1002715
wrḏ to be weary; to grow weary 48260 1002707
wrḏ.w weariness 48300 1002707
wrḏ.w weary one 48290 1002707
wrḏ.w Weary one 500889 1002707
wrḏ.t weariness 48270 1002707
wh unsuccessful one (Seth) 852973 1002646
wh sinner 856687 1002646
wh.t failure 851908 1002646
wh.yw unsuccessful ones (designation for enemy) 48360 1002646
whi̯ to escape; to miss; to fail 48330 1002646
whj failure 48340 1002646
whj (bloody) diarrhoea 48370 1002647
whb to pierce 48390 1002643
whb hole (med.) 48400 1002643
whm to burn 48420 1002649
whm heat 48480 1002649
whn to tear down; to decay; to fall apart 48560 1002651
whnn crown (of the head) 48590 1002652
whnn.wtj the two who are on the crown of the head 48610 1002652
whs to slacken; to be worn out 48640 1002655
wḥ.yt family; kin; tribe 48730 1002640
wḥ.wt settlement; village 48650 1002640
wḥꜣ [a skin disease (rash?)] 48670 1002657
wḥꜣ to quarry (stone); to tear out; to pick; to gather 48660 1002662
wḥꜣ stone worker 400572 1002662
wḥꜣ.y harvest; crop 48720 1002662
wḥꜣ.t oasis 48700 1002662
wḥꜣ.t cauldron 48690 1002658
wḥꜣ.tjw oasis dweller 48710 1002662
wḥꜥ to destroy? (a tomb) 48850 1002669
wḥꜥ to sting (of scorpion) 48840 1002667
wḥꜥ Weha-festival (temple foundation festival) 48820 1002668
wḥꜥ to fish and fowl 48800 1002668
wḥꜥ fisher and fowler 48790 1002668
wḥꜥ fisherman and fowler 860971 1002668
wḥꜥ fisherman and fowler 875450 1002668
wḥꜥ fisherman and fowler 855698 1002668
wḥꜥ provision 48810 1002668
wḥꜥ to loosen; to explain; to establish;
return home 48760 1002669
wḥꜥ explanation; commentary 48860 1002669
wḥꜥ to offer; to sacrifice 48770 1002669
wḥꜥ Detached One 858138 1002669
wḥꜥ.w catfish (Synodontis schall) 48830 1002668
wḥꜥ.t [a duck (greater white-fronted goose)] 48870 1002668
wḥꜥ.t supplies; provisions 48900 1002669
wḥꜥ.t scorpion; scorpion venom 48880 1002667
wḥꜥ.t Nile pike 850415 1002668
wḥwḥ to disappear; fading (of inscriptions) 48970 1002662
wḥwḥ to bark (of a dog) 48980 1002641
wḥf to burn 853374 1002645
wḥm to repeat (gen.) 48440 1002650
wḥm to repeat (something said) 851319 1002650
wḥm bull's leg (a piece of furniture) 48470 1002648
wḥm tongue (lit. repeater) 48460 1002650

wḥm further; again 600562 1002650
wḥm to repeat (to do); [aux./modal] 851318 1002650
wḥm.yt repetition 48530 1002650
wḥm.w speaker; herald; transmitter 48540 1002650
wḥm.w speaker; transmitter 855699 1002650
wḥm.wtj repeater 48990 1002650
wḥm.t bull's leg; hoof 48430 1002648
wḥs to cut (off, down); to remove 49010 1002656
wḥs.wt predators? 49020 1002656
wẖ to be dark 49050 1002642
wẖ darkness; night 49060 1002642
wẖ.t darkness 49080 1002642
wẖꜣ columned hall 49090 1002660
wẖꜣ hang down 858478 1002664
wẖꜣ to empty out; to shake out 49100 1002663
wẖꜣ blowing (of a storm) 49110 1002663
wẖꜣ to smoothen? 49260 1002666
wẖꜣ to seek; to get; to desire 49120 1002665
wẖꜣ official letter; decree 49180 1002665
wẖꜣ column; supporting pillar 49200 1002660
wẖꜣ columned hall (a figure in dancing) 49210 1002660
wẖꜣ foolishness 49160 1002661
wẖꜣ fool 49150 1002661
wẖꜣ lotus flower 49230 1002664
wẖꜣ to be foolish 49170 1002661
wẖꜣ.yt columned hall 850417 1002660
wẖꜣ.w claws? 49280 1002659
wẖꜣ.wt scout; patrol 49290 1002665
wẖr to answer a prayer? 49310 1002654
wẖr to work, to process (wood); to struggle; to care (for someone) 49320 1002654
wẖr.yt carpenter's tools (gen.) 49340 1002654
wẖr.t carpenter's workshop; shipyard 49330 1002654
wẖd forbearance; patience 49370 1002644
wẖd to endure; to suffer 49350 1002644
wẖd to suffer; to endure 49360 1002644
wẖd to suffer 851445 1002644
wẖd.y sufferer 49400 1002644
wẖd.w pain (med.); disease trigger 49410 1002644
wẖd.t disease trigger 49390 1002644
ws to finish; to lack; to be empty 49420 1002717
ws height (of a pyramid) (math.) 49430 1002716
ws.w sawer 500233 1002727
ws.t sawdust (med.) 49450 1002727
wš.t splinter 50080 1002718
wš.t destruction (possibly break) 450165 1002718
wsi̯ to saw; to cut 49470 1002727
wsj (small) window; chink 49480 1002717
wsy very; how (emphatic) 49490 1002734
wsn to procreate; to fertilize 49570 1002731
wsn.j procreator 49580 1002731
wsr powerful one (various gods) 851401 1002734
wsr powerful one 49610 1002734
wsr powerful; strong 49590 1002734
wsr to be powerful; to be strong; to strengthen 500010 1002734
wsr powerful one (phallus of Osiris) 49630 1002734
wsr [Weser-scepter] 49640 1002734
wsr oar 49620 1002733
wsr.w strength; wealth 49600 1002734
wsr.wt power 49760 1002734
wsr.t mighty one (fire) 49680 1002734
wsr.t front hawser; prow rope (naut.) 49700 1002734
wsr.t powerful one (rich woman) 49710 1002734
wsr.t powerful one 858850 1002734
wsr.t stake (in the hereafter); canid head symbol 49660 1002734
wsr.t neck 49650 1002734
wsr.t power (eye) 49690 1002734
wšr.t dry land? 401162 1002735
wsr.tj the two uraei 853977 1002734

wsr.tj powerful one 858216 1002734
wsẖ heat (or similar) 49790 1002724
wsẖ to burn; to heat 49780 1002725
wsẖ cargo-boat 49840 1002723
wsẖ to be wide; to be broad; to extend 49800 1002723
wsẖ broad; proud; famous 400135 1002723
wsẖ breadth; width 49820 1002723
wsẖ broad collar 49830 1002723
wsẖ.t breadth (as a measure) 49850 1002723
wsẖ.t [heaven(s)?] 49880 1002723
wsẖ.t barge; sacred bark 49860 1002723
wsẖ.t broad hall; court; chapel 49870 1002723
wsẖ.tj one of the broad hall (a priest) 49890 1002723
wstj official writings 49980 1002737
wstn [a body of water?] 50000 1002736
wstn to stride unhindered 50030 1002738
wš to be empty; to be destroyed; to destroy 50040 1002718
wš to push one's way through 50060 1002719
wš (vacant) place; gap; interruption 50070 1002718
wš.w whose hair falls out 858205 1002718
wšꜣ to pour out 50130 1002742
wšꜣ to fatten (animals) 50110 1002741
wšꜣ feeder (of animals) 50120 1002741
wšꜣ to treat (a tooth) 50140 1002741
wšꜣ.yt One belonging to the midnight hour 500633 1002739
wšꜣ.w darkest part of the night; darkness 50230 1002739
wšꜣ.w slanders (or similar) 50220 1002740
wšꜣ.t [a fattened fowl (wigeon duck?)] 50160 1002741
wšꜣꜣ.w fattened animals 50200 1002741
wši̯ to reduce to bits; to shred; to empty 50250 1002726
wšꜥ to chew; to eat 50270 1002743
wšꜥ.w itching ("eating" as an illness) 50300 1002743
wšꜥ.t itching spot (med.) 50290 1002743
wšwš to smite; to smash; to break 50310 1002718
wšb to answer; to answer for; take revenge; to react 50340 1002721
wšb to feed on (something) 50320 1002721
wšb fighting bull (Month) 854083 1002721
wšb answer 50350 1002721
wšb fighting bull 50360 1002721
wšb representation?; image? 50400 1002721
wšb.yt answer; statement 50460 1002721
wšb.yt small beads (or similar) 50470 1002720
wšb.yt loan ("answer") 50480 1002721
wšb.w response; return 50510 1002721
wšb.w answerer; defender 50500 1002721
wšb.t fighting cow; mourner? (Isis) 50420 1002721
wšb.t mourner 50410 1002721
wšm slaughtering knife 50580 1002730
wšm awn (of an ear of grain) 50600 1002728
wšm to slay; to kill 50570 1002730
wšm to stir, to mix; to blend 50540 1002729
wšm.y One belonging to the awn 858212 1002728
wšn to wring (the necks of birds); to sacrifice 50620 1002732
wšn.w the catch (of fishing and fowling); sacrifice 50630 1002732
wšr to be absent; to lack; without 70028 1002735
wšr dry land; dry area 50650 1002735
wšr to dry; to parch; to lack; to be bald 854502 1002735
wšr to dry; to parch 50640 1002735
wšt.t [an affliction of the eyes (dryness?)] 50680 1002735
wšd to address (someone); to question; to greet 50700 1002722
wg board; plank 850420 1002632
wg.yt twaddle? 50820 1002635
wg.yt a plank (naut.)? 50830 1002632

wg.wt lower jaw 50840 1002635
wgꜣ inundation; flood 50760 1002639
wgꜣ [crushed grain or fruit] 50750 1002635
wgb to cry out; to shout 50850 1002633
wgi̯ to chew 50790 1002635
wgj board; plank 50720 1002632
wgm powder; crushed grain; flour 50880 1002636
wgm to grind (grain) (or similar) 50870 1002636
wgp to crush; to destroy; to break 50860 1002637
wgs to cut open; to gut (animals) 50900 1002638
wgs (gutted?) bird 50910 1002638
wgs Slaughterer 858137 1002638
wgs.w slaughter (fish and fowl) 50930 1002638
wgg to be weak 850126 1002634
wgg shortage; famine?; weakness 50940 1002634
wgg.t harmfulness; complaint 850421 1002634
wt embalmed one 51060 1002744
wt innermost coffin 51000 1002744
wt mummy bandages; bandages 50990 1002744
wt to bandage; to bind 50980 1002744
wt.j embalmer 855700 1002744
wt.j bandager (of wounds) 51010 1002744
wt.j embalmer 51020 1002744
wt.j fettered one 51100 1002744
wt.y embalmer (Anubis) 851721 1002744
wt.w eldest son 51120 1002747
wt.t Oldest one (a serpent goddess) 51080 1002747
wt.t Oldest one (a serpent goddess as a place in the netherworld) 852193 1002747
wt.t fetterer 500412 1002744
wtꜣ.w those who are wrapped (gods in the netherworld) 500271 1002744
wti̯ to be old; to be great 850422 1002747
wtw.tj eldest son 51130 1002747
wtwt binding; fetter 51140 1002744
wtmt to stick firmly? 51150 1002748
wtmtm to collapse?; to stagger? 51160 1002748
wtn to pierce; to break through 51170 1002749
wtn opening; drill; tunnel 859103 1002749
wtẖ to flee 51230 1002746
wtẖ.w fugitive 51240 1002746
wtṯ semen 51290 1002750
wtṯ to create; to beget 51280 1002750
wtṯ creator? (Osiris) 51270 1002750
wtṯ.w offspring; son 51320 1002750
wtṯ.w creator; father 51310 1002750
wtṯ.t offspring 858220 1002750
wṯz standard 450102 1002751
wṯz carrying chair 51350 1002751
wṯz to announce; to extol; to slander 51340 1002751
wṯz to lift up; to carry; to raise; to boast 51330 1002751
wṯz one who elevates (something, ritually) 51380 1002751
wṯz He who elevates 500475 1002751
wṯz.w elevation 854313 1002751
wṯz.w accuser (who elevates (the accusation)) 51460 1002751
wṯz.wt betrayal; accusations 853631 1002751
wṯz.t throne 51360 1002751
wṯz.t sky; heavens 858710 1002751
wṯz.t flame 858222 1002751
wṯz.t Throne (of Horus) (town and nome of Edfu) 51370 1002751
wd.w Slinger 501070 1002619
wd.t shift (of contagious matter, infection?) 51490 1002619
wdi̯ to put; to place 51510 1002619
wdi̯ to cause that 858907 1002619
wdi̯ to push; to throw 500186 1002619
wdp.w steward 860398 1002626
wdp.w butler; attendant 51600 1002626
wdp.w butler; attendant 855519 1002626
wdp.wyt serving maid 51610 1002626

wdf period (of time); delay 28800 1002615
wdfi̯ to hesitate (and similar) 51620 1002615
wdn heavy one (hippopotamus) 51740 1002623
wdn to lay down; to set (the royal titles) 51650 1002623
wdn to install; to enthrone 51660 1002623
wdn to be heavy; to weigh 51670 1002623
wdn to offer; to sacrifice 51690 1002623
wdn offering 850424 1002623
wdn basket (for offering bread) 51710 1002623
wdn [a sacred baboon] 51730 1002622
wdn to cast down (enemies)? 51640 1002623
wdn offering; sacrificial ritual 51700 1002623
wdn.w offerer 51830 1002623
wdn.w burden 51810 1002623
wdn.w weight (on a plumb line) 51820 1002623
wdn.t offering courtyard 51770 1002623
wdn.t offering stand 856881 1002623
wdn.t offering 51760 1002623
wdn.t heavy block of stone 51750 1002623
wdḥ to pour out; to water 51870 1002617
wdḥ clyster (med.); git; sprue 861174 1002617
wdḥ to melt (metal, glass) 51880 1002617
wdḥ to pour; to water; to melt (metal); to manufacture (glass) 854504 1002617
wdḥ.w distribution (of offerings) 51920 1002617
wdḥ.w offering; sacrifice 858795 1002617
wdḥ.w altar; offering stand 400433 1002617
wdḥ.w offering jug 51900 1002617
wdd to cook 51950 1002614
wdd gall bladder 51940 1002613
wḏ palm fiber (for making rope) 52000 1002761
wḏ [a body of water?] 52030 1002761
wḏ stand of the rudder 858121 1002620
wḏ to command; to assign 51970 1002611
wḏ stela 51990 1002611
wḏ.yw pilots? (of Re's solar bark) 52350 1002611
wḏ.yt journey; campaign; expedition 52330 1002620
wḏ.yt steering gear 856154 1002620
wḏ.w command; decree 51980 1002611
wḏ.w [cattle rambling around freely] 52590 1002620
wḏ.t command; decree 52040 1002611
wḏ.t post (for the steering-oar) 52050 1002611
wḏ.t stele 863063 1002611
wḏ.t post (for the steering-oar) 52050 1002611
wḏꜣ to be whole; to be intact 52090 1002627
wḏꜣ wellbeing 52100 1002627
wḏꜣ magical protection? 182070 1002627
wḏꜣ storehouse 52110 1002627
wḏꜣ room in a temple 52120 1002627
wḏꜣ to proceed; to pass (away); to walk (in a procession) 52130 1002628
wḏꜣ.w remainder 450203 1002627
wḏꜣ.w amulet; protective spell 52280 1002627
wḏꜣ.wt remainder 450146 1002627
wḏꜣ.t Wedjat eye (Horus eye); eye 52140 1002627
wḏꜣ.t wedjat measure (parts of the Wdjat eye as a measure for grain) 52150 1002627
wḏꜣ.t heaven; temple roof 52170 1002627
wḏꜣ.t road; way 52200 1002628
wḏꜣ.t remainder; deficiency (from deliveries) 52210 1002627
wḏi̯ to send out; to depart 52300 1002620
wḏj perch; bulti-fish (tilapia nilotica) 52320 1002621
wḏꜥ to separate; to judge; to appoint 52360 1002629
wḏꜥ He who hears well? 52380 1002629
wḏꜥ judgement 52390 1002629
wḏꜥ judge 52540 1002629

wḏᶜ the judged one (Seth) 52400 1002629
wḏᶜ demoiselle crane 52420 1002629
wḏᶜ.w [a part or a processing state of dates (med.)] 52550 1002629
wḏᶜ.w irrigation canal?; canal?; net? 52560 1002629
wḏᶜ.w discharge 52570 1002629
wḏᶜ.wt scribe's ink-shell (made of shell?) 52480 1002629
wḏᶜ.wt severed limb 52500 1002629
wḏᶜ.t separator? (a knife?) 52450 1002629
wḏᶜ.t judgement; sentence 52460 1002629
wḏᶜ.t divorced woman 52470 1002629
wḏᶜ.t ration; piece 450079 1002629
wḏᶜ piece; fragment 450154 1002629
wḏᶜ.yt freshwater clam 850426 1002629
wḏꜣ.w departed ones (the dead) 853562 1002628
wḏᶜ.tj He who belongs to the judgment 500452 1002629
wḏꜣ intact one 858128 1002627
wḏᶜ.w knife, separator 858134 1002629
wḏᶜ.w scribe's ink well (made of shell?) 858135 1002629
wḏᶜ.tj splitter? 858132 1002629
wḏb to turn back; to fold over; to revert 52620 1002612
wḏb [folded cloth] 52610 1002612
wḏb shore; river bank 52640 1002612
wḏb.jw those belonging to the Two Banks 500450 1002612
wḏb.w donation (of produce) 550444 1002612
wḏn width? 52690 1002624
wḏn.w flood 52710 1002624
wḏnj [reed instrument (oboe?)] 52700 1002625
wḏḥ fruit 52740 1002616
wḏḥ weaned child 52730 1002618
wḏḥ to wean (the infant) 52720 1002618
wḏḥ to bear fruit?; to ripen?; to be planted 52750 1002616
wḏḥ.t fruit; yield 550246 1002616
wḏḏ.t what is commanded 52770 1002611

b

bʾ leg 856528 1000002
b.tj lips 859225 1000001
bꜣ to hack up (the earth); to open up; chop up 52890 1000114
bꜣ to endow with a ba(-soul) 52830 1000112
bꜣ to be a ba-mighty; to be endowed with a ba(-soul) 52820 1000112
bꜣ to be ba-mighty; to make ba-mighty 854507 1000112
bꜣ [a bird (a stork)] 52810 1000107
bꜣ leopardskin garment 52880 1000109
bꜣ leopard 52860 1000109
bꜣ leopard skin 52870 1000109
bꜣ [head disease (bald spot, hole)] 52920 1000114
bꜣ ba (might, power as part of the personality) 52840 1000112
bꜣ Ba (sacred ram of Mendes); ram god 52850 1000111
bꜣ.y hole 53190 1000114
bꜣ.y wooden peg?; wooden post? 53260 1000116
bꜣ.y foot wash basin 53180 1000124
bꜣ.y He who is endowed with a Ba(-soul) 500106 1000112
bꜣ.yt She who belongs to Ba (Osiris) (a demon) 53270 1000112
bꜣ.yw Those belonging to the Ba (Ra) 53280 1000112
bꜣ.w a cargo boat 53310 1000108
bꜣ.w Ba-souls (community of gods) 850437 1000112
bꜣ.w [a pot; a jar] 53320 1000110
bꜣ.w might; Ba-power 53300 1000112
bꜣ.w [a wooden instrument (pestle, masher)] 850441 1000116
bꜣ.w moisture (of the human body); perspiration 53340 1000124
bꜣ.wj the two bas (pairs of gods) 53020 1000112
bꜣ.wj Bawi (decanal star) 53030 1000112
bꜣ.t tomb; hole 850440 1000114
bꜣ.t [a wooden instrument (pestle, masher)]

52990 1000116
bꜣ.t bush; shrub 52960 1000115
bꜣ.t [a cereal] 52970 1000115
bꜣ.t throat 850443 1000113
bꜣ.t [a scepter of Hathor] 52980 1000116
bꜣ.tj The Two Bushes (designation of Egypt) 859756 1000115
bꜣꜣ eye 53120 1000115
bꜣꜣ.j inhabitants of holes 854365 1000114
bꜣꜣ.wt virility 53140 1000116
bꜣi̯ to be moist 53170 1000124
bꜣy malt (soaked grain) 53160 1000134
bꜣy [a kind of sweet baked goods] 53150 1000134
bꜣy.t [a kind of sweet baked goods] 53210 1000134
bꜣw hill 850444 1000100
bꜣw hill 850444 1000133
bꜣw.tjw those belonging to the mound (grave) 53370 1000133
bꜣwj offering stand? 53390 1000133
bꜣwj battlefield (of bulls) 53380 1000114
bꜣbꜣ to distribute; to pour out 53430 1000054
bꜣbꜣ hole; cavern 53420 1000114
bꜣbꜣ lance 600644 1000116
bꜣbꜣ.j [a serpent] 867707 1000116
bꜣbꜣ.t [building] 860481 1000114
bꜣbꜣ.t fresh flood water; whirlpool 53450 1000054
bꜣbꜣ.t [a cereal] 53440 1000134
bꜣn(i) the sleepy one 867710 1000127
bꜣni̯ to lie dormant; slumber; drowse 852854 1000127
bꜣḥ [a measure (solid measure?)] 53520 1000116
bꜣḥ to beget 850447 1000116
bꜣḥ phallus 53510 1000116
bꜣḥ.yt under-kilt? (as phallus protection); [fabric name] 53530 1000116
bꜣẖ to sink; to set 850449 1000123
bꜣẖ to rise (of the sun); to shine brightly 53550 1000123
bꜣẖ.yt She of the eastern mountains 500779 1000123
bꜣẖ.w Bakhu (myth. locality in the east where the sun rises) 850448 1000123
bꜣẖ.w Bakhu (in Libya); western mountains 53570 1000123
bꜣẖ.t white of the eye? 53580 1000123
bꜣs [a jar (for unguent)] 53600 1000130
bꜣs measure of capacity (1/2 hin) 850451 1000130
bꜣs to cut out; to devour 53620 1000131
bꜣs.t beaker; pail 53650 1000130
bꜣš jar (measure for unguent) 53680 1000132
bꜣḳ to be bright; to be clear; to be healthy 53730 1000129
bꜣḳ moringa tree?; olive tree? 53700 1000128
bꜣḳ oil of the moringa tree (ben oil)?; olive oil? 53720 1000128
bꜣḳ.t Dazzling-Eye (Egypt) 53770 1000129
bꜣḳ.t oil of the moringa tree?; olive oil? 53750 1000128
bꜣḳ.t clear character; wellbeing 53780 1000129
bꜣḳ.t [an oil jar] 53760 1000128
bꜣk to work; to pay dues; to render (services) 53800 1000126
bꜣk platform; ramp; tribune 53840 1000125
bꜣk servant; underling 53830 1000126
bꜣk.w taxes; deliveries; pay 53890 1000126
bꜣk.w labour; task; performance 53820 1000126
bꜣk.w workers 53930 1000126
bꜣk.wt servants 53940 1000126
bꜣkbꜣk.t equipment? 53960 1000126
bꜣk.t duties; produce 53860 1000126
bꜣk.t servant 53870 1000126
bꜣkꜣ.t plot; district; town 53920 1000126
bꜣg weakness; weariness 53980 1000121
bꜣg to congeal? (med.) 53970 1000120
bꜣgi̯ to be weary 53990 1000121
bꜣgs to dagger; to stab to death 54010 1000122
bꜣgs [a plant (thornbush?)] 54000 1000122

bꜣgs.w dagger 54020 1000122
bꜣgg weakness; impotence 856542 1000121
bꜣgg.t weakness; impotence 856543 1000121
bꜣd Myrrhe [substantive (something to rub)] 54080 1000118
bꜣḏ [name for myrrh or similar] 54050 1000118
bꜣḏ.y [part of sandals (lacing?)] 54090 1000058
bꜣḏ.t ringlet (or similar) 854444 1000118
bj groats (coarsely ground cereals) 54120 1000036
bj.w wasp?; bee?; hornet? 54530 1000033
bj.t bee 54200 1000033
bj.t honey 54210 1000033
bj.t processional bark 54100 1000037
bj.t honey 860123 1000033
bj.t clapnet 54110 1000035
bj.t (Egyptian) alabaster (of Hatnub) 54160 1000043
bj.t Bit (Red Crown of Lower Egypt) 54220 1000033
bj.t Bit (crown goddess of Lower Egyptian) 852172 1000033
bj.tj King of Lower Egypt 54240 1000033
bj.tj King of Lower Egypt (various gods) 853220 1000033
bj.tj beekeeper; honey gatherer 54230 1000033
bj.tjt queen 54260 1000033
bjꜣ example; model 54340 1000042
bjꜣ brazen heavenly waters; firmament 54320 1000044
bjꜣ mineral of meteoric origin (gen.); ore 54300 1000043
bjꜣ (processional) way 54350 1000044
bjꜣ ore (gen.); metal; meteoric iron; copper 54290 1000043
bjꜣ shell (of the primeval egg) 54280 1000044
bjꜣ spear 860355 1000043
bjꜣ.j valuable; brazen; metal 54460 1000043
bjꜣ.j bronze, celestial 873149 1000043
bjꜣ.y One belonging to the sky 852220 1000044
bjꜣ.yt wonders; marvels 54480 1000042
bjꜣ.ytj marvelous one (Amun) 54490 1000042
bjꜣ.w belonging to the heavenly waters 856572 1000044
bjꜣ.w mine; mining region 54510 1000043
bjꜣ.w marvelous things 54440 1000042
bjꜣ.w ore mining 54500 1000043
bjꜣ.wj cymbals 856570 1000043
bjꜣ.wt firmament 856573 1000043
bjꜣ.t character; mood 54410 1000042
bjꜣ.t mining region 54380 1000043
bjꜣ.t amazement; confusion 54400 1000042
bjꜣ.t crystalline sandstone (quartzite) 54390 1000043
bjꜣ.tj ore (gen.); copper 860878 1000043
bjꜣ.tjt brazen one; steadfast one (Thebes as the oldest city) 54430 1000043
bjꜣi̭ to marvel (at) 54470 1000042
bjꜣi̭ to be far from; to remove oneself from 54330 1000044
bjbj cheer; acclamation 54560 1000034
bjbj [an insect (wasp?)] 54570 1000033
bjn to be bad; to be evil 54600 1000040
bjn evil one 54610 1000040
bjn Evil one (Seth) 855485 1000040
bjn bad things 54620 1000040
bjn bad; evil 54605 1000040
bjn.w bad deeds 54660 1000040
bjn.t evil 54640 1000040
bjn.t harp 54650 1000041
bjk falcon ship 54690 1000039
bjk falcon 54680 1000039
bjk falcon 500418 1000039
bjk.t falcon (female) 54700 1000039
bjk.t falcon (Hathor and other goddesses) 54710 1000039
bjk.t Falcon Town 851580 1000039
bjt King of Lower Egypt 852663 1000033
bjtj to be king of Lower Egypt 54250 1000033
bjdj [an affliction of the eye] 54750

1000038
b^{c} to disregard; to neglect 54820 1000137
b^{c} to bubble; to bath 860858 1000135
b^{c} to engender; to produce; to yield 54830 1000135
b^{c} Esteemed one 54790 1000137
b^{c}j rod of palm 54870 1000141
b^{c}y [a term for flood] 54860 1000135
b^{c}b^{c} glazer (faience craftsman) 54910 1000135
b^{c}b^{c} drink 856540 1000135
b^{c}b^{c} to bubble; to bath, to drink 54900 1000135
b^{c}b^{c}.t inundation; current of water; stream (swirl) 54920 1000135
b^{c}n to mount (stones, in gold) 54940 1000058
b^{c}n.t neck; throat 54950 1000142
b^{c}n.tj He with the neck 500364 1000142
b^{c}r sea; river 54970 1000144
b^{c}r to fight 54980 1000143
b^{c}r Baal 54960 1000143
b^{c}r.t Baalat 860150 1000143
b^{c}ḥ [term for birds (metaphor for abundance?)] 55020 1000140
b^{c}ḥ grapevine? 55030 1000140
b^{c}ḥ inundated farmland 55000 1000140
b^{c}ḥ.w abundance 854994 1000140
b^{c}ḥ.w stream of semen (of Sobek, metaphor for the inundation) 55040 1000140
b^{c}ḥ.w flood; inundation 54990 1000140
b^{c}ḥ.t abundance 55060 1000140
b^{c}ḥ.t Abundance 860254 1000140
b^{c}ḥi̯ to be flooded; to flood; to inundate; to have in abundance 55080 1000140
bb [verb (a way to die)] 550424 1000003
bb collar 55340 1000003
bb.yt region of the collar bones? 55430 1000003
bb.wj the two collar bones 55420 1000003
bb.t throat 55370 1000003
bb.t collar; necklace 859345 1000003
bbj [a semi-precious stone (beads?)] 850446 1000115
bbn to wriggle along 55450 1000004
bfn [a scorpion] 55460 1000014
bfn to bark 55470 1000027
bfn dog 55480 1000027
bfn.t [a scorpion (fem.)] 55490 1000014
bn white wagtail; species of heron 55520 1000051
bn [particle of negation] 55500 1000053
bn.tj nipples; breasts (dual) 55550 1000115
bn.tj Benti (baboon as a son of the sun god) 873152 1000116
bn.ty baboonish 867725 1000116
bn.ty Benti (baboon as a son of the sun god) 56180 1000116
bn.w Phoenix (benu-bird) 55590 1000116
bnw phoenix 867722 1000116
bnw potency 856575 1000116
bnw miller? 55620 1000067
bnw.t inflammation; swelling 55640 1000116
bnw.t [perch? for a bird] 55700 1000116
bnw.t heat; oestrum (oestrous phase of female mammal) 55660 1000116
bnw.t millstone 55650 1000067
bnn globule (of myrrh); bead 55850 1000115
bnn to beget; to be erected 55830 1000116
bnn to overflow (of a granary); to swell 55820 1000116
bnn [phallus?] 55840 1000116
bnn to repulse (the Nine Bows) 55880 1000116
bnn Spherical one 501072 1000115
bnn Benen (a serpent) 55860 1000116
bnr.w outside; exterior 55920 1000050
bnn.wt virility; potency 850952 1000116
bnn.t ball 55890 1000115
bnn.t threshold? 55910 1000063
bnj confectioner 56040 1000062
bnj pleasant 854286 1000062
bnj sweetness (milk) 55950 1000062
bnj sweetness (canal) 55960 1000062
bnj sweet 400993 1000062
bnj date 55930 1000062

bnj to be sweet 55940 1000062
bnj.w sweetness; popularity 56070 1000062
bnj.w date juice 55570 1000062
bnj.wt sweetness 867728 1000062
bnjbnj sweet 56080 1000062
bnj.t date wine 55990 1000062
bnj.t date palm 55980 1000062
bnj.t sweets 56000 1000062
bnj.t popularity 56050 1000062
bnj.tj confectioner 56010 1000062
bny [a fruit (corn)] 850457 1000062
bnu̯ to escape; to depart 55510 1000054
bnf gall-bladder 55810 1000059
bnbn to beget; to ejaculate 55750 1000054
bnbn [a beam (made of cedarwood)] 55740 1000116
bnbn Benben (sacred stone); obelisk 55720 1000116
bnbn to flow out (Nile); to swell 55770 1000054
bnbn [a conical loaf of bread] 55730 1000116
bnbn to point upwards; to be erected 55780 1000116
bnbn House of the obelisk (myth. locality in the netherworld) 500131 1000116
bnbn Benben 850461 1000116
bnbn Benben sanctuary in Heliopolis 856233 1000116
bnbn.t pyramidion (capstone of pyramid and obelisk) 55800 1000116
bnbn.t [a loaf of bread] 851819 1000116
bnbn.tj He who belongs to the conical loaf 500647 1000116
bnbny.tj One belonging to the obelisk (sun god) 500134 1000116
bnhm jubilation 56090 1000549
bns to pierce; to gore 56100 1000066
bnš flower crown? 56130 1000065
bnš doorpost 56120 1000064
bng to have abundance (of food)? 56150 1000060
bngzyt [a musical instrument] 56160 1000061
bnd clothing; garment 56240 1000058
bnd to wrap; to clothe 56220 1000058
bnd to fare badly 56200 1000055
bnd.t cucumber garden; cucumber 850454 1000057
bnḏ to discharge (from the body) 56260 1000056
bnḏ.t landing (naut.) 856577 1000056
br open field (at necropolis); outside? 56340 1000050
br [a mullet] 56320 1000073
br transport ship 56310 1000074
br basket 56380 1000115
br [a bead of pigment?] 56370 1000115
br tuft (of an ox's tail) 56360 1000115
br to see 56280 1000115
br eyeball; eye 56270 1000115
brbr knob (upper part of the Upper Egyptian White Crown) 56450 1000115
brr blind man 56480 1000115
brq to sparkle 56530 1000079
brk gift 56560 1000077
brk to offer 56540 1000077
brkt pool 56570 1000078
brg to be happy; to be content 56600 1000076
brg.t [a semi-precious stone (beryl?)] 56610 1000075
brt agreement; pact 56650 1000080
brtj [a semi-precious stone] 56660 1000081
bh.t fan 56680 1000032
bhꜣ fan 56690 1000032
bhꜣ to make turn back; to flee 56700 1000032
bhꜣ.w fugitive 56720 1000032
bhd perfume 56750 1000023
bhd to inhale (fragrance); to breath in 56760 1000023
bhd to fumigate; to smoke thoroughly 56770 1000023
bhd to inhale (fragrance); to breath in; to smoke thoroughly 854508 1000023
bḥ to do compulsory labor; to force

56800 1000020
bḥ to capture? 858410 1000020
bḥ.w compulsory labor 550264 1000020
bḥbḥ lapis lazuli beads 855369 1000019
bḥn biting snake 856553 1000029
bḥn dismemberment (punishment) 56840 1000029
bḥn dog ("barker") 56850 1000027
bḥn to bark 56860 1000027
bḥn.t knife 56870 1000029
bḥni̯ to cut (up, off); to punish 56830 1000029
bḥz calf 56890 1000031
bḥz.t calf (female) 56910 1000031
bḥs to hunt 56920 1000030
bḥd to settle down 858853 1000022
bḥd.w throne; seat 56990 1000022
bḥd.w a place of throne 858715 1000022
bḥd.t Behdet (court M in Edfou) 858626 1000022
bḥd.t necropolis of primordial gods 858694 1000022
bḥd.tj one of Edfu 858498 1000022
bḥd.tj one of Edfou (Horus) 400311 1000022
bḥd.tj Behdety (winged sun disk) 850566 1000022
bḥd.tjt One of Edfu (Hathor) 56980 1000022
bḫn to watch 859593 1000028
bḫn [a screen made of wattle] 859887 1000028
bḫn greywacke (crystalline dark gray sandstone) 57020 1000026
bḫn fortified house; castle; stronghold; fortress 57030 1000028
bḫn pylon (headdress of Hathor and upper part of the sistrum) 57040 1000028
bḫn.t pylon; gateway 57060 1000028
bḫḫ pellets of natron 57070 1000025
bḫḫ to glow 57080 1000025
bḫḫ.y Glowing one (gate in the netherworld) 500324 1000025
bḫḫ.w fiery breath 57100 1000025
bḫḫ.t Glowing one 501079 1000025
bẖ to give birth; to bring forth 57110 1000123
bẖ to shine 57120 1000123
bẖbẖ arrogance 57140 1000123
bz secret; initiation 57170 1000102
bz product (of the fields, of the mountains) 57180 1002609
bz secret image (cult statue) 850478 1000102
bz flame; fire 856590 1000101
bz.y Emerging one (manifestation of Re) 57350 1002609
bz.y Flaming one 856589 1000101
bz.w swelling; turgidity (of stomach) 57370 1002609
bzi̯ to flood out; to emerge; to come forth 57340 1002609
bzi̯ to introduce (someone); to enter 57160 1000102
bzi̯ to burn 856591 1000101
bzi̯ to introduce (someone); to enter; to
flood out; to emerge; 854509 1000102
bzꜣ protection 57300 1000106
bzꜣ [an offering object ("protection" that is being handed over)] 57290 1000106
bzꜣ to protect 57310 1000106
bzꜣ Protection 500726 1000106
bzꜣ.t protectress (Isis) 850476 1000106
bzn gypsum; natron 57460 1000105
bznw to consider; to notice 57480 1000104
bznw gypsum 855785 1000105
bs [golden amulet] 57220 1000106
bs.y Flaming one 500361 1000101
bs.yt Flaming one 57360 1000101
bs.w result; consequence 57400 1002609
bsn.t etching needle; burin 57470 1000085
bsk entrails; heart 57520 1000084
bsk to cut out; to eviscerate 57530 1000084
bsꜣ.w besau-pendant, sporran (as protection made of beads) 57330 1000106
bš vomiting 57550 1000083
bš.w vomit 57610 1000083
bšꜣ [malted barley (for beer production)]

57570 1000088
bšꜣ ax 57580 1000087
bši̯ to spit out; to spew 57600 1000083
bšw [a shiny flint] 57620 1000021
bšṯ to be rebellious 57640 1000086
bšṯ.w rebels 57650 1000086
bšṯ.w rebellion 57660 1000086
bq to spot; to catch sight of 850452 1000068
bq to be stubborn; to be rebellious; to be hostile 57670 1000069
bqbq recalcitrance? 57710 1000069
bqn to stride 57730 1000070
bqnqn standards (carried in front of a god) 57760 1000070
bqnqn.w standards 861481 1000070
bqs.w spine 57780 1001908
bqy to open?; to stay? 57700 1000071
bq^{c} depression (where flood water collects and stagnates) 53790 1000072
bkj [a (pear?) tree] 57900 1000045
bkj [a fruit (of the pear tree?)] 57910 1000045
bkꜣ morning; morrow 57830 1000049
bkꜣ to be (become) pregnant; to make pregnant 57820 1000049
bkꜣ.t pregnant woman 57840 1000049
bkꜣ.t sprout (of a rush); embryo? 57860 1000049
bkꜣ.t mother cow 57850 1000049
bkꜣ.tj [the two testicles] 57880 1000049
bkn excrement (med.) 57920 1000047
bkr throne 57930 1000048
bgꜣ to howl 855211 1000018
bgꜣ to be shipwrecked 850481 1000017
bgꜣ.w shipwrecked man 58010 1000017
bgꜣ.w shouting 58000 1000018
bgz throat 58050 1000016
bgs to injure; to be injured; to be disloyal 450143 1000015
bgs.w damage; harm; turmoil 58060 1000015
bgs.w rebel 856672 1000015
bgs.w rebel 856672 1000015
bt [a mold for making Osiris figures] 58120 1000089
bt.t womb 856565 1000091
btꜣ wrongdoer 58150 1000095
btꜣ to make (oneself) guilty 58140 1000095
btꜣ.w crime; offence; delict 58130 1000095
btꜣ.t disadvantage 58170 1000095
btk rebel (or similar) 58230 1000092
btk to slaughter (enemies) 58250 1000092
btk squalor; dirt 58220 1000092
btk expectoration? 58260 1000093
btk to be grieved? (of the heart) 58240 1000093
btktk to escape (or similar) 58270 1000093
bṯ to run; to leave (somebody) 854510 1000090
bṯ to gather 859834 1000090
bṯ to run 58280 1000090
bṯ to leave (somebody) 58290 1000090
bṯ.y reed worker 58310 1000090
bṯn to resist; to disobey 58350 1000094
bṯn.w rebel 58380 1000094
bd to illumine; to shine 58420 1000007
bd to purify (with natron) 58410 1000007
bd natron (granulated soda) 58400 1000007
bḏ ball; pellet 58530 1000005
bd.w Natron god 854363 1000052
bd.t emmer 58430 1000006
bdš to be weak; to be inert 58470 1000010
bdš.j weary one 856548 1000010
bdš.w weariness; fatigue 856550 1000010
bdš.t weariness; fatigue 856549 1000010
bdš.t Weary one 58490 1000010
bḏꜣ bread mould; mould (pot made of fired clay) 58570 1000012
bḏꜣ stiff roll of fabric; pad (used med.) 58590 1000011
bḏn stick; cudgel 58630 1000009
bḏn.w ball? 856547 1000005

p

p.t heaven(s) 58710 1001760
p.t sky 859338 1001760
p.tjw heavenly ones 855565 1001760

pꜣ.y Flying up one 500384 1001827
pꜣ.yw birds (lit. what flies) 59070 1001827
pꜣ.yw Flying ones 855525 1001827
pꜣi̯ to fly 58780 1001827
pꜣy to beget; to copulate 59030 1001827
pꜣy.t birds (lit. what flies) 59040 1001827
pꜣjp.t keel? (naut.) 59080 1001780
pꜣjs [pellets, granules? (drug)] 852309 1001828
pꜣu̯ to have done (something in the past); to be primeval 58790 1001827
pꜣw original state (of being) 58800 1001827
pꜣw.w duck 867764 1001827
pꜣw.t primeval goddess 59150 1001827
pꜣw.t primeval times 58830 1001827
pꜣw.t burden (metaph.) (med.) 59160 1001827
pꜣw.tj primeval 59170 1001827
pꜣw.tj Primeval one 861271 1001827
pꜣw.tj primeval god 500060 1001827
pꜣw.tjw primeval gods 59140 1001827
pꜣẖ [plant (med.)] 59190 1001824
pꜣẖ to scratch out (eyes) 59200 1001825
pꜣẖ.w scratching 856006 1001825
pꜣẖ.t lion 856425 1001825
pꜣẖd to be turned upside down; to be turned over 59230 1001826
pꜣz to suffer 59240 1001832
pꜣz.wt faint (or similar) 59260 1001832
pꜣz.wt brewers 59270 1001800
pꜣs (scribe's) water-pot 59250 1001830
pꜣḳ [a thin biscuit] 59310 1001829
pꜣḳ [a kind of a cake] 857504 1001829
pꜣḳ.t potsherd; flake (of stone); carapace (also metaph. for the skull) 59350 1001829
pꜣḳ.t thin sheet of metal 59340 1001829
pꜣḳ.t fine linen 59330 1001829
pꜣḳ.t ladder? 59360 1001829
pꜣḳi̯ to be thin 59300 1001829
pꜣṯṯ baboon 873158 1001831
pꜣṯṯ Patjetj (baboon) 59420 1001831
pꜣd to kneel; to run 59440 1000118
pꜣd.w [a med. substance] 875714 1001761
pꜣḏ knee; kneecap 59460 1000118
pꜣḏ pellet (or cone) (of incense) 59470 1001761
pꜣḏ.tjt [a med. substance] 863029 1001761
pj base; pedestal; throne 58650 1001759
pjpj to knead (clay) 59540 1001779
pjpj.t keel?, standard 59550 1001780
pjs to tread in; to stamp 858452 1001781
pjṯꜣ to mock 59580 1000341
py flea 59500 1001778
pꜥ to spew; to spray (sparks) 59600 1001837
pꜥ.w fire; flame 59660 1001835
pꜥ.t [a kind of pastry] 59620 1001833
pꜥ.t Flaming one 59630 1001835
pꜥ.t people; humankind; (social) upper class 59610 1001836
pꜥ.t [bank; area of land] 59650 1001834
pꜥ.t [a fruit?]; [a cereal?] 850684 1001833
pꜥꜣ.t quail 401147 1001840
pꜥpꜥ to shine 59680 1001835
pꜥpꜥ to bear; to be born 59670 1001836
pꜥpꜥ.yt what is spat out? 59700 1001837
pꜥn to be clever (or similar) 59710 1001839
pꜥn Clever one 857503 1001839
pꜥg spit 858449 1001838
pw who? 59750 1001818
pn spindle 59940 1001784
pn.w mouse 60020 1001782
pnꜥ to turn upside down; to capsize; to reverse; to curve 59960 1001787
pnꜥ.y incorrectness; wrongness 59970 1001787
pnꜥ.yt cataract 59980 1001787
pnꜥ.yt threshold; doorstep 59990 1001787
pnꜥ.wt [an injustice; something wrong] 60000 1001787
pnꜥnꜥ to turn over several times; to roll around 60010 1001787
pnn to twist, to reel (a thread) 60060 1001784
pnn to strew (powder) 60030 1001784
pnz to twist; to pull out 60090 1001787
pnz to cut off; to pull out 60070 1001787
pns earth ("turned around", as material)

60110 1001787
pns.t clump (form of a remedy) 60120 1001787
pnq bailer 60140 1001785
pnq to scoop (out); to water 60130 1001785
png to divide 60150 1001783
pnt to squeeze 60160 1001786
pnḏ to scoop (out) 867779 1001785
pr household; domestic staff 550304 1001792
pr outlay; issuing office? 60260 1001795
pr house (gen.); palace; temple; tomb; administration 60220 1001792
pr one who is going out 857528 1001795
pr square (on a game board) 450627 1001795
pr.y domestic servant 61040 1001792
pr.y lone fighter 60940 1001795
pr.y field service person 860218 1001792
pr.y ferocious bull 60950 1001795
pr.yw Emerging ones 500375 1001795
pr.yt houses; properties 61010 1001792
pr.yt One who comes out 501005 1001795
pr.w field (after the inundation) 61170 1001795
pr.w deliveries 61150 1001795
pr.w coming out; procession 61140 1001795
pr.w surplus; excess 61160 1001795
pr.t mourning; sadness 60330 1001795
pr.t people; servants (of a god) 60320 1001792
pr.t domestic servant (fem.) 60340 1001792
pr.t peret-season (winter) 60300 1001795
pr.t procession (of a god) 60280 1001795
pr.t fruit (of a plant); seed; posterity (metaph.) 60310 1001795
pr.t Issuing point of provisions 60270 1001795
pr.tj first day of peret-season 863195 1001795
pri̯ to come forth; to go forth 60920 1001795
prj battlefield 60990 1001795
prj beans 60970 1001791
prj.t fetter (or similar) 859428 1001795
pry bandage; strip (of linen) 60980 1001795
pry.t [designation of the female part of the house] 61020 1001795
prꜥ to be accessible? 61130 1001799
prpr to jump around (or similar) 61220 1001795
prpr to enjoy (food) (or similar) 61230 1001795
prr one who is going forth 857531 1001795
prẖ blossom; sprout 61250 1001794
prẖ to blossom; to unfurl 61240 1001794
prš [red ochre or ochre containing earth (med.)]; juniper berries? 61260 1001796
prš to smite; to smash; to tear 61270 1001797
prṯ to break? 61290 1001798
prḏ to separate 61320 1001793
phr.t [a body of water] 61340 1001773
pḥ to reach; to attack 61370 1001771
pḥ.w marshland; hinterland 61380 1001771
pḥ.w the far north 61470 1001771
pḥ.wj rear 61510 1001771
pḥ.wj marshes 856007 1001771
pḥ.wj back; end 61490 1001771
pḥ.wjt back; end 859978 1001771
pḥ.wyt anus; rectum 61520 1001771
pḥ.ww ends (of the country); end (of the world) 61550 1001771
pḥ.ww northern end 61570 1001771
pḥ.wt marshland 860884 1001771
pḥ.wt anchor rope of ships 61480 1001771
pḥ.wtj rear 857519 1001771
pḥ.wtjt anchor rope of ships; stern warp 857520 1001771
pḥ.t sheaf (of grain) 61390 1001770
pḥ.tj strong 61630 1001769
pḥ.tj lion 61640 1001769
pḥ.tj Strong one 860512 1001769
pḥ.tj physical strength 61400 1001769
pḥ.tjw Those located at the end? 500483 1001771

pḥ.tjt strength 855240 1001769
pḥ.tjt to reach the shore 500336 1001771
pḥrr runner 61600 1001775
pḥrr to run 61590 1001775
pḥtj to be strong 61620 1001769
pḥd to split 61660 1001772
pḥd.tj separator (a serpent) 61650 1001772
pẖꜣ (wooden) bird trap 61780 1001777
pẖꜣ plank 61760 1001777
pẖꜣ to equip 61750 1001777
pẖꜣ to separate; to open (med.); to split 61730 1001777
pẖꜣ log 61770 1001777
pẖꜣ [a cereal] 61710 1001776
pẖꜣ.t field 61800 1001777
pẖꜣ.t ankle shackle 61790 1001777
pẖꜣ.t [designation of the Uraeus] 61810 1001777
pẖpẖ to course (of poison in the body); to tear; to pull out 61870 1001777
pẖpẖ storm; tempest (or similar) 61880 1001777
pẖr circumferential walkway (part of a building) 858691 1001774
pẖr one who crosses 859793 1001774
pẖr area; rural district; circuit; country estate? 61910 1001774
pẖr circulation of offerings; offerings 61920 1001774
pẖr to go around; to turn round; to circulate; to encircle; to traverse 61900 1001774
pẖr.yt orbital period of stars; period 62080 1001774
pẖr.w flushing (of water)? 62090 1001774
pẖr.wj [a boat] 854399 1001774
pẖr.t frontier patrol 61940 1001774
pẖr.t circuit; area; vicinity 867803 1001774
pẖr.t journey 855329 1001774
pẖr.t ambulatory (a space in a temple) 61930 1001774
pẖr.t circulation of offerings 857548 1001774
pẖr.t [a kilt] 61960 1001774
pẖr.t remedy (gen.) 61950 1001774
pẖr.tj traveler (or similar) 61990 1001774
pẖr.tjw one wandering around 859348 1001774
pzḥ bite; sting 62230 1001820
pzḥ to bite; to sting 62220 1001820
pzẖ to be confused; to confuse 62240 1001819
pzz to labour; to exert oneself 62260 1001821
pzz undertaking 62270 1001821
ps cook; baker 62120 1001808
ps [a jug (used as a measure for beverages)] 62150 1001800
ps [a kind of bread] 62130 1001808
ps [measure for herbs, weed] 62140 1001800
ps.w ratio (of grain to the product, for baking, for brewing) 62190 1001800
ps.wt cooking pot 857535 1001808
ps.t cooking 62170 1001808
ps.t Cook 501112 1001808
psi̯ to cook; to bake; to heat 62180 1001808
psẖ platform on the ship's bow 857538 1001807
psg spittle 62350 1001806
psg spittoon 62360 1001806
psg to spit on; to spit at 62340 1001806
psḏ shining 500184 1001804
psḏ shining one 854201 1001804
psḏ to shine 62420 1001804
psḏ nine 62450 1001801
psḏ light 62430 1001804
psḏ spine; backbone; back 62400 1001803
psḏ keel arch? (naut.) 62470 1001803
psḏ.j [linen (nine-strand fabric)] 62460 1001801
psḏ.y helper (or similar) 62540 1001803
psḏ.wj double back plate 62530 1001803
psḏ.t shining one 62480 1001804
psḏ.t Divine Ennead 62500 1001801
psḏ.t Nine Bows peoples 62490 1001801
psḏ.t light 857533 1001804
psḏ.t ennead 550381 1001801
psḏ.t teeth 859664 1001801

psḏ.tj pelican 62520 1001802
psḏ.tj shining one 62510 1001804
psḏi̯ to distance oneself from; turn the back 62410 1001803
psḏn threshing floor 62550 1001803
psḏn.tjw new moon; festival of the new moon 62560 1001805
psḏn.tjw new moon day 850569 1001805
psš share; portion 857536 1001812
psš [a fishtail-shaped knife of flint] 450149 1001812
psš to divide; to share 62280 1001812
psš.w referee; associate; partner 851900 1001812
psš.t half; share; portion 62290 1001812
psš.t portion 867812 1001812
psš.t carpet; matting 62300 1001812
psš.tj [designation of a servant] 854402 1001812
psš.tj the two parts (of the land, Upper and Lower Egypt) 62310 1001812
pšj comb 62600 1001809
pšj pustule? 62590 1001810
pšn fissure; fracture (med.) 62620 1001811
pšn [designation for an adversary] 62640 1001811
pšn to split 62610 1001811
pšš to spread 62680 1001060
pḳ [flood] 860385 1001789
pḳj [an irrigated area in Delta] 62700 1001789
pḳr [a fragrant ingredient in kyphi preparation] 62720 1001790
pgꜣ bowl 62790 1001768
pgꜣ opening; open space; battlefield 854511 1001768
pgꜣ [a chest?] 62800 1001767
pgꜣ to unfold; to open up 62730 1001768
pgꜣ to slaughter (the enemy) 62780 1001768
pgꜣ opening 62760 1001768
pgꜣ battlefield 62770 1001768
pgꜣ.w washing utensil; bowl 62840 1001768
pgg.t frog (amulet) (med.) 62880 1001766
ptpt to tread; to trample 62890 1001813
ptr strip (of cloth) 62960 1001816
ptr window of heaven 62930 1001817
ptr behold! [interjection] 62910 1001817
ptr look; sight 857541 1001817
ptr Onlooker 857540 1001817
ptr to see; to behold 62900 1001817
ptr Beholder 62950 1001817
ptr who? what? 62920 1001818
ptḥ to form; to create 63000 1001814
ptḥ to open 62990 1000676
ptẖ to prostrate (oneself, before so.) 63010 1001815
ptpt resigning one 857539 1001813
ptt [condition of cultivatable fields] 63040 1001813
pdr sack (or measure) 63090 1001764
pds door leaf 858692 1001765
pds to flatten; to destroy 63120 1001765
pds box (for clothing, for documents) 63110 1001765
pds.t small ball; pill 63130 1001765
pds.t [a kind of wood?] 63140 1001765
pdsw.t delta coast 63160 1001765
pḏ to cure; to burn incense 63190 1001761
pḏ [part of a fisher's net?] 63220 1001762
pḏ [measure for ink colour, pigment] 63200 1001762
pḏ to stretch out; to spread out 63170 1001762
pḏ.w [food offering (lit. what is spread out)] 63360 1001762
pḏ.w wide ground; [cult site of Sokar] 852799 1001762
pḏ.w flood; pond 63370 1001762
pḏ.wj lateral walls 63380 1001762
pḏ.t [designation for the sky] 63250 1001762
pḏ.t [a measure for incense] 63240 1001762
pḏ.t [a measure for linen] 63230 1001762
pḏ.t troop (of soldiers) 63290 1001762
pḏ.t bow-people 63280 1001762
pḏ.t bow 63270 1001762

pḏ.tj Archer 501074 1001762
pḏ.tj (slaughtered) ox (an offering) 63260 1001762
pḏ.tj archer 63310 1001762
pḏ.tj barbarian (bow-man) 63300 1001762
pḏ.tjt Archer 501065 1001762
pḏi̯ to grind; to sharpen 63350 1001763
pḏpḏ to be diffused (of perfume) 63390 1001762

f

fꜣ weight 63570 1000357
fꜣ.y bearer 63490 1000357
fꜣ.y [something made of semiprecious stone (string or the like, used as bracelet, necklace or for stringing amulets)] 63510 1000357
fꜣ.y cloth 63520 1000357
fꜣ.y [something (a rope?) made of Wedj-plants] 63500 1000357
fꜣ.w deliveries of food (offerings) (and similar) 63630 1000357
fꜣ.w carrying service 63660 1000357
fꜣ.w threat 63650 1000354
fꜣ.w power; authority; reputation 63640 1000357
fꜣ.t dust? 63430 1000353
fꜣ.t a part of a ship (rope?) 856728 1000357
fꜣ.t freight (of a boat); yield (or similar) 63420 1000357
fꜣ.t serving food 63410 1000357
fꜣi̯ to weigh 63480 1000357
fꜣi̯ to lift; to carry; to raise 63460 1000357
fꜣi̯ to hoist (the sails) 874892 1000357
fꜣi̯ [verb referring to the decay of the corpse (to raise, to bloat)] 63400 1000357
fꜣi̯ to set about (doing) (with infinitive); [aux./modal] 852484 1000357
fꜣy.t raising 63560 1000357
fꜣy.t bearers (of a divine image) 63530 1000357
fꜣy.t portable shrine (for gods) 63550 1000357
fꜣk man with a shaved head 63690 1000358
fꜣk bald spot 856729 1000358
fꜣk to be bald; to be shorn 63680 1000358
fꜣg to cut off (the foreleg) 63700 1000355
fjw to be disgusted? 63730 1000342
fjṯ to deride; to be scornful 63740 1000341
fꜥꜣ hair 852956 1000360
fꜥg [temple of Nekhbet in Elkab] 858995 1000359
fꜥg claw 63770 1000359
fꜥg.jt [epithet of Nekhbet]; [priestess of Nekhbet] 63780 1000359
fn to be weak 63810 1000344
fnḫ carpenter 855573 1000347
fnḫ carpenter; joiner 63840 1000347
fnḫ to be smart (or similar) 63860 1000347
fnḫ cord? 63850 1000346
fnṯ to become maggoty 63900 1000348
fnṯ snake; worm; maggot 63890 1000348
fnḏ nose 63920 1000345
fnḏ to rage against 63930 1000345
fnḏ.j one with the beak (Thoth) 63960 1000345
fnḏ.j One with the beak 861782 1000345
fẖ to loosen; to move along; to destroy; to cease (doing) 63970 1000340
fẖ.t wig? 63990 1000340
fẖẖ to loosen 63980 1000340
fḳꜣ to jump out quickly 64050 1000356
fḳꜣ reward; gift 64020 1000349
fḳꜣ cake (or similar) 64000 1000349
fḳꜣ to reward 64010 1000349
fḳꜣ to uproot; to eradicate 64040 1000356
fk to be empty; to be wasted; to be bald 64060 1000358
fk.ty one with a shaved head (a priest) 64080 1000358
fgn to defecate 64120 1000339
ft to be disgusted; to become weary 64130 1000350
ftft to leap; to spring (plants) 64170 1000351
ftt [fibrous veg. matter (med.)] 64200 1000351
ftt to obliterate (an inscription) 64190

1000337
ftt.w jumper, diver (name for fish(es)) 64210 1000351
fṯṯꜣ to decay, rot? 858417 1000352
fd to sweat 64240 1000336
fd [a kind of an oil] 64250 1000334
fd.t sweat 64260 1000336
fdi̯ to uproot 64280 1000337
fdfd to apply (an ointment) 64300 1000334
fdḳ to sever; to hack into pieces 64320 1000338
fdḳ slice; portion 64330 1000338
fdḳdḳ to cut up (completely); to destroy 858978 1000338

m

m in; on (temp.) 64365 1001000
m behold!; [particle] 64440 1001496
m in; to; on; from (spatial) 400007 1001000
m in; of; (consisting) of 400082 1001000
m like; as; as (predication) 500292 1001000
m [imperative of the negative verb] 64410 1001009
m by means of; through (instrumental) 64364 1001000
m who?; what? 64430 1001281
m together with 400080 1001000
mꜣ bow (of a boat) 66120 1001476
mꜣ antelope 66130 1001475
mꜣ [a plant] 66140 1001474
mꜣ.w one who sees 851912 1001496
mꜣ.w sight 854706 1001496
mꜣ.t flute 66170 1002917
mꜣ.tj eyes (sun and moon as heavenly eyes) 66220 1001496
mꜣ.tj [pair of endings (of tendons?)] 66230 1002917
mꜣꜣ to see; to look 66270 1001496
mꜣꜣ sight; seeing; supervision; diagnosis 66280 1001496
mꜣꜣ.wt sight 857333 1001496
mꜣꜣ.wt sight; view 857334 1001496
mꜣj lion 66370 1001481
mꜣj sphinx 66380 1001481
mꜣj Lion (a star constellation) 66400 1001481
mꜣj.j lion alike 857335 1001481
mꜣj.t lioness 66420 1001481
mꜣꜥ just; correct; true 66460 1001499
mꜣꜥ a just man 66470 1001499
mꜣꜥ to be just; to be true; to do right 66480 1001499
mꜣꜥ to sail 66510 1001499
mꜣꜥ temple (of the head) 66530 1001499
mꜣꜥ bank 66550 1001498
mꜣꜥ to offer; to present 400136 1001499
mꜣꜥ to guide; to lead 400137 1001499
mꜣꜥ to run a straight line; to coil 500171 1001499
mꜣꜥ correctly; truthfully 500218 1001499
mꜣꜥ place (site) 850060 1001498
mꜣꜥ The right one? 852260 1001499
mꜣꜥ to be true; to do right; to offer; to lead 854512 1001499
mꜣꜥ floodwater 860536 1001499
mꜣꜥ [Maa-canal (waters in the heavens)] 66560 1001498
mꜣꜥ.j the leading one 854782 1001499
mꜣꜥ.w [a kind of wood] 66680 1001497
mꜣꜥ.w validity; rightness; regularity 66770 1001499
mꜣꜥ.w products (of foreign lands); presentation 66780 1001499
mꜣꜥ.w favorable wind 66790 1001499
mꜣꜥ.w [a (wooden) part of a ship] 66800 1001497
mꜣꜥ.w guidance 96860 1001499
mꜣꜥ.t right order; truth; righteousness 66620 1001499
mꜣꜥ.t Maat 66630 1001499
mꜣꜥ.t Maat (solar barque) 66640 1001499
mꜣꜥ.t Maat figure 500390 1001499
mꜣꜥ.tj just men; the righteous (of the blessed dead); vindicated one 500312 1001499
mꜣꜥ.tj the two truths 66650 1001499

mꜣꜥ.tj just; righteous (of the blessed dead); vindicated 66660 1001499
mꜣꜥ.tj truthful one 859759 1001499
mꜣꜥ.tj Maaty (canal at the Giza plateau) 66670 1001499
mꜣꜥ.t(j) [name of a mirror] 66760 1001499
mꜣw new 66150 1001492
mꜣw new 859725 1001492
mꜣw new condition 66810 1001492
mꜣw Renewed one 66960 1001492
mꜣw.t new 66820 1001492
mꜣw.t new land 66830 1001492
mꜣw.t shaft; staff 66840 1002917
mꜣw.t stalk 66850 1002917
mꜣw.t refrain 66860 1001492
mꜣw.t rays; beams 66870 1002917
mꜣw.tj newcomer; novice 66880 1001492
mꜣw.tj [designation for testicles] 66900 1001492
mꜣw.tj Radiant one 500095 1002917
mꜣwi̯ to be new; to become new 66940 1001492
mꜣwi̯ to lighten 66950 1001492
mꜣwr to write 66970 1001493
mꜣwt thought? 853873 1001494
mꜣwṯ to think (up) 67590 1001494
mꜣwṯ the mindful one 500899 1001494
mꜣwṯ (sad) thoughts 854441 1001494
mꜣwṯ.jt the mindful one 500747 1001494
mꜣwḏ [label beside a cage of captured animals]; to carry? 67010 1001491
mꜣwḏ staff; pole; supporting rod 67020 1001491
mꜣwḏ drudgery; soccage 67030 1001491
mꜣwḏ (carrying, counterbalancing) arms 67040 1001491
mꜣwḏ to be decorated; to be forced (to do something) 67050 1001491
mꜣmꜣ doum palm (Hyphaene thebaica Mart.) 67120 1001482
mꜣmꜣ.t He of the doum-palm 857336 1001482
mꜣmꜣ.t doum palm (Hyphaene thebaica Mart.) 854417 1001482
mꜣmꜣw fruits of the doum palm 67130 1001482
mꜣnw western mountains; realm of the dead; the west 67160 1001483
mꜣnw.j belonging to the western mountains 855933 1001483
mꜣr wretched person 67170 1001485
mꜣr misery 67180 1001485
mꜣr to dispossess; to wrong (someone) 67190 1001485
mꜣr to bind; to fetter 855047 1001402
mꜣr bandage?; fetter? 851853 1001485
mꜣr.w maru-temple; pavilion 67210 1001484
mꜣh.t door 67220 1001478
mꜣḥ to clap (the hands) 67230 1001480
mꜣḥ wreath; grape; garland 67240 1002763
mꜣḥ clapper 67250 1001480
mꜣḥ.t clapper?; clapping? 450626 1001480
mꜣẖ corn sheaf 67270 1001477
mꜣẖ.y He of the corn sheaf? 500717 1001477
mꜣẖ to burn (up) (of heart, lit. to be afraid) 67280 1001479
mꜣz knife 67290 1001495
mꜣz to slaughter 67300 1001495
mꜣs to kneel 67310 1001487
mꜣs to sink down (of heart) 67320 1001487
mꜣs [a dance posture] 67330 1001487
mꜣs.yw kneelers 67410 1001487
mꜣs.t knee (of a human); hock (of an animal) 67370 1001487
mꜣs.t garment of fur?; knee-length kilt? 67380 1001487
mꜣs.t shoal; sandbank 67390 1001487
mꜣs.tjw those belonging to the knees? 67420 1001487
mꜣš [a duck] 854630 1001486
mꜣš.t [a duck] 854631 1001486
mꜣḳ.t ladder 67450 1001190
mꜣty.t mourner 67550 1001490
mꜣṯ granite 67580 1001488
mꜣṯ to praise 67600 1001489
mꜣṯr to mourn for (a dead person)? 67660

1001490
mꜣṯr.t mourner 67650 1001490
mꜣṯr.t auricula tree (Calatropis procera) 67670 1001490
mꜣd.yw waiters (servers of food) 67710 1001491
mj Come! 860703 1001317
mj as if; if (conjunction) 67830 1001318
mj to bring 67760 1001321
mj come! 67770 1001317
mj take! 67780 1001320
mj like; according to 67820 1001318
mj.y likewise 68170 1001318
mj.w likewise; the same 867905 1001318
mj.wj such a one 68230 1001318
mj.wtj equal 867914 1001318
mj.t [a (funerary) boat] 67900 1001316
mj.t path; road 67910 1001319
mj.tj alike; similar 851710 1001318
mj.tj the equal (of); the like (of) 67930 1001318
mj.tj copy 67940 1001318
mj.tj likeness (of statues) 67950 1001318
mj.tjt the like; the same 67960 1001318
mj.tw the same (as) 68220 1001318
mjꜣz spine(s) (or similar) 68160 1001495
mjꜥ.t [a house?] 68200 1001329
mjw tomcat 68250 1001327
mjw.j tomcat-like 857359 1001327
mjw.t lament; mourning; grief 856483 1001327
mjw.t cat 854443 1001327
mjm.t [a plant (med.)] 68310 1001323
mjw.tj cat-like one 68280 1001327
mjmj [a cereal (durra?)] 68320 1001324
mjn landing (i.e. death; dying) 401137 1001366
mjn today 850961 1001325
mjn today 68330 1001325
mjn [grape juice]; mash 68350 1001326
mjn.t daily diet 68360 1001325
mjn.t [a water] 68370 1001326
mjn.t mooring post; post 70140 1001366
mjn.t stake 854852 1001367
mjn.t country estate; area, field 68380 1001326
mjn.tjw those belonging to the irrigation basins 500433 1001326
mjn.tjw those belonging to the poles 854448 1001366
mjni̯ to protect 70080 1001366
mjni̯ to stake 854513 1001366
mjni̯ to gift; to connect, to bind (man and woman) 70070 1001366
mjni̯ to moor; to steer; to die (metaph.) 70060 1001366
mjnw.t harbor 68450 1001366
mjnb ax (tool, weapon) 68460 1001029
mjnb.yt ax 68300 1001029
mjz.t liver 68520 1001328
mjtr miter (a worker in the palace) 850152 1001428
mjtr.t miteret (women's title) 68570 1001428
mjdꜣ [edible part of a butchered bull] 68580 1001322
mꜥꜣꜥ uprights (of a ladder) 68620 1001499
mꜥnẖ.t tassel (as necklace) 68820 1003020
mꜥnẖ.t staff 68830 1003020
mꜥnẖ.tj he with the tassel 68840 1003020
mw water 69000 1001468
mw field of water 859785 1001468
mw seed (metaphorically for son) 69210 1001468
mw.y urine; (bodily) fluid 69200 1001468
mw.yt moisture; urine 69240 1001468
mw.w [a kind of a ritual dancers] 69100 1001467
mw.t mother 69040 1001473
mw.t trough (of a coffin, of a sarcophagus) 69080 1001473
mw.t weight of the scale 69060 1001473
mwi̯ to wet; to be wet 69220 1001468
mwj [pun with water] 69230 1001468
mwmw raw, uncooked? 69280 1001468
mwnf guard; protector; assistance 69290 1002685
mwt death 69310 1001469

mwt dead person; spirit of the dead 69320 1001469
mwt to die; to be dead; to vanish 69300 1001469
mwt.t dead person; spirit of a dead person 69330 1001469
mwᶜd council 853912 1001470
mfẖ sledge 69350 1000340
mfẖ to sift (grain) 69360 1000340
mfkꜣ turquoise-like 69370 1000343
mfkꜣ to be glad; to rejoice 69380 1001296
mfkꜣ.t Land of turquoise 69440 1000343
mfkꜣ.t green of plants 69420 1000343
mfkꜣ.t joy 69430 1001296
mfkꜣ.t turquoise 69410 1000343
mfkꜣ.t turqouise-coloured (metaph., for papyrus) 69460 1000343
mfkꜣ.t Turquoise (Hathor) 69390 1000343
mfkꜣ.tj Turquoise-like one 854425 1000343
mfkꜣ.tjw Turquoise coloured one 69470 1000343
mfd to traverse (a land) 69480 1000970
mmj giraffe 69540 1001340
mn to remain; to endure; to be established 69590 1001349
mn remaining is; amount left is 69600 1001349
mn to ascertain; to examine 70110 1001349
mn [a jug (for wine, beer)]; [bowl (incense burner)] 69630 1001344
mn remainder; equation; compensation 853600 1001349
mn [a kind of fabric] 69640 1001342
mn to be ill; to suffer (from); to injure 69660 1001347
mn to displace 69720 1001348
mn battle ground 859627 1001349
mn sufferer 69670 1001347
mn so and so; someone; man (gen.) 69610 1001349
mn nonexistence; loss 69570 1001629
mn nonexistent; [particle (expression for nonexistence)] 69560 1001629
mn.y corveé laborer (carrying stones) 70130 1001349
mn.w trees; plantation 70450 1001350
mn.w mace 70480 1001349
mn.w thread 70510 1001349
mn.w [birds (pigeons?)] 851863 1001382
mn.w monument(s) 70420 1001349
mn.w suffering 70400 1001347
mn.w quartz; [a semiprecious stone (of different colour)] 70490 1001345
mn.w [waterway with plants] 70470 1001350
mn.w jug 500968 1001344
mn.wj coal fire 69940 1001343
mn.wy [a measure for fabric] 69650 1001342
mn.wy rich in monuments 70560 1001349
mn.t disease; suffering 69770 1001347
mn.t melting fire 69820 1001343
mn.t swallow; pigeon? 69780 1001382
mn.t so and so; someone (fem.); woman (gen.) 69750 1001349
mn.t sky; heaven 69840 1001349
mn.t the like; contents 69760 1001349
mn.t thigh (of a human); haunch (of an animal); tights (gen.) 69800 1001346
mn.tj Miserable one (serpent) 69930 1001347
mn.tj lap (that the child sits on) 69890 1001346
mn.tj [bowl] 69880 1001341
mn.tj mountain ranges (to the east and west of the Nile) 69900 1001349
mnj.w herdsman 70310 1001367
mnj.w shepherd 855126 1001367
mnj.w shepherd 861591 1001367
mnj.w [a shrine] 70320 1001369
mnj.w daybed 863006 1001366
mnj.wj the one of the shrine 854999 1001369
mnj.t Menat (Hathor) 70180 1001368
mnj.t [singer (at Dendera and Edfu)] 70190 1001368
mnj.t pasture (for geese) 70160 1001367
mnj.t menat-necklace 70170 1001368

mnjwj [epithet of Anubis] 70340 1001367
mny.t root 70220 1001349
mny.tj [a farmer] 70250 1001367
mnᶜ to nurse; to bring up 70350 1001386
mnᶜ.j nurturer; educator 70380 1001386
mnᶜ.y Nurses' Lake (in the sky) 854729 1001386
mnᶜ.t milch cow 70370 1001386
mnᶜ.t property 70390 1001385
mnᶜ.t nurse 70360 1001386
mnw statue 70430 1001349
mnw.t pigeon 70550 1001382
mnwr incense 70580 1001383
mnwr to purify 70590 1001383
mnwr country in the east 70600 1001383
mnbj.t lion couch; estrade 69980 1001351
mnpḥ skin / fur of the white saber antelope [a gown] 70630 1001373
mnfꜣ.t infantry; soldiers 70670 1001355
mnfr.t bracelet; anklet 70690 1001542
mnm.t bed 70700 1001611
mnmn to beget 70720 1001348
mnmn to move about; to shift; to fluctuate 70710 1001348
mnmn.y begetter 859929 1001348
mnmn.w The one who moves 500804 1001348
mnmn.t herd; cattle 70730 1001348
mnn mina (a measure of weight) 70780 1001371
mnn.w fortress 70790 1001349
mnn.t [part of a granite sarcophagus]; [part of a tomb]) 70820 1001349
mnnn asphalt; resin; pitch 70810 1001372
mnnw annals 70800 1001349
mnh.w rampart 867941 1001519
mnhp begetter (divine epithet) 70860 1001581
mnhp morning 70880 1001581
mnhp [an aphrodisiac plant] 70870 1001581
mnhp phallus with rump (for procreation) 70890 1001581
mnhz watcher 70900 1001591
mnhḏ scribe's palette 70910 1001563
mnḥ youth; stripling; young animal 70940 1001365
mnḥ to make young; to become young 858862 1001365
mnḥ evil fate 70970 1001356
mnḥ to slay; to butcher 70960 1001361
mnḥ wax 70920 1001364
mnḥ to rejoice (or similar) 70950 1001360
mnḥ papyrus plant 70930 1001357
mnḥ.j papyrus shaped 71010 1001357
mnḥ.t gift; tribute 71050 1001363
mnḥy.t Menhit (Slaughteress (uraeus goddess)) 71020 1001361
mnḫ chisel 71060 1001359
mnḫ to chisel 71070 1001359
mnḫ to be splendid; to make splendid; to be effective 71080 1001358
mnḫ splendid; excellent 400111 1001358
mnḫ effective; splendid 400110 1001358
mnḫ splendid one 856481 1001358
mnḫ string of the amulet? 71130 1001362
mnḫ to string (beads); to put on (an amulet) 71120 1001362
mnḫ [designation for food] 71100 1001358
mnḫ to rejoice 71110 1001360
mnḫ.j properly; neatly 850986 1001358
mnḫ.w excellence; virtues 71240 1001358
mnḫ.t neatly 850987 1001358
mnḫ.t excellence 71140 1001358
mnḫ.t excellent one 71160 1001358
mnḫ.t cloth; garment; mummy bandage 71170 1002686
mnḫ.t clothing (feast) 851035 1002686
mnḫ.tj army tenants 600248 1001365
mnḫ.tj Clothed one 500997 1002686
mnz.tj legs 71270 1001384
mnsꜣ to cause ejaculation 71310 1001377
mnsꜣ ejaculation 854465 1001377
mnš cartouche 71330 1001376
mnš [(cartouche-shaped) wooden bowl] 71340 1001376
mnš to brand (with the cartouche) 71350 1001376
mnšd The tearer? (Apophis) 71390

1002047
mnḳ to complete; to retaliate; to grant 71400 1001374
mnḳ to reward 71410 1001374
mnḳb cool place; palace 71500 1001844
mnḳb fan 71490 1001844
mnḳry.t [pendant in the shape of a snake's head] 71530 1001375
mnkꜣ provider 860293 1001266
mnkby.t [pendant in the shape of a snake's head] 71540 1001370
mnkr.t bull's tail (royal regalia) 71550 1001709
mnt.t diorite (diorite-gneiss) 71580 1001378
mnty doorkeeper 71610 1001380
mntꜣ holly grove of the abaton 71590 1001381
mntꜣ.j one belonging to the grove (Osiris) 71600 1001381
mnṯ grain sieving? 71630 1001379
mnd.t tax; gifts; tribute 71710 1001354
mndf.tj [Creator of the flood] 71700 1000183
mnḏ chest; breast; udder 71720 1001353
mnḏ.j bib 857571 1001353
mnḏ.t cheek; eye; eyebrow 71721 1001352
mnḏ.t walls (of a crucible) (lit. cheek) 71730 1001352
mnḏm basket 71740 1001530
mr hoe 71870 1001402
mr to bind 71880 1001402
mr to attach (oneself to) 71900 1001402
mr bond; fetter 855067 1001402
mr pyramid 71780 1001399
mr to ache; to be ill; to suffer 71790 1001401
mr ill; distressing; painful 851222 1001401
mr a sick man 71800 1001401
mr illness; pain 71810 1001401
mr bull 71940 1001394
mr pasture 71850 1001395
mr milk jug 71890 1001398
mr canal 71840 1001395
mr canal (med.) 863036 1001395
mr to run aground; to strand 72510 1001403
mr love 856667 1001407
mr.y the beloved (of) 400005 1001407
mr.y fighting bull; bull 72490 1001394
mr.y beloved 72480 1001407
mr.yt the beloved one 550321 1001407
mr.ytj one who lives on the shore [designation for crocodiles] 650038 1001395
mr.w desert 72640 1001396
mr.w servants; underlings; weavers; parties 71860 1001402
mr.w strips of cloth; bundle; bunch (as a measure of vegetables) 72120 1001402
mr.wt meret-serfs; underlings (coll.); weavers 72040 1001402
mr.t board 72080 1001393
mr.t [chest; box (for linen)] 72090 1001392
mr.t throat; gullet (or similar) 72060 1001400
mr.t illness; evil 72000 1001401
mr.t eye 72070 1001397
mr.t bundle of clothes? 72010 1001402
mr.t black cow 72030 1001394
mri̯ to love; to wish 72470 1001407
mrj speed 859104 1001409
mrj groom 72520 1001408
mrjjnt a container? 72580 1001410
mry.t bank; shore; quay 72540 1001395
mry.tj beloved one 72550 1001407
mry.tj the beloved one 851631 1001407
mryn noble person 72570 1001879
mrw cedar (from Lebanon) 72620 1001418
mrw dam; harbour 72630 1001395
mrw.t love; popularity; wish 72650 1001407
mrw.tj beloved 72660 1001407
mrw.tjt beloved one 72560 1001407
mrw.tjt the beloved one (various goddesses) 72680 1001407
mrw.tj beloved 859329 1001407
mrr flame 72730 1001414
mrr.yt lumps (of incense) 72770 1001414
mrr.t street; block of houses 72740 1001395

mrr.tj beloved one (of the king) 72750 1001407
mrḥ pitch 72800 1002709
mrḥ to decay; to pass away 72810 1001405
mrḥ to paint 72820 1002709
mrḥ to anoint 72790 1002709
mrḥ lance 72830 1001404
mrḥ.t fat (gen.); unguent 72840 1002709
mrẖ.t memorial stone 800020 1001938
mrẖ.t [an astronomical instrument] 72910 1001938
mrẖ.t [observation with an astronomical instrument?] 72920 1001938
mrḥ.tj oil trader 855555 1002709
mrẖm the one who works with the salt 854479 1001406
mrsw cider? 72940 1001416
mrsw [a kind of a vessel for cider?] 72950 1001416
mrš to be bright red 72960 1001415
mrk to provide; to offer; to present 73000 1000077
mrkbt chariot 73010 1001411
mrkḥ.t pyre; stake 73020 1001961
mrt chin 73040 1001417
mh.t forgetfulness; negligence 73050 1001307
mhi̯ to forget; to be forgetful 73070 1001307
mhj.t milch-cow 73090 1000714
mhw.t family; kin 73130 1000882
mhw.t [a positive social characteristic] 73140 1001313
mhw.tj kin 73150 1000882
mhwj [a liquid (med.)] 73160 1000714
mhn box 73180 1000666
mhr associates of Seth 73270 1001310
mhr milk jar 73210 1000714
mhr braver [military officer commanding troops and handling logistics] 73260 1001310
mhr milker (dairy worker) 73240 1000714
mhr to milk; to suckle 73220 1000714
mhr suckling; child 73250 1000714
mḥ care 73370 1001306
mḥ to fill; to be full 73290 1001302
mḥ to be full; to fill; to hold; to seize; to line (with stone) 854514 1001302
mḥ to do (something) diligently (with infinitive); to start 852598 1001302
mḥ to hold; to seize 73300 1001302
mḥ to inlay (with stone) 73310 1001302
mḥ nest 73400 1001302
mḥ child 73350 1001300
mḥ ell; cubit; cubit rod (yardstick) 73330 1001300
mḥ to coil around (of snakes); entwine (garlands); adorn 73440 1002763
mḥ.j water (of the Nile); flood 73760 1001305
mḥ.y caretaker; guardian 73720 1001306
mḥ.y filler (of the eye) (Thoth) 73810 1001302
mḥ.yt north wind 73860 1001301
mḥ.yt fishes (gen.) 73880 1001305
mḥ.w drowned one? 73920 1001305
mḥ.w filling 850371 1001302
mḥ.w (crown of) Lower Egypt 73470 1001301
mḥ.w one floating on the water (Osiris) 851362 1001305
mḥ.w hunter; fish spearer 73960 1001305
mḥ.w Lower Egypt 73940 1001301
mḥ.w grain of Lower Egypt 860404 1001301
mḥ.wj Lower Egyptian; northern 74000 1001301
mḥ.t [part of a wooden boat (strap?)] 73550 1001305
mḥ.t full eye 73490 1001302
mḥ.t field 860274 1001305
mḥ.t marshes of the Delta 73520 1001305
mḥ.tj northern 73560 1001301
mḥ.tj north 73561 1001301
mḥ.tjt She of the North 500788 1001301
mḥ.tjt north 73570 1001301
mḥ.tjw northerners 73580 1001301
mḥꜣ back of the head 73700 1000846

mḥꜥ.w flax fibre 854482 1001315
mḥꜥ.w flax 450266 1001315
mḥi̯ to care for; to be concerned about 73360 1001306
mḥi̯ to be in water; to swim; to float; to drown; to sail 73740 1001305
mḥj to flee 73780 1001308
mḥy.t flood 73840 1001305
mḥy.t papyrus 73850 1001305
mḥw refugee 73950 1001308
mḥw plot of land 73970 1001302
mḥw.t fullness; filling 857351 1001302
mḥw.tj son (as heir); advocate 74030 1001306
mḥwn poultry farm 74010 1000809
mḥwn butcher 860311 1001361
mḥn to coil; to encircle 74060 1001309
mḥn encircling one; uraeus serpent 857353 1001309
mḥn coil 859277 1001309
mḥn Serpent (a game, a board game) 74080 1001309
mḥn Encircler (a serpent) 74070 1001309
mḥn.j belonging to the serpent board game 860556 1001309
mḥn.yt encircler (king's uraeus) 74110 1001309
mḥn.yt uraeus (designation of various goddesses) 853213 1001309
mḥnk intimate? 855703 1000624
mḥnk rewarded person; intimate 74120 1000624
mḥs [an external illness affecting the head] 74140 1000736
mḥs sterile; impotent 74150 1000736
mḥsḥs [designation of a person] 74160 1000736
mḥḏrt fish pond 74170 1001304
mḫ to respect (someone) (or similar) 74200 1001303
mḫ to suffocate; to dam 74220 1001314
mḫꜣ to make level; to match; to be like 74280 1000883
mḫꜣ to skewer 74290 1000883
mḫꜣ to make fast; to bind 74230 1001314
mḫꜣ wreath (or similar) of figs (as measure) 74250 1001314
mḫꜣ builder's hut; wood depot (of the temple of Amun) 74260 1001314
mḫꜣ fetter; rope 74240 1001314
mḫꜣ.wt customs stations on the river 74340 1000883
mḫꜣ.wt result (of weighing) 74330 1000883
mḫꜣ.t balance 74300 1000883
mḫnm.t jasper 74400 1000628
mẖnm.t pool 854483 1000632
mḫnt forehead; front 74410 1000657
mḫr.yt storehouse 550175 1000706
mḫr.w storage (domain) 855370 1000706
mḫsf peg 74470 1000748
mḫt [chariot parts] 74480 1001311
mḫtb.t armband [a golden ornament] 74490 1001312
mḫtbtb armband 74500 1001312
mḫtm ring 855928 1000780
mḫtm.t pinfold 74510 1000780
mḫtm.t sealed box 74520 1000780
mẖꜥḳ.t razor 865712 1000926
mẖꜥḳ.t razor 74580 1000926
mẖn.t ferry-boat 74610 1000620
mẖn.tj ferryman 74630 1000620
mẖr granary; storehouse 74650 1000709
mẖr pasture 74660 1000709
mẖr.w deposit 74670 1000709
mẖr.w necessities; provisions; offerings 74680 1000709
mẖt.w bowel; entrails 74690 1000446
mz floral offerings 74720 1001471
mz carrier 74710 1001471
mz to bring about; to approach; to go; to proceed to 74700 1001471
mzw.t [an offering of grain] 75040 1002838
mzwr drinking place 75220 1002842
mzḥ crocodile 75590 1001472
mzḥ Crocodile 854101 1001472
mzḥ.t female crocodile 75600 1001472
mzmz to put on? 75380 1001471
mzš to core sth; to dissolute 854863

1002832
ms to venerate 74810 1001422
ms grain (as levy) 74780 1001420
ms child 74750 1001430
ms creator 74740 1001430
ms calf 74770 1001430
ms.yt supper (a festival) 74990 1001430
ms.yt foal 74980 1001430
ms.w produce 75050 1001430
ms.t apron (made of jackal skin)? 74830 1001430
ms.t dame; maid 74840 1001430
msꜣḏ.t nostril 76170 1002761
msi̯ to give birth; to create 74950 1001430
msjꜣ.t appreciation; characteristic 75010 1002125
msjw.t she who gives birth (mother) 75020 1001430
msyw.t accusation 650070 1001132
msw.t supper 75090 1001450
msw.t descendants 75060 1001430
msw.t manifestation (or similar) 75080 1001430
msw.t birth; childbirth 75070 1001430
msw.tj descendant 855388 1001430
msbb to turn towards; to serve; to debate 75270 1001423
mspr.t frame? 75330 1002232
mspr.tjw [a kind of a worker] 75360 1002232
msn swimmer on the harpoon leash 75420 1000085
msn to hammer 75490 1000085
msn spinner (epithet of goddess) 75410 1001434
msn to spin; to twist (thread) 75400 1001434
msn.j knife 75500 1000085
msn.w harpooner 75510 1000085
msn.w Harpooner 857373 1000085
msn.t [type of fabric] 75450 1001434
msn.t Mesenet (room I in Edfu) 858629 1000085
msn.tj harpooner (priest at Edfu) 75480 1000085
msn.tj harpooner (epithet of Horus and the king) 75470 1000085
msnḥ to turn around 75520 1002199
msntj foundation ditch 75560 1002215
msẖ [a large vessel, for oil and wine] 75630 1001427
msẖ.t [a body of water?] 75640 1002723
msẖ.t arm 75750 1002104
msẖ.t [a measure for oil]; [large vessel for wine and oil] 75740 1001427
msẖꜣ to rejoice 75650 1002109
msẖꜣ [a sacred beetle] 75670 1002109
msẖꜣ waterway 860102 1002111
msẖꜣꜣ.t [a sacred beetle]; clearing goddess 75690 1002109
msẖᶜ splendor (of gods) 75700 1000920
msẖn residence (of gods) 75710 1000621
msẖn.t abode (of gods); birthplace; birth bricks 75720 1000621
msẖt.w [adze (as used in the Opening-of-the-mouth ritual)] 75760 1002104
mss ribbon?; belt? 75810 1001442
mss tunic; shirt (Galabiya) 600233 1001442
mss.t tunic (Galabiya) 75820 1001442
msḳ [weapon?] 75860 1001436
msḳ [metalworking activity (to emboss?)] 75870 1001436
msk.tjt nocturnal solar bark 75920 1002132
msk.tjt nocturnal solar bark 853782 1002132
mskꜣ leather; hide 75890 1001433
mskj rumor? 75910 1002127
msktw bracelet 75930 1001432
mstꜣ [a liquid] 75980 1001449
mstj [a small galley propelled by oars] 76020 1001446
mstj [a basket] 76010 1001446
mstp.t sled (for transporting coffin or shrine); portable shrine 76120 1002329
mstr office; chancellery 76060 1001448
mstr.t [apron from the fabric] 76070 1001447
msth trap; snare 76080 1001445

msṯ.w offspring 76030 1001443
msṯ.wt offspring 76110 1001443
msṯ.wt Offspring (Hathor) 76040 1001443
msṯ.wtj offspring 854735 1001443
msṯ.wtjt offspring 868004 1001443
msṯ.t (work) obligations 800070 1001444
msd to clothe 76130 1002036
msd.t thigh; haunch 76160 1001098
msd.t clothing 76140 1002036
msdm.j one who prepares eye-paint 76200 1002048
msdm.t black eye paint (galena) 76190 1002048
msḏ.yt that which is hateful; hate 76220 1001426
msḏ.w rival? 650045 1001426
msḏi̯ to hate; to dislike 76210 1001426
msḏr ear 76230 1002054
msḏr.t ear 860133 1002054
msḏḏ.t [designation for a rival] 76240 1001426
mš to cut open; to gut (fish) 76250 1001421
mš [substantive (pond? fish processing site?)] 76260 1001421
mšꜣ.t [body part (anus?)] 861168 1002379
mšꜣb watering place 76290 1001452
mšꜣy [a chariot part (made of leather)] 76280 1001451
mšꜥ to cut off 76340 1002413
mšꜥ to march 76330 1001453
mšꜥ journey; march 600594 1001453
mšꜥ expedition; campaign 76320 1001453
mšꜥ commissions; processes (gen.); rules 76360 1001453
mšꜥ workforce; combat force 76300 1001453
mšꜥ member of a workforce 400345 1001453
mšꜥy.tj envoy; messenger 139150 1001453
mšꜥ.w traveler 76380 1001453
mšꜥ.t combat force 76370 1001453
mšꜥ.t [provisions?] 76390 1002413
mšp to endeavour?; to strive? 76420 1001435
mšpn.t [a skin illness] 76430 1000679
mšr to happen in the evening 76440 1001438
mšr [a piece of furniture (table?)] 76450 1001437
mšr.w evening; (evening) twilight; supper 76470 1001438
mšr.wt dinner 76500 1001438
mšrw [plain; wetland] 76490 1001440
mšrr to attach; to affix 76510 1001439
mšš [part of a boat] 76520 1001441
mšš [wood] 860933 1001441
mškb [title of an official] 76540 1001431
mšṯ [a piece of jewelry] 76570 1002314
mšd to apply 76580 1002047
mšd.t ford (on the Orontes) 76620 1001424
mšdd.t comb 76630 1001425
mḳmḳ to think 856670 1001387
mḳmḳ to sleep, to rest 76660 1001387
mḳn.t washboard? 76680 1001388
mḳr [a vessel (situla?)] 76710 1001390
mḳr staff; rod 76690 1001389
mḳs to comminute? 76770 1001391
mḳs.t disintegration 76780 1001391
mk sustain 858664 1001332
mk festival 76850 1003034
mk to drive (boat) 76810 1001330
mk [a boat] 76800 1001330
mk.w sustenance; food 76840 1001332
mk.t (correct) position; (proper) place 76890 1001331
mk.t place of execution (or similar) 76900 1001331
mk.t overlay 76920 1001334
mk.t protectress 858560 1001334
mkꜣ to attend to something 76970 1001338
mkꜣ pedestal; base 857360 1001339
mkꜣ to flatten; to level 76980 1001339
mkꜣ.t supporting base; bier 76990 1001339
mkꜣ.tj the one on the bier (Osiris) 77010 1001339
mki̯ to overlay (with gold and similar) 76820 1001334
mki̯ to protect; to ward off; to respect

77020 1001334
mkw protector 77030 1001334
mkw.t protection; magical protection 76880 1001334
mkw.tj protector 76930 1001334
mkmr.t fishnets 77040 1001335
mkr [a boat] 77050 1001336
mkr.j merchant 77060 1001336
mkḥꜣ to neglect; not care about 77110 1001333
mkḥꜣ back of the head 77100 1001333
mks [a scepter]; [a cult object of the king (document bag?)] 77120 1001334
mktr tower 77140 1001337
mgꜣ youthful soldier 77170 1001299
mgꜣgꜣ ululation? 77270 1000430
mgr to roast; to grill 600648 1001297
mgrg liar (Seth) 77220 1000400
mgrt cave 77240 1001298
mgsp crate; basket 77260 1000415
mt suppository (med.) 77320 1001456
mt [something unpleasant (poison?)] 550415 1001469
mtꜣ to skewer 77380 1001465
mtꜣy.t [a skewer] 77400 1001465
mtj to be precise; to be correct; to be modest 400854 1001456
mtj correct; precise 77420 1001456
mtj very 858168 1001456
mtj correctness 77680 1001456
mtj reliable one 853566 1001456
mtj cord? 77440 1001456
mtj.t suitability 868013 1001456
mtw.t poison 77490 1001463
mtw.t semen (sperm); son (metaph.) 77480 1001463
mtw.t liquid 854515 1001463
mtw.tj Poisonous one (gatekeeper in the netherworld) 851469 1001463
mty right quantity 77430 1001456
mty.t rectitude of the character 77460 1001456
mtpn.t dagger sheath 77520 1002525
mtmt to discuss 77540 1001454
mtmt gossip 77550 1001454
mtn to inscribe; to name 77610 1001458
mtn to cut into pieces 77580 1001457
mtn tax list 77570 1001458
mtn to reward; to recompense 77560 1001458
mtny.t ax; knife 77590 1001457
mtnw products (of lands) 77600 1001458
mtnw.t reward; recompense 77620 1002508
mtr flood; floodwaters 77690 1001460
mtr presence; vicinity 77650 1001462
mtr to be present; to witness; to instruct 77640 1001462
mtr.w [solders (scouts)] 77780 1001462
mtr.w witness 77760 1001462
mtr.w testimony 77770 1001462
mtr.t midday 77710 1001461
mtr.t testimony; admonition; instruction 77700 1001462
mtrẖ.t strainer 77800 1002540
mtḥn.t girl 77810 1001455
mtḏj lash 77820 1001455
mṯꜣ insolent person 77880 1001464
mṯꜣ phallus 77840 1002582
mṯꜣ to cloak 856424 1002593
mṯꜣ [designation for the followers of Seth] 77850 1001464
mṯꜣ to challenge 77860 1001464
mṯꜣi̯ to deliver; to present 77890 1001466
mṯꜣm [a woman's garment] 77910 1002593
mṯwn battlefield 77920 1002565
mṯpn.t dagger sheath 855071 1002525
mṯpr.t [a tool (chisel?)] 77940 1001459
mṯn road; path; (correct) path (through life) (metaph.) 77960 1002508
mṯn guide 77970 1002508
mṯn to assign 77950 1001458
mdw word; speech; matter 78150 1001293
mdw staff; sacred staff (standard) 78130 1001292
mdw.y He who belongs to the staff 500649 1001292
mdw.w caller (who sets the rhythm for work); speaker 78210 1001293

mdw.t [for forming abstract nouns] 550067 1001293
mdw.t word; speech; matter 78030 1001293
mdw.tj speaker 78180 1001293
mdwi̯ to speak; to badmouth; to claim 78140 1001293
mdn to rest; to be relaxed 78220 1001288
mdn rest; quite; calm 600462 1001288
mdn sharpener 78240 1000219
mdns quite; calm; silence; rest 854403 1001288
mds knife 78310 1000275
mds to be sharp; to do violence 78280 1000275
mds violent one 78290 1000275
mds to mark 78300 1000275
mds.t violence 855651 1000275
mds.w energetic 78320 1000275
mḏ deep; to be deep 78360 1001284
mḏ ten 78340 1001283
mḏ.t byre 78380 1001284
mḏ.t binding; hobble 78370 1001285
mḏ.t oil, unguent (used in cult) 78390 1001282
mḏ.tj person who prepares unguent 78400 1001282
mḏ.tj [a boat ("Tener"?)] 850603 1001283
mḏꜣ block (of pressed dates as a unit of measure) 78430 1000299
mḏꜣ.w adversary 78510 1000299
mḏꜣ.t chisel 78480 1000299
mḏꜣ.t cover 500684 1000299
mḏꜣ.t papyrus book; letter; document 78470 1000299
mḏꜣ.t wooden peg 78500 1000299
mḏꜣ.t mummy bandages 860241 1000300
mḏꜣj [an offering] 78540 1000299
mḏꜣy.t [a kind of cloth] 78570 1000300
mḏꜣb to scoop 78580 1001294
mḏꜣb.t scoop (for bailing a boat) 78590 1001294
mḏꜣb.t [part of the ship] 78600 1001294
mḏꜥ to subdue 855235 1001295
mḏꜥ.w purse-net 857429 1000325
mḏw.t depth; height 78610 1001284
mḏnb.w boundary, limit 78270 1000222
mḏri̯ to fall over 78640 1001290
mḏri̯ to turn (to) 78650 1001290
mḏrn [a metal tool] 78660 1001291
mḏḥ to wind around (the head); to be entwined 78690 1001287
mḏḥ to make ready all-around 854517 1001287
mḏḥ bandeau; band 78680 1001287
mḏḥ belt; strip of cloth 78670 1001287
mḏḥ to hew (wood); to timber 78700 1001286
mḏḥ.t carpentry 78710 1001286
mḏḥ.w carpenter 78740 1001286
mḏḥ.w carpenter 855574 1001286
mḏq [a vessel (for beer)] (syll.) 78750 1001289
mḏq.t [a vessel (for beer and oil)] (syll.) 78760 1001289
mḏd to hit; to press hard; to follow (something); to pierce 78770 1001285
mḏd dues (taxes and services) 78780 1001285
mḏd.w preparation; measure 868028 1001285
mḏd.wt adjustment 857343 1001285
mḏd.t share, stake 78790 1001285
mḏdf.t (chisel (used in the Opening-of-the-Mouth ritual)) 854641 1000183

n

n [particle in discontinuous negation n ... js] 400261 1001627
n [particle of negation] 78890 1001627
n [particle of negation] 850806 1001627
n to 78870 1001507
nʾ.t town; city 80890 1001746
nʾ.t town residents 868052 1001746
nʾ.t the city 80910 1001746
nʾ.tj town; local 81070 1001746
nʾ.tjt female resident of an urban area 868055 1001746
nʾ.tjt the one from town 81090 1001746

n'.tjw townsmen 81110 1001746
n.j to 850787 1001507
n.t item 78990 1001507
n.t Red Crown (of Lower Egypt) 79000 1001506
n.t [serpent] 868037 1001506
n.t water; flood 79020 1001725
n.tj the one who is (exists) - crocodile (a name for Sobek) 89860 1001507
n.tjt that (conj.) 550018 1001507
n.tjt She of the western floods 500671 1001725
n.y therefore 79970 1001507
nꜣy.t weaving workshop 79620 1001724
nꜣw breath 79680 1001749
nꜣw Naw (foreign troops? scouts? hunters? 79690 1001742
nꜣb.t tresses (or similar) 79710 1001747
nꜣb.tj [one with the tress who is in Amduat] 79720 1001747
nꜣp tresses 79730 1001747
nꜣp.t tress 857392 1001747
nꜣš cursed 79740 1001748
nꜣš.wtj [a serpent?] 852810 1001748
ni̯ to rebuff; to drive away 79810 1001627
nj.t wrong-doing 79830 1001627
nj.tjw The evil one 500462 1001627
njꜣ [illness affecting the nose (head cold?) (med.)] 79930 1001749
njꜣ.w ibex 79960 1001601
njꜣ.wj like an ibex 857469 1001601
njꜣj fan? 650032 1001749
njw [a jug] 80020 1001714
njw ostrich 80010 1001599
njw.y lance; spear 80060 1001627
njwjw to be festive 80110 1001600
njwy come to a standstill (the flood) 80080 1001725
njm who? 83990 1001281
njnj injury? 80190 1001627
njnj to turn away 852225 1001627
njnj greeting (as posture) 80180 1001632
njnj to turn away from; to move 80170 1001627
njs calling 80220 1001092
njs to call upon; to reckon (math.) 80210 1001092
njs [Papyrus blossom?] 854375 1001597
njs Calling one 854165 1001092
njs.w one who calls 80240 1001092
njk to punish; to be punished 80270 1001596
njk evil-doer 80280 1001596
njk Punisher 80290 1001596
njk.yt Punisher 500905 1001596
njk.t Punisher (a knife) 80300 1001596
njtjt to hesitate; to hinder 80310 1001598
ny while not (particle of negation) 850808 1001627
ny [noise made by a newborn child as a sign of its viability (med.)] 79820 1001625
nꜥ to announce? (death) 80350 1001750
nꜥ kindness; compassion 80360 1002925
nꜥi̯ to twist (a rope) 80420 1001755
nꜥi̯ to travel 80410 1001754
nꜥi̯ to be mild; to pity 80340 1002925
nꜥ.y One who travels there 860446 1001754
nꜥ.y ropemaker 80430 1001755
nꜥ.t traveler 80380 1001754
nꜥꜣḏ.t [excrement of a person suffering from a stomach problem] 80390 1003076
nꜥy.t mooring post 80450 1001754
nꜥꜥ smooth cloth 80470 1002925
nꜥꜥ to be smooth; to smooth 80460 1002925
nꜥꜥ an unblemished one (animal); the best (of something) (field) 80480 1002925
nꜥw a kind of a snake ("twister") 852793 1001755
nꜥw The twister (personification of the snake) 80510 1001755
nꜥw.t a kind of a serpent 857388 1001755
nꜥw.tj a kind of a snake 857389 1001755
nꜥw.tj traveler (sun god) 80530 1001754
nꜥr catfish 80570 1001756
nꜥrn soldiers; special detachment 80630 1001757
nꜥẖ bundle (unit of measure) 80640 1001753

nꜥš to be strong 80650 1001758
nꜥg door crack? 80690 1001751
nꜥg to pulverize (med.) 80680 1001752
nꜥg.w flour (or similar) 80700 1001752
nw wrong?; weakness? 80770 1001625
nw [pleasant-smelling substance, from Punt] 80790 1001715
nw water 84930 1001725
nw this; these (demons. pron., pl.) 500046 1001722
nw this (demons. pron.) 80730 1001722
nw hunter; scout 80830 1001718
nw time; moment 80840 1001723
nw to hunt 30510 1001718
nw to return; to bring back 80880 1001734
nw [a (bronze) vessel] 80710 1001716
nw desert? 80740 1001718
nw to be weak 80760 1001625
nw to clothe; to wrap 80870 1001724
nw to spend time (to do sth.) 80850 1001723
nw hunter 855708 1001718
nw.y water (gen.); (flood) water(s) 81240 1001725
nw.yt water; flood; wave 81260 1001725
nw.w primeval waters 500005 1001725
nw.w Nun 500006 1001725
nw.wj one who belongs to the primordial water 854860 1001725
nw.t sky; temple roof (metaph.) 80950 1001720
nw.t thread; yarn (for weaving); cord 80980 1001724
nw.t ray of light 81060 1001719
nw.t [a kind of cloth] 80990 1001724
nw.t time 81040 1001723
nw.t adze 80970 1001717
nw.t oval; mist ball of scarab? 81020 1001721
nw.t bundle (of flax) 81010 1001724
nw.t quarry (taken hunting); product (of the desert) 450471 1001718
nw.tjw God of hours 81300 1001723
nwꜣ to see; to look; to watch 80800 1001742
nwꜣ sight 80810 1001742
nwꜣ adze (instrument for the Opening-of-the-mouth ritual) 81180 1001741
nwi̯ to take care of; to collect 81230 1001735
nwi̯ to return 854081 1001734
nwi̯ to call (gesture of greeting (or similar)) 80750 1001733
nwn Disheveled-one 81320 1001736
nwn to dishevel (the hair, in mourning) 81310 1001736
nwnw.t floodwater 855999 1001725
nwr to shake; to tremble 81340 1001737
nwḥ to drink; to make drunk 81440 1001732
nwḥ to bind (enemies) 81410 1001730
nwḥ drunkenness 81450 1001732
nwḥ rope (gen.) 81400 1001730
nwḥ twisted (of the horns)? 81420 1001730
nwḥ to copulate 81430 1001730
nwẖ to boil; to be scorched 81460 1001731
nwz ingot; lump?; sheet? (as a measure (by weight) of metal) 81470 1001740
nws [a crown worn by Re] 81480 1001738
nwd unguent cook 81550 1001729
nwd agility 81520 1001728
nwd.y Waverer 81610 1001728
nwd.w inaccuracy (or similar) 81600 1001727
nwd.t oil-press bark 81580 1001729
nwd.t weakness; inaccuracy 81560 1001727
nwd.t swaddling clothes 81570 1001728
nwd.t ointment 81590 1001729
nwd.tj unguent cook 852185 1001729
nwḏ to dangle 81620 1001728
nwḏ.w antilope 81640 1001726
nwḏ.wt Dangler 857491 1001728
nwdi̯ to press out (oil); to cook (unguent) 81540 1001729
nwtwt to totter 854337 1002745
nwṯ to tremble 81500 1001739
nb every; all 81660 1001509
nb creator; builder 82560 1001513
nb broad collar 81670 1001514

nb lord 858944 1001510
nb lord; master; possessor (owner) 81650 1001510
nb.y swimmer (Osiris) 82500 1001515
nb.yw Swimmers (in the netherworld) 82670 1001514
nb.wj the two lords (Horus and Seth) 81910 1001510
nb.wt melting; pouring 857417 1001514
nb.wt Islands (of the Aegean) 81920 1001508
nb.wtj inhabitants of the Aegean (Basket countries) 853384 1001508
nb.t lady; mistress 81740 1001510
nb.t basket 81730 1001508
nb.t soft parts (of the body) 81760 1001515
nb.t isle 857406 1001508
nb.tj the two ladies (king's title "Nebty") 400065 1001510
nb.tj queen 860538 1001510
nb.tj gilded one (Nemti) 854847 1001514
nb.tj the consort of Osirs (in Edfou) 81830 1001510
nb.tj uraeus pair 81810 1001510
nb.tj The Two Ladies (Nekhbet and Wadjet) 81800 1001510
nb.tj The two Ladies (the two crowns of Upper and Lower Egypt) 852407 1001510
nb.tj He who belongs to the basket 500999 1001508
nb.tjj the one belonging to the two mistresses (the king) 81850 1001510
nbꜣ spindle 82460 1001520
nbꜣ carrying pole 82430 1000116
nbꜣ to tie? 82480 1001520
nbꜣ wig?; hair of a wig?; braid? 155420 1001520
nbꜣ [horn-shaped object] 82440 1001520
nbꜣ.t [post (used at foundation ceremony] 82470 1000116
nbꜣbꜣ to throb? 82490 1000054
nbi̯ to swim 82530 1001515
nbi̯ to melt (metal); to cast (metal) 82520 1001514
nbi̯ to fashion; to model; to gild 82550 1001514
nbj flame 82590 1001516
nbj saliva 82620 1001518
nbj to be aflame 82580 1001516
nbj Burning one 861790 1001516
nbj.wj The two flames 500727 1001516
nbj.t reed 82640 1001517
nbj.t Flame 500455 1001516
nbj.t flame 82650 1001516
nbj.t the flaming one 861201 1001516
nbjbj to be hot (med.) 82720 1001516
nby.w protector 82700 1001513
nbw gold 81680 1001514
nbw goldsmith 82540 1001514
nbw grain; golden grain 81710 1001514
nbw sin 82730 1000096
nbw golden one (deceased, as Osiris in relation to Hathor) 450654 1001514
nbw Gold (Hathor) 81690 1001514
nbw gold (the sun) 81700 1001514
nbw.j golden 854316 1001514
nbw.j belonging to gold 450625 1001514
nbw.t [a heavenly cow, associated with Hathor] 81770 1001514
nbw.t Ombos 81780 1001514
nbnb to protect 82760 1001513
nbnb [coming of the inundation] 82770 1000054
nbnb Protector 500438 1001513
nbs burning 858439 1000101
nbsbs to catch fire; to inflame 82830 1000101
nbd [an instrument] 82880 1001512
nbd basketwork 82870 1001512
nbd to wind around; to coil 82850 1001512
nbd tresses; curls 82860 1001512
nbd to band (with metal) 82890 1001512
nbḏ evil one (Apophis, Seth) 82940 1001511
nbḏ evil; destructive 82930 1001511
nbd.j plaiter; hairdresser 82920 1001512
nbd.t plait (of hair); tresses 82910 1001512

nbd.t dice snake 852315 1001511
nbḏ.t destructiveness 855650 1001511
nbḏbḏ to hop, to jump (of the Horus eye) 82960 1000005
npꜣ umbilical cord 82980 1001639
npꜣ umbilical cord (Apophis) 82970 1001639
npꜣ to water; to make wet 82990 1001638
npꜣ to shiver; to tremble 854651 1001827
npꜣ.t [a small cake] 83000 1001822
npꜣpꜣ to flutter? (with the meaning to shake) 83010 1001827
npn Corn 500251 1001795
npn.t grain 83110 1001795
npnp.t hem 83120 1001636
npr grain 83140 1001795
npr.t step (of the stairs); stairs 83170 1001795
npr.t edge; bank 83160 1001795
npr.tjw inhabitant of the shores 500571 1001795
npḥ.w [part of human lower abdomen]; udder (of cows) 83190 1001771
npḏ to slaughter 83220 1001637
npḏ.y knife 83240 1001637
npḏ.t butcher's knife 857479 1001637
npḏ(w) slaughterer 857477 1001637
nf that (demons. pron.) 83270 1001537
nf breath 83260 1001536
nf wrong; wrong-doing 83280 1001537
nf to be evil 858443 1001537
nf.y wrongful 850750 1001537
nf.w sailor 855709 1001536
nf.wj sailor; skipper (title) 83420 1001536
nf.t wind 868085 1001536
nf.t fan 83300 1001536
nf.t [a disease of cattle] 83310 1001536
nfꜣ to blow (from the nose) 83350 1001536
nfꜣ.w snorter 857440 1001536
nfi̯ to blow (on); to breathe 83380 1001536
nfj darkness?; fog? 83390 1001536
nfꜥ to take out; to remove 83400 1001545
nfw.t wind; breath 857437 1001536
nfnf flood water(s) 83430 1001536
nfr to be good; to be perfect 83470 1001542
nfr nefer (crown of Upper Egypt) 83630 1001542
nfr to make beautiful 83480 1001542
nfr good one; beautiful one 83500 1001542
nfr good 83510 1001542
nfr beauty; goodness 83520 1001542
nfr [heart with windpipe (hieroglyph)] 83460 1001543
nfr grain 83540 1001542
nfr phallus 83560 1001542
nfr to be good; to be beautiful 854519 1001542
nfr young man, recruit 852023 1001542
nfr wine; beer 83550 1001542
nfr the perfect one 851970 1001542
nfr good; beautiful; perfect; finished 550034 1001542
nfr well; happily 400458 1001542
nfr [negative word] 550123 1001542
nfr jar 83650 1001538
nfr horse 83580 1001542
nfr lotus (of Nefertem) 83610 1001542
nfr.yt tiller (naut.) 83890 1001541
nfr.yt end; limit 83880 1001542
nfr.yt Neferyt (cow goddess) 854664 1001542
nfr.w radiance of the sun 83600 1001542
nfr.w goodness; good being 400468 1001542
nfr.w beauty 400467 1001542
nfr.w good things; valuables 83920 1001542
nfr.w deficiency 83940 1001542
nfr.w good things; precious; beauty; the goodness; good being 854638 1001542
nfr.w ground-level; base 83930 1001542
nfr.w best quality (relating to cloth) 83530 1001542
nfr.w young men (of the army); recruits 83910 1001542
nfr.w offering 859229 1001542
nfr.wt beauty 857449 1001542
nfr.wt cows 83710 1001542
nfr.wt bark of goodness 857448 1001542

nfr.t beautiful one 83660 1001542
nfr.t [netherworld] 83700 1001542
nfr.t prow-rope? (naut.) 83730 1001540
nfr.t what is good 83680 1001542
nfr.t maiden 83670 1001542
nfr.t fire, glow 83590 1001539
nfr.t beautiful one 853340 1001542
nfr.t [designation for the sky] 857446 1001542
nfr.t pelvis (anatomical) 83750 1001542
nfr.t grave 83690 1001542
nfr.t [crown of Upper Egypt] 83720 1001542
nft to slacken; to loosen 83950 1001544
nftft to leap (away) 83960 1001544
nfdw.t [illness] 863810 1000345
nm winery (winepress?); brewery 84030 1001608
nm [a large vessel, for grain and beverages] 84020 1001608
nm to rob; to steal 84010 1001610
nm knife (for butchering) 84000 1001615
nm produce of the fields (as offerings) 84040 1001609
nm.t something occupied? 400947 1001610
nm.t place of slaughter 84050 1001615
nm.t dwarf 84070 1001607
nm.tj butcher 868130 1001615
nm.tjw Executioner 84090 1001615
nmj to shout 84140 1001616
nmj Wanderer? (a snake) 854368 1001614
nmj to traverse; to travel 84130 1001614
nmj dwarf 852814 1001607
nmj [transitive verb] (what Seth did to Osiris) 84160 1001615
nmj.y Shouter 500352 1001616
nmj.w [a kind of a boat] 84180 1001614
nmj.t bier; bed 84170 1001611
nmj.t Wanderer? (a snake) 854369 1001614
nmᶜ to lay out (a bed, with linen); to face (a wall with limestone) 84230 1001623
nmᶜ to be biased 84240 1001622
nmᶜ to (go to) sleep 84220 1001611
nmnm to move to and fro; to quiver 84300 1001614
nmnm.w sleeping 84320 1001611
nmḫ to be poor 84350 1001612
nmḫ poverty 853886 1001612
nmḫ Waise? 500415 1001612
nmḫ.yt free woman (of lower social status) 84360 1001612
nmḫ.w orphanhood 84340 1001612
nmḫ.w poor man; orphan; free man (of lower social status); 84370 1001612
nmḫf nephrite [stone for heart scarabs] 79200 1001613
nms cloth; nemes-headcloth (of the king) 84380 1001619
nms to wrap (in bandages) (ritual) 84390 1001619
nms [cult object (document case?)] 84400 1001619
nms to dazzle; to illumine 84440 1001619
nms.yt Those who wear a hood 84110 1001619
nms.w [illness of the vulva] 84480 1001377
nms.t ingot (of standard weight and/or form) (or similar) 84460 1001618
nms.t [a kind of a weight unit] 84470 1001618
nms.t [a jug] 84450 1001617
nmt stride 84500 1001620
nmt to go; to stride through 84490 1001620
nmt.t stride; course 84510 1001620
nmt.t [a kind of a stone vessel] 84530 1001621
nmt.t [a stone used for vessels (white quartzite?)] 84520 1001621
nmt.t location 858693 1001620
nmtj [a stone used for vessels (white quartzite?)] 84540 1001621
nmw dwarf 84270 1001607
nn [flood water] 84620 1001725
nn schist? [a stone for making divine statues] 84890 1001628
nn [a kind of a food] 84610 1001624
nn [particle of negation (Late Middle Egyptian)] 851923 1001627

nn darkness 84580 1001725
nn [particle of negation] 851961 1001627
nn [negative word, distinct from n] 84550 1001627
nn Darkness (god) 84590 1001725
nn.y to bow down 84860 1001632
nn.y tired one 854307 1001630
nn.yt weary one (a dead person) 84870 1001630
nn.yw inert ones (the dead) 84900 1001630
nn.yw [a beverage] 84910 1001725
nn.yw Tired ones 854132 1001630
nn.w child 84560 1001625
nn.w [designation of a person] 84710 1001631
nn.wt roots 84730 1001349
nn.t lower heaven 84660 1001626
nn.t [a plant used to make baskets] 84670 1001632
nn.t rope?; coils? 84680 1001632
nn.t hanging net 84960 1001632
nn.t Darkness (goddess) 84650 1001725
nn.t one of the lower heavens 858207 1001626
nn.tj what belongs to the lower heaven 855547 1001626
nn.tjw those of the lower heaven 500177 1001626
nni̯ to be weary; to be inert; to subside 84820 1001630
nnj to be youthful; to be a child 854644 1001625
nnj.w bed 84940 1001630
nnjb [an aromatic tree (styrax?)] 84920 1001634
nny [a serpent] 84840 1001632
nnw weariness 84700 1001630
nnw.t inertia [noun (a condition)] 84720 1001630
nnm to stray 84980 1001614
nnšm spleen 85010 1001635
nr specific moment; date 85100 1001643
nr [s scepter (or similar)] 85030 1001646
nr herdsman; protector 85020 1001646
nr.w terrible one (with ref. to gods and the king) 85150 1001645
nr.w fear 85160 1001645
nr.t [amulet] 859210 1001646
nr.t vulture 85040 1001646
nr.t year 858633 1001643
nr.t vulture 858897 1001646
nri̯ to protect; to tend 85090 1001646
nri̯ to fear (someone); to overawe 85070 1001645
nry to be defensive? 85080 1001646
nry.t sanctuary (or similar) 85120 1001646
nrw.t sprain; dislocation (med.) 85180 1001645
nrw.t fear 85170 1001645
nrw.tj terrible one 857481 1001645
nrw.tjt terrible one 868160 1001645
nrḥ to blaspheme; to abuse verbally 600265 1001644
nrḥrḥ to inflame; to irritate 859231 1001937
nh to protect 85200 1001519
nh to shake 85210 1001553
nh protecting snake 859452 1001519
nh.y [name of a book as an amulet] 85390 1001552
nh.w loss; lack 85420 1001570
nh.t protection 85240 1001519
nh.t sycamore; tree (gen.) 85290 1001552
nh.t magic book 85280 1001519
nh.t Sycamore (place and/or sanctuary of Hathor at Giza) 850633 1001519
nh.t guardian snakes 85250 1001519
nh.t protection; refuge (metaph., of persons) 85220 1001519
nh.t [protective substance (med.)] 85260 1001519
nhꜣ to exile 864992 1001594
nhꜣ the expeller 500444 1001594
nhꜣ.w those who are in silence 85350 1001594
nhi̯ to avoid; to escape 85380 1001570
nhj some; a little 85370 1001575
nhp to protect 85500 1001580
nhp generative power?; virility? 85540

1001581
nhp to beget; to copulate 85460 1001581
nhp to rise early in the morning 85470 1001581
nhp to look after 85480 1001580
nhp to jump up; to revive; to cast down 85450 1001581
nhp to get away from; to escape from 85440 1001581
nhp lid 865367 1001580
nhp protector 85510 1001580
nhp to leap; jump away 854520 1001581
nhp protection 859453 1001580
nhp to mourn 85490 1001580
nhp Protector 85520 1001580
nhp.w early morning 85570 1001581
nhp.w guardian 853113 1001580
nhm gladness; rejoicing 85610 1000549
nhm to rejoice 85580 1000549
nhm to tremble; quake; shout 85620 1000549
nhmhm to roar (or similar) 85630 1000549
nhn.y rejoicing?; acclamation? 855962 1000619
nhnh to quake (with fear) 85660 1001553
nhr terrifer (Seth) 85710 1001585
nhr to flee?; to sail? 85690 1001586
nhr dread, terror 854745 1001585
nhr fugitive 85700 1001586
nhr.t wickedness (of Seth) 85720 1001585
nhr.ty sacred well? 85760 1001584
nhrhr be satisfied with oneself 85750 1000730
nhz one who is awaken 85770 1001591
nhzi̯ to awaken; to be awake 85790 1001591
nhzj wakeful one 868169 1001591
nhd to tremble; to be infuriated 85810 1001565
nhd weakness, trembling 85820 1001565
nhd Dreadful One 85840 1001565
nhdh to be horrified 85860 1001565
nhdh tremor; horror (or similar) 85850 1001565
nhdhd to tremble (med.) 85870 1001565
nḥ guinea-fowl? (as a divine being) 85900 1001551
nḥ request; prayer 85880 1001572
nḥ.y supplicator 86070 1001572
nḥ.wj as is required 85940 1001572
nḥ.t prayer; plea 85920 1001572
nḥꜣ flame? 500898 1001593
nḥꜣ to be fierce; to be unruly; abnormal 85950 1001593
nḥꜣ dangerous waters 852179 1001593
nḥꜣ fierce one 85960 1001593
nḥꜣ [an illness] 85980 1001592
nḥꜣ.t trachoma; a sadness 86000 1001592
nḥi̯ to ask for; to pray for 86050 1001572
nḥb to harness an animal 86140 1001561
nḥb taxable people 86180 1001561
nḥb to give; to loan 86130 1001561
nḥb to cause (strife); to establish (a festival) 86160 1001561
nḥb yoke 86150 1001561
nḥb.yt unifier 500854 1001558
nḥb.w yoke oxen 86260 1001561
nḥb.wt lotiform columns 86330 1001557
nḥb.t lotus blossom; lotus bud 86230 1001557
nḥb.t lotus-bud scepter 86220 1001557
nḥb.t neck; nape of the neck 86210 1001558
nḥb.tj one with lotus-bud scepter 86350 1001557
nḥp to shape; to create 86370 1001579
nḥp potter's wheel 450065 1001579
nḥp potter's wheel 86360 1001579
nḥp creator (divine epithet) 86380 1001579
nḥp molded 86390 1001579
nḥp.t ball of dung 45000 1001579
nḥp.tj potter 86420 1001579
nḥfk to extract milk 860183 1000502
nḥm to take away; to rescue 86430 1001576
nḥm.w rescuer 86450 1001576
nḥm.n surely; assuredly 650030 1001576
nḥm.t lotus bud 86440 1001557
nḥni̯ to rejoice 86480 1001578
nḥḥ olive oil 86600 1001568

nḥḥ eternally 86580 1001566
nḥḥ eternity 86570 1001566
nḥḥ eternity 86590 1001566
nḥḥ hippopotamus 86610 1001567
nḥḥ.wt hippopotamus? 854342 1001567
nḥr to be like; to resemble 86500 1000697
nḥr.w [a kind of bread] 86520 1001582
nḥrḥr to rejoice 86560 1000708
nḥti̯ to trust; to be confident 86680 1001590
nḥd [an ingredient (med.)] 86730 1001562
nḥd to roar; to bellow out; to raise one's voice 858085 1001564
nḥd to be strong 86700 1001564
nḥd.t [kind of myrrh] 86740 1001562
nḥḏ.t fang(s); tooth (teeth) 86750 1001564
nḫ to protect; to help 86760 1001552
nḫ protection 400968 1001552
nḫ to confirm (the special status of land ownership) 86780 1001552
nḫ.w protector 854700 1001552
nḫ.w safely 868178 1001552
nḫ.w protector; defender (divine epithet) 86990 1001552
nḫ.wt lamentation; complaint 87000 1001571
nḫꜣ knife (of flint) 86820 1000852
nḫꜣ to be pendulous (of the female breasts); dangle 86830 1001595
nḫꜣ flagellum 86810 1001595
nḫꜣ.w fish-shaped pendant (jewelry) 86850 1001595
nḫꜣḫꜣ to tousle? 874331 1000910
nḫꜣḫꜣ flagellum 86890 1001595
nḫꜣḫꜣ to be pendulous (of the breasts); dangle 86880 1001595
nḫi̯ to lament; to complain 86920 1001571
nḫi̯ to endure 86930 1001569
nḫjḫi̯ to endure; to survive; to grow older 852228 1001569
nḫy.t protector (goddesses) 86960 1001552
nḫb blazing one 857493 1001560
nḫb lotus 87020 1001556
nḫb heifer? 856238 1001555
nḫb to assign; to decide 87040 1001559
nḫb stipulation 87050 1001559
nḫb to burn; to illuminate 858447 1001560
nḫb fresh field (freshly determined arable land) 87060 1001559
nḫb.t blazing one 87110 1001560
nḫb.t titulary (of the king); designation 87100 1001559
nḫbi̯ to dance 87090 1000456
nḫbw night lighting? 87170 1001560
nḫbḫb to open (door; door-bolt) 87190 1000457
nḫf to pour 87200 1000496
nḫf cold sweat 87210 1000496
nḫn to be a child; to become a young child 87260 1001577
nḫn [a kind of a sacred place] 87230 1000621
nḫn.t little girl 87280 1001577
nḫn.t youth (abstract) 87300 1001577
nḫn.t little girl (Hathor) 87290 1001577
nḫn.w Child 861819 1001577
nḫn.w brood (of Renenutet) 87320 1001577
nḫn.w child 859268 1001577
nḫn.w child 87250 1001577
nḫn.w childhood; youth 87330 1001577
nḫn.wy opponents 87350 1000621
nḫnm altar? 856001 1000630
nḫnḫ to skid; to slam 87380 1001554
nḫr [something harmful] 87390 1000706
nḫr stream?; canal? 87400 1001583
nḫrḫr to be sad 87420 1000706
nḫḫ to become old; to endure 87470 1001569
nḫḫ enduring one; adolescent 87460 1001569
nḫḫ old one 87480 1001569
nḫḫ to be new born 87440 1001569
nḫḫ Enduring-one (a star) 87500 1001569
nḫḫ cling to? 858448 1001569
nḫḫ youth 87450 1001569
nḫt Mighty one (a constellation) 87590 1001589
nḫt [something on which the risen king

should stand for] 87550 1001589
nẖt strong one 858952 1001589
nẖt to be strong; to strengthen 87560 1001589
nẖt able; very 550230 1001589
nẖt strong; victorious 400031 1001589
nẖt strong one 87580 1001589
nẖt.j giant 87690 1001589
nẖt.w captives; hostages 87640 1001589
nẖt.w strength; victory 87620 1001589
nẖt.w stronghold(s) 87630 1001589
nẖt.t stiffness (limbs) 872162 1001589
nẖt.t stiffness (of joints) (med.) 87600 1001589
nẖt.t reinforcements 87610 1001589
nẖ spittle 87710 1001573
nẖ spittle 855192 1001573
nẖꜣẖꜣ to disturb 858446 1000860
nẖi̯ to spit out; to eject 87700 1001573
nẖw.t what is spit out 87730 1001573
nẖnm [one of the seven sacred oils] 87760 1000625
nẖẖ spittle 87780 1001573
nzw king; king of Upper Egypt 852664 1001668
nzp to smooth out (bread when baked) 88150 1001744
nzp wounds 88180 1001743
nzp knife 88160 1001743
nznzn to destroy 88210 1002819
nznzn to pass away 88200 1002819
nzr.t Flame 88240 1001745
nzr.t the fiery one 860581 1001745
ns to carve 88190 1001650
ns to sink in 87810 1001652
ns bloodbath (or similar) 858082 1001054
ns tongue 87800 1001654
ns to go; to travel 87820 1001652
ns.wt [a javelin] 88030 1001654
ns.t [flood] 860386 1001657
ns.t Base (part of brick ramp) 87880 1002003
ns.t seat; throne 87870 1002003
ns.tj what belongs to the thorn 851582 1002003
nsb.tj one who licks 854283 1001655
ns.ty seedlings? 87890 1001647
ns.tjw those belonging to thrones 857004 1002003
ns.tjw [javelin] 860949 1001654
ns.tjw [a plant] 87990 1001647
ns.tjt [javelin] 860950 1001654
nsꜣ knife 87950 1001650
nsꜣ.wj rowlocks 87930 1001669
nsi̯ to open (or similar) 856262 1001657
nsj [a demon responsible for an illness] 87960 1001658
nsy.t [an illness caused by a demon] 87970 1001658
nsw to lick sth.? 88000 1001654
nsw.y to rule as king 88070 1001668
nsw.y serfs 88050 1001668
nsw.yt queen 88080 1001668
nsw.yt kingship 88090 1001668
nsw.t [injury to a vertebra of the neck] 88020 1001650
nswt king (of Upper Egypt) 851639 1001668
nswt king; king of Upper Egyp 88040 1001668
nsb.w flame 500306 1001655
nsbi̯ to devour; to lick 88100 1001655
nsby.t to devour; to lick 88130 1001655
nsbs to burn, to consume? 88140 1001655
nsr Burning one 500414 1001665
nsr rage; wrath 88250 1001665
nsr to burn up; to shrivel 88270 1001665
nsr fire; flame 88280 1001665
nsr.t flame 88300 1001665
nsrsr Island of fire 70013 1001665
nsrsr the burning one 88340 1001665
nss to do damage to (or similar) 88350 1001666
nssḳ [an affliction of the head (hair loss?)] 88360 1001667
nsḳ to stab, to sting; to bite 88370 1001664
nsḳ needling 859063 1001664
nsk to put in proper array 88380 1001659

nš to shudder 88470 1001653
nš spittle 88410 1001573
nš grain 860462 1001648
nš grain (of sand) 88490 1001648
nš to drive away; to expel 88460 1001651
nš to haul out 854521 1001651
nš to gather (grain) together 88440 1001648
nš rager? (hippopotamus as a Sethian animal) 88480 1002203
nš to comb 88390 1001649
nš.w [a discharge (med.)] 88510 1001651
nš.t hairdresser 88500 1001649
nšw.t hairdressing 88400 1001649
nšbšb to refresh oneself? 88610 1002721
nšp to inhale; to pant? 88620 1001663
nšp gate (or similar) 88640 1001662
nšf fang? 852795 1002070
nšf.wt liquids?; liquid food? 88650 1002070
nšfšf to drip 88660 1002070
nšm to crop 88670 1002145
nšm.y flow 861166 1002153
nšn raging one (Seth; Montu) 88800 1002203
nšn [offering of birds] 88730 1002732
nšn sharp (or similar) 88810 1002203
nšn.j storm; rage 88790 1002203
nšn.t furious one (Hathor-Sakhmet) 88760 1002203
nšn.t fury 88750 1002203
nšn.tj raging 88770 1002203
nšni̯ to rage; to be furious 88780 1002203
nšz drop of poison 88870 1002372
nšzz.t droplet 852769 1002372
nšnš to tear up (documents) 88830 1002203
nšnšn to rage (against enemies) 88840 1002203
nšš.w damp air 88890 1001573
nšd to pick (plants) 88910 1002047
nšd to lacerate; to tear 88900 1001656
nšḏ to comminute 450164 1001656
nšd.y jeweler; lapidary 88940 1002047
nḳᶜ [a specially formed loaf] 88980 1001642
nḳᶜ to scratch 88990 1001642
nḳᶜ.wt notched sycamore fig 89040 1001642
nḳᶜ.wt the cutting (as pain) 854710 1001642
nḳf to beat; to tear (heart) 89080 1001640
nḳm to be sad; to suffer 89100 1001869
nḳm.t sadness 89110 1001869
nḳr gold dust (or similar) 89140 1001641
nḳr to sieve 89120 1001641
nḳr sprinkler (of gold) (Horus of Edfu) 89160 1001641
nḳr sieve 89130 1001641
nḳr to sprinkle (with gold) 89150 1001641
nḳrḳr to hurry 89170 1001894
nḳdd to sleep 89190 1001855
nk to copulate (all nuances) 89200 1001603
nk.w fornicator 89240 1001603
nk.t injured eye 89220 1001605
nkꜣ to consider; to think (about sth.) 89260 1001272
nkꜣkꜣ to revive? 89270 1001266
nkjkj to make pregnant 89280 1001603
nkp.t [an edible plant] 89300 1001606
nkftr [an oil] 89320 1001602
nkn hide (as material of a shield) 89350 1001604
nkn harm; injury 89340 1001605
nkn to wound 89330 1001605
nkn one who injures 89360 1001605
nkn.t injury (injured eye) 857472 1001605
nkn.t wounded eye 855985 1001605
nkn.t knife 859629 1001605
nkk homosexual 89420 1001603
nkk.t wounded eye 89430 1001605
ng.y cackler 500623 1001546
ng.t breach (in a dam) 89490 1001547
ngꜣ to kill; to cut up 89500 1001550
ngꜣ cord (used to tighten a net) 89540 1000445
ngꜣ to lack; to be lacking 89530 1000445
ngꜣ.yt defloration 89570 1001547
ngꜣ.w long-horned cattle 89590 1001549
ngꜣ.w absence (of) 89550 1000445

ngꜣgꜣ to be pendulous (of the breasts); swell? 89600 1000431
ngi̯ to break open 89630 1001547
ngy.t crime 860299 1001547
ngb to refract; to remove 89660 1000364
ngbgb to turn aside 89670 1000364
ngmgm to conspire 89680 1000380
ngs to overflow 89700 1001548
ngsgs to overflow 89710 1001548
ngg to cackle; to screech 89720 1001546
ngg cackler 857451 1001546
ntꜣi̯ to run; to hurry? 89790 1001711
nty [a fabric?] 89830 1001521
ntꜥ to organize 89970 1001713
ntꜥ to desert; to divorce 90220 1001712
nti̯ to be oppressed 89820 1001704
ntf to besprinkle; to wet 90030 1002435
ntn.t diaphragm 90050 1001706
ntn.t skin 90060 1001706
ntš to besprinkle 90100 1001710
nṯ to tie together; to fetter 90180 1001700
nṯ tongue 90190 1001701
nṯ spittle? 90200 1001701
nṯb to parch 852755 1001702
nṯn.t dirt (or similar) 90250 1001705
nṯnṯ spittle 854712 1001701
nṯr god 90260 1001709
nṯr [a plant] 90270 1001708
nṯr.j Canal of the god (waters in the netherworld) 90480 1001709
nṯr.j [a kind of divine cloth] 90490 1001709
nṯr.j Divine (a phyle of funerary priests) 90570 1001709
nṯr.j (divine) fabric 860853 1001709
nṯr.j divine; sacred 400281 1001709
nṯr.j magic cord 90500 1001709
nṯr.j divine one; sacred one 90410 1001709
nṯr.j natron 90510 1001709
nṯr.j [amulet] 859230 1001709
nṯr.j beer; beer jug 90460 1001707
nṯr.j heart (of gods; of kings) 90450 1001709
nṯr.j holy palace 90420 1001709
nṯr.j the divine one (designation of a censer) 90470 1001709
nṯr.jt divine one 854110 1001709
nṯr.jw [a priest of Re] 90580 1001709
nṯr.jw mistress of the stars (Isis-Sothis) 90590 1001709
nṯr.y [a mirror] 90560 1001709
nṯr.yt [a substance related to natron (med.)] 90540 1001709
nṯr.yt [a festival, preliminary to the festival of Sokar] 90550 1001709
nṯr.yt [a divine staff] 90530 1001709
nṯr.wj the two gods (Horus and Seth, Ra and Tatenen) 851539 1001709
nṯr.wt divine state 90610 1001709
nṯr.t divine eye 90320 1001709
nṯr.t [a garment, perhaps made of a feline's pelt] 90290 1001709
nṯr.t goddess 90280 1001709
nṯr.t sacred-eye(s) 90310 1001709
nṯr.tj Two Goddesses (double uraeus) 90330 1001709
nṯr.tj [adze used in the Opening-of-the-mouth ritual] 90340 1001709
nṯr.ty the two divine eyes 853664 1001709
nṯri̯ to be divine; to make divine 90400 1001709
nṯri̯ to purify (with natron); to be pure (through natron) 90520 1001709
nṯḥṯḥ to smile 90620 1002446
nṯẖ [a musical instrument] 90630 1001703
nṯṯ to bind; to tie up (foes) 90670 1001700
nṯṯ rope; cord 90680 1001700
nṯṯ.t the bound one 501051 1001700
ndj [a name for the sun god] 90700 1001552
ndj to fell (someone or something) 90690 1002619
ndb to hear 90770 1000154
ndb wind (or similar) 90780 1001527
ndb the whole earth 859000 1001525
ndb to wound (with the horns) 90750 1002928
ndb to swallow; to consume (drink and eat) 90760 1000154

ndb.yt bunt? (of a sail) 90790 1001527
ndb.wt foundations (or similar) 90810 1001525
ndbdb to sip 90820 1000154
ndfdf to cry; to tear (of the eye of Horus 90840 1000183
ndm throne (or similar) 90850 1001529
nḏ to protect 90940 1001552
nḏ protector 90950 1001552
nḏ flour 90900 1001523
nḏ to ask for (advice); to consult 90910 1001522
nḏ to confer (an office); to appoint 90920 1001522
nḏ thread 90960 1001521
nḏ to punish; to bring to justice 90930 1001552
nḏ to grind; to crush 90880 1001523
nḏ to protect; to punish 854522 1001552
nḏ protector 853694 1001552
nḏ appointment (for something) 91060 1001522
nḏ.y to be hostile towards 91310 1000288
nḏ.yt badness 91320 1000288
nḏ.w protection 91110 1001552
nḏ.w miller 90890 1001523
nḏ.wt questions 857425 1001522
nḏ.wt grinding woman (i.e. fem. miller) 91340 1001523
nḏ.wt maid servants (or similar) 91040 1001523
nḏ.t cosmetic palette 91020 1001523
nḏ.t flour 850683 1001523
nḏ.t subjects 550362 1001552
nḏ.t protectress (Isis; Hathor) 90990 1001552
nḏ.t protection 91000 1001552
nḏ.t rope 857423 1001521
nḏ.tj protector 864989 1001552
nḏ.tj agitator? 91030 1001522
nḏ.tj protector 91080 1001552
nḏ.tj protector 853693 1001552
nḏ.tjt protectress 91090 1001552
nḏꜣ to parch (with thirst) 91230 1001535
nḏꜣ thirst 91240 1001535
nḏꜣ.t irrigation; water 91260 1001535
nḏꜣḏꜣ [to be watery? (med.)] 91290 1001535
nḏꜣḏꜣ [designation for water] 91300 1001535
nḏw.yt malice? 91360 1000288
nḏm to sit down; to settle; to be pleased 91460 1001530
nḏm to be sweet; to be pleasant 500020 1001530
nḏm sweetness; pleasantness 91420 1001530
nḏm carob tree; fruit of the carob tree 91400 1001530
nḏm sweet; pleasing 91410 1001530
nḏm pleasingly 850399 1001530
nḏm.t kindness (or similar) 91480 1001530
nḏm.t [a fruit?] 91470 1001530
nḏmm.t sexual pleasure 28980 1001530
nḏmnḏm sexual pleasure 91580 1001530
nḏmnḏm to copulate with 91590 1001530
nḏnḏ advice; counsel 91610 1001522
nḏnḏ to consult (with someone); to ask (for advice) 91600 1001522
nḏnḏn enflame 91620 1000218
nḏr grip 91640 1000260
nḏr chip; ostracon 91650 1001531
nḏr to smooth (wood); to carpenter 91630 1001531
nḏr.y seizer 91680 1000260
nḏr.wt the moving ones 854151 1001532
nḏr.wt [part of a bed (frame?)] 91690 1001531
nḏr.t imprisonment 91660 1000260
nḏri̯ to follow 861185 1001532
nḏri̯ to hold fast; to seize 91670 1000260
nḏrw.t contraction?; agglomeration? 863005 1000260
nḏḥḏḥ [relating to a heart condition (med.)] 91740 1000194
nḏḥꜥḏḥꜥ.t [a kind of a plant] 91710 1000204
nḏs junior; commoner 91770 1001534
nḏs at the low level 865685 1001534
nḏs small; little; weak 91760 1001534

nḏs to be small 853877 1001534
nḏs.w low estate 91810 1001534
nḏs.t littleness (or similar) 91790 1001534
nḏs.t the younger 91771 1001534
nḏs.tj [epithet of Osiris] 91800 1001534
ndsds to hash? 855349 1000275
nḏsḏs to burn 91840 1000276
nḏdḏd to endure 91870 1000178
nḏdnḏd to endure 91860 1000178

r

r [preposition] 91900 1001078
rʾ goose (gen.) 92640 1001997
rʾ water's edge 92620 1001998
rʾ activity; action 92680 1001998
rʾ stock of; item (in lists) 92630 1001998
rʾ [small measure of capacity] 92600 1001998
rʾ opening; door 92570 1001998
rʾ utterance; speech 92580 1001998
rʾ a third 92610 1001998
rʾ mouth 92560 1001998
rʾ item; part 92590 1001998
rʾ.w openings? [part of a ship] 92690 1001998
rʾ.wj two-thirds 600203 1001998
rj.t coil? 852803 1001952
rj.t side 93230 1001956
ry.t ink 93190 1001954
ry.t heaven 93220 1001953
ry.t pus (or similar) 93200 1001955
rꜥ Re 400015 1001999
rꜥy.t Raet (fem. counterpart of the sun god Re) 93340 1001999
rꜥy.t sun goddess 862769 1001999
rꜥw sun (the king) 853477 1001999
rꜥw sun 93290 1001999
rꜥw.w Re-Gods 860277 1001999
rw Lion 500396 1001987
rw lion 93390 1001987
rw lion 860603 1001987
rw straw, reed 857648 1001988
rw.yt [administrative building]; [law court] 93610 1001995
rw.wt departure 851902 1001995
rw.t Lioness 857644 1001987
rw.t outside 93440 1001995
rw.t gateway; door 93420 1001995
rw.t (false)door 93410 1001995
rw.t dance (or similar) 93450 1001994
rw.t tribunal 93430 1001995
rw.tj Pair of Lions 861786 1001987
rw.tj dancer 856025 1001994
rw.tj stranger 93490 1001995
rw.tj pair of lions 500389 1001987
rw.tj outside 650022 1001995
rwi̯ to cease from 853689 1001995
rwi̯ to dance 856215 1001994
rwi̯ to go away; to expel; to drive off 93540 1001995
rwj.t [a dance] 93570 1001994
rwy.t [part of a false-door (architrave)] 93590 1001995
rwy.t straw 93630 1001988
rwy.t [discharge? (med.)] 93600 1001995
rwny.t heifer 93660 1001970
rwrw.t den (of a lion) 93680 1001987
rwhꜣ evening 93690 1001993
rwḥ to trespass 600032 1001992
rwd stairway; tomb shaft 93730 1001990
rwd stairway; tomb shaft 93800 1001990
rwḏ to be firm; to prosper; to succeed 93780 1001991
rwḏ to control; to administer 93840 1001991
rwḏ strong; firm 400633 1001991
rwḏ bowstring; cord 93760 1001989
rwḏ neat; efficient 860132 1001991
rwḏ firmness; strength 93790 1001991
rwḏ shore 93830 1001991
rwḏ.w agent; inspector 93850 1001991
rwḏ.t success (or similar) 93870 1001991
rwḏ.t bowstring?; whip's lash? 93860 1001989
rwḏ.t hard stone (gen.); sandstone 93880 1001991
rbnbn to be pleased 93990 1000062
rbš cuirass (of leather) 94010 1001926

rbš to arm oneself 855625 1001926
rm fish (gen.) 94160 1001963
rm.y Weeper (sun god) 94190 1001965
rm.yt Weeper (i.e. mourner) 94210 1001965
rm.yt tear 94200 1001965
rm.w weeper 94230 1001965
rm.w weeping 94220 1001965
rm.wt weeping 855602 1001965
rmi̯ to weep; to bewee 94180 1001965
rmm weeping 858630 1001965
rmn support (i.e. column; pillar) 94320 1001966
rmn side (of rowing women) 94260 1001966
rmn upper arm; shoulder 94240 1001966
rmn [measure of area (1/2 aroura)] 94300 1001966
rmn rank 94340 1001966
rmn [a measure of length] 94280 1001966
rmn [measure of length (5 palms)] 94290 1001966
rmn upper arm; shoulder; side; half 854523 1001966
rmn bearer; support 94310 1001966
rmn side; half 94250 1001966
rmn to decay (of walls) 94330 1001966
rmn.yt domain; department 94420 1001966
rmn.w Carrier 854764 1001966
rmn.w companion 856017 1001966
rmn.wj Double-Arm 501058 1001966
rmn.wj arms of balance 857627 1001966
rmn.wt of the same rank; equal 94430 1001966
rmn.wtj companion 868286 1001966
rmn.wtj carrier; companion 94440 1001966
rmn.wtt companion 856018 1001966
rmn.t [part of the reliquary shrine of Osiris] 94360 1001966
rmni̯ to carry; to support 94400 1001966
rmny.t domain; land of a domain 94410 1001966
rmrm to chastize 94470 1001964
rmrm Chastizer 94480 1001964
rmrm.t [a field] 94490 1001966
rmṯ human being; man 94530 1001967
rmṯ people; personnel 450402 1001967
rmṯ.t humankind; people 94550 1001967
rmṯ.t women 853446 1001967
rmy.tj Tearful (Osiris) 500090 1001965
rn name 94700 1001968
rn young one (of animals) 94720 1001970
rn.y calf 94810 1001970
rn.t young one (fem.) (of animals) 94740 1001970
rnw.t motherless girl 94830 1001970
rnp youth 852345 1001971
rnp colt 94900 1001971
rnp fresh water 94870 1001971
rnp young bull (Montu) 94910 1001971
rnp youth 94880 1001971
rnp rejuvenation 94860 1001971
rpw to rot 94100 1001974
rpw.w putrefaction 857633 1001974
rnp.wj youth 94950 1001971
rnp.wj youthful; vigorous 94850 1001971
rnp.wt fresh things (plants and fruit) 95030 1001971
rpw.t figure of a woman; statue of a woman 94110 1001973
rpw.t Repit (a goddess); statue (of a woman); woman of high status; 94030 1001973
rnp.t year 94920 1001971
rnp.t yearly sustenance; festival of the year 500284 1001971
rpw.tj the two ladies (Isis and Nephthys) 851932 1001973
rnpi̯ to be young; to become young (again) 95000 1001971
rnn to nurse; to rear (a child) 95100 1001970
rnn to rejoice; to praise 95040 1001969
rnn youth 95080 1001970
rnn [a kind of cattle] 95060 1001970
rnn to embrace 854524 1001970
rnn to embrace 95090 1001970
rnn.wt joy; exultation 95220 1001969

rnn.t maiden 95130 1001970
rnn.t young hippos 95120 1001970
rnn.t wet nurse; attendant 95140 1001970
rnn.t fortune 95150 1001969
rnn.t cows; heifers 95110 1001970
rns [beads (or similar)] 95230 1001972
rr time 95240 1001977
rr.j swine (gen.); boar 95350 1001976
rr.t sow 95300 1001976
rrm.t mandrake? 95400 1001978
rhb embers 95420 1001942
rhd.t caldron (of metal) 95500 1001943
rhn to lean (on); to rely (on) 95430 1001944
rhn to have (no) success at? 95440 1001944
rhni̯ to wade 95450 1001945
rhni̯ to flee 95460 1001945
rhnj ram (of Amun); criosphinx 95470 1001946
rhnj waste 95480 1001947
rḥ.w comrades; mates 95540 1001935
rḥ.wj the two rivals (Horus and Seth) 95550 1001935
rḥ.t dame; mistress 859001 1001935
rḥb [a vessel] 95570 1001941
rḥḥ to burn 95560 1001937
rḥrḥ to be cheerful (of heart) 95580 1001937
rḥs [a kind of baked goods] 95610 1001948
rḫ knowledge; opinion 95640 1001938
rḫ knowledgeable one 860504 1001938
rḫ know how to do; be able to do 852475 1001938
rḫ to know 95620 1001938
rḫ to know (sexually) 95650 1001938
rḫ wise man 95630 1001938
rḫ.j acquaintance 95790 1001938
rḫ.t acquaintance 95670 1001938
rḫ.t wise one 95660 1001938
rḥ.tj two women 95510 1001935
rḫ.tj two women weavers 854485 1001939
rḫ.tj [designation of Isis and Nephthys] 95690 1001939
rḫ.yt common folk; humankind; subjects (of the king) 95820 1001938
rḫy.t amount 95800 1001938
rḫḫ.j well-known; famous 95860 1001938
rḫs to slaughter; to butcher 95870 1001949
rḫt to wash (clothes) 95890 1001951
rḫt list; amount 95680 1001950
rḫt.j washer 95930 1001951
rḫt.j washer 855716 1001951
rḫt.wt washerwoman 868307 1001951
rzf the catch (fish and fowl); disarray 96160 1001996
rs to wake; to watch 95940 1001981
rs guard; watchman 95950 1001981
rs guard (place where Re and Osiris are being protected) 852848 1001981
rs.j south 96011 1001980
rs.j southern 96010 1001980
rs.jw southerners 96070 1001980
rs.w Guarding Ones 500430 1001981
rs.w south wind 96120 1001980
rs.w the watch (of sentries); vigilance 96110 1001981
rs.t captured enemies? 95960 1001981
rsy.t the watch (of sentries); guard post 96060 1001981
rsy.t guardian (of goddesses) 96040 1001981
rš coryza 96170 1001979
rš.w joy 96180 1001984
rs.wt dream ("wakening (in sleep)") 96130 1001981
rs.wt Southern 500787 1001980
rs.wt south 96150 1001980
rš.wt joy 96220 1001984
rs.wtj Southerner 856024 1001980
rsj entirely; quite; at all 96030 1001982
ršj peak; summit 96200 1001983
ršu̯ to rejoice 96210 1001984
ršrš joy 96280 1001984
ršrš to rejoice 96270 1001984
rḳ counterweight 96300 1001975
rḳ.w enmity 96340 1001975
rḳ.w opponent 96330 1001975

rḳ.t intractable 96310 1001975
rḳi̯ to turn aside; to defy 96290 1001975
rḳw.t resistance (of a swelling?) 96350 1001975
rḳrḳ to stop; to remove; to leave 856232 1001975
rḳrḳ resistance 855367 1001975
rḳḳ.t enmity; resentment? 857634 1001975
rk to stop 96400 1001960
rk time 96390 1001958
rkḥ Burning (a festival) 96460 1001961
rkḥ fire 96450 1001961
rkḥ to light (a fire); to burn up 96440 1001961
rkḥ.y Fiery one 96370 1001961
rkḥ.yt Burning one (2nd night hour) 96380 1001961
rkḥ.t Burning one 861200 1001961
rkḥ.t burning one (designation for goddesses) 501113 1001961
rkrk astragalus? 96430 1001957
rkrk to creep 401172 1001959
rkrk.yt creep 873167 1001959
rks harnessed team 96490 1001962
rg.t compartment 96520 1001933
rgi̯ to stop; to remove 856676 1001934
rtḥ fortification 96550 1001986
rtḥ to confine; to restrain 96540 1001986
rtḥ to bake 800009 1001985
rtḥ baker 96530 1001985
rtḥ.t bakery 96560 1001985
rtḥ.tj baker 96570 1001985
rtḥ.tj metal craftsmen? 500234 1001986
rd foot; footprint 96600 1001928
rd to grow 96610 1001929
rd plants 96620 1001929
rd.t plant 854724 1001929
rd.w [a growing bird] 96630 1001929
rd.wj obligation; functions; transfer; position; art; wise 96640 1001928
rd.yt plant; herb 96720 1001929
rdy.t cord 96710 1001989
rdw stairway; steps 97130 1001990
rdm.t cypress grass 97150 1001936
rdn.y laudanum 852318 1001931
rdrd [a kind of bread] 97170 1001927
rḏi̯ to cause; to allow 550028 1001930
rḏi̯ to give; to put; to place 96700 1001930
rḏi̯ to give; to cause 851711 1001930
rḏw fluidity 97200 1001932
rḏw forewaters 856561 1001932
rḏw.t efflux 857620 1001932
rḏrḏ [term for grain] 97210 1001927

h

hʾ courtyard 97220 1000841
hꜣ blaze 97270 1000847
hꜣ.y descended one 853536 1000882
hꜣ.w descent 856774 1000882
hꜣ.w wild birds 852142 1000863
hꜣ.w corvée; duty 97260 1000882
hꜣ.w corvée worker 97500 1000882
hꜣ.tjw crew (phyle) on duty 97290 1000882
hꜣꜣ Descending One 856765 1000882
hꜣi̯ to attack (the enemy) 97360 1000882
hꜣi̯ to descend; to fall; to strike 97350 1000882
hꜣi̯ to throw; to strike 860784 1000882
hꜣj to beget 97400 1000851
hꜣj husband 97770 1000851
hꜣy.t ceiling; heaven 97430 1000855
hꜣy.t portal; portico 97420 1000855
hꜣy.t bakery (or similar) 97440 1000847
hꜣw neighborhood; environment 97460 1000882
hꜣw affairs; belongings 550026 1000882
hꜣw kindred 97480 1000904
hꜣw proximity; surrounding; time; property 854526 1000881
hꜣw time; life-time 97470 1000881
hꜣw need 97490 1000882
hꜣb letter; communication 550085 1000870
hꜣb to send 97580 1000870
hꜣb.t journey 856771 1000870
hꜣb.w messenger 97610 1000870
hꜣm.w poultry 97630 1000893
hꜣmw to slow down? 97650 1000987
hꜣn.w waves; flood 97670 1000641

hꜣnꜣ O that...! 97660 1000641
hꜣr to be pleased? 858420 1000893
hꜣr.t herd (of desert animals) 97680 1000892
hj to cheer; to whoop 853667 1000520
hj.w Hiu (a hostile serpent, ass, gazelle) 97850 1000518
hj.w Monster (donkey); evil snake 97860 1000518
hj.w [Seth as an ass and as a gazelle] 97800 1000518
hjw.t [creature threatening the dead] 97870 1000524
hjhj to rejoice 600455 1000520
hjhj cheer; rejoicing; acclamation 856804 1000520
ḥjḥj to seek 101930 1000521
hjms to approach humbly 97880 1000522
hy Cheering one 501126 1000520
hy [interjection] 97760 1000520
hy jᶜy; gladness 97780 1000520
hy to make fast (the tow-rope) 97810 1000519
hyn [a kind of land or boundary] 97890 1000822
hyn dwelling; house 860377 1000822
hyt.t burial chamber? 97900 1000882
hw.tj sailer; ship's hand, crew 97980 1000799
hwhw to run away 97940 1000796
hwš to miss; to disregard 600374 1000813
hwt to lament; to complain 97950 1000816
hwt flame; fire 97960 1000815
hwt lamentation(s) 97970 1000816
hwt to burn 854725 1000815
hwt.wt burning (med.) 97990 1000815
hwṯn [a fish] 98000 1000817
hb the trampled one (Seth) 853107 1000471
hb.t netherworld 860419 1000471
hb.t place of execution 98070 1000471
hb.w intrusion 98150 1000471
hbj Ibis 854102 1000458
hbj.t ibis (fem.) 98090 1000458
hbu̯ dance 98080 1000471
hbu̯ plow 98010 1000471
hbu̯ to tread; to traverse; to trample 98020 1000471
hbn [an antilope] 98160 1000460
hbnj ebony 98180 1000462
hbhb to traverse; to tread; to pervade (med.); to remove (enemies) 98210 1000471
hbḳ thicket? 98230 1000464
hbḳ to beat up; to triturate 98220 1000464
hp to wrest from; escape 98250 1001581
hp cord 98260 1000674
hp law; regulation 98240 1000674
hp to act rightly? 853896 1000674
hf to hull (med.) 98350 1000498
hm roar (warlike) 98380 1000549
hm to be hot (diseased state) 98370 1000547
hm.tt cartage; remuneration 856827 1000538
hmh saliva (or similar) 98460 1000544
hmhm to roar; to rumble 98480 1000549
hmhm [a crown] 98490 1000549
hmhm roar 98470 1000549
hmhm.t roar; war-cry 98500 1000549
hmhm.tj Roarer 98510 1000549
hmhm.tj [designation of evil creatures] 98520 1000549
hms cord 98530 1000561
hmṯ [a serpent] 98540 1000565
hmṯ.t [a serpent] 98550 1000565
hn one who is bowing down (Seth) 853106 1000641
hn.y bark of jubilation 855841 1000619
hn.w jubilation 98730 1000619
hnꜣ sweet 859652 1000595
hnꜣ.y [a sweet] 98660 1000595
hni̯ to rejoice 98720 1000619
hnj.wt Rejoicing one 98670 1000619
hnjnj to rejoice 98680 1000619
hnw [a jar]; hin (unit of measure, ca. ½ liter) 98700 1000666
hnw box; cavity (of the body, chest, skull) 98560 1000666

hnw supporter; relative 98760 1000668
hnw.y [epithet of Anubis] 98650 1000666
hnwy.t [part of the djaret-fruit (med.)] 98790 1000595
hnn to nod; to assent to 98810 1000641
hnn fallow deer 98830 1000636
hnn.t doe 98840 1000636
hnhn.yt water mass 856845 1000586
hnhn.w Henhenu-bark [a solar bark] 98880 1000586
hr wooded highlands? 98920 1000698
hr to dispel completely 98910 1000705
hr.t contentment; peace 98990 1000730
hrj to milk? 99010 1000714
hrw day 99060 1000732
hrw due today (grain for harvesting) 99070 1000732
hrw.yt journal; legal document 99160 1000732
hrw̭ to be pleased; to be at peace 99050 1000730
hrw̭ peaceful; pleasing; content 400109 1000730
hrp to sink; to be immersed 99170 1000720
hrp.yw Drowned ones 99180 1000720
hrm to include; to close 99210 1000717
hrhr to satisfy oneself 856208 1000730
hrṯṯ to do stealthily 99250 1000729
hh blast (of fire); heat (of fire) 99260 1000516
hh to exult 99270 1000520
hhj to deafen; to benumb 99290 1000517
hhy.t [a form of deafness (med.)] 99300 1000517
hsmḳ storming (of the king joining battle) 99340 1000752
hskt [bad way of walking] 99350 1000751
hḳ [illness] 859894 1000688
hḳ to break, to crack? 99360 1000688
hḳs to damage; to harm 99370 1000691
hḳs.wtt injured eye 99390 1000691
hkj [a serpent] 99400 1000528
hkr.t [a female serpent] 99410 1000528
ht to wander about 854727 1000769
ht.w [an animal (in spells)] 99460 1000759
ht.t [a female animal (in spells)] 99450 1000759
htj to bore (with a drill) 99480 1000766
hty.t borer (bit) (of a carpenter's drill) 99490 1000766
htm ravaging; destroying 97540 1000779
htht [a canal] 99520 1000766
htht to dig up 99500 1000766
htht to traverse (the heavens); to rush 99530 1000769
hṯt Screamer (baboon) 99560 1000788
hṯt screaming; noise 99580 1000788
hṯt to scream (of baboons); to rejoice 99570 1000788
hd to quarry (stone) 99610 1000478
hd One who returns whack 862904 1000478
hd to attack; to prevail over 99600 1000478
hd to confront; to attack; to break 854527 1000478
hd assault 99620 1000478
hd.t thorn? (of the acacia) 99640 1000478
hdm.w footstool; throne 99680 1000487
hdn hand broom 865385 1000488
hdn [a plant (rabbit ear?)] 99700 1000488
hdn.j [epithet of Thot] 99710 1000488
hbn.t [a bulbous vessel (a measure of capacity)] 98170 1000459
hdhd to charge (of the army) 99730 1000478
hdr.t [a collar] 97750 1000493

ḥ

ḥꜣ He who belongs to the tomb 500463 1000862
ḥꜣ to go ashore; to run aground (naut.) 100180 1000861
ḥꜣ back of the head 100110 1000846
ḥꜣ [relating to the foundation of buildings] 100100 1000846
ḥꜣ back (of something); exterior 100120 1000846
ḥꜣ lament? 100060 1000884
ḥꜣ behind; around 100130 1000846

ḥꜣ behind (in prepositions) 100150 1000846
ḥꜣ round about 400511 1000846
ḥꜣ (a)round 100140 1000846
ḥꜣ to stretch out (wings protectively) 100230 1000846
ḥꜣ.j surrounding; being behind 100660 1000846
ḥꜣ.y protector; helper 100670 1000846
ḥꜣ.yt nakedness 100790 1000703
ḥꜣ.w naked man 101050 1000703
ḥꜣ.w increase; surplus 101060 1000846
ḥꜣ.w mourner 856776 1000884
ḥꜣ.w grape harvest 101090 1002662
ḥꜣ.w except 800061 1000846
ḥꜣ.wtj first 101180 1000849
ḥꜣ.wtj naked man 100900 1000703
ḥꜣ.wtjw ancestors 101200 1000849
ḥꜣ.t [an amulet shaped like the forepart of a lion] 100360 1000849
ḥꜣ.t bow, forepart 873176 1000849
ḥꜣ.t [choice (cuts of meat)] 100340 1000849
ḥꜣ.t [waters] 100330 1000849
ḥꜣ.t tomb 100280 1000862
ḥꜣ.t forepart; beginning; foremost; best 100310 1000849
ḥꜣ.t [a kind of waterfowl] 100250 1000843
ḥꜣ.t Forward (a phyle) 100380 1000849
ḥꜣ.t [designation for water] 100370 1000849
ḥꜣ.t worry 100260 1000884
ḥꜣ.t [designation for wine] 100350 1000849
ḥꜣ.t before 100320 1000849
ḥꜣ.t food? 100290 1000849
ḥꜣ.tj being in front 868364 1000849
ḥꜣ.tj heart 100400 1000850
ḥꜣ.tj [heart-shaped medal, for non-military achievement] 100410 1000850
ḥꜣ.tjj vessel ('belonging to the heart') 863789 1000850
ḥꜣ.tjt prow rope 100450 1000849
ḥꜣ.tjw [fine-quality linen] 101040 1000849
ḥꜣ.tjt best oil 100440 1000849
ḥꜣ.tw those who shine (demons) 101750 1000887
ḥꜣi̱ to support 856205 1000703
ḥꜣi̱ to mourn; to screech; to dance (at the funeral) 100650 1000884
ḥꜣi̱ to bare; to be naked 100710 1000703
ḥꜣy to overflow 100690 1000805
ḥꜣy one who shines (sun god) 100750 1000887
ḥꜣy to illumine; to light up 100730 1000887
ḥꜣy to come 100680 1000805
ḥꜣy light 100740 1000887
ḥꜣy flood 100700 1000805
ḥꜣy.w [designation of a bird of prey] 100960 1000805
ḥꜣy.t light 100800 1000887
ḥꜣy.t one who shines (Hathor) 100810 1000887
ḥꜣy.t malady 100820 1000911
ḥꜣy.t sheet of shallow inundation water overlying the ground 100770 1000805
ḥꜣy.t restlessness (from sleep) 100840 1000911
ḥꜣy.t rectangle? 100850 1000846
ḥꜣy.t bandage 863014 1000849
ḥꜣy.t [room in a temple, shrine or sanctuary] 100870 1000862
ḥꜣy.t embalming hall 100880 1000862
ḥꜣy.t what shines (the sky) 100780 1000887
ḥꜣy.t Mourner 100760 1000884
ḥꜣy.tj the two lights (sun and moon) 100910 1000887
ḥꜣy.tj [designation of the two royal serpents] 100920 1000805
ḥꜣy.tj He who belongs to what shines (sun god) 100930 1000887
ḥꜣy.tj [a person who is hostile] 868373 1000805
ḥꜣy.ty mourner 500559 1000884
ḥꜣy.ty the two mourners (Isis and Nephthys) 100890 1000884
ḥꜣy.tjt one who shines (goddesses; Hathor) 100940 1000887
ḥꜣᶜ.y turmoil 100990 1000911
ḥꜣᶜ.yt turmoil 101000 1000911

ḥꜣꜥ.wtj creator of strive 856766 1000911
ḥꜣꜥꜥ to touch (of a boat on land) 101010 1000911
ḥꜣw.t face (of a god) 101130 1000849
ḥꜣwy.t stake?; pole?; box? 101270 1000906
ḥꜣb bird catcher 550435 1000869
ḥꜣb festival 103300 1000872
ḥꜣb turquoise 103340 1000871
ḥꜣb to fish 850109 1000869
ḥꜣb tent; kiosk 103290 1000872
ḥꜣb triumph 876143 1000872
ḥꜣb catch (of fish, of fowl) 103350 1000869
ḥꜣb.j participants of a festival 868376 1000872
ḥꜣb.yt festival offerings 103590 1000872
ḥꜣb.yt festival pavilion 103570 1000872
ḥꜣb.ytj one who is festive 550080 1000872
ḥꜣb.wj pair of gods 401173 1000872
ḥꜣb.t [part of a tomb; niche; festival kiosk] 103420 1000872
ḥꜣb.t triumphant 856772 1000872
ḥꜣb.t program (for a ritual service) 103410 1000872
ḥꜣb.t bird catcher 859013 1000869
ḥꜣbi̯ to mourn 103320 1000873
ḥꜣbi̯ to be in festival 103560 1000872
ḥꜣbi̯ to make a festival 854980 1000872
ḥꜣbi̯ to triumph 103310 1000872
ḥꜣp Veiled one 501184 1000898
ḥꜣp [secret place?] 101310 1000898
ḥꜣp to hide; to keep secret 101300 1000898
ḥꜣp [a priest] 101320 1000898
ḥꜣp.wtj scout 101370 1000898
ḥꜣp.t hiding place 101330 1000898
ḥꜣm (yield of the) net; catch 101420 1000895
ḥꜣm to fish; to catch 101400 1000895
ḥꜣm.w fisherman 853529 1000895
ḥꜣm.t [designation for fishnet] 101440 1000895
ḥꜣm.t path, road (or similar) 101450 1000892
ḥꜣḥꜣ to support 868391 1000886
ḥꜣḥꜣ [heart ailment] 101510 1000850
ḥꜣq captive (taken in war) 101540 1000890
ḥꜣq plunder 101530 1000890
ḥꜣq to plunder; to capture 101520 1000890
ḥꜣq.w plunderer 101560 1000890
ḥꜣq.w booty maker 858991 1000890
ḥꜣq.t plunder 101550 1000890
ḥꜣk to truncate 101570 1000889
ḥꜣk [the shorter parallel side of the trapeze] 101580 1001128
ḥꜣk.t trapeze 101600 1001128
ḥꜣg to be glad 101610 1000879
ḥꜣgꜣg to rejoice 101630 1000879
ḥꜣt to be bleared (of the eyes) 101640 1000899
ḥꜣtj covering; garment 101680 1000899
ḥꜣtj [eye illness (bleariness)] 101670 1000899
ḥꜣtj to wrap; to coat; to encompass 858803 1000899
ḥꜣtj cloudiness 101690 1000899
ḥꜣtj.j the one who is blurred 856783 1000899
ḥꜣd trap (esp. for fish) 101770 1000877
ḥꜣd to be overwhelmed 101790 1000486
ḥꜣd to trap (fish) 101780 1000877
ḥꜣd.t basket; container (as a unit of capacity for vegetables) 101810 1000877
ḥꜣd.t [a basket (also as a measure of capacity for vegetables)] 101800 1000877
ḥꜣd.t agitation 101820 1000875
ḥy inspector 101880 1000805
ḥy flood 102760 1000805
ḥw food 102280 1000794
ḥw striking one 855342 1000805
ḥw [the great sphinx of Giza] 102300 1000793
ḥw driver; slugger; shepherd 102320 1000805
ḥw Hu ("Utterance") 500190 1000798
ḥw utterance 102270 1000798
ḥw the food 854333 1000794

ḥw.yt chipped (from the millstone) 102800 1000805
ḥw.yt stroke; blow 102790 1000805
ḥw.w (class of) bulls; cattle (gen.) 102450 1000805
ḥw.wtj one who belongs to estates 852043 1000795
ḥw.t One who beats 102360 1000805
ḥw.t pig 102420 1000805
ḥw.t rain; flood 102400 1000805
ḥw.t (larger) house; estate; temple 99790 1000795
ḥw.t rain 855566 1000805
ḥw.t verse 102410 1000795
ḥw.tjw those belonging to an estate 102440 1000795
ḥw.tj(t) He / She of the mansion 857035 1000795
ḥw.tt mine; quarry 99810 1000805
ḥwꜣ to rot; to putrefy 102640 1000819
ḥwꜣ.w stench (of purification) 102660 1000819
ḥwꜣ.wtj he who belongs to the stench 102700 1000819
ḥwꜣꜣ.t rotten materials 102680 1000819
ḥwꜣꜣ putrefaction 857040 1000819
ḥwi̯ to rain 102750 1000805
ḥwi̯ to flow; to flood 102740 1000805
ḥwi̯ to strike; to drive; to tread 102730 1000805
ḥwi̯ to beat; bump; to enter; flow; water 854530 1000805
ḥwi̯ to gather (crops, the harvest) 102840 1000805
ḥwj happy song 102770 1000807
ḥwy.tj shining light 102830 1000887
ḥwꜥ to be short 102920 1000820
ḥwꜥ dwarf ("short man") 102930 1000820
ḥwꜥ the short one 852813 1000820
ḥww washer? 102990 1000805
ḥww to proclaim 102260 1000798
ḥww.t report; announcement 855147 1000798
ḥww.tj messenger 103000 1000798
ḥwn childhood; youth 103060 1000809
ḥwn young man (priest's title in Dendera) 103030 1000809
ḥwn to become young; to be rejuvenated 103040 1000809
ḥwn [a cut of meat] 103070 1000808
ḥwn youthful 103050 1000809
ḥwn.w child; youth; young man 103020 1000809
ḥwn.w young crocodile 103110 1000809
ḥwn.w pupil 857045 1000809
ḥwn.w the young one 500417 1000809
ḥwn.wt pupil 852272 1000809
ḥwn.wt young lioness 855867 1000809
ḥwn.wt young lioness (Tefnut) 103090 1000809
ḥwn.wt girl; maiden 103080 1000809
ḥwn.wt maiden (goddesses) 500613 1000809
ḥwn.wtj the two maidens (uraei) 103100 1000809
ḥwrꜥ to rob; to plunder 103170 1000812
ḥwrꜥ robber (Seth, as a crocodile) 103180 1000812
ḥwrꜥ robber 856681 1000812
ḥwrw to speak evil? 103200 1000811
ḥwrw to be wretched; to be weak 103190 1000811
ḥwrw wretched; weak 400950 1000811
ḥwrw humble man; wretch 103150 1000811
ḥwrr poverty? 103220 1000811
ḥwtf to rob; to plunder 103270 1000805
ḥp.t [crown; diadem] 104050 1000685
ḥp.tj [extreme limits (of the earth)] 104080 1000685
ḥp.tj [designation of gods] 104070 1000523
ḥpw.tj runner 104130 1000523
ḥpp to be held back 104140 1000523
ḥpḥp to be held back 104160 1000523
ḥpg to dance 104200 1000677
ḥpt to embrace; to enclose 104230 1000685
ḥpt reel? (of thread; of twine) 104240 1000685
ḥpt embrace; armful 104220 1000685

ḥpt.w mast step (naut.) 104300 1000685
ḥpt.w crosspieces at the door 104290 1000685
ḥpt.w Embracer 500325 1000685
ḥpd to open (the mouth) 104320 1000676
ḥfn one hundred thousand 104440 1000506
ḥfn.w hundred thousand 104460 1000506
ḥn to be fresh; to provide with 105920 1000598
ḥn to go speedily; to journey 105930 1000602
ḥn to draw back from 105940 1000602
ḥn to go speedily; to journey 854531 1000602
ḥn [a protective container] 105880 1000605
ḥn to equip; to protect; to command 105900 1000605
ḥn [a bird] 105950 1000584
ḥn to look at (or similar) 105970 1000604
ḥn to hail 105980 1000603
ḥn to obstruct 105890 1000599
ḥn to grow (of lotus) 105860 1000598
ḥn [waters, or basin?] 856836 1000598
ḥn order, mission 851162 1000605
hn.w jubilation 98730 1000619
ḥn.w jar; chattel(s) 106280 1000585
ḥn.w jubilation 106330 1000603
ḥn.w military commander 853138 1000605
ḥn.w ribs 865700 1000605
ḥn.w rising? (of the wind) 106150 1000602
ḥn.wt mistress 854850 1000605
ḥn.wt mistress; lady 106350 1000605
ḥn.wt order 868460 1000605
ḥn.wtj servant 853139 1000605
ḥn.t [waters (in the sky)] 106060 1000598
ḥn.t Pelican goddess 500197 1000591
ḥn.t pool; lake 106050 1000598
ḥn.t palm; irrigation channel 106090 1000598
ḥn.t pelican 106020 1000591
ḥn.t [sanctuary of Neith] 106030 1000605
ḥn.t orders; command 106000 1000605
ḥn.tj the one belonging to the Henet waters 855121 1000598
ḥn.tj ends; limits 106120 1000605
ḥn.tj kingfisher? 106080 1000584
ḥn.tw commander (mil.) 107440 1000605
ḥny.t spear; javelin 106190 1000670
ḥnᶜ together with 106200 1000672
ḥnᶜ therewith 106240 1000672
ḥnᶜ [preposition] 850800 1000672
ḥnᶜ and 550300 1000672
ḥnᶜ.j therewith; nearby 850771 1000672
ḥnᶜ.w accumulation 106260 1000672
ḥnw obstruction? 106310 1000599
ḥnw [a crown] 106320 1000605
ḥnw [plant] 875732 1000598
ḥnw.t casket 106360 1000599
ḥnw.t horn 106370 1000667
ḥnw.t [obstruction? (med.)] 106390 1000599
ḥnw.t [a jug (for beer, for wine)] 106340 1000665
ḥnw.tj Horned one 856857 1000667
ḥnwy.t grain usury 106460 1000599
ḥnb to drive away (from) 106490 1000608
ḥnb to survey 106470 1000607
ḥnb arable land 106480 1000607
ḥnb.y Measurer 500215 1000607
ḥnb.w [designation of the sun's rays] 106580 1000606
ḥnb.w [a kind of a solar bark] 106660 1000606
ḥnb.t measured parcel of land; garden 106540 1000607
ḥnb.t bread ration 106530 1000607
ḥnb.tj who belongs to the lot of land 500651 1000607
ḥnb.tjt one which belongs to the lot of land 500853 1000607
ḥnb.tjt farmland? 106570 1000607
ḥnbꜣbꜣ ball-shaped (of a swelling; med.) 106630 1000115
ḥnbb wind 106680 1000608
ḥnbb to slay (offering animals) 106690 1000608

ẖnbb to mingle with people; to enter 123400 1000609
ḥnf to worship 106720 1000508
ḥnj [a plant of the marshes (sedge?)] 105850 1000598
ḥnmw go around? [creeper - TLA] 106740 1000626
ḥnmm.t sunfolk (of Heliopolis); humankind 106750 1000633
ḥnmnm to speak badly of sb. 106770 1001614
ḥnmnm to sneak 106760 1001614
ḥnmnm.w Sneaker (snake) 856849 1001614
ḥnn [part of a date (med.)] 106820 1000635
ḥnn phallus 106810 1000638
ḥnn hoe 106790 1000640
ḥnr to squint? 106860 1000531
ḥnr clouding; darkening 854746 1000531
ḥnry [nickname of the goddess Hathor] 106890 1000531
ḥnrg to quake; to be embarrassed 106910 1000651
ḥnḥn vitality 106960 1000598
ḥnḥn to tear up 858516 1000640
ḥnḥn to hinder; to detain 106930 1000602
ḥnḥn dawdler 857000 1000598
ḥnḥn from forgetting (or the like of the name) 106950 1000599
ḥnḥn [an affliction of the legs (med.)] 106940 1000602
ḥnḥn.t [a swelling (med.)] 106970 1000598
ḥnḥn.yt She who is detained 500885 1000602
ḥns narrow; constricted 106990 1000654
ḥns to be narrow; to be constricted 400975 1000654
ḥnḳ foam; ferment? 107070 1000644
ḥnḳ.t beer 110300 1000644
ḥnk to present (a gift); to offer 107110 1000624
ḥnk cluster? (of dates) (as a unit of measure) 107160 1000624
ḥnk donated land; donation 107180 1000624
ḥnk [an offering vessel] 107120 1000624
ḥnk papyrus float 107150 1000623
ḥnk pigtailer 856846 1000623
ḥnk [kind of an offering] 107140 1000624
ḥnk.yt with braided hair 107050 1000623
ḥnk.yt bed; bed linens? 107240 1000623
ḥnk.yt (diplomatic) gifts 107250 1000624
ḥnk.w scale-pan (of a balance) 107260 1000624
ḥnk.t bedchamber 107210 1000624
ḥnk.t companion 107200 1000624
ḥnk.t braided lock of hair 107220 1000623
ḥnk.t offerings; donation 107190 1000624
ẖnk.t [a garment] 858288 1000622
ḥnk.tj He with (braided) sidelock 107040 1000623
ḥnk.tj braided one (uraeus) 107300 1000623
ḥnk.tj provided with a hair braid; pigtailed 854751 1000623
ḥnk.tj pigtailer 856847 1000623
ḥnk.tjw Those with braided hair (pl.) 853605 1000623
ḥnk.tjt pigtailed 856848 1000623
ḥnk.tyt one with braided hair (Hathor; Isis) 107310 1000623
ḥnk.tyty the two with braided hair (Isis and Nephthys) 853606 1000623
ḥng slaver 868472 1000617
ḥngg gullet 107350 1000617
ḥngg to rejoice 107340 1000879
ḥnt greed 851907 1000660
ḥnt scale?; spike? 855842 1000659
ḥntꜣ breastbone; sternum 107370 1000663
ḥntꜣ an animal (porcupine?) (med.) 107360 1000663
ḥntꜣsw lizard 107380 1000664
ḥnti̯ to be covetous; to be greedy 107400 1000660
ḥntj an animal with spines (porcupine?) (med.) 107410 1000663
ḥntj [a boat] 106140 1000663
ḥntj greedy one 107390 1000660

ḥnty Greedy one (crocodile) 851645 1000660
ḥnṯ.t slaughter 855001 1000661
ḥnṯ.tj butcher 858541 1000661
ḥnṯ.tj butcher 107480 1000661
ḥnṯ.tjw Those who butcher 500355 1000661
ḥnṯi̯ to butcher (animals); to kill (enemies) 107470 1000661
ḥr at (the time of); in (temp., duration) 400091 1000697
ḥr face; sight 107510 1000697
ḥr because 107530 1000697
ḥr steering rope 107540 1000701
ḥr to be ready; to make ready 107560 1000704
ḥr on; upon; up 400090 1000697
ḥr face (a mirror) 107600 1000697
ḥr canal? 108370 1000695
ḥr diameter 107580 1000697
ḥr.j supervisor; chieftain 108310 1000697
ḥr.j [part of the head] 108320 1000697
ḥr.j being upon; being above; uppermost 108300 1000697
ḥr.j lid (of a smoking device) 108450 1000697
ḥr.j the upper (mortuary temple with pyramid) 108330 1000697
ḥr.jw [those who are above (birds)] 108480 1000697
ḥr.jw [those who are above (stars)] 108470 1000697
ḥr.yw enemies 859816 1000713
ḥr.jt topmost 108380 1000697
ḥr.yt fear; dread 108390 1000713
ḥr.w people 107760 1000697
ḥr.w terror; dread, respect 109010 1000713
ḥr.w upper part; top 108990 1000697
ḥr.wj two faces 86177 1000697
ḥr.t the distant one 856921 1000712
ḥr.t rope 856905 1000701
ḥr.t heaven 107670 1000697
ḥr.t offering table 107710 1000697
ḥr.t path 107660 1000697
ḥr.t tomb; necropolis 107640 1000697
ḥr.t roof (of a temple) 107680 1000697
ḥr.t high inundation 107650 1000697
ḥr.t upper side 107630 1000697
ḥr.tj Heavenly one 500280 1000697
ḥr.tt lump (of semi-precious stone) 107740 1000699
ḥri̯ to dread; to instill dread 108360 1000713
ḥri̯ to be far (from); to remove (oneself) 108340 1000712
ḥri̯ to fly (to heaven) 108350 1000712
ḥry.t dung 108410 1000734
ḥry.t melting oven 108400 1000715
ḥrp dagger; short sword 109060 1000718
ḥrr to roar 109080 1000723
ḥrr.t flower 109110 1000722
ḥrr.t small creeping and/or crawling creatures 109120 1000725
ḥrr.tj He who belongs to the flower 500497 1000722
ḥrḥr to guard; to keep 109180 1000707
ḥrs.t carnelian 109190 1000727
ḥrs.t rage 109200 1000727
ḥrst to make red (eyes, with rage) 109210 1000727
ḥrti̯ to travel overland 107720 1000697
ḥḥ Heh 500031 1000513
ḥḥ Heh (subdivision of a phyle) 109260 1000513
ḥḥ inundation water 109240 1000805
ḥḥ Heh (symbol of time) 853978 1000513
ḥḥ million 109250 1000513
ḥḥi̯ to go; to tread 109290 1000521
ḥz.y statue 109630 1000829
ḥz.y the praised one 856479 1000829
ḥz.y praised one 109750 1000829
ḥz.yt praised one 109660 1000829
ḥz.w praised one 109760 1000829
ḥz.w spell 852082 1000829
ḥz.t forearm; animal leg 109350 1000824
ḥz.t water jar; ewer (in ritual use) 109330 1000826
ḥzꜣ dough; paste; mucus (med.) 109510 1000838

ḥzꜣ to be wild 852665 1000839
ḥzꜣ fierce 109520 1000839
ẖzꜣ carrying pole 450162 1000837
ḥzꜣ Nil god?; god of dough? 109500 1000838
ḥzw.t favor; praise 109800 1000829
ḥzw.tj favorite 68730 1000829
ḥzy.tj favorite 109670 1000829
ḥzi̯ to praise; to favor 109620 1000829
ḥzi̯ to turn back; to turn away (the evil-doer) 109640 1000830
ḥzp [corn Osiris] 109990 1000835
ḥzp garden (plot); meadow 109980 1000835
ḥzp.t garden product 858669 1000835
ḥzmn Amethyst-region (Wadi el-Hudi) 400018 1000832
ḥzmn amethyst 110070 1000832
ḥzmn to cleanse; to purify 110030 1002811
ḥzmn menstruation 110040 1002811
ḥzmn to drink; to eat 110050 1000834
ḥzmn bronze 110060 1000833
ḥzmn natron 110020 1002811
ḥzmn one who works with natron 600346 1002811
ḥzmn.y washstand pitcher 110130 1002811
ḥzmn.w one who cleans his mouth with natron 110100 1002811
ḥzmn.w [a meal] 110110 1000834
ḥzmn.t menstruating woman 110090 1002811
ḥzz.t what is praise worthy 110180 1000829
ḥzk.w [a priest of Osiris in Abydos] 110250 1000831
ḥs to stain 858423 1000736
ḥs to be cold 109690 1000739
ḥs excrement 109370 1000736
ḥs he who is cold 109700 1000739
ḥs closed (with a string) 600609 1000738
ḥs.y frost, cold 109710 1000739
ḥs.w singer 109430 1000750
ḥs.w singer 855743 1000750
ḥs.t singer 855744 1000750
ḥs.t singer 109400 1000750
ḥs.t song; singing 109390 1000750
ḥsꜣ thread 109550 1000757
ḥsi̯ to sing; to make music 109680 1000750
ḥsb to slaughter 109890 1000744
ḥsb accounting; distribution 450206 1000742
ḥsb fracture (of a bone) (med.) 109830 1000741
ḥsb enlistee (for compulsory work) 109880 1000742
ḥsb [to hunt with a throwstick] 109840 1000744
ḥsb one quarter of an aroura 109860 1000742
ḥsb to break 109820 1000741
ḥsb ground 860396 1000742
ḥsb to count; to reckon; to distribute 109870 1000742
ḥsb cross band 109850 1000740
ḥsb.w accounting; reckoning 109940 1000742
ḥsb.w square fields (to be drawn on the floor) 109950 1000742
ḥsb.w worker 109960 1000742
ḥsb.w Slaughtered(-steer) (11th nome of LE) 450272 1000744
ḥsb.t calculation 868520 1000742
ḥsb.t portion (of quota achieved) 109910 1000742
ḥsb.t knife 109920 1000744
ḥsb.t quota 550010 1000742
ḥsk "The cutter" (demon) 110210 1000753
ḥsk "what is cut off" (the head) 110230 1000753
ḥsk to cut off (the head); to cut out (the heart) 110200 1000753
ḥsk butcher 856932 1000753
ḥsk.t knife 110220 1000753
ḥḳꜣ ruler 853727 1000693
ḥḳꜣ ruler; chief 110360 1000693
ḥḳꜣ to rule; to govern 110340 1000693
ḥḳꜣ.t uraeus 110420 1000693
ḥḳꜣ.t [a priest] 110430 1000693

ḥḳꜣ.t bushel (a corn measure, 10 hin) 110440 1000692
ḥḳꜣ.t (crook-like) scepter 110380 1000693
ḥḳꜣ.t ruler 110390 1000693
ḥḳꜣ.t rulership 110400 1000693
ḥḳꜣ.tj double-bushel (20 hin) 600004 1000692
ḥḳr famine 110570 1000689
ḥḳr hungry man 110550 1000689
ḥḳr hunger 110560 1000689
ḥḳr to be hungry; to fast (med.) 110540 1000689
ḥḳr.w famine 110600 1000689
ḥḳr.t those who are hungry 110590 1000689
ḥkꜣ to bewitch 110680 1000530
ḥkꜣ.yt magician 162370 1000530
ḥkꜣ.yw Bewitchers 500345 1000530
ḥkꜣ.w magic spell 110661 1000530
ḥkꜣ.w magic; magical power 110660 1000530
ḥkꜣ.w magician 110700 1000530
ḥkꜣ.w The magical one (crown of Upper Egypt) 110710 1000530
ḥkꜣw.t magic 110720 1000530
ḥkn Necklace (depicting a lioness) 855173 1000525
ḥkn activity of drug preparation [verb] 110760 1000526
ḥkn to praise 110740 1000527
ḥkn [a med. substance] 110770 1000526
ḥkn door-bolt (in the shape of a lion) 110790 1000525
ḥkn.y the praised one 110850 1000527
ḥkn.w Praiser 400259 1000527
ḥkn.w praise 110860 1000527
ḥkn.w [a sacred oil] 110870 1000526
ḥkn.w One who praises 110810 1000527
ḥkn.w [a med. substance] 110800 1000526
ḥkn.wtt Praiser (a serpent) 110830 1000527
ḥkn.t Praiser 500676 1000527
ḥknkn to exult 860344 1000527
ḥkk to swallow sth. (or similar) 110910 1000616
ḥgꜣ joys 110940 1000512
ḥgꜣ.w festival place 110970 1000512
ḥt [part of the eye (duct?)] 111010 1000760
ḥt comb 111000 1000762
ḥtꜣ shabby; worn (of clothing, for example) 111040 1000792
ḥtꜣ.w sail 111070 1000791
ḥtꜣ.w blotches (on the face) (med.) 111060 1000792
ḥtꜣ.wt sail 111080 1000791
ḥtj smoke (rising from the offering table) 111130 1000776
ḥtj.t [part of the eye] 861075 1000760
ḥty.t Breather 111170 1000789
ḥty.t throat 111160 1000789
ḥty.t needle 869408 1000789
ḥty.t end piece (terminal; of a broad collar?) 111100 1000789
ḥtw throat 855517 1000789
ḥtp god of offering 856944 1000783
ḥtp the content one 852773 1000783
ḥtp mercy 111250 1000783
ḥtp Contented one 111290 1000783
ḥtp offering (gen.) 400524 1000783
ḥtp basket 111300 1000783
ḥtp blood 111330 1000782
ḥtp to be pleased; to be content 111230 1000783
ḥtp floral offering 111310 1000783
ḥtp [harmful action?] 111340 1002928
ḥtp food offerings 854532 1000783
ḥtp incense 111320 1000783
ḥtp offering table 111210 1000783
ḥtp to make gift 859941 1000783
ḥtp food offerings 111220 1000783
ḥtp.t offerings 111360 1000783
ḥtp.t priestess 111380 1000783
ḥtp.t peace 111370 1000783
ḥtp.t bundle (of herbs) as offering 111410 1000783
ḥtp.t bowl (for bread) 111400 1000783
ḥtp.y provided with offerings 111520 1000783
ḥtp.y priest 111530 1000783

ḥtp.yt Merciful one 111550 1000783
ḥtp.yw the peaceful one 111560 1000783
ḥtp.w setting (of the sun) 500193 1000783
ḥtp.w peace; contentment 111260 1000783
ḥtp.wj Two offering tables 500890 1000783
ḥtp.tjw [ones who have to do with offerings] 111430 1000783
ḥtp.tjw [ones who are provided with offerings] 500212 1000783
ḥtm what should be destroyed 111640 1000779
ḥtm to destroy; to be destroyed 111600 1000779
ḥtm to provide with; to complete 111590 1000779
ḥtm destruction 500195 1000779
ḥtm provider 858510 1000779
ḥtm destroyer 111620 1000779
ḥtm the one to be destroyed 111630 1000779
ḥtm to pay (a debt) 111610 1000779
ḥtm.yw Destroyed ones 111760 1000779
ḥtm.yt place of execution (in the netherworld) 111750 1000779
ḥtm.yt annihilation? 853539 1000779
ḥtm.w destroyer 853092 1000779
ḥtm.wt The destroying one 111740 1000779
ḥtm.wt She who provides 111770 1000779
ḥtm.t [animal native to Syria (hyena? bear?)] 111680 1000777
ḥtm.t chair 111700 1000778
ḥtm.tj [designation of Apophis] 111720 1000779
ḥtr [basketwork] 600478 1000785
ḥtr team of horses; steeds; chariotry 111810 1000785
ḥtr pair 600012 1000785
ḥtr bird cage 111880 1000785
ḥtr revenue; wages 111840 1000785
ḥtr twin 111790 1000785
ḥtr yoke of oxen; team (gen.) 111800 1000785
ḥtr lashings 111850 1000785
ḥtr to bind together 111860 1000785
ḥtr to tax; to assess 111830 1000785
ḥtr.w tax collector 111910 1000785
ḥtr.w door jambs 111820 1000785
ḥts to bury; to conceal 111960 1000786
ḥts to complete 111940 1000786
ḥts [object given by the king to a god] 111930 1000786
ḥṯ [a block of stone] 112030 1000767
ḥṯ to overlay; to inlay 112010 1000767
ḥṯ.w The hyenas (domain) 851409 1000764
ḥṯ.t hyena 112040 1000764
ḥṯꜣ [a kind of bread] 112070 1000790
ḥṯṯ to lift someone 112130 1001125
ḥṯṯ.w baboons 855103 1000788
ḥṯṯ.t mast-step? (naut.) 112150 1000787
ḥṯṯ.t armpit 112140 1000787
ḥdy to spread out 112170 1000486
ḥdy to become limp 112180 1000486
ḥdb to overthrow; to prostrate; to halt (at) 112200 1002928
ḥḏ white land 112380 1000477
ḥḏ mace 112290 1000476
ḥḏ oryx 859467 1000477
ḥḏ to be white; to be bright 112301 1000477
ḥḏ light 112320 1000477
ḥḏ jawbone 112370 1000477
ḥḏ bones 112350 1000477
ḥḏ white; bright 112300 1000477
ḥḏ silver; silver (as medium of exchange) 112330 1000477
ḥḏ damage 112400 1000485
ḥḏ [a goose or duck] 112360 1000477
ḥḏ chapel 112340 1000477
ḥḏ.y the shining one 112190 1000477
ḥḏ.yt slaughter; execution; damage 112680 1000485
ḥḏ.w milk 112730 1000477
ḥḏ.w onions 112710 1000477
ḥḏ.w [a med. substance] 863031 1000474
ḥḏ.w [a med. substance (aromatic resin?)] 112720 1000474
ḥḏ.w destroyer 853560 1000485

ḥḏ.t White Crown (personified) 501050 1000477
ḥḏ.t [a med. substance] 112510 1000474
ḥḏ.t white (of the eye) 112450 1000477
ḥḏ.t [a med. plant] 112490 1000474
ḥḏ.t [a plant] 112480 1000474
ḥḏ.t honey 859672 1000477
ḥḏ.t White one (hippopotamus goddess) 112520 1000477
ḥḏ.t daylight 112410 1000477
ḥḏ.t white cloth; white clothing 112420 1000477
ḥḏ.t milk; [a beverage, lit. white stuff] 112460 1000477
ḥḏ.t White One (goddesses) 112430 1000477
ḥḏ.t White (crown of Upper Egypt) 112440 1000477
ḥḏ.t white one (woman grinding grain) 112160 1000477
ḥḏ.t the white one [mark of the sacred animal] 112530 1000477
ḥḏ.tj white sandals 112540 1000477
ḥḏy west wind 112700 1000495
ḥḏw.yt lamp (or similar] 112770 1000477
ḥḏw.yt spawn 855217 1000477

ẖ

ẖ to be young 112980 1000804
ẖ.t fire; flame 113020 1000447
ẖ.tj Fiery One (a serpent) 113040 1000447
ẖ.tj fiery 868574 1000447
ẖ.tjt fiery one (serpent, Sachmet) 113050 1000447
ẖꜣ leaf 113100 1000856
ẖꜣ [waters in the sky] 113190 1000842
ẖꜣ hall; office 113180 1002660
ẖꜣ road; path 113230 1000883
ẖꜣ thousand 113110 1000857
ẖꜣ to be young 113140 1000858
ẖꜣ.t khat-headcloth 113280 1000845
ẖꜣ.t [a collar-like necklace] 113270 1000845
ẖꜣ.t disease; illness 113480 1000852
ẖꜣ.tj demon causing illness 855596 1000852
ẖꜣ.tjw demons of diseases; demons with knifes 113640 1000852
ẖꜣẖꜣ winnowing field [a field in the hereafter] 114230 1000910
ẖꜣẖꜣ to winnow, to scatter 114220 1000910
ẖy how? 114520 1000977
ẖy height 114470 1000821
ẖy child 852398 1000804
ẖy child 114450 1000804
ẖy high-lying land 114480 1000821
ẖy Flood (the "high") 114490 1000821
ẖy air? 114500 1000805
ẖy oh! 114510 1000977
ẖy...ẖy just as ... so 114570 1000977
ẖy.t acclamation 858998 1000821
ẖy.t little girl 874154 1000804
ẖy.t shelter 114530 1000804
ẖy.t sky; roof 114550 1000821
ẖy.t size (of a figure) 114540 1000821
ẖy.t little girl 113000 1000804
ẖy.t [goddess who lifts up the sky] 114560 1000821
ẖyi̯ to be high; to mount up 114460 1000821
ẖz ritual 120580 1000825
ẖzꜣ.w [a plant used for fuel] 120680 1000836
ẖzꜣ.w [part of a plant (med.)]; [oak apple?] 120670 1000836
ẖzꜣj bribe 120650 1000840
ẖzẖz [a myrrh] 121050 1000823
ẖzd putrefaction (in the limbs of Osiris) 121090 1000827
ẖzd swelling (boil?) 121080 1000827
ẖw Protector 858339 1000804
ẖw protégé; child 856185 1000804
ẖw [a fan] 114930 1000804
ẖw protection 114940 1000804
ẖw oneness; uniqueness 113070 1000797
ẖw protector 856186 1000804
ẖw.t heavens 115000 1000804
ẖw.t protection; exemption (from assessment) 114970 1000804
ẖw.t king's palace; sanctuary 114990

1000804
ẖw.tjw Protective Deities 115020 1000804
ẖwi̯ to be exempt from 114920 1000804
ẖwi̯ to prevent (from doing something) 852623 1000804
ẖwi̯ to protect; to prevent 115110 1000804
ẖww baseness; wrongdoing 115150 1000804
ẖwn to pierce 115170 1000810
ẖwn to be hurtful 115180 1000810
ẖwẖ.t [a boat] 115240 1000803
ẖwz.w [a kind of a structure - hut] 115290 1000818
ẖwzi̯ to pound; to build 115270 1000818
ẖws to slaughter (offering animal) 115260 1000814
ẖwd richness 115330 1000801
ẖwd to be rich; to enrich 115310 1000801
ẖwd rich man 115320 1000801
ẖwd palanquin 115350 1000800
ẖwd to fish? (with a net) 115340 1000802
ẖwḏ.w [a category of fisherman] 115370 1000802
ẖwd.t carrying chair 115360 1000800
ẖb dancer 115380 1000456
ẖb to annihilate 115410 1000451
ẖb to down; to subdue 122840 1000453
ẖb.t reduction? (med.) 115430 1000457
ẖb.t place of execution 115450 1000451
ẖb.t dance 401139 1000456
ẖb.t fire 115460 1000451
ẖb.tj executed one 851557 1000451
ẖb.tjw Foe (also as a designation of Apophis) 115950 1000451
ẖbꜣ to destroy; to diminish 115490 1000473
ẖbꜣ loss 115500 1000473
ẖbꜣ in spite of? 115510 1000473
ẖbꜣ.tw despite 115540 1000473
ẖb+ to deduct; to reduce 115570 1000457
ẖbi̯ to dance 115560 1000456
ẖbi̯ to gather (tribute); to exact (dues) 115590 1000457
ẖby.t massacre 115610 1000451
ẖby.t dancers 115600 1000456
ẖbb massacre 115640 1000451
ẖbb dance 401138 1000456
ẖbn to distort; to be criminal 115660 1000461
ẖbn.t crime; guilt; falseness 115670 1000461
ẖbn.tj criminal 115680 1000461
ẖbr business, trading partner 115700 1000465
ẖbr to join together 859942 1000465
ẖbẖ to slink into 115720 1000452
ẖbẖb to hobble 115730 1000457
ẖbẖb to slink into 861711 1000452
ẖbẖb to trample; to slay 115750 1000451
ẖbẖb to slay 115760 1000451
ẖbẖb to move; push away 858554 1000457
ẖbẖb.t destruction 500400 1000451
ẖbz.t tail 115780 1000472
ẖbz.wt divine beard 115920 1000472
ẖbz.wtjw bearded man 115870 1000472
ẖbs wrongdoer (or similar) 115850 1000469
ẖbs to plough (through water) 115830 1000467
ẖbs ploughlands 115820 1000467
ẖbs (artificial) light (lamp; candle) 113860 1000468
ẖbs to illuminate 115800 1000468
ẖbs [a bird (cormorant?)] 115860 1000467
ẖbs violence? 115840 1000469
ẖbs to hack up (the earth); to plough 115810 1000467
ẖbs.yt hoe 115910 1000467
ẖbt to punish (the enemy) 115940 1000451
ẖbt.j The one belonging to the flame 854000 1000451
ẖbḏ hateful one 852759 1000454
ẖbḏ to damage 855504 1000454
ẖbḏ to be displeased with; to be hateful 115990 1000454
ẖbḏ.w hateful one 858259 1000454
ẖbḏ.t what is hateful 115980 1000454
ẖp the deceased 116000 1000678
ẖp.y the moving one 116070 1000678
ẖp.yt death 858305 1000678

ḫp.yw [gods who follow Osiris] 116130 1000678
ḫp.w [an eye disease] 116140 1002223
ḥp.t [crown; diadem] 104050 1000685
ḫp.t journey 858304 1000678
ḫpi̯ to die; to do away with 116060 1000678
ḫpi̯ to fly up 500265 1000678
ḫpi̯ to travel; to encounter (someone) 116050 1000678
ḫpj.w passing away 116120 1000678
ḫpp strange 116160 1000681
ḫpp to be strange 859324 1000681
ḫpp passerby; stranger 116150 1000678
ḫpp.w strange words 116170 1000681
ḫpp.wt strange things 116180 1000681
ḫppwj flowers (lotus?) 116190 1000680
ḫppwj [pellets? of myrrh] 116200 1000680
ḥpḥp to be held back 104160 1000523
ḫpr to begin (doing): [aux./modal] 500446 1000682
ḫpr to create 854383 1000682
ḫpr to come into being; to become; to occur 116230 1000682
ḫpr to bring into being; to bring about 70024 1000682
ḫpr.y creator (a divine serpent) 116360 1000682
ḫpr.w mode of being; form; transformation 116300 1000682
ḫpr.w those who live now 116290 1000682
ḫpr.t event (lit. that which happens) 116270 1000682
ḫprj child 116340 1000682
ḫprr scarab 500094 1000682
ḫprr [dung beetle; scarab] 116410 1000682
ḫprš Blue Crown 116420 1000683
ḫpš armory 116480 1000684
ḫpš to conquer 116470 1000684
ḫpš scimitar; battle ax 116460 1000684
ḫpš "he whose arm is strong" (the creator god) 116510 1000684
ḫpš strong arm; power; strength 116450 1000684
ḫpš Great Bear (the constellation) 116440 1000684
ḫpš foreleg; thigh 116430 1000684
ḫpš to be efficient 116500 1000684
ḫpš.y armed with a sword (king) 116520 1000684
ḫpd buttock(s); rear part 116550 1000675
ḫf to flood 855088 1000496
ḫf to see; to perceive 116580 1000499
ḫfꜣ to feed 854806 1000507
ḫfꜣ.t food 116610 1000507
ḫfꜣ.t candlestick?; lamp? 854697 1000509
ḫfꜣꜣ.t riverbank 116620 1000510
ḫfꜣi̯ to lighten 116590 1000509
ḫfꜥ fist; grasp 116640 1000511
ḫfꜥ to seize; to grasp 116630 1000511
ḫfꜥ bundle (i.e. a fist-full, of arrows) 116650 1000511
ḫfꜥ.t Seizer (a serpent) 116670 1000511
ḫfḫf to shatter (a statue) 116710 1000340
ḫfḫf to cause to overflow 116700 1000496
ḫfḫf.w Place of origin (of the north wind) 116730 1000496
ḫfḫf.t outburst 116720 1000496
ḫfḫfj to stream 116740 1000496
ḫfnn.wt [fruits] 116690 1000504
ḫft when; at the time of 400129 1000505
ḫft at the time of; at the same time 400128 1000505
ḫft in front of (someone) 116760 1000505
ḫft in accordance with (a command) 400127 1000505
ḫft [preposition] 116761 1000505
ḫft when; while 116770 1000505
ḫft.j enemy 116800 1000505
ḫft.jj hostile; enemy 856170 1000505
ḫft.w accordingly 116840 1000505
ḫft.t enemy 116810 1000505
ḫm shrine; sanctuary 116930 1000543
ḫm dusted one? 116870 1000537
ḫm [a relic] 856275 1000543
ḫm [pulverized ingredient in incense] 116880 1000537

ẖm to be dry (as dust) 116860 1000537
ẖm [stone worker] 117110 1000537
ẖm to not know; to be ignorant of 116910 1000543
ẖm ignorant man 116920 1000543
ẖm destruction 858267 1000555
ẖm.yw over thrower 117070 1000555
ẖm.w those who do not know (Egypt) 117170 1000543
ẖm.w dry grains 860314 1000537
ẖm.w sacred images 116960 1000543
ẖm.w dust 117160 1000537
ẖm.wt destruction 868634 1000555
ẖm.wt sacred images?; sacred beings? 116970 1000543
ẖmꜣꜣ to be convulsed?; to have a convulsion? 116990 1000582
ẖmꜥ.w debris 400986 1000555
ẖmꜥ.t blade (or handle?) (of an oar) 117130 1000583
ẖmꜥi̯ to seize; to grasp 117090 1000583
ẖmi̯ to consume; eat 117050 1000553
ẖmi̯ to overthrow; to demolish; to oppose 117020 1000555
ẖmm destroyer 858271 1000555
ẖmn eight 117240 1000557
ẖmn.j 8-thread weave (a quality of linen) 117200 1000557
ẖmn.yw Ogdoad (of Hermopolis) 117250 1000557
ẖmn.nw the eighth one 854321 1000557
ẖmn.t ogdoad 117220 1000557
ẖmnnw.t eight-thread garment 858273 1000557
ẖmẖm to not know; to negate 858766 1000543
ẖmt to stab 117310 1000569
ẖmt to treble; to do thrice 117290 1000568
ẖmt [a part of the bark "the third"] 117320 1000568
ẖmt spear; harpoon 117300 1000569
ẖmt companion 860850 1000566
ẖmt the thinker? 117360 1000534
ẖmt to plan; to intend 117340 1000534
ẖmt.w three 117280 1000568
ẖmt.nj [a liquid diluted by a third?] 117380 1000568
ẖmt.nw [third month of the year] 117400 1000568
ẖmt.nw third one 117390 1000568
ẖmt.nw third 117410 1000568
ẖn to be foolish 117540 1000597
ẖn to direct (one's hand against) 117490 1000600
ẖn dance; music 860452 1000618
ẖn fool 854618 1000597
ẖn rebel 117500 1000589
ẖn revolting 117510 1000589
ẖn speech; utterance; matter 117520 1000593
ẖn Choral singing (clap beat) 117460 1000618
ẖn to lour 108100 1000589
ẖn.yt music makers 117700 1000618
ẖn.ywt those making music 858931 1000618
ẖn.w Music-maker 117740 1000618
ẖn.w storeroom 117790 1000621
ẖn.w porter 850588 1000592
ẖn.w child 117780 1001577
ẖn.w percussionist (of Hathor) 117750 1000618
ẖn.wt music-maker (sistrum player) (of Hathor) 117820 1000618
ẖn.t the quiet place 117550 1000621
ẖn.t extra gift 117570 1000590
ẖni̯ to make music 117690 1000618
ẖni̯ to flatten; to settle; to stop 117680 1000621
ẖnw dorsal fin (synodontis) 117800 1000669
ẖnp to drink water 117870 1000643
ẖnp [a kind of baked goods] 117880 1000642
ẖnp to steal; to catch; to present 117850 1000643
ẖnp to take in air (i.e. breathe) 117860 1000643

ẖnf to take sth. 117960 1000613
ẖnf.w [a baked goods] 118020 1000614
ẖnf.wt [a baked goods] 118030 1000614
ẖnf.t fire 868655 1000614
ẖnfꜣ arrogance? 117990 1000615
ẖnfꜣ to be aggressive? 118000 1000615
ẖnfi̯ to burn 854701 1000614
ẖnfy fire 118010 1000614
ẖnm to rear 118080 1000630
ẖnm friend 118060 1000629
ẖnm to treat (with an ointment) (med.) 118070 1000629
ẖnm friendly; glad 850992 1000629
ẖnm infant 868658 1000630
ẖnm to scent; breathe in; delight; be happy 854533 1000629
ẖnm to breathe in (a pleasant smell) 118040 1000629
ẖnm keeper of a divine child 118090 1000630
ẖnm to gladden; to be glad 118050 1000629
ẖnm.w friendly 850984 1000629
ẖnm.w smell 118230 1000629
ẖnm.t harlot 118110 1000629
ẖnm.t kiss ("smell") 118120 1000629
ẖnm.t nurse 118130 1000630
ẖnm.t jasper 118140 1000628
ẖnm.t nurse 857705 1000630
ẖnm.tj nurse (who rears a divine child) 118200 1000630
ẖnm.tjt nurse (as applied to goddesses) 118220 1000630
ẖnms mosquito (or gnat?) 118280 1000634
ẖnms [a beer] 118270 1000629
ẖnms friendship 118250 1000629
ẖnms friend 118260 1000629
ẖnms to be friendly with 118240 1000629
ẖnms.t friend 118290 1000629
ẖnn.t fowl 118310 1000637
ẖnr to be hoarse 118410 1000647
ẖnr to scatter; to disperse 118390 1000648
ẖnr fangs 118380 1000532
ẖnr prisoner 118330 1000649
ẖnr reins 118360 1000645
ẖnr person belonging to the ẖnr 851029 1000618
ẖnr criminal 118340 1000649
ẖnr the institution of ẖnr 118350 1000618
ẖnr to restrain 118320 1000649
ẖnr spike (for splitting stone); chisel 118370 1000646
ẖnr.yt female musician belonging to the ẖnr 118490 1000618
ẖnr.t labour camp; fortress; council chamber 118470 1000649
ẖnr.tj official of the labor camp 401029 1000649
ẖnr.tt plotting 118500 1000649
ẖnrj roar 118510 1000652
ẖnrf insult; abuse 118530 1000650
ẖnẖn to establish oneself 118580 1000621
ẖnz to move in two directions 500246 1000671
ẖnz to traverse (a region); to travel through 118590 1000671
ẖnz.w Wanderer 118700 1000671
ẖns To-and-Fro canal 854079 1000656
ẖns [a gold amulet] 118620 1000656
ẖns rolled-up curtain (of matting) 450240 1000656
ẖns double doors 118630 1000656
ẖns.wj skin of the double bull 856230 1000656
ẖnš stinker 856666 1000655
ẖnš sweating 853385 1000655
ẖnš to stink 118730 1000655
ẖnš [plant] 854821 1000653
ẖnt brow; face; front 118790 1000657
ẖnt jar-stand; sideboard 118780 1000658
ẖnt in front of 850802 1000657
ẖnt (head) cold; congestion (med.) 118820 1000657
ẖnt in front of; foremost of; out of 119040 1000657
ẖnt in (some time) 500014 1000657
ẖnt.j foremost; in front 119050 1000657
ẖnt.j forepart; south 119060 1000657

ẖnt.j entrance hall 119070 1000657
ẖnt.j canal 119120 1000657
ẖnt.j one who is in front 119110 1000657
ẖnt.j what is in front (gen.) 119030 1000657
ẖnt.j [characteristic of a crocodile] 119090 1000657
ẖnt.j something located frontally 854347 1000657
ẖnt.jw gods who are in front 119340 1000657
ẖnt.jw person from the far south 119330 1000657
ẖnt.jt beginning of something 118900 1000657
ẖnt.jt one in front 859638 1000657
ẖnt.jt something of the best quality 118890 1000657
ẖnt.yt voyage southwards 119150 1000657
ẖnt.w earlier; previously 119350 1000657
ẖnti̯ to sail upstream; to travel southwards 119140 1000657
ẖnti̯ to be in front of 119130 1000657
ẖntš to be glad; to make glad 119390 1000662
ẖntš to walk about freely 119380 1000662
ẖntš joy 119400 1000662
ẖnd to tread 119430 1000612
ẖnd to plait; to (en)twine 119450 1000611
ẖnd to bend (a staff, during manufacture) 119420 1000611
ẖnd lower leg (calf) 119440 1000612
ẖnḏ shin; (bull's) shank 119560 1000610
ẖnd.w seat (stool, chair, throne); stairway 119540 1000611
ẖnd.w "runner" (job designation) 119480 1000612
ẖnd.w bent timbers (naut.) 119490 1000611
ẖnd.wt the (female) weavers 119470 1000611
ẖr to (someone) 80012 1000694
ẖr tomb; necropolis 119620 1000706
ẖr street; road; quarter 119570 1000700
ẖr to fall; to fell 119610 1000706
ẖr with 850795 1000694
ẖr hostile 119970 1000706
ẖr also, but, then etc. 119600 1000694
ẖr.j located at 119860 1000694
ẖr.j descendant 857322 1000709
ẖr.jt descendant 860283 1000706
ḥr.yt fear; dread 108390 1000713
ẖr.yt animals for sacrifice; butchery 119890 1000706
ẖr.w enemy 119960 1000706
ẖr.w low-lying land 119980 1000706
ẖr.t state; wish 500185 1000694
ẖr.t matter; requirement; possession 854534 1000694
ẖr.tj [sic lege]to kill 120490 1000706
ẖr.tw utterance; oracle 119940 1000731
ẖr.tw sistrum 119950 1000702
ẖry [myrrh] 119870 1000735
ẖrw voice; sound; quarrel 120010 1000731
ẖrw noisy one 856179 1000731
ẖrw The voice (a domain) 852555 1000731
ẖru̯ to say; to tell 600211 1000731
ẖrw.y noise maker 860993 1000731
ẖrw.y noisy one 120070 1000731
ẖrw.yw troops 119910 1000706
ẖrw.yw hostility; war 120090 1000706
ẖrw.yt enemy 120110 1000706
ẖrw.yt hostility; war 120080 1000706
ẖrwrw discord 120100 1000706
ẖrp to bring; to provide 120160 1000719
ẖrp to govern; to control; to administer 120150 1000719
ẖrp to be forward of 120170 1000719
ẖrp director 855078 1000719
ẖrp director 120190 1000719
ẖrp to set out (in the morning) 120180 1000719
ẖrp [herep-scepter] 120140 1000719
ẖrp.w mallet 120250 1000719
ẖrp.wt dues; taxes 120320 1000719
ẖrp.t levy (in the form of cattle) 120210 1000719
ẖrp.t steering rope 120230 1000719

ḫrp.t Taxpayers 120220 1000719
ḫrr watercourse; channel 859155 1000724
ḫrr Noisy one 120400 1000731
ḫrḫr fighter? 858315 1000706
ḫrḫr to upset; to overturn 120420 1000706
ḫrḫr.t destruction? 858314 1000706
ḫrḫr.t destruction 120440 1000706
ḫrš bundle(s) 120460 1000726
ḫrš.t bundle 120470 1000726
ḫrq.t slippery ground 120480 1000721
ḫrd veils; thin cloth 120500 1000711
ḫḫ neck; throat 120510 1000514
ḫḫ to weigh 120530 1000515
ḫḫ neck collar 860285 1000514
ḫsbḏ serpent of the lapis lazuli colour 120740 1000745
ḫsbḏ artificial lapis lazuli 120730 1000745
ḫsbḏ to make blue coloured 860286 1000745
ḫsbḏ [a plant of lapis lazuli color] 859153 1000745
ḫsbḏ lapis lazuli; substitutes for lapis lazuli 120700 1000745
ḫsbḏ lapis lazuli-like; of blue colour 120720 1000745
ḫsbḏ.t one of the lapis lazuli colour (Hathor; Isis) 120710 1000745
ḫsbḏ.tj one of the lapis lazuli colour 120760 1000745
ḫsf to punish 650004 1000748
ḫsf to oppose (in court) 120791 1000748
ḫsf [door of heaven] 120910 1000748
ḫsf answer (to a letter) 120870 1000748
ḫsf to spin (yarn) 450465 1000748
ḫsf spindle 120780 1000748
ḫsf offender 851854 1000748
ḫsf to meet; to draw near; to answer 120800 1000748
ḫsf to repel 120790 1000748
ḫsf to turn around 120810 1000748
ḫsf to remove body hair 120830 1000748
ḫsf.w Repeller 501073 1000748
ḫsf.w approach 120900 1000748
ḫsf.w refuse? 858321 1000748
ḫsf.t punishment 120880 1000748
ḫsfi̯ to sail upstream 120960 1000748
ḫsr to dispel; to drive away 121030 1000754
ḫsr one who distributes 858331 1000754
ḫsdḏ [a kilt] 121120 1000746
ḫsdḏ to grow mouldy 121130 1000747
ḫšb to mutilate 121160 1000743
ḫšḫš rubble 121170 1000749
ḫt through; throughout 121230 1000761
ḫt [rod (linear measure of 100 cubits)] 121210 1000770
ḫt [an administrative unit (land register?)] 121220 1000765
ḫt [an ethereal oil] 121270 1000770
ḫt wood (gen.); tree; stick 121200 1000770
ḫt.j located behind it 868709 1000761
ḫt.jw [a kind of measurement] 121630 1000883
ḫt.y Retreating One 121550 1000761
ḫt.w followers 121590 1000761
ḫt.w threshing floor 121610 1000772
ḫt.w dais; platform; terrace 121600 1000772
ḫt.wj crop, cereal? 121620 1000763
ḫt.wt wooden things 121300 1000770
ht.t [a female animal (in spells)] 99450 1000759
ḥṯ.t hyena 112040 1000764
ḫt.t parcel 121290 1000765
ḫt.t carving; inscription 121910 1000773
ḫti̯ to carve; to inscribe 121520 1000773
ḫti̯ to see 121540 1000775
ḫti̯ to rove around 853931 1000761
ḫti̯ to retreat 121510 1000761
ḫtm to seal; to put a seal on 121710 1000780
ḫtm ring 121700 1000780
ḫtm precious 150290 1000780
ḫtm chest; storehouse (sealed) 121720 1000780
ḫtm bread; offering meal 859355 1000780
ḫtm lock 121730 1000780
ḫtm seal 121750 1000780
ḫtm fortress 121740 1000780

ḫtm (images of gods) with inscriptions 121790 1000780
ḫtm seal; sealing; sealing cylinder 121690 1000780
ḫtm.yt closure? 121850 1000780
ḥtm.w destroyer 853092 1000779
ḫtm.w sealer 150350 1000780
ḫtm.w inscriptions 121780 1000780
ḫtm.w seal maker; sealer? 121840 1000780
ḫtm.t treasure (lit. what is sealed) 850597 1000780
ḫtm.t contract 121830 1000780
ḫtm.tj sealer 855793 1000780
ḫtm.tj sealer 850589 1000780
ḫtm.tjt sealer 850146 1000780
ḫtḫt to turn back; to drive away 121890 1000761
ḫṯn garlic? 121920 1000781
ḫṯḫṯ to pound 121930 1000768
ḫd [canal in the Memphite nome] 121950 1000484
ḫd stream 121940 1000484
ḫd north 859285 1000484
ḫd.t land register (or similar) 121980 1000475
ḫdi̯ to flow 122010 1000484
ḫdi̯ to travel downstream; to travel northwards 122000 1000484
ḥḏr.t [a small animal (hyena?)] 112860 1000492
ḫḏw [fish] 122050 1000802

ẖ

ẖꜣ to break up; to batter 122400 1000860
ẖꜣ.t marshes; lagoon 122270 1000853
ẖꜣ.t corpse 122220 1000848
ẖꜣ.t oxyrhynchus fish 122210 1000853
ẖꜣ.t [a mineral (lit. quarried thing] 122230 1000860
ẖꜣ.t quarry 122280 1000860
ẖꜣ.tj mash dweller 852200 1000853
ẖꜣ.tj storm 122690 1000860
ẖꜣ.tj he of the corpses 858232 1000848
ḥꜣ.tjj vessel (‘belonging to the heart’) 863789 1000850
ẖꜣ.tjj stormy 865226 1000860
ẖꜥ to disgrace (a woman); to empty (so./sth.); deprive 854536 1000916
ẖꜥ to empty sth. /so. 122720 1000916
ẖp.w figure; image 122870 1000673
ẖꜥꜥ [a jug] 122740 1000673
ẖꜥꜥ.w piece; ration 122760 1000673
ẖꜥw [a jug] 122770 1000673
ẖꜥm to approach; to reach 122780 1000922
ẖꜥḳ barber 122810 1000926
ẖꜥḳ barber 855324 1000926
ẖꜥḳ razor 122830 1000926
ẖꜥḳ to shave 122800 1000926
ẖꜥḳ.tskin (shed by a snake) 122820 1000926
ẖpꜣ pellet? 122890 1000686
ẖpꜣ navel 122880 1000686
ẖpꜣw.t scar (as a result of a tumor) 122910 1000686
ẖpy sun disk encircled by a pair of uraei 122920 1000682
ẖpꜥ to chew (med.) 122930 1000687
ẖpꜥ.w [a med. substance to be chewed] 122950 1000687
ẖpn to be fat 122970 1000679
ẖpn.t fattened (domestic) fowl 855580 1000679
ẖms to bend (the back, in respect) 123000 1000563
ẖms spear point 123030 1000563
ẖms [incense] 123020 1000562
ẖms ear of grain 123010 1000563
ẖn [a bandage (med.)] 100970 1000587
ẖn [a sack] 123080 1000588
ẖn to approach 123110 1000596
ẖn to be swollen (from the stomach) 123060 1000639
ẖn tent 123090 1000588
ẖn related party; friend 853897 1000596
ẖn.w Oarsman 500731 1000620
ẖn.w oarsman 123300 1000620
ẖn.w provisions 123180 1000588
ẖn.w oarsman 123130 1000620
ḥn.wt mistress 854850 1000605
ḥn.wt mistress; lady 106350 1000605

ḥn.wt order 868460 1000605
ẖn.wt music-maker (sistrum player) (of Hathor) 861112 1000618
ẖn.t ferryboat 858280 1000620
ẖn.t hide; skin; tube (of skin) (med.) 123140 1000588
ẖn.t water-procession 123160 1000620
ẖny.t crew of rowers 123240 1000620
ẖnw interior 123270 1000588
ẖnw interior; living place; residence 854537 1000588
ẖnw [a body of water] 123290 1000586
ẖnw home; abode 123280 1000588
ẖnw.jw what belong to the household 123250 1000588
ẖnw.t desert fountain; cistern? 850909 1000586
ẖnw.tj inner 200018 1000588
ẖnw.tj inner layer (of the skin) 123390 1000588
ẖnw.tjw people who wear animal skin 123320 1000588
ẖnm to join; to unite with 123420 1000631
ẖnm housemate; dependents 123430 1000631
ẖnm to build; to construct 123450 1000631
ẖnm.w herd 123580 1000631
ẖnm.w [group of animals] 854538 1000631
ẖnm.w marsh fowl; swarm (of waterfowl) 123440 1000631
ẖnm.ww creators 500383 1000631
ẖnm.t well; watering place 123550 1000632
ẖnm.t nurse 123500 1000631
ẖnm.t basin? (for irrigation) 123560 1000632
ẖnm.t one who unites (waxing moon) 123520 1000631
ẖnm.t [dwelling of the sacred crocodile in Ombos] 123530 1000632
ẖnm.t strainer 123540 1000631
ẖnm.tj nostrils 123570 1000631
ẖnmj.t [water in the nome of Hierakonpolis] 123690 1000632
ẖnn to trouble; to decay (med.) 123700 1000639
ẖnn rower 858290 1000620
ẖnn dust; rubble 123740 1000639
ẖnn to be inflamed (med.); to decay 123720 1000639
ẖnn.w disturbance 123760 1000639
ẖnn.w brawler 123730 1000639
ẖnnn irrigation basin? 123800 1000586
ẖnẖn to the side of, in the company of 123820 1000596
ẖnẖn to approach 123810 1000596
ẖnk.t [a garment] 858288 1000622
ẖr [a part of a plant] 123890 1000774
ẖr as a result (reason); [causal] 851509 1000709
ẖr storeroom 852288 1000709
ẖr under 850794 1000709
ẖr.j being under: lower 124220 1000709
ẖr.y beneath 851459 1000709
ẖr.jw humankind 124240 1000709
ẖr.jw reptile 860469 1000709
ẖr.jw relatives; underlings (of a household) 123930 1000709
ẖr.jt lower sky 869000 1000709
ẖr.w base; bottom; under-side 124420 1000709
ẖr.wj testicles 124430 1000709
ẖr.t belongings; share; requirements 123940 1000709
ẖr.t hereafter 123950 1000709
ẖr.t country of provisions 859943 1000709
ẖr.tjw basement 124470 1000709
ẖrm.t causeway? 854473 1000716
ẖrd child 124480 1000710
ẖrd child; young people 854539 1000710
ẖrd to be a child 124510 1000710
ẖrd daughter 124500 1000710
ẖrd young (of an animal) 124490 1000710
ẖrd.w childhood 124540 1000710
ẖrd.wt childhood 858312 1000710
ẖrd.t childhood 124520 1000710
ẖz coward; vile person 124610 1000828
ẖz weak; vile 400267 1000828

h̠z the miserable one (Seth) 852832 1000828
h̠z.yt cowardice 124640 1000828
h̠zi̯ to be weak 124600 1000828
h̠sꜣ to be unanointed 124570 1000758
h̠sꜣ wig 857922 1000758
h̠sꜣ “unanointed one”?; “weak one”? (Osiris) 124630 1000758
h̠sꜣ.yt [a kind of a balsam] 124590 1000758
h̠ss corner (of a building) 124670 1000755
h̠sw eyelid 124660 1000756
h̠ḳs to be injured 124710 1000690
h̠ḳs.t injured eye (of Horus) 124720 1000690
h̠kr adornment 124740 1000529
h̠kr the adorned one 124760 1000529
h̠kr to adorn; to be adorned 124730 1000529
h̠kr.y jewelry maker 856568 1000529
h̠kr.yt [designation of the white crown] 124840 1000529
h̠kr.yt insignia 124850 1000529
h̠kr.t adornment (uraeus) 124790 1000529
h̠tb to overthrow 124890 1000481
h̠tb to dip into (med.) 124900 1000771
h̠th̠t inquirers (mil.) 124910 1000479
h̠th̠t to examine 124920 1000479
h̠dr to feel uncomfortable? 124980 1000494

z

z door bolt 125000 1002787
z man 125010 1002788
zb.y uraeus 131500 1002791
zb.w [something wooden (board, beams)] 852468 1002789
z.t northern pintail duck 125060 1002851
z.t woman 125040 1002788
zꜣ son 125510 1002853
zꜣ phyle (of priests) 125581 1002862
zꜣ protection 125600 1002862
zꜣ phyle (of priests) 854541 1002862
zꜣ eighth of an aroura 125520 1002852
zꜣ amulet 125610 1002862
zꜣ troop (of soldiers, of workmen) 125580 1002862
zꜣ to ward 125550 1002862
zꜣ.w magician 126280 1002862
zꜣ.w one belonging to the phyle 400556 1002862
zꜣ.w guardian 855948 1002862
zꜣ.w guardian 126300 1002862
zꜣ.wt custody 126390 1002862
zꜣ.wtj guardian 126410 1002862
zꜣ.wtj guardian 861593 1002862
zꜣ.wtt sons and daughters 125900 1002853
zꜣ.t daughter 125630 1002853
zꜣ.t daughter 860541 1002853
zꜣ.tj son (in: son of Geb; of the king) 125660 1002853
zꜣ.tj the two daughters 125650 1002853
zꜣꜣ guardian 858344 1002862
zꜣꜣ.y sneaker 401125 1002856
zꜣi̯ to linger; to creep 126320 1002856
zꜣy.t protectress 126190 1002862
zꜣw to break; to be broken 126330 1002863
zꜣw beam; baulk 126360 1002863
zꜣw captive? [abusive name of Apophis] 126310 1002862
zꜣu̯ to prevent 851821 1002862
zꜣu̯ to guard; to heed; to guard against 126290 1002862
zꜣw.t lumbal area 126400 1002862
zꜣw.t beam 857007 1002863
zꜣw.tj sneaker? 852807 1002856
zꜣb dignitary 126620 1002854
zꜣb to traverse (like a jackal) 126610 1002854
zꜣb jackal 126600 1002854
zꜣb to flow; to drip 126590 1002854
zꜣb.wt wisdom 852031 1002854
zꜣr bonds 126890 1002858
zꜣr.t [a garden plant] 126790 1002857
zꜣš to open (ears) 127290 1002820
zꜣṯ libation stone 127630 1002861
zꜣṯ to pour out; to make a libation 127610 1002861
zꜣṯ libation 127620 1002861

zꜣt.t incense 127550 1002860
zꜣṯ.w Offering (domain) 853160 1002861
zꜣṯ.w ground; floor; earth 127650 1002861
zꜣg.t [a fabulous animal (griffin?)] 127510 1002855
zj departure 856192 1002807
zj to go 127740 1002807
zjn to rub (in); to rub (out) 128320 1002808
zy who? what? 127760 1002789
zw.t [a kind of a wheat] 129420 1002838
zw.tjt [a kind of a wheat] 850978 1002838
zwn arrow 130090 1002840
zwꜣ to cut (down, off) 129730 1002846
zwꜣ.t chopper 855501 1002846
zwn.w physician 130260 1002841
zwn.w [a vessel] 130250 1002839
zwn.w physician 855957 1002841
zwnu̯ to suffer 130270 1002841
zwr to drink 130360 1002842
zwr drinking bowl? 130390 1002842
zwr drinking bowl 130370 1002842
zwr drinking bout; carousal 600362 1002842
zwr.t [a beverage] 130400 1002842
zwr.t watering place 130410 1002842
zwr.tj one who slurps 860650 1002842
zwrw.t [a bird] 130490 1002843
zwš strip; ball (of material) 130760 1002844
zwš massing (as an illness symptom) 130770 1002844
zwš rope (on harpoon) 129910 1002844
zwš to lump; to twist together 130750 1002844
zwš.t [a rope] 450010 1002844
zwṯ to roll (a flour ball, fattening geese) 130910 1002845
zb.t wrong; evil 131040 1002791
zb.t reward; remuneration 131020 1002791
zb.t heir 131050 1002790
zb.t expedition 400805 1002791
zb.t cargo; transport 131030 1002791
zb.tj one who passes by (serpent) 858725 1002791
zb.tjw oppressors 131700 1002791
zbꜣ flutist 450260 1002795
zbꜣ to blow (i.e. play a woodwind instrument) 131160 1002795
zbi̯ to go; to conduct; to send; to attain 131460 1002791
zbi̯.tw in order that 131670 1002791
zbb leader; chief 855456 1002791
zbn to slip; to steer (a ship) off course; to make fall 131760 1002793
zbn walking path; running route 852805 1002793
zbn.w [a fish] 131830 1002792
zbnbn to wander 131840 1002793
zbzb to drive away 132050 1002791
zbṯ laughter 131660 1002794
zbṯ to laugh 132270 1002794
zp remainder; remnant 132330 1002824
zp matter; affair; conduct 132300 1002822
zp worm-like clot 132340 1002825
zp time; occasion 132310 1002822
zp case; matter; essence; time 854543 1002822
zp remedy; means 132320 1002822
zp.yt remainder; remnant 132730 1002824
zp.w harvest grain 860460 1002824
zp.w case of illness 132480 1002822
zp.t threshing floor; heap of grain 132380 1002824
zpꜣ writhing; to be wrinkled (or similar) 132620 1002825
zpꜣ [verb of movement, applied to the intestines (med.)] 132660 1002825
zpꜣ centipede 132630 1002825
zpꜣ carrying chair; steps 132650 1002825
zpꜣ.t centipede 857288 1002825
zpi̯ to remain over; to be left (abandoned); to be left out (excluded) 132710 1002824
zpy [as an element during Osiris mysteries] 132720 1002825
zpy.t gobbet 132740 1002824
zpp remainder 132780 1002824
zpp.y remainder 132790 1002824

zpz The tousled one 133090 1002823
zpz to tousle 133080 1002823
zpzp to tousle 133120 1002823
zpzp [a kind of illegal deed] 133130 1002823
zf to cut up; to slaughter 133410 1002797
zf knife; sword 133400 1002797
zf to be fake; to do an injustice 852226 1001164
zf to be mild; to be merciful 133390 1002796
zf friendliness; mildness 851877 1002796
zf.j one who cuts 133590 1002797
zf.w the mild one 853454 1002796
zf.wt slice 856190 1002797
zf.t sword; knife 133420 1002797
zfn gentleness 133630 1002796
zfn to be gentle; to be merciful; to make calm 133620 1002796
zfn.w kind person 133690 1002796
zfn.y gentle one 133700 1002796
zfṯ to slaughter; to cut off 133940 1002797
zfṯ slaughter 133960 1002797
zfṯ butcher 133950 1002797
zfṯ butcher 854261 1002797
zfṯ.t sacrifice 133980 1002797
zfṯ.yw Butcher 134010 1002797
zfzf to break 133860 1002797
zfzf bad slaughter 133850 1002797
zmn natron [element used during the ritual] 135070 1002811
zmn to linger?; to remain? 135080 1001349
zmn to examine (the quality of bread) 450451 1001349
zmꜣ to beget 134220 1002814
zmꜣ to unite; to join 134180 1002814
zmꜣ to eat 859249 1002814
zmꜣ lung 134170 1002814
zmꜣ Unifier 134230 1002814
zmꜣ bed 134280 1002814
zmꜣ.y compeer 134580 1002814
zmꜣ.yt band; troop 134600 1002814
zmꜣ.yt hogging beam? 134620 1002814
zmꜣ.yw confederates; associates; enemies 134610 1002814
zmꜣ.w combination; alloy (in reference to metals) 134680 1002814
zmꜣ.w branches; twigs 134450 1002814
zmꜣ.wj darkness 134740 1002814
zmꜣ.wtj [characteristic of a king] 134710 1002814
zmꜣ.wtj confederate 134720 1002814
zmꜣ.t [throne] 134310 1002814
zmꜣ.tj Compeer 861285 1002814
zmꜣ.tj testicles 134320 1002814
zmꜣ.tj road; path 134350 1002814
zmy.t desert; necropolis 134780 1002812
zmy.tj One who belongs to the two deserts 500423 1002812
zmzr.w [a gate] 855515 1002813
zn plowshare 136140 1002819
zn cutting edge (of the sword)?; sharpening? 850921 1002819
zn to open 136070 1002819
zn.yw those who passed away 136650 1002819
zn.t senet (board game) 136150 1002819
zn.tj likeness 136180 1002819
znḭ to cut off 136120 1002819
znḭ to come close to; to exceed; to resemble 136080 1002819
znḭ to pass (by); to go (by); to separate 136590 1002819
znḭ get close to; surpass; pass; happen; cut off; cut off; be similar to 854546 1002819
znb battlement 136890 1002815
znb to overthrow; to destroy 136900 1002815
znb.t rampart 136910 1002815
znbꜣ failure? 851036 1002816
znbꜣ to get out of control 137170 1002816
znf to bleed 137260 1002817
znf blood 137250 1002817
znf.yw bloody ones 500159 1002817
znḥm locust 858385 1002818
znḥm locust; grasshopper 137910 1002818
znn copy (of a document); record 137570

1002819
znn chariot soldier; warrior 137560 1002819
znn image; likeness 137580 1002819
znnj bad luck 137670 1002841
znnj to suffer; to be distressed 137660 1002841
znzn to cut through 138190 1002819
znzn.t conflagration 138100 1002819
znš to open 855474 1002820
znš gate; corner 858387 1002820
znṯ to be rebellious; to be lustful 138530 1002821
znṯ.w rebels 138610 1002821
zr double-ram gate (in heavens) 138890 1002827
zr ram 138880 1002827
zr.w pellets of incense 139130 1002826
zr.wj the two rams 856198 1002827
zr.t a decan star 138910 1002827
zr.t sheep; ewe 138900 1002827
zrm.t [beer made of dates] 139490 1002828
zrt.w knife 858394 1002829
zḥ council; counsel 140260 1002799
zḥ tent; hall 140250 1002799
zḥ.t herd of sheep (treading seed into the earth) 140270 1002801
zḥ.y counselor; man of good council 140420 1002799
zḥzḥ to rub down; to trample 141060 1002801
zḥzḥ [a bird] 141050 1002798
zḥzḥ (to sound like Zehzeh bird) 855028 1002798
zẖzẖ to run; to hurry 143040 1002800
zḥzḥ.y trampler 141080 1002801
zẖ.t blow 141420 1002803
zẖ.tj smiter (king in battle) 141430 1002803
zẖi̯ to hit; to smite; to beat 141400 1002803
zẖm sanctuary 142100 1000543
zẖn random event 142460 1002804
zẖn to unite 142450 1002804
zẖn stock? 142490 1002804
zẖn [a part of the body of an offering animal] 142470 1002804
zẖn seeker 856200 1002804
zẖn reed-float 142480 1002804
zẖn swelling 142540 1002804
zẖn.w comprehensive one 142640 1002804
zẖn.w [a kind of a prediction] 853457 1002804
zẖn.w [the name of an area] 860491 1002804
zẖn.w search 142620 1002804
zẖn.t pole; support 142500 1002804
zẖn.tj inventory 142610 1002804
zẖni̯ the one who extends 142680 1002804
zẖni̯ to embrace; to seek out; to meet 142440 1002804
zẖz to tear out (the eye of Horus); to pull up (papyrus) 142980 1002805
zẖz to run; to hurry 142990 1002800
zẖz.w runner 143000 1002800
zẖ.y deaf person 143410 1002802
zẖ.yt deaf one (woman) 855579 1002802
zẖꜣ scribe's equipment 144250 1002806
zẖꜣ to write; to paint 600375 1002806
zẖꜣ.yt writings 144670 1002806
zẖꜣ.yt female scribe 144680 1002806
zẖꜣ.w a god who writes 856031 1002806
zẖꜣ.w scribe 550055 1002806
zẖꜣ.w writing; record; depiction 450097 1002806
zẖꜣ.w scribe 855553 1002806
zẖꜣ.w writing material 600376 1002806
zẖi̯ to make deaf 550303 1002802
zẖi̯ to be deaf 854862 1002802
zẖi̯ to be deaf 143400 1002802
zz.w dust?; ashes? 143740 1002847
zz.wj the one belonging to the ashes 855601 1002847
zzi̯ to punish 856224 1002850
zzḥ to destroy (enemies) 144140 1002848
zzḥꜣ vessel (gen.) 144150 1002849

zš to open 144300 1002820
zš writing; writings 144270 1002806
zš threshold 144310 1002820
zš to spread; to strew 144320 1002820
zš to cause to pass away (e.g., anger, through the sound of the sistrum) 144350 1002831
zš a rope 144380 1002830
zš run 859855 1002831
zš to pass (by) 144330 1002831
zš marsh land; pond; nest 144360 1002833
zš.w swamp fowl 144430 1002833
zši̯ to tear out; to pull out 850590 1002832
zšj to nest 144660 1002833
zšp polisher 144840 1002835
zšp to polish; to smooth 144830 1002835
zšn lotus blossom 145220 1002834
zšn lotus flower application (made of copper) 865373 1002834
zšn.t lotus pond 856199 1002834
zšn.t lotus-bark [a kind of a boat] 145440 1002834
zšnn Lotus flower 145390 1002834
zšzš.t a rope 145590 1002837
zšš one who rattles 500365 1002836
zšš to tear out (papyrus) 145600 1002832
zšš sistrum 859774 1002836
zšš to play the sistrum 145610 1002836
zšš.t sistrum 145620 1002836
zk to dig out (a pool) 146380 1002809
zkn to be greedy 858372 1002133
zkr to journey? 146900 1002810
zkzk [a snake] 146970 1002809

s

s [a goose] 125090 1002000
s folded cloth 856026 1002002
s.t [in abstract sense] 125140 1002003
s.t throne 400492 1002003
s.t residence 400493 1002003
s.t place; seat; position (rank) 125100 1002003
s.t place; seat; position (rank); throne; living place 854540 1002003
s.tj successor; deputy 125120 1002003
s.tjt successor? 125130 1002003
sꜣ outside 125680 1002378
sꜣ stall; byre 125710 1002378
sꜣ back; back (of something) 125670 1002378
sꜣ after 600052 1002378
sꜣ flush (of water) 125980 1002378
sꜣ to lay on back? 125790 1002378
sꜣ wall 858698 1002378
sꜣ.w divided by cutting? 866969 1002401
sꜣ.w satiety 126440 1002393
sꜣ.wj gold two-thirds fine 125880 1002380
sꜣ.wt building ("walls") 125890 1002378
sꜣ.t prudence; wisdom 850780 1002409
sꜣ.t satiety 125840 1002393
sꜣ.t wall 125800 1002378
sꜣꜣ the wise one 126220 1002409
sꜣꜣ the wise one 853654 1002409
sꜣꜣ wise man 126170 1002409
sꜣꜣ wisdom 851310 1002409
sꜣꜣ to be wise; to be prudent; to understand 126160 1002409
sꜣi̯ to be sated; to sate 126200 1002393
sꜣi̯ to prepare; to equip 650033 1002393
sꜣw [part of a construction] 126450 1002407
sꜣwi̯ to gladden 126530 1002917
sꜣwi̯ to keep an eye on 126540 1002917
sꜣwi̯ to lengthen; to gladden 126520 1002917
sꜣp to create a pond 126730 1002397
sꜣp.t lotus leaf 126740 1002397
sꜣp.t incense holder (in the form of a lotus leaf) 860926 1002397
sꜣb to make tarry 126630 1002867
sꜣb colorful 126650 1002387
sꜣb.w [a bird with colorful plumage] 126720 1002387
sꜣb.t speckled snake 126680 1002387
sꜣb.t dappled cow 126670 1002387
sꜣbi̯ to gladden (the heart) 126640 1002871
sꜣm to let burn up 126750 1002898
sꜣm.t disheveled hair (a sign of mourning) 126780 1002395

sȝhd to cause to quake 126940 1002891
sȝhh.w grumbler? 126930 1002890
sȝḥ neighbors 126990 1002391
sȝḥ (human) toe 126950 1002391
sȝḥ to endow 127000 1002391
sȝḥ framework 127050 1002391
sȝḥ toes 126960 1002391
sȝḥ grant of land 127010 1002391
sȝḥ to reach; to arrive (at a place) 126980 1002391
sȝḥ.yt those who approach 127090 1002391
sȝḥ.t in the vicinity of 65440 1002391
sȝḫ to ram (the neck vertebra) 127100 1002859
sȝḫ knife 127130 1002859
sȝḫ to glorify; to make excellent 127110 1002885
sȝḫ spiritual state; glorified state 127120 1002885
sȝḫ.w glorification 869123 1002885
sȝḫ.w (ritual) recitations 127220 1002885
sȝḫ.t one who glorify 127160 1002885
sȝḫ.t (ritual) recitations 127150 1002885
sȝḫ.t [characteristic of a knife] 127170 1002859
sȝḫȝḫ to make green 127200 1002892
sȝḫm.w [a bat] 127230 1002392
sȝr the wise one 865547 1002409
sȝr to sieve 126840 1002401
sȝr to be wise 126800 1002409
sȝr needy man 126820 1002906
sȝr wish; need 126810 1002906
sȝr.t wish 126870 1002906
sȝr.t understanding; wisdom 126860 1002409
sȝšr.t [a pastry] 127320 1002910
sȝsȝ to drive back; to repel 127250 1002378
sȝsȝ to force (a boat over the rapids) 127270 1002378
sȝsȝ to apply (oil to someone) 127260 1002378
sȝq assembler [a divine ferryman] 127400 1002399

sȝq to pull together; to be wary of 127330 1002399
sȝq to ruin, to devastate so./sth. 127390 1002904
sȝq mat 127380 1002399
sȝq incense roaster? 127340 1002399
sȝq.tj assembler 857738 1002399
sȝq.tj [construction worker] 127430 1002399
sȝqḥ to strengthen? 127490 1002905
sȝg to cover with vegetation 127520 1002881
sȝgb to irrigate 127530 1002883
sȝt dirt 127590 1002405
sȝt to be dislocated (med.) 127560 1002406
sȝt to defile 127570 1002405
sȝṯ cargo boat; tow boat 127640 1002404
sȝd to strangulate 127670 1002390
sj to limp? 127800 1002114
sjȝ knowledge (personification) 500191 1002125
sjȝ to recognize; to perceive 127840 1002125
sjȝ perception; mind 127850 1002125
sjȝ.w [sacred falcon] 127920 1002123
sjȝ.t [a bird-shaped amulet] 127900 1002123
sjȝ.t [a fringed cloth of linen] 127890 1002124
sjȝ.tj the one with a fringed cloth 856069 1002124
sjȝm to make well-disposed 128310 1001188
sjȝṯ to cheat; to mutilate (somebody) 127960 1001196
sjȝṯ.j cheater; mutilator 127970 1001196
sjȝṯj [sacred leg of Osiris] 127980 1001196
sjʿr to make ascend; to present 128000 1001209
sjʿr.t [epithet of the snake goddess of Buto; uraeus] 128010 1001209
sjw [a waterway in the heavens]) 128060 1001137
sjwi̯ to say something loudly 128050 1001132

sjwꜥ throne 859471 1001158
sjwꜥ to inherit something 128080 1001158
sjwr to make pregnant; to make conceive 128090 1001148
sjwr.tj one who is engendered 857670 1001148
sjwḥ to be violent 128120 1001136
sjwḥ to flood 128110 1001137
sjbꜣ make dance 861020 1000953
sjp to assign; to revise; to inspect 128130 1001066
sjp to deliver 97121 1001066
sjp inspection; inventory 128140 1001066
sjp to transfer; to deliver; to revise; to examine; to visit 854525 1001066
sjp.tj inspection; inventory 128160 1001066
sjp.tj inventory; register 858645 1001066
sjpp to examine 854810 1001066
sjf to insult 128260 1002116
sjft [a kind of jar] 128290 1002069
sjm fog, haze, humidity (or sim.) 128300 1002117
sjn the fast one 128380 1002119
sjn to run; to hurry; to bring (something) quickly 128370 1002119
sjn courier 128430 1002119
sjn clay (material for seals) 128340 1002118
sjn hurry 854358 1002119
sjn.t canoe (fast-moving boat) 128400 1002119
sjn.t sealing (of clay); clay vessel 128410 1002118
sjni̯ to wait 128360 1001040
sjnm to devour 128480 1001043
sjnd to make sad 128490 1001033
sjr [activity connected with the heart] 128500 1002120
sjhm to restrain; to refrain 851873 1000987
sjs six 128520 1002121
sjs.j six-weave linen 128530 1002121
sjs.w house of six chambers? 857784 1002121
sjs.nwt Sixth-day festival 857783 1002121
sjsj to hurry 128560 1002807
sjtj trial (when calculating) 171100 1002122
sjṯn to subordinate?, to compel? 128630 1001121
sjṯn.w to be rebellious 869129 1001121
sjzj to lessen (a burden) 128550 1001166
sjqr to enrich; to make excellent 128590 1001074
sjkn to destroy 128600 1000998
sjd tray; tray with a "heap" (of bread) 128650 1002115
sjdi̯ to mortify; to make powerless 128640 1000961
sꜥꜣ great 128670 1003078
sꜥꜣ to tremble 128710 1000303
sꜥꜣ pregnancy (amniotic sac) 856445 1003078
sꜥꜣ gunwale; thole board 128690 1003070
sꜥꜣ frightening 128680 1003078
sꜥꜣi̯ to make great; to increase 128660 1003078
sꜥwꜣ to let ferment 128740 1003067
sꜥb to saw off (wood); to castrate (cattle) 128760 1002415
sꜥb castrated bull 128770 1002415
sꜥb to equip; to adorn 128780 1002942
sꜥb to cleanse; to purify 128750 1002932
sꜥb ornament 128790 1002942
sꜥbꜣ to instruct 857653 1002942
sꜥbꜣ to be frightened (fig.) 128810 1002942
sꜥpi̯ to allow to pass by 128820 1003030
sꜥfn to cover; to veil 857654 1002966
sꜥm to inlay; to overlay (with gold) 128850 1002994
sꜥm to swallow; to wash down (medicine) 128840 1002994
sꜥm.w remedy to be swallowed 862961 1002994
sꜥn.w Glorifying one 853997 1003024
sꜥni̯ to embellish 128900 1003024
sꜥnḫ to sculpt 128930 1003022
sꜥnḫ to make live; to perpetuate; to nourish

128910 1003022
sꜥnḫ one who sustains 128940 1003022
sꜥnḫ sculptor 128920 1003022
sꜥnḫ endowment; revernue 128950 1003022
sꜥnḫ.w Life sustainer 851895 1003022
sꜥnḫ.t she who preserves (maat) 128960 1003022
sꜥnḏ narrowing; reduction; decrease 863022 1003017
sꜥnḏ to lessen 128970 1003017
sꜥr [a constellation] 129010 1001209
sꜥr to make ascend 128980 1001209
sꜥr scrub country?; barley field? 129000 1002418
sꜥr.t wool 129060 1002420
sꜥry ewer on a stand 129020 1001209
sꜥrq to destroy (enemies) 129040 1003044
sꜥrq to complete; to end 129030 1003044
sꜥrq Wring out (laundry) 129050 1003044
sꜥḥ mummy; form 129130 1002416
sꜥḥ to mark; to wrap in bandages; to be venerated 129110 1002416
sꜥḥ bandage (around the head) 129100 1002416
sꜥḥ noble; dignitary 129120 1002416
sꜥḥ rank; dignity 129070 1002416
sꜥḥ [special neck ornament of the high priests of Memphis] 129090 1002416
sꜥḥ.tj the two noble ones (Isis and Nephthys) 129150 1002416
sꜥḥꜣ make ready for battle; let fight 852719 1002988
sꜥḥꜥ to erect; to set up; to make stand 129190 1002990
sꜥẖ to burn up 129230 1002979
sꜥẖi̯ to make rise (the heavens) 129220 1002981
sꜥšꜣ policeman; escort 129280 1003056
sꜥšꜣ to repel 129270 1003056
sꜥšꜣ protective rite 129290 1003056
sꜥšꜣ to make numerous; to multiply 129260 1003060
sꜥšꜣ.w mass of people 858699 1003060
sꜥsꜥ to damage? 129240 1002414
sꜥgꜣ to make capsize 129360 1002974
sꜥḳ [designation of the temple porter] 129320 1003034
sꜥḳ to make enter; to send in 129310 1003034
sꜥḳ something at the beginning? 861169 1003034
sꜥḳ.y recruit?; conscript? 129350 1003034
sꜥḳꜣ to direct; to set on the way 129340 1003036
sꜥḏ to make hale 129380 1002948
sꜥḏꜣ to ruin 129390 1002960
sw 1/16 arure (area measurement) 863861 1002341
sw time; day; date 129450 1002348
sw day (of the month, in dates) 129460 1002348
sw time; day; date; day of the month 854542 1002348
sw [a plant] 129470 1002340
sw.t danger? 129620 1002343
sw.t sedge plant 129610 1002340
sw.t a piece of meat (of beef, as an offering) 129630 1002342
swꜣ.w passer by (a demon) 129830 1002765
swꜣ.w journey 29300 1002765
swꜣ.w district; area; vicinity 129790 1002765
swꜣ.wt passer by (a female demon) 855623 1002765
swꜣ.t past 129770 1002765
swꜣ.tjw ones who pass by (stellar gods) 129820 1002765
swꜣi̯ to pass 129740 1002765
swꜣi̯ keep (sb./sth.) away 129800 1002765
swꜣjt [a piece of meat] 129810 1002342
swꜣḥ to make endure; to endure 129860 1002763
swꜣḏi̯ to make green; to refresh 129890 1002764
swꜣš to pay honor to; to praise 129900 1002771
swꜣḏ to make green; to make prosper 129930 1002761

sw3ḏw3ḏ to make green 129960 1002761
swy [a name for a crocodile] 129980 1002370
swꜥi̯ to leave alone 130000 1002775
swꜥb to cleanse; to purify 130010 1002777
swꜥb [designation for natron] 130020 1002777
sww to be harmful 129520 1002343
swb3 to open (someone's face) 130040 1002610
swbb to draw back 130060 1002351
swbẖ to shine; to illuminate 857996 1002605
swbg make blossom 130070 1002604
swmt to make thick 130080 1002674
swn one who suffer; needy one 853383 1002841
swn to open 130130 1002679
swn to know of something 130140 1002365
swn to trade; to buy 130110 1002366
swn compliment; flattery 859730 1002364
swn to recognize 130150 1002365
swn condition? 852791 1002693
swn.yt the suffering 130230 1002841
swn.w fish pond 130190 1002363
swn.w tower; fortress 130170 1002362
swn.t trade; price 130160 1002366
swni̯ to drive on?; to make hurry? 850325 1002689
swnf to make (the heart) rejoice 130340 1002685
swnwn flattery 130330 1002364
swnwn to flatter 130320 1002364
swnn [epithet of Horus] 130350 1002365
swr [chariot equipment] 130450 1002367
swr to increase; to make great 130430 1002712
swr.t barrel bead (of carnelian) (an amulet) 130470 1002368
swrḥ to anoint 130500 1002709
swrḏ to make (someone) weary 130520 1002707
swh3 to break (naut.) 650021 1002357
swhi̯ to praise; to yell 130540 1002356
swḥ to enwrap 130570 1002354
swḥ a kind of garment 130560 1002354
swḥ wind 130600 1002355
swḥ.t egg 130630 1002353
swḥ.t (inner) coffin 130650 1002353
swẖ evening offering? 851131 1002642
swẖ3 to spend the night 130680 1002642
swẖ3 to talk wrong; invalidity; ineffectiveness 851604 1002661
swẖ3 to harm 130690 1002661
swsẖ to widen; to extend 130740 1002723
swsr to make strong; to make rich 130730 1002734
swšr to parch; to dry 130790 1002735
swšr.w drying; drying agent 861722 1002735
swg3 to be foolish 130800 1002352
swg3 underaged child 130810 1002352
swgm powder; grind 855631 1002636
swgg to deprive (someone of something); to damage 130820 1002634
swt embalmed? [epithet of Osiris] 130880 1002744
swt gust of wind 130850 1002369
swti̯ to make great 130860 1002747
swtwt to walk about; to travel 130890 1002745
swtwt journey 600319 1002745
swḏ to hand over; to bequeath 130950 1002611
swḏ3 notification; communication 852937 1002627
swḏ3 to make whole; to protect 130960 1002627
swḏ3 to convey; to go 130970 1002628
swḏ3 protective spell 857716 1002627
swḏ3 to pass away (to die) 130980 1002628
swḏb to bring back; to answer 869216 1002612
swḏb to wound; to twine 852149 1002612
swdf to delay; to make (someone) wait 130930 1002615

swdn to give oneself airs? 130940 1002623
swdwd to bandage; to wrap 130920 1002619
sb [edible part of cattle] 131090 1002006
sb.t reed 131120 1002008
sbꜣ to learn 131220 1002028
sbꜣ star 131180 1002027
sbꜣ sun shade 131270 1002027
sbꜣ star amulet 854091 1002027
sbꜣ to teach; to tend 131210 1002028
sbꜣ surveying instrument? 131240 1002028
sbꜣ door; doorway; portal 131200 1002026
sbꜣ pupil 131230 1002028
sbꜣ wise; smart 856678 1002028
sbꜣ.y he of the portal 500386 1002026
sbꜣ.yw the starry ones 131400 1002027
sbꜣ.yt the starry one 131380 1002027
sbꜣ.yt [observation instrument] 863201 1002028
sbꜣ.yt teaching; instruction; punishment 131390 1002028
sbꜣ.w teaching 131330 1002028
sbꜣ.w teacher; instructor 131320 1002028
sbꜣ.wtj teacher 860917 1002028
sbꜣ.wtj the punisher? 131420 1002028
sbꜣ.t gate 869219 1002026
sbꜣ.t star 131280 1002027
sbꜣ.tj pupil 131310 1002028
sbꜣy to be star-like; to sparkle like a star 131370 1002027
sbꜣg to make weary 869222 1000121
sbꜣgi̯ to make weary 131450 1000121
sbꜣḳ Illuminating one 861298 1000129
sbꜣḳ to look at (god) 855476 1000129
sbꜣḳ to make bright; to make serene 131430 1000129
sbꜣḳ.t heavenly eye (sun, moon) 132160 1000129
sbꜣḳḳ to substantiate; to witness; certify; to commend 131440 1000129
sby.t head wind 131570 1002017
sbꜥḥi̯ to make abundant 131690 1000140
sbwꜣ to raise (up) 131720 1000100
sbj joke 853499 1002794
sbj to rebel against 131520 1002017
sbj rebel 131530 1002017
sbj.w hostility 131610 1002017
sbj.t outrage 131560 1002017
sbj.t rebels 131550 1002017
sbjn to alienate; to talk down 131680 1000040
sbbꜣ.yw instructor 131740 1002028
sbn bandage (especially of mummies) 131770 1002018
sbn to crown 131780 1002606
sbn.t nursing cow; breastfeeding one 131820 1000054
sbnj to make pleasant 131850 1000062
sbnn to fertilize 131810 1000116
sbnn.wt virility 857658 1000116
sbr shoots (of a tree); clusters (of grapes) 131870 1002023
sbhꜣ to make to flee 131890 1000032
sbḥ wind 140630 1002013
sbḥ cry; shriek 131910 1002013
sbḥ to cry out 131900 1002013
sbẖ to spread (poison in the limbs) 131960 1002014
sbẖ pot 131950 1002014
sbẖ to enclose (with the arms); to enfold (in the arms) 131940 1002014
sbẖ.t portal; portico 131970 1002014
sbẖ.t pylon-shaped pectoral amulet 131980 1002014
sbẖ.tj he who belongs to the portal 132000 1002014
sbẖn mat 132010 1000028
sbš to make vomit; become clear, sober 132060 1000083
sbš.w something disgusting; emetic 132090 1000083
sbgs to hurt; to damage 132230 1000015
sbkꜣ to make pregnant 132190 1000049
sbḳ splendid; wise 401163 1002022
sbḳ wise one 501137 1002022
sbḳ leg 132110 1002021
sbḳ to become knowing; to be wise 132120 1002022

sbt.t flower 132240 1002024
sbtj wall; rampart 132260 1002025
sbtty.t [a kind of a plant] 132250 1002024
sbdš to make weak 132290 1000010
spꜣ.w swarm (birds) 132700 1001827
spꜣ.t nome; district 132420 1002239
spꜣ.t nome; district 132430 1002239
spꜣ.t nome; district; estate district; desert 854544 1002239
spꜣ.tj what belongs to a nome 854859 1002239
spꜣi̯ to make fly 132670 1001827
spꜣḫd to turn upside down 856050 1001826
spḥ to attain 132970 1001771
spḥ to postpone, to avert (death) 132960 1001771
spḥ to lasso 132950 1002227
spi̯ to bind together (a papyrus boat or skiff) 132750 1002227
spnᶜ to overturn 132800 1001787
spr rib 132820 1002230
spr sheet (of metal) 132860 1002231
spr to appeal to 132840 1002232
spr [a vegetable] 132850 1002229
spr to arrive at; to reach 132830 1002232
spr achieve (to do); ability (to do); [modal] 852612 1002232
spr.w petitioner 132900 1002232
spr.w request 132890 1002232
spr.wt ship's rib? 132920 1002230
spr.t plea; petition 132870 1002232
spr.tj petitioner 132880 1002232
spri̯ to make come out 132930 1001795
spḥ.w lasso catcher (demon) 133000 1002227
spḥ.w lasso 132990 1002227
spḥ.t ribs (of the deceased, of an offering animal) 132980 1002227
spẖꜣ to purge; to make (the skin) sleek? 133010 1001777
spẖr to copy; to register; to draw 133040 1001774
spẖr to brandish (weapons); to cause to circulate (the wind) 133030 1001774
spẖr.w writing; record 133050 1001774
sps to build 133110 1002233
sps to dance 133100 1002234
spt to slaughter 133150 1002238
sptẖ to make writhe (on the ground, like a snake) 133160 1001815
sptẖ.w serpent; reptile 133170 1001815
spd to be sharp; to make sharp 500142 1002226
spd efficacious one (sun god) 133290 1002226
spd sharp; skilled 133190 1002226
spd [a kind of an object] 133210 1002226
spd to be effective; to be skilled 500143 1002226
spd efficacy? 133280 1002226
spd provision; grain ration 133240 1002226
spd [a kind of a wood] 133260 1002226
spd sharp 133180 1002226
spd.w the sharp one 855077 1002226
spd.w sharpness 857835 1002226
spd.t triangle 133300 1002226
spd.t efficacy 851287 1002226
spd.t [women in the entourage of a goddess] 133320 1002226
spdd to equip 133370 1002226
sf yesterday 851674 1002062
sf yesterday 133440 1002062
sf.t friendliness; mildness 133500 1002796
sfꜣ to hate 133520 1002072
sfꜣ to neglect; to be slow 133530 1002072
sfꜣ.t hatred 133560 1002072
sfꜣ.w hated; something you don't want to eat 874520 1002072
sfi̯ to mix 133580 1002065
sfy child; lad; son 133600 1002071
sfn to cause trouble 133650 1000344
sfn.w annoying 133660 1000344
sfr griffin 133730 1002254
sfẖ seven 133760 1002064
sfẖ waste 133820 1000340
sfẖ what is laid aside; offering 133790 1000340
sfẖ to loosen; to release 133780 1000340

sfẖ [ceremony of the mortuary cult] 97050 1000340
sfẖ excretion; urine 133800 1000340
sfẖ strap (of sandals) 133830 1000340
sfẖ.y watch; guardhouse 133840 1000340
sfẖ.wj seven wave cloth 857771 1002064
sfẖ.nw seventh 854324 1002064
sfẖ.t excretion; urine 857661 1000340
sfẖfẖ to release 857662 1000340
sfẖẖ to loosen; to release 852044 1000340
sfsf ashes 133880 1002061
sfsf to offer [water] 133890 1002065
sfsf to burn 133870 1002061
sfg to be hidden 133920 1000340
sfkk [verb (to suffer? to punish?)] 133910 1000358
sfṯ [one of the seven sacred oils] 133990 1002069
sm pleasure 854837 1002144
sm situation? 853500 1002144
sm deed; event; pastime 134050 1002144
sm occasion? attention? worry? 134060 1002144
sm altar 134090 1002144
sm to respect 134030 1002144
sm high priest of Ptah at Memphis 134080 1002144
sm image; likeness 134100 1002144
sm sem-priest 134020 1002144
sm sem-priest 856043 1002144
sm to respect; to provide; to help 854545 1002144
sm to be happy 134070 1002144
sm to help; to provide 134040 1002144
sm.y weeded 134940 1002141
sm.y respected one 134790 1002144
sm.w plants; vegetables; pasture 134140 1002141
sm.wj one who belongs to the plants 500646 1002141
sm.wj [a kind of a priest] 134150 1002144
sm.t straw mat 134120 1002141
sm.t respect 134130 1002144
smꜣ wild bull 854781 1002175
smꜣ scalp; temple (of the head) 134360 1002175
smꜣ sacrifice; sacrificial steer 134380 1002175
smꜣ stolist 852746 1002174
smꜣ wild bull 134390 1002175
smꜣ to slaughter 134370 1002175
smꜣ.t wild cow 134440 1002175
smꜣ.t killing knife 856077 1002175
smꜣ.t wild cow 134430 1002175
smꜣ.tj stolist 860895 1002174
smꜣꜣ to make see 134570 1001496
smꜣꜥ to do right; to put in order; to correct 134630 1001499
smꜣꜥ to pray (to) 134640 1001499
smꜣꜥ prayer(s) 134650 1001499
smꜣwi̯ to renew; to renovate 134750 1001492
smꜣr to impoverish 134770 1001485
smj reporter 134810 1002156
smj whips 134930 1002157
smj shouting (of the infant) 134910 1002156
smj report; accusation 134830 1002156
smj to report 134820 1002156
smj cream; soured milk 134840 1002155
smj.w cordage 134920 1001318
smj.w [a god's bark] 134900 1002814
smj.t indictment 851903 1002156
smj.tj regulator 134880 1002156
smy.t the one who prosecutes 134890 1002156
smjn natron 134960 1002811
smꜥ rope (from plant fibers) 135000 1002177
smꜥ stake (for pushing the ship) 134980 1002177
smꜥ to push 860824 1002177
smꜥ [term for the legs of the falcon ("stake")] 134990 1002177
smꜥ.t staff [a scepter] 135010 1002177
smꜥr to cleanse; to make fortunate; to dress 135020 1001503
smwn probably; surely 135040 1002172

smn image (of a god) 135150 1001349
smn to resign from office 135210 1001349
smn to stay; to dwell; to last 135110 1001349
smn value; price (of grain) 135160 1001349
smn to stay; to remain 851677 1001349
smn order; attachment; fixture 135120 1001349
smn Nile goose 135180 1002160
smn to make firm; to make endure; to establish 135100 1001349
smn [designation for offering] 135170 1001349
smn.w rungs of the ladder 135270 1001349
smn.w supports (of the sky) 135280 1001349
smn.t lioness 135220 1002161
smn.t sky; heaven 865235 1001349
smn.t establishment 135230 1001349
smn.tj explorer; prospector 135250 1001349
smn.tjt mourning woman 857574 1002162
smn.tjt mourning woman 135260 1002162
smnw ordinance? 135330 1001349
smnmn to make move 135340 1001348
smnn to establish; to erect; to fasten; to fix 854830 1001349
smnḫ to make excellent; to make effective; to embellish; to endow 135360 1001358
smnḫ appearance, shape (of the moon) 135370 1001358
smnḫ.t Semenkhet (one who makes excellent) 135380 1001358
smnḫ.t food; offerings 135390 1001358
smr friend; courtier 856044 1002164
smr friend; courtier 135420 1002164
smr to cause pain; to make ill 135440 1001401
smr.t friend; companion (the queen) 135480 1002164
smr.t female friend 869276 1002164
smhi̯ to cause to forget 135500 1001307
smḥ [large transport ship] 135530 1001305
smḥ to finish; to complete a boat 135520 1001305
smḥ branch 135540 1001305
smḥ [a kind of a ship] 856080 1001305
smḥ.j left; left side 135580 1002152
smḥ.j left hand 135590 1002152
smḥ.j left 600521 1002152
smḥi̯ [an action concerning the ship] 859472 1001305
smḥi̯ to water; to flood; to let swim 135570 1001305
smḫ to forget; to ignore 135600 1000543
smḫꜣ to correct (a manuscript) 135620 1000543
smz to go (somewhere) 135630 1001471
sms mallet 135640 1002167
sms nestling 135670 1001430
sms [a cut of beef] 135650 1002165
sms to be old; to become old 135730 1002168
sms seniority 135660 1002168
sms.yt she who delivers 135710 1001430
sms.w the oldest one 500187 1002168
sms.w oldest; older 135720 1002168
sms.w creation 856048 1001430
sms.w elder 856128 1002168
sms.w elder 400263 1002168
sms.w elder 852249 1002168
sms.w the older one 861521 1002168
sms.t the old one 869285 1002168
sms.t the eldest (daughter) 135690 1002168
smsi̯ to deliver; to create 135700 1001430
smswn [myrrh vessel] 135740 1002170
smswn libation water 135750 1002170
smsm to praise 135780 1002144
smsm the oldest 135760 1002168
smšr to spend the evening; to have dinner 135810 1001438
smk.t beam; girder 135830 1002158
smt The hearing one 135890 1002171
smt to hear; to overhear 135840 1002171
smt.t The hearing one (Spy) 856082 1002171

smtmt listen, listen around 135930 1002171
smtr to examine; to make inquiry 135940 1001462
smtr judge (or similar) 135900 1001462
smtr inquiry; interrogation 135950 1001462
smd [a star] 135990 1002146
smd sistrum 136000 1002150
smd eyebrow 135970 1002148
smḏ to make deep 136060 1001284
smd.t beads 136040 1002147
smd.t personnel; staff; underlings 136030 1002149
smd.t something written at the edge 136020 1002148
smd.t workplace?; service? 136050 1002149
smd.t slab 136010 1002151
smḏd to make obedient 600635 1001285
sn to join 136220 1002183
sn two-pronged fork 136200 1002183
sn brother 136230 1002183
sn to smell; to kiss 136240 1002188
sn.w siblings 136310 1002183
sn.w gift (from the field) 136350 1002181
sn.w bread; offerings 136340 1002181
sn.w tongue 136360 1001654
sn.w two 136210 1002183
sn.w doors; gates 136370 1002183
sn.wj The two (two gods as a couple) 853665 1002183
sn.wj twin calves 136390 1002183
sn.wj the two; the two contenders 136380 1002183
sn.wt brethren; siblings 136800 1002183
sn.wt serpentine 136440 1002187
sn.wt offerings? 136470 1002181
sn.wt senu-sanctuary 136430 1002187
sn.nw to be second 136500 1002183
sn.nw the second 136480 1002183
sn.nw second best; inferior 136490 1002183
sn.nw second (companion, fellow); replica 550359 1002183
sn.nwt companion 857809 1002183
sn.t sister; beloved 136260 1002183
sn.t polishing stone 136270 1002187
sn.t flag pole 136280 1002184
sn.tj the two sisters (mostly Isis and. Nephthys) 851924 1002183
sn.tj testicles 136300 1002183
sni̯ to loosen; to free oneself from something 136630 1002202
snjk to destroy 136680 1001596
snꜥi̯ to be mobile 136690 1001754
snꜥꜥ powder? (i.e., something ground fine); mixture 450172 1002925
snꜥꜥ to make smooth; to grind 136700 1002925
snꜥḫ.w angler 136720 1002221
snꜥḫ.t fishhook 136710 1002221
snꜥš to strengthen 865238 1001758
snw poverty 136740 1002202
snw to free oneself from someone 136730 1002202
snw [a pleasant-smelling plant] 136760 1002188
snwꜣ to see 136750 1001742
snwr to make tremble (med.) (or similar) 136830 1001737
snwḥ to make drunk 136840 1001732
snwḥ to impassion 136850 1001732
snwẖ to boil; to burn 136860 1001731
snwḏ to thrust aside 136880 1001728
snb to burn 137000 1002815
snb to heal 136940 1002193
snb to be healthy; to heal 851676 1002193
snb to build 137030 1002815
snb air; breath 137040 1002193
snb to be healthy 136930 1002193
snb fringe 136960 1002190
snb [a plant associated with Lower Egypt (papyrus?)] 136970 1002190
snb ḥealth 136950 1002193
snb.t heaven; sky 137080 1002192
snb.t [a boat (papyrus skiff)] 137090 1001120
snbꜣbꜣ to make restless? 137180 1000054
snbb to exchange greetings 137190 1002193

snbb to cool (by the wind) 137200 1002193
snf one which makes you breathe 855995 1001536
snf previous year 137300 1002198
snfi̯ to let breathe; to comfort 137270 1001536
snfi̯ to empty; to unload 137280 1001536
snfr ornamentation 137360 1001542
snfr to make beautiful; to embellish 137350 1001542
snfḫfḫ to loosen; to release 137390 1000340
snm to be sad 137420 1001616
snm to grab 137430 1001610
snm flood of rain 137440 1002208
snm greed 137410 1002692
snm to feed (someone); to consume (food); to eat 137400 1002692
snm mourning; grief 500524 1001616
snm.w food supply 137490 1002692
snm.t food supply 137470 1002692
snmḥ prayer 137540 1001612
snmḥ [fraud on the scales] 137520 1001612
snmḥ to pray; to make supplication 137530 1001612
snn.wt veneration 137650 1002188
snni̯ to calm; to soothe 137630 1001630
snr.tj sudden blindness? 137730 1001645
snri̯ to terrify 137710 1001645
snrw = slw [basket, or sim.] 137720 1001880
snh registry; revision 137770 1001574
snh.t the registrant? 137750 1001574
snhi̯ to register; to assemble (i.e. to muster (troops)) 137760 1001574
snhp to promote sexual activity 137800 1001581
snhp to set in motion (med.) 137790 1001581
snhmhm to rejoice 137810 1000549
snhzi̯ to wake 137820 1001591
snhd cause to palpitate? 137830 1001565
snḥ to tie up; to fetter 137850 1002199
snḥ fetter(s) 500330 1002199
snḥ.tt fettering 137890 1002199
snḥꜣ to frustrate?; to make dangerous 137900 1001593
snḥm to prevent 137920 1001576
snḫ to bring up (a child); to make young; cause to be protected 137930 1001569
snḫy.t age 137950 1001569
snḫbḫb to draw back (the door bolt) 137960 1000457
snḫn to make young; to educate 137970 1001577
snḫn to guide (so. with sayings) 137980 1001577
snḫn.w rejuvenating one 856049 1001577
snḫḫ to rejuvenate 138000 1001569
snḫt to make strong; to strengthen 138010 1001589
snḫt.w stiffness (med.) 138020 1001589
snẖ.t phlegm 138040 1001573
snẖꜣẖꜣ to disturb 138050 1000860
sns hairdresser? 138060 1002212
sns.w praise 138070 1002213
snsi̯ to worship; to praise 138090 1002213
snsn to smell; to breathe 138130 1002188
snsn to associate with; to fraternize 138150 1002183
snsn rotten; stink (from the corpse) 138170 1002188
snsn brotherhood (characterization of the relationship between rulers) 138160 1002183
snsn to worship 138110 1002213
snsn praise 138120 1002213
snsn close friend 138180 1002183
snsn breathe 138140 1002188
snsn.t smell; perfume 138210 1002188
snš to unstopp (the ears) 138230 1001651
snšn to frighten 138260 1002203
snšmšm to sharpen 138250 1002145
snšnš to extricate (oneself) 138270 1002203
snq breast (of a nurse) 137160 1002211
snq to suckle 138280 1002211
snk the dark one 138360 1002207

snk to be dark 138350 1002207
snk to sink (into darkness) 138330 1002207
snk greed (of water) 138380 1002207
snk.y dark one (the sun god in the netherworld) 138450 1002207
snk.w darkness 138440 1002207
snk.wj who belongs to darkness 857572 1002207
snk.t the dark one 138400 1002207
snk.t darkness 138410 1002207
snk.t longing? 852150 1002207
snk.t.t [a name of a female deity] 138430 1002207
snk.tj darkness 138420 1002207
snkn injure; damage 857674 1001605
snkn.t injury; hindrance 401300 1001605
snk(n)tj.w harmful ones [a divine being] 138480 1001605
snktkt gossip? 138490 1001261
sngꜣ to despoil 138500 1001547
snṯ custom 138560 1002215
snṯ foundation (of a temple); (ground) plan (of a temple) 138540 1002215
snṯ limbs, body 138550 1002215
snṯ.t [shrine on a cult bark] 450241 1002215
snṯ.t foundation; plan (for a building) 138580 1002215
snṯ.y deckhouse; cabin (of a cult bark) 138640 1002215
snṯi̯ to found 138620 1002215
snṯy.t body (i.e., group?) (of the dead) 138630 1002215
snṯr to cense; to purify 138650 1001709
snṯr incense 138670 1001709
snṯr censing? 138660 1001709
snṯri̯ to make divine 138690 1001709
snḏ dreadful one 138750 1002197
snḏ roast goose 138720 1002197
snḏ to fear 138730 1002197
snḏ fear 138740 1002197
snḏ.t fear 138770 1002197
snḏ.t frightening one (Hathor) 138780 1002197
snḏ.w frightened one; timid one 138790 1002197
snḏꜣḏꜣ.w [watery substance (med.)] 138810 1001535
snḏm seat; dwelling 138840 1001530
snḏm to make pleasant; to revive 138820 1001530
snḏm to make oneself comfortable; to rest 138830 1001530
snḏm to make pleasant; to rest 851678 1001530
snḏm.t one who is installed? (Hathor, as the uraeus at the forehead of the king) 138850 1001530
snḏnḏn cause to inflame 138860 1000218
snḏs diminishment; decrease; reduction 138870 1001534
sr hair (of a woman, of an animal) 138980 1002259
sr nobleman; official 138920 1002248
sr prophesier 855669 1002251
sr giraffe 138940 1002251
sr to spread 139020 1002259
sr sheep fat? 139040 1002827
sr nobleman; official 855554 1002248
sr dirt 139010 1002259
sr to visit 138970 1002252
sr tambourine-like drum 138990 1002251
sr to sever? 139180 1001995
sr to strike a drum 139000 1002251
sr to foretell; to make known 138950 1002251
sr the one who is in charge 852375 1002248
sr to cough 863037 1002251
sr.y order 860970 1002248
sr.w the noble one 857005 1002248
sr.w grey goose 139140 1002246
sr.w anklet 139240 1002259
sr.t body of magistrates 139060 1002248
sr.t metal (hair?) pin 139120 1002250
sr.t grey goose 139090 1002246
sr.t thorn; spine 139070 1002250
sr.t [srt] captive (noble) woman 139900 1002247

sr.t the noble one 860190 1002248
sri̯ to be noble; to lead; to command 138930 1002248
sry.t standard 139210 1002260
sry.t cough 139220 1002251
srw to turn 139260 1001995
srw [command to hire people] 139270 1002248
srwi̯ to remove 139300 1001995
srwẖ to foster 857845 1001991
srwẖ to foster; to treat (med.) 139310 1001991
srwḏ to make endure; to make strong 139340 1001991
srwd.t awesomeness? 139330 1001991
srwḏ.t equipment? 851109 1001991
srp.t lotus leaf 139370 1002397
srp.t lotiform fan 139360 1002397
srf the hot one 857841 1002254
srf [term for water] 139420 1002255
srf property 139400 1002255
srf to make rest; to rest 139410 1002255
srf to warm; to be warm 139380 1002254
srf warm 550417 1002254
srf to refresh 139430 1002255
srf rest; relief 650020 1002255
srf warmth 139390 1002254
srf.t rash? (as a symptom of illness) 139450 1002254
srf.t warm bread 857844 1002254
srm.t [a body of water] 139540 1001965
srmi̯ to make weep 139510 1001965
srnpi̯ to make young; to rejuvenate 139560 1001971
srẖ.y accuser 139680 1001938
srḥ.w stream? 860883 1002257
srḥ.t stalks (of onions); bunches (of onions) (as a unit of measure) 139580 1002258
srẖ [something from gods as protection against disease] 139610 1001938
srẖ [designation of Thot] 139620 1001938
srẖ (bad) reputation; accusation 139600 1001938
srẖ memorial stone 139670 1001938
srẖ reliquary 856423 1001938
srẖ to make known (information); to complain; to accuse 139590 1001938
srẖ authority 851146 1001938
srẖ palace facade; throne 139660 1001938
srs to awake; to wake up 139720 1001981
srs.t [epithet of Sachmet] 139700 1001981
srsr to proclaim; to comfort 139740 1002251
sršu̯ to make happy 139760 1001984
šršr to be disturbed; upset 859050 1000706
srḳ snow 139820 1002139
srḳ to rip open; to slay 139810 1002263
srḳ to open; to make inhale 139770 1002263
srḳ.y breather 139890 1002263
srḳ.w breathing 139880 1002263
srḳ.t Selkis 139850 1002262
srḳ.t scorpion 139870 1002262
srḳ.t Selkis (constellation in the northern sky) 139860 1002262
srd to make grow; to plant 139920 1001929
srd [a plant] 139930 1001929
srd to gleen 139910 1001929
srdd [sprout? young branch?] 139960 1001929
srdd collection 875723 1001929
srḏ to chisel; to hammer 139970 1002253
shꜣ to confound; to defraud 140050 1000882
shꜣ to damage 140020 1000882
shꜣ to confound; to defraud 140060 1000882
shꜣ satiation 140040 1002393
shꜣ to confound; to defraud 858549 1000882
shꜣ turmoil 140010 1000882
shꜣ.t drum 140080 1000882
shꜣ.tj he was made fall (Seth) 853090 1000882
shꜣi̯ to bring down; to make fall 140090 1000882
shbu̯ to abuse? 140120 1000470
shp to govern (the Two Lands) 140140 1000674
shp.w behavioral norm 140150 1000674
shru̯ to make content; to satisfy 140180 1000730

shrp to plunge; to immerse 140200 1000720
shrr peacemaker ("who makes content") 851901 1000730
shtht to dispel; to scatter 853568 1000769
shd to punish; to curb 140230 1000478
shd to punish 869357 1000478
shd.t coercion 140240 1000478
sḫ royal dome 140280 1002085
sḥꜣ.w [symptom of illness affecting the uterus] 140380 1000846
sḥꜣ.w wailers 140400 1000884
sḫꜣ.w memorandum 141700 1002109
sḫꜣ.w remembrance; memory; memorial 141690 1002109
sḥꜣ.wt group of wailers 856045 1000884
sḥꜣ.t herd of donkeys 140370 1002108
sḥꜣ.tj donkey boy 450655 1002108
sḥꜣi̯ to strip; to reveal 140390 1000886
sḥꜣbi̯ to make festive 140620 1000872
sḥꜣp to conceal 140410 1000898
sḥjḥj to scour, to roam? 141020 1000521
sḥꜥi̯ to acclaim 140460 1000920
sḥꜥꜥ to make glad 140470 1000920
sḥw grouping (of personnel); assembly 140560 1000805
sḥw collection; assemblage; summary 140550 1000805
sḥw dirt 140480 1002105
sḥw wrapping 140500 1000805
sḥwꜣ to make decay; to despair 140530 1000819
sḥwꜣ.w putrefaction product 863039 1000819
sḥwi̯ to collect; to assemble 140540 1000805
sḥwꜥ to shorten (time) 140570 1000820
sḥwn to constrict 140580 1000809
sḥwn rejuvenate (the moon) 140590 1000809
sḥwr to vilify; to reproach 140600 1000811
sḥwr curse 852704 1000811
sḥbs cover (face with balm) 140660 1000466
sḥpt embrace 140670 1000685
sḥfꜣ [wooden part of boat or house] 140680 1000506
sḥm resolution 870269 1002094
sḥm contusion 140730 1002094
sḥm to pound; to crush 140710 1002094
sḥm trituration (mixture of finely powdered substances) (med.) 140720 1002094
sḥm.y pestle 140770 1002094
sḥm.t mortar 869369 1002094
sḥmi̯ to put a stop to 140700 1000556
sḥmy.t flooding 140750 1000554
sḥmu̯ to let one become skilled 140740 1000570
sḥmsi̯ to sit; to let yourself be seated 857667 1000564
sḥn order; commission 140790 1000605
sḥn commander (Thoth) 140820 1000605
sḥn [structure associated with Min-Horus] 140850 1000605
sḥn to repel 140880 1000602
sḥn benefit; endowment; allocation 140800 1000605
sḥn crown 140870 1000605
sḥn commander; officer 140810 1000605
sḥn to command; to provide 140780 1000605
sḥn to crown; to adorn 140860 1000605
sḥn.yt product 140930 1000605
sḥn.t [structure associated with Min, with Amun] 140890 1000605
sḥn.tj one who hurry back 860652 1000602
sḥnḥn to let it retreat 140950 1000602
sḥns to narrow 140960 1000654
sḥr he who exorcises evil (protector of Osiris) 140970 1000712
sḥr to remove 856046 1000712
sḥri̯ (to drive away; to exorcise (evil); to make distant) 140980 1000712
sḥrr.t one who is removed 140990 1000712
sḥḥ to be engaged (as servant) 141010 1000521
sḥzi̯ to enchant, to invoke 141040 1000829

sḥqꜣ to install as ruler 141090 1000693
sḥqr to starve; to make hungry 141100 1000689
sḥtp [a kind of incense] 141140 1000783
sḥtp to propitiate; to please; to satisfy 141120 1000783
sḥtp offering table 141160 1000783
sḥtp [a kind of bread] 141150 1000783
sḥtp [a part of a plant] 863435 1000783
sḥtp.y the pleased one [name of the deceased Osiris] 141180 1000783
sḥtp.y arm-like censer 141170 1000783
sḥtm to destroy 141190 1000779
sḥtm.w destroyer 141210 1000779
sḥtm.wt destruction 857668 1000779
sḥd [a star] 141220 1002087
sḥd to be covered with stars 141230 1002087
sḥd.w [part of heaven] 141240 1002087
sḥḏ clearing (by burning) 141270 1000477
sḥḏ to make bright; to illuminate; to shine 141250 1000477
sḥḏ light 141260 1000477
sḥḏ inspector 856130 1000476
sḥḏ brightness 857664 1000477
sḥḏ inspector 141280 1000476
sḥḏ.w illuminator (sun god) 141320 1000477
sḥḏ.w [a symptom of illness] 141340 1000477
sḥḏ.t chest 141310 1000476
sḥḏ.t illuminator (Hathor) 141290 1000477
sḥḏ.t inspector 141300 1000476
sḥḏi̯ to punish 500435 1000485
sḥḏy.t palace; shrine (i.e. god's palace) 141360 1000477
sḥḏw.t light 141370 1000477
sḥḏw.tj He who belongs to light 500718 1000477
sḥḏn to vex 141390 1000489
sẖ.w breadth 141540 1002723
sẖ.w gallbladder 141440 1002083
sẖ.w courtyard 141550 1002723
sẖ.t field 859040 1002723
sẖ.t field; marshland; country 141480 1002723
sẖ.tj he who belongs to the marshland 141510 1002723
sẖ.tj peasant; fieldworker 141500 1002723
sẖ.tjt [cow goddess] 141520 1002723
sẖ.tjw [a kind of cattle] 141870 1002723
sẖ.tw [god of fields] 141860 1002723
sẖꜣ to remember 141620 1002109
sẖꜣ darken 141650 1002642
sẖꜣ [a piece of nautical equipment (rope?)] 141660 1002107
sẖꜣꜥ to get ready 141750 1000910
sẖꜣẖ to hasten 141760 1000880
sẖꜣẖ.tj courier 850124 1000880
sẖyi̯ to raise up 141780 1000821
sẖꜥ appearance (of gods in procession) 141800 1000920
sẖꜥi̯ to make appear; to appear 141830 1000920
sẖꜥr to enrage 141850 1000928
sẖwꜣ to deny 141920 1002106
sẖwi̯ to protect 141880 1000804
sẖwi̯ cause to protect 876563 1000804
sẖwn to dispute 141930 1000810
sẖwn.w riot 141950 1000810
sẖwzi̯ to equip 141960 1000818
sẖwd to make rich 141970 1000801
sẖbẖ to slink into 141980 1000452
sẖbẖb to cause to part 854354 1000457
sẖp to laud 142000 1002098
sẖp.w bringers (of cattle, of boxes) 142020 1000678
sẖp.wt swimmer on harpoon 142030 1000678
sẖpi̯ to conduct; to bring 141990 1000678
sẖpr offspring; ward 142060 1000682
sẖpr to create; to bring into being; to rear (a child) 142050 1000682
sẖpr.w creature 142070 1000682
sẖpr.w increment; acquisitions 600610 1000682
sẖf to write down 142080 1002089
sẖm Power 500441 1002093

sẖm sword 142150 1002093
sẖm the mighty one 854304 1002093
sẖm (divine) power; (divine) image 142140 1002093
sẖm [a kind of a building (place of worship?)] 852146 1000543
sẖm sekhem-scepter 142130 1002093
sẖm [watery area in heaven] 142120 1002090
sẖm book of spells 855216 1002093
sẖm mighty 400331 1002093
sẖm might 142180 1002093
sẖm to be mighty 142160 1002093
sẖm to founder? 142230 1000555
sẖm to play sistrum 142200 1002091
sẖm sistrum 142190 1002091
sẖm to be mighty; to prevail over 142170 1002093
sẖm to be mighty; to prevail over 851679 1002093
sẖm.yt sistrum player 142380 1002091
sẖm.w powerful beings (i.e. cult images) 142400 1002093
sẖm.wj [name for two mirrors] 142300 1002093
sẖm.t power; might 142240 1002093
sẖm.t powerful one 858646 1002093
sẖm.t [term for fire] 142270 1002093
sẖm.tj two powerful ones (the double crown) 142280 1002093
sẖm.tj mighty 142290 1002093
sẖm.tj two powerful ones 859592 1002093
sẖmjj sistrum player 142390 1002091
sẖmẖ to amuse 142410 1002095
sẖn [a divine bark] 142550 1002096
sẖn resting-place 142510 1000621
sẖn to go to law; to contend 142520 1000621
sẖn dance? 142570 1000618
sẖn.yw resting 142690 1000621
sẖn.w companion 142630 1002804
sẖn.t daybed 142600 1000621
sẖni̯ to alight; to rest; to dwell 500096 1000621
sẖni̯ to alight; to rest 851680 1000621
sẖni̯ to lie down (with so.); to sleep (with so.) 855049 1000621
sẖni̯ to alight; to bring to rest 142660 1000621
sẖnm smell 851531 1000629
sẖnš to irritate 142710 1002097
sẖnš to make stink 142700 1000655
sẖnt.jw excellent linen fabric 854822 1000657
sẖnti̯ to advance; to promote 142720 1000657
sẖnti̯ to take southwards 142740 1000657
sẖntš to make rejoice 142760 1000662
sẖr lumber; wooden utensils 850926 1002100
sẖr to overthrow; to cast down 142780 1000706
sẖr plan; condition; nature; conduct 142800 1002101
sẖr foe 142790 1000706
sẖr waste (from crops) 142820 1000706
sẖr.y counselor 861829 1002101
sẖr.y advisor 142890 1002101
sẖr. y captain; plan maker 142870 1002101
sẖr.y advisor 142880 1002101
sẖr.t overthrow, massacre 142840 1000706
sẖr.t roll of papyrus; scroll 142830 1002101
sẖrẖr to drive back (lions) 142930 1000706
sẖẖ width; breadth 142960 1002723
sẖsf to collate; check; oppose; face 854547 1000748
sẖsf collation 143020 1000748
sẖsf to collate 143010 1000748
sẖsf to oppose 143030 1000748
sẖt [a stretch of water] 143090 1002102
sẖt bird trap; net; noose 450571 1002104
sẖt brick 97070 1002103
sẖt to make ready 854548 1002104
sẖt to grasp (something) 143070 1002104
sẖt to weave; to form (bricks, in a mould) 143060 1002103
sẖt to trap (with a net, a snare) 143050 1002104

sẖt.j castrated one 143200 1002103
sẖt.j bird catcher 143180 1002104
sẖt.j weaver 143110 1002103
sẖt.j weaver 143190 1002103
sẖt.jt bird catcher 143220 1002104
sẖt.w flesh of snared wild-fowl? 143230 1002104
sẖt.t trapping place 857936 1002104
sẖti̯ to rush; to run 143210 1000761
sẖti̯ to recede 143130 1000761
sẖti̯ to take back 143120 1000761
sẖtẖt to drive back 143240 1000761
sẖd to rebuke 143280 1002088
sẖd to be upside down 143250 1000484
sẖd Upside-down walker 876569 1000484
sẖd blame 856669 1002088
sẖd.y evildoer 143290 1002088
sẖd.yt evildoer 863945 1002088
sẖd.w Those who are upside down (the damned, in the netherworld) 143300 1000484
sẖdi̯ to flow to sth. 143270 1000484
sẖdi̯ to make sail northwards 143260 1000484
sẖdẖd to be upside down 143310 1000484
sẖ.t barley [a kind of a cereal] 143330 1002082
sẖ.t [a kind of a beverage] 143340 1002081
sẖꜣ to pull 143360 1002111
sẖꜣ.t (to pull?) 143370 1002111
sẖꜣꜣ to land (a boat); to row 450518 1002111
sẖꜣk to strain; to squeeze out 143390 1002110
sẖꜥ to gild 143440 1002113
sẖꜥ [an amuletic pendant?] 143460 1002113
sẖꜥ Hare (Seth) 855191 1002112
sẖꜥ dagger 143450 1002413
sẖꜥ.t hare 143470 1002112
sẖb to swallow (something liquid); to quaff 143480 1002086
sẖb.w drinking portion 143490 1002086
sẖpn to fatten (cattle) 142040 1000679
sẖm to be hasty; to be impetuous 143540 1002092
sẖnn to arouse; to stir up 143580 1000639
sẖnn to make decompose (med.) 143600 1000639
sẖnn ruin? 143610 1000639
sẖnk.t sieve 143620 1002110
sẖrd to rejuvenate 143690 1000710
sẖkr to decorate; to adorn 143700 1000529
szꜣi̯ to discard (clothing) 143770 1002856
szwnu̯ to destroy; to punish 143890 1002841
szwr to soak 143900 1002842
szbi̯ to send 143910 1002791
szbṯ to make laugh 143940 1002794
szf to sound friendly 143990 1002796
szn to cause to resemble? 144060 1002819
szn to open (doors) 144070 1002819
ss to burn 143720 1002847
ss net 143730 1001171
ss.w to enclose? 143860 1002300
ssꜣ provisions; sustenance 143780 1002393
ssw enclosure 143840 1002300
ssbj to provoke (a revolt); to incite 143920 1002017
ssbq to honor someone 143930 1002022
sspd to make ready; to supply 143970 1002226
sspd to enliven 143960 1002226
ssf ashes 144010 1002061
ssf to burn up 144000 1002061
ssm.t horse 144020 1002280
ssn to breathe; to smell 144080 1002188
ssnb to heal; to keep healthy 144100 1002193
ssnḏ to frighten 144110 1002197
ssẖ to widen; to extend 855127 1002723
ssẖm to strengthen 144160 1002093
sskꜣ [an ingredient in unguent] 144190 1002277
sskꜣ from the drug Seseka intoxicated 852028 1002277
sskꜣ temple 144180 1002278
sst ankle 144200 1002298

ssḏꜣ.t protective spell 144240 1002057
sš.t rope 144410 1002271
sšꜣ to beseech? 144590 1002304
sšꜣ to beseech 144640 1002304
sšꜣ to change sb.'s mind 144610 1002305
ssꜣi̯ to satisfy 143800 1002393
sšwꜣ to deprive (someone of something) 144780 1002358
sšwi̯ to lift up 144790 1002360
sšwi̯ to empty 144810 1002358
sšwi̯ to dry 144800 1002358
sšp [term for wine] 144880 1002288
sšp milk 859240 1002288
sšp [a bright cloth]; [a bright garment] 144870 1002288
sšp light 144860 1002288
sšp to be bright; to make bright 144850 1002288
sšp [a shining object] 854743 1002288
sšp.y bright one 144940 1002288
sšp.t cucumber? 144920 1002287
sšp.t bright one (Hathor) 144900 1002288
sšp.t brightness 857856 1002288
sšp.t [a kind of a golden amulet] 144930 1002288
sšp.t [term for heaven] 144910 1002288
sšp.t bright (white) cloth 857855 1002288
sšm butcher (lit. one of the whetstone) 145080 1002284
sšm swab 145060 1002153
sšm whetstone 145070 1002284
sšm division; specification 145000 1002153
sšm guidance; state of affairs; conduct 144990 1002153
sšm butcher (lit. one of the whetstone) 855520 1002284
sšm manifestation (of a god); nature (of a god) 145010 1002153
sšm.w statue; image; likeness 145120 1002153
sšm.w leader (a god) 145030 1002153
sšm.w leader; guide 145140 1002153
sšm.w retinue 145130 1002153
sšm.wt leader; guide (uraeus, goddesses) 145190 1002153
šsm.wt inflammation (med.) 157530 1002282
sšm.t [a kind of a bark] 859775 1002153
sšm.t guidance; proof (math.) 145090 1002153
sšmi̯ to lead; to guide 144980 1002153
sšmm to warm (someone); to head (something) 145200 1002159
sšn anger 145260 1002205
sšn to spin; to weave; to twist 145240 1002286
sšn storm 145270 1002286
sšn to demolish; to tear down 145250 1002205
sšn.yt ruins (used as material for building) 145380 1002205
sšn.w ruins (used for building) 860879 1002205
sšn.w cordage (naut.) 145330 1002286
sšn.w [a kind of a fish] 145340 1002285
sšn.t rope 145320 1002286
sšn.t lotus pond 145420 1002834
sšni̯ to grieve? 853573 1002205
sšni̯ to make it round? 852227 1002200
sšntj bird of the lotus pond 145450 1002834
sšnṯ to cause a quarrel 856055 1002214
sšr thing; action; method 145520 1002296
sšr to stroke; to milk 854550 1002293
sšr to stroke; to spread (with something) 145460 1002293
sšr grain 851818 1002289
sšr [an offering (what's milked?)] 145490 1002293
sšr to milk 145470 1002293
sšr.w a linen fabric 145530 1002290
sšrr to reduce 145540 1002264
sšrr.t a kind of loaf 857709 1002264
sšsꜣ to make wise 145550 1002303
sšš.t road; path 145650 1002297
sššj to prepare a bed 145660 1002297
sštꜣ to clothe; to swaddle 145790 1002337
sštꜣ (secret) image (of a god) 145710

1002337
sštꜣ secret 145690 1002337
sštꜣ secret; confidential matter; (religious) mystery 145700 1002337
sštꜣ to make secret; to be secret 145680 1002337
sštꜣ [a fruit] 850976 1002299
sštꜣ libation water 145780 1002337
sštꜣ [a mummy bandage] 145730 1002337
sštꜣ.y mysterious one (the sun god) 145800 1002337
ssd thunderbolt 145830 1002274
ssd to whistle 145850 1002274
ssd flash; lightening 500150 1002274
ssd leather pouch 145890 1002275
ssd to tremble; flash; to lighten fast 145840 1002274
ssd window? 145880 1002273
ssd bandage; headdress; diadem 145860 1002275
ssd to tie (jewelry ribbon); decorate (with) 145870 1002275
ssd.t shrine (of the falcon) 145910 1002273
ssdi̯ to make leave; to remove 450163 1002047
sḳ to cut (flowers) 145940 1002242
sḳ.t fish trap 145950 1002240
sḳꜣ pedestal (for chapels); gallery 145970 1001918
sḳꜣ increase; rising 145980 1001918
sḳꜣi̯ to make high; to exalt 145960 1001918
sḳꜣꜥ to make pour forth; to vomit (med.) 146030 1001924
sḳꜣb to double 146000 1001884
sḳꜣḥ to whitewash; to plaster 146010 1001917
sḳꜣs to bind; to fetter 146020 1001922
sḳb.w cooling 146050 1001844
sḳbb to cool; to refresh 146060 1001844
sḳbb.wj cool room (for food); bathroom 146080 1001844
sḳbḥ to refresh; to give ease to 146110 1001844
sḳfn to bake (bread) 146120 1001860
sḳn to harm 146130 1001886
sḳni̯ to make strong 550241 1001886
sḳni̯ to make fat; to enrich 146140 1001886
sḳnd to enrage 146180 1001885
sḳr to strike; to step out; to present 146190 1002244
sḳr wound; injury 146210 1002244
sḳr to strike; to step out; to present 854551 1002244
sḳr captive; prisoner 146200 1002244
sḳr to unbolt 146220 1002244
sḳrḳr to roll around (in bed, of a feverish patient) 146260 1001895
sḳsn to make sth. miserable 146270 1001909
sḳd boat builder? woodcutter? 146310 1001852
sḳd slope (of a pyramid) 146290 1001852
sḳd oarsman 146280 1001857
sḳd to make build 146300 1001852
sḳd to sail 857677 1001857
sḳd.wt journey; sailing 146340 1001857
sḳd.t ship crew 146330 1001857
sḳdi̯ to travel; to travel (by boat) 146360 1001857
sḳdd to let sleep 146370 1001855
sk to wipe (out, away) 146400 1002131
sk sinking 858508 1002132
sk lance 146460 1002129
sk ruin 852792 1002132
sk accusation 146420 1002127
sk to be a star in the sky 146410 1002130
sk.j [a toilette utensil] 146690 1002126
sk.j flour 146730 1002128
sk.yt battlefield 859239 1002132
sk.w fray; battle 146580 1002132
sk.t [a headache] 146520 1002132
sk.tj [a boat] 146540 1002132
sk.tj military officer 146570 1002132
skꜣ to plough; to cultivate 146610 1002137
skꜣ plough ox 146630 1002137

skꜣ crops 146620 1002137
skꜣ plough ass 146490 1002137
skꜣ.t ploughland 600215 1002137
skꜣp to cover 146670 1001277
ski̯ to destroy 146710 1002132
ski̯ to pass (time) 146720 1002132
ski̯ to perish 146700 1002132
ski̯ to perish; to destroy 854552 1002132
ski̯ to grind 146430 1002132
skm Gray-haired one 869969 1001226
skm to make complete; to finish 146770 1001226
skm to make dark; to blacken 146800 1001227
skm balding; greying (of the hair) 146790 1001226
skm to grow old; to be wise 146780 1001226
skm.yw The old ones 146830 1001226
skm.w gray-haired one 501142 1001226
skmkm destruction 65650 1001226
skn to make unpopular (or similar) 146870 1002133
skn greedy one 650002 1002133
skn to be greedy; to be voracious 146840 1002133
skp to filter 146760 1002135
sksi̯ to make bow down 146940 1001252
sksk to destroy 147010 1002132
sksk light 146990 1002130
sksk [baboon worshiping the sun] 147000 1002130
sksk to illumine 146980 1002130
skki̯ to eclipse 147030 1001225
skt [a military officer (scout?) (guard?)] 147040 1002132
sg to open a way; to break a trail 147080 1002075
sg sacking 34680 1002074
sg.wt astonishment 147140 1000371
sgꜣu̯ to degrade 147130 1000445
sgi̯ to be amazed; to stare 147100 1000371
sgb shrieking; shouting 147160 1002633
sgb to shriek; to shout 147150 1002633
sgbyn [a body of water] 147180 1002076
sgmḥ (cult) spear (of Horus at Edfu) 147210 1002077
sgmḥ to make see; to glimpse 147200 1000379
sgnn to make weak; to enfeeble 147220 1000390
sgnn oil; ointment 147240 1000390
sgnn [Additive in beer preparation] 147250 1000390
sgnn to annoint; to perfume 147230 1000390
sgr silence; stillness 147270 1000396
sgr to silence 147260 1000396
sgr fortress 147280 1002080
sgrḥ to pacify; to make peaceful; to satisfy 147300 1000404
sgrg yard arm? (naut.) 147310 1000402
sgrg to make ready 147320 1000402
st necklace? 859280 1002309
st necklace stringer 450483 1002309
st.y the blazing one 500262 1002321
st.yt sperm 855635 1002321
st.yt descendants 861260 1002321
st.yw jar stand 147850 1002310
st.w the firing one 147420 1002321
st.w arrow; dart 147890 1002321
st.w target 147900 1002321
st.t [a slimy substance (med.)] 147400 1002321
stꜣ to heat; to set afire 147450 1002584
stꜣ flame; lamp 147460 1002584
stꜣ.t lamp; censer 147490 1002584
stꜣḥ to bewitch; to confuse 859158 1002588
sti̯ to pour 147630 1002321
sti̯ to pour 147610 1002321
sti̯ to scatter 147600 1002321
sti̯ to throw 147590 1002321
sti̯ to knot 147640 1002319
sti̯ to shoot; to throw; to pour 147570 1002321
sti̯ to illumine; to light up 147660 1002321
sti̯ to look at intently 147670 1002318
sti̯ to shoot out (semen) 147620 1002321

sti̯ to kindle; to set fire to; to glitter 147650 1002321
stj leg (esp. of Osiris) 147710 1002322
stj.t shrine; temple 147730 1002321
sty shooter 147790 1002321
stw.t light; rays 147910 1002321
stw.tj radiant one 500329 1002321
stwꜣ to move 147930 1002574
stwꜣ to elevate 147940 1002574
stwr to protect; to keep clean 147950 1002568
stwt to praise; to smooth over 147980 1002570
stwt to make like; to make resemble 147970 1002570
stwt to bring (something) 148000 1002570
stwt.j outcome 148020 1002570
stwti̯ to collect; to assemble 147990 1002570
stp strip (of cloth); rag 148100 1002325
stp choice; select 148090 1002328
stp to rapture 855648 1002328
stp to be ruined 853590 1002328
stp goose, or similar 148060 1002326
stp to drip; to absorb liquid 855636 1002328
stp to work with the adze 148030 1002328
stp to pick out; to choose 148070 1002328
stp to refuse; to resist (med.) 148080 1002328
stp to set off; to cut up 148050 1002328
stp.w selected pieces of meat 858700 1002328
stp.w choice 148170 1002328
stp.t incident 148150 1002327
stp.t choice things 148140 1002328
stp.t cut (of meat) 550337 1002328
stp.tj the disassembled one (Seth) 853082 1002328
stf overflow (of fermenting beer) (or similar) 148250 1002435
stf water, liquid pouring out 148260 1002435
stf to pour sth. 148240 1002435
stfnn to rejoice 148300 1002439
stm to destroy 148310 1002487
stm to comfort 148320 1002487
stnw.y charburner? 148350 1000145
stnm to lead astray; to confuse 148360 1002512
stnm.w misguided 851876 1002512
str.w necklace maker 148470 1002330
sthi̯ to pervert; to cause obstruction 148480 1002453
stḫ to open (a door, a door bolt) 148500 1002317
stši̯ to be carried away 148540 1002555
stkn to make approach 148550 1002482
sṯ.w sower 148680 1002321
sṯ.t [jug, for beer]; [jug, as a measure of capacity] 148600 1002307
sṯ.t [bread mold] 148610 1002306
sṯ.t [bread] 148630 1002306
sṯ.t censing 148660 1002321
sṯ.t [a kind of a material] 148640 1002308
sṯꜣ jar 148700 1002334
sṯꜣ passage; cavern; ramp 148750 1002338
sṯꜣ to pull; to flow; to move to 148730 1002338
sṯꜣ to drag; to pull; to usher in 148720 1002338
sṯꜣ [a body of water] 148780 1002333
sṯꜣ secretion (med.) 148790 1002336
sṯꜣ to weave; to spin 148760 1002338
sṯꜣ [a kind of cloth] 148770 1002338
sṯꜣ [a dance position] 858980 1002338
sṯꜣ (stretchable (dough) (med.) 148740 1002338
sṯꜣ.yw tower 148910 1002338
sṯꜣ.w dragging 148870 1002338
sṯꜣ.w attack; wounding 148860 1002338
sṯꜣ.t tower 501144 1002338
sṯꜣ.t necropolis 148850 1002338
sṯꜣ.t hole 148810 1002338
sṯꜣ.t [a (wooden) chest on a sled] 148820 1002338
sṯꜣ.t aroura 148840 1002338
sṯꜣ.t offering 148830 1002335

sṯꜣ.tjw tower 148920 1002338
sṯꜣi̯ to prepare; to form 148900 1002589
sṯꜣm to fertilize farmland 148940 1002593
sṯꜣm clothing; bindings 148950 1002593
sṯꜣm to bind up (an injury); to clothe 148930 1002593
sṯꜣz to reknit (something) 149430 1002600
sṯꜣz to lie stretched out (on the back) 149440 1002600
sṯꜣz.y lying extended on the back 501071 1002600
sṯi̯ to pluck (fowl) 149480 1002320
sṯj fragrance; stench 148990 1002311
sṯbn to transport 857713 1002431
sṯp to leap up 149150 1002329
sṯn.w kind of a swelling 855649 1002508
sṯn.w White Crown 149240 1002508
sṯn.w height 149310 1002508
sṯn.w crowned one 149250 1002508
sṯn.t one who is crowned (Sothis) 149230 1002508
sṯni̯ to raise; to crown; to be highlighted; differ; release (from) 854556 1002508
sṯni̯ to be distinguished (from someone) 149290 1002508
sṯni̯ to expand 858663 1002508
sṯni̯ to distinguish; to crown 149280 1002508
str to make jewelry 148400 1002330
sṯr to wrap up 149340 1002331
sṯr.t upper eyelid 149360 1002331
sṯḥn to make bright; to make dazzling 149370 1002457
sṯz staff; support 852151 1002751
sṯz.w clouds 149470 1002751
sṯz.w raising up 149460 1002751
sṯzi̯ to make (bulls) fervent 149420 1002751
sṯzi̯ to raise; to lift up 149390 1002751
sṯzi̯ to bring up (vomit?) (med.) 149400 1002751
sṯtf to baste 149500 1002560
sd to be clothed 149540 1002036
sd tail 149520 1002035
sd section; column (of a text) 149570 1002029
sdꜣ to tremble 149660 1000303
sdꜣ cattle egret 149650 1002055
sdꜣ.w trembling 149670 1000303
sdꜣdꜣ to tremble; to make tremble 149680 1000303
sdꜣdꜣ trembling 149690 1000303
sdwꜣ to spend the morning (doing something); to make early 149720 1000296
sdwn to fall to pieces (of a boat); to spring (of planks) 149730 1000292
sdwẖ to embalm 149740 1000287
sdb to eat; to chew 149770 1000154
sdb to be softened 856299 1002040
sdb [a kind of a garment] 149760 1002038
sdb [fringed hem of a linen sheet] 149750 1002038
sdb excessive eating 856680 1000154
sdbḥ to supply; to equip 149780 1000160
sdbḥ equipment 149790 1000160
sdf [a unit of measure, for figs] 149810 1002043
sdm eye-paint 149840 1002048
sdm to paint (the eyes) 149830 1002048
sdm.t knife (lit. what is sharpened) 149850 1000210
sdmj to attach (lit. to make touch) 149870 1000213
sdni̯ to punish 149880 1000232
sdḥ to reduce; let it sink; drown 149910 1000194
sdḥ to ease? (misery) 149920 1000194
sdẖ to commit sacrilege 29520 1000194
sdẖ hidden 149940 1000194
sdẖ to hide 149930 1000194
sdšr to make red 149970 1000280
sdšr.w reddening 149980 1000280
sdq to cut 150000 1000250
sdg hidden things 150020 1000188
sdgi̯ to hide 150010 1000188
sdgi̯ to make see 150040 1000189
sḏ fracture (of a bone); rupture (med.)

150120 1002037
sḏ to break; set out; to solve; dissolve 150110 1002037
sḏ Breaker 857754 1002037
sḏ.w loincloth 600584 1002034
sḏ.t water breakthrough 150130 1002037
sḏ.t fire; flame 150140 1002031
sḏ.tj child 858943 1002032
sḏ.tj child; foster child 150150 1002032
sḏ.tjt girl; foster child (female) 869996 1002032
sḏ.tjt girl; foster child (female) 150160 1002032
sḏꜣ end? (of the kingdom of the dead) 500597 1002628
sḏꜣ to be healthy; to be safe and sound 150240 1002627
sḏꜣ to amuse (trans.) 150230 1002056
sḏꜣ [necklace with seal cylinder] 150280 1002057
sḏꜣ to take away 150220 1002628
sḏꜣ to go; to travel 150210 1002628
sḏꜣ.w protection 150310 1002627
sḏꜣ.wt seal; sealing 150320 1002057
sḏꜣ.t valuables; treasure (lit. what is sealed) 150300 1002057
sḏꜣm to make (land) fertile 150380 1000313
sḏꜣm to speak boastfully (of something) 150390 1002060
sḏꜣm to lie with (a woman) 150370 1000313
sḏꜣm.t hoe 150410 1002059
sḏꜣs to be prosperous 108200 1002056
sḏwi̯ to slander 150420 1000288
sḏb obstacle; impediment; evil 150450 1002039
sḏb to make live; to restore (to life) 150440 1000155
sḏb to hold back; prevent 150480 1000167
sḏfꜣ temple endowment 150520 1000186
sḏfꜣ to provide with (food, e.g.); to endow 150510 1000186
sḏfꜣ to prepare (weapons, for battle) 150530 1000186
sḏm to hear; to listen 150560 1002049
sḏm servant 863378 1002049
sḏm servant 150590 1002049
sḏm questioning 150570 1002049
sḏm.j hearer 150680 1002049
sḏm.yw judges (lit. listeners) 150700 1002049
sḏm.yt gossip 150690 1002049
sḏm.w the hearer 851875 1002049
sḏn to lift up; to carry 150710 1002050
sḏnf ibex 150730 1002051
sḏr sleeper 150870 1002054
sḏr strong 150790 1000260
sḏr sleeping one 852797 1002054
sḏr [a med. liquid] 150760 1002052
sḏr to spend the night; [aux./modal] 851684 1002054
sḏr apartment (of the Residence) 150800 1002054
sḏr to secure (a city); be steadfast 150770 1000260
sḏr mat 150750 1002054
sḏr to lie; to sleep; spend the night 150740 1002054
sḏr.yt sleeping place; (state of being) bedridden; intercourse 150820 1002054
sḏr.yt intercourse 150840 1002054
sḏr.yt defeat 150890 1002054
sḏr.yt (state of being) bedridden 150830 1002054
sḏr.w the sleeping ones 851893 1002054
sḏr.t (festival of) laying (Osiris to rest) 150850 1002054
sḏr.t sleeping draught 150860 1002054
sḏḥ shin; lower leg 150900 1002044
sḏsr to consecrate; to sanctify 150930 1000279
sḏd to recount; to talk 150940 1000173
sḏḏ image; form 151000 1002042
sḏd.w tale; conversation 150950 1000173
sḏdꜣ to fatten 150960 1000182
sḏdi̯ to make permanent 150980 1000178
sḏdm to make envious 150990 1000179

š

š the lake 860126 1001062
š basin; offering bowl 151050 1001062
š work?; workplace? 151030 1002004
š lake; district; garden (with pool) 151010 1001062
š chair; support 151020 1002001
š lake; district; garden (with pool) 854557 1001062
šꜣ to command; to ordain 151220 1002382
šꜣ animal (of Seth) 856056 1002394
šꜣ to go aground (naut.) 151200 1002383
šꜣ marsh; meadow 151110 1002381
šꜣ tree (gen.); vine(s) 151120 1002381
šꜣ wine (jars?) 151150 1002381
šꜣ plants; vine(s) 151130 1002381
šꜣ.yt what is ordained; taxes; dues 151400 1002382
šꜣ.w fate 860007 1002382
šꜣ.w worth; suitable 151560 1002382
šꜣ.w excrement (med.) 151290 1002379
šꜣ.w to be useful 852483 1002382
šꜣ.w weight; worth 151310 1002382
šꜣ.w coriander 151280 1002381
šꜣ.w destiny 151300 1002382
šꜣ.wt coriander 151330 1002381
šꜣ.wt shallows 151600 1002383
šꜣ.wtj value; power 856308 1002382
šꜣ.t talon; foot (of a bird of prey) 151250 1002384
šꜣ.t upper chest 151240 1002385
šꜣ.t flat-bottomed boat 151260 1002383
šꜣj pig 151350 1002394
šꜣj.t sow 151410 1002394
šꜣꜥ to begin; to be the first (to do something) 151460 1002411
šꜣꜥ beginning 857729 1002411
šꜣꜥ primeval waters [canal in the 15th nome of Upper Egypt] 151510 1002411
šꜣꜥ until 151470 1002411
šꜣꜥ to begin; to start 851685 1002411
šꜣꜥ until 853916 1002411
šꜣꜥ container (for storage of grain) 151480 1002410
šꜣꜥ.t primeval goddess (e.g. Hathor, Seshat) 151530 1002411
šꜣꜥ.t primordial land 860546 1002411
šꜣꜥ.t storeroom 151550 1002410
šꜣꜥ.tw until that (conj.); as soon as (conj.); [terminative] 853914 1002411
šꜣꜥzẖ [a spice?, from Punt] 400814 1002412
šꜣb.w meals; food 151690 1002388
šꜣb to be blind? 151640 1002223
šꜣb.t [a boat] 151670 1002386
šꜣb.tj shabti 153120 1002388
šꜣm to be hot; to burn 151770 1002159
šꜣm.w dirty laundry 151800 1002396
šꜣm.w [a med. liquid] 151810 1002396
šꜣmy.t water (of the laundryman) (med.) 151820 1002396
šꜣr.w [an eye affliction] 151860 1002400
šꜣs to travel; to go; to tread on 151900 1002403
šꜣš to avoid; to go through 151950 1002402
šꜣs.w striding 151920 1002403
šꜣs.t journeyings 151910 1002403
šꜣšꜣ [a fruit (med.)] 151960 1002377
šꜣšꜣy.t upper chest; bosom 152040 1002385
šꜣšꜣy.t [a necklace] 152050 1002385
šꜣšꜣꜥ [kernels, fruit] 152060 1002377
šꜣw to cauterize (med.) 151570 1002408
šꜣwy.t [a kind of a plant] 151320 1002381
šꜣḳ (leather) bag? 152070 1002398
šꜣḳ container for arrows (box?) (quiver?) 152100 1002398
šꜣd to dig; to dig out 152150 1002389
šꜣd.t pit 857732 1002389
šy [euphemism for crocodile] 152180 1001062
šꜥ field ("detached") 152290 1002413
šꜥ [scribe's implement] 152250 1002413
šꜥ to cut; to cut off 152200 1002413
šꜥ.wtj wash basin 152500 1002421
šꜥ.t [a med. substance (barley dough?)] 152370 1002421
šꜥ.t slaughtering; terror; evil 152300 1002413

šꜥ.t document; letter; book 152350 1002413
šꜥ.t knife 152310 1002413
šꜥ.tj butcher 500026 1002413
šꜥy sand 152280 1002421
šꜥy to be grainy (sandy) 152420 1002421
šꜥy.t sandbank 152430 1002421
šꜥy.t [a storeroom] 152450 1002410
šꜥr prison; gate 152540 1002417
šꜥr to promise 859187 1002419
šꜥr calculation; scheme; threat; promise 152550 1002419
šꜥd sword 152610 1002415
šꜥd to cut (off, down) 152600 1002415
šꜥd log; beam 152630 1002415
šꜥḏ to cut off 450452 1002415
šw protection; sunshade 152770 1002345
šw [a jug, for beer] 152780 1002339
šw needy man 152680 1002358
šw dryness 855583 1002358
šw to shine (with light) 152760 1002347
šw sunlight; sun 152750 1002347
šw blank sheet of papyrus 152700 1002358
šw dry pieces of wood? 152740 1002358
šw need; lack 600209 1002358
šw.w dry land 152920 1002358
šw.w hay; dry rush grass 152940 1002358
šw.t neighbors; helpers? 152850 1002345
šw.t feather; plumage 152830 1002344
šw.t blank sheet of papyrus (med.) 152870 1002358
šw.t side (as a part of the body) 152840 1002346
šw.t emptiness 450167 1002358
šw.t empty eye 152890 1002358
šw.t ship's shade? 152900 1002345
šw.t shadow 152880 1002345
šw.tj the double plume; Two Feather Crown 860191 1002344
sw.tjt [full replacement for the horus eye?] 129670 1002342
šw.tjt fan-bearer 152910 1002345
šw.tjt the feathered one 854197 1002344
šwꜣ to be poor 152970 1002358
šwꜣ.w poor man 153020 1002358
šwꜣ.w poverty 600647 1002358
šwꜣ.t impoverishment 153010 1002358
šwi̯ to soar up; to raise up 153030 1002360
šwi̯ to be empty; to be devoid of 152720 1002358
šwi̯ dried; dry 152730 1002358
šwi̯ to be empty; to be devoid of 152670 1002358
šwj.w ascent 860999 1002360
šwy.w [decoration? of a coffin] 153100 1002344
šwy.t desert; dry spot 153070 1002358
šwy.t trade 857563 1002361
šwy.tj merchant; trader 153090 1002361
šwb persea tree 153110 1002350
šwb.tj [a jar] 153130 1002349
šwšy.t dryness; drought 153160 1002358
šb piece of meat 153210 1002721
šb [an aromatic plant] 153220 1002010
šb.w remuneration, payment; retribution 856686 1002015
šb.w food; main meal 153330 1002721
šb.t meat offering 153260 1002721
šb.t [ritual object, which king offers to a goddess] 153300 1002005
šb.t [an edible vegetable (cucumber?) (melon?)] 153290 1002007
šb.t value; price; wage 153250 1002015
šb.t [a mash (med.)] 153270 1002015
šb.tj rib-joints (as food) 153380 1002009
šb.tjw [primordial creative beings] 153320 1002721
šbi̯ to mix; to mingle; to replace 153350 1002015
šby.w shebyu-necklace 153370 1002016
šbb tube, i.e. reed 153410 1002011
šbb gullet; esophagus 153420 1002011
šbb a bit to eat 153460 1002721
šbb to mix; to mash 153430 1002015
šbb mastic 153450 1002010
šbb.t (beer) mash 153470 1002015
šbb.t brew? 870035 1002015

šbn mixed; various 153500 1002015
šbn to mix; to mingle 153490 1002015
šbn [multicolored components of neck collar etc.] 153510 1002015
šbn [ingredients in kyphi] 153520 1002015
šbn.t various? 153530 1002015
šbšb to divide correctly; to apportion; to set out (a design) 153560 1002015
šbšb to brew; to mix 153570 1002015
šbšb brewer? 153580 1002015
šbd stick (to beat) 153600 1002012
šp prize 153640 1002376
šp to flow out; to depart 153630 1002224
šp to throw; to bound? 153650 1002225
šp to be blind; to blind 153620 1002223
šp.w blind person 854346 1002223
šp.w blindness 857832 1002223
sp.t base (column, stele) 132450 1002222
sp.t lips; edge; bank; shore 132440 1002222
šp.t intestinal disease [an affliction of the anus (hemorrhoids?)] 153670 1002224
šp.t blindness 153660 1002223
špj to blow up; fill with air 852498 1002237
špn [a kind of an illness of the urinary tract] 153700 1000679
špn to be well fed 851309 1000679
špn [a plant (poppy?)] 153710 1000679
špn.t [a jug, as a measure for beer] 153740 1002228
špn.t voluptuous woman 153720 1000679
špn.t [a beverage] 153730 1002228
špnn poppy seeds? 153750 1000679
šps statue; likeness 153820 1002235
šps tomb-chapel 153810 1002235
šps.j splendid; noble 400546 1002235
šps.j libation vase 153890 1002235
šps.w noble 153870 1002235
šps.w glory; riches; costly offerings 153880 1002235
šps.w [a priestly title] 858556 1002235
šps.wt noble women 859274 1002235
šps.ww the nobles 855194 1002235
šps.t statue; image 856427 1002235
šps.t magnificent one 153850 1002235
šps.t [a ritual jar] 153860 1002235
šps.t noblewoman 153840 1002235
šps.t [a female priestly title] 858557 1002235
šps.t favorite 169300 1002235
špsi̯ to be dignified; to honor 851690 1002235
špsi̯ be dignified 153780 1002235
špss noble (an esteemed person) 153900 1002235
špss noble; splendid 550395 1002235
špss to be dignified 153910 1002235
špss to make splendid; to enrich 153920 1002235
špss to be dignified 851689 1002235
špss riches; wealth; precious things 153940 1002235
špss.t noblewoman 153950 1002235
špt to be angry 153970 1002236
špt hedgehog fish 153960 1002237
špt anger; discontent 153980 1002236
šptj to be blown up (med.) 153990 1002237
špty.t (urinary) bladder 154000 1002237
šf having the ram's had; handsome 860289 1002066
šf respect?; honor? 154030 1002066
šf.yt truth [synonym for maat] 154090 1002066
šf.yt majesty; respect 154080 1002066
šf.ytj respected one 154110 1002066
šf.w [a substance (slime?) (med.)] 154060 1002070
šf.wt swelling 154170 1002070
šf.t ram (of Amun, of Khnum) 154050 1002066
šfꜥ to fight 154130 1002073
šfi̯ to respect 859866 1002066
šfu̯ to swell; to be swollen 154160 1002070
šfn to touch 154190 1002067
šfn.w bushes; undergrowth 154200 1002068
šfšf.t respect; awe 154240 1002066
šfšf.t [a med. substance] 154250 1002070

šfšf.t ram's head 154230 1002066
šfšfy.tj greatly-respected one 154260 1002066
šfd to grasp; to sieze 154280 1002063
šfd.w sheet of papyrus; scroll of papyrus 154290 1002063
šfdy.t bier 154310 1002063
šm servant (of a deity) 154350 1002153
šm father in law 856309 1002142
šm.y corridor (in a temple) 154670 1002153
sm.yt herbage 134870 1002141
šm.yt stake; palisade 154650 1002153
šm.yt heat; summer 154660 1002159
šm.w shemu-season (summer) 154850 1002159
šm.w heat 154460 1002159
šm.w one who goes, servant 856079 1002153
šm.w [a kind of spells]; omen; oracle 853456 1002143
šm.w waterway 450456 1002153
šm.w harvest; crop 154860 1002159
šm.wj legs; walking tools 859179 1002153
šm.ww summer ships 154880 1002159
šm.t walking; gait; business 154400 1002153
šm.t mother in law 154440 1002142
šm.t fever; inflammation 154430 1002159
šm.t path (on land, in the sky) 154410 1002153
šm.t [walk with statues] 154420 1002153
šmꜣ to be strange; be abnormal 863021 1002176
šmꜣ to wander; to move around 154540 1002176
šmꜣ to stray around 154550 1002176
šmꜣ to wander; move around; stray around 854558 1002176
šmꜣ foreigner (i.e., a non-Egyptian); wanderer 154570 1002176
šmꜣ.y strangeness; abnormality (a symptom of the disease) 154610 1002176
šmꜣ.w flowers 154590 1002173
šmi̱ to go; to traverse 154340 1002153
šmi̱ go (to do) 852485 1002153
šmy storehouse 154640 1002153
šmᶜ Upper Egyptian grain 154800 1002180
šmᶜ [heraldic plant of Upper Egypt (flowering sedge?)] 154700 1002180
šmᶜ thin (linen) cloth; [a thin material] 600027 1002178
šmᶜ to be slender 154710 1002178
šmᶜ to make music 154730 1002179
šmᶜ thin; slender 154720 1002178
šmᶜ.j Upper Egyptian 154790 1002180
šmᶜ.yt musician 154810 1002179
šmᶜ.w oil of Upper Egypt 154840 1002180
šmᶜ.w crown of Upper Egypt 154690 1002180
šmᶜ.w musician; singer; chantress 154770 1002179
šmᶜ.t snake (ureus) of Upper Egypt 154740 1002180
šmᶜ.t thin (linen) cloth 154750 1002178
šmw movements 154450 1002153
šmm hot one 154900 1002159
šmm to be hot; to become hot (feverish) 154890 1002159
šmm heat 154910 1002159
šmm.t stable; storehouse 154940 1002153
šmm.t fever; inflammation 154920 1002159
šmm.t street 154930 1002153
šmr.t bow (weapon) 154970 1002163
šmr.tj bowman 154980 1002163
šms to follow; to accompany; to bring 155000 1002169
šms.w following; suite 155040 1002169
šms.w retainer 155030 1002169
šms.w retainer, follower 853223 1002169
šms.wt following; suite 155060 1002169
sms.ww old ones 856246 1002168
šms.t retainer (fem.) 155020 1002169
šms.t follower (fem.) 870050 1002169
šms.t [instrument of punishment] 155010 1002166
šn [protective symbol behind figures of the king] 155180 1002200

šn circuit of the world 155200 1002200
šn [indefinitely huge number] 155190 1002200
šn ocean 155210 1002200
šn shen-ring 155170 1002200
šn [a body of water, in compounds] 155220 1002200
šn weak one; disabled? 853480 1002205
šn tree (gen.) 155240 1002189
šn tree (gen.) 155250 1002189
šn bad 155270 1002182
šn crocodile 155590 1002200
šn.w troubles; need 155360 1002205
šn.w rope 155930 1002186
šn.w net(s) 155940 1002186
šn.w summoners; reciter 155380 1002203
šn.w circuit; circumference 155350 1002200
šn.w official inquiry 852182 1002203
šn.w tax inspection; fee 853888 1002203
šn.w official inquiry 155370 1002203
šn.wj tree garden 156000 1002189
šn.wt date palm inflorescence? 156020 1002189
šn.wt encircling? 155400 1002200
šn.wt the jaws? 156010 1002200
šn.wj tree garden 156000 1002189
šn.wt date palm inflorescence? 156020 1002189
šn.wt encircling? 155400 1002200
šn.wt the jaws? 156010 1002200
šn.t circling 855502 1002200
šn.t hundred 155320 1002185
šn.t spell; conjuration 155300 1002200
šn.tj two (grieving) sisters (Isis and Nephthys) 155340 1002205
šni̯ to be round; to surround; to encircle 155450 1002200
šni̯ to inquire; to question (someone) 155490 1002203
šni̯ to fight; to quarrel 155460 1002201
šni̯ to suffer 155480 1002205
šni̯ to pass in review 155280 1002203
šni̯ to stink 856218 1002204
šni̯ to curse; to exorcise; to conjure 155500 1002200
šni̯ to ask; examine; look through; check; recite; discuss; summon 854559 1002203
šni̯ to be infested (with crocodiles) 155230 1002200
šnj [a tree or fruits of this tree] 450467 1002189
šnj inquirer 155580 1002203
šnj to knock down 155520 1002201
šnj (something) rotten (of fish) (med.) 155530 1002204
šnj to compel 155470 1002201
šnj hair 155510 1002206
šnj [a vessel] 155560 1002200
snj.w [a measure of value]; piece of silver (of specific weight) 136670 1002819
šnj.w grass 155390 1002206
šnj.t hailstorm; storm 155570 1002201
šny [a workman] 155540 1002219
šn^c water spout in lion-form 155700 1002219
šn^c enemy 155720 1002219
šn^c breast 155740 1002218
šn^c constipation (med.) 155750 1002219
šn^c storm cloud 155760 1002201
šn^c [a small fish] 155770 1002217
šn^c to hold; to hold back; to be shy 854560 1002219
šn^c [unit of value, equivalent to a weight of silver] 155810 1002220
šn^c to value 550094 1002220
šn^c to hold back 155690 1002219
šn^c to turn back; to detain 155680 1002219
šn^c.w police task 155870 1002219
šn^c.w storehouse 155900 1002219
šn^c.w personnel (of the storehouse) 155780 1002219
šn^c.w deckhouse 155840 1002219
šn^c.w policeman?; guard 155850 1002219
šn^c.w hindrance 155860 1002219
šn^c.wt [a kind of forced labor] 155910 1002219

šnᶜ.t storehouse 155830 1002219
šnᶜ.tj [unit of value, equivalent to a weight of silver] 155920 1002220
šnw food offering 155950 1002200
šnw.t court; entourage (of the king, of a god) 155980 1002200
šnw.t granary; storeroom 155970 1002200
šnw.tj courtier? 857817 1002200
šnb trumpet; tube (for kohl) 156030 1002194
šnb.t chest; front fuselage; throat 156060 1002191
šnb.tj falcon (also Horus) [in a form of breast amulet] 156070 1002191
šnp [a reed] 156090 1002210
šnp [woven shenep-reeds (as a mat, a garment)] 156110 1002210
šnn illness; grief 156150 1002201
šnn.t quarrel 857825 1002201
šnrf to be disheveled 156220 1002138
šnš to be smelly; to be brackish 156250 1002204
šnš to tear up 156240 1002201
šnšn to tear up 156260 1002201
šnt.t enclosure 156280 1002200
šntj [an affliction of the liver] 156380 1002205
šntj hair 156340 1002206
šntj heron 156350 1002206
šnṯ abuse 156410 1002214
šnṯ to revile; to oppose; to punish 156400 1002214
šnṯ policeman; hundreds 155330 1002214
šnṯ.j Rebel (Seth) 156460 1002214
šnṯ.y enemy; foe 156470 1002214
šnṯ.y enmity 156480 1002214
šnṯ.yw enemies; foes 156490 1002214
šnṯ.w shield? 156420 1002214
šnṯ.t strife; quarrel 156430 1002214
šntꜣy.t widow 156300 1002216
šntꜣy.t Shentayet (a heavenly cow) 156310 1002216
šnḏ acacia 156500 1002195
šnḏ.wt king's kilt; kilt (gen.) 156540 1002196
šnḏ.t acacia thorn (med.) 156520 1002195
šnḏ.t acacia 156510 1002195
šnḏ.tj wearer of the kilt [a kind of a priest] 156530 1002196
šr [a body of water] 156560 1002245
šr.t nose; nostril(s) 156610 1002249
šrj little 600257 1002264
šrj the little; the younger (junior) 400731 1002264
šrj child; son; lad 156650 1002264
šrj the minor one 853893 1002264
šrj to stop; to block up 156670 1002261
šrj.t girl; daughter 156680 1002264
šrj.t junior (after personal name) 853881 1002264
šrw.t constipation 156730 1002261
šrm to lay down (weapons); to seek peace 156800 1002140
šrm peace; greeting 156780 1002140
šrm to lay down arms; to seek peace 156790 1002140
šrm.t delivery; provisions 156810 1002332
šrr to cry out; to shout 156840 1002265
šrr to be little; to be meagre 156570 1002264
šrr little 156820 1002264
šrr.j the little one; child; son 852250 1002264
šrḥ brook; stream 156860 1002257
šrš to be quick; to rush 156870 1002266
šrgḥ feelings 859156 1002256
šḥq dust cloud 156900 1002099
šz bowl 156910 1002372
šzp gift? 157180 1002376
šzp palm (measure of length) 157200 1002376
šzp image; likeness; sphinx 157210 1002376
šzp receipt; commencement 853890 1002376
šzp to be acceptable 157170 1002376
šzp to receive; to take possession of 157160 1002376

šzp.yw the imprisoned one 157390 1002376
šzp.w core 157320 1002376
šzp.t lashing (naut.) 157290 1002375
šzp.t chamber; summer house 157250 1002376
šzp.t leather straps 157280 1002375
šzm.t [a belt] 157410 1002373
šzm.t malachite 157430 1002374
šs rope 156930 1002271
šs alabaster; alabaster vessels 156950 1002268
šš to build (temple) 157760 1002272
šš incompetent 856310 1002269
šš fool 861315 1002269
šš to turn (rope) 157750 1002271
šš nest 854815 1002270
šs.yt [green pigment (med.)] 157140 1002267
šs.t alabaster (and objects made of alabaster) 157000 1002268
šsꜣ bubalis antilope 157080 1002301
šsꜣ to be wise; to be skilled; to be conversant with 157030 1002303
šsꜣ.w wisdom; skill 157090 1002303
šsꜣ.w diagnosis; prescription 157100 1002303
šsꜣ.w tongue 157110 1002303
šsꜣ.t nightfall 157060 1002302
šsm to be red; to be inflamed 157480 1002282
šsm to be strong; effective 157490 1002283
šsm leather scroll? 157470 1002281
šsm [something of the dead that is to be released] 157460 1002279
šsr [to prepare the fireplace?] 157600 1002296
šsr to utter; to express 157640 1002294
šsr utterances; specifications 157650 1002294
šsr to shoot down 858464 1002291
šsr to slay 157580 1002291
šsr to shine 157670 1002292
šsr arrow 157560 1002291
šsr sacrificial bull 157590 1002291
šsr.t sanctuary 157680 1002294
šš.t knife 157770 1002413
šḳ ring 157790 1002241
šḳ [a container for arrows (quiver?)] 157810 1002241
šḳb rhinoceros 157820 1002243
šgr [a body of water (ditch? dyke?)] 157910 1002078
šgr [a wooden box] 157900 1002079
škn watering place 157860 1002134
škr [a mineral] 157870 1002136
št tax payer? 859883 1002313
štꜣ hidden water 158010 1002337
štꜣ copse; scrub 158000 1002337
štꜣ to be secret; to be hidden; to be mysterious 157940 1002337
štꜣ secret; hidden; mysterious 400452 1002337
štꜣ small child 158030 1002337
štꜣ quarry; mine; hill 157960 1002337
štꜣ.y the hidden one 158150 1002337
štꜣ.yt cellar; hidden room 600289 1002337
štꜣ.w secrets; (religious) mysteries 158120 1002337
štꜣ.wt mysterious one (fem.) 857997 1002337
štj.w stroke oar? 158220 1002312
štꜣ.t egg 158100 1002337
štꜣ.t secrets 158050 1002337
štꜣ.t womb; belly 158090 1002337
štꜣ.t hidden one (Nekhbet and others) 158080 1002337
štꜣy.t secret? (related to the underworld) 158160 1002337
šty [term for the deceased] 158180 1002337
šty.t leader; stroke (of a bank of oarswomen) 158200 1002312
štjw [term for the underworld] 158260 1002337
štb crate? (for fowl) 158300 1002316
štb to shut in; to enclose 158290 1002316
štm rebellion; hostility 158360 1002324
štm to be quarrelsome; to be hostile 158350

1002324
šṯ satchel 158410 1002314
šṯ to decorate; to cloth 158380 1002314
šṯ vestment; garment 158390 1002314
šṯ.w turtle 158430 1002315
šṯ.wj the turtle like one 857862 1002315
šṯ.wt she-tortoise 857865 1002315
šṯy.t [sanctuary of Sokar] 158440 1002323
šṯy.t rectum 856429 1002323
šṯw.t domed roof 158450 1002315
šd tutor 158480 1002046
šd vulva 158530 1002034
šd cushion (of leather) 158470 1002033
šd liturgies 158550 1002046
šd mortar 158520 1002034
šd [a kind of a messenger] 158500 1002046
šd [a kind of timber used for building boats] 158510 1002045
šd young brood (of birds) 158490 1002046
šd magician; reciter 869177 1002046
šd potter 158540 1002045
šd.y field; meadow; parcel of land 158780 1002045
šd.y catch (of fish; of fowl) 158850 1002047
šd.y ditch 158770 1002045
šd.yt flooded parcel of land 158820 1002045
šd.w skin; water skin 158640 1002033
šd.w field; meadow; parcel of land 158860 1002045
šd.w lacings? (naut.) 158650 1002045
šd.w artificial lake; pool 857753 1002045
šd.wt field; meadow; parcel of land 158870 1002045
šd.t well; water hole 158600 1002045
šd.tj excavators 860727 1002045
šdi̭ to read; to recite 158740 1002046
šdi̭ to suckle; to educate 158750 1002046
šdi̭ to rescue 158730 1002047
šdi̭ to dig; to carve 158720 1002045
šdi̭ to take; remove; remove; to offer (gifts) 158710 1002047
šdy.t rubble 158810 1002045
šdy.t nurse (a divine cow; also epithet of Hathor) 158800 1002046
šdwj [inner animal body part] 158880 1002034
šdr.t ravine; chasm 158900 1002053
šdšd [bolster-like protuberance on the front of divine standard] 158940 1002045
šddt payment; expenditure 158960 1002047
šḏ.t a dough (for baking bread) 158970 1002030

ḳ

ḳꜣ tall; high; loud 158990 1001918
ḳꜣ the high one 158980 1001918
ḳꜣ.yt [palanquin] 861034 1001918
ḳꜣ.yt high field; high-lying land; height 159160 1001918
ḳꜣ.tj that belongs to the high one 854776 1001918
ḳꜣꜣ hill; high ground 159060 1001918
ḳꜣi̭ to be tall; to be high; to be loud 159110 1001918
ḳꜣj [a beverage] 159120 1001919
ḳꜣj seeds (as feed for fowl) 159150 1001923
ḳꜣj.t high boat 857583 1001918
ḳꜣꜥ to vomit; to pour out 159200 1001924
ḳꜣꜥ.w vomit; spit out 159210 1001924
ḳꜣw height; length; volume (of voice) 159010 1001918
ḳꜣw flour? cake? 159230 1001923
ḳꜣw foreman? 400393 1001918
ḳꜣw.w swelling? 856012 1001918
ḳꜣb belly, intestine 857580 1001884
ḳꜣb interior; middle 650065 1001884
ḳꜣb windings 159260 1001884
ḳꜣb intestines 159270 1001884
ḳꜣb to fold over; to wind; to double; to multiply 854562 1001884
ḳꜣb to fold over; to wind 159240 1001884
ḳꜣb to double; to multiply 159250 1001884
ḳꜣb coil, bend 870119 1001884
ḳꜣb? to mortify? 858177 1001884

q3b.y one who winds [a kind of a snake] 159340 1001884
ḳ3b.yt twisted one 500988 1001884
ḳ3b.t knee? 159300 1001884
ḳ3b.t chest 159290 1001913
ḳ3r sack; bundle 159370 1001921
ḳ3r vagabond 858170 1001921
ḳ3r.t door bolt 159380 1001920
ḳ3ri̯ to stay; to deposit 850645 1001921
ḳ3rr vagabond 858171 1001921
ḳ3ḥ to bind 159420 1001916
ḳ3ḥ to tame (horse) 858209 1001916
ḳ3ḥ saddle 858208 1001916
ḳ3ḥ Nile clay; mortar (of clay) 159410 1001917
ḳ3ḥ.yt Nile clay 159450 1001917
ḳ3s rope ladder 159490 1001922
ḳ3s rope (as fetters, as rigging (naut.)) 159480 1001922
ḳ3s to bind (a victim); to string (a bow 159470 1001922
ḳ3s binder 859476 1001922
ḳ3ḳ3 to look upwards 159560 1001918
ḳ3ḳ3 hill 870140 1001918
ḳ3d [a kind of a plant] 159620 1001061
ḳ3d to cry 159630 1001915
ḳ3d [a kind of a bird] 857581 1001061
ḳ3d.yt [a small animal (med.)] 159660 1001061
ḳ3d.t [a creeper plant (med.)] 159650 1001061
ḳj form; shape; nature 159670 1001866
ḳjs vomit 159730 1001867
ḳjs to vomit; to spew out 159720 1001867
ḳjs.w vomiting 857590 1001867
ḳjs.wt efflux 159760 1001867
ḳꜥḥ to bend (the hand, the arm) 159810 1001925
ḳꜥḥ arm; shoulder 159830 1001925
ḳꜥḥ [papyrus sheet] 159900 1001925
ḳꜥḥ.w corner; bend 159840 1001925
ḳꜥḥ.t shoulder (of beef) 159910 1001925
ḳꜥḥ.t side? 159930 1001925
ḳꜥḥ.t district 159920 1001925
ḳwpr henna 159950 1001910
ḳwr gold worker?; miner? 159970 1001912
ḳwr barge; cargo boat 159980 1001911
ḳwr.j stevedores (from ships); unloader (from ships) 860227 1001911
ḳb to pour a libation 160070 1001844
ḳb [a kind of a woodworking for coffins] 160040 1001841
ḳb.w prevalence 160110 1001842
ḳb.t [a term for a temple]; naos 160100 1001844
ḳb.t coolness 160090 1001844
ḳby [a kind of a jar (for water, for beer)] 160130 1001844
ḳbꜥ to joke 160150 1001847
ḳbb cool; calm 550102 1001844
ḳbb to be cool; to be calm 160170 1001844
ḳbb coolness; calmness 160180 1001844
ḳbb cool wind 160190 1001844
ḳbb.wt cool water 870143 1001844
ḳbb.t cool water 160200 1001844
ḳbb.t throat 160220 1001843
ḳbḥ to pour a libation; to present libations 160260 1001844
ḳbḥ water pourer 860401 1001844
ḳbḥ lower leg (with foot) 160230 1001845
ḳbḥ to die 160280 1001844
ḳbḥ to be cool; to cool 160250 1001844
ḳbḥ to be cool; to cool; to pour a libation; to present libations 854563 1001844
ḳbḥ water pourer 160270 1001844
ḳbḥ [a watery area in heaven] 160380 1001844
ḳbḥ.yt libation vessel 160400 1001844
ḳbḥ.w watery region (mythological) 160350 1001844
ḳbḥ.w Cool one 160410 1001844
ḳbḥ.w watery region (habitat of birds) 160340 1001844
ḳbḥ.w water fowl 160360 1001844
ḳbḥ.w libation water; water 160330 1001844
ḳbḥ.w libation vase 160320 1001844
ḳbḥ.w coolness 160310 1001844

ḳbḥ.wj one who belongs to the watery area 854352 1001844
ḳbḥ.wj temple (in Egypt) 859947 1001844
ḳbḥ.wj what belongs to the watery area 854779 1001844
ḳfꜣ.t fame; reputation 160440 1001862
ḳfn to bend down 160450 1001861
ḳfn to build 160490 1001860
ḳfn [a baked good] 160480 1001860
ḳfn to bend, grasp someone's hand 160460 1001861
ḳfn to bake; to clot (blood) 160470 1001860
ḳfn.y baker 160510 1001860
ḳfḳf.t call; name 160530 1001862
ḳmꜣ to throw; create; produce; devise; hammer (metal); float 854564 1001876
ḳmꜣ form; appearance; nature 160590 1001876
ḳmꜣ to mourn 160610 1001875
ḳmꜣ reeds 160630 1001873
ḳmꜣ (sacred) bull 160640 1001876
ḳmꜣ to throw 160550 1001876
ḳmꜣ throwstick 160540 1001876
ḳmꜣ [Method of preparing Qemechu bread] 160560 1001876
ḳmꜣ creator 160580 1001876
ḳmꜣ to hammer out (metal) 160600 1001876
ḳmꜣ to wrestle 160650 1001876
ḳmꜣ to create; to produce; to devise 160570 1001876
ḳmꜣ.y young? 870263 1001876
ḳmꜣ.w winnower 160700 1001876
ḳmꜣ.w [a class of soldier] 160710 1001876
ḳmꜣ.w something thrown (into the water) 853627 1001876
ḳmꜣ.w creator (or creation) 857592 1001876
ḳmꜣ.t product 160660 1001876
ḳmꜣ.tj [a garment? of the king at the sed-festival] 160760 1001876
ḳmꜣ.tj the two mourners 160680 1001875
ḳmꜣ.tj image of the god in the temple 160750 1001876
ḳmy [anointing oil] 160810 1002371
ḳmy.t gum; resin 160800 1002371
ḳmy.tj what belongs to gum mountain 860755 1002371
ḳmḥ barb of harpoon 860192 1001872
ḳmḥ twig; foliage 160830 1001872
ḳmḥ.w [a kind of bread] 160840 1001871
ḳmqm [a kind of a timpani] 160850 1001868
ḳmd lamentation 600643 1001870
ḳmd to mourn 160870 1001870
ḳmd to think of; to be concerned 160860 1001870
ḳn strong warrior 160940 1001886
ḳn to keep away (from so./sth.) 161010 1001881
ḳn to complete; to finish 160990 1001881
ḳn fat (med.) 160900 1001886
ḳn to be fat 870155 1001886
ḳn strong lion (a water spout shaped like a lion's head) 160950 1001886
ḳn plant of the field 160960 1001878
ḳn mat 160980 1001878
ḳn strong; brave; capable 550122 1001886
ḳn force; bravery 856313 1001886
ḳn cease (to do) 852594 1001881
ḳn to weave 161000 1001883
ḳn to beat; to injure 160910 1001882
ḳn end; first quality 600621 1001881
ḳn.yw weaver 161280 1001883
ḳn.yt bodyguard 161230 1001886
ḳn.w many; numerous 161060 1001886
ḳn.w [ref. for sterile arable land] 161090 1001878
ḳn.w the many 161070 1001886
ḳn.t valor; strength 161030 1001886
ḳn.t achievement? 851298 1001881
ḳn.t damage; injury 870158 1001882
ḳn.t whole grain size? 161050 1001881
ḳn.t [a plant (med.)] 856566 1001878
ḳn.t fat (symptom of an eye illness) 161020 1001886
ḳni̯ to be brave; to be capable; to conquer;

to make strong 854565 1001886
ḳni̠ fat; to be fat 160890 1001886
ḳni̠ to be brave; to be strong; to be capable 161150 1001886
ḳni̠ to conquer; to make strong 161160 1001886
ḳnj sheaf; bundle 161300 1001890
ḳnj [a plant (med.)] 161140 1001878
ḳnj [a ceremonial garment] 161200 1001890
ḳnj embrace 161180 1001890
ḳnj to embrace 161170 1001890
ḳnj to hurt? 161220 1001882
ḳnj.w evil deed; injury; lack 160970 1001882
ḳnj.w chair; throne; carrying chair 161290 1001889
ḳnj.w sheaf carrier 853381 1001890
ḳnj.w [term for bird(s) of the marshes] 161310 1001888
ḳnj.w portable shrine 161320 1001889
ḳnj.t yellowish [characteristic (figurative term for a mineral)] 161260 1001891
ḳnj.t [a yellow pigment] 161270 1001891
ḳnj.t [an injury to the eye (med.)] 161250 1001882
ḳnb to bind; to bend; to subjugate 161330 1001884
ḳnb.t court (of magistrates) 161350 1001884
ḳnb.t corner; angle 161340 1001884
ḳnb.tj magistrate; an officer of a court 161390 1001884
ḳnb.tj what belongs to the court 161380 1001884
ḳnr desert; desert edge 161420 1001918
ḳnn predominance 850878 1001886
ḳnḳn chastisement 855208 1001882
ḳnḳn [a cut of meat] 161460 1001882
ḳnḳn to beat; to pound up (med.) 161450 1001882
ḳnḳn.yt mallet? 161500 1001882
ḳnḳn.wj Beater [a divine being (scribe of Osiris)] 161510 1001886
ḳnd raging one (esp. Horus, Sobek) 161540 1001885
ḳnd to rage; to become angry 161530 1001885
ḳnd anger 161530 1001885
ḳr [to blacken?] 860315 1001905
ḳr.tj the twin caverns (at Elephantine) 161610 1001902
ḳrᶜ.w shield 161670 1001907
ḳrᶜ.w shield bearer 161680 1001907
ḳrf to contract; to draw together 161690 1001897
ḳrf bag 851023 1001897
ḳrf.w (facial) wrinkles (med.) 161730 1001897
ḳrf.t bag 161710 1001897
ḳrf.t contractions (med.) 161720 1001897
ḳrm.t ashes 161740 1001899
ḳrn.t foreskin; uncircumcised penis 161760 1001900
ḳrr storm; storm cloud 161770 1001903
ḳrr frog 161780 1001904
ḳrr [storm-snake?] 161830 1001903
ḳrr to fire (pottery); to cook (food) 161810 1001905
ḳrr [a boat] 161790 1001901
ḳrr burnt offering 161820 1001905
ḳrr He-of-the-cavern 161870 1001902
ḳrr.t cavern 161860 1001902
ḳrr.t hole; cavern 854566 1001902
ḳrr.t hole 161850 1001902
ḳrr.t offering place (at the tomb) 161840 1001902
ḳrr.tj rotary pan 161620 1001902
ḳrr.tj He-of-the-cavern 500137 1001902
ḳrḥ.t [primordial goddess in a form of a serpent] 161910 1001898
ḳrḥ.t pottery; pot 161890 1001898
ḳrḥ.t primeval creature; ancestor 161900 1001898
ḳrḥ.t uterus? stomach? 161920 1001898
ḳrs to bury 161940 1001874
ḳrs burial 161950 1001874
ḳrs.w coffin 161980 1001874
ḳrs.wt burial 854326 1001874

ḳrs.t burial 161960 1001874
ḳrs.tjt burial equipment 161970 1001874
ḳrḳr to spread over (of the inundation) 162000 1001895
ḳrḳr quivering? 161990 1001895
ḳrḳr.t hole 852048 1001902
ḳrḳr.t beads; lump 857704 1001895
ḳrṯ [a kind of a young animal] 859143 1001906
ḳrḏn ax; pick ax 162060 1001896
ḳḥ light 162090 1001863
ḳḥ to break stones (as punishment) 600384 1001864
ḳḥ (solar) ring halo 859650 1001863
ḳḥ bright 859649 1001863
ḳḥ.t [part of heaven] 162120 1001863
ḳḥj [characteristic of the Moon] 162130 1001863
qḥn cauldron? 162140 1001865
ḳḥḳḥ to hammer; to chisel 162150 1001864
ḳḥḳḥ.w worker with hammer (metalworker working in the quarry) 162160 1001864
ḳs harpoon tip 162190 1001908
ḳs bone 162200 1001908
ḳs to harpoon; to bone 860563 1001908
ḳs.tj sculptor; carver 855576 1001908
ḳsn the bad one 858513 1001909
ḳsn painful; irksome; difficult 162230 1001909
ḳsn difficulty; bad luck; annoyance; exertion 856685 1001909
ḳsn to be difficult; to be in difficulty 550033 1001909
ḳsn.t trouble; misfortune 162240 1001909
ḳḳ nuts; doum-palm nuts 162280 1001892
ḳḳ to eat 162310 1001893
ḳd to form; to fashion; to build 162420 1001852
ḳd nature; form; character 162430 1001852
ḳd circuit 162440 1001857
ḳd.w potter; builder; sculptor 861184 1001852
ḳd.w potter; builder; sculptor 162500 1001852
ḳd.t [a coniferous, resin-producing tree] 162480 1001848
ḳd.t kite (a measure of weight) 162490 1001849
ḳd.t sleep 162470 1001855
ḳd.tj builder 860726 1001852
ḳdi̯ to go around; to surround; to return 162530 1001857
ḳdw.w essence; character 162560 1001852
ḳdw.t drawings; outlines 162550 1001852
ḳdw.t surroundings 162540 1001857
ḳdb to rent (a field) 162570 1001854
ḳdb rent; lease 550092 1001854
ḳdb.yt [term used for marking a field (lend on lease)] 862838 1001854
ḳdf altar; table 162590 1001856
ḳdf to pick; to collect 162580 1001856
ḳdfw gleanings 162600 1001856
ḳdr.t incense 162620 1001859
ḳdḳd to stroll 859424 1001857
ḳdd sleep 162650 1001855
ḳdd to sleep 162450 1001855
ḳdd to carry out a revision 162660 1001857
ḳḏ thornbush 162690 1001851
ḳḏ plasterer 162680 1001850
ḳḏ gypsum; plaster 162670 1001850
ḳḏ to go around; to run 162700 1001853
ḳḏm handful (as a measure) 600590 1001858
ḳḏmḳm to grasp 863669 1001858

k

kꜣ food; provisions 162890 1001266
kꜣ [appearance of wound secretions] 875705 1001271
kꜣ ka; spirit; essence 162870 1001266
kꜣ so; then 162840 1001272
kꜣ [formative element of verbal forms] 400415 1001272
kꜣ to say 162850 1001272
kꜣ name 162900 1001266
kꜣ to appear as a bull? 162940 1001266
kꜣ male serpent; bull-snake (i.e. a powerful

serpent) 162950 1001266
kꜣ bull 162930 1001266
kꜣ bull (manifestation of gods, also of king) 500667 1001266
kꜣ bull 851433 1001266
kꜣ.j what belongs to Ka 850254 1001266
kꜣ.wj worker 859747 1001268
kꜣ.wt works 163070 1001268
kꜣ.wtj worker; porter 163280 1001268
kꜣ.wtj worker; porter 853549 1001268
kꜣ.t female Ka 860248 1001266
kꜣ.t cow 862899 1001266
kꜣ.t vagina; vulva 162990 1001267
kꜣ.t thought 162980 1001272
kꜣ.t work 163010 1001268
kꜣ.t work; product 163020 1001268
kꜣꜣ leopard-patterned? 163200 1001280
kꜣw.t blister 163270 1001271
kꜣi̯ to think about; to plan 163220 1001272
kꜣy.t excrement (of a gazelle, of a lizard) (med.) 163250 1001279
kꜣj [a Nubian boat] 163240 1001273
kꜣwt to carry; to support 163290 1001268
kꜣp censer 163300 1001277
kꜣp to cense; to fumigate 163310 1001277
kꜣp to catch birds? 163370 1001277
kꜣp royal nursery (institution for schooling elite youths) 163380 1001277
kꜣp incense 163320 1001277
kꜣp shelter 163330 1001277
kꜣp to cover; to roof over 163340 1001277
kꜣp to cover; to roof over; to hide 854567 1001277
kꜣp to hide; to take cover 163360 1001277
kꜣp bandaging material 850651 1001277
kꜣp.w roof; cover; lid 163430 1001277
kꜣp.w birdcatcher 163460 1001277
kꜣp.w hidden one (crocodile) 163470 1001277
kꜣp.w Hidden one (a demon causing illness) 163440 1001277
kꜣp.t incense 163400 1001277
kꜣp.t incense burning 163390 1001277
kꜣp.t linen cover (for a pot) (med.) 163410 1001277
kꜣpꜣp to cover up 163490 1001277
kꜣf flint 164090 1001269
kꜣm vineyard 163520 1001274
kꜣm.wtt ear of wheat?; [barley?] 163550 1001274
kꜣmn blind person 163580 1001275
kꜣmn to be blind; to blind 163570 1001275
kꜣn.w vineyard 163590 1001274
kꜣn.w gardener; vintner 163600 1001274
kꜣr, kꜣj chapel; shrine 163620 1001278
kꜣr.y gardener 163650 1001274
kꜣri̯ to be enshrined 856212 1001278
kꜣhs to be harsh; to be overbearing 165240 1001270
kꜣkꜣ.t blister (med.) 163720 1001271
kj to yell; to lament 163730 1001223
kj.w shout of acclamation 163800 1001223
kj.wj others; the masses 163840 1001264
kj.wj foes; hostile forces 500393 1001264
kj.wj enmity 855087 1001264
kj.t shout of acclamation 163740 1001223
kjw to bow 163820 1001224
kjw summons 163810 1001223
ky [a monkey] 163830 1001222
ky another 400645 1001264
ky another 163760 1001264
ky.t [a monkey] 163750 1001222
ky.t another 162830 1001264
ky.t another one 853029 1001264
kwšn [part of a chariot harness] 163920 1001263
kb.wj soles 163950 1001235
kbs basket 164010 1002576
kp palm (of the hand); sole (of the foot) 164020 1001235
kp sole (of the foot) 164030 1001235
kp waterhole 858346 1001235
kf knife 164100 1001215
kf.y revealing one 500353 1001215
kf.t trustworthiness? 164080 1001215
kf.t flap (of a wound) 863016 1001215
kfꜣ to be discrete 164130 1001215
kfꜣ hinter-parts; base; bottom (of a jar)

164110 1001216
kfꜣ root [a part of a plant (med.)] 164120 1001216
kfꜣ trunk 855920 1001216
kfꜣ.t pedestal?164170 1001216
kff to suck (med.) 164250 1001214
kfi̯ to gape (wound) 164210 1001215
kfi̯ to open 858347 1001215
kfi̯ to uncover; to remove 164200 1001215
kfꜥ to requisition 163880 1001217
kfꜥ to plunder; to capture 164220 1001217
kfꜥ booty; captives 164230 1001217
kfkfꜣ to be discrete 853452 1001215
km black 401218 1001227
km pile of burning charcoals 164300 1001227
km black 164320 1001227
km pupil (lit. black (of the eye)) 164330 1001227
km black leather 164340 1001227
km to complete 164370 1001226
km completion; duty; profit 164380 1001226
km.y [a kind of a serpent] 164590 1001227
km.y black one (Osiris, Min) 164560 1001227
km.t Black-land (Egypt) 164430 1001227
km.t black (arable) land 850767 1001227
km.t completion; final account? 164450 1001226
km.t [a big jar made of granite] 164470 1001227
km.t black cattle (divine herd) 164420 1001227
km.tj Egyptians 164440 1001227
kmy.t conclusion (of a book) 164580 1001226
kmm black; dark 164311 1001227
kmm to be black; to be dark 164310 1001227
kmr [a dancer] 164650 1001228
kmrj tusks; ivory 164660 1001229
kn.t dislike (of someone)? 164710 1001230
knj to complain; to lament 164720 1001230
knj to call; to complain 164730 1001230
knj to complain; to lament; to call; to complain 854568 1001230
knj.w slander 164750 1001230
knw.y complainers 164770 1001230
knw.t female complainer 500242 1001230
knm to wrap in 164780 1001231
knm.t darkness 164830 1001231
knm.tj one belonging to darkness 164870 1001231
knm.tj the dark one (star) 164880 1001231
knnr lyre 164760 1001232
knḥ to grow dark; to make dark 164900 1001429
knḥ porch; shrine 164910 1001429
knḥ.w darkness 164920 1001429
kns abdominal region 164950 1001233
knt [a garment (cloak?)] 165010 1001234
kr saddle (for a donkey) 600048 1001239
kr [a small boat (cargo ship)] 165030 1001236
kr.tj Horns (at the crown of Amun) 165040 1001238
krj prison 165050 1001241
krp to efface (inscriptions) 165060 1001244
krm.t [jewelry of Nubian slaves] 165070 1001243
krḥt basket; bushel 165090 1001240
krs to jump 165110 1001246
krs sack 165100 1001245
krk couch; bed 165130 1001242
krkr heap of stones 165140 1001237
krt slaughter 165160 1001248
krṯ whip cords?; cloth strips? 165170 1001247
krṯ young animal 859143 1001249
khꜣ to rage furiously 165180 1001221
khꜣ to rage furiously; to cast a shadow; to raise (the voice); to utter 854569 1001221
khꜣ to raise (the voice); to utter (a bellow) 165200 1001221
khꜣ to cast a shadow 165190 1001221

khb raging one (Seth) 165230 1001219
khb to harm (someone); to be violent; to roar 165220 1001219
kḥs chair 854765 1001220
kḥkḥ old man 859037 1001218
kḥkḥ to become old; to grow old 165310 1001218
kḥkḥ the old one 863735 1001218
kḥkḥ.t the old one (fem.) 165330 1001218
kz to run freely? 165370 1001265
kz [to hang down arms?] 165390 1001252
ks.w bowing(s); obedience 165450 1001252
ksi̯ to bow down; to bend down; to be prostrate 165430 1001252
ksw.t bowing, reverence 857304 1001252
ksm antagonist 165490 1001253
ksm to defy; to browbeat; to profane (a temple) 165480 1001253
ksks (Nubian) dancer 165530 1001251
ksks [a footed basket] 165540 1001250
ksks to dance; to perform 165520 1001251
ksks.t dancer 165550 1001251
ksks.t [a basket] 600025 1001250
kšw [a plant] 165590 1001254
kk.w darkness 165680 1001225
kk.w [a term for a flood water] 165700 1001225
kk.wt darkness 165710 1001225
kk.wtj dark one [a kind of a snake] 855319 1001225
kki̯ to be dark; to shade 165620 1001225
kt.t louse? 165910 1001261
kt.t little girl 169320 1001261
ktw.t cauldron(s) 165770 1001262
ktw.t hearth stones; cauldron 165760 1001262
ktp sword 165790 1001260
ktm.t gold 165800 1001258
kth̲ other 853259 1000977
ktkt quiet 500007 1001255
ktkt to tremble; quake; steal 165810 1001256
ktkt to beat 165840 1001256
ktkt eclipse 165850 1001255
ktt little one 165890 1001261
ktt trifle 165900 1001261
ktt small; trifling 165730 1001261
ktt to be small; to be trifling 165880 1001261
kt̲m divination; omen; decision (based on augury) 165950 1001257
kt̲n charioteer 165960 1001259

g

g.wt the amazement; the stare 855817 1000371
gꜣ to chant 166020 1000425
gꜣ to wound 166010 1000432
gꜣ [a heron] 166060 1000429
gꜣ to smear (with ointment) 166030 1000439
gꜣ.w lack; need 166220 1000445
gꜣ.wt lack; need 166250 1000445
gꜣ.wt bundle; dues 166280 1000445
gꜣi̯ to revile 166130 1000440
gꜣi̯ to moisten 166150 1000439
gꜣi̯ to overthrow 166110 1000440
gꜣy jar; bowl; flask 166140 1000441
gꜣy.t [a measure] 860119 1000442
gꜣw to crash down (the enemy) 166230 1000440
gꜣu̯ to be narrow; to be constricted; to lack; to deprive 166210 1000445
gꜣb.w [a kind of an employee] 166400 1000433
gꜣj.t chapel; shrine 166180 1000443
gꜣb.t arm 166370 1000433
gꜣb.t leaf; (lotus) petal 166380 1000434
gꜣb.tj eyelash 166390 1000434
gꜣḥ to press out the juice 166470 1000438
gꜣḥ to be weary 166480 1000437
gꜣḥ.w weariness 856734 1000437
gꜣḥ.w fatigue; solidification; exhaustion 856733 1000437
gꜣgꜣ to chatter 166600 1000430
gꜣh̲ shoulder 166490 1000436
gꜣš rush; reed 166570 1000444

gi̱ to be astonished 855608 1000371
gj.w [an aromatic plant] 166660 1000373
gjf vervet (long-tailed monkey) 166670 1000374
gjf.t vervet (long-tailed monkey) 166680 1000374
gy.t [a plant] 166650 1000373
gw to rejoice 852253 1000425
gw [a bull] 166700 1000423
gw [bandage] 875741 1000428
gw [a horse] 166720 1000424
gw.w singer 852091 1000425
gwꜣ to tighten; to be close 166730 1000428
gwꜣ [a tool] 850639 1000428
gwꜣ to besiege 166740 1000428
gwꜣ.t sarcophagus (of the Apis bull) 858488 1000427
gwꜣ.t chest; box 166760 1000427
gwꜣwꜣ to capture 166770 1000428
gwn haversack 166790 1000428
gwš to be crooked; to turn away 166820 1000426
gwš to be crooked (med.) 166810 1000426
gwtn to bind; to replenish 166840 1000428
gb to incline; to bow 166860 1000361
gb.w damage 166960 1000364
gbꜣ side (of a room) 166910 1000365
gbꜣ arm 166900 1000365
gbꜣ to blind 166920 1000367
gbꜣ to accompany [to walk side by side?] 166930 1000365
gbꜣ.w payment 166940 1000366
gbi̱ to be weak; to be deficient; to damage; to cheat 166950 1000364
gbb Geb 167010 1000363
gbb earth 167020 1000363
gbb fatigue 850911 1000364
gbb [a goose] 167000 1000362
gbb field 167030 1000363
gbb ground; field 854570 1000363
gbgb to be lame 167060 1000364
gbgb a lame person 167070 1000364
gbgb floatsam 855595 1000361
gbgb to overthrow (the enemy) 167050 1000364
gbgb.t heap of corpses 167090 1000364
gp to overflow; to inundate 167120 1000393
gp to be clouded (med., fig. for a heart condition) 167100 1000393
gp to overcloud; to be cloudy 167130 1000393
gfgf [a kind of a bread, or cake] 858489 1000435
gm power 167150 1000376
gm.t black ibis 167160 1000375
gm.w weakness; daze 167180 1000377
gm.wt weakness 855819 1000377
gmꜣ temple (of the head) (med.) 167200 1000381
gmi̱ to find; to discover 167210 1000380
gmḥ to catch sight of; to look 167270 1000379
gmḥ [specially shaped stone as part of a doorway] 167290 1000379
gmḥ [a term used for eye] 167280 1000379
gmḥ.t plaited hair 167310 1000378
gmḥ.t widow 167330 1000378
gmḥs.w [a bird of pray] 167360 1000379
gmgm to smash; to break; to tear 167370 1000376
gmgm to feel; to fumble around 167380 1000377
gn strongman 167410 1000384
gn to be respected; to be mighty 167400 1000384
gn stand 450115 1000383
gn.w stand 167470 1000383
gn.wt annals; records 167490 1000385
gn.t record 167440 1000385
gnf to rebuff; to repel 167520 1000386
gnn to be weak; to be soft 600572 1000390
gnn [soft part of a plant product (med.)] 167560 1000390
gnn [an edible plant (legume?)] 167580

1000382
gnn to be weak; to be soft 167540 1000390
gnn weak one 167550 1000390
gnn.w weakness 856747 1000390
gnn.w fat 167610 1000390
gnn.t the weak one (delivering woman) 167590 1000390
gnn.t weakness 167600 1000390
gnẖ to serve; to be subjected 167650 1000388
gnẖ to stud; to mount 167620 1000388
gnẖ to stick; to fix 167630 1000388
gnẖ wing(s) 167640 1000389
gnẖ.t star 167660 1000388
gngn.t [a plant of the Wadi Natrun] 167700 1000382
gngntj lute 167720 1000387
gns outrage; violence 167670 1000392
gnš to select; to distinguish 167690 1000391
gr also; furthermore 167740 1000394
gr to be silent; to end 167750 1000396
gr silence 167760 1000396
gr also; furthermore 167730 1000394
gr fishes 167770 1000396
gr.w silent one 167800 1000396
gr.t furthermore 167790 1000394
gr.tj kidneys 168180 1000395
grb property 860251 1000397
grb to cut (a piece of wood serving as a chariot part) 167830 1000398
grm to drag away 167860 1000405
grḥ to complete; to be satisfied with; to finish 167880 1000404
grḥ [one of the 8 primordial gods] 167910 1000403
grḥ tax arrears 167890 1000404
grḥ night 167920 1000403
grḥ ending 167900 1000404
grḥ.yt darkness 167950 1000403
grg equipment 168020 1000402
grg lie; falsehood 168040 1000400
grg to establish; to equip; to organize 168000 1000402
grg to hunt; to lay (a trap) 167980 1000402
grg exaltation 168060 1000399
grg to be ready 168010 1000402
grg hunter 167990 1000402
grg settlement 168030 1000402
grg rumors 168050 1000400
grg.y liar 168150 1000400
grg.w The foundations (domain) 853430 1000402
grg.t dowry 168170 1000402
grg.t settlement; foundation; newly arable land 550075 1000402
grg.t catch 168080 1000402
grg.t liar (female) 168100 1000400
grg.t trap; net 168120 1000402
grgy.t rib 168160 1000401
grqr gossiper? 167970 1000396
grt husk? 863678 1000406
gḥs gazelle 168210 1000372
gḥs.t gazelle 168230 1000372
gs side 168250 1000407
gs to anoint 168280 1000410
gs to treat (leather) 855556 1000413
gs to mourn 168240 1000411
gs side 168250 1000407
gs side; half 854572 1000407
gs leather-worker 168290 1000413
gs half 168260 1000407
gs.y neighbor 168320 1000407
gs.w half-loaf (offering) 168330 1000407
gs.w ointment 168340 1000410
gs.t mourner 858490 1000411
gs.t run; course 168310 1000414
gs.tj (testicles) 168680 1000407
gsꜣ bag 168540 1000420
gsꜣ favorite? 859413 1000421
gsꜣ to be inclined; to go wrong 168510 1000421
gsꜣ [an antilope] 168530 1000419
gsꜣ to destroy; to annihilate 855203 1000421
gsꜣ.t [leather cover (as robe or bag)] 855165 1000420

gsꜣ.t inclined bed 168520 1000421
gsi̯ to run 168550 1000414
gsp to equip? 500087 1000416
gsp cavetto 858729 1000415
gsr finger ring 863456 1000417
gsgs to overflow 168640 1000414
gsgs to put in order; to regulate 168630 1000412
gstj scribe's palette 168670 1000418
gš migrating bird 168690 1000409
gš to pour off; to pour away 858492 1000408
gš [a body of water] 168700 1000408
gš [dregs or lees] 858493 1000408
gš [vessel] 865331 1000408
gg.t kidneys 168710 1000370
ggw.w the amazement; the stare 856740 1000371
ggw.t the amazement; the stare 852232 1000371
ggwi̯ to marvel; to be amazed 852231 1000371
gt.t cistern 863681 1000422
gḏ arms 168780 1000368
gḏm to grasp 168790 1000369

t

tʾ bread (gen.) 168810 1002425
tꜣ (main) gateway; (main) door (of a temple) 168910 1002580
tꜣ to be hot; to burn 854574 1002584
tꜣ earth (as a material) 400576 1002581
tꜣ to be hot 168890 1002584
tꜣ (arable) land; ground 400577 1002581
tꜣ to burn 168900 1002584
tꜣ earth; land; ground 854573 1002581
tꜣ kiln 168880 1002584
tꜣ [a measure of surface area] 450772 1002581
tꜣ earth; land; ground 168860 1002581
tꜣ land (with geo-political reference); Egypt 400096 1002581
tꜣ.yt bakehouse? 859243 1002584
tꜣ.yt heat 169400 1002584
tꜣ.w hothead 168940 1002584
tꜣ.w heat 168950 1002584
tꜣy.t (main) door (of a temple) 169420 1002580
tꜣy.t fabric; mummy bindings; sail; curtain 169450 1002590
tꜣyt foe; enemy 169410 1002591
tꜣw [divine garment] 169470 1002590
ṯꜣu̯ to steal 174470 1002589
tꜣf pottery kiln 169480 1002587
tꜣḥ to kill 169550 1002588
tꜣḥ rioters (troublemakers by talking) 169560 1002588
tꜣḥ to sink 169530 1002588
tꜣḥ inhabitants of Delta 169570 1002588
tꜣḥ to plunge; sink; confuse; to blur 169520 1002588
tꜣḥ.w foes 169620 1002588
tꜣḥ.t dregs (med.) 169590 1002588
tꜣḥ.t irrigation runnel? 169600 1002588
tꜣḥ.t female inhabitant of Delta 169580 1002588
tꜣj.tjt [a kind of textile, tissue] 854438 1002590
tꜣš boundary; border; region 169650 1002597
tꜣš to demarcate; to divide 169660 1002597
ti̯ to trample 169700 1002476
tj to pound 169700 1002476
tj.t [Isis blood - symbol] 169740 1002472
tj.t fraction 169760 1002473
tj.t lower part of the Udjat eye 169750 1002473
tj.t pestle 169670 1002476
tj.t [a kind of a measure of incense] 169770 1002470
tj.t [a chamber in temple] 169800 1002469
tj.t image; form; sign 169790 1002474
tjꜣ to moan; to scream; to jubilate 169890 1002480
tjꜣ song of praise 863156 1002480
tjꜣ one who celebrates 852087 1002480
tjꜣ acute pain 169880 1002480
tjꜣ.t [a mineral] 450169 1002471

tjs to fix; to mount with 170030 1002479
tjšs to grind; to crush 170060 1002553
tjtj to trample 170080 1002476
tjtj [term for legs] 858889 1002476
ty steppe 852604 1002575
twꜣ to put a claim (on someone); to appeal; to support; to elevate 854575 1002574
twꜣ pillar 170180 1002574
twꜣ [an erected serpent] 170190 1002574
twꜣ culmination? 170200 1002574
twꜣ lintel (or jamb?) 170290 1002574
twꜣ to support; to elevate 170140 1002574
twꜣ to put a claim (on someone); to appeal (to someone) 170130 1002574
twꜣ bearer 170150 1002574
twꜣ man of low station; inferior 170120 1002574
twꜣ.w swellings (med.) 170250 1002574
twꜣ.w claim 851301 1002574
twꜣ.w wrong; evil 170240 1002573
twꜣ.wt [one of the 7 holy oils] 170270 1002572
twr to reject; to repulse 170340 1002568
twr to show respect to 170350 1002568
twr Respected one 856122 1002568
twr purifier 170390 1002567
twr purity; purification 170380 1002567
twr Pure (a body of water in the hereafter) 170400 1002567
twr to purify; to be pure 170370 1002567
twr to stay away (from something); stick to (something) 170360 1002568
twrj.t [a staff] 170420 1002569
twhr (foreign, Asiatic) warrior 173060 1002563
twt likeness? 170460 1002570
twt complete 170490 1002570
twt statue; likeness; image 170470 1002570
twt entire; complete 400242 1002570
twt to be like; to be sufficient; to be complete 170480 1002570
twt.w likeness 170520 1002570
twt.wj the two who are matching 855632 1002570
twtj̑ to collect; to assemble 170500 1002570
tb to pay 170650 1002428
tb.t [a measure] 170620 1002428
tb.t box 170630 1002426
tb.t payment; reward 170610 1002428
tbn to drum 170720 1002432
tbn tambourine-like drum 170710 1002432
tbn head; top 170670 1002430
tbn bone marrow 170690 1002430
tbs to stab 170760 1002434
tbs heel 170750 1002433
tbtb to hoist 170810 1002429
tbtb to carry 170830 1002429
tp on; at the top of; at (local) 170900 1002520
tp head; beginning (of a region) 170860 1002520
tp tip; top (of mountain, of a building, etc.) 170861 1002520
tp principle (to do something); type of calculation (adm.) 600414 1002520
tp itself, yourself etc. 600416 1002520
tp best (of) 450189 1002520
tp headman; chief 600413 1002520
tp at; in; to (temp.) 600417 1002520
tp major 600415 1002520
tp person 170870 1002520
tp beginning (of a period of time) 170880 1002520
tp.j best linen 171480 1002520
tp.j first 550180 1002520
tp.j best 171470 1002520
tp.j principal; first 171460 1002520
tp.j being upon; having authority over 171450 1002520
tp.y the one with the head 171500 1002520
tp.y big woods 171490 1002519
tp.jt first (fine oil) 170960 1002520
tp.jt great; top 858040 1002520
tp.jt [a beam of wood] 108910 1002519
tp.jt uraeus 170930 1002520
tp.jt White Crown (of Upper Egypt)

170940 1002520
tp.jt first 860916 1002520
tp.w (the best) fields 853070 1002520
tp.wj double-headed one 501083 1002520
tp.t head (as a part of the body) 170920 1002520
tp.t fine thread 872573 1002520
tp.tj [part of a boat] 40340 1002519
tp.tj first (in a series); best 170980 1002520
tpꜣ.w [a fruit] 171410 1002531
tpꜣ.w [an affliction of the head] 171390 1002532
tpꜣ.w [a part of the skull] 171380 1002532
tpꜣ.w [an ingredient (med.)] 171400 1002533
tpꜣ.wt [an ingredient (med.)] 171420 1002533
tpj [an ox] 171520 1002524
tpnn cummin 171690 1002527
tpnn.t [an ingredient (med.)] 171700 1002527
tpr to breathe 600420 1002529
tf to spit out 171740 1002435
tf spittle 171750 1002435
tfꜣ saw 171760 1002442
tfi̯ to remove forcefully; to repulse 171780 1002436
tfn joy 171850 1002439
tfn dent (in metal objects) 171860 1002437
tfn orphan 171830 1002438
tfn.t orphan 171870 1002438
tfnn to rejoice; to be glad 171900 1002439
tftf to be confused 171950 1002436
tftf to spit out; to trickle 858891 1002435
tm to complete 172010 1002487
tm to be complete 172000 1002487
tm not to be; [negative verb] 171990 1002487
tm to cease; to perish 171980 1002487
tm everything 172020 1002487
tm to be over 854578 1002487
tm.jw the vain ones (enemies of Osiris) 172240 1002487
tm.w everyone; humankind 172070 1002487
tm.wt totality; completeness 858018 1002487
tm.t sledge 172040 1002488
tmꜣ sack 172160 1002497
tmꜣ troop (of soldiers) 172170 1002500
tmꜣ mat (gen.) 172150 1002497
t̠mꜣ to be strong; to be mighty 175440 1002499
tmꜣ.yt mat 172210 1002497
tmꜣ.ytj who is on the Mat 858020 1002497
tmꜣ.wt pocket (of skin) (med.) 172200 1002497
tmꜣ.t ancestress; mother 172190 1002498
tmm to close (a wound) (med.) 172260 1002487
tmm to close (the mouth) 172250 1002487
tmm [a wooden chest] 172270 1002492
tmz to turn (the face to someone) 172310 1002496
tmt to powder (med.) 172320 1002495
tmt.w powder (med.) 172330 1002495
tmtm pulverize (med.) 172340 1002495
tmtm grinder 862948 1002495
tmtm undoing 172350 1002487
tnj old man 172430 1002510
tnj big; outstanding 172450 1002510
tnj to measure oneself (with so.) 172470 1002510
tnj (external) signs of age (med.) 172440 1002510
tnj to grow old; to be old 172420 1002510
tnj [term for a king in battle] 172460 1002510
tnbẖ to be confused 172520 1002502
tnm furrow 172550 1002512
tnm to avert; to go astray 172530 1002512
tr misbehavior, unclean 172730 1002542
tr to be doomed to; to be destined for 172710 1002537
tr time; season 172700 1002537
trj door 172820 1002541

trj [honorific epithet of the King] 172770 1002543
try.t impurity 172830 1002542
trꜥ worm (Apophis) 860986 1002552
trr oven 172850 1002546
trr to race?; to go for an outing? 172860 1002547
th sacrilege; transgression 172900 1002453
th.w transgressor 172910 1002453
thi̯ to go astray; to transgress; to damage 172920 1002453
thb.w concentration (med.) 172970 1002447
thm perforation; puncture (wound) 172990 1002455
thm to water 173020 1002454
thm to perforate (med.); to penetrate; to drive (cattle) 172980 1002455
thm to stir (in the kettle) 173000 1002454
thm to cook something 173010 1002454
tḥwꜣ peas 852327 1002467
tḥs to squash; to crush; to pulverize 173090 1002465
tḫ Plummet? (Thoth?) 173140 1002444
tḫ drunkenness 859951 1002452
tḫ plummet (of a balance) 173100 1002444
tḫ heavy drinking 173120 1002452
tḫ fat, fattened 173130 1002443
tḫ.w drunkard 173160 1002452
tḫ.t drunkenness 173150 1002452
tḫi̯ to be drunk; to become drunk 173110 1002452
tḫb turtle 859679 1002450
tḫb bloating; blister (med.) 173220 1002449
tḫb [moist secretion?] 169640 1002449
tḫb to dip; to moisten; to irrigate 173210 1002449
tḫbs [a basket] 173230 1002451
tḫn ibis (as Thoth's sacred animal) 173250 1002456
tḫn to injure; to damage 173320 1002458
tḫn obelisk 173240 1002461
tḫn to hide; to be hidden 173270 1002460
tḫn to enter 173290 1002460
tḫn door, door leaf 173310 1002460
tḫn to protect 173280 1002460
tḫn injury (to the eye) (med.) 173260 1002458
tḫn high statue? 173300 1002461
tḫnḫn to spread wings (over so.) 173330 1002460
tḫr [part of chariot] 173340 1003902
tḫs to slaughter; to dismantle 173350 1002464
tḫtḫ disorder 854420 1002445
tḫtḫ to confuse; to confound 173370 1002445
tš.w deserters; wanderers 173450 1002555
tšꜣ to squash (grain for beer) 173470 1002557
tšꜣ to spilt open 173480 1002557
tši̯ to be absent from; to be missing; to flee 173490 1002555
tšmm [a crocodile] 173520 1002556
tštš to squash; to crush 173540 1002557
tštš mutilated one 173550 1002557
tkꜣ to illumine; to burn 173610 1002484
tkꜣ.w flame; torch; candle 173620 1002484
tkꜣ.t illumination 173660 1002484
tkn to be near; to draw near 173680 1002482
tkn.j assailant 860291 1002482
tkn.w neighbours 851306 1002482
tkn.w approacher 858012 1002482
tks to reach (a place); to run through 173710 1002482
tks to be fixed; to settled, to be stigmatized 173720 1002482
tkšš to kick someone 173730 1002481
tkk attack 850939 1002481
tkk to attack; to injure 173740 1002481
tkk Attacker (a serpent) 854366 1002481
tkk attacker 173750 1002481
tkk.t attacker (stinging insect (wasp?)) 173760 1002481
tktk attacker 173780 1002481
tktk to attack 173770 1002481

tqr huge; mighty 173570 1002534

ṯ

ṯ.t timber (for boat building) 173890 1002422
ṯ.t clerks; staff 173850 1002424
ṯ.t staff; crew; clerks 854579 1002424
ṯ.t books 173860 1002423
ṯ.t people; crew 173840 1002424
ṯ.t table (for food) 173870 1002422
ṯꜣ pellet; drop 173960 1002579
ṯꜣ fledgling; chick 173950 1002583
ṯꜣ nestling (epithet of Horus) 174140 1002583
ṯꜣ to sort out (during the flax harvest) 174070 1002589
ṯꜣ [part of a chariot (handgrip?)]174010 1002589
ṯꜣ.y man; male 174240 1002582
ṯꜣ.y male 174250 1002582
ṯꜣ.y the male 856255 1002582
ṯꜣ.yt tweezer(s) 174320 1002589
ṯꜣ.w carrier; trainee 174450 1002589
ṯꜣ.w collection (of writings) (med.) 174460 1002423
ṯꜣ.wj (young) crocodile 174150 1002583
ṯꜣ.wt theft 174520 1002589
ṯꜣ.wt stolen goods; stolen property (as a refund value); confiscated 174500 1002589
ṯꜣ.t fledgling 858001 1002583
ṯꜣ.t the chicks (for children) (coll.) 850972 1002583
ṯꜣ.tj vizier 174090 1002585
ṯꜣ.tjt female vizier 174100 1002585
ṯꜣi̯ to take; to sieze; to don (clothing) 174260 1002589
tꜣy to resist 169390 1002591
ṯꜣy to scold; to reproach 174280 1002589
ṯꜣy reproach; fault 174290 1002589
ṯꜣw boatman 450354 1002598
ṯꜣw air; wind; breath 174480 1002598
ṯꜣw.t sail 174510 1002598
ṯꜣb.t loan (of grain); agricultural surplus 174570 1002586
ṯꜣbb corn ear 174580 1002586
ṯꜣpr to swell 854336 1002595
ṯꜣm to cloak; to cover (with skin) (wound healing) 174590 1002593
ṯꜣm foreskin 174610 1002593
ṯꜣm cloak; swaddling clothes; bandages 174600 1002593
tꜣm.w [noun (worm?); excrements?] 169490 1002592
ṯꜣms to eat; to devour 174650 1002594
ṯꜣr to protect (someone) from (crocodile) 174660 1002596
ṯꜣr to make fast [from the good preparation of the headrests] 174690 1002596
ṯꜣr to exercise protection over 174680 1002596
ṯꜣr [a shelter] 174700 1002596
ṯꜣr [act of the King ascending the throne] 174670 1002596
ṯꜣr.t [an enclosed structure] 174750 1002596
ṯꜣr.t cabin [an enclosed structure] 174720 1002596
ṯꜣr.t fortress [an enclosed structure] 174730 1002596
ṯꜣr.t silo; granary 174760 1002596
ṯꜣz vertebra; spine 176810 1002600
ṯꜣz neck 176820 1002600
ṯꜣz tooth 176830 1002601
ṯꜣz to command; to be ruler 176850 1002599
ṯꜣz saying; utterance; phrase 176860 1002600
ṯꜣz knot 856104 1002600
ṯꜣz.w commander 177110 1002599
ṯꜣz.t vertebra; backbone 176930 1002600
ṯꜣz.t [an ivory chariot appertenance (knob? boss?)] 176940 1002600
ṯꜣzṯꜣz [a kind of a fabric] 862887 1002600
ṯj.t thyme 174850 1002475
ṯjf to flee 174800 1002477
ṯjs [preparing? dough for beer making] 174820 1002478
ṯw.t share (what belongs (to you)) 174920 1002561

ṯwꜣ resistance 174950 1002565
ṯwj.t crown? 174960 1002564
ṯwfj papyrus flowers; papyrus marsh 174970 1002562
ṯwn contribution; gift 175000 1002566
ṯwn to reward 175010 1002566
ṯwn to gore; to attack 174980 1002565
ṯwn.w fighting bull 175020 1002565
ṯwn.w distinction 175030 1002566
ṯb [a bread (sole-shaped)] 851384 1002427
ṯb crate (for fowl) 175070 1002426
ṯb to be shod; to provide with sandals 175090 1002427
ṯbw sole; sandal(s) 175120 1002427
ṯbw sandalmaker 856144 1002427
ṯbw sandals 175150 1002427
ṯbw.t sole (of the foot); sandal 175160 1002427
ṯbn to be quick 175200 1002431
ṯbhn to leap (of animals) 175220 1002431
ṯpnpn to be glad 175250 1002526
ṯpr scribe 175260 1002528
ṯprṯ (bronze-clad Hittite) chariot 175270 1002530
ṯpḥ.t cavern; (snake's) hole; chapel (of a temple) 175280 1002522
ṯpḥ.tj cave dweller 855316 1002523
ṯpg barracks 175290 1002521
ṯfrr to be blue 855714 1002440
ṯfrr lapis lazuli 855713 1002440
ṯfrr.t Tefreret (lapis lazuli land) 855712 1002440
ṯftn to rush; to progress 855232 1002441
ṯftn to rush 175370 1002441
ṯm to be ashamed 175420 1002489
ṯmḥ to avoid; to divide 175500 1002491
ṯmḥ.y [a kind of red ochre] 175520 1002490
ṯms to be red 175540 1002493
ṯms to bury; to cover 175530 1002494
ṯms redness (med., as a symptom of illness) 175550 1002493
ṯms.w injury; harm 175580 1002493
ṯms.t [a kind of a plant] 863012 1002493
ṯms.t red-colored strip of cloth 175570 1002493
ṯms.tj [term for Horus] 854334 1002493
ṯmss.t [a kind of a red thing?] 175600 1002493
ṯmṯm [container?] 175630 1002486
ṯn venerable one 401002 1002508
ṯn raised one 858936 1002508
ṯn warder; guardian; frontier guard 175670 1002501
ṯn.w cliffs (along the river, forming a boundary) 175660 1002508
ṯn.w dignity 175810 1002508
ṯn.t distinguished; different 175690 1002508
ṯni̯ to rise; to distinguish; to be distinguished 175750 1002508
ṯni̯ to observe; to watch closely 175790 1002508
ṯnj where? whence? whither? 175740 1000844
ṯnj to be weak 175780 1002509
ṯnj honour; worship 175760 1002508
ṯnw each; every 175840 1002518
ṯnw to count; to control 175820 1002518
ṯnw number; quantity 175830 1002518
ṯnw every time that 550066 1002518
ṯnw.t census (of the dead, a religious festival) 175870 1002518
ṯnw.t count; quantity 175850 1002518
ṯnw.t cattle count 175860 1002518
ṯnf to drink; to dance 175890 1002504
ṯnf [a weight (in recipes, for cereals)] 175900 1002505
ṯnf to measure; to appraise; to summarize 175920 1002505
ṯnf.yt sack; bag 175950 1002505
ṯnf.t [a vessel] 175940 1002503
ṯnm cauldron; pit 175960 1002511
ṯnr mound; hill 176080 1002485
ṯnr mighty one 176060 1002514
ṯnr might; mighty deeds 176070 1002514
ṯnr to be strong; to grow strong; to preserve 176050 1002514
ṯnr strong; energetic; effective 550245

1002514
ṯnrk [a kind of a bier] 176110 1002515
ṯnḥ to blink; to observe; to wink 176120 1002506
ṯnḥr [a kind of a falcon] 176140 1002507
ṯnt.t [sacred cattle (of Hathor)] 175710 1002516
ṯntꜣ.t throne dais 176160 1002517
ṯntꜣ.t throne dais 176180 1002517
ṯntꜣ.tj the one belonging to the throne dais (Osiris) 858888 1002517
ṯr.w red (blood) 176230 1002536
ṯr.w [a mineral, from Elephantine, containing ochre] 176220 1002536
ṯr.wt redness 856119 1002536
ṯr.t willow 176250 1002538
ṯr.t finely ground wheat flour 176430 1002535
ṯry.t [goddess of willow] 176280 1002538
ṯryn body armor 176290 1002550
ṯrʿ [a field] 176310 1002551
ṯrwrw to delight in sth. 176330 1002549
ṯrp to stumble 176360 1002545
ṯrp white-fronted goose 176350 1002545
ṯrf [a dance] 176370 1002539
ṯrm to move (quickly); to wink; to hurry 851501 1002544
ṯrm wink 856121 1002544
ṯrm to blink; to wink; to observe 176380 1002544
ṯrry siege mound 176400 1002548
ṯhꜣ lame man 176450 1002468
ṯhb to jump 176460 1002448
ṯhm to tempt; to mortify 176480 1002455
ṯhm to hunt 176470 1002455
ṯhṯh lame one 176490 1002468
ṯḥ.w joy 176530 1002446
ṯḥw to rejoice 176520 1002446
ṯḥn to be bright; to gleam; to dazzle 400374 1002457
ṯḥn to be bright; to gleam; to dazzle; to exhilarate 854580 1002457
ṯḥn to be bright; to gleam; to dazzle 176570 1002457
ṯḥn to open (an infected area) (med.) 176550 1002459
ṯḥn brightness 176590 1002457
ṯḥn [term for flowers] 176600 1002457
ṯḥn to encounter; to engage (an enemy, in battle) 176560 1002459
ṯḥn to brighten; to amuse 176580 1002457
ṯḥn.y dazzling one (the sun god) 176690 1002457
ṯḥn.t faience; glass 176620 1002457
ṯḥn.t [a pendant of faience pearls] 176610 1002457
ṯḥn.t gleamer (goddesses, esp. Hathor) 176660 1002457
ṯḥn.t [an unguent]; gleamer? 176650 1002457
ṯḥnḥn to gleam 176720 1002457
ṯḥnn to rejoice 176710 1002446
ṯḥr injury; mockery 176730 1002462
ṯḥḥ to rejoice; to hail 176740 1002446
ṯḥḥw.t rejoice; exultation 176750 1002446
ṯḥs to stretch (e.g., leather) 176760 1002466
ṯḥs.t [a kind of metal - copper; bronze?] 176770 1002463
ṯz taxes; dues; delivery 176880 1002751
ṯz support 176890 1002751
ṯz sandbank 176840 1002751
ṯz.w reprehensible 176900 1002751
ṯz.w extension (of the neck); accumulation (med.) 177260 1002751
ṯz.t taxes 176980 1002751
ṯz.t rank 177000 1002751
ṯz.t heaven; roof 177010 1002751
ṯz.t ridge (of hills); (mountain) range 176960 1002751
ṯz.t image of an enemy (to be destroyed) 177040 1002751
ṯz.t mourning woman 177020 1002751
ṯz.t complaint; accusation 177030 1002751
ṯz.t One who is elevated 860615 1002751
ṯz.t [a case for a sekhem-scepter] 176920 1002751
ṯz.t transport 855640 1002751
ṯz.t chest (on legs?) 176990 1002751

ṯz.tj one who is in the chest (Osiris) 177070 1002751
ṯz.tjw image of an enemy (to be destroyed) 177100 1002751
ṯz.tjt image of an enemy (to be destroyed) 860994 1002751
ṯzi̯ to raise; to elevate 177200 1002751
ṯzi̯ to rise up; to go up (to a place) 600467 1002751
ṯzi̯ to elevate 854581 1002751
ṯzi̯ to elevate 852063 1002751
ṯzi̯ to blame; to suspend 177210 1002751
ṯzi̯ to accumulate (things) 177220 1002751
ṯzm greyhound 855040 1002577
ṯzm hound 177290 1002577
ṯzm to build 177300 1002578
ṯzm.t hound 177330 1002577
ṯzm.t battlements; (defesive) surrounding walls 177340 1002578
ṯs to sit 177080 1002554
ṯsw anticipation? 177270 1002554
ṯkr tower gate 177400 1002483
ṯt to dissolve; to let loose; to remove 177440 1002559
ṯt.jw staff; crew? 177470 1002424
ṯtf to flow; to overflow; to surge (water) 177480 1002560
ṯtf to flow; to overflow; to surge (water); to be flooded 854582 1002560
ṯtf to overflow; to be flooded 177490 1002560
ṯtṯt quarrel 177540 1002559
ṯtṯt to quarrel; to scold 177530 1002559
ṯṯ sparrow 177580 1002558

d

dꜣ to copulate 856558 1000302
dꜣ to tremble (med) 177620 1000303
dꜣ to escape; to disappear; to pass out? 177610 1000303
dꜣj.w [a linen garment] 600206 1000311
dꜣj.w wad of linen; bale of cloth 177680 1000311
dꜣw.t trembling 177700 1000303
dꜣb fig; fig tree 177710 1000304
dꜣb.yt [a beverage made from fig] 859247 1000304
dꜣgy.t bat 859221 1000228
dꜣr to subdue; to suppress 177740 1000319
dꜣr.tj Coerced (Seth) 853085 1000319
dꜣz [equipment for bowstring] 177770 1000320
dꜣz to bind; to tie 177780 1000320
dj.j 50 square meter fabric 850975 1000206
dj.w the Five 855796 1000206
dj.w five 177840 1000206
dj.wt five parts 177860 1000206
dj.wt fiver (winnower); troop of five workers 177870 1000206
dj.nw fifth 854323 1000206
djdj (red) ochre 177900 1000208
dy here; there 177830 1000207
dwꜣ to rise early 177920 1000296
dwꜣ to praise; to worship 177930 1000296
dwꜣ to enjoy; to appreciate 858661 1000296
dwꜣ.yt (early) morning; tomorrow 178120 1000296
dwꜣy.t garden 178130 1000296
dwꜣ.w adorer 178020 1000296
dwꜣ.w song of praise; hymn 178010 1000296
dwꜣ.w in the morning; tomorrow 400078 1000296
dwꜣ.w tomorrow; the morrow 600406 1000296
dwꜣ.w (early) morning 178000 1000296
dwꜣ.w the worshipers 854155 1000296
dwꜣ.wj morning sun 178110 1000296
dwꜣ.wj morning light 856725 1000296
dwꜣ.wj of the morning 178100 1000296
dwꜣ.wt [female divine being (dancer)] 178030 1000296
dwꜣ.t netherworld; nether chamber (crypt) 177640 1000296
dwꜣ.t praise 177960 1000296
dwꜣ.t adoratrice (of a (particular) god) 177970 1000296
dwꜣ.t Duat (Heavenly area where the sun

rises) 177650 1000296
dwꜣ.t abyss 177670 1000296
dwꜣ.t burial chamber; cave 177660 1000296
dwꜣ.t Duat (personified underworld) 854004 1000296
dwꜣ.tj (one who) is in the netherworld 500223 1000296
dwꜣ.tj one who belongs to the netherworld 500101 1000296
dwꜣ.tjt He of the netherworld 500928 1000296
dwꜣ.tyw those from the underworld 853472 1000296
dwꜣtj to praise 177990 1000296
dwn usually; regularly; farther 852346 1000292
dwn to stretch out; to be stretched out; to endow 178160 1000292
dwn libation offering 859682 1000292
dwn food offerings 178200 1000292
dwn.w extension 855814 1000292
dwn.tj triumphator 178220 1000292
dwr [a unit of measure for fruit] 178260 1000293
dwḏw flour 450193 1000181
db horn; tusk 178290 1002928
db.w bank 178360 1000152
dbꜣ to fall down 178370 1000168
dbj hippopotamus 178280 1000161
dbj.y hippopotamus thongs 178430 1000161
dbj.t hippopotamus 178320 1000161
dbb.t constipation 178510 1000157
dbdb to attack? 178930 1002928
dbdb to beat (of the heart) (med.) 178910 1002928
dbdb to stab; to cut up 178920 1002928
dbdb to slurp (blood) 178940 1000154
dbn deben (weight); deben (measure, ca. 91g) 178610 1000163
dbn round 178550 1000163
dbn clay (also med.) 178620 1000163
dbn to go round (a place); to travel round; to encircle 178560 1000163
dbn a kind of a round field 178570 1000163
dbn round-topped wooden box 178580 1000163
dbn ring; circle 178520 1000163
dbn helmet 178600 1000163
dbn to be round 178540 1000163
dbn.j He-who-is-in-the-box (Osiris) 178700 1000163
dbn.w circumference 178660 1000163
ḏbn.w hartebeest (antelope) 183620 1000162
dbn.wj one who goes round (sun, moon) 178690 1000163
dbn.t eyebrow?; eyelashes? 856625 1000163
dbn.t lock of hair 178630 1000163
dbn.tj two who go round (the sun and moon) 178650 1000163
dbnbn to go round (in circles) 178710 1000163
dbnbn wanderings; vicissitudes 178720 1000163
dbḥ to need; to ask for; to requisition 178750 1000160
dbḥ the pleading one 861065 1000160
dbḥ.yt [a plot of land?] 852152 1000160
dbḥ.w requirements; needs (gen.) 178830 1000160
dbḥ.w offering foods 178840 1000160
dbḥ.w requests; necessities 178760 1000160
dbḥ.t inundation ("need") 860366 1000160
dbḥ.t altar (for the funeray meal) 178810 1000160
dbḥ.t need; equipment 178800 1000160
dbḥw complaint; reclamation 178890 1000160
dp to taste; to bite into 178970 1000245
dp lump? (med.) 178960 1000244
dp.w steering oar? 179070 1000242
dp.w boat (gen.) 179060 1000242
dp.w [a part of a ship's mast?] 179080 1000242
dp.t taste 179020 1000245

dp.t boat (gen.) 179040 1000242
dp.t loin; lumbar region 179030 1000243
dpy crocodile (gen.) 179100 1000249
dpẖ execution block? 179120 1000246
dm to be sharp 600468 1000210
dm to pronounce (a name); to mention (by name) 179190 1000210
dm to sharpen 179170 1000210
dm worm 179200 1000211
dm to pierce; penetrate 179180 1000210
dm.t knife 179210 1000210
ḏm.t [a building as the seat of a god, metaph. for throne] 184030 1000209
dm.wt cut; bite; injury (general) 179220 1000210
dmꜣ [a colorful apron] 179250 1000213
dmꜣ to stretch 850991 1000213
dmꜣ to bind together 179230 1000213
dmꜣ to clot (med.) 179260 1000213
dmꜣ.w one who binds 179310 1000213
dmꜣ.t wing 179290 1000213
dmj to touch; to be joined to; to cleave to 179320 1000213
dmj town; quarter of a town; landing place; wharf 179330 1000213
dmj.w townspeople 179380 1000213
dmj.t town; quay 179370 1000213
dmḏ to unite; to (re)assemble; to be (re)assemled 179420 1000213
dmḏ two knotted strips of stuff 179410 1000213
dmḏ total 179430 1000213
dmḏ summation (in accounts) 179440 1000213
dmḏ.yt assembly 179580 1000213
dmḏ.yt grand total 550065 1000213
dmḏ.yt [recurring fixed or appointed time] 179590 1000213
dmḏ.wj the two united ones 179520 1000213
dmḏ.wt crowd 179530 1000213
dmḏ.t [a golden ring?] 179470 1000213
dmḏ.t collection (of recipies); pharmacopoeia 179460 1000213
dmḏ.t [an amulet?] 859208 1000213
dn to cut off; to kill 179620 1000219
dnꜥ to refill (with water) 179640 1000241
dn.yt one who cuts 179760 1000219
dn.w patch (made of stone in a monolith) 179660 1000219
dn.wt families 179670 1000217
dni̯ to allocate (something to so.) 179710 1000232
dni̯ to dam (ater); to revet (earthen banks) 179680 1000232
dni̯ to hold back; to restrict 179690 1000232
dni̯ to soak 179630 1000232
dnj [ḏnj] fifth day 179740 1000233
dnj dam; dyke (as boundary of a field) 179700 1000232
dnj.w share; portion 179850 1000232
dnj.wt shouting; shriek 179860 1000234
dnj.t share; portion 179800 1000232
dnj.t dam; dyke 179780 1000232
dnj.t family 179770 1000217
dny.t land register 179810 1000232
dnrg [a fruit (melon?);] 600464 1000238
dnḥs.t [a metal tool (knife?)] 179890 1000231
dns heavy one (Seth, as hippopotamus) 179920 1000240
dns to be weighty; to be heavy; to be irksome 179910 1000240
dns.w weights (of a net) 179950 1000240
dng dwarf; pygmy 179980 1000228
dng to be deaf 179970 1000229
dndn The angry one 854364 1000225
dndn anger; rage 180040 1000225
dndn to cut 180080 1000219
dndn rager (Seth) 180070 1000225
dndn to be angry; to rage 180050 1000225
dndn to traverse 180020 1000226
dndn.t the angry one [Hathor] 180090 1000225
dndny.t angry one 180120 1000225
dnẖnẖ to protect 179900 1001552
dr to protect (from) 180150 1000266

dr to drive away; to repel; to remove 180130 1000266
dr to spread; to smooth; to overlay 650023 1000267
dr clothing; garment 180170 1000264
dr to dress 180160 1000264
dr.t (cattle) prod 180180 1000263
dr.tj exterminator (Seth) 853086 1000266
drf writing; script; document; papyrus roll 180250 1000269
drf [to paint black line of the eyebrow] 180240 1000269
drp provider 865577 1000271
drp a land of supplies 859954 1000271
drp to offer; to feed; to present 180220 1000271
drp.w offerings 180230 1000271
drdrw leveling 180270 1000267
dhn to bow to; to touch (the ground with the forehead) 180280 1000197
dhn to appoint 180290 1000199
dhn.t forehead 180320 1000197
dhn.t cliff; mountain spur; rock (cultic) 180330 1000196
dhn.t (mountain) ridge 859955 1000196
dḥ to hang down; to be low 180350 1000194
dḥ depth; lowest part 180360 1000194
dḥ.w prostration; hanging down 856646 1000194
dḥꜣ straw; chop 180380 1000202
dḥꜣ to pounce (on something) 180390 1000203
dḥr to be bitter 180440 1000200
dḥr.t bitterness; sickness 180450 1000200
dḥtt testicles 180470 1000194
dḥdḥ to hang down 180480 1000194
dẖ to hide 180520 1000194
dẖ to crush; to prostrate 180530 1000195
dẖ.wt stone blocks; (piece of) rock 180550 1000195
dẖn to beat time 180570 1000198
dẖn to condescend 180590 1000195
dẖn rhythm maker 180580 1000198
ds knife 180620 1000275
ds to cut; to be sharp 180630 1000275
ds flint 180610 1000275
dsds the one who cuts 860655 1000275
dšr red one (Seth, as a hippopotamus) 180780 1000280
dšr [a red steer, as an offering] 180770 1000280
dšr impurity; dirt 180760 1000280
dšr flamingo 180680 1000280
dšr reddening (med.) 180700 1000280
dšr to be red; to become red 180690 1000280
dšr Red one 855803 1000280
dšr [a tree and its wood] 180720 1000280
dšr [a red plant] 180730 1000280
dšr greed for blood; anger 180750 1000280
dšr the red one 856707 1000280
dšr red; angry 550232 1000280
dšr.w desert dwellers? 400757 1000280
dšr.w the red one 858938 1000280
dšr.w schrot? 180900 1000280
dšr.w redfish 180880 1000280
dšr.w The red one (Seth) 180890 1000280
dšr.w blood; redness 180870 1000280
dšr.t Red crown of Lower Egypt 501048 1000280
dšr.t red 857575 1000280
dšr.t red cow 856715 1000280
dšr.t mischief; wrath (of the Red Crown) 180800 1000280
dšr.t [an oil] 180810 1000280
dšr.t [a red pot] 180820 1000280
dšr.t Red (crown of Lower Egypt) 180830 1000280
dšr.t desert; foreign country 180850 1000280
dšr.t blood 180790 1000280
dšr.t fire; flame 180840 1000280
dšr.tj the one who is reddish (angry Seth) 853080 1000280
dšr.tj red one (the sun god) 180860 1000280
dšr.tjw bloody victims? 180910 1000280
dšrr.t the little red one 854858 1000280

dq to chop; to grind 861175 1000250
dq.w powder; flour 180940 1000250
dqᶜ to shape? (an oar) 180930 1000256
dqw to be barefoot 180920 1000255
dqr to attach 180970 1000253
dqr to banish? 180980 1000251
dqr to attach; to dispel 854588 1000253
dqr fruit (gen.) 180950 1000252
dqr to reap 858413 1000252
dqrw essence; essential element? (of a god) 181000 1000254
dg the one who looks [guardian of Osiris] 181150 1000189
dg to visit; to go 181040 1000187
dgꜣ.yt glimpse 851290 1000189
dgꜣ.yt cut of meat; jerky 181110 1000192
dgꜣ.w razor 181120 1000192
dgi̯ to hide; to be hidden 181130 1000188
dgi̯ to behold; to see 181140 1000189
dgm to be speechless; to be unconscious 181200 1000191
dgm castor-oil (ricinus) plant 181210 1000190
dgm ricinus oil 181220 1000190
dgm.t unconsciousness 181230 1000191
dgs foot print 181260 1000187
dgs to step; to enter 181250 1000187
dgdg to walk over; to trample down 181270 1000187
dd to copulate; to unite 855348 1000172
dḏw to grind 181330 1000181

ḏ

ḏ.t djet-servant 181440 1000147
ḏ.tj the eternal one 852605 1000147
ḏ.y gift; provision 177820 1001930
ḏ.t djet-servant 181440 1000147
ḏ.tj the eternal one 852605 1000147
ḏ.y gift; provision 177820 1001930
ḏ.t serf 181430 1000147
ḏ.t flood 181390 1000147
ḏ.t viper; cobra 181340 1000146
ḏ.t body; bodily form; self 181350 1000147
ḏ.t estate; funerary endowment 181420 1000147
ḏ.t eternity 181400 1000147
ḏ.t phallus 181370 1000147
ḏ.t eternal 181401 1000147
ḏ.t [a term for the youth of a city] 181380 1000147
ḏꜣ dja-priest 181520 1000299
ḏꜣ fire drill 181490 1000301
ḏꜣ linen (clothing) 181530 1000300
ḏꜣ.y cell or wall 181790 1000297
ḏꜣ.y [a large riverboat] 181770 1000299
ḏꜣ.yw ferryman 400687 1000299
ḏꜣ.yw opponent 181880 1000299
ḏꜣ.ywt offence; wrongdoing; disgusting (gen.) 181810 1000299
ḏꜣ.yt linen (clothing) 181850 1000300
ḏꜣ.yt opponent 181820 1000299
ḏꜣ.w [linen, for clothing] 182040 1000300
ḏꜣ.w evening or night 182060 1000299
ḏꜣ.w magical protection? 182070 1000299
ḏꜣ.w foot of mast? 600463 1000299
ḏꜣ.wtj foe 181960 1000299
ḏꜣ.wtt adversary 857289 1000299
ḏꜣ.t [a boat] 400952 1000299
ḏꜣ.t fire drill 856598 1000301
ḏꜣ.t crossing 856599 1000299
ḏꜣ.t tomb 181620 1000297
ḏꜣ.t remainder; deficiency 181670 1000299
ḏꜣ.t linen (clothing) 181610 1000300
ḏꜣ.t remainder; deficiency 181670 1000299
ḏꜣꜣ braid 181700 1000321
ḏꜣi̯ to extend (the arm); to turn to; to oppose 181750 1000299
ḏꜣi̯ to cross (a body of water); to ferry 181780 1000299
ḏꜣi̯ to reach out (for food, milk); to devour 181740 1000299
ḏꜣjw hump 181950 1000298
ḏꜣy.t [a kind of an architectural element]; wall 181870 1000297
ḏꜣᶜ vetchling [a substance (med.)] 182020 1000323
ḏꜣᶜ frying pan; gridiron 182030 1000322

ḏꜣb to greet 182090 1000305
ḏꜣp bench 182110 1000314
ḏꜣf to burn up 182120 1000309
ḏꜣf burned meat (med.) 182130 1000309
ḏꜣfḏꜣf to burn up 182140 1000309
ḏꜣm offspring; youths; generation 182160 1000313
ḏꜣm young cattle 182170 1000313
ḏꜣn.w young people 182210 1000313
ḏꜣr helper 182240 1000315
ḏꜣr to cook (with water) 182230 1000318
ḏꜣr requirement 182220 1000316
ḏꜣr.t scorpion 182270 1000317
ḏꜣjs spell; utterance 182000 1000312
ḏꜣjs to negotiate; to counsel 181990 1000312
ḏꜣjs.w councilor; sage 550443 1000312
ḏꜣt.t [a female opponent] 181680 1000299
ḏꜣd to cut off (offering animal] 182290 1000307
ḏꜣḏ.yt wet? 861517 1000308
ḏꜣd.w audience hall 182310 1000306
ḏꜣḏꜣ foe 182370 1000299
ḏꜣḏꜣ assembly; council; magistrates 182320 1000298
ḏꜣḏꜣ to build; to install 182350 1000297
ḏꜣḏꜣ [building in front of a temple (bark station?)] 182340 1000297
ḏꜣḏꜣ hostile 182380 1000299
ḏꜣḏꜣ head; tip 182330 1000298
ḏꜣḏꜣ.w pot 872144 1000298
ḏꜣḏꜣ.wt courses (of a brick wall) 182460 1000297
ḏꜣḏꜣ.t offering table 500245 1000298
ḏꜣḏꜣ.t surrounding area (med.) 182400 1000298
ḏꜣḏꜣ.t assembly; council; magistrates 182390 1000298
ḏꜣḏꜣ.t harp 182410 1000298
ḏꜣḏꜣtw (divine) assessor 182430 1000298
ḏꜥ to spear fish 182530 1000325
ḏꜥ to lie desolate 182540 1000324
ḏꜥ to be stormy; to break wind (med.) 182490 1000324
ḏꜥ storm; wind 182480 1000324
ḏꜥ.wt to spear fish 182560 1000325
ḏꜥb coal-black 182620 1000326
ḏꜥb to blacken 182610 1000326
ḏꜥb.t charcoal 182660 1000326
ḏꜥm fine gold; white gold; electrum 182710 1000329
ḏꜥm gold (Hathor) 182720 1000329
ḏꜥm [a scepter] 182700 1000327
ḏꜥm [a staff] 860855 1000328
ḏꜥm golden 182730 1000329
ḏꜥm.wtj he of the djam-scepter 182750 1000327
ḏꜥq to shout; to call (for help) 182790 1000330
ḏꜥqt shouting 182800 1000330
ḏꜥr to seek; to investigate; to take thought of 182760 1000332
ḏꜥr to take thought of; to care about 182770 1000332
ḏw The evil one 853091 1000288
ḏw bad; evil 600473 1000288
ḏw grind; flour 850682 1000181
ḏw knife 182880 1000286
ḏw evil person 853567 1000288
ḏw evil; bad; sinister 182840 1000288
ḏw mountain 182830 1000290
ḏw bad 182860 1000288
ḏw.wj two mountain ridges (flanking the river) 182920 1000290
ḏw.wt papyrus plant (the erected one) 181460 1000290
ḏw.t mountain 182890 1000290
ḏw.t [a vessel]; [a measure of volume] 450473 1000284
ḏw.t evil; dirt 182900 1000288
ḏw.t [a stinging insect] 183060 1000285
ḏw.tj evil one 182910 1000288
ḏwi̯ Evildoer 858530 1000288
ḏwi̯ to be bad; to be evil 600472 1000288
ḏwi̯ to raise; to lift up 182990 1000290
ḏwi̯ to call 182980 1000289
ḏwj.w [a pottery jar] 183020 1000284
ḏwj.w call 183010 1000289

ḏwᶜ knife? 183040 1000286
ḏws to defame 183050 1000294
ḏwt twenty 183070 1000295
ḏwḏw The ugly one 861808 1000288
ḏwḏw bad one 183100 1000288
ḏwḏw bad 183090 1000288
ḏb.w income 183130 1000153
ḏb.t brick; sheet; ingot 183120 1000150
ḏbꜣ [a ritual garment] 183250 1000168
ḏbꜣ [a multi-colored kilt] 183240 1000168
ḏbꜣ [a scepter] 183210 1000165
ḏbꜣ to sew 858680 1000168
ḏbꜣ harpoon rope 183230 1000166
ḏbꜣ to replace; to reimburse; to repay 183170 1000168
ḏbꜣ [a fabric] 183260 1000168
ḏbꜣ harpoon 183220 1000166
ḏbꜣ papyrus reed float (for fishermen) 183150 1000166
ḏbꜣ to outfit; to clothe; to adorn 183180 1000168
ḏbꜣ food offerings 183200 1000169
ḏbꜣ to be blocked; to block 183190 1000167
ḏbꜣ.w [a wooden box] 450152 1000169
ḏbꜣ.w burial goods? 859246 1000168
ḏbꜣ.w leafage 183380 1000168
ḏbꜣ.w leaves; foliage 183370 1000168
ḏbꜣ.w compensation; payments 183350 1000168
ḏbꜣ.t equipment 857428 1000168
ḏbꜣ.t robing room (in the palace) 183300 1000168
ḏbꜣ.t shrine; sarcophagus 183310 1000168
ḏbꜣ.t base (of a shrine) 183320 1000169
ḏbꜣ.tj the equipped one 859244 1000168
ḏbꜣ.tj adorner?; robing priest 183340 1000168
ḏbꜣ.tj rewarder 858651 1000168
ḏbꜣy.t [a dress] 183400 1000168
ḏbᶜ seal; signet 183510 1000170
ḏbᶜ ten thousand 183450 1000170
ḏbᶜ finger 183430 1000170
ḏbᶜ door-hinge tenon?; ring for a door bolt? 450303 1000170
ḏbᶜ finger (as a measure of lengh); pinch 183440 1000170
ḏbᶜ one who seals 852567 1000170
ḏbᶜ to seal; to lock 183460 1000170
ḏbᶜ to point the finger at (in reproach) 183480 1000170
ḏbᶜ.w blame; reproach 183550 1000170
ḏbᶜ.w sealing; labelling 183580 1000170
ḏbᶜ.wt seal; seal impression 183530 1000170
ḏbj army 183410 1000149
ḏbjjt fish-nets? 183420 1000167
ḏbw [a cut of meat] 183590 1000164
ḏbb [a body of water] 183600 1000156
ḏbb to close; to block 183610 1000157
ḏbḥ.w fisherman 183650 1000159
ḏbqbq to dive (head-first) 183660 1000158
ḏbg dive (head-first) 183670 1000158
ḏbgḏq to dive (head-first) 183680 1000158
ḏbḏb to crush (by treading) 183690 1000167
ḏpḥ apple 183730 1000247
ḏpq dancer 183750 1000248
ḏpq.t dancer 860166 1000248
ḏf drop 600602 1000183
ḏf to be ruined (a building) 183810 1000184
ḏfꜣ to provision 183870 1000186
ḏfꜣ to wipe 183860 1000185
ḏfꜣ provision; sustenance 183850 1000186
ḏfꜣ.y well-provided man 183910 1000186
ḏfꜣ.t provisions 183890 1000186
ḏfi̯ to sink in; to descend into chaos 183920 1000184
ḏfn to hurry 863702 1000186
ḏfn provider 183940 1000186
ḏfn ancestor 183930 1000186
ḏfny.t ancestress 183950 1000186
ḏfḏ iris (including the pupil) 183970 1000183
ḏfḏf droplet 183990 1000183
ḏfḏf to tear (of the eye); to drip 183980 1000183
ḏfḏf.t tearing (as an affliction of the eye)

184000 1000183
ḏfḏf.t droplet 859909 1000183
ḏfḏfw incomplete document? 184020 1000186
ḏmꜥ to mourn; to complain 858545 1000216
ḏmꜥ papyrus (scroll, sheet) 184040 1000215
ḏmꜥ mourn; misery? 184060 1000216
ḏn to be hot 859927 1000218
ḏn to thresh 184090 1000220
ḏn.tj [a term for a sun god] 500126 1000218
ḏn.w threshing floor 184220 1000220
ḏnb to bend 184240 1000222
ḏnb dwarf 184250 1000221
ḏnb to turn back 184260 1000222
ḏnn to struggle; to be tormented 184310 1000236
ḏnn breathtaking arrogance; bristling (of hair) 184300 1000236
ḏnn linen? 859910 1000300
ḏnn agony, torture; hard work 855207 1000236
ḏnn.t skull; head 184340 1000235
ḏnr branch 184350 1000237
ḏnr rod; whip 859911 1000237
ḏnrm to try hard 184360 1000239
ḏnḥ to pinion 184380 1000230
ḏnḥ oar blade 184400 1000230
ḏnḥ wing 184370 1000230
ḏnḥ upper part of the (hind-)leg 184390 1000230
ḏnḥ [a term for prisoners] 66060 1000230
ḏnd anger; rage 184410 1000223
ḏnd fury 856652 1000223
ḏnd to be angry 184420 1000223
ḏnd.t Raging one 871064 1000223
ḏnḏn to strike (a percussion instrument) 184480 1000220
ḏnḏn.t raging fame 184490 1000225
ḏnḏr brushwood (as fuel) 600567 1000227
ḏr to hinder; to finish 184570 1000262
ḏr when; because 184550 1000262
ḏr end; limit; boundary 184530 1000262
ḏr to beat (a drum) 184580 1000265
ḏr since (spatial, temp.) 184540 1000262
ḏr [a male calf] 184520 1000258
ḏr [a grave in a foreign land] 184610 1000259
ḏr wall 856665 1000262
ḏr to end up as 184560 1000262
ḏr until the end; in the end 851460 1000262
ḏr.w obstacle 185000 1000262
ḏr.w kite (bird of prey) 184740 1000261
ḏr.w walls? (of a house) 184730 1000262
ḏr.w end; limit; boundary 184990 1000262
ḏr.t hand; handful (as a measure of volume) 184630 1000260
ḏr.t kite; falcon 184660 1000261
ḏr.t hand (Hathor) 856247 1000260
ḏr.t wailing woman (lit. kite) 184670 1000261
ḏr.t [small calves] 184650 1000258
ḏr.tj falcon 184690 1000261
ḏr.t hand; handful (as a measure of volume) 184630 1000260
ḏr.t kite; falcon 184660 1000261
ḏr.t hand (Hathor) 856247 1000260
ḏr.t wailing woman (lit. kite) 184670 1000261
ḏr.t [small calves] 184650 1000258
ḏr.tj falcon 184690 1000261
ḏr.tjt (fem.) falcon (esp. Hathor) 184700 1000261
ḏr.tjw ancestors; roots 184980 1000262
ḏri̯ to be hard?; to be stolid? 850133 1000260
ḏrj efficient; very; solid 851617 1000260
ḏrj solid; firm; stout 184860 1000260
ḏrj.t wall?; floor? [made from ivory and ebony]184900 1000260
ḏrj.tj pylon 184950 1000260
ḏry.t dwelling; chamber 184910 1000260
ḏrꜥ to subdue; to overthrow 184960 1000273
ḏrꜥ.t plank (made of cedar wood) 184970 1000272
ḏrw.y paint (gen.); [a pigment] 185040

1000270
ḏrw.w side (of the body); flank 185060 1000262
ḏrw.t coffin 185010 1000262
ḏrwt façade; hall? 185030 1000262
ḏrt necessity; ration 185090 1000262
ḏrḏ leaf (med.) 185150 1000268
ḏrḏr to be foreign; to behave hostilely 600474 1000259
ḏrḏr stranger; foreigner 650046 1000259
ḏrḏr strange; foreign 185160 1000259
ḏḥᶜ to bind firmly together? 185280 1000205
ḏḥᶜ leather; (leather) lacings 185270 1000205
ḏḥtj lead (metal) 185320 1000201
ḏḥḏḥ [a monkey] 185350 1000193
ḏs self 185370 1000274
ḏs person 185360 1000274
ḏsy.t (loud) lamentation 185400 1000282
ḏswi̯ to call; to recite 185420 1000282
ḏsf to repair (a net) 185440 1000277
ḏsf net 856701 1000277
ḏsr [a piece of furniture] 185540 1000279
ḏsr [a staff (or scepter?)] 185530 1000279
ḏsr [an incense] 185520 1000279
ḏsr [a snake] 185510 1000279
ḏsr [a priest] 185490 1000279
ḏsr Splendid-one 185500 1000279
ḏsr splendid; sacred; holy 550229 1000279
ḏsr to be holy; to be splendid 185470 1000279
ḏsr to clear; to separate from 185460 1000281
ḏsr [a measure of length, equaling 4 palms] 185560 1000281
ḏsr.yt [10. gate of the Underworld] 185720 1000281
ḏsr.w consecration 856422 1000279
ḏsr.w splendor; sacredness 185650 1000279
ḏsr.t Shilded one 185610 1000281
ḏsr.t [Moon eye] 185620 1000279
ḏsr.t sacred ground 185600 1000281
ḏsr.t [a strong ale (made from the djeseret-plant?)] 1855901000278
ḏsr.t sacredness 856714 1000279
ḏsr.t [a plant (med.)] 185630 1000278
ḏsr.t [a table (for offerings)] 185640 1000279
ḏsr.t remote land 871088 1000281
ḏsḏs alter ego 185760 1000274
ḏt olive tree; olives; olive oil 185770 1000283
ḏd The lasting one 859261 1000178
ḏd Djed-column (a symbol of eternity) 185830 1000178
ḏd to say; to tell 185810 1000173
ḏd column 185840 1000178
ḏd back bone 185850 1000178
ḏd stability; duration 400140 1000178
ḏḏ flower; rosette 186370 1000171
ḏd Enduring-one 185890 1000178
ḏd.w Enduring-one 860560 1000178
ḏd.w slanderer 861036 1000173
ḏd.t stability; duration 185920 1000178
ḏd.t Djedet 185910 1000178
ḏd.t Osiris' coffin 185950 1000178
ḏdꜣ fat 186080 1000182
ḏdꜣ fat 186100 1000182
ḏdꜣ to ripen; to swell; to grow fat 186090 1000182
ḏdi̯ constantly; without interruption 853876 1000178
ḏdi̯ to make endure 185870 1000178
ḏdi̯ to endure 186110 1000178
ḏdjdi̯ to endure 854356 1000178
ḏdy.t [Epithet of Isis and Nephthys] 186120 1000178
ḏdb sting (of an insect) 186150 1000175
ḏdb to sting 186140 1000175
ḏdb to collect; to assemble 186160 1000174
ḏdb.y Piercer (a snake) 186230 1000175
ḏdb.t scorpion 186200 1000175
ḏdf to stand upright; to shudder 186240 1000176
ḏdm to be stinging (med.) 186270 1000175
ḏdm to heap 186280 1000174

ḏdm to sting 186260 1000175
ḏdm.yt Piercer 501080 1000175
ḏdm.t heaps 186290 1000174
ḏdḥ to well up 186300 1000177
ḏdḥ to block 859928 1000177
ḏdḥ to shut up; to imprison 186320 1000177
ḏdḥ.w prison 186330 1000177

Index of roots of Semitic origin

Transcr. Translation	ID lexeme	DRID	Deep Root[1]
jjr stag?; ram?	21420	1000993	jjr horned animal
jbr stallion	23790	1000947	jbr stallion
jbšt [a kind of bread or biscuit]	23960	1000949	jbšt [a bread]
jpt [bread, biscuit]	24490	1001070	jpt brea
jnrn oak	27670	1001052	jln oak
jnhmn pomegranate	27690	1001036	jnhmn pomegranate
jnḳfḳf.t [a wooden part of a chariot]	27930	1001050	jnḳfḳf [a wooden part of a chariot]
jr lion?; wild beast?	28180	1001076	jr lion
jrj ram	28540	1001082	jrj ram
jrjr guide; leader	29530	1001083	jrjr guide
jrẖ [a semi-precious stone]	29890	1001080	jrẖ [a semi-precious stone]
jrḳbs rock crystal	29900	1001086	jrḳbs rock crystal
jhr tent	30350	1000990	jhr tent
jswt long plank (of coniferous wood)	31380	1001109	jswt long plank
jsbw shelter?; hut?	600286	1001096	jsbw hut?
jsbr [a Syrian plant (juniper?)]	31430	1001093	jsbr juniper?
jsbr whip	31420	1001094	jsbr whip
jsbt seat (gen.); chair; base	31390	1001095	jsbt seat
jspt quiver (for arrows)	31490	1001102	jspt quiver (for arrows)
jšf to burn; to scorch (a town)	31980	1001100	jšf to burn
jṯm [metal part of a whip]	33680	1001115	jṯm [metal part of a whip]
jṯr captive	33720	1001122	jṯr captive
ybr stream	23800	1002784	ybr stream
ym sea	24730	1002786	ym sea
yd^{c} skilled, smart	33920	1002785	yd^{c} skilled
^{c}yn well	862932	1003069	^{c}yn well
^{c}mdy supports (chariot parts)	37980	1002997	^{c}mdy supports
^{c}nn singing	860115	1003025	^{c}nn singing
^{c}ršn lentils	39590	1003050	^{c}ršn lentils
^{c}rḏ to terrify (the enemy); to hold on to	39800	1003042	^{c}rḏ to terrify (the enemy)
^{c}šḳ to oppress	41170	1003058	^{c}šḳ to oppress
^{c}gn ringstand	41730	1002969	^{c}gn ringstand
^{c}grt wagon (drawn by oxen)	41770	1002970	^{c}grt wagon
^{c}gsw belt	41800	1002971	^{c}gsw belt

1 That is to say, the envisaged, hypothetically reconstructed form which might exist in Egyptian, after borrowing the lexeme from a Semitic language; it is not the Semitic root per se.

^{c}dn [a cereal (wheat?)]	41850	1002956	^{c}dn wheat?
^{c}dt conspiracy?	41860	1002959	^{c}dt conspiracy?
^{c}ḏr helper	42240	1002958	^{c}ḏr helper
^{c}ḏr [part of a chariot]	42250	1002957	^{c}ḏr [a part of a chariot]
b^{c}r sea; river	54970	1000144	b^{c}r big water
b^{c}r to fight	54980	1000143	b^{c}r Baal
b^{c}r Baal	54960	1000143	b^{c}r Baal
b^{c}r.t Baalat	860150	1000143	b^{c}r Baal
bbj [a semi-precious stone]	850446	1000115	bꜣ = bn little spheric object
bnd to wrap; to clothe	56220	1000058	bnd to wrap
br open field (at necropolis)	56340	1000050	bnr = bl outside
bnr.w outside; exterior	55920	1000050	bnr = bl outside
brt agreement; pact	56650	1000080	brt agreement
brḳ to sparkle	56530	1000079	brḳ to sparkle
brk gift	56560	1000077	brk gift
brk to offer	56540	1000077	brk gift
brkt pool	56570	1000078	brkt pool
brg to be happy; to be content	56600	1000076	brg be happy
brg.t [a semi-precious stone]	56610	1000075	brg [a semi-precious stone]
brtj [a semi-precious stone]	56660	1000081	brtj [semi-precious stone]
bšꜣ ax	57580	1000087	bšꜣ ax
bḳy to open?; to stay?	57700	1000071	bḳy to open?
bkj [a (pear?) tree]	57900	1000045	bkj [tree]
bkj [a fruit (of the pear tree?)]	57910	1000045	bkj [tree]
bḏn stick; cudgel	58630	1000009	bḏn stick
phr.t [a body of water]	61340	1001773	phr [a pond]
prj beans	60970	1001791	pr beans
prẖ blossom; sprout	61250	1001794	prẖ to blossom
prẖ to blossom; to unfurl	61240	1001794	prẖ to blossom
prš to smite; to smash; to tear	61270	1001797	prš to smash
prṯ to break?	61290	1001798	prṯ to break?
pgꜣ [a chest?]	62800	1001767	pgꜣ box
ptr strip (of cloth)	62960	1001816	ptr bandage?
pdr sack (or measure)	63090	1001764	pdr measure?
mw^{c}d council	853912	1001470	mw^{c}d council
mn.w quartz; [a semi-precious stone]	70490	1001345	mn quartz
mn^{c}.t property	70390	1001385	mn^{c} property
mnn mina (a measure of weight)	70780	1001371	mnn mina
mnn.t [part of a sarcophagus]; [part of a tomb])	70820	1001349	mn to stay
mnḥ.t gift; tribute	71050	1001363	mnḥ tribute
mnd.t tax; gifts; tribute	71710	1001354	mnd tribute
mhr braver [military officer]	73260	1001310	mhr braver

mẖt [chariot parts]	74480	1001311	mẖt [a chariot part]
mrj speed	859104	1001409	mrj speed
mrj groom	72520	1001408	mrj groom
mrjjnt a container?	72580	1001410	mrjjnt [a container]
mryn noble person	72570	1001879	mryn noble person
mrḥ lance	72830	1001404	mrḥ lance
mrḥm the one who works with the salt	854479	1001406	mrḥm the one who works with the salt
mrsw [a kind of a vessel for cider?]	72950	1001416	mrsw cider?
mrsw cider?	72940	1001416	mrsw cider?
mrḳḥt [catch?; retreat?]	72970	1001413	mrḳḥt to catch?
mrḳḏn [a metal tool]	72980	1001412	mrḳḏn [a metal tool]
mrkbt chariot	73010	1001411	mrkbt chariot
mḥḏrt fish pond	74170	1001304	mḥḏrt fish pond
msẖ [a large vessel, for oil and wine]	75630	1001427	msẖ [a vessel]
msẖ.t [a measure for oil]; [a large vessel]	75740	1001427	msẖ [a vessel]
msḳ [metalworking activity (to emboss?)]	75870	1001436	msḳ a metalworking
mstj [a small galley propelled by oars]	76020	1001446	mstj basket
mstr office; chancellery	76060	1001448	mstr chancellery
mstḥ trap; snare	76080	1001445	mstḥ trap
mšꜣb watering place	76290	1001452	mšꜣb watering place
mšr [a piece of furniture (table?)]	76450	1001437	mšr [a piece of furniture]
mšrw [plain; wetland]	76490	1001440	mšrw [plain]
mšrr to attach; to affix	76510	1001439	mšrr to attach
mškb [title of an official	76540	1001431	mškb [title of an official]
mšdd.t comb	76630	1001425	mšd(d) comb
mḳr [a vessel (situla?)]	76710	1001390	mḳr [a vessel]
mḳr staff; rod	76690	1001389	mḳr [a staff]
mkr.j merchant	77060	1001336	mkr merchant
mkmr.t fishnets	77040	1001335	mkmr fishnet
mktr tower	77140	1001337	mktr [a tower]
mgrto roast; to grill	600648	1001297	mgr to roast
mgrt cave	77240	1001298	mgrt cave
mgsp crate; basket	77260	1000415	gsp basket
mṯpr.t [a tool (chisel?)]	77940	1001459	mṯpr [a tool]
mḏrn [a metal tool]	78660	1001291	mḏrn [a metal tool]
mḏḳ [a vessel (for beer)] (syll.)	78750	1001289	mḏḳ [a vessel]
mḏḳ.t [a vessel (for beer and oil)]	78760	1001289	mḏḳ [a vessel]
nʿrn soldiers; special detachment	80630	1001757	nʿrn unite of soldiers
nʿš to be strong	80650	1001758	nʿš to be strong

nwṯ to tremble	81500	1001739	nwṯ to tremble
nm^c to (go to) sleep	84220	1001611	nm to sleep
nrḥ = lḥ to blaspheme; to abuse verbally	600265	1001644	nrḥ to blaspheme
nhr to flee?; to sail?	85690	1001586	nhr to flee?
nhr fugitive	85700	1001586	nhr to flee?
nḥš [an ingredient (med.)]	86670	1001587	nḥš medical ingredient
nḫr stream?; canal?	87400	1001583	nḫr canal
nsk to put in proper array	88380	1001659	nsk to put in proper array
nkp.t [an edible plant]	89300	1001606	nkp [a plant]
nkftr [an oil]	89320	1001602	nkftr [an oil]
nṯ^c to desert; to divorce	90220	1001712	nṯ^c to divorce
nṯḫ [a musical instrument]	90630	1001703	nṯḫ [musical instrument]
rbš cuirass (of leather)	94010	1001926	rbš to arm oneself
rbš to arm oneself	855625	1001926	rbš to arm oneself
rhd.t caldron (of metal)	95500	1001943	rhd [a caldron]
rḥb [a vessel]	95570	1001941	rḥb [a vessel]
rḥs [a kind of baked goods]	95610	1001948	rḥs [a baked good]
ršj peak; summit	96200	1001983	ršj peak
rks harnessed team	96490	1001962	rks harnessed team
rg.t compartment	96520	1001933	rg compartment
rdn.y laudanum	852318	1001931	rdn laudanum
hr wooded highlands?	98920	1000698	hr highland
hrṯṯ to do stealthily	99250	1000729	hrṯṯ to do stealthily
hsmḳ storming (of the king joining battle)	99340	1000752	hsmḳ storming
hskt [bad way of walking]	99350	1000751	hskt [bad way of walking]
htm ravaging; destroying	97540	1000779	htm to destroy
hdm.w footstool; throne	99680	1000487	hdm throne
ḥmr donkey	854615	1000559	ḥmr donkey
ḥmḏ vinegar; wine of a poor quality	105840	1000552	ḥmḏ vinegar
ḥny.t spear; javelin	106190	1000670	ḥny spear
ḥnr to squint?	106860	1000531	ḥnr = ḥl to darken
ḥnrg to quake; to be embarrassed	106910	1000651	ḥnrg to quake
ḥr canal?	108370	1000695	ḥr canal?
ḥry.t dung	108410	1000734	ḥry dung
ḥrp dagger; short sword	109060	1000718	ḥrp dagger
ḥtr [basketwork]	600478	1000784	ḥtr [basketwork]
ḥṯ to overlay; to inlay	112010	1000767	ḥṯ to place in
ḫrt wadi	114160	1000895	ḫrt wadi
ḫꜣtrw mongoose	114370	1000901	ḫꜣtrw mongoose
ḫbr business, trading partner	115700	1000465	ḫbr to join together
ḫnr = ḫl to be hoarse	118410	1000647	ḫl to be hoarse

ḫnr = ḫl fangs	118380	1000532	ḫl to sting
ḫnr = ḫl spike; chisel	118370	1000646	ḫl spike
ḫnrj = ḫlj roar	118510	1000652	ḫlj roar
ḫnrf = ḫlf insult; abuse	118530	1000650	ḫlf insult
ḫr street; road; quarter	119570	1000700	ḫr road
ḫrr watercourse; channel	859155	1000724	ḫrr watercourse
ḫrḳ.t slippery ground	120480	1000721	ḫrḳ slippery ground
ḫrd veils	120500	1000711	ḫrd veils
ḫṯn garlic?	121920	1000781	ḫṯn garlic?
s^{c}r scrub country?; barley field?	129000	1002023	s^{c}r scrub country?
s^{c}r.t wool	129060	1002420	s^{c}r wool
swbb to draw back	130060	1002351	swbb to draw back
swr [chariot equipment]	130450	1002367	swr [chariot equipment]
sbr shoots (of a tree); clusters (of grapes)	131870	1002023	sbr branch
smk.t beam; girder	135830	1002158	smk beam
snrw = slw [basket, or sim.]	137720	1001880	snrw = slw [a product of Nubia]
sr.t captive (noble) woman	139900	1002247	sr captive (noble) woman
srḥ.t stalks (of onions); bunches (of onions)	139580	1002258	srḥ stalks (of onions)
srḳ snow	139820	1002139	šlg snow
sḫnš to irritate	142710	1002097	sḫnš to irritate
skt [a military officer (scout?) (guard?)]	147040	1002132	ski̯ to perish
sg to open a way; to break a trail	147080	1002075	sg to open a way
sg sacking	34680	1002074	sg sacking
sgbyn [a body of water]	147180	1002076	sgbyn [a body of water]
sgr fortress	147280	1002080	sgr fortress
š^{c}r prison; gate	152540	1002417	š^{c}r gate
š^{c}r to promise	859187	1002419	š^{c}r to promise
š^{c}r calculation; scheme; threat; promise	152550	1002419	š^{c}r to promise
šwb.tj [a jar]	153130	1002349	šwb [a jar]
šbd stick (to beat)	153600	1002012	šbd stick
šnb trumpet; tube (for kohl)	156030	1002194	šnb trumpet
šnrf = šlf to be disheveled	156220	1002138	šlf to be disheveled
šrm to lay down (weapons); to seek peace	156800	1002140	šlm peace
šrm peace; greeting	156780	1002140	šlm peace
šrm to lay down arms; to seek peace	156790	1002140	šlm peace
šrm.t delivery; provisions	156810	1002332	šlm delivery
šrgḥ feelings	859156	1002256	šrgḥ feelings

šḫḳ dust cloud	156900	1002099	šḫḳ dust cloud
škn watering place	157860	1002134	škn watering place
šgr [a body of water (ditch? dyke?)]	157910	1002078	šgr [a body of water]
šdr.t ravine; chasm	158900	1002053	šdr ravine
ḳwr gold miner	159970	1001912	ḳwr gold miner
ḳbᶜ to joke	160150	1001847	ḳbᶜ to joke
ḳr, ḳrj visitor; alien; vagabond	858170	1001921	ḳꜣri̯ to stay
ḳrᶜ.w shield	161670	1001907	ḳrᶜ shield
ḳrᶜ.w shield bearer	161680	1001907	ḳrᶜ shield
ḳrm.t ashes	161740	1001899	ḳrm ashes
ḳrn.t foreskin; uncircumcised penis	161760	1001900	ḳrn foreskin
ḳrḏn ax; pick ax	162060	1001896	ḳrḏn ax
ḳdr.t incense	162620	1001859	ḳdr incense
ḳḏ thornbush	162690	1001851	ḳḏ thornbush
ḳḏ plasterer	162680	1001850	ḳḏ plaster
ḳḏ gypsum; plaster	162670	1001850	ḳḏ plaster
ḳḏ to go around; to run	162700	1001853	ḳḏ to run
ḳḏm handful (as a measure)	600590	1001858	ḳḏm to grasp
ḳḏmḏm to grasp	863669	1001858	ḳḏm to grasp
kꜣm = krm(n) vineyard	163520	1001274	kꜣm garden
kwšn [part of a chariot harness]	163920	1001263	kwšn [part of harness]
kbs basket	164010	1002576	kbs basket
kp = kb palm (of the hand); sole (of the foot)	164020	1001235	kp = kb palm of hand, sole of foot
kp = kb sole (of the foot)	164030	1001235	kp = kb palm of hand, sole of foot
kmr [a dancer]	164650	1001228	kmr [a dancer]
kmrj tusks; ivory	164660	1001229	kmrj ivory
knnr lyre	164760	1001232	knnr lyre
knt [a garment (cloak?)]	165010	1001234	knt [a garment (cloak?)]
kr saddle (for a donkey)	600048	1001239	kr saddle
krj prison	165050	1001241	krj prison
krp to efface (inscriptions)	165060	1001244	krp to efface
krḥt basket; bushel	165090	1001240	krḥt [a basket]
krs to jump	165110	1001246	krs to jump
krs sack	165100	1001245	krs bag
krk couch; bed	165130	1001242	krk bed
krkr heap of stones	165140	1001237	kr heap of stones
krt slaughter	165160	1001248	krt to cut
krṯ whip cords?; cloth strips?	165170	1001247	krṯ cords (for whip)
kḥs chair	854765	1001220	kḥs chair
ktp sword	165790	1001260	ktp scimitar

ktm.t gold	165800	1001258	ktm gold
kṯm divination; omen; decision (based on augury)	165950	1001257	kṯm boasting
kṯn charioteer	165960	1001259	kṯn charioteer
gw [a horse]	166720	1000423	gw [a bull]
gwn haversack	166790	1000428	gwꜣ to tighten
gwš to be crooked; to turn away	166820	1000426	gwš to be crooked
gns outrage; violence	167670	1000392	gns violence
gr.tj kidneys	168180	1000395	gr kidney
grb to cut (a piece of wood serving as a chariot part)	167830	1000398	grb to cut (wood)
grgy.t rib	168160	1000401	grg rib
gsr finger ring	863456	1000417	gsr finger ring
tnm furrow	172550	1002512	tnm to go astray
trj door	172820	1002541	trj door
tr^{c} worm (Apophis)	860986	1002552	tr^{c} worm
trr oven	172850	1002546	trr oven
trr to race?; to go for an outing?	172860	1002547	trr to run
tḥs to squash; to crush; to pulverize	173090	1002465	tḥs to squash
tẖr [part of chariot]	173340	1003902	tẖr [part of chariot]
ṯpr scribe	175260	1002528	ṯpr scribe
ṯprṯ (bronze-clad Hittite) chariot	175270	1002530	ṯprṯ (bronze-clad Hittite) chariot
ṯpg barracks	175290	1002521	ṯpg barracks
ṯḥr = ṯrḥ injury; mockery	176730	1002462	ṯrḥ injury
ṯnr = ṯl mound; hill	176080	1002485	tl mound
ṯrry siege mound	176400	1002548	ṯrrj siege mound
ṯryn body armor	176290	1002550	ṯryn body armor
ṯrt finely ground wheat flour	176430	1002535	ṯr fine flour
ṯkr tower gate	177400	1002483	ṯkr tower gate
dnrg [a fruit (melon?)]	600464	1000238	dnrg a fruit
dd to copulate; to unite	855348	1000172	dd to copulate
ḏ^{c}ḳ to shout; to call (for help)	182790	1000330	ḏ^{c}ḳ to shout
ḏ^{c}ḳt shouting	182800	1000330	ḏ^{c}ḳ to shout
ḏw.t [a stinging insect]	183060	1000285	ḏw [an insect]
ḏbj army	183410	1000149	ḏb army
ḏbb [a body of water]	183600	1000156	ḏbb [body of water]
ḏbḳbḳ to dive (head-first)	183660	1000158	ḏbg to dive
ḏbg dive (head-first)	183670	1000158	ḏbg to dive
ḏbgḏḳ to dive (head-first)	183680	1000158	ḏbg to dive
ḏpḥ apple	183730	1000247	ḏpḥ = tpḥ apple
ḏpḳ dancer	183750	1000248	ḏpḳ dancer
ḏpḳ.t dancer	860166	1000248	ḏpḳ dancer
ḏnn to struggle; to be tormented	184310	1000236	ḏnn to struggle

ḏnn breathtaking arrogance; bristling (of hair)	184300	1000236	ḏnn to struggle
ḏnn agony, torture; hard work	855207	1000236	ḏnn to struggle
ḏnr branch	184350	1000237	ḏnr branch
ḏnḏr brushwood (as fuel)	600567	1000227	ḏnḏr brushwood
ḏr helper	182240	1000315	ḏr helper
ḏr^{c} to subdue; to overthrow	184960	1000273	ḏr^{c} to subdue
ḏr^{c}.t plank (made of cedar wood)	184970	1000272	ḏr^{c} plank
ḏrḏr strange; foreign	185160	1000259	ḏr foreign
ḏt olive tree; olives; olive oil	185770	1000283	ḏt olive tree
ḏḏ flower; rosette	186370	1000171	ḏḏ flower

Selected bibliography

Allen, James P. 1984. *The Inflection of the Verb in the Pyramid Texts* (Bibliotheca Aegyptiaca II), Malibu.

— 2013. *The ancient Egyptian language: an historical study*, Cambridge.

— 2014. *Middle Egyptian: an introduction to the language and culture of hieroglyphs*, Cambridge.

— 2017. *Grammar of the ancient Egyptian Pyramid Texts. Vol. 1: Unis* (Languages of the Ancient Near East 7), Winona Lake (IN).

— 2020. *Ancient Egyptian phonology*. Cambridge.

Andreu-Lanoë, Guillemette. 1987. Les titres de policiers formés sur la racine šnᶜ, in: *Cahiers de Recherches de l'Institut de Papyrologie et d'Égyptologie de Lille* 9, 17–23.

Anselin, Alain. 2008. Un mot bꜣ.t, du grain – une racine céréalicole transphylique, in: *i-Medjat* 2, [15] – [16]. http://www.culturediff.org/mediasources/epublis/i-Medjat/iMedjat2.pdf.

Baer, Klaus. 1985. Compatible Phonemes in Adjoining Positions within Nominal and Verbal Roots of Old Egyptian. Unpublished handout accompanying a lecture held on August 31st, 1985 at the IV International Congress of Egyptologists in Munich.

Bendjaballah, Sabrina & Chris H. Reintges .2009. Ancient Egyptian verbal reduplication: typology, diachrony, and the morphology-syntax interface, in: *Morphology* 19, 135–157.

Bogdanov, Ivan V. 2021. Egyptian kinship term mwt 'mother' as a metaphor for an object or concept (1–5) [in Russian], in *Indo-European Linguistics and Classical philology XXV (1), Proceedings of the 25th Conferencein Memory of Professor Joseph M. Tronsky*, St. Petersburg, 99–135.

Brein, Brein. 2009. Root Incompatibilities in the Pyramid Texts, in: *Lingua Aegyptia* 17, 1–8.

Brovarski, Edward J. 2012. Studies in Egyptian lexicography III: CG 20506 and the word for "bed canopy", in: *Bulletin de l'Institut Français d'Archéologie Orientale* 112, 77–95.

Brunner, Hellmut. 1965. Die Hieroglyphen für „räuchern", „bedecken", „Handfläche" und die ihnen entsprechenden Wörter, in: *Nachrichten von der Akademie der Wissenschaften in Göttingen: Philologisch-Historische Klasse* 3, 79–96.

Cannata, Maria G. 2007. Cannata, in Maria G. Cannata (ed), *Current research in Egyptology 2006 (Proceedings of the seventh annual symposium which took place at the University of Oxford, April 2006)*, Oxford, 21–42.

Cannuyer, Christian. 1983. Les formes dérivées du verbe en ancien égyptien. Essai de systématisation, in: *Göttinger Miszellen* 63, 25-35.

— 2010. *La girafe dans l'Égypte ancienne et le verbe* : *étude de lexicographie et de symbolique animalière*, Acta Orientalia Belgica, subsidia 4, Bruxelles.

Collombert, Philippe. 2010. 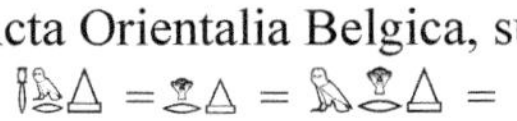 = (m)ḥr, "pyramide"?, in: *Göttinger Miszellen* 227, 17–22

Czermak, Wilhelm. 1931. *Die Laute der ägyptischen Sprache; eine phonetische Untersuchung: die Laute des Alt- und Mittelägyptischen*, Schriften der Arbeitsgemeinschaft der Ägyptologen und Afrikanisten in Wien 2, Wien.

— 1934. *Die Laute der ägyptischen Sprache; eine phonetische Untersuchung: die Laute des Neuägyptischen*, Schriften der Arbeitsgemeinschaft der Ägyptologen und Afrikanisten in Wien 3, Wien.

Černý, Jaroslav. 1976. *Coptic etymological dictionary*, Cambridge.

Deines, Hildegard von & Hermann Grapow. 1959. *Wörterbuch der ägyptischen Drogennamen*, Grundriss der Medizin der alten Ägypter 6, Berlin.

Deines, Hildegard von & Wolfhart Westendorf 1961. *Wörterbuch der medizinischen Texte: Erste Hälfte (A-r)*, Grundriss der Medizin der alten Ägypter 7/1, Berlin.

— 1962. *Wörterbuch der medizinischen Texte: Zweite Hälfte (h–D)*, Grundriss der Medizin der alten Ägypter 7/2, Berlin.

Derchain-Urtel, Maria Theresia. 1973. Das n-Präfix, in: *Göttinger Miszellen* 6, 39–54.

Edel, Elmar. 1955. *Altägyptische Grammatik I*, Analecta orientalia 34, Roma.

— 1964. *Altägyptische Grammatik II*, Analecta orientalia 39, Roma.

Ehret, Christopher. 2004. Third Consonants in Ancient Egyptian, in: *Egyptian and Semito-Hamitic (Afro-Asiatic) Studies in Memoriam W. Vycichl*, ed. by G. Takács, Studies in Semitic Languages and Linguistics 39, Leiden, 33–54.

Erman, Adolf. 1911. *Ägyptische Grammatik: mit Schrifttafel, Litteratur, Lesestücken und Wörterverzeichnis: Dritte völlig umgestaltete Auflage*, Porta Linguarum Orientalium 15, Berlin.

— 1928. *Ägyptische Grammatik: mit Schrifttafel, Paradigmen und Übungsstücken zum Selbststudium und zum Gebrauch in Vorlesungen: Vierte, völlig umgestaltete Auflage*, Porta Linguarum Orientalium 15, Berlin.

Erman, Adolf & Hermann Grapow (eds.). 1926–1961. *Wörterbuch der Aegyptischen Sprache*. Berlin.

Falk, David A. 2018. "My putrefaction is myrrh": the lexicography of decay, gilded coffins, and the green skin of Osiris, in: *Journal of Ancient Civilizations* 33/1, 27–39.

Feichtner, Max Karl. 1932. Die erweiterten Verbalstämme im Ägyptischen, in: *Wiener Zeitschrift für die Kunde des Morgenlandes* 38/1–2, 195–228.

Frandsen, Paul John. 1992. On the root nfr and a 'clever' remark on embalming, in: *The heritage of ancient Egypt: studies in honour of Erik Iversen*, ed. by J. Osing & E. K. Nielsen, CNI Publications 13, Copenhagen, 49-62.

Friedman, Florence. 1985. The root meaning of ꜣẖ: effectiveness or luminosity, in: *Serapis* 8, 39-46.

Gaboda, Péter J. 1989. A p-prefix in Egyptian, in: *Studia in honorem L. Fóti*, Studia Aegyptiaca 12, Budapest, 93–117.

Germer, Renate. 2008. *Handbuch der altägyptischen Heilpflanzen*, Philippika 21, Wiesbaden.

Goedicke, Hans. 1955. Alternation of ẖ and ḏ in Egyptian, in: *Zeitschrift für ägyptische Sprache und Altertumskunde* 80, 32–34.

Goldenberg, Gideon. 1997. Conservative and Innovative Features in Semitic Languages, in *Afroasiatica Neapolitana: Papers from the 8th Italian Meeting of Afroasiatic (Hamito-Semitic) Linguistics, Naples, January 25–26, 1996*, ed. by A. Bausi & M. Tosco, Studi Africanistici, Serie Etiopica 6, Naples, 3–21.

Graefe, Erhart. 1971. *Untersuchungen zur Wortfamilie bjꜣ-: Inaugural-Dissertation zur Erlangung des Doktorgrades der Philosophischen Fakultät der Universität zu Köln*, Köln: [n.publ.].

Greenberg, Joseph H. 1950. The Patterning of Root Morphemes in Afroasiatic, in: *Word* 6, 162–181.

Grossman, Eitan & Polis Stéphane. 2012. Navigating polyfunctionality in the lexicon: semantic maps and ancient Egyptian lexical semantics, in: *Lexical semantics in Ancient Egyptian*, ed. by E. Grossman, S. Polis & J. Winand, Lingua Aegyptia, Studia Monographica 9, Hamburg, 175–225.

Grunert, Stefan & Ingelore Hafemann (eds.). 1999. *Textcorpus und Wörterbuch. Aspekte zur ägyptischen Lexikographie*, Probleme der Ägyptologie 14, Leiden.

Gundacker, Roman. 2011. On the etymology of the Egyptian crown name mrsw.t: an "irregular" subgroup of m-prefix formations, in: *Lingua Aegyptia* 19, 37-86.

Hafemann, Ingelore. (ed.). 2003. *Wege zu einem digitalen Corpus ägyptischer Texte: Akten der Tagung „Datenbanken im Verbund"*, Thesaurus linguae aegyptiae 2, Berlin.

Hannig, Rainer. 1995. *Großes Handwörterbuch Ägyptisch - Deutsch: die Sprache der Pharaonen (2800–950 v. Chr.)*, Kulturgeschichte der Antiken Welt 64, Mainz am Rhein.

Hodge, Carleton T. 1997. The Trickle Down Approach, in: *Humanism, Culture, and Language in the Near East. Studies in Honor of Georg Krotkoff*, ed. by A. Afsaruddin & A. H. Mathias Zahniser, Winona Lake, 337–343.

Hoch, James E. 1994. *Semitic words in Egyptian texts of the New Kingdom and Third Intermediate Period*, Princeton (NJ).

Jansen-Winkeln, Karl. 1996. „Horizont" und „Verklärtheit": zur Bedeutung der Wurzel ꜣẖ, in: *Studien zur Altägyptischen Kultur* 23, 201–215.

Johnson, Janet H. (ed.). 2001. *The Demotic Dictionary of the Oriental Institute of the University of Chicago*, Chicago. https://oi.uchicago.edu/research/publications/demotic-dictionary-oriental-institute-university-chicago.

Junge, Friedrich. 2005. *Late Egyptian grammar: an introduction*, Oxford.

— 2008. *Einführung in die Grammatik des Neuägyptischen*, Wiesbaden.

Kammerzell, Frank. 1998. The sounds of a dead language. Reconstructing Egyptian phonology, in: *Göttinger Beiträge zur Sprachwissenschaft* 1, 21–41.

Koemoth, Pierre P. 1993. La "racine" wꜣb: du mythe à la métaphore, in: *Studien zur Altägyptischen Kultur* 20, 109–123.

Kramer, Ruth. 2018. Nonconcatenative Morphology in Coptic, in: *Phonology at Santa Cruz* 7. https://escholarship.org/uc/item/0765s94q.

Loprieno, Antonio. 1995. *Ancient Egyptian: A Linguistic Introduction*, Cambridge.

Loret, Victor. 1893. La racine , in: *Recueil de travaux relatifs à la philologie et à l'archéologie égyptiennes et assyriennes* 14, 106–120.

Malaise, Michel & Jean Winand. 1993. La racine grb et l'Amon-grb, in: *Chronique d'Égypte* 68, 12-28.

Meeks, Dimitri. 1974. Notes de lexicographie (§1), in: *Revue d'Égyptologie* 26, 52–65.

— 1977. Notes de lexicographie (§2–4), in: *Revue d'Égyptologie* 28, 87–96.

— 1978. Notes de lexicographie (§5–8), in: *Bulletin de l'Institut Français d'Archéologie Orientale* 77, 79–88.

— 1998a. *Année Lexicographique. Égypte ancienne. Tome 1 (1977)* (2eme édition), Paris.

— 1998b. *Année Lexicographique. Égypte ancienne. Tome 2 (1978)* (2eme édition), Paris.

— 1998c. *Année Lexicographique. Égypte ancienne. Tome 3 (1979)* (2eme édition), Paris.

— 1999. Dictionnaires et lexicographie de l'égyptien ancien. Méthodes et résultats, in: *Bibliotheca Orientalis* 56, 569–594.

— 2002. Aspects de la lexicographie égyptienne, in: *Bibliotheca Orientalis* 59, 5-18.

Molen, Rami van der. 2000. *A hieroglyphic dictionary of Egyptian Coffin Texts*, Probleme der Ägyptologie 15, Leiden.

Müller-Wollermann, Renate 1987. Die sogenannte ober- und unterägyptische Gerste, in: *Varia Aegyptiaca* 3 (1), 39–41.

Orel, Vladimir E. & Olga V. Stolbova. 1995. *Hamito-Semitic Etymological Dictionary: Materials for a Reconstruction*, Handbook of Oriental Studies: Section 1; The Near and Middle East, Leiden.

Oréal, Elsa. 2012. Discourse markers between grammar and lexicon: two ancient Egyptian cases for (de)grammaticalization, in: *Lexical semantics in Ancient Egyptian*, ed. by E. Grossman, S. Polis & J. Winand, Lingua Aegyptia, Studia Monographica 9, Hamburg, 227–245.

Osing, Jürgen. 1976. *Die Nominalbildung des Ägyptischen I-II*, Sonderschrift, Deutsches Archäologisches Institut, Abteilung Kairo 3, Mainz am Rhein.

— 1997. Zum Lautwert von 𓄿 und 𓂝, in: *Studien zur Altägyptischen Kultur* 24, 223–229.

Petráček, Karel. 1969. Die Struktur der altägyptischen Wurzelmorpheme mit Glottalen und Pharyngalen, in: *Archív Orientální* 37/3, 341–344.

Peust, Carsten. 1999. *Egyptian phonology: an introduction to the phonology of a dead language*, Monographien zur Ägyptischen Sprache 2, Göttingen.

— 2000. Über ägyptische Lexikographie: 1. Zum Ptolemaic Lexikon von Penelope Wilson; 2. Versuch eines quantitativen Vergleichs der Textkorpora antiker Sprachen, in: *Lingua Aegyptia* 7, 245–260.

— 2006. Nochmals zur Lesung der Kopf-Hieroglyphe, in: *Göttinger Miszellen* 208, 7–8.

— 2018. Zur Depalatalisierung in ägyptischen Verbalwurzeln, in: *Lingua Aegyptia* 26, 167–183.

— 2020. Review: Allen, James P. 2020. Ancient Egyptian phonology. Cambridge: Cambridge University Press, in: *Lingua Aegyptia* 28, 333–353.

Plas, Dirk van der & Joris Frans Borghouts. 1998. *Coffin texts word index*, Publications Interuniversitaires de Recherches Égyptologiques Informatisées 6, Utrecht.

Quack, Joachim F. 1997. Review: Hannig, Rainer 1995. Großes Handwörterbuch Ägyptisch - Deutsch: die Sprache der Pharaonen (2800-950 v. Chr.). Kulturgeschichte der Antiken Welt 64. Mainz am Rhein: Philipp von Zabern, in: *Bibliotheca Orientalis* 54/3–4, 328–334.

— 2003a. Zum Charakter der „zweiradikaligen" Verben des Ägyptischen, in: *Selected comparative-historical Afrasian linguistic studies: in memory of Igor M. Diakonoff*, ed. by M. L. Bender, G. Takács & D. L. Appleyard, LINCOM studies in Afro-Asiatic linguistics 14, München, 167–174.

— 2003b. Zum Lautwert von Gardiner sign-list U 23, in: *Lingua Aegyptia* 11, 113–116.

Ratcliffe, Robert R. 2001. Analogy in Semitic morphology. Where do new roots and new patterns come from?, in: *New Data and New Methods in Afroasiatic Linguistics: Robert Hetzron in Memoriam*, ed. by A. Zaborski, Wiesbaden, 153–162.

Reintges, Chris H. 1994. Egyptian root-and-pattern morphology, in: *Lingua Aegyptia* 4, 213–244.

Roquet, Gérard. 1973. Incompatibilités dans la racine en ancien égyptien, in: *Göttinger Miszellen* 6, 107–117.
Rössler, Otto. 1971. Das Ägyptische als semitische Sprache, in: *Christentum am Roten Meer I*, ed. by F. Altheim & R. Stiehl, Berlin, 263–326.
Rundgren, Frithiof. 1953. The Root šft in the Modern Ethiopic Languages (Tigrē, Tigriña, and Amharic) and Old Egyptian ḫfty, Coptic šft, in: *Orientalia Suecana* 2, 19–25.
Satzinger, Helmut. 1994. Das ägyptische „Aleph"-Phonem, in: *Zwischen den beiden Ewigkeiten. Festschrift Gertrud Thausing*, ed. by M. Bietak et alii, Wien, 191–205.
— 1999. Egyptian 'Ayin in Variation with d, in: *Lingua Aegyptia* 6, 141–151.
— 2007. Modifizierung ägyptischer Verbalwurzeln durch Reduplikation, in: *Wiener Zeitschrift für die Kunde des Morgenlandes* 97, 475–489.
— 2010a. Scratchy sounds getting smooth: the Egyptian velar fricatives and their palatalization, in: *CAMSEMUD. Proceedings of the 13th Italian Meeting of Afro-Asiatic Linguistics held in Udine, May 21st-24th, 2007*, ed. by F. M. Fales & G. G. Grassi, History of the Ancient Near East / Monographs 10, Padova, 239–245.
— 2010b. On the predominant triliterality of Egyptian verbal stems, in: *VIII Afro-Asiatic Congress (Naples, 2008)*, ed. by S. Baldi, Studi Magrebini VI, Naples. https://homepage.univie.ac.at/helmut.satzinger/Texte/Triliterality.pdf.
— 2017. A lexicon of Egyptian lexical roots (project), in: *Afroasiatica romana: "proceedings of the 15th meeting of Afroasiatic linguistics" 17–19 September 2014, Rome*, ed. by A. Agostini & M. G. Amadasi Guzzo, Roma, 213–223.
Satzinger, Helmut & Danijela Stefanović. 2012. The Middle Kingdom ḫnmsw, in: *Studien zur Altägyptischen Kultur* 41, 341–351.
Schenkel, Wolfgang. 1965. Die Wurzel bnj 'süß', in: *Mitteilungen des Deutschen Archäologischen Instituts, Abteilung Kairo* 20, 115–115.
— 1993. Zu den Verschluß- und Reibelauten im Ägyptischen und (Hamito)Semitischen: ein Versuch zur Synthese der Lehrmeinungen, in: *Lingua Aegyptia* 3: 137–149.
— 1995. Die Lexikographie des Altägyptisch-Koptischen, in: *Studi epigrafici e linguistici sul Vicino Oriente antico, Nuova Serie* 12, 191-203.
— 1999. Textdatenbanken und/als virtuelle Wörterbücher, in: *Textcorpus und Wörterbuch: Aspekte zuir ägyptischen Lexikographie*, ed. by S. Grunert & I. Hafemann, Probleme der Ägyptologie 14, Leiden, 35–50.
— 2005. Die ägyptische Nominalbildungslehre und die Realität der hieroglyphischen Graphien der Sargtexte: die Nominalbildungsklassen A I 5 und A I 6, in: *Lingua Aegyptia* 13, 141–171.
— 2008. Die ägyptische Nominalbildungslehre und die Realität der hieroglyphischen Graphien der Sargtexte II: Weitere Nominalbildungsklassen mit einer Endung -w/y/i (A II 5–10, A III 4–6 und A I 7/8/10), in: *Lingua Aegyptia* 16, 153–170.
Schneider, Thomas. 2003. Etymologische Methode, die Historizität der Phoneme und das ägyptologische Transkriptionsalphabet, in: *Lingua Aegyptia* 11, 187–199.
Schwechler, Coralie. 2020. *Les noms des pains en Égypte ancienne: étude lexicologique*, Studien zur Altägyptischen Kultur, Beihefte 22, Hamburg.
Schweitzer, Simon D. 2008. Aus der Arbeit am Ägyptischen Wörterbuch: einige Ghostwords (I), in: *Göttinger Miszellen* 219, 87–93.
— 2009a. Aus der Arbeit am Ägyptischen Wörterbuch: einige Ghostwords (II), in: *Göttinger Miszellen* 222, 69–75.

— 2009b. Bildwörterbuch des Ägyptischen: eine neue Komponente im Thesaurus Linguae Aegyptiae, in: *Göttinger Miszellen* 223, 73–78.

— 2011. Aus der Arbeit am Ägyptischen Wörterbuch: einige Ghostwords (III), in: *Göttinger Miszellen* 230, 59–71.

— 2012. Aus der Arbeit am Ägyptischen Wörterbuch: einige Ghostwords (IV), in: *Göttinger Miszellen* 233, 75–77.

Smith, Henry S. 1982. The treatment of roots in the lexicography of ancient Egyptian, in: *L'Égyptologie en 1979: axes prioritaires de recherches 1*, Paris, 71–73.

Stroot-Kiraly, Eva. 1989. L'offrande du pain blanc, in: *Bulletin de la Société d'Égyptologie* 13, 157–160.

Takács, Gábor. 1995. Egyptian sbꜣ 'tar', sbꜣ 'to teach,' their origin and related questions, in: *Folia orientalia* 31, 177–188.

— 1999. The "aleph problem" in ancient Egyptian, in: *Rocznik Orientalistyczny* 52/1, 101–121.

— 1999-2008. *Etymological dictionary of Egyptian, 3 vols.*, Handbuch der Orientalistik, erste Abteilung: Der Nahe und Mittlere Osten 48, Leiden.

— 2015. Layers of the oldest Egyptian lexicon I, in: *Rocznik Orientalistyczny* 68/1, 85–139.

— 2016a. Layers of the oldest Egyptian lexicon II, in: *Rocznik Orientalistyczny* 69/1, 59–124.

— 2016b. Layers of the oldest Egyptian lexicon VIII: Numerals, in: *Journal of Language Relationship* 14/2, 119–151.

Thausing, Gertrud. 1932. Über ein ḥ-Präfix im Ägyptischen, in: *Wiener Zeitschrift für die Kunde des Morgenlandes* 39, 287–294.

Vernus, Pascal. 2009. Le préformant *n* et la détransitivité: Formation $nC_1C_2C_1C_2$ versus $C_1C_2C_1C_2$. A propos de la racine √gm 'notion de trituration', in: *Lingua Aegyptia* 17, 291-317.

— 2015. La racine √*gm*, notion de 'rencontre, contact avec', et ses radicaux dérivés (*gmḥ*, *ngmgm* et *gmgm*), in: *Lotus and laurel: studies on Egyptian language and religion in honour of Paul John Frandsen*, ed. by R. Nyord & K. Ryholt, Copenhagen, 418–430.

Vycichl, Werner. 1983. *Dictionnaire étymologique de la langue copte*, Leuven.

Warburton, David A. 2007. Texts, translation, lexicography, & society: a brief note, in: *Lingua Aegyptia* 15, 263-279.

— 2008. The theoretical implications of Ancient Egyptian colour vocabulary for anthropological and cognitive theory, in: *Lingua Aegyptia* 16, 213–259.

— 2011. Darkness at dawn: methodology in Egyptological lexicography, in: *Lingua Aegyptia* 19, 287–320.

Ward, William A. 1969. The Semitic root HWY in Ugaritic and derived stems in Egyptian, in: *Journal of Near Eastern Studies* 28/4, 265–267.

Werning, Daniel A. 2004. The sound values of the signs Gardiner D1 (head) und T8 (dagger), in: *Lingua Aegyptia* 12, 183–204.

— 1973. Observations on the Egyptian biconsonantal root pꜣ, in: *Orient and Occident: essays presented to Cyrus H. Gordon on the occasion of his sixty-fifth birthday*, ed. by H.A. Hoffner, Kevelaer; Neukirchen–Vluyn, 207–212.

— 1974. The Semitic biconsonantal root sp and the common origin of Egyptian čwf and Hebrew sûp: "marsh(-plant)", in: *Vetus Testamentum* 24/3, 339–349.

— 1975. The biconsonantal root *bꜣ and remarks on bilabial interchange in Egyptian, in: *Zeitschrift für ägyptische Sprache und Altertumskunde* 102, 60–67.

— 1985. Reflections on methodology in Egypto-Semitic lexicography, in: *Palestine in the Bronze and Iron Ages: papers in honour of Olga Tufnell*, ed. by J.N. Tubb, University College London, Institute of Archaeology. Occasional publication 11, London, 231–248.

— 1986. Some remarks on the root *gbi/gbgb*, "to be weak, lame, deprived", in: *Zeitschrift für ägyptische Sprache und Altertumskunde* 113, 79–81.

Watson, Wilfred G. E. 1979. Consonantal patterning in Egyptian triliteral verbal roots, in: *Glimpses of ancient Egypt: Studies in honour of H. W. Fairman*, ed. by J. Ruffle, G.A. Gaballa & K.A. Kitchen, Warminster, 100–106.

— 2010. Current work on Egyptian lexicography, in: *Historiae* 7, 91–96.

Weill, Raymond. 1931. La racine 𓇋, *i* "être": génératrice de formes verbales et de noms de personnes, in: *Bulletin de l'Institut Français d'Archéologie Orientale* 30, 593–618.

Westendorf, Wolfhart. 1977. *Koptisches Handwörterbuch: bearbeitet auf der Grundlage des Koptischen Handwörterbuchs von Wilhelm Spiegelberg*, Heidelberg.

Wilson, Penelope. 1997. *A Ptolemaic lexikon: a lexicographical study of the texts in the temple of Edfu*, Orientalia Lovaniensia Analecta 78, Leuven.

Winand, Jean. 1985. Structure et lexicologie: la racine ptr et ses implications, in: *Göttinger Miszellen* 88, 69–76.

— 2003. A dictionary between lexicon and grammar: interplay of verbal Aktionsart and grammatical aspects, in: Wege *zu einem digitalen Corpus ägyptischer Texte: Akten der Tagung „Datenbanken im Verbund" (Berlin, 30. September - 2. Oktober 1999)*, ed. by I. Hafemann, Berlin, 277–296.

— 2017. Identifying Semitic loanwords in Late Egyptian, in: *Greek influence on Egyptian-Coptic: contact-induced change in an ancient African language*, ed. by E. Grossman, P. Dils, T. S. Richter & W. Schenkel, Lingua Aegyptia, Studia Monographica 17, Hamburg, 481–511.

— 2018. Understanding the Egyptian Lexicon with(out) Comparison. Rethinking the Origins. Brown University, 14 April 2018. https://orbi.uliege.be/bitstream/2268/222417/1/Brown%202018%20Lexicon%2020180412.pdf.

Zaborski, Andrzej. 1994. Exceptionless incompatibility rules and verbal root structure in Semitic, in: *Semitic and Cushitic Studies*, ed. by G. Goldenberg & Sh. Raz (eds.), Wiesbaden, 1–18.

— 1998. La linguistique chamito-sémitique cinquante années après l'essai comparatif de Marcel Cohen, in: *Actes sur le 1ère congrès chamito-sémitique de Fès, 12–13 mars 1997*, ed. by M.G. El Medlaoui & F. Saïd Saa, Fès, 23–35.

Lingua Aegyptia – Studia Monographica

ISSN: 0946-8641

1 Frank Kammerzell, *Panther, Löwe und Sprachentwicklung im Neolithikum.*
1994 (hardcover, 100 pages), out of print

2 Gerald Moers (ed.), *Definitely: Egyptian Literature: Proceedings of the symposion "Ancient Egyptian literature: history and forms", Los Angeles, March 24–26, 1995.*
1999 (hardcover, X+142 pages), out of print

3 Dörte Borchers, Frank Kammerzell & Stefan Weninger (eds.), *Hieroglyphen – Alphabete – Schriftreformen: Studien zu Multiliteralismus, Schriftwechsel und Orthographieneuregelungen.*
2001 (hardcover, VI+270 pages), ~~€ 49~~, now € 30

4 Stephan Jäger, *Altägyptische Berufstypologien.*
2004 (hardcover, X+340+xlvi+XCIV pages), out of print

5 José M. Galán, *Four Journeys in Ancient Egyptian Literature.*
2005 (hardcover, V+186 pages), out of print

6 Anthony Spalinger, *Five Views on Egypt.*
2006 (hardcover, VIII+176 pages), out of print (PDF online)

7 H.J. Polotsky, *Scripta Posteriora on Egyptian and Coptic,*
edited by Verena M. Lepper & Leo Depuydt.
2007 (hardcover, VI+230 pages), ~~€ 49~~, now € 35

8 Petra Andrássy, Julia Budka & Frank Kammerzell (eds.), *Non-Textual Marking Systems, Writing and Pseudo Script from Prehistory to Modern Times.*
2009 (hardcover, VIII+312 pages), out of print (PDF online)

9 Eitan Grossman, Stéphane Polis & Jean Winand (eds.),
Lexical Semantics in Ancient Egyptian.
2012 (hardcover, vi+490 pages), € 69 (subscribers' price: € 59)
ISBN: 978-3-943955-09-5

10 R.B. Parkinson,
The Tale of the Eloquent Peasant: A Reader's Commentary.
2012 (hardcover, xii+384 pages), € 59 (subscribers' price: € 49)
ISBN: 978-3-943955-10-1

11 Gerald Moers, Kai Widmaier, Antonia Giewekemeyer, Arndt Lümers & Ralf Ernst (eds.),
Dating Egyptian Literary Texts.
"Dating Egyptian Literary Texts" Göttingen, 9–12 June 2010, Volume 1
2013 (hardcover, xiv+653 pages), € 95 (subscribers' price: € 79)
ISBN: 978-3-943955-11-8

12 Andréas Stauder,
Linguistic Dating of Middle Egyptian Literary Texts.
"Dating Egyptian Literary Texts" Göttingen, 9–12 June 2010, Volume 2
2013 (hardcover, xx+568 pages), € 85 (subscribers' price: € 69)
ISBN: 978-3-943955-12-5

13 Marc Brose,
Grammatik der dokumentarischen Texte des Mittleren Reiches.
2014 (cloth, xx+553 pages), € 85 (subscribers' price: € 69)
ISBN: 978-3-943955-13-2

14 Andréas Stauder,
The Earlier Egyptian Passive. Voice and Perspective.
2014 (cloth, xviii+448 pages), € 69 (subscribers' price: € 59)
ISBN: 978-3-943955-14-9

15 Eitan Grossman, Stéphane Polis, Andréas Stauder & Jean Winand (eds.),
On Forms and Functions: Studies in Ancient Egyptian Grammar.
2014 (cloth, vi+366 pages), € 59 (subscribers' price: € 49)
ISBN: 978-3-943955-15-6

16 Julia Budka, Frank Kammerzell & Sławomir Rzepka (eds.),
Non-Textual Marking Systems in Ancient Egypt (and Elsewhere).
2015 (cloth, x+322 pages), € 59 (subscribers' price: € 49)
ISBN: 978-3-943955-16-3

17 Eitan Grossman, Peter Dils, Tonio Sebastian Richter & Wolfgang Schenkel (eds.),
Greek Influence on Egyptian-Coptic: Contact-Induced Change in an Ancient African Language. DDGLC Working Papers 1
2017 (cloth, viii+534 pages), € 89 (subscribers' price: € 69)
ISBN: 978-3-943955-17-0

18 Kristina Hutter,
Das sḏm=f-Paradigma im Mittelägyptischen: Eine Vergleichsstudie verschiedener Grammatiken.
2017 (paperback, x+289 pages, incl. 47 tables), € 49 (subscribers' price: € 39)
ISBN: 978-3-943955-18-7

19 Gaëlle Chantrain & Jean Winand (eds.),
Time and Space at Issue in Ancient Egypt.
2018 (paperback, viii+242 p.), € 55 (subscribers' price: € 39)
ISBN: 978-3-943955-19-4

20 Marwan Kilani,
Vocalisation in Group Writing: A New Proposal.
2019 (paperback, vi+150 p.), € 39 (subscribers' price: € 29)
ISBN: 978-3-943955-20-0
ISBN (OPEN ACCESS PDF): 978-3-943955-90-3 | doi.org/10.37011/studmon.20

21 Gaëlle Chantrain,
Eléments de la terminologie du temps en égyptien ancien.
2020 (paperback, xxxiv+344 p.), € 59 (subscribers' price: € 49)
ISBN: 978-3-943955-21-7

22 Kathrin Gabler, Rita Gautschy, Lukas Bohnenkämper, Hanna Jenni, Clémentine Reymond, Ruth Zillhardt, Andrea Loprieno-Gnirs & Hans-Hubertus Münch (eds),
Text-Bild-Objekte im archäologischen Kontext: Festschrift für Susanne Bickel.
2020 (cloth, xxii+293 p., 23 colour, 60 b&w illustrations), € 65 (subscribers' price: € 49)
ISBN: 978-3-943955-22-4

23 Simon Thuault,
La dissemblance graphémique à l'Ancien Empire: Essai de grammatologie cognitive.
2020 (paperback, xx+376 p., illustrations), € 59 (subscribers' price: € 49)
ISBN: 978-3-943955-23-1

24 Matthias Müller,
Grammatik des Bohairischen.
2021 (paperback, xxiv+936 p.), € 49 (subscribers' price: € 45)
ISBN: 978-3-943955-24-8

All prices include German VAT.

www.widmaier-verlag.de | orders@widmaier-verlag.de

North American distributor: www.isdistribution.com